GunDigest
2015

Edited by
JERRY LEE

Published by

Gun Digest® Books, an imprint of F+W Media, Inc.
Krause Publications · 700 East State Street · Iola, WI 54990-0001
715-445-2214 · 888-457-2873
www.krausebooks.com

To order books or other products call toll-free 1-800-258-0929
or visit us online at **www.gundigeststore.com**

CAUTION: Technical data presented here, particularly technical data on handloading and on firearms adjustment and alteration, inevitably reflects individual experience with particular equipment and components under specific circumstances the reader cannot duplicate exactly. Such data presentations therefore should be used for guidance only and with caution. Gun Digest Books accepts no responsibility for results obtained using these data.

ISSN 0072-9043

ISBN 13: 978-1-4402-3912-0
ISBN 10: 1-4402-3912-6

Cover & Design by Tom Nelsen

Edited by Jerry Lee & Chris Berens

Printed in the United States of America

John T. Amber

LITERARY AWARD

I t is our pleasure to announce that Paul Scarlata is the recipient of the 33rd Annual John T. Amber Literary Award. The award is presented in recognition of his excellent story, "The Remarkable Ross," which was published in last year's 68th Edition of *Gun Digest*. Paul presented a very thorough and well-researched story on the confusing and complicated history of the straight-pull, bolt-action Ross rifle in the early decades of the 20th century. The infamous Canadian rifle was plagued with controversy and problems during its years of service in many different variations from 1903 to about 1940. Several soldiers were seriously injured due to failures of the rifle's pull-bolt design, but the gun's creator, Sir Charles Ross, blamed the incidents on faulty maintenance procedures. Politics and favoritism also played a role in the interesting tale of the Ross rifle.

We asked Paul to tell us a bit about his life and his interest in firearms.

"I guess my ending up as a member of the firearms media was a foregone conclusion. My father, an avid hunter and fisherman, taught my two brothers and myself a respect for the outdoors, wildlife and firearms at an early age. Many of my happiest memories are of those days the four of us spent afield pursuing small and large game and deep-sea fishing. I often tell people that my childhood resembled a Hemingway novel.

"In my teens I developed a fascination for the, then inexpensive, military surplus firearms flooding the market. Over the years I accumulated – and sold off – several collections until I began specializing in Krag-Jorgensens. A fascinating, if expensive, hobby.

"I graduated college with an MA in Russian and Middle Eastern history and a minor in journalism, and over the years I worked as a teacher, medical office manager and business owner. After a life-changing event in my 40s, a divorce, the opportunity presented itself for me to pursue a career that involved two things that I loved – firearms and history.

"With the urging of my daughter and the help of my brothers, one an engineer for a major firearms/ammunition company and the other a photographer, I began submitting articles to various

Paul and one of his beloved Krag-Jorgensen rifles. Photo by Becky Leavitt

firearms publications – and almost starved to death for three years! But my perseverance paid off and my work has been published by gun and military history magazines in the U.S., Switzerland, Finland, Russia, the Netherlands, Great Britain, South Africa, New Zealand and Australia. I have also had three books on classic bolt-action military rifles published, all of which have proven successful.

"Today I continue to contribute to publications in the U.S. and around the world and am about to begin my fourth book. In my leisure time I am an active Action Pistol shooter, a sport that I share with my fiancée and photographer – Becky, and continue to pursue the Holy Grail of Kragdom – an all original U.S. M1892 rifle!"

The John T. Amber Award is presented each year to a *Gun Digest* contributor whose work demonstrates significant

Paul Scarlata

knowledge of the subject matter through experience and research, and also for the ability to express it in a way to inform, inspire and entertain the reader. Each recipient receives a handsome plaque and a $1,000 honorarium. The award is named for the late John Amber, who served as the editor of *Gun Digest* from 1951 to 1979 and is fondly remembered by many readers and industry people for his knowledge and love of fine firearms. Amber died in 1986 on his Creedmoor farm in Illinois at the age of 82.

Congratulations Paul. We look forward to seeing your stories in future editions of *Gun Digest*.

Jerry Lee
Editor

WELCOME
to the 2015 69ᵗʰ Edition of *Gun Digest*!

It's hard to believe another year has gone by and that this edition of "The World's Greatest Gun Book" is in bookstores and gunshops all over the country. Or, these days, on a truck or plane headed to someone's front door from gundigeststore.com, Amazon or some other online retailer.

From its early years, *Gun Digest* has set the standard for firearms-related journals and as editor, it is my goal to continue that tradition. We have put together a mix of stories, field reports, gun tests and reference sections that cover a wide range of the shooting sports from some of the top writers in the field. This edition has stories on everything from investing in machine guns to a women's-only African safari; from historical articles on Webleys, Rolling Blocks and Enfields, to tests on a modern-day sniper rifle and the latest Glock; and from holsters of the Hollywood Westerns to the handgun that's number one in battlefield fatalities. (It's not a 1911.)

We are very proud to add Dick Williams' byline to our ever-expanding list of *Gun Digest* contributors. Dick has been published in many gun magazines for years and is recognized as a leading expert in the field of handgun hunting. He has taken a number of big-game animals in Alaska, Africa and Australia, as well as all over the United States. Dick's story in this edition is about the very first .44 Magnums from Smith & Wesson and Ruger.

It's great to welcome back two writers whose names haven't been seen on our table of contents page for many years: Garry James and Nick Sisley. Garry has been associated with *Guns & Ammo* magazine for decades, having served as editor in the past and now as senior editor and contributor. He frequently appears as a host or guest on various gun-related television shows and is a regular contributor to the NRA's *American Rifleman* magazine. Garry's contribution to this edition is about the early .303 British rifles that were made for black-powder cartridges. No one, and I mean, no one, knows more about early English and French military rifles than Garry James.

Nick Sisley is Mr. Shotgun to many readers of gun books and magazines over the last 40-plus years. He has written thousands of magazine articles, eight books, is an NSCA, NSSA and NRA shotgun instructor, and a private pilot with many ratings. In this edition of *Gun Digest*, Nick covers the fine products of the Connecticut Shotgun Manufacturing Company, and reviews the Caesar Guerini Invictus over/under. You can find a lot of Nick's thoughts and opinions at www.shotgunlife.com/author/Nick-Sisley.html.

Highlights of This Edition

For many years Wayne van Zwoll has hosted safaris to Africa for women hunters. In his "Safari Sisters" story, he says he discovered long ago that neither machismo nor magnums are required for a successful hunt. He tells us that women tend to be more careful in shooting big game, partly because they are inexperienced, but also because they aren't reluctant to acknowledge their inexperience, unlike many male hunters. To quote Wayne, "Circumstantial evidence suggests many men think they were born shooting bull's-eyes." And "…such fellows commonly attempt shots beyond their ability." That sounds like good advice for some of us.

Many of us recall the golden age of Western movies and television shows in the middle of the last century. Those formative years are when I'm sure many of the readers of *Gun Digest* developed an interest in guns. Most of us will recall that along with the sixguns of the Hollywood cowboys were all those wonderful leather rigs in which they were carried. My friend Rick Hacker is a walking, talking encyclopedia of the guns and gear of Western films and TV programs. His story on Arvo Ojala takes us back to "those thrilling days of yesteryear" (sorry, I couldn't resist it), and tells us how a champion fast-draw shooter became an artist in leather whose holsters appeared in virtually every TV Western. Rick also reveals which famous TV scene you have probably seen many times that features Arvo Ojala.

Values of many types of machine guns have skyrocketed in recent years and Frank James provides a fascinating look at the subject in this edition. Frank is a recognized expert on the subject and has owned and fired many full-auto weapons. In addition to his fine book on the Heckler & Koch MP5 submachine gun (published by Gun Digest Books/Krause in 2003), he has written hundreds of articles on machine guns for many gun

magazines in the U.S. and Europe. By the way, Frank suffered a severe stroke in early 2013 but as we go to press in June, he is recovering quite well and hopes to be back at the keyboard soon.

Many gun books and magazines have articles about the different shooting schools around the country that teach the skills needed for personal defense and the various competitive disciplines. But the FTW Ranch in Texas has a training program that is different, one that is designed specifically for hunters. Buck Pope took one of the courses and reports on what he and other students learned in "Shooting School for Hunters." The 12,000-acre ranch in the Texas Hill Country also offers hunting opportunities.

Terry Wieland's "Shooting Stars" story is on the history and development of the 7mm Sharpe & Hart cartridge and the Schultz & Larsen rifles chambered for it in the years following World War II. The 7x61 S&H was the only alternative to the 7mm Weatherby Magnum during the 1950s and developed quite a following. Then the 7mm Remington Mag. came along in 1962 and soon became America's favorite big seven. Terry tells a good story about Philip Sharpe's dream and clarifies some confusing claims and statements that have been published in the past.

Other highlights of this edition include Jon Sundra and his favorite cartridge. He quotes Jack O'Connor telling him one time that no one wanted him to ever change his mind about his favorite cartridge, the .270. Jon tells us about his own favorites and how they have changed over the years. John Taffin gives us a look at the history and lots of photos of the great .44-40 WCF and its compatible pairings of sixguns and rifles. And James and Kathleen House celebrate 50 years of the Ruger 10/22, America's favorite rimfire.

We hope you enjoy this edition of what we like to call "The World's Greatest Gun Book." A lot of people have put in a great deal of effort to get it into your hands.

State of the Industry

The firearms industry continues to grow and prosper in this time of a slow recovery in the overall economy. The $6 billion industry has experienced growth for several years with a good sign being that many new shooters are young, more female and more urban, due obviously to interests in personal defense and home protection products.

The industry still faces many attempts at the state and federal level to further restrict the ownership of certain kinds of firearms. The good news is that violent crimes committed with guns have decreased steadily over the last five years. This is in spite of the fact that more people are buying more guns than ever before. It is also true that no matter what you see or hear in the mainstream media, accidents with firearms account for less than one percent of all accidental fatalities in the country.

Attendance at the industry's SHOT (Shooting, Hunting and Outdoor Trade) Show in Las Vegas in January 2014 once again set a new record. More than 67,000 people involved in the business of marketing firearms and associated products attended the four-day event, which is closed to the general public.

More and more firearms manufacturers are on the move. Remington has a new plant in Huntsville, Alabama, and will be relocating several of its other production facilities there: Para USA from North Carolina, LAR from Utah, DPMS from Minnesota, Bushmaster from New York, as well as production of the R1 pistol from New York. Other companies that are expanding some of their production to more gun-friendly and tax-friendly states are Kahr Arms from New York, and several from Connecticut including Mossberg, Ruger, Colt and Stag Arms. Beretta USA is moving some of its facilities from Maryland to Tennessee and has already relocated part of its company to Virginia.

At one time almost every major gun manufacturer in the U.S. was in "gun valley" of Connecticut and New York, but for a variety of reasons—mainly political and economic—those days are no more.

Standard Catalog of Ruger Firearms

Shameless Plug: *Standard Catalog of Ruger Firearms* by yours truly will be published by Gun Digest Books in the fall of 2014. It is the latest addition to the series of Standard Catalogs devoted to the products of a single firearms manufacturer and the first one on the guns of Sturm, Ruger & Co. Previous editions have covered the guns of Colt, Winchester, Smith & Wesson, Browning and others. Included in *Standard Catalog of Ruger Firearms* are articles on the founding of the company by William B. Ruger and Alexander Sturm in 1949, stories and photographs of the rarest and most collectible Rugers, plus production dates and serial numbers for virtually every model. The history of each model and its variations is included, from 1949 to the present, plus many color photographs, complete specifications and estimated current values for different condition grades on today's collectible and used gun market. Another section features reprints of early articles about the company's most famous firearms from the pages of *Gun Digest* over the years. If you're a Ruger aficionado, we hope you check out this new publication. Here's a look at the introduction to *Standard Catalog of Ruger Firearms*.

There have been few individuals involved with the American firearms history who have made a real difference to the industry—individuals who possessed an inventive mind and knew how to get things done, but also understood how to make a business become successful and grow. Their names are familiar to anyone who is a student of the gun.

Samuel Colt, Horace Smith, Daniel B. Wesson, Eliphalet Remington, Oliver Winchester, John M. Marlin, John Browning and Arthur Savage were sons of the 19th century. The companies that bear their names are still going today, many generations after they were founded.

One other name should be added to that list of visionary giants in the word of firearms, William Batterman Ruger. He started his company in 1949, in the middle of the 20th century just a few years after World War II in a small building now affectionately known as the Red Barn in the tranquil little New England town of Southport, Conn. Sturm, Ruger & Co. has been one of the biggest success stories in the industry, reaching a point where it can be said to be the only full-line manufacturer of rifles, shotguns, revolvers and auto pistols, all made in the U.S.A. From the first .22 pistol 65 years ago to the almost 200 firearms in the latest catalog, the company has offered a gun for every need for the average shooter. Within these pages will be found historical information, specifications, photos and estimated values of the guns of Bill Ruger.

Gun Digest-The Magazine

Many readers of this annual publication do not know that there is another *Gun Digest* published by the same company, *Gun Digest the Maga-*zine. I asked the magazine's editor-in-chief Doug Howlett for a description and some background.

"**For 70 years**, *Gun Digest* has served as the preeminent source of information on firearms both new and old, firearm values and on-point reviews by the top writers in the firearms industry as they personally test the most popular guns of the day. As an off-shoot of that success, the publishers of *Gun Digest* morphed the former *Gun List* classified tabloid into a more recently redesigned *Gun Digest the Magazine*, an 18 times-a-year publication that boasts the same type of great firearms and shooting gear reviews and information familiar to annual readers, combined with up-to-date gun and accessory classifieds and complete gun show listings familiar to readers of the old *Gun List*. Now *Gun Digest* fans don't have to wait an entire year to read the best information on firearms, but can get it right in their mailbox or from their favorite newsstand every three weeks.

"'We Know Guns, So You Know Guns' isn't just a tagline with *Gun Digest the Magazine*; it's what makes this publication unique among firearms titles. *Gun Digest's* team of editors and writers—some of the most recognized in the business—not only deliver detailed reviews of the latest guns and shooting accessories to hit store shelves, they offer the tactics and insight needed for shooters of every skill level—from novice to hardcore veteran—to improve their own knowledge of, ability with and level of fun, safety and preparedness with firearms. Each issue also offers in-depth interviews with the most compelling personalities in the shooting world, as well as profiles of the most awesome shooting destinations located around the country. Whether it's rifle, handgun, shotgun, collectible, historical, reloading, tactical, concealed carry or simply cutting edge, if it has to do with shooting, it can be found in the pages of *Gun Digest the Magazine*. Visit our website at gundigest.com for more details on how to subscribe, and follow us on Facebook at facebook.com/gundigest to be a part of the most dynamic online community of shooting enthusiasts in the world."

—Doug Howlett

Acknowledgements

A tip of our hat to Managing Editor Chris Berens for his editorial support, for keeping us on schedule, and on our toes watching out for typos and grammatical no-nos. We want to again this year acknowledge Tom Nelsen's creativity and artistic skills in making Gun Digest look as good as it does.

About the covers

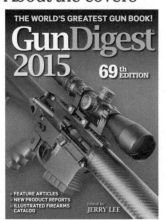

FRONT COVER:

The modern sporting rifle continues to grow in popularity as more shooters discover how well the AR platform performs in the hunting field. DPMS is leading the way with its new GII Hunter, a smaller, lighter and more technically advanced .308 with a receiver that's only slightly larger than that of a 5.56 NATO model. At 7¾ pounds with a 20-inch barrel, it's light enough to carry all day, yet it is stronger than other .308 AR designs. Features include a redesigned extraction system, dual ejectors, contoured steel feed ramps, and a completely redesigned gas delivery system that eliminates the possibility of gas leakage during operation. Several tactical variations of the GII are also offered by DPMS. The scope is a Nightforce NXS 2.5-10x42 Compact.

BACK COVER:

On our back cover is Benelli's newest autoloading shotgun, the handsome Ethos with its engraved nickel-plated receiver and AA-grade walnut stock; the 50th Anniversary Ruger 10/22, based on the submission of a design contest winner; the unique Taurus View revolver with its see-through sideplate; and Remington's R51 9mm pistol, resurrecting a model name from out of the past.

Gun Digest Staff

Jerry Lee, Editor
Chris Berens, Managing Editor

CONTRIBUTING EDITORS
John Haviland: Shotguns
Kevin Muramatsu: Handguns/Autoloaders
Jeff Quinn: Handguns/Revolvers
Wm. Hovey Smith: Blackpowder

Larry Sterett: Ammunition, Ballistics & Components
Tom Tabor: Optics
Tom Turpin: Custom and Engraved Guns
Wayne van Zwoll: Rifles

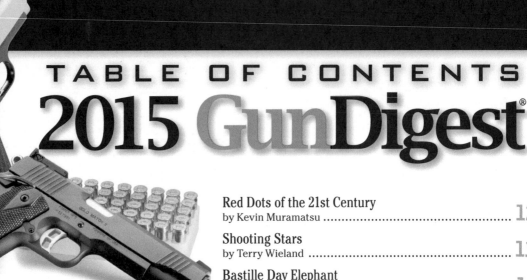

TABLE OF CONTENTS
2015 GunDigest®

FEATURES

2015 FIREARMS CATALOG

Rifles of the Safari Sisters

BY **Wayne van Zwoll**

Julie's .280 bullet deflected on a limb, but expert tracking and a fast shot finished this kudu.

Machismo earns no points on safari, where accuracy and hunting skills trump recoil. Just ask the Safari Sisters.

Noon's sun is ferocious; still, my Zeiss turns up several red hartebeest on the *vlei*. We swing wide through the thorn. Downwind, Emily gets as low as the grass allows, palms the bolt and grabs the sticks. She's sweating; the heat has little to do with that. She breathes deeply and levels the Browning. The old bull moves, now clear of the others but quartering.

Wait. *Wait!* Minutes drag by – or seconds. The hartebeest turns slightly, then lurches at the strike.

Sub-Saharan Africa is a tough neighborhood. Animals there grow up durable. "They take a lot of killing," we're told. "Aim well forward. Break a shoulder." Sound advice – especially as many of the big antelopes carry their vitals up front between the shoulders. "Don't fret about meat. Bring the beast down."

Dutifully, hunters on their first safari bring plenty of firepower. Africa is magnum country, sure as ice on the crest of Kilimanjaro.

But what about recoil? Few shooters perform at their best with hard-kicking

rifles. I don't. And I'm much bigger in frame than the women I've hosted on safaris for nearly a decade. Outfitting them might seem a challenge if you cotton to guns that belch mightily and hurl themselves viciously against your clavicle.

For me, recoil has all the appeal of Obamacare, and I've become adept at avoiding it. Killing big, tough animals with rifles of civil demeanor requires no more from you than does killing them with rifles that buck violently and leave your ears ringing.

"A .308 or a .30-06," I say. "If you shoot better with a lighter cartridge, use that. Choose a proper bullet and send it to the right place." I've repeated that advice many times, after offering it to a youngster on his first elk hunt 25 years ago.

The young man could have used his father's .30-06. After all, elk are tough. But at my urging he chose the 6mm Remington he shot more comfortably. Early the first morning we spied a herd, sneaked within 150 yards and bellied onto the frozen Utah hill. "Tight in the crease," I whispered needlessly. The rifle settled over a pack, the teenager launched a 95-grain Nosler. The elk collapsed.

The next season in that same unit, a fellow with a .300 Magnum opened up on another elk. The stricken bull struggled up a butte as the shooter followed with a barrage. The animal's legs gave way, but it clung to life, struggling on. Nearly a box of ammunition later, the last softpoint found vitals at over 400 yards.

Now, there's nothing inhumane about belted .30s. And I can't say the recoil of that rifle kept the first shot off the mark. Still, the biggest elk I've seen shot fell to .30-06s. Of elk I've seen crippled, most were hit with more powerful rounds.

In Africa, animals as big as elk drop readily to the likes of the .30-06. Many on our safaris have fallen to the .270, partly because most women who don't bring their own rifles are loaned a .270.

"Kudu!" We creep forward, a bloody evening sun to our backs. The bull is a flicker of movement ghosting through thin thorn. Leslie slides the Sako onto the sticks, bracing her slight, 110-pound frame. I feel her pulse – or is it mine? The barrel quivers as her finger tightens. Leslie has never shot an animal. The blast jerks the rifle from its rest, but she recovers quickly, closing the bolt on a fresh round. The bull vaults through a gap in the thorn. His legs wilt, and he noses into the winter-hard earth.

Such one-shot kills are the rule on our High Country Adventures Safaris. The .270 has no magic; nor do the 130- and 150-grain softpoints we carry for that Sako. But the women who use them are careful.

"No. I'll wait." Cathy smiles, as if losing her rifle in transit on her first safari doesn't matter. She has now gone three days without it, politely declining the .270. And my '06. Time is passing quickly.

She demurs. "There's lots of game. I'll just watch."

Left: Emily took this heavy-horned kudu with a Browning rifle in .270 WSM, with .30-06-level recoil.

Below: Tamar used a .270 on this impala. The suppressor reduced noise and recoil but added a bit of length and weight.

Even a zero check at the range (here in Namibia) gives better results when rifles don't kick hard.

One of the most versatile cartridges, even in sub-Saharan Africa, is the civil .270 Winchester.

Few men I know would take this setback with such equanimity. You might have concluded, as I'd come to think, that she cared little about killing game. You'd have been half right. She didn't care that she had *first crack* at game, though she knew I couldn't guarantee last-hour success.

With just two days left to hunt, Cathy's rifle arrived. Three dead-center hits later, she had killed a kudu, a gemsbok and a blue wildebeest. I saw genuine delight in her grin. Her Remington 700 .30-06 had little to do with those one-shot kills. Credit instead her serenity. I can't recall ever seeing Cathy tense. Nothing rattled her. As cool behind the scope as at a luggage counter filling out claims forms, she calmly executed each shot.

OK, Cathy had logged more range time than most Safari Sisters. And some of them have literally shaken with excitement as the crosswire swung onto the shoulder of their first African game.

Gemsbok are famously hard to kill. They're big, hardy, determined. The lungs lie tucked between the shoulders. When I spied a bull quartering toward us on the fringe of a pan, Donna took my silent cue and eased her Sako ahead on the sticks. The animal moved cautiously; Donna began to shake. *Not yet!* At 90 yards it paused, but the angle was wrong. *Uh-uh.* By now the rifle was chattering on the hardwood. I whispered a low "Easy. We have time. Relax." I can't say she heard me.

At last the bull turned. Still the rifle vibrated. Then, with visible resolve, Donna gripped the neck of the sticks and stilled the .30-06. A second later the blast blew tiny leaves from the thorn by the muzzle. The gemsbok galloped off, but not before the "whup" of a solid hit floated back. We eased forward. The bull lay dead just a few steps from where she'd shot it, perfectly.

The .30-06 is no pipsqueak. Indeed, when it appeared more than a century ago, the '06 was the most powerful infantry round in the world. For another decade, it remained more potent than

Whatever the load, marksmanship counts! Sticks steady rifle and nerves for that first-round hit.

every other smokeless big-game cartridge in common use in North America! Frisky loads in lightweight rifles hit you with nearly 20 foot-pounds of recoil. Small-framed shooters can find that intimidating. But since the postwar trend to magnums has upped the power ante, hunters have come to endure even more violence.

When you trigger a rifle, a small bomb goes off in front of your nose. Hard to ignore that, even if you don't think about pressures of 60,000 pounds per square inch accelerating lead shrapnel from zero to Mach 3 in a short eye-blink. Recoil not only belts you on the gums and pounds your shoulder – it reminds you the explosion would take your head off if the rifle didn't contain it. Now, you may not *think* that, but your body responds reflexively. Reducing recoil helps you shoot better because it absolves you of such instinctive action. The roll of distant thunder doesn't make us jump. If each clap brought a lightning bolt that hit us with

The .30-06 still tops most lists of all-around hunting cartridges. New bullets enhance it.

Keeping Scopes Modest Too

For most hunting you need little magnification in a riflescope – 3x or 4x will do fine. But beginners have a hard time keeping variable-power scopes at the low end. Once, after a Safari Sister shot a gemsbok, she and I approached through tall grass. Spotting the bull, I hissed, "Get ready." A gemsbok's lunge can gut a lion. This bull was dead – fortunately for my friend, who couldn't find the beast in her scope, dialed to 9x.

Another lady brought to Africa a rifle she'd carried in the high desert of the Intermountain West. Her first shot in Namibia came at 80 yards. The bullet landed a few inches off, in part because the field of the 6-18x sight was filled by shoulder and rib, also because the shot had to be taken offhand, with little time to steady the rifle on the sticks. Every heartbeat bounced the reticle all over the animal. High-power scopes also add unnecessary weight and bulk. A young lady who'd borrowed a long-barreled .270 for her first safari bought a lightweight Kimber 84M for the next. She scoped it with a slender 1.5-5x scope. Her new rifle relieved her of two pounds dead weight but killed a nyala, a bushbuck and a zebra with dispatch.

voltage enough to light a stadium, we'd leap at the slightest burp from above. To claim some loads are "good for women" is to say men don't flinch. This is the purest hokum. At a range bench not long ago I watched one veteran shooter close his eyes and turn his face from the comb as he yanked the trigger. "I'll have to check that bedding," he said, frowning over scattered holes in the target. "That's sometimes helpful," I replied.

You can, of course, carry a cartridge too light for the game. I did a few years back, when in South Africa hunting eland. The 6.5 Creedmoor is a marvelous round, flat-shooting and civil. I'd killed several animals with it, including an elk

A happy young lady's first African game! One shot with a .270 at 90 yards took the bull for 13-year-old Thea.

Though this eland fell to Wayne's 6.5 Creedmoor, he considers it light for such big animals.

Left: The .270 is comfortable at the bench, where all hunters must spend some time without flinching.

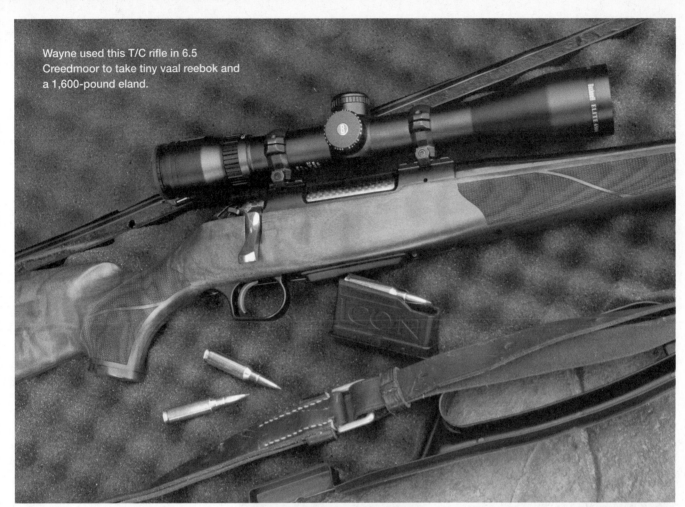

Wayne used this T/C rifle in 6.5 Creedmoor to take tiny vaal reebok and a 1,600-pound eland.

at extreme range. A big eland is twice as heavy as a big elk, but I figured a careful shot with my Creedmoor, out of the T/C rifle, would deck an eland. My chance came after an approach on my belly toward two bulls browsing in thin thorn. At 70 yards, I slinged up to kill the nearest. But it was quartering sharply away – not a good lie. I declined. Then the wind shifted. The bulls moved. When the second eland paused at just a slight angle, I held in line with the off-shoulder and fired.

Trailing turned up little blood. My tracker worked his magic into rocks that gave up fewer prints as the bull climbed. But the waning sign slowed us as the sun sank low and scarlet. Dispirited, we halted. Then, hoofbeats! Across a draw, perhaps 100 yards away, the eland broke cover. I swung, fired offhand, missed, cycled the bolt and anchored the animal with a follow-up shot as it entered the bush. It was dead when we arrived. My first bullet, an hour earlier, had landed well, centering the far lung. It tired itself in the massive shoulder. But each eland lung is the size of a big Styrofoam cooler.

Three gentle but effective 6.5s: From left: 6.5x55 Swedish, .260 Remington, 6.5 Creedmoor.

Hornady
#81494 6.5 CREEDMOOR
140 gr A-MAX®

Remington.
PREMIER® BALLISTI
260 REMINGTO
120 GR. NOSLER BALLISTIC

WINC
6.5 x 55
140 GR. SOF

"When a man hits a target they call him a marksman. When I hit a target, they call it a trick. Never did like that much."
— Annie Oakley

Above: Oakley in her twenties (1880s)

Right: Annie Oakley shooting a shotgun in front of dozens of spectators. Pinehurst, NC

Annie Oakley

A Girl Like No Other

The notion that women need help choosing rifles and killing game has less credence now than when men alone went afield. You could say the shift started with Annie Oakley, an extraordinarily gifted shot whose celebrity derived from beating men at their own game.

Born in a cabin in Darke County, Ohio in August 1860, Phoebe Ann Moses had a hard childhood. But subsistence hunting would propel her to fame. She shot her first squirrel at age 8. Soon she was killing quail on the wing with her .22 and dominating turkey shoots. At a local match she beat visiting sharpshooter Frank Butler – who apparently didn't know his opponent would be a 15-year-old girl. A year later they married, and Annie joined Frank's traveling show under the stage name of Annie Oakley. When exhibition shooter Captain A.H. Bogardus left Buffalo Bill's Wild West Show, Annie got on that docket, aiming into a mirror to shoot over her shoulder at glass balls Frank threw in the air.

Petite at 100 pounds, and sweet-tempered, Annie became an audience darling. Sioux Chief Sitting Bull called her *Watanya* cicilia, or "Little Sure-Shot." The German

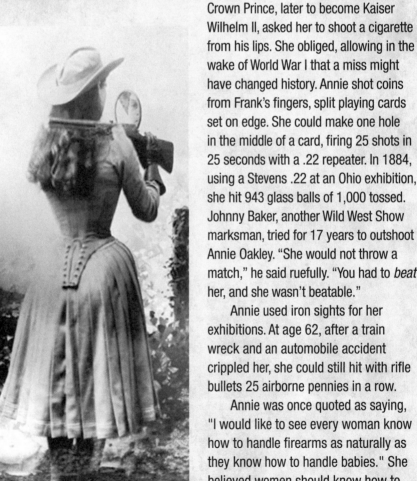

Crown Prince, later to become Kaiser Wilhelm II, asked her to shoot a cigarette from his lips. She obliged, allowing in the wake of World War I that a miss might have changed history. Annie shot coins from Frank's fingers, split playing cards set on edge. She could make one hole in the middle of a card, firing 25 shots in 25 seconds with a .22 repeater. In 1884, using a Stevens .22 at an Ohio exhibition, she hit 943 glass balls of 1,000 tossed. Johnny Baker, another Wild West Show marksman, tried for 17 years to outshoot Annie Oakley. "She would not throw a match," he said ruefully. "You had to *beat* her, and she wasn't beatable."

Annie used iron sights for her exhibitions. At age 62, after a train wreck and an automobile accident crippled her, she could still hit with rifle bullets 25 airborne pennies in a row.

Annie was once quoted as saying, "I would like to see every woman know how to handle firearms as naturally as they know how to handle babies." She believed women should know how to defend themselves. It is believed that in her lifetime she trained nearly 15,000 women on how to use a gun.

After its extractor broke, Sarah made three one-shot kills with her .260, including this hartebeest.

Fine shooting with a mild cartridge brought Kelsey this red hartebeest, her first African game.

Janice used a Remington Model Seven in .300 WSM to kill this exceptional nyala at 110 yards.

One 120-grain 6.5 bullet had simply cut too small a channel to cause quick death.

Still, cartridges of that ilk are deadly on most plains game. One Safari Sister carried her .260, a lovely featherweight rifle from New Ultra Light Arms. But at our first-day range-check of scope zeros, an ambitious handload worked up in a cooler climate blew the .260's extractor. We had a back-up rifle, but Sarah wanted to use her own. I crawled out on a long limb: "You're a careful shooter. The rifle is just not a repeater now. Center the first shot; you won't need an extractor." Sarah made the best of her handicap, downing a gemsbok, a red hartebeest and a tremendous kudu with one bullet apiece.

Over the last decade, Safari Sisters have brought rifles much like those you'll find in deer camps stateside. Remington's 700 outnumbers other models, with the Tikka T3, Ruger 77, Winchester 70 and Remington Model Seven also popular. Some belong to husbands, boyfriends. No pink stocks. The range of cartridges is pretty

A tense half-hour in thick thorn gave Tritia a close offhand shot with her .30-06. She made it count!

Springbok don't require powerful rounds, but you'll need a rifle that handles big antelopes too.

narrow. The .30-06, .270 and .308 predominate. Of course, a few magnums have shown up. Emily downed her hartebeest, and a heavy-horned kudu with a .270 WSM. Teri used the .300 Winchester she carries for mule deer. Shannon knew her .300 Weatherby had more horsepower and recoil than she needed. But, "a friend urged me to take it. I couldn't say no."

This friend evidently had a mean streak. A couple of years after our safari, Shannon called to say he'd coaxed her into firing his .338 Ultra Mag. from the bench. "I should have known better," she sighed.

But most women are advised *not* to indulge punishing recoil – oddly enough, by men brandishing artillery with enough horsepower to disable a Panzer. In the 1960s, such chauvinism appeared on T-shirts: "Get women, children and Chevys off the street." Not to disparage GM. Any automobile can be branded with the weakness of women and the frailty of youth.

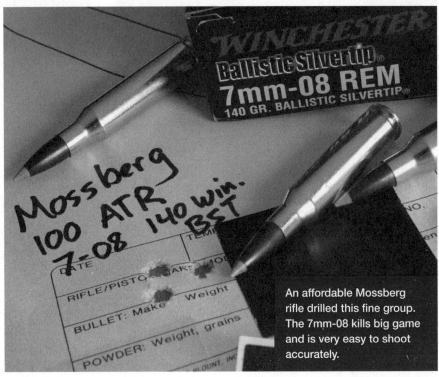

An affordable Mossberg rifle drilled this fine group. The 7mm-08 kills big game and is very easy to shoot accurately.

On a hunt, however, horsepower doesn't win prizes. Indeed, many of the *least effective* shots I've observed afield have been triggered by men with fire-breathing rifles. On the eve of one mule deer hunt, over a couple of thick fingers of Scotch, a loquacious chap told me he routinely rolled running bucks 500 yards out. "Flat-shooting magnum, this. And I don't miss."

Next morning he crippled a beautiful buck at 125 steps. I tracked it as a group of his colleagues formed an arc across a flat ahead of me. The deer met a merciful end.

I'd be painting with too broad a brush to say hunters who prefer magnum cartridges shoot poorly or irresponsibly at game, or that women shoot better than men. Still, in my experience, hunters who tout the most potent rifles are least apt to kill with one shot. Many in the magnum crowd seem to assume a big

stick offsets mediocre marksmanship. In fact, I've heard as much: "My Ultimate-SuperMag will knock an animal down no matter where it's hit." Logic tells you this is balderdash.

First, bullets do not knock beasts to earth. A truck can. Ditto a falling tree. But animals stricken by bullets fall when they become too weak to stand, or when supporting bones are broken or the nervous system damaged so it can't control supporting muscles. A shooter of scientific bent tested this notion by gripping handles welded on a thick steel plate barely supported by a table's edge. He had confirmed the steel would stop softpoint bullets from a .458 Winchester Magnum. Using that rifle, a pal then fired at the plate, which instantly absorbed 5,000 foot-pounds of energy. The intrepid fellow holding it from behind was not knocked down. Of course, his trial carries the caveat: "Do not try this at home."

Only hits to the vitals kill humanely. Bullets that open reliably but retain most of their weight as they plow deep channels make ordinary cartridges deadly. Few animals weighing less than a ton can long survive a well-placed hit from a .30-06-class cartridge.

Women on our safaris have taken this to heart. They're uniformly careful with their shooting, in part because they're inexperienced – also because they *acknowledge* they are. Circumstantial evidence suggests many men think they were born shooting bull's-eyes. Loath to serve an apprenticeship behind a rifle, such fellows commonly attempt shots beyond their ability. "Women," observed a veteran PH, "mind fundamentals. They try to make each shot good, so they practice only good habits." He added that women "tell you when recoil hurts, when they're too tired to hold the rifle still. Men put their egos on the line."

A quick shot from her .30-06 tumbled this aged warthog for Dori. No time to get nervous!

A truly outstanding Namibian gemsbok! Encountered on an impala hunt, it dropped to one .30-06 bullet.

The Ideal Non-Magnum?

You needn't brook the recoil of even a .30-06 to hit big game hard at distance. Our first high-velocity .25-caliber rifle, Charles Newton's .250, was developed in 1912. It fired a 100-grain bullet at 2,800 fps, an 87-grain at 3,000. Ned Roberts took the high-speed notion farther in the 1920s by necking the 7x57 Mauser case to .25. The .25 Roberts was a joint effort with A.O. Neidner and F.J. Sage. By 1930 it had appeared in Griffin & Howe rifles. In 1934 Remington adopted it as the .257 Roberts, acceding to E.C. Crossman, who suggested the groove-diameter name. Remington moved the shoulder forward and increased its angle to 20 degrees.

The .257's mild disposition prompted Jack O'Connor to predict at the close of World War II that this cartridge would soon rank among the three most popular. He was wrong. The Roberts didn't match the .222 or .22-250 as a varmint round, and heavier bullets of the day didn't have the profile to retain energy far away. By the early '50s Winchester-Western had an accurate 87-grain spitzer, Remington a 100-grain pointed Core-Lokt. But Winchester's .243 was then in the works. The .244 Remington (essentially a Roberts necked down) arrived at the same time, later gaining traction as the 6mm Remington. They all but buried the .257 Roberts.

Captain Crossman praised the Roberts as a "super .250." Whelen thought the .257 Roberts adequate for black bear and caribou. O'Connor considered it superb for mule deer and bighorns. Warren Page observed darkly that the .257 was too short to match .25-06 performance, too long for short-rifle actions. He was right.

A .257 revival has accompanied new, more efficient bullets and friskier loads. These carry more than twice as much energy to 300 yards as the .44 Henry, scourge of the Confederate Army, brought to the muzzle!

They deliver more at 200 yards than most .30-30 loads at 100. And they fly as flat as 150-grain bullets from a .270. While the .243, 6mm, .260 and 7mm-08 are worthy competition, the .257 remains an overlooked prize.

.257 ROBERTS BALLISTICS

117-grain SST (Hornady)					
	muzzle	100 yds.	200 yds.	300 yds.	400 yds.
Velocity, fps	2946	2705	2478	2265	2057
Energy, ft-lbs	2253	1901	1595	1329	1099
Arc, inches	-1.5	+1.7	0	-7.6	-21.8

120-grain Nosler Partition (Federal)					
	muzzle	100 yds.	200 yds.	300 yds.	400 yds.
Velocity, fps	2780	2560	2360	2160	1970
Energy, ft-lbs	2060	1750	1480	1240	1030
Arc, inches	-1.5	+1.9	0	-8.2	-24.0

Remington's 7mm Magnum has little more recoil than a .30-06, yet shoots flatter. Very versatile!

Because women recognize that lethal hits have less to do with hardware than with marksmanship, it's easy to steer them to affordable rifles and ammo that are comfortable to shoot.

The 7mm-08 is one cartridge I expected to show up more often. It outperforms traditional loads in the 7x57mm, a 130-year-old safari veteran that in the hands of men like W.D.M. Bell, has killed game as big as elephants. Amber's 7mm-08, a Remington Model Seven, was fresh out of the box when she arrived in Namibia. "A gift from my parents." Serious about shooting it well, the young lady killed a gemsbok with one well-directed bullet, then focused her hunt on a warthog. Alas, old boars can be frustratingly elusive. They stay in thick bush, move little during the day and are easily spooked. But midweek we got a break. With her PH, Amber stole across an opening to waylay a huge boar slipping to water at thorn's edge. Her bullet struck a bit far back but angled forward. We took the track cautiously. A wounded pig can shred your legs in one rush. We found the boar down but breathing. When Amber fired again, the animal burst into action. Tusks an ivory blur in a tornado of dust, it lashed out. We jumped clear; Amber fired again. And again! Her 7mm-08 duly broken in, Amber grinned over one of the biggest warthogs I've ever seen!

We've lost few animals on women-only safaris. Still, as on any hunt, a bullet barely off the mark can mean a long trail. Dori's .30-06 downed a superb kudu and tumbled a thick-tusked warthog without a hitch. But then she stalked a blue wildebeest in fading light. Her bullet landed mid-rib. We didn't find the bull until the next morning. It had died hard. Dori shed tears. Hunters understand her reaction; people who deride hunting can't imagine how anyone who'd stalk game can care about its welfare.

When another woman lost a kudu, another a zebra, and others followed for hours to anchor poorly hit warthog, gemsbok and impala, the gloom at camp was palpable, if temporary. Neither rifles nor loads were to blame, of course. The shooter alone decides to fire, and when.

Responsibility for clean kills seems to weigh most heavily on women new to hunting. For some, the very idea of killing is a psychological challenge. Taking a life is a big thing. You can't put life back. I empathize. Hunters reluctant to kill impress me; those who fire with robotic indifference don't. Still, the kill is part of hunting. It could be argued that until you've killed, you've not completed a hunt. Certainly, until

Are You Big But Not Tough?

Having fired both gentle and violent rifles for 50 years, I've come to appreciate women and youth more, recoil less. I have more fun with .22 rimfires than with *uber*-magnums whose blast rattles rocks on adjoining hillsides. Still, my 36-inch arms and skillet-size hands aren't served by stubbed-off stocks with short, thin grips. And rifles fashioned without thought to weight distribution depress me. Balance matters in fly rods, tennis racquets, golf clubs. Certainly in upland guns. Why should rifles handle like fluorescent light fixtures? Balance, in weight and line, makes svelte rifles fit big-and-tall shooters. A slim, responsive grip needn't be close-coupled, or a short barrel muzzle-light. Sleek, comely rifles that leap to the cheek, point like a wish and bring recoil to heel before it hammers face and clavicle are like Italian sports cars. They're not big, but a lot of big people find them irresistible.

The eye for balance that makes an automobile look and feel alive can give rifles the same vitality. They're nimble, yet easy to shoot accurately. As you strip ounces, felt recoil increases. But featherweight rifles needn't kick brutally. A stock comb shaped to move off your face and a buttpad that cushions the blow and is proportioned to spread it, help you fire lightweight rifles as comfortably as if relying on mass alone to absorb kick. When a rifle rides naturally in your hands with a low center of gravity and a slight tilt to muzzle – when balance and proportion dictate design – recoil won't ruin your day.

Bearing down on a sight-in target, Donna readies her Remington. It gave her three fine trophies.

you've had the chance to kill you can't decide to take a life – or decline a shot. Unless, after much effort, you've put game in the scope, you cannot know the imperatives of a predator that define hunting.

Late one afternoon Teri and her PH were easing toward a distant gemsbok when a kudu suddenly appeared in a small opening. She settled her .300 on the sticks and fired. The animal spun and vanished in the thorn. A certain kill, we thought. But Teri hadn't allowed for the slightly quartering presentation and her bullet had damaged only the near shoulder. The PH, an excellent tracker, pressed that animal, but when it jumped from several beds we couldn't manage a lethal shot. With shooting light almost gone, the kudu collapsed just long enough for a finisher.

In the same way, Donna planted a softpoint just in front of a kudu's heart. The animal sunfished, dashing into cover already in dusk's shadow. We followed fast. I hesitated when the bull appeared, briefly – and lost my chance. The next time spiral horns popped into view I fired right away, killing the kudu as it leaped. Shot angle matters, as the vitals are a three-dimensional target, not a shadow on the ribs.

Heavy, deep-penetrating bullets can be driven faster from magnum rounds, so

they have an advantage on beefy animals like zebras and eland. Magnums may also have a slight edge in cover, where deflection can scuttle a shot. Still, the only way to ensure straight flight in thickets is to shoot *between* the branches.

Last spring in a section of dense Namibian thorn, Julie waited, her Remington on sticks, PH at her elbow. I crouched, eyes glued to an alley to their left. A big kudu lived here. We'd heard a stick snap. In that unfathomable way native hunters sense the presence of game, this PH *knew*. Half an hour passed. The bull became a horn tip, then the glint of an eye. At 26 yards, closer than we'd expected, he came clear of the bush. Julie triggered her .280 and the animal rocketed away. I saw in that instant, a hitch in its step. But the PH spied what I had not – a wrist-thick limb centered and torn asunder by a bullet. "A miss."

But the branch had been close to the rib and that off-beat snapshot of the kudu's step played back in my mind. We searched the track; I found a drop of blood. Little daylight remained so we trailed at top speed. A couple of kilometers on, the bull jumped. My bullet quartered through both lungs and we heard the crash. Julie's .280 softpoint, expanded by the branch, had deflected sharply. With less than three

yards to travel before striking the kudu it had strayed to a hind leg, just above the hock.

The Mossberg rifle I carried that day, incidentally, was a 7mm Magnum. I'm sure a .308 or even a lesser round would have dispatched the kudu. It probably would have brought Sallie's zebra to bag too. She'd paunched it, on an open plain that pulled the animal quickly out of range as she fired again. Clearly hit, the zebra plodded toward distant bush. The PH ranged the stallion at 500 yards. "Too far," I said. With no time or cover for a sneak, I dropped to my knees and began a direct approach, crawling fast. A couple of minutes later he paused at thorn's edge, now 420 yards out. I flopped prone, sling taut. Holding a foot into a light wind and adding two feet of elevation, I fired. The zebra collapsed.

For such tasks, cartridges that drive stout bullets fast and flat have a decided benefit. On the other hand, first-shot precision trumps all. And the cream of a hunt is still inside 100 yards. Quarter-mile shots come when you botch the close ones.

You don't need magnums to kill animals that fall routinely to the .30-06. Intelligent bullet choice and careful shooting yield humane kills consistently. Just ask the Safari Sisters.

The CLASSIC .44

BY **Dick Williams**
PHOTOS BY **JOHN DOUKAS**

MAGNUM

One writer's five-decade journey with the fabulous .44

ne of the good things about being older is that I've lived moments in history younger folks have only read about. Starting this article, for example, did not require any 21st century computerized "googling," but rather a stroll through my memories and a trip to my gun vault. As a young teenager I was already a longtime victim of the "gun bug" and read gun magazines voraciously, particularly anything about the newly introduced .44 Magnum. For me it was strictly a fantasy trip since any cartridge larger than a .22 Long Rifle was beyond my experience and budget. Little did I know what a huge role the .44 Magnum would play in my life.

In 1956 both Smith & Wesson and Ruger began the production of revolvers chambered for Remington's .44 Magnum, the new king of handgun cartridges. Smith's Model 29 double action was first to hit the stores, followed closely by Ruger's Blackhawk single action. The S&W was the company's "N" frame revolver, but with a stretched cylinder that filled the frame window as opposed to the shorter cylinders of the .357 Magnum. Ruger built their .44 on the existing Blackhawk, which at the time was the old style Flattop. While Smith offered the gun in three different barrel lengths, one of which was 6½ inches long, the Blackhawk was initially available only with a 6½-inch barrel; a limited number of Blackhawks were later made with 7½-inch and 10-inch barrels. At the time, having never fired or even handled either brand of gun, I knew with the absolute certainty of youth that 6½ inches was the perfect barrel length for a .44 Magnum. And while I would own a variety of .44 Magnums in different barrel lengths over the next several decades, I held that viewpoint through the mid-1960s when I finally acquired my first two .44 Magnums – one from Smith, one from Ruger, and both with 6½-inch barrels.

Ruger produced the .44 Magnum Flattop until 1962 at which time three significant (to me) things happened. First, I became a 2nd Lt. in the USAF, which meant I had an income, a portion of which I planned to spend on .44 Magnums. Second, Ruger discontinued production of the .44 Flattop but continued to offer the big Magnum in the company's larger Super Blackhawk, which had been introduced in 1959. Third, Ruger introduced the integral frame ribs on all centerfire Blackhawks. These were the "ears" that protected the

A pair of 50-year commemorative .44 Magnums from the original manufacturers that introduced the caliber to the world. When you hunt wild boar on the Tejon Ranch in southern California in the summer, you may find good use for a couple of CCI .44 Magnum shotshells on the resident rattlesnake population.

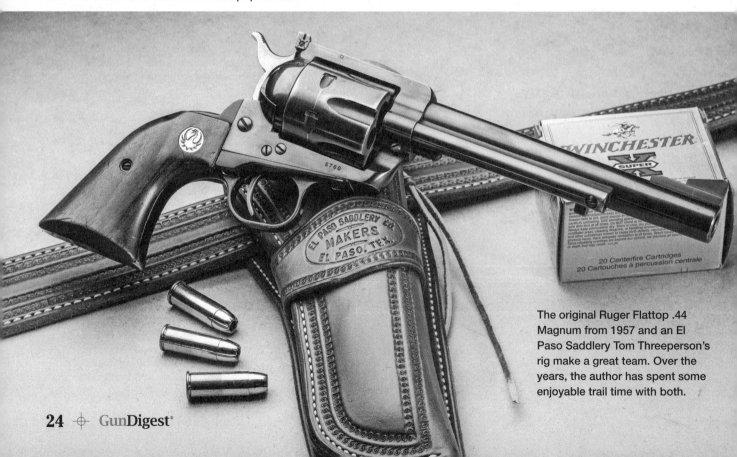

The original Ruger Flattop .44 Magnum from 1957 and an El Paso Saddlery Tom Threeperson's rig make a great team. Over the years, the author has spent some enjoyable trail time with both.

rear sight, and their introduction meant the end of the original Ruger Flattop.

Fortunately, there were some .44 Flattops in the distribution pipeline so new guns were still found in stores. More important for me, .44 Magnum revolvers, particularly the Flattops with their lightweight aluminum alloy frame, weren't all that popular since they administered a beating on anyone who shot full magnum loads. I found one on the used gun market and subsequently became acquainted with a variety of .44 Special handloads. That Ruger and I spent a fair amount of recreational time together (but not nearly as much as I would have liked) in various terrain around the country, and I never felt ill equipped. In collecting the range data for this article decades after the Flattop's discontinuation, and despite the physical abuse I've absorbed from shooting bigbore revolvers over the years, I was quite pleased to see how manageable the original lightweight magnum was when shooting the factory loads shown in the accompanying table. I wouldn't want to take the gun through a five-day defensive training program with factory magnum loads, but for hunting or any hostile social engagement of limited

duration, the old Flattop could still get the job done.

Sometime midway through the 1960s, I read an article by Bob Petersen of Petersen Publications about a brown bear hunt on Kodiak Island using a Smith & Wesson .44 Magnum with a 6½-inch barrel. It was one of two gun articles from that time frame that had a huge influence on my handgun interests, and I became obsessed with obtaining a Smith .44 Magnum. With a 6½-inch barrel, of course.

By the '70s I had become a civilian and was spending more time camping and hunting. For strictly daylight events, I preferred the crisp sight picture presented by the Ruger's black sights. The reduced lighting of early morning or late afternoon outings favored the red plastic insert of the Smith's front sight. All of my .44 Magnum shooting was handled by one bullet and two handloads. The Ruger produced 1,000 feet per second with the Lyman hard cast Keith bullet over Unique powder, while the Smith yielded 1,200 fps with the same cast bullet over a subsequently discontinued ball powder, Winchester 630. The Ruger handled rabbits, javelina and other small

game in Colorado and Arizona while the Smith took several deer and antelope in Colorado and Wyoming.

When Ruger installed the transfer-bar system in all newly manufactured Blackhawks in 1973, it had no immediate effect on me. I still had my old Flattop and was accustomed to loading the six-shot cylinder with only five rounds, keeping an empty chamber under the lowered hammer for safety. Interestingly, this was exactly 100 years after Colt had begun teaching Americans the concept of loading single-action revolvers with five rounds instead of six. You'd think the ability to safely load an extra round would have been embraced by all, but that was not the case. To this day, there are devout single-action traditionalists who consider the transfer bar system an abomination. The fact that the new feature changed the Blackhawk's (and Super Blackhawk's) appearance by deleting one of the externally visible frame screws didn't bother me. Some of the early six-shooters did have rather rough triggers, but any reasonably competent gunsmith could take care of that quickly and easily. New Rugers I've tried in the last several years have come from the factory

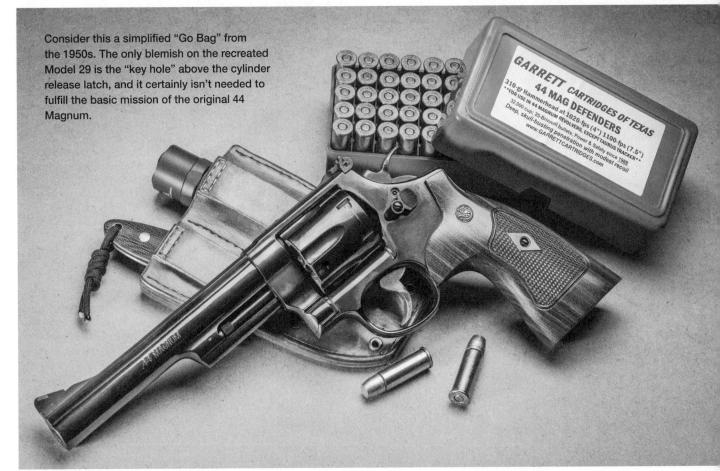

Consider this a simplified "Go Bag" from the 1950s. The only blemish on the recreated Model 29 is the "key hole" above the cylinder release latch, and it certainly isn't needed to fulfill the basic mission of the original 44 Magnum.

Both the S&W stainless Classic 629 (top) and the 1957 Ruger Flattop (bottom) produced nice groups using modern .44 Magnum ammunition. Reminds one of the old saying, "These dogs can still hunt!"

with much improved triggers, including the re-released Flattops introduced after the year 2000. More on that later.

In the mid '70s, handgun metallic silhouettes arrived on the scene and my shooting world blossomed. My favorite event was the production gun standing class, and while I tried a number of different guns in this, the outstanding performer was the 6½-inch barreled Smith & Wesson. I would love to have used the Ruger, but by then I had cut its barrel to 4¾ inches to make it handier for outings in the high Rockies, and any external modifications on production guns were prohibited. No matter, the Smiths (I had bought a second, nickel-plated Model 29 with 6½-inch barrel) excelled, and the silhouette matches did wonders for my shooting skills in the hunting fields.

My .44 Magnums did a lot of competitive shooting in the late '70s and into the '80s. The Denver area had another magnum match, which involved shooting a series of targets that became gradually smaller as the match progressed. Targets were placed at 100 yards and the first three targets were shot offhand. On the final target – the smallest – shooters were allowed to sit and rest their backs against the shooting bench. If you were behind going into the last stage, it wasn't likely you'd be able to catch up because once braced, several competitors were able to clean the stage. It was a useful event for anyone planning on handgun hunting, as it was in the late '70s that Colorado legalized hunting big game with handguns.

That was the same time the International Practical Shooting Confederation appeared on the scene in our area, and having never been to a "run-and-gun" shooting event, I showed up with my 6½-inch Smith & Wesson. Talk about feeling out of place; I was like Elmer Fudd attending a formal dinner party wearing his red plaid hunting jacket. There were a couple of long-range targets in the match, so I didn't totally embarrass myself, but it was an early lesson in choosing the right gun for the right mission. I dug out my 1911 for future close-range action events, but to this day, it's almost always a .44 Magnum that accompanies me when civilization gets left behind.

In the early '80s, Smith & Wesson made some internal changes to beef up the Model 29s. Handgun silhouette competition provided the first real durability tests for the big .44 and there were numerous reports of problems associated with prolonged use of magnum loads. Prior to this, most owners (even Dirty Harry) practiced with .44 Special ammo and only loaded up with magnums for the serious work like hunting, or in Harry's case, for decisive felony stops. The internal changes were a big improvement. Somewhere in that same time frame, the 6½-inch barrel length on S&W .44 Magnums changed to an even 6 inches. I was older and more mature by this time, so I didn't get too upset by this change. Besides, unless two guns are held side by side, I have trouble telling the difference between the two models.

Into the '80s, I drifted away from handgun silhouette shooting, partly because I had two teenage kids involved in weekend athletic events and partly because the family wanted to do more high-country camping on the remaining weekends. But my handgun hunting became even more intense, with fall big-game hunts for deer, antelope and elk, plus a couple of small-game hunts every year in Arizona. While I did use some specialized single-shot handguns on many of those trips, the true sidearm on almost every outing was still either the Ruger Flattop or the S&W .44 Magnum. This continued through the late '80s when disaster struck. There was a job change that required me to move back to California. Just before leaving Colorado, I ran into some silver-tongued devil at a gun show who talked me into selling my chopped Ruger Flattop. To top it off, I traded the 6½-inch Smiths toward some newer model Model 29s. I returned to California a broken man!

I was doing some freelance professional gun writing by then ("professional" meaning I was now getting paid for articles), so most of my shooting and hunting was done with handguns approved for articles. Many of those guns were not .44 Magnums, but rather the new super powerful magnum revolvers – .454, .475, etc. – or some very interesting

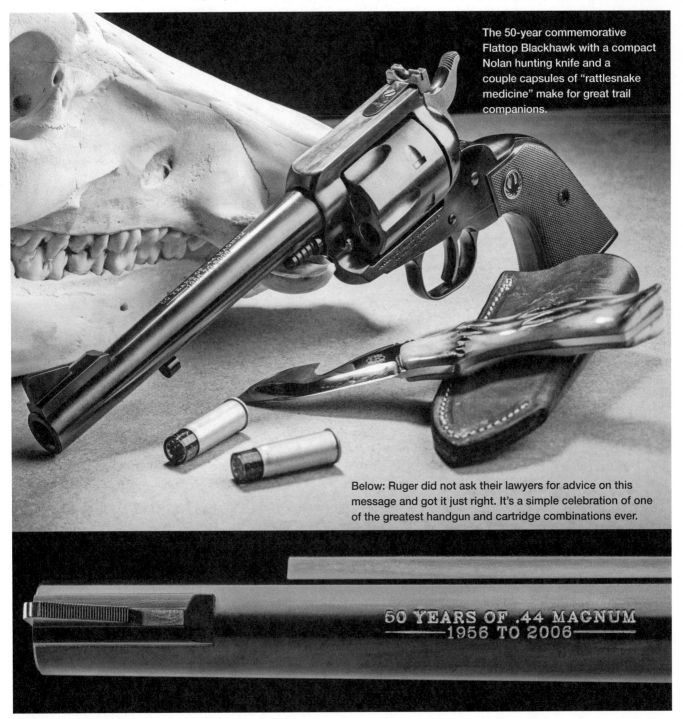

The 50-year commemorative Flattop Blackhawk with a compact Nolan hunting knife and a couple capsules of "rattlesnake medicine" make for great trail companions.

Below: Ruger did not ask their lawyers for advice on this message and got it just right. It's a simple celebration of one of the greatest handgun and cartridge combinations ever.

50 YEARS OF .44 MAGNUM
—1956 TO 2006—

SHOOTING COMPARISONS

Velocities from a Chrony chronograph 10 feet from muzzle, ambient temperature 66 degrees. Guns used were an original Ruger Flattop .44 and a new Model 29 from S&W's classic series.

.44 Magnum

Load	Velocities (fps)	
	Ruger	S&W
Federal 240 gr. Hi-Shok	1,358	1,309
Garrett 310 gr. Hard Cast	1,053	1,038
Hornady 225 gr. FTX	1,431	1,437
Winchester 240 gr. Hollow soft point	1,306	1,241

.44 Special

Load	Velocities (fps)	
	Ruger	S&W
Blazer 200 gr. JHP	807	757
Winchester 200 gr. Silvertip HP	767	739
Load	5 Shot group size at 25 Yards	
Garret 310 gr. Hard Cast	2.6"	2.4"
Blazer 200 gr. JHP	2.5"	2.7"
Winchester 200 gr. Silvertip	2.1"	2.0"

high-performance single-shot handguns. However, there were also some writing assignments on both Ruger and S&W .44 Magnums, which gave me some opportunities to get acquainted with the new generation .44s from both companies. Smith & Wesson added some very useful attributes like full-barrel-length under lugs that helped reduce muzzle flip and rubber grips that helped absorb felt recoil. They also rounded the backstrap, a boon for short-fingered people like me. When the 5-inch barrel with rounded backstrap and full under lug was introduced, I knew instantly I'd found my new favorite double-action .44 Magnum – or rather it had found me.

Ruger was not making a Blackhawk in .44 Magnum then, but they did round the Dragoon-style triggerguard on the Super Blackhawk, which was both instantly visible and highly effective in preventing the beating the middle finger of my shooting hand used to take with heavy loads. The new .44s were so interesting I acquired some customized versions of both brands that are among my favorite firearms to this day. And while I stayed busy shooting, hunting and sort of collecting, there was still that big hole in my memory and my gun vault. You don't just get rid of irreplaceable classics and go on with life like nothing has happened.

The 50-year commemorative Model 29 proudly bears the gold inlaid S&W logo. Gun and caliber are two of the all-time great achievements in handgunning.

The modern Model 629 from S&W isn't just about memories. Whatever the weather, you can carry it afield all day in one of Galco's modern shoulder holsters safely stored under your rain parka.

A few years into the new millennium I was saved. Both Ruger and S&W brought out classic reproductions of the Flattop and the Model 29. I don't think it was in my honor, but the Smith & Wesson featured a 6½-inch barrel and the Ruger Flattop had my new favorite barrel length, 4¾ inches. In 2006, both companies celebrated the 50th anniversary of the .44 Magnum with commemorative editions. The Model 29 was almost original, as was the Flattop, and both guns had 6½-inch barrels!

While both companies did a good job recreating the original look, there were some differences with both guns, the most obvious being the engraving. Ruger put a gold colored written message on the barrel, and no, it wasn't the old legal department message to read the manual before you think of touching the gun. It simply says "50 YEARS OF .44 MAGNUM" and right below that "1956 – 2006." The Flattop also has the modern transfer-bar system and a steel grip frame that makes it a bit heavier than the original .44 Flattop, but both these changes contribute to the gun's shootability, and I'm OK with them. So far I've been unable to take the gun on a field trip since the

.44 is one of two guns in a set of Flattop Commemoratives, both of which have the same serial number. The other is a Flattop Blackhawk .357 Magnum with a 4¾-inch barrel, and I haven't put a round through it yet either.

Like the Ruger, the commemorative Smith & Wesson has some gold inlaid engraving, in this case a S&W logo on the right side panel behind the cylinder. Above the logo is printed, "50th ANNIVERSARY SMITH & WESSON," and below the logo is "1956-2006 .44 MAGNUM." The gun has the original target hammer and trigger along with wood S&W logo grips that expose the backstrap and are slightly thinner than the wood grips on the original Model 29s. The only blemish (and it's a big one in the eyes of many Smith fans) is the "key hole" in the left side panel that allows the action to be locked up with the factory supplied key. I used the word "blemish" because it's hard to believe that anyone would punch an ugly hole in such a beautiful gun on purpose. Another example as to why lawyers should not be allowed to design firearms! Still, like the Flattop, I haven't been able to drag the Smith out for a shooting session yet. My resolve is weakening on both

guns, and I think the right occasion will see the guns sending rounds downrange in the near future. In the meantime, I've shot noncommemorative remakes of both guns joyously, and have even put some loving bumps and scratches on the short-barreled Ruger Flattop on hog hunts at Tejon Ranch and in Texas.

Most of my .44 Magnum dreams have been fulfilled in the 58 years since the caliber was first introduced. Numerous deer, antelope, hogs, javelina and rabbits have fallen to my favorite magnum on hunts within the continental U.S. An Alaskan brown bear and caribou fell to handguns in other calibers, but one deer was taken with a .44 Magnum from a boat in the inland channels. Some heads and hides of African plains game decorate my man-cave, although the Cape Buffalo sadly is not among them. This single disappointment has been tempered by a successful Australian hunt for Asian Buffalo that also accounted for numerous down-under hogs. I may never take that African buff or even go hunting again with either of my two classic .44s, but as long as I feel younger than I am, who knows? It's a reasonably sure bet we haven't had our last outing.

THE EVER-CHANGING

The author started his hunting career with the 7mm Rem. Magnum, this one built around the Swedish Carl Gustaf barreled action.

BY **Jon R. Sundra**

PERFECT CARTRIDGE

A writer's evolution in his search for the ideal big-game cartridge

Long ago in a galaxy far, far away…

Actually, it wasn't that long ago or far away that I had a conversation with Jack O'Connor at what I believe was the last Remington Writers' Seminar he attended before his death in January of 1978. So I'm talking early to mid-70s. We were discussing rifle cartridges, and of course Jack's beloved .270 immediately came up.

Basically, what Jack told me was that he kinda regretted that so many of his readers so closely associated him with the .270. A lot of it was his fault, he said, because he had written so glowingly about it, but he told me he considered the 7mm Remington Magnum better, and the .30-06 more versatile. What he regretted was that whenever he'd say something

to that effect, his readers reacted like he was committing heresy. "It's like I'm not allowed to change my mind, even though technology is constantly bringing us new guns and new cartridges."

That conversation with Jack comes to mind whenever I write about how my idea of the perfect cartridge has evolved over the years. By "perfect" I mean perfect for me. I must confess that my 50-year odyssey has been remarkably consistent – some would say boringly so, in that it has been limited almost exclusively to one caliber, the 7mm. But that is not without the perspective and field experience garnered having used every game caliber from 6mm to .416 on game ranging from groundhogs to elephants.

Why 7mm, and not .30 or .270? It was simply a nonempirical conclusion I had

come to in my late teens and early 20s, based on having devoured every gun magazine in print for a period of four or five years. I literally had the ballistics charts memorized! No one writer had any more influence on me than another, but it was 1962 when Remington rolled out its 7mm Magnum that my love affair with the bore size began. I want to say that under different circumstances, I could just as easily have become a .30-caliber guy, but that wouldn't be truthful. At that time the 7mm was still considered a "foreign" caliber and hadn't achieved much acceptance here in .30-caliber America. I guess that's why I was so predisposed to it.

It's not like I didn't have experience with other calibers at the time, but what I did have was very limited. Unlike many

The author has used all of these 7mms in the field (left to right): 7mm-08, 7x57mm, .284 Win., .280 Rem., 7mm Rem. Magnum, 7mm Weatherby Magnum, 7mm Dakota, 7mm WSM, 7mm Rem. SAUM and 7.21 Lazzeroni Tomahawk.

Sundra took this double-shovel caribou with a 7mm JRS built on a Sako action. It's one of four rifles he has owned that were so chambered.

of my colleagues who grew up on farms or ranches where they were able to start shooting and hunting at an early age, I had no such opportunities growing up on Cleveland's east side. It was not until graduating from high school and getting my driver's license that I was able to get out into the hinterlands of northern Ohio and hunt groundhogs. During a 3½-year hiatus between high school and college I had managed to scrape up enough money to have acquired a Marlin Levermatic in .256 Win. Magnum. I eventually replaced the Marlin with a Remington 722 in .257 Roberts, and soon thereafter had it rebarreled to .22-250, which was a wildcat at the time. By then I was an avid handloader.

Also by then, 1961, I had entered Ohio State University and was in the process of putting together a 6mm Remington.

Maybe it was just my natural contrariness, but the .243 Winchester was all the rage in those days as being the perfect dual-purpose caliber. I, however, saw the floundering .244 Rem./6mm Rem. as the superior cartridge, assuming it was built on a standard-length action, fitted with a 1:10-inch twist barrel, and throated to allow seating 100-grain bullets out where they belonged. Which is what I did. I bought a commercial Mauser action and had Flaig's in Millvale, Pa. barrel it for me. I then stocked it myself using a Fajen Regent semishaped and inletted stock. I couldn't realistically plan on hunting anything but deer for at least awhile after graduation, so the 6mm was the ideal caliber for me at that time in my life. It served me well on varmints, predators, whitetails, mule deer and black bear until 1968; by then I had graduated

and was living in western Pennsylvania and had made hunting trips to Wyoming, Montana and Quebec.

But, like I said before, it was four years earlier in late 1962 that a seminal moment arrived for me with the introduction of the 7mm Remington Magnum. If the word "sexy" could be applied to a rifle cartridge, this was it. Not only did it look fast, it was fast. The big, belted case pushed a 150-grain bullet out at 3,260 fps. Those were the days when factory ballistics were established in 26-inch barrels, accompanied by a dash of optimism. When 24 inches became the standard in 1970-something, that figure was reduced to 3,100 fps. But then so too were the stats for all other commercial cartridges, so the performance edge over popular rounds like the .270 and .30-06 was still there. I was so enamored with the cartridge that I doodled pictures of it in the margins of my college textbooks. I still have one of those books.

By the time I made what I considered my first genuine big-game hunt—a caribou hunt in Labrador in 1968 —I had built up my first of what would eventually be four 7mm Mags. The first was on a BSA action from Herter's; one was a stock Ruger No. 1B; one was on a Sako action; and yet another was on a Carl Gustaf barreled action.

By the mid `70s and after having made my first African hunt, I became disenchanted with the 7mm Mag., but not because it failed me in any way. On the contrary, everything I pointed it at simply dropped either in its tracks or within a short distance. And I'm talking big stuff like kudu, gemsbok, hartebeest and zebra. It just reaffirmed my belief that for anything short of dangerous game, a 7mm bullet of 140 to 160 grains, depending on the critter, was enough gun. Whether or not I realized it at the time, I had developed a minimalist attitude about cartridges. I never wanted to be undergunned, but packing a .300 Magnum for deer or a .375 for elk simply didn't appeal to me, even though it would have completely eliminated any questions about cartridge adequacy.

Nope, the reason I became disenchanted with the 7 Mag was because I believed the belted case, which had become so synonymous with magnums in those days, had outlived its usefulness. Its whole raison d'etre was to provide a definitive forward surface for purposes of headspace, nothing more.

Back around the turn of the 20th century, large-caliber cartridges had long, sloping shoulders that precluded their use as a datum line for headspacing. Rimmed cases were the answer, but with the emergence of Mauser's box magazine, the rimmed cases of the day would not allow cartridges to slide against one another. The belt, which only protrudes .010" was enough to provide a definite stopping surface for a chambered cartridge, yet not enough to impede cartridge feed from magazine to chamber.

For the nonhandloader, the presence of a belt makes absolutely no difference whatsoever, but from the handloading standpoint, a beltless case is actually better for minor technical reasons we haven't the space to go into here.

In 1978 I again left for Africa, this time with a standard .280 Remington. It wasn't quite the equal of the 7 Mag, but I felt the 150 fps difference was no big thing. Again, everything I pointed it at dropped—kudu, gemsbok, zebra, wildebeest, etc., and nothing required tracking.

In 1979 I had a Ruger Model 77 barreled in .284 Winchester, a case I always thought to be of superior design. It was the first commercial cartridge to use a 35-degree shoulder, which I thought was ideal. I, of course, based it on a standard length rather than a short action, and had it throated accordingly. Unfortunately, I learned the .284's severely rebated rim can cause feeding problems in a staggered-row box magazine. The rifle was finished at the last minute and I didn't have time to really test its feeding reliability before leaving for Africa. That

little oversight almost got me eaten by a lion, but for all the other plains game in Zambia, it performed with typical 7mm lethality, including a 1,500-pound eland that dropped after running only 40 yards.

Two years earlier, in preparation for my first safari to Rhodesia, Cape buffalo was on the agenda and for that chore I wanted to use a .375. But I didn't like the fact that the H&H version, with its sloping case body and slight shoulder, didn't take full advantage of the available case capacity. Just as I was about to decide between the old .375 Weatherby and the wildcat .375 Mashburn, Remington announced its 8mm Rem. Magnum. Suddenly I had a readily available "improved" H&H case, i. e., with a minimum body taper and a

Once again, the 7mm did a fine job anchoring this handsome Kudu on one of the author's African hunts.

This nice Zambian Buff (or Sable) fell to Sundra's .375 JRS. He now considers the .375 Ruger to be a better and more practical cartridge.

sharp shoulder. I simply necked it up from .323 to .375. Thus was born the 375 JRS.

The rifle I chose was another Ruger No. 1 in .375 H&H, which I simply had rechambered. That cartridge was capable of pushing a 300-grain bullet close to 2,700 fps, which was a damn sight better than the 2,530 the H&H could deliver. I have since come to favor the .375 Ruger as the best medium-bore cartridge for all African big game, with the exception of elephant. It will do everything my .375 JRS can do and then some, and in a standard-length action. It would also be my choice for Alaska's big bears.

Upon returning from my first safari to Zambia, where I used the aforementioned .284 Win., I decided to go back to the .280 Remington, but an improved version thereof, the .280 RCBS. How-

In 1977 Remington took the .375 H&H Magnum case at left and improved it by reducing body taper and sharpening the shoulder. The result was the 8mm Rem. Magnum, which became the basis for Sundra's .375 JRS. He now considers the beltless, standard-length Ruger version at right to be the perfect .375.

ever, I immediately realized that simply improving the .280 Rem. case — reducing the body taper and sharpening the shoulder — increased case capacity by just a couple of grains, which translated to a scant 50 fps over the stock .280. So I set out to design another wildcat to take maximum advantage of the .280 case.

Starting with the stock .280 Remington case, I simply specified to the Clymer people to cut me a reamer that would result in a case that would have a .015-inch body taper, and extend a 35-degree shoulder forward to where I'd have a .300-inch neck. The net result was a case that had about 6 percent greater capacity than the .280 Ackley Improved.

Over the next decade I built three rifles, one on a Remington 700 action, one on a Sako and one on a Model 70. All have magazines long enough that I could seat bullets up to 160 grains to where there was very little infringement on powder space. All were throated accordingly and all three would yield 3,100 fps with a 150-grain bullet from a 24-inch barrel. I used those guns almost exclusively for the next decade to take game on four continents.

By the early 1990s, beltless cases of magnum capacity finally came upon the scene. Most were based on an improved

Starting with the stock .280 Rem. at left, Jon went to the .280 Rem. Improved RCBS, then the .280 Ackley Improved, then designed his own 7mm JRS. He says his version maximizes the .280 Remington's case capacity, yet has a neck length of more than one caliber, and an optimum shoulder angle of 35 degrees.

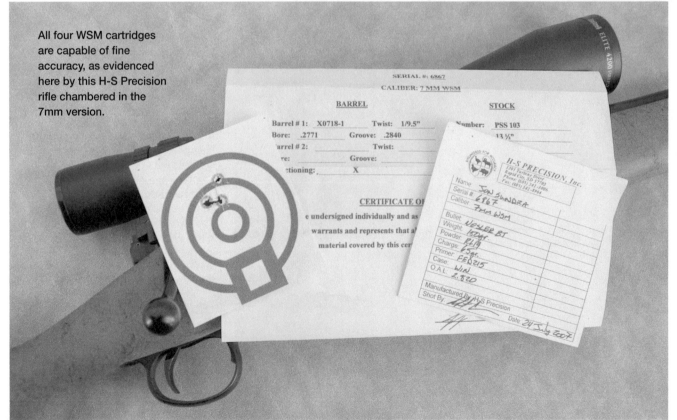

All four WSM cartridges are capable of fine accuracy, as evidenced here by this H-S Precision rifle chambered in the 7mm version.

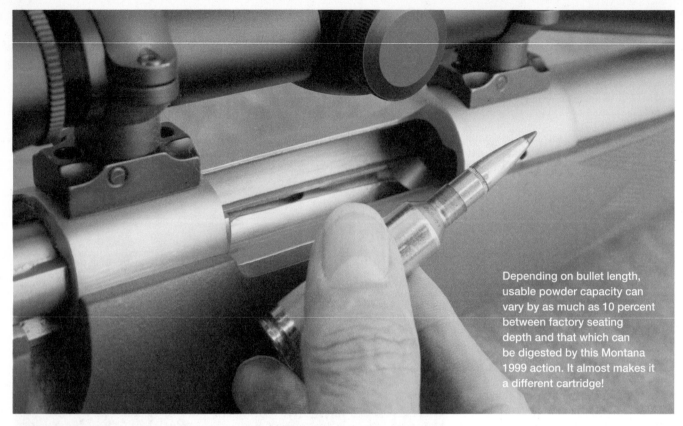

Depending on bullet length, usable powder capacity can vary by as much as 10 percent between factory seating depth and that which can be digested by this Montana 1999 action. It almost makes it a different cartridge!

The factory 7mm WSM at left is loaded to the maximum overall cartridge length of 2.8 inches. Next to it is a Hornady 154 gr. SST and a 150 gr. Barnes TSX. Note how deeply they must be seated to fit a short action. At right is the length accepted by the Winchester and Montana short actions.

version of the British .404 Jeffery case, which had a head diameter of .540-.550, with slightly rebated rims of .532, so that they matched existing belted magnum bolt faces. Imperial Cartridge of Canada was the first to offer a line of cartridges based on such a case, followed by Dakota Arms and John Lazzeroni. All required either standard or magnum-length actions. I soon had a Ruger No. 1 barreled in 7mm Dakota, then rebarreled again in the mid-90s to Lazzeroni's short-action 7.21 Tomahawk. John was the first to introduce a line of short, beltless magnums, preceding Winchester by several years.

All the aforementioned machinations were the result of my searching for what could be the perfect cartridge for me. That search came to an end in 2001 when Winchester introduced its .300 WSM (Winchester Short Magnum). Before you could buy a Winchester Model 70 or Browning A-Bolt chambered in .300

Above: Three of Jon's 7mm rifle battery (top to bottom): a Montana Rifle Co. 7mm WSM, a Bansner 7mm WSM on a Model 70 short action and a custom Ruger No.1 in 7.21 Lazzeroni Tomahawk. All are wearing 6X fixed-power scopes – Nikon, Sightron and Leupold.

Left: The author has never found the 7mm bore wanting in nearly 50 years of hunting non-dangerous game with it almost exclusively. This Cooksen's Wildebeest fell to a 7mm WSM built on a Ruger standard-length action.

optimal bullet seating. Thankfully, there are two: Winchester's own short Model 70 and the Montana Rifle Company's Model 1999, which is a hybrid version of the Winchester. Both have magazines that allow overall cartridge lengths of 3-1/8 inches. I've owned several such 7mm WSM rifles, some based on standard-length actions as well, all throated accordingly, and all were able to coax 3,150 fps for 150-grain bullets through 24-inch barrels.

For more than 10 years now, nothing has come along that has made me change my concept of the perfect cartridge, but even at that, it takes a specific rifle to make it so. How can you get any nebbier than that!

I, of course, continue to field and bench test every new rifle and cartridge that does come along, but like I said, nothing thus far has changed my mind. Sure, there are more potent 7mms and .30s out there, but maximum velocity has never been my criteria. If it were, I'd be shooting the 7mm Ultra Mag. No, there's more to it than that.

To me, cartridge efficiency, case design, bullet selection, trajectory, energy retention, all contribute to the equation. When I punch in all those factors and hit compute, for me it comes out 7mm WSM every time.

WSM, I had necked it down to 7mm and soon thereafter took it to Africa in 2002. Winchester, of course, rolled out its 7mm version that same year.

When I said "could be" the perfect cartridge, the factory-loaded WSMs do not bring out the full potential of the case because they're all factory loaded to a cartridge length of 2.8 inches to fit the magazines of your typical short magnum action. As such, even medium-weight bullets (150 grain in 7mm) have to be seated to where they seriously infringe on usable powder space. Every millimeter the base of the bullet juts down into otherwise usable powder

space, you in effect make the case smaller than it is. Being the efficiency weenie I am, that has always been unacceptable.

Now there are many who would say, just barrel any standard-length action and as a handloader you can seat the pills as shallow as you want. But then there are others who would say that in doing so you defeat the whole premise behind the short magnum. Both are legitimate concerns.

What's required, then, to realize the full potential of any short magnum is the perfect action; one with a bolt stroke and magazine length that allows

THE HOLSTERS OF ARVO OJALA

The real "Fastest Gun in the West" and his Hollywood holsters

BY **Rick Hacker**

U nless you've been living under a tumbleweed, you know that the American frontier was largely a land of myths. In fact, the wildest thing about the Wild West was the yarns it could spin about itself, especially when it came to legends of high-noon showdowns and gunmen who were "faster than greased lightning." In the real West, if an hombre were naïve enough to call you out on the streets at 12 o'clock with your sixguns buckled on, you'd show up a little early, wait for him behind a barricade of wooden crates, and cut him down with both barrels of a sawed-off shotgun the minute he stepped into view.

That's not to say there weren't some gunfighters who could hit what they aimed at and do it in fairly short order. James Butler "Wild Bill" Hickok and Luke Short are two who immediately come to

This studio publicity photo, taken in 1959 on the Warner Bros. backlot shows many of the studio's top Western TV stars of the day. Left To Right: Will Hutchins (Sugarfoot), Peter Brown (Lawman), Jack Kelly (Bart Maverick), Ty Hardin (Bronco), James Garner (Bret Maverick), Wayde Preston (Colt .45), John Russell (Lawman). All are wearing Arvo Ojala holsters.

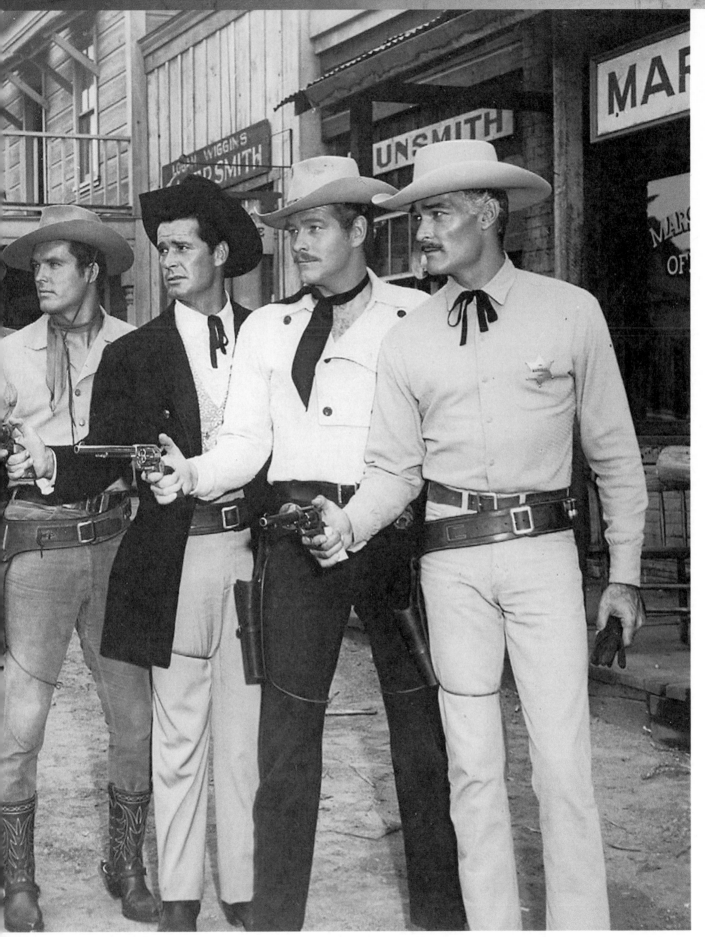

Right: The author has had years of experience using Ojala holsters. Here he is in the late 1950s or early '60s with his first Ojala holster (albeit worn on a gunbelt made by a local shoe shop). Today, with a different second-generation Colt single action and a different pre-'64 Winchester 94 carbine, Hacker still wears an Ojala holster, in fact, he has more than one. Color photo by Joan Hacker.

Arvo Ojala, in a late 1950s publicity photo taken on the *Gunsmoke* Dodge City set.

ARVO OJALA

ley, as a young boy Ojala would practice his marksmanship by shooting the heads off of rattlesnakes, he recalled years later. Whether or not this was another western legend doesn't matter, because his extreme skill with a sixgun is a matter of record, as witnessed in person and on film.

The first time I met Arvo was on the set of a western being filmed just outside Phoenix, Ariz. A few years earlier I had organized a fast-draw group in high school called the Arizona Young Guns, and had just returned from performing a trick shooting demonstration for the *Lew King Rangers*, a popular Phoenix television program on KPHO. As this was during a time when (from 1958 through 1961) the three top-rated TV shows were *Gunsmoke, Have Gun, Will Travel* and *Wagon Train*, and it was possible to

watch back-to-back westerns on network television every day of the week, Arvo was well known among the fast-draw crowd. After all, he was the guy who faced down Matt Dillon every week during the opening scene of *Gunsmoke*, and taught Hugh O'Brian in *The Life and Legend of Wyatt Earp* how to yank his 12-inch Buntline Special from its elongated holster with the same polished speed as if unsheathing a rapier.

At that first meeting, Arvo taught me the basics of his fast draw technique. During our lesson, he drew his single-action Colt and fired three shots so rapidly they sounded like one, thumbing the first shot as the barrel cleared leather, raking the hammer against the drop of his holster for the second shot, and fanning the third. Naturally all of this was done with studio 5-in-1 blanks – the only thing

mind. There were others, of course, but none of them were what one would call "fast guns," as personified by the dime novels of the era and later, to an even greater extent by Hollywood. And yet, it was during the Golden Age of Television Westerns – a period that began on June 24, 1949 with *Hopalong Cassidy* on NBC, and ended on Sept. 1, 1975 with the final episode of *Gunsmoke* – that viewers not only saw, but were often able to emulate some of fastest and fanciest gunwork that never existed in the Old West.

Part of the reason the old-time gunfighters weren't as fast on the draw as many of their celluloid successors was that they simply did not have the holsters that made a fast draw possible. And while some would-be gunfighters coated the insides of their holsters with grease and trimmed away leather to get their sixshooters into action quicker, these embellishments could work against them when mounted on a galloping horse or taking a tumble during a barroom brawl and finding their sixgun was no longer there.

And yet, there was one individual who finally made the legend of the fast draw a reality. His name was Arvo Ojala, and it has been verified that he could draw, fire and hit his target with a Colt Single Action Army in one-sixth of a second. Born of Finnish parents (the correct pronunciation of his last name is Oh-JAH-La) and growing up on their apple farm in Washington's Yakima Val-

Shown here is a rare basket-weave-stamped Ojala holster.

anyone in his or her right mind would ever use for fast draw.

In addition to his reflexes, the key to Arvo's speed with a single action was the holster he created and eventually patented. In the 19th century West, the gun belt was normally looped through the holster, which was worn high on the hip. By the time of the B-westerns of the early 20th century, the buscadero rig had made its appearance. This was a wider gunbelt, which featured a slotted drop through which the holster was threaded, thus keeping it stationary on the belt. But between the late 1940s and early 1950s Ojala had been bringing the buscadero to a new level of sophistication, inspired by the need for a gun rig dedicated solely to the art of fast draw.

Aware of the growing popularity of westerns and the tremendous inroads of television as a household medium, Arvo came to Hollywood in 1950, where his gun expertise enabled him to find work as a stuntman along with bit parts as a gunslinger. One day, while spinning his single action in and out of the holster in-between takes, Arvo was approached by a producer who asked him to be the gun coach on his next western. Thus began Arvo's career as a preeminent Hollywood fast-draw artist. But it wasn't so much in front of the camera that Arvo found fame – it was with his sixgun skill off the screen, a dexterity made even more dramatic thanks to a unique holster he finally perfected in 1952, the Hollywood Fast Draw Holster, a gun rig that had the potential of speeding up even the slowest draw in real time, without having to resort to trick photography or cutaways.

Unlike other rigs, Arvo's Hollywood Fast Draw Holster was a slimmed-down buscadero-style rig constructed of double leather, which gave it durability. The holster, which featured a three-inch drop, was gracefully sculpted to leave the triggerguard and hammer completely exposed. Although many users of his rig wore their guns low in traditional Hollywood gunfighter fashion, Arvo designed his gun belt to be worn straight across the waist so that it didn't sag (other than a slight dip caused by the weight of the gun), thus placing the gun close to the shooter's hand, so that precious seconds weren't wasted reaching for it. Perfectly positioned, when the thumb of the relaxed gun hand was extended 90 degrees to the side, it would rest across the deepest curve of the hammer.

The other secret to Arvo's fast-draw

Arvo Ojala's 1958 booklet, *The Secrets of the Fast Draw* illustrated his step-by-step techniques. Note in the photo sequence that the trigger finger stays outside the triggerguard before the gun clears the holster. Ojala's technique keeps movement to a minimum while stressing safety through the draw.

technique was a steel lining sandwiched between the double leather of the upper cylinder portion of the holster and extending through the drop. The steel lining kept the holster leather from coming in contact with the cylinder. This not only resulted in a friction-free draw, it permitted the single action to be cocked while the gun was still holstered and before the draw was completed, thus enabling the gun to be fired the instant the muzzle cleared leather. At the start of the draw, the gun hand sweeps back, with the thumb contacting the hammer and bringing it to full cock as the bottom three fingers grasp the grip and draw the gun, with the trigger finger positioned outside the guard and along the frame as the gun is drawn and leveled, at which point the trigger finger enters the guard and touches off the shot. Of

course, Arvo's technique is only done with blanks – never with live ammo. And needless to say, a well-tuned gun is paramount to a fast draw.

The result was that no more precious seconds were wasted drawing the gun first and then cocking the hammer; or getting the gun snagged by a tight holster. In addition, the steel-lined drop enabled the holster to be perfectly positioned, ideally angling the grip out and slightly away from the gunbelt. Arvo filed for a patent on this design on Aug. 29, 1956, and on April 29, 1958 he was granted patent number 2832519. Even so, Arvo was not the first to feature a metal-lined fast-draw holster. In the 1940s trick-shooter Ed McGivern used a steel-reinforced S.D. Myers buscadero rig for exhibition work, and later, famous Hollywood outfitter Edward H. Bohlin

incorporated steel linings in some of his fast-draw rigs. But unfortunately for Bohlin, the noted "Saddlemaker and Silversmith To The Stars" never patented his steel-lined holsters and as a result, Arvo became the first to legally protect the idea, thereby winning a 1960s lawsuit by Bohlin.

But the controversy didn't end there. Two of Arvo's original craftsmen – Andy Anderson and Alfonso Piñeda – eventually left Arvo and started fast-draw holster companies of their own (with the late Andy Anderson's Walk And Draw rigs perhaps being more notable, while today Alfonso's son Omar continues making many of the original patterns in which metal linings are often used - www. alfonsosgunleather.com). Plus, during the 1960s the no-longer-existing Pony Express Sports Shop on Ventura Boule-

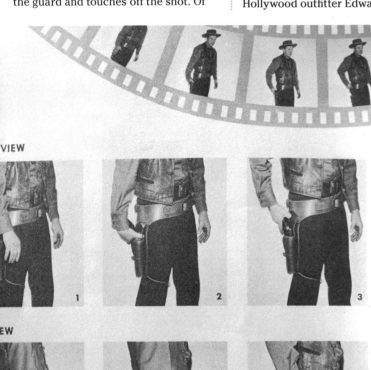

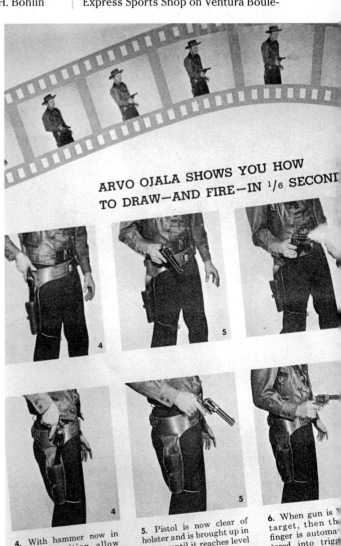

ARVO OJALA SHOWS YOU HOW TO DRAW—AND FIRE—IN 1/6 SECOND

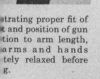

...strating proper fit of ...t and position of gun ...tion to arm length, ...arms and hands ...tely relaxed before ...g.

2. Wrist bent toward gun until thumb is horizontal with the hammer-spur. The first joint of thumb pressing hammer back. The trigger finger alongside of trigger guard, to prevent accidental firing. The last three fingers grasping the gun butt.

3. Thumb continues backward pressure on hammer while gun is being drawn.

4. With hammer now in *full cock* position, allow thumb to slip off hammer to help grip gun butt. Trigger finger is held alongside trigger guard for safety.

5. Pistol is now clear of holster and is brought up in an arc until it reaches level on target. NOTE: Trigger finger is still outside of trigger guard for safety, which also aids in pointing the gun accurately and quickly for "fast draw hip shooting".

6. When gun is ...target, then th... finger is automa... tered into trigg... and trigger is sq... firing). Your... slightly bent fo... natural balance...

vard in Encino, Calif. produced a limited number of fast-draw rigs that featured a leather-covered steel strip encircling the outside of a single-thickness holster, which also had a metal strip sewn into the drop. Ironically, the Pony Express rigs were made by a Bohlin employee in his spare time.

But it was Arvo's holsters that were eventually seen on practically every TV western, including *Gunsmoke* – in which James Arness wore a number of different rigs before finally settling on an Ojala belt and holster, *Colt .45* – with Wade Preston sporting a double Ojala rig offset by two silver rampart Colt medallions, and *Have Gun, Will Travel*, starring Richard Boone as the mythical Paladin, who opened every show with a close-up of his 7½-inch black Ojala holster embellished with a silver chess knight. Indeed, Ojala's rigs soon came to symbolize the television western as much as the Warner Brothers backlot or the rolling hills of the Iverson Ranch, where many of those oaters were filmed.

Above: Prior to the introduction of the Ojala holster, most Western rigs in the 1930s to the '50s were offshoots of the Mexican buscadero B-Western style, as reproduced here with silver embellishments by Jim Lockwood of Legends in Leather.

Left: Ojala's competition included the steel-lined Andy Anderson Walk & Draw rig and Ed Bohlin's Quick-Draw Holster, circa 1958-61, which featured a spring-tension hammer thong and Bohlin's uniquely cut "low slung" gun belt.

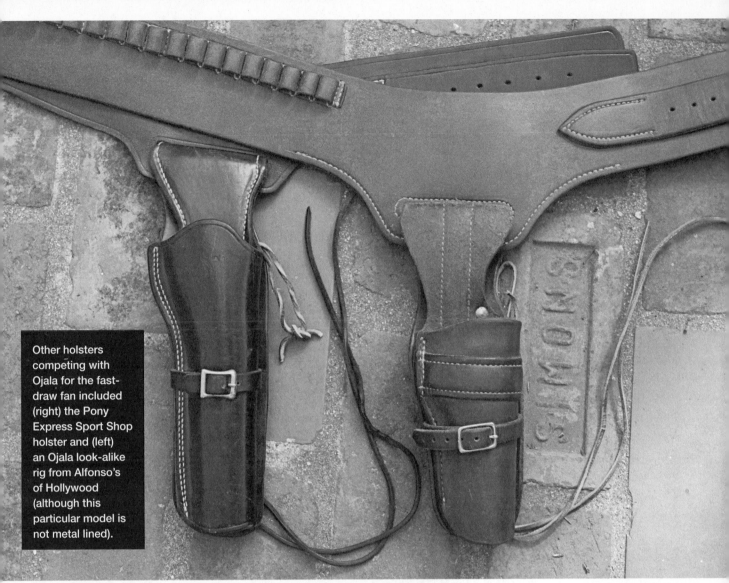

Other holsters competing with Ojala for the fast-draw fan included (right) the Pony Express Sport Shop holster and (left) an Ojala look-alike rig from Alfonso's of Hollywood (although this particular model is not metal lined).

Initially there were three holster sizes made for the SAA, one for each of the three standard SAA barrel lengths. However, as demand grew, Arvo simplified things by only producing two basic holsters, one that would fit both 4¾ and 5½-inch barrels, and another for the 7½-inch Colt. Although Arvo's Hollywood Fast Draw Holster was designed for the Colt Single Action Army, rigs for other guns including double actions, as well as slings and belts, were eventually produced. In addition, holsters were also made for the Ruger Blackhawk, which soon became the fast-draw gun of choice due to its sturdier action, although the Micro rear sight had to be replaced with a smooth steel plug to prevent lacerated thumbs.

This is the back of the rarely seen Pony Express Sport Shop fast-draw rig. Note the stitching on the back of the holster's drop that secures the steel band.

But no matter what the gun, there was only one basic style for the fast-draw holster, Arvo's classic straight-hang single gun rig known as Model No.1, constructed of double thickness, neat's-foot oil treated Grade-A leather with steel insert, a leather safety loop that could be slipped over the hammer to keep the gun from falling out, and a leather tie-down to anchor the holster during the draw (although the holster-to-belt fit was so tight the tie-down was rarely needed,

One of the most recognized Ojala holsters in TV Western history was the black silver knight-embellished rig worn by Richard Boone as Paladin in *Have Gun, Will Travel*. Shown in the photo with the 7½-inch Colt is a metal-lined replica of the Paladin rig made by Alfonso's of Hollywood.

and it sometimes made mounting a horse and even walking difficult). As an aside, during the walk-and-draw contests of the '50s and '60s, in which contestants walked towards each other with a red light between them that was connected to a split-second sound-activated electronic timer (obviously only blanks were used), the shooter who was stepping with his right leg forward when the red light flashed – signaling time to draw – had the advantage, as the tied down holster would be in a muzzle-forward position, making it faster to draw and fire from the hip. This inspired Andy Anderson to develop his famous Walk And Draw holster, in which the gun rode high on the belt, without a tie-down, and with the muzzle angled forward.

It also inspired Arvo to eventually come up with the Model No. 1-25 for competition fast draw, with an Ojala holster that positioned the single action's muzzle forward at a 15-degree angle, and with a pronounced cutaway scallop in the front of the holster for faster clearance. Double rigs of both styles of Ojala rigs were produced, although single rigs are more commonly encountered. In later years, Arvo also made a few "One Piece"

In his role as Matt Dillon on *Gunsmoke*, James Arness wore a number of different gun rigs before finally settling on the Arvo Ojala Model No. 1. The long drop of the holster paired with the 7½-inch barrel of the Colt SAA was in perfect proportion to his height of six feet, seven inches.

The early Ojala holsters (left) were cut straight across the throat, while later models (right) incorporated a slight dip for quicker gun clearance. You can see these changes as you watch the progression of the *Have Gun, Will Travel* opening sequences over the years, as more than one holster was used in the series.

rigs in which the belt and holster were cut and stitched from a single piece of leather. But no matter the style, all Ojala fast-draw rigs featured gently contoured belts that conformed to the shooter's waist, thus insuring a comfortable fit.

Bullet loops, which numbered 25 across the back of the gun belt, were for .44 or .45 calibers, or .38 and .357 Magnum, as the actual loop sizes for similar calibers were the same (i.e., a .44 caliber loop could be made to fit a .45 cartridge, and a .38 loop would work for a .357 Magnum). Eventually, however, Ojala produced belts marked with bullet loops for each caliber individually. Later, with the advent of the Ruger Single Six and the Colt Scout, correspondingly smaller holsters were made for these guns and the belts would contain enough .22 loops to hold a full box of rimfires. But no matter the caliber, bullet loops could be special ordered in any configuration and one occasionally encounters Ojala gunbelts with six bullet loops just forward of the holster, or with three loops placed over the holster position. I often thought these would have been the most practical arrangements, as it alleviated the necessity of having to reach around your back for more ammo. But then, part of the Ojala rig's visual appeal was that solid row of cartridges encircling the shooter's waist.

At first the rigs were offered in black or tan, with black rigs retaining a tanned coloring on the inside back of the belt and on the inside back skirt of the holster. But soon a russet color and a roughout finish were added. In addition, a small number of stamped and hand-carved holsters were made on special order. One of the most noted examples is the double-dyed floral carved rig for a 7½-inch barreled Colt Peacemaker worn by Lorne Greene in his role as Ben Cartwright on *Bonanza*. And in answer to the trivia questions as to why none of the *Bonanza* Ojala rigs had bullet loops, the reason given by the producers was that the show was to have been set in the 1860s, before the advent of cartridge revolvers. The fact that the entire Cart-wright family was using Single Action Armies obviously did not equate with Hollywood logic.

Arvo started making holsters in his garage but contracted some early work to Ed Bohlin's shop, which was located at 931 North Highland in Hollywood (no longer there and now relocated to Dallas, Texas). Of course, this was before the Bohlin lawsuit. However, fast draw was not only becoming a way of life for TV westerns, it was becoming a way of life for the country, as it was rapidly developing into a national sport. Competitions – using blank ammunition for timed events and wax bullets when targets were involved – were springing up in backyards, on TV programs and at community gatherings. Soon demand for his holsters caused Arvo to move opera-tions out of his Woodland Hills home and into a small red building located at

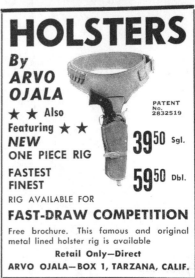
An early ad from the August 1961 issue of *Guns* Magazine.

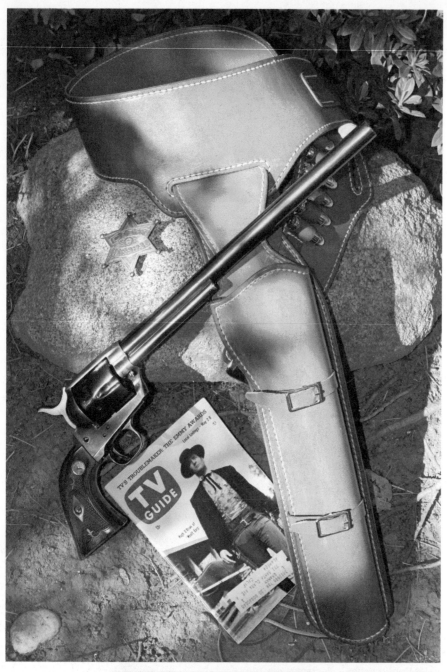

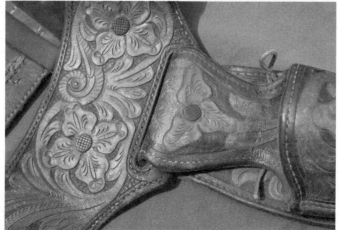

Carved Ojala holsters are rare. This heavily worn and dyed rig was worn by Lorne Greene in his role as Ben Cartwright on the long-running *Bonanza* TV series. Photo courtesy of Little John's Auction Service, Anaheim, Calif.

Although Ojala made a limited number of holsters for the 12-inch Colt Buntline Special, they are scarce, as not many shooters wanted to pack such a long-barreled sixgun. However, Jim Lockwood of Legends in Leather created this accurate reproduction for the author using an original Ojala pattern. The author's second-generation Buntline Special .45 is fitted with Altamont fleur-de-lis rosewood grips.

4726 North Lankersheim Boulevard – and later at 3873 North Lankersheim – in North Hollywood, not far from the movie studios and near where Universal City is today. A concrete freeway expressway and onramp now marks the spot where the old Hollywood Fast Draw Holster Company once stood.

Nor is there any evidence of Arvo's fast-draw studio on the 8500 block of Sunset Strip, where he taught aspiring gunslingers – actors and non-actors alike – during the heyday of the Hollywood westerns. Arvo once told me that two of his most successful pupils had been Sammy Davis Jr. and comedian Jerry Lewis. While Davis performed his sixgun expertise during numerous television appearances (including two memorable episodes of *The Rifleman* – "The Most Amazing Man" and "Two Ounces of Tin"), I actually witnessed Jerry Lewis demonstrate his amazing Ojala-taught dexterity with a nickeled Colt SAA on stage in Las Vegas. Lewis mesmerized the audience as he drew, flipped, spun and tossed his 4¾-inch barreled Peacemaker, finally ending his act – in true comedic style – with the gun holstered butt-down, and the barrel facing backwards.

During the height of the fast-draw sport, Arvo's company was turning out as many as 500 holsters a day. In 1959, at the first annual Colt-sponsored National Fast Draw Championship held at the Sahara Hotel in Las Vegas, Ojala holsters were everywhere – inside the winner's circle and out. His holsters were so much in demand that in 1960 he sold the rights to make and market his famous fast-draw rig to the Daisy Manufacturing Company, which published a fast-draw booklet that emulated Arvo's own instruction manual, and produced a line of single-action BB pistols to go with their Ojala holsters. Meanwhile, on the screen, Arvo's holsters were on practically everyone's hips, from James Garner in *Maverick* to Clint Walker in *Cheyenne*. And not only did he outfit these shooting stars in gunleather, he taught them how to draw – and to look good doing it.

In addition to his TV work, Arvo served as gun coach and technical advisor for numerous western motion pictures, including *The War Wagon*, *Silverado* and *Back To The Future III*, and taught his fast-draw skills to generations of Hollywood gunslingers, including Kevin Kline, Kevin Costner, Marilyn Monroe, Paul Newman and Robert Redford. His on-camera appearances included some less-than-stellar films, such as *Oregon Trail* and *The Return of Jack Slade*. Much more impressive were his guest appearances on programs such as Jack Parr, Johnny Carson and *What's My Line*. However, the majority of his film work was anonymous, as in many cases when a shot of a gunfighter making a fast draw was needed, it was actually a close-up of Arvo's hand that was shown.

So it's not surprising that Arvo's most memorable television role is one in which he isn't readily identified, even though today most fans know he is "the man in black," ready to throw down against James Arness as Marshall Matt Dillon during the opening sequence of *Gunsmoke*. Arvo got paid $100 for this now-famous showdown, which ran for eight years, until the show's producers realized that if they only showed Arness and not Ojala, they wouldn't have to pay the gun coach residuals every time the program aired. Nonetheless, the Dec. 7, 1961 issue of Australia's *TV Times* magazine referred to Arvo as "The Gunfighter Who Never Wins."

In later years Arvo – always the entrepreneur – produced a variety of commemorative items, including silver plated bullets and key chains, belt buckles (including two runs of bronze buckles by artist Al Shelton in 1980), and a number of limited-edition engraved Colt single actions, including a pair that was presented to Ronald Reagan (interestingly, the boxes for these guns were eventually auctioned off separately from the guns themselves). He also

In 1980 Arvo Ojala commissioned noted Western artist Al Shelton to cast a limited edition of individually numbered commemorative belt buckles. Afterwards, an additional 100 unnumbered buckles were cast. They are no longer available.

Arvo Ojala and Frank Sinatra check their single actions on the set of the 1963 movie, *4 For Texas*. Photo courtesy of the Arvo Ojala family.

John Bianchi's Frontier Gunleather pays tribute to Ojala with this limited edition James Arness Commemorative, made in the Ojala style.

Ojala holsters used in motion pictures and television typically are stamped with the studio or prop house name, such as this early left-handed rig from Stembridge Gun Rentals at Paramount Studios. It was worn by Michael Landon, who played Little Joe on the *Bonanza* TV series. Also note the unusual double sampling of Ojala's "Pat. Pend." and patent stamps. Photo courtesy of Little John's Auction Service, Anaheim, Calif.

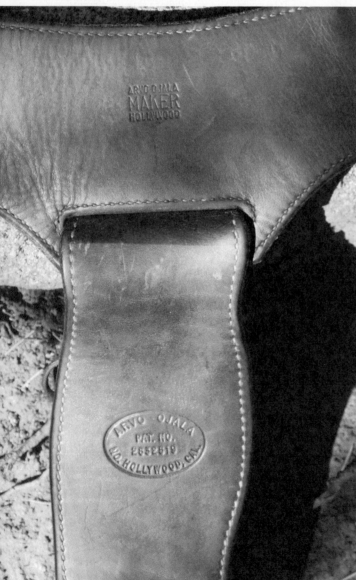

Left: One of the author's fast-draw rigs from the early 1960s bears both a pre-patent and a patent number stamping.

Below: During the 1960s Colt granted permission for their serpentine logo to be used on a select number of Ojala rigs.

promoted a number of products, and I recall seeing Arvo and one of his daughters, Valerie, demonstrating fast draw for a gun safe company in the '90s at the industry's Shooting Hunting Outdoor Trade (SHOT) Show.

Sadly, Arvo Ojala passed away on July 1, 2005, at the age of 85 at his home in Gresham, Ore. But just as the TV westerns and movies live on, so do his holsters; up until recently they were made by his son Erikk but are now being produced by another one of his daughters, Inga (*www.arvoojalaholstercompany. biz*). However, it is the originals that have become collectible and command the most attention. But a quick perusal of the Internet reveals much misinformation, so here are a few facts on the collectability of Arvo's holsters:

First, just because it is an Arvo Ojala holster does not mean it was used in the movies. Although many were, most of Arvo's holsters were purchased by western fans, collectors and shooters, including fast-draw aficionados. In addition, the Hollywood studios invariably marked their holsters with the studio or prop house name, such as Stembridge or Ellis Mercantile. Plus, movie holsters usually suffered more abuse on the set in one month than most holsters were subjected to in a year. Beware of a "movie" holster that looks too new. And always ask for providence if the seller claims it was used in Hollywood.

When buying an Ojala holster beware of fakes or holsters that have been repaired. For one thing, with the exception of custom or presentation rigs, all original Ojala holsters used nickeled North & Judd buckles, which were marked with an anchor on the reverse side. The billets (the leather strip that fastens through the buckle) started out with five holes but Arvo soon changed that to seven holes, with the middle hole meant to be used to fasten the belt. This center hole is also what the CH stands for on the stamping on Ojala belts. And to the best of my knowledge, Arvo stamped all of his personal rigs with his initials, so if buying a holster purported to have belonged to him, get documentation.

Unfortunately, many people selling Ojala holsters on the Internet do not describe the stampings under the billet. Although these stampings are not always consistent, they are a means of identifying the waist size and the caliber of the rig. There are exceptions, but typically the three or four numbered stampings represent the serial number of the rig, although these weren't always numerically accurate. That is, a belt numbered 1479 might – or might not – indicate it was the 1,479th rig produced. The two-digit number followed by the letters CH was the waist size; thus a belt stamped 36CH means that a person with a 36-inch waist would buckle on the rig using the center hole. The second set of numbers was the caliber of the bullet loops – .38, .44, etc.

In attempting to date Ojala holsters, the earliest rigs featured a squared-off "Arvo Ojala MAKER Hollywood" stamping. Holsters made from 1954 or '56 up to 1958 would have a similar stamping with a "Pat. Pend" mark underneath. Those belts and holsters made after 1958 will be stamped with "Arvo Ojala Pat. No 2832519 No.Hollywood, Ca" in an oval. Later this was changed to the same oval stamping but omitted the "No." so that it just reads "Arvo Ojala Pat. No 2832519 Hollywood, Ca." One of the least-encountered stampings was produced during the early 1960s when Arvo was performing fast-draw exhibitions in Las Vegas in conjunction with Colt, during which time a limited number of his rigs were stamped "Made in U.S.A." along with the rampant Colt logo and Arvo's name and patent number in an oval.

Yes, there were other fast-draw artists of the era, most notably Dee Woolem, who began slapping leather at Knott's Berry Farm amusement park in southern California and went on to national fame

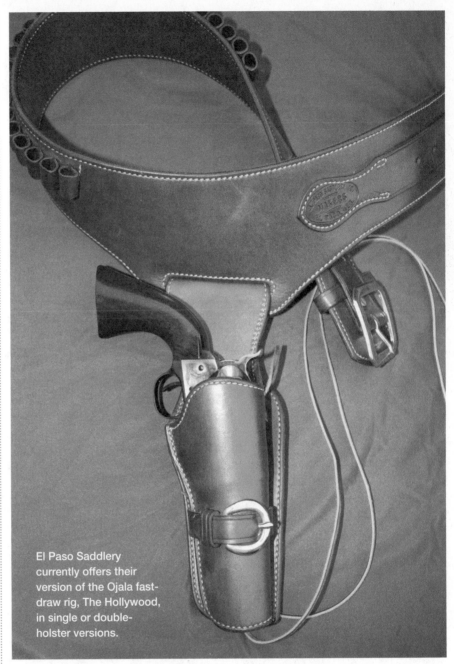

El Paso Saddlery currently offers their version of the Ojala fast-draw rig, The Hollywood, in single or double-holster versions.

as a four-time fast-draw champion; Tandy Leather sold his holster kits. And Rodd Redwing, a Chickasaw Hollywood gun coach who could draw a gun, throw a knife, and have the bullet hit the exact spot as the blade and at nearly the same time. But it was Arvo Ojala, observing actors on the backlots of Warner Brothers and other studios, who became aware that many actors playing TV cowboys wanted to be "the fastest gun in the West." In the real Old West this might not have given anyone more than a modicum of immortality. But in Hollywood's "reel" Old West, such a title could open the swinging bat-wing doors to Western stardom.

Thus, Arvo used his skill – and his holster – to achieve fame not only for himself, but for others. And yet, it is interesting to note that even though James Arness took lessons from Arvo, you never see him draw his 7½-inch barreled hogleg during *Gunsmoke's* famous weekly showdown. There is simply the classic opening scene and then a cut to Arness bringing his Colt into frame and firing a single shot. But listen closely and you'll hear a distant shot of Arvo actually shooting first – just a split second before Arness pulls the trigger. Perhaps that was Arvo's subtle way of saying, "I may not be on camera, but I really am the fastest gun in the West."

The classic
American-made shotgun
is alive and well in the Nutmeg State.

CONNECTICUT
SHOTGUNS

BY **Nick Sisley**

Lou Frutuoso (left) explains the features of the company's A-10 American sidelock to a customer.

What started out as a project in a home workshop to recreate the great Winchester Model 21 side-by-side shotgun has become a company with 50 employees who manufacture hundreds of finely made double shotguns every year. Connecticut Shotgun Manufacturing Company does not turn out the number of firearms like Remington, Browning or Beretta, but this was never the long-term game plan. The guy who started it all is Antony Galazan.

Tony still heads up the business. A wizard of an engineer/machinist, he was hardly wet behind his figurative ears before he was making gauges to measure bores and chokes, gun-related tools and fixtures, as well as creating all manner of machine refinements that professionals 20 years his senior had yet to figure out. Always interested in guns, Galazan's machine wizardry led him to gun shows where he would buy firearms of all types, especially the most desirable ones – those that had been discontinued, and then restore them to like-new condition—and, of course, sell them at a bit of a profit. This all started in the 1970s.

By the late 1980s, Winchester was wrapping up its Custom Shop in New Haven, Conn. Galazan had already set up shop in New Britain, so in those intervening 16 or so years Antony was learning his trade—building guns, learning about guns, mastering so many guns' innards. His education had been so complete that Galazan took over the Winchester Custom Shop work. With that venture, he completed all manner of guns that had been started by the Custom Shop, plus built some from scratch.

One of the key Winchester guns that drew Tony's attention like iron filings to a magnet was the Winchester Model 21 side-by-side. Winchester would no longer make them. Galazan saw intense interest from sophisticated shotgun shooters all across America. Connecticut Shotgun started building Model 21s, right from scratch. From the tiniest screw to the most difficult to make part, this company makes the 21 that was so loved by Winchester's John Olin and many others of

the 1930s and beyond. This side-by-side is known as the CSMC Model 21.

Some say the Model 21 is one of the strongest, if not the strongest, side-by-side actions ever designed. Manufacture of the originals was largely between 1931 and 1988, during which time about 32,500 were built. Compare this with less than 6,000 Model 32 Remington over/unders. Both shotguns were introduced at about the same time. Additionally, perhaps another 1,000 Model 21s were manufactured by the Winchester Custom Shop through 1988.

In addition to the basic model—mostly made in 12 or 20 gauge—a very few 28s and .410s were built. I recall seeing one highly engraved and gold adorned Model 21 .410 in the Winchester Museum in Cody, Wyo. Who could put a price on such rarity? The Winchester 21 was produced in a number of higher grades, and Connecticut Shotgun produces several of these higher grades even today. In addition to the higher-grade Winchester 21s there were Skeet, Trap and Duck (with 3-inch chambers) models.

At about the time Connecticut Shotgun started making Model 21s, Galazan came to an agreement with Savage, the company that owned the rights to produce Fox shotguns. The original lower-rung Fox Sterlingworth was manufactured

from 1910 to 1942. There was also a Sterlingworth Deluxe, a Sterlingworth Skeet and the so-called Super Fox. From there, grades went up in quality, and it's several of these models that Connecticut Shotgun manufactures today. As with the bring-back of the Winchester Model 21, the resurrection of the A.H. Fox is similar, with the handwork of skilled craftsmen doing all the finishing.

The Fox can be had brand new in five different grades: CE with fine scroll and game scenes as well as fine hand checkering; the XE Grade with more and finer scroll, game scenes and checkering; the DE Grade with deeper cut scroll and game scenes; the FE Grade with not only more intricate engraving but gold inlays as well; and finally the Exhibition Grade—really a museum-type piece due to its beauty and execution by the artist's hands. These A.H. Fox side-by-sides are offered in 16, 20, 28 and .410.

Similarly, the CSMC Model 21 is offered in several different grades, each available in 12, 16, 20, 28 and .410. The two smaller gauges can be had on a full-size receiver, or one scaled to gauge. All Model 21s are built to the customer's stock specifications. Like every shotgun produced at this facility, this is not a "finishing" plant. Every part is made here and every bit of work done on Galazan guns is done inside the New Britain

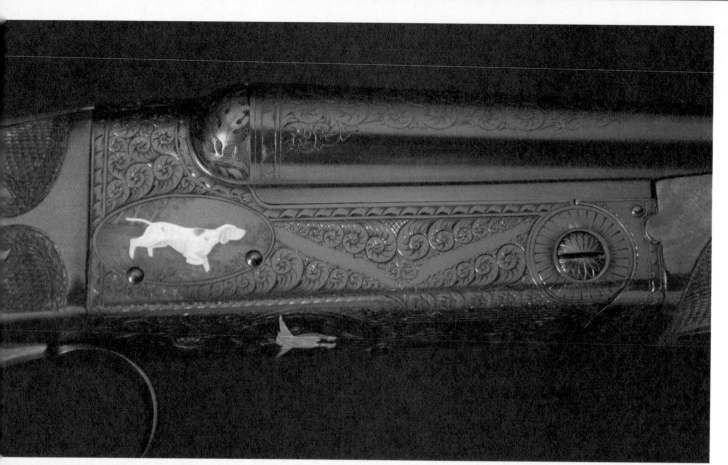

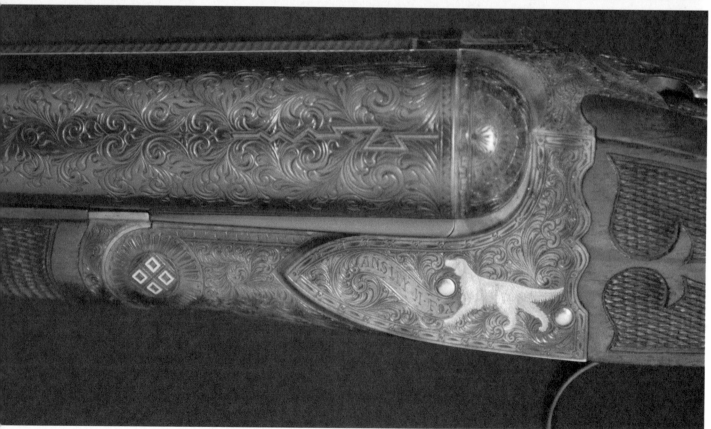

This is the quality of workmanship on the CSMC Model 21 side-by-side—the Grand American version.

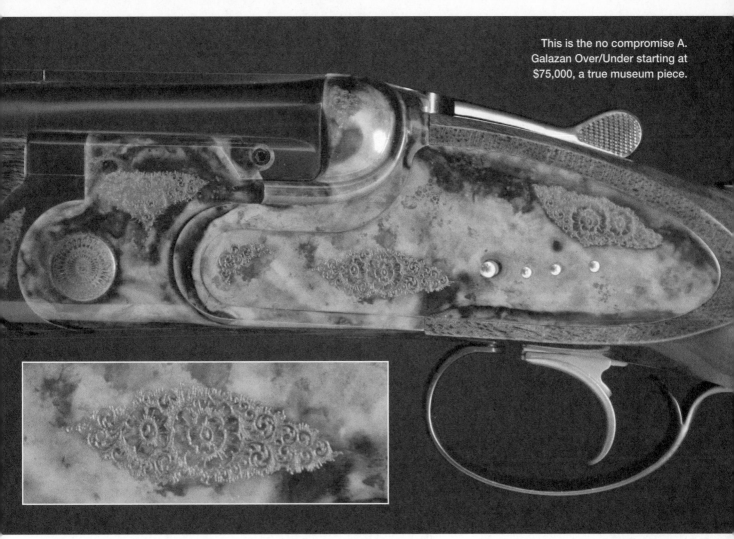

This is the no compromise A. Galazan Over/Under starting at $75,000, a true museum piece.

building. Four CSMC Model 21 grades are offered: Standard or 21-1, 21-5, 21-6 and Grand American. You can go to the company's website for more insight into the Model 21 and other side-by-side and over/under shotguns: *www.connecticut-shotgun.com.*

From re-creating the Model 21 and the A.H. Fox, Tony Galazan's next project was to produce his own best-of-the-best guns – both a side-by-side and an over/under. The A. Galazan Over & Under compares to the finest Italian-made Fabbri, and the A. Galazan Side-by-Side compares to the finest English side-by-sides. Both are no-compromise shotguns that the most noted sportsmen in the world would love to own, even if they can't afford these very special pieces of art. Prices start in the $75,000 range without engraving, similar to the price of a Fabbri or a Purdey, and these impeccable Galazan shotguns are made completely in the U.S.A., under that one roof in New Britain.

Remington Arms purchased the rights to build the Parker side-by-side shortly before World War II, and retains those rights today. But Remington does not have a facility that can make the Parker, especially the AA, so they contracted with Galazan to do it. Connecticut Shotgun doesn't make very many Parkers each year, but they do make them, only in 28 gauge, to the tune of $49,000 each. The fact that Tony Galazan has brought back the Model 21, the A.H. Fox and the Parker certainly says a lot about this man.

By around 2005 Galazan was thinking that it was time to bring out a totally new American-made shotgun, but one that thousands of Americans could afford. No doubt a great deal of thinking went into what type of double gun to produce, how to make it, what gauge to bring it out in, what cosmetics should become a part of such a gun, and more.

This was a time period in America where the interest in side-by-side shotguns had risen significantly, as well as interest in smaller gauges, plus an interest in the beauty of round-body actions.

This "launch" was thus a side-by-side, in 20 gauge for starters with a round-body action. Dubbed the RBL (Round Body Launch) this model was first offered in 2007.

The RBL is still being made—about 5,000 so far in 20 gauge, around 6,000 total, as it is now offered in all gauges. Currently the 20-gauge RBL sells for $3,795, and there's a Reserve Edition with more engraving, plus the Gallery model that starts at $8,000, which does not include engraving or other special requested features.

The gun's hammers, sears and trigger feature a specially developed gold and titanium coating to prevent corrosion and wear. The initial RBL standard features were 20 gauge, 28-inch barrels with five screw-in chokes, 2X walnut, French gray receiver, ejectors, receiver of 41-40 steel, flat V springs and splinter fore-end. Optional add-ons could include a case-hardened receiver, wood upgrades, assisted opening system and more. These guns were first offered at $2,799

This is the Rose & Scroll Edition of the A-10 American—a true sidelock.

in 2007—an exceptional buy for a finely made American round-body side-by-side. No wonder so many were sold. Even on the used market a Standard Grade RBL in 20 gauge can sell for as much or more than that original $2,799 asking price. There's also a Sporting Clays Edition of the RBL—12 gauge, adjustable comb stock, raised vent rib, quick interchange recoil pad, bone and charcoal case-hardened receiver, competition beavertail fore-end and a weight balancing system.

In 2003, Lou Frutuoso had come on board at Connecticut Shotgun, and he eventually became the company's Number Two Man. After graduating from Central Connecticut State University he spent 10 years working in the manufacturing field, then another decade as Operations Manager for a venture capital outfit. Lou told me that when he started working for Galazan he thought he knew a lot about shotguns. However, the last 10 years working for Tony has been a "real revelation" with regard to how little Lou knew and how much he has learned. Frutuoso interviews a lot of prospective new employees, many of whom think they know a lot about shotguns. Very few know enough to become a part of the Connecticut Shotgun Team.

Both Antony Galazan and Lou Frutuoso are shooters and hunters. Tony belongs to and shoots at the famous Pauling Mountain Club. He travels to Great Britain when he can. Lou belongs to East Haddam Fish & Game Club – shoots there as often as he can – plus he makes his annual pilgrimage for pheasants to Winter, S.D.

One very good quote I got from Lou was, "Tony and I are both so passionate about what we do. We leave work and all we think about at home is work. To both of us, work is like breathing. We have to do it. We love to work."

With the RBL launch successfully under the company banner it was natural to expect that an over/under priced within range of thousands of shotgunners would be next. Thus came the A-10 American—not just another over/under, but one that was a true sidelock, with hand-detachable sideplates, the trigger workings a part of each sideplate. Remarkably, prices for the A-10 American true sidelock are less than $8,000. No one was, or is making a sidelock over/under or side-by-side for $8,000. For most true sidelocks – add another zero!

The A-10 American was offered initially in both 12 and 20 gauge. If you want a 20 on a 20-gauge frame, add $500 to the above price. While the hand-detachable sidelock is perhaps the most important feature of this model there are many others, for instance the gold/titanium plating of the sear, hammers and trigger, as mentioned previously for the RBL. This coating is included on the A-10. A new barrel technology called Cryo Pattern is also incorporated. It's a deep freeze process that relieves stress to the metal. Also added is Tough Bore, the company's proprietary treatment of the bores for added hardness, meaning that these A-10s are safe with steel and other hard nontoxic shot. Five screw-in chokes are included. American black walnut is used for the stocks. The current A-10 American Standard model features a case-hardened receiver, which previously was a $250 upgrade in price.

The first upgrade over the Standard A-10 is the Deluxe, which has a different and more intricate engraving pattern— price $9,000. The Rose & Scroll Edition features 100 percent scroll and rosette engraving, one I think is particularly attractive, priced at $10,000 for the 12 and 20 gauge—add $500 for the 20 bore on a 20-gauge frame. Extra options on most all A-10 models include a second set of barrels, wood upgrades, matching pairs and more. Brand new is an A-10 American .410, made on a baby-size .410

The side-by-side that started the more popular-priced line of guns at Connecticut Shotgun, the RBL (Round Body Launch), which has been very successful.

receiver, as well as a 28-gauge A-10 fitted to a 20-gauge receiver. There is also a Sporting Clays version of the A-10 American with adjustable comb stock, ported barrels, competition adjustable rib, adjustable recoil pad, stock weight balancing system, target pistol grip swell and under fore-end weight balance system. Galazan dubs this one "The Hammer." Also check out the photos of the A-10 American Platinum Edition, the highest priced A-10.

Acceptance of the A-10 must have been at least as good as expected, because the company's next launch was another O/U, the Inverness. This over/under, like the RBL side-by-side, features a round body on a trigger-plate action. I bought an Inverness so I've written about it elsewhere and have described its looks as "elegant." It appears there's David McCay Brown (Scottish maker of extremely fine over/unders and side-by-sides) influence in the Inverness. This one comes only in 20 gauge, at least so far, and the receiver is color case-hardened. I should interject here that all Connecticut Shotgun case color is not done with chemicals. The process is with charcoal, a time consuming and special procedure. The receiver and other metal parts are not merely dipped in a chemical solution to get the color effect.

Further, the Inverness receiver gets 100 percent scroll and bouquet engraving coverage. Similar engraving adorns the top tang, opening lever, fore-end iron and triggerguard. The barrels get the Cryo and Tuff Bore treatment already covered for the A-10 American. These guns weigh in at 6 pounds, 8 ounces or less, have 28-inch or 30-inch barrels, ejectors, single selective trigger, vent rib, classic two-point checkering to the grip and fore-end, and a straight grip is priced the same as the standard somewhat open pistol grip. These are hunting guns, not competition target guns. Turkish walnut is used and op-

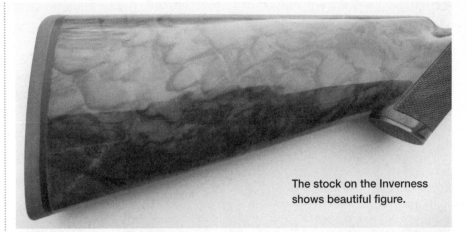

The stock on the Inverness shows beautiful figure.

The fore-end on the Inverness has the rounded shape much like that on the Browning Lightning.

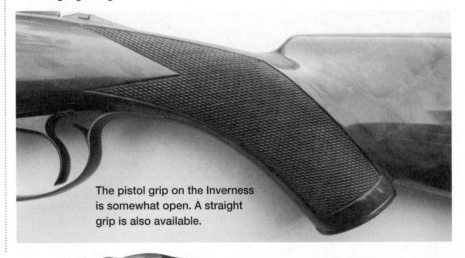

The pistol grip on the Inverness is somewhat open. A straight grip is also available.

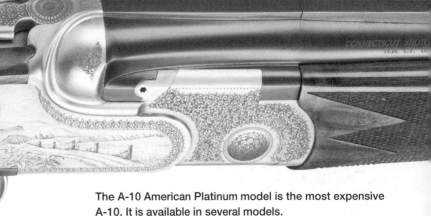

The A-10 American Platinum model is the most expensive A-10. It is available in several models.

Connecticut Shotgun's Gun Room is a treasure trove of thousands of used shotguns—all top quality and mostly double guns.

tions include wood upgrades and a leather-covered recoil pad. The styling around the fences, the styling of the opening lever, the elegance of the round-body receiver, all combine to make the Inverness one great looking smoothbore. There's also the Inverness Deluxe Edition – this one with a bright nitride receiver and a lot more deep cut engraving than on the Standard Inverness.

Priced currently at $5,000—if you had gotten in on the first 500 orders you could have received a $1,000 discount for paying up front (it took about a year to get mine made), plus another $1,000 discount if you were a previous Connecticut Shotgun customer—bringing the price down

to $3,000 plus shipping, an unbelievable price for an over/under of this quality and beauty—and very important to many—all made in America.

This brings us to the most recent Galazan intro, the Model 21 over/under. Yes, an over/under patterned after the venerable Winchester Model 21 side-by-side. The Model 21 O/U will be offered in three grades—similar to the CSMC 21 side-by-side—Standard or 21-1, 21-6 and the Grand American.

Let's talk about the Standard model 21 O/U. This one is built on a low-profile shallow frame in 20 gauge with 3-inch chambers, barrel lengths of 26- to 32-inches, vent rib, American walnut, straight or pistol grip, automatic safety, ejectors, steel shot compatible, stock dimensions of 14 3/8" x 1 3/8" x 2½" and a weight of approximately 6 pounds, 5 ounces with 28-inch barrels.

This is the Inverness Deluxe Edition with deep and intricate engraving on a bright receiver.

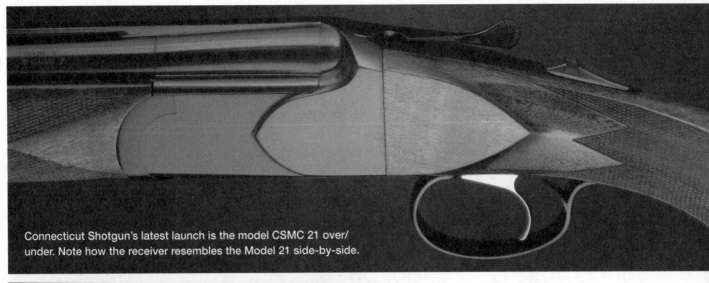

Connecticut Shotgun's latest launch is the model CSMC 21 over/under. Note how the receiver resembles the Model 21 side-by-side.

This is the Grand American version of the new CSMC Model 21 over/under.

The Standard Grade has no engraving on its blued receiver, which looks very similar to the Model 21 side-by-side receiver. This model is priced at $3,995, but if you pay up front you get a $1,000 price reduction. It will take about a year to get your Model 21 O/U from the factory.

In addition to being a company that makes only fine double guns, Connecticut Shotgun sells all of the guns I've talked about here, direct and only direct. Thus, you cannot get a new RBL, A-10 American, Inverness over/under or Model 21 O/U from your local gun store or any other gun shop. This is another unique aspect of the Galazan touch. The advantage for the American buyer to this is what? There is no middleman. There is no cost of shipping across the Atlantic or Pacific Oceans. There's no markup by a company that does the importing. There's no markup for a distributor or a gun dealer. This all-sales-direct policy for its new guns is why Connecticut Shotgun can give outstanding quality at a great price.

Yet another unique aspect about this company is its Gun Room. Galazan takes in a lot of shotguns on trade. But the company also goes out and buys shotguns and rifles from estates and other sellers. For example, Galazan currently has 400 of the guns from the Robert Petersen estate on consignment from the NRA, all of them high-grade, high-quality guns. They also have many of the guns of former *Outdoor Life* firearms editor Jim Carmichael in their Gun Room. Where are you going to ever see more than 2,000 high-quality used shotguns and rifles? On the CSMC website the Gun Room is billed as "The largest selection of high-grade guns ever assembled."

The company website is also replete with many of these fine shotguns and rifles, but it's the Gun Room that needs to be on the to-do list of every serious shotgunner who lives in the vicinity. The Gun Room is open Thursdays and Fridays 11:00 am to 7:00 pm, Saturdays from 11:00 am to 4:00 pm, and other times by appointment.

Finally there's the Connecticut Shotgun catalog. It is mailed out to customers automatically, but anyone can request a catalog. In additions to the guns, it has page after page of company products like trunk-type gun cases, all manner of bags for shooters, sophisticated gun cleaning accessories, gunsmith turn screws, clothing, jewelry, knives, gun racks and more.

Antony Galazan has never set his sights on selling thousands of shotguns a year. His total focus has been on all made-in-the U.S.A. double shotguns, only the finest quality shotguns will leave his shop, and innovation in both products and methods of manufacture. Connecticut Shotgun is definitely a unique American gun company.

BRITAIN'S
BLACK-POW
.303

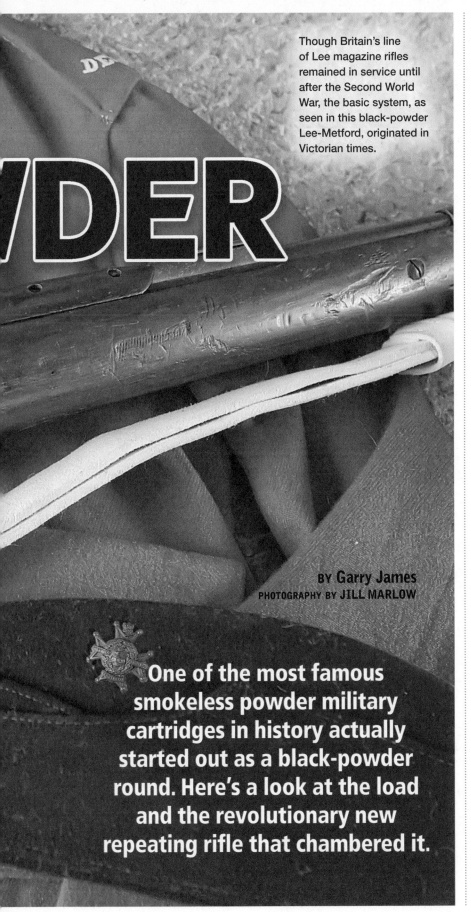

Though Britain's line of Lee magazine rifles remained in service until after the Second World War, the basic system, as seen in this black-powder Lee-Metford, originated in Victorian times.

BY Garry James
PHOTOGRAPHY BY JILL MARLOW

One of the most famous smokeless powder military cartridges in history actually started out as a black-powder round. Here's a look at the load and the revolutionary new repeating rifle that chambered it.

By the mid-1880s, it was becoming manifestly evident that the smallbore, bolt-action repeater was the top choice for general service military longarms. A number of different systems were devised whole cloth or adopted from earlier ones, resulting in groundbreakers such as the French Model 1886 Lebel, German Model 1888 Commission Rifle, Italian Model 1891 Terni, Japanese Type 22, Russian Model 1891 Mosin-Nagant, American Model 1892 Krag-Jorgensen and one of the best – Britain's 1888 Mark I Lee-Metford.

Curiously, while a number of its contemporaries were introduced with smokeless powder loads, the Metford's designers decided that a black-powder load was suitable for Her Majesty's forces – at least as a stopgap.

The Lee-Metford, like its two single-shot predecessors the Snider and Martini-Henry, had its origin in the United States. James Paris Lee was a naturalized American citizen whose parents emigrated from Scotland to Canada in 1836. Though initially following his father's occupation of watchmaking, firearms were his real passion and by the time he moved to Wisconsin in 1858 he had taken up gun making and design full time.

While Lee didn't invent the box magazine, there is no question he perfected it. His circa 1879 Remington-Lee bolt-action rifle was tested by the U.S. Navy, and though not used by the American military in any great numbers, this revolutionary rifle caught the eye of British authorities. In 1880, versions of the rifle chambered for the .577-450 Gatling variation of the British service round and fitted with Martini-Henry barrels, bested a number of foreign and domestic rifles in early trials. Further testing continued throughout the 1880s with altered Remington-Lees, as well as with production .45-70 and .43 Spanish models.

Early on, sentiment leaned towards the adoption of a .402 service round, but the success of a .303-caliber cartridge by Swiss designer Col. Eduard Rubin caused some rethinking. Plans for the larger caliber were dropped and further testing ordered for the .303.

Finally in 1888, prototype Lees fitted with barrels featuring the seven-groove rifling of William E. Metford were tested using the .303 Rubin round, and in December of that year the first Lee magazine rifle was officially adopted into British service.

The Lee-Metford, as well as some later Lee-Enfield rifles, employed a magazine cutoff, which blocked cartridges from being fed from the magazine. This was a common 19th century practice used by many countries, which allowed rifles to be fired single shot, with the ammo in the magazines kept in reserve.

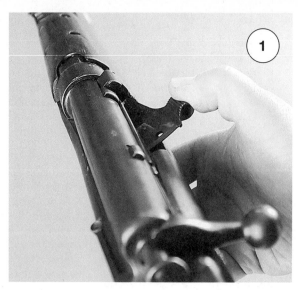

(1)

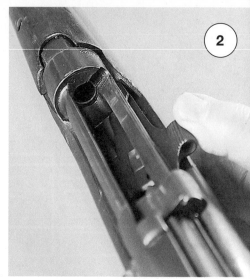

(2)

This .303 round had a drawn brass case and round-nosed, 215-grain cupronickel-jacketed bullet. The cartridge was Boxer primed and incorporated a compressed black-powder charge of 71½ grains. Though ordnance officials planned on using smokeless powder pending the acceptance of a suitable pro-pellant, it was decided to be prudent and stay with black powder for the moment.

Britain's first general-issue repeating rifle, the "Magazine Lee-Metford Rifle Mark I" was a unique arm. Featuring rifling devised by William Ellis Metford, it had an eight-shot, sheet-steel metal box magazine, which protruded from the stock in front of the triggerguard. The magazine was detachable, though it was linked to the rifle and not intended to be routinely removed.

The bolt, while not as strong as many later Mauser designs, was fine for the pressures developed by the .303 round. Locking was effected by means of a lug

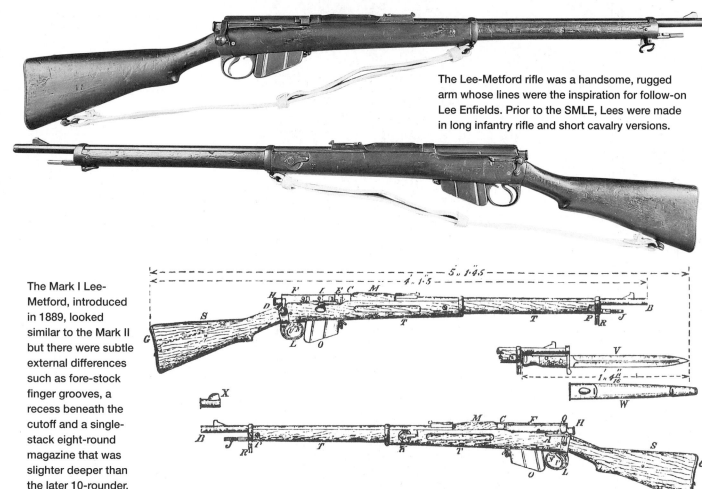

The Lee-Metford rifle was a handsome, rugged arm whose lines were the inspiration for follow-on Lee Enfields. Prior to the SMLE, Lees were made in long infantry rifle and short cavalry versions.

The Mark I Lee-Metford, introduced in 1889, looked similar to the Mark II but there were subtle external differences such as fore-stock finger grooves, a recess beneath the cutoff and a single-stack eight-round magazine that was slighter deeper than the later 10-rounder.

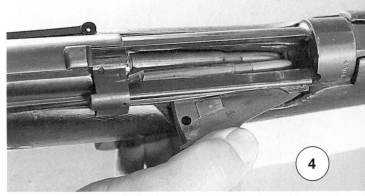

that engaged a recess in the receiver and a solid rib that was secured against a shoulder. The bolt head was a separate piece that threaded onto the bolt body, and by snapping it out of a rail on the receiver, the bolt could be freed and removed rearwards out of the receiver. The gun locked on closing and proved to be one of the smoothest military bolt actions ever – one that

could be manipulated with considerable rapidity. A rear-mounted cocking piece allowed the Metford to be armed or disarmed with the bolt closed. Though the gun was a repeater, it was fitted with a sliding cutoff that permitted single-shot firing. The rounds in the magazine were then held in reserve.

The Mk I's barrel-mounted rear sight was graduated to 1,900

yards, though it was also equipped with a long-range dial sight on the left side of the stock. This was marked to an optimistic 3,500 yards.

Overall length of the rifle was 49½ inches and the barrel measured just over 30 inches. Like the Lee-Metfords and Enfield that would follow it, the Mark I Metford had a two-piece walnut stock. The butt was secured to the

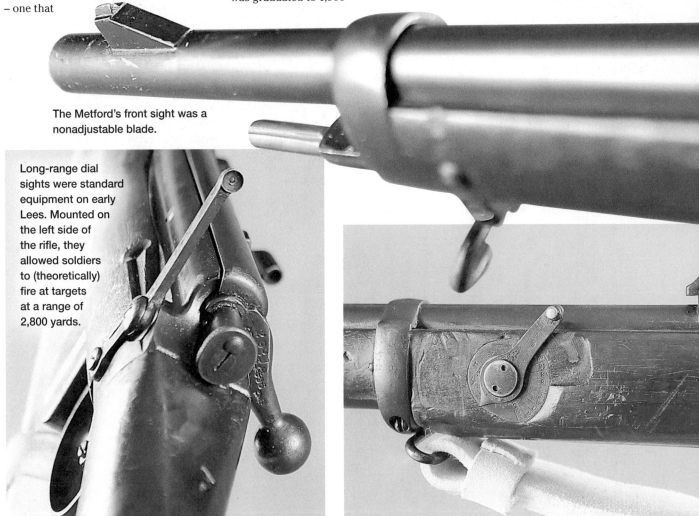

The Metford's front sight was a nonadjustable blade.

Long-range dial sights were standard equipment on early Lees. Mounted on the left side of the rifle, they allowed soldiers to (theoretically) fire at targets at a range of 2,800 yards.

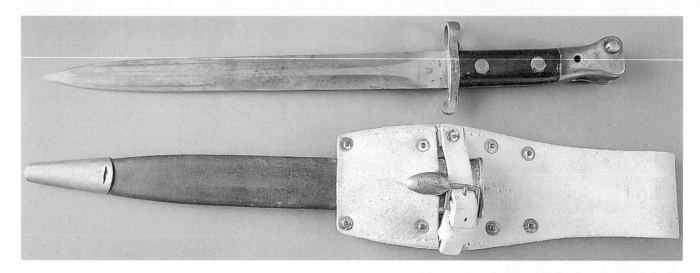

receiver by means of a long bolt that passed through it. The grooved fore-end was secured by a combination of screws and barrel bands. A cleaning rod was housed under the barrel. To use it, two sections had to be screwed together.

A Pattern 1888 bayonet featuring a nine-inch sword blade and grip with walnut panels was introduced with the Metford, and in a couple of different versions that would be used with all the Metfords and Long Lees.

Military arms were marked on the left side of the socket with a Queen's Crown over "VR," for Victoria Regina, the place of manufacture (Enfield B.S.A. – Birmingham Small Arms Co., Sparkbrook or L.S.A. – London Small Arms Co.) Beneath this was the date of manufacture and the "Mark."

Above: The Pattern 1888 bayonet was standard issue for the Lee-Metford. There were two "marks" of this short-bladed weapon.

Right: The socket of our evaluation Lee-Metford has markings that include a crown and the initials "V.R." (Victoria Regina) as well as its place and date of manufacture and the rifle's "mark" designation.

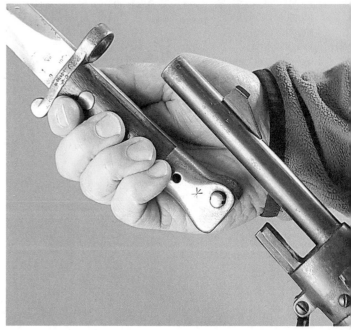

Bayonets attached to the Lee-Metford by means of a muzzle ring and latched groove that slid over a rail on the front band. They were easy to fix and unfix.

In early 1892, a number of small changes were made to the Lee-Metford. Modifications on this Mark I* (a "Mark" signified a major change, while a "*" indicated only a minor one) involved the elimination of a rear-mounted safety lever in favor of a half-cock notch on the cocking piece which was also found to be problematic, and the arrangement was changed to a cocking-piece-mounted lever in some later Lees; along with the substitution of a brass stock identification for a steel one and re-graduation of the rear sight to 1,800 yards and the dial sight to 2,900 yards.

A year later a Mark II Metford was authorized. Its most important feature was a 10-round magazine, upping the Lee's capacity by two rounds. Other mods included a brass buttplate, improved bolt, sturdier nose cap, simplified cutoff and the elimination of finger grooves. In addition, the ID disc was jettisoned, the elongated tang on the new buttplate serving as a marking place for unit designations. Two years later a Mark II* rifle was released that included a safety catch on the cocking piece. As the Mark II had a compartment in the butt for a cleaning pull-through and oil bottle, the rod beneath the barrel was now solely intended for stuck cartridge case removal. Eventually, it was removed altogether.

In late 1891, Britain's first smokeless powder rifle load was officially adopted—and its acceptance would ultimately sound the death knell for the Lee-Metford. The "Cartridge, S.A., Ball .303 inch Cordite (Mark I)" featured the black-powder round's drawn brass case and 215-grain bullet, but was charged with 31 grains (60 strands) of Cordite, an extruded propellant fashioned from nitroglycerine, guncotton and mineral jelly. The composition of the Boxer primer was also changed.

While the relatively smoke-free Cordite was a real advantage on the battlefield – it boosted the muzzle velocity of the .303 from 1850 fps to 1970 fps – it unfortunately burned much hotter than the black powder, and soon it was found that Metford rifles and carbines were experiencing distressing bore erosion.

Ordnance technicians set to work to modify the Lee's rifling to take better advantage of the new round. What emerged was a more angular, deeper five-groove rifling that would not be damaged by the new propellant. Termed "Enfield" after the site where it was

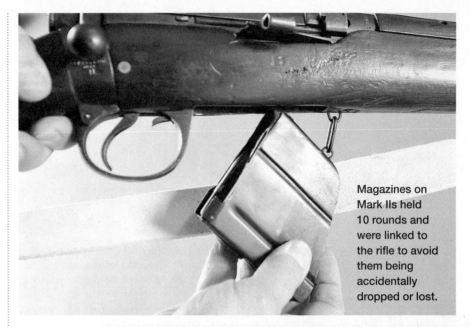

Magazines on Mark IIs held 10 rounds and were linked to the rifle to avoid them being accidentally dropped or lost.

The Mark II's safety consisted of a simple midpoint notch on the cocking piece. It was a tad awkward to manipulate and was ultimately replaced with a more positive system.

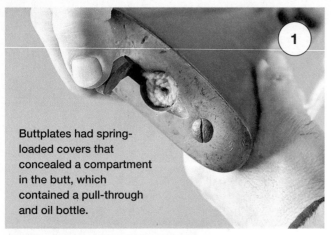

① Buttplates had spring-loaded covers that concealed a compartment in the butt, which contained a pull-through and oil bottle.

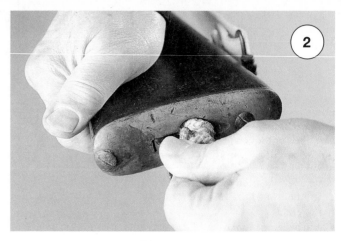

②

British student volunteers at St. Edward's School, Oxford, with Lee-Metford and Long Lee-Enfield rifles c. 1914-15.

(Author's collection)

developed, this rifling heralded the beginning of a firearms legend, but it also marks the end of our developmental history of the Lee-Metford.

Despite the fact the Mark I Lee-Enfield was approved in 1895, stocks of Metfords were manufactured until 1896 and kept in service while production and issue of the new arm could be brought up to speed (as well as kept as a supplementary arm well into the 20th century). Accordingly, many Metfords saw service in India and other places in the Empire for a good number of years; most notably in the Sudan in 1898 at the Battle of Omdurman, where in the hands of British regulars it helped achieve a lopsided defeat over the Khalifa's forces, with the British killing 11,000 and wounding

16,000 of the enemy. Their own casualties were a mere of 48 killed and 328 wounded.

SHOOTING THE BLACK-POWDER LEE-METFORD

I've always been fascinated by the fact the modern .303 started out relying on a then-800-year-old propellant, so I was curious to see just how it would perform. Accordingly, I rounded up a nice condition Mark II Lee-Metford (no mean task, as Metfords are quite tough to come by nowadays) and had some ammunition rustled up by Bob Shell of Shell Reloading, using Privi Partizan .303 cases, Winchester large rifle primers, Hawk Precision Bullets' 215-grain,

Below: The Lee-Metford's rounded rifling (below right) was found to be unsuitable for use with smokeless powder cartridges and was replaced by the more angular Enfield style (below left).

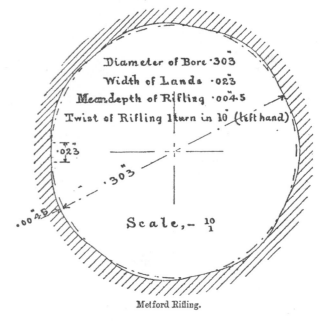

Enfield Rifling.

Metford Rifling.

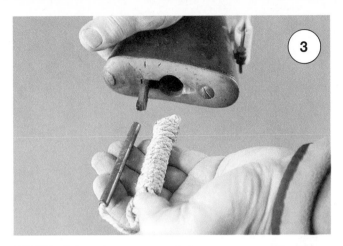

③

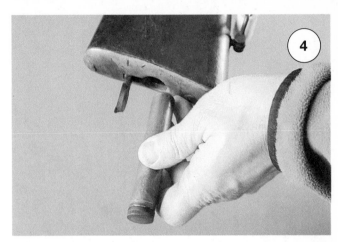

④

311 RT bullets and a compressed charge of 55-grains of Hodgdon FFg black powder.

Why only 55 grains you may ask? Try as he may, that was all Bob could squeeze into the cases, but as the original Brit brass probably had a bit more internal area and the factory had a special method of forming the 71½-grain load into a pellet, this is understandable.

Our 1895-dated Sparkbrook-built Mark II was fired at 50 and 100 yards from a rest. Bullets chronographed at an average of 1480 fps, some 370 fps less than the period round, so it didn't surprise me when the strikes were about 10 inches low at 50 yards and 12 inches low at 100. With the rear sight set to 450 yards the bullets hit at point of aim and gave good results (in a clean bore), with groups at 50 yards running in the 2½-inch range and those at 100 yards, 2¾ inches. It was interesting, but not surprising, to find out that accuracy dropped off considerably after about 20 rounds due to the black-powder fouling, some spreads widening out to five or

The Mark II Lee-Metford's rear ladder sight was graduated from 100 to 1,800 yards. Wind-gauge lines were engraved on the side of the slide's V-notch.

A new Bob Shell black-powder .303 (left) compared with an original period round. Both cartridges have a 215-grain, .311 bullet.

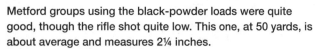

Metford groups using the black-powder loads were quite good, though the rifle shot quite low. This one, at 50 yards, is about average and measures 2¼ inches.

This rested, 100-yard group measuring 2¾ inches was fired early in the range session. Spreads degenerated considerably as black-powder fouling built up.

Our original evaluation Lee-Metford handled beautifully and was a joy to shoot. Recoil was relatively light with the black-powder loads, though they did throw out a good volume of smoke and flame.

Like all Lees, the Metford's action was smooth and reliable. Feeding and ejection was flawless.

six inches. Smoke was considerable, but recoil, quite manageable.

For a control I also tried some British-issue 174-grain c. 1967 Mark VII Cordite .303s and 150-grain Hornady STs in the Metford. Amazingly, they hit in exactly the same spots as the black-powder loads, and groups with both types of ammo were just about the same, giving the edge to Hornady. I talked this over with Bob and neither of us had an adequate explanation other than the fact that sometimes these older guns can present Quixotic results. The gun had an excellent bore and functioned perfectly.

I'm still not quite what all this proves, other than the fact the Metford, in the black-powder mode, was a formidable arm – at least for the first three or four magazine's-full, after which time the groups, while not match-grade, would have probably been OK for combat. I do have a Long-Lee Enfield in my collection and it is a tack driver, even after extended firing, so there is no question it was an improvement over the Metford.

Still, Britain was well served by its first magazine rifle. As well as being a formidable arm in its own right, it paved the way for a family of bolt-action re-peaters that would continue in use as a service rifle with the parent nation past the midpoint of the 20th century, and considerably longer with other nations. You can't ask for a much better legacy than that.

A stalwart group of soldiers of the 1st Bn. King's Royal Rifles pose for the photographer with their Mark I Metfords during the Chitral Relief Expedition of 1895.

Sources

Shell Reloading
Bob Shell
REL4350@aol.com
(480) 983-7078

Hawk Precision Bullets
info@hawkbullets.com
(856) 297-2800

.44-40
SIXGUNS & LEVER GUNS

Singing the praises of one of the great cartridges in American history.

Harkening back to the 1870s are this Uberti Winchester and Colt Third Generation, both chambered in .44-40.

BY **John Taffin**

In 1860, B. Tyler Henry received a patent for a truly landmark rifle. With a lever operated action and the .44 rimfire copper cartridge case, the Model of 1860 or .44 Henry was born. This was a tremendously important firearms advancement coming at a time when the single-shot muzzleloader ruled. There is much truth to the advertising saying that a man armed with a Henry rifle and on horseback simply could not be captured.

With its 17-round capacity, this first true lever gun and first true .44 cartridge offered previously unheard of firepower. The 1860 Henry had a bronze alloy frame and loaded not through a gate, as subsequent centerfire lever guns, but rather loaded through a tube from the front much like many of today's .22 lever-action rifles. The repeating capability was a giant step forward, but the method of loading was a serious drawback, as the rifle could not be subject to immediate use if it was being reloaded during a gunfight. Additionally, there was no forearm to protect the tubular magazine from dents and dings.

Mr. Henry was Oliver Winchester's shop foreman and when Winchester eventually lent his name to a rifle, the first official Winchester came forth as the 1866, or as it was soon called due to its brass frame, the Yellow Boy. By adding a forearm and using King's patent to provide a loading gate, Winchester set the stage for a whole line of great lever guns. The 1860 Henry followed by the 1866 were both great steps forward, but the best was yet to come – and that best brings us to the year 1873 and the now legendary Winchester 1873's arrival. The Winchester frame was now made of iron, and then steel in the 1880s, instead of the brass/bronze alloy used in the 1860 and 1866 rifles.

The actions of the 1860, 1866, and 1873 models are all basically the same design using what is known as a toggle link action. The toggle link operating the action was certainly not very strong by today's standards, however all three rifles used relatively low-pressured black-powder shells. One of the great advantages of the toggle link action was its incredible smoothness. Operating the lever of any of the first Winchesters seems almost effortless and feeding of cartridges

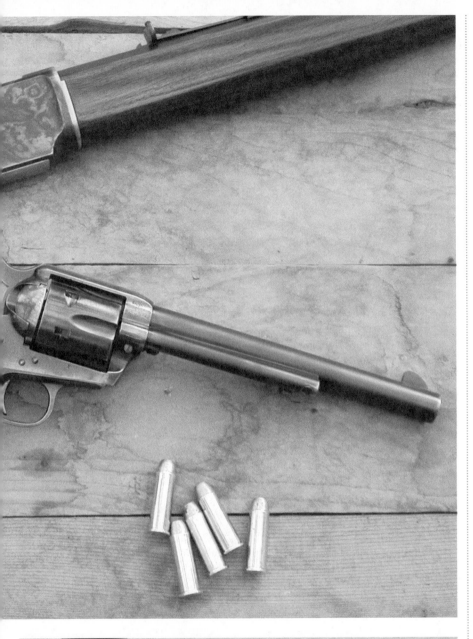

The Winchester 1873 and Winchester 1866 .44-40s are both offered in replica form by Uberti of Italy.

coming straight back from the magazine tube, straight up the lifter, and then into the barrel as the lever is closed is almost a spiritual experience.

The 1860, 1866 and 1873, and especially the latter, were to the shooters of that time what the AR15 is to so many shooters today. High capacity, easy handling, easy shooting, accurate and especially, dependable. Today many law-enforcement officers carry ARs in their cars; back then many a lawman had an 1873 Winchester chambered in .44 WCF in his saddle scabbard.

The ammunition for the 1873 Winchester was no longer a rimfire as the .44 Henry, but a centerfire – the .44 Winchester Center Fire – which used an inside lubricated bullet rather than the outside lubricated bullet of the .44 rimfire. The .44 WCF, more commonly called the .44-40, differed in two other ways from the Henry. The case was lengthened to 1.3 inches and instead of being a straight-walled .44 the .44 WCF had a tapered case with a slight bottleneck. The .44 WCF in the Winchester 1873 arrived the same year as the .45 Colt in the Colt Single Action Army and it is very close to being a .45 case necked down to .44. This may have been done for greater case capacity, ease of chambering or both. Whatever the reason, the .44-40 is one of the all-time great cartridges.

Buyers of the 1873 Winchester had many custom options available. The Model 73 could be purchased as a rifle with a 24-inch round or octagon barrel, or special ordered with longer barrels; the carbine came with a 20-inch barrel while the musket had a 30-inch barrel. Buttstocks could be ordered in straight grip or pistol grip configurations with a curved or shotgun-style buttplate; stocks could be standard walnut or extra-fancy wood, and set triggers were also available in the single or double variety. Magazines were normally full-length, but abbreviated magazines were available as were Trapper versions with a barrel shorter than the now legal minimum of 16 inches. In addition to a round or octagon barrel, one could have a combination of both.

Approximately 80 percent of all Model 1873 Winchesters were chambered in .44-40. Winchester selected individual rifles that were above average in accuracy, and those became "One of One Hundred" or "One of One Thousand" examples set at premium prices.

The .44 rimfire of the 1860 and 1866 used a bullet of approximately 200 grains

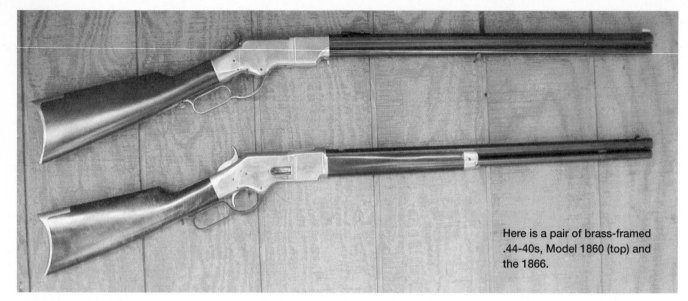

Here is a pair of brass-framed .44-40s, Model 1860 (top) and the 1866.

with a muzzle velocity at about 1100 fps. But with the coming of the longer and larger .44 WCF cartridge case using 40 grains (the "40" in .44-40) of black powder, muzzle velocity was increased to 1250 fps. By today's standards, that is not very powerful for a rifle, but it is about the equivalent of a heavily loaded .44 Special sixgun. It proved to be potent enough for whitetail deer and black bear, and many more than one grizzly was taken down with the .44 WCF. Men on the frontier knew how to make do with what they had.

The Winchester 1873 would go on to be made for half a century, from 1873 all the way through 1923, with just under three-quarters of a million being produced. If we use the year 1900 as the start of rifles suitable for smokeless powder, the beginning serial number that

year was 541,329. However, any original Winchester 1873 should be checked by a competent gunsmith before being fired.

The 1873, with its toggle link action, was basically enlarged to become the Model 1876, which was chambered in such cartridges as the .45-60 and .45-75, still with the same action. A few years later it was time for a change, and that change was the newer and stronger action of the 1886 design of John Browning, which was chambered in such cartridges as the .45-70, .45-90 and .50-110. The next step by John Browning was to miniaturize the 1886 into the Model 1892. This progression is overly simplified but it works for our purposes.

John Browning's first lever gun, the massive and powerful 1886 Winchester, was a great rifle but overly powerful

and large for most uses. So Browning combined the best attributes of the 1873 and 1886 by downsizing the '86 into a modernized version of the Model 1873 and chambered in the same .44 WCF. Instead of the toggle link action of the 1873, the Model 1892 had the much stronger double locking bolts of the 1886.

When the Model 1873 emerged the West was still very wild and it was used mostly as a battle rifle for lawmen, outlaws and frontiersmen. However, it was never adopted by the U.S. Army, which stayed with their more powerful single-shot rifles. By the time the Model 1892 arrived the West was considerably tamer and it became the rifle of the farmer, the rancher and the hunter. The .44 WCF Model 92 rides easily in saddle scabbards or pickup trucks or even

The author in the field with the Uberti Model 1873.

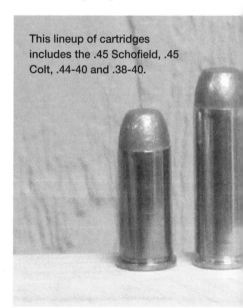

This lineup of cartridges includes the .45 Schofield, .45 Colt, .44-40 and .38-40.

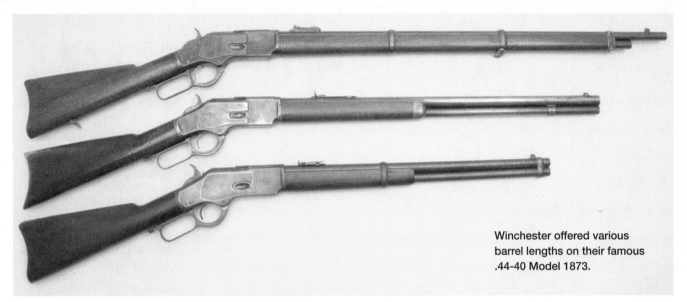

Winchester offered various barrel lengths on their famous .44-40 Model 1873.

carried by hand. It shoulders easily, lines up naturally, shoots accurately, and does so with very light recoil. It is not the rifle when long-range shooting is expected and was never meant to be. As a close-range battle rifle it still will fill the bill.

When I started shooting seriously in the 1950s, lever gun fanciers were grabbing up Model 1892s for conversions to both .357 and .44 Magnums, and Arizona's Ward Koozer did a brisk gunsmithing business with these conversions. They made excellent companions to the new magnum sixguns from Ruger, the .357 and .44 Blackhawks, but it seemed a shame to convert the grand little .32-20s and .44-40s to the magnum chamberings. With so many conversions being done, the supply of original shooter-grade Model 1892s began to dry up. Luckily today we have a whole line-up of Winchester Model 1892s in replica form available in .44 WCF.

Another "Model 1892" emerged and sold for $39.95 in the 1950s. This was the El Tigre produced in South America under special licensing from Winchester. I have experience with only one El Tigre and it is an excellent rifle, rivaling the quality of the real Model 1892. The El Tigre was built as a military rifle and as such has a 22-inch barrel, sling swivels and a ladder-type rear sight. Though, I don't think there is much use for the 1,000 yards marked on the sight.

The Model 1892's production would last until 1931 with over one million being manufactured. Just as with the Model 1873, the Model 1892 was available as a carbine with a 20-inch barrel, a rifle with 24 inches and a musket with 30. The special options of the Model 1873 also carried over into the 1892 with both round and octagonal barrels offered, several styles of sights, standard walnut or fancy grade stocks, and crescent or shotgun style buttplates.

Winchester was not the only firm offering .44-40 rifles. Marlin also made a .44-40 lever gun, the Model 1894, from the same year as the model number until 1935. In some ways and for some uses, Marlin's .44-40 is probably an even better rifle than the Winchester 1892, as it has side ejection of spent cartridges instead of the top ejection of the Winchester. This is especially handy for anyone who wishes to scope a lever gun. It has been said the idea of ".44-40" came from Marlin as they did not want to write "Winchester" or "WCF" on their rifle barrels. The 1894 Marlin .44 resurfaced in 1969 and has been made in both .44 Magnum and .44-40, with both round and octagon barrels available in several barrel lengths.

Several years ago, too many to think about now, Brian Pearce, Bob Baer and I met with the powers that be at Marlin during a SHOT Show to discuss firearms Marlin should be building. We asked for octagon barrels and a return to some of the old chamberings. As a result of that meeting Marlin brought back the .38-55 and the .44-40 in octagon barrel form, as well as offering octagon barrels in .45 Colt, .357 Magnum and .44 Magnum. When my wife and I were both competing in Cowboy Action Shooting we used a pair of Marlin .44-40s. I had hers cut to 19 inches, which still allowed the magazine tube to hold 10 rounds. It not only made an excellent gun for competition, it is also good for close-range hunting with its tang sight and very strong action.

Today we are far removed from the original Winchester Model 1873 and Model 1892 .44-40s. However the 1860 Henry, 1866 Yellow Boy, 1873 Winchester and the 1892 Winchester all are now readily available in excellent replica form from Italy, Japan or South America, and chambered in the now legendary .44-40. Not only are these lever guns readily available, they are of excellent quality. Metallurgy today is certainly better than it was in the middle of the 19th century, but the 1860, 1866 and 1873 replicas still utilize the old toggle link action and are for standard loads only. On the other hand, the original 1892 Winchester, with its twin locking bolts is a very strong rifle.

I keep things simple these days and mostly load the .44-40 with 8 grains of Unique or Universal and use the Oregon

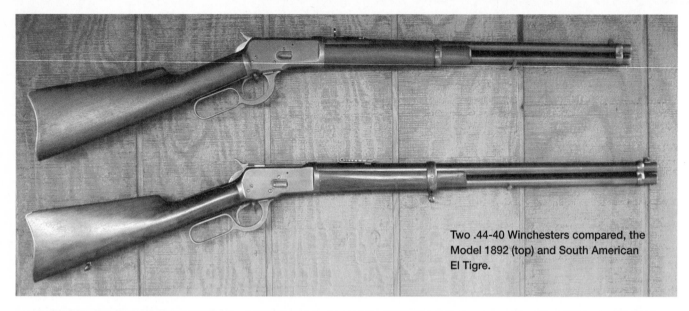

Two .44-40 Winchesters compared, the Model 1892 (top) and South American El Tigre.

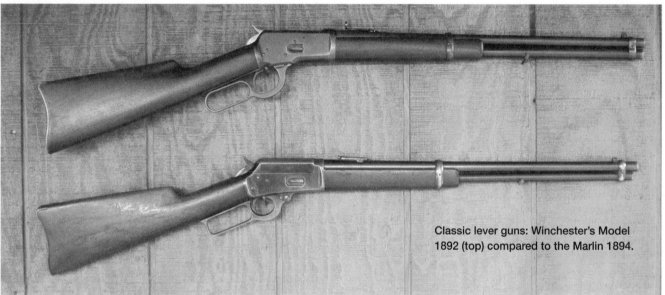

Classic lever guns: Winchester's Model 1892 (top) compared to the Marlin 1894.

Trail Laser Cast 200-grain or 225-grain RNFP .44-40 bullet. These are mostly used in sixguns and the toggle link lever actions. If I need more energy I switch to the Model 1892 replicas and use 200- to 215-grain cast hollowpoints, or 200-grain JHPs over 10 grains of Unique or Universal.

I load the .44-40 on a RCBS Pro 2000 Progressive Press and have found Starline to be the strongest brass. By placing approximately 100 cases in a shallow cardboard box and liberally applying spray cartridge lube, they are ready to be loaded. I have also found reloading the .44-40 works much better if one uses four dies instead of three, as seating and crimping separately prevents crumpling the front edge of the brass. By using a progressive press the extra operation does not require any extra effort.

Replica lever guns are or have been available from many sources. Some that come immediately to mind are Cimarron, EMF, Navy Arms, Taylor's & Co. and Uberti. Very few of us will ever be allowed to even handle much less shoot a real 1860 Henry or 1866 Yellow Boy, and even if we did have one .44 rimfire ammunition is very difficult to find and also quite expensive when it is located. However, thanks to replicas we can all enjoy true copies of these historic and legendary, and I might add, extremely important piece of firearms history; all now chambered in a shootable version chambered in .44-40.

The modern version of the 1860 Henry is true to the original replica. "That damned Yankee rifle that you loaded on Sunday and fired all week," is offered by Navy Arms in at least three versions, all with 24-inch barrels and holding 13 rounds. The brass-framed Military Henry Rifle is available in .44-40, as is a case-colored receiver version and also a third option with a blued receiver. Sights consist of a brass blade front matched up with a long-range, flip-up, ladder-style rear sight. With the rear sight down in its normal position, the Navy Arms 1860 Henry is right on the money at 50 yards. All three versions weigh right at nine pounds. Several versions of the Model 1866 are also available and Cimarron's .44-40 Model 1866 Carbine has a beautiful brass receiver, curved brass buttplate and a 19-inch round barrel.

Anyone who can hold one of these rifles in their hands and not have their soul, spirit and heart stirred by the historical significance of such a great firearm is in emotional trouble! Sight down the barrel, feel a gentle nudge against the shoulder as a .44 WCF round is fired, operate the lever and experience the almost sensual feeling of the new round being chambered. The 1860, 1866 and the 1873 all chamber differently than subsequent lever guns with the cartridge coming straight up and into the chamber with a smooth feeling that no other rifle can duplicate.

The Model 73 Winchesters are made by Uberti of Italy and also offered by several importers. There is the 24" Rifle with octagon barrel, the round barrel 19-inch Carbine, the Sporting Rifle with pistol grip stock and choice of a 24-inch or 30-inch barrel – all available in .44-40; and my favorite – the 1873 Border Model. Navy Arms says its version of this model, the original 1873 Short Rifle, was very rare and available on special order only. It was very popular

in the Southwest along the Mexican Border during the 1870s and 1880s, and it is easy to see why – as this is a very handy and easy to use lever gun. The 1873 Border Model has a brilliantly case-colored receiver mated up with a red colored wood forearm and buttstock, and blued barrel and crescent shaped buttplate.

The 1873, as well as the 1860 and 1866, make a most distinctive sound in operation that endears itself to its user much

The .44-40 can easily be loaded on the RCBS Progressive Press.

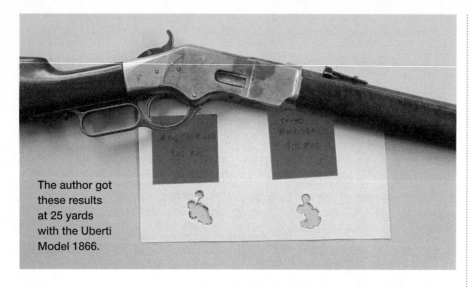

The author got these results at 25 yards with the Uberti Model 1866.

These groups were shot at 50 yards with a tang-sighted Winchester Model 1892.

The author loves being on the range with the Winchester Model 1892.

like the clicks of a Colt Single Action as the hammer is drawn back. Especially with its short but heavy octagon barrel, the 1873 balances very well and comes right up on target.

The slickest Winchester ever, the Model 1892, is being made again by Winchester. It's offered in a carbine model with a large-loop lever in .44-40, as well as .357 Mag., .44 Mag. and .45 Colt. There's also a Short Rifle with a steel crescent buttplate, but it is not available in .44-40. The Model 92 is also offered in replica form by several importers with such models as the standard Rifle Model with a 24-inch octagon barrel and the choice of either a blued or case-colored receiver with real American walnut forearm and buttstock. Joining the rifle is the 20-inch round-barreled carbine, the most popular version of all the original Model 1892s as seen by millions of audiences in four decades of John Wayne movies. My Navy Arms Model 92 Short Rifle is a mate to the above mentioned '73 Border Model Rifle. Navy Arms says of these carbines that the originals were ordered by the Eagle Hardware Co. of Eagle Pass, Texas, and marketed as "Texas Specials." This Model 92 comes with a full octagon barrel, one inch longer than the 1873 Border Rifle at 20 inches.

The Model 1873 may not be what we would consider a strong action; the Model 1892, however, is a very strong action and as such can be used for many more varied activities than the 1873. It also deserves better sights, such as a gold bead front mated up with a Lyman #66 receiver sight. In my old Lyman Cast Bullet Manual there are loads for the .44-40 in the Winchester 92 consisting of a 205-grain cast bullet at 1900 fps, a 215-grain gas check at 1850 fps and a 200-grain jacketed bullet at 2100 fps! All loads were assembled with #2400 powder. Times change, powders and primers change, and I don't believe I want to push the 1892 that hard.

The South American made Rossi M92 in .44-40 is a less expensive alternative to the original Model 1892 Winchester with a retail price about one-third as much as a good used original Winchester 1892, and about half as much as the imported replica 1866 or 1873 rifles. Sights are the standard elevation adjusting style on the rear mated up with a front post fitted into the barrel band. The rear sight can be adjusted laterally by tapping the sight to the right or left in its dovetail slot. A

KAPINE 430211 HB
33.0 GOEX FFg

tang sight or receiver sight would be a much better choice.

Is there room for a .44-40 lever gun in the midst of all the long-range rifles we have today? I'm way past the age of wanting to get beat up by rifles and greatly appreciate the lack of recoil in a .44-40, the smoothness of the action, and just as it did in the few decades preceding and following 1900 – it is still certainly powerful enough to serve as a short-range deer rifle. Whether carried in a pickup truck or on horseback or just used for plinking – it's still one of the handiest rifles ever offered.

It did not take long for someone at Colt to realize the cartridge case for the .44 WCF at a length of 1.3 inches was awfully close to the 1.285 of the .45 Colt, and that users of Winchester 1873s would probably be very interested in having a sixgun using the same ammunition. Just how potent was the .44 WCF in a sixgun? The original brass was what we now refer to as balloon head instead of modern

solid head brass, and had greater case capacity. When I came up with some of the old-style brass I duplicated the original load of 40 grains of black powder under a 200-grain cast bullet. Using a modern magnum pistol primer, this load clocks out of a 7½-inch Single Action Army right at 1000 fps. That is more powerful than the modern .40 S&W and most .45 ACP loads.

Today lever-gun/sixgun combinations abound in .357 Magnum and .44 Magnum, even .45 Colt, and to a much lesser extent in .41 Magnum. Actually, the first combination started in late 1869 as the first Smith & Wesson Model No. 3s were chambered in .44 rimfire. The Army wanted a centerfire cartridge so the .44 S&W American emerged in the Model No. 3 S&W American sixgun. But in the last quarter of the 19th century the main combination was in .44 WCF. Today, with the ease of acquiring replicas, the .44-40 combination has made a comeback. I certainly feel well armed with a Marlin

This Colt Frontier Six-Shooter from the 1880s still shoots very well with carefully crafted black-powder loads.

The author relaxing with a pair of First Generation Colt Frontier Six-Shooters.

1894 or a Winchester or replica 1892 chambered in .44-40 and backed up by a short-barreled Colt New Frontier .44-40.

The standard barrel lengths of the Colt Single Action Army revolver were 4¾, 5½ and 7½ inches, often referred to, respectively, as the Civilian, Artillery and Cavalry Models. Those Colt Single Actions chambered in .44-40 or .44 WCF or .44 Winchester Centerfire, as preferred, were marked on the barrel with "COLT FRONTIER SIX SHOOTER." When the Bisley Model of 1896 was so chambered, "(BISLEY MODEL)" was added in front of the above inscription, and by 1923 ".44-40" had been added behind the same inscription on the Single Action Army. Of the approximately 357,000 Colt Single Action Army sixguns produced from 1873 to 1941, approximately 150,000 were .45 Colts and about 71,000 were chambered in .44-40, making it the second most popular chambering.

One of the most famous Colt Frontier sixshooters in existence is the 7½-inch nickel-plated .44 used by Theodore Roosevelt. When Roosevelt's mother and wife died in the same house on the same day leaving him as a widower with a newborn baby, it was more than he could handle. He had not yet become Col. Theodore Roosevelt of the Rough Riders or the man who would someday become one of our greatest presidents. When this terrible tragedy struck he ran away to the Dakotas and became a rancher, leaving his young daughter with his sister. That experience in the Dakotas had a great deal to do with making Theodore Roosevelt into the man most of us know. As a rancher, Roosevelt dressed in buckskins and carried his fully engraved and ivory stocked .44 Colt crossdraw-style in a carved leather holster. Today, anyone can have a Theodore Roosevelt Colt as Cimarron offers an authentic replica of this most beautiful .44.

In addition to the Single Action Army, Bisley Model and the Flat-Top Target versions, Colt also chambered their Model of 1878 in .44-40. The 1878 was Colt's first bigbore double-action sixgun and except for the double-action mechanism and Smith & Wesson-style grip frame, the Model of 1878 operated the same as the Single Action for loading and unloading. That is, it had a loading gate and an ejector rod. Barrels were marked the same as on the Single Action Army. In the late 1890s Colt would introduce the swing-out cylinder, double-action New Service revolver also chambered in .44-40.

It took a long time for me to locate a 7½-inch Colt New Service .44 WCF at a reasonable price, but the wait was worth it. It is an excellent sixgun, easy shooting and quite accurate. Any outdoorsman in the time between the two World Wars was certainly well armed with a .44 Colt New Service.

Three years after Colt introduced the double-action Model of 1878, Smith & Wesson countered with their Double Action First Model and then followed with the .44 Double Action Frontier in 1886. Chambered in .44-40, the Double Action Frontier would last until just over 15,000 were manufactured by 1913. As with all other Smith & Wesson Frontier revolvers, these are black-powder guns with the frames made before 1900. Remington

Here are two prime examples of First Generation Colt Frontier Six-Shooters, circa 1897 and 1903, with leather by Will Ghormley.

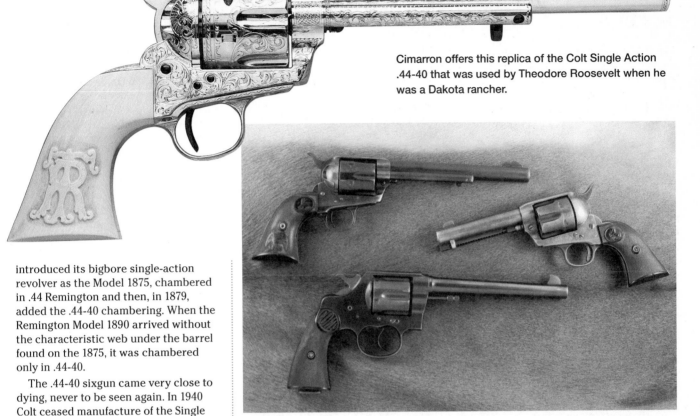

Cimarron offers this replica of the Colt Single Action .44-40 that was used by Theodore Roosevelt when he was a Dakota rancher.

From top to bottom: A Third Generation Colt Single Action, First Generation Colt Single Action and Colt New Service double action, all in .44-40.

introduced its bigbore single-action revolver as the Model 1875, chambered in .44 Remington and then, in 1879, added the .44-40 chambering. When the Remington Model 1890 arrived without the characteristic web under the barrel found on the 1875, it was chambered only in .44-40.

The .44-40 sixgun came very close to dying, never to be seen again. In 1940 Colt ceased manufacture of the Single Action Army and said it would never be produced again. With the coming of television and many hours every day filled up watching Westerns, the time was right for the Colt Single Action Army to return – and return it did – however it did so without the .44-40. The original run of Colt SAAs from 1873 to 1940 included at least three dozen chamberings. With the return of the Colt Single Action in late 1955, only the .45 Colt and .38 Special were cataloged, and then later the .357 Magnum and .44 Special were added.

These sixguns are known as Second Generation Colts. The .44-40 was never chambered in standard catalog versions of the second run of Single Actions. However, Colt made a special version offering the Frontier Six-Shooter Commemorative .44-40 in 1973, along with the Peacemaker Centennial .45 Colt, and then chambered the .44-40 in both the Single Action Army and New Frontier in the Third Generation sixguns. In replica form it has been offered not only in the Single Action Army but also the Bisley Model, the S&W Schofield, the Remington 1875 and 1890 Models, and Ruger's Vaquero. Even Smith & Wesson offered a .44-40 Commemorative on their N-frame and a special edition of Ruger's Super

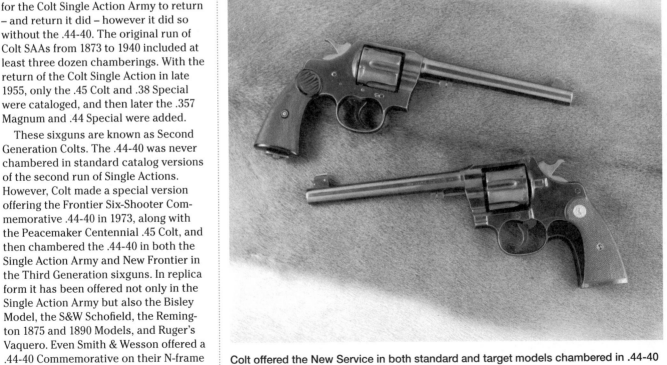

Colt offered the New Service in both standard and target models chambered in .44-40 or .44 Special.

The author has found that the Smith & Wesson Frontier Double Action .44-40 can shoot to minute-of-man.

S&W FRONTIER DA .44-40 BLACK DAWGE 200 769 FPS

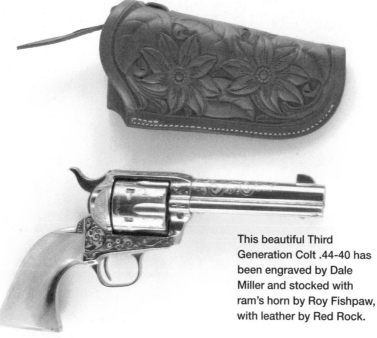

This beautiful Third Generation Colt .44-40 has been engraved by Dale Miller and stocked with ram's horn by Roy Fishpaw, with leather by Red Rock.

Blackhawk Convertibles had a second cylinder chambered in .44-40.

Replica firearms really began with the American manufacturer Great Western in 1954 and its rendition of the Single Action Army. Even though the Great Westerns disappeared in the early '60s, they set the stage for replicas from Italy through such companies Cimarron, EMF, Navy Arms and Taylor's to provide shooters with a large catalog of authentically styled single actions. I have several .44-40 Single Actions from these companies as well as a very special pair from AWA (American Western Arms). These two .44-40s have octagon barrels – one 10 inches and the other 7½, are beautifully blued and finished, and are fitted with one-piece mesquite stocks by special friend and sixgunsmith Jim Martin. Jim was very active in Fast Draw competitions, always using a 7½-inch Colt .44-40. My two AWA sixguns are not only excellent shooting .44-40s, they also came with extra cylinders chambered in .44 Special.

Colt used the same barrels on the .44 Specials as it did on the .44-40s even though it only produced about 500 of the Specials prior to World War II. During the Third Generation run of both Colt Single Actions and New Frontiers this was also true, so either the .44 Special or .44-40 can be easily fitted with an extra cylinder of the other chambering. In fact, I have several such combinations as well as a 7½-inch New Frontier .44 Special, which has been fitted with not only a .44-40 cylinder but one in .44 Russian as well. Ruger .357 Magnum Three-Screw Flat-Top Blackhawks can also be easily converted to .44-40/.44 Special by rechambering two Ruger cylinders and fitting a Colt Third Generation .44-40 New Frontier barrel. The old Rugers have the same thread pattern on their frame as the Colt Third Generation barrels, namely 24 tpi.

Custom sixgunsmiths David Clements and Brian Cosby have built .44-40s for me using Colt New Frontier barrels and Ruger Three-Screw .357 Blackhawks. I was able to supply David with two cylinders and a 4¾-inch barrel so it is a convertible in .44-40 and .44 Special, while Brian used a supplied 7½-inch .44-40 New Frontier Colt barrel and rechambered my Ruger cylinder to .44-40. Both of these make excellent, relatively lightweight, easy-to-pack .44-40s, while the Clements gun is an excellent example of what a Perfect Packin' Pistol should be. Today Ruger offers their New Model

Brian Cosby built this .44-40 on a Ruger Three-Screw .357 Blackhawk using a Colt New Frontier barrel.

One of the author's favorite Perfect Packin' Pistols by David Clements on a Ruger Three-Screw .357 Blackhawk with a Colt New Frontier barrel, and fitted with two cylinders in .44-40 and .44 Special.

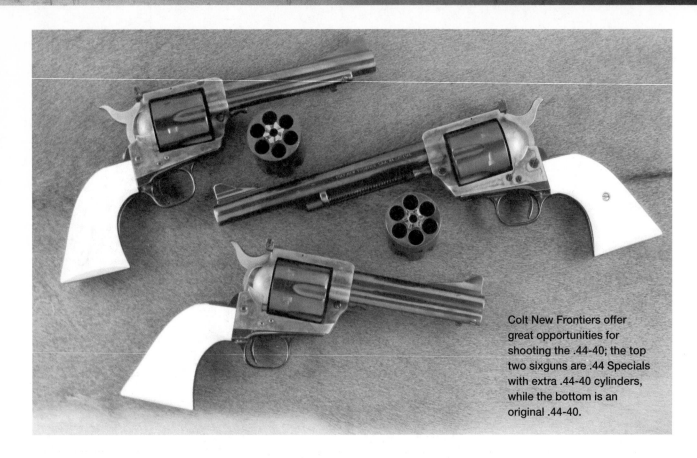

Colt New Frontiers offer great opportunities for shooting the .44-40; the top two sixguns are .44 Specials with extra .44-40 cylinders, while the bottom is an original .44-40.

SPECIALLY SELECTED .44 WCF/.44-40 LOADS
.44-40 COLT NEW FRONTIER 3ᴿᴰ GENERATION 4¾" BARREL

Load	MV	5 Shots at 20 Yards	
Lyman #42798 (.428")/9.2 gr. Unique	981 fps	1 ⅛"	
Meister 200 (.427")/7.1 gr. HP38	803 fps	1 ⅜"	
Meister 200 (.427")/6.2 gr. Red Dot	831 fps	1 ¾"	
Oregon Trail 200 (.429")/8 gr. Unique	771 fps	1 ½"	
Oregon Trail 200 (.427")/9 gr. Universal	833 fps	1 ¼"	
Oregon Trail 225 (.427")/8 gr. Universal	871 fps	1 ½"	
Oregon Trail 200 (.429")/6.5 gr.Trail Boss	713 fps	1 ¾"	

.44-40 COLT NEW FRONTIER 3ᴿᴰ GENERATION 5½" BARREL

Load	MV	5 Shots at 20 Yards	
Lyman #427666 (.428")/9 gr. Unique	921 fps	1 ⅛"	
Lyman #42798 (.428")/9 gr. Unique	1016 fps	1 ¼"	
Oregon Trail 200 (.429")/8 gr. Unique	821 fps	1 ⅛"	

NAVY ARMS 1860 HENRY .44-40, 24" OCTAGON BARREL

Load	MV	10 Shots/25 Yds	10 Shots/50 Yds
Oregon Trail 200/8 gr. Unique	1127 fps	2"	3 ¾"
Oregon Trail 225/8 gr. Unique	1038 fps	1 ⅝"	3 ¾"

SPECIALLY SELECTED .44 WCF/.44-40 LOADS (CONTINUED)
NAVY ARMS 1873, 19" OCTAGON BARREL BORDER MODEL SHORT RIFLE

Load	MV	5 Shots at 50 Yards	
Black Hills 200 .44-40	1151 fps	1 ¼"	
Oregon Trail 225/8 gr. Unique	1181 fps	1 ⅜"	
Oregon Trail 225/7 gr. WW231	1074 fps	1 ⅛"	

MODEL 1892 WINCHESTER .44-40 20" BARREL

Load	MV	3 Shots at 50 Yards	
Hornady 200 JHP/20 gr. H4227	1256 fps	1 ¼"	
Remington 200 JFP/22 gr. H4227	1537 fps	1 ¾"	
Remington 200 JFP/8 gr. Unique	1056 fps	2"	
Remington 200 JFP/9 gr. Unique	1197 fps	2"	
Speer 200 JFP/10 gr. Unique	1366 fps	2 ¼"	
Speer 225 JHP/10 gr. Unique	1309 fps	2"	
AA LTD 205 RNFP/8 gr. Unique	1193 fps	1 ⅝"	
Burgess 200 RNFP/8 gr. Unique	1191 fps	1 ¾"	
Oregon Trail 200 RNFP/10 gr. Unique	1390 fps	2"	
Oregon Trail 225 RNFP/10 gr. Unique	1360 fps	1"	

ROSSI M92 .44-40 20" BARREL

Load	MV	3 Shots at 50 Yards	
Oregon Trail 200 RNFP/7 gr. WW231	1076 fps	⅞"	
Oregon Trail 200 RNFP/5.3 gr. N100	1017 fps	1 ¼"	
Oregon Trail 200 RNFP/4.8 gr. Clays	927 fps	1"	
Oregon Trail 200 RNFP/9 gr. Herco	1244 fps	2 ½"	
Oregon Trail 200 RNFP/7 gr. Universal	876 fps	1 ⅜"	
Oregon Trail 200 RNFP/5 gr. Bullseye	1020 fps	⅞"	
Oregon Trail 200 RNFP/8 gr. Unique	1195 fps	1"	
Oregon Trail 200 RNFP/8.5 gr. Universal	1145 fps	1 ⅜"	
Oregon Trail 200 RNFP/10 gr. Unique	1377 fps	2"	
OregonTrail 200 RNFP/5 gr. Goex FFg	1220 fps	1 ¼"	
Oregon Trail 200 RNFP/36.5 gr. Goex FFFg	1311 fps	2"	

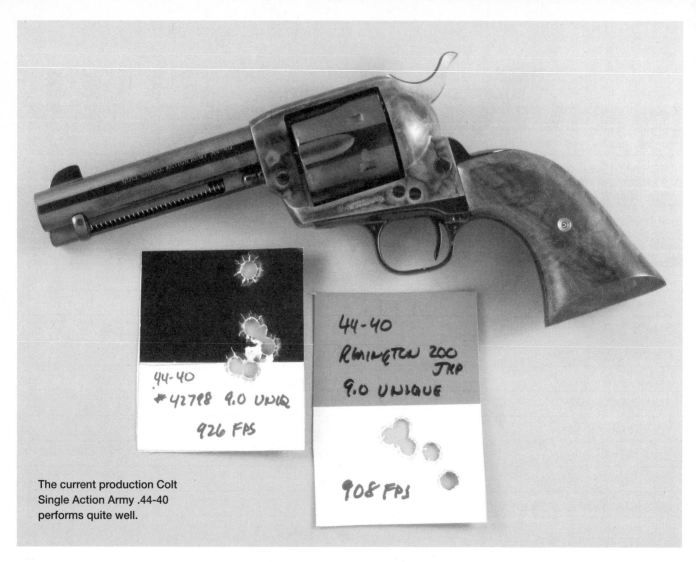

44-40

#42798 9.0 UNIQ

926 FPS

44-40
REMINGTON 200
JHP
9.0 UNIQUE

908 FPS

The current production Colt
Single Action Army .44-40
performs quite well.

Flat-Top Blackhawk in .44 Special. Perhaps someday they will add an auxiliary cylinder in .44-40.

Nestled among many of my most cherished possessions is a Texas Longhorn Arms West Texas Flat-Top Target that originally was maker Bill Grover's personal sixgun. This 7½-inch Single Action started life as a .44 Magnum and then after selling it to me, Bill fitted it with .44-40 and .44 Special cylinders. I used all three on a hunting trip with him in Texas to take three different animals. He then made one more cylinder for it in .44 Russian before he passed on, and we never did get the fifth cylinder done which was to be in .44 Colt. Unlike Grover's Improved Number Five Single Actions, which duplicate Elmer Keith's grip frame from his No. 5 SAA, this grip frame is more like an 1860 Army and makes shooting heavy loads very comfortable. The West Texas Flat-Top Target is a large-framed single action about the size of a Ruger Super Blackhawk, so it

allows heavier loads to be developed and used in .44-40 brass.

There are many who will label the .44-40 as antiquated, totally out of date and useless. I often feel the same labels could be hung on me; perhaps that is why I feel such a kinship with it.

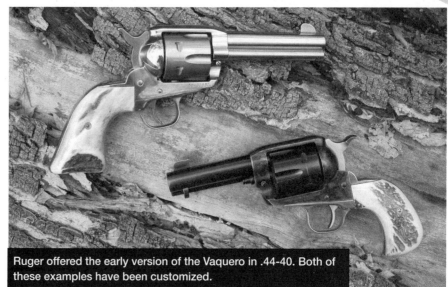

Ruger offered the early version of the Vaquero in .44-40. Both of these examples have been customized.

THE MACHINE GUN INVESTOR

Going Full Auto, For Fun and Profit

BY **Frank W. James**

The German MG-34 was the first mass-produced, general-purpose belt-fed machine gun and as such it represents a milestone in automatic weapons design. This well-preserved and well-equipped, fully transferable example was sold by Cowan's Auctions in October 2013 for $43,125.00.

Photo courtesy Cowan's Auctions

The beginning of the 21st century has been characterized by economic turmoil and uncertainty. The lackluster performance of investments in real estate, stocks and bonds has only made such investments uncertain and dismal, when compared to their performance a decade ago. Additionally, bank interest rates on certificates of deposit have sunk to the lowest levels seen in decades, out of fear of potential inflation due to a lopsided national deficit. All of these factors that affect an individual's search for a safe place to put his cash assets.

Where can the investor with liquid resources best protect this hard-earned equity and safeguard their family's future? As crazy as it may sound, the answer for some is the purchase of an NFA-registered machine gun or, in some cases, guns.

FIRST, THE LAW

The first thing anyone researching this subject must do is to understand the federal law, their state law and in some cases, their local ordinances and regulations. The federal law starts with the 1934 National Firearms Act (NFA), which

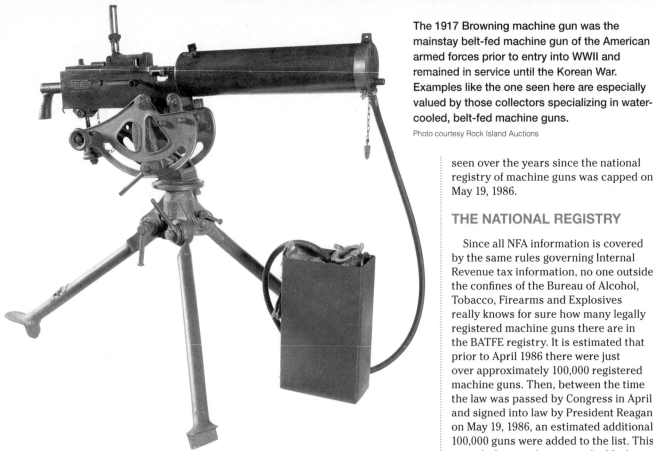

The 1917 Browning machine gun was the mainstay belt-fed machine gun of the American armed forces prior to entry into WWII and remained in service until the Korean War. Examples like the one seen here are especially valued by those collectors specializing in water-cooled, belt-fed machine guns.

Photo courtesy Rock Island Auctions

seen over the years since the national registry of machine guns was capped on May 19, 1986.

THE NATIONAL REGISTRY

Since all NFA information is covered by the same rules governing Internal Revenue tax information, no one outside the confines of the Bureau of Alcohol, Tobacco, Firearms and Explosives really knows for sure how many legally registered machine guns there are in the BATFE registry. It is estimated that prior to April 1986 there were just over approximately 100,000 registered machine guns. Then, between the time the law was passed by Congress in April and signed into law by President Reagan on May 19, 1986, an estimated additional 100,000 guns were added to the list. This period of time is known as the Machine Gun Rush. Since then some guns have been culled from the list because of improper registrations, but most authorities believe there are just over 200,000 legal machine guns in the registry, and most of these are available for civilian ownership.

FORM 4 REGISTRATION FORMS

All machine guns eligible for civilian possession in the NFA registry are

was modified with the 1968 Gun Control Act and then the May 19, 1986 Firearms Owners Protection Act. The 1934 NFA law established that all firearms capable of firing more than one shot with a single trigger pull must be registered with the federal government and pay a $200 NFA tax. This registration requirement also included sound suppressors (often referred to as silencers), and short-barreled rifles and shotguns.

In recent years, weapons like cane guns, smoothbore hand-guns, short-barreled shotguns made with a pistol grip and no buttstock, and hand-guns with a forward vertical grip have been classified as "Any Other Weapon," which remains a subcategory of weapons and firearms covered by the NFA registration requirements.

Individuals in the United States can currently possess legally registered NFA items in approximately 33 states, and the regulations within these states are not uniform with each other. Some states will allow the civilian ownership of machine guns, if they are registered under the provisions of the federal NFA require-ments, but will not allow the possession of silencers or sound suppressors. Other

states will allow machine guns, but will not allow the possession of a "sawed-off" or short-barreled shotgun.

With these many distinctions in mind and, for this article, we are concerned only with legally registered machine guns and their values, which have increased steadily since 1986. In some cases, these increases have been spec-tacular in their appreciation and in other cases more mundane, but in all cases significant equity appreciation has been

The German MP-40 was the mainstay of the Nazi war machine and well over a million were produced during WWII. Original examples that were registered prior to or during the 1968 amnesty period have demonstrated sterling performance in asset appreciation. More affordable, but fully transferable examples were made from parts kits and American receivers in the years prior to the 1986 ban on new machine guns.

Photo courtesy Rock Island Auctions

Although most WWII military Thompson submachine guns range in value from $10,000 to well over $20,000, this example broke the record when Cowan's Auctions sold it during their October 2013 auction for $29,900.00! It's in perfect condition and small details like the original canvas sling certainly helped it reached this record value.

Photo courtesy Cowan's Auctions

registered on a BATFE Form 4. There are other forms for other types of transfers but for our purposes here, and speaking solely for nondealer civilian ownership, only those guns registered on a Form 4 are eligible for civilian ownership. Special Occupational Tax payer (SOT) dealers in legal machine guns can possess guns that are forbidden for civilian possession, such as pre-ban and post-ban dealer samples, but the BATFE requirements for the NFA dealer are far more involved, including the fact that each dealer is routinely inspected for compliance with these regulations. (The terms pre-ban and post-ban dealer samples refer to guns available only to SOT dealers and the specific enactment date of May 1986. Most post-ban dealer samples require a letter from a law enforcement agency requesting a demonstration of that specific weapon before the SOT

dealer can possess the weapon in his inventory.)

As to why machine guns have continuously appreciated in value, many like comparing ownership of registered machine guns to that of real estate because in both cases the production of "new" real estate or "new" registered machine guns is virtually impossible.

Jack Lewis, the resident machine gun expert at Cowan's Auctions in Cincinnati, Ohio, says the machine gun market is very similar to the diamond market, but the difference is that instead of the mining companies restricting the supply, the federal government does. Another difference is that the diamond firms, although they control the supply, also add to it in a continuous fashion while the government makes every effort not to do so.

What effect does all this have on the value of registered guns available to the civilians able to possess these items? In the late 1980s, shortly after the law went into effect and the registry was closed to the addition of more Form 4 machine guns, a registered-receiver replica HK MP5 was selling for around $2,500. Seven years ago that same gun had increased in value to $12,500 and today the value of that firearm can be anywhere from $25,000 to $32,000, depending upon condition.

CONDITION, CONDITION, CONDITION

The value of real estate always centers on location. A similar situation exists for firearms, as any collector will tell you, and here it is the condition of the firearm. What shape is it in and how close to being virtually new is it? Additionally, is it a historic firearm? Did someone famous or, in some cases, infamous own or possess this weapon at some point in its history? And, if so, how well documented is this history? What accessories or spare parts and packaging accompany the gun as it is offered for sale?

Some things that might normally be ignored or considered trivial can have a profound impact on the overall price of

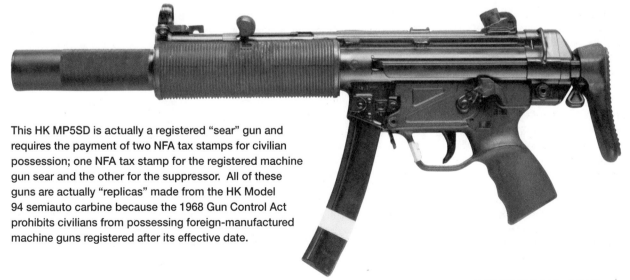

This HK MP5SD is actually a registered "sear" gun and requires the payment of two NFA tax stamps for civilian possession; one NFA tax stamp for the registered machine gun sear and the other for the suppressor. All of these guns are actually "replicas" made from the HK Model 94 semiauto carbine because the 1968 Gun Control Act prohibits civilians from possessing foreign-manufactured machine guns registered after its effective date.

This Kreighoff Waffenfabrik FG-42 was a select-fire battle rifle that was produced during WWII for German paratroopers. It fires a full-power 7.92x57mm cartridge and was not made in large numbers. No one knows for sure how many are registered with the NFA branch of the BATFE, but it can't be many. This example is fully transferable and was sold by Cowan's Auctions in October 2013 for $143,750!

Photo courtesy Cowan's Auctions

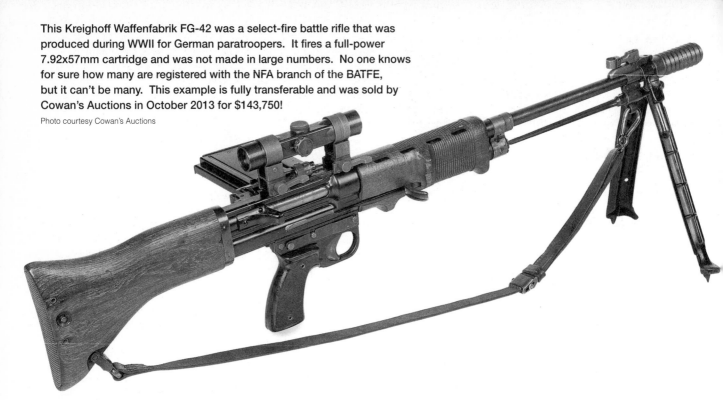

a firearm. As an example, during World War II approximately 824,000 M1 and M1A1 Thompson submachine guns were manufactured. After the war many were given to various local law enforcement agencies and many of these guns were registered either by these same agencies as legal machine guns, or as legal "dewat" or registered de-militarized machine guns. (A registered dewat machine gun can be made operational because it was registered prior to the May 19, 1986 cutoff date.)

As such, these guns currently run in value from $10,000 up to $19,000, depending upon the individual condition. However, during the Cowan's Auction October 2013 sale, a pristine WWII Auto-Ordnance M1A1 Thompson sold for $29,900. Its condition was perfect, but one of the more trivial aspects to this particular gun was the fact it came with an original issued cloth sling. These slings are very hard to locate and this little added feature, together with the gun's overall perfect condition, yielded a sale price that was almost double that of the average condition M1A1 Thompson.

Another factor in terms of condition is if the gun is a conversion—which is a machine gun made from a semiauto version of the original and registered prior to the cutoff date. And how good was the work performed in doing the conversion?

For instance, all the fully transferable registered Form 4 HK MP5s are actually

replicas. They had to be because the 1968 Gun Control Act forbade the importation and sale to civilians of foreign-made machine guns after its effective date. If the guns were registered prior to 1968, they are permitted for civilian possession, but the MP5 didn't start arriving into this country in any number until the mid- to late 1970s. There were guns in existence prior to 1968, but they didn't have all the features commonly associated with the MP5 submachine gun seen in the last 20 years.

The MP5s currently registered on Form 4s are guns that were built from the civilian-legal HK Model 94 semiautomatic 9mm carbine. Manufacturers like Bill Fleming, Billistics, Curtis Higgins of S&H and many others converted these guns and registered them. Some of these guns were detailed to such an extent that they are complete duplicates of the original, to the point that all parts will easily interchange. Most, however, are what are known as "sear guns."

Due to the design of the lower trigger group on the roller locked MP5, HK53, HK33 and G-3 firearms, the upper receiver is the actual firearm because it is the serial numbered part, but a full-auto sear can be installed in the lower receiver/trigger group. This, together with the installation of a full-auto bolt carrier, converted the gun to select-fire capability. During April and May of 1986 when the machine

gun rush was on, many of these Title II manufacturers concentrated on making only the full-auto capable HK sear and registered them as the actual machine gun, because these sears could be installed without alteration to the original "firearm," the upper receiver. A few registered sears were also made for the FN-produced FNC semiauto carbine in 5.56x45mm because the situation there was very similar.

Today, you will find Form 4 HK MP5 replica submachine guns offered for sale with "swing-down" lowers. They were converted in a fashion to be just like the originals and have what the Technology Section of the BATFE considers a machine gun receiver. Most of these guns are registered receiver guns but I have seen guns made in this fashion that were registered sear guns, because supposedly they were registered before the BATFE clarified their positions on these features.

Most sear guns however still have the features of the semiauto upper receivers because the BATFE eventually ruled that converting these guns to be identical with the original design would create another machine gun that was not registered prior to the 1986 cutoff date. If this is starting to sound confusing, you are beginning to understand the intricacies of these guns, their features and the NFA rules and regulations that govern their possession.

Yet, even the sear guns have been escalating in price because if you have just one registered sear with the HK roller locked guns, you can move that sear to other HK firearms with a similar design. That means you can have an MP5 sear gun, remove the lower receiver/trigger group with the registered sear, change the ejector and install it on an HK93 to create a select-fire HK33—or move it to a HK91, change the ejector once again, and create a select-fire G-3 replica. It is this versatility that drives the interest in registered HK sears and their values.

Back in the late 1980s and early '90s, these sears were not considered as worthwhile as the swing-down lower receivers and most sold for around $600 (plus the $200 NFA tax and any state sales tax) apiece. Today, with the increased value of registered machine guns and the versatility offered by a registered sear, the sears now command as much as a fully transferable registered gun, which currently is in the $18,000 to $25,000 range.

SCARCITY

Scarcity is also another factor in determining the value and financial appreciation of a machine gun. Although no one knows for sure, knowledgeable collectors estimate there are fewer than a dozen fully transferable German Kreighoff FG-42 machine guns in the NFA registry. Even the German war records indicate that in comparison to other weapons of the Nazi war machine, these guns were made in small numbers, but an extremely fine example FG-42 was sold by Cowan's Auction in October 2013 for the astonishing price of $143,750.00!

Although they are not scarce, Cowan's Auction also sold a Steyr produced MP-40 for $48,000 during their April 2013 auction. This particular gun was highly finished and the equivalent of a presentation-grade gun, while the standard MP-40 was made in the millions at relatively low cost to equip the German forces during WWII.

DRAWBACKS AND NEGATIVES

With any investment there are negatives and pitfalls. The big one with NFA registered machine guns is not so much the paperwork requirements, but waiting for that paperwork to be processed. All Form 4 transfers have to be approved by the BATFE in Washington, D.C., and the application has to be accompanied by two sets of the transferee's fingerprints and two passport-style photos. Additionally, the application must be signed by the Chief Law Enforcement Officer (CLEO) where the applicant resides. This can be a problem in some areas because as a matter of policy, some CLEOs refuse to sign these applications.

Currently, the approval of a Form 4 transfer is taking nine months or longer. Some believe this is the result of the increased interest and sales of registered suppressors and silencers, which have overwhelmed the NFA section of the BATFE with an avalanche of Form 4 applications. Add in the occasional governmental shutdown and budget restrictions due to sequestration, and the process seems to take forever to the person who has just laid out many thousands of dollars for a commodity that he cannot possess until the federal government grants its sanctified approval.

One factor influencing the value and potential appreciation of any registered machine gun is its caliber. Years ago many advanced collectors deemed the British Vickers water-cooled, belt-fed machine gun to be the epitome of machine gun collecting and their prices at the time reflected that view. Today however, the situation has changed somewhat for the simplest of reasons; relatively inexpensive military surplus .303 British ammunition no longer exists, and in a practical sense is unavailable. Despite the financial potential to owning any legal machine gun, it is not as much fun to own if you can't find ammo to shoot in it.

The drought in military surplus .303 British ammunition has affected the values of all the historic machine guns chambered for this round and remains a concern for any potential investor. If there is an area of the machine gun market that has gone soft, it would have to be the older guns chambered for calibers that are simply unavailable in most any form or volume, such as the 8mm Lebel, 6.5 Arisaka or the 6.5 Carcano. Some would suggest reloading if you can locate a sufficient quantity of virgin boxer primed brass, but it's hard to envision reloading 300 to 400 rounds per hour for a gun that shoots 600 rounds per minute.

For years many machine gun collectors considered the water-cooled Vickers belt-fed machine gun to be the epitome of machine gun collecting. The problem that no one ever foresaw was a worldwide shortage of reasonably priced .303 British military surplus ammo. These guns now sell at auctions between $11,500 and $19,000.

Photo courtesy Cowan's Auctions

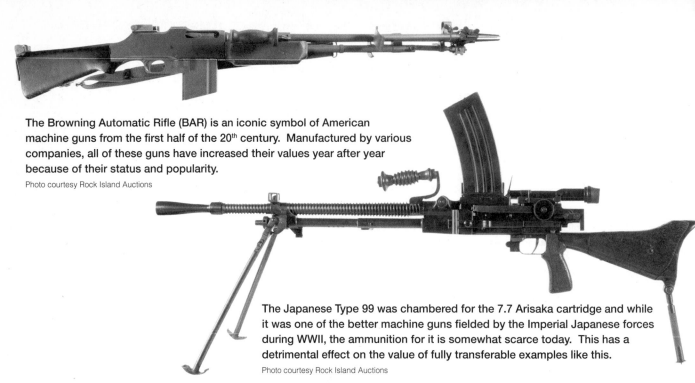

The Browning Automatic Rifle (BAR) is an iconic symbol of American machine guns from the first half of the 20th century. Manufactured by various companies, all of these guns have increased their values year after year because of their status and popularity.

Photo courtesy Rock Island Auctions

The Japanese Type 99 was chambered for the 7.7 Arisaka cartridge and while it was one of the better machine guns fielded by the Imperial Japanese forces during WWII, the ammunition for it is somewhat scarce today. This has a detrimental effect on the value of fully transferable examples like this.

Photo courtesy Rock Island Auctions

WHO BUYS THESE THINGS?

Many Class III dealers believe the actual number of people interested in submachine guns and select-fire rifles is about twice the size of those interested in the heavier belt-fed, tripod-mounted guns. Ammunition availability and cost factors into this as well because the pistol-caliber submachine guns chambered for 9x19mm or .45ACP are the most popular, with the select-fire rifles chambered for 5.56x45mm and 7.62x51mm coming a close second.

There are also entry-level NFA machine guns, if you will. The MAC-10, MAC-11, Reising and Sten tube guns would fit into such a category. All of these submachine guns are valued at the lower end of the market and are more affordable, but then their potential financial appreciation rate is lower as well.

Jack Lewis, of Cowan's Auctions, explained he has witnessed trends over the years in gun collecting. Years ago, firearms used in the American Civil War were the in thing, but that trend has

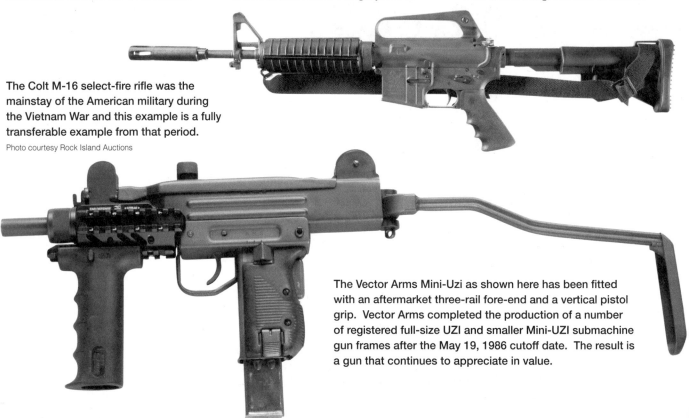

The Colt M-16 select-fire rifle was the mainstay of the American military during the Vietnam War and this example is a fully transferable example from that period.

Photo courtesy Rock Island Auctions

The Vector Arms Mini-Uzi as shown here has been fitted with an aftermarket three-rail fore-end and a vertical pistol grip. Vector Arms completed the production of a number of registered full-size UZI and smaller Mini-UZI submachine gun frames after the May 19, 1986 cutoff date. The result is a gun that continues to appreciate in value.

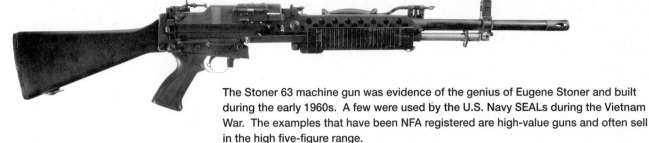

The Stoner 63 machine gun was evidence of the genius of Eugene Stoner and built during the early 1960s. A few were used by the U.S. Navy SEALs during the Vietnam War. The examples that have been NFA registered are high-value guns and often sell in the high five-figure range.

Photo courtesy Rock Island Auctions

softened and Lewis feels the same could be said for the "One of One Thousand" Winchesters and their like. However, NFA Class III guns have stood the test of time and with the economic factors being what they are, interest has been steadily increasing in recent years.

Lewis said, "For the machine gun dealer or those licensed to sell Class III weapons, these customers are a very professional group of people. They are educated and knowledgeable about the subject matter and the legal procedures. The Class III customer can be divided into one of three groups: those interested in hand-held weapons like submachine guns and select-fire rifles, those interested in belt-fed weapons and those who are only interested in water-cooled guns.

"They include royalty from offshore because one of the bidders on the FG-42 in the October auction was a king from a Middle Eastern country. You find more professional people in this category of gun collecting than any other, and the reason is they know where they want to put their money and they understand the potential for financial growth."

It is worth noting that the FG-42 did not go to the king, but to an American buyer. Registered NFA items can be exported if shipped to the proper authorities in the designated country, but once exported they can never be brought back into the United States, which is another factor in the exclusivity of this investment.

A FUN INVESTMENT

Some voice reluctance to owning a legal machine gun because of the extensive registration and the fear that the government will confiscate them at some point. My feelings are that legal machine gun owners are the canary in the coal mine. If any administration would move against this highly regulated and tightly controlled segment of the gun community, those outside it would move in such a way to make further confiscation of any firearm extremely unacceptable politically, labor intensive and counterproductive.

Additionally, people who own multiple examples of these devices are those with the greatest financial assets and are often the heavy contributors to both major political parties. Jack Lewis feels their wrath would be vented highly effectively on their representatives at the local and regional level, and no politician worth his salt wants to anger those who are good financial contributors.

Presently, informed observers believe that NFA weapons, on average, are appreciating somewhere between 6 and 11 percent each and every year. Obviously, some more than others and some less than average, but overall many feel that is the average rate of appreciation. I think the neatest thing about this form of financial investment is the fact that often these guns are living history and have a connection to events that preceded me, but remain the stuff of legend and heroics.

Besides that, they are a lot of fun to drag out of the gun vault and shoot full-auto a couple of weekends a year. You can't do that with a certificate of deposit or a share of stock regardless of its dividend or rate of return.

References:

Cowan's Auctions
6270 Este Avenue
Cincinnati, Ohio 45232
(513) 871-1670
www.cowanauctions.com

Rock Island Auction Company
7819 42nd Street West
Rock Island, Illinois 61201
(800) 238-8022
www.rockislandauction.com

Things that enhance the value of an already expensive fully transferable machine gun are the extras that go with it. This MG-42 is mounted on a Lafette tripod and is fitted with the anti-aircraft ring sight. All of these details add to the value as the gun appreciates over time.

Photo courtesy Rock Island Auctions

For lawmen and citizens considering a 9mm-class pistol for defense, the .38 Super offers an important third choice.

THE .38 SUPER
TOO GOOD TO DIE

For all of its long history, this cartridge is as modern as tomorrow.

BY Jim Wilson

The .38 Super has also enjoyed a popular place among action-shooting enthusiasts.

One of the misconceptions about the .38 Super cartridge is that it was designed because lawmen of the day needed a cartridge that would be more effective against the gangsters who had taken to driving cars and wearing bulletproof vests. While this may be true in one sense, it sort of puts the cart before the horse.

You see, the cartridge was designed by John M. Browning and introduced by Colt in 1900 for their Model 1900 auto-loading pistol. At that time the cartridge was called the .38 ACP and drove a 130-grain bullet at slightly over 1,000 fps.

By the time the Model 1911 pistol came along and production quotas were finally being met, it was determined that this new pistol could handle velocities and pressures that previous models simply could not.

Along about the latter half of the 1920s Colt began to consider beefing up the .38 ACP cartridge to give it more power and, in 1929, they brought it out as the .38 Super. In today's jargon it would have been termed the ".38 ACP +P." In fact, the .38 Super was the same bullet and same cartridge case as the .38 ACP. Nothing had changed except the powder. However, it drove that 130-grain bullet at

a good 1,300 fps.

You could say that the .38 Super is America's 9mm cartridge because it uses the same .356" bullets as the 9mm. The cartridge consists of a semirimmed case that is .9" in length and requires a 1:16" rifling twist. And today, SAAMI specs list the maximum pressure as being 36,500 psi. The "+P" listing that we see on boxes of today's .38 Super ammunition was first added in 1974, simply to differentiate it from the original 1900 loading.

Now back to those gangsters. By the 1920s and '30s, gangsters were still following the old traditions of bank robbery first set out by the James boys,

Traditionally, the .38 Super is found in the 1911 platform, which includes lightweight and all-steel Commanders.

For comparison: the .38 Super on the left with the 9mm and .45 ACP.

the Youngers and the Daltons. About the only real difference in their techniques was that they were using cars instead of horses. They'd hit a bank in a whirlwind attack, shoot anyone that resisted, then jump in their cars and get as far away from the scene of the crime as they possibly could. The other modern addition to this time-honored bank robbery method was the fact that many of them now wore the thick, bulky, bulletproof vests that had become available.

The modern police pistol calibers of the day included the .38 Special, .44 Special, .45 Colt and .45 ACP. It was quickly learned that none of these did a very impressive job of penetrating car bodies or the bulletproof vests. But, it was found that the 130-grain FMJ load of the .38 Super had enough penetration to get the job done in most cases. Of course, since cops drove cars and wore vests too, the .38 Super also became the darling of the crooks. John Dillinger and Baby Face Nelson both liked the .38 Super and even had 1911s customized with shoulder stocks and altered to fire fully automatic.

In 1934 on a dusty Louisiana farm road, Clyde Barrow and Bonnie Parker met their fate at the hands of a determined team of lawmen. Now, I never knew Capt. Frank Hamer, but his son, Frank Jr., was a friend of mine. The son confirmed to me that his father always carried his engraved Colt single action, in .45 Colt, but he also pointed out that Capt. Hamer was a big believer in carrying two guns when things looked like they might get serious. Frank Hamer Jr. said that throughout the Bonnie & Clyde investigation, his father's second gun was a Colt Government Model in .38 Super, worn under his suit coat in a shoulder holster. Whether or not he fired it on that fateful day in Louisiana, however, is doubtful.

One of the interesting parts of the .38 Super story that has never been fully investigated is the relationship between that cartridge and the Texas Rangers. Up until fairly recent times, the Texas Rangers were never issued firearms, but were expected to provide their own. By the early 1900s, the venerable Colt

Peacemaker had begun to give way in the Ranger ranks to the Colt 1911 auto. And an unknown number of these were chambered for the .38 Super cartridge.

My old friend Lee Trimble served as a Texas Ranger and a Special Texas Ranger from about 1920 through World War II. In the early days, working along the Rio Grande in Big Bend country, Lee relied on a pair of .44 Special Smith & Wesson revolvers. But, just prior to the start of the war he went to work for Frank Hamer, guarding the shipyards in the Houston-Galveston area. In the place of his .44 revolvers, Trimble chose to carry a pair of .38 Super Colt autos in A.W. Brill holsters.

Company A, Texas Rangers, the company that worked the Houston area, seemed to have a particular fondness for the .38 Super. It could have been that their old captain, Hardy Purvis, had some influence on this. In 1962, Company A Ranger Ed Gooding used his Colt .38 Super in a vicious shootout with two burglars in a Houston warehouse, killing one and seriously wounding the other. And as late as the 1970s, .38 Super autos were often given as retirement gifts when a Texas Ranger left the service. Clearly, the relationship between the Texas Rangers and the Colt .38 Super deserves further research.

Another area of popularity for this cartridge was in Mexico, and Central and South America. Many of those countries decreed that citizens could not own a pistol chambered for a military cartridge, which of course, left out the 9mm and .45 ACP. For that reason, the .38 Super has always had a following south of the Rio Grande. It is a little known fact that Col. Jeff Cooper, the guru of the .45 auto, always carried a 1911 in .38 Super when teaching and working in those countries. At least one of his .38 autos is still a prized possession of the Cooper family.

For all that, the .38 Super never gained the popularity and place among American cartridges that it probably deserved. I think that there are two major reasons for this lack of interest.

The first is that the .357 Magnum cartridge, and guns chambered for it, was introduced in 1935. Even with the soft lead bullets of the first magnum ammunition, the .357 proved to be a much better performer in all respects, due to the increased power. That and the fact that law enforcement of that era was duly and solidly wedded to using double-action revolvers. They could have the power and the reliability of the DA revolver… what's not to like?

The second factor that led to the lack of popularity of the .38 Super was the fact that the cartridge just did not prove as accurate as other pistol cartridges. It turns out that this really should have been blamed on the gun and not the cartridge.

Back in 1900, Colt designed the Model 1900 pistol so that the cartridge case headspaced on the semi-rim, not the case mouth, as in later pistol cartridges. The barrel and feed ramp of the Model 1900 pistol were designed so that they gave adequate support to this arrangement. For some reason, when Colt went to the Model 1911 pistol they did not change this arrangement, even though the new gun's barrel and feed ramp did not offer that same necessary support. It wasn't until Irv Stone began to manufacture drop-in barrels for the .38 Super Colts that the problem was resolved. Since the 1980s, all modern .38 Super pistols are manufactured so that the case headspaces on the case mouth, and accuracy has been competitive with other autoloading cartridges.

Still, throughout all of this, the .38 Super soldiered on. The bull's-eye shooters figured out that they could use the Colt 1911 in .38 Super as a basis for modifying the pistol so that it would fire the .38 Special target load. Pistol-smiths like Bob Chow and Jimmy Clark made a good living modifying the pistols for this formal target competition.

With the advent of IPSC competition, the .38 Super got another boost. Since this shooting discipline was supposed to simulate combat and defensive shooting, the ammunition used was required to score at a certain power level in order to make Major Class. Gamesmen quickly found that a heavy loaded .38 Super, using one of Irv Stone's Bar-Sto barrels, would do just that. And it would do it with less felt recoil than the .45 ACP.

Today, the ammunition manufacturers have pretty well standardized on .38 Super loads with slightly less velocity than the original. For example, most of the loads using a 124-grain bullet will run at about 1,250 fps, comparable to many .357 Magnum loads. However, some of the smaller ammunition companies specialize in .38 Super loads offering higher performance. Double Tap, Buffalo Bore and Cor-Bon are good examples. Their 115-grain loads will run in excess of 1,400 fps. The 124 and 125-grain ammunition will clock in the neighborhood of 1,350 fps. And the 147-grain will produce something like 1,150-1,200 fps. The .38 Super may be one of our oldest auto cartridges, but today's handgunner will still find ammunition to fit just about every need.

There are still quite a few guns being manufactured in the caliber, the vast majority being built on the 1911 platform. Colt, Taurus, Springfield Armory, Para, Les Baer, Ed Brown and Nighthawk

Historically, the .38 Super was the choice of quite a few Texas Rangers and other lawmen.

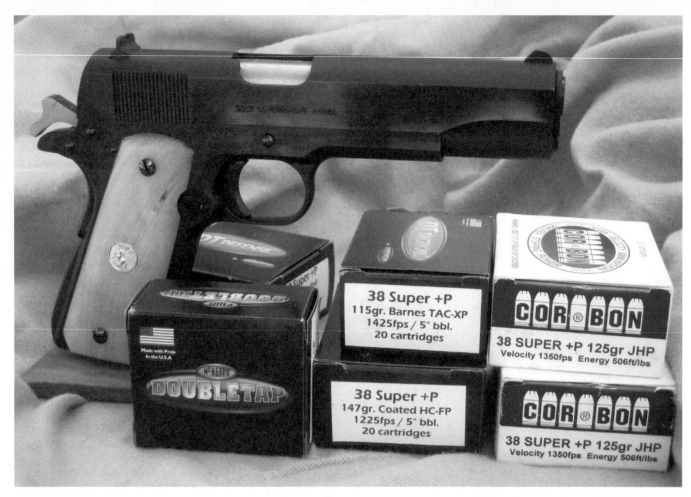

Above: A small sampling of the high-performance .38 Super ammo that is currently available.

All modern .38 Super barrels headspace on the case mouth and the cartridge gives good accuracy, as this five-shot group will attest.

Custom to name a few, all include the .38 Super in their list of offerings. An added advantage is that there are a huge number of accessories offered for the 1911 pistol and most of them will work just fine if your 1911 happens to be in .38 Super.

Of course, there are those who will spend a good deal of time arguing the merits and comparison of the 9mm, .38 Super and .357 Sig cartridges. For the most part, this is a harmless endeavor and if it pleases them, it pleases me. However, it is pretty much like arguing the difference between the .30-06 and the .270; a deer hit with either one won't be able to tell the difference. The same is true of these three 9mm cartridges in a defensive situation. Delivered properly, the crooks won't complain.

For all of its long history, the .38 Super cartridge is just as modern as tomorrow. It is chambered in America's most popular autoloading handgun. It continues to give good service in the field, in defensive uses and in action-shooting competition. Come to think of it, .38 ACP +P would not have been a good name for it. "Super" seems to fit it quite nicely.

THE 10/22 TURNS

50

America's favorite .22 hits the half-century mark.

BY James E. House and Kathleen A. House

CUSTOMIZE THE

RUGER
10/22

BROWNELLS

Comprehensive Do-It-Yourself Guide to Upgrading America's Favorite .22

NO GUNSMITH REQUIRED

James E. House & Kathleen A. House

The Ruger 10/22 autoloader has become the benchmark against which other rimfire semiautomatic rifles are compared.

Some products reflect an excellence of design that becomes synonymous with the company that produced them. Although Sturm, Ruger & Company Inc. is a relative newcomer in the field of firearms manufacturing, it has established itself as a company that produces excellent firearms that are durable and represent good value. One of the products that has gone a long way toward establishing the reputation of the company is the .22 LR autoloader known as the Model 10/22, which celebrated its

50th anniversary in 2014. Even though the 10/22 performs well, it is the fact that so much can be done to modify the 10/22 that has helped make it an American icon. It is truly a "tinker-toy" rifle that can be configured to suit almost any taste or purpose, and has spawned numerous producers of aftermarket accessories.

Sturm, Ruger & Company Inc.

From a modest beginning 65 years ago, Ruger has become the largest manufacturer of firearms in this country. The initial product, a .22-caliber semiautomatic pistol that sold for $37.50, was introduced in 1949. Other manufacturers may also produce handguns, rifles and shotguns, but Ruger manufactures a very comprehensive line of firearms that includes all variations of these types, all made in the USA. The handguns include numerous models of rimfire semiautomatics and a wide variety of centerfire semiautos. Ruger revolvers have from the beginning included both rimfire and centerfire single-action models, and the current offerings of this type are numerous. Double-action revolvers are also well represented by models that are suitable for sporting and law enforcement uses.

In recent years Ruger has also produced double-barrel shotguns in both over/under and side-by-side models. Centerfire rifles are currently offered in a bewildering array of models that include the bolt-action Model 77 Mark II Hawkeye series, the new American Rifle, as well as the single-shot No. 1, and several models of semiautomatics. Throughout the years many models have been introduced and discontinued including the lever-action Model 96/44 (.44 Magnum), 96/22M (.22 WMR) and 92/22 (.22 LR). Ruger also produces outstanding bolt-action rifles in .22 LR, .22 WMR and .17 HMR. The .17 Mach 2 was also briefly in production but was not a success for Ruger or other manufacturers.

Whereas these offerings include something for almost any shooter, it should be made clear that the first rimfire rifle offered by the Sturm, Ruger & Company was the .22 semiautomatic that has arguably become the most successful rimfire rifle of all time. That little rifle is known as the Model 10/22 Carbine and was introduced a half-century ago in 1964. In the intervening 50 years over 5 million 10/22s have been produced. Moreover, the 10/22 continues to be produced in numerous versions that span the range of plinking, target and tactical models.

With a firearm as long-lived and successful as the 10/22, there are numerous dates that are significant with regard to the variants produced and when certain changes were made. The accompanying table provides a timeline that summarizes some of the most important dates related to events in the life of the 10/22. In addition to the events listed, there are many others in which minor changes were made in sights, markings and other features that are too numerous to list in detail in this brief survey.

Ruger 10/22 Versions

Although they will be discussed in more detail later, this section presents an overview of the several versions of the 10/22 that are available at the present time. The original Ruger 10/22, known as the Carbine, has distinctive styling. Being a true carbine and having a barrel that measures only 18.5 inches, it also sports a stock that has carbine styling. The buttplate is curved and the forearm is circled with a barrelband. Loosely speaking, a 10/22 Carbine bears some

Year	Event
1964	Ruger 10/22 Carbine introduced
1966	Sporter version (noncheckered) introduced
1966	International version (noncheckered) introduced
1967	Canadian Expo version of the 10/22
1969	International version discontinued
1972	Deluxe Sporter introduced
1981	Hardwood stock replaced walnut
1986	Stainless steel/laminated stock version introduced
1994	International version reintroduced (checkered)
1996	Target model 10/22T introduced
1997	Stainless steel/composite all-weather version
1998	Ruger 10/22 Magnum introduced
2000	Heavy barrel/thumbhole stock version
2004	Introduction of 10/22 Rifle version
2004	40th Anniversary Edition of the 10/22
2005	Introduction of 10/22 Compact Rifle
2006	Ruger 10/22 Magnum discontinued
2009	Tactical models introduced
2012	Takedown version introduced
2013	Takedown with threaded barrel and suppressor

resemblance to the military M1 Carbine. However, in addition to the Carbine version of the 10/22 there are also variants known as the Rifle (introduced in 2004), which has a 20-inch barrel, and the version with a heavy 20-inch barrel that is known as the 10/22 Target (introduced in 1996). In September 2005 Ruger announced the introduction of yet another version of the 10/22. This version, officially known as the 10/22 Compact Rifle, has a 16.5-inch barrel and a scaled-down stock that gives a length of pull of only 12.5 inches. The 10/22 Compact Rifle has a stock that resembles that of the Rifle in that there is no barrelband, and the buttplate is flat rather than curved like that on the Carbine.

Although current Ruger 10/22 products include the Carbine, Target, Sporter, Tactical, Takedown and Compact Rifle models, there have been a very large number of small changes over the years. These include changes in sights, stocks and other parts, but the basic design has remained the same. It is neither possible nor necessary to give a complete description of these variants, although that information would certainly be of interest to the serious collector. The most complete catalog of 10/22 variants in the first 30 years of its production is the book by William E. Workman (1994), *The Ruger 10/22*, from Krause Publications. A wealth of information on the entire

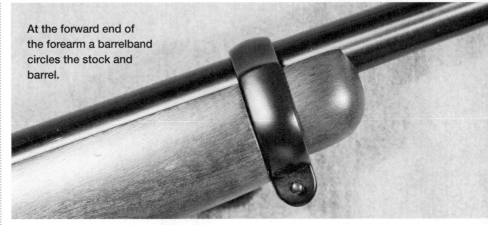

At the forward end of the forearm a barrelband circles the stock and barrel.

Ruger product line is also presented in R.L. Wilson's *Ruger and His Guns* (Simon & Schuster, 1996). These books are required reading for collectors and others who are serious about the Ruger 10/22. (Editor's note: To this list we must add the excellent book by James and Kathleen House, *Customize The Ruger 10/22,* published by Krause Publications/ Gun Digest Books, 2006, from which this article was excerpted and updated by the authors.)

There are also a number of variants that were prepared exclusively for a particular distributor but were never Ruger catalog items. For example, one of these has a 22-inch stainless steel barrel and checkered hardwood stock. This

variant was marketed through Wal-Mart by Lipsey's, a large firearms distributor located in Baton Rouge, La. On some Internet chat rooms owners refer to it as the "Wal-Mart version" of the 10/22. As this is being written, several distributors are marketing numerous versions of the Ruger 10/22 that differ in type and finish of stock, metal finish and other features. Over the years there have been other short runs of 10/22s produced that had special characteristics. For example, the 40th Anniversary 10/22 that was produced in 2004 had a large medallion embedded in the right side of the buttstock to commemorate the event. A brother-in-law of mine has a Ruger 10/22 with stainless steel barrel and laminated stock that was marketed with a 4X scope

The buttplate of the 10/22 has the unique carbine style.

THE RUGER 10/22 MODELS

Model	Length, in.	Bbl. Length, in.	Weight, lb.	Stock
Carbine	37	18.5	5	Hardwood[a]
Sporter	37	18.88	5.75	Walnut
Target	38.5	20	7.5	Laminated
Rifle[b]	38.5	20	5	Hardwood
International[b]	37	18.5	5.6	Walnut
Compact	33.5	16.12	4.5	Hardwood
Tactical	34.50	16.12HB[c]	6.88	Composite
Tactical	36.25	16.12SB[d]	4.30	Composite
Takedown	37	18.5SS	4.67	Composite
Takedown	36.75	16.62[e]	4.67	Composite
Magnum[b]	37.25	18.5	6.5	Hardwood

[a] Variants have blue barrel with hardwood or synthetic stock, or stainless barrel with synthetic stock. [b] Discontinued models. [c] Heavy barrel, 0.920". [d] Standard-weight barrel. [e] Threaded blue barrel with suppressor

This version of the 10/22 was widely available through Wal-Mart stores. It has a 22-inch stainless steel barrel and checkered hardwood stock.

and sling with the Ruger logo embossed in it. Apparently, this package was offered through a large chain of stores but never appeared as a catalog item.

The 10/22 Carbine

The original Ruger 10/22, the Carbine, was offered with a walnut stock and 18.5-inch blue steel barrel. Over the years of production it has been produced in many other forms that include some having stainless steel barrels and laminated, composite or hardwood stocks. Current versions of the carbine include those with a blue barrel and hardwood or composite stock, one having a stainless barrel and composite stock, and one having a blue barrel and composite stock that has a laser sight attached to the forearm. A large number of "distributor exclusive" versions are also available through several major distributors of Ruger firearms. These include some that are similar to previously offered factory versions. It is not surprising that over the 50 years since it was introduced, the 10/22 has undergone many changes, most of which are minor.

Although the Ruger 10/22 broke with tradition in many areas, perhaps the most unique was the fact that it uses a 10-round rotary magazine that is completely enclosed in the action. This results in a clean profile with a magazine that does not protrude from the bottom of the action – precisely where it is natural to hold the rifle while it is being carried in one hand. This cartridge reservoir is novel, but that is not sufficient to explain why the 10/22 is held in such high esteem. No, it is the fact that the Ruger rotary magazine enables it to rank among the most reliable .22 autoloaders that has endeared it to so many shoot-

An adjustable folding rear sight is used on most versions of the 10/22 Carbine.

The front sight on the 10/22 Carbine is a bead on a post that is held in a dovetail groove.

The rotary magazine does not protrude from the bottom of the action.

For many years the Ruger scope base accommodated mounts that clamp in the grooves along the edges (top), but current scope rails will also accommodate Weaver-type rings.

The Ruger 10/22 has always had a receiver made of aluminum alloy. Although this is true of the 10/22 in .22 LR, the discontinued .22 WMR version has a steel receiver. If you fire both the .22 LR and the .22 WMR rifles, you will quickly see that they are in some respects different rifles. Because of this they should be considered separately.

Although the 10/22 comes with excellent open sights, the accuracy of any rifle is easier to demonstrate by adding a scope. However, because the receiver has a slightly rounded profile it is not possible to have grooves milled in it to accommodate scope mounts. Instead, the top of the receiver has four dummy screws that fill the holes where the screws that attach a scope rail can be fastened. For many years the standard scope rail had grooves along the sides that resemble those milled into the receivers of most rimfire rifles. Beginning in 2004, all versions of the Ruger 10/22 were shipped with a scope rail that not only has grooves along the sides but also has transverse grooves that enable the enormously popular Weaver-type scope rings to be attached. The new scope rail thus increases the options that are available for the types of mounts that can be used to attach a scope to a 10/22. The steel receivers of the 10/22 Magnums have raised sections that have milled into them the curved notches similar to those found on the centerfire Ruger rifles. So, mounting a scope on one of the older 10/22s in .22 WMR caliber is an entirely different situation.

The 10/22 Deluxe Sporter

A personal favorite of the authors' is the version designated as the 10/22 DSP, which is known as the Deluxe Sporter. It

ers. The action is legendary for long life and reliability, and the 10/22 also has an excellent reputation for accuracy among rifles of this type. These attributes are responsible for many 10/22s being found in remote areas where the owners need a reliable rifle for pest control and small-game hunting.

The Ruger 10/22 Magnum has scope bases that are part of the receiver to which Ruger rings can be clamped.

With a checkered walnut stock, the Ruger 10/22 Deluxe Sporter is a handsome rifle.

A target crown is used on the .920-inch hammer-forged barrel of the Ruger 10/22 Target.

has the same length barrel as the Carbine, but has a checkered walnut stock with sling swivels installed. Another attractive version is known as the 10/22 International, which has a full-length Mannlicher-style stock. It has been introduced and discontinued twice.

The 10/22 Target

Rimfire shooting sports such as benchrest and silhouette competitions demand a rifle that is much more accurate than the factory Ruger 10/22 Carbine. Although many shooters modify their carbines, Ruger decided to offer a more capable rifle, and the 10/22 Target

was the result. It features a .920-inch diameter, hammer-forged barrel, a heavy target-style stock and an improved trigger. These attributes go a long way toward removing the necessity of adding aftermarket parts for many shooters.

Although I never actually thought of the Ruger 10/22 Target as beautiful, it is impressive. With a 20-inch barrel measuring almost an inch in diameter and an attractive brown laminated stock, the Target weighs 7.5 pounds. It comes with no sights because this rifle begs to have a scope attached and to be challenged. Target versions of the 10/22 are available with either blue or stainless steel barrels and laminated stocks, and both come

with target-type crowns. Functioning of the 10/22 Target is identical to the other variants of the model.

The 10/22 Compact Rifle

Recognizing the need to provide equipment for smaller shooters, Ruger introduced a scaled-down version of the 10/22 in September 2005. The resulting model, known as the 10/22 Compact Rifle, features a blued barrel measuring 16.12 inches and a shortened hardwood stock that gives a 12.5-inch length of pull. The stock has a regular flat

Since it was introduced in 1996, the 10/22 Target has developed an excellent reputation as a highly accurate rimfire.

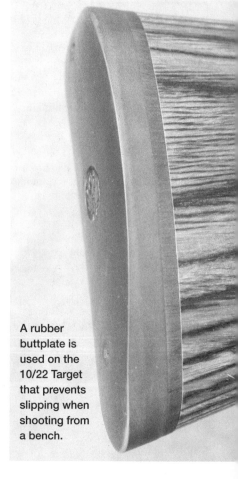

A rubber buttplate is used on the 10/22 Target that prevents slipping when shooting from a bench.

buttplate, and gone is the barrelband. In many ways, the Compact resembles the Rifle version with a shorter stock and barrel.

Sights on the Compact consist of a front sight on a low ramp and a blade rear sight. Along the top of the front sight there is a fiber-optic insert, and the rear sight has fiber-optic inserts on either side of the notch. As with all current 10/22s, Ruger supplies a scope base with the Compact that can accommodate either tip-off or Weaver-type rings.

In 2004 Ruger produced 10-shot magazines made of clear plastic for the 10/22. These magazines have a red rotor. It is the clear magazine that is standard on the Compact model. Altogether, the 10/22 Compact is a handy, sturdy autoloader that will travel well. It is convenient not only for shooters of small stature, but also anyone who wants a compact rimfire rifle, and that takes in a lot of territory.

The Ruger 10/22 Tactical

Ever aware of the changing market, Ruger responded with the introduction of the 10/22 Tactical in 2009. There are two versions of the Tactical model, one featuring a black Hogue OverMolded stock and a blue heavy barrel that is just over 16 inches in length. The other has a black composite stock and a standard-weight barrel. Weights of these models are 6.88 pounds for the heavy-barrel model and 4.3 pounds for the version with a standard-weight barrel. The heavy-barrel model is provided with a folding bipod. Functioning and accommodation of accessories are identical to other 10/22 versions.

The Ruger 10/22 Takedown

There is a lot of interest in rifles that can be made smaller for easier transport and packing. Ruger responded to that demand by offering the 10/22 Takedown Model in 2012. The Takedown is available in two versions, both of which feature black composite stocks and blue barrels. One version features a standard 18.5-inch barrel whereas the other, introduced in 2013, has a barrel measuring 16.62 inches in length that has a threaded muzzle with a suppressor attached. Both versions utilize a two-piece stock that comes apart at the front of the action.

The Takedown Model is composed of two subassemblies, one comprised of the buttstock and action and the other

In late 2005 Ruger introduced the 10/22 Compact Rifle (right), which is a smaller version of the 10/22 Rifle (left).

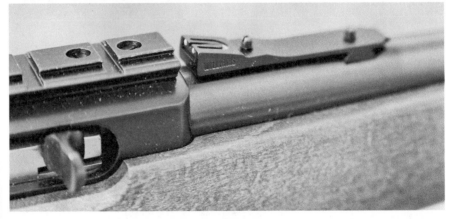

The rear sight on the 10/22 Compact Rifle has a fiber-optic insert that gives a green dot on either side of the notch.

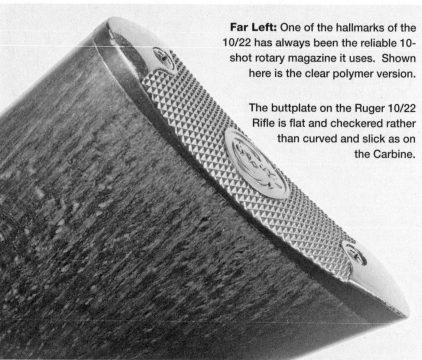

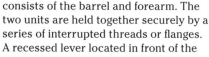

Far Left: One of the hallmarks of the 10/22 has always been the reliable 10-shot rotary magazine it uses. Shown here is the clear polymer version.

The buttplate on the Ruger 10/22 Rifle is flat and checkered rather than curved and slick as on the Carbine.

consists of the barrel and forearm. The two units are held together securely by a series of interrupted threads or flanges. A recessed lever located in front of the magazine serves as a locking device, and it must be pushed forward to unlatch the units. Rotating the units one-quarter turn relative to each other separates the locking flanges so that the halves of the rifle can be pulled apart. The Ruger Carbine and Compact models are of convenient size, but the Takedown version makes it possible to have a Ruger 10/22 that can have even smaller dimensions.

For smaller shooters, the Ruger Compact gives excellent performance and the same possibilities for customization.

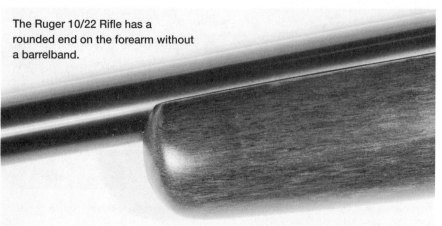

The Ruger 10/22 Rifle has a rounded end on the forearm without a barrelband.

The Ruger 10/22 Rifle

Introduced in 2004, the Ruger 10/22 Rifle represents a sort of combination of the Deluxe Sporter and Carbine versions but with some unique features. First, the Rifle has a 20-inch barrel rather than the 18.5-inch barrel used on the Carbine and Deluxe Sporter. Like the Carbine and Deluxe Sporter versions, the barrel of the Rifle is fitted with open sights. Second, the stock is slimmer than those used on either the Carbine or Sporter. One of the aesthetic deficiencies of the 10/22 Carbine has always been that the stock is rather fat in the cross section. This is necessitated by the rotary magazine, which is approximately twice as wide as a clip that holds stacked rimfire cartridges. However, the stock of the Carbine is fairly thick throughout its entire length. On the Rifle version the stock is slimmer and especially so in the areas of the grip and the forearm. With its longer barrel and slim stock, I developed a love at first sight relationship with the 10/22 Rifle. It would be some time before I owned one, but it was worth the wait. It seems that the 10/22 Rifle was offered only with a hardwood stock and a blued steel barrel. This model has been discontinued but it

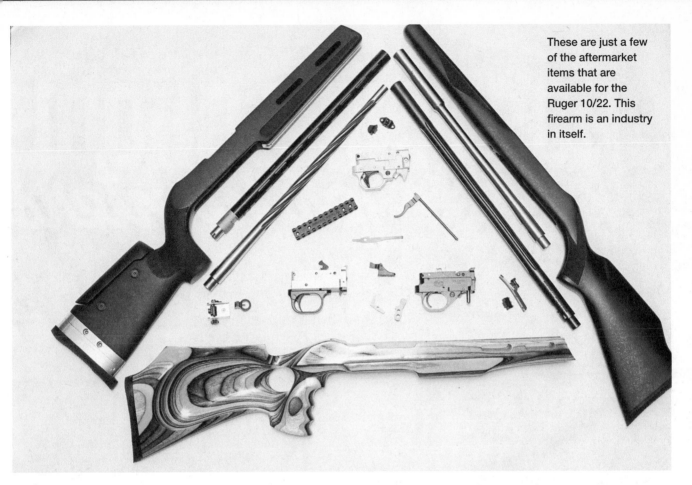

These are just a few of the aftermarket items that are available for the Ruger 10/22. This firearm is an industry in itself.

is still listed as a "distributor exclusive" by Williams Shooters Supply.

Enhancing the Ruger 10/22

It is unlikely that there is any machine produced by a factory, even using modern manufacturing techniques, which could not be made better in some way. Manufacturers must make decisions based on availability of materials, cost-related issues and marketability of the end product. A custom shop may not be forced to operate under all of these constraints, and the owner of a Ruger 10/22 certainly does not have to. Almost everything except the receiver housing is replaceable. Moreover, components are available that exceed the capabilities of the original factory parts in many instances. The owner of a 10/22 can customize his or her rifle to almost any degree desired. As good as the 10/22 is in factory form, it can be made better. Aftermarket products of virtually every type are available for the 10/22, and you can turn your rifle into an elegant tack-driving machine.

The replacement of barrels and stocks on Ruger 10/22s is so common that several companies offer accessory kits that consist of a stock and barrel combination. Stocks range from elegant sporter types to tactical models with pistol grips, handguards and folding buttstocks. Laminated stocks are also available in various color combinations. One popular type of aftermarket stock is known as the thumbhole model, and several styles are produced. In general, stocks are produced with barrel channels that are cut to fit either a factory barrel or a heavy barrel having a diameter of .920 inch.

When it comes to barrels for the Ruger 10/22, the term smorgasbord comes to mind. Some barrels have contours that match that of the factory Carbine barrel so they can be used with the factory stock. Probably the most popular style of aftermarket barrel is not tapered but has a uniform diameter of .920 inch. Within this general type, the buyer can choose from those having a blue finish or those made of stainless steel. Another type of barrel has the same configuration as the factory barrel for most of its length except for the last four inches or so the diameter increases to .920 inch. This allows the use of the factory stock or a stock that has a barrel channel of the same size. Finally, there are several barrels available that have an outside diameter of .920 inch, and have an inner sleeve made of steel encased in a sleeve of aluminum or carbon fiber composite. These barrels are light in weight, but they can be used with a stock that is designed for use with a heavy barrel.

Because of the array of items produced for the Ruger 10/22, not all of the aftermarket products available can be described here. Those that are described are certainly representative of most of the accessories that are available, but it is not a complete list. Before you embark on customizing your 10/22 study the catalogs and websites of the numerous manufacturers. You may find that there are many more options available than you ever imagined, as it is a very large market indeed. After all, the Ruger 10/22 is that kind of machine, and it would be very difficult to outgrow this little rifle.

This article was excerpted from Standard Catalog of Ruger Firearms (Gun Digest Books, 2014) including revised and updated portions from Customize the Ruger 10/22 by James E. and Kathleen A. House (Gun Digest Books, 2006).

By **Buck Pope**

SHOOTING SCHOOL *for hunters*

Hunter marksmanship training at its finest

This past December I had an opportunity to attend a four-day marksmanship training course for hunters at the FTW Ranch located just out of Barksdale, Texas. The ranch is located deep in the Texas Hill Country a couple of hours west of San Antonio. The FTW (Fallow Trophy Whitetail) Ranch was founded by Tim Fallon, an avid big-game hunter who has hunted extensively around the world. He saw a need for a hunter marksmanship school back in 2006 and since then the training facility has grown into a full-scale operation over a good portion of the 12,000-acre ranch.

In addition to hunter marksmanship training, the FTW Ranch offers year-round hunting for a large variety of exotic animals, plus trophy whitetail deer when in season. Today, this totally modern facility offers the best in training for the more than 450 guests who come to the ranch each year. Tim himself is an instructor, and he also has several other highly trained marksmanship instructors, who are typically ex-military such as Navy SEALs and U.S. Marine Corps snipers.

A variety of courses are available to fit the needs of each student. The objective is to teach the proper skills and techniques to make you a much better marksman for hunting game, and also to enhance your skills as a hunter in the field, no matter what or where you're hunting. The course attended was the SAAM Hunt Combo, which is a four-day course. SAAM stands for "Sportsman's All-terrain All-weather Marksmanship."

The class I attended included eight students. Sturm, Ruger & Company has a policy of sending some of its high achievers to the ranch every year and this time five of its employees were in the class. Then there was a grandfather-grandson team and myself. The school can handle as many as 24 students at a time, if necessary. I took a special interest in our youngest student. His name is Connor Smith and at 15 years old has had some prior experience hunting with his grandfather, Glen Hill. His grandfather thought this would be an excellent training experience on how to learn the proper methods and techniques of

The great room at FTW Ranch headquarters displays some spectacular trophies from around the world, as well as exotics and native whitetails taken at the ranch.

The first day's training was mostly in the classroom where topics included various hunting rifles, ammunition, scope adjustments, trigger control and overall shooting techniques. Instructor Doug Prichard also stressed the rules of gun safety.

hunter marksmanship as well as pick up some hunting skills. In addition to taking the course myself, I wanted to follow and observe Connor as he went through the training.

The first day of the course was spent mostly in a classroom where the students can listen, learn and participate. The SAAM Hunt Combo entails 18 to 22 hours of SAAM Training with the days split between in-class instruction and precision shooting on the range. In addition, we would do some hunting in the early morning and evening hours. I would be hunting for a trophy whitetail deer and the others would be hunting wild boar and varmints. We each received a SAAM Handbook, which followed the class training and was full

of extra data and tips for shooting and hunting, along with medical information for our hunts.

The very first thing our instructor Doug Prichard addressed was safety – the number one most important part of the course. Four safety rules are followed at all times:

1. Guns are always loaded; treat them that way.
2. Never let the muzzle point at anything you're not willing to destroy.
3. Keep your finger off the trigger until your sights are on the target and you are ready to shoot.
4. Be sure of your target and what is behind it.

Incidentally, the policy at the FTW Ranch is that "Everyone is a Range Safety Officer."

Prichard talked about today's hunting rifles, bore sizes and types of barrels, twists, receivers and stocks. He also talked about various types of guns and their applications. Next he discussed such things as measuring bullet drop, bullet drift and the most commonly used terms like minute of angle (MOA) and mill radian (Mils). We each received a "Range Card" that was to be referenced throughout the course showing our rifle caliber, bullet type, velocity and necessary range data we would need to shoot the course. It was our ballistics bible of data for the course to assist our calculations on how to get the bullet on

Yds	Moa	Clks 1/4	Inch Drop	Wind@10 MOA-Inch		MOA 200 HZD		Yards
100	Zero	Zero	Zero	0.75	1			
150	0.50	2	1	1.00	2	1.8		285
200	1.50	6	0	1.25	3	3.6		355
250	2.50	10	3	1.50	4	5.4		420
300	3.50	14	6	2.00	6	7.2		480
350	4.75	19	11	2.50	9	9		535
400	6.25	25	19	3.00	12	10.8		585
450	7.75	31	28	3.50	16	12.6		635
500	9.25	37	39	4.00	20	14.4		680
550	11.00	44	52	4.50	25	16.2		720
600	12.75	51	68	5.00	30			
650	14.50	58	85	5.50	36	**Buck Pope**		
675	15.50	62	95	5.75	39			
700	16.75	67	107	6.00	42	**Full X Wind Holds**		

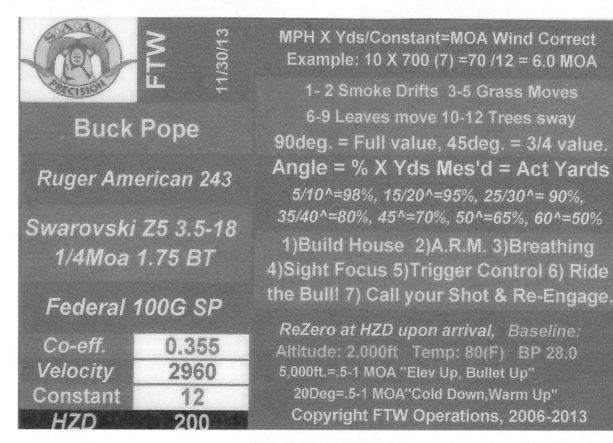

FTW 11/30/13

Buck Pope

Ruger American 243

Swarovski Z5 3.5-18
1/4Moa 1.75 BT

Federal 100G SP

Co-eff.	0.355
Velocity	2960
Constant	12
HZD	200

MPH X Yds/Constant=MOA Wind Correct
Example: 10 X 700 (7) =70 /12 = 6.0 MOA

1- 2 Smoke Drifts 3-5 Grass Moves
6-9 Leaves move 10-12 Trees sway
90deg. = Full value, 45deg. = 3/4 value.
Angle = % X Yds Mes'd = Act Yards
5/10^=98%, 15/20^=95%, 25/30^= 90%,
35/40^=80%, 45^=70%, 50^=65%, 60^=50%

1)Build House 2)A.R.M. 3)Breathing
4)Sight Focus 5)Trigger Control 6) Ride
the Bull! 7) Call your Shot & Re-Engage.

ReZero at HZD upon arrival, Baseline:
Altitude: 2,000ft Temp: 80(F) BP 28.0
5,000ft.=.5-1 MOA "Elev Up, Bullet Up"
20Deg=.5-1 MOA"Cold Down,Warm Up"
Copyright FTW Operations, 2006-2013

Here is the author's Range Card, a "ballistics bible" of data that each student received for their individual rifle and caliber.

the target in different conditions.

Prichard also talked about scopes, the different types and the functions of each, including adjusting your scope and eliminating parallax. He also explained HZD (Hunter Zero Data) and establishing a "baseline zero" on your scope for hunting conditions. We learned a lot about ballistics, the effects of gravity and weather conditions, including how to determine wind speed. All of this data is important to the hunter and are factors that can, and will, affect accurate shot placement. We also discussed recoil among the various calibers and the need to use a shoulder recoil pad, which was provided, along with a shooting glove, ear protection and hand towel. As each shooter was going to be firing anywhere from 160 to over 200 rounds, even a light-recoiling caliber can become a discomfort without a shoulder pad.

As we would be doing a lot of prone shooting, each rifle was equipped with a Harris Bipod. I was shooting the bolt-action Ruger American Rifle in .243 Winchester. It was topped with a Swarovski Z5 3.5-18x44 scope featuring the BRX reticle. The ammunition was Federal's Power-Shok 100-grain Soft Point rated at 2,960 fps.

The next session was called the "Seven Shooting Fundamentals of Marksmanship." The lesson started out with body position and ended up with calling

The author's Ruger American Rifle in .243 Winchester with a Swarovski Z5 3.5-18x44 scope. There's nothing wrong with spending more for your scope than for your rifle.

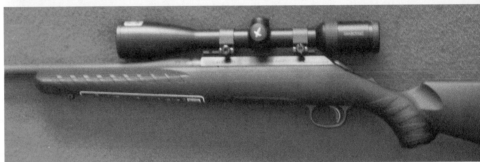

a shot. Each session builds on the prior session and all are critical to becoming a proficient marksman. One question that came up was: what is considered an accurate rifle? Assuming a bolt-action scoped rifle, a one-inch group at 100 yards is still defined as the ideal accuracy for most hunting applications. We also discussed muzzlebrakes and their advantages and disadvantages, and how dry-firing a rifle can enhance breathing and trigger release skills. Trigger control and pull are critical to accurate shooting. It was suggested that a 2½- to 3-pound trigger pull was about ideal for a hunting rifle.

Connor, who is an honor student in high school, had no problem following all the technical data and doing the calculations. He was a quick learner.

Our next session covered how to properly maintain and clean your rifle. The instructor for this phase was Gene Hauenstein, and he went through a six-step procedure to properly clean your rifle and scope. The ranch has a separate building that is set up just for this purpose.

At this point we were basically done with the majority of the classroom material and the next step was to head to the range and get our rifles sighted in. At the range, the safety rules were reviewed once again. We were shown the proper prone position and asked to do some dry-firing to get familiar with our rifles. This was certainly a Ruger event, as each shooter had either an American or target model. It only took a few rounds to get on paper, then I made

The youngest student in the class was 15-year-old Connor Smith, here getting tips on prone shooting.

Proper gun care and maintenance are important. Here students learn the right way to clean their rifles.

several adjustments and let my rifle cool off for my final sight-in, which is always a good idea. After waiting a bit, I shot a one-inch, five-shot group. Before long we all had our rifles sighted in at 100 yards. One thing that I really liked about the training at the ranch is that you do a lot of shooting while being closely observed

The author's five-shot, one-inch group at 100 yards. It appears to be only four shots but the fifth is in one of the other bullet holes.

by the instructors so they can coach you in the proper shooting techniques.

We all had shooting sticks to shoot from and they were a great aid. I brought along my Bog-Pod three-legged sticks and it was amazing how much they helped. I have hunted for more than 50 years and I always carry a pair of shooting sticks when in the field. Shot placement is critical in the clean harvesting of game, and every effort should be made to make certain that each bullet goes where you want it to go.

I myself am not a proponent of long-distance shooting at game, which now seems popular with some hunters. Shooting targets at long range is fine, but as a hunter, your first obligation is to get as close as you can to make that accurate shot. If you can't do that, then let the animal walk. To me, it's just that simple. FTW Ranch has a number of ranges and each one offers certain objectives, different conditions and target challenges. We continued with various shooting sessions and shot targets from 100 yards, 200 yards, 300 yards and on out as far as 550 yards. We each had to use our Range Card to make the necessary elevation clicks on our scopes to be able to hit the target. We also had another instructor, Larry Summerfield join us along with Fredo, who would also assist where needed. We shot at metal targets and you could hear the hit when it was

made even at the long ranges, which made it a lot of fun. We also practiced various other shooting positions – such as sitting, kneeling and the most difficult, offhand or standing. Plus, we again utilized our shooting sticks in numerous positions and the instructors showed us a few tips, in addition to how a second pair of sticks can be used to help steady your position.

One thing that really stood out for me was just how far 300 yards really is. One of the problems I had while shooting was keeping on the rifle after the shot, as I have a bad habit of raising my head to see what I shot. This is due to years of not doing it right. At FTW, students are trained to make the shot and immediately chamber another round and stay on the stock without taking your eyes off the target. I watched Connor do this perfectly. He was a good student and I would say he was also one of the better shooters in our class, even at his young age of 15.

The last day of shooting was high up in a canyon at a location named Crusader Range. There is a large rock next to the range with a plaque in honor of our troops that reads, "For all who served! Especially for those Who Gave All." This would be a competition shoot across the canyon at metal plates and a variety of animal plates at ranges from 100 to over 700 yards. In addition to the distances,

Instructor Gene Hauenstein shows this student the correct way to shoot in the sitting position.

The author on a stand, shooting his Ruger .243 for a group.

we had to factor in the wind with a limited amount of time to make the shots. Everyone shot well and several shot very well. As for Connor, he was in the top group of shooters. This was the grand finale for the course, and a challenge it surely was.

In the off hours, the majority of us went hunting in the early morning and evening. Doug was my guide, and finally on the morning of the last day we located the buck I was after. He was in a stand of trees and, according to my Swarovski Range binoculars, was

410 yards away. However, he was very smart and wouldn't leave the cover. We could see just enough of him off and on to know he was a shooter buck. But, he would not come out into the opening in front of him. He was definitely a wise old buck and wasn't taking any chances. Our

The Crusader Range has targets that range from 100 to more than 700 yards, a real test of marksmanship. The range is dedicated to those who have served in our military.

Typical terrain on the FTW Ranch for hunting whitetail and a large variety of exotic game.

The author took this trophy Fallow deer the prior year, one of the many exotic species found on the ranch.

The dangerous-game course allows students to shoot a charging elephant target. Here the author is using a Ruger Guide Gun in .375 Ruger caliber topped with a Swarovski Z6 1.75-6X scope.

Grandfather and grandson, Gene Hill and Connor Smith. The FTW Ranch is a perfect place for one generation to pass along the tradition of hunting, and the skills required to be a true sportsman.

I really enjoyed this Hunter Marksmanship course. It is an action-packed four days that's full of great training. The FTW Ranch also offers handgun hunter training, if requested, offering another fun option with a lot of shooting to develop the correct skills.

The last evening we had a special steak dinner, after which Tim Fallon and his staff presented each of us with a certificate for completing the course. That last evening I asked Connor how he liked the course and what had he gotten out of it? He had a great big smile on his face as his proud grandfather stood next to him. He said the ranges were outstanding, he really liked all the shooting he got to do and that he is a much better shot now after learning so much from the instructors. He said he hadn't realized just how important trigger squeeze is in making the shot. Well said, Connor, well said.

SOURCES

FTW Ranch
1802 Horse Hollow Road
Barksdale, Texas 78828
830-234-4366
www.ftwoutfitters.com

Ruger Firearms
www.ruger.com

Swaroski Optik
www.swarovskioptik.com

plan for the evening hunt was to sneak back into that canyon and wait him out. Hopefully he would come out of the thick brush on the distant hillside. But as darkness settled in, that old buck never showed, and thus ended my hunt. In the end, he had outsmarted us and won the challenge.

While at the FTW Ranch I was also able to spend some time on the Dangerous Game Course firing the Ruger Hawkeye rifle in .375 Ruger at the charging elephant target. This would be an excellent warm up for a person going on a dangerous-game safari. This course also lets you shoot at standing and running buffalo targets, and is a great chance to gain the marksmanship skills required to accurately place your shots on dangerous game.

Why Not the WEBLEY?

The development and eventual rejection of the classic British revolver

BY **John Malloy**

The last of the big .455 Webleys, the Mark VI, had an exemplary service record and the .38 caliber Webley seemed a logical replacement. However, the smaller-caliber Webley was not chosen.

The large-caliber Webley service revolver was adopted by the British government in 1887. The big .455-caliber military Webleys served across the far-flung British Empire, fought in the Boer War, and gave exemplary service through World War I. They earned a reputation for ruggedness, power and unfailing reliability.

After World War I, British military planners decided that a lighter, smaller-caliber revolver would suffice. Webley had made such revolvers for commercial sales. The firm was naturally eager to receive a contract to provide the smaller guns for military use. The Webley design should have been a sure thing for adoption. However, the design chosen for service was a different revolver, to be

The strong Webley stirrup latch, which made a hinge-frame revolver as strong as one with a solid frame, was used with the "WG" series, here a 7½-inch target version. WG revolvers predated the military Webleys.

made by a government factory. Why not the Webley?

British military men of the time must have been puzzled. They knew that Webley's big .455 revolvers had given dependable service for decades. Certainly the firm could provide a smaller, .38-caliber revolver that could fit any specifications the government desired. Indeed, it seemed a mystery that a scaled-down Webley design was not chosen. And, as we shall discover, it is related to a number of other mysteries.

It is very difficult, at any distance in time, to be able to say with certainty why something did *not* happen. It would seem as if the specifications and procedures for selecting a new sidearm should be clear, and should be available in historical records. Yet, as a number of historians have noted, many types of British records were destroyed by World War II bombings, fires and other causes. In this particular case, the unusual aspects of the selection procedure may not have even produced such records.

We can still gain insights that may help us understand the situation. We can study secondary sources of information in the form of published works by knowledgeable researchers. We can relate the guns to the history of the time. We can evaluate the mechanical, handling and accuracy characteristics of the guns themselves.

WEBLEY REVOLVERS

By the mid-1800s, the British government had realized the value of handguns that could fire more than one shot. In 1854, the first British service revolver, the .36-caliber Colt 1851 Navy, was adopted in time to see Crimean War service. The Colt revolver was chosen because it worked, and because it was the only choice available in the numbers the British wanted. The British firearms industry had some way to go to catch up with American mass-production techniques. However, some British manufacturers—Webley in particular—were working toward doing just that.

A decade prior to the adoption of the Colt, in 1845, Philip Webley had acquired the firearms business of William Davis. Before long, Webley recognized the possibilities of revolvers. The business grew and in 1853, along with his brother James, the firm released a single-action percussion revolver of their own design. The Webley firm became a family concern as Philip Webley's sons also entered the business.

Around 1865 Webley first offered hinge-frame revolvers. However, it was their line of solid-frame cartridge revolvers that brought them early recognition. In 1867, the solid-frame Webley RIC model was adopted as the official sidearm of the Royal Irish Constabulary.

Webley's solid-frame revolvers did not exhibit great innovation, but were very well made. In addition, Webley was one of the first British gunmakers to understand and work toward the American system of fully interchangeable parts. The company continued their design development and produced a revolver with a "rebounding" hammer mechanism in 1876, and an improved hinged frame design in 1877.

The British government made a study of their available sidearms in 1879. They found a mixture of Adams, Colt, Tranter and Webley revolvers, no one of which was completely satisfactory as a sidearm for all of their military services. Work began at the Royal Small Arms Factory (RSAF) at Enfield Lock to create a standard revolver. By 1882, an interesting Enfield revolver had been developed, and it was adopted that year. The unusual design had a modified hinged-frame operation that when opened, pulled the cylinder forward to extract fired cases, but not loaded rounds. Unfortunately, it was heavy and not particularly easy to use. In the words of one historian, it was met with "not much enthusiasm."

The Webley firm soon brought out a new hinge-frame design with a superior latching mechanism. Henry Webley had worked with gunsmith John Carter to earn an 1885 patent on this strong "stirrup latch" mechanism. Webley's use of this latch was later challenged by Edwinson C. Green, who claimed that Carter was aware of his own 1883 development of a similar latch. The Webley firm was apparently able to reach some sort of arrangement with Green. The company introduced an advanced new revolver, with a hinged frame, simultaneous extraction, retracting hammer and the strong Green-type latching mechanism. Plus, all parts were fully interchangeable. Precise fitting and the strong latch made the new fast-loading hinged-frame Webley equal in strength to a solid-frame revolver. Although Edwinson Green had not been involved in the design, Webley's revolvers that used the stirrup latch were generally known as Webley-Greens, and at some point were designated "WG" on the barrel and frame. Though, recent historians seem to downplay the Green connection, and often refer to the WG marking as "Webley Government." This is mysterious terminology, as the WG was never adopted by the government.

At any rate, the big, smooth-working WGs, when compared with the clumsy official Enfields, became very popular with British army officers, who purchased their own sidearms. Sir Robert Baden-Powell, who became the army's youngest general after his amazing defense of Mafeking during the Boer War, reportedly carried a .455-caliber Webley-Green revolver. (As an aside, Baden-Powell was well known as an outdoorsman and shooter, and was the founder of the Boy Scout movement. When the Boy Scouts came to America in 1910, the first Handbook included a Merit Badge for Marksmanship.)

Webley made the WG revolvers for commercial sales and sold many to British officers, but as we know, the Webley-Green was never formally adopted into British service. A large government contract would, of course, be a desirable thing for the company. Webley still continued development and had come up with a slightly lighter, slightly more compact design that used fewer parts. The WG revolvers had sideplates on the frame. In those early days of British manufacture of fully interchangeable parts, a perfectly fitted sideplate was a difficult item to manufacture. The new Webley design did away with the sideplate, inserting a smaller number of parts from the top or bottom of the frame.

THE MILITARY WEBLEYS

The new Webley military revolver was a good one. In 1887, the British War Office ordered 10,000 of them. (To be chronologically accurate, it was at the time this lucrative order was placed that Edwinson Green made his claim to the stirrup latch). The military service Webleys were in general service by 1892 and went through a series of six variants, or Marks, during their decades of usage.

The Mark I, as the first military service Webley was designated, was originally planned to be a .442-caliber revolver. The caliber was changed to .455 so that the same ammunition could also be used in the older Enfield revolvers. The big black-powder .455 cartridge, with its 265-grain bullet, would also provide ammunition for the privately purchased Webley-Greens being carried in service.

The Mark I was more compact than the WG. Clever design allowed a single V-type mainspring to operate the entire internal mechanism and reduced the number of lockwork parts, making the gun easier to service under field conditions. With its 4-inch barrel, it weighed about 35 ounces. The Mark I was the only military Webley with a hump at the upper rear of the birdshead grip. Compact and powerful, it gave the British a satisfactory military revolver at a time when a heavy-duty sidearm was needed for a country with a widespread empire.

It may be of interest that the year 1887, the year of introduction of the Webley Mark I, was also the year of publication of the first Sherlock Holmes story by Arthur Conan Doyle. In these stories, which continued into the 1920s, Holmes had a big-bore revolver and his fictional biographer, former army surgeon Dr. John Watson, often carried and used his unidentified "service revolver" to good effect. Extremely popular, the Sherlock Holmes stories served to increase interest in what sort of service revolvers actually were in use.

The Mark I was a good sidearm, but early service use showed ways it could be improved and some features were revised. The slightly modified Webley Mark II was adopted in 1894. Visually similar to the Mark I, it could be distinguished by the smooth curve of the rear grip strap of its birdshead grip, which omitted the hump of its predecessor. Mechanically, the Mark II had a heavier firing pin and hammer, and its breechface was a replaceable hardened insert.

The first of the Webley military revolvers, the Mark I, with its 4-inch barrel. It was compact and powerful, and used the strong stirrup latch.

The Mark I Webley hinge-frame revolver gave British troops a compact, powerful new revolver that was easy and quick to load and unload.

The Webley Mark III was similar in size and function to the earlier Marks I and II, but introduced an easy cylinder-removal mechanism attached to the holster-guide "wings" in front of the cylinder. This cylinder removal system was used on all subsequent British revolvers.

Webley's Mark III was adopted in 1897. Its major distinction was an improved method of retaining the cylinder and allowing its easy removal for cleaning. Marks I and II had a single large screw that held the cylinder in the barrel unit. The Mark III had a clever pivoting latch made as part of the "holster guide" wings. Made with standard 4-inch barrels, some are also found with 6-inch barrels. Many officers and many military shooting teams preferred the longer barrels. 1897 was the year that the Webley firm expanded by merger, and the new company name "Webley & Scott" may be found on revolvers from that date on.

The Mark IV, which was adopted at the beginning of the Boer War in 1899, is visually quite like the preceding Mark III. The primary difference was in the grade of steel used. Reportedly, a different grade of steel was employed to give greater strength for the smokeless-powder cartridges that had slowly replaced the earlier black-powder loads. Again, although they were standard with 4-inch barrels, some were made as 6-inchers.

WORLD WAR I

Mark V Webleys were introduced just prior to the beginning of World War I, in 1913. Reportedly, the cylinder was made stronger and was a slightly larger diameter. As England became involved in the First World War in August 1914, all the different Marks in storage were readied for service. All previous Marks, when appropriate, were improved with the most current parts as they were serviced. In some cases, identifications were modified with stars added to the original model numbers to indicate the modifications, such as fitting earlier models with later cylinders.

The final variation of the .455 Webley service revolver, the Mark VI, was adopted during the First World War and was the variant made in the greatest numbers. Introduced in 1915, it was the only military Webley .455 revolver with a squared, flat-butt grip. It had perhaps the best grip of any revolver used during that war. The Mark VI military Webley was made almost exclusively with a 6-inch barrel.

The Webley contract for Mark VI revolvers ended after World War I. However, the Royal Small Arms Factory (RSAF) at Enfield Lock continued the manufacture of the Mark VI until 1926. An explanation for this production was that it kept the factory, located south of London, in operation during the postwar military cutback. The revolvers made by RSAF are identical to those made by

The Webley Mark III revolvers were standard with 4-inch barrels (below), but were also available with 6-inch barrels (above). This 4-inch variant has the heavier "cavalry" hammer. Mark IV and Mark V guns were visually very similar.

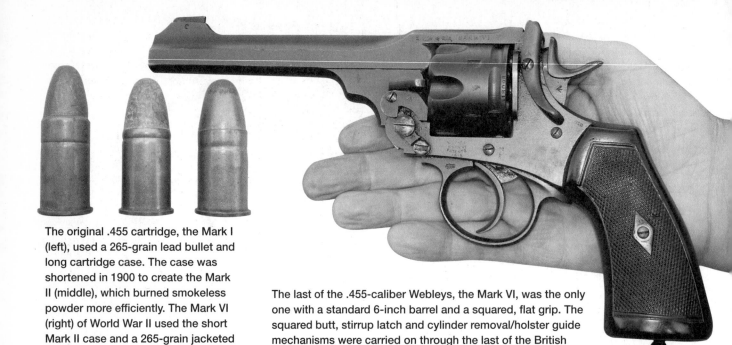

The original .455 cartridge, the Mark I (left), used a 265-grain lead bullet and long cartridge case. The case was shortened in 1900 to create the Mark II (middle), which burned smokeless powder more efficiently. The Mark VI (right) of World War II used the short Mark II case and a 265-grain jacketed bullet.

The last of the .455-caliber Webleys, the Mark VI, was the only one with a standard 6-inch barrel and a squared, flat grip. The squared butt, stirrup latch and cylinder removal/holster guide mechanisms were carried on through the last of the British .38-caliber revolvers.

the Webley factory, but are marked with Enfield markings rather than Webley markings.

The Mark VI, with its 6-inch barrel, was a big sidearm – about 11½ inches long, 5¾ inches high and weighed about 38 ounces. The gun's size and weight were factors that would soon be considered negatively.

THE .455 CARTRIDGE

The .455 cartridge had been a good one for Great Britain's colonial conflicts. Its slow-moving 265-grain unclad lead bullet, starting out at the leisurely pace of about 650 to 700 feet per second, achieved its effectiveness through momentum, rather than energy. Three major variants of .455 cartridges intended for the Webley revolvers were used. Starting out as the Mark I cartridge, a black-powder load, it was gradually changed to smokeless (cordite) powder beginning in 1892. In 1900, to improve the burning of the smokeless powder, the case length was shortened to create the Mark II cartridge. Ballistics were essentially the same. There were other short-lived versions adopted, which were soon discontinued. The Webleys, using primarily the Mark II cartridge, served well across the British Empire and also proved their value during the trench warfare of World War I.

The last .455-cartridge variant, the Mark VI, was later adopted in 1939 as World War II loomed. It had a 265-grain

jacketed bullet to conform to Declaration 3 of the Hague Convention of 1899.

The .455 had served well through the colonial period, the Boer War and World War I. But the world was changing. The Great War had changed many things and the .455 was no longer held in the same high regard.

THE AFTERMATH OF WORLD WAR I

England had suffered Zeppelin bombing attacks during the war, but was relatively undisturbed compared to the continental European countries. However, England had other worries. Communism, little known before the war, now was a force to be feared. It held power in Russia, which constituted almost one-sixth of the earth's land surface. Closer to home, Irish rebel groups were threatening the stability of English life. British politicians worried about violent upheavals by armed people. They responded by attempting to control human actions by controlling inanimate objects—they passed laws to restrict firearms.

The Firearms Act of 1920 required licensing of all firearms except shotguns. Restrictions on handguns, initiated previously in 1903, were increased. From that time on, British law virtually barred ordinary individuals from owning common handguns. The 1920 Act put harsh controls on the manufacture of all rifled arms, devastating the British firearms

industry in the world market. With sales of firearms reduced and an onus placed on firearms ownership, the market for skilled workers in the firearms trade grew smaller.

As generally happens after a war, less attention was given to military service. Recruits, mostly now from large cities, came into service with little knowledge or background of guns and shooting.

It was in this climate that British military planners decided that the big .455 Webley was too big, too heavy and kicked too hard to be used by soldiers with little background experience. The resulting thinking was that a smaller, lighter sidearm should be adopted. The move to change to a smaller revolver began in 1922. The cartridge chosen was the relatively low-powered .38 Smith & Wesson (.38 S&W).

The process by which the decision in favor of a smaller revolver was made is not readily evident from commonly available references. Neither is the process for the determination of the particular cartridge selected. American students of firearms have wondered why the .38 S&W cartridge was chosen over the more powerful .38 Special. However, from the British standpoint it was a logical choice.

The .38 S&W, introduced around 1877, had been chambered in British-made revolvers since before 1900. The Johnny-come-lately .38 Special was only introduced in America at the turn of the century, and even by 1922 was rarely

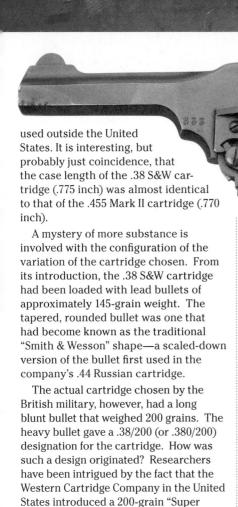

The results of early British development of a .38-caliber revolver led the Webley firm to the development of the Webley Mark IV .38 revolver; however, it was not adopted by the British government. This specimen, with a 4-inch barrel, was made commercially and served as a police revolver.

used outside the United States. It is interesting, but probably just coincidence, that the case length of the .38 S&W cartridge (.775 inch) was almost identical to that of the .455 Mark II cartridge (.770 inch).

A mystery of more substance is involved with the configuration of the variation of the cartridge chosen. From its introduction, the .38 S&W cartridge had been loaded with lead bullets of approximately 145-grain weight. The tapered, rounded bullet was one that had become known as the traditional "Smith & Wesson" shape—a scaled-down version of the bullet first used in the company's .44 Russian cartridge.

The actual cartridge chosen by the British military, however, had a long blunt bullet that weighed 200 grains. The heavy bullet gave a .38/200 (or .380/200) designation for the cartridge. How was such a design originated? Researchers have been intrigued by the fact that the Western Cartridge Company in the United States introduced a 200-grain "Super Police" load for the .38 S&W cartridge in about the same general time frame. Were the British and American cartridges the result of joint development? Did one copy the other? Such questions are beyond the scope of our specific investigation. However, they add to the number of small mysteries that surround the decision to reject the Webley .38. Even more were to come.

Velocity was a leisurely 650 feet per second. Early testing

seemed to bear out the effectiveness of the heavy .38 bullet as a satisfactory man-stopper, approaching that of the .455. The reasoning of British Ordnance, however, may leave a ballistics student scratching their head: "The quality of efficiency depends to some extent on the massive soft lead bullet and the relatively low velocity rather than on any inherent magic in the caliber." Although the strange wording of the concept seemed to indicate that lowering the velocity increases the stopping power, the tests of the soft lead bullet as a satisfactory man-stopper probably had some validity. Julian Hatcher wrote favorably about the performance of the Western "Super Police" load, as previously stated, one virtually identical to the British .38/200.

Once the cartridge had been chosen, exactly what happened? Webley had

Mark II and Mark III (company designations, not military) .38-caliber revolvers already in production, and apparently offered them to the Royal Small Arms Factory at Enfield Lock for evaluation. It appears that Webley engineers also worked in consultation with the RSAF staff, but the details of this arrangement are not clear. The upshot was that the Webley .38-caliber design was improved into the Mark IV (again, a company designation).

The .38-caliber Webley Mark IV had traditional Webley features and a grip similar to that of the .455 Mark VI.

The Royal Small Arms Factory at Enfield Lock however, began production of a different design. What had happened? Authorities offer a variety of comments in published references.

Chamberlain (1974) noted, "These (Enfield-made) revolvers resemble the Webley & Scott company's Mark IV .38, the basic design offered by Webley for service adoption..." Ward (1984) provided some fragmented insights into the course of testing, and Webley & Scott's participation: "The earliest trials were on the two revolvers supplied by Webley's." Boothroyd (1970) stated, "(the Enfield revolver was) chosen to replace the Webley .455... Webley & Scott carried out the development work..." Ezell (1981) offered, "Webley & Scott was commissioned to carry out these experiments... Unhappy with Webley & Scott's progress, Enfield took control of the project in 1926, and continued to modify the basic revolver design until an acceptable one was approved..." Batchelor and Walter (1988) were more blunt: "After spurning the... .38 Mark IV Webley revolver, the government designers had produced a near-facsimile for British service...(a) discreditable episode..." Dowell (1987) stated, "(Webley) was commissioned to prepare designs and carry out experiments... the Government Enfield .38-caliber revolver was ultimately accepted and produced in the government factory at Enfield Lock, around 1928."

From these comments we get some idea of the rivalry, behind-the-scenes intrigue, power struggles and conflicting ideas. Putting everything together into its simplest form, the story may go something like this:

Webley & Scott, quite logically, had been given the nod to come up with a suitable .38-caliber service revolver. Webley already made .38-caliber revolvers and it seemed obvious that the firm could produce a suitable design. However, the company was to work with the staff at Enfield.

So, a decision may have already been made that the final design would be produced at Enfield. This opens the door to speculation that there was some interagency rivalry between Webley and RSAF. This possibility seems borne out by the fact that the military .455 Mark VI was continued in production after World War I by Enfield, not by Webley. In a period of downsizing the British government wanted its own facility to remain in service.

However, at least in the early stages, people from Webley and Enfield apparently worked together. Webley's outcome was the Mark IV .38, a scaled-down version of the .455 Mark VI, with some actual improvements.

However, the Webley .38 was not the design that was adopted. For whatever reasons, the British government gave the responsibility for the final design to the RSAF to complete. The RSAF staff eventually came up with a revolver design that was in very many ways similar to the Webley .38-caliber revolver. The Enfield .38 revolver had the Webley hinge frame and stirrup latch design, but it had many differences. No parts will interchange between the two types. The production of the new Enfield revolver was begun in 1929-1930, and the design was formally adopted in 1932 as the Pistol, Revolver, No. 2 Mark I.

According to an uncredited Internet source, Webley & Scott sued the

British government for costs involved in research to finalize their Mark IV .38 design (and possibly the resulting Enfield design?). The RSAF contested this action, claiming that the Enfield design was one originated by them, with "assistance" from Webley & Scott. The Webley suit was denied. However, the British Royal Commission on Awards to Investors eventually awarded Webley & Scott a lesser amount.

So, we have at least some idea as to why the Webley was not chosen. Can we chalk this up to rivalry between a commercial manufacturing facility and a government manufacturing facility, with the final decision being made by the government? Does this seem reasonable? Can we learn anything further from an examination of the guns themselves?

THE WEBLEY MARK IV .38

The Webley Mark IV .38 that was generated as a possibility for government service consideration was basically a scaled-down version of the last .455 revolver, the big Webley Mark VI. With a 5-inch barrel, it was 10 inches long and 5½ inches high. Weight was about 27 ounces.

Webley offered an improved grip for the .38-caliber Mark IV that closely resembled the excellent grip of the .455-caliber Mark VI. In fact, is it so close that some have suggested that it is exactly the same as the bigger-frame .455. The grip of the .38 is close to, but not exactly the same as the earlier

pin of the .455 had been made as part of the hammer, and a damaged firing pin required replacement of the hammer.

Although the stirrup latch of the .38 worked in the same fashion as did those on the .455s, the dimensions changed. The smaller frame required making the dimensions smaller, but the resulting stirrup latch had a built-in problem—the distance from the pivot point to the end of the thumbpiece was about .90 inch, about the same dimension as that from the pivot point to the top of the latch, which was approximately .85 inch. This gives a short lever arm for the thumb to push with decreased mechanical advantage, and the revolver is much more difficult to open than the larger .455. The same relative dimensions of the Mark VI .455 measured 1.20 inches to .80 inches. Such measurements gave the thumb a great deal of mechanical advantage. In addition, the last part of the latch opening pushes the hammer back, so the required pressure grows greater just before the final opening of the latch. It is obvious that the .38's shorter opening lever arm was of some importance. Long strings of firing would show this to be a negative aspect in the Mark IV Webley design.

Another small feature related to cylinder removal was carried over from the .455 revolvers. To remove the cylinder, a small screw on the left of the frame is removed. This screw locks a lever in place. When freed, the lever can be turned counterclockwise.

The cylinder retainer (made as part of the holster-guide wings) turns to free the cylinder, which can be easily removed for cleaning. This is

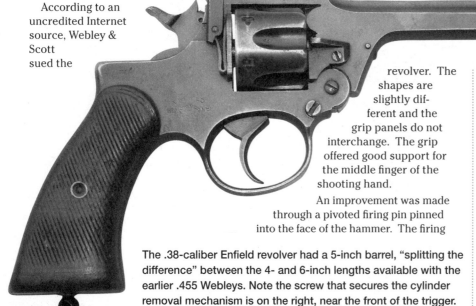

revolver. The shapes are slightly different and the grip panels do not interchange. The grip offered good support for the middle finger of the shooting hand.

An improvement was made through a pivoted firing pin pinned into the face of the hammer. The firing

an effective system, but does increase the chance of losing the small screw. The Enfield .38-caliber revolver solved this problem by having the screw enter the frame from the right, with only the tip protruding to the left to hold the lever. Thus, it only had to be partially unscrewed to free the lever.

Although not adopted for military service, the Webley Mark IV .38 was a strong and generally satisfactory revolver. It was sold on the commercial market and marketed to police forces, generally with a 4-inch barrel, and was well received for police use. The commercial Webley .38 revolvers were well-made, nicely finished revolvers. Their triggers and grip frame front and back surfaces were grooved.

The .38-caliber Enfield revolver had a 5-inch barrel, "splitting the difference" between the 4- and 6-inch lengths available with the earlier .455 Webleys. Note the screw that secures the cylinder removal mechanism is on the right, near the front of the trigger. This is an improvement over the Webley design.

THE ENFIELD .38 REVOLVER

The revolver chosen over the Webley and made by the government's Royal Small Arms Factory at Enfield was adopted as the Pistol, Revolver, No. 2 Mark I. It was officially adopted in 1932, although production had actually begun by 1929. Obviously based on the Webley design, it had a number of changes. A 5-inch barrel was chosen, "splitting the difference" between the 4-inch and 6-inch lengths of the .455s. Dimensions with a 5-inch barrel were roughly 10¼ inches in length and 5¼ inches high. Weight was about 28 ounces. Although very slightly larger, it was, in effect, about the same general size as the Webley .38.

Enfield had gone back to the sideplate type of frame construction, a reminder that the "WG" Webley had used that system. Such construction allowed easier assembly at the factory. However, in the field it was not as great an advantage as the stirrup latch had to be removed from the gun before the sideplate could be removed.

The shape of the grip was not bad. But, like contemporary American Colt and S&W revolvers, there is substantial space behind the triggerguard that does not allow the third finger of the shooting hand to properly support the weight of the revolver. The revolver has to be firmly gripped to keep it in proper position for firing. The grip panels were of checkered or grooved wood.

The stirrup latch is actually much better proportioned than that of the .38-caliber Webley for opening the gun. From pivot to thumbpiece end is about 1.1 inch, and from pivot to latch top is .8 inch, giving the thumb the advantage of the longer lever arm. The Enfield No. 2 Mark I is easier to open than the Webley Mark IV because of that difference. It can be imagined that over a long period of firing, men might well prefer the Enfield to the Webley.

Still, there was not a great deal of difference in the general handling and performance of the guns. We must suspect that an intergroup rivalry between the manufacturing components of RSAF and Webley played a large part in the selection of the Enfield.

Has this answered our mystery as to the selection of the Enfield revolver? Or is there more to be learned about these guns? It may be instructive to consider what happened with the production of the Enfield .38 after its adoption.

We know that the Enfield No. 2 Mark I was officially adopted in 1932. However, it did not remain in its original form for very long. By the middle '30s, double-action-only variants with no hammer spurs had been made for testing. In 1938 the original design was modified into the No. 2 Mark I* (Number Two Mark One Star) by replacement of the original hammer to one with no spur. This new standard revolver did not allow single-action use.

The story we see repeated in firearms literature is that British tank crews kept snagging the hammers of their Enfield revolvers as they climbed in and out of the vehicles. Because of this situation, the hammer spurs were removed. Rather than manufacture separate variants for tank crews and other troops, all Enfield revolvers were made as double-action-only.

Such a story should raise substantial questions to students of firearms. On what did they snag? Were holsters not issued? Did the traditional flap holsters not cover the hammers? We have encountered another small mystery; one that may be larger than it first appears.

The Enfield .38 revolver chosen by the British government was officially adopted in 1932 as the Pistol, Revolver, No. 2 Mark I. The features of the cylinder removal/holster guide system and the stirrup latch are similar to those of the Webley revolvers.

There is a school of thought that tank crews snagging the hammers had little or nothing to do with the removal of the single-action hammers. The War Department had apparently been sold on the idea of double-action-only shooting by W. E. Fairbairn and other British shooting instructors since about 1919.

About the same time in America, exhibition shooters were becoming popular. Some of them

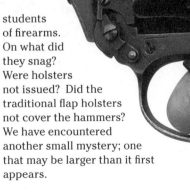

Gripping the No. 2 Mark I in shooting position normally left space between the shooter's middle finger and the frame of the revolver. This lack of support was later addressed (with limited success) by different grips for the No. 2 Mark I*.

specialized in fast shooting with double-action revolvers. American shooters Elmer Keith and J. Henry "Fitz" Fitzgerald demonstrated practical fast-draw revolver shooting at Camp Perry in 1919. Even before World War I, about 1912 or 1913, Ed McGivern of Montana was giving rapid-fire exhibitions with revolvers.

McGivern used both Colt and Smith & Wesson revolvers, but his most outstanding records were set with S&Ws. Fitzgerald worked for Colt and did all his fast double-action shooting with Colts. Elmer Keith generally favored S&W double-action revolvers. Keith's firearms writing became popular in the early 1920s and promoted the new ideas of different ways to shoot handguns. It is interesting to note that all these men apparently had large, beefy hands, and at least in this early period, used the revolvers with relatively small factory grips.

Were British planners aware of any of this? We can only speculate. But somehow, British planners became interested in double-action-only revolver use.

We can imagine their thinking: Double-action shooting at short range had been shown by experts to be amazingly accurate and very effective. With a double-action-only revolver as standard issue, training would be simplified as only a few operations needed to be learned, and accidental discharges would be reduced (no one would forget that the hammer was cocked, because it could not be). Such thinking would suppose that military planners no longer considered British soldiers capable of using a revolver effectively in different situations

as a weapon in battle. A sidearm was considered only suitable for short-range defense purposes. In such cases, it may have been reasoned, double-action-only (DAO) ought to be fine.

But consider if this ties in with our original question of the rejection of the Webley .38. If British military leaders in the early 1920s had indeed come around to the idea of adopting a revolver to be used as a DAO, could that have influenced their decision toward a revolver that could be readily used in such a configuration? The shape and construction of the Enfield .38 frame is much more like that of a contemporary Smith & Wesson or Colt than that of a Webley. The cylinder turning and locking mechanisms of the Enfield .38 also are very much like those of the American revolvers. They are very different than the Webley mechanisms.

Did the American success with close-range DAO shooting have any part in the decision

to use a similar shape and lockwork as American revolvers? Could this factor have any part in the decision to reject the Webley design?

At any rate, the Enfield .38 was adopted as a fairly conventional hinge-frame revolver using the strong Webley latching mechanism. Before long, it had been changed into a double-action-only revolver, a rarity in military history.

Several references state that lighter mainsprings were installed in No. 2 Mark I* revolvers to reduce the double-action pull down to 11 pounds. That may have been the intention, but I have seen no evidence of this. I have measured double-action trigger pulls of a number of Enfield revolvers, and they all ran around 14 or 15 pounds. For this writer, the DAO Enfield is a difficult gun to shoot well.

One final modification was made. To speed production during World War II the internal hammer-block safety (the device that would keep the gun

WWII revolvers made at the Enfield Royal Small Arms Factory (RSAF) usually were lightly stamped and painted with black enamel. Markings are generally difficult to distinguish.

In 1938, the Enfield No. 2 Mark I* was adopted (a wartime internal change made it the Mark I**). A double-action-only version of the revolver adopted six years earlier, it had a spurless hammer and thick Bakelite grips.

The early .38 Smith & Wesson cartridge (left) traditionally used a lead bullet of about 145 grains. The .38/200 Mark I load planned for the British .38 revolvers (center) used a longer, heavier 200-grain bullet. In 1937 the less effective Mark II (right) was adopted, using a 178-grain jacketed bullet.

The lack of finish on this Albion-made revolver suggests that these were apparently not painted, as were the wartime guns made at Enfield.

The markings of this Albion-made No. 2 Mark I** indicate it was made in 1943. Albion markings stand out somewhat better than wartime Enfield markings.

from firing if dropped forcefully on its hammer) was omitted. This was the final variation adopted in 1942 and designated No. 2 Mark I** (Number Two Mark One Star Star). Astoundingly, earlier variants were converted to the Mark I** configuration as they were serviced. It is apparently difficult for collectors to find an unaltered Mark I or Mark I* nowadays.

Initial use of the Enfield .38 as a DAO revolver exhibited a problem. Rapid fire made the revolver shift in the hand with the recoil of successive shots. There was too much space behind the triggerguard. The thick hands of the American exhibition shooters apparently accommodated such space. As time went on, Americans would make adapters or special grips that would fill the excess space between the middle finger and the revolver frame. The British used another idea. Thick Bakelite grips were fitted that had a wide groove near the upper portion of both grip plates. These grooves have been called thumbrests, but they are not. The shooter's firing-hand thumb and trigger-finger knuckle fit into the grooves on opposite sides of the grip, and attempted to arrest the pivoting movement created by the recoil.

PRELUDE TO WAR AGAIN

As the 1930s continued, British planners feared that the unclad lead bullet might be in violation of the 1899 Hague Convention's Declaration 3, which addresses the use of bullets that expand or flatten easily in the human body. In 1937 the original Mark I .38/200 cartridge was replaced by the .38-caliber Mark II cartridge. The Mark II dispensed with the 200-grain lead bullet and used a heavily jacketed 178-grain bullet. The Mark II was the standard .38-caliber cartridge used by the British during World War II. It was regarded as being decidedly inferior in stopping power to the original lead bullet load.

British soldiers were destined to go into battle using an inferior cartridge for which the gun had not been designed. The original gun, of course, was itself changed to the spurless-hammer No. 2 Mark I* in 1938, the year following the substitution of the cartridge. The DAO Enfield .38 revolver and its marginal cartridge were apparently not popular with knowledgeable soldiers.

There were other factors brewing during this prewar period. Like most of Europe, England was affected by the worldwide economic depression of the 1930s. While crime increase in Britain was relatively slight, British leaders addressed it in what was becoming their standard response – more gun control. The 1937 law applied additional restrictions – already harsh on handguns – to most rifles, and also to shotguns with barrels less than 24 inches long. It was to prove a poor time to further disarm British subjects.

WORLD WAR II

The Second World War officially began on Sept. 1, 1939 with the German *blitzkrieg* attack on Poland. Within days Great Britain and France had declared war on Germany. By May 1940, Germany had conquered Poland, Norway, the Netherlands and Luxembourg. On May 28, Belgium surrendered. The Belgian surrender left the British forces in Europe in a desperate situation. They retreated to Dunkirk on the coast of France and 300,000 troops were picked up by a flotilla of every sort of vessel that could provide rescue.

The Dunkirk evacuation in 1940 had saved the British Army, but had meant the loss of all British arms and equipment left on the French shore. Firearms of all sorts were in short supply. Great Britain faced a potential German invasion across the channel at any time. British troops and civilians alike stood almost defenseless in the face of such a threat.

In the United States, posters were distributed entreating Americans to "Send a Gun to Defend a British Home," explaining that "British civilians, faced with the threat of invasion, desperately need arms for the defense of their homes." Americans, perhaps shaking their heads that British gun laws had disarmed those British civilians, sent quantities of their personal firearms to England.

Hitler's decision not to invade gave the British time to re-arm their military forces. The .455 Webleys that had been replaced by the Enfield .38s were brought out of storage, refurbished if necessary, and put back in service. The .455 Webley cartridge (in its Mark VI jacketed-bullet form) went back into production to supply them. The Royal Small Arms Factory was unable to meet the demand for .38-caliber sidearms and a contract for No. 2 Mark I** revolvers was awarded to Albion Motor Works in Glasgow, Scotland. An estimated 24,000 were made by Albion. A small number were also made in Australia by the Howard Auto Cultivator firm. Guns made by these last two manufacturers can be readily identified by markings on the right side of the frame. The wartime Enfield-made revolvers were stamped very lightly and then finished with black enamel. Markings are generally difficult to read.

Smith & Wesson "Victory" revolvers (the Military & Police model chambered for the .38 S&W) were acquired from America. These revolvers were generally provided with a dull finish, and came in barrel lengths between 3 and 6 inches.

In a final twist of irony, a contract for revolvers was given to Webley & Scott. The Webley Mark IV .38, which had been rejected in favor of the Enfield, was adopted as a substitute standard in 1942. The wartime Webley .38s, all with 5-inch barrels, were marked "War Finish" on the frames, in what amounted to an apology for their rough exteriors.

Everything that would shoot was used for some purpose during the war. Revolvers not used in the combat zones served to arm guards in the rear areas and on the home front, and served other functions. This would

A final irony—the .38-caliber Mark IV revolver, which had been rejected for British military adoption, was later adopted during WWII as a substitute standard sidearm.

be the last time Great Britain would use revolvers in any quantity. New arms—the submachine gun and the semiautomatic pistol—entered the scene of British military arms.

AFTER WORLD WAR II

After the end of the war most nations considered updating their armament. The Sten submachine gun used the 9mm Luger cartridge, and it seemed logical to adopt a handgun using that same cartridge. The Browning Hi-Power had been made in Canada during the war, and was eventually adopted in 1957 as the standard sidearm of British forces. Upgrading their armament meant that obsolete equipment, including firearms, could be sold to bring in funds for new items.

The now-obsolete British revolvers, the Webley .455s, the Webley and Enfield .38s, were sold—along with rifles and other surplus equipment—on the world market. Most of the guns came to the country with the greatest degree of personal freedom—the United States.

This "Golden Age of Surplus," a decade that lasted from about 1957 until the Gun Control Act of 1968, allowed Americans the opportunity to purchase and shoot the firearms of many countries.

The Webley Mark IV .38 was made during WWII only with a 5-inch barrel. It was about the same size and weight as the Enfield .38. The same operating instructions applied to both revolvers.

Webley Mark IV .38s produced during WWII were stamped "WAR FINISH" perhaps as a form of apology for the rough machining.

SHOOTING THE BRITISH REVOLVERS

Can actually handling and shooting the British revolvers give us any additional insights into why the Webley .38 wasn't chosen? It seemed a reasonable way to conclude this investigation was to consider this. There were few *collectors* of British arms when the British revolvers first appeared on these shores. Americans bought them at low prices as *shooters*. And shot them! In some cases, modifications to the guns and a lot of shooting have lowered their potential collector value. Such "using" guns, however, give us perhaps a better idea of how they would have served their users under wartime conditions.

There was very little ammunition available when the first wave of .455 revolvers came to this country. American ingenuity soon got the big Mark VI revolvers shooting by simply facing the back of the cylinders off in a lathe until there was a space of .009 inch between the rear of the cylinder and the recoil shield of the frame. This spacing allowed the use of .45 ACP cartridges in contemporary three-round half-moon clips. The less common .45 Auto Rim cartridges could also be used individually. Concern about the .455 bore being too big turned out to be misplaced. The Webleys had seven-groove bores that were difficult to measure, but authorities such as Hatcher (1952) let us know that they were just fine for .452-inch .45-caliber bullets.

The .38-caliber revolvers that came in could, of course, use factory .38 S&W cartridges, which were more common then compared to nowadays.

Handloaders found that the .38 Webley and Enfield revolvers had bores very slightly oversize for available .357-inch .38 Special bullets. However, most handloading was done with lead bullets, which expanded easily. The guns seemed not to know the difference, and shot just fine.

I was fortunate to have been around during the "Golden Age" of surplus guns and purchased my first British revolver, a Mark VI Webley .455, in 1963. I have kept records of just about every gun I have fired since 1966. Going back through my old notebooks was a trip down memory lane. Over the years, I had acquired a baker's dozen of variations of the immigrant British revolvers and was surprised to recall how often I shot them. I made notes of scores, groups and personal opinions of the handling and "feel" of a number of the guns.

I was basically a revolver shooter back then, and shot Bullseye Pistol competition. I had target revolvers that I used regularly. However, for fun I sometimes used surplus handguns to see how well I could do with them under the pressure of competition. My notes show that I occasionally used my Mark VI for match shooting. I couldn't duplicate the scores of my usual target guns, but I was impressed that the Webley scores were not *that* far behind.

For recreational shooting, all the British revolvers back then were inexpensive and fun to shoot. I expected them to shoot well, and did not notice much difference in practical accuracy. Early shooting was usually done with

You won't see this very often. The writer learned that a careful home craftsman could convert a DAO Enfield No. 2 Mark I** to cock and fire in single-action mode. The conversion of this revolver allowed single-action accuracy comparisons with .38-caliber Webley and No. 2 Mark I revolvers.

one hand, bull's-eye style. However, Jeff Cooper's influence was spreading and two-handed shooting became more common.

The .455 Mark I, Mark II and Mark VI cartridges (left to right) used in the .455 Webleys are here compared with the author's Mark I-equivalent handload in a .45 Auto Rim case (far right). The handloads were used in military Webleys that had been converted to .45 ACP.

The British .38/200 cartridge (left, here made by Kynoch) and the U.S. .38 Smith & Wesson Super Police load (middle, made by Western) are compared with the author's equivalent 195-grain handload (right). This handload was used to evaluate and compare the various British .38 revolvers.

Needless to say, it was hard to make any realistic comparison of accuracy between the Enfield .38 No. 2 Mk I** and the Webley Mk IV .38. The long double-action-only trigger pull of the Enfield obviously made some difference, though. Enough to make a person wonder: exactly what were the internal mechanical differences between the original Enfield and the DAO version? It turned out that the primary difference was that a new spurless hammer without a full-cock notch had been installed. Could a full-cock notch be added to the spurless hammer? Yes, it was possible. Careful measurement and careful removal of enough metal to create a notch, and wow! I had a Mark I** that I could fire in single-action mode. Eventually, I found that the best way to cock the hammer was to start pressure on the trigger until the hammer began to move back, then grasp the hammer with the thumb and forefinger of my left hand and draw it to full cock.

I learned that the Webley and Enfield revolvers, fired single action, were roughly comparable in accuracy, at least when fired by me. Firing the Enfield double action, as it was intended, opened up the groups. I also made notes that the thick grips of the Enfield hurt my hand during recoil when doing extensive shooting. However, I noted that the Enfield seemed somewhat easier to trigger double action than the Webley .38.

My old notes gave me some insights, but the shooting sessions were not fired under uniform conditions. Perhaps now at this present time, I could still reassemble a group of representative revolvers and load ammunition approximating

that for which the guns were originally designed to use. Consistent ranges, positions and loads would allow a more systematic evaluation and tell more about how the guns compared. A tough job, but somebody ought to do it!

To condense a long story, I loaded quantities of cartridges as close to the original loadings as I could, for both the .455 and .38-caliber British revolvers. I made many trips to the range and shot a number of targets from a variety of positions. Without much surprise, the results of my recent shooting were pretty much the same as the results of shooting back then. The .455s shot as well as I had remembered. The groups from .38-caliber Webley and Enfield revolvers fired under the same conditions were comparable to each other, and were in pretty much the same league as the groups from the .455s.

So, personally I put to rest the idea that accuracy, or lack thereof, of the Webley .38 revolver entered into the decision to reject it for service. What then, were the deciding factors?

CONCLUSION

In the selection of a military sidearm we would expect a listing of measurable specifications and performance standards to be met. We would anticipate that records of testing would be kept. Such documents, if they exist, seem to not be readily available.

From secondary sources, a number of factors seem to have been at work in the adoption of the .38-caliber revolver. There seems to have been a latent rivalry

between the government manufactory and the commercial manufacturer. The government, while protecting its own arms manufacturer, created restrictive firearms laws that harmed the civilian arms industry. The 20th century saw the loss of skilled firearms industry workers, and the growth of a citizenry no longer familiar with firearms. The strange fascination of British planners with double-action-only shooting also had an effect on the final outcome—the last official British military revolver ever produced.

In this strange mix of factors, available information precludes any single reason for the rejection of the Webley .38 revolver.

"Why not the Webley?"

It seemed such a simple question.

SELECTED BIBLIOGRAPHY

Barnes, Frank C., 1963, Military Handguns for Sporting Use in *Gun Digest, 18th Edition (1964)*, p.112-123

Barnes, Frank C., 1965, *Cartridges of the World*: Follett, Chicago

Batchelor, John, and John Walter, 1988, *Handgun*: David & Charles, Devon, UK

Boothroyd, Geoffrey, 1970, *The Handgun*: Bonanza, New York

Chamberlain, W.H.J., 1974, The Marks of Enfield Lock, in *Gun Collector's Digest*, p.151-159.

Chamberlain, W.H.J., 1977, Webley Service-Pattern .455 Caliber Revolvers, in *Gun Collector's Digest, Vol. II*, p.49-55.

Dowell, William Chipchase, 1987, *The Webley Story*, Commonwealth Heritage Foundation

Ezell, Edward C., 1977, *Small Arms of the World, 8th edition*: Stackpole, Harrisburg, PA

Ezell, Edward C., 1981, *Handguns of the World*: Stackpole, Harrisburg, PA

Hatcher, Julian S., 1935, *Textbook of Pistols and Revolvers*: Small-Arms Technical Publishing Co., Plantersville, SC

Hatcher, Julian S., 1952, .455 Barrel Dimensions (Dope Bag item): *American Rifleman*, v.100, no.2 (February 1952), p.56

Hoffschmidt, E. J., 1954, Enfield Revolver No.2 Mk1 and Mk1*: *American Rifleman*, v.104, no.1 (January 1956), and p.30-31

Hogg, Ian V., 1977, *The Encyclopedia of Infantry Weapons of WWII*: Thomas Y. Crowell, New York

Hogg, Ian, and John Weeks, 1992, *Pistols of the World, 3rd Edition,* DBI Books, Northbrook, IL

Labbett, Peter, 1970, British Military Cartridges in *Gun Digest, 25th Edition (1971)*, p.328-333.

Riordan, Dennis, 1970, Webley Mark IV Revolver, *American Rifleman,* v.118, no.5 (May 1970), p.44-45.

Riordan, Dennis, 1976, Webleys at War in *Guns Annual Book of Handguns*, v.7 (Summer 1976), p.16-19, 87-88

Smith, W.H.B., 1943, 1945, *A Basic Manual of Military Small Arms*: Military Service Publishing Company, Harrisburg, PA

Smith, W.H.B., 1944, The Enfield Double-Action: *American Rifleman*, (August 1944), p. 24-25.

Smith, W.H.B., and Joseph Smith, 1968, *Book of Pistols and Revolvers*, Stackpole, Harrisburg, PA

Ward, Wilfrid, 1984, The Gun That Followed the Famous Webley .455 in *Gun Digest, 39th Edition (1985)*, p.76-85

Ward, Wilfrid, 1989, The Englishman and the Revolver in *Gun Digest, 44th Edition (1990)*, p.43-51

• THE EVOLUTION OF RED-DOT SIGHTS •

RED DOTS OF THE 21ST CENTURY

BY Kevin Muramatsu

he Leatherwood/Hi-Lux company makes several different sizes of red dots. bove to the left is an ES1x50TP, which s a very large 50mm lens model, and hen just below is the 25mm ES-1x25, ith a lens diameter half the size. eneath those are the new Max-Tac series.

he first red-dot "scope" I ever saw was a weird-looking thing that my uncle picked up at a gun show someplace, and this was back in the mid to late '80s; don't quite remember just when exactly. It looked nothing like today's models, being the first of three or four generations of development. It looked like some moron had a see-through scope mount and had put some

sort of cheap-looking laser gun on top of it. It literally looked like the scopes that the rebel soldiers on Princess Leia's ship had on top of their blasters as the Stormtroopers blew in the hatch and attempted to take the ship with minimal casualties.

The laser scope thingy on top was a primitive fiber optic that gathered the photons and pumped them into the see-through section at the bottom. Like

modern red dots, the light then reflected off the inside of the front lens and back through the rear lens. I distinctly recall that it required pretty bright light to work well, but also that it had a very crisp dot that (assuming sufficient light) was very easy to see. It used no batteries and was completely passive. Of course the lenses were non-magnifying. Without getting too deeply into the science involved, and there is some considerable

Right: This is one of the early red-dot scopes that used fiber-optic tech to illuminate the dot. The tube with the clear tip is the light gatherer and the adjustments are made to this tube. What is apparently a riser below it is actually the glass tube through which the shooter's gaze passed.

The M21 is the classic Meprolight red-dot sight, but it isn't really a red dot; it's more like an amber dot. This unit does not use batteries but utilizes ambient light, collected with the fiber-optic light pipes that run around the front of the housing. When the light is not so bright the Tritium inside serves to illuminate the dot quite well, thank you. This is the standard optic on the IDF's Tavor rifle.

Right: Here is a rather fragile and inexpensive red dot designed for use with air rifles, BB guns and maybe .22 rimfires. It was something like $20 at Wal-Mart.

C-MORE also has a micro line, the RTS2 seen here and the STS. The RTS2 has a manual 10-setting brightness adjustment and a large round window, while the STS has an auto-brightening/off/max-power switch with a more square, traditional window.

amount, red-dot scopes work using reflected light to form the reticle, as opposed to the standard riflescope that is refractory, bending light to enlarge an image, or to make it look closer.

Red-dot sights are commonly called reflective or reflex sights for this reason. The image of the target passes right through the lens as it would if the lens were plain old glass. The inner surface of the lens is coated with a substance that reflects back a certain color, in most cases red, but allows all others through. This red light is reflected off this lens and goes back to the shooter's eye. The red light comes from, in most cases, a red light emitting diode (LED) that is mounted inside the housing, but some models use lasers rather than LEDs. Most are battery powered. Some are illuminated with Tritium, others fiber optics, though more often a combination of some or all of these. Some are housed in a tube like a traditional scope, others in a more open type of housing. They come in large and small sizes and everything in between. Now that we know how they work generally, let's look at a few specifically.

Aimpoint

Aimpoint was the first big name in the red-dot market, and to be fair even with all the recent competition, probably is still the biggest. It doesn't hurt that this Swedish company's products were adopted by the U.S. Army. The CompM2 is the normal designation for the military's M68 Close Combat Optic. Why is it called a Close Combat Optic and why a red dot for that purpose?

Think of it this way. The great thing about optics, whether they are the traditional scopes or the newer red dots, is that you only have to place one thing on the target, the reticle. With open sights you must align two objects with the target – the front and rear sights. It is inherently easier and faster to place one object on the target than to place two. We all know that the first guy that shoots has a tremendous advantage. The CCO allows the shooter who has it

Left: Here we see an Aimpoint, looks like a CompM2 or M3, mounted on a .22 pistol. This configuration is popular, since it is mounted on a part of the receiver that does not reciprocate.

Below: The newest incarnation from Aimpoint is this CompM4, which replaces the older CompM2 as the military's M68 Close Combat Optic.

to very quickly place the aiming object, in this case a dot, on the target. There is no magnification, so there is no change in perspective to deal with when transitioning from the naked eye to looking through the tube in the red-dot scope, and this makes the target acquisition even faster.

The CompM2 exists in a cheaper version, the CompML2. The difference lies in the ability of the M2 to be used with night vision equipment via ultralow settings, whereas the ML2 – which lacks these intensities, does not have that capability. Of course the ML2 is cheaper as a result, 10-20 percent or so, but it looks identical to the M2. Other lines included the C-Series that also shared the look, but was lesser in some respects. The newer M3 supersedes the ML2 and M2 with updated technology. When I read an ML2 box for the first time I thought I had found a typo on the box. 10,000 hours of battery life? Yeah right. To be fair, 10,000 hours was on low power, with the high power being only around 1,000-2,000 hours. And then I was impressed. When the M3 came along with 50,000 hours it was almost a profound middle finger to the rules imposed by physical reality, then not to be

outdone by the M4 at 80,000 hours. You just leave it on and change the battery every year or two on your birthday. Earlier models like the M2 and M3 used DL1/3N batteries, which you pretty much had to order online or get at Radio Shack. Newer models use AA or CR123 batteries, which are much more common.

These optics are waterproof to an insane depth and fogproof (as any optic ought to be), very impact resistant and come in a variety of sizes suited to different disciplines. There are models designed for hunting, competition and tactical purposes, even including very small units such as the Micro T1 and H1. You will also find that the general styling and look of the Aimpoint has been, ahem… is flatterized a word? It is now.

EOTech

An often-obtained alternate to the traditional red-dot sight as espoused by the Aimpoint and its clones and flatterizers, is the Holosight. Using holographic technology, the Holosight forms a reticle by means of a laser rather than an LED. The general nature of the reflective or reflex sight is still intact, however. The

standout point of the Holosight is that the reticle is viewable from any part of the window, as long as any part of the window is visible. If the entire window of the sight except for the bottom left corner is broken and gone for example, you can still use that little remaining corner to aim with.

Even better, the Holosights, like the Aimpoints, use readily available batteries such as AA and CR123. This reminds me, if you haven't seen a CR123 lithium battery, they are very commonly used in optics and tactical lights. Otherwise, you will find them used in a number of SLR cameras. Either way, you can find them right next to the AA and AAA batteries at Wal-Mart. The EOTech products are quite rugged, with a protective canopy that encircles the housing. Bushnell for a time sold Holosights as well, but these were manufactured by EOTech and were quite similar, only lacking the canopy. A streamlined hunting version was also sold by Bushnell, but it seems they were only on the market for a few years. Holosights are not the most expensive of

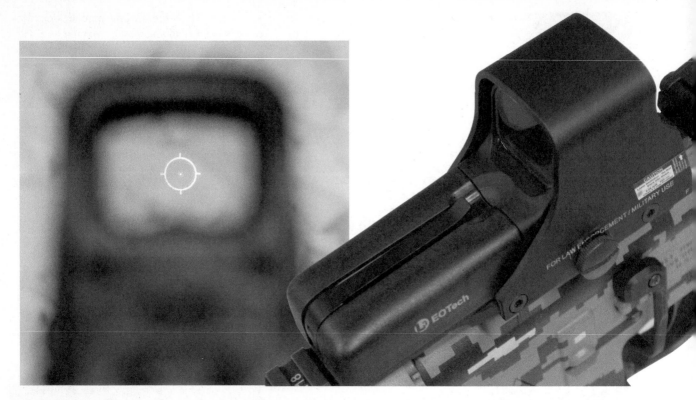

The basic EOTech Holosight, the Model 512. This unit is powered by two AA batteries in the housing just in front of the lens window. It does take up a lot of rail space because of this housing, but fortunately, the housing also contains an integral mounting clamp. With some red dots you have to buy the mounting equipment extra; with the Holosights, you don't. Also shown is the standard circle/dot reticle of the EOTech Holosight. Other styles are available but this is the most common.

products, running between $400 and $600, excepting the EOLAD model that also includes a laser that tops $1,000. EOTech also has a line of micro red-dot sights that more closely match the traditional LED equipped optics. Of course, the EOTech line has its own set of flatterizers too, and the distinctive boxy silhouette of the Holosight is clearly a source of inspiration for other offerings in the realm of red-dot tech.

JP Enterprises

JP makes a small unit called a JPoint that is classified as a "micro" red dot. In design it is very close to the Docter Optics micro red-dot optic, which is really the granddaddy of the micro series. The Docter sights were and still are quite strong and durable, with glass lenses and aluminum housings. They run on a button battery, as do just about all the optics in this classification, usually a CR

2032 or something very much like it. This is the same battery that powers most optics, whether micro, mini, full-size red dots and even illuminated reticle riflescopes.

People realized that putting an optic of appreciable weight on a slide tended to throw the fine balance of cartridge pressure or recoil force, slide mass (now increased) and recoil spring out of whack. In fact most early mounts, and still some nowadays, in order to work were affixed to the pistol's frame with the mount then encircling the slide. This kept the sight off the slide and the potential negative side effects as a result. Traditional tube styles are still always mounted this way on handguns.

The JPoint has an acrylic lens and a plastic housing and weighs half an ounce. The weight reduction has made this optic the next best thing to weight-

Here is a JP Enterprises JPoint mounted on top of a JP flattop scope mount. The standard topstrap of the rear ring has been replaced with a topstrap that incorporates a mounting platform for the JPoint.

less and so mounting it on a slide has minimal to no effect on the function of the pistol. Of course, making it more lightweight makes it fun to use on a long gun too and it makes an excellent secondary optic. The JPoint has been around for a while now and is one of many micro red dots. Virtually all share the same basic design with some more robustly made, others less so, and they often even have the same footprint so the mounts for one can fit many other brands. If you are a mouth-breathing knuckle-dragger who can't help themselves from banging nice expensive things against harder, heavier, cheaper things – JP also sells a guard housing that will protect the sight from incidental damage. In contrast, The Docter is about $100 more expensive and many people happily pay for the glass lens and aluminum housing without too much problem, but the result of building with those materials is that it has a certain amount of additional mass, in this case just a hair under an ounce. Another common example is the Burris FastFire and its several generations. This one weighs almost five ounces and is priced in-between the JPoint and Docter, but is also the most common of the three. Plus, there are many others with their own unique combination of features such as the Trijicon RMR, the EOTech MRDS, in addition to a veritable host of flatterizers.

The micro red dots are most commonly seen as a primary sighting device on a handgun and it is mostly evident in competition use. Open class shooters always have an optic on their pistols and they are often of the micro type like the JPoint. Other times the more traditional tube style like the Aimpoints or Bushnell Trophy types are found. On handguns, red dots are very useful and can definitely hasten the target acquisition of the pistol. On rifles or other long guns the micro red dot is almost always used as a secondary optic. Why use two scopes you ask? If your excuse for poor accuracy is bad eyesight and you purchase a magnifying optic for whatever shooting you are doing, then it makes sense to use a secondary non-magnifying optic to replace the iron sights that you claim you can't see anymore. So you usually see micro units sitting on top of a traditional riflescope, perhaps canted to the side, or frequently mounted at an angle on the receiver or handguard. Indeed, when a shooter wants to transition from a long-range shot to a close-range shot, all he has to do is slightly lift his head or rotate the rifle on his shoulder to bring the

micro red-dot secondary into play. This is supremely helpful for anyone shooting at anything – be it deer, other people, Communists or competition targets.

For the most part, micro red dots require a mount to attach to a pistol or rifle and many have integral Picatinny rail clamps on them, many do not. The JPoint, for example, follows the classic approach to this and screws down to a mount, which then is affixed in one of several ways to the firearm. You will find scope mounts that have topstraps designed to accept these sights, the most

The C-MORE Tactical and its related cousins, the Railway and Scout were designed for the AR-15 series of rifles. This open style without an enclosed tube is popular and lightweight, and eventually led to the micro red-dot type that has become common today.

common and obvious being JP's JPFTSM and the Burris P.E.P.R. The P.E.P.R. ships with standard topstraps and also a set of straps that have Picatinny rails incorporated into them; in fact you can

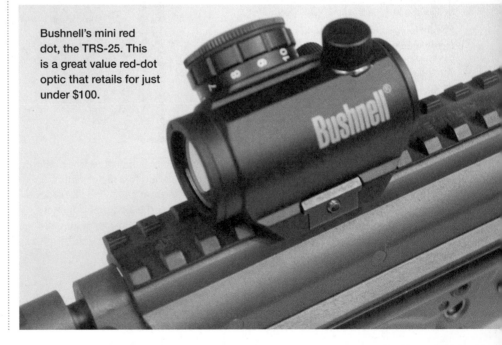

Bushnell's mini red dot, the TRS-25. This is a great value red-dot optic that retails for just under $100.

Many companies manufacture simple but efficient red-dot scopes like this Bushnell Trophy. Most have multiple reticles and some have multiple colors. The only complaint here is that most also come with crummy rings that should probably be replaced with something that has better heat treatment, or is just made of better aluminum.

purchase one of several handy packages from Burris that combine a variable low-power riflescope with a P.E.P.R. mount and FastFire red dot. There are also a number of micro bases that are designed to fit into rear sight dovetails on various guns, completely replacing them. On the other hand, pistol slides are machined with a cut-out for the sight to slide into, and this allows the front sight to still be used, and brings the dot down much closer to bore line, pretty much right where the rear sight was to begin with. The two pistols that come to mind immediately are the Smith & Wesson M&P and the FNH FNX-45 Tactical.

Interestingly, some, like the JPoint, have no on or off switch nor does it have a manual intensity adjustment. It relies on an ambient light sensor to self-adjust to the environment, and includes a cap to cover the sight when not in use, to keep the battery from running out when it is just sitting around. When you're ready, just pop the cap off and go.

Bushnell

The final type of red dot I'd like to mention is what I call the mini red dot. This style is just like the larger tube styles such as the Aimpoints, Bushnells, Tascos, Barskas, Hi-Luxes and Tru-Glos. Just smaller. The minis almost always have integral Picatinny mounts, are generally only a couple inches in size, and are in the $100-$200 range on average.

One of the best examples is the Bushnell TRS-25. It is low mounted and has a rheostat type of on/off/intensity dial and uses the ever-present CR 2032 button battery. Other similar designs include the Aimpoint H-1 and T-1, and the Vortex SPARC.

Now that we've covered what's out there, let's look at a few examples of red-dot optics in the natural environment.

Here the JPoint is mounted to a platform that can be fitted to a pistol slide, replacing the rear sight. The "B" is code for Bo-Mar, as this platform is meant to fit into standard Bo-Mar sight cuts common on many 1911s.

EXAMPLE 1:

John is a competition shooter and he really, really likes 3-gun shooting. He enjoys shooting in the open division (as many optics as you like) and when he gets to feeling big in his britches he will also shoot limited (one optic on any one of your three guns). So he mounts a JPoint on his Glock 17L after paying for a cut-out to be scraped out of the slide. On his rifle he mounts a variable riflescope that costs as much as his car and a dual illumination Trijicon RMR stuck on the side of it. On his shotgun he mounts another JPoint halfway down the vent rib. No matter what he's shooting at, he is shooting with a red dot. Okay, he's using the riflescope for ranged shots but everything else, the red dots.

EXAMPLE 2:

Richard is a proctologist that likes to upland bird hunt. He trades the local gun dealer a colonoscopy for a nice Benelli 12-gauge Montefeltro shotgun and gets the Burris Speedbead for it. This is a FastFire III attached to a mount designed to fit between the stock and receiver of the shotgun. The red dot then sits right in front of your face as you shoot. Simply lead the bird with the dot and shoot. Richard has bad eyes and can't really see the standard bead sights on the gun, so the Speedbead is a great solution, and after a couple thousand rounds of practice Richard can hit almost as many grouse as he misses.

EXAMPLE 3:

Andy is a county sheriff's deputy and stows a personally owned AR-15 in his county-supplied iron horseless carriage. Should he ever need to use it, the AR has an Aimpoint Comp M3. He knows that the little red dot is where the bullet will hit, and he knows he can shoot more precisely and more quickly than he could with just the iron sights that are on the gun, though he still has the option use them. He also likes the idea that the battery will last until the next Ice Age begins and he simply leaves the thing on, but just in case,

This Aimpoint CompC3 is a civilian version of the military/LE CompM3. It looks the next best thing to identical to the M3 but does not have a few nice features that one would find on the M3, and that most civilians would never use. This picture shows the optic without a mounting platform.

he changes the battery on the first of every month whether it needs to be changed or not.

EXAMPLE 4:

Tricia has a Beretta Storm carbine and being a *Battlestar Galactica* fan, she wanted to have her own version of one of the firearms in that show. Hence, the CX4 Storm with Aimpoint sight. She can't have the short, weird-looking barrel, but the rest she can have and so she bought it. She doesn't need it for her job and she doesn't shoot in matches, just informally at the range.

This is a Sightmark Green Mini Shot. It is a microsized optic with its own Picatinny rail. The sight must be removed from the mount to change the battery.

This red dot has an unknown provenance other than that it came from some factory in China. Several recognizably named companies use it under their own brand name. It has the option of different reticles such as dots, circle dots or others, and some can even switch between green and red colors. It uses a rheostat and CR 2032 battery.

EXAMPLE 5:

Mike is a gunshop owner and carries one of those FNX-45 Tacticals on his hip when on the job. He wanted something to fight back with if he had a hold-up, and a pistol is always on hand when, or hopefully, if he needs it. It's big. It's a .45. And with the micro red dot on top, a fast shooter.

A more conventional red-dot design reminiscent of the EOTech Holosight, the M5 from Meprolight uses a battery to light up its reticle. It helpfully positions its power switch at the rear left corner, making it easy to manipulate with the left hand.

EXAMPLE 6:

Tak grew up in Japan where he had no access to guns. Real guns anyway. He got his fill of airsoft, but when he moved to the U.S. one of the first things he did was purchase a real Remington 11-87 because he wanted to shoot some clays and he also wanted to shoot him some venison. His buddy Steve lets him hunt on his property, which is heavily wooded. Tak is also very impatient and doesn't like to sit and wait for a buck to stand in front of his sights, nor does he see the honor in that. He's a stalker, and when he's walking his way through the deer trails

Vortex has a mini red dot called the SPARC. A really nice feature, it comes with both short and high mounting spacers so you can use it right out of the box either on a low bore mount like an AR or CX4, or on a higher bore gun like an FAL or traditional hunting rifle.

he only gets time for one very quick shot if he sees something, and the Holosight on his slug gun lets him get an effective shot off almost every time.

So you see, red dots have a multitude of uses. Most people still do not use them or, for that matter, even consider using them. This is a shame because they can be a gloriously effective hit-multiplier for the shooter. They are easy to use, mount in virtually the same manner as any riflescope, and can be had in a vast range of quality, features and cash investment. I'd like to have mentioned more models since there are many that did not figure into this article. Just type "red-dot sight" or "reflex sight" into your Internet search page and start your research from there.

SHOOTING STARS

Schultz, Larsen, Sharpe, Hart and a short-lived dream.

BY **Terry Wieland**

The Schultz & Larsen M65DL in .358 Norma in Alaska. The .358 Norma is the perfect cartridge for moose and big bears. It became a favorite in Alaska and the Yukon.

The story of Schultz & Larsen rifles in the United States is inextricably linked with the career of Philip B. Sharpe, late captain of ordnance in the U.S. Army, and his dream of a factory cartridge bearing his name, chambered in a factory rifle.

As Frank de Haas wrote of Sharpe in the 1984 edition of his classic *Bolt Action Rifles*, "Rifleman, shooter, reloader, and writer…(he) was all of them and more. It was Sharpe's writing and (the 7x61 Sharpe & Hart) that brought the name of Schultz & Larsen to the attention of the American hunter-rifleman."

Sharpe was an influential figure in the world of shooting from the 1930s until his death in 1961. The author of two massive books, *Complete Guide to Handloading* and *The Rifle in America*, Sharpe was a respected ballistician, consultant to gunmakers and ammunition companies, and served on the technical staff of the NRA. As a personal friend of both Harry M. Pope (the "Old Master") and Major Douglas B. Wesson, he was involved in Smith & Wesson's development of the .357 Magnum in the 1930s, as well as improvements to rifle and handgun ammunition of all types. He was also heavily involved in long-range target shooting, military firearms and the emergence of the sporting bolt-action in America.

Although Sharpe was a hunter, his real interest lay in the technical side of rifles. He watched developments in big-game cartridges, especially the widespread efforts to produce a magnum 7mm hunting cartridge in the years before World War II, and concluded that a big seven was the ideal cartridge for North America.

Where Sharpe diverged from his contemporaries was his contempt for wildcat cartridges, and one need not delve very far into his writing to realize this. Wildcats, he wrote, "blossom daily and die weekly, leaving no trace of their passing, doing little except muddy the waters of genuine progress."

During World War II Sharpe served in Europe on an Army team investigating small-arms manufacturing. There he met some prominent figures in the European arms trade, contacts that would be critical to his plans after the war. He also, according to his own account, saw an experimental 7mm French cartridge that he believed could be the basis for that "ideal hunting cartridge" he dreamt of producing.

Apparently he never saw the cartridge itself, but rather an experimental rifle, handmade sometime before 1914. He extrapolated the specifications of the cartridge from the rifle's chamber. It was relatively short with a wide base, minimal body taper, sharp shoulder and a long neck. It was rimless, but otherwise resembled Holland & Holland's .275 Magnum and the even earlier .280 Ross. Back in the U.S., Sharpe teamed up with his friend Richard Hart, formed Sharpe & Hart Associates, and began serious development work. The result was the 7x61 Sharpe & Hart, a belted cartridge and charter member of what became the family of short, belted magnums that sprouted in the 1950s.

Originally, Sharpe did not want a belted cartridge. He found, however, that .300 H&H brass provided the best basic case from which to make his brainchild. One day, as Richard Hart was removing the belts on a lathe and experiencing a high failure rate due to poor concentricity, it occurred to him it would be easier to just leave them on. Sharpe concurred, and thus was born the 7x61 as we know it.

In an appendix to the fourth and final edition of *The Rifle in America*, which appeared in 1958, Sharpe explains in detail the history of the cartridge's development. By his account, he and Hart spent seven years from 1947 to 1954, expended thousands of rounds and invested $10,000 in development work. Frank De Haas wrote that Sharpe never knew when to stop. Having proven something once, he would then embark on endless experiments to confirm it. This may account for such an extraordinary financial expenditure on a cartridge that in its final form so closely resembles the .275 H&H, that one suspects technological plagiarism.

But then, Ned Roberts took even longer (and spent the same ubiquitous $10,000) developing the cartridge that became the .257 Roberts, which to put it bluntly, was a necked down 7x57 and nothing more.

Philip Sharpe knew, however, that if he was to persuade an ammunition company to adopt his cartridge and produce brass and ammunition, he required more than just an outline. He needed a solid design supported by professional test data.

For ammunition, he called on an acquaintance from his days in Europe, Amund Enger, president of Norma Projektilfabrik of Sweden. Norma wanted to break into the North American market, which after 1945 represented the only serious potential for growth. On his visits to the U.S., Enger frequently visited Sharpe's farm, also known as the Philip B. Sharpe Ballistic Laboratories Inc., in Pennsylvania. After seeing the work in progress he offered to make a run of experimental brass, removing the drudgery of converting the .300 H&H. Later, when the cartridge was finalized this grew into commercial production, with Sharpe & Hart Associates as the importer. Early boxes of Norma ammunition carry that label.

Sharpe sprang his creation upon the shooting world long before he had either rifles or ammunition to sell, but later insisted that hunters seized upon it and by the time he began importing components, there were "hundreds of thousands" of 7x61 S&H rifles in use. That must have been a typographical error, or perhaps he was trying to decide between "hundreds" and "thousands" and it came out both. Whatever the explanation, it was a wild exaggeration. But then, Sharpe was somewhat given to that, all the while as he loudly condemned wildcatters' outlandish claims.

Sharpe's stated ballistic performance for the 7x61 S&H was also substantially off the mark, and this later led to credibility problems for both he and Norma. He had developed a load using a 160-grain Sierra bullet, which when chronographed from the 32-inch bull barrel of his pressure gun delivered velocity of 3,100 feet per second.

Norma was asked to duplicate that load. Later, muzzle velocity of factory ammunition from the 25-inch barrel of a factory rifle measured around 2,900 fps. This in itself was pretty good, but it fell below the magic 3,000 fps mark, the goal of every hot-rod cartridge since it was reached by the .280 Ross (1908) and .250-3000 (1915).

* * *

But those problems were in the future. With the ammunition question answered, Sharpe went looking for a riflemaker. Being a devotee of fine rifles and admirer of European quality, it is no surprise that he looked to Europe rather the U.S. But money was also a factor – labor costs were substantially lower in postwar Europe than in New Haven or Chicopee Falls.

With dozens of fine German and Austrian rifle makers sitting idle, Schultz & Larsen of Denmark was not an obvious choice, but the name did not come up by accident. Among the rifles Sharpe brought back from Europe was an unidentified but extremely accurate target .22, which Sharpe's friend and well-known target shooter Eric Saetter-Lassen immediately identified as a Schultz & Larsen.

This small Danish company, located in the town of Otterup, was founded in 1889 by Hans Schultz. It specialized in target rifles, both rimfire and large-bore, and during the war manufactured machine gun parts and sniper rifles. Since 1945 Schultz & Larsen had been struggling, making target rifles on surplus Mauser 98 actions. By the early 1950s, however, things were improving and they had begun making a bolt-action target rifle called the M54. The model was named for its year of introduction, a custom the company would follow henceforth.

At Sharpe's behest, Schultz & Larsen began work on a bolt-action hunting rifle and they started with a clean slate. They did not want just another Mauser 98 derivative, such as the FN Supreme or Winchester Model 70. S&L's designers studied the question and with Sharpe's advice and suggestions, arrived at a design, which in its individual features was highly unusual.

First, its locking lugs were at the rear. There were four and they created an action that was extremely strong. It was also very smooth. Without the need for

locking-lug raceways running the length of the action, the bolt could fit snugly with no wobble. With no locking-lug recesses required in the receiver ring there was a tight, exact fit of barrel, ring and bolt face.

There is no question about strength, but having the lugs at the rear left the action open to criticism from handloaders, who later maintained that the bolt allows excessive case stretching with high-powered loads. This bugaboo dogged the Schultz & Larsen M54J and all subsequent models.

Schultz & Larsen made a tactical error at that point in calling the new design a "54." The addition of the "J" for *Jäger*, or hunter, meant little to North American dealers and rifle buyers. As Schultz & Larsen's importer, Sharpe later complained there was endless confusion with orders as to whether they wanted the M54 target or the completely different M54J hunting rifle.

There was no doubt about one thing, and that was that the M54J was a massive, strong action. When Roy Weatherby created his huge .378 Weatherby cartridge in 1953, he built his first few .378s on the Schultz & Larsen M54J. Any action that could accommodate the .378 Weatherby was obviously larger than necessary for the 7x61 S&H, which meant the rifles were bulky and heavy. As well, its in-line (rather than staggered) box magazine

gave the rifle a deep, ungainly look. Prodded by Sharpe, Schultz & Larsen began redesigning the action to make it more attractive to American shooters.

Frank de Haas wrote that there was an interim action made for Weatherby to fit the .378, called the Super Magnum M56A. It was even longer and heavier than the 54. These massive actions are seldom seen, but the extra length was carried over into the next modification, which was the S&L M60.

The M60 was the first model imported in real quantity. It was chambered only in 7x61 S&H and came to be identified with Phil Sharpe. The M60 had a much different appearance than the M54J. Its staggered box magazine held five rounds, which eliminated the deep fore-end and allowed Schultz & Larsen to outfit it with a stock of the California school, with trim lines and a pronounced Monte Carlo comb.

* * *

The Schultz & Larsen rifles evolved over a 15-year period from 1954 to 1968, and they did so both technically and aesthetically. The major technical changes from model to model were the safety, the magazine and the cocking mechanism. Aesthetically, the stock became modern and streamlined, the shotgun-style triggerguard of the M54J was replaced by a milled floorplate triggerguard similar to the FN Mauser, and the magazine became a staggered box rather than in-line, which eliminated the deep, ungainly belly of the early rifle.

The M60 largely settled the style that Schultz & Larsen rifles would employ for the next decade, but it was replaced almost immediately by the M65, and shortly after that by the M65DL (for DeLuxe). These model changes were not major, but more in the way of technical tinkering. A later generation might call this "continuous improvement" and applaud it in Toyotas, but to riflemen of the 1960s it was confusing.

More confusing is the fact that Frank de Haas, in his description of the Schultz & Larsen rifles, ignores the fact that there was both an M65 and an M65DL, with distinct differences between the two. And although the model numbers equated roughly to the year of introduction, the M60 was made for three years *before* 1960 and was replaced by the M65 around 1961. It became the 65DL in 1965. Some of the changes de Haas attributes to the M68DL were actually made in the 65DL.

The Model 65 was an interim model between the M60 and the M65DL.

Sharpe and Schultz & Larsen were fighting several battles simultaneously. One had to do with appearance and changing tastes—or what they saw as the "taste of the future." Early on they settled on the Weatherby look as the coming thing. The second battle was price, and that would only get worse as economic conditions changed. The third was ballistics. If they were going to compete with Weatherby, then the velocity-mad crowd would compare the numbers closely. From the start Schultz & Larsen was at a disadvantage because the 7x61 S&H trailed the 7mm Weatherby by a good margin; later cartridges, notably the .308 Norma and .358 Norma, were also not as hot as comparable Weatherby rounds.

All of that, however, was yet to come.

With the M65DL Schultz & Larsen established its look. The somewhat plain but tasteful appearance of the M60 was replaced by the much more California style of the M65DL. It had a rosewood fore-end tip and grip cap with white spacers, and the fore-end tip angled back toward the barrel. S&L did not use particularly flashy walnut on their rifles, but they were beautifully shaped and inletted, and distinguished by an inlaid ivory disk in the rosewood grip cap, echoing Weatherby's signature diamond.

In fact, Schultz & Larsen saw the rising star of Weatherby as their main competition. Both were selling sizzle in their cartridges and glitz in their designs. Weatherby had designed its own action by this time, the famous Mark V, with its nine locking lugs, produced by J.P. Sauer & Sohn in Germany. Both rifles were expensive: In 1962, when a Model 70 Standard Grade was selling for $139, a Weatherby Mark V cost $285. The *1962 Gun Digest* lists the rifle as a "Sharpe & Hart" with a price of $160, which suggests Sharpe was attempting, at least initially, to compete with Winchester. It didn't last. Three years later the Model 70 was still $139 and the Weatherby $285, but the Schultz & Larsen (as it was now billed) was $245.

Both companies were on a collision course with rising wage rates in Europe. Low postwar wages that made high quality and skilled workmanship available at a bargain were giving way to union-demanded increases. Eventually the inflation of the 1970s, caused by spiraling oil prices, would put an end to European manufacturing for Browning (Belgium) and Weatherby (Germany).

Schultz & Larsen was on the other end of that stick. Unlike Browning and Weath-

The Schultz & Larsen Model 65DL in 7x61 S&H.

erby, they could not switch production to Japan. Instead, the high European costs simply priced them out of the U.S. market.

In the meantime, Schultz & Larsen suffered a major blow. In 1961 Philip B. Sharpe died suddenly, ostensibly of a heart attack, and Sharpe & Hart Associates died with him. Schultz & Larsen, which had been laboriously establishing a name in America through their free pistols (they were the only major competitor to Hammerli) and target rifles, was now left on its own to promote its hunting rifles.

Throughout their association with Sharpe, Schultz & Larsen had maintained a close relationship with Norma. This continued through 1959 when Norma introduced its .358 Norma belted magnum, and S&L immediately offered the M65 chambered for it. A year or two later it was followed by the .308 Norma Mag-

Original Schultz & Larsens had a round ivory insert in the rosewood. The new rifles are more ornate.

num. All three cartridges were offered in the M65DL. Alas, in the velocity-oriented 1960s all three were seen as less powerful than the Weatherby cartridges, while at the same time, the Schultz & Larsen rifles were just as expensive. It was a no-win situation.

With Sharpe's death, Schultz & Larsen was free to attack the problem however it saw fit, with no contractual obligations limiting chamberings. Their answer was the M68DL, the last modification and iteration of the series to be imported to the U.S. The M68DL was essentially the 65DL but chambered in every magnum cartridge that might appeal to American shooters, and a number of non-magnums as well. They included the .22-250, .308 Winchester and .458 Winchester Magnum.

Most significantly, in a move that would have broken Sharpe's heart, it was offered in the 7mm Remington Magnum.

* * *

The 7mm Remington Magnum is the most successful of all the short belted magnums introduced in those years, and perhaps of all time. Although it appeared on the scene a year after Sharpe's death, it played a major role in the demise of his dream.

With the Remington Model 700—strong, extremely accurate and inexpensive—and the 7mm Remington Magnum—accurate, powerful, inexpen-

sive and readily available—Remington trumped Sharpe and Schultz & Larsen, on every front. Now, those who wanted a conventional Big Seven had Remington, and those with more money and *avant-garde* tastes had Weatherby.

The last year the Schultz & Larsen was listed in *Gun Digest* was 1972. The numbers from that year make an interesting comparison. The standard Winchester Model 70 was up to $174 and the Weatherby to $299, but the S&L M68DL was a whopping $485! And that was before the spiraling inflation from the 1975 oil embargo. The rifle was offered in 13 different chamberings (de Haas quotes 20) from .22-250 to .458 Winchester; with both the 7x61 S&H and the 7mm Remington Magnum; and both the .308 Norma and .300 Winchester Magnum, but –perplexingly—not the .358 Norma. The importer was listed as R.C. Fessler & Co. of Los Angeles.

For American shooters, that was the end of the line. And not long afterwards, it was the end of the line for the original Schultz & Larsen company. It folded in the late 1970s and its machinery was sold off. A barrel maker in Oregon purchased some of the equipment including rifling machines, and at least one is still in use in the U.S. As with many old European names, Schultz & Larsen was later resurrected in 1994, although not in Otterup (its original home in Denmark) and not making the same rifles. The new

centerfire Schultz & Larsens utilize a multilug bolt similar to the Weatherby Mark V. They've never been exported to the U.S., although they have been available in the United Kingdom and New Zealand. They exhibit the same luxurious finish as the original Schultz & Larsens, and bear a superficial resemblance.

Looking back on the history of Schultz & Larsen in the U.S., which ran from the early '50s into the 1970s—roughly a 20-year span—the rifle would seem to be a bit player compared with the career of the Mannlicher-Schönauer, which was imported for 75 years, or the commercial Mausers. Unlike those two rifles there is no real collector interest in Schultz & Larsen. They weren't very big, weren't around that long, and Denmark is not at the top of anyone's list of rifle-making countries.

Still, starting with the M60, the Schultz & Larsen rifles had a lot to offer, and they still do. Let's start with the characteristics of the action itself.

Its rear locking lugs may have contributed to case stretching, but in my experience this only becomes noticeable when you push pressures beyond sensible limits. If you want a 7mm Weatherby you should buy one, not take a 7x61 S&H and try to push velocities beyond its capabilities.

On the other hand, without raceways for front locking lugs, the action can be considerably stiffer and stronger, able to

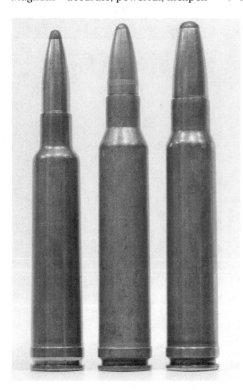

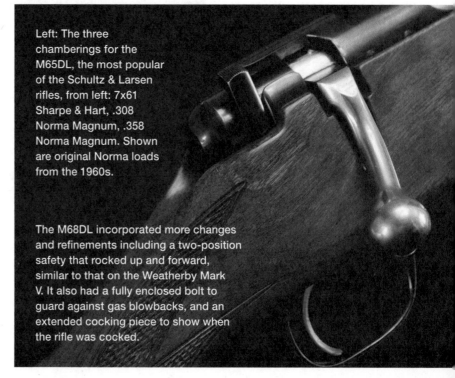

Left: The three chamberings for the M65DL, the most popular of the Schultz & Larsen rifles, from left: 7x61 Sharpe & Hart, .308 Norma Magnum, .358 Norma Magnum. Shown are original Norma loads from the 1960s.

The M68DL incorporated more changes and refinements including a two-position safety that rocked up and forward, similar to that on the Weatherby Mark V. It also had a fully enclosed bolt to guard against gas blowbacks, and an extended cocking piece to show when the rifle was cocked.

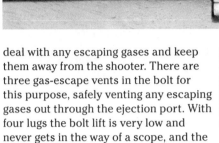

deal with any escaping gases and keep them away from the shooter. There are three gas-escape vents in the bolt for this purpose, safely venting any escaping gases out through the ejection port. With four lugs the bolt lift is very low and never gets in the way of a scope, and the bolt throw is shorter.

The Schultz & Larsen receiver is a full-length cylinder with only its ejection port open to the elements, rather than the whole top of the action. The port has been criticized as difficult to load through, but the fact is, that is not and never was its intended purpose. You load a Schultz & Larsen by dropping one cartridge through that port and closing the bolt to chamber it. You then apply the safety, turn the rifle over, open the floorplate and drop three more rounds into the magazine. As long as they are staggered, the order doesn't matter (unlike a conventional Mauser-style box) and you snap the floorplate closed. You do not try to load the magazine through the ejection port.

Through its various models, cosmetics aside, the Schultz & Larsens did not change much. The barrel length did vary, beginning long at 26 inches and gradually moving through 25 inches in the M65DL 7x61 S&H, to 24 inches for all calibers in the M68DL.

One major difference from model to model was the safety catch. The designers never seemed to be satisfied, changing from vertical wings to horizontal wings, from wings on the left to wings on the right. All worked well. In the early rifles it was a three-position safety; later it evolved into a two-position—*not* an improvement.

As you would expect from a firm famed for its target guns, all the Schultz & Larsen rifles were precise and accurate. Initially, it was offered in a single-shot configuration and some early benchrest rifles were built on it. With its solid-cylinder receiver, it offered in a factory rifle the stiffness that some benchresters achieved by fitting action-length cylindrical shrouds to Remington

Above: The new rifles retain the old style of model identification in semiscript forward of the bolt release.

The Schultz & Larsen M100DL.

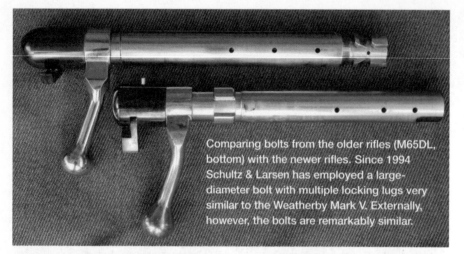

Comparing bolts from the older rifles (M65DL, bottom) with the newer rifles. Since 1994 Schultz & Larsen has employed a large-diameter bolt with multiple locking lugs very similar to the Weatherby Mark V. Externally, however, the bolts are remarkably similar.

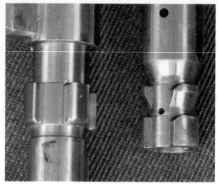

Locking lugs of a M65DL (left, four lugs at rear) and the M100DL (six lugs at front of bolt).

722s.

We can get an idea of exactly where these rifles fit into the world of North American big-game hunting by looking at who bought what, and where they were used.

If there is a Schultz & Larsen enclave in North America, it is in Canada's Yukon Territory. Early on, writers noted how many Yukoners seemed to be buying the 7x61, and when the .358 Norma came along they snapped it up as well. The .358 Norma is tailor-made for moose and the big bears at any range, and there are still quite a few of these rifles to be found in the Yukon, with their owners hoarding brass and loading their own.

That, however, seems to be it.

In terms of numbers, based on the rifles that become available on the used gun market, more 7x61 S&H rifles were sold than all the other calibers combined, with the .358 Norma in second place and the .308 Norma a distant third. This is not based on any scientific analysis, only on personal experience of being interested in these rifles for 50 years, and watching for them on used-gun racks and Internet listings.

It also seems the M65DL outsold all the other models, by far. So, if you go looking for a Schultz & Larsen, you are more likely to find one in good shape at a reasonable price, as a 7x61 S&H M65DL than any other. Conversely, if you want

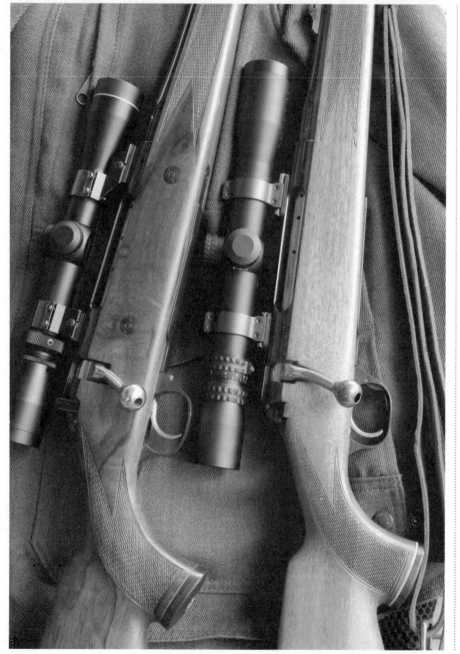

New and old: The Schultz & Larsen Model 100DL (left) beside a M65DL. The newer Schultz & Larsens produced by the resurrected company since 1994, are made in the style of luxury European hunting rifles with fine walnut stocks. They retain some features of the old 65 and 68, including immaculate interior finishing and beautiful workmanship.

one in .358 Norma Magnum, you may look for a while. Most of us who own them searched a long time and no one is anxious to part with them.

As a working gunsmith, Frank de Haas had a deep appreciation of the technical virtues of the Schultz & Larsen. His assessment is worth quoting:

"Sharpe stressed the advantages of the rear position of the locking lugs. He was correct in claiming that this allowed for a shorter bolt travel and a shorter overall action length…and that the rear locking lugs made for a stronger and safer action that is less likely to develop headspace.

"In the Schultz & Larsen design I can agree with him."

In the later models, however, the action was longer and heavier than need be, negating this advantage to some extent. Any action that will accommodate the .378 Weatherby is simply too long for the 7x61 S&H, to say nothing of the .22-250, and the rifles were always a pound or two heavier than necessary.

For workmanship and quality, de Haas had nothing but praise.

"No one makes a more precision crafted rifle than Schultz & Larsen, and the design of the action is as sound as any other action I can name," he wrote. "All their lives, American riflemen have been reading and hearing that a turnbolt action with locking lugs on the front is the only action design worthwhile, all of which is a fallacy.

"A machining tool mark can hardly be found, and there are no buffed off corners or edges."

Overall, the fit and finish of the Schultz & Larsens were as good as it gets.

* * *

Sharpe's death in 1961 and the advent of the 7mm Remington a year later really spelled the doom of both Sharpe's cartridge and the Schultz & Larsen rifle in America. Without Sharpe, the whole project lost its driving force and guiding light.

Around 1970 a Texas firm began importing a Japanese-made rifle, the Golden Eagle 7000, about which little is known except that it was more or less a copy of the Schultz & Larsen, but lacked the precise workmanship and immaculate finishing.

Norma Projektilfabrik, having invested both time and money in the development of the 7x61 S&H, was unwilling

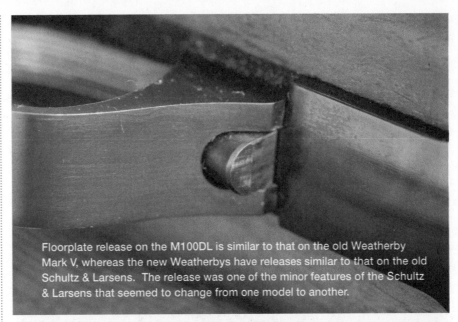

Floorplate release on the M100DL is similar to that on the old Weatherby Mark V, whereas the new Weatherbys have releases similar to that on the old Schultz & Larsens. The release was one of the minor features of the Schultz & Larsens that seemed to change from one model to another.

The Model 65 had yet another style of safety—this one a wing very similar to the early Winchester Model 70.

to give up on it. Phil Sharpe's specs for the cartridge case were unnecessarily stout, and sometime in the 1970s Norma redesigned the interior to give more powder space without altering the exterior dimensions or increasing pressures beyond the capability of existing rifles. They renamed the cartridge the 7x61 Super, and made factory ammunition loaded with a 154-grain bullet rather than the previous 160, thereby finally achieving the magical 3,000 fps.

The 7x61 was always a fine cartridge, and still is in either form. Handloaders should be careful, however, in using data for the later, roomier cartridge in early Sharpe & Hart brass.

In a philosophical moment Frank de Haas asked three questions about Sharpe, the cartridge and the rifle: Was the 7x61 a success? Was the rifle? Was the Schultz & Larsen ever accepted by Americans on equal terms with the Winchester Model 70 or Remington 700?

The answer to all, with regret, was no. And today all three—Sharpe, cartridge and rifle—are largely forgotten. Yet, as de Haas says, the early death of Phil Sharpe was "a great loss to all riflemen the world over." He certainly deserves to be remembered, his books deserve to be read, and his baby – the 7x61 Sharpe & Hart, deserves to be loaded and shot in the beautifully made rifles he helped create.

THE BASTILLE DAY
ELEPHANT

The Culmination Of A Half-Century Quest

BY **Tom Caceci**

*The elephant carries
a great big trunk;
He never packs it
with clothes.
It has no lock
and it has no key,
And he takes it
wherever he goes.*

—*Children's nursery rhyme*

The Caprivi strip is divided into tribal regions whose quotas for elephant are set by Conservancy officials, agents of the Ministry of Environment, the hunting industry and conservation groups. This is the entrance to the Sikunga Conservancy Office. The headquarters of each conservancy maintains a staff of game rangers, conducts anti-poaching patrols and distributes meat to the various villages participating in the conservancy operations. Fees paid by hunters are a primary source of conservancy financing.

I started hunting better than half a century ago as a 13-year-old in southeastern New York, where gray squirrels were abundant and a single-shot 20 gauge was available. Over the course of my life I've "worked my way up," so to speak, on most of the game animals and birds native to eastern North America. But from the beginning – perhaps because at that age I was also reading *Tarzan* books – I've always wanted to hunt in Africa.

As I gained age, experience and income I was finally able to "scratch the itch" for the first time in 2004, with a plains game safari in South Africa. Since then I've managed enough hunts to become sated with the various

antelope species. I'd shot a lot of very nice trophies including a huge eland bull, but I wanted a new challenge. I wanted an elephant. And on a 2013 safari in Namibia that particular "itch" got scratched, big time.

Namibia is huge, about the size of Texas plus Oklahoma, and sparsely populated. It's an acutely environmentally conscious nation that nevertheless recognizes big game for what it is: a renewable and fully sustainable natural resource, as well as a huge source of hard currency. Hunters are welcome and entry into the country with guns is a routine matter handled within minutes upon arrival. Hunting seasons are generous, free-roaming game is fantastically

Accommodations at Sobbe Camp were unpretentious and rather rustic, but very comfortable. This hut is built of reeds tied together, a common method of construction in the area.

Hot water is provided by wood-fired heaters that the camp staff keeps going. At times the water in the huts is scalding, but at the end of a day in the bush a hot shower is very welcome.

abundant (the hunting areas are almost entirely free of high game fences, unlike South Africa), prices are moderate and infrastructure is excellent. Namibia is by far the cleanest and safest and most stable country in sub-Saharan Africa as well. In short, it's as close to a true Hunter's Paradise as this earth provides. A hunt there usually costs less than one in Alaska, with a much higher success rate, a greater variety of species and far more comfort. Elephant hunting isn't cheap, but it's within the reach of most ordinary people who really want to do it.

A word about African elephants is in order: no matter what you may be told, they aren't endangered, though perhaps 40 years ago they were. The elephant population in most of sub-Saharan Africa today is in good shape; several countries, including Namibia, have a healthy surplus of animals that must be cropped off every year to keep the herd in balance with the land's carrying capacity.

I booked my hunt for a location in the eastern Caprivi Strip, the long, narrow "tail" that extends from Namibia's northeastern corner and is bordered by the Zambezi and Chobe Rivers. This is definitely "The Real Africa," where land is held in common by various tribes. It's dotted here and there with small villages of reed huts, whose inhabitants are mostly pastoralists or fishermen.

The eastern Caprivi is administratively subdivided into tribal conservancy areas; each sets a yearly quota of elephants to be harvested, with consultation of the Ministry of Environment and Tourism, the hunting industry, conservation organizations such as World Wildlife Fund, and tribal authorities. Safari companies periodically bid for concessions within the conservancies to lease large areas for exclusive use. The companies also buy the conservancies' yearly game quotas in advance, and in turn sell the game to foreign hunters.

The hunting business is very tightly regulated; conservancy game rangers are present on every hunt to see to it that the rules are followed. The conservancy authorities distribute the cash as well as the meat of animals taken to the local villages (USDA rules flatly prohibit importation of meat from any African game animal). Non-exportable tusks are serial numbered and stored in a government warehouse. Namibia's sustainable-use model has been a great success and has an additional benefit – the constant presence of safari guides and hunters is a real deterrent to ivory poachers.

Huntable elephants in Namibia break down into exportable "trophy" animals and "own use," i.e., non-exportable ones. Trophy elephants are very, very expensive, but the non-exportable ones actually can cost less than some plains game species. Paying the high trophy price allows you to bring the ivory back on a CITES[1] permit. "Own use" doesn't mean a small elephant, either. Many very nice bulls get taken on non-exportable tags.

I arrived in Windhoek, the capital city of Namibia, and was met by my PH, Cornie. We then drove directly to the Caprivi with an overnight stop; easily 12 hours time on mostly paved roads, traveling the entire length of the Strip to a base camp near the northeast corner of Mudumu National Park. The actual hunting area was another two or three hours east of that in the triangle where Namibia, Zambia and Botswana lie adjacent to each other. The camp was at Sobbe in the Sikunga Conservancy, as far east in the Caprivi as you can go.

This sort of base camp is rustic but comfortable, with running water (brought in by truck from 10 kilometers away!) and flush toilets. Electricity was available several hours a day when the generator was running. We ate mostly game meat prepared by the camp cook, including some of my elephant, as well as some zebra schnitzel.

The hunting area is totally flooded in summer, but in winter things dry out enough that one can drive over the flattened grass. There are no real roads; at best a few wandering tracks run between villages, so we were bush-bashing in four-wheel drive the whole time. At riverside villages redolent with the aroma of drying fish, we stopped to

ask if anyone had seen elephant. Many of them cross the Chobe River to feed from a vastly overpopulated and overgrazed national park in Botswana.

On July 14 we'd spent the entire day looking for elephant spoor, at one point getting into a soft patch that bogged down even the 4x4 Land Cruiser. It was touch and go whether we'd get it out of the muck at all. By dint of jacking up the rear wheels and stuffing huge quantities of grass in the holes, enough traction was generated to make it out. Otherwise I suppose we'd still be there! Well, maybe not, we might have been eaten by the miscellaneous carnivores that are pretty common in the region. Yes, there are lions.

After we got the Cruiser out of the mud, we finally spotted some tracks. We followed them for quite awhile, until shortly after 5:00 p.m., then made visual contact with a herd of 50 or so elephants about 1,000 yards away. We dismounted, moved downwind from them and started a stalk from perhaps 300-400 yards, Cornie constantly checking the wind with his ash bag.

As we crept closer the herd moved into a little patch of scrubby forest. This was to our advantage as it screened us from their vision. We moved very slowly

Elephants wade across the Chobe River from Botswana to feed on the Namibia shore. The Botswana side is a National Park that's completely overgrazed, and there is little for them to eat. So they "emigrate" to Namibia on a regular basis, as do buffalo. This can be a hazardous undertaking for the smaller species – huge crocodiles abound in the Chobe!

to within 40 yards, at which point there was a bit of a shift in the wind. They probably got a whiff of us, because they started to get restless, moving slowly through the scrub, from our left to right. That was when I spotted THE elephant, MY elephant, the one I'd waited more than 50 years to meet. He was a big, old bull with a couple of younger "askaris" in escort. While there were many others in the herd, I had eyes only for him – "target fixation" had fully set in.

The elephants were getting very upset because they knew something was wrong, so we didn't dare get closer. The PH set up the shooting sticks and when the bull moved into a clear shooting lane, I put the red dot on his right side and fired. Half a second later the PH shot. This is standard practice – the PH's main job is to keep the client alive, so once the client has fired, everyone shoots until

the animal is down. At that point the herd went nuts and began to stampede farther off to our right.

Now, my PH has a little dog, Fox, whose job is tracking wounded animals. Fox instinctively runs after moving game when the shots go off and since he's a fox terrier, he is totally unaware of the fact that he weighs at most 20 pounds. This was not only my first elephant, it was also Fox's. He went tearing off into the herd barking his fool head off, with Cornie yelling at him to come back, without any luck. Fox is courageous, but he must understand the saying that "discretion is the better part of valor." After 30 seconds or so of dodging feet the size of serving platters, he decided that escape was a good idea. How he managed to avoid getting trampled I'll never understand, but he did, and came back with his little stub of a tail between his legs.

Above Left: This bullet was recovered when processing the bull. It was the insurance shot, fired to be sure he was dead before approaching too closely. The Hornady 400-grain DGS projectile penetrated several feet of bone and muscle in a perfectly straight line without deformation. That's exactly what a dangerous-game bullet is supposed to do, and the Hornady ammunition performed outstandingly well on this elephant and on a partner's Cape Buffalo.

My Shaw .416 Remington Magnum with an Aimpoint Micro H1 red-dot sight affixed. The red-dot sight is rapidly becoming the favorite optic for dangerous-game hunting, as it's fast on target, instinctive in use and offers a single sight plane with infinite eye relief. For older eyes, the difficulty of focusing on the rear and front sights and the target simultaneously is eliminated. The red dot can also be used with both eyes open.

The culmination of a half-century quest! The elephant was taken with an E.R. Shaw Mark VII rifle chambered in .416 Remington.

By the time Fox returned the bull had moved out of sight, and then I heard someone yell, "He's down!" The bull had gone perhaps 100 yards, turned around, and hit the ground. We very cautiously approached him as he lay on his left side. Everything happened so fast it was a bit dreamlike – not 15 seconds could have elapsed from the time the bull paused in the little clearing to the moment when I fired. There's a vivid image seared into my visual cortex of the sighting dot on his shoulder; I remember hearing my shot go off (I usually don't) but I didn't feel any recoil.

My bullet hit higher than had I intended, taking him through the lungs. I don't much like shooting off of sticks and at the short range of 40 yards I might have done better with an offhand shot, but what was done was done. Once the first bullet hit he was a dead elephant walking, anyway. The second and third

bullets hit him behind the right shoulder. I fired an insurance shot into the back of his head, and that was that.

He was a very large, elderly bull – about six tons and perhaps 45 years old – well past his prime who would likely never have sired another calf. He had one broken tusk and one intact one, weighing approximately 35 and 40 pounds respectively. He was, in short, a perfect candidate for culling. His meat will provide 300 villagers with a year's worth of protein and fat, and every inhabitant of the village received some of my cash. I have photos and memories and a lifetime goal achieved, and that's enough for me.

My rifle was an E.R. Shaw Mark VII chambered in .416 Remington, equipped with an Aimpoint Micro HS-1 red-dot sight. I ordered the rifle two years ago specifically for this hunt. It was loaded with Hornady's 400-grain solid Dangerous Game series ammunition. This

is pretty much the perfect setup for elephant hunting – very fast to get on target and the .416 Remington has plenty of punch. The bullet from the insurance shot was later recovered by the skinners and it was totally undeformed, and had retained 100 percent of its weight. I couldn't have asked for better performance from my equipment.

The 14th of July, Bastille Day in France, commemorates the beginning of the French Revolution. For me, Bastille Day will henceforth also be a day of commemoration – of a dream fulfilled and of gratitude for a great hunt.

FOOTNOTE

1. Convention on International Trade in Endangered Species. Ivory from a trophy can be brought to the USA (at vast additional cost) but once it's here you can't do anything with it: it can't be sold or traded, it can only be looked at and admired. A replica tusk, indistinguishable from the Real Thing, can be made for a few hundred dollars.

EVOLUTION OF THE
BERETTA
MILITARY PISTOL

L'evoluzione di Beretta le Pistole Militari, from the Alpine Front to Afghanistan

BY **Paul Scarlata**

PHOTOS BY **PAUL BUDDE, MICHAEL HUGHES AND BECKY LEAVITT**

It's a well-known fact that certain small arms have distinctive features that immediately identify their nation of origin. The same can be said for certain private gunmakers who continually use certain mechanical or styling features that immediately identify their manufacturer. Perfect examples of this are the semiauto pistols produced by the Italian firm of Fabbrica D'Armi Pietro Beretta SpA.

In 1526 a gunsmith by the name of Bartolomeo Beretta of the town of Gardone in the Brescia region of northern Italy was paid 296 ducats to manufacture 185 arquebus barrels for the Arsenal of Venice. Bartolomeo's son, Jacomo, and grandson Giovannino both became master gun barrel makers while another grandson, Lodovico, was involved in the fabrication of gun locks.

At the middle of the 16th century, Val Trompia had 50 mines, eight smelters, 40 smithies and produced in excess of 25,000 guns a year. By 1698 the Berettas were the second largest barrel producer out of more than 30 in Gardone, producing in excess of 2,800 gun barrels.

But Gardonese firearms began falling out of favor and so, beginning in 1797, the Berettas supplied barrels to firearms factories in nearby Brescia,

which produced 40,000 guns a year. In 1815 Pietro Antonio Beretta toured Italy making connections with gun dealers, and in 1832 gave the firm the name it carries to the present day.

In the 1850s Pietro's son Giuseppe refocused the business on the production of sporting guns and by 1870 annual production had increased to 8,000 guns a year. Beretta also became the agent for several non-Italian manufacturers including Colt, Remington, Smith & Wesson and Winchester. In the 1870s Beretta once again entered the military firearms market when it received a contract from the Italian government to produce the Fucile di Fanteria Modello 1870 (a.k.a. Vetterli) for the new nation's army.

Italy's entry into World War I on the Allied side found them, as it did most of the belligerent nations, dreadfully short of small arms for their rapidly expanding armed forces. The standard handgun of the Italian army was the Pistola Automatica Modello 1910 (the "Glisenti"), a native design that fired the Cartucce 9mm per Pistola Mo. 910 that, while dimensionally identical to the 9mm Parabellum, was loaded much lighter.

Also in service were large numbers of Modello 1874 and 1889 revolvers, while the navy issued the Mauser C96

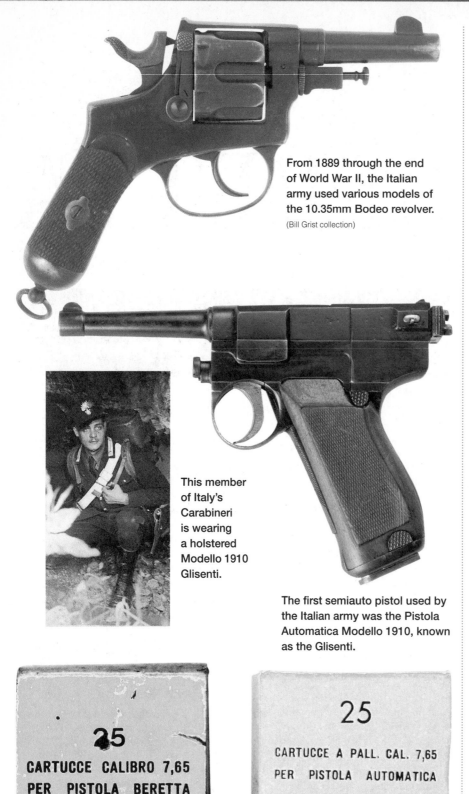

From 1889 through the end of World War II, the Italian army used various models of the 10.35mm Bodeo revolver.

(Bill Grist collection)

This member of Italy's Carabineri is wearing a holstered Modello 1910 Glisenti.

The first semiauto pistol used by the Italian army was the Pistola Automatica Modello 1910, known as the Glisenti.

25
CARTUCCE CALIBRO 7,65
PER PISTOLA BERETTA
LOTTO G.F.L. 23 1-65

25
CARTUCCE A PALL. CAL. 7,65
PER PISTOLA AUTOMATICA
LOTTO DI CARTUCCE GFL 1 5 67
LOTTO DI PROPELLENTE   35

Two boxes of Italian issue Cartucce Calibro 7,65 per Pistola Beretta (.32 ACP). The box on the left was made by Fiocchi.

(John Moss collection)

"Broomhandle" pistol. The Modello 1910 was only produced at one facility, Metallurgica Bresciana gia Tempini, and could not be made in sufficient numbers to meet demand, forcing the government to turn to Italy's other private firearms manufacturers.

At the request of the Italian government the Beretta factory designed a simple blowback operated, semiauto pistol chambered for the Glisenti's 9mm Mo. 910 cartridge. While based upon ideas pioneered by John M. Browning and pistols already being produced for the French army by the Basque firm Gabilondo y Urresti of Eibar, Spain, Beretta engineer Tullio Marengoni designed a pistol that had several distinctive features.

One, which was to become a Beretta trademark, was an open top slide that exposed most of the barrel except for a bridge near the muzzle with the front sight. Ejection of spent cases was straight up through an ejection port located midway along the top of the side. This pistol was fired by a concealed hammer and utilized a single-column, detachable box magazine retained by a heel-type catch. A safety lever of the Eibar pattern was located on the left side of the frame and when applied locked the trigger, in addition it was used to hold the slide open when dismantling the pistol. A second safety, a pivoting lever, on the rear of the frame was added at the insistence of the Italian army.[1]

The Italian army was in no position to be fussy and Marengoni's pistol was quickly adopted as the Pistola Automatica Beretta Modello 1915. But the small-frame pistol had trouble standing up to the operating pressures of the Mo. 910 cartridge and in 1917 Beretta offered the army a similar pistol chambered for the popular 7.65mm Browning (.32 ACP; Cartucce Calibro 7,65 per Pistola Beretta). Italian collectors refer to this pistol as the Model 1915/17.

While some may question the use of the 7.65mm Browning as a military handgun cartridge, it must be remembered that, in general, the Continental military establishment did not view the pistol as a true combat weapon – but rather a badge of rank or authority that would rarely be used and then only as a last ditch, defensive weapon. For this reason, light weight and compactness were valued above stopping power and 7.65mm pistols saw wide use by European military and police.

SPECIFICATIONS: PISTOLA AUTOMATICA BERETTA MODELLO 1915	
Caliber:	Cartucce 9mm per Pistola Mo. 910*
Overall length:	5.85 in.
Barrel length:	3.3 in.
Weight (unloaded):	20 oz.
Magazine:	7 rounds (8 in 7.65mm)
Sights front:	blade
Sights rear:	v-notch
Grips:	checkered wood

* - beginning in 1917 it was chambered for the Cartucce Calibro 7,65 per Pistola Beretta

According to Italian arms authority Gianluigi Usai, approximately 15,600 9mm Modello 1915 pistols were produced, 300 of which were sold on the civilian market after the war. Production numbers for the Model 1915/17 were in the area of 60,000 units, numbers of which were also sold on the post-1918 civilian market.

The Model 1915 and 1915/17 were seen as wartime expedients and once the war was over Signores Marengoni and Giovanni Beretta worked together to improve the design for the commercial market. The resulting Model 1915/19, also referred to as the Model 1922, replaced the round post barrel mount where the barrel was lifted straight up out of the frame, with a T-shaped slot mount. This required a larger opening in the top of the slide so the ejection port was lengthened to meet the open-top slide producing the open-topped style still used by Beretta to this day. The Model 1922 was chambered for the 7.65mm Browning and the Italian air force and navy both purchased small numbers of the new pistol, while others were supplied to various Fascist security and militia organizations. But the Italian army wanted a pistol chambered for the 9mm M. 910 cartridge and so the following year Beretta attempted to supply it.

The new pistol incorporated the Model 1915/19 improvements but the internal hammer was replaced with an external ring hammer, which would become another Beretta trademark. After trials, the Italian army found it suitable and adopted it as the Pistola Automatica Beretta Modello 1923 and purchased approximately 3,000 units

while others were supplied to various Fascist government agencies. Others were sold on the civilian market, while foreign sales included 4,000 pistols sold to Bulgaria in 1926 and 600 purchased by the Buenos Aires (Argentina) Provincial Police.

The Model 1923 frame and slide did away with the sharp corners and squared-off profile of the earlier pistols, making it much more ergonomic. The grip frame was significantly longer than earlier models even though the magazine only held seven rounds. A heel-type magazine catch was used and a large lanyard attachment loop was mounted on the lower left grip frame.

Small numbers of Model 1923s had a groove for a shoulder stock holster machined into the bottom of the grip frame. The shoulder stock was a leather holster with a hinged folding steel arm riveted to the spine, the end of which slipped over the butt of the pistol and locked in place.[2]

SPECIFICATIONS: PISTOLA AUTOMATICA BERETTA MODELLO 1923	
Caliber:	9mm Cartucce per Pistola Mo. 910
Overall length:	7 in.
Barrel length:	3.5 in.
Weight (unloaded):	28 oz.
Magazine:	7 rounds
Sights front:	blade
Sights rear:	v-notch
Grips:	grooved wood or stamped steel

Beretta continued to improve their pistols and introduced the Modello 1931, a 7.65mm pistol that featured a more streamlined slide, ergonomic grip and another feature that would become a Beretta trademark – a magazine floorplate with a curved finger rest extension that provided a full, three-finger grip. The Italian navy purchased in excess of 3,000 units. After approximately 6,500 had been produced, the frame was redesigned with an arched backstrap that provided far superior ergonomics to all the earlier Beretta pistols.[3] This model is sometimes referred to as the Modello 1932.

The first 7.65mm Beretta used by the Italian army was the Pistola Automatica Beretta Model 1915/17. The frame-mounted safety was also used as a takedown lever.

The Model 1915/19 (also known as the Model 1922) was the first Beretta to feature the fully open topped slide. Note the metal grip panels, pivoting safety lever and the large navy crest on the frame.

With the adoption of the Model 1931, the Italian armed forces had a total of seven different pistols in service: the Mauser C96, Glisenti Modello 1910 and Beretta Models 1915, 1915/17, 1922, 1923 and 1931. Plus there were large numbers of ancient 10.35mm Bodeo revolvers and M.7 Roth and M.12 Steyr pistols received as reparations from Austria after WWI. These handguns required six different cartridges to be carried in inventory to say nothing of a confusing collection of spare parts. The lot of an Italian army ordnance officer was not a happy one!

In the early 1930s the Italian government expressed an interest in adopting a standard pistol for all branches of the armed forces. In keeping with the European preference for smaller handguns, it was decided that the Model 32 would best serve their purposes, but they wanted it chambered for a "more authoritative" cartridge.

The resulting Pistola Automatica Beretta Modello 1934 is dimensionally and mechanically identical to the Model 32, except it was chambered for the 9mm Corto (.380 ACP) and the plastic grips had steel backings to increase the weight to help hold down recoil. In 1935 the Italian government placed an order with Beretta for 150,000 pistols.

SPECIFICATIONS: PISTOLA AUTOMATICA BERETTA MODELLO 1934	
Caliber:	Cartucce 9mm per Pistola M.34
Overall length:	6 in.
Barrel length:	3.75 in.
Weight (unloaded):	23.5 oz.
Magazine:	7 rounds
Sights front:	blade
Sights rear:	v-notch
Grips:	plastic with steel backings

In keeping with the finest traditions of intra-service rivalry, the Italian air force declined to accept the new pistol, announcing they wanted a lighter handgun for their air crews. Accordingly, Beretta produced the Modello 35, which differed only in being chambered in 7.65mm, having a slightly lighter slide and no steel backings for the grip panels. The navy found the Model 35 more to their liking also and placed an order with Beretta.

Model 1934 and 1935 pistols will be found marked "RE" (Regio Esercito) for the army, "RM" (Regia Marina) for the navy, or "RA" (Regia Aeronautica) for the Air Force. The latter always in the form of an eagle wearing a royal crown for the royal air force. Both were issued to Italy's paramilitary gendarmerie, the Carabinieri, and local police forces. Police pistols may be marked "PS" (Pubblica Sicurezza).

Pistols manufactured during the Fascist Era are marked with their year of manufacture in two forms: the conventional Julian date in Arabic numerals and the date in the Fascist Era in Roman numerals. The Fascist calendar commenced on Oct. 28, 1922, so a pistol from 1937 may carry either "XV" or "XVI" as its Fascist year.

The immediate predecessor to the very popular Model 1934 was the Model 1931. Note the navy marking disc inletted into the grip panel.

Both the Model 1934 and 1935 proved very popular with the Italian armed forces. In addition, Germany, Romania and Finland all placed orders with Beretta. In German service they were known as the 7.65mm oder 9mm Pistole 671(i) and were issued to all branches of the armed forces, especially in the Mediterranean theater.

The Romanians placed an order for 61,000 pistols in August 1940 although shortages of raw materials – and late payment – resulted in only 40,000 being delivered. Romanian pistols are identical to Italian issue except the slide is marked "CAL. 9 SCURT" (9mm Short) instead of "CAL. 9 CORTO."

During the 1939-40 Winter War against the USSR, Finland purchased a wide variety of pistols including the Beretta Model 1915/17 and 1922 (Pistoolit M/15 ja M/19 Beretta). In 1941 the Finns purchased an additional 4,000 Model 1934 and 1935 Berettas (Pistooli M/35 Beretta), some of which remained in service until the 1980s. Finnish pistols will be found marked "SA" (Suomen Armeija – Finnish Army) inside a rounded square on the frame in front of the safety lever.[4]

Captured pistols proved very popular with Allied soldiers who often carried them as backup

Four boxes of Italian military issue Cartucce 9mm per Pistola M. 34.

(John Moss collection)

weapons and brought thousands home as souvenirs. The Model 1934 and 1935 remained in service with the postwar Italian armed forces well into the 1960s and with Italian police even longer.

The Model 1934 and 1935 also proved popular on the post-WWII civilian market and with many European, Middle Eastern and African police forces.[5] Production of the Model 1935 ended in 1967 with approximately 525,000 being made while manufacture of the Model 1934 continued until 1991 with slightly more than one million units leaving the factory. To say that Beretta's Model 1934/35 pistols were merely successful would be a gross understatement.

In 1950 Beretta assigned the redoubtable Signore Marengoni the task of designing a pistol chambered for the 9mm Parabellum cartridge. The pistol he developed retained, externally, all of the traditional Beretta characteristics: a single-action trigger, external ring hammer, open top slide, finger rest extension on the magazine baseplate and an ergonomic grip frame that provided excellent handling.

The high-pressure 9mm Parabellum required a locked breech, and to achieve this Marengoni utilized a system similar to that on the Walther P38. The barrel and slide are locked together by the wedge being cammed up by ramps on the frame rails so that dual lugs on its rear engage recesses on either side of the slide. When fired, the barrel and slide recoil together a short distance whereupon a floating plunger on the rear barrel lug impacts on the frame and releases the locking wedge, allowing it to drop down and disengage the lugs from the slide, which then continues rearward extracting and ejecting the spent case.

An Italian officer during World War II is wearing a holstered Model 1934 pistol.

A recoil spring on a full-length guide rod under the barrel pulls the slide forward, stripping the next round from the magazine and chambering it. As the barrel and slide go into battery the wedge is cammed up so the lugs can engage the slide, locking the two units together. A slide stop moves up under pressure from the magazine follower to lock the slide open when the magazine is empty. An external slide stop lever allows the slide to be released to chamber a new round.

The open-topped slide has the front sight mounted on the typical Beretta bridge near the muzzle and the single column, eight-round magazine's finger rest extension provided a full purchase, while a long grip tang that prevents

The Model 1934 is one of the best known of the Beretta pistols. Note the open top slide, rowel-type hammer and Eibar-type safety. This pistol is marked "RE" for the Regio Esercito – Royal Army, and was made in 1942, the 20th (XX) year of Mussolini's reign.

"bite." Originally Beretta planned to offer pistols with a choice of lightweight alloy or steel frames, but the alloy prototypes suffered accuracy and durability issues and were subsequently dropped.

The Pistola Automatica Beretta Modello 1951, also known as the Mo. 1951, was not released on the market until 1957 when it was adopted by the Italian armed forces. A commercial version, the Brigadier, was produced for sale on the civilian market. Beretta offered the Brigadier chambered for the 7.65mm

World War II Italian pistol cartridges: (left to right) Cartucce 9mm per Pistola M. 910, Cartucce Calibro 7,65 per Pistola Beretta, Cartucce 9mm per Pistola M.34, and Cartucce NATO a Pall. Cal. 9mm Parabellum.

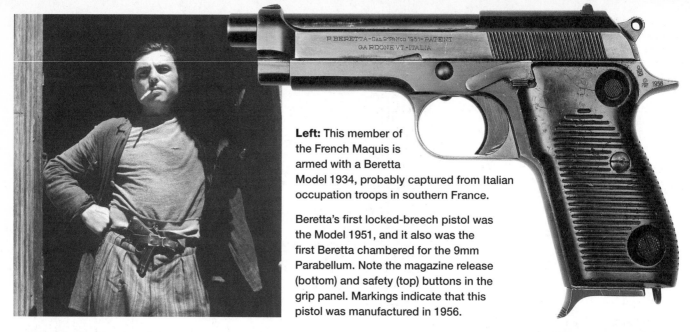

Left: This member of the French Maquis is armed with a Beretta Model 1934, probably captured from Italian occupation troops in southern France.

Beretta's first locked-breech pistol was the Model 1951, and it also was the first Beretta chambered for the 9mm Parabellum. Note the magazine release (bottom) and safety (top) buttons in the grip panel. Markings indicate that this pistol was manufactured in 1956.

Parabellum (.30 Luger) for sale in those countries like Italy that prohibited civilian ownership of firearms chambered for current military cartridges.

SPECIFICATIONS: PISTOLA AUTOMATICA BERETTA MODELLO 1951

Caliber:	Cartucce NATO a Pall. Cal. 9mm Parabellum [6]
Overall length:	8 in.
Barrel length:	4.5 in.
Weight (unloaded):	31 oz.
Magazine:	8-round detachable box
Sights front:	blade
Sights rear:	square notch
Grips:	plastic

Unlike earlier Beretta pistols, the Model 1951's magazine release button was located at the bottom of the left grip panel, while the manual safety, a button located at the top rear of the grip, was pushed from right to left to make the pistol safe.[7] And unlike many European military pistols, there was no magazine-disconnect safety.

The Mo. 1951 proved to be a rugged, powerful pistol and was adopted by the Italian armed forces, Carabinieri, Guardia di Finanza and the Pubblica Sicurezza. Like Beretta's earlier pistols, the Model 1951 sold well on the international market with both Israel and Egypt adopting it in the 1960s. Additional sales were made to Pakistan, Libya, Haiti, Nigeria, Tunisia and Yemen.

The Egyptian government obtained a license to produce the Model 1951 as the "Helwan" at the Maadi Military & Civil Company. Some of these were fitted with larger sights and utilized a heel-type magazine release. Iraq also obtained a license to manufacture the Mo. 1951 at the Al-Qādisiyyah Establishments. Known as the "Tariq," it was the standard pistol of the Saddam Hussein-era army and police.

Beretta also produced a small number of selective-fire versions known as the Modello 951R ("R" for Raffica or "burst" in Italian). It had a heavier slide, slightly longer barrel, a fold down pistol grip in front of the trigger guard and a selector lever on the right side of the frame above the trigger. Extended 10 and 15-round magazines were used and it had a cyclic rate of fire of approximately 1,000 rpm, which made it very difficult to handle in full-auto mode. Small numbers were used by the Italian army's special forces, the Carabinieri and Pubblica Sicurezza. Reportedly a few were sold to the Pakistani National Police. The Mo. 1951 was replaced in Italian service by the Beretta Model 92, although some are reportedly still in service with reserve forces.

In the 1970s a new breed of pistol began capturing the attention of military and law enforcement agencies around the world. Baptized the "Wondernine," these pistols shared a number of features: DA/SA triggers, high-capacity magazines and were chambered for the

A motorcycle officer of the Polizia Stradale is sharply dressed with his holstered Model 1951 pistol.

(Gianluigi Usai collection)

9mm Parabellum cartridge. With the intention of capturing a share of this new market a design team led by Carlo Beretta, Giuseppe Mazzetti and Vittorio Valle began working on a Beretta Wondernine. The result was an alloy-frame, DA/SA pistol with a 15-round magazine, and which still retained Marengoni's trademark open-top slide, ring shaped hammer and finger-rest magazine floorplate. Introduced on the market in 1975 as the Modello 92, it attracted immediate attention from armies and police forces around the world.

Like the Model 1951, the first Model 92s had the magazine release at the bottom of the left grip panel and utilized a frame-mounted safety that did not decock the hammer. Production began in May 1976 and ended in February 1983 with approximately 52,000 pistols leaving the factory.

At the request of a number of agencies, in 1984 Beretta relocated the magazine release behind the trigger and fitted an ambidextrous, slide-mounted, decocker/safety lever. This, the Model 92S, was adopted by a number of Italian law enforcement agencies.

With the establishment of NATO, the armies of the member nations attempted to standardize their weapons and ammunition. While the former proved only partially successful, the latter was achieved fairly quickly with the standardization of the 7.62mm NATO for rifles and light machine guns, the .50 BMG for heavy machine guns and the 9mm Parabellum for pistols and submachine guns—with one exception. While the U.S. Army had expressed interest in a 9mm pistol since the 1950s, many in the American military had an innate dislike for the cartridge. There was also a belief that any pistol would be of little real value in future wars so why go through the trouble and expense of adopting a new one? U.S. soldiers continued to carry aging 1911 pistols until they just plain wore out.

Eventually it was realized that it was no longer practical to keep rebuilding the aging stock of 1911s. In 1979 the Joint Services Small Arms Planning Commission was formed and the Air Force was authorized to test handguns from Beretta, Colt, Smith & Wesson, Fabrique Nationale, Heckler & Koch and Star. In 1981 the Commission stated the Beretta was their choice.

The Army contested the decision, which led to such an uproar that in 1983 a congressional committee insisted upon a new series of trials to be conducted by the Army rather than the Air Force. Pistols submitted by S&W, Beretta, SIG Sauer, H&K, Walther, FN and Steyr were tested and while the SIG Sauer P226 was

The M92 was one of the first high-capacity "Wondernines" and used a 15-round, double-column magazine.

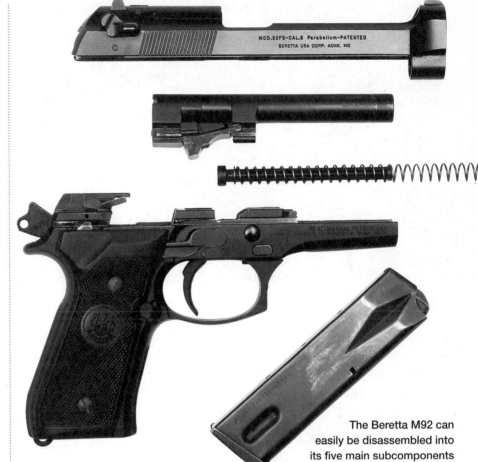

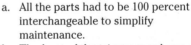

The Beretta M92 can easily be disassembled into its five main subcomponents in a few seconds.

found to be as suitable as the Beretta, the Italian company presented a lower bid and so was declared the winner.[8] In 1988 there was a third series of trials—which several manufacturers boycotted—that resulted in the Beretta being declared the winner for a third time.

At the request of the U.S. Army, Beretta modified the basic Model 92 pistol to produce the Model 92F:

a. All the parts had to be 100 percent interchangeable to simplify maintenance.
b. The front of the trigger guard was curved to allow finger support for easier aiming.
c. The bore was hard chromed to protect it from corrosion and to reduce wear.
d. A new finish called Bruniton, provides better corrosion resistance than plain blued finish.

In 1990, the Beretta Model 92F, under the designation Pistol, Semiautomatic 9mm M9, was adopted as the standard sidearm of all branches of the U.S. armed forces. Today the pistol is produced at the Beretta USA facility in Accokeek, Md., for military, police and commercial sale.

Teething problems led to several changes of the basic design resulting in the Model 92FS, which has an enlarged hammer pin that fits into a groove on the underside of the slide that prevents the slide from flying off the frame to the rear if it cracks. This was in response to reported defective slides during U.S.

American military personnel are seen here training with the M9 Beretta. The group of Marines are on a mission with tactical lights mounted on their M9A1 pistols.

military testing, which were apparently caused by high-pressure 9mm ammunition.

In 2009, the U.S. government signed a contract with Beretta for 350,000 M9 pistols. Service in Iraq and Afghanistan has shown that the M9 is a rugged, accurate and reliable handgun. And despite continuing criticism—mostly from dyed-in-the-wool fans of the 1911 pistol —the M9 will continue as the standard issue sidearm of U.S. armed forces well into the foreseeable future.

SPECIFICATIONS: PISTOL, SEMIAUTOMATIC, 9MM, M9	
Caliber:	9mm Ball NATO M882
Overall length:	8.5 in.
Barrel length:	4.9 in.
Weight (unloaded):	33.6 oz.
Magazine:	15-round detachable box
Sights front:	blade
Sights rear:	square notch
Grips:	plastic

In 2010, the U.S. Marines adopted the M9A1 which features a Picatinny rail for mounting tactical lights, lasers and other accessories. It also has more aggressive front and backstrap checkering, a beveled magazine well for easier reloading, a reversible magazine release and PVD coated magazines for improved functioning in sandy environments.

Following in the tradition of the Model 951R, Beretta has produced limited num-

bers of the Model 93R. Based upon the Model 92, it offers the option of semiauto or three-round burst fire, has a longer, ported barrel, a folding metal fore grip and can accept a folding metal buttstock. It is used by Italian counterterrorism forces such as the Nucleo Operativo Centrale di Sicurezza and Gruppo di Intervento Speciale, the Honduran National Police and several other law enforcement agencies.

SPECIFICATIONS: BERETTA MODELLO 93R	
Caliber:	Cartucce NATO a Pall. Cal. 9mm Parabellum
Overall length:	9.5 in.
Barrel length:	6.14 in.
Weight (unloaded):	41.3 oz.
Magazine:	15 or 20-round detachable box
Sights front:	blade
Sights rear:	square notch
Grips:	plastic

Beretta offers variants of the Model 92 in a number of calibers. To address the requests of North American police agencies the Model 96 series is chambered for the .40 S&W cartridge. For sale in countries that forbid civilians to own firearms chambered for current military cartridges – such as Italy and Mexico – the Model 98 is available in 9x21mm and in limited numbers, 7.65mm Parabellum (.30 Luger).

In addition to the Italian and U.S. armed forces, the Beretta 92 has been adopted by dozens of armies around the world as widely varied as Albania, Monaco, Malaysia, Peru, Slovenia, Pakistan and Bangladesh. It has been produced under license in the USA (M9 & M9A1), Brazil (Pist Mod 92), France (PAMAS G1), Egypt (Helwan 920) and South Africa (Vektor Z88). Other, unlicensed variants have been produced in Brazil (Taurus PT92), Turkey (Yavuz 16), Taiwan (Type 75) and Spain (Llama 82).

The Model 92 has been used by too many police forces to list here. It was one of the first semiauto pistols to find acceptance with American police and was adopted by the State Police and Highway Patrols of Connecticut, North Carolina, Maryland, Tennessee and Indiana.

Like its younger brothers, this Model 1915/19 showed it could put rounds where I wanted them.

When fired from a rest at 10 yards, the Model 1934 produced this perfectly centered group measuring only 1.5 inches.

These 25-yard targets fired by the author with the M92 and Model 1951 shows both were capable of extremely pleasing accuracy.

Test Firing Beretta Military Pistols

I thought it would be interesting to compare the performance of four Beretta military pistols for this article. Fellow collectors Bill Grist and Tim Hawkins provided me with samples of the Model 1915-19 and Model 34 pistols. Both were in very good condition, and the former bore large Regia Marina markings,

indicating it was one of 200 produced for the Italian navy, while Tim's was a Regio Esercito pistol made for the army in 1942. Steve Kehaya at Century Arms kindly sent me one of the Model 1951 pistols his company recently imported. A search of my gun safe revealed an Italian-made Model 92 of recent vintage.

Test firing was performed with .32 ACP, .380 ACP and 9mm Parabellum ammo provided by Winchester and Remington.

Our quartet of *Pistole italiane* were test-fired for accuracy from an MTM K-Zone Rest, the Model 1922 and 1934 pistols at 10 yards and the Model 1951 and Model 92 at 25. I fired three five-shot groups with each, the average of which can be seen on the nearby chart. The Model 1951 and M92 performed almost identically, with both shooting to point of aim and showing they were capable of producing sub two-inch groups, if I did my part.

Both the Model 15-19 and 1934 had rather decent triggers, but their sights—especially those on the former—left much to be desired. But to my surprise, both shot to point of aim. The Model 1934 proved a real winner when one of its groups measured a mere 1.5 inches.

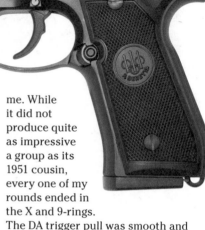

Test firing results:

Pistol	Group Size
Modello 1915-19	2.6 in.
Modello 1934	2.3 in.
Modello 1951	3 in.
Model 92	2.8 in.

As is my usual practice, I set up a number of combat targets and ran each Beretta through a series of offhand drills at seven yards, firing them with supported and unsupported (one-handed) grips. I'm sure the latter method would have met with the approval of a pre-1960s Italian army *istruttore di tiro*.

Once again the Model 15-19 surprised me with its performance. Despite its rather less than optical ergonomics, I was able to put all but three rounds into the X and 9-rings of its target.

I was also very impressed with the performance of the Model 1934. Despite its tiny sights and short grip tang, ergonomics were first rate; it had a very nice SA trigger and recoil was sharp but controllable. Of the 30 rounds I sent downrange, only one impacted outside of the X and 9-rings.

Right: The M92 Beretta has long been a popular sidearm with law enforcement agencies in the United States.

As the Pistol M9, the Model 92FS Beretta is the standard handgun of the U.S. armed forces. Note the well-known Beretta "trademarks" like the open top slide, ring-shaped hammer, finger rest extension on the magazine base pad and ergonomic grip.

The Model 1951 proved the Cinderella story of the day. The SA trigger was excellent as were the ergonomics and recoil control. And while the sights were not as user friendly as the Model 92, it proved to be the best shooter of the day, tearing a ragged hole in the center of the target with only four rounds wandering outside the X-ring.

I have been shooting Model 92s for years and so it presented no surprises to me. While it did not produce quite as impressive a group as its 1951 cousin, every one of my rounds ended in the X and 9-rings. The DA trigger pull was smooth and stage-free while the SA had some take-up before a crisp let-off. The grip was the most comfortable of all the pistols and it had the best controls.

All in all I was suitably impressed with *le nostre quattro pistole italiane*. And while some may accuse me of being prejudiced in their favor because my last name ends with a vowel, I found it easy to understand why Beretta pistols have been, and continue to be, so popular with soldiers, law enforcement agencies and civilian shooters around the world. *Arrivederci!*

The author would like to thank the following for supplying items used to prepare this article: Steve Keyaha, Dina Sanders, Doss White, Dionigi Maladomo, Gianluigi Usai, Tim Hawkins, Bill Grist, John Moss, John Rasalov, Jim Tosco, Winchester Ammunition and Remington Arms Company.

When comparing the M92FS (top) and Model 1951, the family resemblance is obvious.

FOOTNOTES

1. See www.carbinesforcollectors.com/Italianauto.html for a photo.

2. http://www.carbinesforcollectors.com/Italianauto.html

3. Italian navy pistols often had a brass disc with "RM" (Regia Marina) and an anchor inletted in the left grip panel.

4. Palokangas, Markku. MILITARY SMALL ARMS IN FINLAND 1918 – 1988. The Arms History Society of Finland, 1991. Pages 144 – 147.

5. Post-war Modello 1935 pistols usually lack the lanyard attachment loop.

6. Prior to the adoption of the Modello 1951 pistol, the Italian army only used the 9mm Parabellum in submachine guns. It was known as the "Cartucce 9mm per Moschetto Automatico Beretta Mo. 38."

7. Late production Modello 1951s had the pushbutton safety replaced with a 1911-type thumb lever.

8. In 1993 the SIG Sauer P228 was adopted as the Pistol, Compact, 9mm, M11 for those personnel who needed a smaller, lighter sidearm.

A PAIR OF FIRST-YEAR 20-GAUGE CLASSICS — THE A-5 AND THE SUPERPOSED

BROWNING'S
First Twenties

BY **Nick Hahn**

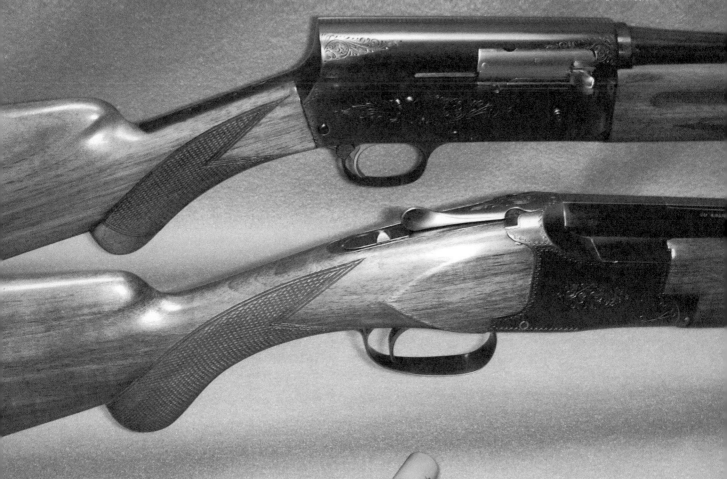

When a gun manufacturer introduces a new shotgun, it is almost a foregone conclusion that it will first be offered in 12 gauge. Only after the market has been tested for a while does the maker come out with other gauges. It's rare, but sometimes a manufacturer will debut a new model in several gauges. The introduction of a new model chambered only in one of the smaller gauges is not all that common, but it has happened.

For instance, way back in 1912, the Winchester Model 12 was first introduced in 20 gauge, to be followed with a 12 and 16 gauge a couple of years later. The Remington Model 17 likewise was introduced in 20 and was never made in 12.

Bill Ruger introduced his Red Label over/under in 1977 as a 20 gauge, with a 12 not arriving until some six years later. More recently, Smith & Wesson attempted to re-enter the shotgun market with its Turkish made Gold Elite side-by-sides, and they were initially made only in 20 gauge. Kimber also introduced both of its Turkish-made shotguns, the side-by-side Valier and over/under Marias in 20 gauge.

So, while the introduction of new model shotguns in a smaller gauge is not new, generally speaking, shotguns are first introduced to the market in 12, because that's the most popular and best-selling bore size.

Browning has always been known for its conservatism. From time to time the company does try to break that mold by introducing a somewhat radical design, such as the Cynergy over/under that was introduced a decade ago, but in general, Browning is pretty conservative. Ever since the beginning, when it came to shotguns, they were always introduced first in 12 gauge. If the market did not treat the new shotgun kindly, then it usually ended with the 12.

Such was the fate of the Double Auto, which appeared on the American scene in the early 1950s and lasted for about 17 years, but in 12 only. There was a light-weight model called the Twentyweight Double Auto, but it too was a 12 gauge. Two experimental 20s were made, but never put in production. Part of the problem, I believe, is that the Double Automatic was somewhat radical in design and American shooters did not take to it.

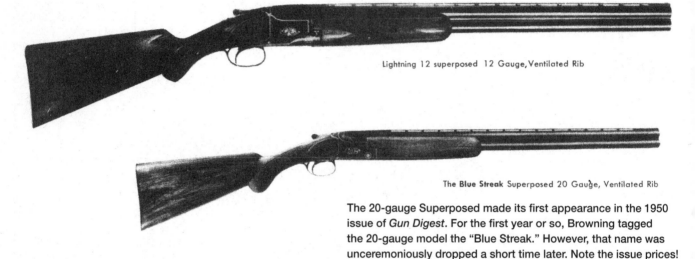

Lightning 12 superposed 12 Gauge, Ventilated Rib

The **Blue Streak** Superposed 20 Gauge, Ventilated Rib

The 20-gauge Superposed made its first appearance in the 1950 issue of *Gun Digest*. For the first year or so, Browning tagged the 20-gauge model the "Blue Streak." However, that name was unceremoniously dropped a short time later. Note the issue prices!

Superposed: 12 gauge. Single selective trigger, automatic ejectors, single sighting plane. Chambered for 2¾" shells.
Stock: 14¼"x1⅝"x2½" field stock dimensions.
14⅜"x1½"x1⅞" trap stock dimensions. French walnut. Hand checkered.

Barrel Lengths

	26½"	28"	30"
Choke	Skeet & Skeet	Imp. Cyl. & Mod.	Mod. & Full
	Imp. Cyl. & Mod.	Mod. & Full	Full & Full
	Mod. & Full	Full & Full	

Available in both raised matted rib and ventilated rib models.
Gun Weight from 7 to 7½ pounds depending upon barrel length and rib.
Specifications: Over-all length 45" with 28" barrels. Taken down length action and stock 20". Barrel depends upon length.

Barrel Lengths

	26½"	28"
Choke	Imp. Cyl. & Mod.	Imp. Cyl. & Mod.
	Mod. & Full	Mod. & Full
	Full & Full	Full & Full

Available in both raised matted rib and ventilated rib models.
Gun Weight approximately 6½ to 6¾ pounds depending upon barrel length and rib.
Specifications: Over-all length 44" with 28" barrels. Taken down length action and stock 19". Barrel depends upon length.

Prices of 12 and 20 Gauge	
Superposed with Raised Matted Rib	$219.00
Superposed with Ventilated Rib	244.00

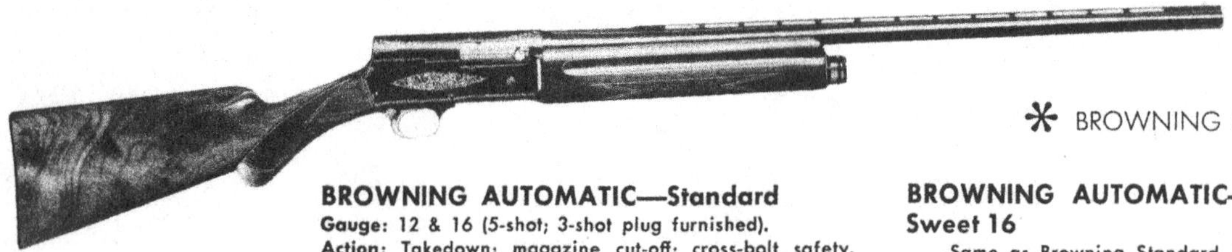

The 20-gauge A-5 first appeared in the 1959 issue of *Gun Digest*. It was called the "Light 20," although only the word "Twenty" was engraved on the receiver. To this day, that is how most people refer to the model. Note the asterisks and the side notes that indicate "new gun" and that it is a "Browning 20-gauge auto."

✱ BROWNING 20 GAUGE AUTO

BROWNING AUTOMATIC—Standard
Gauge: 12 & 16 (5-shot; 3-shot plug furnished).
Action: Takedown; magazine cut-off; cross-bolt safety.
Barrel: 26" (Imp. C., Cyl.); 28" (Mod., Full); 30" (Full).
Stock: 14¼"x1⅝"x2½". French walnut, checkered. Half pistol grip.
Weight: About 8 lbs. in 12 ga. 7¼ lbs. in 16 ga.
Features: Engraved receiver; double extractors; barrel and guide ring forged together.
Price: Plain barrel $144.75
Price: Hollow matted rib barrel 154.75
Price: Ventilated rib barrel 164.75

BROWNING AUTOMATIC—Light 20
Same as Browning Standard Auto except: 26" bbl. (Skeet, Imp. C. and Mod.), 28" bbl. (Mod. and Full). Wgt., under 6½ lbs.
Price: Plain barrel $144.75
Price: Ventilated rib barrel 164.75

BROWNING AUTOMATIC—Light 12 & Sweet 16
Same as Browning Standard Automatic except: 26" barrel (Mod., Imp. C., Cyl.) 28" (Full, Mod.) only in Sweet 16. Weight 12 ga., about 7¼ lbs.; 16 ga. about 6¾ lbs.
Price: Plain barrel $134.75
Price: Hollow matted rib barrel 144.75
Price: Ventilated rib barrel 154.75

BROWNING AUTOMATIC Magnum 12
Same as Browning Standard Auto except: 32" bbl., Full choke only. Recoil pad on 14"x1⅝"x2½" stock. Wgt., 8¼-8½ lbs.
Price: Plain barrel $140.00
Price: Ventilated rib barrel 160.00

Some models never even got to the experimental stage in smaller sizes. Both the A-500R and A-500G autoloaders only appeared briefly as 12s, never in any other bore size. Interestingly, the B-2000, which lasted only eight years, less time than the Double Automatic, was made in 20 gauge as well almost right from the start. The 20 appeared only a couple of years after the 12 made its debut. The same thing was true of the Citori and the BSS when they were introduced. The 20s followed shortly. But that was because the models, especially the Citori, were already in existence in 20. The first Citori was an existing Miroku model, so no special tooling had to be made. The BSS was a modified version of another existing model, so to bring it out in 20 did not require much retooling or change. But if you go back to some of Browning's original models, it is a very different story.

The venerable old Browning humpbacked A-5 first came off the production line at the Fabrique Nationale factory in Belgium in 1903. The first shipment to the U.S. arrived in 1905, all in 12 gauge. Four years later, in 1909, the first 16 gauges came off the assembly line, but the 20 gauge didn't see the light of day until 1958, more than a half century after the first 12 was made.

There are many reasons why it took Browning so long to come up with a 20-gauge A-5. For one thing, the 16 was a more popular bore size than the 20 during the first half of the 20th century. Another reason was that the 16-gauge A-5, which was lightened considerably in 1936 as the "Sweet Sixteen," was a great seller for Browning. Anyone wanting a smaller gauge, lighter gun, bought the Sweet Sixteen. Then, of course, World War II had an impact. It put a hold on many Browning projects when the Nazis occupied Belgium. But before the war, there just weren't any other autoloading shotguns that could compete with Browning's quality and reputation.

The Remington Model 11 was Browning's closest competitor in America, and the Remington was made in 12, 16 and 20 gauge. However, the Model 11 in 20 was no lightweight. It weighed as much, perhaps a bit more, than Browning's Sweet Sixteen so there really wasn't much for Browning's front office to worry about. The Remington Model 11 was advertised at 6¾ pounds for a 20 gauge without a rib, the same weight as the Sweet Sixteen. In reality, most Model 11 20s were closer to 7 pounds.

Many years ago I shot ducks with an old gentleman who called his Sweet Sixteen "Widgeon." He said the 12 gauge I was shooting should be called "Mallard" because it was bigger, thicker. He said an A-5 20 would be a "Teal" because it was smaller and more slender.

At the end of the war, Remington vastly modified and modernized their autoloader and in 1949 came out with the Model 11-48. The 11-48 was made in 12, 16 and 20 gauge. The 20 weighed less than Browning's Sweet Sixteen, and it also cost less. Additionally, new imports from Italy – the Franchi 48AL and the Breda, two modernized versions of the Browning autoloader – appeared on the market in the 1950s. They were both lighter than the A-5 and available in 20. The Franchi in particular was exceptionally lightweight, and caught the attention many of upland gunners.

Not long after the end of World War II shotgun ammunition was improved considerably and the newer 20-gauge rounds became as effective as the old 16 gauge of the prewar era. The popularity of the 20 gauge soared while the 16, although still popular and number two in sales, began to sag a bit. It was time for Browning to do something about the situation, so Val Browning, son of the great John M. Browning, redesigned the old A-5 and scaled it down for a 20 gauge. Val had done this before, back in 1936 when he redesigned and lightened the 16 gauge and came up with the highly successful Sweet Sixteen model.

The new "Twenty" was introduced in 1958 and became an immediate success. Although Browning advertised it as weighing less than 6¼ pounds, to reach that weight you had to get a gun with a short, plain barrel, and hope the wood

was not very dense. It did weigh less than 6½ pounds with a ribless barrel, sometimes dipping down to 6¼, but rarely below that weight unless you went for a 24-inch barrel. Nevertheless, it was a great success and the Twenty remained unchanged, except for the shape of its grip in 1968, until it was discontinued in 1997.

The Browning Superposed over/under made its first appearance in America in 1928 as a 12-gauge gun. It was made only in 12 through all the pre-World War II years, although Val Browning had developed a scaled-down 20-gauge version and there may have been some very rare 20-gauge Superposeds in Europe before the war. However, it wasn't until after the war, in 1949, that the first 20-gauge models arrived in America. Initially they were available in just one grade, the so-called Grade I with minimal engraving. They were delightful little guns and immediately caught the fancy of upland gunners. Unlike the A-5 20 gauge, which remained the same throughout its life except for a change in grip shape and the change of manufacture to Japan in 1976, the Superposed 20 underwent some changes almost immediately. First, the engraving pattern was increased only two years after its introduction. Then in 1955, the Lightning grade was introduced. The Lightning had been available in 12 gauge before the war, but production was stopped after the war. In 1955, both the 12 and the 20 were avail-

A 20-gauge Superposed has long been a favorite choice of upland bird hunters everywhere.

able in the Lightning grade.

The Lightning was a lightened version of the Superposed. In 12 gauge, there was sometimes as much as a pound difference in weight between the Standard and the Lightning. This was especially true of the prewar 12-gauge Lightnings, which were available without a rib and could weigh as little as 6¾ pounds. In 20 gauge the difference was not that great, although the Lightning 20s tended to be lighter by anywhere from ¼ to ½ pound than the Standard 20s.

Interestingly, the very early 20 gauges could be as light as the Lightning because their wood tended to be much slimmer. My first-year 20-gauge Superposed weighs six pounds, six ounces, and this is with 28-inch barrels and a solid rib! An average Lightning 20 with 26½-inch barrels and a ventilated rib will weigh six pounds, four ounces,

about two ounces lighter than my gun. As Art Isaacson, a former Browning employee and Browning firearms expert told me, there really wasn't all that much difference. The Lightning models used hollowed-out buttstocks and slimmer forearms. If a standard model happened to have wood that was not very dense, it could weigh the same – even without the hollowed-out buttstock.

Additionally, some of the very early pre-Lightning 20s had hollowed-out buttstocks. In many ways the early 20s were much more attractive than the later models. They had very slim wood, making the guns look sleek and lightweight. Sometimes you can find some of the more imaginative sellers advertise the early 20s as being stocked in "Holland & Holland" style with "slim wood."

The 20-gauge Superposed later appeared in an even lighter version called

the Super Light, with not just slimmer wood but also metal shaved and thinner barrels. But such was not the case with the 20-gauge A-5. A magnum 20 version did appear in 1968, a beefier gun, actually weighing a bit more than even the Sweet Sixteen. But the Twenty – popularly referred to as the "Light Twenty" – did not undergo any changes to speak of, except as mentioned earlier, the shape of the grip and the change of manufacture location to Japan. However, there were some so-called "Super Light" A-5s made by FN that were never imported by Browning. These were alloy-framed A-5s that weighed much less and were made in Belgium at the FN factory in the 1970s, just about the time Browning switched the manufacture of A-5s to Japan. But, they were only sold in Europe.

As with just about all products in the modern era, the first models seem to receive much more care and attention. Later models might be superficially more attractive, glitzier, but chances are that some manufacturing shortcuts were taken to save costs.

The first-year 20 Superposed was a very simple affair. The engraving pattern was sparse, but deeper cut and of very good quality. The wood, although not fancy, tended to be much better, showing some attractive grain, unlike the later "blonde" wood that showed up in the 1960s. For some reason many seem to think that this very plain, light colored wood is somehow superior, and actually seek out the guns with blonde wood.

The main difference appears to be in the finishing of both metal and wood. The early guns seem to show much more

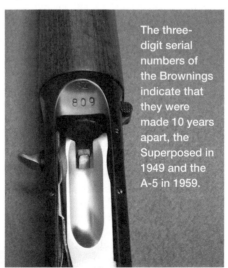

The three-digit serial numbers of the Brownings indicate that they were made 10 years apart, the Superposed in 1949 and the A-5 in 1959.

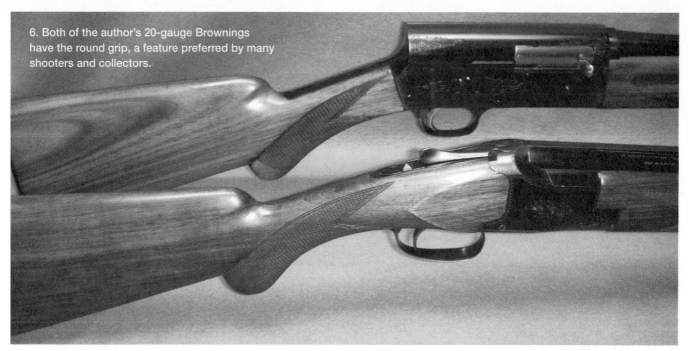

6. Both of the author's 20-gauge Brownings have the round grip, a feature preferred by many shooters and collectors.

care in metal polishing and fitting. The wood was oil finished before the war but finished with lacquer after the war. It had a nice subdued finish, not the glossy finish found on later guns when polyurethane replaced the traditional lacquer finish. The checkering was also finer and of better quality, or so it seems.

Until the early 1960s the A-5 receivers were rust blued in a very deep finish, giving them a nice, rich appearance. However, the later hot-bluing process was still done very well and actually there was very little difference in durability and appearance. However, all in all, the earlier guns were better finished. Naturally, the first-year production guns demonstrate this better than any other year models. There isn't a dramatic difference, but there is enough, especially with the Superposed compared to the A-5.

My two first-year 20-gauge Brownings are not all that different from the later production guns, but there are differences. Both guns have three-digit serial numbers. The first batch of 20-gauge Supers was made in the late spring of 1949 and shipped to America in May 1949. The initial shipment consisted of a total of 22 guns serial numbered from 242 to the 500s. The guns were not consecutively numbered for the most part and came off the assembly line that same month. My gun, numbered in the 700 series, was made shortly after that and was in a batch of five guns that shipped two months later. Somewhere around 1,000 20 gauges were produced

the first year, supposedly serial numbered from one to 1,700 with gaps here and there. The lowest serial numbered 20-gauge Superposed gun to reach America was 242, and no one seems to know what happened to those guns that were numbered before 242. No doubt there is a number one and others somewhere. But here in America, the first guns to arrive were already numbered at 242 or higher.

The 20 gauge A-5s had a higher number than the Superposed, numbered in the 800s. But then there were a lot more 20-gauge A-5s made the first year than the Superposed 20. Records show that only one 20-gauge gun was made in 1958, followed by 4,694 guns in 1959. However, guns made in 1959 are stamped with the prefix of 8Z indicating the year of manufacture as 1958. Browning does not have detailed records of when or where the A-5s were shipped – at least they couldn't tell me. At any rate, despite its higher number, my 20-gauge A-5 with an 800-range serial number was obviously made early during the first year of production when you consider that there were a total of 4,694 made that year. Whatever the case may be, like the Superposed 20, it is a very early 20-gauge A-5.

Are these guns all that rare and collectible? Well, that depends. Perhaps the Superposed 20 is more collectible since fewer were made and it is older than the A-5 20 by some 10 years. Normally, when you do find a Superposed 20 that was made in 1949,

it is usually pretty worn or has had some changes made to it, most of the time it has been re-blued. Mine is still in its original finish, so I suppose it isn't as common. The same thing applies to the 20-gauge A-5, perhaps even more so, since A-5s were less expensive and were considered to be working guns and used heavily, sometimes carelessly. A die-hard Browning collector would consider them as collector's pieces, but I enjoy shooting them. After all, that is why they were made – to shoot and not just sit in a gun cabinet or a safe.

Belgian Brownings are still quite common on the used gun market. The Superposed, in the opinion of many, is still not overpriced like some of the other classic shotguns. This applies primarily to the Grade I 20 gauge, which can still be found for anywhere from $2,000 to $3,000 in good to excellent condition. Unfortunately, the Superposed higher grades have skyrocketed in price. The Pigeon Grade (Grade II) usually sells for between $3,500 to $7,500 in good to excellent condition, and the Diana Grade, probably the most desirable of the higher-grade Brownings, can go for anywhere from around $6,000 up to $10,000, and even more for mint condition.

These prices, as already stated, are for 20-gauge models. Values are much higher for the 28 gauge and .410 bore. The 12-gauge guns are much lower priced and more common, and therefore may be considered even better bargains.

But for many of us, there's nothing like a 20.

THE TWENTY

BY Gary Zinn

REMEMBERING DAD'S MODEL 12

There is a well-worn old shotgun in my gun locker. It is a 20-gauge Winchester Model 12 with a modified choke and 26-inch barrel. I haven't shot it for several years now, but I will keep and treasure it as long as I live, for two reasons. First, it holds memories for me of many days I spent hunting with it. Second – and most

importantly – it was my father's prized possession, which he indirectly bequeathed to me.

I have checked the Winchester manufacturing records and determined that this gun was built in 1923. I'm sure that's the year dad bought it, special-ordered through a store in our locality. It was the first firearm he ever owned.

I came to understand how much he treasured it because he would tell me stories of his adventures when he had hunted with it – which was, unfortunately, for all too brief a time. Dad always insisted that after I had used the "Twenty" (as we always called it), I had to clean it thoroughly, whether I had shot it or not. This was special treatment, for during most of my youth the only other working gun in our home was a .22 rifle that only got a few swabs run through its barrel a couple times a year.

My parents married in 1924. During the next eight years they added a daughter and three sons to their family, and then I arrived 12 years later. Meanwhile, a tragedy occurred in 1930—my father's eyesight began to fail. He and one of his brothers had served in the Army during World War I. They fought in France, where dad once encountered mustard gas. He was not seriously poisoned – or so it seemed at the time – and returned home to a normal life after the war. But the eventual deterioration of his eyesight was eventually attributed to the gas poisoning he had suffered. Dad's sight finally stabilized at a point where he could, wearing thick glasses, read large newspaper headlines. But his hunting days were done.

During the years that followed a unique relationship developed between my father and his sons. I came to understand this gradually. For instance, I would take the Twenty hunting and come home with some squirrels. Dad would always help me clean them and while we were doing this chore he would ask me about my outing: "Where did you go? What did you see – any grouse, any deer? How did you get a shot at this squirrel? Did you see any sign of that fox we heard howling down the ridge the other evening?"

I finally realized that dad was still enjoying the pastime of hunting, but now vicariously through me. I checked with my older brothers and they confirmed that it had been the same as they were growing up. We were his tenuous link to something he had enjoyed immensely but could do no longer.

Sadly, dad died of a heart attack in 1970. My mother survived him by a quarter century and during her waning years she began distributing special family possessions among her children and grandchildren. When she asked me if there was anything that I would especially like to have, I answered immediately: "Mom, the only thing

I want is the Twenty." And so I have it. Thank you for understanding, Mom.

The last time I hunted with the Twenty was a special day, because it was truly a trip down memory lane. My eldest nephew now owns and lives on the small West Virginia farm where I grew up. I was visiting there one autumn weekend and decided to spend an afternoon hunting. I took the Twenty and hiked up to the ridge that crosses the back of the farm and then meanders some two miles southward across neighboring properties. This was my favorite hunting area when I was growing up and as I walked through the woods many memories of other days spent there came to mind. I saw several squirrels, flushed a couple of grouse, watched a hawk that was hunting much harder than I, and kept bumping into a doe with two half-grown fawns. I didn't shoot at any of the small game – I was enjoying the outing too much to disturb things with a lot of noise. The highlight of the day was when I slipped up on a flock of wild turkeys. I simply stood still and watched them feed along ahead of me until they wandered out of sight over the ridge. It's not often that one can watch undisturbed turkeys going about their business.

As evening fell and I was making my way out of the woods I began thinking about how I would have described all of this to Dad. If he had been waiting back at the house he would certainly have expected a full and detailed report. He would have liked to hear about the turkeys especially, because they were nonexistent in our neighborhood during most of his lifetime, so he never had the experience of seeing them in the wild.

"There were over a dozen of them, Dad. They were right in front of me as I watched them."

ADVENTURES AND MISADVENTURES

Here are a few of my experiences with the Twenty, some of which were spectacular – others not so much.

The Wile E. Coyote squirrel: One day I was hunting along the ridge beyond our farm. I was walking along one edge of a pipeline right-of-

way when I saw a squirrel run up the trunk of an oak tree on the other side. He quickly climbed to where a dead limb jutted out of the tree. For some reason he began running up that limb and as he did I mounted the Twenty, swung ahead of him, and touched off. At the shot the squirrel continued running flat out up the limb and at its end he continued into the air, feet still flying. Suddenly he stopped moving, seemed to suspend for a moment, and then fell like a brick, looking exactly like the cartoon character Wile E. Coyote running off the edge of a cliff.

The easiest limit ever: One opening day I walked into the woods just before daylight and picked a spot to wait for the squirrels to start moving. Just as full light came I spied one in a nearby hickory tree. I shot him and the tree instantly came alive with squirrels running in all directions. Without taking a step, I fired until the Twenty was empty (six shells) and then walked over and pocketed my limit of six squirrels. It's never that easy – except that one time.

The day I couldn't miss: After graduate school, I returned to my alma mater, West Virginia University, to teach forestry. I once invited a colleague of mine, along with one of our graduate students, for a day

of hunting on my home turf. The colleague, Bruce, and I had met in graduate school and had hunted together many times. Bruce knew I was not a great wing shot because when we had hunted grouse or woodcock together he typically outshot me three or four birds to one.

All small game was in season, so we decided to bust the brush for targets of opportunity. My day started out well when I neatly rolled a rabbit on a dead run. Next I picked off a grouse that flushed in front of me, followed by another rabbit. Then I hung back for a while and let my companions have some of the fun.

The climax of the day came when we unexpectedly flushed a covey of quail from a briar patch. Bruce and the student got one each, while I scored a neat double.

That was my day – five shots with three birds and two rabbits in the bag. "Have you been practicing?" Bruce asked. "No," I replied, "and I can't explain what happened, but I sure enjoyed it!"

And just when I thought I had a sure thing: Two incidents where I thought I had it covered connect in my memory because they happened within 50 yards of each other, though at different times.

I was rabbit hunting in an abandoned pasture that had reverted to brush and saplings. While walking along a narrow deer trail I flushed a rabbit that scooted out on the trail directly in front of me. Easy shot – just point the Twenty so the muzzle covered his bobbing tail and fire. That's what I did, but the rabbit ran on, untouched. I just stood there wondering what had happened – until I noticed that a sapling 10 feet in front of me had doubled over at belly height. My entire shot string had hit it squarely. That was one lucky wabbit.

Another time, one the edge of that same field was a fence with a woodlot on the other side. I was walking along the fence when I flushed a grouse. He cleared the foliage and then set his wings and glided away into the open (they *never* do that!). I swung through him and pulled the trigger. Click! Broken firing pin—one lucky bird.

Something I didn't know about the Model 12: I had been hunting with the Twenty for a couple of years and was getting quite comfortable with it. One day I was sitting in a mature forest watching for squirrels. Eventually I saw one working his way through the treetops, coming my way. I watched him as he jumped into a very tall tree just to my right. He scampered through the crown and was heading along a limb from which he could jump to the next tree. I decided to shoot just as he made the jump. The squirrel was almost directly overhead when I shot. Boom! Boom! Boom! Boom! The next thing I knew I had shot four times! Somehow I never even touched the squirrel.

I thought something was wrong with the gun, so I carefully unloaded the remaining shells and headed home. When I told Dad what had happened, he laughed so hard that tears came to his eyes. When he caught his breath he said. "I never thought to tell you. That gun doesn't have a trigger sear disconnector." "What the heck does that mean?" I asked crossly, peeved that he was having so much merriment at my expense. "Mind your tongue, boy, and I'll tell you. It means that if you don't release the trigger as you pump the action, the gun will fire again as soon as the bolt closes."

You're never too young to learn. I had learned how to use the Twenty as an automatic weapon!

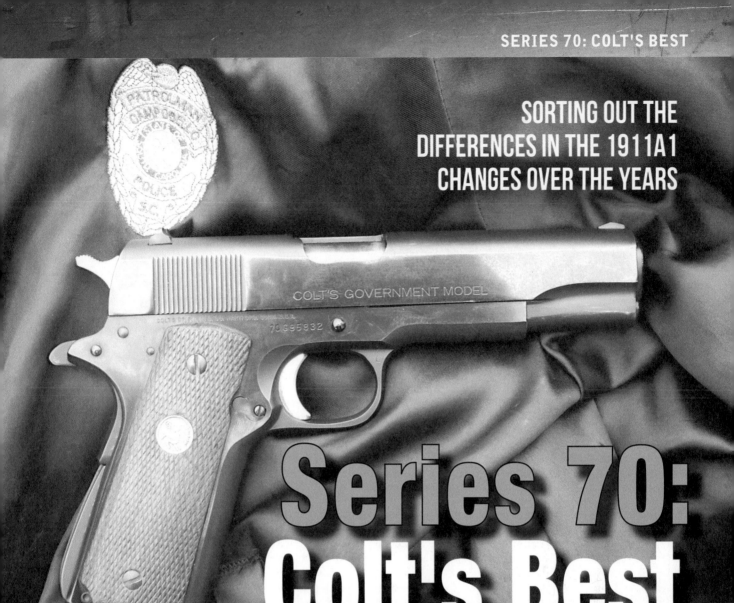

SORTING OUT THE DIFFERENCES IN THE 1911A1 CHANGES OVER THE YEARS

COLT'S GOVERNMENT MODEL

70G95832

Series 70: Colt's Best

BY **Robert K. Campbell**

For those who favor the "Hammer of the Century" there is nothing like a Colt 1911 pistol. Its straight-to-the-rear trigger compression, well-designed controls, low bore axis and comfortable grip frame that comprise the "Golden Ratio" of handgunning, define the 1911.

Colt was the first with the most in 1911 when the U.S. Army adopted the original 1911. But nothing is perfect and after World War I, certain complaints regarding handling were addressed. Scalloped finger grooves on the frame at each side of the triggerguard shortened the trigger reach. This eliminated the tendency of short fingers to press the frame when squeezing the trigger. The trigger was replaced with a shorter type and the mainspring housing was changed from a flat to an arched style to give the pistol

a better point, and address a tendency to shoot low. The sights were modified. The result was the 1911A1. Today we call the pistol 1911 but the modern versions are 1911A1s.

Military and commercial production strayed little from 1927 to 1970. In 1970, a general tightening up and improvement in fit and finish resulted in the Colt Mark IV, Series 70. This model was the answer to a demand for a better 1911. The primary difference in the Series 70 was the collet bushing. This was a barrel bushing with fingers that grasped the barrel more tightly. In my experience, as time and round count went up, the pistol could become more accurate as the bushing grooved into the barrel. The Series 70 would not out-perform a pistol with a properly fitted National Match barrel and bushing, but the new Colt had promise.

The Series 80

In the early 1980s Colt introduced the Series 80 1911. This handgun added the positive firing pin block. Once the competing 1911 manufacturers introduced the firing pin block, Colt had to do so as well or forget institutional sales. The Series 80 featured improved sights (finally!) and a feed-ramp redesign that ensured the pistol would feed hollow-point ammunition. With the introduction of a stainless steel version, Colt had their best service pistol yet.

In the Series 80 handguns Colt eliminated the sometimes trouble-prone collet bushing. The Series 80 is a good gun, but the Series 70 soon had a cult following, with good examples commanding a premium over the Series 80. On another front, for the first time Colt was facing real

The Colt 1991A1 is also a good pistol, although plain. This example is fitted with Lance Larson Katana grips and is a .38 Super.

competition in the 1911 market. The competitor was not as refined as the Colt but it worked well and was similar to the GI 1911A1. Colt responded with the 1991A1. The 1991A1 cut costs with plastic grips and a matte finish. It is a very serviceable, if not attractive pistol. Colt had reintroduced the flat mainspring housing and long trigger in the Series 80. The premise was that it is easier to fit a beavertail safety to the flat mainspring housing, which is true because everyone desired a beavertail safety.

In the 1990s, this is where Colt stood: The Series 80 was the flagship. The 1991A1 was intended to compete with the Springfield GI pistol and inexpensive imports. The 1991A1 pistols originally were supplied with inexpensive grip panels that did not support the plunger tube, but Colt fixed that. The latest variations are finished rather nicely and feature good quality wood grip panels. The public is willing to pay a little more for a nicer Colt and current 1991A1 pistols are attractive handguns. The older matte finish pistols are often found at an attractive price and are bargain workhorses.

Colt was competing with the GI pistol with the 1991A1, but also had to address stiff competition from handguns with advanced features such as low-profile combat sights, extended controls and a beavertail grip safety. Colt responded with the XSE. The firing pin block, trigger action, springs and barrel bushing are the same as the modern Colts. But the intrinsic accuracy of each is the same, though control in rapid fire may be better with the XSE due to the frame cut-out and beavertail grip safety. Practical accuracy is also improved due to superior sights. But the pistols are each still Colts.

There remained a demand for pistols without the Series 80 firing pin block. These handguns are still known as Series 70 pistols. Others waxed poetic in their call for a Colt that harkened back to the heyday of production. Bright Colt blue finish, Series 70 lockwork, short trigger and original arched mainspring housing were all on the wish list.

The Series 80 firing pin block does not preclude achieving a good trigger action but when the trigger must be light and crisp there are complications. The Series 70 pistol featured the short trigger and arched mainspring housing that some of us prefer. This combination, I feel, is better suited for fast work and combat shooting, while the long trigger and flat mainspring housing may be better suited for target work. The addition of target triggers and beavertail safeties to defensive pistols has resulted in the widespread use of the long trigger and flat mainspring housing combination. The icing on the cake for our dream pistol would be a Colt finished like the old days.

While other makers have done a lot with the 1911 and produced excellent handguns, nothing stirs the heart like the little pony on the slide. When a sense of history and emotional attachment are important – it has to be a Colt.

The New Series 70

Colt has given us just that pistol in the new Series 70. This Series 70 does not use a collet bushing. The pistol is tight enough but easily field strips with just the fingers. The finish is a nice Colt blue and the grips are excellent examples of high-grade checkered stocks superior to the originals. The top of the slide is finished in a dull blue that is attractive and nonreflective. This is a true Series 70 action with no firing pin block. Trigger compression is smooth and breaks at a decent 4.25 pounds, which is a good all-around trigger for personal defense, IDPA matches or informal target work. An excellent addition to the Series 70 is a set of high-profile sights as used on the 1991A1. Overall, the new Series 70 is a very nice handgun by any standard.

How does the new Series 70 compare with the old? I feel qualified to comment as I have extensive experience with a dozen originals, including several purchased new in the box back in the day. While the Series 70 was usually a good handgun, I upgraded to the Series 80 as my service pistol as soon it became available. Original Series 70 production included some nice pistols, but quality control issues soured my opinion of the model. I would never run to the gun show with cash in hand to obtain an original while the new Colt is available. The original had the

The XSE is a high-end pistol with good features. It is a Colt to the core, but the Series 70 will still appeal to the traditionalist.

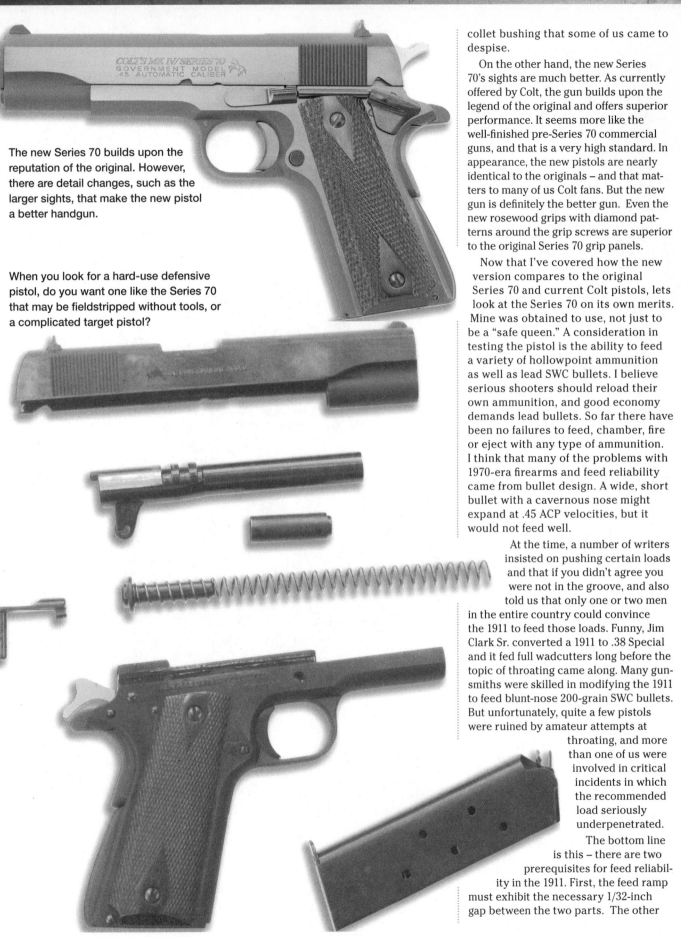

The new Series 70 builds upon the reputation of the original. However, there are detail changes, such as the larger sights, that make the new pistol a better handgun.

When you look for a hard-use defensive pistol, do you want one like the Series 70 that may be fieldstripped without tools, or a complicated target pistol?

collet bushing that some of us came to despise.

On the other hand, the new Series 70's sights are much better. As currently offered by Colt, the gun builds upon the legend of the original and offers superior performance. It seems more like the well-finished pre-Series 70 commercial guns, and that is a very high standard. In appearance, the new pistols are nearly identical to the originals – and that matters to many of us Colt fans. But the new gun is definitely the better gun. Even the new rosewood grips with diamond patterns around the grip screws are superior to the original Series 70 grip panels.

Now that I've covered how the new version compares to the original Series 70 and current Colt pistols, lets look at the Series 70 on its own merits. Mine was obtained to use, not just to be a "safe queen." A consideration in testing the pistol is the ability to feed a variety of hollowpoint ammunition as well as lead SWC bullets. I believe serious shooters should reload their own ammunition, and good economy demands lead bullets. So far there have been no failures to feed, chamber, fire or eject with any type of ammunition. I think that many of the problems with 1970-era firearms and feed reliability came from bullet design. A wide, short bullet with a cavernous nose might expand at .45 ACP velocities, but it would not feed well.

At the time, a number of writers insisted on pushing certain loads and that if you didn't agree you were not in the groove, and also told us that only one or two men in the entire country could convince the 1911 to feed those loads. Funny, Jim Clark Sr. converted a 1911 to .38 Special and it fed full wadcutters long before the topic of throating came along. Many gunsmiths were skilled in modifying the 1911 to feed blunt-nose 200-grain SWC bullets. But unfortunately, quite a few pistols were ruined by amateur attempts at throating, and more than one of us were involved in critical incidents in which the recommended load seriously underpenetrated.

The bottom line is this – there are two prerequisites for feed reliability in the 1911. First, the feed ramp must exhibit the necessary 1/32-inch gap between the two parts. The other

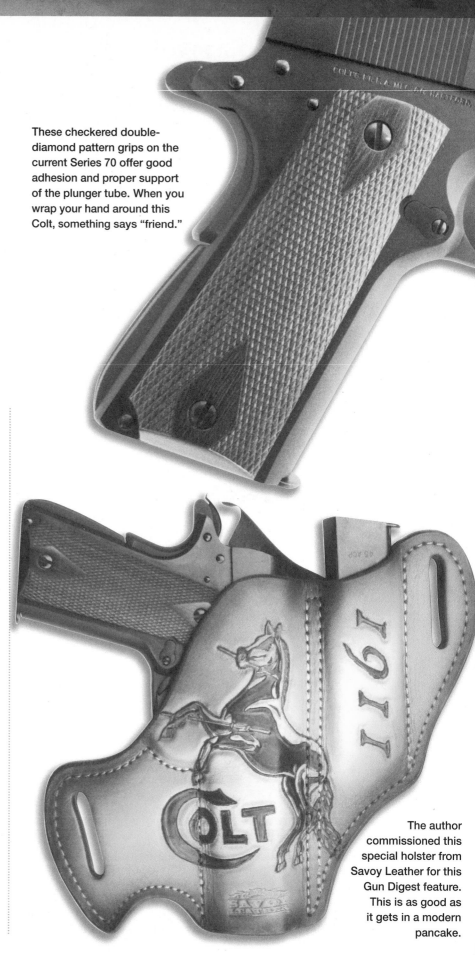

These checkered double-diamond pattern grips on the current Series 70 offer good adhesion and proper support of the plunger tube. When you wrap your hand around this Colt, something says "friend."

The rear sight of today's Series 70 is a marked improvement over the GI sight. It is large enough for rapid acquisition and the rear notch is large enough for a rapid flash sight picture. The front post is also a great design, not too tall, but large enough for good shooting.

requirement is that the loaded cartridge has an overall length of 1.25 inches. When these requirements are met feed reliability is assured.

A slight cause for concern could be the original-style ejection port. This design worked well for many years, but it was also the subject of lowering or scalloping in most modern slide designs. The spent case ejects just fine, but administrative handling and a loaded cartridge case is more difficult to eject. It is a Series 70 after all. An important consideration with the Series 70 is to never use a shock buff if the pistol is destined for personal defense use. With the shock buff, the slide will not retract sufficiently to clear a loaded cartridge from the chamber if the magazine is locked in. In the case of a dud round, this could leave one in quite a predicament.

When firing the pistol for groups from a solid bench rest it was obvious Colt struck the ideal balance between tightness and reliability. The pistol is plenty accurate for all-around defense and IDPA use. It doesn't rattle when shook and the locking lugs slide effortlessly together. Someone with vast experience had their hands in the engineering of this pistol.

The author commissioned this special holster from Savoy Leather for this Gun Digest feature. This is as good as it gets in a modern pancake.

As for reliability, the new Series 70 is a Colt and should prove to be as reliable as a machine can be. I have never experienced a problem with the Series 80 firing pin block in an unaltered Colt, but I have experienced a failure in a high-round count pistol from another maker that used the Colt Series 80 design drop safety. Just for the record, the Series 70 eliminates four parts in comparison to the Series 80. These are the frame-mounted trigger-bar lever and plunger, and the slide-mounted firing pin plunger and driving spring. Simplicity is much better for reliability.

The pistol was proofed with the loads I use most often. A combination of the Oregon Trail 200-grain SWC and enough Titegroup powder for 890 fps proved the single most accurate combination. This load is sensibly less hot than hardball, and the gun will last forever shooting this combination. Next, the pistol was fired with Black Hills 230-grain ball ammunition. This pistol, unlike most originals, did not demand a break-in but came out of the royal blue Colt box running. Hardball is a good general-purpose load. It is proven in interpersonal combat, has good penetration, adequate accuracy and good feed reliability. Finally, the pistol was proofed with a modern defense load. It doesn't get any better than the Black Hills 185-grain TAC +P. A wide mouth, solid copper hollowpoint and +P velocity confirmed the Series 70 will handle modern ammunition as far as both feed and cycle reliability go.

At a long 25 yards from a solid benchrest position, the pistol turned in a best group for five shots of 2¼ inches with the 200-grain handload. The Black Hills TAC load was nearly as accurate at 2½ inches, and the ball load broke just under 3 inches. The Series 70 is most definitely accurate enough to address any foreseeable threat. The pistol is comfortable to fire, well-balanced and lively in the hand, as a 1911 should be. It is fast from leather as there is nothing extraneous about it and no light rail. This is a serious combat pistol with impeccable lineage.

When carrying the Series 70, I decided something different was necessary. The strong-side pancake holster is a good choice for concealed carry when a covering garment may be worn, and it preserves a good balance of speed and retention. The holster illustrated from Savoy leather has more than a little show but gets the job done in enviable fashion, plus it's comfortable on the hip and handles the 39-ounce Colt well.

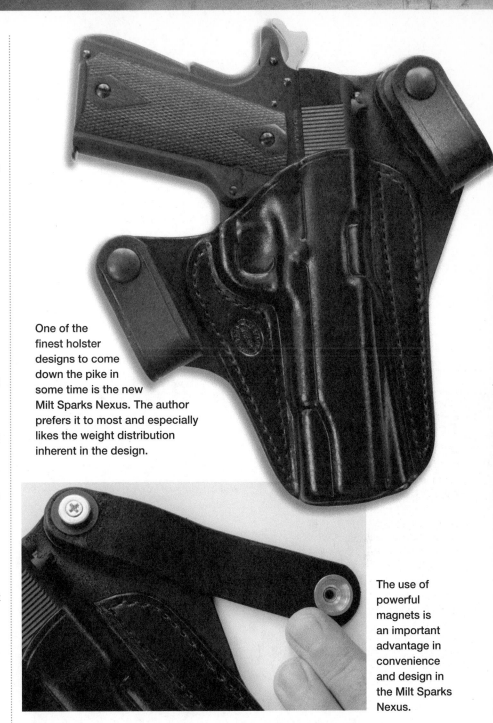

One of the finest holster designs to come down the pike in some time is the new Milt Sparks Nexus. The author prefers it to most and especially likes the weight distribution inherent in the design.

The use of powerful magnets is an important advantage in convenience and design in the Milt Sparks Nexus.

When weather and local mores demand greater concealment, the inside-the-waistband holster is ideal. I have used the Milt Sparks Summer Special for decades. However, I recently elected to go with a newer design in the search for more comfort and a different draw angle. The Milt Sparks Nexus spreads the weight of the pistol out on the belt nicely and the draw is a bit easier for those with aging rotator cuffs. Neodymium magnets are used in the belt loops. These ultra strong magnets are easier to align than snaps and neatly solve some of the problems associated with belt loops. Colt and Milt Sparks seem to just naturally go together well. In common with the Series 70 pistol, this holster reeks of class and style and is far better than anything we had in 1970.

If you desire a first-class pistol that harkens to the grand old days of Colt production, the Colt Series 70 is the gun. If you want a rugged self-defense pistol without peer and nothing but a 1911 will suit you, the Series 70 is your gun. It just doesn't get any better than that.

Engraved Guns

Our Annual Review of the Finest Examples of Beauty and Artistry in the World of the Custom Gun

BY **Tom Turpin**

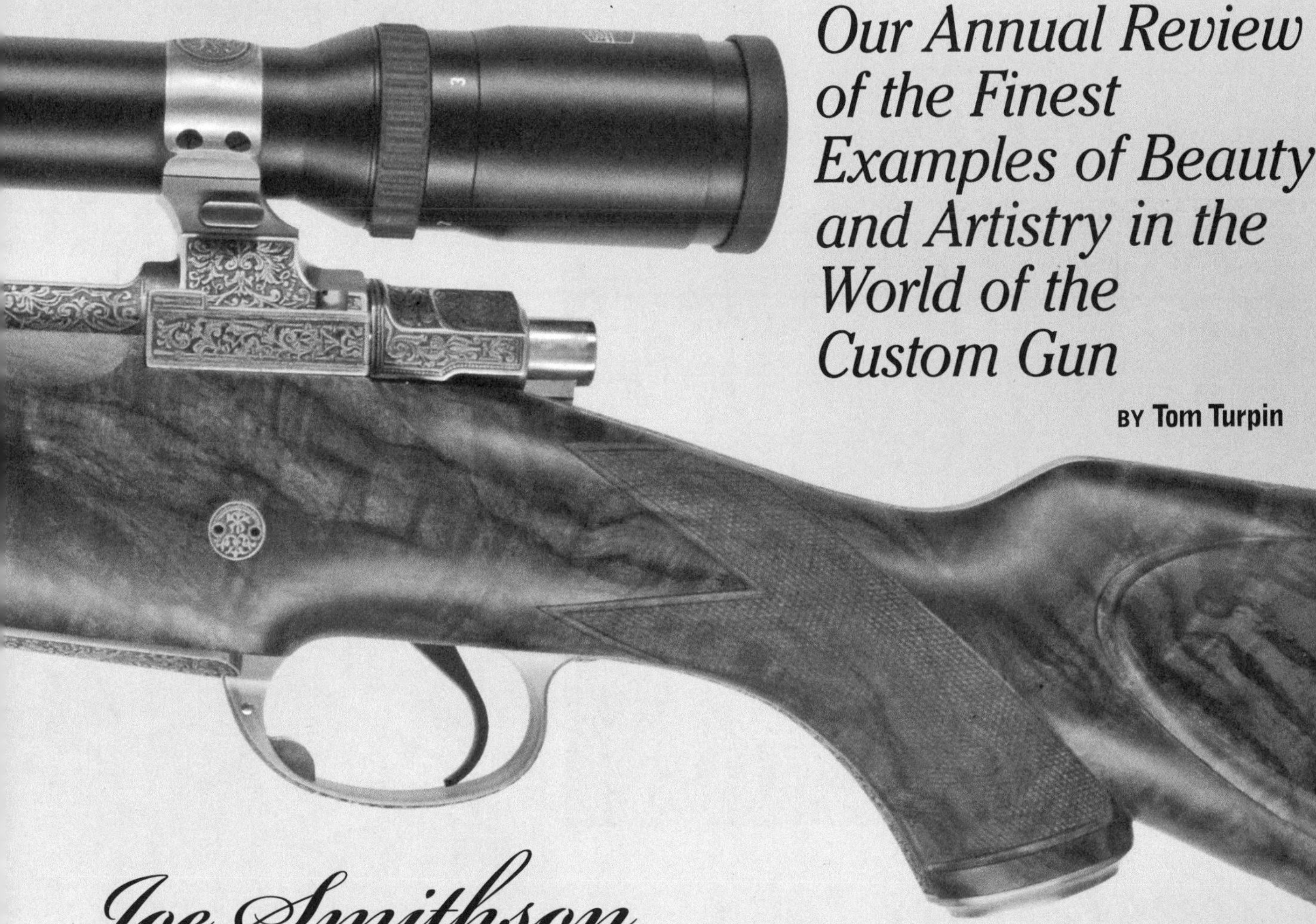

Joe Smithson

Joe has been making guns full-time, since 1985. He attended the Trinidad State Junior College gunsmithing program and followed that with working under the supervision of gunsmithing legend Jerry Fisher. He has been crafting the highest quality guns and rifles in his own shop for more than 20 years now. His is a one-stop shop, with both wood and metalwork done in-house. He also developed and makes a quick detachable scope mounting system known everywhere fine rifles are appreciated. His son Brett has joined him in his Utah shop, and is working side-by-side with his dad. The accompanying photos show an example of his current outstanding work. The fantastic engraving was done in Italy by Frederique Lepinois.

Photos by Brett Smithson

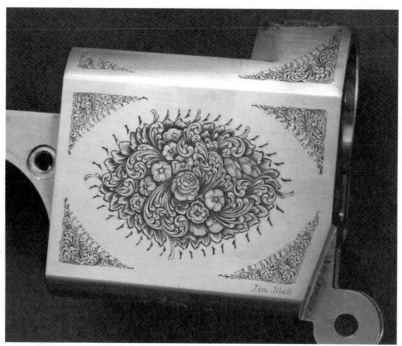

Jim Blair

Jim Blair is a Master Engraver, recognized as such by none less than both FEGA and the Colt Firearms Company. His engraving is highly tailored to his client's wishes. He normally works with one of three variations of scrollwork – a modified arabesque, banknote or English scroll. However, he will go outside these traditional types of scrollwork to satisfy a client's wishes, as he can do almost anything in the engraving world. He prefers to give the scroll a life of its own, and usually does just that. He goes where it, and his client, leads him. The accompanying photo is an example of his work. It is a beautiful example of English rose and scroll, a pattern that Purdey is usually credited for developing.

Photo by Sam Welch

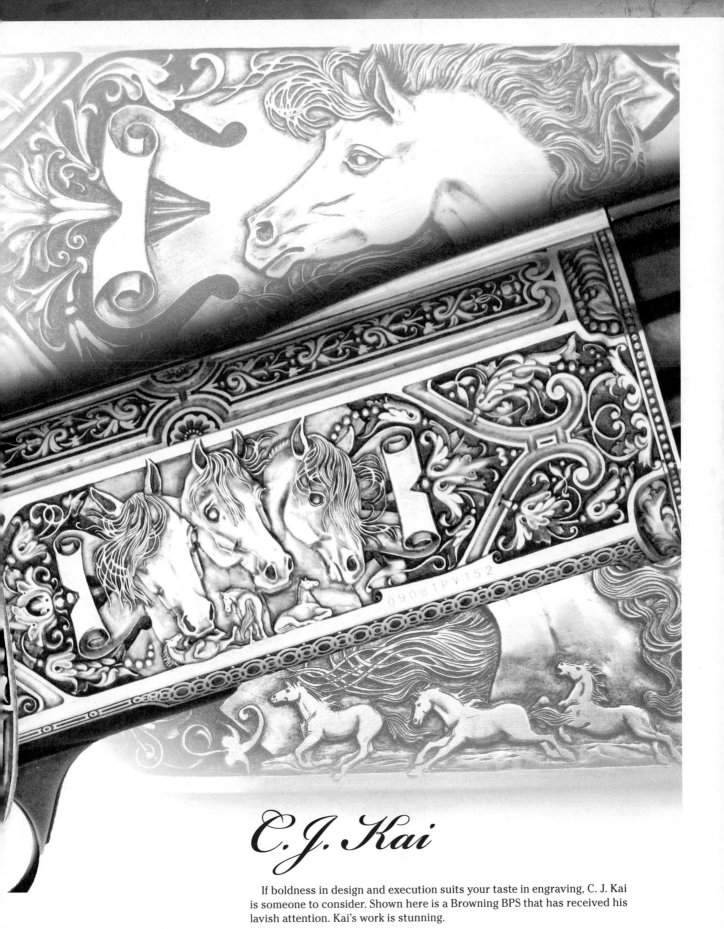

C. J. Kai

If boldness in design and execution suits your taste in engraving, C. J. Kai is someone to consider. Shown here is a Browning BPS that has received his lavish attention. Kai's work is stunning.

Photo by Yi Lin Hu

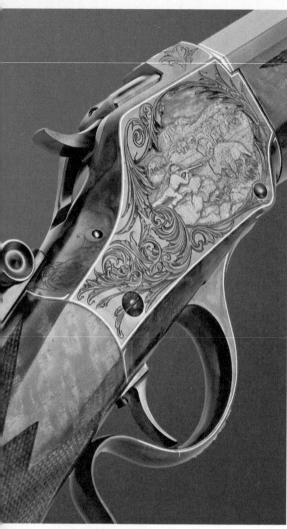

FEGA Auction Project

This Model 1885 Winchester .45-70 features metalwork by Steve Heilmann and a Gary Goudy stock. It was originally crafted for the late Don Allen. The Firearms Engravers Guild of America (FEGA) obtained the rifle and used it as a fund-raising project. In addition to the work done by Heilmann and Goudy, Ron Smith designed the engraving layout, Sam Welch did the gold line work, Mike Dubber the barrel lettering, Jim Blair did the scrollwork and Bob Strosin the screw engraving. Barry Lee Hands then did the deep relief etching on the action sides, which were detailed by Lee Griffiths and Weldon Lister.

Photos by Eric Eggly

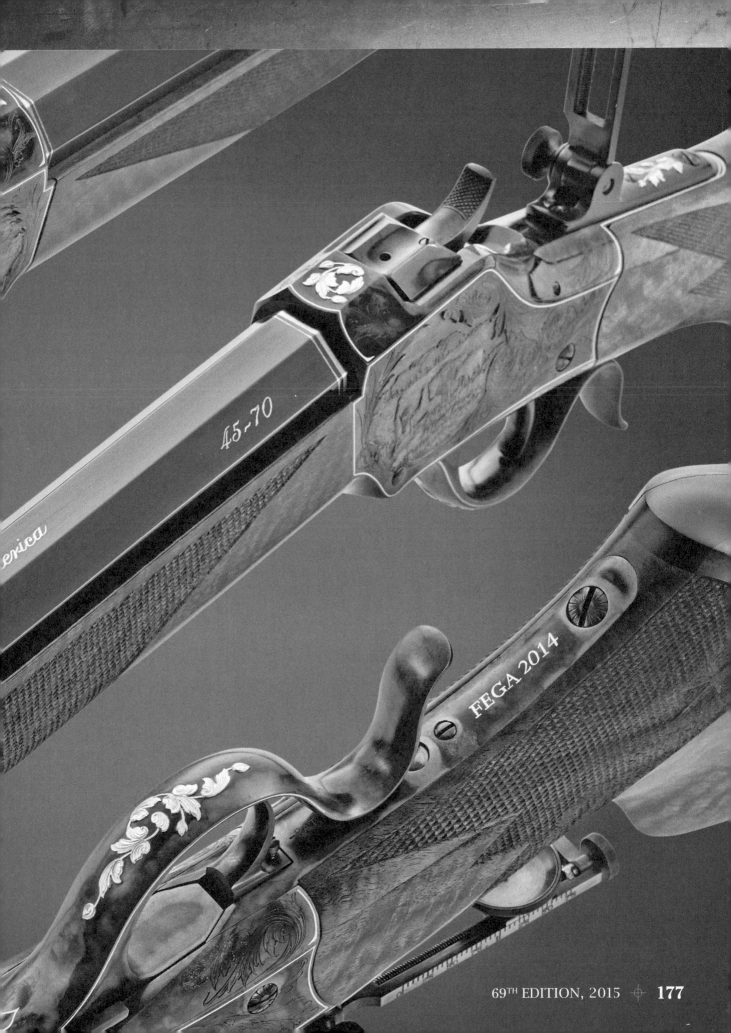

45-70

erica

FEGA 2014

James Anderson

Talk about turning a sow's ear into a silk purse, this one fits the description. Custom gunmaker James Anderson started with a Brno Model 1 from the early '50s and essentially rebuilt it. He reworked and modified the floor metal, moved the trigger back, modified the magazine for trimmer lines, made a new bolt handle and stocked the rifle in a nice piece of California English walnut. According to the owner, it shoots lights out for a .22 RF.

Photos by James Anderson

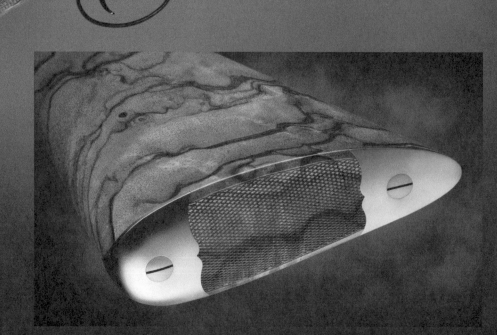

Martin Rabeno

Marty Rabeno is a founding charter member of FEGA and has served as an officer in the organization numerous times since its founding. In 1993, he was chosen by U.S. Repeating Arms Company to engrave what they considered to be the most important Model 94 ever manufactured. This was their Centennial Model 1894-1994, the only rifle ever manufactured by Winchester to have the factory designation "1 of 1." Though he is a master of most any form or style of engraving, he seems to be exceptionally gifted in mid-19th to mid-20th century styles, particularly those from that period of Winchesters. There is one big difference, however—his work is far superior to any I've seen on period originals. Shown here is an example of his stunning work on a Winchester lever gun.

Photos by Sam Welch

Robert Strosin

Bob Strosin has been engraving professionally since 1978. He is a member of the American Custom Gunmakers Guild (ACGG) and a certified Master Engraver in the Firearms Engravers Guild of America (FEGA). He engraves full-time and is mostly self-trained, although he has attended several sessions of the Grand Masters classes at the GRS Training Center that have helped to refine his skills. The engraved and gold inlaid Fox double shotgun shown here is representative of his exceptional talent.

Photos by Sam Welch

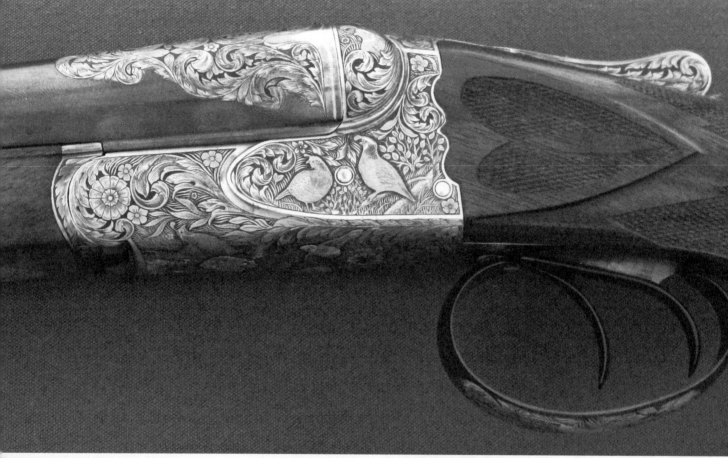

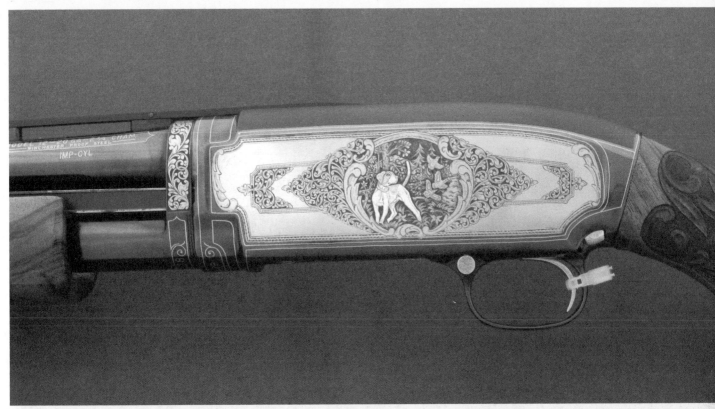

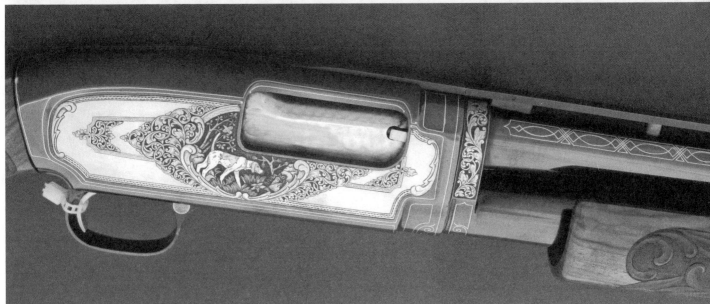

John Barraclough

John has been many things in his life, including a professional engraver. He has also been a jockey, avocado farmer, interior designer and I believe he did a bit of boxing in his youth. Originally from England, he immigrated to the USA in 1951. He became involved with the NRA Summer School Engraving program in Trinidad, Colo., in 1980, and has been teaching the basic and advanced engraving classes at Trinidad and Lassen Colleges each summer since. Shown here is an example of his artistry on a 20-bore Winchester Model 12 shotgun.

Photos by Sam Welch

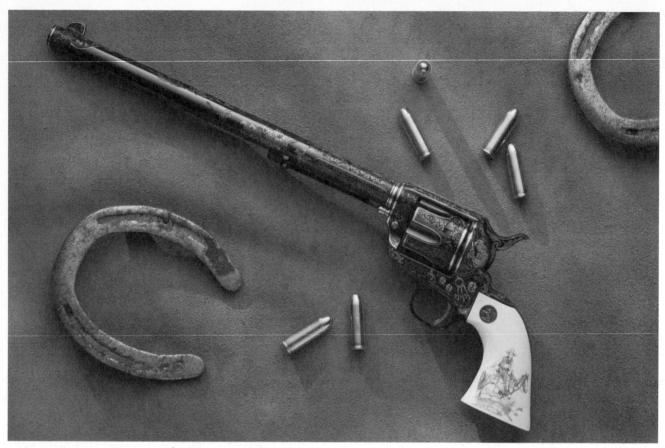

Mike Dubber

"Tex & Patches" Colt. Dubber began this project with a Colt 2nd Generation Model Buntline made in 1957. The "Tex & Patches" theme was developed from images on a painting by artist Frank L. Schoonover. Dan Chesiak made the ivory grips while Dennis Holland color scrimshawed the grips with images from the Schoonover painting. Dubber then engraved the Buntline with profuse gold inlay work throughout. Reliable Electroplating gold plated the trigger, cylinder pin and external screws, and Doug Turnbull did the genuine Colt Royal Blue, timed the cylinder and performed the final assembly.

Photo by Mike Wheatley

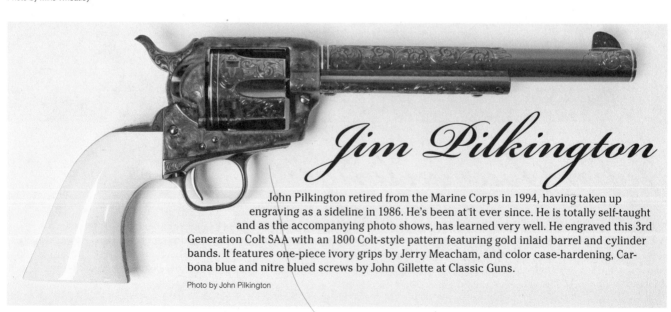

Jim Pilkington

John Pilkington retired from the Marine Corps in 1994, having taken up engraving as a sideline in 1986. He's been at it ever since. He is totally self-taught and as the accompanying photo shows, has learned very well. He engraved this 3rd Generation Colt SAA with an 1800 Colt-style pattern featuring gold inlaid barrel and cylinder bands. It features one-piece ivory grips by Jerry Meacham, and color case-hardening, Carbona blue and nitre blued screws by John Gillette at Classic Guns.

Photo by John Pilkington

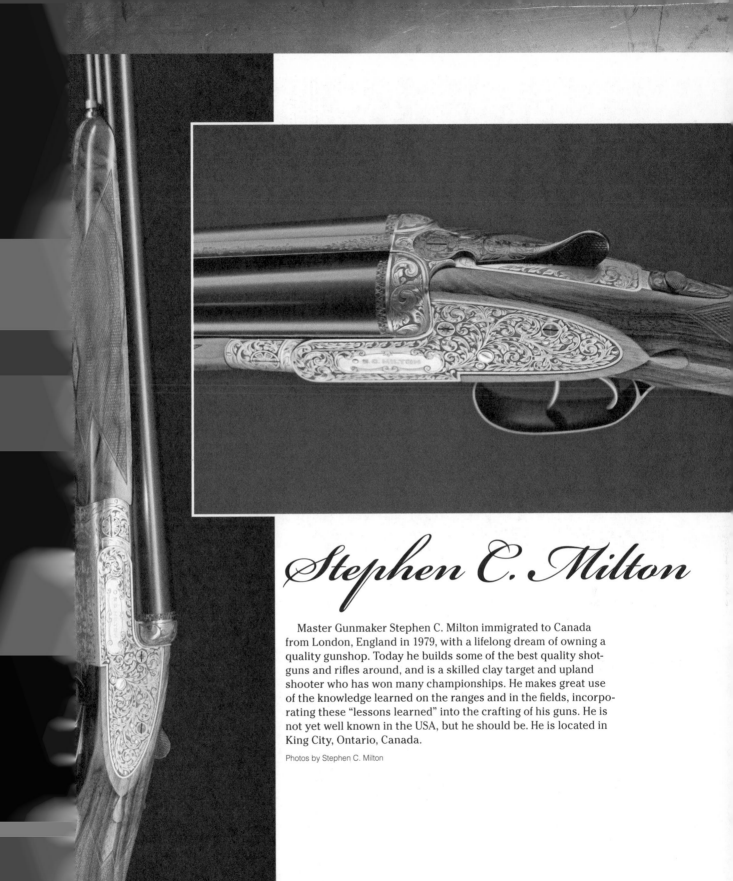

Stephen C. Milton

    Master Gunmaker Stephen C. Milton immigrated to Canada from London, England in 1979, with a lifelong dream of owning a quality gunshop. Today he builds some of the best quality shotguns and rifles around, and is a skilled clay target and upland shooter who has won many championships. He makes great use of the knowledge learned on the ranges and in the fields, incorporating these "lessons learned" into the crafting of his guns. He is not yet well known in the USA, but he should be. He is located in King City, Ontario, Canada.

Photos by Stephen C. Milton

Lee Helgeland

This rifle is about as magnificent as they come. Lee started with a prewar Model 70 .375 H&H action and a stick of simply fantastic California English walnut, and this is the result. He replaced the prewar safety and shroud with one made by Tom Burgess, fashioned the quarter-rib, added a curved, leather-covered recoil pad and fashioned custom bases for stock Leupold rings. Barry Lee Hands performed the engraving.

Photos by Victoria Wojciechowski of Creative Visions

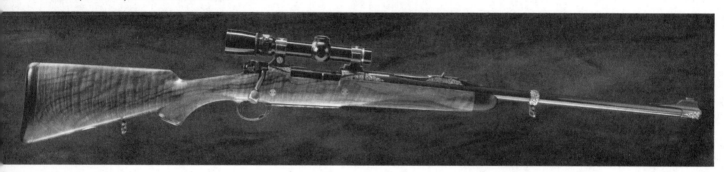

Gary Goudy/Barry Lee Hands

This pair of shotguns was a personal project of Gary Goudy. He acquired the barreled actions from the late Don Allen when he was importing a few shotguns from Italy. He called them Dakota Legends. Like the shoemaker's kid's shoes, the barreled actions lounged in Gary's safe for a bunch of years before he got around to stocking them. It is an almost identical pair of guns, the almost being that one is a 12 bore and the other a 20. Once the guns were stocked, he sent them to Barry Lee Hands for his exquisite floral motif engraving and gold inlay. The results speak for themselves.

Photos by Gary Goudy

Weldon Lister

Weldon is a third-generation engraver. He began apprentice training under his father, Master Engraver W.E. "Bill" Lister, who had apprenticed under his uncle, Austin Lee Lister in the late 1940s. Texas engraver Frank Hendricks, who learned his engraving skills in Germany, also played a role in Weldon's engraving education. The example of his engraving prowess shown here, a Winchester Model 21 shotgun, shows a definite Germanic influence. Weldon also told me he didn't want to do any more oak leaves for a while. Any classic country music fans out there might also remember Bill Lister as a member of the Hank Williams band back in the good old days.

Photos by Weldon Lister

In Praise of the

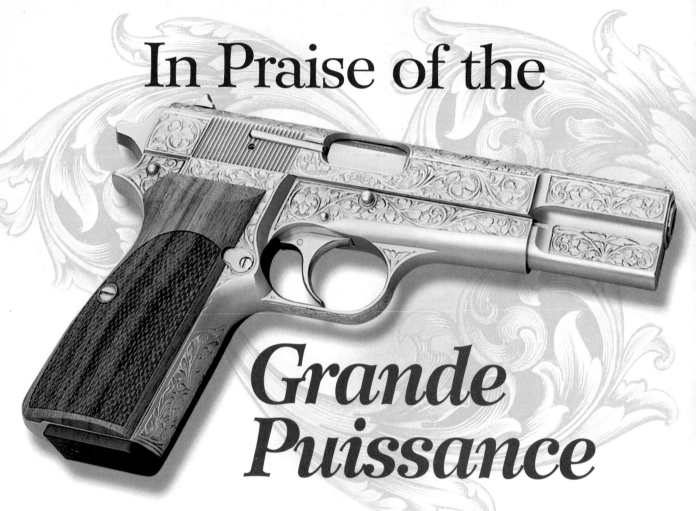

Grande Puissance

From the French for Major Power, Super Power, or High Power, in gun talk *Grande Puissance* is a name of respect for the Browning Hi-Power pistol. **BY Nick Hahn**

John M. Browning, that genius from Utah, is probably responsible for more modern gun designs than any other man to this day. Some of Browning's designs are so enduring that they are still used more than a century later, with little or no modifications whatsoever. The over a century old 1911 pistol is still very much in use today, and the recoil-operated semiautomatic shotgun, the A-5, although discontinued by Browning in 1998, is still manufactured with minor modifications by Franchi of Italy. Talk about enduring designs! Even the Winchester Model 94 lever action that was discontinued for a short while has been resurrected and now is made by Miroku in Japan.

Of all John Browning gun designs, the most recognizable are the 1911 pistol and the A-5 shotgun. The A-5, made by FN in Belgium, was marketed under the Browning label here in America for almost a century, while the Remington Model 11 and other Browning copies were made and sold for almost as long. The legendary 1911 is generally known as a Colt, though several companies made them during World War II. Today it is made by a dizzying number of companies. Still, everyone seems to recognize it as Browning's design.

Browning always tried to improve on all of his initial designs. The A-5 was the first commercially successful semiautomatic shotgun on the market, and it sold like the proverbial hot cakes when it first appeared. But, rather than trying to improve on his

A Hi-Power Renaissance Model, one of the most beautiful pistols found anywhere. From the Custom Shop at the Fabrique Nationale factory in Belgium, this variation is known as the Argent.

original design because of all the talk at the time about limiting the magazine capacities of repeating shotguns, Browning decided to go the other route. He simply worked on a twin-barreled shotgun to eliminate any possibility of having magazine capacity restriction problems later. Thus, the Superposed was born, rather than an improved version of the A-5, he just came out with an over/under shotgun. Some say that had he lived longer, he might have designed an improved version of the A-5. Who knows?

Browning did live long enough to come up with a mechanically improved version of the 1911 pistol. Yes, I know, the 1911 has a cult following that no other handgun has to date. Just read the countless articles that are published each month about the 1911. In fact, look at all the books that have been written about the 1911 just in the past decade.

It seems that every handgun manufacturer of any note has their version of the 1911, except for Beretta and Glock. But, setting aside the incredible popularity of the 1911 today, John Browning did

try to improve on the design when he began work on what was to become the P-35, popularly known as the Browning Hi-Power. Devout 1911 lovers will send a lynch mob after me for saying this, but the Hi-Power is an improvement over the venerable old 1911. Why else would Browning change some of the 1911 features, if it was not for improvement?

The Fabrique Nationale (FN) P-35 became an immediate success in Europe where it was adopted by several countries' military services. During World War II it had the distinction of being used by both the Axis forces and the Allies. The Germans quickly realized that the P-35 was a better handgun than some of their own, and as soon as they occupied Belgium, the FN-made P-35s were assigned to their troops. In the meantime, Canadian engineer John Inglis reverse engineered the P-35 and began to churn out the Canadian versions, which were supplied to the British and Canadian troops as well as over 200,000 to the Nationalist Chinese. By the time World War II was over, just about all of

the western European nations started to adopt the P-35 Hi-Power. In a relatively short time, it developed a reputation for extreme reliability and shootability among most of the countries in the free world. By the 1970s, there were well over 80 countries that adopted the P-35 as their official sidearm.

FN initially sold Belgian-made P-35s to Argentina, but later, at their request set up a factory to produce the pistol in South America. Argentina switched from the Colt 1911 *(Sistema Colt Modelo1927)* to the newer P-35 which they called FM for *Fabrica Militar.* Israel long favored the P-35s and purchased them from FN in large quantities and ultimately produced their own version, which was marketed in America as the Kareem. It was only recently, in the last decade or so, that Israel switched to another handgun. Even Hungary reverse engineered the popular P-35 to produce a cloned version by FEG. So there was no shortage of P-35 fans around the world. In fact to this day, despite a plethora of high-capacity "wonder-guns" available, the P-35 and its

FOR THE FIRST TIME IN AMERICA
Genuine BROWNING Pistols

FOREIGN ARMS

The very first Hi-Power mention in Gun Digest was in the 1955 edition. Note the amazing price tags, $74.50 for standard and $200 for the heavily engraved Renaissance. Today the retail for the standard is over $1,000 and a Renaissance will cost you between $2,500 and $3,500.

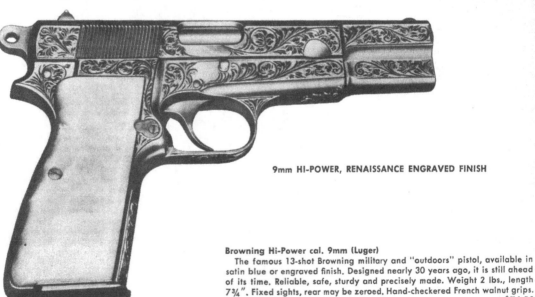

9mm HI-POWER, RENAISSANCE ENGRAVED FINISH

Imported by Browning Arms Co., St. Louis, Mo.

To most of the world, *Browning* is the synonym for "automatic pistol." Basic Browning designs have been imitated in every country—and hardly improved on. The Chinese, attaching mystic value to the word *Browning* often stamped their imitations with BROWNINGS PATENT BROWNINGS PATENT BROWNINGS PATENT, but even magic cannot improve the original excellence of the genuine Browning pistols.

The Hi-Power stands well among the large-caliber pistols of sporting and military circles. The 380 is perhaps the most widely imitated of the pocket arms, and embodies the renowned 3 safeties of Browning construction—grip, thumb, and magazine disconnector safeties. The 25 is the "Baby"—small enough to fit in a change pocket without sagging! For close-in protection, for

Browning Hi-Power cal. 9mm (Luger)
The famous 13-shot Browning military and "outdoors" pistol, available in satin blue or engraved finish. Designed nearly 30 years ago, it is still ahead of its time. Reliable, safe, sturdy and precisely made. Weight 2 lbs., length 7¾". Fixed sights, rear may be zeroed. Hand-checkered French walnut grips.
Price, blue..$74.50
Renaissance engraved, plated, "Nacrolac" pearl grips, price....200.00

The 380 model is a hammerless, 6-shot pocket pistol. Weight 20 oz., length 6 inches. Hard rubber grips. Shown in case (below), price..........$44.50
Renaissance engraved, plated, "Nacrolac" pearl grips, price.....115.00

The 25 (shown to scale in the 3-pistol set, left) is 6-shot, and extremely light and concealable—weight 9.7 oz. Cocking indicator at rear of slide tells whether gun is cocked, an important safety. Thumb and magazine safeties, also. Price with single case....................................$29.95
Renaissance engraved, nickeled, "Nacrolac" pearl grips, price.... 75.00

A lineup of different finishes on Hi-Powers, from the top: A highly engraved chromed Renaissance, a silver chrome model, a high-polish blue model with adjustable sights, and a classic matte blue model with fixed sights and ring hammer.

progeny, clones and copies, still enjoy tremendous popularity outside of the United States.

In the United States, the P-35 Hi-Power appears to be popular only among certain circles. It is considered outmoded and outdated by many who prefer the more modern high-capacity striker-fired guns mostly made with polymer frames. Considering how mistrustful American shooters were of any guns that were made of anything other than steel in the recent past, it is amazing how quickly everyone took to the newer polymer-frame handguns.

The power of the press, or I should say the pen, has no limits. When gun writers started singing the praises of the "newer" guns, naturally everyone wanted one. Obviously, if the new guns with polymer or alloy frames were acceptable to gun writers, it was acceptable to the average gun owner. Shooters are susceptible to trends and fashions just as everyone else, and today's trends and fashions lean heavily on the side of the new type of handguns. But, there are some shooters who appreciate and prefer the classic style of handgun. For those individuals, the P-35, better known as the Hi-Power in America, is still a highly desirable gun – not as a collectible piece, but as a shooter.

The P-35 began its life in a rather roundabout way. Shortly after the end of World War I, the French government approached FN for a new type of handgun, one that would have a 15-round magazine capacity. The original gun was designed as the French model Grande *Rendement* of 1922, which translates into English as the great or large output or capacity. It went through several design changes and at one point even appeared briefly as a 16-round version. However, its final design was a product of Diendonne Joseph Saive, the brilliant FN designer, who refined the gun after Browning's death. It was the last pistol designed by John M. Browning, but it was tweaked and refined by Saive into the gun it is today.

It appeared in its final version in 1935 with a name change to the *Grande Puissance* (great or high power) or GP-35 as it was called then, and later became known simply as the P-35. *Grande Puissance* referred to the large magazine capacity, which in the first models held 14 rounds. Of course the original 1935 version has undergone changes since its first appearance. The first noticeable change was the extractor, which was initially internal, like on the 1911, but changed to the external in 1965-66. In the intervening years there have been other changes here and there, mostly cosmetic. But overall, the pistol stayed the same.

Americans did not see this pistol in any quantity until almost a decade after the end of World War II. Most Americans were first exposed to this gun when they saw the Canadian versions being used by the British, Canadian and other Commonwealth troops. Also, some P-35s were "liberated" from German troops and brought back by returning GIs. But in 1954, Browning Arms Company began importing the Belgian-made P-35 in the civilian version, which was the same gun as the military version, but given a high

polish and blued rather than the plain finish. Browning called this new import the Hi-Power, resurrecting its original name of *Grande Puissance* and simply using the English translation. FN at this point decided to call their civilian guns Hi-Power and even thought of calling the military version the Model 1946 after the war. The civilian version was a straightforward piece with fixed sights, checkered walnut grips, highly polished and beautifully blued, priced at $74.50. From the start, it was also offered in a three-gun cased set: a 9mm Hi-Power with a Model 1955 .380 ACP and a Baby Browning .25 ACP at $148.95. Along with the Hi-Power, Browning began importing the .380 and .25 pistols. Prior to this,

Browning had not been importing any handguns. Also offered were all three guns as Renaissance Models that were highly engraved and beautifully finished versions. The Hi-Power Renaissance Model cost $200, and a three-gun cased set was $390. (Editor's note: Today a mint condition Renaissance set can bring close to $10,000.)

Despite these seemingly bargain prices by today's standards, in 1954 $74.50 was a pretty steep price tag for a single handgun. Colt's 1911s were priced at $64.60 that year and Smith & Wesson's new Model 39 was yet to be priced. Three years later in 1957 Colt raised its price to $74.50 and Smith & Wesson finally put a price tag on their Model 39

A somewhat rare factory alloy-frame lightweight weighing in at one pound and 6.8 ounces, or about 23 ounces.

The current production Mark III model comes with fixed sights and composite grips.

This is the Hi-Power Standard currently being made by FN and marked "Made in Belgium" and "Assembled in Portugal." The latter reference is required by U.S. import regulations.

at $70. Browning very wisely kept the price of their Hi-Power at $74.50, same as the Colt.

The Hi-Power was always one of Browning's best selling guns. Ironically, its biggest competitor has always been the Colt 1911, what you might call its ancestor. Accordingly, the price of the Hi-Power seemed to be always tied to the Colt's. By the 1960s, the Browning Hi-Power was considered the premium auto pistol available to American shooters.

Like most guns, it was not without its faults. The sights, as they came from the factory, were about useless, tiny and for all practical purposes nonfunctional. The safety was an abomination, almost impossible to engage or disengage without shifting your grip so full thumb pressure could be applied. Browning did not change anything for a number of years. An adjustable sight version was introduced with a high-sitting rear sight and an unusually high front, both of which ruined the sleek lines of the otherwise handsome pistol. Those who wanted something better went to the aftermarket for sights and safeties for the Hi-Power, just as 1911 shooters did with their stock

guns. However, Browning finally changed some of the things on the guns to suit the needs of shooters, starting around 25 years or so ago. From about mid- to late-1980s Browning started to supply the Hi-Power with better sights and a sensible ambidextrous safety. For a short period in the 1980s the Hi-Power was available in what is known as the Mark II version, which even had a raised rib like Colt's Gold Cup. Today, all Hi-Powers come with good fixed sights and good safeties. The adjustable-sight version is better, although still not perfect, but the sights are set lower for a more stream-lined appearance.

Throughout almost 70 years there have been a variety of different versions of the Hi-Power. Although the initial imports into the United States were plain fixed-sight models, in Europe this gun had appeared in various guises. Tangent sights were one of the first variations. The tangent sight models actually were meant for the shoulder-stock versions, which converted the pistol into a short carbine, like the Lugers and Mauser broomhandles that were similarly configured. The Canadian Inglis company pro-

duced a majority of its shoulder-stocked versions for the Chinese market.

In the 1970s, both the Belgian FN and Argentine FM models were also made in the shortened Detective versions. These were basically P-35s with shortened slides and barrels, and the frame remained the same, just as with Colt's Commander. However, Browning never imported the shortened versions. Also, in the late 1970s and early 1980s FN produced some alloy-framed lightweight P-35s. These were primarily made for the European police contracts, although some civilian models were also made. The lightweight guns are delightful for those who want a carry piece. A number of these lightweight guns were imported in the mid-1990s by some surplus gun importers. They were mostly police contract guns that were battered from rough handling, but very little actual use. Initially they were sold at bargain prices because they looked rough, but once the importers discovered how rare these pieces were the prices skyrocketed. FN supposedly made only a few thousand of these guns and they were traded in when just about all of the European police departments switched to new models. The alloy-framed P-35 weighs less than the much smaller steel-framed Walther PP.

Unfortunately for American fans of the Hi-Power, as with the shortened Detective versions, Browning never saw fit to import the alloy-framed guns. Incidentally, at the same time the alloy-framed P-35s were being made, FN also made alloy-framed A-5 autoloading shotguns, which they dubbed as Super-lights. These too were never imported by Browning. It appears that Browning had become "gun shy" of alloy-framed guns after the experience with the Double Automatic shotgun, which did not sell all that well in America. Browning's front office was convinced that the American shooters did not like alloy-framed guns. Now, however, it appears that Browning has decided that the American public is ready for alloy-framed guns as its autoloading shotguns all now have alloy frames. However, it is doubtful that FN would make more alloy-framed P-35s. A pity, because it is truly a great gun for carrying, but FN seems to be preoccupied with producing new types of handguns, including polymer-frame versions.

Today, if you want a shortened Hi-Power your best solution is to locate an Argentine Detective model at a reasonable price. The FN versions are much more difficult to locate and would be rather costly. If you are looking for an alloy-frame Hi-Power, buying one of the used alloy-frame police contract imports is probably the best solution, although it will still be pricey and the gun will need some cleaning-up. Aside from that, the only alternative is to go custom. Cylinder & Slide Inc. and some others make Hi-Powers on custom alloy frames, and they also make the shortened (both in length and height) versions, but you will have to pay quite a bit.

For the American market, Browning has tried different types of Hi-Powers. The first attempt to get a piece of the competition market with a Hi-Power was the introduction of the Competition Model in the late 1980s. It was a Hi-Power with a longer 6-inch barrel, rather roughly finished with a "beer can" adjustable rear sight and Pachmayr rubber grips. Nothing special and it was not an especially successful attempt at producing a competition version of the Hi-Power. It was rather surprising that Browning couldn't come up with a better rear sight than the stamped metal version they put on the Competition Model.

Since that time, there have been a number of other versions that Browning tried to market in America. There was the tangent sight model, which they called Capitan and the Practical version that is actually pretty decent. The Practical model comes with a hard chromed frame to give the gun a two-tone effect. It has good fixed sights, ambidextrous safety, and Pachmayr wrap-around grips like the older discontinued Competition Model. The standard finish now seems to be the rougher matt epoxy coating rather than the old high-polish blue. You can still get the high-polish version, but it will cost more. Also, plastic grips became standard while the walnut grips are found only on the high-polished models for a greater price.

Through the years, there have been various different versions, nickel plated, chromed, two-tone, rough finished, epoxy coated, etc. Considering that for the first 45 years or so of its life as the Browning Hi-Power it was only available in the standard blued version or the highly engraved Renaissance model, so it is interesting to see the variety that Browning has tried to offer in the last 25 years or so.

Today, the standard Hi-Power is more or less what is called the Mk III version with good fixed sights, ambidextrous safety, plastic grips and black matte epoxy finish. Next in line would be a gun configured the same way, but with high-polish blue and walnut grips, followed by the more expensive Standard model, which would be the one with adjustable sights. The older Practical model would have fit somewhere in between the Mk III and Standard versions. Today's Hi-Powers are available in .40 S&W as well as 9mm.

Sometime around the mid 1970s FN set up a plant in Portugal and started to assemble some of its guns there with parts that were made in Belgium. I believe the first gun to go through this process was the then new shotgun, the B-2000. I may be wrong, but at least with the guns that were found in gun stores at the time, the B-2000s were the first ones to appear with the stamping of "Made in Belgium and Assembled in Portugal."

Shortly, the Hi-Powers began to show this marking on the right side of the slide. There are those who insist that guns marked as "Made in Belgium" only are superior to those that are marked "Assembled in Portugal." It seems to these folks the addition of the wording, "Assembled in Portugal" somehow degrades the quality of the gun. If truth be known, just about all of the Belgian FN-made guns, with the exception of the Custom Shop guns such as the Superposed, are now assembled in Portugal.

FN guns sold in Europe and elsewhere don't have the "Assembled in Portugal" markings that appear on guns sold in the United States. That is because U.S.

An adjustable-sight model with high-polish blue finish and walnut grips, and a fixed-sight model with matte blue finish, ring hammer and composite grips.

import laws require that the firearm be marked as to where it was made and assembled. In Europe many guns are imported in the white from one country and assembled in another, and simply marked as being made wherever the final finishing took place. A gun that was assembled with parts that were made and finished in one country but assembled in another would still be marked only as being made where the parts were made and finished. If the finishing was done in another country, then the gun would more than likely be marked as made where the finishing was done!

Such is the case with many English shotguns today, which are imported in white from Italy and finished and assembled in England, and are marked as being made in England. So the P-35s, although assembled in Portugal like the ones sold as Hi-Powers in America, are only marked as being made in Belgium if they are for sale in the rest of the world. Here in America they have to be stamped with the additional wording because of our laws.

If you want a Hi-Power for shooting rather than collecting, buy the one that is marked "Assembled in Portugal," especially if it is one of the newer guns built on the Mk III frame with good sights and an ambidextrous safety. It will cost less than the one marked "Made in Belgium" only, unless it is a European-market gun, but it will be just as serviceable a gun and as far as quality is concerned, there will be no difference between the two.

There is also much talk among those who own and shoot Hi-Powers about the difference in quality of frames that were made before the appearance of newer versions like the Mk III. The guns that were made before the appearance of the newer versions are referred to as having forged frames, not cast, like the newer frames. I don't know if the forged frame is superior or not, but the newer frame was developed to better withstand the higher pressures of the .40 S&W cartridge, at least according to Browning. So I don't quite follow the reasoning that the older forged frames are better. I believe it has more to do with the perception that many have about forged versus cast frames, just as there was for a long time a bias against alloy-frame guns, be they pistols or shotguns.

As mentioned earlier, there were basically three things that were negative about the Hi-Power in the past: terrible sights, impossible safety and hard trigger pull. The trigger pull could usually be corrected by removing the magazine safety, a useless device in the opinion of many. The sights and safety had to go for an aftermarket fix. But once these three features were corrected, it was a wonderful pistol. The current Hi-Power comes with good fixed sights and an extended ambidextrous safety. It essentially comes out of the box with only one weakness, the hard trigger pull, which can be corrected most of the time with the simple removal of magazine safety. So in many respects today's Hi-Power is a much better gun straight out of the box than the older version, as far as shoot-ability is concerned.

I am not a collector nor am I an expert on Hi-Powers. I am just a shooter and admirer of this pistol. I have owned and shot these guns for more than 40 years, and have admired them ever since seeing and handling one for the first time in the mid-1960s. I came into possession of my first Hi-Power in 1970 when my brother Jim gave me one. It was the old ring-hammer T-series gun, beautifully finished with high-polished blue. Jim had installed adjustable Micro sights on the gun. This was before Micro started mounting the sights lower. The old target sights were somewhat awkward looking and were made for bull's-eye shooting. It was a nice gun, shot very well, but somewhere along the line I traded it off for something else. A few years later I got heavily into IPSC, shooting Colt .45 ACP 1911s, but then decided to try a 9mm Hi-Power. I got another Hi-Power, sent the slide off to Micro Gun Works and had their adjustable sight mounted low and put on an extended safety. The gun shot beautifully.

None of my Hi-Powers, starting with the first one in 1970, ever jammed or gave me any mechanical trouble. I have owned several since that first one, including the current crop. None have malfunctioned, not once. I can't say the same thing for the Colt 1911s that I have owned and shot.

Like the 1911, the Hi-Power was developed as a battle pistol. As such, it had to be robust, reliable and easy to handle. It is all of those things and more. It has one of the best ergonomically designed grips of any handgun, single or double stack. Most double-stack handguns feel awkward or "fat." The Beretta Model 92/M9 is a great battle pistol, but its grip is too fat even for someone with large hands. The Hi-Power somehow manages to have a grip that feels just right.

As with all mechanical things, it too can break down and I am sure there are those who have experienced problems with this gun. No doubt there are broken down Hi-Powers found in military armories and gunsmith shops around the world. But the vast majority of those guns that ended up in that condition are due to neglect or improper and excessive use and lack of care. Any gun if abused and not properly cared for will break. You'd be amazed how many 1911s with their legendary durability ended up in junk piles of armories or gunsmith shop trash bins.

For me, the Hi-Power is by far one of the most reliable, if not the most reliable auto pistol that I have ever owned or shot. There are those who say that the Hi-Power is not durable, that it cannot take a pounding. I find that to be somewhat confusing. Why in the world would all of those nations that adopted the Hi-Power for their military and police use this gun if it were not durable? There are also those who say that +P ammo should never be used in a Hi-Power. Most European ammunition is loaded at or close to +P level, and their militaries do not differentiate between the hot ammo that is used for submachine guns and ammo that is used for pistols, so the Hi-Powers used by those nations are shot with the hot ammo. Unless the critics of Hi-Powers have put their guns through torture tests with excessive loads, or have shot thousands upon thousands of +P-type ammo through the gun, I can't think of how they came up with their conclusions. Any gun, even when listed as safe for use with +P ammo, will show metal fatigue and break down if excessively used. Normal use should not affect such guns negatively.

I shot a lot of German GECO 9mm hardball ammunition when I used a Hi-Power in IPSC. The ammo was marked *"maschinepistole patronen"* or machine-pistol (submachine gun) cartridges. My Hi-Power did not fall apart and was as good as new after thousands of rounds of hot ammo. I imagine if I continued to shoot hot ammo in that gun for years, it would have developed wear and problems. But for normal use, it was just fine.

For those who wish to shoot hot ammo in a Hi-Power, a simple precautionary step will ensure that the gun won't develop excessive wear and possibly break down. Replace the recoil spring with a heavier spring. A heavier spring will pre-

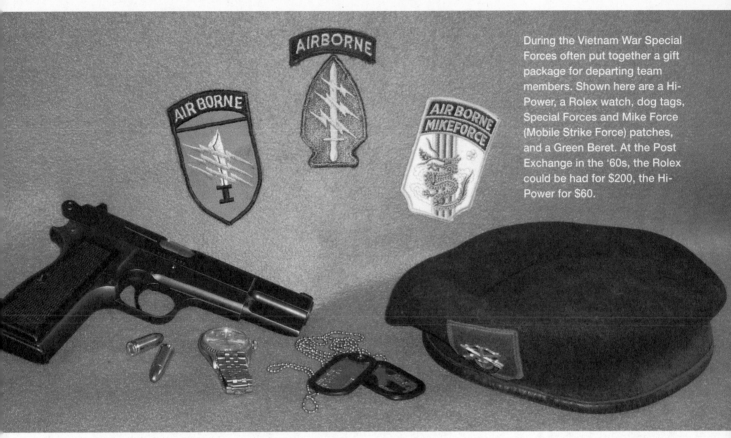

During the Vietnam War Special Forces often put together a gift package for departing team members. Shown here are a Hi-Power, a Rolex watch, dog tags, Special Forces and Mike Force (Mobile Strike Force) patches, and a Green Beret. At the Post Exchange in the '60s, the Rolex could be had for $200, the Hi-Power for $60.

vent the slide from battering excessively and cracking or causing other problems. Many users of Colt Gold Cups in IPSC did the same thing. They replaced the recoil spring with a heavier one if they planned to use hot loads. Those who didn't take these precautions developed problems, whether they were shooting Colt's Gold Cups or Hi-Powers. Change the recoil spring if you are going to use heavy loads. It is the same as shifting the friction ring on the A-5 before shooting heavier shotshell loads.

Unfortunately, the Hi-Power will never gain the popularity that it deserves among American shooters. The followers of Jeff Cooper's school may cling to their single-action auto pistols, but they will insist that nothing but a .45 ACP will do for a defensive round. Those who accept the 9mm as a defensive round by and large want double actions, preferably with polymer frames.

There was a time, however, when the Hi-Power was considered to be the ultimate battle pistol in some circles. Back in the 1960s and early 1970s, before the handgun market was saturated with high-capacity double-action "wonder guns," the Hi-Power was considered to be the supreme combat handgun by some. At the time when the war in Vietnam raged and the U.S. Army Special Forces

was deeply involved in Southeast Asia, it was a popular practice with some Special Forces operational teams to present a Browning Hi-Power and a Rolex watch to departing team members. These items were purchased from military exchanges (BXs/PXs) in Saigon or other places that had large exchanges, so they were purchased tax free and cost about 1/3 less than the stateside retail prices.

Just to give you an idea, at the peak of Special Forces involvement in Vietnam in 1968, the Browning Hi-Power retailed stateside for $104.50, at the military exchanges you could pick one up for around $60. The Rolex watch cost much more, around $200, but with everyone on the team chipping in the cost was easily covered. Each member contributed around $20 to purchase the gun and the watch. There was another high-capacity double-action handgun available at the time, the Smith & Wesson Model 59, which was used by some Navy SEAL teams. But it was the Browning Hi-Power that everyone lusted after, at least in the Army Special Forces.

The standard issue sidearm was the .45 ACP 1911 during the Vietnam era. Members of conventional units in the Army, Navy, Marines or Air Force used handguns that were issued, whether they were .45 ACP 1911s or .38 Special S&W re-

volvers. The special operations units, like the Navy SEALs or Army Special Forces could and did use different handguns (I am not sure about Marine Force Recon). In the Army Special Forces everyone was issued a sidearm, so everyone carried a handgun. Also, unlike in conventional units, Army Special Forces allowed the use of personal handguns that were not issued. Some preferred to carry personal handguns instead of the issue 1911s. Given a choice, I can't think of a single person in my unit who would not have selected a Browning Hi-Power if it were available. But I can only say this for my unit, not for the Navy, Marines, Air Force, or other Army units for that matter.

Today, some half a century later, and with an incredible variety of excellent handguns available, the Hi-Power takes a back seat to others as a first choice for the Army Special Forces soldiers. Although the Beretta M9 is the issue weapon and carried by most, for those who prefer personal handguns the Glocks appear to be the top choices. In fact, the standard issue handgun for Special Operations Detachment Delta now is the Glock 17. But the Browning Hi-Power has not been forgotten. There are still some who consider it to be the premier battle pistol.

THE HEYM-MARTINI ODYSSEY

A LONG AND WINDING ROAD TO A GREAT RIFLE

A full-length view of a Heym-Martini rifle, this one chambered for the .416 Rigby cartridge. The rifle, as pictured, weighs just less than 11 pounds including the scope and mounts. The super dense stick of European walnut used for the stock also adds a bit of weight. Also shown is a rare collector's item, a Heym custom knife. This is the only one the author has ever seen.

BY **Tom Turpin**

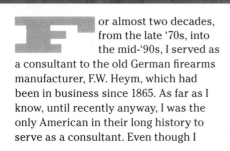

or almost two decades, from the late '70s, into the mid-'90s, I served as a consultant to the old German firearms manufacturer, F.W. Heym, which had been in business since 1865. As far as I know, until recently anyway, I was the only American in their long history to serve as a consultant. Even though I previously knew of their existence, I was first personally introduced to the company in 1975.

Rolf Heym, the last of the Heym sons running the family-owned company, passed away unexpectedly in 1972, leaving his widow to manage the company. She knew nothing of firearms and their manufacture so she promoted the long-time Technical Director of the company to the position of Geschäftsführer, or Managing Director.

While he had the best interests of the company at heart and he really tried to operate the company profitably, he did not have the managerial experience and training to manage it efficiently. Finally, Frau Heym began a search for a trained

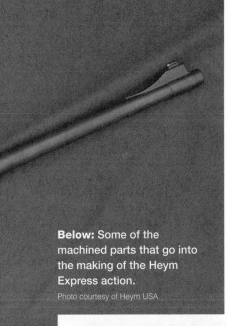

Below: Some of the machined parts that go into the making of the Heym Express action.

Photo courtesy of Heym USA.

Above: The Heym crew at the factory in Germany responsible for turning out the production Heym-Martini rifles. Up front holding the rifle is the owner of Heym, Mr. Thomas Volkmann. On the left is Mr. Chris Sells of Heym USA, who imports and markets the rifles in the U.S., and is also responsible for much of the design work on rifles destined for the U.S. market.

Photo courtesy of Heym USA.

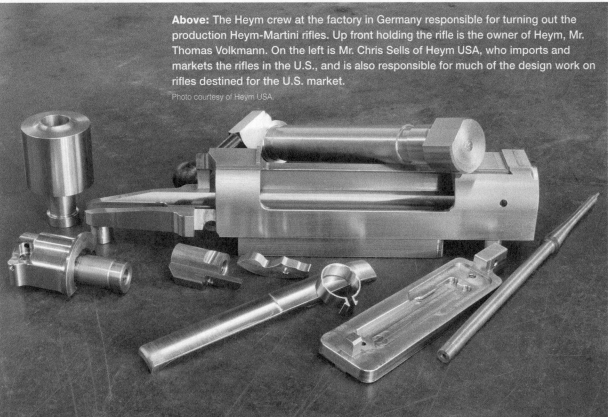

and experienced manager. She found one running a farm implement manufacturing facility. He accepted her offer and moved to Münnerstadt. His name was Peter Bang, an apropos name for the managing director of a firearms factory, don't you think?

Herr Bang was a university-trained management expert, with the German equivalent of an MBA degree. He knew accounting, taxation, human resources, negotiations and all the other management skills required to operate a successful manufacturing business. What he did not know anything about was the product his company was producing. The previous technical director promoted to managing director knew all about the product and making it, but had no management skills. Frau Heym appointed them as co-managing directors, but there was no doubt as to which held the trump card. Herr Bang was fully in charge, but relied heavily on the technical expertise of Herr Horst Rödder in producing the products.

A close-up view of the Heym Express action, around which the Heym-Martini rifle is fabricated. This production rifle features the "new" three-position safety and flange design. The bridges on the action are machined to accept Talley scope rings and all rifles are fitted with a stock thru-bolt behind the recoil lug. This particular rifle has a Trijicon 1.25-4x24 AccuPoint scope mounted in Talley quick-detachable scope rings, a pretty perfect combination for a dangerous-game rifle.

Heym previously had some success in marketing its firearms in the United States, mostly in the years between World War I and World War II, but very few were sold under the Heym name since they resumed making firearms after WWII. One of Herr Bang's goals with the company was to reintroduce the Heym name and products into the U.S. marketplace. That's where I came into the picture. Herr Rödder was very knowledgeable about the European clientele, but knew nothing of the American hunting methods or firearms preferences. He proved to be, inadvertently I think, a thorn in my side in doing my job. He had two sayings, and he always voiced one or the other when we were trying to accomplish something. They were, "wir haben nie so gemacht," or, "wir haben immer so gemacht." The translation being: we have never made it that way, or, we have

always made it that way. Adaptability was not Herr Rödder's strong suit.

I report this not to be critical of the man as he was doing what he thought best for the company, but he had no experience in this new (for him) market. Fortunately, Peter was much more compromising in his thinking.

How I got the job itself is an interesting story. A terrific German friend of mine was renowned Gravurmeister (Master Engraver) Erich Boessler. Erich had followed Heym across the east/west border from Suhl, sneaking over in the dead of night. Heym made it across in 1945, Erich a few years later. He worked for Heym as an in-house engraver for a period of time before striking out on his own. Up until his passing in the late 1990s, he still did a few special projects annually for Heym.

I returned to Germany in 1975 for a tour of duty with the U.S. Army, having

known Erich from a previous tour when we had met and become friends. As soon as I got my household under control, my kids in school, etc., I scheduled a visit with Erich and his lovely wife Herta. Unknown to me, Erich met with Peter and scheduled me for a 30-minute visit with Peter in his office at Heym. Erich knew what Peter wanted to accomplish with the U.S. market, and felt that I could assist. To make a long story short, my scheduled 30-minute meeting lasted over five hours. After the meeting Peter asked for my help.

The end result was my acceptance of the responsibility for redesigning the existing line of appropriate Heym firearms to be more acceptable to American shooters and hunters, and to come up with new models for the same purpose. I also agreed to work two shows each year in the U.S. – my real job permitting – the SHOT Show and the

Safari Club International Convention. That started in 1979.

My first task was to redesign the SR-20 line of bolt-action rifles from their distinctly Teutonic appearance—a real turnoff for most American shooters—into a more classic and acceptable styling for the U.S. market. The SR-20 was the biggest seller in the Heym inventory and was the closest thing they made to a mass-produced product. Even so, much handwork was involved in each and every rifle.

The rifle was, in essence, a modified and refined Mauser 2000, 3000 and 4000 series of rifles, previously marketed in the U.S. under the name of Mauser-Bauer. None of those rifles ever saw Oberndorf. All were crafted in Münnerstadt by Heym for Mauser. They were also

available at an extra cost in left-hand models. Few rifles were available for the southpaw at the time, which made it a big selling factor for Mauser-Bauer and later for Heym's SR-20.

The other Heym models available were mostly all various forms of combination guns, and did include a couple models of O/U double rifles. The largest cartridge chambered in the double rifle was the 9.3x74R, similar to the .375 H&H flanged, but not quite as potent. My recommendation was to leave those models alone. In my view there was such an extremely limited market for them in the U.S. that it didn't justify redesigning them. I thought it much smarter to spend the very limited design and development funds on totally new products specifically for the American market.

About the same time as all this was going on, Jim Bell started Brass Extrusion Laboratories Ltd. (B.E.L.L.) and began offering brass cases and loaded ammunition for the old British Nitro Express cartridges. This development did two things: it resurrected the market for old English and other continental double rifles that had been gathering dust in a closet somewhere, and it created an entirely new market for the production of a modern manufactured double rifle using vastly improved materials. When I learned of the ammo development, I informed Peter and we started the wheels rolling to produce a bigbore, side-by-side double rifle.

It took awhile, but the result was the Heym Model 88-B Safari, a very successful addition to the Heym line, and

This is the prototype rifle crafted by Ralf Martini using a Heym Express action and Heym hammer-forged barrel. The rifle was sent to the Heym factory in Germany and used to create the factory production rifles. The prototype is chambered for the .375 H&H Magnum cartridge. The three-position safety and shroud were changed on the factory production rifles.

This Heym-Martini made a considerable splash at my local range. With a nearby military base, along with scads of Border Patrol Agents due to our close proximity to the U.S./Mexican border, most of the rifles and handguns showing up on the range were military/LE types. To say that this one stood out in the crowd is an understatement.

the best-known Heym product in the USA today. The market is stronger these days for that rifle than it has ever been.

From the very beginning I wanted a Heym large-caliber express rifle, with the action basically copied from the original magnum version of the Mauser Model 98 action. I discussed the concept early on with Peter, and while he agreed in principle, and agreed to devote some effort to the project when market conditions permitted, he placed it on the back burner.

Not long thereafter, Peter's contract came up for renewal. In the intervening years Frau Heym had remarried and her new husband, who also knew nothing about manufacturing firearms, was increasingly getting involved in the decision making within the plant. Peter was the kind of guy that, as Managing Director, he was either in charge, or he was out. There was no in-between. He later told me that it took but five minutes to agree on his compensation package, the usual obstacle in contract negotiations, but they could not agree on the management of the activities of the factory. He resigned. When he

left, nothing had been done on the new Mauser express rifle clone project, much to my disappointment.

After a few months and one replacement, in and out the door quickly, a new Managing Director, Horst Reinold, took the reins. Not long after that the Technical Director, Horst Rödder, retired. His replacement was a young büchsenmachermeister (master gun maker), Franz Würger. The new regime kept me onboard as a consultant. As it turned out, Horst was a bit more accommodating to the idea of the "new" Mauser project. That was music to my ears.

In my collection of rifles was an original John Rigby rifle that was built around a magnum Mauser square-bridge action and once had belonged to the writer Jack Lott. It featured typical British styling that, with a few exceptions, I wanted to emulate in a Heym model. After making arrangements with Heym to do the import paperwork and pick up my rifle from the German authorities at the Frankfurt airport, my Rigby and I took a plane ride to Germany. I needed a schnitzel fix anyway, and this provided

a good justification to get one. Traveling with a firearm, while not easy, was much simpler in those pre-TSA/9-11 days. There were no problems encountered.

It took several days at the factory to go over all the specifications for the new model. The technical guys took all the measurements they needed from my rifle, and we discussed the styling in great detail. When I left the plant on my way back home my expectation was to see pretty much a modern clone of my Rigby within about six to eight months, just in time for the show season. Alas, I failed to take into account the German fascination with engineering, often at the expense of everything else, and their international reputation for inflexibility. Having worked with them for a long time and also having been married to one for quite a long time, though no longer, I should have known better. But, I've never been accused of being a quick learner!

Several months later, just a few weeks before the SHOT Show where we intended to introduce the Heym Express rifle to the U.S. market, I received a package of photos in the mail from the old country.

With the anticipation of an expectant father in the waiting room, I tore open the package for my first look. I can't ever remember being more disappointed and disillusioned than I was that day.

The rifle in the photos bore absolutely no resemblance to my Rigby – none, zero, nada! It was quite obvious that Heym had paid absolutely no attention to my requests, and I might as well have stayed home and saved the travel costs. The only good thing resulting from the trip was my schnitzel fix was alleviated. I almost resigned on the spot and sent off a fax to Horst that I'm sure he had to handle with asbestos gloves.

When I had the opportunity to see the first rifle, and had cooled down a bit and could look it over somewhat objectively, the Heym guys actually did a pretty good job on the metalwork. The action was clearly a Mauser derivative. They changed the safety and shroud for some reason known only to the Teutons, but I could live with it temporarily. The action itself was fine, in fact superb. The real problem was with the bottom metal and the stock design.

Franz Würger came up with a real lulu of a bottom metal design. Instead of bedding the stock traditionally with the large integral recoil lug under the front receiver ring, a very successful and foolproof design, Franz decided to bed the action recoil lug into the bottom metal unit. He then put two smaller recoil shoulders in the bottom metal unit, one on either side of the magazine box, which he bedded into the pistol grip area of the stock. His reasoning—I haven't the foggiest notion.

In order to provide sufficient strength in the stock to accommodate the bedding system it had to be bigger, thicker and heavier. Compared to my Rigby, the supposed model for the rifle, the Express looked and handled like a sledgehammer. I tried to convince the Heym management to go back to the drawing board with the rifle, but to no avail. Not long afterward the company went through substantial turmoil, resulting in my leaving the company. They went through several ownership changes and finally declared bankruptcy.

Fast-forward a couple years. Heym, or what was left of it, was acquired by a new owner, downsized substantially, moved from the old plant in Münnerstadt to a brand new facility in Gleichamberg, not far from where the old company had started in 1865, and pretty much started all over again as a leaner and meaner company. The new owner, Thomas Volkmann, eventually found a new importer for the U.S. market in Chris Sells, who added Heym USA to his existing Double Gun Imports business. As the name of his company implies, Chris was particularly interested in the Heym double rifle production.

Working together, Chris and Thomas built the U.S. operation into a very successful concern with the 88B Safari double rifle as the backbone of the sales. It took a few years to get all the wrinkles ironed out, and during that time most all the emphasis was on the double. Chris convinced Heym to make a number of subtle, but very desirable changes to the 88B.

Once calm seas arrived though, metaphorically speaking, and things were functioning as they should, Chris started looking at new product ideas. He resurrected my old idea from years before, to produce a Heym bigbore express-type rifle chambered for dangerous-game cartridges. He started with the existing, but mostly dormant action that Heym had already developed.

Ralf Martini, a German-born gunmaker working in Canada, crafted very stylish custom express rifles that were just what

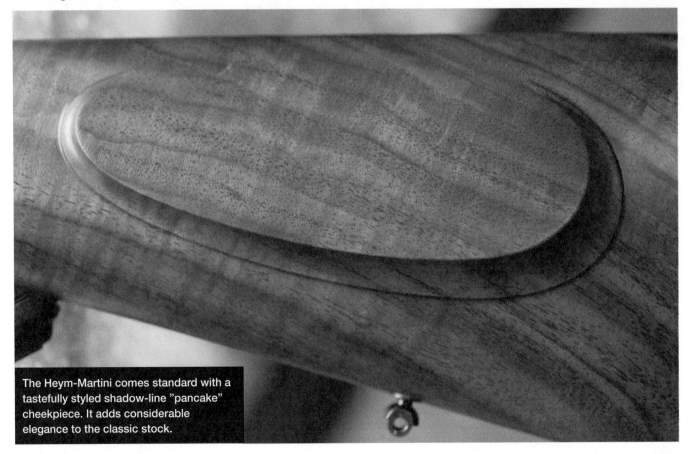

The Heym-Martini comes standard with a tastefully styled shadow-line "pancake" cheekpiece. It adds considerable elegance to the classic stock.

Jeff Turpin putting this Heym-Martini .416 Rigby to the test at the range. We found it to be very accurate with groups running around 3/4 inch. We usually shot groups with two of the three holes touching, but we couldn't get all three together. Because of the cost and availability of ammo we didn't do exhaustive shooting of the rifle. Still, we shot it enough to know this rifle is ready for Africa.

Shown here is a pretty typical three-shot group fired at 100 yards with the Heym-Martini. While this group is excellent, measuring well under MOA, it could have been much better had the shooter not flubbed the second shot slightly. Even so, .774 inch center-to-center ain't bad!

Heym-Martini Exp
416 Rigby
Federal Safari Factory
Ammo 400 Gr.
.774" C to C

Chris had in mind for Heym. Chris got an action from Heym and sent it to Ralf with instructions to build a rifle around it. Ralf did, and the Heym-Martini Express rifle was born. At long last, my dreams of many years earlier had come to pass. When the prototype was completed Chris sent it to me to play with for a short while. Chambered for the .375 H&H, it had everything that I had asked for on my trip to Germany with my Rigby years before, and then some. It felt like old home week.

I did not write about the prototype. I'd been burned a time or two in the past, writing about a prototype that differed considerably from the production version when it finally came out. I wanted a production rifle, made in the Heym plant in Germany by Heym employees, and not the prototype that Ralf had handcrafted in his shop in Canada. I wanted to see the production rifle before getting too enthused. It was well worth the wait.

Chris finally sent me a production rifle to play with. It was a long time coming, as he couldn't keep one long enough. As soon as he got one in from the plant in Germany it went out immediately into the hands of a customer, which of course, was great news for Chris. He finally got one long enough to send to me for a short while. Happily, it was chambered for the .416 Rigby, a proper cartridge for such a rifle. The rifle came to me fitted with an excellent Trijicon scope. Wisely, the double square bridges on the production rifle were milled to accept Talley scope rings. That's a great move since the ring bases are integral with the action steel and there are no base screws to come loose under fairly stiff recoil.

The prototype rifle had a safety on the bolt shroud as it should, and it was a three-position safety. However, it was one of Heym manufacture from years

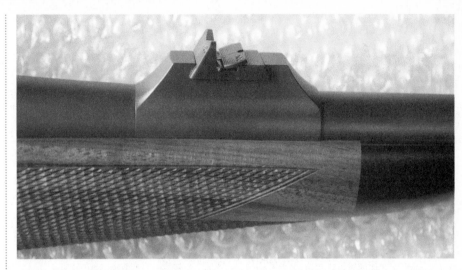

Each Heym-Martini comes standard fitted with a barrelband rear sight base, and one standing and one folding leaf express sight.

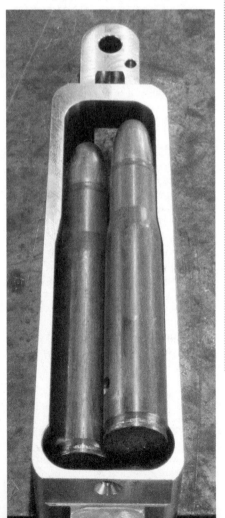

The Heym-Martini is available in four calibers: .375 H&H, .404 Jeffery, .416 Rigby and the .458 Lott. The magazine box for each rifle is machined caliber specific.

Photo courtesy of Heym USA.

back and not exactly eye pleasing. Neither was the shape of the shroud. It was more streamlined in shape, and looked nothing like a Mauser shroud should look. Fortunately, the safety and shroud were changed to a more acceptable form on the production rifle.

I had on hand some Federal .416 Rigby factory ammo, but had no time to order in an assortment of ammunition from different manufacturers for my testing. Both Norma and Hornady, and perhaps another two, also load excellent factory ammo for the Rigby. Typical factory ballistics, regardless of the manufacturer, are a 400-grain bullet at 2,400 feet per second. That is plenty for anything short of a T-Rex or M1 Abrams tank.

The test rifle I received was stocked with a nice dense piece of European walnut with perfect grain flow for such a rifle. It made it an attractive stock, not flashy or overbearing, and pretty ideal for the rifle. It is a fairly heavy rifle weighing around 11 pounds complete with scope and mounts. The .416 Rigby is not as ferocious in recoil as some cartridges, but one certainly knows that it didn't misfire when it goes off. The added weight makes it pleasurable to spend time with at the range, on and off the bench.

It has been my experience that large-bore rifles tend to be very accurate. This Heym .416 is no exception. My son Jeff

and I took it to the range and put a few rounds through it. We, by no means, conducted an exhaustive range session with it, for a number of reasons. That the ammo runs a bit short of about 10 bucks per shot was one reason. Another is getting hammered from the bench is not the most pleasant way to spend an afternoon. Still, we shot it enough to know that at 100 yards it is a sub-MOA capable rifle. Our best group measured .774 inch, with two of the three holes touching. The shot that landed out of the group was most likely a result of the shooter and not the rifle or ammo.

The Heym-Martini Express is available in four chamberings: .375 H&H, .404 Jeffery, .416 Rigby and .458 Lott. Considering the number of bigbore cartridges out there that might seem a bit miserly. However, Heym does it right (this time) and the magazine box in each rifle is machined caliber specific. That is, each chambering has it's own box that will fit no other cartridge. Each chambering will hold four cartridges in the magazine, plus of course, one in the chamber. As a matter of practicality they settled on four chamberings that should, for most shooters anyways, take care of anything. It also comes with a 24-inch hammer-forged barrel, barrelband front sight ramp and front sling swivel stud, express sights and steel grip cap.

It took a lot of time and many changes, and the invaluable help of Chris Sells to finally get what I set out to achieve those many years ago. My only regret is that we were unable to get it right the first time around.

BY Mike Thomas

SNUBNOSE SPECIALS

A Retired Detective Reflects On The Classic .38 Snubbies From Colt And Smith & Wesson.

This article was developed for active enthusiasts interested in various aspects of the small-frame, 2-inch barrel .38 Special revolvers manufactured for decades by Colt and Smith & Wesson. It is not a formal discourse for collectors; such aspects as every variation, series, obscurities, sight blade widths and correct screws won't be touched upon here. That's best left to those versed in such particulars.

The Colt snubnose .38 Special six-shot cylinder (left) at 1.4 inches in diameter is only about .1 inch larger than the cylinder of the five-shot Chiefs Special.

No introduction is necessary for the .38 Smith & Wesson Special cartridge that had already gained status and popularity long before Colt introduced the Detective Special in 1927. Over the years, this revolver and its later Cobra variant have been chambered for "punier" cartridges. The availability of some of these chamberings continued well past the mid-twentieth century, but the more powerful .38 Special versions were preferred by most buyers of snubnosed guns.

The original Colt Detective Special was basically a Police Positive Special with a 2-inch barrel. It was to be a handgun that had virtually no competition for a long while. Even after the competition's arrival, the Detective Special continued to retain a healthy position in the market, at least for a time.

Since their inception, snubnose revolvers have had great appeal to many who carry a concealed handgun on their person as a matter of daily business in both public and private sectors— primarily plainclothes law enforcement officers and agents, private security personnel, private investigators and the like. To a lesser extent, such guns were also in demand by the citizenry, including small business owners. Most defensive needs could be adequately addressed with the Detective Special. It can rightfully be assumed that the criminal segment

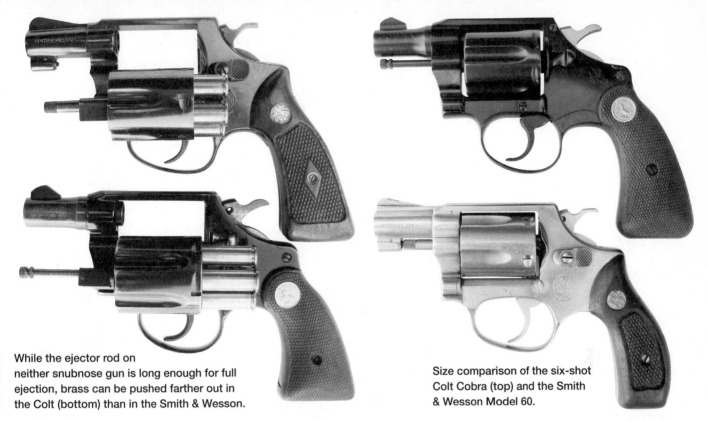

While the ejector rod on neither snubnose gun is long enough for full ejection, brass can be pushed farther out in the Colt (bottom) than in the Smith & Wesson.

Size comparison of the six-shot Colt Cobra (top) and the Smith & Wesson Model 60.

also found usefulness in these easily concealed handguns.

The year 1950 was quite noteworthy in the specialized domain of snubnose .38s. Both Smith & Wesson and Colt came forth with major announcements: the introduction of the S&W Chiefs Special and the Colt Cobra, a lightweight, alloy-framed Detective Special.

The Chiefs Special was a five-shot revolver designed to be as small as possible yet with the capability of handling the comparatively long .38 Special cartridge. With a nominal weight of around 19 ounces, it was a couple of ounces lighter than the six-shot Detective Special. The Chief measured approximately 6¼ inches in length by 4-3/8 inches tall, while the Colt was 6¾ by 4-3/8 inches. The cylinder diameter of the Colt (1.4") was about one-tenth of an inch greater than that of the Smith & Wesson. Because of the 2-inch barrels neither revolver had full-length ejector rods, but the Colt was a bit longer than that of the S&W. This made it easier and quicker to eject empty brass. On paper, weight and dimensions of the two revolvers were remarkably close.

The newer Colt Cobra shared the dimensions of the Detective Special, but had an aluminum alloy frame that reduced overall weight to about 15 ounces, making it 30 percent lighter than

its predecessor and 20 percent lighter than even the smaller-proportioned Chiefs Special. Anyone who has carried a concealed firearm on a regular daily basis is well aware of how much difference there is in what some might consider a few insignificant ounces.

Smith & Wesson countered with the Airweight in 1952, an alloy-framed Chief that weighed around 12½ ounces. Other descendants of the original Chiefs Special that also came about in the 1950s included the Centennial (completely concealed hammer with grip safety) and the Bodyguard (with extended top frame that shrouded all but the tip of the hammer spur). Both models were also available in Airweight versions. In 1965, the Model 60 Stainless Chiefs Special was introduced, the first stainless steel revolver from Smith & Wesson.

Colt introduced the Agent in 1955, a Colt Cobra with a shortened grip frame. Advertised weight was 14½ ounces. While Colt never built a revolver with a shrouded frame to cover the hammer, the manufacturer did market an alloy shroud that fit its small-framed guns. It could be factory ordered on a revolver or purchased aftermarket. Drilling and tapping three small holes in the frame were necessary for installation.

Colt advocates touted the six-round capacity of the Detective Special as an

advantage over the five-shot cylinder of the S&W. Chiefs Special fans preferred the more compact revolver. To many, however, the difference is hardly worthy of debate.

Some years ago, most law enforcement officers were required to be armed off-duty as well as during working hours. When I went to work for the Dallas Police Department in 1970, such a policy was in effect. The rules regarding handguns were quite simple; the department issued uniformed officers a 4-inch barreled Colt or Smith & Wesson .38 Special revolver. Chiefs and plainclothes personnel were primarily issued Model 36 Chiefs Specials, though some K-frame Smith & Wesson snubnosed guns were also included in the mix. However, being large and heavy when compared to the J-frame revolvers, they were likely not very popular. Personal guns for on-duty use by uniformed officers were allowed as long as they had 4-inch or longer barrels and were chambered in .38 Special or larger. The same went for the plainclothes and undercover personnel except for the snubnose revolvers previously mentioned. Choices were Colt or Smith & Wesson only.

Semiautomatics by Colt, Smith & Wesson or Browning were permitted in 9mm Luger or larger, with the Colt Government Model .45 ACP being the

Various Smith & Wesson J-frame .38 Special snubnose guns (clockwise from top left): nickel Model 36, nickel Model 49 Bodyguard shrouded frame, Model 60 Stainless, blue Model 36 square butt.

most popular. Guns for off-duty use had to be of "any reliable make, .32 caliber or larger." With no criticism directed toward Sturm, Ruger & Co., that company's handguns intended for law enforcement came along well after Colt and Smith & Wesson had been major suppliers of the market for decades.

DPD kept records on department issued guns only, not personal firearms. Most officers carried some sort of Chiefs Special for off-duty use. While merely a guess, probably 20 percent carried a Colt Detective Special or one of its variants; same for on-duty plainclothes detectives.

Law enforcement has since seen significant changes in several areas. One of these deals with the notion that revolvers are generally considered obsolete. Regardless of whether this trend was based on an accurate assessment or erroneous belief, new personnel have little or no experience with revolvers. The semiautomatic transition began about 25 years ago and was all but completed within a few years. To initiate a semiauto vs. revolver debate is inappropriate here, but there are some important points to consider regarding snubnose guns. To a lesser extent, these same factors may

apply to .38 Special revolvers in general.

For decades, many criminal careers were abruptly shortened by law enforcement personnel who often used nothing more than standard-velocity 158-grain roundnose .38 Special ammunition. In a 4-inch barrel revolver, this would mean 800 to 850 feet per second muzzle velocity at best. Subtract up to 100 fps for a 2-inch snubnose gun. Having never really understood the meaning of vague and ambiguous terms like "knockdown power," I'll leave that interpretation to others. Despite criticisms, it is a fact that the .38 Special has made a decent accounting of itself in terms of effectiveness for a long time.

What about civilian use of snubnose .38s? One may assume the appeal to such guns for private citizens was the same as for law enforcement – practical and easy to conceal. There was one additional element that was important to those who were not "gun people," and that was the revolver's foolproof, simple operation.

Most police officers at least test-fired any gun they carried just to make sure it functioned, though this was not necessarily so with civilian purchasers. Descriptions in gun classified ads like "in the box, appears to be unfired" are good

indications that some civilian buyers never fired their snubnose revolvers. They assumed the guns worked; there was no need to fire them. Their major concern was the sense of security that went along with having a loaded handgun in a nightstand, glove box or pocket. Business owners who dealt with sizeable amounts of cash were also in this category.

A healthy market continues for snubnose .38 Special revolvers. The proliferation of civilian concealed carry laws in recent years has in no small way contributed to the demand. Smith & Wesson still produces a wide variety of the J-frame guns, but sadly, Colt has been out of the double-action revolver market since 1998. Its last revolver was the Detective Special II.

Shooting the Snubnose Revolver

Unfortunately, an inexperienced shooter often buys a snubnose as a first handgun, a decision that is usually a mistake. For several reasons these guns are best utilized by experienced handgunners. The small size, low weight and very short sight radius serve to amplify a shooter's lack of skill. This often leads to an unfair evaluation of the snubnose as being inaccurate. A larger, heavier revolver is more forgiving in terms of an inconsistent grip, less-than-perfect trigger control, recoil and recovery from the same. Also, the greater distance between front and rear sights allows for slight errors in sighting that affect a bullet's point of impact far less than with a 2-inch barrel.

A ruler and a postage scale indicate there is not a great deal of difference between the Colt Detective Special and the Smith & Wesson Chiefs Special. However, the fingers, hands and extended arms of many shooters indicate otherwise. Colt stocks (call them "grips" if you wish) are somewhat larger than the more compact and more easily concealed round-butted J-frame stocks. Many find the Colt's to be more comfortable for shooting. For years, S&W marketed an optional square grip frame on the Chiefs Special for this reason. Some aftermarket stocks were made large; a Chief so equipped was easier to shoot but more difficult to conceal.

While handgun shooting technique and instruction is beyond the parameters of this article, the best suggestions would be reading all one could find on the subject and seek the guidance of an experienced handgunner. Basic instruction needn't be anything more than just that, and one can then practice and progress at a comfortable pace with constant attention to safety and the avoidance of bad shooting habits. Of the latter, flinching is often a problem that quickly creeps in when the inexperienced shoot these guns.

Snubnose revolvers have considerably more recoil than their larger and heavier counterparts. However, it is tolerable, particularly in the all-steel guns, and with standard pressure ammunition rather than +P cartridges. The lightweight models are, of course, less comfortable to shoot. Double-action trigger pulls are fairly heavy, but can

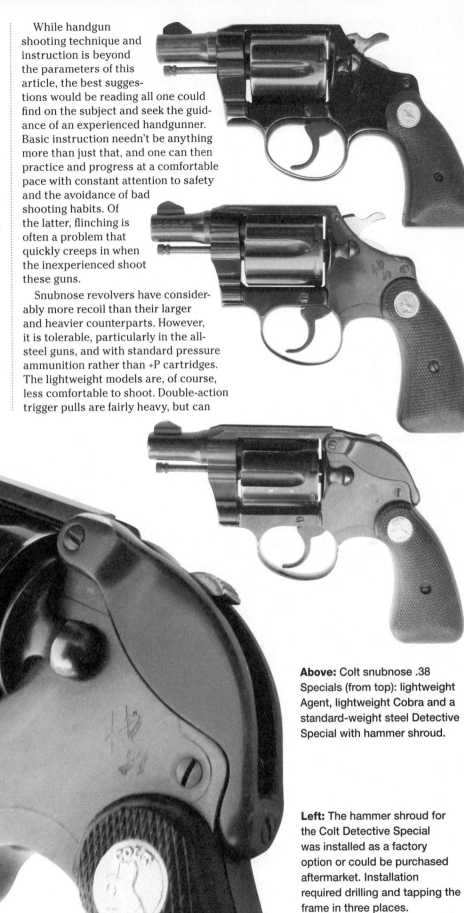

Above: Colt snubnose .38 Specials (from top): lightweight Agent, lightweight Cobra and a standard-weight steel Detective Special with hammer shroud.

Left: The hammer shroud for the Colt Detective Special was installed as a factory option or could be purchased aftermarket. Installation required drilling and tapping the frame in three places.

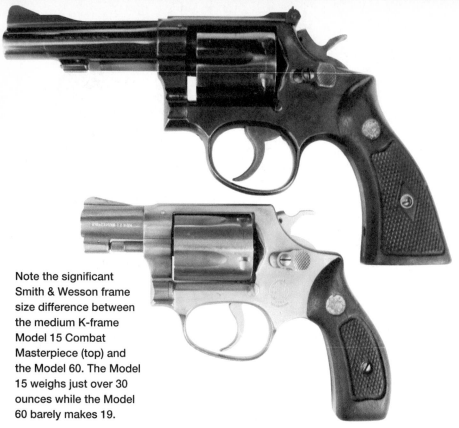

Note the significant Smith & Wesson frame size difference between the medium K-frame Model 15 Combat Masterpiece (top) and the Model 60. The Model 15 weighs just over 30 ounces while the Model 60 barely makes 19.

be well managed with practice. Some shooters make the mistake of trying to fire too many rounds during one trip to the range. Any shooting after fatigue sets in is a waste of time and ammunition, and snubnose .38s provide a shooting workout; they are not plinking guns. One

box of ammunition expended per session is plenty.

Regarding ammunition, the choice for use in a snubnose .38 is a bit more critical than it would be for a larger revolver. Sights are reportedly regulated for heavier bullets at standard velocity.

I've found this to be roughly true, mostly at distances of 15 to 25 yards. Many snubnose guns shoot the popular lighter bullets (110-125 grains) low, often six to eight inches low at 15 to 25 yards. For defensive use that may be tolerably close, but ultimately that's a decision for the shooter. At very close ranges, however, it's of little consequence.

The argument with respect to the use or non-use of +P ammunition in snubnose .38s will likely go on forever. Most self-anointed Internet "authorities" should be considered unreliable sources. The best suggestion for one advocating the use of +P in a particular revolver is to simply contact the gun manufacturer to find out if the product is rated for such ammo. Velocity suffers in short-barrel firearms and sometimes the difference between standard-pressure loads and +P is not as great as some would like to believe. Also, whether +P or not, many hollowpoint bullets cannot be depended upon to reliably expand at modest velocities.

While not often mentioned, it would be a wise move to select at least three or four commercial loadings for evaluation. Shoot at 15 and 25 yards and stick with whatever provides the best combination of accuracy, closeness of point of bullet impact vs. point of aim and acceptable recoil. A secondary consideration should be +P or standard. It's better to hit with standard-pressure ammunition than to miss with +P.

Other important factors sometimes ignored are muzzle flash and fast recovery from recoil. Snubnose guns can produce considerable muzzle flash, which can often go unnoticed except in very low light situations. The flash, coupled with recoil can hinder recovery for subsequent shots. Some ammunition makers advertise products that produce less recoil and lower muzzle flash. These would certainly merit consideration when making selections.

As for shooting practice with a snubnose revolver, some advocate practicing at very close distances simply because, "It's a snubnose and you can't hit anything with one anyway." There is little or no benefit in practicing at three, seven or 10 yards. Granted, most defensive shooting incidents occur at very close range, but shooting targets at such distances does little to improve one's shooting skills. It does, however, serve to hide a shooter's shortcomings. At 15 and 25 yards one's deficiencies become blatantly evident. Learning to shoot and practicing at the longer

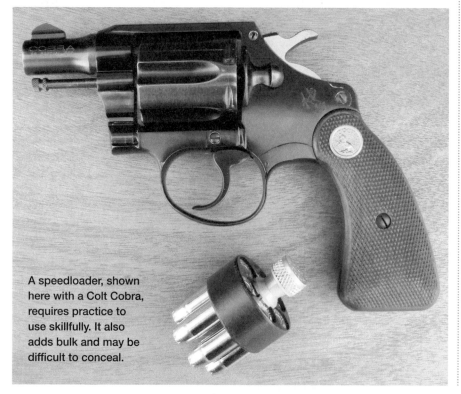

A speedloader, shown here with a Colt Cobra, requires practice to use skillfully. It also adds bulk and may be difficult to conceal.

FAVORITE HANDLOADS

For 30 years most of my articles, several of which have appeared in the pages of this publication at one time or another, have dealt with the technical aspects of handloading. Try as I might, I couldn't turn this one into a handloading piece. However, for those readers who are also handloaders I'm including a few favorite cast-bullet .38 Special loads I have used in many revolvers, including various snubnose models. They're safe, standard pressure (not +P) recipes that are accurate and comfortable to shoot, and are proven loads popular with many shooters. Use any sorted .38 Special brass in good condition. Standard (not magnum) small pistol primers of any brand work fine.

Commercial variations of these bullets will also work, but powder charges should be reduced for initial load development. Undersize bullets or those cast of a hard alloy may cause bore leading and poor accuracy.

Bullet	Powder	Muzzle Velocity
Lyman #358311		
• 158-grain roundnose		
• .358" diameter cast of wheel weight alloy	3.5 grains Alliant Bullseye powder	840 fps (4-inch barrel)
(same as above)	4.3 grains Winchester 231 powder	850 fps (4-inch barrel)
Hensley & Gibbs #51		
• 158-grain semi-wadcutter	4.3 grains Winchester 231 powder	860 fps (4-inch barrel)
• .358" diameter cast of wheel weight alloy	4.3 grains Winchester 231 powder	730 fps (2-inch barrel)

DISCLAIMER: Any and all loading data found in this article or previous articles is to be taken as reference material *only*. The publishers, editors, author, contributors and their entities bear no responsibility for the use by others of the data included in this article or others that came before it.

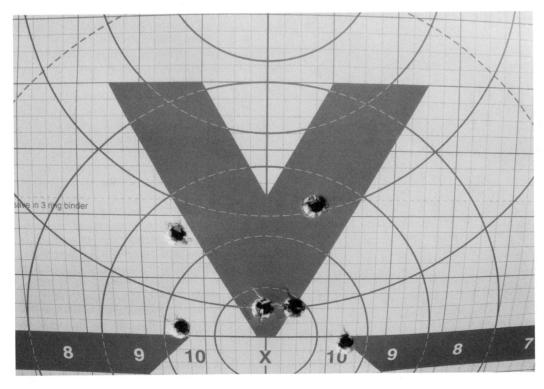

The snubnose revolver's small size and short sight radius do not lend themselves to target-grade accuracy, but with practice reasonable groups are attainable, and are accurate enough for the gun's intended purpose.

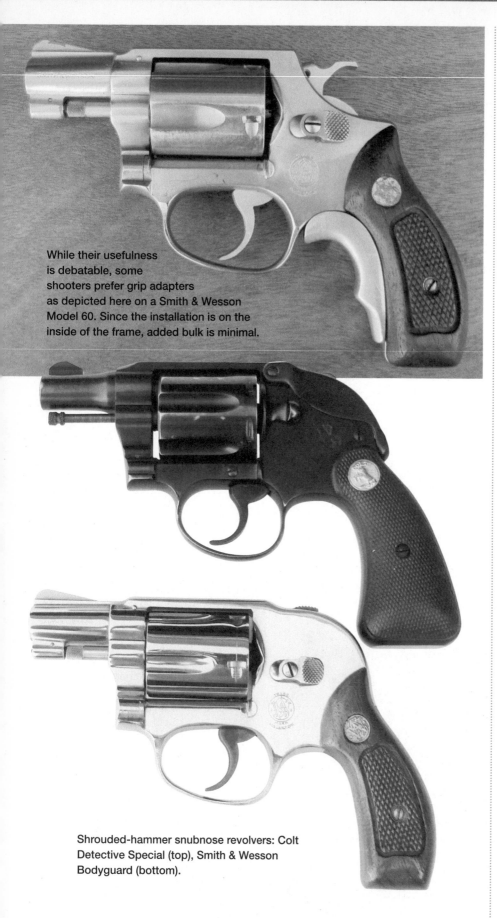

While their usefulness is debatable, some shooters prefer grip adapters as depicted here on a Smith & Wesson Model 60. Since the installation is on the inside of the frame, added bulk is minimal.

Shrouded-hammer snubnose revolvers: Colt Detective Special (top), Smith & Wesson Bodyguard (bottom).

ranges eliminates the need for practice at shorter distances, other than to check point of impact vs. point of aim.

Laser grips, night sights, fast reload devices and other gadgetry can be found useful to varying degrees, but like the snubnose .38s, such accessories are not for beginners. A wise decision would be to expend available funds on ammunition and range practice to the point that shooting basics become ingrained. If a burning desire for aftermarket gizmos goes unquenched after shooting skills are mastered, only then should optional equipment be considered. This approach works out much better than the other way around. Regardless of the ads and sales gimmicks that serve to sell merchandise, none of the products being hawked will transform an inexperienced handgunner into a proficient one.

Depending on one's needs a holster may or may not be a necessary acquisition. However, a holster may be required for a concealed carry qualification course. A big advantage of a snubnose .38 is the fact that it can easily be carried concealed on a person without the use of a holster and instead in a coat pocket, waistband, etc. Of course, some may not "carry" a gun at all, instead preferring to have one within reach.

I was a vice detective for many years. Such an assignment was (and probably remains) 100 percent undercover work. A handgun not only had to be small, but well concealed to the point that the carrier could pass a cursory (fortunately sloppy!) pat-down search by some street hustler. Holsters are of little use for such duty. I tried an ankle holster briefly but found it worthless due to pain from prolonged wear.

Most of the time I carried a 2-inch Smith & Wesson Chiefs Special as it came from the box. A brief trial with aftermarket rubber grips may have made the gun a bit easier to qualify with, but added to overall bulk. With no regret, I replaced them with the original tiny S&W wood stocks.

What about grip adapters? While these items have enjoyed a renewed popularity in recent times, I question whether it's from actual usefulness or simply a fad. They do add an appealing look to many revolvers and there are claims that they provide a better grip. That may be true for some shooters. My experience with grip adapters has been on J-frame S&W revolvers only and my conclusion is one of indifference. However, since they are on the inner frame area (rather than the

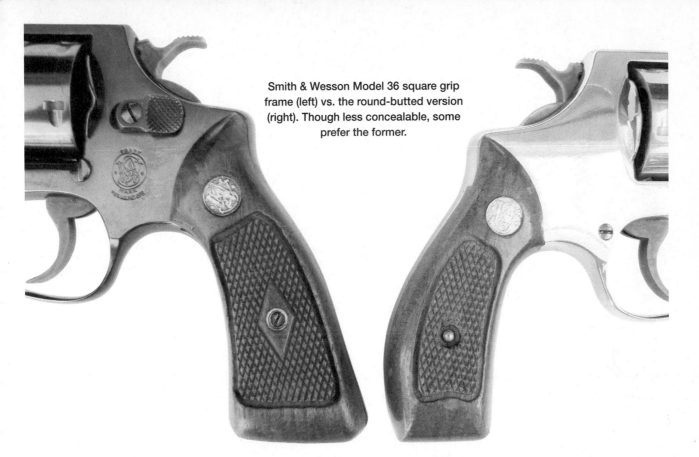

Smith & Wesson Model 36 square grip frame (left) vs. the round-butted version (right). Though less concealable, some prefer the former.

outer), they add almost nothing to the overall bulk of a revolver.

Never did I feel undergunned or find a snubnose Chief lacking in any way. Most of the detectives I worked with were similarly armed, though a few carried Colt snubnose guns. I'm unaware of any shooting incidents involving vice detectives where bad guys got up and ran off after being struck by anemic bullets fired from short-barrel .38 Special revolvers.

Speedloading devices have been around for years. Some like them; others can't see a need. Depending on several factors, they are often too bulky for adequate concealment. In my experience, the time and effort required for familiarization and practice with such implements is about the same as that necessary to master fast manual loading.

Glow-in-the-dark "night sights" and laser grips may have a place in the specialized niche of snubnose .38s if used by experienced handgunners. Mistakenly, like the unskilled rifleman who thinks a light trigger pull and a high magnification scope will offset his shortcomings, revolver sighting contraptions are not learning tools. It's also important for a shooter to remember that reliance on any device requiring battery power to function can easily become a liability at the worst possible moment. Again, money for such items, especially for the beginner, is far better spent on ammunition and learning to shoot well.

While I am a snubnose .38 enthusiast and have had long experience with them, I sincerely hope that no one has been led to believe that the small-frame Colt and Smith & Wesson revolvers are the best choice for any situation requiring a handgun. Far from it. These guns are specialized tools and are perfectly adequate for their designed purpose. Despite technological advances over many years, the usefulness of the small-frame snubnose .38 is no less now than it was generations ago.

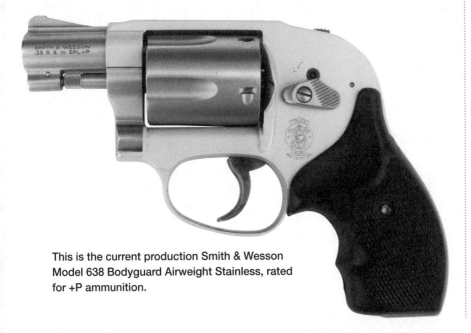

This is the current production Smith & Wesson Model 638 Bodyguard Airweight Stainless, rated for +P ammunition.

THE GUNS OF

CZ

BY Brad Fitzpatrick

CZ Upland Ultralight: Russell Edwards of Kentucky's Winghaven Lodge uses the Upland Ultralight on a timber duck hunt. The large red fiber-optic bead is easy to see in low light conditions like this.

HERE'S A QUICK LOOK AT SOME OF THIS COMPANY'S OUTSTANDING FIREARMS

Since it began producing firearms in a small machine shop in 1936, Ceska zbrojovka, or CZ, has grown into one of the world's largest gun companies with an extensive lineup of handguns, rifles and shotguns that continues to grow. By many standards, a gun company with a history dating back to 1936 isn't that old. But CZ has undergone major changes throughout their relatively short history. The company, which is located in the Czech Republic, opened its doors in the town of Strakonice as a machine shop for the production of military weapons, a decision that came from the nation's National Defense Council. Originally the company produced only military arms, from aircraft machine guns to military pistols and smallbore rifles.

In the years that followed, the company that would later become CZ underwent rapid change. Nazi occupation came shortly after the doors opened, and at the end of World War II the company began producing both civilian and military arms once more. Corporate restructuring resulted in the company acting as a machine shop for the production of mechanical parts for aircraft and tractors. CZ merged with Agrozet Brno, a company perhaps best known in big-game hunting circles as the name that appeared on the CZ's now-famous Mauser-style dangerous game rifle, the Brno 602, but in 1988 CZ and Brno parted ways. In 1990, the company expanded its production space for civilian and sporting guns, and since that time CZ's firearms have gained worldwide appeal.

Today CZ is one of the companies at the forefront of modern firearms production. Virtually unheard of two decades ago, CZ now has a growing number of fans in the United States that appreciate their durable, innovative guns. Here's a look at some of the outstanding firearms CZ has to offer.

Handguns

The CZ 75 is one of the most successful handguns of the modern era and it is the weapon of choice for law enforcement and military officers around the world. This short-recoil operated semiauto first appeared in the mid-1970s and it was a major hit immediately. The 75 has proven to be very reliable and accurate, thanks in no small part to its superb balance. Today, CZ offers over a dozen variants of the 75, including

The P-09 has a polymer frame and a magazine capacity of 19 rounds in 9mm. It is also available threaded for a suppressor and has a decocker that can be converted to a manual safety.

CZ's 75 has been around for almost 40 years and today there is a wide variety of different options. The 75 Compact, shown here, is a short-recoil operated semiauto that is small enough for concealed carry.

several small versions ideal for personal defense. For those who are shopping for a concealed carry gun, the CZ 75 Compact has all of the features you'd expect from the full-size gun like SA/DA operation, a large manual safety and decocker, and a wide, double-stack grip. The 75 Compact comes with a steel frame, which is slightly heavier than other carry pistols in the CZ line (about 33 ounces), but that weight helps reduce recoil. If you're looking for a lighter carry gun, the CZ P-01 in 9mm is ideal. The alloy frame reduces weight, and at 28 ounces unloaded the P-01 is large enough to reduce recoil and shoot accurately but still light enough for carry. There's also a conversion kit to turn your 9mm or .40 S&W 75 into a .22 for cheap, low-recoil practice.

Competition shooters also have several options available as well, including the IPSC-ready CZ-75 Tactical Sport. Designed for competition, the Tactical Sport offers competition-ready features like an extended magazine release and competition hammer. The magazine well is large so that it is easy to make rapid mag changes during the heat of competition, and the front and rear straps have heavy checkering for a secure grip. If you want to step up another level, try the CZ 75 TS Czechmate. This semiauto pistol is designed for IPSC Open or Limited division competition and it offers a long list of features like an ambidextrous slide racker, four-port compensator, four magazines (three 20-round, one 26-round) and much more. The price for the Tactical Sport is $1,310, and the feature-loaded Czechmate sells for $3,317.

The P-09 is one of the best full-size, high-capacity, polymer-frame 9mms on the market. It's very well balanced, accurate, and the grip is comfortable. In addition, the P-09 has a large magazine capacity – 19 +1 in 9mm – so you'll cut down on time between reloads and you'll always know that you've got plenty of firepower on tap. The P-09 also comes with a decocker that can be transferred to a manual safety, and there are new versions

The CZ 550 action has a full-length claw extractor. The Magnum version, shown here, is chambered for powerful magnums like the .375 H&H and the .416 Rigby, and it's one of the best production dangerous-game rifles on the market.

that come with a flat dark earth frame, and another version that is threaded for suppression. MSRP on the P-09 ranges from $530 to $577, making it one of the best buys in full-size polymer guns.

Dan Wesson, which is owned by CZ, is offering a full lineup of 1911 handguns for every need and budget. Some of

the standouts in that lineup are the Razorback RZ-10, which is chambered in the mighty 10mm Auto and comes with defensive sights, cocobolo grips, a 5-inch ramped match-grade barrel, a smooth front strap and much more. The Razorback is an ideal gun for defense (for those who can handle the recoil) and will

also serve as a close-range hunting gun. Also from Dan Wesson is the compact ECO, a 25-ounce concealed carry 1911 available in either 9mm or .45 ACP. It has a solid one-piece guide rod and a flat recoil spring rated for an incredible 15,000 rounds. MSRP on the Razorback is $1,350 and the ECO is $1,662.

Rifles

CZ is known for producing high-quality rimfires that are versatile and extremely accurate. The CZ 455 rimfire line of bolt-action rifles continues to grow and gain praise from shooters as well as the media. A few decades ago virtually every major firearms maker offered a line of bolt-action .22s, but since that time the number of high-quality, accurate, reasonably priced rimfire bolt guns have dwindled. CZ offers one of the most extensive lineups of .22 bolt actions, and there is a 455 to fit virtually every need. In addition, the 455 rifle allows the shooter to switch stocks and barrels, so you can purchase a single rifle and fire .22 LR, .22 Magnum and .17 HMR loads simply by switching to the appropriate barrel. The 455 Training Rifle in .22 LR features a 24.8-inch barrel with high-quality adjustable iron sights, perfect

The compact Kevlar Carbine is accurate and durable. Chambered in calibers like the .30-06 it's a versatile, reliable big-game rifle that's perfect for a variety of game.

for teaching a new shooter (MSRP $374). The 455 American features a straight-comb walnut or synthetic stock and has integral 11mm dovetail bases machined into the receiver for scope mounting. In addition, there's a new version that is threaded and ready for suppression. Look for the standard 455 American to retail for about $385 to $438, and you can get a rifle that includes both a .22 LR barrel and a .17 HMR barrel for $557. The threaded version sells for $421, and there's a 455 Tacticool that has a heavy 16.5-inch barrel and a black painted laminate stock with a wide fore-end for $549. The 455 Varmint Precision Trainer has a Manners composite stock and the 455 Varmint Evolution has a blue/gray thumbhole laminate Boyds stock, and both come with heavy target barrels and adjustable triggers. Retail for the Varmint Precision Trainer is $940, and the Varmint Evolution sells for about $565.

CZ's 550 action, which features a full-length Mauser-style claw extractor, is legendary. This year, CZ offers a variety of 550 rifles for everything from precision varmint shooting to dangerous game hunting. The 550 Varmint Tacticool comes with a Boyd's Foliage Green Laminate stock, a 25.6-inch barrel and integrated 19mm dovetail optic mounts. It has CZ's adjustable trigger and is available in .308 Win. for the price of $924. The CZ Kevlar Carbine is one of the best short-barreled woods rifles available and features a set trigger, a Kevlar stock and easily adjustable iron sights, making it a versatile carbine for hunting all varieties of big game (MSRP $1,080). For really big game, CZ offers their successful Safari Classics line, which is available in a wide variety of wood and Kevlar-stocked models in calibers like .375 H&H Magnum, .416 Rigby, .458 Lott and others. The Safari Classic line is popular with hunters who pursue the largest game because it offers the company's controlled-round feed action, express sights and set triggers. MSRP for the Safari Classics rifles range from about $1,200 up to $3,300 for the Express models.

The new CZ 557 is built to the same standards as the 550 line but incorporates a push-feed design instead of the full-length claw extractor. The 557 Standard model is available in .243 Win., .30-06, .308, .270 and 6.5x55 Swedish Mauser, and retails for $792. In addition, there is a version of the Sporter with a Manners synthetic stock that is impervious to weather and rough handling that sells for $1,268. The Sporter Carbine has a 20.5-inch barrel and iron sights, perfect for close-range work or running shots on game like driven boar, and it sells for $812. All of the 557 rifles come with machined bases that accept 19mm dovetail rings, providing a secure platform for your optic of choice.

Shotguns

CZ offers an extensive lineup of shotguns for just about every need, including the classic Ringneck and Bobwhite side-by-sides. The Bobwhite is a boxlock action with two triggers and a straight grip, while the Ringneck features classy false sideplates, a single trigger, ejectors and a round-knob pistol grip. Both guns come with five different choke tubes – Full, Modified, Improved Modified, Improved Cylinder and Cylinder – to meet all your upland hunting needs. The 612 lineup of pump guns now includes a Home Defense version, a Big Game version with a smoothbore barrel and Weaver-style cantilever optic rail, and a new youth version, all which range in price from $304 to $428, making these hard-working pumps the ideal budget gun.

The 550 American Safari Magnum is a great dangerous-game rifle. It's also available in a European-style Safari Magnum version with a curved stock that is perfect for using iron sights.

Below: The Express version of the 550, which is available through Safari Classics, is offered in a variety of specialized dangerous-game chamberings like the .404 Jeffery and the .450 Rigby. It's a purpose-built dangerous-game gun with folding express sights and a well-figured walnut stock.

The appropriately named Ringneck side-by-side double is a good-looking, reliable upland gun that is available in a variety of gauges including 16 and 28. The Bobwhite model is similar but has a straight stock and double triggers.

The Upland Ultralight weighs in at about six pounds and is the perfect gun for all-day wingshooting trips. The simple, black anodized receiver is very durable, and with five choke tubes standard, it's perfect for any hunting situation.

In their semiauto line, CZ offers a variety of different 12 and 20-gauge models in their 712, 720, 912 and 920 line. One of their newest additions is the 712 Practical, which is designed specifically for 3-gun competition and features a 6-position adjustable stock, comes with five choke tubes and has a hefty 9-shot capacity. The 712 Practical employs the same gas-powered action and lightweight alloy receiver found on other CZ semiautos. MSRP is $699.

CZ also offers a wide variety of over/unders that include the Upland Ultra-light, a no-frills, lightweight field gun with a tough black anodized receiver and chrome-lined barrels. The Upland Ultralight has a tang-mounted safety, a Turkish walnut stock and comes with five choke tubes for $762, making it one of the best bargains in upland over/unders. Best of all, the Upland Ultralight weighs around six pounds, making it a great gun to carry during long days afield.

CZ also announced the production of their new Lady Sterling over/under, which is built and designed specifically for women shooters. The Lady Sterling features a high comb and pitch designed to allow female shooters to comfortably mount and fire the gun. The Lady Sterling comes with extractors, 28-inch barrels, a single selectable mechanical trigger and weighs 7.5 pounds. From the ground up the Lady Sterling was designed for the serious competitive female shooter, and it retails for $1,281.

To learn more about the guns of CZ, visit the company's website at www.cz-usa.com.

NEW GENERATION AIRGUNS

THIS AIN'T YOUR OL' RED RYDER BB GUN

The Crosman Benjamin Marauder PCP is a great rifle for hunting small game including rabbits, squirrels, even marmots and raccoons. The author was impressed at the accuracy of the .25-caliber pellet rifle.

BY **Thomas C. Tabor**

I grew up in the era when virtually every respectable boy and even many girls considered their BB gun their best friend. Like young Ralphie in the classic movie *A Christmas Story*, I too dreamed of someday being the owner of a new Daisy Red Ryder BB Gun. But when my dream finally came to fruition the rifle wasn't new, nor was it even a Red Ryder. My first BB gun came to me as a well-used hand-me-down possessing the dubious distinction as having once been owned by my much older brother. Apparently he had moved on to what he thought at the time to be cooler things in life, quite likely that being members of the opposite sex.

I'm not sure how old I was at the time, maybe 6, or possibly 7. Like most BB-wielding kids of that era, inside my pants pocket was always a container of shiny new BBs. If you are about my age you will surely remember that the BBs always came in a small, red colored cylindrical tube. When the sides of the tube were squeezed together it resulted in the end pouching out, thereby freeing its contents. If I remember right, at that time a tube cost a nickel or a dime, which in either case was a whole lot of money for a family trying to eke out a living on a tiny 40-acre dairy farm. In those days my spindly little arms weren't strong enough to even cock the rifle, but that was only a minor impediment to the adventures that the rifle brought me. Once I'd fired it I would typically have to head back to the house or barn to find someone to cock the gun again for me. After that I would continue on my imaginary safari looking for dangerous game in the form of any snake, lizard, frog, small bird or even a tadpole that dared to show itself.

Ironically, I don't remember ever hitting one of those critters. The power, or better put, the lack of power that rifle possessed made it necessary for me to hold well over the top of my intended target before my stubby finger would squeeze the trigger. Once the trigger was pulled I would watch the little copper colored BB slowly arcing it way in the general direction of its prey, only to send the critter scurrying for the safety of its nearest sanctuary.

Today's New .177 & .22 Airguns

Those days on the farm as a youngster were certainly great times that culminated into a lifetime of shooting enjoyment for me. But those wimpy attempts at launching a BB through the air, or in some case a lead pellet, are now well behind us. Today's new

The Crosman Benjamin Marauder .25-caliber rifle is also available with a synthetic stock.

No offense to the ol' Daisy of my past, which I truly loved, but the new pellet rifles now being produced far outshine those early BB guns in both accuracy and overall performance.

sophisticated generation of air-powered rifles are now capable of producing muzzle velocities close to that of a .22 rimfire rifle, and have reached a point that they can in some instances be quite effective for hunting such tenacious and hard-to-kill critters as feral hogs, coyotes and turkeys.

For many years the .177 pellet rifles have been the most popular chambering. My .177 Gamo rifle, (www.gamousa.com) called the Varmint Hunter, has served me well and is a fine example of the progress made in the area of airguns. I primarily use that rifle for pest control and for plinking. It came from the factory well equipped with a 4x32mm scope, a laser sight and even a light for night shooting. Capable of sending a 7.5-grain pellet on its way at a remarkable 1,000 fps, at moderate range it provides very good results on small critters like squirrels and starlings. And if I wanted to boost the velocity even higher I could switch to some of the lighter pellets likes the Gamo Raptors, Gamo Lethal Hunting Pellets, Platinum Power Pellets or comparable products from other manufacturers. In some cases these lighter pellets have the capability of increasing the muzzle velocity by as much as 30 percent.

Like many airgun companies, Gamo has a variety of rifles and pistols to select from including manual cocking systems, CO2 powered units and pre-charged pneumatics (PCP). These are most often available in the typical choices of .177 and .22 calibers. The .177-caliber pellets cost less than the larger diameter ones, so that is an asset worthy of consideration if you plan to do a lot of shooting. However, as pellet rifles have started to creep more into actual hunting scenarios many shooters prefer the somewhat less common larger calibers, maybe something in the neighborhood of a .25 caliber. Understandably, the pellets for these larger calibers will cost more, but the additional killing potential that they provide is necessary when it comes to hunting the larger animals.

The most common airguns today fall into three design categories. These include the spring-propelled guns, which can either come in the form of single pump or multipump design; CO2-powered units, which most often take small 12g CO2 cylinders; and the pre-charged pneumatics (PCP) that must be charged by an outside air source. Obviously the single-pump spring-charged airguns, like my ol' farm Daisy, are quicker to use (that is if your arms are strong enough to cock the gun yourself) than the multipump spring-style guns. But, the multipump designs come with the option of being able to vary the velocities and energy based on how many times the gun is pumped.

The CO2-powered units have been around for quite a few decades, but their popularity seems to be diminishing a bit in recent years. I believe the reasons for this are primarily due to the cost of the CO2 canisters and the fact that this style airgun is heavily dependent upon warm weather. CO2 rifles simply fail to work well as the mercury begins to drop.

On the other hand, the popularity of the PCP models seems to be on the increase. But as the name suggests, the drawback to this design lies in the fact that the guns must be pre-charged with air. There are several ways of accomplishing that task. Possibly the most convenient way is to use a hand-operated pump, but if you are opposed to the exercise needed to pump the gun up to the substantial levels needed, which can sometime involve a formidable amount of effort, there are a couple of alternative charging techniques you might consider. Some manufacturers sell high-pressure compressed air tanks specifically intended to replenish the air supply of the PCPs. Once one of these tanks has been filled to capacity, in many cases by a paintball facility, you can head to the field with the ability to repeatedly recharge your rifle whenever needed with little effort. Another method would be to use a scuba diving tank for the alternate filling supply. In this case a specialized adapter would be necessary to make the connection

After connecting up the pump to the airgun the pumping can begin.

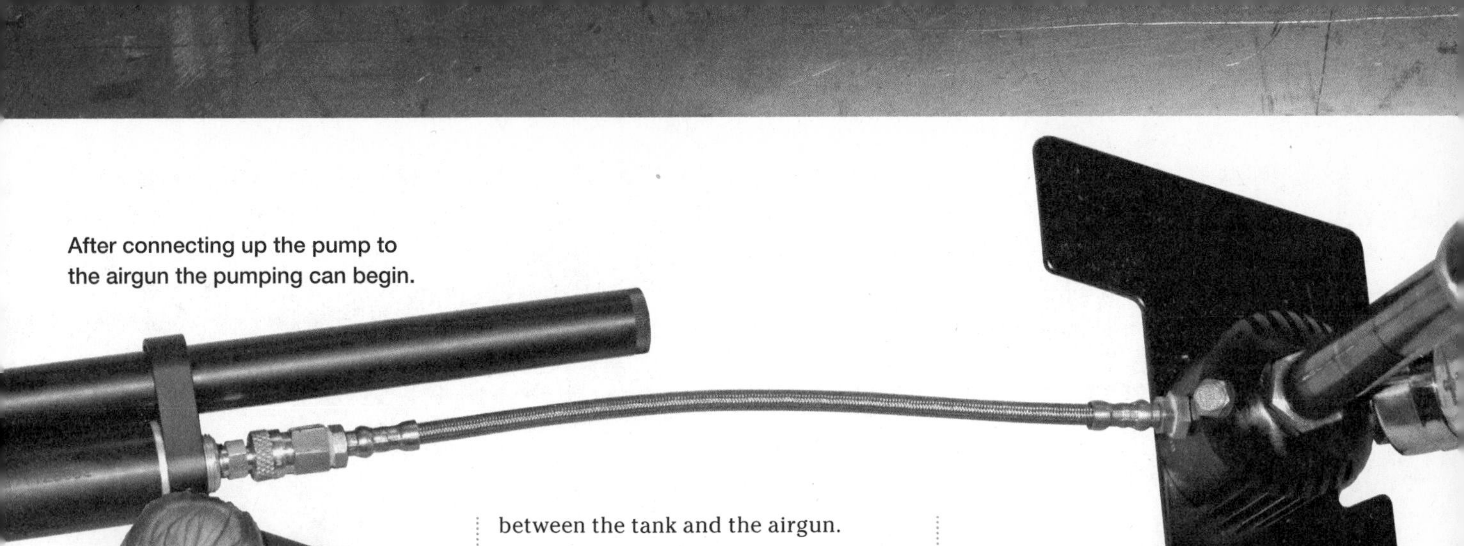

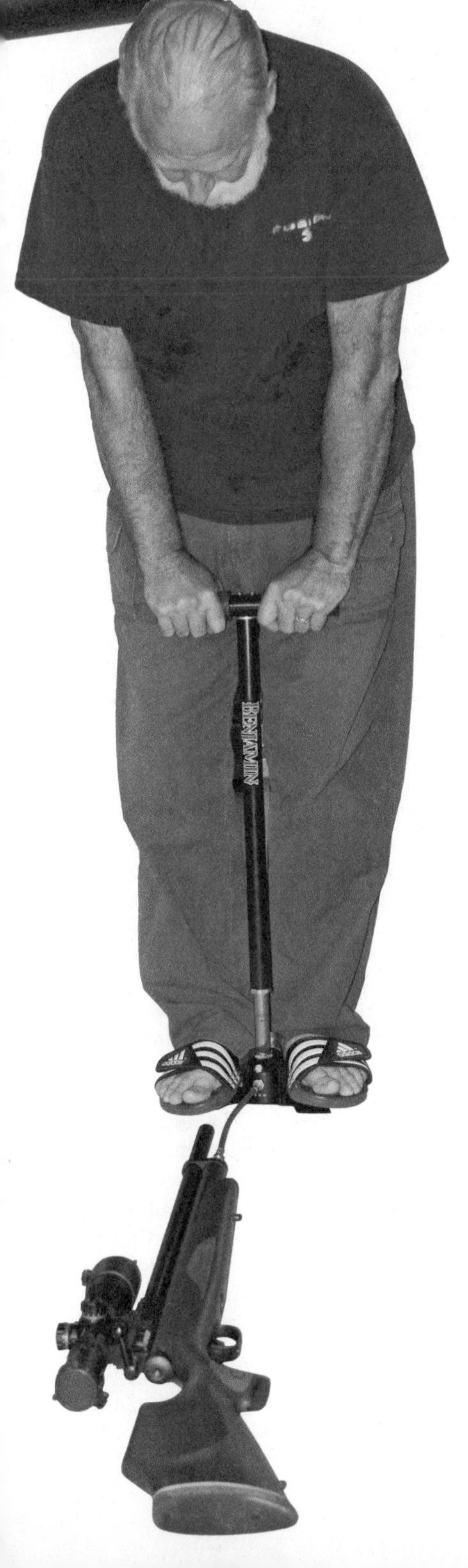

between the tank and the airgun.

Obviously, when it comes to an airgun intended for hunting purposes accuracy is crucially important. But equally important is the fact that the gun must be capable of delivering an adequate amount of energy on target in order to effectuate a quick and humane kill. In most cases this means that the shooter must be capable of consistently hitting either the brain or heart/lungs area of the animal. For game like rabbits, marmots, turkeys and similarly sized animals you can expect the brain to be about the size of a quarter. The heart and lungs area is frequently a little larger, but all air-rifle shooters would do well to use that one-inch shooting standard as an indicator of maximum effective range. In other words, if you are unable to keep all your shots consisting grouping within the size of a quarter, it would best to reduce your range until you can do so. That distance should be considered your maximum hunting range.

Just like with other styles of rifles, energy is largely a product of velocity and bullet weight, or in this case velocity and pellet weight. Pyramyd Air (www.pyramydair.com), a leading supplier of airguns and related products, recommends eight ft-lbs of energy on target when hunting small game the size of squirrels and cottontail rabbits. If your rifle is only capable of 12 ft-lbs of energy at the muzzle it would be wise to limit your hunting range to about 25 yards. For larger game the size of marmots and turkeys, Pyramyd Air recommends about 20 ft-lbs of energy on target. Generally, lighter pellets produce higher muzzle velocities, but may deliver less energy on target. The chart below provides a rudimentary example of how velocity, pellet weight and pellet diameter all play a role in the effectiveness and performance of airguns.

A strange but interesting side note about pellet weight vs. velocity is that heavier pellets fired from a PCP air rifle will typically produce slower velocities than lighter pellets, but the power of those pellets usually will increase. That is not the case when shooting a spring-powered airgun. In that case, shooting heavier pellets from a spring-powered gun, both the velocity and power will be reduced more so than the lighter pellets.

Bigger Bore & More Power, Crosman's .25 Caliber

The .177 and .22-caliber pellets have been the standard for many decades in airguns, but recently there has been a movement in the direction of larger and more powerful air rifles. This has opened up great new possibilities for the airgun hunter. A great rifle that meets those

Pellet Diameter (inch)	Pellet Weight	Muzzle Velocity	Muzzle Energy
.177	8 grains	822 fps	12 ft-lbs
.177	9 grains	1,000 fps	20 ft-lbs
.22	14 grains	621 fps	12 ft-lbs
.22	16 grains	750 fps	20 ft-lbs

Crosman's Benjamin Marauder PCP .25 pellet rifle is an impressive weapon that has great potential as a hunting rifle for small game.

Unlike many other pellet guns the Crosman Benjamin .25 caliber comes with a self-indexing eight-shot magazine. This is a great feature in a hunting pellet rifle.

requirements is the Crosman Benjamin Marauder PCP (www.crosman.com) chambered in .25 caliber, which sends a whopping 28-grain pellet on its way at speeds purported by the factory to be 900 fps. I had the pleasure of testing one of these rifles a couple of years ago, and I liked it so well that it now has become

my airgun weapon of choice in many cases, especially when it comes to rabbit hunting and pest control around my rural Montana home. Its unique design includes a self-indexing, eight-round magazine. By simply working the bolt of the rifle another pellet is automatically and quickly fed into the rifle chamber

and ready to be fired. When fully charged to 2,900 psi I found this rifle to be capable of firing up to 40 rounds without needing to be recharged with air.

When a comparison is made between the .177-caliber pellet guns and the Crosman .25 caliber, the difference is a substantial one. While most .177-caliber pellets weigh between 5 and 7.5 grains, the pellets for the Crosman .25 caliber tip the scales at a whopping 28 grains. That means that it would take about four to six of the .177s to equal the weight of a single .25-caliber pellet. And when the Crosman .22-caliber pellet rifle is compared to the .25 Crosman Benjamin we find the larger bore delivers a whopping 80 percent more kinetic energy on target. At 45 ft-lbs of energy I found my .25 produced devastating results on small game like rabbits.

A concern some shooters might have with pre-charged pneumatic airguns is whether the velocities would necessarily change from shot to shot as a result of changes in the chamber pressure of the rifle. In other words, would the muzzle velocity of the first shot be greater than say, shot number 30? I had the same concern so I ran a few of my own checks us-

To fully charge the Crosman Benjamin it needs to be pumped to a fill capacity of 2,900 psi.

ing a chronograph to record the muzzle velocities, and found that even after 40 rounds had been fired the consistency of the velocity was very good. While I did detect some degradation of the accuracy beginning at about shot number 34, I came away very satisfied with the overall consistency of both the velocity and the accuracy. The complete results of that testing can be seen in the chart entitled Crosman Benjamin .25 Marauder.

Accuracy is clearly an important consideration with any firearm and the Crosman Benjamin .25 certainly demonstrated its capabilities in this area out to about 50 yards. After that distance the trajectories start to wane significantly. But along with a potential for good accuracy, a hunting rifle must have the capability to penetrate deep enough to produce adequate damage to the vitals of the animal. Ideally, penetration and bullet performance should be tested by shooting into a block of ballistic gelatin, but not having any, I had to settle on an alternative, ironically that being a pile of old phonebooks. Even though this wasn't necessarily my preferred media, I felt it would still provide an adequate understanding of how well the pellets were penetrating and possibly even provide me a basis for comparison.

I began by placing the phonebooks at a range of 25 feet. At that distance the .25 caliber pellet penetrated 612 pages for a penetration depth of about 7/8 inch. Following that I moved the phonebooks out to 50 yards and found that the pellet stopped at page 569, providing a depth of penetration of 3/4 inch. At that distance the pellet expanded very well, measured .350 inch and it only lost about .1 grain of its original weight. I'd sighted the rifle in to impact 3/4 inch high at 50 yards and found that at 25 feet the pellet impacted at the center of the target, indicating that the pellet was likely still climbing as it approached the 50-yard mark. But when I tried to stretch the range out, that same 50-yard +3/4-inch scope setting resulted in the pellets being down a full 20 inches at 100 yards. Nevertheless, the three-shot group I fired at 100 yards measured only about an inch across and formed an almost perfect cloverleaf design. Obviously, I wouldn't consider 100 yards an acceptable range for hunting purposes. At that distance the energy would also be severely waning, and if you misjudged the distance by only a few feet it would likely result in either a missed target, or worse yet, wounded game.

In order to draw a comparison be-

CROSMAN BENJAMIN .25 MARAUDER			
Velocity Test			
Shot No.	Pressure(psi) (50 yards)	3-Shot Group (fps)	Muzzle Velocity
1			742
2	3,000	1"	745
3			738
4			745
5	2,900	1/2"	753
6			752
7			756
8	2,800	1/2"	756
9			756
10			756
11	2,750	3/4"	760
12			765
13			770
14	2,700	9/16"	767
15			762
16			778
17	2,500	7/16"	775
18			777
19			771
20	2,400	1-1/16"	788
21			786
22			787
23	2,200	1-1/8"	784
24			781
25			774
26	2,000	1"	611
27			774
28			766
29	2,000	3/4"	759
30			754
31			747
32	1,900	1-1/16"	584
33			736
34			725
35	1,800	2-1/4"	717
36			712
37			702
38	1,400	2-5/8"	695
39			686
40			537
41	1,100	1-5/8"	652
42			641

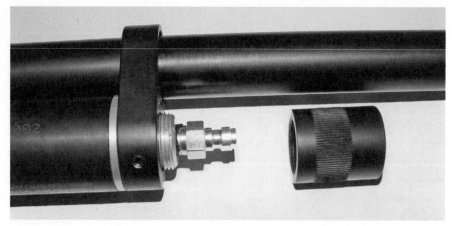

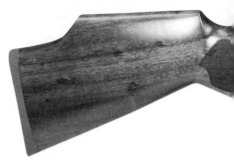

Top Left: When charging the Crosman Benjamin .25 caliber with air, the cap must be removed to expose the nipple connection.

Left: Once the cap of the Crosman has been removed the pump hose connection can be made.

tween the penetration of Crosman 28-grain .25-caliber pellets and the much smaller 7.5-grain .177-caliber pellets fired from my Gamo single-shot break-barrel rifle, I decided to run the .177 through the same series of tests. At 25 feet the little 7.5-grain pellet only penetrated 223 pages for a depth of 3/16 inch, and at 50 yards it performed even less impressively with the pellet stopping at page number 137 for a total penetration depth of only 1/4 inch. The trajectory was pretty pathetic as well compared to the .25. It actually took me three shots before I'd finally elevated the crosshairs high enough to even make contact with the pages of the phonebook. But while the .177 clearly didn't perform all that well under those conditions, no one should discount the potential use of the .177 under other lesser extremes. The .177 has a place in shooting and that place is at short range – and if used for hunting purposes – on small game.

For Even Bigger Tougher Game

It is quite natural for most shooters to relate pellet guns to the long-running

When the Crosman Benjamin Marauder PCP rifle was sighted in at 50 yards to shoot 3/4 inch high (top left target) this essentially produces a dead-on point of impact at the close range of 25 feet (bottom left target).

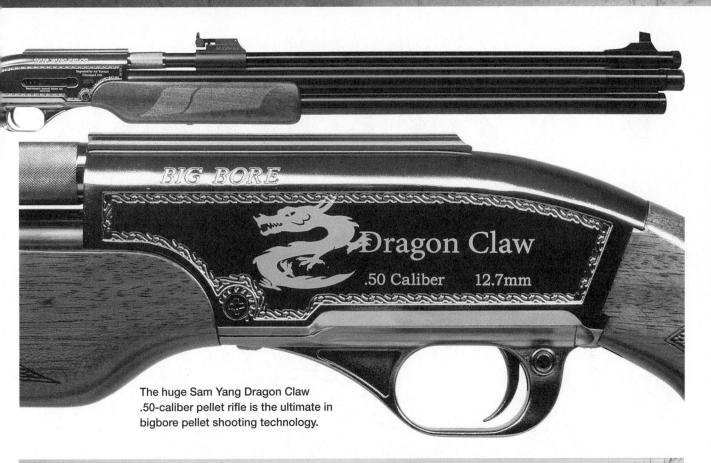

The huge Sam Yang Dragon Claw .50-caliber pellet rifle is the ultimate in bigbore pellet shooting technology.

A BB gun is a great way to train young children in the safe handling of guns and get them accustomed to shooting. The author's 6-year-old granddaughter received this pink-stocked Daisy as a Christmas present.

standard bores of .177 and .22, but aside from Crosman's .25 and a few other rifles so chambered, there is a whole world of larger bores available from companies like Evanix and Sam Yang. Evanix has a varied selection of 9mm chambered rifles and Sam Yang offers even larger bores in calibers like .357, .45 and even a couple called Dragon Claws, which launch huge .50-caliber pellets on their way. These massive .50s come with the capability of producing a whopping 230 ft-lbs of muzzle energy, and reportedly are capable of a muzzle velocity of 879 fps. These bigbore pellet rifles could be a good dose of medicine when it comes to hunting larger, tougher species of game like feral hogs, foxes, bobcats and coyotes.

Even though airguns in various configurations have been around for many decades, it has only been in recent years that they have been considered as a viable alternative to the conventional powder-burning weaponry for hunting purposes. Obviously airguns will never totally replace the cartridge-fed powder-burning firearms. But in some areas of the country where firearm restrictions have crippled the sport, or when hunters simply want to try something a bit different, airguns, particularly the new bigger bore designs, can provide real food for thought.

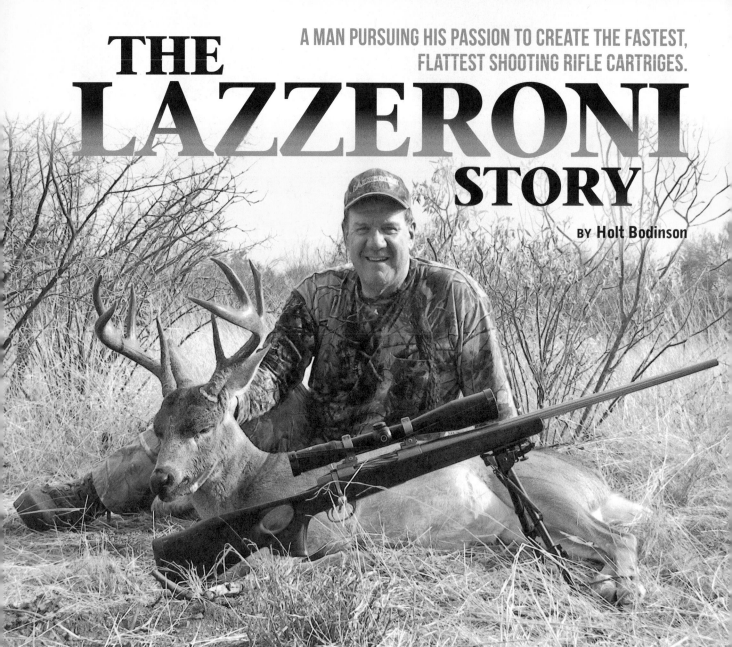

THE LAZZERONI STORY

BY **Holt Bodinson**

Ever heard of the Spitfire, Phantom, Tomahawk, Patriot, Galaxy, Flash, Scramjet, Blackbird, Firebird, Warbird, Titan, Saturn and Meteor? No, they're not a new family of advanced missiles, drones, aircraft or navigation systems, but they're just as remarkable. These are the whimsical names of the original high-performance, short and full-size beltless magnums that John Lazzeroni developed from scratch over a period of months, and then chambered and marketed them in some equally high-tech rifles that bear his name today. Across from the main post office in Tucson, Ariz., is a modest office building housing the J&M Corpora-tion. Based on a wall full of original

patents, John Lazzeroni and his J&M staff (www.jmcorp.com) manufacture and market much of the world's highest quality motorcycle audio systems includ-ing helmet intercom headsets, CB radio and cellular telephone systems, speaker kits and more. Given the increasing popularity of the motorcycling sport, J&M's two-wheeling audio business has thrived. In doing so, it has afforded Lazzeroni the time and money to pursue his other pressing passions of big-game hunting and ballistic experimentation.

Not surprisingly, Lazzeroni credits Roy Weatherby as his original inspiration for pursuing ultra-performance hunting cartridges. Long before Weatherby rolled out the .30-378 as a stock factory

cartridge, Lazzeroni was necking down the cavernous case (basically the .416 Rigby case cinched with a belt) to 7mm, .308 and .338 calibers, and the smaller .257 Weatherby case to .243 caliber.

While he liked the performance of his Weatherby-based wildcats, Lazzeroni didn't care for the belted cases and the long, free-bored Weatherby throats. So he decided in the mid-1990s to design and market his own family of nonbelted, high-performance cartridges and a rifle in which to chamber them. It wasn't an easy mission.

If you're outside the industry, consider what's entailed in developing just one new commercial cartridge. To achieve a specific level of ballistic performance,

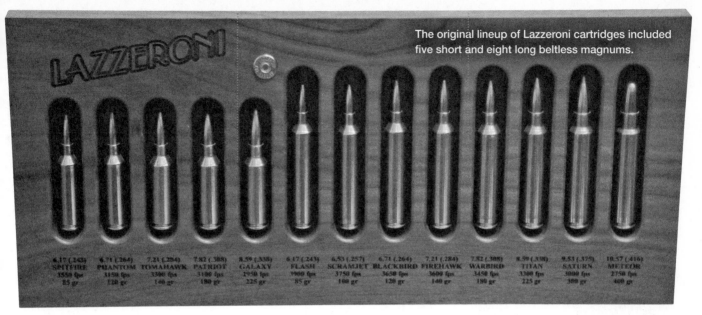

The original lineup of Lazzeroni cartridges included five short and eight long beltless magnums.

| 6.17 (.243) SMTFIRE 3550 fps 85 gr | 6.71 (.264) PHANTOM 3150 fps 120 gr | 7.21 (.284) TOMAHAWK 3300 fps 160 gr | 7.82 (.308) PATRIOT 3100 fps 180 gr | 8.59 (.338) GALAXY 2950 fps 225 gr | 6.17 (.243) FLASH 3900 fps 85 gr | 6.53 (.257) SCRAMJET 3750 fps 100 gr | 6.71 (.264) BLACKBIRD 3650 fps 120 gr | 7.21 (.284) FIREHAWK 3600 fps 140 gr | 7.82 (.308) WARBIRD 3450 fps 180 gr | 8.59 (.338) TITAN 3300 fps 225 gr | 9.53 (.375) SATURN 3000 fps 300 gr | 10.57 (.416) METEOR 2750 fps 400 gr |

the internal capacity and external dimensions of the cartridge case must be calculated. A manufacturer to draw the case must be found and financial arrangements confirmed. Reamers and headspace gauges to chamber barrels and cut reloading dies must be made. Throat dimensions, rifling twists and barrel lengths must be fed into the equation. Pressure data must be collected using a strain gauge system like Oehler's Model 43 Personal Ballistic Laboratory, and then checked and confirmed by an independent testing laboratory like H.P. White, which will then supply standard-pressure rounds to calibrate the Oehler strain gauge system for further ballistic development. Then – having put all that time and expense into the project – if the results aren't what you were shooting for, the whole process has to begin all over again.

Once the final product is achieved, then the real expense hits home with a minimum investment of $100,000 to a case-making firm to draw commercial quality brass. Then case dimensions have to be supplied to die and reamer manufactures, and if you want firearm manufacturers to be able to chamber your cartridges, the cartridges must go through the rigorous approval process of SAAMI and the European C.I.P.

In the span of only 18 months Lazzeroni rolled out not one, but four completely original cartridges with whimsical names and calibers expressed in millimeters: the 6.53 Scramjet (.257), 7.21 Firehawk (.284), 7.82 Warbird (.308) and the 8.59 Titan (.338). The original case dimensions were interesting indeed.

The common case used for both the Warbird and the Titan hinted at its Rigby and Weatherby antecedents. The case head measured .580 inch; the 30-degree shoulder had a diameter of .560 inch, while the overall length of the case was 2.790 inches with a .020-inch taper. The length of the case neck measured a long and useful .300 inches.

John Lazzeroni at the moment he broke 4,000 fps with the 7.82 Warbird and a 130-grain plated bullet, as measured on his Oehler chronograph.

Only the highest quality components go into a Lazzeroni rifle.

Both calibers are still in production and their ballistics are impressive. Loaded to a maximum lot mean pressure of 66,000 psi, the Warbird (.308) with a 27-inch barrel can be handloaded to generate 3,775 fps with a 150-grain bullet, 3,550 fps with a 180-grain and 3,358 fps with a 200-grain bullet. In fact, in 1999 with a 130-grain, electroless nickel/Teflon (NP3) plated Barnes X-Bullet the Warbird crashed through the .30-caliber, 4,000 fps barrier with a velocity of 4,047 fps, later stepped down to 4,000 fps and briefly offered as a factory load. The ever popular Titan (.338) is no slouch either with factory loads delivering 3,550 fps with a 185-grain bullet, 3,300 fps with a

225-grain and 2,965 fps with a 285-grain bullet.

On the lighter end of that original, four-caliber Lazzeroni lineup were the Firehawk (7mm) and the Scramjet (.257). As Lazzeroni early on pointed out in his literature, if you can't tolerate the recoil of a particular cartridge but still want exceptional field performance, drop down a caliber—a prime example would be going from a .30-caliber magnum to a 7mm-caliber magnum.

Both the Firehawk and the Scramjet cases turned out to be quite unique. They do share their larger team members overall length of 2.790 inches, a 30-degree shoulder, a case taper of .020 inch and useful .300-inch length neck,

but there the similarity ends. The Firehawk (7mm), which has been superseded today by the Firebird, is an interesting case study in the complexities of designing an original cartridge.

Lazzeroni was looking for a 7mm case design that would generate 3,600 fps with a 140-grain bullet. Hitting the drawing boards, he came up with an original case that would do just that. The only problem was that it had a bastard head size of .548 inch. It was neither fish-nor-fowl in the world of common cartridge head sizes. The Firehawk cartridge also required a unique bolt face and a unique shell holder, but that didn't deter Lazzeroni. He was pushing the envelope on another front at the time.

Above: The $895 Lazzeroni/Sako was offered in 7.21 Firehawk and 7.82 Warbird.
Below: The most affordable short-magnum rifle offered was the Lazzeroni/Savage in 7.82 Patriot for $499.99.

During that same 18-month cartridge design window he was also designing what would become the Lazzeroni line of high-tech rifles. Like his cartridges, the design of his rifles was uncompromising, and fortunately the resources he needed were close at hand in Arizona.

Working with Rock McMillan of Phoenix, Ariz., he designed a distinct magnum action in both right and left-hand configurations, featuring a helically fluted bolt with a heavy-duty extractor and both pin and mechanical ejectors. The trigger he selected was one of Arnold Jewel's incomparable models. The custom bottom metal held two rounds and featured a straight-feed magazine.

He turned to another Phoenix craftsman for his barrels—benchrest barrel maker Gary Schneider, who's button-rifled, stainless steel barrels are renowned for their accuracy.

The receiver, bolt and bottom metal received an electroless nickel/Teflon (NP3) finish and the barrel a black polymer finish provided by Robar of Phoenix.

For the stock design he worked with the Harry Lawson firm in Tucson to develop an ergonomic, hybrid design combining the best features of an offhand silhouette stock, a conventional sporting stock and a classic thumbhole stock. The stock models were then provided to Kelly McMillan of McMillan Fiberglass Stocks in Phoenix for commercial production.

The final rifles were assembled using all the tricks of the accuracy trade including pillar bedding and fully

Sierra's new 350-grain .375 MatchKing bullet is delivering 1/2-inch groups at 300 yards in Lazzeroni's 9.53 Saturn.

The author with a first-generation Lazzeroni rifle featuring a hybrid silhouette/sporter stock.

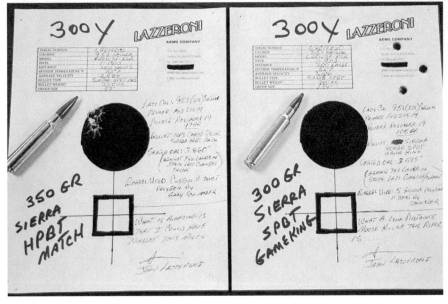

floated barrels. They were guaranteed to shoot a minute of angle or better, and they were pricey. The thumbhole and standard stock models cost $3,695 with one-inch and 30mm rings included, and performance demanding hunters bought a lot of them.

Just as Lazzeroni got his line of long magnums going in the marketplace, the shooting world was turned on its head with the introduction of the Remington and Winchester short magnums. The resulting short magnum ad copy was seductive – shorter, lighter rifles giving full-size magnum performance, and shorter powder columns providing more uniform ignition, smaller deviations and greater accuracy. In the face of the short magnum craze, what do you do as an entrepreneur? You rollout your own line of superior short magnums – and that's exactly what Lazzeroni did.

He took his long magnum cases, cut 3/4 inch out of the middle section of each one and brought to the market not one, not two, but five new short magnums. Again they shared some whimsical names and metric designations, but they were hot numbers. The 7.17 Spitfire (.243) delivered an 85-grain bullet at 3,550 fps; the 6.71 Phantom (.264), a 120-grain bullet at 3,150 fps; the 7.21 Tomahawk (.284), a 140-grain at 3,390 fps; the 7.82 Patriot (which, being a .308 was the most successful of the Lazzeroni shorts), a 180-grain at 3,100 fps; the 8.59 Galaxy (.338), a 225-grain at 2,950 fps.

Having set new standards for ballistic performance and furthering consumer expectations in the hunting firearms world, Lazzeroni was still challenged by the cost of his rifles and ammunition and the lack of interest from the firearms industry to chamber any of his superior cartridges – so he did it himself.

In 1999 he contracted with Sako to chamber their Model TRG-S with a stainless steel barrel in 7.21 Firebird (7mm) and 7.82 Warbird (.308). Lazzeroni ordered 1,000 in 7.82 Warbird and 200 in 7.21 Firebird. With a retail price of $895, the Lazzeroni/Sako's sold off overnight.

Turning to Savage, he contracted for 500 Model M16Ls chambered in his most popular short magnum, the 7.82 Patriot (.308). With a retail price of only $499.99, the Savages sold well but not as well as the Sakos. To Lazzeroni, it was an indication that the short magnum craze was winding down.

Much to his disappointment, neither Sako nor Savage would promote the Lazzeroni caliber models through their normal distribution systems. They would sell to him but not to the general public.

Sitting down with Lazzeroni earlier this year, I asked him about the current direction of the Lazzeroni cartridge and rifle lines. He commented that his

The most popular Lazzeroni cartridges sequentially are the 7.82 Warbird, 7.21 Firehawk, 8.59 Titan and 9.53 Saturn.

In 2005 the Lazzeroni rifle line went through a facelift designed to reduce the weight of the original L2000 models.

The current model rifles include the Long Magnum Lightweight, at left, and the Long Magnum Sporter and Thumbhole models below.

Lazzeroni's canted Picatinny rails are screwed and pinned to the action, facilitating maximum scope elevation adjustments.

Lazzeroni stresses that the devil is in the wind when shooting at extended ranges.

big-game hunter market now favors the fast 7mm, .30 and .338 cartridges with heavier-than-normal bullets featuring the very highest ballistic coefficients to retain velocity and energy downrange and to overcome wind drift. Consequently, he's discontinued his short magnums.

He observed that 500-yard kills on big game today are not unusual given the cartridges, rifles and optics now available and the serious target practice put in by conscientious long-range hunters. He even mentioned that with Sierra's introduction of the 350-grain .375-caliber MatchKing and its astonishing ballistic coefficient of .805, his 9.53 Saturn (.375) cartridge was delivering 2,833 fps and 1/2-inch groups at 300 yards in a standard Lazzeroni sporter with a 27-inch Schneider polygon barrel fitted with a Vais muzzlebrake.

I asked him what his most popular calibers were. Not surprisingly, the .30-caliber Warbird ranked first followed by the 7mm Firebird, .338 Titan and .375 Saturn. Those four cartridges plus the .257 Scramjet and the .416 Meteor now constitute the full Lazzeroni line.

And the Lazzeroni rifle line? John mentioned that the line had undergone a major facelift in 2005. The receiver was lightened, the bottom metal was changed from steel to aluminum and the magazine box redesigned to hold three cartridges. The bolt was diamond fluted and the bolt handle drilled out, plus the barrel profile was lightened and fluted.

Today the Lazzeroni rifle line consists of a Light Magnum model with a 26-inch barrel, weighing 7.3 pounds; a Long Magnum Thumbhole model with a 25-inch barrel, weighing 7.7 pounds, fitted with a 20 MOA, canted, Picatinny-style rail screwed and pinned to the receiver for maximum elevation scope adjustments; a Long Range Magnum Sporter model with a heavyweight 28-inch barrel and an overall weight of 8.8 pounds, furnished with a detachable five-round magazine and a canted Picatinny rail; finally, there's a Long Range Magnum Tactical model with a fully adjustable tactical stock, detachable magazine, canted Picatinny rail, 26-inch barrel and an overall weight of 10.9 pounds. All models are supplied with both 30mm and 34 mm scope rings, which indicates that hunters who buy Lazzeroni rifles also invest in premium optics.

And Lazzeroni ammunition? The brass is now made by Hornady and the quality is second to none. Bullets? Lazzeroni offers a proprietary line of electroless nickel/Teflon (NP3) plated Barnes solid copper bullets in 7mm, .308 and .338 calibers as components, as well as loaded in factory ammunition. The NP3 bullets, like all Lazzeroni products, have a unique moniker – LazerHeads. Being chemically bonded to the jacket material, the NP3 coating will neither scratch off nor wipe off. The purpose of the coating is to improve shot-to-shot uniformity in pressure and to minimize fouling. Other coated bullets loaded in Lazzeroni factory ammunition include Sierra and Swift A-Frame.

One final note. The Lazzeroni catalog is available at www.lazzeroni.com. It not only covers the complete Lazzeroni line, but also includes an excellent five-part article by John Lazzeroni on the essential components and skill sets required for successful long-range hunting.

I've often thought about John Lazzeroni in the same way I think of Roy Weatherby or Charles Newton. These are advanced amateurs, quite outside the mainstream of the firearms industry, whose passion and determination to create a better cartridge and firearm, coupled with their entrepreneurial skills, set new standards for ballistic performance in the commercial world while ever improving our performance in the hunting fields we love.

THE REMINGTON SPACE GUN

BY L.P. Brezny

SHOOTING THE XM2010 MSR (MODULAR SNIPER RIFLE)

When Gary Eliseo and others started turning to all-metal, free-floating-barreled long-range rifles for shooting competition events in both target and benchrest matches, it was a game changer in many respects in terms of the future look and feel of the modern centerfire rifle. In short, "tube guns" are here to stay, and becoming more popular all the time.

During the writing of my second edition of *Gun Digest Book of Long-Range Shooting*, I spent some extensive amount of time researching and shooting rifles marked by this new direction in hard-hitting, long-range hardware design. During the course of my testing I was offered a brand-new rifle as put forward by Remington Arms and, as such, contracted with the U.S. Army and others to be pressed in the direction of a dedicated special-use, ultra long-range weapon system. The gun was the now designated XM2010, or known in the ranks as "The Space Gun," and due to

Author shooting the XM2010 at the 1,000-yard bench. With correctly doped sights this was an easy task in terms of this outstanding long-range sniper rifle.

its unique features and appearance the name stuck right from the get go.

In short order my old friend Jessica Kellam with Remington press relations came up with a complete XM2010 in its drag case, with all the bells and whistles designed into this new gun system by

the Big Green machine. When the FedEx truck rolled up my road with only a single box in the back cargo bed – being transported by no less than two drivers with a pile of paperwork in hand – I knew this was not my daddy's deer rifle, but something very high priced and special in its triple-brass-padlocked black box. At once my little part of the gun world went on complete high alert.

The XM2010 was sent complete with the outstanding and world-class M-6 Leupold sniper scope, which also made use of the Horus reticle system, very massive custom rings and bases, with quality flip-style lens caps to match. Equipped with a Harris Bipod rest and an AAC (Advanced Armament Corp.) suppressor, the rifle was field ready to go to work downrange, and that is exactly where it

was headed after I quickly rounded up an assortment of .300 Win. Mag. ammo for some steel target work. This rife is capable of swapping barrels for unitizing the installed .300 Win., the .338 Lapua, .338 Norma or 7.62x51mm NATO (.308 Winchester). Quick changes are possible in the event that a mission calls for a different cartridge to be employed by snipers in the field.

This new rifle features a totally free-floating handguard (tube-gun style), a titanium receiver frame and bedding system hard bolted to the action, and a folding and completely adjustable butt-stock. Just about everything on the rifle from the muzzle to the buttplate is still in the patent pending stages of protection by the Remington Arms Company. Price per rifle? I didn't even ask.

Field Test

Immediately, the rifle was transported to a local, private club range near my home in Piedmont, S.D. My rancher friend Greg Iverson had allowed our SASS-based cowboy action and black-powder club to build a 600-yard range using steel plates as targets, and with the addition over the years of a full 1,000-yard element to the range it was the letter perfect location to set up and touch off the new Remington super gun. If anything was missing in terms of the test event it was that I didn't have any change-out barrels in .338 Lapua or Norma to run rounds downrange with.

Day one of shooting was accomplished alone to allow me to gather my thoughts and retain a level head lacking distrac-

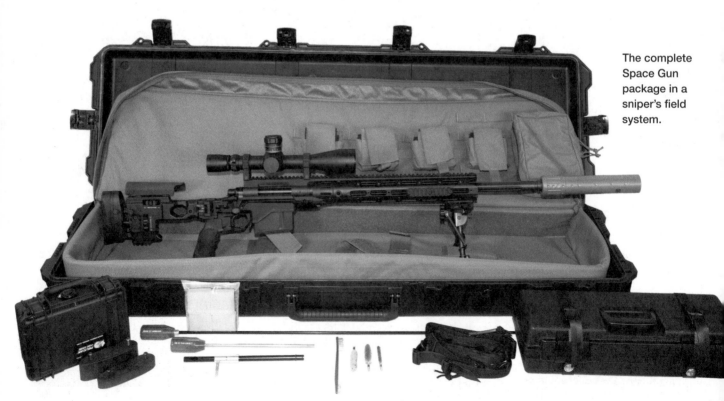

The complete Space Gun package in a sniper's field system.

tions when doping the Leupold M-6 glass sights. The rifle was zeroed judging by the 150-grain .300 Win. Mag. round in a Century Arms marketed Russian brand sent downrange for group effect. I was not shooting groups as such, but turned at once with a known zero established to the 600-yard steel gong target. Now I chambered a Hornady 165-grain SST InterLock, checked my Horus reticle mil-dots for holdover and at 2.5 mils sent a round out over the prairie. With a vapor trail cutting a spiral line across the sky the return slap on steel indicated that the bullet had founds its mark. The shot had been completely painless in that the suppressor had generated the sound of a .22 LR at the most, and with a 17-pound rifle on the bench recoil was nonexistent as well. By way of the outstanding two-pound X-Mark Pro trigger measured by my Timney trigger pull scale, shooting this rifle was just about effortless.

With three Hornady rounds downrange, and not wanting to use this outstanding big-game ammunition on steel targets, I turned back to my Century Arms Hot Shot brand 150-grain bullets. In less than another half-dozen rounds down range, 600 yards was about to become just a bit boring. I had not recorded a single miss on steel at 600 yards, and by setup time on day two with about 13 cowboys looking on, the real test of the system had come.

Word had gotten around that the Remington sniper rifle had arrived, and with a pile of 150-grain Century Arms ammo I would allow any and all that wanted to shoot the big gun an opportunity to do so. The rules were simple: At the 600-yard gong the shooter was required to chamber a single round, establish a sight picture exactly to the mark I indicated with the Horus reticle mil-dot holdover point, and simply touch off the XM2010 with a spotter in standby chasing the vapor trail in his optics system. A point in fact is that the 150-grain pills leaving the rifle almost silent to the 600-yard mark allowed about half a sentence to be stated before the bullet got to the

target. In effect the spotter, and at times shooter, was calling the shot with the rifle settled down lacking any felt recoil. The whole scene was a bit abstract and surrealistic to be sure. While shooters included a 13-year-old boy who didn't know how to sight the scope at all, and a cowboy with one eye and a bad left shoulder to boot, not one of a total of nine shooters ever missed a first-round hit on the steel.

On day three it was my old partner Jerome Besler and me, and we had moved back to the 1,000-yard bench so we could put some designed effort into the second phase of testing. The rifle, as designed, was built to accommodate the new military .300 Win. Mag. round developed by Black Hills Ammunition at Rapid City, S.D. Jeff Hoffmen – owner, sniper and expert in long-range shooting had developed this round that could stay with the .338 Lapua and Norma rounds, but his company was not manufacturing the new cartridge as it had gone to the lowest bidder. Word has it around the old range coffee pot that the manufacturer that received the military contract was not able to get Jeff's ballistics downrange, so the whole deal could still come back to Black Hills Ammunition in the end. You have most likely gotten this information first here in *Gun Digest*.

Now shooting Norma .300 Win. Mag. in 165-grain Oryx bullets, as well as the Hornady 165-grain SST fodder, I made a guess at the degree of holdover based on reticle mils. There was also the fact that I had been shooting out to 1,000 yards all summer with varied rifles and loads while working on my new book. So I was quite relaxed with the rifle cradled across my left arm on the bench as I dropped two pounds off that totally outstanding trigger. Jerome watched the shallow rise to the target as the bullet cut a white trail of high-velocity humidity that ended a bit low, but well centered on the steel plate. "We have a mark," was my first comment, and now at the corrected mil-dot holdover point (5.6 mils) the 1,000-yard steel was about to get pounded. I had used some Whiz Wheel data that had been previously applied to my .308 Win., the Horus reticle configurations and the excellent optics of the Leupold M-6 to dope in the glass sight. Once a range card zero is established, this rifle can more or less shoot itself, at least in dead early morning air. However, the wind came up as wind always will on the Dakota open prairie. Now the rules changed after both Jerome and I pasted the daylight out of the target's center. Each and every hit had been a dead-on killer if required, and at no time had we turned to electronic hand-held gizmos or

The author at the 1,500-yard gong. This range in western South Dakota can exceed 2,000 yards if required, a good test bed for the Remington XM2010.

This is the intended purpose of the Remington XM2010 rifle.

ballistic programs to produce accuracy or hard data at that indicated range.

With a slight breeze crossing my left ear, I estimated a 5-mph, 30-percent crossing value airflow was about to start to turn bullets a bit. Watching the short, late-fall prairie grass bend at the 1,000-yard mark also indicated that there may have well been more wind downrange than what we were experiencing at the starting line. I pulled 3/10 of a mil into the wind with the Horus reticle system, while still holding the correct mil setting for bullet drop. At the shot Jerome called miss as the bullet lifted Dakota dry dirt

and dust into the air in a dead-on perfect elevation line, but the bullet drifted to the right. With a correction at a full mil left the second round returned a solid ding against the raw-steel plate. Again we ran a series of rounds downrange with very effective results. But when the Dakota winds started gusting to over 10 mph it didn't take long to change conditions at all, so it was time to fold up shop and save the valuable ammo for another day in the field.

At no point did I spend a massive amount of time to try and shoot the XM2010 for a dead-center sub-MOA

group. In my opinion, and after interviewing a number of current and past snipers for my new book, I have come to the conclusion that far too much emphasis is being placed on group size and not downrange accuracy by the shooter behind the rifle. Groups can count for a lot, but minute of man, deer or coyote counts for much more.

The XM2010 is not perfect in that the stock requires folding to remove the bolt, the magazine rattles when empty and it is strictly a static-position rifle, however, it fit well into the bed of my Polaris RZR during field testing. In other words the big gun requires wheels. Tube guns in general are becoming outstanding static-position long-range or target rifles, but I would not trade my sporter-stocked Weatherby Back Country in .257 Weatherby for it when hunting at deer camp. These "Space Guns" are not well suited as hunting rifles at all in my opinion. What the XM2010 can do is assist in adding to the growing volumes of information gun builders are turning to when advancing high-performance firearms design.

Why was it built? There is a simple answer—to keep the mortar crews of the Taliban outside an effective strike range by way of a special rifle that can deliver the mail via the .300 Winchester Magnum at a reasonable cost per round. I have a feeling that we are about to see a great deal of this rifle's design applied to future benchrest 400 to 600-yard rifles, as well as those ultra long-range 1,000-yard match rifle systems.

A local cowhand took his turn and drilled 600-yard steel with the first round downrange.

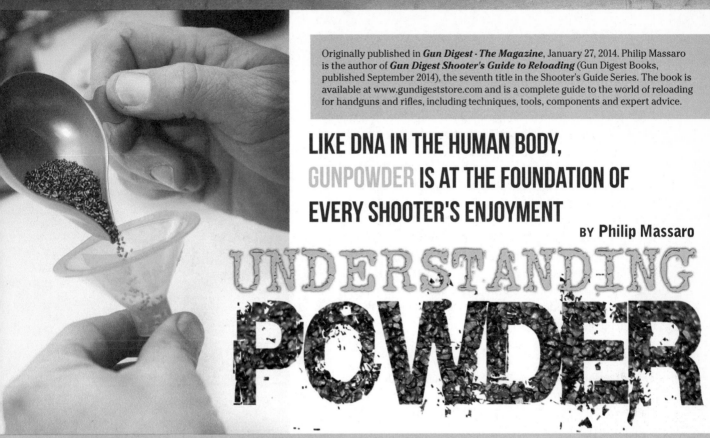

Originally published in *Gun Digest - The Magazine*, January 27, 2014. Philip Massaro is the author of *Gun Digest Shooter's Guide to Reloading* (Gun Digest Books, published September 2014), the seventh title in the Shooter's Guide Series. The book is available at www.gundigeststore.com and is a complete guide to the world of reloading for handguns and rifles, including techniques, tools, components and expert advice.

LIKE DNA IN THE HUMAN BODY, GUNPOWDER IS AT THE FOUNDATION OF EVERY SHOOTER'S ENJOYMENT

BY Philip Massaro

UNDERSTANDING POWDER

Warm apple pie, evergreens in November, a puppy's breath, my wife's perfume: these are among my favorite scents. All of them pale in comparison to the wonderful acrid scent of burnt gunpowder. You either know or you don't.

But what is that magic stuff? That mystical dust that makes a maraca sound when you shake your favorite cartridge? Some shooters never need or want to answer this question, but being the curious human I am, I had to know. Hours spent in my youth, thumbing through my dad's reloading manual initially confused more than enlightened, so allow me to shed a little light on this wonderful substance.

Friar Roger Bacon was the first European to record the mixture for gunpowder back in the 13th century, although it is a widely held belief that Chinese culture had it long before that. Regardless, that blissful blend of sulphur, charcoal and saltpeter called black powder certainly changed the world. It ruined the effectiveness of metal armor, diminished the security of the castle, and leveled the playing field between strong, brave soldiers and their more diminutive and cowardly counterparts.

Black powder has not really changed in its makeup over the last century and is still going strong. However, it burns dirty and leaves a corrosive residue throughout the rifle's or pistol's bore which must be removed quickly to prevent rusting and pitting. There are cleaner-burning substitutes available that have made the job of cleanup easier. Hodgdon's Pyrodex and 777 are among these. Black powder is generally measured by volume, not weight, and the substitutes are measured this way as well. Black powder is graded and identified by the coarseness or fineness of the granules; Fg is the very coarse cannon and shotgun powder, FFg and FFFg are more fine and used in many rifles and pistols, and the finest, FFFFg is usually reserved for priming the flintlock action. I must note that it is NEVER safe to use substitute in any load of black powder.

Progress was made in the scientific field of powder in the 1840s, when nitric acid was put upon cellulose to produce nitrocellulose. This was known as guncotton. It was capable of producing pressures and velocities much greater than its black powder counterpart, and it took a bit to develop steel that could withstand the pressures generated. Later, in 1887, Alfred Nobel invented nitroglycerine. This, when mixed with nitrocellulose,

Phil's Favorites- Three powders I have grown to love.

Hodgdon's H380

Myth has it that Mr. Bruce Hodgdon used this surplus U.S. Military powder in his then wildcat .22-250 with a 55-grain bullet, with a charge weight of 38 grains, to achieve ridiculous accuracy. It was so accurate that he decided to use the load data in the naming of this powder. It is one of the true spherical powders available and its performance in the .22-250 is unparalleled. However, as a medium-burn-rate powder, it has a multitude of uses. I've had great results using it in the .250-3000 Savage, .308 Winchester, and in the .375 Ruger topped with a 300-grain Barnes TSX. Because of the grain structure it doesn't take up as much room in the case as some other powders. H380 makes a lot of sense in cases like the (quickly fading) .284 Winchester and the benchrest sweetheart 6.5-284, where bullets are often seated very deep into the case. My .308 Winchester is very happy when loaded with H380 and 180-grain bullets, as it gives very consistent velocity readings and accuracy that is more than sufficient for the hunting applications I use a .308 for.

IMR4350

When DuPont announced the release of their (at that time) very slow burning 4350 powder, shooters rejoiced! It allowed the handloader to produce the velocities they wanted from the bigger cases with longer barrels. It was, and still is, a classic powder, one capable of hair-splitting accuracy. Although it is not considered slow burning in comparison to the newer magnum-case powders, it is a very versatile choice. It has been a choice for factory loading of the .270 Winchester and .300 H&H Magnum at various times. I love it in the .243 Winchester and the .30-06 with 180-grain bullets. It is my personal choice for the .300 Winchester Magnum with a 180-grain bullet, and I love what it does in my .375 H&H Magnum using 300-grain projectiles. It burns a little too slow for the smaller cases, but any case based on the '06 design or the H&H belted magnum can be well served by good ol' 4350!

Reloder 25

When I need to stuff a voluminous case full of powder and launch a projectile at very high velocities, more often than not I reach for a canister of Alliant's Reloder 25. It is very slow burning, and helps the over-bore "beast" cartridges, with their long barrels, achieve their full velocity potential. It is my powder of choice for the 7mm and .300 Remington Ultra Magnums, the .30-378 Weatherby Magnum and in the safari classic .416 Rigby. Powder charges in these cases can approach or exceed 100 grains of powder, and require a magnum rifle primer to consistently ignite those huge powder charges. Col. LeFrogg's .30-378 can push a 180-grain bullet over 3,300 feet per second using Reloder 25 for those reach-out-and-touch-'em shooting situations. It is also a good choice for those interested in the .338 Lapua Magnum for long-range work.

Store your powder in a place that is cool, dry and away from direct sunlight. Keep it in the original container to avoid any mix-up.

created a plasticized substance that was a stable compound. Cordite, an early British version of this compound, was the propellant du jour for many of our classic cartridges. One of cordite's little peculiarities was the fact that it was very sensitive to temperature fluctuation. The cartridges that were developed in England and Continental Europe often had pressure increases when brought to Africa and India. The heat of the tropics showed the flaws (hotter temperatures equaled higher pressures), from extraction troubles to cracked receivers, and this is why some of the huge cases like the .416 Rigby and the .470 Nitro Express came about. They needed that case volume to keep the pressure low.

Our modern single-base and double-base smokeless powders have resolved that issue, and the temperature sensitivity has been minimized. Single-base powders are usually comprised mostly of nitrocellulose; double-base powders are a mixture of nitrocellulose and nitroglycerine. The powder is coated with a deterrent and a stabilizer; the deterrent slows the burn rate to a desired amount, and the stabilizer slows down the self-decomposition of the compound.

The shape of the powder granules is usually one of three types: flake, stick or spherical. Flake powder is usually shaped like miniature pancakes. Many shotgun and pistol powders are made in this configuration. Alliant's Green-Dot, Red-Dot, Bullseye and Unique, and IMR Hi-Skor 700X and 800X are examples of flake powder. They are faster burning in part due to the large amount of surface area common to this shape. Stick powder is one of the most popular rifle powder shapes. The compound is rolled into long spaghetti-like rods and cut to the desired length. Examples of stick powder include IMR4064, IMR4350, Hodgdon's Varget and H4831, and Alliant Reloder 19 and 25. Spherical powder is a round ball, or a slightly flattened round ball. It takes up less space than stick powder, and can help achieve good velocity in a case with limited capacity. Some of the spherical powders include Hodgdon's H380 and BL-C(2) (read as Ball-C-Two), Winchester's 760 and Accurate Powder's No. 9. Many different powders have the same shape and color, so you don't ever want to try and visually identify an unknown lot of powder.

Powder is measured in *grains*, not to be confused with grams, which is a metric unit of weight. There are 7,000 grains to the pound. Depending on the cartridge being loaded (and especially pistol cartridges), a variation in powder charge of as little as one-tenth of a grain can make the difference between a safely loaded cartridge and a dangerous one that produces excessive pressures. **IT IS IMPERATIVE THAT YOU STRICTLY ADHERE TO THE LOAD DATA PUBLISHED BY REPUTABLE MANUFACTURERS WHEN LOADING CARTRIDGES OR SHOTSHELLS!** I cannot stress that point enough. The various reloading manuals are a product of months or years of pressure testing under strict laboratory conditions, and an attempt to exceed the published values can result in your untimely demise. Start at the published minimum charge weight and carefully increase the charge, stopping when you see the first sign of excessive pressure.

The powders available to the handloader are referred to as "canister-grade" powder. They are each unique in their burn rate. "Fast" burning powders are (generally) used in shotshells, small-case rifle cartridges, straight-walled rifle cases and many of the pistol cartridges. The "medium" burn rate cartridges work well in the standard rifle cartridges and some of the bigger caliber magnums. The newly developed "slow" burning powders really shine in the huge over-bore cases. The velocity kings like the .30-378 Weatherby Magnum, 7mm STW, .338 Remington Ultra Magnum and .270 Winchester Short Magnum all develop their high speeds from very slow burning powders that develop the high pressure necessary to push their bullets so fast.

Today's powders go by many different names, so it can be confusing and sometimes bordering upon dangerous. Some are just names like Retumbo, TiteGroup, Varget, Red Dot or Unique. Some are just numbers, such as (Accurate Arms) No. 5, (Winchester) 760 and 748. Some are a combination, such as IMR7828, H380, N160, Reloder 15, etc. It is important that you are pretty well versed in the different powders, so as to avoid confusion and possible injury. An example: There are three different powders, from three different manufacturers, that contain "4350" in their name. IMR4350 (Improved Military Rifle), H4350 (Hodgdon) and AA4350 (Accurate Arms) all have slightly different burn rates **AND ARE NOT INTERCHANGEABLE.** Strict attention must be paid to ensure that you have the

right powder in hand that the reloading manual specifies. This rule must be followed.

Storing powder is not a big deal. Common sense should prevail. It should be stored in a cool place, with no risk of open flames and no exposure to direct sunlight. Store your powder in a storage box that will keep it dry, yet in the event of a powder fire will not generate pressure. Never store powder in a gun safe – if you do, you've just made a large bomb! Always store powder in its original container – never try to re-label another container. I mark the date of purchase and the date I opened the container, so as to use the powder in the order in which it was purchased.

Choosing a powder can be time consuming. Often, the reloading manuals will offer several selections per cartridge/bullet combination, and will sometimes highlight or recommend the powder that worked best *in their test rifle or pistol*. All barrels are different, and while the most accurate load in the manual may work well in your firearm, sometimes you may need to experiment. Not all manuals test every powder that would be suitable for your cartridge, so inevitably you will end up owning more than one manual.

Some powders can be used in many different applications. For example, among pistol cases I use Unique and Tite-Group in many different cartridges, from 9mm Luger to .40 Smith & Wesson to .45 (Long) Colt, with great results. The .308 Winchester is the first cartridge I learned to load for. My dad, Grumpy-Pants, insisted that a 165-grain bullet on top of his chosen charge weight of IMR4064 was the only way to go in the .308, and anything else was near blasphemy. According to G.P. at that time, there was no other powder, or cartridge, for that matter. His choice for the .308 was certainly a good one, but it wasn't the only one. I have used IMR4064 (because we had a ton of it!) in .22-250 Remington, .243 Winchester, 6.5x55 Swedish, .270 Winchester, 7x57 Mauser, .308 Winchester, .30-06 Springfield, .300 Winchester Magnum, .350 Remington Magnum, .35 Whelen, .375 H&H Magnum and my sweetheart .416 Remington Magnum. This doesn't mean that this is the only powder that will work, nor the best powder in each of those cartridges. It just means it is a powder that has a very wide range of applications. There are many powders capable of being this widely used.

Conversely, a single cartridge may be served well by a large number of

Stick powder is one of the most popular rifle powder shapes. The compound is rolled into long, thin rods and cut to the desired length.

different powders. The venerable .30-06 Springfield, that classic of classics, can be fed a wide range of powders, with a wide range of burn rates, and still provide great results. For example, depending upon bullet weight, consider the following powders which are all well suited for use in the .30-06: IMR3031, IMR4064, IMR4320, IMR4350, IMR4895, IMR 7828; Hodgdon VARGET, H414, H380, H4350 and BL-C(2); Alliant Reloder 15, Reloder 17, Reloder 19, Reloder 22, Reloder 25 and 4000-MR; Winchester 748 and 760, you get the idea.

Read the manuals and choose wisely. It may take trying several types of powder before you find that accuracy you so desire, but that's a big part of the fun of being a handloader!

GUNPOWDER AND RECOIL

BY **Brad Miller**

Recoil is that nasty thing that happens when guns go bang. Sir Isaac Newton made it official in 1687 in his seminal work *Mathematical Principles of Natural Philosophy* when he described the Third Law of Motion that for every action there is an equal and opposite reaction. Of course, people discharging firearms at the time had already figured that out. But as we know about anything in the natural world, it doesn't officially exist until some scientist says it does. So in that sense, recoil is Sir Isaac Newton's fault. Or something like that.

Here's another problem, and it's all about us. We have a nervous system. And nervous systems get a little nervous around loud noises and things that whack them. Every time we pull the trigger we get a bang and a whack, and we come to anticipate that a bang and a whack will happen every time we pull the trigger. That's called learning. We're like Pavlov's dogs, except we don't salivate, we flinch. And flinching is bad because it happens before the gun goes bang and that throws off our shot.

So, how do we fix that? The same way you get to Carnegie Hall: practice, practice, practice—to not flinch. That can work but it takes a steely mind and doesn't work for everyone or every time. Most of us have discovered that the tendency to flinch increases with more recoil. So keeping recoil down reduces the chance of flinching, and less recoil is simply more pleasant.

Sometimes more recoil is the goal. Some semiautomatics won't cycle reliably with low-recoil ammunition. If you have a compensator on your gun, you know that some ammunition works the compensator better than others.

With factory ammunition you're stuck with whatever is available. But not so for handloaders. They can tailor their ammunition to regulate recoil and gun function. This is where it's good to understand how gunpowder affects recoil.

How do you select gunpowder based on recoil? Two guides are useful.

One is burning rate. Gunpowders have different burning rates: fast, medium, slow—that sort of thing. The general rule of thumb is to use faster burning gunpowder to reduce recoil, and a slower one to increase it.

But here's the thing: different burn rate charts have different rankings for some gunpowders. Table 1 shows the powders used in this article. Note the disagreement on where they are ranked by different manufacturers. This muddies the notion of using burn rate as a guide since it's not obvious which chart to use for this purpose.

Fortunately there is another rule of thumb to follow: charge weight. It might be a better guide to predict recoil because it's more specific, and as we know, it's all about the details—just ask Sir Isaac Newton.

The general idea is that it takes less weight of a faster burning gunpowder than a slower burning gunpowder to achieve the same velocity, and a lower charge weight means less recoil. Here's the reasoning. As gunpowder burns, it produces gas. Gas pressure is what pushes the bullet down the bore. The gas volume also contributes to the recoil. More gunpowder equals more gas equals more recoil. Many

Gunpowder	Hodgdon	Vihtavuori	Western Powders
Hodgdon Titegroup	14	5	9
Vihtavuori N320	24	7	12
Winchester 231	29	5	7
Alliant Power Pistol	33	12	18
Vihtavuori 3N38	48	16	22
Accurate No. 7	50	17	21
Hodgdon Longshot	52	13	-

Table 1. The Vihtavuori and Western Powders guides do not list the gunpowders sequentially like Hodgdon does, but on "lines," and some powders are on the same line indicating a comparable burning rate. The number indicates which line they were on, with line 1 being the fastest burning gunpowder(s). The Western Powders chart does not list Longshot.

FIGURE 1

Three or four charge weights were prepared for each gunpowder. The use of multiple charge weights produces data that can be evaluated mathematically with linear regression. For example, recoil and gunpowder charge

Before | FIGURE 2

mathematical formulas that calculate recoil include the weight of the gunpowder.

The key point is that the velocity is the same. Comparing recoil characteristics of gunpowders is only valid when they produce the same velocity. So if a gunpowder requires more charge weight than another gunpowder to produce the same velocity, it should also produce more recoil.

This principle was put to the test by comparing the relative recoil of several gunpowders with different burning rates and charge weights in two semiautomatic pistols, one with a compensator. Compensators are interesting beasts. They reduce muzzle rise by redirecting gas – Newton's Third Law again – and change the perception of recoil in an odd way.

Handgun recoil has at least two elements: rearward force and muzzle rise. The gun pushes back on the hand, but the hand also pivots due in part to the gun's bore axis being above our arm axis. Some folks equate recoil with muzzle rise alone. For example, some shooters who fire a compensated pistol for the first time remark that it has "no recoil." Well, that's not correct, even though muzzle rise is greatly reduced. These people obviously aren't familiar with Sir Isaac Newton's work.

Two customized Para Ordnance .38 Super pistols were used for the test. One was a standard configuration with a 5-inch Kart barrel, and the other had a 5.5-inch Bar-Sto bull barrel with a three-port compensator and a lightened slide (Figure 1).

Recoil was measured with a Ransom Rest, which is a device that tests a handgun's mechanical accuracy. The rocker arm that holds the gun rotates upward when the gun fires, similar to when the gun is handheld (Figure 2). The Ransom Rest does not measure recoil force per se, but measurements of the arm's movement can be used to compare *relative* differences in recoil. The distance that the gun moved vertically was measured.

Remington 115-grain jacketed hollowpoint bullets were seated to 1.245 +/- .002 inches overall length in fired Remington .38 Super +P nickel-plated cases with CCI

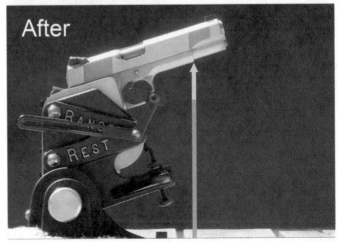

After

FIGURE 3

LS = Longshot;
PP = Power Pistol;
TG = Titegroup.

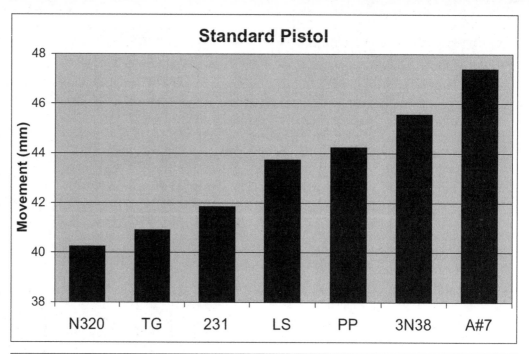

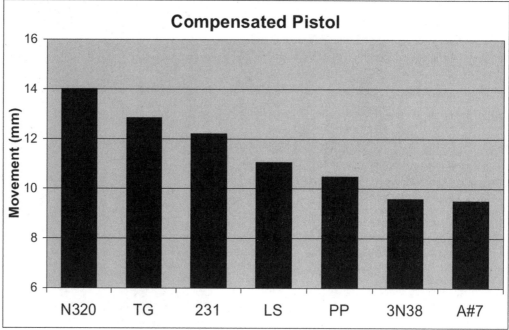

weight can be calculated for a specified velocity even if the tested charge weights did not produce that specific velocity.

Charge weight and velocity are linearly associated, which can be seen in loading manuals that show charge weights in velocity increments, such as the Hornady and Sierra manuals. Linear means that the values (measurements) are arranged along a straight, or mostly straight, line, which indicates change at a constant rate. For example, a gunpowder might produce a 50 fps increase in velocity for every .3 grains added. Mathematical formulas that calculate recoil also

produce a linear output. Ransom Rest movement is also linear, so this mathematical method is ideal.

A total of 540 rounds were fired from the Ransom Rest. The velocities spanned a range from 1,200 to 1,350 fps.

Gun movement for 1,250 fps is shown in Figure 3 with the powders shown in the order of their relative recoil. N320 had the least recoil and Accurate No. 7 (A#7) had the most recoil in the standard pistol.

The results with the compensated pistol ranked the gunpowders in the same order, but with a twist. The recoil effect was reversed. That is, N320 now produced the most

FIGURE 4

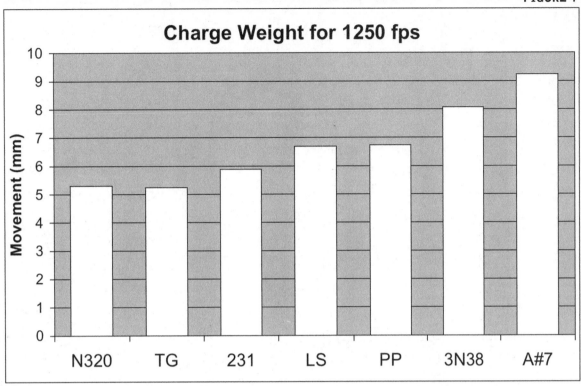

Charge Weight for 1250 fps

gun movement, while A#7 produced the least. Why is the recoil effect reversed in the compensated pistol? The same factor that contributes to more muzzle rise in the standard gun now contributes to less muzzle rise in the compensated gun. That factor is charge weight. Remember, more gunpowder equals more gas. More gas blasting out of the top of the compensator produces more downward force.

The compensated pistol moved far less than the standard pistol, anywhere from one-third to one-fifth as much depending on the gunpowder. Remember, some of the reduced muzzle rise is likely due to the additional weight of the compensator and heavier bull barrel.

Charge weights for 1,250 fps in the standard pistol are shown in Figure 4 with the gunpowders listed in the same sequence as Figure 3. Charge weights for 1,250 fps were nearly identical for both pistols. Higher charge weights produced more rocker arm movement in the standard pistol, and less movement in the compensated pistol. There was one exception. Titegroup's charge weight of 5.38 grains was slightly less than that of N320 – 5.41 grains, even though Titegroup produced more movement in the standard pistol, and less movement in the compensated pistol. But the difference in charge weight was only .03 grains, which in practical terms is nothing.

The results show that, indeed, charge weight predicts recoil better than burning rate.

The differences in recoil between some closely ranked gunpowders was very small. So if you're switching powders to one that has only a small difference in charge weight, the difference in recoil might not be very noticeable. And if the new load's velocity is only slightly different than the old one, any gain from using a different powder might be masked by the difference in velocity. Larger differences in charge weight between powders are more likely to yield noticeable differences in felt recoil.

What can we conclude from all this?

First, we have some control over recoil with the appropriate powder selection. How you load your ammunition depends on what you want it to achieve: velocity, felt recoil, gun function, etc. Second, burn rate is not the best predictor of recoil. Add to this that not even the experts can agree on where to rank a gunpowder's burning rate, and you're left with an inherently imperfect method. Third, charge weight is better for predicting recoil. A greater charge weight for the same velocity produced more recoil. Titegroup was an exception and serves as a good example of other, not-so-obvious differences between gunpowders. After all, there are scores of different powders and their formulations vary with respect to energetic composition as well as other components such as stabilizers, flash suppressants and so on, which influence their weight and burning characteristics. No doubt there are other gunpowders that break the rules, too. Fourth, compensators utilize gas volume to help reduce muzzle climb.

And finally, after all this, if you've learned only one thing about recoil, it should be this – it's Sir Isaac Newton's fault.

5 Biggest Challenges

TO LONG-RANGE ACCURACY

Learn to read the conditions, adjust your aim and make every shot find its mark.

BY **Dave Morelli**

ne of the things I really like about long-range shooting is the challenge of getting everything just right over and over for consistent precise hits way out there. Although the definition of long range changes every year, 1,000 yards is still a good poke even with rifles that are capable of consistent extreme long-range accuracy. It also depends on how precise your shot needs to be for the task at hand. Hunting for elk at 500 to 700 yards, the precision needed is far more forgiving than a police sniper crossing hairs on a hostage taker at 100 yards. Both shots have to be made as precise as possible, and the shooter will always have some obstacles that have to be addressed to keep from spoiling the shot. To become a reliable long-distance shooter, capable of striking your target every time, a shooter must first learn to handle several key challenges.

1 Distance

Accurately determining the distance to a target and properly adjusting the elevation of the shot is the first thing a shooter must be able to address. Usually a rifle will be sighted to a given distance. Personally I like 100 yards with most rifles, but a varmint hunter might sight his .22-250 at 300 yards while a military sniper might zero his at 600. No matter where the gun is sighted-in to, when the target is farther away, or even sometimes much closer, elevation correction will be needed to compensate rise or drop in the bullet as it travels before or beyond it's zeroed distance.

As a bullet leaves a barrel, it's immediately acted upon by gravity pulling it toward earth. As it gets farther from the barrel, it gets closer to the ground. When a rifle is sighted at 100 yards, the bullet will pass through the point of aim (POA), which is where the crosshairs and bullet intersect at the target. As the bullet continues past that point it will continue to drop at a repeatable rate. This can be calculated for any given yardage and must be adjusted with the turret of the scope or using the hash marks on some reticles to adjust for the bullet's drop at the distance the target is situated.

It's critical to understand the performance characteristics of the cartridge you are shooting. When I am working up a load, I use a chronograph to record its velocity. Knowing the velocity after it's sighted at 100 yards, I can feed the velocity, bullet weight and ballistic

TOP LONG-RANGE CALIBERS

.22-250

For coyotes at longer ranges I prefer a smaller bullet to minimize fur damage. Normally I shoot coyotes either by calling or stalking and shots are well under 300 yards with most 100 yards or less. However, there are times that coyotes hang up 600 or more yards out and have absolutely no interest in coming to a call. For them, I worked up a load for my .22-250 with Nosler's 80-grain HPBT bullet. This load comes out of the 26-inch barreled rifle I built at 2,900 fps and shoots a ragged hole at 100 yards. This bullet requires a fast twist of 1:9 or less to stabilize and my rifle has a 1:8 twist. The rifle has a heavy barrel that I don't really want to pack around all day, but it gives those frustrating coyotes something else to worry about when they are mousing in a distant field and ignoring or wary of my calls.

coefficient into a ballistic program such as Nightforce Optics's Ballistic Software (nightforceoptics.com) and it will build a drop compensation chart with the minute of angle (MOA) corrections to adjust the scope for a POA hit at whatever distant range I select on the chart. With a drop compensation chart, I, or any shooter, must then precisely determine the distance to the target.

Estimating range can be a tricky skill, and while most people, with practice, can determine fairly accurate estimates out to about 300 yards, beyond that, even the practiced shooter is only guessing. Out to 300 yards, even if the shooter misjudges the distance to the target by 40 to 50 yards, as long as it is an elk- or deer-sized target, a centerfire load shouldn't drop so much that it would result in a miss. However, for longer ranges or more precise shots at shorter distances, I depend on a laser rangefinder like the quality products from Leica or Leupold to obtain a precise reading. Laser rangefinders provide the actual range of the target from the shooter, not estimates, with the touch of a button. Every shooter should own one.

So now that we have a chart for our drop compensation and the laser to give us precise range, all we have to do is range the target, correct the scope, put the crosshairs on the POA and every bullet will go where we tell it. Well that's partly true, as long as all the environmental conditions stay exactly the same, at least theoretically.

2 Environmental Conditions

Environmental conditions will also definitely affect bullet performance. Temperature, elevation, humidity and barometric pressure will have an effect and change cartridge performance at long ranges. As a set of general rules, warm air tends to be thinner than cold air meaning a bullet in warm air will meet less resistance. Heat can also adversely affect the barrel temperature with each additional shot, which can affect bullet flight after it travels down the barrel. Although many people assume humid air is denser, dry air molecules are actually heavier than water molecules meaning less humidity can actually negatively impact bullet flight more. Likewise, thinner air at higher elevations or with decreased barometric pressure will impede bullet flight less.

Although there are powders that burn consistently in a wide variance of temperatures the effect of the different air densities on the bullet traveling through the atmosphere will change its velocity and thus its trajectory. These too can be calculated using a ballistic program or through shooting in different conditions and recording the results. Calculations with a ballistic program should be confirmed on the range and further adjusted as necessary before required to make an important shot at long range or precise shorter distances. Keeping careful records of each shooting practice will give the shooter info to create a card for that rifle and round. This information can be quickly put into the scope at the shot for a precise first round hit. As always the information that the ballistic program calculates should be shot in real time for minute changes and recorded.

3 Wind

Wind is perhaps one of the biggest obstacles a long-distance shooter must contend with and can be trickier than elevation. Distance is distance no matter where you are, but wind changes constantly even in the same location. I have shot matches where the wind was estimated and compensated for but at the exact moment of the shot it completely quit. The shooter must constantly be aware of this and may have to adjust the scope at the time of the shot. One technique, if time allows, is to just wait until the wind dies to make the shot.

The challenge to wind is there are two calculations. One is estimating the speed, the other is estimating the correction, whether it is with the turrets or hold over. Both must be precise and well practiced for consistent hits in wind. A wind meter provides the shooter a precise way to estimate wind. Meters from companies like Kestrel also have weather stations built right in and will give the shooter other important info like barometric pressure, temperature, altitude, etc. They are a good piece of

An angle cosine indicator is a great tool for long-distance shooters when taking shots at steep uphill or downhill angles.

SARA NORMAN

.308 WIN.

The .308 is a proven workhorse and there is a wealth of information and components for it. It is without a doubt, my favorite all-around caliber for most long-range shooting situations. The very first rifle I owned was a .308 and my profession has had me behind one so much it seems there is a ballistic card taped to my eyelids. Whether it starts its journey from an M-14, AR, or bolt gun its mild recoil and awesome power make it a great all around caliber. The cartridge is still a military and police sniper mainstay and 1,000-yard precision is proven again and again in the field and on the range. There is a multitude of bullet weights available, and it will digest a large variety of powders giving the reloader just about any purpose round they want to build. I like my .308's with a 1:10 twist as I usually shoot 175-grain HPBT for competition and target shooting and the 180-grain for game, such as elk and deer.

equipment for the long-range shooter and hunter.

The meter is only capable of giving the shooter the speed and direction where it is sitting—usually where the

shooter and rifle are. Other signs at the target have to be observed to confirm what the wind is doing where the bullet will travel. Most shooting competitions have flags at different distances to the

target but this is not always so and there are never flags in the field. The shooter will have to be able to estimate wind using vegetation or other natural things in the environment that move in the breeze. The police sniper in an urban environment might be able to use decorative flags or advertisement signs along with trees and vegetation to calculate wind. Mirage can also be used to calculate wind speed and direction up to 12 to 15 mph.

Direction of the wind also is important. Obviously which way the wind is going will indicate which way the bullet will drift but also important is the angle that the wind is contacting the bullet. Direct wind at 90 degrees to the bullet path will have the most effect. Wind from 10 to 15 degrees of either side of the 12 o'clock or six o'clock areas will have no value or no appreciable effect on the bullet flight. Wind striking the bullet at a 45 degree angle to the bullet path will have a half value or will affect the bullet flight half as much as a full

The Answer my Friend is Blowing in the wind

ESTIMATING WIND SPEED

Wind correction has been the cause of more misses in the hunting field than it's given credit for. The first step to correcting for wind is estimating its speed and value. A wind meter will be the most precise gauge for determining speed and will help provide the value of effect on the bullet path. However, many times there won't be time or one will not be available. If one is available, hold it next to the rifle so the fan blade is parallel to the bore to determine wind speed perpendicular to the bullet's flight. The wind value also will be included because the wind hitting the fins at an angle will not spin the blades like a 90-degree wind.

If a wind meter is not handy, natural flags in the woods like trees, shrubs and grass will help the shooter estimate the speed. A 3 to

5 mph wind will be felt lightly on the face, a 5 to 8 mph wind will make leaves in the trees agitate continuously, while an 8 to 12 mph wind will blow dust into the air. When the wind hits 12 to 15 mph, small trees will sway and bushes will blow from side to side. Even if you have the availability of a wind meter, like one from Kestrel, it's good to note visual indicators between you and the target to determine variances over the full distance of the shot. Comparing velocities in the meter with the actions of the shrubbery will help estimate the wind downrange when all you have is the movement of the shrubs.

Another way of estimating wind is with mirage. Mirage is the wavy effect that heat makes as it is rising from the ground. This method is accurate up to about 12 mph. Mirage is visible with the naked eye but can be magnified with the spotting scope. To see mirage focus the scope on the distant target and then rotate the focus to blur the target. The heat shimmer barely noticeable with the naked eye becomes amazingly clear. If the mirage rises straight up there is no wind. If the mirage tips about 60 degrees, the wind is 1 to 3 mph and direction is the way the top is leaning. Forty-five degrees will indicate the wind is about 4 to 7 mph, and mirage parallel to the ground is 8 to 12 mph. Next calculate the value it will have on the bullet path and adjust your aim accordingly. To become proficient, practice shooting on windy days and keep detailed notes of every shot. – D.M.

A wind meter is the most precise gauge for determining speed and helps provide data on how it will affect a bullet's path.

SARA NORMAN

value. These can be calculated down to ¼ or 1/8th values for more precision.

Once the speed and direction are estimated the effect on the bullet at the desired range must be dealt with. Once the wind is properly estimated feed the info into a ballistics program to determine the correction for the wind in MOA. The shooter can compensate for this either by using the turret or manually correct using the reticle of the scope. This is why I am fond of the Mil Radian-type reticles like the ones in the Leupold Mark 4 scopes. These lines make it easier to do precise holdovers for wind and elevation.

Another accurate method for calculating cor- rection for wind can be determined using a simple formula:

Range in 100 yards x wind speed in mph divided by 15 (Math constant) = MOA windage

Math Constants are:
600 yards divide by 14
700 yards divide by 13
800 yards divide by 13
900 yards divide by 12
1,000 yards divide by 11

An example would be a 300 yard shot in 10 mph wind looks like this 3 x 10 divided by 15 = 2 MOA

Got it?

TOP LONG-RANGE CALIBERS

.300 WIN. MAG.

The 300 Winchester Magnum has all the attributes of the .308 with more punch at 1,000 yards. It will handle the heavier bullets better at longer ranges and I have found the 200-grain Sierra HPBT to be a favorite. I can safely get the 200 grainer kissing out the muzzle at 2,950 fps and the rifle delivers a 3/8 minute group. Recoil is a bit more but not unmanageable and in the 12-pound rifle and scope I own, I can shoot it all day without a bruise. Again I like the 1:10 twist here because I mostly shoot heavier bullets from this caliber.

4 Inclination

Another overlooked obstacle, at least until you miss a trophy animal because of it, is inclination. Inclination is the up or down angle the shot is taken at. In general shots will print high whether a shot is taken at a steep up or down angle. This is because the line of sight that the range is estimated at is different than the actual distance the bullet is affected by gravity. The amount of up or down can be calcu- lated using the amount of angle and the distance.

At shorter hunting distances on a big boiler room this can be quickly addressed by holding off a little low, but for more precise compensation, such as a sniper making a high angle shot at 100 yards or better it should be figured into the shot. This angle of the shot can be fed into a ballistic program to figure the yardage corrections with the angle of the shot figured in. Even better, use a laser rangefinder that automatically calculates the angled distance for you.

5 Cartridge Performance

Cartridge performance also comes into play when estimating range correction or calculating adjustments in your

aim. Cartridge velocity must be consistent from shot to shot with the selected bullet so that corrections will also be precisely the same every time the scope or aim is adjusted. Quality match ammo or reloads must be tested for constant velocity and performance. The

shooter must become comfortable with the rifle and ammo and confident in their consistently. Avoid using inferior or bargain ammo as it may not perform as reliably throwing calculations off and resulting in seriously blown shots at long range.

There are other factors that affect bullet travel but these are some of the biggies. By mastering these factors and recording results every time we shoot, we can be confident that our calculations will be precise and the shot will be true.

*Originally published in *Gun Digest - The Magazine*, April 8, 2013 edition.

TOP LONG-RANGE CALIBERS

.338

For extreme long range the three big 338s have become popular producing awesome punch and consistent stability out 1,400 yards and farther. The three popular ones of the times are the .338 Remington Ultra Magnum (RUM) [see article pg. 31], .338 Edge and the .338 Lapua. These three are very similar in performance and discussing which is best will usually turn into an argument between fans. There are some features of each that might influence which is best for the shooter.

Recoil is not as bad as some whiners would make you think, and they all have the same variety of bullet weights, though I like using the heavier ones. The .338 RUM, which I shoot, is a factory cartridge. The brass is available ready to use and loaded rounds with limited bullet weights are available in the sport shop. The hand loader can create a good long-range loading by working with Sierra and Nosler 300-grain HPBTs or Hornady's 285-grain bullet. The 250-grain bullets also perform well.

The .338 Edge is less popular, but still a fine cartridge; however, it is not factory loaded yet and may never be. It's created by necking up a .300 RUM cartridge to 338. Although the .300 RUM brass is readily available it has to be formed in the Edge dies when resizing. I'm not aware of any factory rifles being made in this caliber so it would also have to be fired through a custom rifle—more trouble than many shooters will want to deal with.

Lastly, the .338 Lapua is a wonderful cartridge that is gaining popularity quickly in the professional and civilian markets—particularly where competitions are concerned. It's powerful with all the performance attributes of its counterparts and is available as a factory load by select manufacturers. It also fires with slightly more velocity than the others. Availability is sometimes a problem in some areas, but not if you order direct or online. More rifle manufacturers are also producing rifles in this caliber, and despite my fondness for the .338 RUM, it is the more popular of the three .338 variations.

The 3 DEADLIEST Gunfighting

By the numbers, the infamous Luger has been involved in more combat kills and casualties than any other handgun. The author believes it is the best pointing and most accurate military pistol ever issued.

LIEST
Pistols of All Time

The Luger, the 1911A1 and Single Action Army

BY **Jim Dickson**

The three greatest gunfighting pistols of all time, based on the number of kills and casualties made with them, are the Luger, the M1911A1 and the Colt Single Action Army. The circumstances surrounding these exploits are not likely to ever be duplicated again so their positions seem safe for all time.

THE LUGER

Used worldwide in the first part of the 20th century, the Luger saw its greatest action in German hands during the two World Wars. It was during the First World War that it earned the distinction of being the only pistol that was a major tactical weapon capable of winning a war. But for the entry of the United States in the war, it likely would have tipped the scales in Germany's favor.

The story is rarely told today, as the victors write the history books and the losers' exploits are often deliberately left out whenever the history re-writers can get away with it. Such is the case with the story of the Luger.

While World War I was defined by barbed wire, machine guns and artillery, combat in the trenches was an incredibly close-quarters battle. Entrenching tools and knives often had the advantage over rifles and bayonets in the crush of battle in the confined spaces of the trenches. This is where a pistol is best. Even at the closest quarters you can hold off your enemy with your left hand while you shoot him with the pistol in your right.

It was reported that the British and the French were reluctant to issue pistols to all of their rank and file because the soldiers were mutinying in large numbers. Also, the pistol was still an officer's badge of rank and something that just wasn't shared with enlisted men.

The German army had a different attitude. It was run like a very strict authoritarian family. Mutiny was never a consideration. When the troops needed

Angled views of the Luger with its unique toggle-operated action, open and closed.

pistols the Fatherland set out to supply them, despite the fact that the Luger pistol cost three times as much to manufacture as the Mauser rifle.

The Luger proved up to the challenge. It took in stride the mud, dust and sand maelstrom that was a WWI artillery barrage and kept on working when the famed Smith & Wesson Triple-Lock Revolvers were jamming. It would continue firing when its barrel was bulged from being clogged with mud. A Browning-style gun with the slide over the barrel is jammed solid until a new barrel can be installed when its barrel is bulged. This feature saved so many German lives in the First World War that when the P38 was designed, the army specifications demanded a fully exposed barrel on it. All the Luger needs for reliability is a magazine spring that is as strong as you can get in the magazine and proper ammo—standard velocity ammo of the proper overall length. Hot loads cycle the action too fast for the magazine to feed cartridges in position to chamber before the bolt rides them

down. This was never a problem with German army issue ammo.

A larger problem was the fact that the average German soldier was not a pistol shooter. The Luger handled that problem better than any pistol before or since. The Luger is the best pointing pistol ever made, bar none. Just point at the target and you hit it. It is as simple as that. It is also the most accurate pistol you will ever find. Most any good Luger will shoot a 10mm group with 9mm ammo at 25 yards.

Armed with the Luger the German troops proved a terror in trench fighting. Every stormtrooper was issued one regardless of rank, and production was geared up to equip every combat soldier by late 1918 or 1919. The Luger was a key factor in the new stormtrooper tactics as well as the new infiltration strategies of General Von Hutier and Colonel Bruchmuller, which had knocked Russia out of the war. The intensity of the trench fighting and the number of kills made by the Luger was staggering.

World War II saw more intense fighting with the Luger often being used against Russian human-wave assaults. Sometimes it was the officer's only weapon and sometimes it was the last thing he had loaded magazines for. At those close ranges one could hardly miss. Once more the tally went up drastically. Add to these figures the numbers of the other countries' armies that used the Luger and you get a number far exceeding any other pistol.

THE 1911A1

The number two spot in numbers of enemies killed should go to the M1911A1 .45. During the first part of the 20th century Americans took great pride in their skill with a pistol. There have always been American soldiers who prefer the pistol to the rifle at close range, "close range" being a relative term that some will take out to 100 yards or more. Nothing is faster on target than a pistol and that fact has saved the life of many a pistoleer in combat.

Ramping up pistol production took priority over rifle production when America entered WWI. Unlike the French and British, the Americans were quick to issue pistols to anyone who needed one. WWII saw more handgun use with house-to-house and jungle fighting all within easy pistol range. Americans got their first look at human-wave assaults with the Japanese banzai charges in the Pacific Theater. They experienced them again in Korea when the Chinese communists obeyed their Russian advisors and launched the same sort of human-wave assaults Russia had used against Germany in WWII. The M1911A1 has also seen close-quarters fighting in Vietnam and subsequent wars.

The M1911A1 is the most reliable pistol in harsh conditions that is possible to make. I have seen an M1911A1 throw sand out of every joint with the first shot and keep on firing. An unaltered military M1911A1 will tolerate more rust, dust, sand and mud than any pistol ever made and continue to fight. Its FMJ 230-grain bullet is a sure fight stopper with a hit to the vitals. It is a natural pointer, and with a little practice many shooters can't seem to miss with it. My Betty has shot every coin out of the air with one as long as I had pocket change to throw for her. While it comes in second to the Luger in the number of people killed with it, the M1911A1 remains the ultimate fighting pistol.

Some readers will disagree with the author's number two ranking of what many call the "World's Greatest Fighting Pistol." But remember, he is using historical numbers of kills and casualties.

A well-worn, pitted Remington Rand M1911A1 from WWII that will still shoot 2½-inch groups at 25 yards all day long. There is play in the slide to allow plenty of room for dirt and sand, but it does not hurt its accuracy one bit. It has never jammed under any conditions. This is a gun to stake your life on.

The Model 1873 Colt Single Action Army revolver with a 4¾-inch barrel in .45 Colt, the classic gunfighter's weapon of the Old West.

COLT SINGLE ACTION ARMY

Finally, we come to the classic gunfighter's revolver, the Colt Single Action Army .45 Model of 1873. The old cowboy sixgun is what the public thinks of when they think of a gunfighter's gun, although its tally of kills is below that of the Luger and M1911A1.

Most of its kills were racked up on the frontier where many a pistoleer insisted

it was as accurate as a rifle out to long carbine ranges, and would proceed to prove it to any doubters.

Today's shooters often can't get the same results because they don't grip it and cock it correctly. If you cock it like you would a double-action revolver with the thumb held lengthways behind the hammer, it will throw your grip low to the round bottom of the gun, and it will tend

to shoot to one side or another without ever pointing very well.

The correct way is to lay the thumb crossways on the hammer and cock it as you would one of the old cap-and-ball Colts with the vertical hammer. This throws your grip high. You should have the cocked hammer forced against the top of your hand, with the ball of the hand behind the trigger finger squeezing one of the flat Colt logo panels, and the thumb squeezing against the other. Put the first joint of the trigger finger over that narrow trigger, and if possible touch the tip of the trigger finger to the tip of the thumb. This puts the gun's backstrap against the center of the palm of your hand. Squeezing the flat logo panels aligns the sights with whatever you are pointing at, and squeezing the trigger at the same time converts the act of pulling the trigger into a steadying affect, instead of disrupting the aim.

This is the only pistol I have shot like this. Many people say the single action rolls back in the hand with recoil. I have never felt any recoil nor have I experienced the gun moving in my hand with this grip. This is an old gunfighter's secret and I believe I'm the only writer ever to put it in print.

The 19th century design of the SAA does have its limitations. Since it lacks a hammer bar safety like later revolvers, it must be carried with the hammer down over an empty chamber for safety. This is accomplished by loading one chamber, skipping one, loading four and then cocking. You can now lower the hammer down on an empty chamber.

Since it is almost as slow to reload as a cap-and-ball revolver using paper cartridges, you don't want to take this gun into a gunfight where you have more than five opponents. However, it is so fast and sure with those five shots that you will find it an excellent choice for five or fewer enemies. The .45 Colt, like the .45 ACP, was designed to stop a 1,500-pound cavalry horse with one shot, which it does easily. Obviously, man stopping comes easy with either caliber.

These pistols all share an ease of accuracy due to the best pointing characteristics possible. They are all very reliable in service use – with the M1911A1 being the most reliable pistol of all time. Even today there is no handgun approaching its level of effectiveness in combat. Anyone planning on using a pistol for gunfighting should confine his search to these three.

Cocking the Colt Single Action Army is done with the thumb laid crossways over the hammer so the hand remains positioned as high as possible for accurate pointing.

The old gunfighter's secret grip is necessary to make the Colt Single Action point its best. The palm of the hand is against the backstrap, not beside it. The grip is as high as possible with the hammer spur digging into the back of the hand. The flat Colt logo panels at the top of the grip are squeezed between the thumb and the ball of the hand at the base of the trigger finger, both of which are angled downward. The trigger is hooked by the first joint of the trigger finger, while the tip of the trigger touches the tip of the thumb. Squeezing the flat logo panels aligns the gun with whatever you are pointing at, and squeezing the trigger is converted into a steadying force instead of a disruptive force – enabling the shooter to get the maximum accuracy from the gun and cartridge.

Young Guns

Want to make shooting the safe, positive and thrilling experience it should be for your son or daughter? Start with a compact rifle or shotgun that fits them.

BY Doug Howlett

It's probably one of the most contentious and misunderstood decisions in all of shooting: What's the best type of gun/caliber/gauge to start a young shooter out so that they learn good marksmanship skills, maintain the highest level of safety and develop a lifetime love for the shooting sports? From arguments over which action type is better to whether it's best to start them with small rimfire calibers or smaller gauges or get them out shooting and hunting with the gun they'll use for the game or type of shooting they'll eventually do, there is plenty of room for interpretation. Ultimately, a lot of it comes down to the individual child or even young adult learning to shoot.

Where hunting is concerned, a lot of kids are started out on a .22 Long Rifle or .410 shotgun—the latter a true disservice to the child unless all he will be hunting is squirrels or maybe the occasional rabbit, says Kurt Derwort, a Virginia gunsmith, retired armorer for the Navy and a Double Distinguished Shooter.

The load is so limited and constriction tight as to make it a poor choice for ducks, deer or turkeys unless you expect the animal to always come within point-blank range, something that can lead to frustrating hunts and potentially wounded animals. A 20-gauge shotgun offers the best blend of low recoil and lighter gun weights without severely handicapping downrange energy and knockdown.

Where rifles are concerned, Derwort says a .22 is ideal for teaching the basics of trigger control and proper aiming technique (and until this current spate of frantic ammo purchases, were much less expensive, too), but when looking to actually hunt anything beyond the smallest game, switching over to a .243, 7mm-08 and even 7.62x39 or .308 are top choices.

TOP 5 TIPS

START 'EM OFF RIGHT

The quickest way to ruin a young shooter and turn them toward a life of skateboards, video games and mall food is to make their first forays into firing a gun scary, pressure-filled and uncomfortable. To ensure your son or daughter develops a love for your favorite activity, follow these tips from expert shooter Kurt Derwort.

1 Keep it Fun. Don't expect a kid to shoot at paper for three hours as if they are preparing for combat. "You've got to keep it fun and interesting or you're going to lose their interest," Derwort says. Change up the types of targets you're using to keep them interested and having fun. Balloons are a great choice as everyone loves to see stuff pop and explode. Derwort also likes charcoal briquettes. "They are the most awesome targets," he says. "They explode upon impact and wash into the ground with rain so there is nothing you have to pick up afterward."

2 Don't Overgun a Young Shooter. If they have never fired a gun at all, every kid should be started with a .22. The low-recoil and limited "bang" won't frighten them as they are figuring out what shooting is all about. Rimfires are usually smaller and lighter so they are easier for small shooters to handle and the shooting skills they learn with the .22 are easily transferable to heavier calibered centerfires or even shotguns when they are ready to make the transition.

3 Make Sure the Gun Fits. Just like a jacket that's too big or sneakers that don't fit, a poor fitting shotgun will erode proper shooting stance and can actually increase the discomfort of felt recoil. You want to make sure the shooter can reach the trigger without having to stretch their arm or alter the way their face and buttstock should align. Don't have a youth model handy and don't want to cut a perfectly good stock to fit? Buy an inexpensive synthetic replacement stock and put it on the gun. You can always switch back after your hunter or shooter grows up.

4 Perfect Practice Makes Perfect. It's a blast, literally, to go out and just crank off rounds at targets, but while a little free reign is good, maintain some level of structure that allows them to see how well they are improving and becoming better shots. After all, you want to be sure they are developing the skills necessary for good marksmanship. Always shoot from a rested position from a firm, safe rest to ensure good technique and proper aim.

5 Be Safe. Safety is paramount every time you're in the presence of firearms and particularly when handling them. Begin every session having them go over the tenets of safe gun handling: Keep the muzzle down range or safely pointed; keep the safety on until ready to shoot; keep fingers off the trigger until ready to shoot and treat every firearm as if it is loaded at all times. Point out when they do something wrong and make them take a time out from shooting when they slip up.

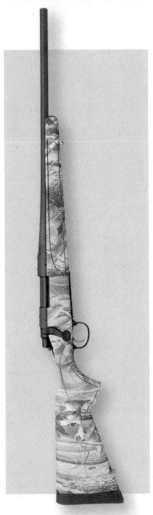

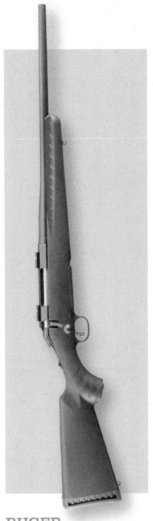

REMINGTON MODEL 700 SPS COMPACT

The Model 700 is one of the most ubiquitous rifle lines in history so of course, Remington is going to have one designed for young or small stature shooters. The 700 SPS (Special Purpose Synthetic) Compact shortens the length of pull, trims 4 inches from the barrel and shaves a ¼ pound of weight compared to standard-sized models. The synthetic stock can take scratches and being dropped for years and still deliver in the performance department. The 7mm-08 version (it also comes in .243) paired with the company's Managed Recoil 7mm-08 ammo is a good choice for young hunters. ($639, www.remington.com)

SAVAGE MODEL 11 TROPHY HUNTER XP-YOUTH

Savage's light-shooting bolt-action Model 11, chambered in .223, .243, 7mm-08 and .308, is available in both right- and left-handed models, to create a gun that will truly fit your young shooter. The rifle features a matte black synthetic stock and forend with a matte black carbon steel barrel, a detachable four-round magazine and Savage's AccuTrigger, which allows for simple adjustments to the weight of the trigger pull. The rifle comes complete with a premounted Nikon 3x9-40mm BDC reticle scope, which when used with Nikon's ballistic software, helps determine the appropriate drop at any range. ($675, www.savagearms.com)

RUGER AMERICAN COMPACT

For our little patriots out there, the Ruger American is 100 percent American made and features Power Bedding integral bedding blocks, a three-lug 70-degree bolt, an adjustable trigger and flush-fit, four-round rotary magazine. The Compact variation is chambered in .243 or 7mm-08, weighs a mere 6 pounds and delivers a comfortable 12½-inch length-of-pull. The stock is black composite with a textured and tapered forend for improved grip by small hands. ($449, www.ruger.com)

NEW ENGLAND FIREARMS COMPACT HANDI-RIFLE

For those adults who prefer the safety of a single-shot for their new hunting partner, New England Firearms owns the category. The NEF Compact Handi-Rifle weighs in at less than 7 pounds and boasts a comfortable 11¾-inch length of pull for smaller shooters. The .243 chambered model features a Monte Carlo hardwood stock with a walnut veneer. Mounts are included or you can buy the gun already outfitted with a 3x9-32mm scope. ($266 w/o scope, $305 scoped, www.hr1871.com)

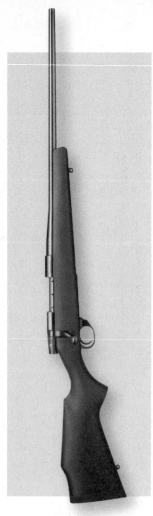

WEATHERBY VANGUARD YOUTH/COMPACT

Weatherby's economical Vanguard line includes the Vanguard Youth/Compact so today's young shooter can enjoy the same quality older Weatherby aficionados appreciate. The gun weighs 6¾ pounds, a length of pull of 12½ inches and an overall length of nearly 39 inches. The Youth/Compact features a synthetic stock or added weight reduction and durability, while the trigger is fully adjustable and comes factory tuned. Youth-compatible chamberings include .243, .308 and 7mm-08. ($643, www.weatherby.com)

MOSSBERG 500 SUPER BANTAM COMBO

Not every young shooter plans to pursue game or targets with a rifle, and where a trusty shotgun is needed, Mossberg answers by pairing up a fully interchangeable 22-inch field barrel and 24-inch ported and fully rifled Slugster barrel to create the Model 500 Super Bantam Combo. With both barrels, this could be the only gun a young hunter needs. Chambered for 3-inch, 20-gauge rounds, this pump-action weighs 5¼ pounds with a 12 to 13 inch length-of-pull depending on how you set up the adjustable stock. Available in Mossy Oak Break-Up Infinity (shown) matte and Realtree AP. ($518, www.Mossberg.com)

MARLIN XT-22YSR

For developing perfect shooting skills in truly young shooters, few firearms can compare to the .22 rimfire. While the once cheap ammo has skyrocketed like everything else, don't expect the madness to last, and when it subsides, Marlin's XT-22YSR will be a choice that will deliver shooting fun for your child's entire life. It features a shorter stock (12-inch length-of-pull), shorter trigger reach, smaller grip and a raised comb for easier aiming. The bolt-action .22 has a 7-round nickel-plated clip magazine, synthetic stock and 16-inch stainless steel barrel with a fast 1:16 twist. ($254, www.marlinfirearms.com) **GDTM**

As for shotgun actions, he likes a pump, because subsequent shots don't automatically go to battery as they do in a semiauto, yet the child has the ability to produce quick follow-up shots when required. Using a break-open, single-shot would simply leave them undergunned when more than one shot is needed. For rifles, he prefers a bolt action.

"A good bolt gun allows you to cycle the rifle while it's still on the bench, more so than a lever gun, meaning the shooter doesn't have to lift his head completely off the stock and loose sight of the target. It also provides more options for scopes and sights."

Most importantly, be sure the gun fits. A good fit ensures a better stance and shooting form, which will reduce felt recoil and poor shooting results. Fortunately, today's manufacturers boast a plethora of youth and compact models, perfect for getting today's young sportsman off to the perfect start.

* Originally published in Gun Digest - The Magazine, April 22, 2013 edition.

THE MYSTERY OF THE

THESE TWO REMINGTON ROLLING-BLOCK RIFLES PROVIDE A CONVOLUTED HEADACHE FOR THE MODERN COLLECTOR

Photo Courtesy NRA National Firearms Museum nramuseum.com

EGYPTIAN AND GREEK
REMINGTONS

BY **George Layman**

ALL PHOTOS COURTESY OF THE CHRIS LENER COLLECTION UNLESS MARKED OTHERWISE

It's the same line we have heard at gun shows for decades, "They all look the same… it's probably a Spanish Model… yeah, it's all worn down and must be an Egyptian Model." Comments such as these still go on, but not as often as they once did. With new reference works and research on the Remington military rolling block booming at its highest like never before, collectors, dealers and others are begin-

ning to challenge the once-hackneyed clichés and are demanding factual answers. It is not our intention here to delve into the rocky but successful road to fame of the military Remington rolling block, but rather decipher two specific variations of this family of firearms, which made their international debut on the battlefields of Western Europe.

When the Franco-Prussian War began in the summer of 1870, France was com-

pelled to arm its troops with the latest ordnance against the highly disciplined and very well-equipped Prussian army. With its military basically limited with the inefficient Model 1866 Chassepot rifle, the French president of the New Republic, Adolphe Thiers, was forced out of desperation to turn to foreign suppliers across the Atlantic. At the commencement of hostilities one of Remington's chief salesmen, Samuel

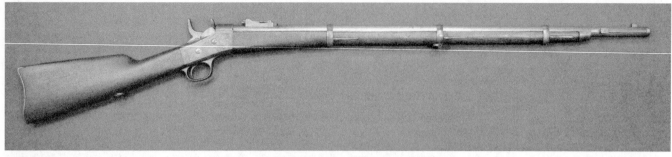

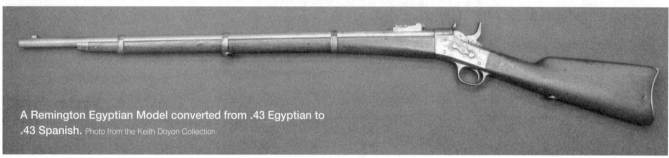

A Remington Egyptian Model converted from .43 Egyptian to .43 Spanish. Photo from the Keith Doyon Collection.

Norris, was in the Netherlands and almost immediately began hounding the French to accept several hundred of the new 11mm-caliber Remington rifles. The French eventually took up the offer and expressed great satisfaction. The resulting hodgepodge of metallic cartridge rifles of various calibers was a headache that contributed to the logistical nightmare the French would soon experience. Through persistence and slick persuasion, the now flourishing American firm of Remington and Sons soon became a chief supplier in arming France throughout the conflict.

Having won a silver medal just three years earlier at the Paris Exposition for its Remington-Rider breech-loading system, the efficient and reliable Remington rifle was sorely required – and without delay. Known in modern collector terms as simply the "rolling block," by 1870 it was already in the hands of Denmark, Sweden, Spain and a few nations of Latin America. Furthermore, on June 30, 1869, Egypt signed a contract in London with Remington for some 60,000 rolling-block rifles. In addition, the government of Greece had recently contracted with Remington for almost 13,500 rifles, which included 1,000 carbines. France had excellent credit at the time of the war and would pay top dollar for Remington rifles and other small arms, but their expeditious needs soon put a strain on the Remington factory, forcing them to dedicate all efforts to the precarious French situation on a 24/7 basis.

In terms of sheer numbers, it appears that in popularity the Remington Egyptian Model topped all other rolling-block rifles received by France in the period between October 1870 and the war's end in May 1871. Some 149,957 were purchased, more than double the number procured by Egypt almost a year and a half prior. Why the .43-caliber Egyptian Model was obtained in such large numbers might be attributed to Remington's anticipation of a large follow-up order by the Egyptian government, with all the tooling and raw material that was apparently in a ready production stage. It should be noted that the original Egyptian contract specified that the rifles "will be chambered for the Vienna Cartridge," a meaning arguably subject to varied interpretations. As it stands, the 11mm or .43 Egyptian Remington rolling block and cartridge were by far the largest of their genre in circulation with French forces during the war with Prussia. The 1876 Remington catalog even advertised them as the "French Model" on the commercial market.

All pre-August 1870 Remington military rolling-block rifles have the "concave" breechblock axis as shown on the open action of this early Egyptian Model. Note the machine markings left on this example, indicating the factory was hastily producing this variant during the hectic months of the short Franco-Prussian War.

The Remington Egyptian Model was equipped with a 35⅛-inch barrel and a saber bayonet lug. Those manufactured prior to August 1870 had what is known as a concave breechblock, with all subsequent production modified to a simpler to produce, flat breechblock base. The extractor on all 1870 and 1871 production arms utilized the screw-retained horizontal bar extractor.

The markings on many of the early Egyptian Model Remington rifles varied with most having a "B" stamped on the left frame and barrel flat. A small but unknown number were stamped with a "KM" on the left frame, barrel, hammer and breechblock flat. A single example owned by the author also has the "KM" stamped on the barrelbands as well, and is the only such example viewed to date. The basic cosmetics of the Egyptian Model bears a slight resemblance to most others of its ilk, with one in particular that is near identical – the elusive Remington Greek Model.

Until the recent past the background of this once practically unidentifiable variant was a mystery to collectors. Its story is a convoluted one and is often coined, "the Remington rolling block that almost wasn't." In the past, the author had a document that specified the Greek Defense Minister Spyros Milios approved an order/contract in 1869 for 13,500 Remington rifles and 1,000 carbines. It appears that since this contract was practically undertaken on the eve of the Franco-Prussian War, it is here that things turn misty. Research has indicated that when Remington became France's chief arms supplier and learned the French would pay 100 francs ($20) per rifle in lieu of the standard 75 francs ($15), as well as pay their bills quickly, it appears outright greed superseded common business ethics and integrity.

Remington lusted for Frances's profitable business so badly that they even persuaded the Greek government into canceling their entire contract! Once the Greeks caught on to what the plan was, they stipulated that they wanted a percentage of Remington's windfall profit from the sale. Remington concurred, but was still receiving more than they would have from the financially shaky Greek government. For the French however, the purchase of the 9,202 Greek Model Remington rolling-block rifles was a near disaster.

The rifle was originally chambered for the 10.75x58R Russian cartridge, which is more commonly known as the

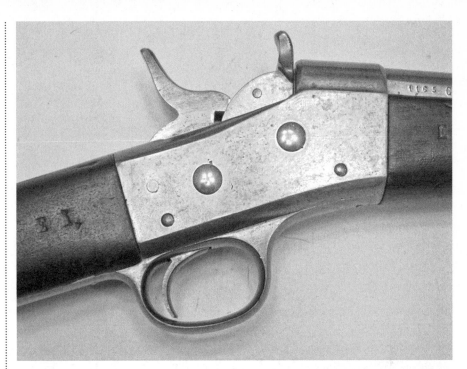

This view of the right frame has French unit markings as well as being serial numbered on the side of the chamber. Such marked examples of Franco-Prussian War era Remington Egyptian Model rolling-block rifles are rarely seen on the U.S. collectors market, but are more frequently encountered in Europe.

A close-up of the French serial number on the right side of the chamber on the Egyptian Model.

.42 Berdan and has a smaller case and bullet diameter than the .43 Egyptian Remington. French supply officers were issuing some eight or more different types of ammunition and the situation was nearly total bedlam, especially for soldiers in the field. It appears there was a shortage of .42 Berdan shipments from the United States, which essentially meant French soldiers were issued the Greek Remington rolling block and sometimes issued the wrong ammunition, such as .43 Egyptian, .43 Spanish Remington or at times nothing at all. Neither of the aforementioned will fit in the Greek Model Remington, however, it is possible for the .43 Spanish to be made to chamber in a .42 Berdan rolling block, as we shall later see.

There appears to have been so much confusion regarding the Greek Model rifle, that French ordnance ended up stamping a "G" in a circle on the left buttstock, indicating they were the Greek variation. For

A little known feature on many early Remington military rolling-block rifles is the tiny, roll-stamped patent markings of Feb. 11, 1868, which are found on the ring of both rear and front sling swivels. This patent was issued to Remington engineer, Joseph Rider, who refined the rolling block in its final stages.

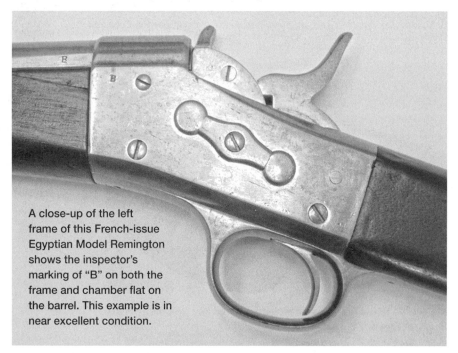

A close-up of the left frame of this French-issue Egyptian Model Remington shows the inspector's marking of "B" on both the frame and chamber flat on the barrel. This example is in near excellent condition.

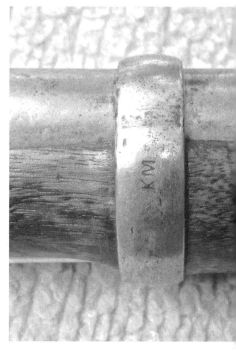

the modern collector, they can be readily observed on those rifles having a visible circle G cartouche. Most importantly, they may positively be identified by the presence of a crown on the left hammer and breechblock flat, as well as on the left frame, barrel flat and each barrelband. Originally, the Greek Remington was designed to use a French Chassepot-style bayonet with a secondary tenon opposite the saber bayonet lug. It appears these

were ground or sweated off by the Remington factory and the only example observed with this feature is the sample in the Remington Arms Company collection in Ilion, N.Y. Those that appear from time to time on the collector's market are devoid of the secondary tenon lug.

Overall, this rifle failed due mostly to the extremely limited quantities of ammunition that were shipped during the short war between France and

Prussia. It should be noted that in April 1873, the Greek Remington rifles were sold at public auction in France and were among 6,640 surplus arms from the Franco-Prussian conflict. More were sold at auction once again on Sept. 15, 1878. There is, however, a very mysterious twist to these rifles.

At least 11 specimens have been examined by the author, all of which had the aforementioned Greek contract

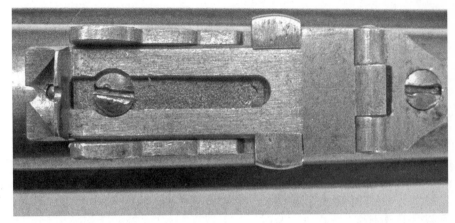

Above: Both the early Remington Egyptian and Greek Model Remington rifles have a nearly identical rear sight. And both also have the same two-line Remington tang markings that end with April 17, 1866, which is the date of the second Remington-Rider patent. The example shown on this Egyptian Model is somewhat faint from wear.

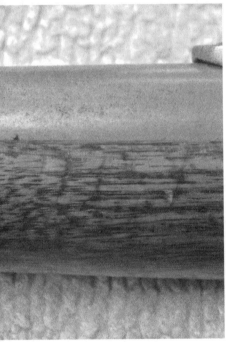

Left: This is the "KM" marked barrelband from an Egyptian Model Remington that was shipped to France during the Franco-Prussian War of 1870. This is somewhat of an enigma, as it is not clearly known why such markings on this model occasionally appear. The author believes it may be the Greek Model re-chambered for the Egyptian cartridge and identified by the factory representing a modification.

Photo by Catherine M. Druckenmiller

markings, with the exception of a single deviation—the rifles had been re-chambered for the .43 Egyptian cartridge. None had the "G" in a circle, with most having a faint but distinct "J.O.B." inspector's cartouche (Jeremy O. Bush, a former Springfield Armory inspector employed by Remington), a marking which is normally located on the left side of the butt on the very early Remington Egyptian Model rifles.

Several collectors have contacted me in the past regarding this caliber question and have found it bewildering, however, it appears to have been an attempt by Remington to remedy the .42 Berdan ammunition dilemma experienced by France. These particular variations observed were in remarkably clean condition, and were all in the white with no evidence of having been finished with case colors or blued barrels. Also a

deep "E" cartouche was present adjacent to the middle barrelband, which likely is meant to indicate "Egyptian" for ammunition identification purposes.

Whether these were part of the remaining 3,800 rifles from the Greek contract and re-chambered at the Remington factory to be readied for shipment to France is unknown. What *is* known is that the war finished before they could have been shipped. There is also a distinct possibility that some, if not all, of the .42 Berdan Greek Remington rolling-block rifles converted to .43 Egyptian were among those advertised as the "French Model" in the 1876 factory catalog.

There is, however, yet another caliber modification to the Greek Remington rolling-block rifles. It appears many of those sold at auction in France were purchased by the New York based arms dealer Schuyler, Hartley and Graham, who in fact were one of Remington's chief agents. In the .42 Berdan chambering, there was little marketability for the

Remington rolling block due to this cartridge being used almost exclusively by Russia. In addition, imperial Russia showed only token interest in the Remington, with but a few samples being in their hands. The primary ace in the hole in this respect was that dimensionally, the .42 Russian Berdan cartridge was practically identical to Remington's hottest product, the Spanish Model in its own .43 caliber chambering.

The .43 Spanish Remington uses a slightly larger .439-diameter bullet as opposed to the .42 Berdan's .430. But, the .42 Berdan will chamber and can be safely fired in the .43 Spanish Remington rifle. The biggest problem though was that the reverse is not true. The longer and minutely larger bullet diameter of the .43 Spanish will not seat entirely in a .42 Berdan chamber.

With thousands of the former Greek Model Remington rolling-block rifles on hand, the military arms dealers who purchased the rifles from the French had their subcontractors perform a minor gunsmithing operation to remedy the problem. All that was required was a simple "bushing" known in modern terms as "throating." This procedure extended the .42 Berdan chamber approximately one-eighth of an inch, which allowed the longer .43 Spanish cartridge to snugly chamber. The end result was that the Greek Remingtons, in essence, transformed into the "Spanish Model," the hottest commodity Remington had ever offered. The Schuyler, Hartley and Graham company sold several thousand of these "bushed" Greek rifles for the "Spanish Cartridge," and recorded these conversions as such in their sales registers during the mid-1870s to early 1880s. Among the documented countries that bought them were Costa Rica, Venezuela, Cuba and others. Oftentimes they are listed as sold together with saber bayonets, with some having the bayonet lug modified to the "combination lug," allowing either the saber or lower cost angular bayonets to interchange.

For today's collector, discovering a Remington Greek Model in its original .42 Berdan caliber is practically impossible as nearly the entire lot returned to the United States was converted to use the supremely popular .43 Spanish cartridge. Then again, some will be found reamed out to the .43 Egyptian cartridge leftover from the final days Franco-Prussian War. The conversion of the Greek Model to an Egyptian or Spanish Model brings us to just one more case of transformation.

Let us regress once again to the Egyptian Model Remington. Certainly we have seen that along with being sold to the country of its namesake, the French were also very fond of this rifle and cartridge. At the end of the Franco-Prussian War the French indeed were not averse to making a profit on their surplus, often selling to the highest bidders in both the U.S. and Europe. In reality they ended up infuriating Samuel Remington, who saw the postwar French as profiteering interlopers, especially while disposing of thousands of their Egyptian Remington surplus rifles to various Middle Eastern customers. Such a move may have indeed hurt Remington's business to a degree, as by 1878 there were thousands of Remington Egyptian Model rolling-block rifles sitting on ships in Liverpool. With the Egyptians' credit souring, the rifles lay stagnant awaiting clearance to be shipped to Alexandria. The result was that several thousand had to be returned to the United States and ended up back at Remington or in its agents' hands once again.

So, what to do with another large quantity of Remington rolling-block rifles in a caliber that no country in the Western Hemisphere wanted was another headache for the now financially strained company. Since a ready market for the Remington Spanish Model awaited in Latin America, several thousand leftover Egyptian Model Remington rifles would almost follow a similar path of the Greek variants—conversion.

In reality, this was not something entirely new. The Schuyler, Hartley and Graham sales records indicate that as early as May 1870 there were entries of "Remington Egyptian Rifle Bushed for Spanish Cartridge" sold to Cuba, Colombia, Nicaragua and other nations

The left side of the frame, chamber flat and barrelbands on the Greek Model were marked with a crown as shown here. Both the hammer and breechblock have this crown marking as well, but many surviving examples find these to be very worn from use.

Another feature similar to both the Egyptian and Greek Model Remington rolling-block rifles is the full-length saber bayonet lug on the right side of the muzzle. Note that the front sight was fitted to a dovetail which allowed windage adjustment if needed.

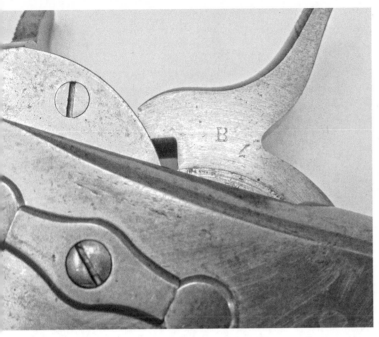

Here we have a detailed view of both the hammer and breechblock flats, which also were stamped with the initial of the last name of inspector Jeremy O. Bush, whose cartouche may sometimes also be seen on the rear of the left buttstock of surviving Egyptian Model Remington rifles in above-average condition. As these markings are apt to disappear over time, they are quite faint here as well.

To aid French ordnance personnel during the Franco-Prussian War, an "EC" was occasionally marked on the stock or forearm to indicate Egyptian Caliber, and to assure the correct ammunition was issued by supply officers.

A side view of the Greek Remington rear sight that is practically the same as the Egyptian Model, aside from numerations used when the leaf is raised. The sights of the rifles that were converted from .42 Berdan to .43 Spanish were not modified, as both cartridges had nearly identical ballistics.

Shown is the buttstock of a Greek Model Remington that was sold back to U.S. importers after the Franco-Prussian War and re-chambered to .43 Spanish bought by Venezuela. It was re-stamped with a local serial number of 1241.

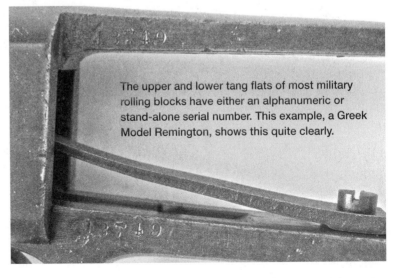

The upper and lower tang flats of most military rolling blocks have either an alphanumeric or stand-alone serial number. This example, a Greek Model Remington, shows this quite clearly.

of Latin America. It is evident that even a year after the 1869 Egyptian contract and during the Franco-Prussian War, Remington and its agents were doing their best to satisfy a continual need of .43 Spanish rolling-block rifles for willing and waiting customers in the Southern Hemisphere. Apparently, overproduction of the Egyptian Model deemed this a profitable move.

This author also believes that a few years prior to being christened the .43 Egyptian, Remington may have hoped this number would have become the "universal Remington cartridge" for all customers of the rolling block. In any case, an in-house letter from Schuyler, Hartley and Graham dated September 1879 requested 8,000 Egyptian Remington rifles be "transformed" to use the Spanish cartridge and the combination bayonet stud. The Egyptian "transformed" Remington rolling block is yet another variation similar to the Greek Model that collectors were unable to properly identify for years. Since the base of the .43 Egyptian cartridge is a larger .594 diameter compared to the .579 of the .43 Spanish, it was necessary to shorten the Egyptian barrel from 35⅛ inches to 33¾ inches to allow re-reaming of the Egyptian barrel to the smaller

This left-hand view of the Remington Greek Contract Model is nearly identical to the Egyptian variant, with the early horizontal bar extractor screw at the top of the action.

specifications of the Spanish cartridge. In addition, the forearm and cleaning rod had to be reduced in length with the end result being a shorter three-band

The open action on this Remington Greek Model shows it was manufactured after August 1870, as it is equipped with the improved flat breechblock axis. This is one method to estimate the production date of an early military rolling block that has the two-line tang address and patent marking.

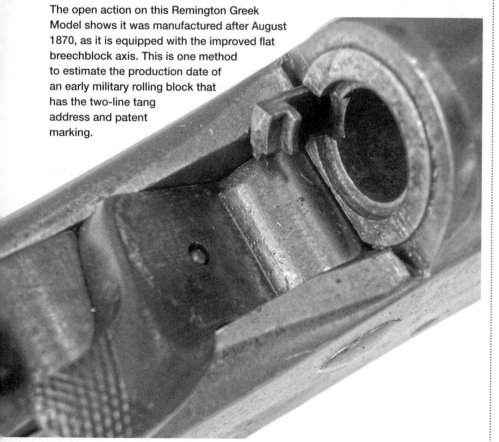

rifle. Furthermore, the rear sights on these "transformed Egyptian/Spanish Model" conversions also reveal that the sight base is set back to a mere 1½ inches from the receiver ring, making for an unusual looking military rolling-block rifle.

A large majority of these conversions have been observed with the short combination bayonet lug, which required breaking the silver solder on the lug, cutting it back and re-sweating into place. Close examination on such rifles will reveal the metal showing a "trail" where the original long lug was once placed. All in all, both the Remington Greek and Egyptian Model rolling-block rifles were indeed a pair that for years was puzzling to rolling-block collectors, and evaded identification until just the past decade. Remington and its agents continued to sell them off in this configuration well after the E. Remington & Sons bankruptcy of 1887.

The bottom line is that the Remington Spanish Model in its own .43 caliber, regardless of minor differences, was indeed the most popular and widespread military rolling block produced by America's oldest firearms manufacturer. Only until recently, however, have the pieces of this Remington puzzle been put into the proper perspective, at last.

BY **Wayne van Zwoll**

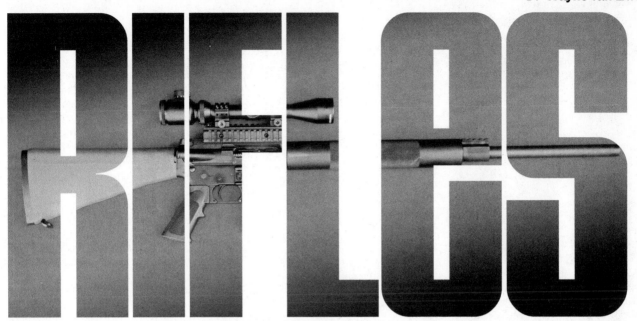

RIFLES

SPORTSMEN OUTNUMBER BLACK OPS SNIPERS, DESPITE TRENDS IN RIFLE FORM. NEW MODELS SERVE BOTH CAMPS!

In the first of our annual Reports from the Field, Wayne van Zwoll covers the new crop of rifles hitting dealers' shelves this year.

ANSCHÜTZ 1727 IN .17 HMR

Biathlon competition demands quick cycling of rifle actions, and shooters can ill afford to shift position to reload. The new 1727 Anschütz sporter, introduced last year but only recently available, brings biathlon speed to the hunting field. A flick of your index finger opens the breech of this straight-pull rifle; a tap of your thumb shuts it. No need to move your arm or take your eye from the sight. The 1727's two-stage match trigger adjusts to 1¼ pounds, so you can take advantage of the great reach and inherently fine accuracy of the .17 HMR cartridge. The checkered European-style walnut stock is well fitted and nicely finished. Anschütz competition rifles are renowned for accuracy (my Model 1413 posted winning scores in many prone events). This repeater will print half-minute groups. (www.anschuetz-usa.com)

ARSENAL, INC. SLR-104FR

It's touted as the first factory-built Bulgarian 5.45x39.5 rifle with a side-folding stock to sell in the U.S. The new SLR-104FR has a stamped receiver, with a U.S.-made trigger group and a side-mounted scope rail that accepts Arsenal's latest SM-13 mount. A hammer-forged, chrome-lined barrel comes with a removable muzzlebrake, bayonet and accessory lugs. In black or desert tan, the SLR-104FR features a hinged polymer or metal stock and retails for $1,099. (www.arsenalinc.com)

BLASER R8 PROFESSIONAL SUCCESS

Since Blaser (blah'-zer, not blay'-zer) appeared in 1957, this German firearms firm has become one of the most respected. Its F3 over/under shotgun, in competition and field versions, ranks among the world's best. The R93 straight-pull bolt rifle has a superb trigger, and an improbably short receiver. You can cycle this action faster than you can work

Blaser's versatile R8 handles even the giant .500 Jeffery. Magazine and trigger group detach as a unit.

Blaser, Mauser and Sauer rifles are tested in facilities like this indoor 300-meter range in Germany.

any turn-bolt. The R8 (arrival, 2008) is the R93's successor and retains its signal features: hammer-forged barrel, telescoping, radial-head bolt, screwless scope mounts and single-stack magazine tucked into a compact trigger group. The thumbpiece that cocks the R8 is the only safety. Shove it up and forward; you're ready to fire. To decock, push the tab ahead while pressing down. Let it return to the rear. The R93 and R8 are the only bolt rifles you can carry safely at the ready, as they're not cocked until you're ready to fire.

The R8's bolt locks like the 93's but even more securely. Tests to pressures

of 120,000 psi have damaged gauges before the rifles failed. Barrels are treated to plasma nitriding to boost surface hardness. Saddle-style scope rings clamp directly into precisely machined dimples so you can remove the scope and replace it without losing zero. Barrels are just as carefully fitted. You need only the supplied T-handle Allen wrench to switch barrels or remove the buttstock.

An even better magazine arrived with the R8. Pinch a pair of tabs bracketing the guard and the magazine, with the trigger group, falls into your hand. You can top-load the stack without removing

the box or load it in your hand. One box accommodates all cartridges for which the R8 is chambered (more than two dozen, .223 to .416 Remington Magnum). Switchable innards work for families of cartridges. For example, a stop limits the bolt throw for rounds shorter than the .30-06. The rifle was designed for a wide range of cartridges, it even handles the giant .500 Jeffery! A polymer cup protects the magazine assembly while it's out of the R8; an insert seals the receiver.

R8s sold in Europe come with a trigger pull of 1½ pounds. Stateside hunters get a crisp break at 2½. Shooting a .375 and a .30-06, I was impressed by the R8's minute-of-angle groups when hot. Both rifles took African game for me. On targets at 600 yards a .300 Winchester R8 performed as well as a turn-bolt match rifle. I've also used the newest R8s, a series labeled the Professional Success, on big game. They have elegantly sculpted synthetic stocks of thumbhole design in green, brown and black. Even traditionalists should think them handsome, as detailing is worthy of an Italian sports car. On two versions, classy leather panels replace checkering. The full-stocked Stutzen is fetching indeed! (www.blaser-usa.com)

BROWNING AB3, AND A NEW X-BOLT

Remember the BBR? Since it appeared in 1978 to replace the lovely High-Power series with its commercial 98 Mauser actions, Browning has introduced several three-lug variations. The A-Bolt arrived in 1985, the X-Bolt in 2008. Both boast low, 60-degree bolt lift. The X-Bolt has a clever spool magazine and is clearly Browning's new flagship. For 2014 the firm has a line extension: the X-Bolt Eclipse Hunter rifle, with a laminated gray thumbhole stock. In typical Browning fashion, it's available in a wide range of standard and magnum chamberings, .243 to .300 Winchester. Price: just over $1,000. Browning's stable also includes the new AB3, a synthetic-stocked A-Bolt rifle that retails for $600. It comes in .270 and .30-06 with a 22-inch barrel, 7mm Remington and .300 Winchester Magnum with a 26-inch tube. Weight: 6¾ to 7¼ pounds. The AB3 has a detachable box magazine and a bolt-lock override. (www.browning.com)

Since its re-introduction, Browning's T-Bolt has appeared in new versions, one with a maple stock.

BROWNING T-BOLT MAPLE SPORTER AND COMMEMORATIVE SEMI-AUTO .22

Introduced in 1965, the straight-pull T-Bolt .22 rifle was built for a decade in Browning's Belgian FN plant. It was dropped for a time, then reintroduced eight years ago. Besides its Miroku manufacture, the new T-Bolt incorporated several changes. In 2008 it appeared in .17 HMR and .22 WMR. In its most appealing form with a walnut stock, the T-Bolt is one of my favorite .22 rifles. With a receiver machined from steel bar stock, it has a cat-quick action and a clever 10-shot "double helix" detachable box magazine that fits flush. The tang safety is convenient and positive. The three-lever trigger design breaks cleanly. For 2014 you can choose a Target or Sporter version, synthetic or walnut stock. And there's also a Maple Sporter. I'm told, however, that only a limited run of this handsome 5½-pound T-Bolt is scheduled to satisfy dealer orders. Inquire at your dealer now if your taste in rifles parallels mine.

John Browning's autoloading, bottom-ejecting, takedown .22 appeared many moons ago. A most distinctive rifle in profile and function, it carries its cartridges in a buttstock tube. The slender 16½-inch barrel, with the fore-end, can be easily and quickly removed by hand. The receiver is truly svelte, with no unnecessary bulk or weight. Beautiful checkered walnut still marks this rifle, even in an industry largely won over by black polymer. Choose the Grade I or Grade II Semi-Auto – or, this year, the 100th Anniversary model with gold inlays, deep engraving, fancy wood. Production will be limited. (www.browning.com)

CHIAPPA 39 AND M6

Italian-built rifles on American patterns have sold well the last couple of decades, partly because they're fine stand-ins for scarce and costly originals in Cowboy Action events. But hunters and plinkers have also found great bargains here. Among the most appealing in the 2014 catalogs is Chiappa's 39, a reproduction of the iconic Marlin 39. Its origins date to Annie Oakley's day. Annie adored lever-action Marlin .22s, and she shot them with jaw-dropping skill. True to its namesake, Chiappa's 39 features one-screw takedown. It has an 18½-inch barrel and full-length magazine, with barrelbands at fore-stock and front ramp. The receiver is case-colored, the stock walnut.

For backcountry hikes or fishing trips, or travel by canoe or bush plane, a lightweight, compact survival rifle should be in your kit. For 2014 Chiappa lists the M6, a hinged-breech rifle/shotgun combination with a .22 barrel under a 20 gauge. It collapses into an 18½-inch package. Compartments in its synthetic stock hold cartridges and a cleaning kit. Double triggers and an under-lever opener make the M6 operable with cold fingers. Rails accept optics and accessories. You get iron sights too, of course. (www.chiappafirearms.com)

CMMG MK4 RCE

There's no "AR" in that daunting name, but the MK4 RCE is just that. Its forged M4 upper and AR15 lower are of machined 7075-16 alloy. A Magpul CTR adjustable stock complements an RKM 14 KeyMod free-floating handguard. The stainless, 16-inch 5.56mm barrel has a fast 1-in-7 rifling twist for the long, heavy bullets shooters need to score well at a distance. A full-length 1913 Picatinny rail and the company's own nitride-finished muzzlebrake are standard. CMMG installs a Geissele Automatics SSA two-stage trigger. The rifle (also available in .300 AAC Blackout) weighs 6½ pounds empty. Loading the 30-round Magpul magazine adds a pound. (www.cmmginc.com)

CZ MODEL 557

The rugged CZ 550, with its stout Mauser claw extractor and chamberings to .505 Gibbs, has no match for mass and

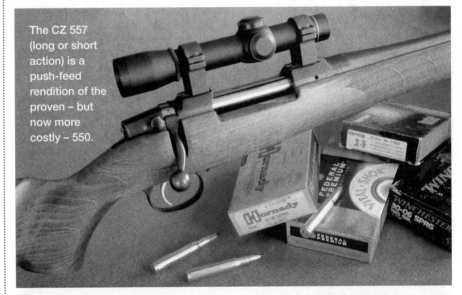

The CZ 557 (long or short action) is a push-feed rendition of the proven – but now more costly – 550.

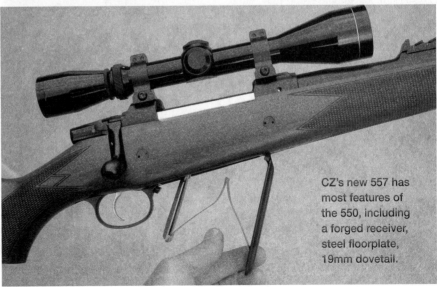

CZ's new 557 has most features of the 550, including a forged receiver, steel floorplate, 19mm dovetail.

Legacy Sports now lists a Howa 1500 rifle with Zeiss Terra 3-9x42 scope. Pick from 13 chamberings!

muscle among commercial bolt guns. It's one of the best values to boot! Now CZ has an even more affordable bolt action. The push-feed 557 has a bolt-face extractor and plunger ejector. But in most other aspects, it's a twin to the 550. The receiver is machined from a steel billet and has 19mm dovetails for scope mounts. The fixed four-shot magazine has a hinged steel floorplate. Its 22-inch barrel is cold-hammer-forged and lapped. A two-detent safety permits the bolt to function at either position, and the trigger is fully adjustable for take-up, weight and over-travel. An early 557 that came my way registered a smooth, crisp pull of just over three pounds. CZ offers this new rifle with short actions in .243 and .308, and long actions in 6.5x55, .270 and .30-06. The wood stock has a straight comb and attractive machine-cut checkering. (By the way, CZ lists it as walnut, and production stocks may well be. But my sample seems to be dark-stained birch.) List price: $792. You can get the 557 in two other configurations; the Carbine has a 20½-inch barrel with open sights and retails for $812. A Manners Sporter has a top-shelf synthetic stock that trims eight ounces from the 7¼-pound weight, but hikes the price to $1,268. (www.cz-usa.com)

DESERT TECH MDR

You may have known Desert Tech as Desert Tactical Arms, founded in 2007. Last year the name changed, but the firm is still coming up with innovative products. The new Micro Dynamic Rifle, really a carbine, is of bullpup design. Its 16½-inch barrel, available in five chamberings, can be changed quickly in the field. A 10½-inch barrel is also avail-able. The ambidextrous action boasts forward ejection, a full-length rail, and a behind-the-grip magazine. With standard barrels, the MDR weighs 7½ pounds. (www.deserttech.com)

HOWA "PACKAGE RIFLES" FROM LEGACY SPORTS

The smooth, sturdy, economical Howa bolt action has been used by Smith & Wesson, Weatherby and other firms as the heart of rifles marketed under those names. But it has long lived undisguised in the firearms lines of Legacy Sports International. Legacy has also packaged it with Nikko-Sterling scopes. In 2014, you can get a Howa 1500 rifle with a factory-mounted 3-9x42 Zeiss Terra. This scope, new to the Zeiss stable last year, has many features of top-end Zeiss optics, and quality worthy of the brand. Hunter Zeiss Walnut Package rifles give you a choice of 13 chamberings from .223 to .375 Ruger. The action carries a forged, twin-lug bolt, a three-position safety and a two-stage match trigger that on my sample 7mm Magnum rifle breaks silkily at an even three pounds. The walnut stock is nicely checkered and fitted; it has a satin finish. Retailing at $1,103 for standard chamberings with 22-inch barrels, and $1,131 for magnums with a 24-inch barrel, the rifle and scope weigh nine to 9¼ pounds. Stainless versions list for $1,241 and $1,255 respectively. For hunters who prize durability, a Hogue-stocked, Zeiss-scoped package is also available. It's a few ounces heavier, but prices start lower at $965. You get the same chamberings and the stainless option – plus a limited choice of fluted barrels. (www.legacysports.com)

KIMBER ADIRONDACK – AND THREE NEW TACTICALS

The svelte Kimber 84M action is the basis for the firm's newest rifle: the Adirondack. At just four pounds, 13 ounces, this synthetic-stocked, pillar-bedded stainless repeater is also its lightest. The 18-inch fluted barrel, in 7mm-08 or .308, is threaded for a muzzlebrake, which is also available from Kimber. The fluted two-lug bolt has a Mauser-style extractor for controlled feed and a three-position M70-type safety. That bolt, with modifications, also appears in three new heavy Kimber rifles. The Patrol Tactical,

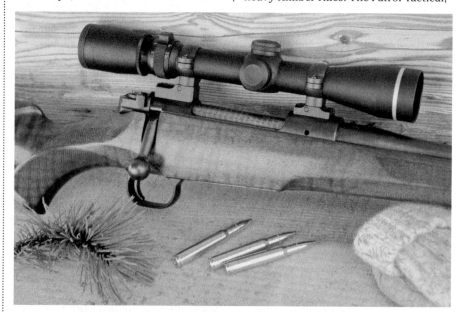

The new six-lug Mauser M12 has a clean, sculpted American look, open port, three-position safety.

Advanced Tactical II and Advanced Tactical SOC all come in .308. But they're available as well in .300 Winchester, which requires the 8400 action – an upsized 84M. The Patrol has a Manners MCS-T6 stock of reinforced carbon fiber. It's black, the steep grip with palm swells on both sides. The Tactical II wears a folding Manners stock – an MCS-TF4 with adjustable comb. Both it and the Advanced Tactical SOC come with an adjustable, folding aluminum stock, sport fore-end rails and tan stock finishes. These two rifles accept detachable five- and 10-round box magazines and are guaranteed to put three shots into a half minute of angle. Barrels in .300 Winchester measure 26 inches(Patrol) and 27 inches, a couple of inches longer than those in .308. Weights: 9¾ pounds for the .300 Magnum Patrol, 11¼ pounds for the Tactical II, 12 pounds for the Advanced Tactical SOC. Subtract 10 ounces for .308 rifles. (www.kimberamerica.com)

MAUSER M12

It appeared at the 2013 SHOT Show but became available only late last year. Unlike its legendary forebear, the 1898, the new Mauser M12 was not born of battle. It evolved with hunters in mind. It is slim and conservatively profiled, with a straight-comb stock in walnut or synthetic and a smooth, six-lug action. The bright-polished damascened bolt runs full-diameter to a head machined away for three pairs of lugs that lock into the barrel. Bolt lift is 60 degrees. The recessed bolt face has two plunger ejectors, an extractor mounted in a forward lug. To my delight, the bolt handle is vintage Mauser – simple, elegant and straight. It drops to the top center of the trigger bow, where it's easy to reach but doesn't bruise your knuckle on recoil. The ball is of nonslip polymer. Mauser adopted the M70-style three-position safety for the M12 and a red striped pin protrudes from the bolt shroud when the rifle is cocked. The trigger is gracefully curved with a pull that adjusts to a crisp two pounds.

A dozen chamberings include Europe's 6.5x55 and 7x64, 8x57 and 9.3x62 – but also our .22-250, .243, .270, .308 and .30-06. All wear 22-inch barrels. The Magnum M12 comes with a 24½-inch barrel in 7mm Remington, .300 and .338 Winchester. A brushed steel floorplate with Mauser logo caps the flush-fitting polymer magazine, secured by a latch recessed behind the front guard screw. You can order spare magazines – with

black polymer floor, if you like. I was pleased to see the box, which holds five standard rounds and three magnums, can be loaded when in the rifle, and that the M12's port is as roomy as the 98's. Toss a handful of cartridges at that maw, and it'll gobble them up.

Last fall I carried an M12 in .270 with upgraded wood. (You'll save pennies with the plain walnut or synthetic options.) I liked the tasteful cheek-rest, the crisp sculpting around the magazine, the close fit of wood to steel. The M12 shouldered eagerly, centering my eye in the Leupold.

Weather on the Austrian peaks kept us guessing, but at last, through a window in freezing fog, I spied the chamois our guide wanted to take from the mountain. A 200-yard shot through the shoulders

killed it instantly. I'd like to have stayed longer in this spectacular country – then to take that Mauser M12 home. Alas, I could do neither! (www.mauser.com)

MCMILLAN ALIAS

Appropriately named, the Alias bolt rifle has many guises. Interchangeable barrels and a long list of component options and accessories allow use of one action to build many rifles. The CS5 is configured as a "concealable suppressed sniper system," with a 12½-inch stainless barrel in .308, 1-in-8 twist. This 10½-pound rifle measures less than 24 inches disassembled, the adjustable stock detached. Multiple rails permit use of a variety of sights and accoutrements. The action accepts detachable box magazines. Install a longer barrel, in 6.5

The author field tested the Mauser M12 in the Austrian Alps and took this chamois with a .270 at 200 yards.

McMillan's short-action Alias, available in several cartridges from 6XC to .308 Palma, is modular and takes many forms and accessories.

Creedmoor, 6x47 Lapua or .308, and you have the Star Tactical rifle. Target-length barrels in those chamberings, 6XC, .260 or .308 Palma, plus a prone-style butt-stock and a "competition" fore-end make the Alias into a match rifle. A full-length rail with 20 minutes elevation gain suits it to long-range shooting. The twin-lug bolt and fully adjustable Anschütz trigger deliver very fast lock time. While unconventional in form, the Alias is eminently practical – and beautifully finished. (www.mcmillanUSA.com)

MONTANA RIFLE COMPANY SCR AND PRINCESS WARRIOR

Just outside of Kalispell, you'll find the Montana Rifle Company – recently expanded and equipped with new CNC equipment to manufacture a growing line of bolt rifles. They're built on the firm's 1999 action, a clone of the Winchester Model 70. The success of MRC is due in large part to the business next door, a barrel-making enterprise started and run by Brian Sipe. Montana Rifle Company operates under Brian's son Jeff, who's introduced a couple of new rifles for 2014. The SCR, or Seven Continent Rifle, is a synthetic-stocked muscle-gun for cartridges as big as the .338 Lapua, .416 Rigby and .505 Gibbs. The Princess Warrior, especially for women, features a long or short action, left- or right-side bolt. A long list of chamberings includes the 6XC and .280 Ackley. I've carried Montana rifles in Alaska and Africa.

The .375 is one of my go-to guns for big game. The Montana Rifle Company, unlike some of its competitors, has not abandoned walnut stocks or iron sights. The AVR (American Vantage Rifle) and XVR (Xtreme Vantage Rifle) introduced last spring feature irons on stiff barrels in .35 Whelen, .375 Ruger, .375 H&H, .416 Remington, .416 Ruger, .458 Winchester and .458 Lott. (www.montanarifleco.com)

NESIKA SPORTER, LONG RANGE AND TACTICAL

Adored by benchresters, Nesika actions now appear in three more conventional rifles. They're built in the brand's new home – Dakota's shop in Sturgis, S.D. Priced from $3,500 to $4,500, the Sporter, Long Range and Tactical rifles feature actions of 15-5 stainless steel machined to tolerances of .002 inch. Bolts are machined from one piece of chrome-moly steel and they complement Timney triggers. Douglas stainless air-gauged barrels and Bell and Carlson Medalist synthetic stocks, with bedding blocks, are appropriately contoured for each rifle. Nesika's Sporter weighs eight pounds, the Long Range model 9¾ pounds, the Tactical 13¾ pounds. Leupold QRW scope bases come with the lighter rifles. A 1913 Picatinny rail with 15-minute elevation gain accompanies the Tactical model – which has an AAC Blackout muzzlebrake and suppressor adapter. Six Sporter chamberings range from 7mm-08 to .300 Winchester Magnum. Choose the 7mm Remington or .300 Winchester Magnums for your Long Range rifle. Tactical barrels are bored to .300 Winchester and .338 Lapua Magnums. Nesika also sells actions only, in several configurations. (www.nesikafirearms.com)

REMINGTON/TRACKING-POINT 20/20 RIFLE

Last year Remington tapped a young firm called TrackingPoint to equip three of its rifles with a sight that delivers a heads-up computer display such as you'd find in a fighter aircraft. The sight appeared first on a bolt gun tricked out by TrackingPoint as its own. This "Precision Guided Rifle" wore a complex sight that told the shooter when to fire. In fact, an

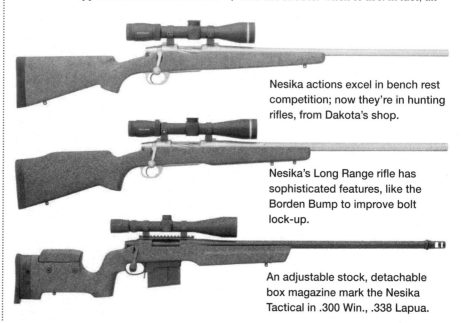

Nesika actions excel in bench rest competition; now they're in hunting rifles, from Dakota's shop.

Nesika's Long Range rifle has sophisticated features, like the Borden Bump to improve bolt lock-up.

An adjustable stock, detachable box magazine mark the Nesika Tactical in .300 Win., .338 Lapua.

Remington's 20/20 project with TrackingPoint produced packages with M700 and AR-type actions.

The TrackingPoint sight is essentially a 3-21x rangefinding scope – but you don't look *through* it. Instead of a target image enhanced by lenses, this device yields a digital image on a screen. An integral laser rangefinder reads the range as you "tag" a target. Meanwhile, atmospheric conditions are monitored by TP's computer, which has already adjusted for bullet drop so you can hold center. The sight adjusts for rifle cant and vertical shot angle 54 times per second! It even compensates for target movement.

Here's the process: Power on with the button at the rear of the scope. A button opposite lets you pick "traditional" mode to see the target with a mil-dot reticle, or "advanced" mode to engage electronics (target tracking and ballistic computing). In the advanced mode you'll see a white dot in the scope field. Place that dot on the target and press the "tag" button atop the scope. The laser unit reads the range and displays it in the scope field. Once the white dot turns red, you're locked onto the target. Place the blue X in your scope field over the dot. When the X also turns red, your shot will hit the target. If you must adjust for wind drift, first estimate wind value, then press the wind tab in the direction of the blow until you see the appropriate number in mph. The sight will then compensate for drift of the programmed bullet.

To change magnification from 3-21x, press the power rocker on the scope.

You can set the desired level of precision from half minute to four minutes. Obviously, if you set it for the highest level of precision you'll have to hold the rifle very still, or the "fire" signal won't stay on long enough for a trigger squeeze. A more generous setting, say, three minutes, gives you the go-ahead as long as the shot is within three minute of center – practical for shooting big game out to 350 or even 400 yards. Rifle and sight can be used without the computer assist if you wish.

I've tested TrackingPoint's ranging and computer functions on steel targets out to 800 yards, getting first-round hits easily until the wind picked up. Then the long shots were just as tough as with traditional sights, because I couldn't program downrange wind I couldn't read. What the TP sight is built to do, it does well enough. The pixilated image takes getting used to, and it becomes too dark to be practical at the edge of legal shooting light. Also, you mustn't tag the target until you're ready to fire. Move-

electronic link to the trigger permitted the rifle to fire *only when the sight was aligned for a sure hit!* The price of this magic? $28,000. "We want to sell rifles," said the Remington crew. "Do you make an entry-level sight?" Perhaps because TrackingPoint's CEO at the time once worked at Remington, he understood. His design team came up with a utility version of this computer sight that does everything you'd expect of its parent, except control the trigger. You do that.

You can't buy the sight separately. The 20/20 system is just that. Affixed to an otherwise ordinary rifle, a TP sight must be programmed to that rifle and specific load. Remington pairs the sight with three rifles: 1) Model 700 LR .30-06, 2) Model 700 SPS Tactical .308, 3) Bushmaster Varminter .223. It works with these Remington target and hunting loads: 1) .30-06 168-grain MatchKing, 168-grain Barnes TTSX, 180-grain Core-Lokt Ultra Bonded, 2) .308 168-grain MatchKing, 150-grain Core-Lokt Ultra Bonded, 168-grain Barnes TTSX, 3) .223 69-grain MatchKing, 55-grain AccuTip Varmint, 55-grain TSX.

Wayne fires a Remington 700 with the TrackingPoint sight. An "X" lights up when you're on target.

Rock River's LAR-8 isn't new, but the big action has spawned other rifles in .308-size rounds.

RRA's new 9½-pound LAR-8 X-1 in .308 has an 18-inch barrel with 1-in-10 twist. It comes in tan or black.

Rock River's new LAR-15 X-1 in .223 has spawned similar rifles in 6.8 SPC (shown here) and .458 SOCOM.

ment, such as when you tug the rifle into your shoulder or bump it as you thumb the safety off, cancels the tag.

I killed a stag with the TrackingPoint sight on a Remington 700 in .308. It was an easy shot at just 147 yards. But the sight put the 150-grain Core-Lokt Ultra where I wanted it. Remington lists the 20/20 system – your choice of any of the three rifle/sight combinations – for $4,995. (www.remington.com)

ROBAR SR21

Remington's Model 700 rifle is justifiably popular. Now Robar makes it better with semicustom features. (The new SR21 can also be fashioned from Savage's short bolt action.) You furnish the heart of the SR21 (long or short mechanism in the 700), Robar then installs a stainless, competition-grade, 24-inch barrel. Its gunsmiths follow with a series of "accurizing" steps to ensure the finished rifle meets Robar's stringent half-minute accuracy guarantee. The receiver gets a Picatinny rail with a 20-minute slope for long shooting. The SR21 trigger adjusts from two to five pounds. A floating modular

fore-end pairs up with the Magpul PRS buttstock and MIAD grip (other AR grips also fit). There are two 1913 five-inch rails up front. QD swivel studs attach at 3, 6 or 9 o'clock. The bolt and most internal parts wear an NP3 finish. Available in .308, .300 Winchester and .338 Lapua, the

11-pound SR21 accepts AICS magazines. (www.robarguns.com)

ROCK RIVER ARMS

Among the best known and most respected names in AR-type rifles, Rock River Arms has added new configurations to its LAR-15 (5.56mm) and LAR-8 (7.62mm) models. These X-1 versions feature stainless, heavy, fluted 18-inch barrels with RRA Beast or Hunter muzzlebrakes. The RRA TRO-STD rifle-length floating handguard is paired with a low-profile gas block under a full-length Picatinny rail. The LAR-15 X-1 has a .223 Wylde chamber that accommodates both .223 and 5.56 loads. The 1-in-8 rifling twist in its cryo-treated barrel is suited to heavy bullets for long-range shooting. Rock River claims three-quarter-minute accuracy for this 7¾-pound model. The larger LAR-8 X-1 weighs 9½ pounds, has 1-in-10 rifling twist and should deliver one-minute accuracy. X-1 rifles come in tan or black with a RRA Operator 2 or CAR buttstock and Hogue rubber grip. Price for the LAR-15 X-1 in black: $1,450. The LAR-8 X-1 lists at $1,800. Add $50 for the tan option. Rock River has also cataloged X-1 rifles in 6.8 SPC and .458 SOCOM. They're named for the chamberings (not LAR-15) and retail at $1,550 in black. (www.rockriverarms.com)

RUGER SR-762 AND NO. 1 UPDATE

Big news at Ruger this year is the SR-762, a piston-driven AR-style autoloader with a 16-inch cold-hammer-forged,

Wayne shot this buck with a full-stocked Ruger No. 1 RSI, offered for 2014 only in .257 Roberts.

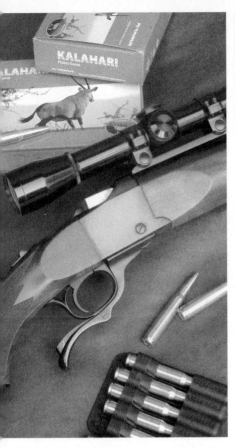

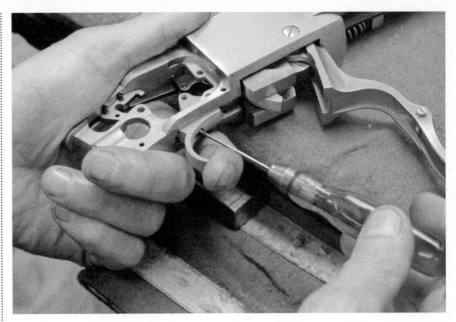

The No. 1's components and assembly have steadily hiked manufacturing costs, limiting production.

SAVAGE 64 FV SR AND 93 FV SR, A SCOPED MARK II FXP

Suppressors have become popular of late, and not only on loud, hard-kicking rifles. A suppressor on the muzzle of a .22 almost mutes the report, and light recoil becomes almost nonexistent. Savage has just announced threaded, suppressor-ready 16½-inch barrels on Model 64 autoloading and Model 93 bolt-action .22s. These synthetic-stocked rifles wear receiver-length rails in lieu of iron sights. The 64 FV SR has a 10-shot detachable magazine, the 93 a five-shot.

Only the 93 is furnished with AccuTrigger. This rifle is also available in .17 HMR and .22 WMR. The 93 lists for: $358. Price for the 64 autoloader: $231.

While box-fed, bolt-action .22 rifles have been around a long time, Savage has hiked the utility of one by adding a scope. The Mark II FXP wears a medium-weight, 21-inch barrel without sights and a 3-9x40 Bushnell scope, already mounted. Like many of its stablemates, the Mark II FXP comes with the Accu-Trigger, a wonderful assist for accurate shooting. At $291, this combination costs more than the .22s of my youth, but that

chrome-moly barrel that's fluted and chrome-lined. Chambered in .308, it has a standard 1-in-10 twist. The flattop upper has a full rail with backup iron sights. A six-position M4-type buttstock complements a smooth Ruger hand-guard tapped for additional rails at 3, 6 and 9 o'clock. Up front, a four-position chrome-plated gas regulator can be adjusted for top performance with any load – or shut off for manual operation. The bolt and rear-radiused carrier are also chromed. Ruger installed a Hogue Monogrip on the SR-762 – one of the most comfortable available. The rifle comes with three 20-round magazines and lists for $2,195.

As predicted, Ruger is dropping last year's chamberings in its No. 1 series of centerfire rifles. The 2014 offerings: Light Sporter (A) - .280 Remington, Medium Sporter (S) - 9.3x62, Varminter (V) - .220 Swift, International (RSI) - .257 Roberts, Tropical (H) - .450-400. Prices on the No. 1 have risen a great deal since the rifle appeared in 1966 at only $265! The hand fitting necessary in assembly and limited demand for this classy single-shot prompted Ruger in 2013 to begin listing only one chambering per submodel, changing each year. Pity! (www.ruger.com)

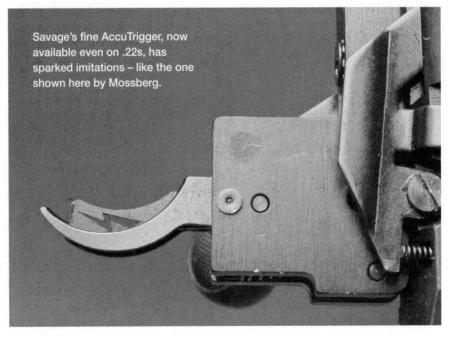

Savage's fine AccuTrigger, now available even on .22s, has sparked imitations – like the one shown here by Mossberg.

For 2014 Weatherby is building 26 special Mark Vs dedicated to the memory of Navy SEAL Chris Kyle.

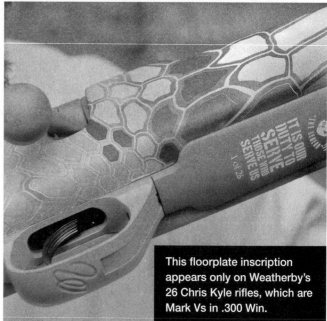

This floorplate inscription appears only on Weatherby's 26 Chris Kyle rifles, which are Mark Vs in .300 Win.

was before three-dollar gasoline and two-dollar chocolate bars. This blued steel rifle wears an olive drab synthetic stock. There's also a Magnum version in .17 HMR and .22 WMR, with the same scope package but a black stock, for $344. (www.savagearms.com)

SHILOH SHARPS 1877

The mechanism is like an 1874's, but lighter. The new 1877 Sharps from Shiloh Sharps has a trim hammer, smaller action plates, a plain hinge pin rather than the signature right side key. There's also less steel behind the barrel for a reason. Developing the original Model 1877, Charles E. Overbaugh, Sharps Rifle Company's chief traveling salesman and exhibition shooter in 1876, had the 1,000-yard Creedmoor match in mind. Long, heavy barrels were favored for a

generous sight radius and to limit barrel whip and recoil. The .45 bore popular in that day (with a 520-grain bullet driven by 105 grains of black powder) required thick barrel walls for adequate stiffness. The 10-pound weight limit thus limited barrel length. Putting the 1874 Sharps action on a diet gave Mr. Overbaugh more ounces in the barrel. Period shooters were keen for this change, which included drilling a hole in the lower part of the breechblock.

With its self-cocking Model 1875 hamstrung by patent disputes, Sharps shifted focus toward what would become its hammerless 1878. At the same time, demand from the Creedmoor clan for a lightweight 1874 mechanism pushed manufacture of the 1877. Nearly 140 years later (at last winter's SHOT Show), Shiloh Sharps of Big Timber,

Mont., unveiled photos of a prototype reproduction of the 1877. "Wait time for a '74 is down below two years," I was told. "So we're ready to launch the new rifle." By April 2013 the prototype was functional. A shooter from the Shiloh shop fired it in the Texas State Silhouette Match. Now Shiloh has display models – "and 18-month delivery." You can get it with straight or pistol grip stock, heavy or standard-weight barrels from 26 to 34 inches, in 10 chamberings from .38-55 to .45/100. As with Shiloh's 1874 rifles, you can add custom touches like an ebony pistol grip, schnabel grip terminus, Rigby rib, cheek rest, tang and globe sights. The base price is a pretty reasonable $2,150, though it climbs fast with extra features, or if you want figured Turkish walnut instead of plain American. (www.shilohrifle.com)

A full-diameter bolt with interrupted-thread lugs still distinguishes Weatherby's stout Mark V action.

Weatherby is adding more Range Certified rifles, all guaranteed to fire sub-minute three-shot groups.

WEATHERBY MARK V CHRIS KYLE LIMITED EDITION

Navy SEAL Chief Chris Kyle became known for his deadly accuracy as a sniper, then wrote two best-selling books: *American Sniper* and *American Gun*. Tragically, Kyle was killed at a Glen Rose, Texas, shooting range by a gunman in February 2013. He left behind a young family. Now Weatherby has built a rifle in his memory. Only 26 of these specially numbered Mark Vs are slated for production. Chambered in .300 Winchester Magnum, each is distinguished by Cerakote Flat Dark Earth metal finish and a synthetic stock with CNC-machined alloy bedding block and Kryptek Highlander camo finish. The 28-inch, #3 button-rifled barrel wears a muzzlebrake. The Chris Kyle Limited Edition rifle has a specially inscribed floorplate and comes with a letter of authenticity signed by Ed Weatherby. A portion of the sale proceeds from these Mark Vs, which list for $3,400, goes to Kyle's family. (www.weatherby.com)

WEATHERBY MARK V TERRA-MARK RC AND ULTRA LIGHT-WEIGHT RC

At Weatherby, "RC" stands for "Range Certified." Rifles so marked are guaranteed to print subminute three-shot groups. Two new bolt guns qualify. The Mark V Terramark and Ultra Lightweight both come in Weatherby chamberings from .240 to .300, plus .270, .308 and .30-06, and 7mm Remington and .300 Winchester Magnums. The Terramark is also bored for the .340, .30-378 and .338-378 Weatherby, and the .338 Lapua. With the Lapua and .378-based chamberings, you get a 28-inch braked barrel. Ditto the Ultra Lightweight in .300 Weatherby. Other barrels are of #3 contour, 24 and 26 inches long. They're fluted, with a brushed stainless finish. The Terramark has a desert camo gelcoat on its hand-laminated synthetic stock. The Ultra Lightweight stock, fortified by a T6 alloy bedding plate, is red-brown under the gelcoat, with black spider webbing. Metal finish on the ULW is traditional blue. Both rifles wear an RC-engraved floorplate and a Decelerator buttpad. All Weatherby Mark V rifles are now made in the Paso Robles, Calif., plant and all wear adjustable triggers. The new RCs retail for $2,400 to $3,000. (www.weatherby.com)

The WBY-X brand, unveiled last year, has grown to include new rifles for youthful shooters.

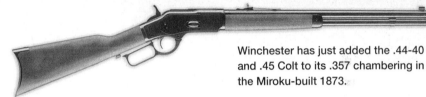

Winchester has just added the .44-40 and .45 Colt to its .357 chambering in the Miroku-built 1873.

WBY-X VANGUARD SERIES 2

Weatherby announced an entirely new line of rifles and shotguns late in 2012. In fact, the line was so different, it didn't bear the Weatherby name. Instead, expanded for 2014, it's called WBY-X. The striking rifles and shotguns so labeled are targeted to a young market. Traditional in substance, they differ in dress. For example, the Vanguard Series 2 rifles are built on the Vanguard actions Weatherby lists in its standard catalog – but WBY-X rifles feature slightly shorter stocks with bold graphics. A quartet of new Series 2 Vanguards strut Kryptek, Blaze and Typhon stock cosmetics. Chambered in .223, .243, .270, .308 and .30-06, three with slender 24-inch barrels weigh 7¼ pounds. The Series 2 Typhon TR (Threat Response) rifle boasts a stiff 22-inch barrel in .223 and .308. A pound heavier than the others, it's priced the same at $749. All four are fitted with two-stage triggers adjustable to 2½ pounds. (www.weatherby.com)

WINCHESTER REPEATING ARMS VINTAGE LEVER GUNS

Built in the Japanese Miroku facility that has produced many Winchester and Browning rifles over the years, new reproductions of Winchester 1873 and 1892 lever actions appear quite faithful in form. To my eye, wood-to-metal fit equals that of the originals. And if not as smooth-shucking as saddle guns cycled hundreds of times in trail dust, the new rifles run with an easy, hitch-free cadence. Like earlier 1886 and Model 71 rifles from Miroku, these may also shoot more accurately than originals. The Model 1873 introduced in .357 Magnum last year now comes with a color case-hardened receiver and crescent butt, and in two additional chamberings: .44-40 and .45 Colt. Each has a 20-inch barrel and a full-length magazine. You can get the Model 1892 Large Loop Carbine in the same chamberings, plus .44 Magnum. Like the '73, it features a straight-grip stock with a muzzle-length tube. Of course, it differs a great deal in design. The Model 1873 descended from the Hunt, Henry and 1866 rifles, before Winchester's Vice President Thomas Bennett discovered John Browning. After he bought Browning's first commercial rifle and built it in New Haven as the Model 1885 single-shot, Bennett encouraged the young Utahn to design a powerful lever action to replace Winchester's 1876. Browning employed the vertically sliding lugs of his single-shot to come up with the stout Model 1886. He followed with the similar 1892, sized for smaller cartridges. It became one of the best-selling Winchesters of all time. Counting the Model 65 variant, more than 1,034,000 original 1892s were built before the rifle was dropped from Winchester catalogs in 1941. The new 1892 has the same fetching profile and fine balance, as well as a very slick action. (www.winchesterguns.com)

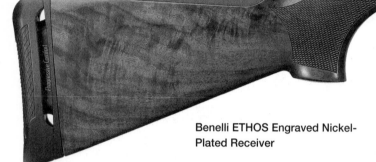

Benelli ETHOS Engraved Nickel-Plated Receiver

Below: The Benelli ETHOS has a hollow stock that houses the Progressive Comfort recoil reduction system of interlocking polymer fingers. The stiffer the recoil produced by a shell, the more fingers mesh together to absorb recoil.

This year's new shotgun models cover the entire range of smoothbore guns – from defense and competition guns to lavish over/unders, to utility hunting and target guns that tame the recoil of magnum 12-gauge shells. The tactical influence continues to permeate the shotgun market to the point that several new shotgun models look more like a jackhammer than conventional shotguns. However, quite a few new shotguns feature a traditional look with svelte lines and walnut.

BENELLI USA

The ETHOS is Benelli's next generation of 12-gauge recoil-operated semiauto shotguns. Benelli says the ETHOS will cycle everything from light 7/8-ounce loads up to stout 3-inch magnums. The new design includes a patented easy-locking system with a detent on the bolt body that ensures the rotating bolt head locks up, even when the bolt is

eased forward. A two-part carrier latch, beveled loading port and redesigned carrier ensure easy shell chambering. Its large bolt release is easy to operate, with or without gloves. The ETHOS

features a replaceable carbon-fiber rib with interchangeable red, green or yellow fiber-optic front sights. Crio choke tubes include cylinder (C), improved cylinder (IC), modified (M), improved

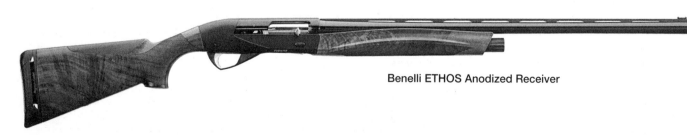

Benelli ETHOS Anodized Receiver

OTGUNS

BY **John Haviland**

Benelli Vinci Tactical

Benelli Performance Shop M2
3-Gun Edition

modified (IM) and full (F). Plus, an anti-seize magazine cap incorporates a synthetic bushing to prevent binding in foul weather or dusty conditions.

ETHOS stocks are European walnut and hollow to accept a recoil reduction system that adjusts to and dampens the recoil of different loads. The Progressive Comfort system is designed with a series of interlocking polymer fingers. The stiffer the recoil produced by a shell, the more fingers mesh together to absorb recoil. I shot the ETHOS quite a few times at clay targets and the system seemed to significantly lessen recoil sting at the point the bolt of the inertia recoil system reached its rearward travel.

Benelli's original Vinci 12-gauge autoloader sports long, graceful lines. The model has been altered to the point that the Vinci Tactical looks like a jackhammer. The Tactical has a buttstock with a vertical grip and corrugated V-Grip surface and a shim kit is included to adjust

drop and cast for a personalized fit. A QuadraFit buttstock is optional and also allows easy adjustment of drop, cast, comb height and length of pull (LOP). A Picatinny rail, ghost-ring rear and red bar front sight add to the tactical look. The Tactical model has a three-round magazine and comes with C, IC, M, IM and F choke tubes.

Like all Benelli autoloaders, the Inertia Driven operating system is the heart of the Performance Shop M2 3-Gun Edition. This tactical competition shotgun incorporates custom parts from Nordic Components. The large Speed Button bolt release eliminates fumbling during quick reloads and the extended bolt handle provides a quick and sure grip while manually cycling the gun. In addition, the M2 3-Gun's loading port has been widened, edges beveled and the carrier modified to assist with the speed and ease of loading the magazine. A Teflon-coated follower in the magazine eliminates shell drag. The barrel is fitted with a HiViz Comp green LitePipe front sight with a .135-inch diameter bead.

Extra LitePipes in different sizes and colors are also included.

Several shotguns from Benelli and its sister companies Franchi and Stoeger are now offered in Realtree MAX-5 camo waterfowl pattern. Benelli models include the Super Black Eagle II, M2 Field in 12 and 20 gauge, Super Vinci, Vinci, Super Nova and Nova. The Franchi models available include the Intensity and Affinity in 12 and 20 gauge. Stoeger models consist of the M3500, M3000, M3020 and P350.

BROWNING

The Browning High Grade Program continues with a pair of full sideplate Citori over/ unders. Those extended sideplates leave plenty of room for engraving, and match up nicely with the gun's case-hardened receiver. Finely checkered and finished high-grade wood is hand fit to Grade III and Grade VI 12-gauge models with 28-inch ventilated rib barrels. The High Grade III Citori receiver features high-relief scroll engraving with a color case-hardened

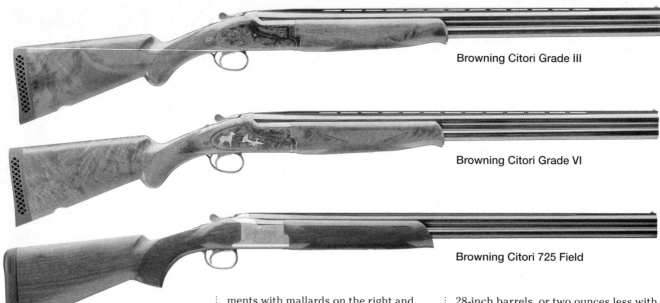

Browning Citori Grade III

Browning Citori Grade VI

Browning Citori 725 Field

finish. The walnut stock and forearm have a gloss finish and 22 lines-per-inch checkering. The Grade III comes in a protective ABS plastic case.

The Grade VI Citori High Grade receiver has a color case-hardened finish with engraving that features gold enrich-ments with mallards on the right and pheasants on the left. The walnut stock and forearm have a gloss finish with 22 lines-per-inch checkering. The Grade VI Citori will be supplied with a Browning High Grade Canvas/Crazy Horse Leather fitted gun case.

A lighter 20 gauge has been added to the Citori 725 Field and Sporting models that weighs six pounds, six ounces with 28-inch barrels, or two ounces less with 26-inch barrels. Browning's FireLite Mechanical Trigger System, full-width hinge pin, tapered locking bolt design, Inflex II recoil pad and Invector-DS choke tube system are all featured. The 725 Field has a receiver finished in silver nitride with engravings of game bird scenes and a gloss oil-finished walnut stock and forearm. The Sporting model also has a silver nitride receiver with gold target engraving and a choice of 28-, 30- or 32-inch barrel lengths. The stock is designed with a close radius pistol grip and palm swell. I shot a 725 Sporting, and while its weight was not all that light compared to other 20-gauge over/unders, it fit very well. I aligned clay targets above the swinging gun's rib, pulled the trigger, and the targets turned into fresh dirt.

Other new Citori 725s are the Trap and Skeet models in 12 gauge. The Trap is available with 30-inch or 32-inch barrels with a high post rib. An adjustable comb stock is optional. And the Skeet is offered with 28- or 30-inch barrels, also with an adjustable comb stock option.

CZ-USA

New additions to CZ's shotgun lineup for this year include pumps, autoloaders and over/unders.

The CZ 600 series pump 12 gauges include the Field with a three-inch chamber, walnut stock and forearm, and chrome finish. The 620 Big Game slug gun has a 22-inch smoothbore barrel with a Weaver-style rail for mounting optics, while its extended rifled choke tube improves the accuracy of Foster-style slugs. The 620 Youth gun has a

The Browning Citori 725 Sporting 20 gauge.

shortened LOP and a 24-inch barrel. This 20 gauge features a three-inch chamber and comes with three interchangeable choke tubes. The 612 Home Defense Combo has a black synthetic stock, an 18½-inch cylinder-bore barrel and a spare 26-inch barrel with a ventilated rib.

3-Gun competitors will love the 712 ALS 12 gauge. Its six-position stock adjusts from 11¼ to 15 inches, and the ATI fluted magazine extends just forward of the gun's 22-inch barrel to hold nine rounds. Five choke tubes are included.

The Sporter Standard Grade Adjustable Rib over/under has a Moneymaker Guncraft rib that adjusts point of impact for shooting everything from sporting clays to trap. Its stock comb also adjusts for a custom fit. The 12 gauge has 30-inch or 32-inch barrels and six interchangeable stainless steel choke tubes are included. The Canvasback Gold over/under is an upgrade of the original Canvasback. Its black chrome receiver is engraved with two golden birds inlaid on each side and the barrels have solid mid-ribs. Other features include a single selectable trigger and extractors that lift shells partially out of the chamber, and it is available in .410, 28, 20 and 12 gauge, all on gauge-specific sized frames. And last but certainly not least, the fine-shooting Lady Sterling model is built on the Upland Sterling 12-gauge receiver with smaller stock dimensions made especially to fit women shooters.

CZ 620 Big Game

CZ 620 Youth

CZ Sporter Standard Grade

CZ Canvasback Gold

CZ Lady Sterling

FRANCHI

Franchi's Affinity Compact 12-gauge autoloader has a 12 ⅜-inch LOP, which can be adjusted with ¼-inch spacers up to 13 ⅜ inches. A shim kit is also included to adjust cast and drop at heel from 2 to 2½ inches, and drop at comb 1½ inch for a highly custom fit. The Compact features a 26-inch barrel with IC and M choke tubes, and an aluminum receiver with steel inserts for strength and to lock up with the barrel. Its synthetic stock and slim forearm keep weight down to 5½ pounds.

Franchi Affinity Compact

Franchi Affinity Sporting

Franchi Intensity Mossy Oak Bottomland

Franchi Intensity Realtree Xtra Green

The Affinity Sporting is now available in a 20-gauge version. The Inertia Driven semiautomatic shotgun features a brushed nickel anodized receiver and 28-inch barrel with a stepped ventilated rib, red fiber-optic front sight and three extended choke tubes. The slender grip of its synthetic stock and slim forearm keeps its weight down at seven pounds. LOP is adjustable from 14 3/8 inches, to 14¼ inches, to 15 inches by switching between three recoil pads of different thicknesses. In addition, drop and cast can be adjusted with a shim kit.

On the more brawny side, the Franchi Intensity handles 3½-inch 12-gauge shells. A slender grip and forearm give the autoloader a trim profile and weight of just 7 1/8 pounds. Its synthetic stock is available in black, or hidden in Realtree MAX-5, Realtree Xtra or Mossy Oak Bottomlands camouflage. The Intensity offers a choice of a 26- or 28-inch barrel with a stepped ventilated rib, red fiber-optic front sight and IC, M and F extended choke tubes. LOP can be adjusted to 14⅜, 14¼ or 15 inches with three different recoil pads, and the drop and cast are set with a shim kit. The Intensity's Inertia recoil system easily cycles shells from 3½-inch magnums down to 1⅛-ounce target loads.

LEGACY SPORTS INTERNATIONAL

The Legacy Escort Gladius models of tactical home defense shotguns are the 20-gauge versions of the Escort MP-P/A pump and MP-S/A semiauto 12-gauge models. These shotguns feature a black polymer stock with a cushioned vertical pistol grip, adjustable comb and a two-round shell holder. Forends are lengthened and include a Picatinny-style Tri-rail. The forend of each Gladius also has a forward down-grip to enhance handling. Receivers are aircraft-grade aluminum alloy with a rail and adjustable ghost ring rear sight to go along with an elevation adjustable fiber-optic front sight. Barrels are cylinder bored and chambered for 3-inch 20-gauge shells, and also include heat shrouds and muzzlebrakes. The semiauto model features Escort's SMART valve technology for fast cycle rates, and the FAST loading system. The pump model has a short-throw handle for quick action. Both models feature five-round magazine tubes.

The Pointer 1000 over/under shotgun is available in 12, 20, 28 and .410-bore, and a Youth model 20 gauge. The 12, 20 and 28-gauge models are chambered for 3-inch magnum loads and come with five choke tubes, while the .410 is chambered for 2¾-inch shells and has fixed C and M chokes. Blued barrels are chrome lined and topped with a ventilated rib and front brass bead. Receivers are nickel-plated and contrast nicely with a Turkish walnut stock and forearm. A single trigger, barrel selector and automatic safety are standard. Plus, the 12-gauge model has ejectors while others are made with extractors.

MOSSBERG

Mossberg is hitching a ride on the celebrated coattails of A&E's *Duck Dynasty* with a Duck Commander series of shotguns endorsed by the Robertson family. The Duck Commander 500 Super Bantam, FLEX, 535 ATS, 835 Ulti-Mag pump guns; and autoloading 930, 935 Magnum and SA20 shotguns all feature a Realtree MAX-5 camouflage pattern, Premium TRUGLO, TRU-BEAD dual-color front fiber-optic sight, Duck Commander logo on the stock, and an American Flag bandana just like the one worn by Willie Robertson. Beards are not included.

The 930 autoloading 12-gauge High-Performance guns have an extended tube magazine with a 13-shot capacity, and a five-shot magazine conversion kit also comes with each gun. One model has a black synthetic stock and

Mossberg Model 500 Super Bantam Duck Commander

Mossberg 535 Duck Commander

Mossberg 500 FLEX Duck Commander

Mossberg 835 Ulti-Mag Duck Commander

Mossberg 935 Magnum Duck Commander

Mossberg 930 High-Performance

Mossberg 930 High-Performance in Kryptek Yeti camo

Mossberg 930 JM Pro (Jerry Miculek Series) 9-Shot

forearm that matches its matte black metal finish, while the other model is concealed in white Kryptek Yeti camouflage.

Three other new 12-gauge shotguns are covered with Kryptek Typhon camouflage. The 930 JM Pro (Jerry Miculek Series) autoloader has a 10-shot extended magazine tube clamped to its barrel. A beveled loading gate provides quicker loading and a fiber-optic front sight aids in faster aiming. The 930 Security model has an eight-shot magazine under its cylinder-bore, 18½-inch barrel, a pistol grip stock and ghost ring rear sight to align with the fiber-optic front sight. And lastly, the 590A1 Security pump shotgun has many similar features, with a six-shot magazine.

REMINGTON

Remington has introduced a few new tactical competition guns based on its 870 pump and VERSA MAX auto.

The 870 Express Tactical Magpul is completely coated with a weatherproof Cerakote Flat Dark Earth coating. Its 18½-inch barrel features a threaded-on muzzlebrake, and a rail on the receiver accepts an adjustable XS Ghost Ring Sight to go along with a white bead front sight. Up next is the 870 Express Tactical Pistol Grip model featuring a Pachmayr pistol grip. With an 18½-inch barrel, the gun's overall length is a short, quick-handling 30 inches. Its pistol grip can be swapped out for the included black synthetic stock. For those looking for a tactical autoloader, the VERSA MAX Competition Tactical's

receiver is covered with durable green Cerakote, and below its 22-inch barrel is an extended magazine, plus an adjustable XS rear express sight aligns a front fiber-optic bead.

Other new models include the VERSA MAX Synthetic Left Hand autoloader, which has a black synthetic stock and forearm, and a 26- or 28-inch barrel with a ventilated rib. HiVis interchangeable fiber-optic pipes are included for the front sight, and a Mossy Oak camo finish is also available. The VERSA MAX Waterfowl Pro has a large bolt handle, bolt release button and safety tab for enhanced operating while wearing gloves. Its ejection port is also larger than the one on a regular VERSA MAX, plus its shell carrier has a gap between it and the magazine to prevent pinching a gloved thumb while

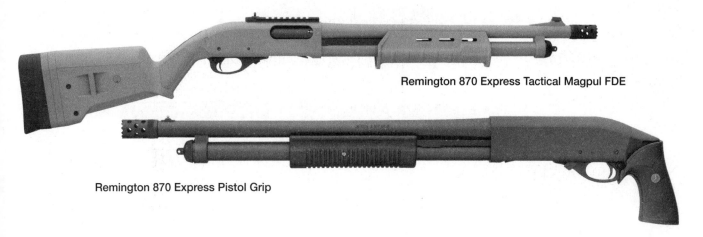

Remington 870 Express Tactical Magpul FDE

Remington 870 Express Pistol Grip

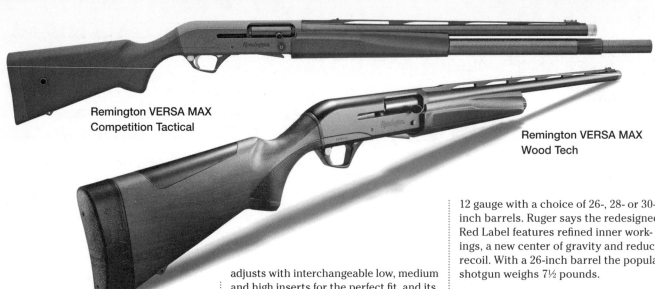

Remington VERSA MAX
Competition Tactical

Remington VERSA MAX
Wood Tech

loading shells into the magazine. HiVis interchangeable fiber-optic sights and a sling are included, and the entire gun is concealed in Mossy Oak Shadow Grass Blades camouflage. For a more traditional look, the VERSA MAX Woodtech features a walnut stock and forearm with soft inserts for a sure grip. Comb height

adjusts with interchangeable low, medium and high inserts for the perfect fit, and its 28-inch barrel accepts an assortment of Pro Bore choke tubes.

RUGER

Ruger first introduced its Red Label over/under in 20-gauge in 1977, and it was produced until the gun quietly disappeared from Ruger's catalog in 2011. The beloved gun is back, initially now in

12 gauge with a choice of 26-, 28- or 30-inch barrels. Ruger says the redesigned Red Label features refined inner workings, a new center of gravity and reduced recoil. With a 26-inch barrel the popular shotgun weighs 7½ pounds.

STOEGER

The M3020 autoloading 20 gauge is Stoeger's latest addition to its line of affordable shotguns. The M3020 is built on the recoil-operated Inertia Driven operating system. Choices of 26- or 28-inch barrels are fitted with a ventilated rib and red fiber-optic front sight. Also included are extra-full turkey, M and IC

Ruger Red Label

Stoeger Double Defense

Stoeger M3020

Stoeger Grand

Winchester Super X3 Long Beard

Winchester Super XP Compact Field

Winchester Super SXP CampField Combo

Winchester Super SXP Extreme Defender

Winchester Super SXP Extreme Marine Defender

choke tubes and a shim kit to adjust the stock drop and cast.

Competition shooters will enjoy the Grand single-shot 12-gauge trap gun, which has a 30-inch barrel with a stepped ventilated rib and fiber-optic front sight. Its automatic safety engages when the lever is pushed to open the action, and when the action opens a shell is extracted, but not ejected. M, IM and F choke tubes are included, and the hardwood stock has an adjustable comb. Weight is seven pounds.

The tactical trend has finally reached every aspect of the shooting sports with Stoeger clamping an accessory rail on the barrels and receiver, and adding a synthetic stock and forearm to its Double Defense side-by-side shotgun.

Its 20-inch barrels are called "tactical-length" and have fixed improved cylinder chokes. The gun has a single trigger, tang-mounted automatic safety and green fiber-optic front sight.

WINCHESTER REPEATING ARMS

Winchester's Super X3 Long Beard autoloader is chambered for the fearsome 12-gauge, 3½-inch shell. This dedicated turkey gun includes a Briley X-Full Long Beard Invector-Plus extended choke tube in a 24-inch barrel. Its pistol grip stock comes with three interchangeable recoil pads to adjust length of pull, and three interchangeable pieces to adjust the comb height for a truly custom fit. Sights

include a TRUGLO fiber-optic front sight, an adjustable folding rear sight and a Weaver-style cantilever base for optics. The gun is finished in Realtree Xtra Green camouflage.

The Super X Pump Compact Field model has a 13-inch LOP to fit perfectly for smaller-statured hunters. This 12 gauge features a three-inch chamber, checkered satin-finished stock and forearm. Black chrome covers the bolt and other metal parts for easy cleaning and long-lasting durability. Plus, its chamber and bore are protected from corrosion and wear with hard chrome. Invector-Plus choke tubes are included, as well as the Inflex Technology recoil pad and easy-cleaning drop-out trigger group.

Cabot Guns now offers perfectly inverted matching 1911 pistol sets fully customized to the exacting specifications requested by the customer.

BY **Kevin Muramatsu**

Semi-Auto Pistols

J ust about every gun company releases a new model or two at strategic times of the year. After all, any business must continue to make something new available to their customers, and in fact, the customer base demands it.

"When are you gonna make that in .45?"

"When are you gonna make that in .308?"

"Is that gonna come in a subcompact version?"

"How about a .380 version for my wife?"

Then, there are the examples where the product is simply expanded or modified for ergonomics, better function or simply because the customer base demands it.

"You know what? If this was in .40 with a single-stack magazine, I'd buy ten of 'em."

"Where's the night sights?"

"Are you gonna have a version with a carry melt? (Heavily broken,

The Pico is the 9mm Nano's little brother. This .380 is extremely thin and conceals six rounds in the magazine.

chamfered or rounded edges for those of you who may not know what a "carry melt" is).

"When are you gonna have this in 9mm?"

"When are you gonna have this in .40?"

"When are you gonna have this in .45?"

"When can I get a Glock 28?"

Finally, there are the examples wherein a firearm was promised a year or more ago and the product still, for whatever reason, has not yet hit the market, or has suffered a crippling recall. This is an infrequent event, and for anyone who has worked in any manufacturing field knows, really should be an expected event on occasion. Despite best efforts, this kind of thing simply happens and it really ought to happen more than it does. The gun industry has gotten pretty good, except with rare examples, of delivering in short order at least a few of the promised goods. So I want to point out to those in anxious anticipation of the pistol that was first covered in the big glossy magazines a year or two ago that sometimes it takes awhile.

Very few manufacturers fabricate every little or big thing in house. When you have to wait for your barrel supplier to fix his tooling because his bar supplier sent him slightly different steel than last time, you cannot fit the barrel to the slide, nor can you fit the bushing to the barrel, or that ramped barrel to the frame, and so the whole process takes a bit longer and it's completely out of the gun manufacturer's control. So there may be one or two pistols in this list that fit this category.

BERETTA

Late in 2013 Beretta announced the Pico. The little brother to the 9mm Nano, the Pico is a very small .380 pistol. A number of alternatively pigmented polymer grips can be purchased if desired. A Pico magazine holds six rounds and each gun ships with one flush magazine and a second magazine with a generous grip extension on the bottom. You also have a choice of standard model or another with a LaserMax Guide Rod Laser sight installed from the factory. Night sights appear to be standard, and the Pico is only 18mm in width. For those who live in 'Merica, that is a bit less than three-quarters inch wide. The Pico retails for $399.

Also new this year is a modification to the long extant Model 92. Of course there have been a number of variants to the 92, but this time we are getting an easily accessorized compact model. The 92 Compact drops about three-quarters inch in overall length and almost one-quarter inch in overall height. It doesn't seem like much, but it doesn't take much to matter when carrying concealed. Furthermore, it has an accessory rail

under the barrel and comes in both Bruniton (black) and Inox (stainless) versions. Capacity is 13 rounds of 9mm and the suggested retail is $775. (www.berettausa.com)

BERSA

The BPCC series of pistols has been expanded a little bit. While Bersa is better known for traditional double-action pistols like the Thunder, they also have been offering a new striker-fired pistol. The BP9 is an attractively thin compact offering in the polymer-framed pistol set. Alternate colors are now available, such as charcoal gray and flat dark earth. Furthermore, the BPCC is now offered in .40 S&W. MSRP is $475. Unfortunately at the time of this writing, the BP40 is still awaiting import approval. Presumably, it will have received such approval by the time the reader skims past this paragraph. (www.bersa.com)

BOBERG ARMS

Boberg Arms has been selling the XR9 pistols for a couple years. Distinguished by the reverse-feeding magazine and set-back barrel, these pistols generate high muzzle velocities and incorporate substantial recoil reduction into the little packages. Being introduced in 2014 is the XR45-S, which upgrades to America's favorite, the .45 ACP. It's a little bigger, as can be expected from the 9mm to .45 jump, but it's still mighty small. MSRP has not been set but is expected to be a few bucks higher than the 9mm, which starts at $995. (www.bobergarms.com)

Boberg follows up their 9mm with the XR45-S. This super compact .45 has super low felt recoil and super high velocity from its "longer than it looks" barrel.

BROWNING

Since Browning introduced the 1911-22 they haven't been able to keep up with the demand. Apparently they can now, as several new models have been introduced. When before we could only get standard and commander-style models, we now have access to pink gripped models, composite frames, guns with rails and beavertails, and combinations thereof. The Black Label models are especially attractive and look just like

The new reduced-in-size Beretta 92FS Compact Rail. It sacrifices two rounds and not quite ¾ inch of barrel length.

The Bersa BP9 CC has been in the country since mid-2013. Expect a near identical BP40 to hit the shores mid-2014, as well as alternate frame colors for the BP9.

The 1911-22 line from Browning has expanded. This is one of the nicer looking Black Label models, with all the nice-to-have features in an 85-percent-size pistol.

The Coonan Classic on the right, with the new Coonan Compact .357 on the left. It loses about an inch of barrel and still holds seven rounds.

a high-end full-size .45, but in .22 LR. As was Browning's intent, these guns were mainly introduced for the purpose of introductory pistol shooting for those folks with small hands, namely young shooters. The grips on these pistols are very small and adults with larger hands may find them to be unusable. Not so for the youngsters, for whom these pistols are perfectly sized. These 85-percent versions of the full-size 1911 pistol range in price from $599 to $679. (www.browning.com)

COLT

The Mustang has been upgraded to a more modern standard in the form of the XSP. While functionally the same as previous models, the XSP weighs in at only 12 ounces. Colt accomplished this in the same way most companies do, by making the frame from polymer. This also allows some more freedom of form and function and so they have also

Colt has revamped the classic Mustang with the XSP. It has a polymer frame and a catchy square triggerguard.

squared off the pistol grip and added an accessory rail. Both will allow the mounting of lights or lasers should the owner desire such an enhancement. Slide serrations are deeper and easier to grasp than previous models; the ambidextrous thumb safety, larger dovetailed front sight and poly frame also have been tweaked for the preferred ergonomics of whoever it was that didn't like the shape of the previous models. $649 is the recommended price tag established by Colt's Manufacturing Company for this .380 ACP pocket pistol. (www.colt.com)

COONAN

The Coonan .357 Magnum pistol is one of the more unique 1911 variants to have come forth from the mind of man. Coonan has a compensated model that takes some of the significant flip out of the very significant muzzle flip associated with shooting this pistol. Add a custom DuraCoat finish and you have a low-recoiling .357 Mag. auto pistol to strap to your hip when you go out coyote plinking. Also, a compact pistol is in the works that is optimized for concealed carry. It takes half an inch off the barrel

and a quarter inch off the grip, leaving a full three fingers for full control. MSRP should be in the $1,100 range, but has not been firmly established as of this writing. (coonaninc.com)

COBRA

The CA pistol has been upgraded to a .45 ACP firing Denali model. Besides being a .45, the frame is now made of polymer for reduced weight. With a lifetime warranty the Denali runs $160. (www.cobrapistols.net)

The Cobra Firearms Denali is a .45 ACP upgrade of the CA pistol. Inexpensive, it is small and concealable.

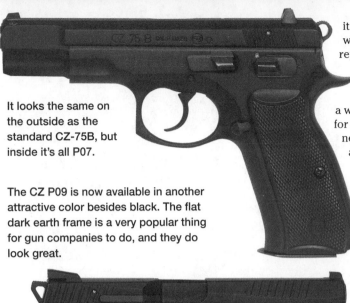

It looks the same on the outside as the standard CZ-75B, but inside it's all P07.

The CZ P09 is now available in another attractive color besides black. The flat dark earth frame is a very popular thing for gun companies to do, and they do look great.

CZ USA

The CZ-75B Omega model has an upgraded trigger assembly. Using the parts from the P09 model, the Omega is much easier to take apart for maintenance. Price is $544.

The Omega series continues with the upgrading of the P07 model. The P09 introduced last year is a full-size, polymer-frame pistol. The P07 now has the upgraded features of the P09 such as forward cocking serrations, a reshaped trigger contour, interchangeable backstraps, and interchangeable decockers or manual safeties, which can be swapped by the consumer. This P07 also has a new finish on the slide to make it more durable. If you want the new updated P07 you will max out at $524. The P09 is also now available in flat dark earth for $596, and in a black suppressor-ready format with threaded barrel for $577. (cz-usa.com)

DIAMONDBACK

The very small Diamondback pistols have been cosmetically upgraded. The slide cocking grooves have been improved, and enhanced texturing has been implemented on the grip frame itself. Attractive wavy serrations replace the old scallopy types, and forward serrations are a welcome addition for many users. The new models start at $394 for the DB380 models and $431 for the DB9 models. Diamondback has also added an AR-style pistol line called the DB15 that starts at $899. More than just basic AR pistols, these DB15s have additional nice-to-have features straight from the factory, such as a railed handguard and Magpul or Stark pistol grips, and olive drab green and dark earth finishes. (diamondbackfirearms.com)

EAA

The Witness Pavona pistol by Tanfoglio is the newest offer from European American Armory. The Pavona was designed specifically with the female market in mind. EAA wanted to stay away from the basic pink color as that has been found to alienate a significant segment of female shooters who find the use of that color condescending. However (and I am saying this from a male perspective) the use of other sorts of bling is apparently still okay, and the Pavona has a pretty cool means of implementing the bling. Small metal flakes are impregnated into the polymer of the frame. Several colors of the polymer are available, such as black, charcoal or sapphire (not an exhaustive list) and all have gold or silver colored flakes in the matrix. The slide is either blued or chromed. Besides the cosmetics, the gun is also optimized for women by incorporating lighter hammer and recoil springs to enable easier slide racking, and the grasping grooves on the slide are also cut quite deeply to allow better grip with less effort. These attractive guns start at $476. (eaacorp.com)

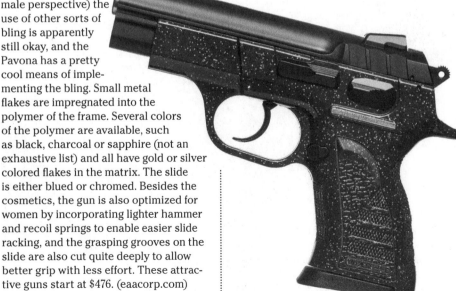

The Diamondback DB15 pistol is a great entry into the AR pistol class. It comes standard with some nice upgrades.

The EAA Pavona has some nice frame color upgrades. This is the black frame with gold flake.

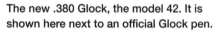

The wonderful FNH FNS pistol has had an upgrade for the playing field in the form of the Long Slide models. Featuring a full 5-inch barrel, the 9mm and .40 S&W Long Slides are ready for the matches they are sure to be used in.

FNH

FN has a long history of firearms manufacturing. I instantly liked the FNP and FNX pistols when they were introduced, and the short-lived Pro-9 and 40 brothers made under the Browning name. Then the FNS striker-fired models were introduced. While available in black and two-tone models, and multiple calibers, the barrels stubbornly remained at the 4-inch length. No longer. Long Slide models in both 9mm and .40 S&W are now on the market with 5-inch barrels. The intended market is the highly competitive competition market. The same capacity as

the standard models remains at 17 for the 9mm and 14 for the .40. FNH-USA suggests dealers charge $749. Of course, street price will be somewhat less. (www.fnhusa.com)

GLOCK

You can't get a Glock 28, ever, (because it does not conform to the stupid Saturday night special law) so Glock has delivered an alternative. Now you can purchase a Glock 42. This is the first Glock chambered in .380 Auto available in the U.S. Without drooling too much, I will say that this falls into the "customer demanded" category. Glock has been subjected to years of clamoring for a subcompact .380 and this is finally the result. The best part, in my opinion, is that unless you have really fat fingers, you can still get your pinky finger on the front strap of the gun as long as the magazine is present. This translates to a much higher degree of controllability. The 42 is less than an inch in width, holds six rounds in the magazine (you can bet some enterprising individual will market an 18-round extension soon), and weighs less than a pound with a full magazine inserted. It is skinny, light and the grip is just tall enough to be easily controllable. It functions in all ways just like any other Glock pistol.

Also, Glock has released another model called the 41 Gen4. This particular monster, again by customer demand, is made for tactical and competition use. It has a 5.31-inch .45 ACP barrel, with the Glock 36 width slide. This makes it a bit skinnier than the standard .45 ACP Glock 21 and follows in the footsteps of last year's Glock 30S, which essentially combines the larger-capacity model 30 frame with the thin model 36 slide. Even though

The new .380 Glock, the model 42. It is shown here next to an official Glock pen.

it has a longer slide and barrel, it actually weighs less than the shorter-barreled Glock 21 Gen4. Like previous Gen4 models, the 41 has replaceable backstraps and nicely aggressive texturing. Thirteen rounds of .45 with the longer barrel will be welcome in many matches and many holsters. The Glock 42 has an MSRP of $475 and the Glock 41 Gen4 has an MSRP of $635. (www.glock.com)

HEIZER DEFENSE

Heizer Defense has the PS1 Pocket Shotgun single-shot pistol, new in 2014. It is a single-barrel, very thin, tip-up-style gun that shoots either .45 Colt or .410 shotgun shells. Overall the size of a smartphone, it is very concealable and contains a reserve ammo compartment

The Heizer Defense PS1 Pocket Shotgun, open and ready for loading.

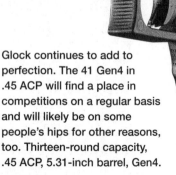

Glock continues to add to perfection. The 41 Gen4 in .45 ACP will find a place in competitions on a regular basis and will likely be on some people's hips for other reasons, too. Thirteen-round capacity, .45 ACP, 5.31-inch barrel, Gen4.

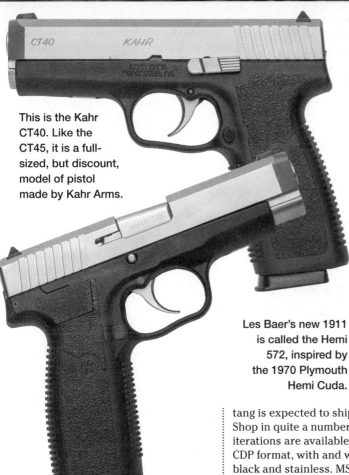

This is the Kahr CT40. Like the CT45, it is a full-sized, but discount, model of pistol made by Kahr Arms.

Kahr's new CT45. It's a little tall, but that's because it is a full-sized .45 pistol.

Les Baer's new 1911 is called the Hemi 572, inspired by the 1970 Plymouth Hemi Cuda.

in the grip that holds two additional .45 Colt cartridges. The suggested retail price is $499. (www.heizerdefense.com)

KAHR

Kahr has introduced two full-size value series pistols in its 2014 catalog. The CT40 and CT45 are both full-length pistols with 4-inch barrels – 4.04 to be precise on the CT45. The CT40 and CT45 each have a price tag of $449. Compare this to their standard contemporaries, the TP40 and TP45 at $697. The savings is gained mostly from less-involved machining and other manufacturing steps. Both models use seven-round magazines. (www.kahr.com)

KIMBER

Continuing the current trend of marketing super-compact .380-caliber pistols is Kimber. Well known for making 1911s of many sizes and chamberings, Kimber's incarnation of the old Colt Mus-

tang is expected to ship from the Custom Shop in quite a number this year. Several iterations are available, such as in the CDP format, with and without laser grips, black and stainless. MSRP starts at $651 for the standard Micro Carry .380 and ends with the Micro CDP (LG) at $1,406. (www.kimberamerica.com)

Like several other companies, Kimber has introduced its own version of the Mustang in the form of the Micro Carry. The model shown is the upgrade to that model called the Micro CDP. This one has "carry melt" and Crimson Trace Lasergrips.

LES BAER

The 1911 Hemi 572 is inspired by Les Baer's own Plymouth Pro Street Hemi Cuda. A 5-inch barrel, front and rear cocking serrations, DuPont S coating on the controls, screws and spring plug, with VZ grips makes this an attractive handgun. It MSRPs for $2,395. (www.lesbaer.com)

Masterpiece Arms' MPA Defender 935SST. This is a mean-looking machine. I want one.

It sort of looks like an AR but it's not. The heavy pistol class welcomes the Masterpiece Arms MPAR pistol to its educational content.

MASTERPIECE ARMS

Masterpiece Arms is known for the reintroduction of the MAC series of pistols. They have added a completely different type of pistol that sort of looks like an AR, but isn't, called the MPAR556. Based upon the similar rifle introduced earlier, the MPAR556 has a non-reciprocating side-charging handle with forward assist, uses AR magazines and comes from the factory with an angled fore-grip. It has all the other black pistol features as well, such as a free-floated handguard tube, the ability to accept accessories on side rails of the handguard, and a full-length top rail that can be used to mount your choice of

sights or optics over the threaded barrel. MPA lists $899 for this model.

The MPA935SST Defender is also new. An 8-inch barrel with adjustable sights, optic mount and angled fore-grip is present on this highly tactical model. $675.99 for this one. (masterpiecearms.com)

PARA

Formerly Para-Ordnance, Para is returning to its old ways and has reintroduced the LDA (Light Double Action) triggers they were known for before the company was purchased by the Freedom Group.

The LDA Officer Crimson Trace incorporates that smooth double-action trigger that made Para famous long ago, with the addition of Crimson Trace Lasergrips, a fiber-optic front sight, and with the near obligatory extended beavertail grip safety and extended thumb safety. The entire forged frame and slide assembly is coated with black Ionbond. For $1,225 you can get it in .45 ACP or 9mm, and in any color you want as long as it's black. (www.para-usa.com)

PSA

PSA has been making Browning Baby pistols for Browning for years and also producing an identical model under their own name, the PSA-25 for a similar period. These wonderful little pistols are one of John Browning's most famous creations. PSA has now introduced a drop-in barrel upgrade that will fit any Baby pistol ever made. This barrel, like the standard barrel, is in 6.35mm, otherwise known as .25 ACP or .25 Auto. The yummy goodness involves the internally threaded muzzle designed to accept a sound suppressor. The barrel comes with a thread protector and is $179.95. (www.precisionsmallarms.com)

REMINGTON

Big Green is returning another old classic to the American public. The first was of course the R1, Remington's 1911, introduced several years ago. New variations continue to materialize periodically to satisfy the 1911 nuts in the gun culture that we all know and love. But that's not what we are going to look at here. Remington is bringing back to us the

The Para light double-action trigger returns with the release of the LDA Officer. This officer-size pistol has all the nice features plus the LDA trigger we have missed for years.

Remington has brought back the R51 in a 21st century package.

The P556xi is a fully modular pistol based on the rifle version of the SIG 556. It can be purchased with the totally gnarly pistol brace.

Model 51 in the form of the new R51. It is not the same as the classic, but it is close enough for those who only ever saw a 51 under glass at a gun show or shop. The R51 continues to utilize the Pedersen block to lock the slide closed. This uses a unique dropping block that not only locks the breech, but also acts to absorb a not insignificant amount of recoil impulse. It also has the benefit of lowering the bore axis, which keeps the muzzle flip more controllable. But there are significant differences. The new R51 is currently available only in 9mm Luger and has an aluminum frame. The original Model 51, which was made from 1918 to 1926, was chambered in .32 ACP and .380 ACP and made entirely of steel. Furthermore, the rather heavy trigger pull of the R51 uses a pivoting trigger rather than the 1911-style stirrup of the classic pistol. This R51 has a very attractive MSRP of only $420. Oh, yeah – the side grip panels can be exchanged with those of a different thickness to better accommodate big hands. (www.remington.com)

RUGER

Ruger has held a strong grip on the .22 LR pistol market as far back as the original Standard model. The Mark III and the .22/45 models are very close descendants of that original, and every year there is at least one new baby born into that extended family. With the recent upsurge in interest in sound suppressors, Ruger, like many other manufacturers of .22 pistols, has several models that come from the factory with a threaded muzzle. A suppressed .22 is one of the most fun things of, like ever, to shoot, and the 22/45 Lite fits well into the fun-to-shoot concept. Not only is the muzzle threaded, but it also has an upper section made from aluminum that is cobalt-color anodized with completely unnecessary yet cosmetically wonderful ventilation holes, a very attractive look. It joins its slightly older brother that had a black anodized fluted aluminum upper. The MSRP is $499 for this little fun gun, which also comes with a thread protector. (www.ruger.com)

SIG SAUER

SIG Sauer guns through the ages have always been traditional hammer-fired designs, almost always with some sort of hammer-drop mechanism. Finally, they have jumped on the

SIG Sauer's new striker-fired pistol in its full-size configuration. A compact version is also available.

striker-fired bandwagon like everybody else in existence, and have offered the really cool SIG P320. Like the earlier P250 it has the ability to change calibers by means of swapping slides and the polymer grip frames. The actual "gun" is the trigger housing. It is available – and convertible to – 9mm, .357 SIG and .40 S&W. Furthermore, it has both the standard full-size profile and a compact option as well. It has just about every conceivable internal passive safety incorporated into its construction, but like most striker-fired guns, has no manual safety of any type. Currently available in any color you want as long as you like black, the MSRP is $713 for either model.

The P556xi is the newest pistol addition to the venerable 550 family. Unlike previous versions, this xi has modularity incorporated into the design, a strength that anything in the black rifle and pistol market nowadays needs to possess. Since this is a pistol column, we'll pretend that the rifles don't exist for a bit and point out that the barrels, bolts, handguards and trigger housings (lower receivers) are all fully interchangeable to allow switching between .223, 7.62x39

The 22/45 Lite Cobalt from Ruger is an attractive, super lightweight .22 pistol.

Not much bigger than the author's hand is the SIG Sauer P938-22. It is mounted on the same frame and slide as the standard P938.

and .300 BLK. This includes the pistol model, which is equipped with an SB15 pistol brace. The handguards come in aluminum, polymer or carbon fiber. Lowers are either standard for AR magazines or Russian style, using AK magazines. The charging handle can be reversed to the left side if desired, and the gas system now has three positions. You're looking at about $1,800 for this one.

The P938 and P238 pistols have been around for a year or three, but there is now a .22 LR version called the P938-22. The pistol can be purchased, or existing P938 owners can purchase the conversion kit as desired. The pistol will MSRP at $656, and the conversion kits at $302

for the standard, and $352 for the longslide target model. SIGLITE night sights are standard, as are rosewood grips and a Nitron finish.

SIG Sauer has been busy. The P290 is now available in .380 ACP, called the P290RS. The slide assemblies of the new .380 can be placed onto the frames of the older 9mm, however, at the time of this writing SIG Sauer does not yet indicate if the slide assemblies will actually be sold as an upgrade to already owned 9mm P290s. Grip panels of various bents will also be available for further personalization. The manufacturer's suggested beginning level for personal currency reduction is $586.

The long available P232 can now be had in .22 LR, standard with a threaded barrel. MSRP is $427. This new classic can be easily differentiated from the old classic by the use of a thumb button magazine release (apparently this is the "American" style) and a slide stop lever. (www.sigsauer.com)

SMITH & WESSON

Since the introduction of the Bodyguard 380 pistol, there were a number of folks who really liked the gun but could have done without the integrated laser. That's OK. Some people just don't like lasers, or prefer to keep things easy and simple with no batteries to change, and for greater ease of holster acquisition. Smith & Wesson has satisfied those customers this year by introducing the M&P Bodyguard 380. This is the same gun minus the laser. Everything else is the same, with all the features one could wish for – manual safety, slide stop, second strike capability and supremely compact size. One minor additional change was to give the slide serrations a fish scale appearance to match the other M&P models. Suggested retail price is only $379. (www.smith-wesson.com)

SPRINGFIELD ARMORY

The XD-S line continues to expand with the 9mm 4.0 single-stack model.

The 9mm Springfield Range Officer comforting the hand of a show person. Fully adjustable sights, low recoil, National Match barrel and bushing, and nice Cocobolo grips show it off.

The enhanced version of the SIG Sauer P290RS. The colored grip panels can be swapped out.

Uselton Arms continues to increase their stock of pistols with explosion-welded frame rails. This is the IA .45 Commander.

Like other XD-S models, it is short with a single-stack magazine, but the barrel is a full 4 inches long to mimic the full-size XD pistols. The price tag falls at $599.

The Range Officer 1911 pistol is now also available in 9mm. Like its bigger-bullet brother it has a fully adjustable rear sight, cocobolo grips and all the usual goodies, including two nine-round magazines. The Range Officer in .45 ACP was a very popular offering from Springfield, so the 9mm version is expected to match that popularity. The MSRP for the 9mm is $977. (www. springfield-armory.com)

STEYR ARMS

The Steyr M-A1 pistol has been on the U.S. market for several years now. Shortly after the M9-A1 and M40-A1 arrived, Steyr also threw the smaller C and S variants at us for more concealability. The L models have a 4.5-inch barrel and Steyr has added a loaded chamber indicator on the back of the slide. This is handy, and unlike a magazine safety, is a good attempt to lawyer-proof a gun that still has great practical utility. A reversible magazine catch and upgraded trigger are also featured. The bad news is not so bad at only $540 MSRP. (www. steyrarms.com)

TURNBULL MANUFACTURING

Doug Turnbull is well known for the excellent firearms restorations he has conducted over the years and continues to do. Relatively recently, new gun manufacturing has been added to the Turnbull repertoire. This year two new 1911 models are released. The first is a Commander-style pistol clearly meant to be carried in a concealed holster, chambered only for .38 Super, with a superb charcoal blued finish. The second is a full government-sized .45 model called the Heritage Edition that incorporates nitre-blued parts such as the screws, pins, trigger, thumb safety and slide stop. Most attractive is the color case-hardened frame of the pistol. The MSRPs of these two beauties are $2,599 for the Turnbull Commander, and $1,995 for the Turnbull 1911 Heritage Edition. (www. turnbullmfg.com)

USELTON ARMS

Uselton Arms is known for the use of what's known as explosive bonding, or explosive welding on their pistols. This process literally uses an explosion to force together two disparate metals, in this case the aluminum or titanium frame with the steel frame rails of the pistol frame. This allows the frame to be lightweight but still have the superior wear characteristics of steel on the frame rails. A new model, the IA Commander is out. A stainless steel slide and aluminum frame with all the usual features are present. The retail price for this IA Commander starts at $3,399. (www.useltonarms.com)

WALTHER

The PPQ is one of Walther's newest pistols, and specifically the first striker-fired model from this company. This year the PPQ M2 is unveiled. M2 you ask? While the 4-inch barreled version has been out for a little while the 5-inch barrel is available now as well. The biggest difference is the replacement of the triggerguard magazine release on the original version with the more traditional button-style release (ambidextrous) that most Americans are more used to. Some minor cosmetic differences are also present but otherwise it's just like the original version in most ways. Of course, the ergonomics continue to be superior with the presence of interchangeable backstrap pieces. Like other manufacturers' 5-inch guns, it is marketed as a superior competition and duty firearm. MSRP for the M2 series begins at $649.

Walther has been making rimfire versions of a number of other companies' centerfire firearms and it is only expected that they would do the same for themselves. The PPQ M2 .22 is the rimfire version of the normal PPQ. Very little external differentiation exists between the two, until you look at the stamps and feel the weight. The PPQ M2 .22 starts at a suggested retail of $449. Unlike most competitors who use 10-round magazines, the Walther is shipped with 12-round mags. (www.waltherarms.com)

Walther's new full-size .22 pistol, the PPQ M2 .22. It has 12-round magazines and a threaded barrel.

REVOLVERS & OTHERS

BY **Jeff Quinn**

or the past couple of years, business has been booming for gunmakers and importers in the United States, with not too many new things happening in the world of revolvers and derringers. The makers have been running wide-open just to meet demand for their existing products. However, with the backlog of firearm orders easing just a bit, we now have a few new variations of products in the world of *Revolvers & Others*.

As more and more citizens are taking to carrying a handgun for protection around the U.S., with most states having at least some kind of concealed carry permit program, and other states requiring no permit at all for a citizen to utilize his or her right to carry a firearm, many are choosing a compact revolver as their carry gun of choice. As I sit here pecking at this keyboard, I have a lightweight concealed-hammer .38 Special in my pocket, where it resides much of its time.

A small revolver is easy to carry, lightweight, powerful and doesn't litter the ground with empty brass should it be necessary to quickly resolve a distasteful and violent social conflict. Some choose a good revolver for its simplicity. The manual-of-arms for a double-action revolver can be taught to a novice quickly, and it is easy to determine whether or not the weapon is loaded. It can also be unloaded easily and quickly by swinging the cylinder out of the frame. With a revolver, there are no magazine springs nor feed ramps to cause problems. There is nothing at all

wrong with a quality semiautomatic, but it is hard to argue with the simplicity of operation and the reliability of a good revolver.

There are also a few new entries into the derringer market this year. The .45 Colt/.410 derringers are very popular, and with good reason. They are powerful, simple and especially in the South and West, will quickly dispatch a venomous snake if it poses a threat. The .410 derringers are also very handy to keep within reach to repel a carjacker, should one jerk your door open and try to drag you from your vehicle. Being tugged around by one's arm is not conducive to good marksmanship, but a load of .410 shot into the face of a carjacker would very likely turn his mind towards seeking medical attention, if he can see to find it. These derringers are compact, relatively lightweight and simple to operate.

For hunting, there are plenty of good choices of revolvers on the market, as well as a few good single-shot pistols, that allow the hunter to harvest game with a quick shot at close range, or to take animals as far out as one can with a rifle.

We will also be looking forward to some new introductions this year in revolvers built for competition, as many shooters of IDPA and other sports take advantage of the smooth and quick shooting qualities of a good double-action revolver. A semiauto performs well in the fast-shooting sports, but I realized many years ago that a good double-action revolver tends to smooth

out the rhythm of a competition that uses multiple targets in a string of fire, allowing a cadence that is harder to maintain with a short, crisp trigger of a semiautomatic pistol.

With that, we will take a look at some of what is available in the world of revolvers, derringers and single-shot hunting pistols.

American Derringer

American Derringer is a Texas-based company that builds several versions of their popular two-shot derringer. They have models that are built primarily out of stainless steel, but also have a lightweight version that uses aluminum for the frame and barrels, with steel liners for the chambers and bores. The American derringers are chambered for some serious cartridges, ranging from the .22 rimfires through the .45 Colt/.410 shotshell combination, well-suited as a close-range defensive weapon for defense from attackers on the street, in the home or on the trail. American Derringer has several special-edition pistols, some engraved if desired. The company is also making in limited quantities the dandy little double-action derringer, chambered for the .22 Magnum, .38 Special and .40 S&W cartridges. (www.amderringer.com)

American Western Arms

AWA imports some very good replica sixguns of the Colt Single Action Army style, as well as a pump-action pistol that looks like a cut-down rifle, but is legally a pistol. Called the Lightningbolt, it is offered in various finishes and is chambered for the .45 Colt. The company also still catalogs the interesting Mateba revolver. The Mateba is a very unusual revolver, and the uniqueness of the revolver is not just in appearance. The Mateba turns upside down the sixgun as we know it. These futuristic looking revolvers feature interchangeable barrels and are chambered for the .357 and .44 Magnum cartridges, as well as the .454 Casull. The Mateba fires from the bottom chamber in the cylinder, lowering the center of the recoil in relation to the shooter's hand for a more straight-back recoil impulse, lessening muzzle jump and making target acquisition between shots faster. (www.awaguns.com)

Armscor

Armscor has entered the revolver market with a .38 Special six-shot revolver that is reminiscent of the old Colt double-action revolver design. Marketed under their Rock Island brand, the Armscor sixgun is a durable, well-built and very affordable double-action revolver with a parkerized finish and black polymer grip. It has fixed sights and is available with either a 2-inch or 4-inch barrel. (us.armscor.com)

Bond Arms

Bond Arms of Texas makes some of the best two-shot single-action derringers ever built. Crafted from stainless steel, the Bond derringers are fitted to very close tolerances, and any set of barrels will fit on any Bond frame without individual fitting. One can order extra barrel sets from Bond in any of its 19 different chamberings. My particular favorite variation of the Bond derringer is the Snake Slayer. The more I carry my Bond Arms two-shot Snake Slayer derringer, the more I like it. It is a relatively light, handy and easily concealed pistol that is ideal for carry in the deep woods in the summertime South, where venomous snakes are encountered on a regular basis. Bond derringers are often regarded as the best that money can buy, top-of-the-line quality in the derringer market, and Bond offers an extensive variety of chamberings from .22 Long Rifle up through .45 Colt/.410 shotshell, covering many popular chamberings in between.

Bond derringers are built primarily of stainless steel, they are very weather resistant. The company offers a variety of barrel lengths and derringers with or without triggerguards are available to suit the buyer's preference. Besides being ideal to use for protection from venomous reptiles, the .410-bore derringers are also a fine personal defense arm for use against carjackers and other two-legged predators. Loaded with 000 buckshot or Winchester's combination PDX-1 load, that compact two-pipe would be a very effective close-range defensive weapon. Bond Arms also offers some high-quality leather holsters in which to carry a derringer. I particularly like the horizontal driving holster. It is ideal to wear while riding in a vehicle, or on an ATV or motorcycle, placing the handgun within reach for a fast and comfortable draw. The company leads the market in the extensive variety of chamberings offered, but their .45 Colt/.410 shotshell versions are very popular these days, not just as a backup to a larger handgun, but for primary carry as well. (bondarms.com)

Charter Arms

Charter Arms is a company that has been producing affordable and reliable revolvers for decades now, with an ever-expanding variety from which to choose. I have owned many throughout the years, and probably still have most of them. One favorite that I carried for a long time was a reliable and accurate companion. It was the .44 Bulldog,

which epitomizes the bigbore belly gun. The Bulldogs are the workhorse of the Charter line. While the .38-caliber revolvers are a dandy choice for personal protection, some knowledgeable folks prefer a bigger bullet, and the Charter .44 Bulldog is in a class of its own. It is a lightweight, reliable five-shot .44 Special, and is relied upon by many for daily carry. Charter revolvers are available in blued steel or stainless, and recently the company has added alloy frames to the lineup for those who want to carry the lightest possible package.

The latest innovation from Charter is the finishes that they apply to their alloy-frame guns. With a variety of colors to choose from, the pink finish has proven to be extremely popular with women in the "Pink Lady" variation of the five-shot .38. In addition to the Pink Lady, Charter now has the "Chic Lady," which comes packaged in a good-looking, alligator-textured pink hard carry case. The company also has a line of revolvers with a mottled finish. I refer to them unofficially as the "Cat" revolvers. The Cougar has a pink mottled finish and the Panther a medium-dark bronze mottled finish. I have handled and shot both of these, and they are indeed good-shooting lightweight revolvers. No matter which caliber or finish is chosen, Charter revolvers are reliable and effective weapons.

For a compact trail gun, the Pathfinder rimfire revolvers are a great choice, riding comfortably in a holster all day,

Bond Arms Backup

at the ready to dispatch small game for the camp pot or to provide economical recreational plinking at targets of opportunity. I have one old Charter .22 Long Rifle revolver that was the forerunner to the Pathfinder; called the Pocket Target. Really just a Pathfinder with another name, this little jewel once belonged to one of my favorite gun writers, Mr. Hal Swiggett, and I am sure it shoots as well today as it did many years ago when he first wrote of this little sixgun. (www.charterfirearms.com)

Chiappa

The Chiappa Rhino is an interesting sixgun that has been in production for a couple of years now. This unique "upside-down" sixgun has the barrel located to fire from the chamber which is lowest in the frame, instead of firing from the top chamber in the cylinder as do most other revolvers. This unique feature makes for an odd-looking revolver that is a delight to shoot. I have had the opportunity to fire a few rounds through a couple of Rhino revolvers. Firing full-power .357 Magnum ammunition, the felt recoil was straight back, helping to keep the sights on target for fast repeat shots. Chiappa has several variations of the Rhino in production now featuring various barrel lengths, and even a model with an accessory rail. The Rhino is available in either a nickel or black matte finish. Chiappa also has a line of rimfire single-action revolvers with various barrel lengths. These are reliable yet inexpensive revolvers with the look of the Colt Single Action

DoubleTap Pocket Pistol

Army sixgun. (www.chiappafirearms.com)

Cimarron Firearms

Cimarron Firearms of Fredericksburg, Texas, continues to market some of the best-quality replicas of sixguns of 19th century design. Featuring a wide assortment of Colt and Remington pattern cap-and-ball and cartridge revolvers, Cimarron also has models of some of the transitional cartridge conversion sixguns that bridged the gap from the weapons that were stuffed with loose powder and ball, to the introduction of the self-contained brass cartridge as we know it today. The company also does not ignore some of the lesser-known revolvers from the 19th century, keeping alive the look and feel of those old revolvers that were around at the time that the Confederate States had a dispute with its neighbors to the north. Without Cimarron's replica of the Leech & Rigdon, such historical firearms would have fallen into obscurity, as most of us will never see an original. Cimarron still has its derringer line as well, offering inexpensive derringers in various chamberings and finishes. The company's replica revolvers are fitted and finished very well, and it offers some variations that are not offered by many of the importers, such as their "Holy Smoker" and "Man With No Name" replica sixguns. (www.cimarron-firearms.com)

Cobra Firearms

Cobra Firearms of Utah is relatively new to revolver manufacturing, but they produce some good-looking pocket revolvers on the five-shot pattern that are similar in size and design to the Smith & Wesson J-frame revolvers. The Shadow is a +P-rated, five-shot .38 Special revolver with a concealed hammer, and looks very much like a Smith & Wesson model 642. These revolvers have stainless cylinders and barrels, and an aluminum frame with a weight of 15 ounces. The company also produces some small and reliable two-shot single-action derringers, marketed under the Cobra name, as well as making those same derringers for other firearms brands. The compact derringers are made in .22 Long Rifle, .22 Magnum, .38 Special, 9mm Luger, .25 Auto, .32 Auto, .380 Auto and .32 H&R Magnum. The Titan model is built of stainless steel and is offered in 9mm Luger or .45 Colt/.410 shotshell. These derringers are available in a variety of colors, and sell at an affordable price. (www.cobrapistols.net)

Colt's Manufacturing Company LLC

The Colt Single Action Army is the most recognized revolver in the world. Even those who have never held a handgun recognize that wonderful sixgun from seeing it on television and in the movies for over a century now. Sam Colt's first successful revolver, the Patterson, set the stage for all revolvers that have followed, including the other cap-and-ball Colt revolvers, and the many revolver designs from other manufacturers. Today, Colt still has the venerable Single Action Army sixgun in production, with demand still far exceeding Colt's ability to fill the orders. Not only is the SAA the most recognized handgun in the world, it is also the most copied revolver design ever produced. The SAA sixguns that it's been shipping for the past few years are as good as any that the company has ever produced, and the reintroduction of the New Frontier was welcome news a couple of years ago. The wonderful SAA is available in three barrel lengths: 4¾, 5½ and 7½ inches, and is chambered in a choice of .357 Magnum, .44 WCF, .45 Colt, .38 Special, .32 WCF and .38 WCF, with some chamberings available only through the Colt Custom Shop. The SAA is available in blued/case-hardened or nickel finishes. Through the Colt Custom Shop, many options are available such as nonstandard barrel lengths and hand engraving. (www.colt.com)

Double Tap Defense

It has been a long time in the making, but the DoubleTap pocket pistol is finally on the market. No longer associated with Heizer Defense, the DoubleTap is in production and is currently chambered for either the .45 ACP or the 9x19mm (9mm Luger) cartridges, with easy, no-tools conversion kits available to switch to either chambering.

Freedom Arms .500 Wyoming Express

It was somewhere around two years ago that I first heard of the DoubleTap derringer. Like most, I was impressed with the thinness of the little pistol, measuring just a bit over five-eighths of an inch across the frame and barrels. Also impressive was its light weight and ability to fire the .45 ACP cartridge. The derringer is lightweight for a .45 ACP pistol and the .45 ACP ported-barrel pistol shown here weighs in at 13.3 ounces on my scale. Weight will vary according to chambering and frame material. The gun shown here is the lighter version, built on an aluminum frame. A slightly heavier titanium frame version is also available, at a higher cost. The titanium pistols weigh two ounces more, and cost an additional $230, so most purchasers will likely go with the aluminum version. All DoubleTap pistols wear stainless steel barrels that have a matte black finish. While on the topic of finish, the anodizing and other metal treatment on this pistol is flawless, showing no tool marks of any kind.

The DoubleTap is a two-shot, hammer-fired derringer. The barrels alternate the firing sequence, firing one barrel, then the other, with each pull of the trigger.

After firing two shots the barrels are tipped up by pulling back on the barrel latches, allowing the barrels to tip open under spring pressure. This pistol hides very easily in a pants pocket, due to its diminutive size and overall thinness. It is not as thick as most wallets that men stuff into their pockets, and barely prints at all. It is the most easily conceal-able .45 ACP pistol on the market, and also the lightest. (www.doubletapdefense.com)

European American Armory

EAA Corp still has their line of imported Single Action Army replica revolvers called the Bounty Hunter. These sixguns are available chambered for the .22 Long Rifle and .22 Magnum cartridges, with an alloy frame and a choice of six or eight-shot cylinders. The revolver is also available chambered for the .357 and .44 Magnums, and the .45 Colt. These centerfire sixguns are built with all-steel frames in a choice of nickeled, blued or case-hardened finishes. Each sixgun has the traditional half-cock loading feature, and a modern transfer bar safety action that permits carrying fully loaded with

a live round under the hammer, without fear of firing if accidentally dropped.

The double-action Windicator revolvers are chambered for the .38 Special cartridge with an alloy frame, or the all-steel .357 Magnum version. Both revolvers have a synthetic rubber grip and a business-like matte blue finish, with a choice of 2- or 4-inch barrel lengths. (eaacorp.com)

Freedom Arms

Introduced about seven years ago now, the Freedom Arms Model 2008 Single Shot pistol is a high-quality single-shot handgun that is made for hunting and long-range target shooting. Current chamberings offered are the .223 Remington, 6.5 Swede, .260 Remington, 7mm BR, 7mm-08, .308 Winchester, .357 Magnum, .357 Maximum, .338 Federal, .375 Winchester and .45-70 Government. Standard barrel length options are 10, 15 and 16 inches, depending upon the caliber chosen, but nonstandard lengths are available as well for a nominal extra cost. What makes this single-shot so comfortable to shoot is the single-action revolver grip style. Shooting with this grip allows the gun to recoil comfortably, with no pain at all to the hands, as is encountered with some single-shot pistols. The barrels are interchangeable, with extra fitted barrels available, allowing the shooter to switch among any of the available barrel and caliber options all on one frame.

The Model 2008 weighs in around four pounds, depending upon barrel and caliber chosen. The barrel is drilled for a Freedom Arms scope mount and the scope stays with the barrel, allowing the interchange of the barrels without altering the sight adjustment. The Model 2008 wears beautiful, expertly fitted laminated wood grips and fore-ends, and are the best-feeling, most comfortable single-shot handgun grips that I have ever handled.

Heading up the Freedom Arms revolver line is the large-frame Model 83. The Model 83 is chambered for the .454 Casull and .475 Linebaugh cartridges, in addition to the .357 Magnum and .500 Wyoming Express cartridges, as well as the .41 and .44 Magnum cartridges. It is also available chambered in the .22 rimfire cartridges, if desired. The Model 83 is available with fixed or rugged adjustable sights. The adjustable-sight guns will also accept a variety of scope mounts. The fixed-sight models have an available dovetail front sight to easily regulate bullet impact, while retaining a low profile and rugged durability.

The Model 97 is Freedom's compact single-action revolver. Built to the same tight tolerances as the Model 83 revolver, the Model 97 is a bit handier to carry all day, and is chambered for the .17 HMR and .22 Long Rifle/Magnum rimfire cartridges, as well as the .327 Federal, .357 magnum, .41 magnum, .44 Special and .45 Colt centerfire cartridges. In addition to these standard handgun cartridges, the Model 97 is also available in Freedom Arms' own .224-32 cartridge, which is a fast-stepping .22 centerfire based on the .327 Federal cartridge case. (www.freedomarms.com)

Heizer Defense

The PS1 Pocket Shotgun pistol is made by Heizer Defense in Pevely, Mo. The Heizer single-barrel derringer is made primarily of stainless steel. The pistol is finished in a matte black, but other various colors will be available later. The Heizer Pocket Shotgun is chambered for the .45 Colt/.410 shotshell, and will shoot any standard-pressure .45 Colt cartridge or any 2½-inch .410 shotshell. The grip portion of the frame is textured with a "HD" pattern for a secure grip, but is not aggressive enough to be abrasive to the hand nor to clothing. The Heizer pistol is thin, measuring less than three-quarters of an inch thick at its widest point, making it the flattest .45 Colt/.410 pistol on the market. This flat profile allows the pistol to be carried almost undetectable in a pants pocket. The edges are rounded and smooth, much like a used bar of soap, making the pistol completely snag-free. The Heizer pistol is a good choice for those needing a concealable defensive single-shot "pocket shotgun." (www.heizerdefense.com)

Henry Repeating Arms Company

Henry Firearms is well known for its American-made rifles, and now the company has its version of a Mare's Leg lever-action pistol in production, chambered for the .22 Long Rifle, .357 Magnum, .44 Magnum and .45 Colt. The .22 rimfire version is a very affordable alternative, both to own and to shoot, compared to the centerfire lever-action pistols available. The centerfire pistols are powerful enough to harvest any game animal. Made like other Henry firearms, these pistols are very reliable and easy to operate. And just like all other Henry firearms, the Mare's Leg firearms are made in the USA. (www.henryrifles.com)

Legacy Sports

Legacy Sports has its 1873 Colt replica sixgun called the Puma Westerner. The Westerner is a reliable and well-built sixgun, chambered for the .357 Magnum, .44 WCF and .45 Colt cartridges, with 4¾-, 5½-, or 7½-inch barrels. The Puma Westerner replica sixguns are offered in a choice of blued and case-hardened finish with walnut grips, nickel finish with walnut grips, or with a stainless finish and white synthetic ivory grips. The Westerner line also includes a very affordable single-action replica chambered for the .22 Long Rifle and .22 Magnum cartridges that would make a good understudy for the larger sixguns, but will be much more affordable to shoot using inexpensive .22 Long Rifle ammo.

The Puma Bounty Hunter lever-action pistol has been a big success for Legacy Sports, replicating the sawed-off lever-action rifle made famous by the old television Western – *Wanted: Dead or Alive*. Nostalgia aside, the Puma Bounty Hunter is a fun, handy lever gun, and scratches the itch of those who have always longed for a mare's leg rifle, without the legal hassle of cutting down a lever-action carbine. The Bounty Hunter is legally a pistol and can be purchased just as easily as any other handgun in most of the U.S. (www.legacysports.com)

Magnum Research

Magnum Research of Minneapolis is now part of the Kahr family of firearms.

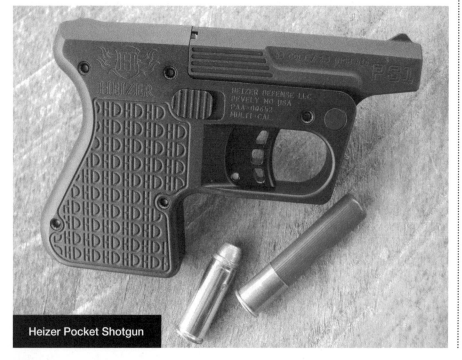

Heizer Pocket Shotgun

Henry Centerfire Mare's Leg

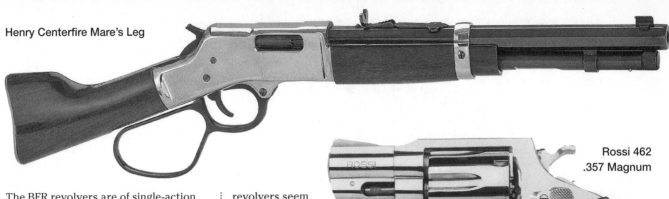

Rossi 462
.357 Magnum

The BFR revolvers are of single-action design, and built to handle a variety of powerful cartridges. These rugged single-action revolvers are built for hunting the largest, most dangerous game in the world, and are fully up to the task. The BFR is available in high-performance calibers like the .460 and .500 Smith & Wesson Magnums, .44 Magnum, .454 Casull, .50 Action Express, .475 Linebaugh and .480 Ruger revolver cartridges, as well as the .30-30 Winchester, .444 Marlin and .45-70 Govt. rifle cartridges. The BFR is also available chambered for the ever popular .45 Colt/.410 shotshell combination, which offers a lot of versatility in a handgun. Built for hunters, these large single-action revolvers are also a lot of fun for those who do not hunt, but just desire a quality single-action revolver for plinking at the range or for protection in the wilderness. (www.magnumresearch.com)

North American Arms

The North American Arms lineup of mini revolvers has been in production for a long time now, and these little revolvers seem to be more popular than ever. NAA does an outstanding job of producing these small revolvers, which are favored by those who need a firearm that is as concealable as possible. These little five-shot revolvers are more often than not bought as deep-concealment handguns. The lightweight firearms are small enough to fit into most any pocket, and are handy enough to always be with you, no matter what the attire or climate. Chambered for the .22 Short, .22 Long Rifle and .22 Magnum cartridges, these little jewels are easy to carry and surprisingly accurate within their intended range.

While most NAA revolvers use a removable base pin for loading and ejection, they also have a swing-out cylinder version called the Sidewinder, which is a new feature for a NAA revolver. The Sidewinder is quicker to load and unload than the other revolvers in the NAA line, and is a dandy little revolver to carry when nothing larger can be concealed, or as a backup to a primary sidearm. (northamericanarms.com)

Rossi

Rossi has been producing reliable and affordable revolvers for decades. These double-action sixguns are available chambered for the .38 Special and .357 Magnum cartridges in either blued or stainless finishes. Rossi was acquired by Taurus a few years ago, and all of the Rossi revolvers are now produced by Taurus in Brazil. They are quality, reliable revolvers built for concealed carry or as duty/hunting guns. Available with short barrels and fixed sights for concealment, or longer barrels and adjustable sights for precision shooting, the Rossi line still means a quality product at an affordable price.

New for this year is the Rossi Plinker .22 rimfire revolver. It has an eight-shot cylinder and adjustable sights. The Plinker is available with either a 4-inch or 6-inch barrel. Rossi USA has introduced their version of the popular mare's leg lever-action pistol, called the Ranch Hand. The Ranch Hand is a six-shot lever gun that is built for pure fun, but also has the power needed for more serious purposes if needed. The Ranch Hand is quality-built, but priced well under its competition. I have one that is chambered for the .45 Colt cartridge, and it is also available chambered for the popular .357 and .44 Magnum cartridges. Rossi also has a single-shot pistol that is built for hunting. Based upon the very popular single-shot rifle action, the

Author shooting the NAA .22 Magnum

Ruger
New Model
Blackhawk .45
Convertible

Ruger
Single-Ten
.22 LR

Ruger
Single-Nine
.22 Magnum

single-shot pistol is reliable, accurate and affordable on most any budget. (www.rossiusa.com)

Ruger

Ruger has a couple of new variations to add to their revolver line this year, as well as bringing back a couple of old favorites. Starting with the Single-Six rimfire revolvers over six decades ago, the company built upon that single-action rimfire design to introduce the Blackhawk and Super Blackhawk centerfire sixguns as time went by. The Ruger Single-Six and Blackhawk revolvers are still in production today, and have expanded to include the very popular new Vaquero line of fixed-sight revolvers. Another very popular sixgun for Ruger is the Flattop .44 Special and .45 Colt, which are reminiscent of the original Blackhawk revolvers of the mid-20th century. The Flattop is also available in a Bisley model with a blued finish, and also as a regular Flattop made of stainless steel.

I regret to report that the .327 Federal cartridge appears nowhere in Ruger's catalog this year. The company had chambered the tough little SP-101, the GP-100 and the Blackhawk for that hot-stepping .32-caliber cartridge, but at least for now, the .327 appears to be if not dead, at least seriously ill.

The Redhawk was recently dropped from Ruger's catalog, but I am happy to report that it is back again. The .44 Magnum and .454 Casull Super Redhawks are still in production, and hopefully we will see a resurgence in interest in the .480 Ruger cartridge.

Of course, Ruger still has the GP-100 in .357 Magnum. This is one of the strongest, most reliable, and most durable double-action .357 Magnum sixguns ever built. New this year is the GP-100 Match Champion, and this is my personal favorite GP-100 that Ruger has ever built. The sides of the barrel are machined flat and the ejector rod shroud is the half-lug style, giving this GP-100 excellent balance – feeling to me a lot like the old Security-Six revolver.

Ruger introduced the polymer-framed LCR five-shot .38 Special revolver a few years ago, and it has been a runaway success. Ruger has sold many thousands of these little pocket revolvers, and now has added an exposed-hammer version of the LCR to the catalog, called the LCRx. This gives the user a choice of shooting the revolver in either double-action or single-action mode. (www.ruger.com)

Smith & Wesson

Smith & Wesson has an extensive line of double-action revolvers available, from .22 rimfires up through the .500 S&W Magnum, and almost every sixgun cartridge in between. The small J-frame five-shot .38 Special revolvers have always been some of the most popular self-defense guns ever produced, and remain so today. The Model 642 is probably still the best-selling revolver in the S&W line, as it is very popular for concealed carry. Lightweight and simple to operate, the J-frame Smiths ride easily in the pocket and can always be within reach if needed. The J-frame Smiths are compact, reliable five-shot revolvers with concealed hammers and lightweight frames, with the rimfire versions holding eight or nine cartridges, serving reliably for those of us who love the .22 Long Rifle and .22 Magnum cartridges. Even the all-steel models carry well. They are easily slipped into the pocket, where they ride comfortably, day in and day out, ready for action when needed.

Moving up in size, the S&W K-frame and L-frame revolvers are the mainstay of the Smith & Wesson duty line. Not many law enforcement agencies still issue S&W revolvers as they did for many decades, but the traditional double-action revolver is as good now as it ever was. These revolvers have served well for many generations of sixgun users, both for defense and for hunting. I particularly am fond of the S&W Classic line, and also the new L-frame .44 Magnum Model 69. This new five-shot double-action .44 should prove to be very popular with hunters and other outdoorsman. Moving up to the N-frame, the classic Models 27 and 29 are still in the lineup, as well as the Models 25 and 57. These are beautiful and functional examples of the timeless double-action revolver upon which Smith & Wesson built their reputation. Large but well-balanced, these .357, .41 and .44 Magnums, as well as the .45 Colt, define the double-action revolver to many shooters, with crisp single-action trigger pulls and butter-smooth double-action trigger pulls. They are reliable, accurate and beautiful. Also new this year from the S&W Performance center is the eight-shot N-frame chambered for the 9x19mm cartridge. The 929 is built for competition with a titanium cylinder and wears a compensator at the muzzle.

Next up in size, strength and power we have the big S&W X-frame guns. The .460 and .500 S&W Magnums are at the

Smith & Wesson Model 69

Smith & Wesson 329PD Backpacker

upper limits of what most would ever consider possible in a handheld revolver, and many shooters are intimidated by the power of these weapons. The large frames and ported barrels handle the recoil well and they are really not painful to shoot, at least with most loads – and like all S&W revolvers they are smooth, reliable and accurate. (www.smith-wesson.com)

Taurus

Taurus USA has continued to introduce new revolvers every year, and the big news from Taurus this year is the View. Like it or hate it, the View does have some unique features, the most notable of which is the clear polycarbonate sideplate, allowing the internal workings of the double-action revolver to be seen. Also interesting is the shape of the grip and the weight of this .38 Special five-shot revolver. Weighing in at only nine ounces, this is the lightest Taurus revolver in the

Smith & Wesson Model 929

Smith & Wesson .500 Magnum

Taurus 992 Tracker

Taylor's Smoke Wagon

Taylor's & Company

Taylor's imports some great-looking and useful replica sixguns, some of which have unique features to make the weapons better-handling and easier to shoot well, such as the new Smoke Wagon. This SAA replica offers a lower hammer spur and larger fixed sights for easier and faster action, and should prove popular with Cowboy Action competitors. Taylor's also has a line of cartridge conversion revolvers, as well as other unique sixgun replicas, like their line of nostalgic and useful cap-and-ball sixguns. (www.taylorsfirearms.com)

Thompson/Center Arms

Thompson/Center keeps plugging along with its proven single-shot pistol design. Starting with the Contender model decades ago, the T/C pistols have evolved into today's Encore and Contender G2 designs – but both are just improvements and refinements of the original Contender pistol. The pistol is offered in just about any chambering that one would want from .22 Long Rifle up through powerful rifle cartridges such as the .45-70 Government, and all the magnum handgun cartridges, including the .460 and .500 S&W Magnums. Thompson/Center offers both wooden and synthetic stocks, and a variety of barrel lengths. The barrels are interchangeable within the same frame group, and these hand-rifles come pre-drilled for scope mounts to take full advantage of the power and accuracy of which these pistols are capable. (www.tcarms.com)

catalog. The company makes a wide variety of quality revolvers that are suitable for concealed carry, hunting and target shooting. From the small lightweight pocket revolvers up through the large-frame magnums, Taurus has a wide selection of revolvers from which to choose. The small-frame snubnose revolvers are available chambered for the .22 Long Rifle, .22 Magnum, .32 H&R, .38 Special and .357 Magnum calibers. They are available in blued, nickel or stainless finishes, mostly with fixed sights, but a couple of models have fully adjustable rear sights. The duty-size 4-inch and 6-inch .357 Magnum revolvers are still in production, with a wide variety of models available. Its large-frame series of hunting handguns chamber the trusted .357 and .44 Magnum cartridges, along with the powerful .454 Casull, and are good choices for hunting medium to large game.

In its extremely popular line of Judge .45 Colt/.410 shotshell revolvers, Taurus now has 12 different models from which to choose. From the small Judge Poly up through the larger versions of the steel-framed Judge, these revolvers are as popular as ever. (www.taurususa.com)

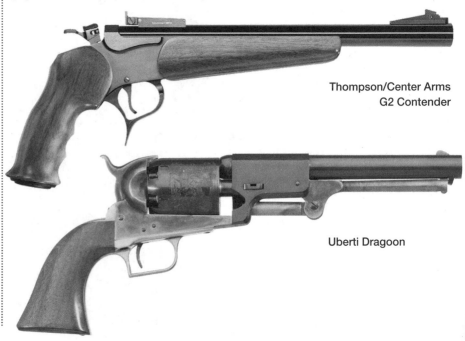

Thompson/Center Arms
G2 Contender

Uberti Dragoon

Traditions Performance Firearms

Traditions Firearms is best known for its muzzleloading rifles, but the company also imports a line of Pietta Single Action Army replica sixguns. The top-of-the-line model is the Frontier, but the Rawhide is basically the same sixgun, only with a matte black finish. Either way, the Traditions sixguns are well built, smooth and reliable. They are also relatively affordable. (www.traditionsfirearms.com)

Uberti

Uberti firearms is the premier Italian producer of quality replica revolver designs, marketing handguns under their own banner as well as manufacturing revolvers for several other replica importers. Uberti offers many different caliber options and finishes, and replicates some of the less popular, but historically accurate designs such as the cartridge conversions, transition model Colts and the Remington 1875 and 1890 cartridge revolvers.

The Cattleman series replicates the Colt Single Action Army design and includes the Callahan Model that is chambered for the .44 Magnum cartridge. This Magnum is offered with original-style fixed sights or as a flattop style with adjustable target sights. In addition to the Callahan, Uberti has these 1873 style sixguns chambered for the .45 Colt, .357 magnum, .44 WCF (44-40) cartridges. Finish options run from a standard blued/case-hardened, to nickel and even a bright charcoal blue finish. Also, quality engraving is offered as an option. The Uberti Stallion is a slightly scaled-down version of the Single Action Army, and is chambered in a choice of six-shot .22 Long Rifle or .38 Special, or a 10-shot .22 Long Rifle. There are also Bisley and bird's head grip models available.

Uberti has fans of the old Remington revolvers covered with their Outlaw, Police and Frontier models, replicating the 1875 and 1890 Remingtons. Uberti has several variations of the S&W top-break revolver including the Number 3 Second Model, as well as the Russian, in both nickel and blued finishes, in addition to fully hand-engraved models. These are available in .38 Special, .44 Russian and .45 Colt chamberings. Uberti also makes an extensive line of quality cap-and-ball revolvers sold under their own brand, as well as being branded by other firearms importers. The chances are very good that if a replica handgun is being

Eagle Grips on Hannah

made at all, you can find it at Uberti. (www.uberti.com)

Customize Your Revolver

Last year, I listed a few of the better custom gun builders available to do custom work on revolvers, from adding sights to building a full-blown one-of-a-kind sixgun. These men are artists in steel, and can pretty much build whatever the customer desires – as long as they can pay for it. Custom gunmakers have pioneered innovations in the industry that have later shown up in production revolvers and single-shot pistols. However, especially with a revolver, a shooter does not have to be wealthy to add some custom touches to their own sixgun, making it special and unique. Having a set of grips crafted from that old walnut tree upon which you played as a kid, or a set of buffalo horn grips for that handgun which you used to drop a buff on that hunt-of-a-lifetime is relatively inexpensive, and there are many craftsmen who will make them for you. Something as simple as having a name engraved or a set of sights installed is also inexpensive. A revolver, like no other weapon excepting maybe an old 1911 or a sleek lever gun, lends itself to this type of personalization better than most any other object known to man. A quality sixgun is everlasting; to be passed down for generations, and adding a bit of oneself to the weapon makes it special, not only for the owner, but for his descendants as well. I imagine that

our grandchildren would rather have our well-worn sixgun that bears a good set of aged stag grips, than to have our polymer Glock 17. Or I at least hope that they would.

Another reason to customize a particular sixgun is that it can be a reminder of another time, or an old friend. I never really got very interested in the Colt Bisley revolver, as with the standard grips fitted to that gun it never fit my hand quite right. However, I have a good friend and fellow Shootist who likes to carry and shoot a Bisley. I seldom get to visit with him anymore and may not ever see him again, as we never know what lies ahead for any of us. His old Bisley is well worn and wears a nice set of stag grips. The grips are thicker than a set of standard Bisley grips, and feel just right in my hand. While at a large gun show last fall, I spotted on a table a good-looking old Bisley Colt, .38 WCF caliber, and negotiated a deal. The finish is worn off and the old Colt has a nice patina to it. I got it home and immediately sent it off to Eagle Grips to be fitted with a set of stag grips, and specified that they be a bit thicker than normal. When the gun arrived back at home I held it, shot it, and immediately named it "Hanna," in honor of my old friend. To a modern "tactical" shooter that old Bisley would not get a second look, but to those of us who live and love old sixguns, it is a handgun which stirs the soul, and to me, it is a reminder of an old friend.

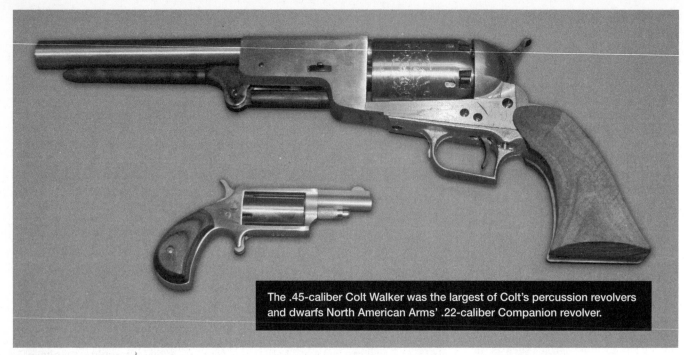

The .45-caliber Colt Walker was the largest of Colt's percussion revolvers and dwarfs North American Arms' .22-caliber Companion revolver.

MUZZLE LOADERS

BY **Wm. Hovey Smith**

It was so cold that my nose-drip froze the instant it touched the stock of the Traditions PA Pellet rifle, which was one of three of the company's muzzleloading rifles that I used this hunting season. The newest was the Vortek StrikerFire Northwest gun and the others were the PA Hunter and the .32-caliber Crockett squirrel rifle that I built from a kit.

My other hunts also included using an original Alonzo Selden Adirondack rifle in New York and Georgia. Young Blunderbuss, which I built last year from a Sportsman's Guide kit, also went along as a backup gun. My experiences with kit gun building projects illustrate that almost anyone can have a hand in making their own muzzleloading guns or returning originals to shooting condition.

I'll look at these guns first, and then discuss what's new in muzzleloading guns and accessories from the 2014 SHOT Show.

Modern Kit Guns

There is an understandable pride in using a muzzleloading gun that you built to win a match or kill a piece of game. Few have the time, tools or skills to make a gun starting from a wooden blank and handmade parts. However, most of us can build a gun from a kit of pre-fitted components.

These kit guns can range in complexity from a single-barreled muzzleloading pistol to the three-barreled Duckfoot pistol (that will amaze almost anyone), percussion revolvers, utilitarian plains rifles, fancy Kentucky long rifles and military patterns from the 15th to the 19th centuries.

Scotch thrift may inspire some to shave a few bucks off a gun's price by doing the wood and metal finishing themselves, but these savings largely evaporate when one considers the cost of the finishing materials, extra tools and time.

Building a kit gun teaches something of the gunmaker's art, lets the owner have exactly the gun that he wants, maintains small motor skills and lets him craft a firearm that is distinctly his. Anyone with sufficient money can have a custom gun built, but that will forever be the gunsmith's gun, even if the buyer owns it for a time. Only if you build it yourself will the gun be truly yours. But of course, there is no shame in having someone else do fabrication steps when you do not have the tools to do them yourself.

Following is a series of experiences that I have had building and using kit guns that include a plain-Jane Trade Rifle, the near-fantastical Duckfoot pistol and Blunderbuss, a Colt Walker pistol and returning an original rifle to shooting condition.

Adventures With Kit Guns

Last year I built and shot a Duckfoot pistol that I ordered from Dixie Gun

Works Inc. and described in *Gun Digest 2014*. Construction steps consisted of working down the grips from a block of wood, polishing the brass frame and bluing the metal barrels. This was accomplished over a period of days using mail-ordered Birchwood Casey stock finishing components, degreaser and cold blue solution.

Both Dixie and Brownell's sell gunsmithing tools and supplies. Dixie also catalogues numbers of gun kits, including those made by Davide Pedersoli, Uberti, Pietta and others. My most recent Dixie kit gun was a Uberti Colt Walker .45-caliber six-shot revolver. The Walker was the largest of Colt's revolving pistols. It is just shy of 16 inches in length and weighs 4½ pounds. As received, the gun was "in the white" with a color cased-hardened ramrod, an as-cast brass triggerguard and roughed-out wooden grips.

A pleasant surprise was that the action was assembled, the gun functioned smoothly and the trigger pull was very nice. I will still polish any rough edges with an oil stone, but the pre-fitted gun saved many hours of meticulous work.

This is the third replica Walker I have owned. I gave up on the other two because of their miserable sights, which did not shoot to the point of aim, and the weak loading-lever retaining springs. When the guns were fired the levers often spontaneously fell, forcing the rammer into an empty chamber and jamming the guns.

Arkansas gunsmith Dykes Reber fitted a new loading lever with a more positive latch and mounted his Weaver sight base, which will allow modern optics to be put on the gun. The Walker will have a black matte nitride finish applied by

H&M Metal Processing of Akron, Ohio. These alterations will improve the gun's functionality and provide the nonreflective finish that I want on a hunting pistol.

Kit Rifles

I have built three rifles from kits. The oldest is a .54-caliber percussion Hawken Trade Rifle made from parts sold by the now-defunct Sharon Rifle Barrel Co. I lived in Tucson during the 1970s and I thought that this rifle would be appropriate for Arizona's mule deer and elk.

Perhaps someday I will take this rifle and participate in Colorado's plains rifle elk season where only rifles of this type are allowed. That would be an appropriate hunt for the rifle loaded with 120 grains of black powder and a hardened .54-caliber ball.

CVA's Hawken rifle was very popular during its long production period, and I built one from a kit in 1980. A nice feature of this kit, which is no longer available, was that the barrel and lock were already blued. The gun-building part of the project was mostly polishing the brass and finishing the stock. This kitchen table gun building was done at intervals after work and took a week to complete. Most of that time was spent allowing the oil finish to dry between coatings.

One of my best kills with this gun was an offhand shot on Ossabaw Island, Ga., at a running hog at about 80 yards. I have often loaned this gun to other shooters, and my friend Paul Presley took his first muzzleloader deer with it.

This gun had one problem though. If it was a humid day and I shot early in the

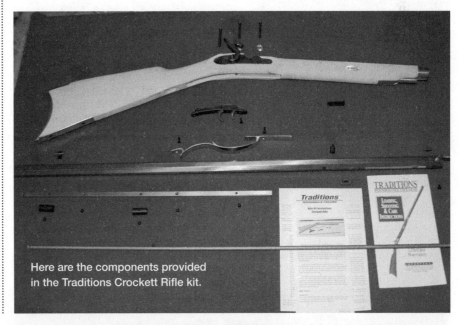

Here are the components provided in the Traditions Crockett Rifle kit.

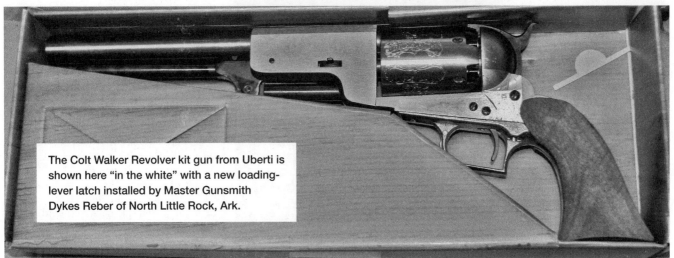

The Colt Walker Revolver kit gun from Uberti is shown here "in the white" with a new loading-lever latch installed by Master Gunsmith Dykes Reber of North Little Rock, Ark.

morning and then attempted to shoot it again in the afternoon, the water of combustion would apparently accumulate in the gun's drum to a sufficient degree to cause a misfire.

Squirrels aplenty I have. I had a long-term hanker for a .32-caliber muzzleloading squirrel rifle, and preparation for this article was my excuse to order Traditions' Crockett Kit. This gun is actually more like a smallish Hawken-style gun than anything Davy Crockett owned, but it is an attractive gun with a brass triggerguard and buttplate.

Work needed to complete the gun included polishing the brass, a small amount of metal fitting, bending the hammer and finishing the barrel. In total, this took about 10 days.

Because the Crockett had more drop in its stock than most modern guns, I found that I shot much better when I braced it against a tree and raised my head off the stock to sight on a squirrel before touching off the set trigger. Offhand shots were much less certain.

Those experiences are described in more detail in my YouTube videos and audio-visual e-book, *Building or Restoring Your Own Muzzleloading Rifle*.

Smoothbores

Smoothbores are the most underappreciated of all muzzleloading arms. These versatile guns can shoot ducks in the morning and kill deer in the evening. I have not accomplished that feat yet, but I have taken squirrels and deer with a .54-caliber blunderbuss that I built from a kit. This kit was made by Traditions

and sold as a one-time offering from The Sportsman's Guide.

I have named the gun "Young Blunderbuss." Although its .54-caliber, cylinder-bored 16-inch barrel shooting a maximum of one ounce of shot proved to have its limitations when used on geese and swans, it cleanly killed an Eastern wild turkey at 25 yards, and drove a round ball through the heart of a 180-pound buck deer at 20 yards. That demonstrated the blunderbuss could, in a pinch, be employed to take game, although almost any contemporary musket or shotgun would have been much more effective.

The lack of sights on the blunderbuss did not prove to be as great of a problem as might be supposed. I carved a persimmon wood stock extension for the comb so that the gun shot to the point of aim. Then, one ounce of shot propelled by 80 grains of Hodgdon's Triple Se7en, and .535 unpatched round balls pushed by 85 grains of powder could be centered on targets at 25 yards. For the final steps I put an oil finish on the stock and the barrel was given a matte black nitride finish from H&M Metal Processing.

Kitchen Table Gun Building

Because I build few guns, I do not have a shop or the tools that every gunsmith would own. I have accumulated sets of chisels, screwdrivers, punches, vise-grips and small power tools including an electric drill and hand sander. Most of the time I hold the parts in a woodworker's vise clamped to an improvised workbench on my back porch. An advan-

tage of owning relatively few tools is that they are portable. I have built kit guns in house trailers, motel rooms as well as at my home.

Regardless of where I work, the steps are the same. These consist of unpacking and inventorying the parts, fitting the metal to the wood, checking the gun's functionality, finishing the wood, bluing or browning the metal, test shooting and making final adjustments to the gun.

My guns go to the woods and duck blinds where they are often exposed to water, snow and salt. As a consequence, I prefer durable, repairable and non-reflective finishes. Most often I use a multicoated oil finish on the stock and a blued or browned finish on the barrel. These finishes require sanding or polishing the wood and metal, applying a coat, sanding or polishing, allowing the parts to dry and repeating the process until the desired finish is obtained.

Hand finishing a gun is a process that takes days and may extend for over a week. When I am done, I put a coat of high-quality paste furniture wax on the wood and apply Thompson/Center Arms' Bore Butter to the barrel and metal parts.

Working On And Hunting With An Original Gun

Sometime between 1860 and 1875 Alonzo Selden, a gunsmith who built double and single-barreled hunting guns in Whitehall, N.Y., completed a half-stocked, .45-caliber Adirondack rifle for one of the area's hunters. When I purchased the gun from Arizona Al in Tucson, it had a fractured stock retained by the cast-on German silver fore-end cap, three plugged holes in the barrel, a replacement triggerguard and non-original set triggers.

"It's a shooter," Al said. "It has a Remington barrel, and I won a whole bunch of matches with it." About a century after the gun was built, I glass bedded the stock and returned it to shooting condition. As Al suggested, I used a patched .451 round ball and the gun gave tack-driving accuracy with a load of 85 grains of FFg GOEX black powder.

Fast forward to 2013 when the Outdoor Writers Association of America was to hold its annual convention at Lake Placid, which was likely in the very mountains where the gun last hunted. I decided to take the Selden rifle back to the Adirondacks for New York's muzzleloading bear season. I also took Young Blunderbuss as a backup gun.

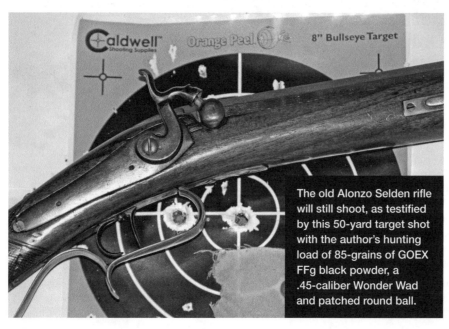

The old Alonzo Selden rifle will still shoot, as testified by this 50-yard target shot with the author's hunting load of 85-grains of GOEX FFg black powder, a .45-caliber Wonder Wad and patched round ball.

A 10-point, 180-pound Georgia buck taken with the Alonzo Selden rifle and a .45-caliber round ball at about 70 yards, and finished off at 20 yards with a shot through the back and heart from Young Blunderbuss using a .54-caliber round ball.

That hunt was not successful because I was going into a new area and could only stay four days. I concluded that I had discovered how to hunt those bears, but it would take a week to 10 days to get the job done.

The Alonzo Selden Rifle And Young Blunderbuss Returns

I resumed my deer hunting when I returned to Georgia. About 70 yards from my stand I saw a buck coming through the pines and shot it when it crossed into a small opening. The round ball penetrated the near shoulder blade, cut a nearly one-inch hole though the spine, passed through the opposite shoulder and was recovered from just under the skin.

I grabbed Young Blunderbuss and climbed down from my stand. It was loaded with 80 grains of Hodgdon's Triple Se7en, 20 grains of Cream of Wheat and a bare .535 round ball retained by a wad. That shot penetrated the deer's ribs, cut through the heart and exited through the sternum of the 180-pound deer. Both the Selden rifle and Young Blunderbuss performed well that day.

Hunts With Production Guns

Returning to my hunts with Traditions' production rifles, Traditions introduced their new Vortek StrikerFire drop-barreled muzzleloader at the SHOT Show last year and sent me the Northwest version of the gun. The StrikerFire differed from most other muzzleloaders in that it was cocked by a sliding cocking piece on top of the gun's wrist. In appearance, the cocking slide looks like an oversized safety with a de-cocker button on top. The slide is pushed forward to cock the gun, and the action is uncocked by pressing the button or opening the gun.

This slide somewhat protects the gun's interior parts from the weather and adds a second safety mechanism to supplement the trigger-block safety on the triggerguard. When uncocked this gun will not fire, even if it is dropped from a treestand.

Other features of this gun include a slim-profile 30-inch barrel, a very nice trigger pull and a built-in storage compartment in the synthetic stock, which also had over-molded rubberized grip panels. With the scope, the entire gun weighed seven pounds, compared to eight for my weight-augmented PA Pellet rifle.

Washington, Oregon and Idaho's regulations for their muzzleloading seasons require that guns have exposed ignitions, use percussion caps or flint ignition, use loose powders and have exposed nipples. To meet these requirements, the StrikerFire Northwest model uses a musket-cap nipple and has a half-moon cutout on the back of the barrel.

Zeroing the gun revealed some perplexing problems, which turned out to be caused by differential pressure applied to the lightweight barrel resting on the end of the bench rest. These problems

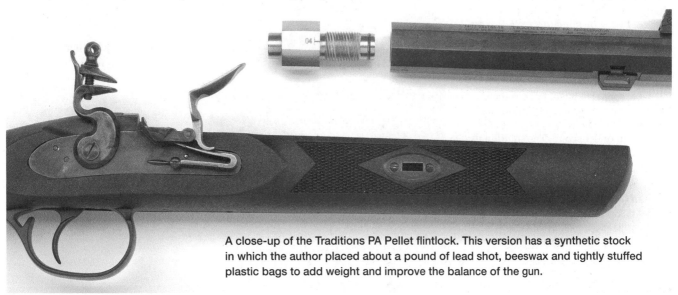

A close-up of the Traditions PA Pellet flintlock. This version has a synthetic stock in which the author placed about a pound of lead shot, beeswax and tightly stuffed plastic bags to add weight and improve the balance of the gun.

The Traditions PA Pellet flintlock
disassembled and ready for cleaning.

disappeared when the StrikerFire was taken off the rest.

The gun performed well with charges of loose black and Triple Se7en powders. It also shot well with black-powder primed pellet loads where 10 grains of FFg were preloaded down the barrel ahead of Triple Se7en pellets. This loading technique simulates the priming charge molded onto Pyrodex pellets and the FFFFg priming of the PA Hunter. This black-powder preload worked with both .45 and .50-caliber Triple Se7en pellets shot from the gun's .50-caliber barrel.

A factor that is unavoidable in the Northwest gun is that combustion gases that were vented from the nipple fouled the bottom of the scope. The solution to this problem was to wrap the rear of the

scope with a strip of aluminum foil held on by electrical tape.

I enjoyed shooting and experimenting with the StrikerFire, but did not get a kill with it this year.

Traditions PA Pellet Rifle

The PA Pellet rifle was designed for Pennsylvania's muzzleloading season. This gun is a flintlock that shoots Pyrodex

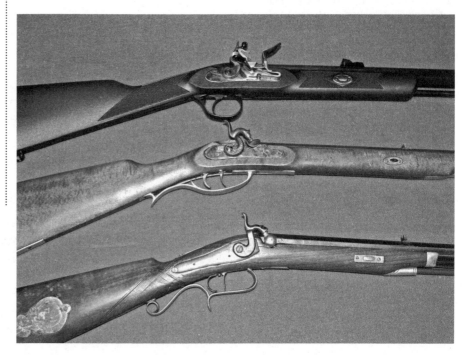

Three of the rifles that the author took to the field. Top is the .50-caliber Traditions PA Pellet flintlock rifle, in the middle is the completed .32-caliber Traditions Crockett kit gun and bottom is the refurbished Alonzo Selden .45-caliber Adirondack rifle.

pellets as well as loose black and substitute powders. The ignition of a priming charge of FFFFg powder provides a jet of flame through the touch hole to ignite the black-powder booster charge molded onto the 50-grain Pyrodex pellet.

Hopefully, the pan's prime would be sufficient to ignite the pellet's booster charge, but I always liked to tease a little powder into the ignition chamber to help ensure success. I have used the same technique on Thompson/Center Arms' Firestorm flintlock as well as with other flintlock rifles.

Since the PA Pellet rifle's introduction, Hodgdon has released new nonsulfur Triple Se7en pellets, and these promise more complete combustion and easier clean up compared to black powder or Pyrodex. I also assumed that more complete combustion of the pellets would be achieved by loading .45-caliber Triple Se7en pellets down the rifle's .50-caliber bore, and pushing some priming powder behind the pellets, would cause everything to go bang.

Range tests validated these assumptions and my hunting load for the season became two .45-caliber Triple Se7en pellets and a hollowpoint 240-grain XTP Hornady sabot.

Eight Georgia hunts produced no deer, and the PA Pellet rifle and this load went to Illinois for its early December muzzleloading hunt. This hunt produced the rain and snow that are typical of many states' muzzleloading seasons.

Physically, my PA Pellet had a black synthetic stock, heavy 26-inch octagon barrel with Traditions' new design of flintlock and a single trigger. I had smoothed up the lock with a stone, added some lead shot and melted beeswax to the hollow buttstock to balance the gun, and found that it preferred sawn agate flints. I finished it off with a jury-rigged sling and the gun was ready to go after some big Midwestern deer.

After finding no deer that I was willing to take, I discharged the gun. While filming in nearly dark conditions the charge ignited normally. The film sequenced showed that the flint continued to spark the frizzen even after the ball had left the barrel. It also demonstrated that the charge was completely burned in the barrel with no flaming fragments exiting the muzzle.

SHOOTING RESULTS

Traditions Vortek StrikerFire Northwest, 30-inch barrel

Bullet	Powder	Velocity	Energy
240 gr. XTP Hunter	100 gr. .45-cal. 3-7 pellets*	1,598 fps	1,361 ft-lbs
250 gr. Smackdown	85 gr. granular FFg 3-7 pellets*	1,451 fps	1,169 ft-lbs
250 gr. Smackdown	100 gr. .45-cal. 3-7 pellets*	1,557 fps	1,346 ft-lbs
300 gr. Full Bore	100 gr. .45-cal. 3-7 pellets*	1,385 fps	1,279 ft-lbs
348 gr. PowerBelt	100 gr. .50-cal. 3-7 pellets*	1,263 fps	1,233 ft-lbs

Traditions PA Pellet Flintlock, 26-inch barrel

Bullet	Powder	Velocity	Energy
240 gr. XTP Hunter	100 gr. GOEX FFg	1,403 fps	1,049 ft-lbs
240 gr. XTP Hunter	90 gr. Pyrodex RS	1,365 fps	993 ft-lbs
240 gr. XTP Hunter	100 gr. .45-cal. 3-7 pellets*	1,522 fps	1,235 ft-lbs
300 gr. Full Bore	100 gr. GOEX FFg	1,263 fps	1,063 ft-lbs

Traditions Crockett Kit Rifle, 28½-inch barrel

Bullet	Powder	Velocity	Energy
.310, .45 gr. round ball	20 gr. GOEX FFFg	1,359 fps	185 ft-lbs

Alonzo Selden Adirondack Rifle, 32-inch barrel

Bullet	Powder	Velocity	Energy
.451, 136 gr. round ball	85 gr. GOEX FFFg	2,140 fps	1,282 ft-lbs

Sportsman's Guide (Traditions) Blunderbuss 16-inch barrel

Bullet	Powder	Velocity	Energy
.535, 220 gr. round ball	80 gr. FFg 3-7 pellets*	975 fps	465 ft-lbs

* Ten grains of FFg black powder loaded behind pellets or about three grains of FFFFg pushed from pan through the touch hole to prime Triple Se7en or Pyrodex pellets.

New Black-Powder Guns And Products For 2014

Diversity in the muzzleloading gun market continued during 2013 with sales of modernized in-line muzzleloaders dominating the market, but with interest continuing in traditionally styled and replica guns. A hammerless muzzleloading rifle was introduced by Traditions last year, and another hammerless gun was announced by a new company, LHR Sporting Arms. This company was started by former Thompson/Center employees who remained in Rochester, N.H., after Smith & Wesson moved T/C's operations to Springfield, Mass.

Most of the "new" guns were those featuring different finishes, re-introduced older models or those having increased performance characteristics. LHR and CVA added nitride finishes on one or more guns, Knight has returned the entry-level Wolverine to production, and Davide Pedersoli now offers a shortened version of its Kodiak double rifle with ghost-ring sights and three new Civil War replica rifles.

Chiappa, Pedersoli, Pietta and Uberti muzzleloaders and cartridge replica guns are sold by Cabela's, Cimarron, Dixie Gun Works, Taylor's and others. Almost any gun that had a significant part in U.S. history is available in replica form.

Chiappa

Although no new muzzleloading guns were introduced, the company reports

good acceptance of its "defarbed" .69-caliber 1842 Springfield (smoothbore $900 and rifled $1,000), .577-caliber 1853 Enfield ($750-$800), 1862 Richmond ($900), 1861 Springfield rifle ($825) and 1862 Richmond carbine ($900). These guns are marked as closely as possible with original stampings, and the Italian proof markings are under the barrel. The .45-caliber Napoleon Le Page pistol ($900) also remains in the company's

lineup. This is a sophisticated percussion target pistol that is one of the most handsome of the world's muzzleloading handguns. (www.chiappafirearms.com)

CVA (BPI) Industries

Application of a black nitride finish, "Ferric Nitrocarburation," to muzzleloading guns provides a chemically inert barrier between corrosive black-powder

NEW

CVA's Accura with different options, including a nitride finish on the middle gun.

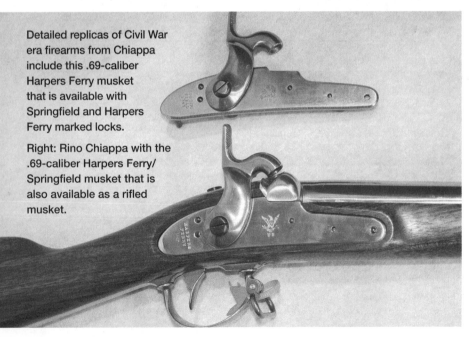

Detailed replicas of Civil War era firearms from Chiappa include this .69-caliber Harpers Ferry musket that is available with Springfield and Harpers Ferry marked locks.

Right: Rino Chiappa with the .69-caliber Harpers Ferry/ Springfield musket that is also available as a rifled musket.

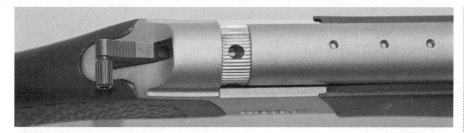

A vented breech plug is employed to make Northwest-legal muzzleloaders from CVA's Accura, Optima and Wolf rifles.

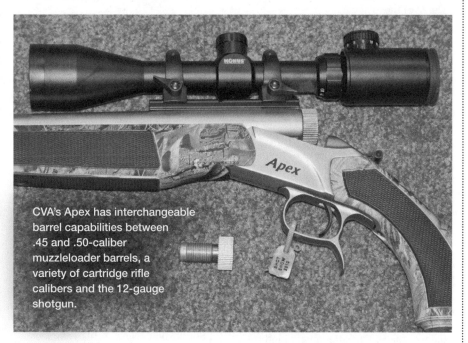

CVA's Apex has interchangeable barrel capabilities between .45 and .50-caliber muzzleloader barrels, a variety of cartridge rifle calibers and the 12-gauge shotgun.

products and the steel barrel. CVA guarantees its nitride treated barrels for life. Although this is a new application for commercially made muzzleloaders, this surface treatment has also been commonly applied to military and police guns.

CVA guns that are available with Nitride rust-proofing include the drop-barrel Accura 6.35 pound Mountain Rifle with a 25-inch barrel, the standard Accura V2 with a 27-inch barrel at 7.3 pounds and the Northwest version of the V2 with exposed ignition. All of these guns are priced at about $600, depending on options.

The mid-range priced Optima remains the best-selling gun in the CVA line. The rifle and pistol versions of the Optima are available in stainless steel with a variety of stock options for between $300 and $400. New for 2014 is an exposed ignition Northwest version of the gun.

Of interest to those in states that allow single-shot rifles to be used during muzzleloading seasons, the Apex rifle offers interchangeable .45 and .50-caliber

muzzleloading barrels along with 11 rifle calibers and a 12-gauge shotgun. The gun with one barrel is priced between $600-$700, and additional barrels are available for about $200 each.

Centerfire guns in the CVA line are the Scout rifle, which is available in stainless steel in rifle calibers ranging from .243 to .35 Whelen, and the Scout pistol in .243, .357 Magnum, .44 Magnum and .300 BLK. These guns are priced in

the $400-$500 range. A less expensive option priced between $300 and $350 is the Hunter Centerfire. This 5½-pound gun's chamberings include the .243, .35 Remington, .35 Whelen and .44 Magnum. (www.cva.com)

Knight

Knight continues to upgrade and reintroduce versions of the late Tony Knight's guns following the company's relocation to Athens, Tenn. The company's production efforts have concentrated on the bolt-action guns in the Knight line, such as the Disc Extreme ($550-$950) and Kevlar-stocked six-pound Ultra-Lite ($900).

More Knight Wolverine ($350) rifles have been sold than any other Knight rifle. The striker-fired mechanism is simple to operate and easy to maintain. The Wolverine is back with a 22-inch, .50-caliber stainless steel barrel, with a weight of 6.9 pounds, and ships with either Full Plastic Jacket, musket cap or no. 11 cap ignition capabilities in a choice of new CarbonKnight or Realtree Hardwoods Green stock. The CarbonKnight stock has the texture of carbon fiber, but is made of a synthetic polymer. There is also a Western version for Idaho, Washington and Oregon with an exposed ignition.

The Bighorn and Littlehorn ($500) are also striker-fired guns. The Bighorn is the heavier at seven to eight pounds, longer-barreled version with a 26-inch barrel. This gun is bored for .50 or .52-caliber bullets and has match-grade barrels with Dyna-Tek coatings for increased corrosion protection. The Littlehorn is designed for smaller-framed shooters and has a shortened stock with a 12.5-inch length of pull and a 22-inch stainless barrel for a total weight of 6.7 pounds. The stocks are available in G2 Camo or Camouflage Pink.

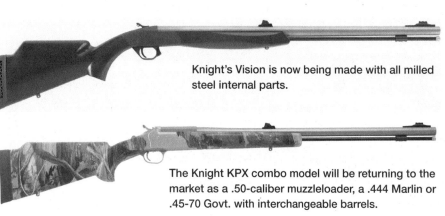

Knight's Vision is now being made with all milled steel internal parts.

The Knight KPX combo model will be returning to the market as a .50-caliber muzzleloader, a .444 Marlin or .45-70 Govt. with interchangeable barrels.

The Vision ($300-$500), Knight's drop-barrel muzzleloader, is now being made with all milled steel internal parts. The .50-caliber rifle uses Full Plastic Jacket ignition, is sold with a composite black stock, 24-inch blued barrel and pre-installed Weaver scope bases. The gun has a total weight of 7.9 pounds.

For those who want cartridge/barrel interchangeability in a drop-barrel gun, the KPX is available as a .50-caliber muzzleloader and with barrels chambered for the .45-70 Govt. or .444 Marlin cartridges. This is a handsome rifle with an all stainless steel barrel and Shadow Gray laminated wood stock. The KPX as a muzzleloader has a 26-inch barrel and weighs eight pounds. The two cartridge barrels are 24-inches long, which reduces the gun's weight to 7.8 pounds. Prices for the new KPX have yet to be determined. (www.knightrifles.com)

LHR Sporting Arms

LHR's first production rifle, the Redemption, is now in stores. This is a 209-primed, black nitride finished drop-barrel, single-shot, .50-caliber muzzle-loading rifle with an aluminum frame and a steel monoblock insert. It also features a steel locking wedge and barrel-pivot pin, external threaded-breech-plug attachment and a thumb-activated sliding cocker/decocker on the wrist of the stock. The Redemption sells for $700-$925 depending on which of three stock options are selected. The rifle is opened by pushing the top lever to one side, which unlocks the single barrel lug. Two optional 209 breech plugs are available to provide optimum performance for loose powder, or up to 150-grains of pelletized powder. The gun is cocked by pushing the sliding cocking mechanism forward, and uncocked by pressing a prominent button on top of the cocking slide. The gun is also equipped with an inertia safety to prevent the gun from

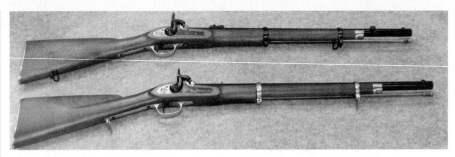

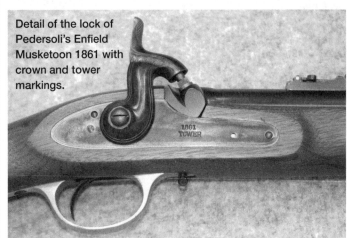

Detail of the lock of Pedersoli's Enfield Musketoon 1861 with crown and tower markings.

Two of Pedersoli's historic replicas include the Enfield Musketoon 1861 (top) and the Cook & Brother Artillery Carbine (bottom) with battle flag and Athens, Ga., markings.

firing should it be dropped after being cocked.

The Green Mountain barrel is held in the frame by a steel monoblock. The breech plug is retained by a threaded collar that screws onto the barrel to hold it in place. This attachment method allows the breech plug to be removed by using a three-function tool that is provided with the gun. This tool also serves as a ramrod extension and palm saver.

Weaver sight bases are mounted on the gun, and a set of front and rear Williams fiber-optic sights are also shipped with it. (www.lhrsportingarms.com)

Davide Pedersoli

Pedersoli continues to produce exacting replicas of many historic civilian

and military arms that encompass American Revolutionary War flintlock guns such as the Brown Bess musket ($1,150), to the Winchester 1886/71 lever-action cartridge rifles chambered for the .45-70 Govt. and .444 Marlin ($1,800-$2,000). New at this year's SHOT Show was a Cook and Brothers Artillery Carbine ($1,000) with Athens, Ga., markings and a browned 24-inch barrel, a Zouave 1863 ($925) and a British .577 Musketoon ($900) with Birmingham, England markings on the stock and English crown stampings on the lockplate.

Directed more towards hunters, a new variant of the Kodiak Express Mark VI ($1,300) double-barrel rifle features shorter, 24.5-inch barrels – compared to 28.5 inches on the older model – ghost-ring sights and a rubber recoil pad. This gun is available in .50, .54 and .58 calibers and its shorter overall length and rapid acquisition sights are designed for hunting wild hogs. (www.davide-pedersoli.com)

F.lli Pietta

Pietta continues to produce a variety of percussion and cartridge revolvers from the Civil War and cattleman periods of U.S. history. Not only do these include a nearly complete line of Colt and Remington percussion revolvers, but also replicas of Dance, Spiller,

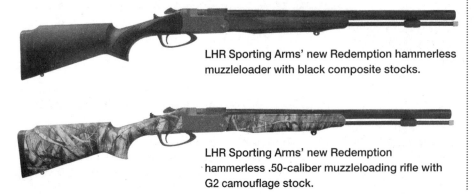

LHR Sporting Arms' new Redemption hammerless muzzleloader with black composite stocks.

LHR Sporting Arms' new Redemption hammerless .50-caliber muzzleloading rifle with G2 camouflage stock.

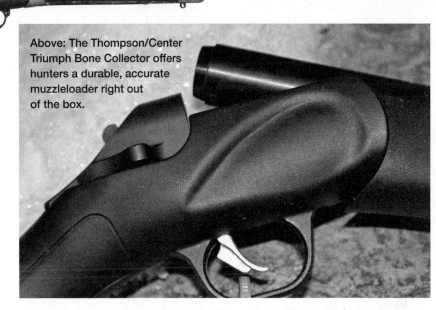

Above: The Thompson/Center Triumph Bone Collector offers hunters a durable, accurate muzzleloader right out of the box.

Starr, LeMat and 1873 Colt Peacemaker cartridge revolvers.

Special variants are produced for hunters, target and cowboy action shooters. One of my favorites is the stainless steel Buffalo with adjustable sights and 12-inch barrel, which was formerly sold by Cabela's and is still offered in a brass-framed version ($250). A new pistol is the 1860 3-inch barrel Snubnose with a birdshead grip that is available in .44 or .36 caliber. This gun puts a lot of power in a small package. It is now carried by EMF and Taylor's & Company and will likely sell in the $300 range.

The Snubnose's birdshead grips are not authentic but make the gun easier to carry, as does the gun's short overall length. The Snubnose and other 1860 model Colts tend to pluck caps off the nipples and jam the gun when they are fired. This can be fixed by filling the hammer notch with a dab of Liquid Weld, and carrying the gun with an empty chamber under the hammer. (www.pietta.us)

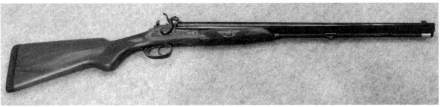

The barrel shroud lock on a Thompson Center Arms rifle provides a low cost, but effective method of locking a budget-priced muzzleloader because the barrel pressure is contained by the breech plug and not the action.

Thompson/Center Arms

The past several years have seen a steady diminution in the number of muzzleloading guns offered by this company in favor of increasing development of the Dimension and Venture bolt-action platforms. The T/C Hawken and Firestorm side-hammer guns have

been discontinued, but the Encore muzzleloader ($550-$900) is still available with a .50-caliber muzzleloading barrel and interchangeable cartridge barrel options. The Pro Hunter XT uses a nearly identical action, but is only sold with a .50-caliber muzzleloading barrel.

I particularly regret the passing of the percussion version of the T/C Hawken rifle. In my opinion there was no better muzzleloader designed for offhand shooting that was available to the average individual than this set-triggered Hawken rifle. I never did like the flintlock version as the lock was touchy and unreliable, but the percussion gun was of fine quality.

T/C's two remaining muzzleloaders are drop-barrel guns using less complex actions. The Triumph is a 6.5-pound rifle with an aluminum frame and under-lever action that is available with a 28-inch barrel for $550-$650. In the low-cost category, T/C has the Impact ($250-$325), which uses a manual sliding hood to lock the pivoting barrel in place. All T/C muzzleloaders are now .50-caliber guns and available with the Quick Load Accurizor design for faster reloading, and Weather Shield coating. (www.tcarms.com)

Traditions

One of the most innovative new muzzleloaders in the past two years has been the Traditions Vortek StrikerFire

Close-up of the action and ghost-ring sight employed on Pedersoli's Kodiak Express Mark VI, which is available in .50, .54 and .58 caliber, and is particularly designed for wild hog hunting.

with its hammerless firing system that is operated by a sliding button on the gun's wrist. For 2014, the gun is available with a 30-inch barrel, CeraKote finish, a match-grade two-pound trigger and Stow-N-Go removable buttpad. The price of the LDR version is between $525 and $625. The StrikerFire LDR will also be offered as a combo-pack with scope and case for about $700.

The Vortek pistol for 2014 will also be sold as a value-priced model with synthetic stocks for $325, compared to about $400 for the conventional wood stock/camo version.

Traditions' extensive line of drop-barrel muzzleloaders includes the Ultralight LDR, which has a conventional hammer and 30-inch barrel ($450-$650), and the 5.15-pound Pursuit Ultralight ($325-$525) and Buckstalker ($225-$350). One bolt-action gun, the Evolution ($300-$350), and one striker-fired gun, the Tracker ($175) remains in the lineup. All of the muzzleloaders mentioned are only available in .50 caliber. Northwest options are available in the StrikerFire, Ultralight, Evolution and Tracker models.

Traditions continues to offer the PA Pellet Accelerator Flintlock ($400-$500), the Deerhunter – including a new left-handed model ($250-$400), in addition to the Hawken, Pennsylvania, Tennessee, Kentucky and Crockett rifles ($500-

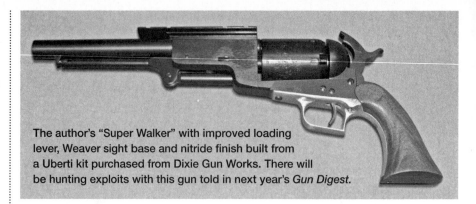

The author's "Super Walker" with improved loading lever, Weaver sight base and nitride finish built from a Uberti kit purchased from Dixie Gun Works. There will be hunting exploits with this gun told in next year's *Gun Digest*.

$800). All but the percussion Crockett .32-caliber squirrel rifle are .50-caliber guns and available with flint or percussion ignition.

Traditions also has three .50-caliber sidelock percussion pistols ($200-$400), but has discontinued the Crockett .32-caliber pistol. The company also continues to offer a line of replica Colt and Remington percussion revolvers made by Pietta including a stainless steel target model with adjustable sights ($550) and a brass-framed Bison with a 12-inch barrel ($325). (www.traditions-firearms.com)

Uberti

This Italian company specializes in making many nearly exact replicas of Colt and Remington percussion revolvers. These guns include the Colt Walker (also available as a kit gun), four .44-caliber Dragoons ($450), two variants of the 1851 .36-caliber Colt Navy ($350), a .31-caliber 1849 Pocket revolver and the 1849 Wells Fargo without a loading lever ($350). In the solid-frame Remington pattern, there's the 1858 .44-caliber Army pistol, including a blued or stainless steel model with an 8-inch barrel ($350-$450).

Largest of the company's revolving arms is the 1858 Remington Army Target Carbine with an 18-inch barrel and permanently attached walnut buttstock ($575). (www.uberti.com)

Powders

All Hodgdon powders, including the GOEX, Reenactor and Old Eynsford brands, are now being sold in plastic bottles instead of the traditional metal containers.

American Pioneer Powder announced a more refined version of its granular powders in a Premium Grade black-powder substitute that is designed to provide

Premium Grade Pioneer Powder offers more consistent performance for greater accuracy.

more consistent performance in a cleaner burning, less-hydroscopic powder up to a maximum of a 100-grain charge.

Bullets

Modern solid brass bullets are expensive compared to their lead alternatives. One way to avoid having to purchase four different packs of bullets to test in your gun is to buy Knight's new .50-caliber sample pack, which contains four different weight sabot bullets. Included in the pack are five each of 220-, 250-, 275- and 300-grain Lehigh Defense Bloodline bullets to test in your gun so you can determine which projectile performs best.

Traditions' Vortek StrikerFire, now offered with a longer 30-inch barrel.

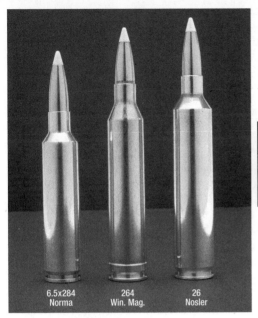

6.5x284 Norma

264 Win. Mag.

26 Nosler

ammunition, ballistics and components

BY **Larry Sterett**

The really big news in ammunition this past year was the introduction of the .26 Nosler cartridge. This totally new round, which resembles a necked-down and shoulder-sharpened 7mm Remington Magnum without a belt, pushes a 129-grain AccuBond LR bullet out the muzzle at 3,400 fps, beating the .264 Winchester by 200 fps with a 130-grain bullet. The .26 Nosler has a maximum overall loaded length of 3.3340 inches, allowing it to function in a standard-length .30-06 size action. This .26 reminds this shooter of an unbelted .264 Barnes Supreme of a half-century or more back, but the Barnes used longer and heavier 6.5mm bullets and would not function through a standard .30-06 size action.

Most 6.5mm (.264 inch) bullets have an excellent ballistic coefficient, as witnessed by the number of governments that have had this caliber as standard issue, such as the 6.5x55 Swedish, which is still used in some target rifles today. The Italian Carcano and Japanese Arisaka 6.5mm cartridges were capable of more than the rifles they were used in could realize. Then there was the 6.5x54mm Mannlicher-Schoenauer, which W.D.M. Bell used so effectively on elephants using a 160-grain FMJ bullet. And we as a nation came close with a 6mm Lee Navy, and the almost .276 Pedersen. Today we have the 6.8mm SPC, 6.5mm Grendel, 6.5x47 Lapua, 6.5-284 Norma, .260 Remington and a lesser-known 6.5x40mm,

and there may be a few others. A couple of decades ago in Pennsylvania there were a number of 6.5mm wildcat cartridges developed for 1,000 yard shooting, but none are recalled that resembled the .26 Nosler. The new .26 has a useable case capacity of 93 grains of water, and has as much velocity at 400 yards as the .260 Remington has at the muzzle.

2nd Amendment Ammunition

One of the new kids on the block is 2nd Amendment Ammunition. This firm currently loads new handgun ammunition in .40 S&W and .45 ACP calibers packaged in tan 20-round boxes with a 2nd Amendment and a "Minuteman" logo prominently displayed. The

Two green-lead bullets, so called because of their similar ballistic properties, these two Zuerillium Alloy bullets are lead free.

cartridges are loaded with jacketed hollowpoint bullets, and the brass cases are headstamped with the caliber and "2nd AMEND." The firm notes "Freedom

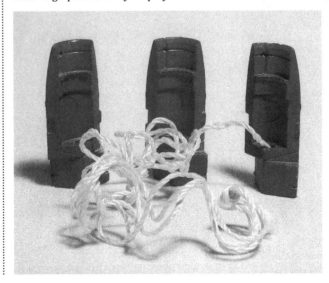

An ABC 12-gauge Multiple Impact Bullet separated to show the interior where the connecting cord is stored. The large hollow tip ensures rapid separation to provide a 14-inch to 24-inch radial spread.

is Never Free," and two percent of the purchase price of each box goes toward defending the Second Amendment. (www.secondammo.com)

Advanced Ballistic Concepts, LLC

Advanced Ballistic Concepts, LLC is promoting the Green Bullet or lead-free bullets produced from Zuerillium Alloy. It's sometimes called Green-Lead, because it has ballistic properties and the look and feel similar to lead, but without the environmental concerns. Suitable for handgun and rifle ammunition, and in pellet form for loading shotgun shells, the Zuerillium projectiles are said to have 100-percent weight retention and reduced barrel friction.

Another ABC concept is the Multiple Impact Bullet, advertised as the ultimate personal and home defense ammunition where first hit advantage is everything. (Isn't it always?) Todd Kuchman, the inventor, calls this design "semi-lethal" as it produces a 14- to 24-inch radial spread pattern at close range, but does not generally produce long-range damage or penetrate extended wall surfaces. Currently, the MIB design is being produced in .45 ACP and 12-gauge loads, with five 12-gauge shells per box, and 10 rounds of .45 ACP per pack. (www.mibullet.com)

Australian Outback Ammo

From the land down under comes a new line of metallic rifle ammunition, Australian Outback Ammo. Packaged in 20-round boxes featuring the colors of the land – blue sky and red soil, with silhouettes of a windmill and 'roos, the Outback ammo is currently available in .223 Remington and .308 Winchester

rounds. Bullets are Sierra or Swift, depending on the intended use. Suggested use for the .308 loaded with a 150-grain Swift Scirocco II BTS bullet to 2,800 fps range is on deer, buffalo, (Australian water, not African Cape) and camels (yes, wild camels). The .223, when loaded with a 55-grain Sierra BlitzKings to the 3,200 fps range, is recommended for use on rabbits, foxes and coyotes.

Since Australia can have rather extreme temperature ranges, the Outback ammunition is loaded via BTI (Ballistic Temperature Independence). According to the firm, a temperature increase of 120 degrees Fahrenheit will produce a velocity increase of less than 100 fps, depending on the caliber and bullet weight. The .308 Swift-Scirocco load at 5 degrees F has a muzzle velocity of 2,817 fps, while the same load at 125 degrees F has a muzzle velocity of 2,853 fps. (www.outbackammo.com.au)

Battenfeld Technologies, Inc.

Battenfeld Technologies, Inc. has a host of new items for handloaders under their various labels. Under the Caldwell Shooting Supplies brand there are two spent brass catchers, a ballistic Precision Chronograph and a Premium Kit accessory. The brass catchers save shooters lots of time by not having to look for those flying cases to use for reloading. The Brass Trap is a separate bag that can be mounted on a camera tripod off to the side, and the PIC Rail Brass Catcher mounts directly on the Picatinny rail of any AR-15 with a flattop rail or rail handguard, and on most AR-10 models also equipped.

Under the Frankford Arsenal Platinum Series brand there's a new seven-liter Rotary Tumbler Kit that

can handle 1,000 5.56mm/.223 cases at a time. To go with the tumbler is a new media – stainless steel pins that clean the cases inside and out, and the primer pockets. There is even a Media Transfer Magnet available to effectively separate the steel pins from the brass cases. Other new items in the Frankford Platinum line for handloaders include a Case Trim & Prep Center, a Precision Scale and a Reloading Stand. The adjustable collet on the Prep Center comes with three collets, six bushings and will handle all shouldered cases from the .17 Remington to the .460 Weatherby. It will trim, chamfer, deburr and clean primer pockets. It can be mounted in any of three positions and its heavy-duty motor is powered by regular 110-volt AC.

The Platinum Precision Scale is AC or battery (four AAA batteries) powered and has a capacity of 1,500 grains, with an accuracy of .1 grain. The scale will measure in grains, grams, ounces and carats. It features an LCD display with blue backlight. There is a smaller DS-750 scale with a capacity of 750 grains. It operates on two AAA batteries.

The new Frankford Platinum Reloading Stand folds completely for storage and is adjustable in height from 28.5 to 45 inches. The width extends from 13 to 39 inches by turning the sides upward, drop-leaf table style. It comes with two small storage bins that mount onto the folding sides. Frankford also has a smaller, nonfolding reloading stand with a hollow plastic base. (www.BTIbrands.com)

Black Hills Ammunition

Black Hills Ammunition has been in business for over three decades and is still introducing new loads. The latest in the new rifle line is the 5.56mm loaded with a 77-grain TMK bullet to 2,750 fps from a 20-inch barrel. In the Gold line the .308 Winchester is now available with a 175-grain TMK bullet loaded to 2,600 fps. Some 17 of the various loads are available with moly-coated bullets, and the Cowboy Action Shooting line features 14 calibers, all loaded with suitable flatpoint lead bullets. True, a couple of the cartridges, .32 H&R and .357 Magnum, weren't around when cowboys were getting blasted on a semi-regular basis, but most of the others were even if only near the end. The .45 Colt and .45-70 Government definitely saw a lot of use over the past 140 years. (www.black-hills.com)

The new Australian Outback rifle cartridges are packaged in boxes that leave no doubt as to their origin.

At the top is a DDupleks Kaviar 26L slug load and on the lower right is an actual synthetic slug with embedded lead pellets. Designed for training use and on steel targets, the slug disintegrates on impact. On the lower left is the new DDupleks Super Target Slug. This 380-grain slug is loaded to a velocity of 1,080 fps to produce 1,000 ft-lbs of muzzle energy.

Bone Orchard Ammunition

Bone Orchard Ammunition features a line of Cowboy Action Shooting cartridges consisted of two handgun loads – .38 Special and .45 Colt; and three 12-gauge loads. Loads for the 9mm Luger, .380 ACP and .45 ACP should be available by the time you read this, and other calibers are planned for production. The handgun loads feature lead bullets and clean, but smokey powder to be authentic, while the 12-gauge Clay Duster loads contain an ounce or 1-1/8 ounces of size 7½ lead shot. (www. boneorchard.us)

Cor-Bon/Glaser Ammunition

Cor-Bon/Glaser Ammunition has been in the business of producing top quality specialized ammunition for over three decades. The current lines include the Self-Defense JHP in handgun and rifle calibers, the DPX Handgun line – which also features some hunting loads, a DPX Rifle line, the Glaser Safety Slug line, Glaser Pow'RBall line, the Thunder Ranch line, the Performance Match line of rifle and handgun calibers, the Hunter line in nine handgun calibers and four rifle calibers, and the MPG Multi-Purpose Green line. Then there's the Expedition Hunter line of bigbore rifle cartridges for use on the "big five" or other equally dangerous game. This last line consists of 14 calibers from the .375 H&H Magnum and .375 Flanged to the .577 Nitro Express. If you shoot a .404 Jeffery, .500 Jeffery or a 3-inch .450/400 Nitro Express, Cor-Bon has your ammunition packaged 10 rounds per box. Most Cor-Bon ammunition is packaged 20 rounds per box, with some packaged 12 rounds per box, and the Glaser Safety Slugs bubble packed in six rounds per card. (www.corbon.com)

DDupleks Ltd.

DDupleks Ltd. has been producing their line of hourglass-shaped steel shotgun slugs for quite some time, resembling the Balle Blondeau. Now they have a new design, the Super Target. Available in standard-length 12-gauge shells, the Super Target design features a pointed steel slug with a cup-type base wad. Intended for use in competition shooting at targets up to 50 meters, it has done well in competition in Europe. The slug weighs 380 grains and is loaded to a velocity of 1,080 fps, producing 1,000 foot-pounds of energy. It should do well on big game where penetration is needed more than expansion.

The other DDupleks slugs – the Monolit 28, Monolit 32, Dupo 28, Hexolit 32 – feature flat or expanding tips and are suitable for game up to the size of bear and moose. All of these slugs are in 12 gauge, except the Monolit 28 is available in 20 gauge, and the D28 is available in 16, 20 and 28 gauge. These last three gauge slug loads are recommended for use on game no larger than deer.

The DDupleks Kaviar 26L is a red-polymer slug embedded with lead shot. Designed for use on steel popper targets or as a training load, the 26L slug weighs 400 grains and is loaded to 1,360 fps. It will disintegrate on contact with a steel target. (www.ddupleks.com)

Federal Premium Ammunition

Federal Premium Ammunition has a new Vital-Shok Trophy Bonded 10mm Auto pistol load. Pushing a 180-grain bullet out the muzzle at 1,275 fps, it brings the 10mm back to the life it was designed to have in the Bren Ten. Nothing new in the shotshell or other cartridge lines, except the .22 rimfires. For shooters who use a suppressed firearm, there is a new .22 Suppressor round loaded with a 45-grain hollowpoint bullet at 970 fps. It is said to function reliably in suppressed semiautomatic firearms.

Under the CCI label, Federal has two new Troy Landry Signature Series rounds, the Mini-Mag HP and the Maxi-Mag HP. The Mini is a .22 Long Rifle round loaded with a 36-grain copper plated hollowpoint bullet to a velocity of 1,260 fps, and the Maxi-Mag is a .22 WMR round loaded with a 40-grain jacketed hollowpoint bullet to a velocity of 1,875 fps. The Mini comes 300 rounds per pack, and the larger Maxi is a 200-round pack.

The current ATK rimfire line of cartridges, all under the CCI label, consists of 30 different loads including the shotshells in .22 WMR and LR, and the .17 HMR rounds. Most of the loads are .22 Long Rifle rounds, but there are three .22 Short loads available and one .22 Long, which CCI states is the only high velocity at 1,215 fps .22 Long load on the market. (www.federalpremium.com)

Forster Products

Forster Products has a new Datum Dial Ammunition Measuring System, which can be used to tailor your handloaded ammunition to a specific firearm. The core components of the system are a body and three interchangeable dies. If the entire Datum Kit is purchased it will include the body with the case dial already mounted, bullet/cartridge dials #1 and #2, and a storage box. This will allow the handloader to measure the relative distance between the base of a case to a datum point on its shoulder angle, and the base of a bullet or cartridge to a point on the bullet's ogive. The #1 bullet/cartridge dial will handle five calibers: .224 (5.56mm), .243 (6mm), .264 (6.5mm), .284 (7mm) and .308 (7.62mm). The #2 dial will handle the calibers .17, .204, .257, .277 and .338. A #3 "blank" dial with five starter holes is available to permit the custom drilling of holes for diameters not provided in the #1 and #2 dials. (www.forsterproducts.com)

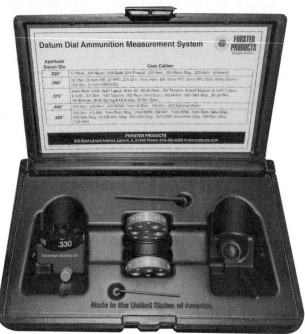

Forster Products' new Datum Dial Measurement System is available in a kit, or as components. It's the ultimate in obtaining maximum accuracy from a rifle cartridge.

Helvetica Trading USA, LLC

Helvetica Trading USA, LLC continues to feature an economical line of reloading equipment including digital scales, reloading trays, two-powder tricklers, hand priming tools, case tumblers, case trimmers, deburring tools, etc., and two reloading presses including the SBP (Smallest Biggest Press), a "C" frame design that will even resize rifle cases. (www.helveticausa.com)

Hodgdon

The *Basic Reloading Manual* from Hodgdon is a 34-page softbound volume with loading data for Hodgdon, IMR and Winchester powders. It contains descriptions of all the various powders plus charts of suggested usage for each in handloading handgun, rifle and shotgun cartridges. For example, only Hodgdon US869 and H50BMG powders are recommended for reloading .50 BMG cartridges. No IMR or Winchester powders are suggested for such use. A Burn Rate Chart, comments on powder storage, warnings, charts of abbreviations used in the manual, and charts of the powder bushings for Lee, Ponsness-Warren, Hornady/Spolar and MEC loading presses are other features of this handy tome.

Loading data is provided for more than 30 rifle cartridges from the .17 Hornet to the .50 Browning Machine Gun, and for 17 handgun cartridges from the .223 Remington to the .500 S&W Magnum. No illustrations of cases or bullets are provided, but for each cartridge the barrel length for data collection is listed, along with case brand, primer brand and size, bullet weight, type and brand, and overall loaded cartridge length. The powder brand, charge weight in grains, muzzle velocity and pressures generated in CUP or psi, are listed for each bullet. All loads are considered maximum, and it is so stated with the warning to not

Geco

Geco ammunition includes the Geco and RWS Rottweil lines of ammunition, and is under the RUAG umbrella. Ammunition bearing the Geco label includes Geco Plus, Geco Express, Geco Softpoint, Geco Plus and Geco Express rifle loads, plus 10 pistol loads and seven revolver loads. There is also a Geco Rifle .22 Long Rifle round pushing a 40-grain bullet at 1,082 fps, and a 12-gauge Coated (Teflon) Competition Slug load. (The coated slug weighs 15/16 ounce, including the plastic tail wad, and leaves the muzzle at 1,476 fps to get on moving targets faster.) These 12-gauge Competition Slugs are packed 100 rounds per box with a carrying handle.

The Geco/RWS-Rottweil line includes the RUAG Copper-Matrix NTF green line of cartridges, plus the MFS line, in addition to the Rottweil EXACT and Laser Plus shotgun slug lines. Both the EXACT

and Laser Plus loads are available in 12 or 20 gauge, high velocity or magnum, depending on the specific load. (www.geco-ammunition.com)

Gorilla Ammunition Company

Gorilla Ammunition, LLC is currently loading premium quality metallic ammunition in three calibers: .223 Remington, .300 Blackout and .308 Winchester. Sierra bullets are featured, and the .223 offerings include rounds loaded with the 55-grain BlitzKing, 69-grain MatchKing or 77-grain MatchKing bullets. The .300 Blackout round is available loaded with a choice of a 125-grain bullet to a standard velocity, or the 220-grain MatchKing to a subsonic velocity. The .308 Winchester is currently loaded with a 175-grain MatchKing bullet. Packaging is in 20-round boxes, with the .223 round also available bulk packed in a Gorilla hardcase. (www.gorillaammo.com)

Hornady American Whitetail

exceed, but reduce all powder charges by 10 percent to start loading.

Loading data for the shotgun cartridges – 12, 16, 20 and 28 gauges, plus .410 bore, lists the shell brand, length and type. The shot charge weight in ounces, powder name, primer brand and size, wad brand and name or number, and the powder charge in grains are listed in the tables, along with the velocity obtained and the pressure generated in psi. Follow the listed data, and DO NOT SUBSTITUTE. Check for another possible powder to use, as substitution could be hazardous to your health. (www.hodgdon.com)

Hornady

Hornady has added a new Custom Lite ammunition line featuring eight rifle calibers from .243 Winchester to .300 Winchester Magnum, and two shotgun slug loads – 12 and 20 gauge. Recoil reduction is said to be from 25 to 43 percent, depending on the particular load, and compared to a standard load with the same weight of projectile. Another new load is the 12-gauge American Whitetail Slug featuring a 325-grain InterLock HP bullet in a rigid polycarbonate sabot.

In the Superformance rifle line two new .375 loads have been added, the H&H Magnum and the Ruger. Each is loaded with a 250-grain GMX bullet. In the Custom Ammunition line loads have been added for the .275 Rigby and the .338 Lapua, the first with a 139-grain InterLock BTSP bullet and the second with a 250-grain InterLock SP-RP bullet. These additions bring the Custom line to 44 cartridges, from the .204 Ruger up to the .450 Bushmaster, with bullet weights ranging from 45 grains to 250 grains.

The Critical Duty handgun cartridge line has a new addition. The .357 SIG

is available loaded with a 135-grain FlexLock hollowpoint bullet to a muzzle velocity of 1,225 fps. Bullets recovered from a variety of mediums indicate good expansion – up to .580 inch – and weight retention – from 95 to 100 percent, except for 77 percent when impacting glass. In fact, of the five loads in this line, the .357 SIG had better weight retention when impacting glass than any of the others including the 9mm Luger and the .45 Auto +P. But the .40 S&W loaded with a 175-grain FlexLock bullet loaded to 1,010 fps did almost as well.

In the Critical Defense line, which consists of 14 handgun loads specially developed for concealed carry handgun, there's a CD Lite .38 Special load with reduced recoil. Loaded with a 90-grain FTX bullet with pink Flex Tip, and packaged in a 25-round box with pink printing and a pink ribbon, it's to help showcase breast cancer awareness. (A portion of the proceeds from the sale of this line goes to help fund breast cancer research.) For those who like to keep a .410 bore around for self-defense, Hornady has a Critical Defense .410 Triple Defense load. This .410 round has a .41-caliber FTX nonjacketed slug stacked atop two .35-caliber round balls. Used in a Judge or similar revolver, the FTX slug actually engages the rifling to ensure greater accuracy. At seven yards all three projectiles should impact the target close to the point-of-aim. Even in a smoothbore shotgun the .410 Triple Defense should do the job at seven yards.

Hornady also has a new 3-inch 20-gauge Heavy Magnum Turkey load. Featuring 1-3/8 ounces of nickel-plated #5 shot in a Versatite plastic wad pushed out the muzzle at 1,200 fps, this load should be deadly out to 50 yards or more. This is the only 20 gauge in the Heavy Magnum family; the other members are 12 gauge.

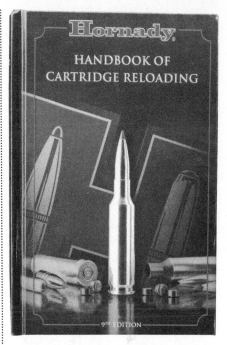

The 924-page *Hornady Handbook of Cartridge Reloading* features dimensioned case drawings of each cartridge for which loading data is provided. This handbook also features an excellent illustrated glossary.

Also new from Hornady are two Custom Lite slug loads, one each in 12 and 20 gauge. The SST slugs are housed in standard-length hulls and felt recoil is said to be from 25 to 40 percent less than standard slug loads.

If you don't have a copy, check your local dealer for the 9th edition of the *Hornady Handbook of Cartridge Reloading*. This 924-page hardbound volume contains 10 sections: Hornady Heritage and Vision, Basics of Reloading, Special Tips, Complete Hornady Bullet Guide, Charts and Conversion Tables, Illustrated Glossary, and of course, Reloading Data for Rifle and Handgun Cartridges.

Loading data in the rifle section is provided for more than 160 different rifle cartridges from the .17 Hornet to the .50 BMG, including such cartridges for which reloading data is not always readily available, like the .20 Tactical, .22 K Hornet, .219 Donaldson Wasp, .219 Zipper, .22-6mm, 7x61 Sharpe & Hart, 7.65x53mm Belgian Mauser, 8mm-06, .416 Barrett and .50 Beowulf. If you handload for the .505 Gibbs or the .500 Nitro Express 3-inch, the data is in this volume.

In the Handgun Loading section data is provided for six dozen handgun cartridges from the .22 Hornet to the .500

Hornady
Critical Duty

Left to right: .22 Hornet, .224-32 FA, .500 Wyoming Express and .500 S&W Magnum cartridges. All four have been used in revolvers, but the last three were actually designed for this use. Of the four, only the .500 Wyoming Express uses a belted case.

S&W Magnum. Some handgun cartridges not often encountered, such as the 6.5 JDJ, .270 REN, 7mm IHMSA, .309 and .338 JDJ #2, .357-44 Bain & Davis, .30 and .357 Herrett, .44 Auto Mag, .445 Super Magnum and .50 Action Express also have data provided.

A dimensioned case drawing for each of the cartridges for which loading data is listed heads the beginning. This is followed by basic data such as barrel make, length, rifling twist, case brand, trim length, maximum length, bullet diameter, primer brand and size, and maximum overall loaded cartridge length. Accompanying this information are a few paragraphs of background on each cartridge.

A photograph of each bullet for which loading data is provided is shown, along with pertinent data including sectional density, ballistic coefficient, diameter, name and type, item number and overall cartridge length when loaded. Loading data includes the name of the powder followed by several charges and the velocities in feet per second that each produces.

The illustrated glossary is excellent, from "accuracy" to "zero." Not every term is illustrated, but those that are are well done. It's a nice touch.

Hornady has several new products for handloaders, with the most outstanding being the Lock-N-Load Control Panel with Safeguard Die. This unit senses any primer issues, low powder levels, and any dropped or double powder charges,

and halts the loading process until the problem is corrected. Another new item is the Lock-N-Load Rifle Bullet Feeder, which is sold as a complete unit for .22-caliber bullets, with a kit available for .30-caliber bullets. The Safeguard Powder Die is available separately, and there's a new Bench Rest Metering Insert to replace the unit in your Lock-N-Load Bench Rest Powder Measure.

For those handloaders who ream and/or turn cartridge case necks, Hornady has a new Neck Wall Thickness Gauge. An accessory to the Concentricity Tool, this gauge features a dial indicator accurate to .0005 inch. It definitely will help identify neck thickness variations. (www.hornady.com)

Kent Cartridge

Kent Cartridge has two new 12-gauge FiveStar Deer Slug loads. The first Kent slug load was introduced in 2013, and the new loads feature a revised and coated rifled slug design said to be effective in both smoothbore and rifled-bore shotguns. The new slug weighs an ounce and sits atop a posted wad column. The slug, in a choice of standard or magnum lengths, has a muzzle velocity of 1,750 fps. Kent also has an extensive line of steel shot – TealSteel, SilverSteel, Fasteel, Upland Fasteel and Velocity Precision Steel Target. Newest is the TealSteel, a magnum waterfowl load in 3-inch hull, moving 1¼ ounces of size 5 or 6 shot at 1,350 fps.

Tungsten Matrix Waterfowl and Upland loads are Kent products. The Waterfowl line includes five 12-gauge loads and two 20-gauge loads, while the Upland line consists of one each in 16 or 20 gauge, in a choice of size 5 or 6 shot. Shot sizes in the Waterfowl TM loads are 1, 3 or 5, depending on the specific load. A single 3½-inch 12-gauge TM load is available with a choice of size 1 or 3 TM shot, while in the Fasteel Waterfowl line there are three 3½-inch loads available. Steel shot charges in these shells include 1¼, 1-3/8 and 1-9/16 ounces of shot sizes BBB, BB, 1, 2, 3 or 4 depending on the specific load. Velocities range from 1,625 fps down to 1,300 fps, respectively.

There are no .410-bore loads in the Kent line of shotshells, but the company's Gamebore line features a couple of loads, one in a 2½-inch hull with 3/8 ounce of shot, and one in a 2-7/8-inch hull with 9/16 ounce of shot. The Gamebore Pure Gold line also includes some paper-hull shells and a number loaded with fiber wads in place of plastic wads. (kentgamebore.com)

Lapua

Available at your local dealer should be copies of *Reloading Guide for Centerfire Cartridges, Edition 12*, from Vihtavuori powders. This 76-page softbound volume is loaded with information and data, starting with a Burning Rate Chart for 11 brands of powders on the inside cover. There are descriptions of the Vihtavuori powders, a discussion of the properties and storage of smokeless powders, tips on safety and a couple of tabled pages at the back for recording personal or favorite loads.

In the reloading data sections starting and maximum loads are listed for more than five dozen rifle cartridges from the .204 Ruger to the .50 Browning. Between are such cartridges as the 6mm BR Norma, 6.5x47 Lapua, 6.5x55 Swedish Mauser/SKAN, .300 Lapua Magnum and 9.3x66 Sako, for which information is not always available in other reloading manuals.

Loading data is also provided for more than two dozen handgun cartridges from the 7mm TCU to the .500 S&W Magnum. Between are such cartridges as the 7mm GJW, 9x21, 9x23 Winchester, .38 Super Lapua, 10mm Auto and .50 AE. Data is also provided for the five most popular Cowboy Action Shooting revolver cartridges.

No bullet or dimensioned cartridge illustrations are provided with either the rifle or handgun cartridge loading data. The test barrel length and rifling twist are listed, along with the primer size, case brand and trim length. The bullet weight, type and brand are listed, followed by the overall loaded cartridge length. The powder charges – VV powders, naturally – are listed in both grams and grains, followed by the velocity in feet per second and meters/second for the starting and maximum loads. Those loads that proved to be exceptionally accurate are darkly shaded. (www.lapua.com)

Lehigh Defense LLC

Lehigh Defense LLC produces some of the most specialized ammunition available. The Maximum Expansion line features solid copper projectiles with cavernous hollowpoints and four razor-sharp petals. These bullets were designed not to expand on dry mediums such as drywall, wood, bone or shell metal, but to expand on contact with a fluid-based medium. Currently rounds are available in seven handgun loads from the .380 Auto (ACP) to the .45 Colt, and one rifle load, the .300 AAC/Whisper. Packaging is 20 rounds per box, except for the .38 Special and the .45 Colt, which are packaged 12 rounds per box. Due to the enormous hollowpoint, bullet weights are lower than usual with a corresponding increase in muzzle velocity. The 9mm Luger round loaded with a 70-grain bullet has a muzzle velocity of 1,650 fps from a 5-inch barrel, with a penetration in ballistic gelatin of 10 inches and an expansion to .66-inch.

Another Lehigh line is the CF for Controlled Fracturing ammunition. Produced from solid copper or brass the bullets have a deep hollowpoint and are designed to fracture or break apart after achieving a predetermined penetration depth. Three fragments from the nose portion of the bullet, plus a fourth – the base section, are designed to penetrate the opposite side to create a better blood trail. Eight loads are currently available in five handgun calibers, from the .38 Special to the .45 Super, and a dozen loads in eight rifle calibers, from the .223 Remington to the .510 Whisper Subsonic. Packaging is 20 rounds per box, with 10 rounds per box for the .45-70 Government and .458 SOCOM cartridges. All the subsonic rounds are loaded to have muzzle velocities of 1,040 fps, while the top velocity is 3,600 fps for the .223 Remington with a 45-grain bullet.

Multiple Projectile Ammunition (MP) has been around for well over a century, with the U.S. military using such loads in the .45 Colt and .45-70 Government cartridges in the late 19th century. However, none of these loads were of the caliber (no pun intended) of Lehigh Defense loads. Three handgun and two rifle calibers are currently available, and each is loaded with three to six solid copper nested projectiles. The total projectile weight is approximately the same as for a standard bullet weight. Weight of the six projectiles in the .45-70 Government cartridge totals 500 grains, while in the .44 Special cartridge the total weight of the four projectiles is 240 grains.

The object of the MP load is to create multiple wounds in a hurry. Thus, in a home defense situation, one shot from a .44 Special MP load could produce four wounds in a playing card area at 15 feet. The .44 Magnum MP load would produce five wounds within the same approximate area. Maximum penetration at 15 feet is approximately a foot or slightly more, according to Lehigh tests.

A third Lehigh ammunition line is the CC (Controlled Chaos). Developed as the result of an animal control agency's request for a no lead .243 bullet capable of generating extensive wound trauma with minimal pass-through energy. The CC bullets differ from those of the CF line by having smaller fracturing particles. The result is less penetration depth but greater initial energy transfer. Currently four rifle calibers – 223 Remington, .243 Winchester, .300 AAC/Whisper and .308 Winchester – are available in the CC line. CC bullets are available in boxes of 100 for the same calibers for handloading, plus a 750-grain .510-caliber bullet in a box of 20 is available, but not in loaded ammunition.

Another Lehigh product is Subsonic (SS) ammunition, loaded to 1,040 fps and combining the Controlled Fracturing and Maximum Expansion technologies. Currently only five rifle calibers from the .300 AAC Blackout/ Whisper to the .510 Whisper are available, all packaged 20 rounds per box. Maximum penetration with this line, according to Lehigh, is with

the .375 Whisper and .510 Whisper loads where the base section has achieved more than 24 inches of penetration in ballistic gelatin.

Some of the Lehigh projectiles are available as components for handloading. These include the 194-grain .308 Maximum Expansion in a box of 50, the Controlled Fracturing (CF) in seven calibers from .224 to .510, in boxes of 50 up through the .338 and in boxes of 20 for the .416, .458, .500 and .510. The Match Solid bullets are available in seven calibers from the .338 to the .510, with only the .338 bullets being available in a box of 50; the others are packed 20 bullets per box. Available weights depend on the caliber, and range from 230 grains in the .338 to 808 grains in the .510. (www.lehighdefense.com)

LKCI Firearms & Ammunition

LKCI Firearms & Ammunition handles some rimfire and centerfire ammunition produced in Russia and an entirely new shotshell line produced in Turkey, in addition to brass-cased 9mm Luger ammunition from Turkey. The Turkish ammunition bears the Sterling label, and the shotshell line is extensive. The 9mm load is pretty much standard, featuring a brass case with a Boxer primer and a 124-grain roundnose, full-metal-jacket bullet. Velocity is over 1,200 fps.

The shotshell line is extensive as mentioned, but whether loads will available in the U.S. has yet to be determined. The competition series of shotshells, mostly in 12 gauge, features loads for trap, skeet and sporting clays use, with shot loads of 7/8, 1, 1-1/16, 1-1/8, 1-3/16 ounces available. Available shot sizes range from 1 to 10 for many loads, and the wad composition may be fiber or plastic, depending on the load.

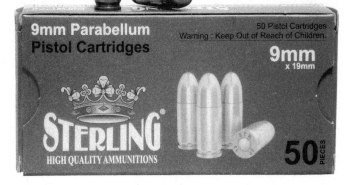

The new Sterling 9mm Parabellum pistol cartridges are packaged 50 rounds per colorful box.

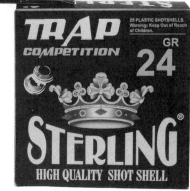

The Sterling shotshell line is packaged with 10 or 25 shells per colorful box, each with a crown logo.

While most of the Sterling shotshell line is comprised of 12-gauge loads, there are shells available in 16, 20, 24, 28 and 32 gauge, plus .410 bore. Shotguns in 24 and 32 gauge have not been produced in the U.S. for nearly a century, although once in a dry spell an old attic-bound specimen appears. If shells were available, these small gauges would increase in popularity and surpass the .410 bore. The 24-gauge shell holds an ounce of shot while the 32 gauge holds

The Sterling Super Magnum 3½-inch shotshells featuring 2½ ounces of shot are packaged 10 rounds per glossy black-colored box.

5/16 ounce, the same as the Sterling .410 bore, but with larger diameter, less pellet deformation and a shorter shot column. Shot sizes for the .410 loads include 1, 3, 5, 7 and 9, a much larger choice than U.S. manufacturers provide. Packaging for most of the Sterling shotshells is 25 per box, with the magnum 12-gauge loads packaged 10 per box, the same as the slug and buckshot loads.

The Sterling slug loads feature Foster-type rifled slugs with plastic base wads. There is also a unique six-fold steel slug with a dished nose and plastic retaining bands. Another different slug load, labeled the Super Slug, resembles a Foster-type slug with a 5mm-diameter copper ball embedded in the nose to force more rapid expansion. Most of the slug loads are 12 gauge, with some 16 and 20-gauge loads, and even a .410-bore slug load with a 5/16-ounce slug. Buckshot loads in 12, 16 and 20 gauge are catalogued, in a choice of plain lead or copper-coated.

The Sterling shotgun line includes a 12-gauge nonlethal series consisting of a blank cartridge, a Roman Candle load featuring three different color – red, white and green – spheres, a nine-ball rubber buckshot load and a defense slug load featuring a 16-grain rubber slug loaded to just under 1,000 fps.

Whether it will be available or not to U.S. shooters, Sterling has a second line of 12-gauge shells bearing the label Kaiser. This line includes a slug load for wild boar, a trap and skeet, three game loads for quail, partridge and francolin or snipe, and a couple of cold weather waterfowl loads. The last two loads were

developed for use in snowy, cold, wet winter weather with temperatures in the minus range. (arsenalexpress.com)

Lyman Products

Lyman Products has a new AR Reloading Handbook intended for those shooters that load extensively for rifles/carbines on AR platforms. It provides the AR shooter with reloading data for nearly all AR-based cartridges, with the exception of some possible "wildcat" designs. In addition to the standard .223/5.56mm, other cartridges include the 6.8mm SPC, .300 AAC/Whisper, 7.62x39mm, .450 Bushmaster, .50 Beowulf and others. Other features of this magazine-size softbound handbook include articles on reloading for suppressors, cartridge interchangeability, loading with cast bullets and more. Each of the calibers for which loading data is provided features a dimensioned drawing of the cartridge, followed by a few paragraphs of useful information. (www.lymanproducts.com)

Magtech Ammunition/Sellier & Bellot

Magtech/Sellier & Bellot has a line of ammunition – sporting, law enforcement and military – that is distributed in more than 90 countries around the world. (S&B has been in business for 189 years.) In the different handgun cartridge lines, the cartridges are available loaded with Bonded Hollowpoint, Solid Copper Hollowpoint, Jacketed Hollowpoint, Jacketed Softpoint, Full Metal Jacketed and lead bullets. The target calibers and Cowboy Action Shooting cartridges are loaded with the roundnose, flatnose, wadcutter or semiwadcutter bullets, depending on the load. Depending on the line, the cartridges available range from the .25 Auto to the .500 S&W.

The S&B rifle cartridge line is extensive, ranging from the .204 Ruger to the .50 BMG, and includes a few not readily available from other brands, including many metric calibers and the .408 Cheytac and .460 Steyr. Bullet weights and brands – S&B, Hornady, Nosler and Sierra – depend on the cartridge line. One of the more interesting bullets is the SPCE, a jacketed softpoint with a unique cutting edge designed into the bullet jacket about midway between the nose and base. The HPC line features a capped hollowpoint bullet that resembles the old Remington Bronze Tip in appearance and the Westley Richards capped bullets in design. The HPC bullets are available in nine cartridges from the .30-06 Springfield to the 8x64mmS.

Shooters that own a drilling and need ammunition for the rifle barrel should check out the S&B line. Many drillings are chambered for the 7x57R, 7.65R, 8x57JRS or 9.3x72R cartridges, and these are all available in one or more of the S&B lines, as is the 5.6x52R (.22 Hi-Power).

In the shotgun line S&B has a series of non-lethal loads featuring rubber buckshot, slugs and balls, plus a breaching round that features a ½-ounce polymer projectile that disintegrates following target contact. Under the Magtech label, but probably produced by CBC, is a line of unprimed brass shotshell cases. A century ago such cases were common, but seldom seen today. Packaged 25 shells per box or 250 shells per case, these brass beauties are available in 12, 16, 20, 24, 28 and 32 gauge, plus .410 bore and a 9.1 gauge. These cases take a large pistol primer and not the regular 209 shotshell primer. (www.magtechammunition.com)

Melior

Another line of shotshells from Spain, and not as well known to U.S. shotgunners as the Saga line, is the Melior line of competition and hunting loads. The vast majority of the loads are 12 gauge, with a couple of 16-gauge loads and three 20-gauge loads as well.

The Melior Competition Super GT shells currently include six 12-gauge loads and one 20 gauge, with available shot sizes ranging from 7-9, with the exception of the 20 gauge Xtreme Steel – which is available in a choice of 2, 3, 4 or 5 shot.

The Melior Field shells are available in three grades: Super GT, Especial Batida and Acero-Steel – plus buckshot and slug rounds. The four – three 12 gauge and one 20 gauge – Acero-Steel loads are new, as are the two Super GT in 16 gauge, and the 12-gauge PM Pigeon load. Available shot sizes for Xtreme Steel 12-gauge shells in the Acero-Steel line include BB, 2, 3, 4, 5, 6 and 7. Shot sizes for the new PM Pigeon load include 4, 5, 6, 7, 8, 9 and 10, the same as for the two new 16-gauge Super GT loads.

The Melior buckshot loads are available loaded with 0 or 00 buck, and the slug loads feature a Brenneke slug and what is termed the "Killer Slug." All Melior shotshells, from Competition to Slug, are standard length at 2¾ inches, and packaged in 10 or 25 rounds per box

depending on the load. (www.melior-icc.com/en/outdoors)

MTM Molded Products Co.

MTM Molded Products Co. has redesigned their AC11 and AC35 Ammo Can. These cans can handle over 30 pounds of stuff like fired brass, reloaded ammunition in bulk and more. With O-ring seals the cans are literally waterproof. The AC-50C Ammo Can is now available in Pack-N-Pink color, in addition to the regular green or black color, and of course Zombie with neon green handle and latches.

MTM has slip-top or flip-top ammo boxes available to fit almost every small-arms cartridge that has been manufactured in the world. Handgun or rifle cartridge, from .17 Hornet to .50 BMG, and .17 HMR to .500 Wyoming Express, MTM probably has an ammo box to fit it. (www.mtmcase-gard.com)

Norma

Labeled the *Precision Reloading Guide For Professional Shooters*, the new Norma Reloading Manual is a hardbound 448-page volume loaded with information. It also features loading data, using Norma brand powders, for seven dozen rifle cartridges from the .222 Remington to the .505 Magnum Gibbs. The first third or so of the manual is devoted to such interesting topics as 111 years of Norma history. Other topics include Norma bullets, how to make a cartridge, reloading for double rifles, exterior ballistics, a discussion of powders and primers, and reloading rifle cartridges step-by-step.

In the loading data section, each cartridge is illustrated with a dimensioned color photograph followed by pertinent data, including barrel length and rifling twist, case brand and volume in grains of water, primer brand and size, and maximum pressure in psi and bars. Several paragraphs are devoted to the background for each cartridge. Each bullet for which loading data is provided is shown in color, along with brand, type, weight, the ballistic coefficient, powder type and minimum and maximum charges, muzzle velocities in feet and meters per second, the bullet number, and the overall loaded cartridge length in inches and millimeters.

While this manual is strictly for handloading using Norma powders, it has data for some interesting cartridges not found in every reloading guide such as the 6XC, the Blaser Magnums – 7mm, .300,

The latest 448-page hardbound *Norma Reloading Manual* features dimensioned color photographs of each cartridge for which loading data is provided. Norma powders are the only powders for which data is provided, but various bullet brands are featured.

.338 and .375 – .404 Jeffery and all the Norma Magnums. A couple of others not always found are the .338-378 Weatherby Magnum and the .500/416 Nitro Express. Following the loading data is a glossary, some conversions tables and a few ruled pages for recording your most accurate or favorite loads. Any handloader using Norma powders needs a copy for reference. (www.norma-usa.com)

Nosler

The Nosler Trophy Grade of ammunition currently features 39 calibers, from the .22-250 Remington to the .375 H&H Magnum, plus four – .204 Ruger, .223 and .22-250 Remington, and .220 Swift in the Trophy Varmint line all loaded with Nosler bullets, of course. In the Defense Handgun line there are six loads in three calibers, 9mm Luger +P, .40 S&W and .45 ACP +P, plus three – .223 Remington, 6.8 SPC and .308 Winchester in the Defense Rifle line. The top Nosler ammunition line, the Safari, currently has 15 calibers from the 9.3x62 Mauser, considered by some hunters to be the best of the medium-power safari cartridges, to the .505 Gibbs. A choice of Partition or Solid bullets, advertised to shoot to the same point-of-impact for the same weight, is

The PCP .308 Winchester round features a metal head and a two-piece synthetic case.

available. Bullet weights range from 250 grains for the 9.3x62 Mauser to 570 grains for the .500 Jeffery or .500 Nitro Express.

Nosler will also custom handload for many of their calibers, using Nosler bullets and brass where available. Powder charges are meticulously weighed and the cases neck-sized, chamfered and checked for correct length. The hand-loaded rounds are visually inspected and polished prior to hand packing in hard plastic boxes. (www.nosler.com)

PCP Ammunition

PCP Ammunition is the latest to attack the problem of obtaining lighter ammunition using a nonmetallic case. PCP uses a patented three-piece polymer case design to lighten the conventional .308/7.62x51mm NATO case by 30 percent, compared to brass. The company currently uses Sierra MatchKing bullets, and .308 Winchester ammunition is packaged 20 rounds per box. (www.pcpammo.com)

ProGrade Ammunition

ProGrade Ammunition is available in 10 grades, from hunting to match, varmint, bear, safari, cowboy and defense grades. With over 250 variations in the complete line of handgun and rifle ammunition, Prograde has practically covered all the bases. The newest grade is the Hog Grade, featuring 10 handgun calibers from the .357 Magnum to .500 S&W Magnum, and 11 rifle calibers from the .223 Remington to the .300 Winchester Magnum. Bullets used include Barnes and Nosler brands, plus some hardcast lead, with weights depending on the caliber. Packaging depends on the cartridge.

In the Cowboy Grade line there are five popular handgun loads and one rifle load – .45-70 Government – all loaded with roundnose, flatpoint lead bullets. The Bear Grade line is a bit larger, with a single

load each for eight different handgun cartridges, from the .357 Magnum to the .500 S&W Magnum, all loaded with hardcast, wide, flatnose gas-check bullets of appropriate weights. The .357 Magnum, for example, is loaded with a 220-grain bullet while the .500 is loaded with a 525-grain hardcast bullet.

The Prograde Safari Grade line features a baker's dozen of calibers from the .30-06 Springfield to the .500 Nitro Express, and more then five dozen loads to chose from. Barnes and Woodleigh bullets are loaded exclusively in the Safari Grade ammo, and eight of the cartridges are in the .400 range and above. Six loads each are available for the .375 H&H Magnum, .375 Ruger, .375 Remington Ultra Magnum, .458 Winchester Magnum and .458 Lott. Load availability for the others in the Safari Grade line range from three to five, except for the .30-06, which is only available in two loads.

The Hunting Grade rifle line is the most extensive, with more then 150 loads possible in 41 calibers from the .243 Winchester to the .45-70 Government. Included are the Weatherby Magnums from the .240 up to the .30-378, the .264 Winchester Magnum, .300 Savage, 7.62x54mmR, 8mm Remington Magnum and the great .358 Winchester. No Norma or Lapua magnums are available, except for the .338 Lapua. There's also an eight-cartridge Hunting Grade handgun line, from the .32 H&R Magnum to the .500 S&W Magnum. (www.progradeammo.com)

Quality Cartridge

Quality Cartridge no longer loads ammunition, but does turn out many unprimed brass cases for approximately 300 different rifle cartridges from the .17 Ackley Bee to the .550 Magnum. Not all case calibers are constantly in stock, but they can be produced, and just because you've never heard of it doesn't mean the firm might not produce it. And if you have a wildcat cartridge design of your own and need cases, check with Quality.

The company also produces brass cases for over 50 different handgun cartridges, from the .17 OTTR to the 11mm German Revolver. Auto Mag owners can find brass at Quality, as can shooters of the Action Express and IHMSA cartridges. If you handload for the 8mm Nambu or .32 French Long for use in the MAS or MAC pistols, Quality has brass.

Packaging of Quality brass is 20 cases per heat-sealed bag for most rifle and handgun cases, with a few of the hand-

gun calibers packed 50 per bag. A few of the rifle calibers are packaged at 200 per bag, and box packing is available at an additional cost. (www.qual-cart.com)

RCBS

RCBS has two new Explorer Reloading Kits – the Standard and the Plus. Both include a Reloader Special-5 Press, Uniflow powder measure, hand priming tool, Nosler 7th Edition Reloading Manual, universal case reloading block, 1,500-grain digital pocket scale and more. The Plus kit just includes more, such as a Powder Trickler-2, an advance powder measure stand, six die lock rings and five popular shell holders – No. 2, 3, 4, 10 and 43.

Another item for handloading in the RCBS line is the Arbor Die Conversion Kit. Replacing the standard die bushing and shell holder in the single-stage Summit press with the Arbor Die set produces two flat, parallel surfaces – ideal for use with arbor dies used by some benchrest shooters. (www.rcbs.com)

Redding Reloading Equipment

Redding Reloading Equipment has several new products for handloaders, including Micro-Adjustable Taper Crimp Dies for five popular cartridges – two rifle and three handgun; Master Hunter Die Sets for 16 different cartridges from the .223 Remington to the .300 WSM. The Hunter sets include a full-length sizing die and a competition seating die. Other new dies available include Bushing Die Sets and Competition Die Sets for the .17 Hornet, and a special .45-70 FTX Profile and Crimp Die.

Standard Redding seating dies using 1/2x20 threads can be upgraded with a new Bullet Seating Micrometer. This is a replacement for the original seating plugs. It can be changed from one die to another and is available in nine sizes each for standard (STD) and VLD bullet shapes. The new die is not for use with the Redding Competition Seating Dies.

Shooters reloading the .17 Hornet and using a Redding Competition Model 10X powder measure can now fit it with a new Drop Tube Adapter to handle .17- and .20-caliber cases. This adapter will fit all Redding powder measures and funnels.

Although case resizing can be done dry, a bit of lubrication makes the process easier and helps extend case life. Redding has had the excellent Imperial

Sizing Die Wax and Imperial Application Media for years. Now they have a new "green," petroleum-free Imperial Bio-Green Case Lube that does not stain and is water soluble for easy cleaning. Also new is an Application Media Convenience-Pak for dry lubing of case necks. (www.redding-reloading.com)

Rio Ammunition

Rio Ammunition has been in the shotshell business for decades, with the parent company, MAXAM, dating back to 1896. While the predominate shotshell loads are 12 gauge, the Rio line also includes 16, 20 and 28 gauge, plus .410 bore. All gauges are standard 2¾-inch length, except for the .410 bore which is available in 2½- or 3-inch lengths, and the 3-inch 20 gauge.

Rio has a steel shot line of 12- and 20-gauge shells with both being available in standard and magnum lengths, and the 12 also being available in two 3½-inch loads featuring 1-3/8 or 1-9/16 ounces of size BBB, BB, 2, 3 or 4 steel shot. Plus, there are five 12-gauge loads and one 20-gauge load featuring bismuth shot.

In addition to other game and buckshot loads, Rio has five 12-gauge and one 20-gauge slug loads, and five less-lethal 12-gauge loads. The slug line includes the time-tested Brenneke, plus an expansive design, an armored design and a star that resembles a hollowpoint Foster with a flat tip and plastic base wad. The Less Lethal line includes polyethylene shot, rubber ball and buckshot, and a beanbag sock loaded with size 7 lead shot with a muzzle velocity of 262 fps.

Rio is well known for its shotshells, but has now also expanded into the metallic cartridge line with the introduction of 5.56mm NATO rounds loaded with a 62-grain FMJ bullet exiting the muzzle at 3,000 fps. Other popular handgun and rifle cartridges are slated for introduction in the future, possibly a few by the 2015 SHOT Show. (www.rioammo.com)

RUAG Ammotec USA, Inc.

RUAG Ammotec USA, Inc. has four lines of ammunition, the lead-free Copper-Matrix, Original Sport, Swiss and Coupled Performance. The Copper-Matrix line features lead-free Sintox primers in reloadable brass cases and frangible copper-matrix NTF bullets. The line currently includes two rifle calibers – .223

Remington and .308 Winchester – five handgun calibers from the 9mm Luger to the .45 Auto, and two 12-gauge shotgun loads. Packaging is in five, 20, 25 or 50-round boxes depending on the caliber, and the boxes feature lots of green color with the word "copper" done in copper-colored ink. Bullet weights depend on the caliber, but the 12-gauge NTF slug weighs 375 grains and the buckshot load contains eight 00-size NTF shot pellets loaded in standard length 2¾-inch hulls.

The Original Sport line contains eight handgun loads for seven cartridges from the .32 Auto to the .45 Auto. Bullets are all FMJ, except for one .38 Special load with a 158-grain lead bullet, and the cases are all Boxer-primed reloadable brass. RUAG engineers modified the FMJ bullet profiles slightly to maximize the bearing surface and improve accuracy. Bullet weights are standard for each caliber.

The Swiss P series actually contains six sublines: P Ball, P Target, P Styx Action, P Armor Piercing, P Tactical and P Subsonic. All types are designed for minute-of-angle accuracy and the four calibers – .223 Remington, .308 Winchester, .300 Winchester Magnum and .338 Lapua Magnum – are available depending on the intended use.

All four calibers in the Swiss P Ball line feature full-metal-jacket lead-core boattail bullets. In the Swiss P Target line

similar bullets are used, but with a slight hollowpoint. Bullets used in the P Styx Action line feature a larger hollowpoint specially machined to insure more rapid expansion. The Swiss P Armor Piercing cartridges feature a bullet-shaped, tungsten carbide core embedded ahead of the lead core in the base of the bullet. This bullet design, in the two .30-caliber cartridges and .338, will penetrate a 12mm thick Amox steel plate at distances of 300, 400 and 500 meters, respectively.

The .223 Remington cartridge is not available in the P Tactical line, which features solid projectiles machined from a special alloy. Each boattail bullet is machined with three relief grooves on the bearing surface, given an aerodynamic ogive and small, flat tip to provide directional stability on impact on glass surfaces.

The .308 Winchester cartridge is available in the P Subsonic line, in two loadings – a 200 grain and a 240 grain – both loaded to a muzzle velocity of 1,040 fps. The bullets used in these loads feature a small hollowpoint for rapid expansion and a special ring of grease at the case mouth to promote uniform movement of the projectile through the barrel from shot to shot.

The MFS Coupled Performance line features two handgun calibers – .380 Auto and 9mm Luger; and five rifle calibers – .223 Remington, 7.62x39mm,

Saga shotshells from Spain are available in a variety of loads for competition and hunting use.

.308 Winchester, 7.62x54mmR and .30-06 Springfield. All cartridges are loaded into zinc-plated steel cases, and with the exception of the .223 Remington and 7.62x54mmR, all have flat-base bullets. The bullets are FMJ in the handgun and rifle loads with four exceptions in the latter line. One loading each in the .223 Remington, 7.62x39mm, .308 Winchester and .30-06 Springfield feature softpoint bullets. Packaging is 20 rounds per box for the rifle cartridges and 50 rounds per box for the handgun cartridges. (www.ruag-usa.com)

Saga Cartridges

Saga Cartridges from Spain have been available for a number of years. Most of the loads are 12 gauge for skeet, trap and sporting clays shooting, but the firm also produces hunting loads, including those loaded with steel shot in sizes from 1 to 7. Another load is the Dispersante, designed for use on medium-size small game such as rabbits. Saga actually has a couple of Rabbit loads – the Rabbit 32 with shot sizes from 6-10, and the Rabbit 34 – with shot sizes from 5-10.

For big game, Saga produces a number of slug loads and at least three buckshot loads. Currently the firm has five different slug loads: a solid point designed for longer distances, a hollowpoint intended for shorter ranges, a star round, an expansive slug composed of two parts designed to break into four parts once it enters game, and the Rubin sabot. The Rubin sabot is a highly modified Brenneke design. All the slug loads are available only in 12 gauge at present.

Although the majority of the Saga shotshells are 12-gauge loads, the firm does produces a few smaller gauge loads in 16 and 20 gauge. Shot sizes available depend on the specific load, and Star slugs are available in both 16 and 20 gauge, and the Brenneke is also available in 20 gauge. (www.saga.es)

Swift Bullet Company

Swift Bullet Company produces the Scirocco II and

A-Frame bullets for loading, and more recently, Blackburn custom triggerguards for Winchester M70 and various Mauser rifle actions, plus trigger assemblies. Several years ago Swift produced their first manual for handloaders. Now, Volume II is about ready, and should be by the time you read this. (www.swiftbullets.com)

Ten-X Tactical

Ten-X Tactical now loads 5.56mm/.223 Remington ammunition with a 45-grain metal/polymer bullet that eliminates damage to steel targets during training exercises. Loaded to a velocity of 3,100 fps from a 24-inch barrel, the round is stated to function well in short barrel, select barrel, and suppressed carbines and/or rifles. (www.TenXTactical.com)

Texas Armament & Technology LLC

Texas Armament & Technology LLC is the U.S. source for Aguila ammunition from Mexico. Aguila first introduced a portion of its rimfire cartridge line more than a decade ago, and using Eley technology the company gained a reputation for producing a quality product. The rimfire 5mm Aguila cartridge is no longer catalogued, but current production includes 18 rimfires, including three Short and two Long rimfire rounds. Except for the SSS Sniper Subsonic round that features a 60-grain bullet at 950 fps, the

Short rounds feature 29-grain lead bullets loaded to 1,095 and 950 fps respectively. The Long rounds – Colibri and Super Colibri – feature 20-grain bullets loaded to 420 and 590 fps, respectively.

The Aguila metallic centerfire line has grown to include 17 handgun loads in 11 popular calibers, and three rifle calibers – .30 Carbine, 5.56mm and 7.62x51mm. Shotshells are being produced in 12, 16, 20 and 28 gauge sizes, plus .410 bore and 8 gauge industrial. Other than the 8 gauge and the 2½-inch .410-bore shotshells, all the Aguila shotshells are standard length – 2¾ inches. The available shot sizes include 0B, 00B, 1B, 2B, 3B, 4B, 0B, 00B, FB, BB, 2, 4, 6, 7½, 8 and 9, depending on the specific load and gauge. Not all loads may available in the U.S. (The 8 gauge industrial shell is loaded with a solid slug for kiln clinker busting.) (www.tx-at.com)

Western Powders, Inc.

Another source of loading data available at your local dealer is the new and expanded Edition 5.0 of *Western Powders Reloading & Load Data Guide*. This magazine-size 81-page softbound features a good bit of useful information such as getting started, reloading basics, tips, general cleaning for firearms; in addition to loading data for more than two dozen handgun cartridges from the 5.7x 28mm FN to the .500 S&W. Also included are such cartridges as the .30 Luger, .38 Super, .357 Maximum-TC, .45 GAP and .475 Maximum. No dimensioned drawings are provided, but the barrel length and rifling twist, primer brand and size, case brand with trim and maximum lengths are listed, along with bullet brand, diameter, weight and type. Starting loads and maximum loads are listed for each bullet weight and powder charge, and the maximum overall loaded cartridge length is listed.

Loading data is also provided for more than nine dozen rifle cartridges from the .17 Hornet to the .550 Magnum, and including data for such cartridges as the .20 VarTarg Turbo, .219 Zipper, .256 Winchester, 6.5mm Remington Magnum, .307 Winchester, 7.65x53 Belgian and .348 Winchester, which you won't find listed in every manual. Basic data, barrel length, rifling twist, overall loaded cartridge length, etc., for each cartridge is provided, similar to the data for the handgun cartridges.

Preceding the two data sections is a handy Powder to Cartridge Reference

The 81-page softbound *Western Powders Reloading & Load Data Guide* is available at your local dealer.

List. Each powder is listed and an X in the column below it indicates whether it is suitable powder to use with a specific cartridge. For example, the only Western powder listed as suitable for reloading the .221 Fireball is Accurate 1680, while for the .17 Fireball, there are six suitable powders – Accurate 2015, 2230, 2460, 2520, and Ramshot X-Terminator and TAC. Inside the rear cover is a Burn Rate Chart for most powders available to American handloaders including IMR, Norma and Tubal. It's a handy reference list. Preceding this is a short section devoted to .50-caliber muzzleloading using Buckhorn 209 powder with a variety of bullet types and weights. Following this is data for loading Blackhorn 209 in more than 20 black-powder cartridges for either hunting or Cowboy Action Shooting. Data is also provided for both handgun and rifle cartridges, from the .32 H&R Magnum to the .50-90. Charges listed are in weighed grains, not volume, and loads for several bullet weights are provided. (www.westernpowders.com)

Winchester Ammunition

Winchester, of the major three sporting ammunition manufacturers, appears to have the most new products this year, with nearly four dozen, depending on how you count. The Train & Defend line of handgun cartridges features four popular handgun cartridges in nickel-plated cases loaded with

jacketed hollowpoint bullets. The Train cartridges are packaged 50 rounds per box with a large "T" and "Train" prominently displayed, while the Defend rounds are packaged 20 per box with a large "D" and "Defend" on the box. Both loads are said to produce less recoil than standard loads in the same caliber.

New shotshell loads include the 12-gauge Long Beard XR Lok'd & Lethal and the Rooster XR Lok'd & Lethal rounds for turkey hunters. The Long Beard loads are available in two sizes, 3½-inch and 3-inch, loaded to 1,200 fps. The former shell is loaded with two ounces of shot in a choice of #4, #5, or #6, and the latter with 1¾ ounces in the same choices. The Rooster rounds in 3-inch and standard 2¾-inch are loaded to 1,300 fps, with 1½ and 1¼ ounces of shot, respectively, in the same shot sizes as the Long Beard rounds. The Shot-Lok technology employs the shot in a hardened resin encapsulating the lead pellets, protecting them during bore travel and launching them nearly as a single projectile. The result is said to produce twice as many pellets in a 10-inch circle out to 60 yards, with 10 percent greater penetration over standard lead loads beyond 50 yards.

Owners of the renowned 1911 autoloader will like the new Win 1911 load. It's available loaded with a choice of 230-grain FMJ or JHP bullets to a velocity of 880 fps from a 5-inch barrel. It was designed with personal defense in mind, and both loads should have the same point of impact.

Competitive shooters in 3-Gun matches should appreciate the new Win3Gun – handgun, rifle and

Winchester Long Beard XR Lok'd & Lethal

shotgun – loads. Three handgun rounds – 9mm, .40 S&W and .45 ACP – one rifle load – 5.56mm – and two 12-gauge shotgun loads – 00 buck and size 7½ lead shot – are available.

Varmint hunters should have a field day with new Winchester loads in five calibers. The .17 Winchester Super Magnum, advertised as the "fastest rimfire in the world," is now available in two new HV (high velocity) loads. One load features a 20-grain bullet at 3,000 fps and the second features a 25-grain bullet at 2,600 fps. The centerfire VarmintX loads include a .204 Ruger with a 32-grain at 4,000 fps, two .223 Remington loads, and one each for the .22-250 Remington and the .243 Winchester calibers. Velocities for the new VarmintX rounds range from 3,240 fps (.223 Rem. with a 55-grain bullet) to 3,850 fps (.243 Win. with a 58-grain bullet).

For deer hunters Winchester has a new Ballistic Silvertip load for the .270 Winchester cartridge. Loaded with a 130-grain polymer Silvertip bullet, it exits the rifle muzzle at 3,050 fps. (www.winchester.com)

Winchester Win 1911

NEW OPTICS

BY Tom Tabor

New trends and innovations seem to be everywhere in the shooting industry today, but nowhere are those advances more pronounced and ground-shattering than in the area of optics. Powerful magnification levels we could only dream of a few years ago seem to be commonplace today; new breakthroughs in night vision equipment are bursting free from their previous bonds; new high-quality rimfire optics are becoming more prevalent than in the past; innovative breakthroughs in being able to snap photos right through the lens of field optics have been developed and improved; creative new ways of judging shot distance has become commonplace in many of our binoculars and scopes; and with the increase in interest in tactical shooting, many manufacturers have come out with exciting new products specifically dedicated

The Aimpoint 9000SC-NV.

to this area of shooting. All of these changes have excited folks like me who get an adrenaline rush when we see these new products and envision how they might help us in the field. While it would be a virtual impossibility to cover all of these great new products, the following is an attempt to wet the reader's appetite as to what is now available.

Aimpoint

Aimpoint, the originator and to some the world leader in electronic red-dot sighting technology, has once again developed breakthrough technology for shooters. Back in 2005 the company ushered in the 9000 series sight, which quickly became accepted in the hunting and shooting communities worldwide. Now they have carried that technology one step further with their new 9000SC-NV. This new Aimpoint addition combines the high-quality technological

The author mounted an Aimpoint 9000SC-NV sight on his custom Remington 700 BDL .243 rifle, and found he liked it a lot.

advancements found in the 9000 series red-dot sights with night-vision capabilities specifically designed for the hunting market. Or as Dave Pasienski, Aimpoint's Director of Commercial Sales put it, "Adding night vision compatibility to a sight that already offers superior low-light and daylight performance, makes this the most versatile hunting optic you can own."

This sight is night vision compatible, meaning it can be used alone, similar to other Aimpoint red-dot sights, or it can be used in conjunction with other night vision enhancing devices. It is a nonmagnifying, parallax-free optic that features a two minute-of-angle (MOA) red dot for fast target acquisition. It is waterproof and allows continuous operation for over five years on a single 2L76 or DL1/3N battery. The main tube is 30mm and it comes with a set of matte blue mounting rings compatible with Weaver-style scope bases or a Picatinny rail system.

I had an opportunity to test one of the new 9000SC-NV sights recently, as well as other red-dot sights produced by Aimpoint, and have found them to all be excellent products. Because the 9000SC-NV and some other sights produced by Aimpoint possess no magnification capabilities, I believe some shooters might feel these sights are best intended for use at short to moderate range, but I became amazed at how accurately they perform at extended range. I wonder if we might have become a bit spoiled over the years by the huge influx of high-magnification optics. MSRP for the 9000SC-NV is $465. (www.aimpoint.com)

Burris

Burris has introduced a new series of tactical optics called the XTR II™, (Xtreme Tactical Riflescopes), which come with a versatile 5x zoom potential. The features include sophisticated reticles and advanced windage and elevation adjustments to assist tactical, competitive and long-range precision rifle shooters. Shooters can choose from front, rear or dual focal-plane designs, and reticle choices consisting of Mil-radian or MOA measurements, trajectory-compensating crosshairs, and either illuminated or non-illuminated. RFP reticles maintain a constant reticle size on all magnification settings, but the crosshairs change with the power. The XTR II scopes come in wide variety of optic dimensions and magnifications ranging from a 1-5x24mm up to an 8-40x50mm. (www.burrisoptics.com)

Bushnell

On Nov. 1, 2013, the huge sporting goods conglomerate ATK announced it had completed the acquisition of Bushnell Group Holdings. Reportedly, ATK paid $985 million for Bushnell and plans to integrate its operation into ATK's Sporting Group, which is anticipated to increase the company's exposure to higher-growth hunting and outdoor lifestyle markets. ATK is a fine company and I personally believe that

Bushnell's new ImageView 8x30mm Binoculars.

the Bushnell products will benefit from this acquisition.

Many hunters and outdoorsmen like the idea of being able to capture pictures of animals in the wild. Unfortunately, hunters are often preoccupied when a trophy critter presents itself. Maybe the hunter is scouring a canyon bottom with his or her binos when unexpectedly that big buck appears seemingly out of nowhere. In this case, is the shooter going to put their binoculars away and get the camera out in hopes that the animal will stay put long enough to snap the picture? The answer to that question is likely "no." Time is of the essence in

The Burris XTR II 5-25x50mm with illuminated reticles.

Below: Available reticles for the Burris XTR II.

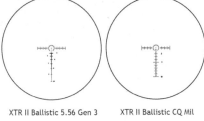

XTR II Ballistic 5.56 Gen 3   XTR II Ballistic CQ Mil

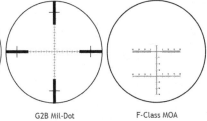

G2B Mil-Dot   F-Class MOA

Bushnell Equinox 3x30mm Night Vision Monocular.

Hawke Rimfire SR Reticle.

Hawke 3-9x40mm Sport HD IR Rimfire Scope.

these types of situations and while it might be nice to capture a photo, much more pressing is squeezing the trigger.

Bushnell has an answer to this problem and it's the ImageView Binoculars. These binos come with many features that sportsmen prefer. It consists of a compact roof prism design weighing only a mere 13.5 ounces, yet has full 8x magnification, BK-7 prisms and the lenses are fully coated. The neat part comes in with the integrated 12 MP digital camera, which has the capability of capturing and storing high-quality still images, or 720p HD video. The system is compatible with up to a 32 GB SD card. Included in the low retail price of $287.95 are a remote shutter cable and USB cable.

Recently there has been an increase in interest for moderately priced night-vision equipment, and that focus hasn't gone unnoticed by Bushnell. The company's new Equinox family of optics has been expanded to include a 3x30mm monocular that uses digital technology to provide crisp, clear images in either green or black-and-white displays with the push of a button. Typically the green display is utilized when facing near total darkness and the black-and-white display is used when minimal ambient light is available. I had the opportunity to personally test one of these units and found it to be a great aid when shooting and animal watching in poor light conditions. Power for this unit is provided by two lithium CR123 batteries. It can be used separately or in conjunction with an auxiliary IR light source, which can be mounted on the monocular's integrated accessory rail. MSRP for the Equinox 3x30mm Night Vision Monocular is $329.99. (www.bushnell.com)

Hawke

Hawke Optics has now joined the fast growing market of quality rimfire scopes with their new 3-9x40mm Sport HD (High Definition) IR (Illuminate Reticle) Rimfire Scope. The unique design of the reticle of this scope marries long-range shooting capabilities with rimfire cartridges – and in particular the .22 LR caliber. When sighted in at 50 yards, the Hawke Sport HD IR Rimfire Scope provides crosshair aiming points from 50 to 200 yards. Marked in increments of 25 yards, this reticle helps to ensure pinpoint accuracy throughout that range. As an added bonus feature, there is no need to memorize the distance

of each marked holding point because those yardage values have been etched directly onto the glass of the reticle. This scope is waterproof, shockproof and nitrogen purged to prevent fogging and comes with the transferable Hawke Worldwide Warranty. Additionally, the Rimfire SR reticle is supported by the Hawke BRC program, which can be downloaded free from the Hawke website. (www.hawkeoptics.com)

Konus Sight-Pro Atomic QR.

Konus Pro T30 3-12x50mm Riflescope.

Konus PTSI 3x32mm Prismatic Sight.

Konus

For over 30 years Konus has provided their customers with high-quality European-designed optics specifically intended for shooters, and with special emphasis given to the hunters and tactical folks. Konus has a number of new products to offer including a tactical model Pro T30 3-12x50mm scope. This scope consists of a 30mm main tube, a sleek and compact design, glass engraved Mil-Dot reticle with dual illumination, comes with mounting rings and is available for an MSRP of $499.99. Also with a 30mm main tube, Konus' new Pro M30 2.5-10x52mm scope comes with lockable tactical turrets (resettable to zero), an anti-canting level bubble, flip-up lens covers and a detachable sunshade. The scope is priced at $629.99. The Konus Sight-Pro Atomic QR was also designed with tactical shooters in mind and includes a 4 MOA red dot, quick-release potential, has unlimited eye relief, one-inch integrated riser, compatibility with Weaver or Pincatinny rail systems and carries an MSRP of $299.99. Konus also offers a new four-color (red, blue, green and black) prismatic model called the PTS1 3x32mm Prismatic Sight that features a 30mm tube, a solid one-piece base capable of being mounted on either a Weaver or Picatinny-style base, and has a 3.15-inch optimum eye relief for $399.99 MSRP. (www.konuspro.com)

Leica

Leica has added two new models to their already successful ER series of riflescopes, which they have dubbed the ER i Models. You can select either the 2.5-10x42 or the 3-12x50 and pick from three different illuminated reticle configurations. These consist of the 4a Classic Hunting Reticle, Ballistic Reticle with stadia lines for long-range shooting and the IBS Reticle, which is MOA based and comes with stadia lines and hash

marks. Also, there is a new, patented bullet drop compensator (BDC) turret available. When equipped with the BDC, the ER i scopes provide shooters a whole new level of long-range shooting capability. Battery life when set on the continuous mode and on the brightest setting is about 40 hours, and more than 210 hours when set on the intermediate setting. And, Leica has incorporated an intelligent "auto on/off" function. When not in a regular shooting position, or when left on unintentionally, the power shuts down to provide even longer battery life.

The eye relief on the ER i models is a bit longer than on many scopes, at just under four inches. This longer distance provides an extra degree of safety from catching the rim of the scope in the shooter's eye when firing lightweight, bigbore rifles, or when shooting at extreme angles – and in some cases it also provides a little better compatibility for certain action types. There are two different mounting systems – the proven rail mount, or the more traditional ring and base system. Depending upon model, reticle and mounting system, the

The Leica ER i 4a Classic Hunting Reticle.

The Leica ER i Ballastic Reticle with stadia lines for long-range shooting.

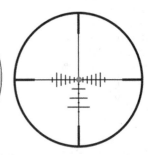

The Leica ER i IBS Reticle, which is MOA based and comes with stadia lines and hash marks.

MSRP for the Leica ER i scopes run from $1,599 up to $2,349. (www.leica.com)

Leupold

Leupold & Stevens continues to expand their very popular binocular lineup with several new models within the BX® series. Those include a new BX-1 Yosemite® 10x30mm, which was specifically designed for smaller faces and hands, making it a great choice for families with young users. MSRP is $129.99. The new compact BX-2 Acadia® is available in either 8x32mm or 10x32mm and offers all the features of the larger models, but in a more compact package, and carries MSRPs of $214.99 and $249.99. The BX-3 Mojave® also received a couple of new additions, including 8x32mm and 10x32mm units. These are lightweight and ergonomically designed, and feature L-Coat™ BAK4 prisms like the other versions, but in a smaller package. MSRP for these new additions are $439.99 and $464.99 respectively. And one of the most recent of the Leupold binocular family to hit the market is the new BX-4 McKinley HD. I had an opportunity to

Rifle mounted Leica ER i 3-12x50mm scope.

Leupold BX4 McKinley 10x42mm Binocular.

Leupold VX-R 4-12x40mm CDS (30mm) Riflescope.

personally test one of the 10x42mm units on a whitetail and hog hunting trip to Oklahoma recently, and found the optics to be crystal clear – it provided me the perfect match for my hunting needs. The lightweight magnesium alloy chassis is durable and rugged, and its second generation water and fog proofing helps to ensures effective use in all types of weather extremes. The BX-4 McKinley HD binoculars are available in either 8x42mm or 10x42mm and carry MSRPs

Leupold RX-1000i TBR DNA Rangefinder.

of $724.00 and $749.00 respectively.

Leupold also continues to expand its very popular FireDot Duplex (Illuminated) Reticle into more scopes. This innovative design marries the standard duplex style crosshair reticle with an illuminated red dot at the center of the aiming point. One of the recent new models equipped with this style reticle is the VX-R 4-12x40mm CDS (30mm), which comes with all the bells and whistles that have made Leupold famous in the business for an MSRP of $789.99.

Rangefinders have nearly become standard equipment for many hunters, and Leupold has many new choices to select from within their RX Digital series. These units are very compact when compared to many of the competition's models, and range in length from only 3.8 inches up to 4.2 inches and weigh a mere 6.8 to 7.8 ounces. I also had the chance to test one of these units – an RX-1000i TBR (True Ballistic

Range) with DNA and found it to be an overall excellent product that locks onto its targets reliably and quickly. The TBR function calculates the equivalent horizontal range (level fire range) from which the shooter can determine the correct aim for the conditions, whether firing a firearm or shooting a bow, and the DNA engine improves the ranging accuracy down to one-tenth of a yard. The MSRPs range from the base RX-600i model at $274.99, up to $499.99 for the RX-1000i TBR with DNA. (www.leupold. com)

Meopta

Meopta is a family-owned, multinational company that has marketplace facilities located in both the U.S. and Europe. Recently the company announced the release of its next generation MeoStar® riflescopes, the R2 line and the first of its scopes to possess 6x zoom capabilities. The new European-made 1-6x24mm RD scope comes with a choice of two illuminated reticles, the K-Dot 2 or 4C-RD. I would describe the K-Dot 2 reticle as a type of fine three-legged semicrosshair design (omitting the uppermost leg of the crosshair), and the 4C-RD being a more traditional style of four-legged duplex crosshair with the uppermost vertical leg being finer than the other legs. Both reticle designs come with the company's new RD8 illumination red dot that is adjustable to eight levels of intensity. The body of the 1-6x24 RD is machined from a solid block of aircraft-grade aluminum alloy and has an anodized scratch-resistant exterior. In order to enhance the light-gathering abilities, Meopta uses its new MeoLux lens coating on the premium quality Schott glass lenses, which enables 99.8 percent light transmission per glass surface and a full 95 percent transmission through the entire scope. The new 1-6x24 RD could be the perfect match for

Meopta S2 82 HD Spotting Scope.

Meopta MeoPix iPhone 5 Adapter for use with the MeoStar Spotting Scope.

Nikon

The Monarch series has essentially become the flagship for Nikon's binocular lineup and the new and enhanced Monarch 5 has elevated that standard in both feel and performance. At almost an ounce less in weight, largely due to the use of a lighter rubber armor coating material, the Monarch 5 has become a serious contender in the "go-to" binocular marketplace. Nikon's ED (Extra-low Dispersion) glass lenses help to effectively compensate for chromatic aberrations, which in turn helps to increase the image contrast and improve the resolution. The overall resolution and contrast through the Eco-Glass lenses are further enhanced thanks to the phase correction coatings and the dielectric high-reflective multilayer prism coatings that help to produce clear, natural looking images and overall better light transmission. There are three new black models available in 42mm: 8x42, 10x42 and 12x42; and three in 56mm: 8x56, 16x56 and 20x56. MSRP for the 42mm models range from $299.95 up to $349.95; and for the 56mm models they carry MSRPs from $749.95 up to $899.95.

An all-new line of riflescopes is also being offered by Nikon – earmarked as its flagship Monarch 7 series. Currently there are two models available: 2.5-10x50mm SF and 4-16x50mm SF. Each features Nikon's Custom XR Turret package along with a glass etched BDC reticle, providing shooters with the option to either dial in a particular distance on the crosshair, or to utilize the

dangerous-game hunting, or wherever close to moderate-range shots are called for. It carries an MSRP of $1,595.

Meopta's MeoStar® S2 82 HD spotting scopes are built to be lightweight and rugged. Couple that with sculpted rubber armor coating and you have a durable and attractive product built specifically for harsh field conditions, with resistance to temperature extremes ranging from -13 to 131 degrees F, and storage potential from a low of -40 to 158 degrees F. The bodies are nitrogen filled to ensure their waterproof and fog proof integrity. The 82mm high-definition, extra-low dispersion, two-part fluoride objective lens element is said to eliminate chromatic aberration (CA), or color fringing, across the entire field of view to ensure brilliant, sharp and more vibrant images

Meopta MeoStar R2 1-6x24mm Riflescope.

than typical non-HD optical systems are capable of achieving. Eyepieces are available in either 30x-60x WA or 20x-70x, which comes with twist-up eyecups to accommodate all sizes of users. Quick-release bayonet mounts automatically lock the eyepiece securely in place and unlock it with only the push of a button.

The MeoStar® S2 82 HD also comes with very close focusing capability at only a mere 13.12 feet, which makes it a very versatile unit for use in the field. The rotating tripod collar allows a smooth 360-degree rotation of the scope body, which makes it convenient and comfortable for the user. Its integrated retractable aluminum sun shade helps to protect the lens from both moisture and stray light. If you are so inclined, Meopta even sells an iPhone adaptor called the MeoPix so you can snap photos through the lens of the MeoStar® S2 82 HD spotting scope. MSRP for the spotting scope is $2,199.98, and for the new redesigned MeoPix iScoping iPhone 5 Adapter it is $71.99. (www.meoptasportsoptics.com/us)

Nikon Monarch 5 12x42mm Binoculars.

Nikon Monarch 7 2.5-10x50mm SF Riflescope.

Over the years Redfield became one of the leading American manufacturers of fine sporting optics for hunters and outdoorsmen. Leupold & Stevens purchased the Redfield brand in 2008. Since that time, Leupold has continued to expand the line of moderately priced Redfield sporting optics, which now includes Revolution, Revenge and Battlezone series riflescopes; Rampage spotting scopes; and Raider rangefinders. In line with that expansion is a couple of new riflescopes. The new Revolution/TAC 3-9x40mm blends the now recognized performance, quality and clarity found in the Revolution Series scopes with characteristics.

The Redfield TAC.22 has interchangeable elevation dials.
(Photo by Tom Tabor)

hold-over points on the BDC reticle. Nikon Custom XR Turret riflescopes allow custom matching of the distances inscribed on the elevation dial to specific ballistics of virtually any cartridge, load and environmental condition. A voucher is included with each scope permitting the purchaser to custom order a turret to match their specific requirements, and additional turrets are available for purchase. MSRP for the Monarch 7 2.5-10x50 SF is $849.95, and $999.95 for the 4-16x50 SF. (www.nikonsportoptics.com)

Redfield

Redfield Gun Sight Company was founded in 1909 by John Hill Redfield.

tactical reticle features stadia lines on the horizontal and vertical crosshairs set at two minutes of angle (MOA) increments to provide quick holdover for elevation, or lateral compensation for wind drift. The heavy, knurled 1/4 MOA knobs provide quick and easy adjustment of the reticle. MSRP for the Revolution/TAC 3-9x40mm is $349.99.

The Battlezone Series of scopes adds a new member to its family, the 6-18x44mm, which is equipped with a BDC (Bullet Drop Compensation) reticle or a Tac-MOA reticle. The pop-up, resettable 1/4 MOA finger adjustments provide an audible click as the adjustments are made. The BDC comes with two adjustable dials calibrated for two of the most popular tactical rifle calibers. The .223/5.56mm NATO dial is set for 55-grain bullets traveling out the muzzle at 3,100 fps, and the .308/7.62mm NATO dial has been calibrated for 168-grain bullets traveling at 2,650 fps. Each reticle is marked in 50-yard increments. MSRP for the Battlezone 6-18x44mm with a Tac-MOA reticle is $374.99.

Also new in the Battlezone Series is the TAC.22 2-7x34mm riflescope dedicated to those shooters that like the inherent advantages of tactical-style optics, and is specifically tailored to meet the needs of the rimfire .22 shooter. This is essentially the first of its kind and comes with two interchangeable elevation adjustment dials, one dedicated to the usual 1/4 MOA incremental adjustments and the other having a Bullet Drop Compensation (BDC) dial calibrated precisely to match a 36-grain hollowpoint traveling out of the muzzle at 1,260 fps. This ammo is commonly available and includes Federal

Redfield Revolution/TAC 3-9x40mm Riflescope mounted on an M&P15 AR.

Redfield Revolution/TAC 3-9x40mm Riflescope.

Redfield Battlezone TAC.22 2-7x34mm Riflescope.

Champion Load #745 and CCI Mini-Mag HP ammunition. The BDC dial is marked from 50 to 150 yards with the parallax set at a rimfire-friendly 75 yards. I mounted one of these scopes on a Ruger 10/22 and found it worked perfectly. While some scopes intended for use on .22s appear overly large, this particular one seemed to match the petite characteristics of the stock Ruger very well. MSRP for the Battlezone TAC.22 2-7x34mm is $189.99. (www.redfield.com)

Steiner

Steiner's new GS3 (Game Sensing) scopes utilize the unique CAT (Color Adjusted Transmission) lens coatings to amplify contrast in the peak human vision sensitivity range. Available in four models: 2-10x42mm, 3-15x50mm, 3-15x56mm and 4-20x50mm, and all are equipped with the company's Plex S2 etched reticle marked for both trajectory bullet drop and wind drift. The GS3 4-20x50mm model features side parallax adjustment and is available with either a Plex S2 or a Plex S7 reticle. The S7 comes with simple hash marks calibrated to provide dead-on aiming from 100 to 500 yards for most common hunting cartridges. The GS3 riflescope features include a versatile mounting length of 5.4 inches (for mounting on short actions or muzzleloaders), 1/4 MOA adjustments (resettable back to zero) and rugged 30mm tubes (milled from solid aluminum stock with no

welds or seams). MSRP: GS3 2-10x42 is $919.99; GS3 3-15x50mm is $1,029.99; GS3 3-15x56mm is $1,029.99; and GS3 4-20x50mm is $1,149.99.

Steiner's new M30r LRF Military 8x30mm Mil-Spec Laser Rangefinder Binocular was designed to be compact and light, and is well suited for military and tactical units. Built to military specifications, the M30r LRF is rugged, reliable and based on the company's battle-proven porro prism design. These binoculars are capable of ranging targets from 27 to 1,680 yards, and in the event of battery failure, or out-of-range targets – Steiner has built in its SUMR ranging reticle. MSRP for the M30r LRF Military 8x30mm binocular is $2,587. (www.steiner-optics.com)

Swarovski

Over nearly one-quarter of a century of production, Swarovski's SLC binoculars have established a reputation synonymous with high quality, ruggedness and reliability. Now expanding that fine line of optics, Swarovski has announced a new generation of SLC binos consisting of three new models: 8x42, 10x42 and 15x56. These are compact in design making them handy when traveling with plenty of luggage, and providing a maximum degree of comfort when carrying even on lengthy outings afield. And if you prefer even more compactness, the company's new CL 8x25mm Pocket Binoculars might be just what you have been looking for in a model that folds up out of the way to fit in your shirt pocket. In this case the exit pupil has been shifted back in order to permit easier use by eyeglass wearers. Correct adjustment of the pupil distance and the twist-in eyecups are important features. When closed, the CL Pocket is a compact pair of binoculars, but when opened they transform into an

Swarovski CL Binoculars.

uninhibited full-size pair of binos that doesn't allow for compromises. As Rob Lancellotti, Swarovski's P.R. Associate, puts it: "The CL Pocket delivers big optic performance from a small, light, easily carried binocular that can be with you for any outdoor activity, as well as indoor sporting events or concerts." MSRP for the CL Pocket Binos is $888.00. (www.swarovskioptik.us)

Trijicon

Trijicon's new VCOG (Variable Combat Optical Gunsight) 1-6x24mm riflescope was designed to meet the rigorous demands of duty or competition while

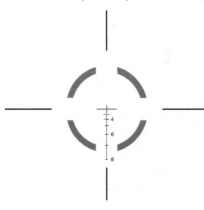

Initially the VCOG will be offered with seven different reticle choices, all of which are located in the first focal plane allowing the ballistic reticle to be used at any magnification.

Steiner's GS3 (Game Sensing) 2-10x42mm Riflescope.

Trijicon's new VCOG (Variable Combat Optical Gunsight) 1-6x24mm riflescope.

giving shooters the flexibility to engage CQB (Close Quarters Battle) targets out to the maximum effective range of most service rifles. The body of the VCOG is machined from a 7075-T6 aluminum forging and given a Mil-Spec, hard-coat anodized finish. It has a full 90 MOA for windage and elevation adjustment in .5-inch click increments at 100 meters. Initially the VCOG will be offered with seven different reticle choices, all of which are located in the first focal plane allowing the ballistic reticle to be used at any magnification. The segmented circle reticle with a centered crosshair can be matched to 175-grain 7.62mm, 55-grain and 77-grain 5.56mm, or 115-grain supersonic 300 BLK loads. The popular horseshoe/dot reticle is available in each of the 5.56 and 7.62 calibers. The VCOG's red illuminated reticle is powered by a single AA battery, which will deliver up to 700 continuous hours of runtime at four of the six settings when a lithium battery is installed. MSRP for the VCOG 1-6x24mm is $2,270. (www.trijicon.com)

Vixen

Vixen has for the first time entered the 6x scope category, with a wider selection in that power range to come in the near future. The company's new VIII 1-6x24 was specifically designed to be a short to mid-range dangerous-game scope, but also fits nicely in 3-Gun competition and tactical CQB applications. It features a one-piece, aircraft-grade aluminum 30mm main tube, and its high-quality performance is meant to compete head-to-head with Europe's very best models. Buyers have the option of purchasing the hunting model, which comes with a center illuminated dot, second focal plane, glass-etched fine duplex reticle; or the tactical 3-Gun version, which sports a standard mil-dot design with illuminated center cross. All Vixen Sport Optical products sold in North America are backed by an unconditional, transferable lifetime warranty. MSRP for the VIII Series

Zeiss Conquest Rimfire 3-9x40mm with Z-Plex reticle.

1-6x24 scope is $1,500. (www.vixenoptics.com)

Weaver

Weaver's very popular series of riflescopes, the Grand Slams, have now undergone a complete transformation both inside and out. Concentrating on enhanced accuracy, reliability and durability, Weaver has improved their Mico-Trac erector system, the one-piece power adjustment and changed the exterior styling. There is a wide range of variable-power Grand Slams available from 2-8x36mm up to several 4-16x44mm models. In each category of magnification there is a variety of reticle style choices to select from. MSRPs for these new Grand Slam models list from $415.95 up to $540.95.

Within the Weaver family of riflescopes, the KASPA line provides a wide variety of choices to select from, many of which are specifically designed with specialized optics, and all at modest prices. There are three new 1-4x24mm models each dedicated for a specific application. For example, there is a model with a reticle intended for use by sluggunners and muzzleloader shooters, one with the turkey hunter clearly in mind possessing a VZT (Vertical Zone Turkey) reticle and a camo body, and the last comes with a standard Dual-X reticle. The Dual-X model carries a MSRP of $239.99, and the other two models both run $259.99. There is also a Tactical KASPA 1-4x24mm scope that comes

Weaver Grand Slam 3-12x is available in both 42mm and 50mm with a couple of reticle choices.

with many of the features of much more expensive tactical scopes, including a 30mm main tube that is nitrogen filled to prevent internal fogging. MSRP for the Tactical 1-4x24mm runs $329.99.

If you like small optics you might have interest in the KASPA Micro Dot Sight. This is a great product that would work well on a handgun, shotgun or AR-style rifle. It would also be ideal for young shooters, 3-Gun shooters or even turkey hunters. MSRP for the KASPA Micro Dot Sight is only $108.45. (www.weaveroptics.com)

Zeiss

For many years it was hard to find a high-quality rimfire scope, but with the increased interest in high-performance rimfire rifles and handguns it has brought with it new opportunities in optics. A prime example of this new trend can be found in Zeiss' rimfire riflescopes. On par with a comparable centerfire scope, this new 3-9x40mm Conquest is the perfect choice for target plinking, or varmint and small-game hunting. It comes with a compact, one-inch main tube and produces bright images with generous eye relief. Set to be parallax free at 50 yards makes it perfect for most rimfire uses, plus it features the Z-Plex (#20) reticle for precise shot placement on small targets. All glass has been multicoated and is anti-reflective to provide super-crisp, bright images even in poor light. Of course the Conquest is waterproof, dustproof and nitrogen filled to prevent fogging, and is covered by Zeiss' Limited Lifetime Transferable Warranty. Suggested retail for the Conquest Rimfire Riflescope is $555.00. (www.zeiss.com/sports)

NOTE: In some locales the use of night-vision equipment is considered illegal for hunting purposes or restricted to the hunting of certain species. For this reason it is strongly recommended that anyone using any night-vision equipment for hunting check with their local game department to determine legality.

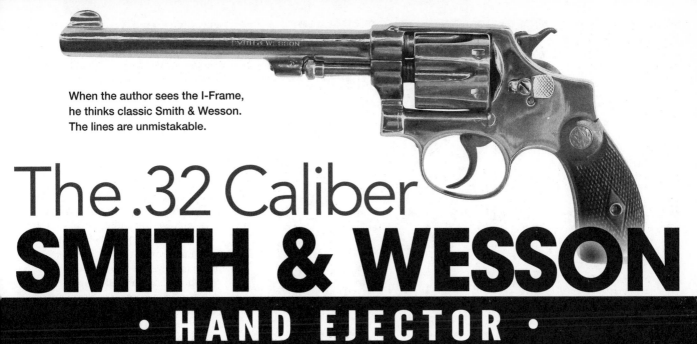

When the author sees the I-Frame, he thinks classic Smith & Wesson. The lines are unmistakable.

The .32 Caliber
SMITH & WESSON
• HAND EJECTOR •

BY **Bob Campbell**

The Smith & Wesson I-Frame, also known as the Hand Ejector, is the most neglected and overlooked of the Smith & Wesson revolvers. Introduced in 1896 and combining a double-action mechanism with a swing-out cylinder it was a sensational step forward at the time.

The Hand Ejector chambered the .32 Smith & Wesson Long cartridge. While not powerful by today's standards, the .32 Smith & Wesson Long is an accurate cartridge that was more powerful than the previous .32 S&W cartridge. The Hand Ejector was a very popular handgun with police agencies because at the time many officers carried their revolver in a deep pocket in the uniform tunic. It was easy to carry and survived for many years as a police and personal defense revolver.

There's not a single shooting involving a .32-caliber revolver in my extensive database and I cannot comment on the cartridge in personal defense situations, but I do know that the .32 could not perform better than

the .38 Special roundnose lead load, which was not a combination that gave great confidence. Still, the .32 served long and well, if not in hot combat, on the mean streets as a badge of office. If the presence of a firearm deters criminals and makes the owner feel better, then the .32 Smith & Wesson is acceptable. My opinion of the cartridge notwithstanding, the old .32 Smith & Wesson Long must have dispatched a few bad actors during its 40-plus years of front-line use.

After World War II Smith & Wesson developed a new version of the small-frame revolver. By deepening the frame and lengthening the cylinder, S&W engineers were able to produce a revolver capable of chambering the .38 Special cartridge, albeit with a five-shot cylinder. The Chief's Special J-Frame was born. Eventually the six-shot .32 was also

produced on the J-frame while the five-shot .38 Special was far more popular. Even today, many old-timers refer to the Chief's Special as a .38 on a .32 frame.

Eventually the I-Frame was replaced by the more modern J-Frame. There were also .22-caliber I-Frames and a five-shot version known as the Terrier that was chambered for the mild .38 Smith & Wesson cartridge. Over the years I have owned quite a few I-Frame revolvers, so I will make a few observations concerning the type.

I have never seen an I-Frame .32 that was not accurate. A combination of quality control at the height of old-school production is one reason. The excellent balance of the cartridge is another. Even the two or three Smith & Wesson I-Frame revolvers I have owned with bulged barrels were quite accurate. For some reason it is far more common to see the

The swing-out cylinder is taken for granted today, but the original Hand Ejector was a sensation in 1896.

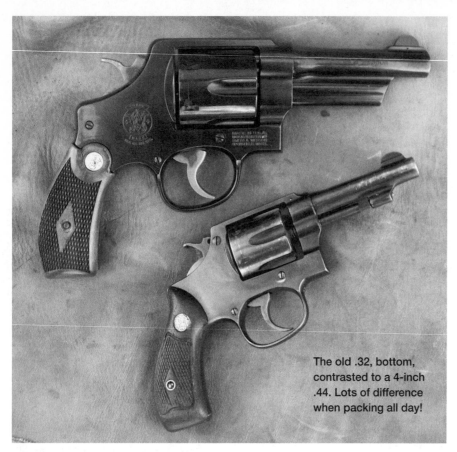

The old .32, bottom, contrasted to a 4-inch .44. Lots of difference when packing all day!

the average 4-inch revolver barrel. With handloading, it is not difficult to push the Magnus brand 100-grain flatnose semiwadcutter to a full 1,000 fps. This makes the .32 a very good small-game cartridge.

Fiocchi offers first-class standard-velocity ammunition. A rule beater is the full-metal-jacket .32 from the same company that is quite accurate. But the most pleasant and accurate .32 Smith & Wesson Long cartridge on the market is the 100-grain full wadcutter offered by Fiocchi. This one is not only hyper accurate, but the flatnose also does the business on squirrels and rabbits.

Manufacturers cannot be raking in much money on a small production caliber such as this, and I am surprised to see Buffalo Bore offer loads for the .32 Smith & Wesson Long. They are right at the top level I have attempted to reach with handloads and each maximizes the caliber. A 115-grain flatnose bullet at 800 fps is a decent pocket-gun load. If I were to draft the old gun into action for personal defense the Buffalo Bore loads are credible. They take the .32 into the bobcat territory, at least at close range. The 100-grain hardcast wadcutter breaks 900 fps and the bullet has plenty of weight to fill the lands and grooves with lead, producing excellent accuracy.

As for the nickel-plated revolver illustrated, the action is tight and crisp. This is the only 6-inch barrel I-Frame .32 I have seen and it is a treasure. The characteristic old-style cylinder latch and color case-hardened trigger and hammer are classic Smith &

.32 with a bulged barrel than any other caliber. Perhaps ammunition was not as reliable as modern loads. One cartridge would misfire without a complete powder burn and push a bullet partway down the barrel, and the next would jam into the previous projectile and bulge the barrel. But, there was not enough pressure to blow the gun. I have seen such a revolver just

this year at a gun show. The I-Frame is becoming difficult to find, particularly in grades above 90 percent, but it is still far from rare.

The .32 Smith & Wesson Long is an accurate cartridge using a bullet with a soft, hollow base that expands to fill the bore. The bullet clocks at 650 fps from

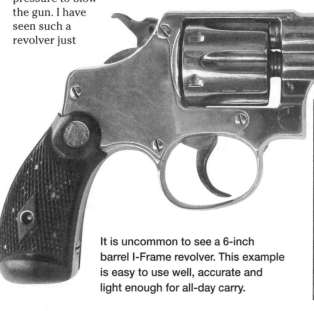

It is uncommon to see a 6-inch barrel I-Frame revolver. This example is easy to use well, accurate and light enough for all-day carry.

Accuracy Results

Cartridge	Group size
Fiocchi 98-grain FMJ	2.8 inches
Fiocchi 100-grain SWC	2 inches
Buffalo Bore 100-grain WC	2.5 inches
Buffalo Bore 115-grain	2.25 inches
Magnus 100-grain SWC/ Titegroup (817 fps)	2.75 inches
Magnus 100-grain SWC/WW 231 (700 fps)	2.45 inches

Note: Based on five-shot groups at 25 yards.

The original Hand Ejector was a well-made revolver and a very pleasant handgun to fire and handle.

Left: There aren't a lot of choices in .32 Smith & Wesson ammunition today, but what is available is very good. The RNL .32, bottom left, is great for target practice. The SWC, right, is for more serious use.

Wesson. Other than the relatively low power of the cartridge, there are no faults. The action is smooth, the sights are adequate, accuracy is excellent and the overall feeling is one of quality.

You can't fault the cartridge's power as you know what you are getting when you deploy the .32 Smith & Wesson Long. I was able to control the revolver easily and fired several offhand double-action groups at seven yards that could be covered with the hand. I fired as quickly as I could bring the sights back on target after recoil – which is hardly a factor with this handgun.

This revolver is more accurate in a mechanical sense than the majority of the .22-caliber I-Frame revolvers we call the .22/32 kit gun. As a lark, I carefully bench-rested this Hand Ejector and fired several groups with six different loads. With the aid of my Hansen's Eagle Eyes shooting glasses, I was able to produce good results shown in the following table.

I included the Fiocchi FMJ cartridge in this experiment. This load is produced primarily for the European market. Just the same, a FMJ load may be appropriate for use in a revolver that may lack the penetration of larger

calibers. I also used one of my own handloads utilizing the Magnus 100-grain SWC over enough Titegroup powder for 800 fps. This is a hefty load that should be used only in tight revolvers. All of these combinations will group five shots into less than three inches at 25 yards, not bad at all for a light, fixed-sight revolver.

The .32 Smith & Wesson Long is a wonderful small-game cartridge that takes rabbit and squirrel without any fuss and bother, and without destroying excess meat. As for personal defense, the choice of a quality revolver that is easy to use well may instill more confidence than is warranted in such a light caliber—but then, what do I know about gun fighting? The I-Frame was an important revolver for Smith & Wesson that will only become more collectible with time. It is one good gun worth having.

The old groove rear sight isn't the most efficient, but when properly lined up gives good accuracy.

THE M1 CARBINE -
SHOOTING WITH A REAL WWII VET

BY **Rick Hacker**

The author's 1943-44 era M1 Carbine was originally purchased for $20 from the NRA and still has all of the original shipping documents.

Although it has assumed a current collectability that might surprise those who used it in combat, the author still shoots his NRA-purchased M1 Carbine regularly. With standard-issue magazines, it has yet to jam.

alk about being at the right place at the right time—the appearance of the M1 Carbine on the eve of our entering World War II had a lot to do with the eventual victory of the United States in that global conflict. In fact, the M1 Carbine's fortuitous existence was due to General Douglas MacArthur's 1938 directive to upgrade the Army's battlefield weapons. As a result, on Nov. 24, 1941, the United States Army signed a contract for Winchester Repeating Arms Company and General Motors' Inland Manufacturing Division to start production on a newly designed "light rifle" that was to be issued to military support personnel. Two weeks later, the Japanese bombed Pearl Harbor.

As a result, United States Carbine, Caliber .30, M1, as it was officially called, went directly from the Winchester and GM assembly lines to the front lines. It eventually became one of the most ubiquitous weapons of WWII, with over 6,221,200 carbines produced between 1941 and 1943 alone, and approximately another 280,000 made by the time military production ceased in 1945. To put this in perspective, the M1 Carbine was even more prolific than the Army's primary battlefield rifle, the M1 Garand.

And yet, the M1 Carbine owed its existence not to a rifle, but to a pistol, the equally celebrated Government Model 1911A1, which at the time was our official military sidearm. But the reality was that many GIs who were issued this .45-caliber semiautomatic couldn't hit a barracks wall with it, even if they were firing from inside the building. Chalk it up to the 1911A1's shallow sights, the purposely designed loose-fitting parts (which nonetheless enabled the 1911A1 to function when dirty and be easily field-stripped) or to the fact that most troops were simply more accurate with a rifle than with a handgun. But packing a nine-pound Garand was not practical for certain logistical support personnel such as medics, mortar crews and radio operators. Even NCOs and officers were issued sidearms rather than being encumbered by the bulkier Garand. But having a pistol was counterproductive if you couldn't hit anything with it. Clearly a compromise had to be found that bridged the gap between the short-range of the 1911A1 and the farther-reaching Garand.

The answer was found in the gas-operated semiautomatic M1 Carbine, with its 18-inch barrel, peep sights and magazine capacity of 15 rounds; later supplemented by a 30-round "banana clip" made specifically for the fully automatic M2 version of the light-recoiling 5½-pound carbine – although both magazines would function in either version of the carbine. Interestingly enough, the basic concept for the M1 Carbine originated with Jonathon Edmund Browning, a half brother to the 1911 inventor John Moses Browning. But the final design was perfected by a team of Winchester's top engineers, including William C. Roemer and Fred Humeston, and was supervised by Edwin

The semiautomatic M1 Carbine was issued with 15-round magazines, but a 30-round magazine (left) was produced for the M2 Carbine, which featured a full-auto selector switch. The magazine could function in either weapon.

Pugsley. In spite of this, via a 1952 movie entitled *Carbine Williams*, Hollywood has led many to believe that the sole inventor of the M1 Carbine was David Marshall Williams, an ex-con played by James Stewart in the title role.

In truth, while "Marsh" Williams did work at Winchester on the initial phases of the carbine's design, his only lasting contribution to the project was the short-stroke gas piston system, which the convicted bootlegger and murderer had invented while in prison. In addition, Williams was difficult to get along with and created dissention among the other engineers at Winchester. He eventually went off on his own to create a different version of the gun, and even though Pugsley admitted it had some advantages over Winchester's design, the war was already under way and production had been started on the "approved" M1 Carbine.

M1 Carbines featured a fixed blade front sight protected by two "ears."

Of course, there was no way the little carbine could handle the standard .30-06 service round of the heftier M1 Garand. Thus, an entirely new .30 cartridge had to be created. In fact, Winchester's Pugsley began development of the Army's desire for a "greater than .27 caliber" cartridge before the carbine was even perfected. He started out with the nearly obsolete .32 Winchester Self-Loading round of 1906, and ended up with a .30-caliber straight-walled cartridge that fired a 110-grain roundnose bullet that exited the barrel at about 1,975 feet per second. So, it was very much on par with the older .32-20, a popular small to medium-game cartridge in its day. Hardly a man-stopper when compared to the .30 Springfield or the .45 ACP, but when fired from the M1 Carbine it had an effective range of 300 yards and would put an enemy down when shots were well placed. In addition, the carbine's 15-round magazine offered much greater firepower than the seven-round pistol it was designed to replace, and in fact, surpassed the eight-round capacity of the Garand as well.

The well-balanced M1 Carbine was extremely shooter-friendly. Recoil was minimal, allowing for quick recovery time, and its sights were quick to line up. The rear sight initially consisted of an L-shaped, folding peep that was changed around 1944 to an adjustable milled (later stamped) aperture. That same year a bayonet-lug sleeve, designed for the M4 bayonet, was added. However, the bayonet attachment didn't see active duty until 1945 after the war was over.

So for all you WWII re-enactors and eagle-eyed film viewers, that means any carbine used during the early stages of the war should not have a bayonet attachment. Of course, many of the earlier guns were retrofitted with bayonet lugs afterwards, most notably for the Korean and Vietnam wars. Yes, the M1 carbine was used by our military as late as the early 1960s, when it was issued to U.S. Air Force Security Police and the Army's Special Forces.

Although both Winchester and Inland produced the majority of carbines during WWII, in order to meet wartime demands other companies were soon conscripted. They were (in order of quantities produced) Hartford, Conn., typewriter manufacturer Underwood-Elliot-Fisher; the Saginaw Steering Gear Division of General Motors, which assembled carbines from parts made by the Irwin-Petersen Arms Company of Grand Rapids, Mich.; National Postal Meter, which previously had only made postal meters and scales; International Business Machines (IBM) of Poughkeepsie, N.Y.; automotive parts maker Standard Products of Port Clinton, Ohio; and Rock-Ola Manufacturing Company of Chicago, which turned its attention from mechanically spinning 78s to making guns for the war effort. Extra receivers were also produced by the Quality Hardware Machine Company of Chicago.

After the Armistice, numerous M1 Carbines were reconditioned, and many continued to see service for decades afterward with our allies overseas. Up until the Obama administration's ill-conceived stoppage of military imports, a number of these guns were returned to America where they now serve the civilian population as small-game getters, plinkers, personal defense weapons and (without import marks) as collectables. I distinctly remember back in 1963 when about 240,000 M1 Carbines were decommissioned and sold to NRA members for a mouth-watering $17.50 each plus $2.50 for shipping and handling. Back then, working my way through school at the A. J. Bayless grocery store in Phoenix, Ariz., I didn't have $20, but my high school buddy Jim did, who promptly had his dad send away for one. It was mailed directly to his home (boy, those were the days) and shortly thereafter we took it out to the desert to see just how fast a magazine full of .30-caliber surplus ammunition could make a jackrabbit run. But that wasn't the first time I had seen one of these war veterans up close and personal.

No, the first time I saw an M1 Carbine (Saturday matinee movies like *Earth vs. The Flying Saucers* and *The Longest Day* notwithstanding) was on the football field of the no-longer-existing West High School in Phoenix, where I was a

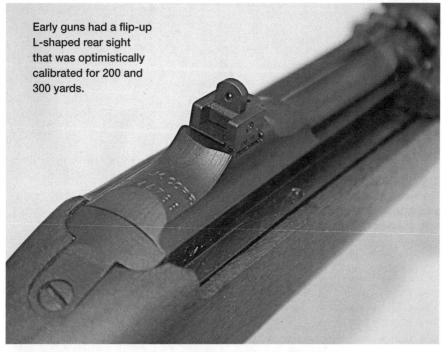

Early guns had a flip-up L-shaped rear sight that was optimistically calibrated for 200 and 300 yards.

Early M1 Carbines featured a stamped steel triggerguard.

Below: The bayonet-lug sleeve was created in 1944, too late to be used on any carbines that saw action during WWII, although many guns were retrofitted with this sleeve afterward. It was designed for the M4 bayonet.

member of the Junior Reserve Officers Training Corps (JROTC). However, as a low-ranking freshmen squad member, I was condemned to drilling with the M1 Garand. But the junior and senior cadet officers got to carry M1 Carbines nattily slung, muzzle up, over their right shoulders. Let me tell you, a 5½-pound carbine versus a 9½-pound rifle makes a big difference on the drill field, especially under a blazing southern Arizona sun when temperatures often climbed to well over 100 degrees. I suspect that was really the impetus behind my motivation to become an officer, a goal that carried over with me throughout ROTC at Arizona State University.

In any case, I finally got to carry an M1 Carbine, although not in the regular Army. By the time I made it to Officer's Candidate School at Ft. Lewis, Wash., they were using different rifles entirely. But many years later, as fate would have it, Jim looked me up. It seemed he needed to raise some cash and decided to sell his NRA M1 Carbine. And like the true friend he was, he wanted to give me first dibs on it. Of course, after all these years Jim wanted more than the $20 he had originally paid for the gun, but that was understandable. A deal was quickly and almost painlessly consummated and at last the gun I had coveted so long ago was mine, complete with all the original NRA and Army Depot shipping papers plus the original cancelled check stub from Jim's father.

My carbine, with its serial number in the 3,550,000 range, was made between

Even when compared to rebuilt M1 Carbines, such as this Rock-Ola from James River Manufacturing (www.jamesriverarmory.com), which features a newly forged receiver and Kreiger/Criterian barrel, the author finds the functioning of the original Winchester design flawless.

May 1943 and February 1944 (specific years are not available) and was subsequently shipped from Red River Arsenal in Texarkana, Texas to Jim's dad on Jan. 24, 1964. Jim had taken good care of it through the years and it still retained its 80 percent arsenal refinish. With factory ammo it consistently shoots 1-1/8-inch groups, which makes it ideal for coyotes and plinking, and it has yet to jam using military surplus magazines.

Today, my carbine has taken on more of a collectible aura, which often makes me think twice about taking it afield. After all, there are great M1 Carbine re-

builds being sold by firms such as Fulton Armory and Miltech, and James River Manufacturing is even producing a Rock-Ola carbine using mostly original military parts, with the exception of barrels and a newly-forged Rock-Ola receiver. Plus, firms such as Auto-Ordinance are offering newly made M1 Carbines in all its guises, including an M1A1 version with folding stock. But somehow, I prefer the timeworn, oil-soaked feel and look of my WWII original. After all, there's something about going shooting with a World War II veteran.

For those who like shooting originals, this early IBM carbine was completely restored by Miltech of Los Altos, Calif. (www.MiltechArms.com) Note the flip-up rear peep sight and stamped triggerguard, denoting its early 1943 manufacture. Miltech carbines are shipped in pine boxes serial numbered to the gun and include a reproduction of the March 17, 1942 Army technical manual.

ROSIE'S .270

BY **Steve Gash**

Light snow fell as I wended my way home from work along Hampden Avenue in 1979, and it was slow going as usual in the Denver rush-hour. It was dark, the temperature was 22 degrees, and the snow was starting to accumulate, not unusual weather for Jan. 18 in Colorado. As I trundled up a slight grade, watching for slick spots, the country music radio station cut to a commercial and my ears perked right up. "For a limited time only," the announcer breathlessly exclaimed. "Ruger Model 77 rifles for less than $175 at the Woolco on South University!"

The buck that launched a big-game hunting career: Rosielea Gash with a Colorado mule deer taken with a Ruger M77R in .250 Savage, October 1977.

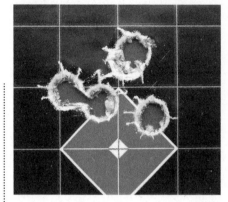

Rosie's Ruger Model 77R in .270 Winchester with a Leupold 4X scope, the quintessential big-game gun. Jack O'Connor would approve.

Most loads don't group this well in the M77, but it's always shot within "minute-of-deer."

By happy coincidence the next intersection was University Boulevard, so I clicked on my right turn signal and headed south, and in a few minutes I was standing at the gun counter at the Woolco. A nice young clerk came right over and said, "How can I help you?"

They had a good inventory of all sorts of guns, and a lot of Ruger M77s in stock. "Do you have one in .270 Winchester?" I asked. As if he knew I was coming, quick as a wink he handed me a brand new Model 77-R off the rack. The American walnut stock was nicely checkered, had some figure here and there, and the dark bluing fairly glistened. But overall it was actually rather plain, obviously destined to be a "working gun," made for a hunter by other hunters.

The price? True to the ad it was less than $175, by a penny. "I'll take it," I said. Since the MSRP for this model in 1979 was $245, this was a pretty good buy. However, while new in the box, Ruger records show that the gun was actually made in late 1977. This no doubt affected the low price; Woolco was unloading older stock. The M77's trim, 22-inch barrel wore no sights so I also bought a Leupold M8 4X scope to mount in the supplied Ruger rings.

The Model 77 was a gift for my wife, Rosielea, to expand her hunting horizons, and was not exactly an "impulse purchase." Rosie had recently started hunting (married to me, what choice did she have?) and had taken a plump 4x4 mule deer with her one and only rifle, a Ruger M-77 in .250 Savage. She was ready to tackle an elk, so I was contemplating a more powerful rifle for her. I thought it should be somewhat more potent than the .250, but without a lot of recoil. A .30-06 or 7mm Magnum would be a logical step up, but there's the recoil problem. The .25-06 Remington was a likely candidate, but similar to the .250; the 7x57mm was also considered.

But all in all, I figured a .270 Winchester would be as Goldilocks said, "just right," and housed in another M-77

it would be like old home week. Thus, the Woolco commercial seemed prescient.

There was some logic to this. In the 1970s Colorado had what they called the "combined season" in which both mule deer and elk could be hunted, with the appropriate licenses, of course. Deer were plentiful in those days, but there weren't nearly as many elk in Colorado then as there are now. Bull licenses were sold over-the-counter, but boy elk were few and far between. Licenses for cow elk and doe mule deer were awarded by drawing, so we both put in for licenses for both species in the drawing, figuring that would up our chances of getting at least one tag for the more numerous female ungulates. We were meat hunters, plain and simple.

Rosie took to the new .270 like a duck, well, you know the rest. She shot it very well, and it was pleasingly accurate. This, I later learned, was before Ruger started hammer-forging its barrels, and sometimes the accuracy of these guns was not terrific. Best of all, the .270's modest recoil didn't muss up Rosie's

locks – an important consideration. She used the .270 pretty much in box-stock condition, although the thin factory buttpad was replaced with a Pachymar No. 325 Deluxe, and the 4X Leupold scope purchased with the gun is still going strong.

Of course, since the .270 is a centerfire cartridge I had to reload for it, and for years Rosie depended on my handloads made with the inexpensive but excellent Speer 130-grain "pre-HotCor" softpoints over a charge of Hodgdon 4831. Velocity was barely 3,000 fps, but game hit with it

Rosie took this plump axis doe with her .270 and one round of Federal Premium 130-grain Trophy Bonded Tip in October 2013.

generally bit the dust. She used this load until we learned that it took a bonded, partitioned, or monolithic "boutique" bullet costing about a dollar apiece to slay a deer or elk.

With the new .270 in hand, a load selected and sighted in, it was on to elk hunting. For this, I handloaded the Nosler 150-grain Partition, and it too, worked just dandy. The .270's first elk, a cow, took one shot through the lungs and fell so fast that we momentarily lost sight of it in the sagebrush.

Then a seminal event in our hunting careers occurred. In the mid-1980s, we surrendered the corporate race to the rats and moved to a 34-acre parcel of riparian woodlands and rolling fields in southwestern Missouri, and white-tailed deer were literally in our front yard. We clung to our meat-hunting ways, so every November we hunted deer. I built each of us a ground blind at the edge of the woods along either side of the meandering creek that bisects our property. We figured it was easier to sit and wait for the deer to come to us than tramp around, making noise and scaring them off.

This has proven a sound strategy and in the ensuing decades we've harvested dozens of deer. Missouri regulations recognize that to control deer populations, you have to shoot does. So, in addition to our free landowner licenses, most years we'd buy an antlerless deer tag or two for a little extra meat. Consequently, Rosie's .270 has whacked quite a few deer. These whitetails grow fat and tasty on the local row crops, so wholesome meat has never been a problem.

Being a gun writer, I tend to use a different rifle every year; I have been known to even switch rifles between deer in the same season. But not Rosie. She says the .270 is all she wants or needs for her hunting.

When the opportunity to hunt hogs in Texas came up in 2009, we jumped at it. I don't remember what caliber I used, but I'll let you guess what the wife used. On that first hog hunt I didn't get anything,

Federal Premium .270 ammo loaded with the 130-grain Trophy Bonded Tip bullet delivers excellent expansion and penetration.

but a 200-pound boar walked out in front of Rosie's blind at about 80 yards. Big mistake. One shot, and four pig feet were pointed skyward. This pig, for the record, was taken with Winchester's then-new 130-grain XP3 factory load.

Next came exotics. As part of my job, I "had to" hunt axis deer in the Texas Hill Country a few years back. Since I drove to the hunt, I brought back several ice chests full of delectable meat. After tasting the axis deer Rosie decreed that we needed more! So now we make a safari for Texas exotics almost every year. On our 2013 foray we got a total of three axis. Mine were taken with .280 Remington handloads and an AR in 6.8 SPC with 120-grain Federal Fusion factory fodder, but by now you know what Rosie used; the only gun she ever uses – her battle-scarred M77 in .270. "If it ain't broke, don't fix it," is her motto. For this hunt she used Federal factory ammo loaded with the 130-grain Trophy Bonded Tip bullet, which has proven to be an excellent all-around big-game bullet.

The appearance of the M77 tells of its past. All sorts of mishaps in the field have resulted in numerous battle scars. Various tumbles, once on a Colorado mountain, and a couple more in Missouri, have resulted in some choice dings in the stock. One time in Texas the front

This 130-grain Trophy Bonded Tip bullet was recovered from a Texas axis deer. Penetration was 19 inches, and the deer dropped instantly.

sling swivel came loose from its stud and the .270's barrel crashed ignominiously onto a granite boulder, putting a scratch in the bluing. But none of this affects its functionality, and the old M77 continues to put game on the table.

In the past when I was feeling particularly brave, I used to suggest to Rosie that she trade the old .270 off on a new one. Before she realized that I was only kidding, such shenanigans produced "the look," well known to all married men.

The popularity of the .270 Winchester seems never to waver, and I expect that this vintage Ruger M77 will continue to serve Rosie as a game-getter for years to come. Thank goodness for a simple ad on the car radio all those years ago.

References

1. *Ruger Model 77 Bolt Action Rifles*, by Ronnie Burke, 1983. Taylor Publishing Co., Dallas, Texas, 100 pp.

2. *Ruger & His Guns*, by R. L. Wilson, 1996. Simon & Schuster, New York, New York, 358 pp.

3. "New Ruger Rifles – Model 77 Bolt Action," by John T. Amber, 1968. *Gun Digest*, 23rd (1969) Edition. The Gun Digest Co., Chicago, Illinois, pp. 79-82.

4. "Testfire Report, The Ruger Model 77 Rifle", by Bob Wallack, 1969. *Gun Digest*, 24th (1970) Edition, The Gun Digest Co., Chicago, Illinois, pp. 178-179.

5. "The Model 77 Ruger Rifle," by Daniel Peterson, 1978. *Gun Digest*, 33rd (1979) Edition, The Gun Digest Co., Chicago, Illinois, pp. 140-145, 312.

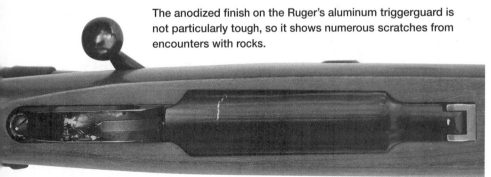

The anodized finish on the Ruger's aluminum triggerguard is not particularly tough, so it shows numerous scratches from encounters with rocks.

BROWNING MODEL 12

BY **Brad Fitzpatrick**

The author used his Browning Model 12 28 gauge to take this Ohio pheasant. Model 12s have been used for upland hunting for over a century, and the Browning version performs just as well as the original.

A near-perfect clone of the "Perfect Repeater."

inchester's Model 1912, later to become known worldwide as the Model 12, was the first commercially successful internal-hammer repeating shotgun, and we owe much of what we believe about shotguns today to this early model. The Model 12 was not, contrary to popular opinion, designed by John Moses Browning, though his work on the Model 97 pre-dated the Model 12 and certainly many of the design elements on the Model 12 trace their lineage back to Browning's exposed-hammer 1897 repeater. Browning would later design shotguns that would bear his name as well as Remington, Ithaca and others. But of

the handful of great guns that appeared in the early 1900s that Browning didn't have a direct hand in, the Model 12 was the most successful.

The original Winchester Model 12 was first introduced in a 20-gauge model with a six-round magazine tube located under the barrel. The receiver is rounded and has a port on the side for loading and ejecting spent shells, and a crossbolt safety is located just ahead of the trigger. If that layout sounds familiar it's because the current design of most pump-action repeating shotguns was based, at least in part, on the lines and styling of the original Model 12. Versions in 12 and 16 gauge would come later, as would a 28 gauge. A scaled-down model, the

42, was designed to accommodate .410 shotshells.

Besides being the favorite field gun of many hunters, the Model 12 would also become a military and law-enforcement weapon, as the Perfect Repeater saw service in both World Wars and was the shotgun of choice for many law-enforcement agencies. The Model 12 seemed ubiquitous; it helped us harvest game for the freezer, protect our nation's streets and our own interests in the trenches of war, as American a product as the Ford sedan or Coca-Cola. But that was about to change.

Everyone who knows the Winchester story remembers the year 1964. By that time, Winchester had realized that other companies, namely Remington, had developed a process by which they could produce guns at a lower cost. This involved making some serious changes to Winchester's traditional formula, primarily dumping the Model 12 in favor of the lighter, cheaper Model 1200 pump with its aluminum receiver and stamped parts. Costs went down, but so did consumer interest. Winchester had always stood for build quality and durability, and consumers were willing to pay a little more for that. When Winchester cheapened their shotguns, the backlash was immediate and powerful. Jack O'Connor and other writers lamented over the cheapening of one of America's favorite gun brands, and sales started to slip. Demand for pre-'64 guns, both rifles and shotguns, rose quickly, as did the prices.

Many American shooters saw the end of production of Winchester's Model 12 and the original Model 70 as the end of quality gunmaking in America, and as a kid I grew up listening to those stories. And while America didn't suddenly quit making good guns, the end of the Model 12's production did signal a shift in the way that guns were produced, and that evolution continues today. But for the Model 12, mass production had indeed ended.

That's not to say that Model 12 production stopped. It slowed, sure, but Winchester's brass realized that by ending large-scale production of the gun, they had dramatically increased demand for the small-scale production versions of the Model 12 that would later be built by U.S. Repeating Arms and Miroku of Japan. Trap and skeet grades were produced, as were pigeon-grade guns with embellishments that seemed out of place on a gun that had earned its reputation in war and in the bottom of duck boats. Over the course of the years, Winchester or Browning produced guns built on the old Model 12 patent in one variation or another, and when these guns came to market demand was high.

As a kid fresh out of college, I attended an auction where the guns that had belonged to one of my shooting mentors, the late Harry Huber, were to be sold. Harry was an accomplished marksman, a competitive bull's-eye shooter and a regular at the Grand American, and he had one of the largest collections of Winchester and Browning guns I've ever seen. One of the guns that interested me most was an original 28-gauge Model 12, a gun that I had only seen once and admired for years. I was broke, as I was

for much of the first few years I was working, and I waited patiently for the gun to come up for bid. I hoped that the crowd wouldn't pounce on it, but the opening bid was double what I could afford to pay. When it sold I was in shock. The gun brought more than any of the other firearms at the auction.

In the late 2000s I stumbled upon a Browning-label Model 12 28 gauge, a gun that looked very much like the one that had slipped away from me at that auction. In fact, the Browning version was actually in better shape than Harry's gun (Huber didn't believe in locking guns in a safe, gold inlays, limited editions, exhibition walnut; they all went to the field). The Browning was a clone of the Model 12, identical to the original except for a few minor cosmetic differences. Best of all was the price. The Browning version was for sale for less than $600, which hooked me. I bought the gun and took it home, certain that the internal workings were made of tinfoil or that the barrel would fall off after the first hunt.

The Browning Model 12 was available in two gauges (20 and 28) and two grades (I and IV), and was built for Browning by Miroku of Japan in the early 1990s. Both the 20 and 28-gauge

An original 12-gauge Winchester Model 12 is shown above the Browning 28-gauge version. The guns are very similar both mechanically and aesthetically, with the primary cosmetic difference being the larger forearm on the Browning model.

From a distance, the Browning Model 12 looks very much like the original Winchester version. The steel receiver is precisely machined, and fit and finish are excellent, as good as the original.

The Browning Model 12 is short enough and light enough to be used on a variety of upland game, and for those who like to shoot skeet and sporting clays with a subgauge pump, it's as good as anything currently available.

versions had fixed modified chokes, and both had 26-inch vent rib barrels. The Grade I gun, which looked most like the field version of the Model 12, differed cosmetically in that it had higher grade wood, a grip cap and a larger checkered forearm – as opposed to the original Winchester field versions that had small forearms with a circular pattern. Internally, Browning/Miroku did away with the trigger disconnect feature that allowed the trigger to be held while the gun was cycled for continuous firing, the pin striking the primer with each successive stroke of the forearm. Other than that, the gun was very similar to the original Model 12, with a solid steel receiver and a barrel that was removed by pressing a plunger and rotating the barrel so that it released from a series of interrupted threads in the receiver.

The Browning Model 12 gained a lot of attention everywhere I carried it, first to the skeet club where someone asked me where I'd gotten the gun and why I was breaking clays with it on a snowy day. The Model 12 Browning handled nicely, and the large, simple brass bead on the front was both classy and functional. Cycling was smooth and solid, and when I did my part it shattered the 108mm targets.

The Browning version is a gun that begs to be taken afield, and it remains my favorite upland hunting gun to this

The steel carrier is designed like the Winchester version, and the small cutout makes it easy to load the magazine.

Above: The Browning Model 12 has a crossbolt safety in front of the triggerguard, true to the original design. However, it doesn't have the trigger disconnect that allows the shooter to pump and fire repeatedly with the trigger depressed.

Top Right: The Browning Model 12 28-gauge (below) has a grip cap, a nice touch that offsets the excellent walnut stock. The gun shown below is the Grade I version; the Grade IV has even better wood and costs a few hundred dollars more.

Right: The Browning Model 12 shares the Winchester's original barrel release system. Simply depress the button, rotate in the receiver, and the interrupted threads allow for the barrel to be removed easily for cleaning and maintenance.

Far Right: The Browning Model 12 comes with a single brass bead and a fixed modified choke. The 26-inch barrel gives the gun excellent balance and is short enough to carry in dense cover.

Today's crop of excellent 28-gauge upland loads makes subgauge guns more effective than ever, and the Browning Model 12 is a classy repeater that works well in the field. In addition, they cost far less than original 28-gauge Model 12s.

day. It's perfect for shooting quail, and it is my go-to rabbit gun, light and easy to shoulder and shoot. Best of all, it costs less than many new pump guns and has a look and feel that hasn't been available in mass-produced shotguns in over 50 years. The steel construction of the original Model 12 Winchesters made them stout, durable guns, but they were also heavy, and the 6½-pound Browning Model 12 is just right for long days afield.

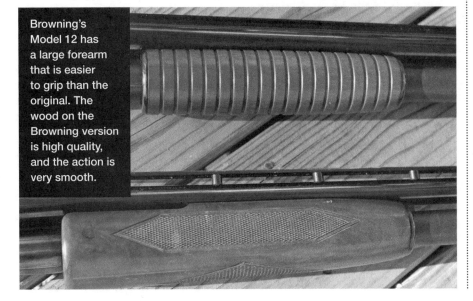

Browning's Model 12 has a large forearm that is easier to grip than the original. The wood on the Browning version is high quality, and the action is very smooth.

In addition, the rise in popularity of 28-gauge guns has made it possible to purchase a variety of different ammo types, so I can shoot light target loads and magnum loads for the field, both of which are readily available. The fit and finish are excellent, and the gun looks good and shoots great.

Today, Browning Model 12s are available from time to time on the used gun market, and if you're willing to do some

searching it's still possible to find one at a reasonable price. For Grade I 28-gauge guns, the costs range from about $500 to $900 dollars for guns in good condition, and the 20-gauge version is available for about the same money, perhaps a bit less. If you step up to the Grade IV version, which has gold-inlaid game scenes and upgraded wood, the price quickly will climb above $1,000. These are excellent guns, and it's nice to be able to carry a gun that has that classic look and feel without the high price tag of the original. (Original Winchester 28-gauge Model 12s in very good to excellent condition command prices of $6,000 or more. –Editor)

The original Model 12 is an iconic firearm that sold well because it was so well designed and solidly built. The Browning Model 12 has those same qualities, and it's more readily available and more affordable. If you like the classic look and feel of the subgauge Model 12 but can't stand the high price, spend some time in search of one of the Browning models. They're still out there, but they're becoming harder to find. I'm thrilled to have the one that I own and you can be sure that if I happen to come across another I'll own that one as well.

Alexander Arms
6.5 Grendel Hunter

BY **Steve Gash**

TEST FIRE

The new Grendel Hunter is the latest sophistication of the high-quality ARs from Alexander Arms. It is decked out with features that make it an ideal modern sporting rifle for medium-sized big game. The new Highlander camo finish is from Kryptek.

The 6.5 Grendel is one of the more purposefully designed accuracy cartridges to ever come down the pike. So when an equally unique rifle for it comes along, accuracy-minded shooters sit up and take notice. New for 2014 is the "Grendel Hunter" from Alexander Arms, an AR with attitude, and the results to back it up.

The 6.5 Grendel cartridge itself is equally impressive. Its goals were simple yet heretofore elusive in all but a few contemporary rounds, i.e., the .22 and 6PPC and similar wildcats. In fact, the 6.5 Grendel can trace its lineage to some of these outstanding cartridges. It was designed from the ground up to provide the optimum combination of power, efficiency and accuracy in America's "modern sporting rifle" – the AR-15. To this end, it has succeeded remarkably.

While the Grendel has been used successfully for hunting a large variety of medium-sized big game and varmints, there was no specific hunting model until now, with the release of the Grendel Hunter model from Alexander Arms (www.alexanderarms.com). The company is headed up by the inimitable Bill Alexander, and is located at the U.S. Army Arsenal in Radford, Va. Bill Alexander is a multitalented engineer who had worked for the British Ministry of Defense.

I caught up with him at a recent industry gig, and talked with him at length about the trials and tribulations that led to the 6.5mm Grendel Hunter. I love talking to Bill because you can't help but learn a bunch of neat, new information.

Bill is one of those people who's so smart it's scary. As he expounds on firearm design, ballistics and especially the 6.5 Grendel, you can almost hear the wheels whirling in his head at a hundred miles an hour, and his enthusiasm and passion are infectious.

When the Cold War ended, Bill said he "turned his attention to ARs. They are great rifles." But he added that he wanted to "make the AR a little more versatile." He saw the need for a flat-shooting, hard-hitting cartridge that would broaden the horizon of the AR rifle, and the Grendel was the result. Bill told me, "I designed the 6.5 Grendel specifically as a hunting cartridge."

Alexander Arms ARs have always been made with the care and precision that result in high-quality guns. There

No sights come on the Grendel Hunter, but its flattop receiver makes the mounting of optics or backup iron sights a snap. The new Leupold VX-6 4-24x52 scope was perfect for wringing out the last drop of accuracy from the AR, and Talley's Tactical 34mm Black Armor rings were rock solid.

isn't much really all that new in the Grendel Hunter except for the finish and, of course, the 6.5 Grendel chambering. Alexander Arms has offered various versions of its ARs chambered for the Grendel since its introduction at the 2004 SHOT Show, and this is the latest iteration.

The fluted 18-inch, stainless steel barrel is matte black, and has six grooves with a right-hand twist of one turn in 8 inches – steep enough for the heaviest bullets that can realistically be launched out of the modest-sized Grendel case. Although the rifle does not come equipped with a muzzle brake or flash hider, the muzzle has 9/16-24 threads so that accessories can be added, if desired, and a thread protector comes as standard.

The handle is a comfortable Ergo Grip, and the collapsible B5 stock allows length-of-pull adjustment from

12½ to 14½ inches; handy when shooting from awkward positions, in heavy winter clothing or at steep angles from a coyote set.

The single-stage trigger is Alexander Arm's Tactical style with skeletonized hammer and disconnector. Pull weight on my test rifle was five pounds, six ounces. Alexander Arms says it's "glass rod" crisp, and they aren't kidding. The flattop receiver is festooned with plenty of M-1913 Picatinny rail slots for the attachment of optics or a rear sight. Provision for a front sight is a MK10 Plus rail section atop the 12½-inch cylindrical, free-floated handguard; three additional attachment

points are spaced around the front of the handguard at 90-degree intervals.

Without sights, the new model weighs in at a comfortable six pounds, nine ounces; with the addition of a relatively lightweight scope, it would easily come in at under eight pounds. The fat, 34mm Leupold VX-6 4-24x52mm scope I used for testing brought the weight to a little under nine pounds. Admittedly, this su-

The Hunter's trigger is what Alexander Arms calls the Tactical Blade Trigger. It broke at five pounds, six ounces, and was as crisp as could be.

The caliber is marked below the Alexander Arms crest on the left side of the receiver. Controls are in the familiar places.

perlative scope was a bit of overkill, but it is certainly high on the "wow" factor.

Probably the coolest feature of this new AR is the finish. It is a camo pattern called Kryptek Highlander, and is very attractive and would look right at home in the field.

For my money, though, the *pièce de résistance* of this outfit is the 6.5 Grendel cartridge itself. This was no haphazard development, and its circuitous history illustrates the amount of thought and experimentation that went into its design. It took many years, but the result is well worth it. Here's a brief chronology.

In 1943, the Russian 7.62x39 was developed for their military. Never content, in the late 1950s, the Russians necked down that round to hold a 5.67mm (.223 inch) bullet for deer hunting, and they called it the .220 Russian.

In 1975, Dr. Louis Palmisano and gunsmith Ferris Pendell developed a .22 caliber target round based on the .220 Russian, and called it the .22 PPC (Pendell Palmisano Cartridge). It went on to achieve phenomenal success in the benchrest game.

Magazines with followers for the 6.5 Grendel are of steel. One 10-round magazine comes standard, with four- and 26-round magazines also available from Alexander Arms.

In 1984, Dr. Palmisano and noted ballistician Bill Davis developed the 6.5 PPC cartridge, also based on the .220 Russian case. This was for use in bolt-action guns by the U.S. Shooting Team in the 1986 World Championships. While the performance of the new round was fine, the team stuck with the 6mm cartridge they were already using at the time.

The 6 PPC, a necked-up version of the .22 PPC, came along in 1988 and has rightfully earned the reputation of "the most accurate cartridge in the

world." Also in 1988, a noted competition shooter, Arne Brennan, started experimenting with the 6.5 PPC, and in 2000, discussed his results with Dr. Palmisano. Brennan has written extensively and authoritatively on the Grendel.

About this time, Bill Alexander became interested in the cartridge. This wasn't his first rodeo, as he had designed several unique cartridges, and the 6.5 Grendel was merely his latest brainchild.

When Bill turned his attention to ARs, he tweaked the case of a cartridge

6.5 Grendel Factory Loads

Factory Load	Bullet Wt. (grains)	Vel	ES (fps)	SD (fps)	COV (%)	Group (mm)	Accuracy (MOA)	M.E. (ft-lb.)
Alex. Arms. Berger HPBT	100	2,704	19	7	0.26	9.0	0.68	1,624
Alex. Arms. TS-X	120	2,457	35	13	0.53	19.5	1.47	1,609
Wolf Gold HPBT	120	2,392	40	10	0.42	10.5	1.07	1,525
Hornady SST	123	2,429	19	7	0.29	9.0	0.68	1,612
Alex. Arms. Hor. SST	129	2,308	53	22	0.95	23.5	1.77	1,526
Alex. Arms. Scirocco	130	2,258	35	16	0.71	22.0	1.65	1,472
						Ave.	1.22	1,561.3

of known accuracy, the 6PPC or 6mm PPC. He necked it up 6.5mm, shortened the neck a bit, and moved the shoulder forward. This increased the powder capacity just enough to increase hunting-weight bullet velocity and downrange punch. Bill also thickened the neck to increase case life in the rough and tumble world of the semiauto rifle. The contributions of Lapua engineer Janne Pohjoispää around 2003 were significant here, too. The end result was the introduction at the 2004 SHOT Show of the 6.5 Grendel cartridge and rifles to shoot it.

It is interesting to note that the name "Grendel" was initially a trademarked cartridge, which precluded it from being produced by any other company and significantly, from being considered by the Sporting Arms and Ammunition Manufacturers' Institute (S.A.A.M.I.) for approval as a factory round. In 2010, Hornady obtained a licensing agreement with Alexander Arms, and began making ammunition and reloading dies. Alexander Arms subsequently released its trademark and Hornady submitted the round to S.A.A.M.I., also in 2010. Final approval was granted June 12, 2012, and the Grendel was off and running. Maximum Average Pressure (MAP) was set at 52K psi; now any company could make Grendel products.

The name Grendel is from the epic Anglo-Saxon poem Beowulf (circa 700-1000 A.D.). As the story goes, the mythical monster Grendel had been ravaging the mead-hall of Herot, killing and eating anyone he finds there. The vicious Grendel is feared by all, except Beowulf, who is not about to take any grief from Grendel, and sets out to destroy him. Finally, Beowulf succeeds in killing Grendel by ripping his arm off. After also

killing Grendel's mother, Beowulf finds Grendel's corpse, and removes his head as a trophy. (Whether or not the head was mounted is not known.) It is perhaps only logical that one of Bill's other cartridges is the ponderous .50 Beowulf.

While metric calibers have never been very popular in the States, the 6.5mm caliber has had an enviable reputation as a game getter for years. The high sectional densities and modest velocities of the long-for-caliber bullets from most 6.5mm rounds result in deep penetration and reliable expansion, without bullet blow-up.

Hunting history is rife with the tales of derring-do with 6.5mm cartridges. W.D.M. Bell whacked many elephants and Werner von Alvensleben slew hundreds of buffalo with what they termed a "small-bore rifle," namely, the 6.5x54 Mannlicher-Schönauer. African hunter John Taylor noted in his 1948 tome *African Rifles and Cartridges* that the 160-grain 6.5mm bullet had about the best diameter-to-weight ratio of any game bullet, although Taylor wasn't a big fan of the 6.5 on larger African game. Today, the 6.5mm is well represented in the cartridge lineup, with the 6.5 Creed-

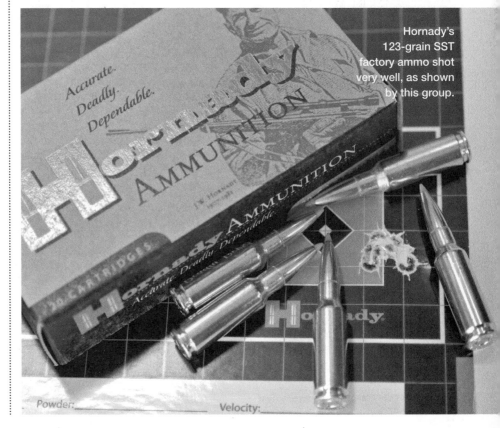

Hornady's 123-grain SST factory ammo shot very well, as shown by this group.

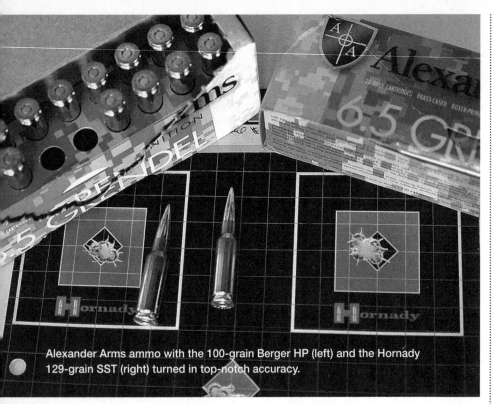

Alexander Arms ammo with the 100-grain Berger HP (left) and the Hornady 129-grain SST (right) turned in top-notch accuracy.

are: 120-grain TS-X (2,457 fps, 1.47 MOA), 129-grain Hornady SST (2,308 fps, 1.77 MOA) and 130-grain Scirocco (2,258 fps, 1.65 MOA).

Finally, for "blasting ammo," Wolf's 120-grain HPBT load from (where else?) Russia, is only $15.99 a box from Alexander Arms, MidwayUSA and other sources. This ammo is brass-cased and Boxer-primed, but the brass is pretty soft and really not suitable for reloading. In the Grendel AR, it registered 2,392 fps and shot a respectable 1.07 MOA average. All of the factory load data are shown in the accompanying table.

Handloading the Grendel is where the fun starts. Most manufacturers of reloading tools make reloading dies, and Alexander Arms offers them, too. With the number of powders and high-tech bullets available, it is easy to tailor ammo for benchrest competition, long-range targets, plinking, varmints and big game.

Frankly, load development in the Grendel is mundane. About the only requirements are a primer in one end of the case, a bullet in the other and a safe powder charge in between. That's about it. It's downright difficult to find a load that won't shoot like gangbusters in the Grendel. The famous PPC case shape, a good barrel, the inherent accuracy of the AR platform and today's quality components all add up to fine performance.

The 6.5 Grendel case takes small rifle primers, and standard caps are all that are required. New cases are available from Alexander Arms, Hornady and Nosler. Alexander Arms cases are made by Lapua, and have the PPC-sized small flash hole, thought to be a component in the PPC accuracy equation.

moor, .260 Remington, 6.5-284 Norma, .264 Winchester Magnum and the brand new .26 Nosler, to name a few.

Factory ammo for the Grendel is relatively plentiful these days. Hornady offers two loads with 123-grain bullets, the A-MAX and SST. I was unable to locate the A-MAX load, but I shot the SST version. It is catalogued at 2,620 fps, clocked 2,429 fps out of the AR's 18-inch barrel, and accuracy averaged a delightful .68 MOA. Hornady's ballistic wizard, Dave Emary, told me that this SST is specifically designed for small- to mid-sized big game, such as antelope or white-tailed deer.

Alexander Arms itself lists five excellent factory loads in its catalog. Bullets are the Hornady 129-grain SST, 123-grain Lapua Scenar, Barnes' 120-grain TS-X, the Nosler 120-grain Ballistic Tip and Swift's 130-grain Scirocco. Although not listed in their 2013 catalog, I shot some Alexander Arms ammo loaded with the Berger 100-grain HPBT bullet. It was the fastest load tested at 2,704 fps, and grouped into .68 MOA. Specs on three additional Alexander Arms loads tested

6.5 Grendel Demonstration Loads

Bullet	Weight (gr.)	Case	Primer	Powder (Type)	Powder (Grs.)	Average Velocity (fps)	Extreme Spread (fps)	Standard Deviation (fps)	ME (ft-lbs)	COL (inches)	Accuracy (MOA)
Nosler Ballistic Tip	100	Hor.	CCI-450	Benchmark	29.0	2,576	38	13	1,474	2.250	0.86
Nosler Partition	100	Alex. A.	F-205	IMR-8208XBR	30.5	2,690	12	6	1,607	2.153	0.94
Nosler Ballistic Tip	120	Hor.	F-205	CFE-223	31.2	2,444	24	12	1,592	2.247	0.99
Hornady SST	123	Hor.	F-205	IMR-8208XBR	28.5	2,419	14	7	1,599	2.240	0.74
Nosler Partition	125	Alex. A.	F-205	CFE-223	30.7	2,385	20	11	1,579	2.229	0.61
Sierra Spitzer	120	Hor.	F-205	AR-Comp	27.0	2,478	20	10	1,637	2.216	1.03
Sierra HPBT GK	130	Hor.	F-205	Norma N-201	31.0	2,374	15	8	1,627	2.112	1.02

NOTES: An Alexander Arms Grendel Hunter AR with an 18-inch barrel and an 8-inch twist was used for all testing. Sight was a Leupold VX-6 4-24 set at 10x. Velocity is at 10 feet. Accuracy is the average of three, five-shot groups at 100 yards from a bench rest. Range temperatures were 55 to 63 degrees F.

ABBREVIATIONS: Abbreviations: SST, Super Shock Tip; COL, Cartridge Overall Length; HPBT GK, Hollow Point Boat Tail Game King.

Load data are readily available in most contemporary loading manuals, and the comprehensive two-volume set of *6.5 Grendel Reloading Handbooks* by Joseph Smith, Paul Scott and Gregory Luli (see references) is a must for all 6.5 Grendel reloaders.

I tested over 40 handloads in the AR, and the average accuracy of all of them was 1.19 MOA; the best 25 percent averaged .76 MOA and for the top 50 percent, it was .87 MOA. Those results are no fluke.

The load table shows just the best loads for seven bullets that demonstrate the superb accuracy of the 6.5 Grendel that the reloader can use as a starting

Alexander Arms Grendel Hunter AR15 Specifications

Model: Grendel Hunter AR15

Type: Direct gas impingement semiautomatic AR-15

Caliber: 6.5 Grendel

Capacity: One 10-round magazine supplied, 4- and 26-round magazines available

Barrel: 18-inch fluted stainless steel, six-grooves, 8-inch twist; muzzle threaded 9/16-24, thread protector provided

Overall length: 36¾ inches

Weight: 6 pounds, 9 ounces (with empty 10-round magazine); 8 pounds, 10½ ounces (with scope and mount, as tested)

Trigger: Blade-type Tactical single-stage trigger, weight of pull 5 pounds, 6 ounces, skeletonized trigger, hammer and disconnector

Sights: None. Flattop receiver standard scope/optic mounts. Leupold VX-6 4-24x52 CDS 34mm scope with T-MOA Reticle (as tested)

Scope Mount: Talley Tactical 34mm Black Armor Rings (as tested)

Finish: Matte black finish on barrel, Kryptek Highlander camo pattern on upper, lower and stock, black Ergo Grip

Handguard: Free-floated 12.5-inch, one MK10 Plus Rail section, four attachment points for additional rails

Stock: Adjustable for length of pull (12½ to 14½ inches)

MSRP: TBD

Maker: Alexander Arms, P.O. Box 1, Radford Arsenal, Radford, VA 24143, 540-639-8356, (alexanderarms.com)

The Grendel Hunter loaded with the Hornady 123-grain SST is perfectly matched for game such as this 132-pound 10-point Missouri whitetail buck.

point for a big-game load. In fact, I am going to pick one of these loads for an upcoming exotic sheep hunt in Texas.

The best powders in my tests were IMR-8208XBR, CFE-223 and Norma N-201. Bullet standouts were the Nosler Partitions and the Hornady SST. Because of the limited capacity of the Grendel case, about the heaviest bullets that are practical weigh 100 to 123 grains. The 129- and 130-grain bullets just take up too much case volume, preventing adequate charges for reasonable velocities. The same goes for the longer lead-free bullets, too. I apologize for not testing the many other great game bullets, such as the Barnes TS-X, Swift Scirocco, but there is only so much light in a day.

These test results pretty much demonstrate why the 6.5 Grendel is firmly established as a super-accurate cartridge. With the addition of the Alexander Arms Grendel Hunter rifle, more hunters can take to the field with what may well be the optimum combination of power, portability, ballistic efficiency and pinpoint accuracy.

REFERENCES

Cartridges of the World, 9th Edition, 1965. pp. 23 and 28.

6.5mm Grendel, Wikipedia.org/w/index. php?title=6.5mm_Grendel.

.220 Russian, Wikipedia.org/wiki/.220_Russian

"6.5 Grendel," by J. Guthrie 2010. Shootingillustrated.com/index.php/1759/6-5-grendel.

6.5 Grendel – Origins and Performance, by Arne Brennan, 2005. 6mmbr.com/65grendel.html/

African Rifles and Cartridges, by John Taylor, 1948. p. 180.

Nosler Reloading Guide, No. 7, 2012. pp. 120, 167, and 240.

Speer Reloading Manual, No. 14, 2007, p. 239.

"6.5 Grendel," by Brian Pearce, *Rifle Magazine AR Special Edition*, Fall, 2013, pp. 46-53.

"Handloading Allows the 6.5 Grendel to Shine," by Lane Pearce. *Shooting Times*, March 2014, pp. 20-22.

6.5 Grendel Reloading Handbook, Vols. I and II, by Joseph A. Smith, Paul Scott, and Gregory Luli, 2013, 56 and 98 pp. Go to "ShootersNotes.com" or the "ar15buildbox" home page for ordering info. Also from Alexander Arms or American Build Box, 10308 Leilani Dr., Sandy, UT 84070.

TEST FIRE

Finally, after all these years, a GLOCK .380

BY Al Doyle

The annual SHOT Show ranks among the largest trade conventions in America. Imagine a week full of guns, gear and gun people, and you have a typical SHOT experience. A select few firearms emerge as up and coming stars every January in the wake of their popularity at SHOT, the industry's Shooting Hunting and Outdoor Trade Show.

The hot item of this year's event weighs less than a pound, and it's quite different than anything else in the company's product line. The Glock 42 in .380 ACP is the firm's first attempt at a pocket pistol, and it's also the first American-made Glock. In a category where minimal weight has become the Holy Grail, this 13.76-ounce package could seem chunky to people who like anorexic pistols.

That might be hilarious to those who carry Model 1911s or Beretta 92s on a

regular basis, but fractions of inches and single ounces count for much in the pocket pistol game. Someone who owns a Rottweiler could care less about the difference between a six-pound toy poodle and a 4.7-pound Chihuahua, but dinky-dog specialists would call it an issue. Likewise, a few ounces on a modern .380 can be a big deal.

First impressions count for much, and the Glock 42's grip and balance scored high in that department. Those who handled the 42 immediately remarked on how well the gun pointed and especially how well it filled the hand. Anyone with hands in the small to medium-large range shouldn't have any problems with getting a comfortable hold – something

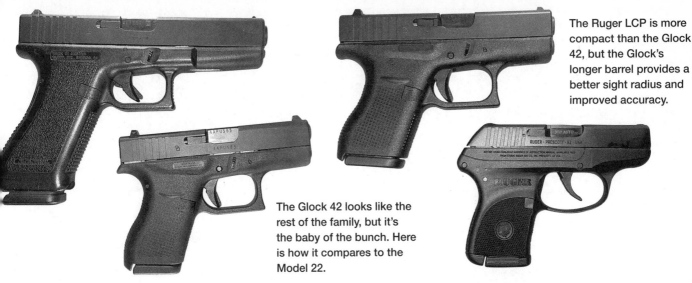

The Ruger LCP is more compact than the Glock 42, but the Glock's longer barrel provides a better sight radius and improved accuracy.

The Glock 42 looks like the rest of the family, but it's the baby of the bunch. Here is how it compares to the Model 22.

that can't be said for many of the currently produced small pistols.

A 10.2-ounce Taurus 738 in an Uncle Mike's pocket holster slips unobtrusively into my front pocket, but the bulge from a Glock 42 is less discreet. What a difference 3.56 ounces can make. There are definitely lighter options in 6+1 capacity .380 ACPs. The Ruger LCP tips the scales at 9.42 ounces, while the Diamondback DB380SC comes in at 8.8 ounces and the Kel-Tec P3AT is even scrawnier at 8.3 ounces. Perhaps the closest thing to a direct comparison is the 12.5-ounce aluminum-frame version of the Colt Mustang.

So why tote a Glock 42 when it means more planning (or possibly an inside-the-waistband holster) to carry than the

competition? Well, guns are made for shooting and this sample came through on the range. The little Glock was cutting nice groups from its first round out of the box.

Trying different brands of ammunition is an absolute must, as the TulAmmo Brass Maxx .380 ACP that shot flawlessly and accurately in the aforementioned Taurus 738 often jammed in the 42. A switch to Prvi Partizan, CCI aluminum-cased Blazers and Winchester .380s resulted in trouble-free ejection, two-inch groups at 25 feet and punching cardboard with ease.

As one gun-savvy tester put it, "I'm not a Glock guy, but I really like the 42. It's not something you would want to use

at 40 yards, but this is a very accurate pistol. It shoots to point of aim." A local farmer who dropped in on this test fire session was pounding out the center of the target after taking just a few rounds to sight in.

What about the ultimate test for a small pistol? The Glock 42 never stuttered on Winchester 95-grain PDX1 Defender hollowpoints. Accuracy was comparable to what was obtained with roundnose ammo. Why was the 42 so accurate? It's those extra ounces and fractions of inches. The 3.25-inch barrel is longer than most other small .380s. Combine that longer radius with typical Glock sights as compared to what sits on the slides of other pocket pistols, and a person might be willing to tote a bit more weight rather than go for the ultimate in concealability.

Pocket pistols are usually carried for dealing with up close and personal encounters of the dangerous kind. When the goon is only feet or inches away, the idea of a proper two-handed stance and deliberately sighting in becomes ludicrous. In such situations, a quick one-handed draw and fire is often the only option. Glock's dual-action recoil springs, combined with the mild-mannered .380 ACP brings the 42's recoil down to minimal levels. Follow-up shots definitely aren't a problem.

Is there a more memorable way to describe the 42's polite handling? I was also playing around with an Italian-made .38 Special single-action revolver after testing the little Glock. A box of cast reloads for Cowboy Action practice was labeled "2.0 grains Bullseye – mouse farts." The Glock 42 kicks like a mouse fart, and the MSRP of $480 doesn't stink.

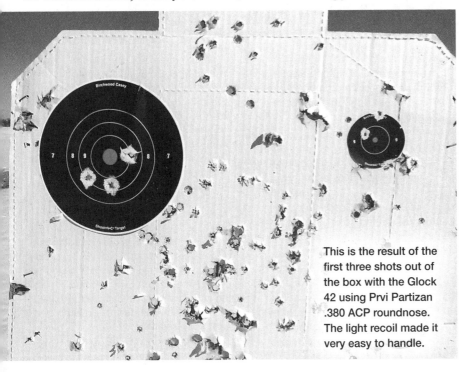

This is the result of the first three shots out of the box with the Glock 42 using Prvi Partizan .380 ACP roundnose. The light recoil made it very easy to handle.

A .44 WCF
Lever-Action Rifle from
Henry Repeating Arms.

A NEW "ORIGINAL HENRY"

BY Jeff Quinn

When Oliver Winchester took over control of the Volcanic Arms Company in late 1856, he moved the operation to New Haven, Conn. He did two things that would change the history of firearms in the world. He changed the name of the company to The New Haven Arms Company, and he hired Benjamin Tyler Henry as his shop foreman. Henry went to work on improving the Volcanic design to fire a .44-caliber rimfire cartridge, and the Henry Rifle was born.

I can imagine that had this occurred today, some politician would go on a rampage about, "why does anyone need 16 cartridges in the magazine?" But thankfully, people were smarter 154 years ago than they appear to be today. The Henry was a real game changer. There were other repeating rifles and carbines introduced about the same time, such as the Spencer, which was built in much higher numbers and adopted by the Union Army, but it had a lower capacity and a slower rate of fire.

The Henry was never officially adopted by the Union, but many of them were purchased by well-financed individual soldiers, and a few units had several in their possession during the war. The Confederates referred to the Henry as, "That damn Yankee rifle that you load on Sunday and shoot all week."

The Henry was the AR-15 of its day. It was expensive to make and expensive to purchase, but was revolutionary in its rate of sustained fire compared to the muzzleloading muskets in use by both armies during The War Between the States.

The Henry also played a significant role in the settling of the American West following the war. For those who could afford one, it offered a lot of firepower compared to other readily available weapons, even the much more prevalent Spencer war surplus carbines and rifles. Along with other Winchester lever guns the Henry played a role in the defeat of Custer's 7th Calvary at the Battle of the Little Big Horn in June of 1876. By that time Winchester rifles had been upgraded with King's patents for an improved magazine and the addition of a loading gate, but the Henry still served well on the battlefield in the hands of the American Indians, as it continued to also do with farmers, ranchers and others who headed West during the latter part of the 19th century.

The Henry is one of the most highly prized and sought-after rifles for well-

The author found that the Henry balances well, just ahead of the receiver, and comes to the shoulder quickly.

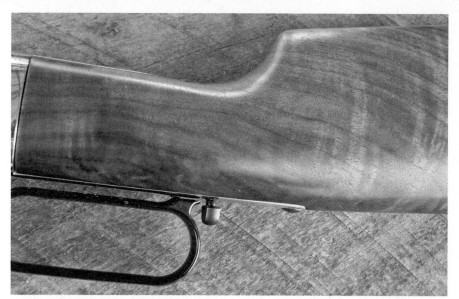

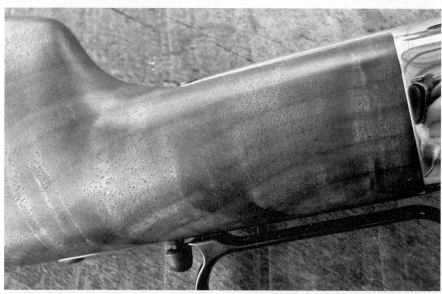

heeled firearms collectors today, with original rifles selling for many thousands of dollars. Italian replicas of the Henry have been available from importers in the United States for a long time now, but after an absence of 148 years the Henry is once again being built in the USA by the company that bears the Henry name; the Henry Repeating Arms Company of Bayonne, N.J.

While the original Henry was chambered for the .44 Henry Rimfire cartridge, which used a 216-grain bullet (pointed or flatnose) loaded over 25 to 26 grains of black powder, that cartridge is long out of production. The new Original Henry rifle is chambered for the .44 WCF centerfire cartridge (.44-40), with only the mechanical changes needed to fire the newer cartridge.

The .44 WCF was introduced by Winchester along with the 1873 Winchester rifle and has endured the test of time, being popular for many years as both a rifle and handgun cartridge. Most ammunition sellers today list the .44 WCF as a handgun cartridge, and it is frustrating to look online for the ammunition listed under rifle cartridges – where it should be – but it is usually listed under the handgun ammunition sections. However, the .44 WCF was introduced in 1873 as a rifle cartridge, and it will always be a

The new Original Henry wears a beautiful American walnut stock with a nicely fitted, polished brass buttplate.

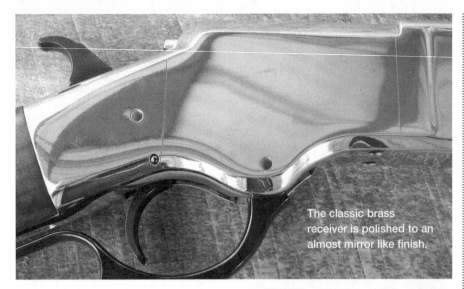

The classic brass receiver is polished to an almost mirror like finish.

Right: The folding rear sight is graduated for engaging targets at extended ranges.

Below: A barrelband front sight base adds to the rifle's authentic design.

The brass breechblock smoothly lifts the cartridges into alignment for loading into the chamber.

rifle cartridge, even though it works well when fired from a revolver.

The Henry Repeating Arms Company has been around for several years now, initially in Brooklyn, N.Y., and now in Bayonne, N.J., with another manufacturing facility in Wisconsin. For their first few years they focused on building some smooth-running rimfire lever-action rifles, along with the semiautomatic AR-7 Survival rifle, a rimfire pump rifle, a full-size .22 magnum bolt action, and the Mini-Bolt .22 which is scaled for smaller shooters. I bought a Henry .22 magnum lever gun for my dad about a dozen years ago, and bought my grandson a Golden Boy .22 LR lever gun two years ago for Christmas. Both are excellent rifles, and made in the USA.

Henry Repeating Arms Company also now makes some excellent centerfire lever-action rifles chambered for the .357 and .44 Magnum cartridges, the .45 Colt, .30-30 and .45-70 cartridges, as well as a Mare's Leg pistol in both rimfire and centerfire versions. Their latest rifle introduction is the one featured here, the Original Henry, offered in a limited-edition engraved model, or the slick-sided standard rifle shown in the photos here.

The new Original Henry is a beautiful rifle, as were the ones made in the 19th century. On the new rifles, of course, the quality of the strengthened brass and steel is much better than the rifles built 15 decades ago. The rifle shown here has a really good-looking piece of American walnut for the buttstock, which is fitted well to the polished brass buttplate and receiver. The 24-inch barrel wears an integral magazine tube, as did the early rifles, and that unit is built of highly polished blued steel.

This was one of the most difficult firearms to photograph with which I have worked in a long time, as it is so well polished that the surfaces reflect light and images like a mirror. There was a time when all quality firearms made in the USA were finished like this, but sadly, new firearms as well finished as this Henry are hard to find. The rifle weighs in at just under 9½ pounds on my scale, with an overall length of 43½ inches. The length of pull measures 13 inches from the center of the crescent buttplate. The trigger pull releases with just under four pounds of resistance on average, with a slight amount of take-up before releasing. The magazine holds 13 .44 WCF cartridges, and has the traditional open bottom and brass follower. The lever, hammer, bolt and trigger are polished

Henry Repeating Arms Co.

HENRY ORIGINAL HENRY
CALIBER .44-40
MODEL H011

Made in America

After 14 decades, the Henry rifle can once again be labeled "Made in America."

dark blued steel, as are the screws. The front sight is a naturally colored steel blade and the rear is a traditional ladder type of blued steel, useful at moderately long range.

This Henry has a very slick action, as did all Henry and Winchester designs up through the 1876. The brass cartridge-lifter design lifts the cartridges straight up from the magazine and the bolt smoothly pushes each cartridge into the chamber. Ejection is just as slick, and this Henry functions perfectly. Shooting this new Henry was a real pleasure. Recoil is

very mild as the weight of the rifle soaks up most all of it, and it is not painful at all to shoot, even when firing from the bench for several hours.

The only ammo that I could find in stock anywhere were two Magtech loads; a sporting load and a target cowboy action load. Both use 200-grain lead bullets, with the sporting load pushing them a bit faster. The sporting load, fired over the chronograph at a distance of 10 feet averaged 1,071 fps. The cowboy load averaged 1,015 at the same distance. My handload, which uses a .429-inch Tennessee Valley

200-grain truncated cone lead bullet, 9.5 grains of Hodgdon Universal powder, Starline case and a WLP primer clocked an average of 1,201 fps at the same distance. The Henry handles these .429-inch bullets as well as it does the traditional .427-inch .44 WCF bullets. Chronograph readings were taken at 541 feet above sea level, with an air temperature of 62 degrees Fahrenheit and a relative humidity of 44 percent.

Accuracy testing was done from a solid bench at a distance of 50 yards, and the Henry proved to be very accurate. Five-shot groups ran from around the 1¼-inch mark, up to three inches. This is as good as I can do using this type of sight, and I am certain that with better eyes and a better shooter these groups would tighten up, at least a bit. Still, I was satisfied with the accuracy exhibited by this new Henry rifle.

I am glad to see the Henry in production once again in the USA, built by a company for whom I have a lot of respect. Their motto is, "Made in America, Or Not Made At All." The new Original Henry rifle has a suggested retail price of $2,300, which in today's dollars, is less expensive than the Henry of 150 years ago. A private in the U.S. Army in 1860 made $11 per month. A new Henry at that time would cost him almost three month's pay. A newly enlisted soldier in the Army today can buy a new Henry for about half that in comparable base pay.

There are also a limited number of engraved Henry rifles, serialized from 1 to 1,000 that have a suggested retail price of $3,495. Number 1 has been donated to raise money for the NRA. All Original Henry serial numbers begin with the initials BTH, in honor of Benjamin Tyler Henry, the inventor of the rifle. The one shown here is serialized BTH01602, and will not be going back to Henry Repeating Arms. This new Henry stirs my soul.

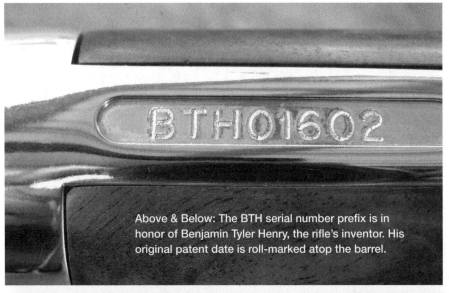

Above & Below: The BTH serial number prefix is in honor of Benjamin Tyler Henry, the rifle's inventor. His original patent date is roll-marked atop the barrel.

HENRY'S PATENT OCT. 16. 1860

TEST FIRE

THE NEW INVICTUS FROM
CAESAR GUERINI

BY **Nick Sisley**

When it comes to over/unders, there are quite a few very strong ones. Locking systems from the likes of Browning, Boss, Perazzi, Krieghoff, Beretta and many others including Caesar Guerini, have held up to the test of time for 100,000 rounds and a lot more. But Caesar Guerini's new Invictus O/U breaks new ground with regard to how long a gun will hold up to shotshell punishment.

First a little background. Caesar Guerini has been around for only a bit more than a decade, but the company has captured a huge share of the over/under market. Their sales record during this period has probably set a benchmark that cannot be broken. Every year

the total production has been sold out.

How did they do this? Number one: they have good products—double guns with numerous models that are ideal for clay target competition, models for hunting, models for high-volume shooting and more. A wide array of different models are listed on the Guerini website, including eight Field, nine Sporting, five Ellipse, three Hi-Rib Sporters, and three Trap guns. Some Field models are built with aluminum alloy receivers – making them super lightweight for hours-on-end-carrying between shots. All these different models have very appealing and differing engraving patterns.

Caesar Guerini was one of the first to bring out a high adjustable comb in

conjunction with a high adjustable rib, i.e. their Impact models. Virtually the entire shotgun industry has followed suit with high rib/high comb guns. Guerini was among the first to come out with a sexy round body receiver, i.e. in its Ellipse EVO models. They have constantly tweaked the engraving patterns, not only changing them but making them more attractive as well. The innovation list goes on.

With all the advancements Caesar Guerini has made, what could they do next to make a better product? Enter the Invictus. During my interview with Wes Lang, president of Caesar Guerini USA, he told me that from the top over/under manufacturers' competition guns, including Caesar Guerini's, they were lasting

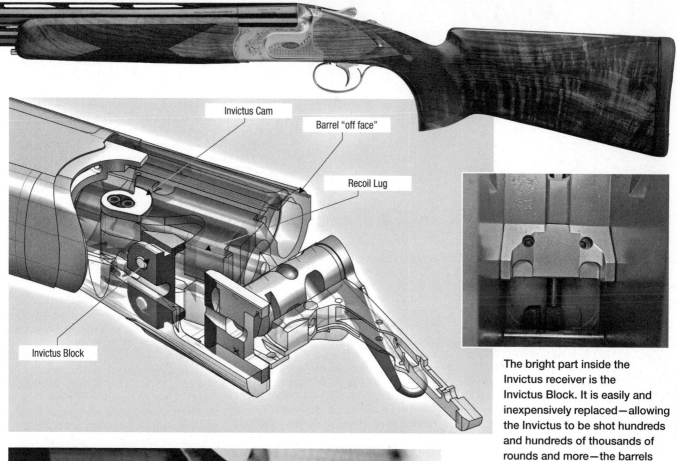

Invictus Cam

Barrel "off face"

Recoil Lug

Invictus Block

Close-up of the Invictus Cam, easy and inexpensive to replace with a slightly larger cam.

The bright part inside the Invictus receiver is the Invictus Block. It is easily and inexpensively replaced—allowing the Invictus to be shot hundreds and hundreds of thousands of rounds and more—the barrels still tight to the breech face.

what I'll call a mythical 500,000 rounds. That figure is certainly a round one, as no two shotguns are alike, no two have the same power of shells shot through them, no two are made exactly the same, some are slammed shut while some are closed gently, some are well lubricated – some not. No two are final-finished exactly the same. Many factors can determine how long a shotgun will last.

Please understand that the 500,000 rounds are suggested so that for the rest of this treatise we have some number for reference. Some competition guns

certainly last more than 500,000 rounds, including Caesar Guerini guns.

I was under the impression, and I'm certain many shotgunners are, that the trunnions or crossbolt and underlocking lugs or pin-type lugs (like those used in the Perazzi, Beretta 680 series, Zoli and others) were what made the true strength of an over/under shotgun. Not so, though all of the above are contributors to an O/U's strength, both have little to do with how long one of these double guns will hold up to incessant pounding.

Check the accompanying schematic drawing. What you are about to read is all new, so it can perhaps be a bit confusing, but stay with me. The "recoil lugs" built into the bottom of the monobloc fit tightly into the area just behind the new Invictus Block. These recoil lugs on the monobloc are the major contributors to a shotgun's strength longevity. In a Perazzi and others, these strength areas are built into the sides of the monobloc and inner sides of the receiver. As those guns close, these two areas mesh tightly together. In the Browning Superposed and Citori, the recoil lugs are built into the bottom of the monobloc and nestle right through the bottom of the receiver. Most O/U manufacturers utilize some sort of a bottom recoil lug or lugs on the base of the monobloc that fit into matching areas in the bottom of the receiver. It's these recoil lug areas that are major factors in an over/under's long-term strength and that contribute to the mythical 500,000 rounds – not the trunnions, nor the crossbolt, underlocking lugs or "pins."

Double guns can be "tightened up" a bit by switching to larger hinge (trunnions) pins and/or larger underlocking

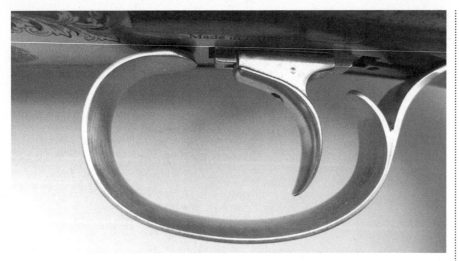

The trigger can be moved back and forth so the shooter can attain his or her perfect grip-to-trigger distance.

bolts, of which there are several types depending upon the manufacturer. Most of these bolts are in the base of the receiver and move forward upon closing; these bolts can also be tapered so they keep moving forward, taking up some wear. But what really wears a double gun out is the rear of the barrels not being tight against the breech face, often called "off the face." This usually happens because of wear on the recoil lugs, or wear on their opposing surfaces, like I've been talking about; these recoil lugs built into the bottom of the monobloc or those of the Perazzi type on the sides of the monobloc. It's Guerini's new Invictus Bolt—plus doing away with the trunnions system—that allows the Invictus to break new ground.

This was accomplished by designing two new locking parts, but the important key to both is that they are replaceable. Let's look at one of these parts at a time. Replacing traditional trunnions is the new part in the accompanying schematic

called the Invictus Cam, one positioned on each side of the receiver, opposing surfaces to these new Invictus Cams are milled into both insides of the inner receiver. Now we have a pivot point, as has previously been provided by trunnions or a crossbolt (á la the Browning and a few others) to swing open and close the barrels. Note the two screws in the Invictus Cam. This cam can be removed if the gun wears, and a slightly larger one added.

But next look at the Invictus Block again. This is positioned in the base of the receiver. It too, has two screws keeping it in place, as you will note. Again, it's the recoil lug at the base of the monobloc that provides most of the strength in the over/under. A gun comes "off the face" when wear in the recoil lug and/or its opposing areas of the Invictus Block. In a traditional O/U there's not much that can be done when this happens and the barrels are off the face. The gun is worn out. Such a gun has served

its purpose, maybe firing those mythical 500,000 rounds (or more – or less) I've talked about.

But what if we could extend that mythical 500,000 to another 500,000, and then another 500,000, and then another 500,000! That's what these two innovative parts do for the Invictus. That means once worn to that 500,000 round point or whenever the barrels are no longer tight to the receiver, by changing out the new parts in the schematic for slightly larger ones, shoot the gun for another 500,000 rounds, or whatever amount of shooting it takes to have the barrels off the face again. Change those parts out again and shoot for another 500,000. During all this you might have to change the locking bolt—an inexpensive fix—but so is changing out the Invictus Block and/or the Invictus Cam.

At last January's SHOT Show, Wes Lang had to explain the Invictus system over and over to gun writers and customers. The way he did a lot of that explaining is as follows. "Trunnions and hinge pins are the hinge point, and are not designed to take all of the recoil forces. Locking lugs or bolts serve to latch the barrels closed, but do not contribute to the strength of the action upon firing. Recoil lugs are the structures that integrate with the action to bar all the forces of a shotgun shell trying to push the barrel and receiver in opposite directions. When the recoil lugs wear to the point that the tolerances no longer allow the barrels to close tightly, there is a gap between the barrels and the breech face called off face. This condition spells the practical end of the road for all double guns, until now. The Caesar Guerini Invictus is the first shotgun to cure the off face condition. By changing out to a slightly larger Invictus Block and larger Invictus Cam, the worn tolerances can be compensated for to the point that the action will again be tight and the barrels no longer off face."

Well, how many of you are interested in a gun that shoots hundreds of thousands of shells before any wear occurs, and then have that gun shoot for thousands and thousands more rounds after an inexpensive fix? Clay target shooters are interested, and most all of us would love to pass a treasured gun on to our heirs, or a person who would genuinely appreciate finally owning a shotgun that you have shot for years and years.

A shotgun that can last through literally millions of rounds certainly has its importance. Would you like a new

The fore-end is slender and rounded in shape, reminiscent of the Browning Lighting fore-end.

A new engraving pattern, designed by Bottega Giovanelli, one of Italy's most prominent engravers of fine firearms, is shown here on the receiver of the Invictus.

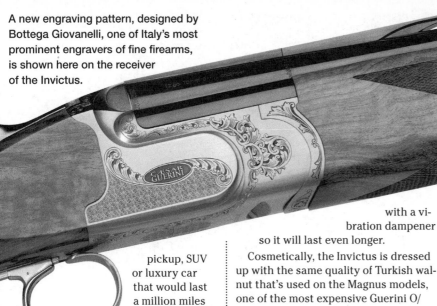

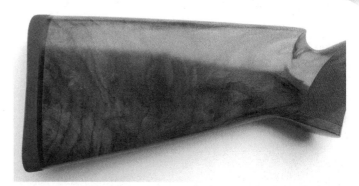

Dr. Gary Trilli handles the new prototype Invictus.

pickup, SUV or luxury car that would last a million miles with minimal maintenance? Who wouldn't! But what if that vehicle's style never changed, and didn't have any new eye appeal? You'd probably still go for that million-mile car; but give it good looks plus special new features and such a purchase would be even more appealing.

Caesar Guerini did not stop at their new Invictus Block innards design that will allow the gun to shoot a million or more rounds. They added more. The receiver is thicker and wider, maybe the thickest and widest in the industry. In actuality, this change may not be a strength issue, but a few more ounces of weight are now between the hands, theoretically more ideal for the gun's handling qualities.

The company also worked the triggers over with newly designed hammers and sears. To those parts a special lubricity coating has been added, resulting in a more precise feel. The push-button release on the fore-end is now equipped with a vibration dampener so it will last even longer.

Cosmetically, the Invictus is dressed up with the same quality of Turkish walnut that's used on the Magnus models, one of the most expensive Guerini O/Us. There's also a new engraving pattern created by world-renowned artisan Bottega Giovenelli. There's more sculpturing to both receiver sides. Check the photo that displays around the fences—that area is beautiful, but it takes time to mill away all that metal.

Barrels remain a deep blue and there are vented side ribs, a metal midbead and a white bead at the muzzle. Sides of the monobloc are well jeweled. The soft rubber recoil pad has rounded edges so the gun will be less likely to hang up during the mount. The trigger can be moved back and forth. The triggerguard is engraved, as well as the top tang. All the features of the previous Guerini sporting guns have been retained, but as you can see a number of new features have been added.

As I was interviewing Wes Lang, I was thinking to myself, "With all this new technology there has to be a big dent to the pocketbook of anyone who wants to buy an Invictus." But I was genuinely surprised to find the Invictus retails for $6,700; a reasonable amount for a gun that will reportedly last through a million rounds and more. And all Caesar Guerini shotguns come with a lifetime warranty. It will be interesting to see how the rest of the shotgun world reacts to this one.

Right: The Turkish walnut wears a hand-rubbed oil finish and is the same grade of walnut used on the Guerini Magnus Sporting, a more expensive Guerini model.

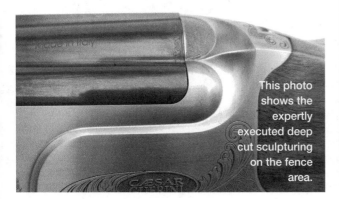

This photo shows the expertly executed deep cut sculpturing on the fence area.

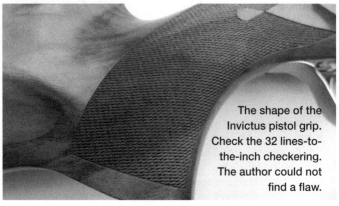

The shape of the Invictus pistol grip. Check the 32 lines-to-the-inch checkering. The author could not find a flaw.

TEST FIRE

The Ruger Bearcat Shopkeeper handled a wide variety of .22 rounds with ease and accuracy.

Ruger Bearcat Shopkeeper

AN OLD-FASHIONED FUN GUN

BY Al Doyle

In an era of laser sights, polymer frames and exotic alloys, revisiting older firearms concepts can be an enjoyable experience. Take one of the numerous single-action revolvers done in steel, add wood grips, and you've got a blast from the past.

What happens when the venerable 19th century-style wheelgun is tweaked a bit? If sales figures for the Ruger Bearcat Shopkeeper in .22 LR are an indicator, minor changes can make a major difference in handling and popular appeal.

The Bearcat debuted in 1959 and its modest weight and dependability are no secret. In addition to trim dimensions, the Bearcat's superb balance and pointability (it almost feels like a natural extension of the hand) have kept it in production for more than a half century. Since the Bearcat has such a proven track record, why mess with

success? The saying "If it ain't broke, don't fix it" seems to apply here.

Lipsey's had a different idea. The Baton Rouge, La.-based firearms wholesaler is known for their extensive selection of "distributor exclusives." These are limited editions of current models that have been given anything from minor changes to significant modifications. It's a segment of the 21st century firearms market that remains unknown to many shooters.

"We work with independent dealers, and they like the Shopkeeper and other Lipsey's exclusives because it gives them something the big box stores don't have," said product development manager Jason Cloessner.

In this instance, the barrel was shortened from 4 to 3 inches, and a "bird's head" grip was added. The Shopkeeper designation was a shrewd bit of marketing, as this handy revolver looks like it would be just right under the counter

of an 1880s general store or saloon. The stainless steel finish is the only feature that doesn't hit the nostalgia button, but it's a popular option for those who see

This honorably discharged young Marine is making the transition to civilian firearms.

The Shopkeeper had some extraction issues straight out of the box on a frigid Wisconsin morning. Everything works fine now that the gun has fired several hundred rounds.

the gun as a holster piece while in the outdoors.

Lipsey's and other large distributors typically come up with concepts for limited-edition pieces. The special models could be entirely original or based on estimated potential demand.

"One thing we do is look at what people are doing with custom guns," Cloessner said. "We try to come up with exclusives that people are already willing to spend a lot of money on customizing." More than a few Bearcats have been modified to appear something like the Shopkeeper, so the concept made sense from a business standpoint.

Looks are always a selling point, but performance is what counts in the long run. So how does the Bearcat Shopkeeper do straight out of the box? Taking a brand-new gun and firing it during a windy and snowy 10-degree Wisconsin morning is far different than a climate-controlled indoor range.

The little revolver gobbled four different brands of rimfire ammunition without a hitch. Despite gloves and shivering bodies, keeping shots in groups of two inches or less at ranges of 25 to 50 feet wasn't a problem. Perform this test in the summer, and there would be some one-inch groups.

Frigid temperatures combined with tight tolerances and the normal break-in period did cause a problem though. We had trouble ejecting brass from two of the six chambers. A needle-nose pliers was used to pull cases out before reloading. The process improved during a second session on the range, and there were no ejection issues during a recent indoor session. Cloessner reports a similar break-in experience with his Bearcat Shopkeeper.

Above: This gentleman specializes in small groups with the Bearcat Shopkeeper.

Right: The little Ruger is accurate even without a high-visibility front sight.

One of the better cowboy action shooters in the state wasn't able to attend the frosty range session, but he examined the Shopkeeper later and provided this review.

"It's very solid and well built, typical Ruger," he said. "Everything is tight on it. The bird's head grip is really nice. It lets you put your pinky under the butt for better control and accuracy. The pointability is excellent. It might not be ideal for someone with large hands, but it's really nice if your hands are average size. This would be the perfect gun if they had a .22 side match at a cowboy action shoot."

But, don't go to Ruger or another manufacturer if you want to a make a run of 100 or 200 Joe Schmoe Limited Edition models of your favorite firearm. This game requires deeper pockets and the ability to move product.

"The Shopkeeper started when we saw a stainless Bearcat that was cut down to a 3-inch barrel with a shortened ejection rod," Cloessner said. "Everybody here fell in love with it, which is a good sign. The minimum number for a distributor exclusive is 3,000, but we told Ruger we'd take 5,000, and we've had trouble keeping them in stock. We'll keep running them as long as they sell. I have a feeling the Shopkeeper will have legs and be around for a few years."

At $679 MSRP, the Bearcat Shopkeeper carries a recommended price just $60 higher than the standard stainless Bearcat. How do I like it? Articles on narrowing one's collection down to a few cherished pieces are a popular theme in firearms circles, and this compact rimfire would definitely make my short list.

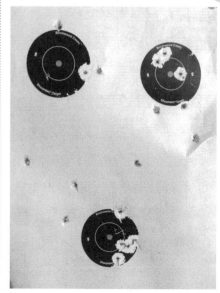

Many manufacturers do not supply suggested retail prices. Others did not get their pricing to us before press time. All pricing can vary dependent on the exact brand and style of ammo selected and/or the retail outlet from which you make your purchase. Pricing has been rounded to the nearest dollar and represents our best estimate of average pricing. An * after the cartridge means these loads are available with Nosler Partition or Swift A-Frame bullets. Listed pricing may or may not reflect this bullet type. ** = these are packed 50 to box, all others are 20 to box. Wea. Mag.= Weatherby Magnum. Spfd. = Springfield. A-Sq. = A-Square. N.E.=Nitro Express.

Cartridge	Bullet Wgt. Grs.	VELOCITY (fps)					ENERGY (ft. lbs.)					TRAJ. (in.)				Est. Price/box
		Muzzle	100 yds.	200 yds.	300 yds.	400 yds.	Muzzle	100 yds.	200 yds.	300 yds.	400 yds.	100 yds.	200 yds.	300 yds.	400 yds.	
17, 22																
17 Hornet	15.5	3860	2924	2159	1531	1108	513	294	160	81	42	1.4	0.0	-9.1	-33.7	NA
17 Hornet	20	3650	3078	2574	2122	1721	592	421	294	200	131	1.10	0.0	-6.4	-20.6	NA
17 Remington Fireball	20	4000	3380	2840	2360	1930	710	507	358	247	165	1.6	1.5	-2.8	-13.5	NA
17 Remington Fireball	25	3850	3280	2780	2330	1925	823	597	429	301	206	0.9	0.0	-5.4	NA	NA
17 Remington	20	4200	3544	2978	2477	2029	783	558	394	272	183	0	-1.3	-6.6	-17.6	NA
17 Remington	25	4040	3284	2644	2086	1606	906	599	388	242	143	+2.0	+1.7	-4.0	-17.0	$17
4.6x30 H&K	30	2025	1662	1358	1135	1002	273	184	122	85	66	0	-12.7	-44.5	—	NA
4.6x30 H&K	40	1900	1569	1297	1104	988	320	218	149	108	86	0	-14.3	-39.3	—	NA
204 Ruger (Hor)	24	4400	3667	3046	2504	2023	1032	717	494	334	218	0.6	0	-4.3	-14.3	NA
204 Ruger (Fed)	32 Green	4030	3320	2710	2170	1710	1155	780	520	335	205	0.9	0.0	-5.7	-19.1	NA
204 Ruger	32	4125	3559	3061	2616	2212	1209	900	666	486	348	0	-1.3	-6.3	—	NA
204 Ruger	32	4225	3632	3114	2652	2234	1268	937	689	500	355	.6	0.0	-4.2	-13.4	NA
204 Ruger	40	3900	3451	3046	2677	2336	1351	1058	824	636	485	.7	0.0	-4.5	-13.9	NA
204 Ruger	45	3625	3188	2792	2428	2093	1313	1015	778	589	438	1.0	0.0	-5.5	-16.9	NA
5.45x39mm	60	2810	2495	2201	1927	1677	1052	829	645	445	374	1.0	0.0	-9.2	-27.7	NA
221 Fireball	40	3100	2510	1991	1547	1209	853	559	352	212	129	0	-4.1	-17.3	-45.1	NA
221 Fireball	50	2800	2137	1580	1180	988	870	507	277	155	109	+0.0	-7.0	-28.0	0.0	$14
22 Hornet (Fed)	30 Green	3150	2150	1390	990	830	660	310	130	65	45	0.0	-6.6	-32.7	NA	NA
22 Hornet	34	3050	2132	1415	1017	852	700	343	151	78	55	+0.0	-6.6	-15.5	-29.9	NA
22 Hornet	35	3100	2278	1601	1135	929	747	403	199	100	67	+2.75	0.0	-16.9	-60.4	NA
22 Hornet	40	2800	2397	2029	1698	1413	696	510	366	256	177	0	-4.6	-17.8	-43.1	NA
22 Hornet	45	2690	2042	1502	1128	948	723	417	225	127	90	+0.0	-7.7	-31.0	0.0	$27**
218 Bee	46	2760	2102	1550	1155	961	788	451	245	136	94	+0.0	-7.2	-29.0	0.0	$46**
222 Rem.	35	3760	3125	2574	2085	1656	1099	759	515	338	213	1.0	0.0	-6.3	-20.8	NA
222 Rem.	50	3345	2930	2553	2205	1886	1242	953	723	540	395	1.3	0	-6.7	-20.6	NA
222 Remington	40	3600	3117	2673	2269	1911	1151	863	634	457	324	+1.07	0.0	-6.13	-18.9	NA
222 Remington	50	3140	2602	2123	1700	1350	1094	752	500	321	202	+2.0	-0.4	-11.0	-33.0	$11
222 Remington	55	3020	2562	2147	1773	1451	1114	801	563	384	257	+2.0	-0.4	-11.0	-33.0	$12
222 Rem. Mag.	40	3600	3140	2726	2347	2000	1150	876	660	489	355	1.0	0	-5.7	-17.8	NA
222 Rem. Mag.	50	3340	2917	2533	2179	1855	1238	945	712	527	382	1.3	0	-6.8	-20.9	NA
222 Rem. Mag.	55	3240	2748	2305	1906	1556	1282	922	649	444	296	+2.0	-0.2	-9.0	-27.0	$14
22 PPC	52	3400	2930	2510	2130	NA	1335	990	730	525	NA	+2.0	1.4	-5.0	0.0	NA
223 Rem.	35	3750	3206	2725	2291	1899	1092	799	577	408	280	1.0	0	-5.7	-18.1	NA
223 Rem.	35	4000	3353	2796	2302	1861	1243	874	607	412	269	0.8	0	-5.3	-17.3	NA
223 Rem.	64	2750	2368	2018	1701	1427	1074	796	578	411	289	2.4	0	-11	-34.1	NA
223 Rem.	75	2790	2562	2345	2139	1943	1296	1093	916	762	629	1.5	0	-8.2	-24.1	NA
223 Remington	40	3650	3010	2450	1950	1530	1185	805	535	340	265	+2.0	+1.0	-6.0	-22.0	$14
223 Remington	40	3800	3305	2845	2424	2044	1282	970	719	522	371	0.84	0.0	-5.34	-16.6	NA
223 Remington (Rem)	45 Green	3550	2911	2355	1865	1451	1259	847	554	347	210	2.5	2.3	-4.3	-21.1	NA
223 Remington	50	3300	2874	2484	2130	1809	1209	917	685	504	363	1.37	0.0	-7.05	-21.8	NA
223 Remington	52/53	3330	2882	2477	2106	1770	1305	978	722	522	369	+2.0	+0.6	-6.5	-21.5	$14
223 Remington (Win)	55 Green	3240	2747	2304	1905	1554	1282	921	648	443	295	1.9	0.0	-8.5	-26.7	NA
223 Remington	55	3240	2748	2305	1906	1556	1282	922	649	444	296	+2.0	-0.2	-9.0	-27.0	$12
223 Remington	60	3100	2712	2355	2026	1726	1280	979	739	547	397	+2.0	+0.2	-8.0	-24.7	$16
223 Remington	62	3000	2700	2410	2150	1900	1240	1000	800	635	495	1.60	0.0	-7.7	-22.8	NA
223 Remington	64	3020	2621	2256	1920	1619	1296	977	723	524	373	+2.0	-0.2	-9.3	-23.0	$14
223 Remington	69	3000	2720	2460	2210	1980	1380	1135	925	750	600	+2.0	+0.8	-5.8	-17.5	$15
223 Remington	75	2790	2554	2330	2119	1926	1296	1086	904	747	617	2.37	0.0	-8.75	-25.1	NA
223 Rem. Super Match	75	2930	2694	2470	2257	2055	1429	1209	1016	848	703	1.20	0.0	-6.9	-20.7	NA
223 Remington	77	2750	2584	2354	2169	1992	1293	1110	948	804	679	1.93	0.0	-8.2	-23.8	NA
223 WSSM	55	3850	3438	3064	2721	2402	1810	1444	1147	904	704	0.7	0.0	-4.4	-13.6	NA
223 WSSM	64	3600	3144	2732	2356	2011	1841	1404	1061	789	574	1.0	0.0	-5.7	-17.7	NA
5.56 NATO	55	3130	2740	2382	2051	1750	1196	917	693	514	372	1.1	0	-7.3	-23.0	NA
5.56 NATO	75	2910	2676	2543	2242	2041	1192	1002	837	693	693	1.2	0	-7.0	-21.0	NA
224 Wea. Mag.	55	3650	3192	2780	2403	2057	1627	1244	943	705	516	+2.0	+1.2	-4.0	-17.0	$32
225 Winchester	55	3570	3066	2616	2208	1838	1556	1148	836	595	412	+2.0	+1.0	-5.0	-20.0	$19
22-250 Rem.	35	4450	3736	3128	2598	2125	1539	1085	761	524	351	6.5	0	-4.1	-13.4	NA
22-250 Rem.	40	4000	3320	2720	2200	1740	1420	980	660	430	265	+2.0	+1.8	-3.0	-16.0	$14
22-250 Rem.	40	4150	3553	3033	2570	2151	1530	1121	817	587	411	0.6	0	-4.4	-14.2	NA
22-250 Rem.	45 Green	4000	3293	2690	2159	1696	1598	1084	723	466	287	1.7	1.7	-3.2	-15.7	NA
22-250 Rem.	50	3725	3264	2641	2455	2103	1540	1183	896	669	491	0.89	0.0	-5.23	-16.3	NA
22-250 Rem.	52/55	3680	3137	2656	2222	1832	1654	1201	861	603	410	+2.0	+1.3	-4.0	-17.0	$13
22-250 Rem.	60	3600	3195	2826	2485	2169	1360	1064	823	627	...	+2.0	+2.0	-2.4	-12.3	$19
22-250 Rem.	64	3425	2988	2591	2228	1897	1667	1269	954	705	511	1.2	0	-6.4	-20.0	NA
220 Swift	40	4200	3678	3190	2739	2329	1566	1201	904	666	482	+0.51	0.0	-4.0	-12.9	NA
220 Swift	50	3780	3158	2617	2135	1710	1586	1107	760	506	325	+2.0	+1.4	-4.4	-17.9	$20
220 Swift	50	3850	3396	2970	2576	2215	1645	1280	979	736	545	0.74	0.0	-4.84	-15.1	NA
220 Swift	50	3900	3420	2990	2599	2240	1688	1298	992	750	557	0.7	0	-4.7	-14.5	NA
220 Swift	55	3800	3370	2990	2630	2310	1765	1390	1090	850	650	0.8	0.0	-4.7	-14.4	NA
220 Swift	55	3650	3194	2772	2384	2035	1627	1246	939	694	506	+2.0	+2.0	-2.6	-13.4	$19
220 Swift	60	3600	3199	2824	2475	2156	1727	1364	1063	816	619	+2.0	+1.6	-4.1	-13.1	$19
22 Savage H.P.	70	2868	2510	2179	1874	1600	1279	980	738	546	398	0	-4.1	-15.6	-37.1	NA
22 Savage H.P.	71	2790	2340	1930	1570	1280	1225	860	585	390	190	+2.0	-1.0	-10.4	-35.7	NA

Cartridge	Bullet Wgt. Grs.	VELOCITY (fps)					ENERGY (ft. lbs.)					TRAJ. (in.)				Est. Price/box
		Muzzle	100 yds.	200 yds.	300 yds.	400 yds.	Muzzle	100 yds.	200 yds.	300 yds.	400 yds.	100 yds.	200 yds.	300 yds.	400 yds.	
6mm (24)																
6mm BR Rem.	100	2550	2310	2083	1870	1671	1444	1185	963	776	620	+2.5	-0.6	-11.8	0.0	$22
6mm Norma BR	107	2822	2667	2517	2372	2229	1893	1690	1506	1337	1181	+1.73	0.0	-7.24	-20.6	NA
6mm PPC	70	3140	2750	2400	2070	NA	1535	1175	895	665	NA	+2.0	+1.4	-5.0	0.0	NA
243 Winchester	55	4025	3597	3209	2853	2525	1978	1579	1257	994	779	+0.6	0	-4.0	-12.2	NA
243 Win.	58	3925	3465	3052	2676	2330	1984	1546	1200	922	699	0.7	0	-4.4	-13.8	NA
243 Winchester	60	3600	3110	2660	2260	1890	1725	1285	945	680	475	+2.0	+1.8	-3.3	-15.5	$17
243 Win.	70	3400	3020	2672	2350	2050	1797	1418	1110	858	653	0	-2.5	-9.7	—	NA
243 Winchester	70	3400	3040	2700	2390	2100	1795	1135	890	685	11	1.1	0	-5.9	-18.0	NA
243 Winchester	75/80	3350	2955	2593	2259	1951	1993	1551	1194	906	676	+2.0	+0.9	-5.0	-19.0	$16
243 Win.	80	3425	3081	2763	2468	2190	2984	1686	1357	1082	852	1.1	0	-5.7	-17.1	NA
243 Win.	87	2800	2574	2359	2155	1961	1514	1280	1075	897	743	1.9	0	-8.1	-23.8	NA
243 Win.	95	3185	2908	2649	2404	2172	2140	1784	1480	1219	995	1.3	0	-6.3	-18.6	NA
243 W. Superformance	80	3425	3080	2760	2463	2184	2083	1684	1353	1077	847	1.1	0.0	-5.7	-17.1	NA
243 W. Winchester	85	3320	3070	2830	2600	2380	2080	1770	1510	1280	1070	+2.0	+1.2	-4.0	-14.0	$18
243 Winchester	90	3120	2871	2635	2411	2199	1946	1647	1388	1162	966	1.4	0.0	-6.4	-18.8	NA
243 Winchester*	100	2960	2697	2449	2215	1993	1945	1615	1332	1089	882	+2.5	+1.2	-6.0	-20.0	$16
243 Winchester	105	2920	2689	2470	2261	2062	1988	1686	1422	1192	992	+2.5	+1.6	-5.0	-18.4	$21
243 Light Mag.	100	3100	2839	2592	2358	2138	2133	1790	1491	1235	1014	+1.5	0.0	-6.8	-19.8	NA
243 WSSM	55	4060	3628	3237	2880	2550	2013	1607	1280	1013	794	0.6	0.0	-3.9	-12.0	NA
243 WSSM	95	3250	3000	2763	2538	2325	2258	1898	1610	1359	1140	1.2	0.0	-5.7	-16.9	NA
243 WSSM	100	3110	2838	2583	2341	2112	2147	1789	1481	1217	991	1.4	0.0	-6.6	-19.7	NA
6mm Remington	80	3470	3064	2694	2352	2036	2139	1667	1289	982	736	+2.0	+1.1	-5.0	-17.0	$16
6mm R. Superformance	95	3235	2955	2692	2443	3309	2207	1841	1528	1259	1028	1.2	0.0	-6.1	-18.0	NA
6mm Remington	100	3100	2829	2573	2332	2104	2133	1777	1470	1207	983	+2.5	+1.6	-5.0	-17.0	$16
6mm Remington	105	3060	2822	2596	2381	2177	2105	1788	1512	1270	1059	+2.5	+1.1	-3.3	-15.0	$21
240 Wea. Mag.	87	3500	3202	2924	2663	2416	2366	1980	1651	1370	1127	+2.0	+2.0	-2.0	-12.0	$32
240 Wea. Mag.	100	3150	2894	2653	2425	2207	2202	1860	1563	1395	1082	1.3	0	-6.3	-18.5	NA
240 Wea. Mag.	100	3395	3106	2835	2581	2339	2559	2142	1785	1478	1215	+2.5	+2.8	-2.0	-11.0	$43
25-20 Win.	86	1460	1194	1030	931	858	407	272	203	165	141	0.0	-23.5	0.0	0.0	$32**
25-35 Win.	117	2230	1866	1545	1282	1097	1292	904	620	427	313	+2.5	-4.2	-26.0	0.0	$24
250 Savage	100	2820	2504	2210	1936	1684	1765	1392	1084	832	630	+2.5	+0.4	-9.0	-28.0	$17
257 Roberts	100	2980	2661	2363	2085	1827	1972	1572	1240	965	741	+2.5	-0.8	-5.2	-21.6	$20
257 Roberts	122	2600	2331	2078	1842	1625	1831	1472	1169	919	715	+2.5	0.0	-10.6	-31.4	$21
257 Roberts+P	100	3000	2758	2529	2312	2105	1998	1689	1421	1187	984	1.5	0	-7.0	-20.5	NA
257 Roberts+P	117	2780	2411	2071	1761	1488	2009	1511	1115	806	576	+2.5	-0.2	-10.2	-32.6	$18
257 Roberts+P	120	2780	2560	2360	2160	1970	2060	1750	1480	1240	1030	+2.5	+1.2	-6.4	-23.6	$22
257 R. Superformance	117	2946	2705	2478	2265	2057	2253	1901	1595	1329	1099	1.1	0.0	-5.7	-17.1	NA
25-06 Rem.	87	3440	2995	2591	2222	1884	2286	1733	1297	954	686	+2.0	+1.1	-2.5	-14.4	$17
25-06 Rem.	90	3350	3001	2679	2378	2098	2243	1790	1434	1130	879	1.2	0	-6.0	-18.3	NA
25-06 Rem.	90	3440	3043	2680	2344	2034	2364	1850	1435	1098	827	+2.0	+1.8	-3.3	-15.6	$17
25-06 Rem.	100	3230	2893	2580	2287	2014	2316	1858	1478	1161	901	+2.0	+0.8	-5.7	-18.9	$17
25-06 Rem.	117	2990	2770	2570	2370	2190	2320	2000	1715	1465	1246	+2.5	+1.0	-7.9	-26.6	$19
25-06 Rem.*	120	2990	2730	2484	2252	2032	2382	1985	1644	1351	1100	+2.5	+1.2	-5.3	-19.6	$17
25-06 Rem.	122	2930	2706	2492	2289	2095	2325	1983	1683	1419	1189	+2.5	+1.8	-4.5	-17.5	$23
25-06 R. Superformance	117	3110	2861	2626	2403	2191	2512	2127	1792	1500	1246	1.4	0.0	-6.4	-18.9	NA
25 WSSM	85	3470	3156	2863	2589	2331	2273	1880	1548	1266	1026	1.0	0.0	-5.2	-15.7	NA
25 WSSM	115	3060	2844	2639	2442	2254	2392	2066	1778	1523	1398	1.4	0	-6.4	-18.6	NA
25 WSSM	120	2990	2717	2459	2216	1987	2383	1967	1612	1309	1053	1.6	0.0	-7.4	-21.8	NA
257 Wea. Mag.	87	3825	3456	3118	2805	2513	2826	2308	1870	1520	1220	+2.0	+2.7	-0.3	-7.6	$32
257 Wea. Mag.	90	3550	3184	2848	2537	2246	2518	2026	1621	1286	1008	1.0	0	-5.3	-16.0	NA
257 Wea. Mag.	100	3555	3237	2941	2665	2404	2806	2326	1920	1576	1283	+2.5	+3.2	0.0	-8.0	$32
257 Wea. Mag.	110	3330	3069	2823	2591	2370	2708	2300	1947	1639	1372	1.1	0	-5.5	-16.1	NA
257 Scramjet	100	3745	3450	3173	2912	2666	3114	2643	2235	1883	1578	+2.1	+2.77	0.0	-6.93	NA
6.5																
6.5 Grendel	123	2590	2420	2256	2099	1948	1832	1599	1390	1203	1037	1.8	0	-8.6	-25.1	NA
6.5x47 Lapua	123	2887	NA	2554	NA	2244	2285	NA	1788	NA	1380	NA	4.53	0.0	-10.7	NA
6.5x50mm Jap.	139	2360	2160	1970	1790	1620	1720	1440	1195	985	810	+2.5	-1.0	-13.5	0.0	NA
6.5x50mm Jap.	156	2070	1830	1610	1430	1260	1475	1155	900	695	550	+2.5	-4.0	-23.8	0.0	NA
6.5x52mm Car.	139	2580	2360	2160	1970	1790	2045	1725	1440	1195	985	+2.5	0.0	-9.9	-29.0	NA
6.5x52mm Car.	156	2430	2170	1930	1700	1500	2045	1630	1285	1005	780	+2.5	-1.0	-13.9	0.0	NA
6.5x52mm Carcano	160	2250	1963	1700	1467	1271	1798	1369	1027	764	574	+3.8	0.0	-15.9	-48.1	NA
6.5x55mm Swe.	93	2625	2350	2090	1850	1630	1425	1140	905	705	550	2.4	0.0	-10.3	-31.1	NA
6.5x55mm Swe.	123	2750	2570	2400	2240	2080	2065	1810	1580	1370	1185	1.9	0.0	-7.9	-22.9	NA
6.5x55mm Swe.*	139/140	2850	2640	2440	2250	2070	2525	2170	1855	1575	1330	+2.5	+1.6	-5.4	-18.9	$18
6.5x55mm Swe.	140	2550	NA	NA	NA	NA	2020	NA	NA	NA	NA	0.0	0.0	0.0	0.0	$18
6.5x55mm Swe.	140	2735	2563	2397	2237	2084	2325	2041	1786	1556	1350	1.9	0	-8.0	-22.9	NA
6.5x55mm Swe.	156	2650	2370	2110	1870	1650	2425	1950	1550	1215	945	+2.5	0.0	-10.3	-30.6	NA
260 Rem.	100	3200	2917	2652	2402	2165	2273	1889	1561	1281	1041	1.3	0	-6.3	-18.6	NA
260 Rem.	130	2800	2613	2433	2261	2096	2262	1970	1709	1476	1268	1.8	0	-7.7	-22.2	NA
260 Remington	125	2875	2669	2473	2285	2105	2294	1977	1697	1449	1230	1.71	0	-7.4	-21.4	NA
260 Remington	140	2750	2544	2347	2158	1979	2351	2011	1712	1448	1217	+2.2	0.0	-8.6	-24.6	NA
6.5 Creedmoor	120	3020	2815	2619	2430	2251	2430	2111	1827	1574	1350	1.4	0.0	-6.5	-18.9	NA
6.5 Creedmoor	120	3050	2850	2659	2476	2300	2479	2164	1884	1634	1310	1.4	0	-6.3	-18.3	NA
6.5 Creedmoor	140	2550	2380	2217	2060	1910	2021	1761	1527	1319	1134	2.3	0	-9.4	-27.0	NA
6.5 Creedmoor	140	2710	2557	2410	2267	2129	2283	2033	1805	1598	1410	1.9	0	-7.9	-22.6	NA

Cartridge	Bullet Wgt. Grs.	VELOCITY (fps)					ENERGY (ft. lbs.)					TRAJ. (in.)				Est. Price/box
		Muzzle	100 yds.	200 yds.	300 yds.	400 yds.	Muzzle	100 yds.	200 yds.	300 yds.	400 yds.	100 yds.	200 yds.	300 yds.	400 yds.	
6.5 Creedmoor	140	2820	2654	2494	2339	2190	2472	2179	1915	1679	1467	1.7	0.0	-7.2	-20.6	NA
6.5 C. Superformance	129	2950	2756	2570	2392	2221	2492	2175	1892	1639	1417	1.5	0.0	-6.8	-19.7	NA
6.5x52R	117	2208	1856	1544	1287	1104	1267	895	620	431	317	0	-8.7	-32.2	—	NA
6.5x57	131	2543	2295	2060	1841	1638	1882	1532	1235	986	780	0	-5.1	-18.5	-42.1	NA
6.5-284 Norma	142	3025	2890	2758	2631	2507	2886	2634	2400	2183	1982	1.13	0.0	-5.7	-16.4	NA
6.71 (264) Phantom	120	3150	2929	2718	2517	2325	2645	2286	1969	1698	1440	+1.3	0.0	-6.0	-17.5	NA
6.5 Rem. Mag.	120	3210	2905	2621	2353	2102	2745	2248	1830	1475	1177	+2.5	+1.7	-4.1	-16.3	Disc.
264 Win. Mag.	100	3400	3104	2828	2568	2322	2566	2139	1775	1464	1197	1.1	0	-5.4	-16.1	NA
264 Win. Mag.	125	3200	2978	2767	2566	2373	2841	2461	2125	1827	1563	1.2	0	-5.8	-16.8	NA
264 Win. Mag.	130	3100	2900	2709	2526	2350	2773	2427	2118	1841	1594	1.3	0	-6.1	-17.6	NA
264 Win. Mag.	140	3030	2782	2548	2326	2114	2854	2406	2018	1682	1389	+2.5	+1.4	-5.1	-18.0	$24
6.5 Nosler	129	3400	3213	3035	2863	2698	3310	2957	2638	2348	2085	0.9	0	-4.7	-13.6	NA
6.5 Nosler	140	3300	3118	2943	2775	2613	3119	2784	2481	2205	1955	1.0	0	-5.0	-14.6	NA
6.71 (264) Blackbird	140	3480	3261	3053	2855	2665	3766	3307	2899	2534	2208	+2.4	+3.1	0.0	-7.4	NA
6.8 REM SPC	90	2840	2444	2083	1756	1469	1611	1194	867	616	431	2.2	0	-3.9	-32.0	NA
6.8 REM SPC	110	2570	2338	2118	1910	1716	1613	1335	1095	891	719	2.4	0.0	-6.3	-20.8	NA
6.8 REM SPC	120	2460	2250	2051	1863	1687	1612	1349	1121	925	758	2.3	0	-10.5	-31.1	NA
6.8mm Rem.	115	2775	2472	2190	1926	1683	1966	1561	1224	947	723	+2.1	0.0	-3.7	-9.4	NA

27

Cartridge	Bullet Wgt. Grs.	Muzzle	100 yds.	200 yds.	300 yds.	400 yds.	Muzzle	100 yds.	200 yds.	300 yds.	400 yds.	100 yds.	200 yds.	300 yds.	400 yds.	Est. Price/box
270 Win. (Rem.)	115	2710	2482	2265	2059	NA	1875	1485	1161	896	NA	0.0	4.8	-17.3	0.0	NA
270 Win.	120	2675	2288	1935	1619	1351	1907	1395	998	699	486	2.6	0	-12.0	-37.4	NA
270 Win.	140	2940	2747	2563	2386	2216	2687	2346	2042	1770	1526	1.8	0	-6.8	-19.8	NA
270 Win. Supreme	130	3150	2881	2628	2388	2161	2865	2396	1993	1646	1348	1.3	0.0	-6.4	-18.9	NA
270 Win. Supreme	150	2930	2693	2468	2254	2051	2860	2416	2030	1693	1402	1.7	0.0	-7.4	-21.6	NA
270 W. Superformance	130	3200	2984	2788	2582	2393	2955	2570	2228	1924	1653	1.2	0.0	-5.7	-16.7	NA
270 Winchester	100	3430	3021	2649	2305	1988	2612	2027	1557	1179	877	+2.0	+1.0	-4.9	-17.5	$17
270 Winchester	130	3060	2776	2510	2259	2022	2702	2225	1818	1472	1180	+2.5	+1.4	-5.3	-18.2	$17
270 Winchester	135	3000	2780	2570	2369	2178	2697	2315	1979	1682	1421	+2.5	+1.4	-6.0	-17.6	$23
270 Winchester*	140	2940	2700	2480	2260	2060	2685	2270	1905	1590	1315	+2.5	+1.8	-4.6	-17.9	$20
270 Winchester*	150	2850	2585	2336	2100	1879	2705	2226	1817	1468	1175	+2.5	+1.2	-6.5	-22.0	$17
270 WSM	130	3275	3041	2820	2609	2408	3096	2669	2295	1564	1673	1.1	0.0	-5.5	-16.1	NA
270 WSM	140	3125	2865	2619	2386	2165	3035	2559	2132	1769	1457	1.4	0.0	-6.5	-19.0	NA
270 WSM	150	3000	2795	2599	2412	2232	2997	2601	2250	1937	1659	1.5	0	-6.6	-19.2	NA
270 WSM	150	3120	2923	2734	2554	2380	3242	2845	2490	2172	1886	1.3	0.0	-5.9	-17.2	NA
270 Wea. Mag.	100	3760	3380	3033	2712	2412	3139	2537	2042	1633	1292	+2.0	+2.4	-1.2	-10.1	$32
270 Wea. Mag.	130	3375	3119	2878	2649	2432	3287	2808	2390	2026	1707	+2.5	-2.9	-0.9	-9.9	$32
270 Wea. Mag.	130	3450	3194	2958	2732	2517	3435	2949	2525	2143	1828	1.0	0	-4.9	-14.5	NA
270 Wea. Mag.*	150	3245	3036	2837	2647	2465	3507	3070	2681	2334	2023	+2.5	+2.6	-1.8	-11.4	$47

7mm

Cartridge	Bullet Wgt. Grs.	Muzzle	100 yds.	200 yds.	300 yds.	400 yds.	Muzzle	100 yds.	200 yds.	300 yds.	400 yds.	100 yds.	200 yds.	300 yds.	400 yds.	Est. Price/box
7mm BR	140	2216	2012	1821	1643	1481	1525	1259	1031	839	681	+2.0	-3.7	-20.0	0.0	$23
7mm Mauser*	139/140	2660	2435	2221	2018	1827	2199	1843	1533	1266	1037	+2.5	0.0	-9.6	-27.7	$17
7mm Mauser	139	2740	2556	2379	2209	2046	2317	2016	1747	1506	1292	1.9	0	-8.1	-23.3	NA
7mm Mauser	154	2690	2490	2300	2120	1940	2475	2120	1810	1530	1285	+2.5	+0.8	-7.5	-23.5	$17
7mm Mauser	175	2440	2137	1857	1603	1382	2313	1774	1340	998	742	+2.5	-1.7	-16.1	0.0	$17
7x30 Waters	120	2700	2300	1930	1600	1330	1940	1405	990	685	470	+2.5	-0.2	-12.3	0.0	$18
7mm-08 Rem.	120	2675	2435	2207	1992	1790	1907	1579	1298	1057	854	2.2	0	-9.4	-27.5	NA
7mm-08 Rem.	120	3000	2725	2467	2223	1992	2398	1979	1621	1316	1058	+2.0	0.0	-7.6	-22.3	$18
7mm-08 Rem.	139	2840	2608	2387	2177	1978	2489	2098	1758	1463	1207	1.8	0	-7.9	-23.2	NA
7mm-08 Rem.*	140	2860	2625	2402	2189	1988	2542	2142	1793	1490	1228	+2.5	+0.8	-6.9	-21.9	$18
7mm-08 Rem.	154	2715	2510	2315	2128	1950	2520	2155	1832	1548	1300	+2.5	+1.0	-7.0	-22.7	$23
7-08 R. Superformance	139	2950	2857	2571	2393	2222	2686	2345	2040	1768	1524	1.5	0.0	-6.8	-19.7	NA
7x64mm	173	2526	2260	2010	1777	1565	2452	1962	1552	1214	941	0	-5.3	-19.3	-44.4	NA
7x64mm Bren.	140	2950	2710	2483	2266	2061	2705	2283	1910	1597	1320	1.5	0.0	-2.9	-7.3	$24.50
7x64mm Bren.	154	2820	2610	2420	2230	2050	2720	2335	1995	1695	1430	+2.5	+1.4	-5.7	-19.9	NA
7x64mm Bren.*	160	2850	2669	2495	2327	2166	2885	2530	2211	1924	1667	+2.5	+1.6	-4.8	-17.8	$24
7x64mm Bren.	175	2650	2445	2248	2061	1883	2728	2322	1964	1650	1378	2.2	0	-9.1	-26.4	$24.50
7x65mmR	173	2608	2337	2082	1844	1626	2613	2098	1666	1307	1015	0	-4.9	-17.9	-41.9	NA
275 Rigby	139	2680	2456	2242	2040	1848	2217	1861	1552	1284	1054	2.2	0	-9.1	-26.5	NA
284 Winchester	150	2860	2595	2344	2108	1886	2724	2243	1830	1480	1185	+2.5	+0.8	-7.3	-23.2	$24
280 R. Superformance	139	3090	2890	2699	2516	2341	2946	2578	2249	1954	1691	1.3	0.0	-6.1	-17.7	NA
280 Rem.	139	3090	2891	2700	2518	2343	2947	2579	2250	1957	1694	1.3	0	-6.1	-17.7	NA
280 Remington	140	3000	2758	2528	2309	2102	2797	2363	1986	1657	1373	+2.5	+1.4	-5.2	-18.3	$17
280 Remington*	150	2890	2624	2373	2135	1912	2781	2293	1875	1518	1217	+2.5	+0.8	-7.1	-22.6	$17
280 Remington	160	2840	2637	2442	2556	2078	2866	2471	2120	1809	1535	+2.5	+0.8	-6.7	-21.0	$20
280 Remington	165	2820	2510	2220	1950	1701	2913	2308	1805	1393	1060	+2.5	+0.4	-8.8	-26.5	$17
280 Ack. Imp.	140	3150	2946	2752	2566	2387	3084	2698	2354	2047	1772	1.3	0	-5.8	-17.0	NA
280 Ack. Imp.	150	2900	2712	2533	2360	2194	2800	2450	2136	1855	1603	1.6	0	-7.0	-20.3	NA
280 Ack. Imp.	160	2950	2751	2561	2379	2205	3091	2686	2331	2011	1727	1.5	0	-6.9	-19.9	NA
7x61mm S&H Sup.	154	3060	2720	2400	2100	1820	3200	2520	1965	1505	1135	+2.5	+1.8	-5.0	-19.8	NA
7mm Dakota	160	3200	3001	2811	2630	2455	3637	3200	2808	2456	2140	+2.1	+1.9	-2.8	-12.5	NA
7mm Rem. Mag.	139	3190	2986	2791	2605	2427	3141	2752	2405	2095	1817	1.2	0	-5.7	-16.5	NA
7mm Rem. Mag. (Rem.)	140	2710	2482	2265	2059	NA	2283	1915	1595	1318	NA	0.0	-4.5	-1.57	0.0	NA
7mm Rem. Mag.*	139/140	3150	2930	2710	2510	2320	3085	2660	2290	1960	1670	+2.5	+2.4	-2.4	-12.7	$21
7mm Rem. Mag.	150/154	3110	2830	2568	2320	2085	3221	2667	2196	1792	1448	+2.5	+1.6	-4.6	-16.5	$21

Cartridge	Bullet Wgt. Grs.	VELOCITY (fps)					ENERGY (ft. lbs.)					TRAJ. (in.)				Est. Price/box
		Muzzle	100 yds.	200 yds.	300 yds.	400 yds.	Muzzle	100 yds.	200 yds.	300 yds.	400 yds.	100 yds.	200 yds.	300 yds.	400 yds.	
7mm Rem. Mag.*	160/162	2950	2730	2520	2320	2120	3090	2650	2250	1910	1600	+2.5	+1.8	-4.4	-17.8	$34
7mm Rem. Mag.	165	2900	2699	2507	2324	2147	3081	2669	2303	1978	1689	+2.5	+1.2	-5.9	-19.0	$28
7mm Rem Mag.	175	2860	2645	2440	2244	2057	3178	2718	2313	1956	1644	+2.5	+1.0	-6.5	-20.7	$21
7 R.M. Superformance	139	3240	3033	2836	2648	2467	3239	2839	2482	2163	1877	1.1	0.0	-5.5	-15.9	NA
7 R.M. Superformance	154	3100	2914	2736	2565	2401	3286	2904	2560	2250	1970	1.3	0.0	-5.9	-17.2	NA
7mm Rem. SA ULTRA MAG	140	3175	2934	2707	2490	2283	3033	2676	2277	1927	1620	1.3	0.0	-6	-17.7	NA
7mm Rem. SA ULTRA MAG	150	3110	2828	2563	2313	2077	3221	2663	2188	1782	1437	2.5	2.1	-3.6	-15.8	NA
7mm Rem. SA ULTRA MAG	160	2850	2676	2508	2347	2192	2885	2543	2235	1957	1706	1.7	0	-7.2	-20.7	NA
7mm Rem. SA ULTRA MAG	160	2960	2762	2572	2390	2215	3112	2709	2350	2029	1743	2.6	2.2	-3.6	-15.4	NA
7mm Rem. WSM	140	3225	3008	2801	2603	2414	3233	2812	2438	2106	1812	1.2	0.0	-5.6	-16.4	NA
7mm Rem. WSM	160	2990	2744	2512	2081	1883	3176	2675	2241	1864	1538	1.6	0.0	-7.1	-20.8	NA
7mm Wea. Mag.	139	3300	3091	2891	2701	2519	3361	2948	2580	2252	1958	1.1	0	-5.2	-15.2	NA
7mm Wea. Mag.	140	3225	2970	2729	2501	2283	3233	2741	2315	1943	1621	+2.5	+2.0	-3.2	-14.0	$35
7mm Wea. Mag.	140	3340	3127	2925	2732	2546	3467	3040	2659	2320	2016	0	-2.1	-8.2	-19	NA
7mm Wea. Mag.	150	3175	2957	2751	2553	2364	3357	2913	2520	2171	1861	0	-2.5	-9.6	-22	NA
7mm Wea. Mag.	154	3260	3023	2799	2586	2382	3539	3044	2609	2227	1890	+2.5	+2.8	-1.5	-10.8	$32
7mm Wea. Mag.*	160	3200	3004	2816	2637	2464	3637	3205	2817	2469	2156	+2.5	+2.7	-1.5	-10.6	$47
7mm Wea. Mag.	165	2950	2747	2553	2367	2189	3188	2765	2388	2053	1756	+2.5	+1.8	-4.2	-16.4	$43
7mm Wea. Mag.	175	2910	2693	2486	2288	2098	3293	2818	2401	2033	1711	+2.5	+1.2	-5.9	-19.4	$35
7.21(.284) Tomahawk	140	3300	3118	2943	2774	2612	3386	3022	2693	2393	2122	2.3	3.2	0.0	-7.7	NA
7mm STW	140	3300	3086	2889	2697	2513	3384	2966	2594	2261	1963	0	-2.1	-8.5	-19.6	NA
7mm STW	140	3325	3064	2818	2585	2364	3436	2918	2468	2077	1737	+2.3	+1.8	-3.0	-13.1	NA
7mm STW	150	3175	2957	2751	2553	2364	3357	2913	2520	2171	1861	0	-2.5	-9.6	-22	NA
7mm STW	175	2900	2760	2625	2493	2366	3267	2960	2677	2416	2175	0	-3.1	-11.2	-24.9	NA
7mm STW Supreme	160	3150	2894	2652	2422	2204	3526	2976	2499	2085	1727	1.3	0.0	-6.3	-18.5	NA
7mm Rem. Ultra Mag.	140	3425	3184	2956	2740	2534	3646	3151	2715	2333	1995	1.7	1.6	-2.6	-11.4	NA
7mm Rem. Ultra Mag.	160	3225	3035	2854	2680	2512	3694	3273	2894	2551	2242	0	-2.3	-8.8	-20.2	NA
7mm Rem. Ultra Mag.	174	3040	2896	2756	2621	2490	3590	3258	2952	2669	2409	0	-2.6	-9.9	-22.2	NA
7mm Firehawk	140	3625	3373	3135	2909	2695	4084	3536	3054	2631	2258	+2.2	+2.9	0.0	-7.03	NA
7.21 (.284) Firebird	140	3750	3522	3306	3101	2905	4372	3857	3399	2990	2625	1.6	2.4	0.0	-6.0	NA
30																
300 ACC Blackout	110	2150	1886	1646	1432	1254	1128	869	661	501	384	0	-8.3	-29.6	-67.8	NA
300 AAC Blackout	125	2250	2031	1826	1636	1464	1404	1145	926	743	595	0	-7	-24.4	-54.8	NA
30 Carbine	110	1990	1567	1236	1035	923	977	600	373	262	208	0.0	-13.5	0.0	0.0	$28**
30 Carbine	110	2000	1601	1279	1067	—	977	626	399	278	—	0	-12.9	-47.2	—	NA
300 Whisper	110	2375	2094	1834	1597	NA	1378	1071	822	623	NA	3.2	0.0	-13.6	NA	NA
300 Whisper	208	1020	988	959	NA	NA	480	451	422	NA	NA	0.0	-34.10	NA	NA	NA
303 Savage	190	1890	1612	1327	1183	1055	1507	1096	794	591	469	+2.5	-7.6	0.0	0.0	$24
30 Remington	170	2120	1822	1555	1328	1153	1696	1253	913	666	502	+2.5	-4.7	-26.3	0.0	$20
7.62x39mm Rus.	123	2360	2049	1764	1511	1296	1521	1147	850	623	459	3.4	0	-14.7	-44.7	NA
7.62x39mm Rus.	123/125	2300	2030	1780	1550	1350	1445	1125	860	655	500	+2.5	-2.0	-17.5	0.0	$13
30-30 Win.	55	3400	2693	2085	1570	1187	1412	886	521	301	172	+2.0	0.0	-10.2	-35.0	$18
30-30 Win.	125	2570	2090	1660	1320	1080	1830	1210	770	480	320	-2.0	-2.6	-19.9	0.0	$13
30-30 Win.	140	2500	2198	1918	1662	—	1943	1501	1143	858	—	2.9	0	-12.4	—	NA
30-30 Win.	150	2390	2040	1723	1447	1225	1902	1386	989	697	499	0.0	-7.5	-27.0	-63.0	NA
30-30 Win. Supreme	150	2480	2095	1747	1446	1209	2049	1462	1017	697	487	0.0	-6.5	-24.5	0.0	NA
30-30 Win.	160	2300	1997	1719	1473	1268	1879	1416	1050	771	571	+2.5	-2.9	-20.2	0.0	$18
30-30 Win. Lever Evolution	160	2400	2150	1916	1699	NA	2046	1643	1304	1025	NA	3.0	0.2	-12.1	NA	NA
30-30 PMC Cowboy	170	1300	1198	1121	—	—	638	474	—	—	—	0.0	-27.0	0.0	0.0	NA
30-30 Win.*	170	2200	1895	1619	1381	1191	1827	1355	989	720	535	+2.5	-5.8	-23.6	0.0	$13
300 Savage	150	2630	2354	2094	1853	1631	2303	1845	1462	1143	886	+2.5	-0.4	-10.1	-30.7	$17
300 Savage	150	2740	2499	2272	2056	1852	2500	2081	1718	1407	1143	2.1	0	-8.8	-25.8	NA
300 Savage	180	2350	2137	1935	1754	1570	2207	1825	1496	1217	985	+2.5	-1.6	-15.2	0.0	$17
30-40 Krag	180	2430	2213	2007	1813	1632	2360	1957	1610	1314	1064	+2.5	-1.4	-13.8	0.0	$18
7.65x53mm Arg.	180	2590	2390	2200	2010	1830	2685	2280	1925	1615	1345	+2.5	0.0	-27.6	0.0	NA
7.5x53mm Argentine	150	2785	2519	2269	2032	1814	2583	2113	1714	1376	1096	+2.0	0.0	-8.8	-25.5	NA
308 Marlin Express	140	2800	2532	2279	2040	1818	2437	1992	1614	1294	1207	2.0	0	-8.7	-25.8	NA
308 Marlin Express	160	2660	2430	2226	2026	1836	2513	2111	1761	1457	1197	3.0	1.7	-6.7	-23.5	NA
307 Winchester	150	2760	2321	1924	1575	1289	2530	1795	1233	826	554	+2.5	-1.5	-13.6	0.0	Disc.
7.5x55 Swiss	180	2650	2450	2250	2060	1880	2805	2390	2020	1700	1415	+2.5	+0.6	-8.1	-24.9	NA
7.5x55mm Swiss	165	2720	2515	2319	2132	1954	2710	2317	1970	1665	1398	+2.0	0.0	-8.5	-24.6	NA
30 Remington AR	123/125	2800	2465	2154	1867	1606	2176	1686	1288	967	716	2.1	0.0	-9.7	-29.4	NA
308 Winchester	55	3770	3215	2726	2286	1888	1735	1262	907	638	435	-2.0	+1.4	-3.8	-15.8	$22
308 Win.	110	3165	2830	2520	2230	1960	2447	1956	1551	1215	938	1.4	0	-6.9	-20.9	NA
308 Win. PDX1	120	2850	2497	2171	NA	NA	2164	1662	1256	NA	NA	0.0	-2.8	NA	NA	NA
308 Winchester	150	2820	2533	2263	2009	1774	2648	2137	1705	1344	1048	+2.5	+0.4	-8.5	-26.1	$17
308 W. Superformance	150	3000	2772	2555	2348	1962	2997	2558	2173	1836	1540	1.5	0.0	-6.9	-20.0	NA
308 Win.	155	2775	2553	2342	2141	1950	2650	2243	1887	1577	1308	1.9	0	-8.3	-24.2	NA
308 Win.	155	2850	2640	2438	2247	2064	2795	2398	2047	1737	1466	1.8	0	-7.5	-22.1	NA
308 Winchester	165	2700	2440	2194	1963	1748	2670	2180	1763	1411	1199	+2.5	0.0	-9.7	-28.5	$20
308 Winchester	168	2680	2493	2314	2143	1979	2678	2318	1998	1713	1460	+2.5	0.0	-8.9	-25.3	$18
308 Win. Super Match	168	2870	2647	2462	2284	2114	3008	2613	2261	1946	1667	1.7	0.0	-7.5	-21.6	NA
308 Win. (Fed.)	170	2000	1740	1510	NA	NA	1510	1145	860	NA	NA	0.0	0.0	0.0	0.0	NA

Cartridge	Bullet Wgt. Grs.	VELOCITY (fps)					ENERGY (ft. lbs.)					TRAJ. (in.)				Est. Price/box
		Muzzle	100 yds.	200 yds.	300 yds.	400 yds.	Muzzle	100 yds.	200 yds.	300 yds.	400 yds.	100 yds.	200 yds.	300 yds.	400 yds.	
308 Winchester	178	2620	2415	2220	2034	1857	2713	2306	1948	1635	1363	+2.5	0.0	-9.6	-27.6	$23
308 Win. Super Match	178	2780	2609	2444	2285	2132	3054	2690	2361	2064	1797	1.8	0.0	-7.6	-21.9	NA
308 Winchester*	180	2620	2393	2178	1974	1782	2743	2288	1896	1557	1269	+2.5	-0.2	-10.2	-28.5	$17
30-06 Spfd.	55	4080	3485	2965	2502	2083	2033	1483	1074	764	530	+2.0	+1.9	-2.1	-11.7	$22
30-06 Spfd. (Rem.)	125	2660	2335	2034	1757	NA	1964	1513	1148	856	NA	0.0	-5.2	-18.9	0.0	NA
30-06 Spfd.	125	2700	2412	2143	1891	1660	2023	1615	1274	993	765	2.3	0	-9.9	-29.5	NA
30-06 Spfd.	125	3140	2780	2447	2138	1853	2736	2145	1662	1279	953	+2.0	+1.0	-6.2	-21.0	$17
30-06 Spfd.	150	2910	2617	2342	2083	1853	2820	2281	1827	1445	1135	+2.5	+0.8	-7.2	-23.4	$17
30-06 Superformance	150	3080	2848	2617	2417	2216	3159	2700	2298	1945	1636	1.4	0.0	-6.4	-18.9	NA
30-06 Spfd.	152	2910	2654	2413	2184	1968	2858	2378	1965	1610	1307	+2.5	+1.0	-6.6	-21.3	$23
30-06 Spfd.*	165	2800	2534	2283	2047	1825	2872	2352	1909	1534	1220	+2.5	+0.4	-8.4	-25.5	$17
30-06 Spfd.	168	2710	2522	2346	2169	2003	2739	2372	2045	1754	1497	+2.5	+0.4	-8.0	-23.5	$18
30-06 M1 Garand	168	2710	2523	2343	2171	2006	2739	2374	2048	1758	1501	2.3	0	-8.6	-24.6	NA
30-06 Spfd. (Fed.)	170	2000	1740	1510	NA	NA	1510	1145	860	NA	NA	0.0	0.0	0.0	0.0	NA
30-06 Spfd.	178	2720	2511	2311	2121	1939	2924	2491	2111	1777	1486	+2.5	+0.4	-8.2	-24.6	$23
30-06 Spfd.*	180	2700	2469	2250	2042	1846	2913	2436	2023	1666	1362	-2.5	0.0	-9.3	-27.0	$17
30-06 Superformance	180	2820	2630	2447	2272	2104	3178	2764	2393	2063	1769	1.8	0.0	-7.6	-21.9	NA
30-06 Spfd.	220	2410	2130	1870	1632	1422	2837	2216	1708	1301	988	+2.5	-1.7	-18.0	0.0	$17
30-06 High Energy	180	2880	2690	2500	2320	2150	3315	2880	2495	2150	1845	+1.7	0.0	-7.2	-21.0	NA
30 T/C	150	2920	2696	2483	2280	2087	2849	2421	2054	1732	1450	1.7	0	-7.3	-21.3	NA
30 T/C Superformance	150	3000	2772	2555	2348	2151	2997	2558	2173	1836	1540	1.5	0.0	-6.9	-20.0	NA
30 T/C Superformance	165	2850	2644	2447	2258	2078	2975	2560	2193	1868	1582	1.7	0.0	-7.6	-22.0	NA
300 Rem SA Ultra Mag	150	3200	2901	2622	2359	2112	3410	2803	2290	1854	1485	1.3	0.0	-6.4	-19.1	NA
300 Rem SA Ultra Mag	165	3075	2792	2527	2276	2040	3464	2856	2339	1898	1525	1.5	0.0	-7	-20.7	NA
300 Rem SA Ultra Mag	180	2960	2761	2571	2389	2214	3501	3047	2642	2280	1959	2.6	2.2	-3.6	-15.4	NA
300 Rem. SA Ultra Mag	200	2800	2644	2494	2348	2208	3841	3104	2761	2449	2164	0	-3.5	-12.5	-27.9	NA
7.82 (308) Patriot	150	3250	2999	2762	2537	2323	3519	2997	2542	2145	1798	+1.2	0.0	-5.8	-16.9	NA
300 RCM	150	3265	3023	2794	2577	2369	3550	3043	2600	2211	1870	1.2	0	-5.6	-16.5	NA
300 RCM Superformance	150	3310	3065	2833	2613	2404	3648	3128	2673	2274	1924	1.1	0.0	-5.4	-16.0	NA
300 RCM Superformance	165	3185	2964	2753	2552	2360	3716	3217	2776	2386	2040	1.2	0.0	-5.8	-17.0	NA
300 RCM Superformance	180	3040	2840	2649	2466	2290	3693	3223	2804	2430	2096	1.4	0.0	-6.4	-18.5	NA
300 WSM	150	3300	3061	2834	2619	2414	3628	3121	2676	2285	1941	1.1	0.0	-5.4	-15.9	NA
300 WSM	180	2970	2741	2524	2317	2120	3526	3005	2547	2147	1797	1.6	0.0	-7.0	-20.5	NA
300 WSM	180	3010	2923	2734	2554	2380	3242	2845	2490	2172	1886	1.3	0	-5.9	-17.2	NA
300 WSM	190	2875	2729	2588	2451	2319	3486	3142	2826	2535	2269	0	3.2	-11.5	-25.7	NA
308 Norma Mag.	180	2975	2787	2608	2435	2269	3536	3105	2718	2371	2058	0	-3	-11.1	-25.0	NA
308 Norma Mag.	180	3020	2820	2630	2440	2270	3645	3175	2755	2385	2050	+2.5	+2.0	-3.5	-14.8	NA
300 Dakota	200	3000	2824	2656	2493	2336	3996	3542	3131	2760	2423	+2.2	+1.5	-4.0	-15.2	NA
300 H&H Mag.	180	2870	2678	2494	2318	2148	3292	2866	2486	2147	1844	1.7	0	-7.3	-21.6	NA
300 H&H Magnum*	180	2880	2640	2412	2196	1990	3315	2785	2325	1927	1583	+2.5	+0.8	-6.8	-21.7	$24
300 H&H Mag.	200	2750	2596	2447	2303	2164	3357	2992	2659	2355	2079	1.8	0	-7.6	-21.8	NA
300 H&H Magnum	220	2550	2267	2002	1757	NA	3167	2510	1958	1508	NA	-2.5	-0.4	-12.0	0.0	NA
300 Win. Mag.	150	3290	2951	2636	2342	2068	3605	2900	2314	1827	1424	+2.5	+1.9	-3.8	-15.8	$22
300 WM Superformance	150	3400	3150	2914	2690	2477	3850	3304	2817	2409	2043	1.0	0.0	-5.1	-15.0	NA
300 Win. Mag.	165	3100	2877	2665	2462	2269	3522	3033	2603	2221	1897	+2.5	+2.4	-3.0	-16.9	$24
300 Win. Mag.	178	2900	2760	2568	2375	2191	3509	3030	2606	2230	1897	+2.5	+1.4	-5.0	-17.6	$29
300 Win. Mag.	178	2960	2770	2588	2413	2245	3463	3032	2647	2301	1992	1.5	0	-6.7	-19.4	NA
300 WM Super Match	178	2960	2770	2587	2412	2243	3462	3031	2645	2298	1988	1.5	0.0	-6.7	-19.4	NA
300 Win. Mag.*	180	2960	2745	2540	2344	2157	3501	3011	2578	2196	1859	+2.5	+1.2	-5.5	-18.5	$22
300 WM Superformance	180	3130	2927	2732	2546	2366	3917	3424	2983	2589	2238	1.3	0.0	-5.9	-17.3	NA
300 Win. Mag.	190	2885	1691	2506	2327	2156	3511	3055	2648	2285	1961	+2.5	+1.2	-5.7	-19.0	$26
300 Win. Mag.	195	2930	2760	2596	2438	2286	3717	3297	2918	2574	2262	1.5	0	-6.7	-19.4	NA
300 Win. Mag.*	200	2825	2595	2376	2167	1970	3545	2991	2508	2086	1742	-2.5	+1.6	-4.7	-17.2	$36
300 Win. Mag.	220	2680	2448	2228	2020	1823	3508	2927	2424	1993	1623	+2.5	0.0	-9.5	-27.5	$23
300 Rem. Ultra Mag.	150	3450	3208	2980	2762	2556	3964	3427	2956	2541	2175	1.7	1.5	-2.6	-11.2	NA
300 Rem. Ultra Mag.	150	2910	2686	2473	2279	2077	2820	2403	2037	1716	1436	1.7	0.0	-7.4	-21.5	NA
300 Rem. Ultra Mag.	165	3350	3099	2862	2938	2424	4110	3518	3001	2549	2152	1.1	0	-5.3	-15.6	NA
300 Rem. Ultra Mag.	180	3250	3037	2834	2640	2454	4221	3686	3201	2786	2407	2.4	0.0	-3.0	-12.7	NA
300 Rem. Ultra Mag.	180	2960	2774	2505	2294	2093	3501	2971	2508	2103	1751	2.7	2.2	-3.8	-16.4	NA
300 Rem. Ultra Mag.	200	3032	2791	2562	2345	2138	4083	3459	2916	2442	2030	1.5	0.0	-6.8	-19.9	NA
300 Rem. Ultra Mag.	210	2920	2790	2665	2543	2424	3975	3631	3311	3015	2740	1.5	0	-6.4	-18.1	NA
300 Wea. Mag.	100	3900	3441	3038	2652	2305	3714	2891	2239	1717	1297	+2.0	+2.6	-0.6	-8.7	$32
300 Wea. Mag.	150	3375	3126	2892	2670	2459	3794	3255	2786	2374	2013	1.0	0	-5.2	-15.3	NA
300 Wea. Mag.	150	3600	3307	3033	2776	2533	3642	3064	2566	2137	NA	+2.5	+3.2	0.0	-8.1	$32
300 Wea. Mag.	165	3140	2921	2713	2515	2325	3612	3126	2697	2317	1980	1.3	0	-6.0	-17.5	NA
300 Wea. Mag.	165	3450	3210	3000	2792	2593	4360	3796	3297	2855	2464	+2.5	+3.2	0.0	-7.8	NA
300 Wea. Mag.	178	3120	2902	2695	2497	2308	3847	3329	2870	2464	2104	+2.5	-1.7	-3.6	-14.7	$43
300 Wea. Mag.	180	3330	3110	2910	2710	2520	4430	3875	3375	2935	2540	+1.0	0.0	-5.2	-15.1	NA
300 Wea. Mag.	190	3030	2830	2638	2455	2279	3873	3378	2936	2542	2190	+2.5	+1.6	-4.3	-16.0	$38
300 Wea. Mag.	220	2850	2541	2283	1964	1736	3967	3155	2480	1922	1471	+2.5	+0.4	-8.5	-26.4	$35
300 Pegasus	180	3500	3319	3145	2978	2817	4896	4401	3953	3544	3172	+2.28	+2.89	0.0	-6.79	NA

31

Cartridge	Bullet Wgt. Grs.	VELOCITY (fps)					ENERGY (ft. lbs.)					TRAJ. (in.)				Est. Price/box
		Muzzle	100 yds.	200 yds.	300 yds.	400 yds.	Muzzle	100 yds.	200 yds.	300 yds.	400 yds.	100 yds.	200 yds.	300 yds.	400 yds.	
32-20 Win.	100	1210	1021	913	834	769	325	231	185	154	131	0.0	-32.3	0.0	0.0	$23**
303 British	150	2685	2441	2211	1993	1789	2401	1985	1628	1323	1066	2.2	0	-9.3	-27.4	NA
303 British	180	2460	2124	1817	1542	1311	2418	1803	1319	950	687	+2.5	-1.8	-16.8	0.0	$18
303 Light Mag.	150	2830	2570	2325	2094	1884	2667	2199	1800	1461	1185	+2.0	0.0	-8.4	-24.6	NA
7.62x54mm Rus.	146	2950	2730	2520	2320	NA	2820	2415	2055	1740	NA	+2.5	+2.0	-4.4	-17.7	NA
7.62x54mm Rus.	174	2800	2607	2422	2245	2075	3029	2626	2267	1947	1664	1.8	0	-7.8	-22.4	NA
7.62x54mm Rus.	180	2580	2370	2180	2000	1820	2650	2250	1900	1590	1100	+2.5	0.0	-9.8	-28.5	NA
7.7x58mm Jap.	150	2640	2399	2170	1954	1752	2321	1916	1568	1271	1022	+2.3	0.0	-9.7	-28.5	NA
7.7x58mm Jap.	180	2500	2300	2100	1920	1750	2490	2105	1770	1475	1225	+2.5	0.0	-10.4	-30.2	NA
8mm																
8x56 R	205	2400	2188	1987	1797	1621	2621	2178	1796	1470	1196	+2.9	0.0	-11.7	-34.3	NA
8x57mm JS Mau.	165	2850	2520	2210	1930	1670	2965	2330	1795	1360	1015	+2.5	+1.0	-7.7	0.0	NA
32 Win. Special	165	2410	2145	1897	1669	NA	2128	1685	1318	1020	NA	2.0	0.0	-13.0	-19.9	NA
32 Win. Special	170	2250	1921	1626	1372	1175	1911	1393	998	710	521	+2.5	-3.5	-22.9	0.0	$14
8mm Mauser	170	2360	1969	1622	1333	1123	2102	1464	993	671	476	+2.5	-3.1	-22.2	0.0	$18
8mm Mauser	196	2500	2338	2182	2032	1888	2720	2379	2072	1797	1552	2.4	0	-9.8	-27.9	NA
325 WSM	180	3060	2841	2632	2432	2242	3743	3226	2769	2365	2009	+1.4	0.0	-6.4	-18.7	NA
325 WSM	200	2950	2753	2565	2384	2210	3866	3367	2922	2524	2170	+1.5	0.0	-6.8	-19.8	NA
325 WSM	220	2840	2605	2382	2169	1968	3941	3316	2772	2300	1893	+1.8	0.0	-8.0	-23.3	NA
8mm Rem. Mag.	185	3080	2761	2464	2186	1927	3896	3131	2494	1963	1525	+2.5	+1.4	-5.5	-19.7	$30
8mm Rem. Mag.	220	2830	2581	2346	2123	1913	3912	3254	2688	2201	1787	+2.5	+0.6	-7.6	-23.5	Disc.
33																
338 Federal	180	2830	2590	2350	2130	1930	3200	2670	2215	1820	1480	1.8	0.0	-8.2	-23.9	NA
338 Marlin Express	200	2565	2365	2174	1992	1820	2922	2484	2099	1762	1471	3.0	1.2	-7.9	-25.9	NA
338 Federal	185	2750	2550	2350	2160	1980	3105	2660	2265	1920	1615	1.9	0.0	-8.3	-24.1	NA
338 Federal	210	2630	2410	2200	2010	1820	3225	2710	2265	1880	1545	2.3	0.0	-9.4	-27.3	NA
338 Federal MSR	185	2680	2459	2230	2020	1820	2950	2460	2035	1670	1360	2.2	0.0	-9.2	-26.8	NA
338-06	200	2750	2553	2364	2184	2011	3358	2894	2482	2118	1796	+1.9	0.0	-8.22	-23.6	NA
330 Dakota	250	2900	2719	2545	2378	2217	4668	4103	3595	3138	2727	+2.3	+1.3	-5.0	-17.5	NA
338 Lapua	250	2900	2685	2481	2285	2098	4668	4002	2416	2899	2444	1.7	0	-7.3	-21.3	NA
338 Lapua	250	2963	2795	2640	2493	NA	4842	4341	3881	3458	NA	+1.9	0.0	-7.9	0.0	NA
338 RCM Superformance	185	2980	2755	2542	2338	2143	3647	3118	2653	2242	1887	1.5	0.0	-6.9	-20.3	NA
338 RCM Superformance	200	2950	2744	2547	2358	2177	3846	3342	2879	2468	2104	1.6	0.0	-6.9	-20.1	NA
338 RCM Superformance	225	2750	2575	2407	2245	2089	3778	3313	2894	2518	2180	1.9	0.0	-7.9	-22.7	NA
338 WM Superformance	185	3080	2850	2632	2424	2226	3896	3337	2845	2413	2034	1.4	0.0	-6.4	-18.8	NA
338 Win. Mag.	200	3030	2820	2620	2429	2246	4077	3532	3049	2621	2240	1.4	0	-6.5	-18.9	NA
338 Win. Mag.*	210	2830	2590	2370	2150	1940	3735	3130	2610	2155	1760	+2.5	+1.4	-6.0	-20.9	$33
338 Win. Mag.*	225	2785	2517	2266	2029	1808	3871	3165	2565	2057	1633	+2.5	+0.4	-8.5	-25.9	$27
338 WM Superformance	225	2840	2758	2582	2414	2252	4318	3798	3331	2911	2533	1.5	0.0	-6.8	-19.5	NA
338 Win. Mag.	230	2780	2573	2375	2186	2005	3948	3382	2881	2441	2054	+2.5	+1.2	-6.3	-21.0	$40
338 Win. Mag.*	250	2660	2456	2261	2075	1898	3927	3348	2837	2389	1999	+2.5	+0.2	-9.0	-26.2	$27
338 Ultra Mag.	250	2860	2645	2440	2244	2057	4540	3882	3303	2794	2347	1.7	0.0	-7.6	-22.1	NA
338 Lapua Match	250	2900	2760	2625	2494	2366	4668	4229	3825	3452	3108	1.5	0.0	-6.6	-18.8	NA
338 Lapua Match	285	2745	2623	2504	2388	2275	4768	4352	3966	3608	3275	1.8	0.0	-7.3	-20.8	NA
8.59(.338) Galaxy	200	3100	2899	2707	2524	2347	4269	3734	3256	2829	2446	3	3.8	0.0	-9.3	NA
340 Wea. Mag.*	210	3250	2991	2746	2515	2295	4924	4170	3516	2948	2455	+2.5	+1.9	-1.8	-11.8	$56
340 Wea. Mag.*	250	3000	2806	2621	2443	2272	4995	4371	3812	3311	2864	+2.5	+2.0	-3.5	-14.8	$56
338 A-Square	250	3120	2799	2500	2220	1958	5403	4348	3469	2736	2128	+2.5	+2.7	-1.5	-10.5	NA
338-378 Wea. Mag.	225	3180	2974	2778	2591	2410	5052	4420	3856	3353	2902	3.1	3.8	0.0	-8.9	NA
338 Titan	225	3230	3010	2800	2600	2409	5211	4524	3916	3377	2898	+3.07	+3.8	0.0	-8.95	NA
338 Excalibur	200	3600	3361	3134	2920	2715	5755	5015	4363	3785	3274	+2.23	+2.87	0.0	-6.99	NA
338 Excalibur	250	3250	2922	2618	2333	2066	5863	4740	3804	3021	2370	+1.3	0.0	-6.35	-19.2	NA
34, 35																
348 Winchester	200	2520	2215	1931	1672	1443	2820	2178	1656	1241	925	+2.5	-1.4	-14.7	0.0	$42
357 Magnum	158	1830	1427	1138	980	883	1175	715	454	337	274	0.0	-16.2	-33.1	0.0	$25**
35 Remington	150	2300	1874	1506	1218	1039	1762	1169	755	494	359	+2.5	-4.1	-26.3	0.0	$16
35 Remington	200	2080	1698	1376	1140	1001	1921	1280	841	577	445	+2.5	-6.3	-17.1	-33.6	$16
35 Remington	200	2225	1963	1722	1505	—	2198	1711	1317	1006	—	3.8	0	-15.6	—	NA
35 Rem. Lever Evolution	200	2225	1963	1721	1503	NA	2198	1711	1315	1003	NA	3.0	-1.3	-17.5	NA	NA
356 Winchester	200	2460	2114	1797	1517	1284	2688	1985	1434	1022	732	+2.5	-1.8	-15.1	0.0	$31
356 Winchester	250	2160	1911	1682	1476	1299	2591	2028	1571	1210	937	+2.5	-3.7	-22.2	0.0	$31
358 Winchester	200	2475	2180	1906	1655	1434	2720	2110	1612	1217	913	2.9	0	-12.6	-37.9	NA
358 Winchester	200	2490	2171	1876	1619	1379	2753	2093	1563	1151	844	+2.5	-1.6	-15.6	0.0	$31
358 STA	275	2850	2562	2292	2039	NA	4958	4009	3208	2539	NA	+1.9	0.0	-8.6	0.0	NA
350 Rem. Mag.	200	2710	2410	2130	1870	1631	3261	2579	2014	1553	1181	+2.5	-0.2	-10.0	-30.1	$33
35 Whelen	200	2675	2378	2100	1842	1606	3177	2510	1958	1506	1145	+2.5	-0.2	-10.3	-31.1	$20
35 Whelen	200	2910	2585	2283	2001	1742	3760	2968	2314	1778	1347	1.9	0	-8.6	-25.9	NA
35 Whelen	225	2500	2300	2110	1930	1770	3120	2650	2235	1870	1560	+2.6	0.0	-10.2	-29.9	NA
35 Whelen	250	2400	2197	2005	1823	1652	3197	2680	2230	1844	1515	+2.5	-1.2	-13.7	0.0	$20
358 Norma Mag.	250	2800	2510	2230	1970	1730	4350	3480	2750	2145	1655	+2.5	+1.0	-7.6	-25.2	NA
358 STA	275	2850	2562	229*2	2039	1764	4959	4009	3208	2539	1899	+1.9	0.0	-8.58	-26.1	NA

Cartridge	Bullet Wgt. Grs.	VELOCITY (fps)					ENERGY (ft. lbs.)					TRAJ. (in.)				Est. Price/box
		Muzzle	100 yds.	200 yds.	300 yds.	400 yds.	Muzzle	100 yds.	200 yds.	300 yds.	400 yds.	100 yds.	200 yds.	300 yds.	400 yds.	
9.3mm																
9.3x57mm Mau.	286	2070	1810	1590	1390	1110	2710	2090	1600	1220	955	+2.5	-2.6	-22.5	0.0	NA
370 Sako Mag.	286	3550	2370	2200	2040	2880	4130	3570	3075	2630	2240	2.4	0.0	-9.5	-27.2	NA
9.3x62mm	250	2550	2376	2208	2048	—	3609	3133	2707	2328	—	0	-5.4	-17.9	—	NA
9.3x62mm	286	2360	2155	1961	1778	1608	3537	2949	2442	2008	1642	0	-6.0	-21.1	-47.2	NA
9.3x62mm	286	2400	2163	1941	1733	—	3657	2972	2392	1908	—	0	-6.7	-22.6	—	NA
9.3x64mm	286	2700	2505	2318	2139	1968	4629	3984	3411	2906	2460	+2.5	+2.7	-4.5	-19.2	NA
9.3x72mmR	193	1952	1610	1326	1120	996	1633	1112	754	538	425	0	-12.1	-44.1	—	NA
9.3x74mmR	250	2550	2376	2208	2048	—	3609	3133	2707	2328	—	0	-5.4	-17.9	—	NA
9.3x74Rmm	286	2360	2136	1924	1727	1545	3536	2896	2351	1893	1516	0.0	-6.1	-21.7	-49.0	NA
375																
375 Winchester	200	2200	1841	1526	1268	1089	2150	1506	1034	714	527	+2.5	-4.0	-26.2	0.0	$27
375 Winchester	250	1900	1647	1424	1239	1103	2005	1506	1126	852	676	+2.5	-6.9	-33.3	0.0	$27
376 Steyr	225	2600	2331	2078	1842	1625	3377	2714	2157	1694	1319	2.5	0.0	-10.6	-31.4	NA
376 Steyr	270	2600	2372	2156	1951	1759	4052	3373	2787	2283	1855	2.3	0.0	-9.9	-28.9	NA
375 Dakota	300	2600	2316	2051	1804	1579	4502	3573	2800	2167	1661	+2.4	0.0	-11.0	-32.7	NA
375 N.E. 2-1/2"	270	2000	1740	1507	1310	NA	2398	1815	1362	1026	NA	+2.5	-6.0	-30.0	0.0	NA
375 Flanged	300	2450	2150	1886	1640	NA	3998	3102	2369	1790	NA	+2.5	-2.4	-17.0	0.0	NA
375 Ruger	250	2890	2675	2471	2275	2088	4636	3973	3388	2873	2421	1.7	0	-7.4	-21.5	NA
375 Ruger	260	2900	2703	2514	2333	—	4854	4217	3649	3143	—	0	-4.0	-13.4	—	NA
375 Ruger	270	2840	2600	2372	2156	1951	4835	4052	3373	2786	2283	1.8	0	-8.0	-23.6	NA
375 Ruger	300	2660	2344	2050	1780	1536	4713	3660	2800	2110	1572	2.4	0.0	-10.8	-32.6	NA
375 H&H Magnum	250	2670	2450	2240	2040	1850	3955	3335	2790	2315	1905	+2.5	-0.4	-10.2	-28.4	NA
375 H&H Magnum	270	2690	2420	2166	1928	1707	4337	3510	2812	2228	1747	+2.5	0.0	-10.0	-29.4	$28
375 H&H Mag.	270	2800	2562	2337	2123	1921	4700	3936	3275	2703	2213	1.9	0	-8.3	-24.3	NA
375 H&H Magnum*	300	2530	2245	1979	1733	1512	4263	3357	2608	2001	1523	+2.5	-1.0	-10.5	-33.6	$28
375 H&H Mag.	300	2660	2345	2052	1782	1539	4713	3662	2804	2114	1577	2.4	0	-10.8	-32.6	NA
375 H&H Hvy. Mag.	270	2870	2628	2399	2182	1976	4937	4141	3451	2150	1845	+1.7	0.0	-7.2	-21.0	NA
375 H&H Hvy. Mag.	300	2705	2386	2090	1816	1568	4873	3793	2908	2195	1637	+2.3	0.0	-10.4	-31.4	NA
375 Rem. Ultra Mag.	270	2900	2558	2241	1947	1678	5041	3922	3010	2272	1689	1.9	2.7	-8.9	-27.0	NA
375 Rem. Ultra Mag.	260	2950	2750	2560	2377	—	5023	4367	3783	3262	—	0	-3.8	-12.9	—	NA
375 Rem. Ultra Mag.	300	2760	2505	2263	2035	1822	5073	4178	3412	2759	2210	2.0	0.0	-8.8	-26.1	NA
375 Wea. Mag.	260	3000	2798	2606	2421	—	5195	4520	3920	3384	—	0	-3.6	-12.4	—	NA
375 Wea. Mag.	300	2700	2420	2157	1911	1685	4856	3901	3100	2432	1891	+2.5	-.04	-10.7	0.0	NA
378 Wea. Mag.	260	3100	2894	2697	2509	—	5547	4834	4199	3633	—	0	-4.2	-14.6	—	NA
378 Wea. Mag.	270	3180	2976	2781	2594	2415	6062	5308	4635	4034	3495	+2.5	+2.6	-1.8	-11.3	$71
378 Wea. Mag.	300	2929	2576	2252	1952	1680	5698	4419	3379	2538	1881	+2.5	+1.2	-7.0	-24.5	$77
375 A-Square	300	2920	2626	2351	2093	1850	5679	4594	3681	2917	2281	+2.5	+1.4	-6.0	-21.0	NA
38-40 Win.	180	1160	999	901	827	764	538	399	324	273	233	0.0	-33.9	0.0	0.0	$42**
40, 41																
400 A-Square DPM	400	2400	2146	1909	1689	NA	5116	2092	3236	2533	NA	2.98	0.0	-10.0	NA	NA
400 A-Square DPM	170	2980	2463	2001	1598	NA	3352	2289	1512	964	NA	2.16	0.0	-11.1	NA	NA
408 CheyTac	419	2850	2752	2657	2562	2470	7551	7048	6565	6108	5675	-1.02	0.0	1.9	4.2	NA
405 Win.	300	2200	1851	1545	1296		3224	2282	1589	1119		4.6	0.0	-19.5	0.0	NA
450/400-3"	400	2050	1815	1595	1402	NA	3732	2924	2259	1746	NA	0.0	NA	-33.4	NA	NA
416 Ruger	400	2400	2151	1917	1700	NA	5116	4109	3264	2568	NA	0.0	-6.0	-21.6	0.0	NA
416 Dakota	400	2450	2294	2143	1998	1859	5330	4671	4077	3544	3068	+2.5	-0.2	-10.5	-29.4	NA
416 Taylor	400	2350	2117	1896	1693	NA	4905	3980	3194	2547	NA	+2.5	-1.2	15.0	0.0	NA
416 Hoffman	400	2380	2145	1923	1718	1529	5031	4087	3285	2620	2077	+2.5	-1.0	-14.1	0.0	NA
416 Rigby	350	2600	2449	2303	2162	2026	5253	4661	4122	3632	3189	+2.5	-1.8	-10.2	-26.0	NA
416 Rigby	400	2370	2210	2050	1900	NA	4990	4315	3720	3185	NA	+2.5	-0.7	-12.1	0.0	NA
416 Rigby	400	2400	2115	1851	1611	—	5115	3973	3043	2305	—	0	-6.5	-21.8	—	NA
416 Rigby	400	2415	2156	1915	1691	—	5180	4130	3256	2540	—	0	-6.0	-21.6	—	NA
416 Rigby	410	2370	2110	1870	1640	NA	5115	4050	3165	2455	NA	+2.5	-2.4	-17.3	0.0	$110
416 Rem. Mag.*	350	2520	2270	2034	1814	1611	4935	4004	3216	2557	2017	+2.5	-0.8	-12.6	-35.0	$82
416 Rem. Mag.	400	2400	2142	1901	1679	—	5116	4076	3211	2504	—	3.1	0	-12.7	—	NA
416 Wea. Mag.*	400	2700	2397	2115	1852	1613	6474	5104	3971	3047	2310	+2.5	0.0	-10.1	-30.4	$96
10.57 (416) Meteor	400	2730	2532	2342	2161	1987	6621	5695	4874	4147	3508	+1.9	0.0	-8.3	-24.0	NA
500/416 N.E.	400	2300	2092	1895	1712	—	4697	3887	3191	2602	—	0	-7.2	-24.0	—	NA
404 Jeffrey	400	2150	1924	1716	1525	NA	4105	3289	2614	2064	NA	+2.5	-4.0	-22.1	0.0	NA
404 Jeffrey	400	2300	2053	1823	1611	—	4698	3743	2950	2306	—	0	-6.8	-24.1	—	NA
404 Jeffery	400	2350	2020	1720	1458	—	4904	3625	2629	1887	—	0	-6.5	-21.8	—	NA
425, 44																
425 Express	400	2400	2160	1934	1725	NA	5115	4145	3322	2641	NA	+2.5	-1.0	-14.0	0.0	NA
44-40 Win.	200	1190	1006	900	822	756	629	449	360	300	254	0.0	-33.3	0.0	0.0	$36**
44 Rem. Mag.	210	1920	1477	1155	982	880	1719	1017	622	450	361	0.0	-17.6	0.0	0.0	$14
44 Rem. Mag.	240	1760	1380	1114	970	878	1650	1015	661	501	411	0.0	-17.6	0.0	0.0	$13
444 Marlin	240	2350	1815	1377	1087	941	2942	1753	1001	630	472	+2.5	-15.1	-31.0	0.0	$22
444 Marlin	265	2120	1733	1405	1160	1012	2644	1768	1162	791	603	+2.5	-6.0	-32.2	0.0	Disc.
444 Mar. Lever Evolution	265	2325	1971	1652	1380	NA	3180	2285	1606	1120	NA	3.0	-1.4	-18.6	NA	NA
444 Mar. Superformance	265	2400	1976	1603	1298	NA	3389	2298	1512	991	NA	4.1	0.0	-17.8	NA	NA
45																
45-70 Govt.	250	2025	1616	1285	1068	—	2276	1449	917	634	—	6.1	0	-27.2	—	NA

Cartridge	Bullet Wgt. Grs.	VELOCITY (fps)					ENERGY (ft. lbs.)					TRAJ. (in.)				Est. Price/box
		Muzzle	100 yds.	200 yds.	300 yds.	400 yds.	Muzzle	100 yds.	200 yds.	300 yds.	400 yds.	100 yds.	200 yds.	300 yds.	400 yds.	
45-70 Govt.	300	1810	1497	1244	1073	969	2182	1492	1031	767	625	0.0	-14.8	0.0	0.0	$21
45-70 Govt. Supreme	300	1880	1558	1292	1103	988	2355	1616	1112	811	651	0.0	-12.9	-46.0	-105.0	NA
45-70 Govt.	325	2000	1685	1413	1197	—	2886	2049	1441	1035	—	5.5	0	-23.0	—	NA
45-70 Lever Evolution	325	2050	1729	1450	1225	NA	3032	2158	1516	1083	NA	3.0	-4.1	-27.8	NA	NA
45-70 Govt. CorBon	350	1800	1526	1296			2519	1810	1307			0.0	-14.6	0.0	0.0	NA
45-70 Govt.	405	1330	1168	1055	977	918	1590	1227	1001	858	758	0.0	-24.6	0.0	0.0	$21
45-70 Govt. PMC Cowboy	405	1550	1193	—	—	—	1639	1280	—	—	—	0.0	-23.9	0.0	0.0	NA
45-70 Govt. Garrett	415	1850	—	—	—	—	3150	—	—	—	—	3.0	-7.0	0.0	0.0	NA
45-70 Govt. Garrett	530	1550	1343	1178	1062	982	2828	2123	1633	1327	1135	0.0	-17.8	0.0	0.0	NA
450 Bushmaster	250	2200	1831	1508	1480	1073	2686	1860	1262	864	639	0.0	-9.0	-33.5	0.0	NA
450 Marlin	325	2225	1887	1587	1332	—	3572	2570	1816	1280	—	4.2	0	-18.1	—	NA
450 Marlin	350	2100	1774	1488	1254	1089	3427	2446	1720	1222	922	0.0	-9.7	-35.2	0.0	NA
450 Mar. Lever Evolution	325	2225	1887	1585	1331	NA	3572	2569	1813	1278	NA	3.0	-2.2	-21.3	NA	NA
457 Wild West Magnum	350	2150	1718	1348	NA	NA	3645	2293	1413	NA	NA	0.0	-10.5	NA	NA	NA
450/500 N.E.	400	2050	1820	1609	1420	—	3732	2940	2298	1791	—	0	-9.7	-32.8	—	NA
450 N.E. 3-1/4"	465	2190	1970	1765	1577	NA	4952	4009	3216	2567	NA	+2.5	-3.0	-20.0	0.0	NA
450 N.E.	480	2150	1881	1635	1418	—	4927	3769	2850	2144	—	0	-8.4	-29.8	—	NA
450 N.E. 3-1/4"	500	2150	1920	1708	1514	NA	5132	4093	3238	2544	NA	+2.5	-4.0	-22.9	0.0	NA
450 No. 2	465	2190	1970	1765	1577	NA	4952	4009	3216	2567	NA	+2.5	-3.0	-20.0	0.0	NA
450 No. 2	500	2150	1920	1708	1514	NA	5132	4093	3238	2544	NA	+2.5	-4.0	-22.9	0.0	NA
450 Ackley Mag.	465	2400	2169	1950	1747	NA	5947	4857	3927	3150	NA	+2.5	-1.0	-13.7	0.0	NA
450 Ackley Mag.	500	2320	2081	1855	1649	NA	5975	4085	3820	3018	NA	+2.5	-1.2	-15.0	0.0	NA
450 Rigby	500	2350	2139	1939	1752	—	6130	5079	4176	3408	—	0	-6.8	-22.9	—	NA
458 Win. Magnum	400	2380	2170	1960	1770	NA	5030	4165	3415	2785	NA	+2.5	-0.4	-13.4	0.0	$73
458 Win. Magnum	465	2220	1999	1791	1601	NA	5088	4127	3312	2646	NA	+2.5	-2.0	-17.7	0.0	NA
458 Win. Magnum	500	2040	1823	1623	1442	1237	4620	3689	2924	2308	1839	+2.5	-3.5	-22.0	0.0	$61
458 Win. Mag.	500	2140	1880	1643	1432	—	5084	3294	2996	2276	—	0	-8.4	-29.8	—	NA
458 Win. Magnum	510	2040	1770	1527	1319	1157	4712	3547	2640	1970	1516	+2.5	-4.1	-25.0	0.0	$41
458 Lott	465	2380	2150	1932	1730	NA	5848	4773	3855	3091	NA	+2.5	-1.0	-14.0	0.0	NA
458 Lott	500	2300	2029	1778	1551	—	5873	4569	3509	2671	—	0	-7.0	-25.1	—	NA
458 Lott	500	2300	2062	1838	1633	NA	5873	4719	3748	2960	NA	+2.5	-1.6	-16.4	0.0	NA
460 Short A-Sq.	500	2420	2175	1943	1729	NA	6501	5250	4193	3319	NA	+2.5	-0.8	-12.8	0.0	NA
460 Wea. Mag.	500	2700	2404	2128	1869	1635	8092	6416	5026	3878	2969	+2.5	+0.6	-8.9	-28.0	$72

475

Cartridge	Bullet Wgt. Grs.	Muzzle	100 yds.	200 yds.	300 yds.	400 yds.	Muzzle	100 yds.	200 yds.	300 yds.	400 yds.	100 yds.	200 yds.	300 yds.	400 yds.	Est. Price/box
500/465 N.E.	480	2150	1917	1703	1507	NA	4926	3917	3089	2419	NA	+2.5	-4.0	-22.2	0.0	NA
470 Rigby	500	2150	1940	1740	1560	NA	5130	4170	3360	2695	NA	+2.5	-2.8	-19.4	0.0	NA
470 Nitro Ex.	480	2190	1954	1735	1536	NA	5111	4070	3210	2515	NA	+2.5	-3.5	-20.8	0.0	NA
470 N.E.	500	2150	1885	1643	1429	—	5132	3945	2998	2267	—	0	-8.9	-30.8	—	NA
470 Nitro Ex.	500	2150	1890	1650	1440	1270	5130	3965	3040	2310	1790	+2.5	-4.3	-24.0	0.0	$177
475 No. 2	500	2200	1955	1728	1522	NA	5375	4243	3316	2573	NA	+2.5	-3.2	-20.9	0.0	NA

50, 58

Cartridge	Bullet Wgt. Grs.	Muzzle	100 yds.	200 yds.	300 yds.	400 yds.	Muzzle	100 yds.	200 yds.	300 yds.	400 yds.	100 yds.	200 yds.	300 yds.	400 yds.	Est. Price/box
50 Alaskan	450	2000	1729	1492	NA	NA	3997	2987	2224	NA	NA	0.0	-11.25	NA	NA	NA
500 Jeffery	570	2300	1979	1688	1434	—	6694	4958	3608	2604	—	0	-8.2	-28.6	—	NA
505 Gibbs	525	2300	2063	1840	1637	NA	6166	4922	3948	3122	NA	+2.5	-3.0	-18.0	0.0	NA
500 N.E.	570	2150	1889	1651	1439	—	5850	4518	3450	2621	—	0	-8.9	-30.6	—	NA
500 N.E.-3"	570	2150	1928	1722	1533	NA	5850	4703	3752	2975	NA	+2.5	-3.7	-22.0	0.0	NA
500 N.E.-3"	600	2150	1927	1721	1531	NA	6158	4947	3944	3124	NA	+2.5	-4.0	-22.0	0.0	NA
495 A-Square	570	2350	2117	1896	1693	NA	5850	4703	3752	2975	NA	+2.5	-1.0	-14.5	0.0	NA
495 A-Square	600	2280	2050	1833	1635	NA	6925	5598	4478	3562	NA	+2.5	-2.0	-17.0	0.0	NA
500 A-Square	600	2380	2144	1922	1766	NA	7546	6126	4920	3922	NA	+2.5	-3.0	-17.0	0.0	NA
500 A-Square	707	2250	2040	1841	1567	NA	7947	6530	5318	4311	NA	+2.5	-2.0	-17.0	0.0	NA
500 BMG PMC	660	3080	2854	2639	2444	2248	13688		500 yd. zero			+3.1	+3.9	+4.7	+2.8	NA
577 Nitro Ex.	750	2050	1793	1562	1360	NA	6990	5356	4065	3079	NA	+2.5	-5.0	-26.0	0.0	NA
577 Tyrannosaur	750	2400	2141	1898	1675	NA	9591	7633	5996	4671	NA	+3.0	0.0	-12.9	0.0	NA

600, 700

Cartridge	Bullet Wgt. Grs.	Muzzle	100 yds.	200 yds.	300 yds.	400 yds.	Muzzle	100 yds.	200 yds.	300 yds.	400 yds.	100 yds.	200 yds.	300 yds.	400 yds.	Est. Price/box
600 N.E.	900	1950	1680	1452	NA	NA	7596	5634	4212	NA	NA	+5.6	0.0	0.0	0.0	NA
700 N.E.	1200	1900	1676	1472	NA	NA	9618	7480	5774	NA	NA	+5.7	0.0	0.0	0.0	NA

50 BMG

Cartridge	Bullet Wgt. Grs.	Muzzle	100 yds.	200 yds.	300 yds.	400 yds.	Muzzle	100 yds.	200 yds.	300 yds.	400 yds.	100 yds.	200 yds.	300 yds.	400 yds.	Est. Price/box
50 BMG	624	2952	2820	2691	2566	2444	12077	11028	10036	9125	8281	0	-2.9	-10.6	-23.5	NA
50 BMG Match	750	2820	2728	2637	2549	2462	13241	12388	11580	10815	10090	1.5	0.0	-6.5	-18.3	NA

Notes: Blanks are available in 32 S&W, 38 S&W and 38 Special. "V" after barrel length indicates test barrel was vented to produce ballistics similar to a revolver with a normal barrel-to-cylinder gap. Ammo prices are per 50 rounds except when marked with an ** which signifies a 20 round box; *** signifies a 25-round box. Not all loads are available from all ammo manufacturers. Listed loads are those made by Remington, Winchester, Federal, and others. DISC. is a discontinued load. Prices are rounded to the nearest whole dollar and will vary with brand and retail outlet.

Cartridge	Bullet Wgt. Grs.	VELOCITY (fps)			ENERGY (ft. lbs.)			Mid-Range Traj. (in.)		Bbl. Lgth. (in).	Est. Price/ box
		Muzzle	50 yds.	100 yds.	Muzzle	50 yds.	100 yds.	50 yds.	100 yds.		
22, 25											
221 Rem. Fireball	50	2650	2380	2130	780	630	505	0.2	0.8	10.5"	$15
25 Automatic	35	900	813	742	63	51	43	NA	NA	2"	$18
25 Automatic	45	815	730	655	65	55	40	1.8	7.7	2"	$21
25 Automatic	50	760	705	660	65	55	50	2.0	8.7	2"	$17
30											
7.5mm Swiss	107	1010	NA	NA	240	NA	NA	NA	NA	NA	NEW
7.62x25 Tokarev	85	1647	1458	1295	512	401	317	0	-3.2	4.75	
7.62mmTokarev	87	1390	NA	NA	365	NA	NA	0.6	NA	4.5"	NA
7.62 Nagant	97	790	NA	NA	134	NA	NA	NA	NA	NA	NEW
7.63 Mauser	88	1440	NA	NA	405	NA	NA	NA	NA	NA	NEW
30 Luger	93	1220	1110	1040	305	255	225	0.9	3.5	4.5"	$34
30 Carbine	110	1790	1600	1430	785	625	500	0.4	1.7	10"	$28
30-357 AeT	123	1992	NA	NA	1084	NA	NA	NA	NA	10"	NA
32											
32 NAA	80	1000	933	880	178	155	137	NA	NA	4"	NA
32 S&W	88	680	645	610	90	80	75	2.5	10.5	3"	$17
32 S&W Long	98	705	670	635	115	100	90	2.3	10.5	4"	$17
32 Short Colt	80	745	665	590	100	80	60	2.2	9.9	4"	$19
32 H&R	80	1150	1039	963	235	192	165	NA	NA	4"	NA
32 H&R Magnum	85	1100	1020	930	230	195	165	1.0	4.3	4.5"	$21
32 H&R Magnum	95	1030	940	900	225	190	170	1.1	4.7	4.5"	$19
327 Federal Magnum	85	1400	1220	1090	370	280	225	NA	NA	4-V	NA
327 Federal Magnum	100	1500	1320	1180	500	390	310	-0.2	-4.50	4-V	NA
32 Automatic	60	970	895	835	125	105	95	1.3	5.4	4"	$22
32 Automatic	60	1000	917	849	133	112	96			4"	NA
32 Automatic	65	950	890	830	130	115	100	1.3	5.6	NA	NA
32 Automatic	71	905	855	810	130	115	95	1.4	5.8	4"	$19
8mm Lebel Pistol	111	850	NA	NA	180	NA	NA	NA	NA	NA	NEW
8mm Steyr	112	1080	NA	NA	290	NA	NA	NA	NA	NA	NEW
8mm Gasser	126	850	NA	NA	200	NA	NA	NA	NA	NA	NEW
9mm, 38											
380 Automatic	60	1130	960	NA	170	120	NA	1.0	NA	NA	NA
380 Automatic	85/88	990	920	870	190	165	145	1.2	5.1	4"	$20
380 Automatic	90	1000	890	800	200	160	130	1.2	5.5	3.75"	$10
380 Automatic	95/100	955	865	785	190	160	130	1.4	5.9	4"	$20
38 Super Auto +P	115	1300	1145	1040	430	335	275	0.7	3.3	5"	$26
38 Super Auto +P	125/130	1215	1100	1015	425	350	300	0.8	3.6	5"	$26
38 Super Auto +P	147	1100	1050	1000	395	355	325	0.9	4.0	5"	NA
9x18mm Makarov	95	1000	930	874	211	182	161	NA	NA	4"	NEW
9x18mm Ultra	100	1050	NA	NA	240	NA	NA	NA	NA	NA	NEW
9x21	124	1150	1050	980	365	305	265	NA	NA	4"	NA
9x21 IMI	123	1220	1095	1010	409	330	281	-3.15	—	5.0	NA
9x23mm Largo	124	1190	1055	966	390	306	257	0.7	3.7	4"	NA
9x23mm Win.	125	1450	1249	1103	583	433	338	0.6	2.8	NA	NA
9mm Steyr	115	1180	NA	NA	350	NA	NA	NA	NA	NA	NEW
9mm Luger	88	1500	1190	1010	440	275	200	0.6	3.1	4"	$24
9mm Luger	90	1360	1112	978	370	247	191	NA	NA	4"	$26
9mm Luger	92	1325	1117	991	359	255	201	-3.2	—	4.0	NA
9mm Luger	95	1300	1140	1010	350	275	215	0.8	3.4	4"	NA
9mm Luger	100	1180	1080	NA	305	255	NA	0.9	NA	4"	NA
9mm Luger Guard Dog	105	1230	1070	970	355	265	220	NA	NA	4"	NA
9mm Luger	115	1155	1045	970	340	280	240	0.9	3.9	4"	$21
9mm Luger	123/125	1110	1030	970	340	290	260	1.0	4.0	4"	$23
9mm Luger	124	1150	1040	965	364	298	256	-4.5	—	4.0	NA
9mm Luger	135	1010	960	918	306	276	253	—	—	4.0	NA
9mm Luger	140	935	890	850	270	245	225	1.3	5.5	4"	$23
9mm Luger	147	990	940	900	320	290	265	1.1	4.9	4"	$26
9mm Luger +P	90	1475	NA	NA	437	NA	NA	NA	NA	NA	NA
9mm Luger +P	115	1250	1113	1019	399	316	265	0.8	3.5	4"	$27
9mm Federal	115	1280	1130	1040	420	330	280	0.7	3.3	4"V	$24
9mm Luger Vector	115	1155	1047	971	341	280	241	NA	NA	4"	NA
9mm Luger +P	124	1180	1089	1021	384	327	287	0.8	3.8	4"	NA
38											
38 S&W	146	685	650	620	150	135	125	2.4	10.0	4"	$19
38 S&W Short	145	720	689	660	167	153	140	-8.5	—	5.0	NA
38 Short Colt	125	730	685	645	150	130	115	2.2	9.4	6"	$19
39 Special	100	950	900	NA	200	180	NA	1.3	NA	4"V	NA

Cartridge	Bullet Wgt. Grs.	VELOCITY (fps)			ENERGY (ft. lbs.)			Mid-Range Traj. (in.)		Bbl. Lgth. (in.)	Est. Price/box
		Muzzle	50 yds.	100 yds.	Muzzle	50 yds.	100 yds.	50 yds.	100 yds.		
38 Special	110	945	895	850	220	195	175	1.3	5.4	4"V	$23
38 Special	110	945	895	850	220	195	175	1.3	5.4	4"V	$23
38 Special	130	775	745	710	175	160	120	1.9	7.9	4"V	$22
38 Special Cowboy	140	800	767	735	199	183	168			7.5" V	NA
38 (Multi-Ball)	140	830	730	505	215	130	80	2.0	10.6	4"V	$10**
38 Special	148	710	635	565	165	130	105	2.4	10.6	4"V	$17
38 Special	158	755	725	690	200	185	170	2.0	8.3	4"V	$18
38 Special +P	95	1175	1045	960	290	230	195	0.9	3.9	4"V	$23
38 Special +P	110	995	925	870	240	210	185	1.2	5.1	4"V	$23
38 Special +P	125	975	929	885	264	238	218	1	5.2	4"	NA
38 Special +P	125	945	900	860	250	225	205	1.3	5.4	4"V	#23
38 Special +P	129	945	910	870	255	235	215	1.3	5.3	4"V	$11
38 Special +P	130	925	887	852	247	227	210	1.3	5.50	4"V	NA
38 Special +P	147/150	884	NA	NA	264	NA	NA	NA	NA	4"V	$27
38 Special +P	158	890	855	825	280	255	240	1.4	6.0	4"V	$20

357

Cartridge	Bullet Wgt. Grs.	Muzzle	50 yds.	100 yds.	Muzzle	50 yds.	100 yds.	50 yds.	100 yds.	Bbl. Lgth.	Est. Price/box
357 SIG	115	1520	NA	NA	593	NA	NA	NA	NA	NA	NA
357 SIG	124	1450	NA	NA	578	NA	NA	NA	NA	NA	NA
357 SIG	125	1350	1190	1080	510	395	325	0.7	3.1	4"	NA
357 SIG	135	1225	1112	1031	450	371	319	—	—	4.0	NA
357 SIG	147	1225	1132	1060	490	418	367	—	—	4.0	NA
357 SIG	150	1130	1030	970	420	355	310	0.9	4.0	NA	NA
356 TSW	115	1520	NA	NA	593	NA	NA	NA	NA	NA	NA
356 TSW	124	1450	NA	NA	578	NA	NA	NA	NA	NA	NA
356 TSW	135	1280	1120	1010	490	375	310	0.8	3.5	NA	NA
356 TSW	147	1220	1120	1040	485	410	355	0.8	3.5	5"	NA
357 Mag., Super Clean	105	1650									NA
357 Magnum	110	1295	1095	975	410	290	230	0.8	3.5	4"V	$25
357 (Med.Vel.)	125	1220	1075	985	415	315	270	0.8	3.7	4"V	$25
357 Magnum	125	1450	1240	1090	585	425	330	0.6	2.8	4"V	$25
357 Magnum	125	1500	1312	1163	624	478	376	—	—	8.0	NA
357 (Multi-Ball)	140	1155	830	665	420	215	135	1.2	6.4	4"V	$11**
357 Magnum	140	1360	1195	1075	575	445	360	0.7	3.0	4"V	$25
357 Magnum FlexTip	140	1440	1274	1143	644	504	406	NA	NA	NA	NA
357 Magnum	145	1290	1155	1060	535	430	360	0.8	3.5	4"V	$26
357 Magnum	150/158	1235	1105	1015	535	430	360	0.8	3.5	4"V	$25
357 Mag. Cowboy	158	800	761	725	225	203	185				NA
357 Magnum	165	1290	1189	1108	610	518	450	0.7	3.1	8-3/8"	NA
357 Magnum	180	1145	1055	985	525	445	390	0.9	3.9	4"V	$25
357 Magnum	180	1180	1088	1020	557	473	416	0.8	3.6	8"V	NA
357 Mag. CorBon F.A.	180	1650	1512	1386	1088	913	767	1.66	0.0		NA
357 Mag. CorBon	200	1200	1123	1061	640	560	500	3.19	0.0		NA
357 Rem. Maximum	158	1825	1590	1380	1170	885	670	0.4	1.7	10.5"	$14**

40, 10mm

Cartridge	Bullet Wgt. Grs.	Muzzle	50 yds.	100 yds.	Muzzle	50 yds.	100 yds.	50 yds.	100 yds.	Bbl. Lgth.	Est. Price/box
40 S&W	125	1265	1102	998	444	337	276	-3.0	—	4.0	NA
40 S&W	135	1140	1070	NA	390	345	NA	0.9	NA	4"	NA
40 S&W Guard Dog	135	1200	1040	940	430	325	265	NA	NA	4"	NA
40 S&W	155	1140	1026	958	447	362	309	0.9	4.1	4"	$14***
40 S&W	165	1150	NA	NA	485	NA	NA	NA	NA	4"	$18***
40 S&W	175	1010	948	899	396	350	314	—	—	4.0	NA
40 S&W	180	985	936	893	388	350	319	1.4	5.0	4"	$14***
40 S&W	180	1000	943	896	400	355	321	4.52	—	4.0	NA
40 S&W	180	1015	960	914	412	368	334	1.3	4.5	4"	NA
400 Cor-Bon	135	1450	NA	NA	630	NA	NA	NA	NA	5"	NA
10mm Automatic	155	1125	1046	986	436	377	335	0.9	3.9	5"	$26
10mm Automatic	155	1265	1118	1018	551	430	357	—	—	5.0	NA
10mm Automatic	170	1340	1165	1145	680	510	415	0.7	3.2	5"	$31
10mm Automatic	175	1290	1140	1035	650	505	420	0.7	3.3	5.5"	$11**
10mm Auto. (FBI)	180	950	905	865	361	327	299	1.5	5.4	4"	$16**
10mm Automatic	180	1030	970	920	425	375	340	1.1	4.7	5"	$16**
10mm Auto H.V.	180	1240	1124	1037	618	504	430	0.8	3.4	5"	$27
10mm Automatic	200	1160	1070	1010	495	510	430	0.9	3.8	5"	$14**
10.4mm Italian	177	950	NA	NA	360	NA	NA	NA	NA	NA	NEW
41 Action Exp.	180	1000	947	903	400	359	326	0.5	4.2	5"	$13**
41 Rem. Magnum	170	1420	1165	1015	760	515	390	0.7	3.2	4"V	$33
41 Rem. Magnum	175	1250	1120	1030	605	490	410	0.8	3.4	4"V	$14**
41 (Med. Vel.)	210	965	900	840	435	375	330	1.3	5.4	4"V	$30
41 Rem. Magnum	210	1300	1160	1060	790	630	535	0.7	3.2	4"V	$33
41 Rem. Magnum	240	1250	1151	1075	833	706	616	0.8	3.3	6.5V	NA

44

Cartridge	Bullet Wgt. Grs.	Muzzle	50 yds.	100 yds.	Muzzle	50 yds.	100 yds.	50 yds.	100 yds.	Bbl. Lgth.	Est. Price/box
44 S&W Russian	247	780	NA	NA	335	NA	NA	NA	NA	NA	NA
44 Special	210	900	861	825	360	329	302	5.57	—	6.0	NA
44 Special FTX	165	900	848	802	297	263	235	NA	NA	2.5"	NA
44 S&W Special	180	980	NA	NA	383	NA	NA	NA	NA	6.5"	NA
44 S&W Special	180	1000	935	882	400	350	311	NA	NA	7.5"V	NA
44 S&W Special	200	875	825	780	340	302	270	1.2	6.0	6"	$13**
44 S&W Special	200	1035	940	865	475	390	335	1.1	4.9	6.5"	$13**

Cartridge	Bullet Wgt. Grs.	VELOCITY (fps)			ENERGY (ft. lbs.)			Mid-Range Traj. (in.)		Bbl. Lgth. (in.)	Est. Price/ box
		Muzzle	50 yds.	100 yds.	Muzzle	50 yds.	100 yds.	50 yds.	100 yds.		
44 S&W Special	240/246	755	725	695	310	285	265	2.0	8.3	6.5"	$26
44-40 Win.	200	722	698	676	232	217	203	-3.4	-23.7	4.0	NA
44-40 Win.	205	725	689	655	239	216	195	—	—	7.5	NA
44-40 Win.	210	725	698	672	245	227	210	-11.6	—	5.5	NA
44-40 Win.	225	725	697	670	263	243	225	-3.4	-23.8	4.0	NA
44-40 Win. Cowboy	225	750	723	695	281	261	242				NA
44 Rem. Magnum	180	1610	1365	1175	1035	745	550	0.5	2.3	4"V	$18**
44 Rem. Magnum	200	1296	1193	1110	747	632	548	-.5	-6.2	6.0	NA
44 Rem. Magnum	200	1400	1192	1053	870	630	492	0.6	NA	6.5"	$20
44 Rem. Magnum	200	1500	1332	1194	999	788	633	—	—	7.5	NA
44 Rem. Magnum	210	1495	1310	1165	1040	805	635	0.6	2.5	6.5"	$18**
44 Rem. Mag. FlexTip	225	1410	1240	1111	993	768	617	NA	NA	NA	NA
44 (Med. Vel.)	240	1000	945	900	535	475	435	1.1	4.8	6.5"	$17
44 R.M. (Jacketed)	240	1180	1080	1010	740	625	545	0.9	3.7	4"V	$18**
44 R.M. (Lead)	240	1350	1185	1070	970	750	610	0.7	3.1	4"V	$29
44 Rem. Magnum	250	1180	1100	1040	775	670	600	0.8	3.6	6.5"V	$21
44 Rem. Magnum	250	1250	1148	1070	867	732	635	0.8	3.3	6.5"V	NA
44 Rem. Magnum	275	1235	1142	1070	931	797	699	0.8	3.3	6.5"	NA
44 Rem. Magnum	300	1150	1083	1030	881	781	706	—	—	7.5	NA
44 Rem. Magnum	300	1200	1100	1026	959	806	702	NA	NA	7.5"	$17
44 Rem. Magnum	330	1385	1297	1220	1406	1234	1090	1.83	0.00	NA	NA
44 Webley	262	850	—	—	—	—	—	—	—	—	NA
440 CorBon	260	1700	1544	1403	1669	1377	1136	1.58	NA	10"	NA

45, 50

Cartridge	Bullet Wgt. Grs.	VELOCITY (fps)			ENERGY (ft. lbs.)			Mid-Range Traj. (in.)		Bbl. Lgth. (in.)	Est. Price/ box
		Muzzle	50 yds.	100 yds.	Muzzle	50 yds.	100 yds.	50 yds.	100 yds.		
450 Short Colt/450 Revolver	226	830	NA	NA	350	NA	NA	NA	NA	NA	NEW
45 S&W Schofield	180	730	NA	NA	213	NA	NA	NA	NA	NA	NA
45 S&W Schofield	230	730	NA	NA	272	NA	NA	NA	NA	NA	NA
45 G.A.P.	165	1007	936	879	372	321	283	-1.4	-11.8	5.0	NA
45 G.A.P.	185	1090	970	890	490	385	320	1.0	4.7	5"	NA
45 G.A.P.	230	880	842	NA	396	363	NA	NA	NA	NA	NA
45 Automatic	165	1030	930	NA	385	315	NA	1.2	NA	5"	NA
45 Automatic Guard Dog	165	1140	1030	950	475	390	335	NA	NA	5"	NA
45 Automatic	185	1000	940	890	410	360	325	1.1	4.9	5"	$28
45 Auto. (Match)	185	770	705	650	245	204	175	2.0	8.7	5"	$28
45 Auto. (Match)	200	940	890	840	392	352	312	2.0	8.6	5"	$20
45 Automatic	200	975	917	860	421	372	328	1.4	5.0	5"	$18
45 Automatic	230	830	800	675	355	325	300	1.6	6.8	5"	$27
45 Automatic	230	880	846	816	396	366	340	1.5	6.1	5"	NA
45 Automatic +P	165	1250	NA	NA	573	NA	NA	NA	NA	NA	NA
45 Automatic +P	185	1140	1040	970	535	445	385	0.9	4.0	5"	$31
45 Automatic +P	200	1055	982	925	494	428	380	NA	NA	5"	NA
45 Super	185	1300	1190	1108	694	582	504	NA	NA	5"	NA
45 Win. Magnum	230	1400	1230	1105	1000	775	635	0.6	2.8	5"	$14**
45 Win. Magnum	260	1250	1137	1053	902	746	640	0.8	3.3	5"	$16**
45 Win. Mag. CorBon	320	1150	1080	1025	940	830	747	3.47			NA
455 Webley MKII	262	850	NA	NA	420	NA	NA	NA	NA	NA	NA
45 Colt FTX	185	920	870	826	348	311	280	NA	NA	3"V	NA
45 Colt	200	1000	938	889	444	391	351	1.3	4.8	5.5"	$21
45 Colt	225	960	890	830	460	395	345	1.3	5.5	5.5"	$22
45 Colt + P CorBon	265	1350	1225	1126	1073	884	746	2.65	0.0		NA
45 Colt + P CorBon	300	1300	1197	1114	1126	956	827	2.78	0.0		NA
45 Colt	250/255	860	820	780	410	375	340	1.6	6.6	5.5"	$27
454 Casull	250	1300	1151	1047	938	735	608	0.7	3.2	7.5"V	NA
454 Casull	260	1800	1577	1381	1871	1436	1101	0.4	1.8	7.5"V	NA
454 Casull	300	1625	1451	1308	1759	1413	1141	0.5	2.0	7.5"V	NA
454 Casull CorBon	360	1500	1387	1286	1800	1640	1323	2.01	0.0		NA
460 S&W	200	2300	2042	1801	2350	1851	1441	0	-1.60	NA	NA
460 S&W	260	2000	1788	1592	2309	1845	1464	NA	NA	7.5"V	NA
460 S&W	250	1450	1267	1127	1167	891	705	NA	NA	8.375-V	NA
460 S&W	250	1900	1640	1412	2004	1494	1106	0	-2.75	NA	NA
460 S&W	300	1750	1510	1300	2040	1510	1125	NA	NA	8.4-V	NA
460 S&W	395	1550	1389	1249	2108	1691	1369	0	-4.00	NA	NA
475 Linebaugh	400	1350	1217	1119	1618	1315	1112	NA	NA	NA	NA
480 Ruger	325	1350	1191	1076	1315	1023	835	2.6	0.0	7.5"	NA
50 Action Exp.	325	1400	1209	1075	1414	1055	835	0.2	2.3	6"	$24**
500 S&W	275	1665	1392	1183	1693	1184	854	1.5	NA	8.375	NA
500 S&W	300	1950	1653	1396	2533	1819	1298	—	—	8.5	NA
500 S&W	325	1800	1560	1350	2340	1755	1315	NA	NA	8.4-V	NA
500 S&W	350	1400	1231	1106	1523	1178	951	NA	NA	10"	NA
500 S&W	400	1675	1472	1299	2493	1926	1499	1.3	NA	8.375	NA
500 S&W	440	1625	1367	1169	2581	1825	1337	1.6	NA	8.375	NA
500 S&W	500	1300	1178	1085	1876	1541	1308	—	—	8.5	NA
500 S&W	500	1425	1281	1164	2254	1823	1505	NA	NA	10"	NA

Note: The actual ballistics obtained with your firearm can vary considerably from the advertised ballistics.
Also, ballistics can vary from lot to lot with the same brand and type load.

Cartridge	Bullet Wt. Grs.	Velocity (fps) 22-1/2" Bbl.		Energy (ft. lbs.) 22-1/2" Bbl.		Mid-Range Traj. (in.)	Muzzle Velocity
		Muzzle	100 yds.	Muzzle	100 yds.	100 yds.	6" Bbl.
17 Aguila	20	1850	1267	NA	NA	NA	NA
17 Hornady Mach 2	15.5	2050	1450	149	75	NA	NA
17 Hornady Mach 2	17	2100	1530	166	88	0.7	NA
17 HMR Lead Free	15.5	2550	1901	NA	NA	.90	NA
17 HMR TNT Green	16	2500	1642	222	96	NA	NA
17 HMR	17	2550	1902	245	136	NA	NA
17 HMR	20	2375	1776	250	140	NA	NA
17 Win. Super Mag.	20 Tipped	3000	2504	400	278	0.0	NA
17 Win. Super Mag.	20 JHP	3000	2309	400	237	0.0	NA
17 Win. Super Mag.	25 Tipped	2600	2230	375	276	0.0	NA
5mm Rem. Rimfire Mag.	30	2300	1669	352	188	NA	24
22 Short Blank	—	—	—	—	—	—	—
22 Short CB	29	727	610	33	24	NA	706
22 Short Target	29	830	695	44	31	6.8	786
22 Short HP	27	1164	920	81	50	4.3	1077
22 Colibri	20	375	183	6	1	NA	NA
22 Super Colibri	20	500	441	11	9	NA	NA
22 Long CB	29	727	610	33	24	NA	706
22 Long HV	29	1180	946	90	57	4.1	1031
22 LR Pistol Match	40	1070	890	100	70	4.6	940
22 LR Shrt. Range Green	21	1650	912	127	NA	NA	NA
CCI Quiet 22 LR	40	710	640	45	36	NA	NA
22 LR Sub Sonic HP	38	1050	901	93	69	4.7	NA
22 LR Segmented HP	40	1050	897	98	72	NA	NA
22 LR Standard Velocity	40	1070	890	100	70	4.6	940
22 LR AutoMatch	40	1200	990	130	85	NA	NA
22 LR HV	40	1255	1016	140	92	3.6	1060
22 LR Silhoutte	42	1220	1003	139	94	3.6	1025
22 SSS	60	950	802	120	86	NA	NA
22 LR HV HP	40	1280	1001	146	89	3.5	1085
22 Velocitor GDHP	40	1435	0	0	0	NA	NA
22 LR Segmented HP	37	1435	1080	169	96	2.9	NA
22 LR Hyper HP	32/33/34	1500	1075	165	85	2.8	NA
22 LR Expediter	32	1640	NA	191	NA	NA	NA
22 LR Stinger HP	32	1640	1132	191	91	2.6	1395
22 LR Lead Free	30	1650	NA	181	NA	NA	NA
22 LR Hyper Vel	30	1750	1191	204	93	NA	NA
22 LR Shot #12	31	950	NA	NA	NA	NA	NA
22 WRF LFN	45	1300	1015	169	103	3	NA
22 Win. Mag. Lead Free	28	2200	NA	301	NA	NA	NA
22 Win. Mag.	30	2200	1373	322	127	1.4	1610
22 Win. Mag. V-Max BT	33	2000	1495	293	164	0.60	NA
22 Win. Mag. JHP	34	2120	1435	338	155	1.4	NA
22 Win. Mag. JHP	40	1910	1326	324	156	1.7	1480
22 Win. Mag. FMJ	40	1910	1326	324	156	1.7	1480
22 Win. Mag. Dyna Point	45	1550	1147	240	131	2.60	NA
22 Win. Mag. JHP	50	1650	1280	300	180	1.3	NA
22 Win. Mag. Shot #11	52	1000	—	NA	—	—	NA

NOTES: * = 10 rounds per box. ** = 5 rounds per box. Pricing variations and number of rounds per box can occur with type and brand of ammunition. Listed pricing is the average nominal cost for load style and box quantity shown. Not every brand is available in all shot size variations. Some manufacturers do not provide suggested list prices. All prices rounded to nearest whole dollar. The price you pay will vary dependent upon outlet of purchase. # = new load spec this year; "C" indicates a change in data.

10 Gauge 3-1/2" Magnum

Dram Equiv.	Shot Ozs.	Load Style	Shot Sizes	Brands	Avg. Price/box	Velocity (fps)
Max	2-3/8	magnum blend	5, 6, 7	Hevi-shot	NA	1200
4-1/2	2-1/4	premium	BB, 2, 4, 5, 6	Win., Fed., Rem.	$33	1205
Max	2	premium	4, 5, 6	Fed., Win.	NA	1300
4-1/4	2	high velocity	BB, 2, 4	Rem.	$22	1210
Max	18 pellets	premium	00 buck	Fed., Win.	$7**	1100
Max	1-7/8	Bismuth	BB, 2, 4	Bis.	NA	1225
Max	1-3/4	high density	BB, 2	Rem.	NA	1300
4-1/4	1-3/4	steel	TT, T, BBB, BB, 1, 2, 3	Win., Rem.	$27	1260
Mag	1-5/8	steel	T, BBB, BB, 2	Win.	$27	1285
Max	1-5/8	Bismuth	BB, 2, 4	Bismuth	NA	1375
Max	1-1/2	hypersonic	BBB, BB, 2	Rem.	NA	1700
Max	1-1/2	heavy metal	BB, 2, 3, 4	Hevi-Shot	NA	1500
Max	1-1/2	steel	T, BBB, BB, 1, 2, 3	Fed.	NA	1450
Max	1-3/8	steel	T, BBB, BB, 1, 2, 3	Fed., Rem.	NA	1500
Max	1-3/8	steel	T, BBB, BB, 2	Fed., Win.	NA	1450
Max	1-3/4	slug, rifled	slug	Fed.	NA	1280
Max	24 pellets	Buckshot	1 Buck	Fed.	NA	1100
Max	54 pellets	Super-X	4 Buck	Win.	NA	1150

12 Gauge 3-1/2" Magnum

Dram Equiv.	Shot Ozs.	Load Style	Shot Sizes	Brands	Avg. Price/box	Velocity (fps)
Max	2-1/4	premium	4, 5, 6	Fed., Rem., Win.	$13*	1150
Max	2	Lead	4, 5, 6	Fed.	NA	1300
Max	2	Copper plated turkey	4, 5	Rem.	NA	1300
Max	18 pellets	premium	00 buck	Fed., Win., Rem.	$7**	1100
Max	1-7/8	Wingmaster HD	4, 6	Rem.	NA	1225
Max	1-7/8	heavyweight	5, 6	Fed.	NA	1300
Max	1-3/4	high density	BB, 2, 4, 6	Rem.		1300
Max	1-7/8	Bismuth	BB, 2, 4	Bis.	NA	1225
Max	1-5/8	blind side	Hex, 1, 3	Win.	NA	1400
Max	1-5/8	Hevi-shot	T	Hevi-shot	NA	1350
Max	1-5/8	Wingmaster HD	T	Rem.	NA	1350
Max	1-5/8	high density	BB, 2	Fed.	NA	1450
Max	1-5/8	Blind side	Hex, BB, 2	Win.	NA	1400
Max	1-3/8	Heavyweight	2, 4, 6	Fed.	NA	1450
Max	1-3/8	steel	T, BBB, BB, 2, 4	Fed., Win., Rem.	NA	1450
Max	1-1/2	FS steel	BBB, BB, 2	Fed.	NA	1500
Max	1-1/2	Supreme H-V	BBB, BB, 2, 3	Win.	NA	1475
Max	1-3/8	H-speed steel	BB, 2	Rem.	NA	1550
Max	1-1/4	Steel	BB, 2	Win.	NA	1625
Max	24 pellets	Premium	1 Buck	Fed.	NA	1100
Max	54 pellets	Super-X	4 Buck	Win.	NA	1050

12 Gauge 3" Magnum

Dram Equiv.	Shot Ozs.	Load Style	Shot Sizes	Brands	Avg. Price/box	Velocity (fps)
4	2	premium	BB, 2, 4, 5, 6	Win., Fed., Rem.	$9*	1175
4	1-7/8	premium	BB, 2, 4, 6	Win., Fed., Rem.	$19	1210
4	1-7/8	duplex	4x6	Rem.	$9*	1210

12 Gauge 3" Magnum (cont.)

Dram Equiv.	Shot Ozs.	Load Style	Shot Sizes	Brands	Avg. Price/box	Velocity (fps)
Max	1-3/4	turkey	4, 5, 6	Fed., Fio., Win., Rem.	NA	1300
Max	1-3/4	high density	BB, 2, 4	Rem.	NA	1450
Max	1-5/8	high density	BB, 2	Fed.	NA	1450
Max	1-5/8	Wingmaster HD	4, 6	Rem.	NA	1227
Max	1-5/8	high velocity	4, 5, 6	Fed.	NA	1350
4	1-5/8	premium	2, 4, 5, 6	Win., Fed., Rem.	$18	1290
Max	1-1/2	Wingmaster HD	T	Rem.	NA	1300
Max	1-1/2	Hevi-shot	T	Hevi-shot	NA	1300
Max	1-1/2	high density	BB, 2, 4	Rem.	NA	1300
Max	1-1/2	slug	slug	Bren.	NA	1604
Max	1-5/8	Bismuth	BB, 2, 4, 5, 6	Bis.	NA	1250
4	24 pellets	buffered	1 buck	Win., Fed., Rem.	$5**	1040
4	15 pellets	buffered	00 buck	Win., Fed., Rem.	$6**	1210
4	10 pellets	buffered	000 buck	Win., Fed., Rem.	$6**	1225
4	41 pellets	buffered	4 buck	Win., Fed., Rem.	$6**	1210
Max	1-3/8	heavyweight	5, 6	Fed.	NA	1300
Max	1-3/8	high density	B, 2, 4, 6	Rem. Win.	NA	1450
Max	1-3/8	slug	slug	Bren.	NA	1476
Max	1-3/8	blind side	Hex, 1, 3, 5	Win.	NA	1400
Max	1-1/4	slug, rifled	slug	Fed.	NA	1600
Max	1-3/16	saboted slug	copper slug	Rem.	NA	1500
Max	7/8	slug, rifled	slug	Rem.	NA	1875
Max	1-1/8	low recoil	BB	Fed.	NA	850
Max	1-1/8	steel	BB, 2, 3, 4	Fed., Win., Rem.	NA	1550
Max	1-1/16	high density	2, 4	Win.	NA	1400
Max	1	steel	4, 6	Fed.	NA	1330
Max	1-3/8	buckhammer	slug	Rem.	NA	1500
Max	1	TruBall slug	slug	Fed.	NA	1700
Max	1	slug, rifled	slug, magnum	Win., Rem.	$5**	1760
Max	1	saboted slug	slug	Rem., Win., Fed.	$10**	1550
Max	385 grs.	partition gold	slug	Win.	NA	2000
Max	1-1/8	Rackmaster	slug	Win.	NA	1700
Max	300 grs.	XP3	slug	Win.	NA	2100
3-5/8	1-3/8	steel	BBB, BB, 1, 2, 3, 4	Win., Fed., Rem.	$19	1275
Max	1-1/8	snow goose FS	BB, 2, 3, 4	Fed.	NA	1635
Max	1-1/8	steel	BB, 2, 4	Rem.	NA	1500
Max	1-1/8	steel	T, BBB, BB, 2, 4, 5, 6	Fed., Win.	NA	1450
Max	1-1/8	steel	BB, 2	Fed.	NA	1400
Max	1-1/8	FS lead	3, 4	Fed.	NA	1600
Max	1-3/8	Blind side	Hex, BB, 2	Win.	NA	1400
4	1-1/4	steel	T, BBB, BB, 1, 2, 3, 4, 6	Win., Fed., Rem.	$18	1400
Max	1-1/4	FS steel	BBB, BB, 2	Fed.	NA	1450

12 Gauge 2-3/4"

Dram Equiv.	Shot Ozs.	Load Style	Shot Sizes	Brands	Avg. Price/box	Velocity (fps)
Max	1-5/8	magnum	4, 5, 6	Win., Fed.	$8*	1250
Max	1-3/8	lead	4, 5, 6	Fiocchi	NA	1485
Max	1-3/8	turkey	4, 5, 6	Fio.	NA	1250
Max	1-3/8	steel	4, 5, 6	Fed.	NA	1400
Max	1-3/8	Bismuth	BB, 2, 4, 5, 6	Bis.	NA	1300
3-3/4	1-1/2	magnum	BB, 2, 4, 5, 6	Win., Fed., Rem.	$16	1260
Max	1-1/4	blind side	Hex, 2, 5	Win.	NA	1400
Max	1-1/4	Supreme H-V	4, 5, 6, 7-1/2	Win. Rem.	NA	1400
3-3/4	1-1/4	high velocity	BB, 2, 4, 5, 6, 7-1/2, 8, 9	Win., Fed., Rem., Fio.	$13	1330
Max	1-1/4	high density	B, 2, 4	Win.	NA	1450
Max	1-1/4	high density	4, 6	Rem.	NA	1325
3-1/4	1-1/4	standard velocity	6, 7-1/2, 8, 9	Win., Fed., Rem., Fio.	$11	1220
Max	1-1/8	Hevi-shot	5	Hevi-shot	NA	1350
3-1/4	1-1/8	standard velocity	4, 6, 7-1/2, 8, 9	Win., Fed., Rem., Fio.	$9	1255
Max	1-1/8	steel	2, 4	Rem.	NA	1390
Max	1	steel	BB, 2	Fed.	NA	1450
3-1/4	1	standard velocity	6, 7-1/2, 8	Rem., Fed., Fio., Win.	$6	1290
3-1/4	1-1/4	target	7-1/2, 8, 9	Win., Fed., Rem.	$10	1220
3	1-1/8	spreader	7-1/2, 8, 8-1/2, 9	Fio.	NA	1200
3	1-1/8	target	7-1/2, 8, 9, 7-1/2x8	Win., Fed., Fio.	$7	1200
2-3/4	1-1/8	target	7-1/2, 8, 8-1/2, 9, 7-1/2x8	Win., Fed., Fio.	$7	1145
2-3/4	1-1/8	low recoil	7-1/2, 8	Rem.	NA	1145
2-1/2	26 grams	low recoil	8	Win.	NA	980
2-1/4	1-1/8	target	7-1/2, 8, 8-1/2, 9	Rem., Fed.	$7	1080
Max	1	spreader	7-1/2, 8, 8-1/2, 9	Fio.	NA	1300
3-1/4	28 grams (1 oz)	target	7-1/2, 8, 9	Win., Fed., Rem., Fio.	$8	1290
3	1	target	7-1/2, 8, 8-1/2, 9	Win., Fio.	NA	1235
2-3/4	1	target	7-1/2, 8, 8-1/2, 9	Fed., Rem., Fio.	NA	1180
3-1/4	24 grams	target	7-1/2, 8, 9	Fed., Win., Fio.	NA	1325
3	7/8	light	8	Fio.	NA	1200
3-3/4	8 pellets	buffered	000 buck	Win., Fed., Rem.	$4**	1325
4	12 pellets	premium	00 buck	Win., Fed., Rem.	$5**	1290
3-3/4	9 pellets	buffered	00 buck	Win., Fed., Rem., Fio.	$19	1325
3-3/4	12 pellets	buffered	0 buck	Win., Fed., Rem.	$4**	1275
4	20 pellets	buffered	1 buck	Win., Fed., Rem.	$4**	1075
3-3/4	16 pellets	buffered	1 buck	Win., Fed., Rem.	$4**	1250
4	34 pellets	premium	4 buck	Fed., Rem.	$5**	1250
3-3/4	27 pellets	buffered	4 buck	Win., Fed., Rem., Fio.	$4**	1325
		PDX1	1 oz. slug, 3-00 buck	Win.	NA	1150
Max	1 oz	segmenting, slug	slug	Win.	NA	1600
Max	1	saboted slug	slug	Win., Fed., Rem.	$10**	1450

12 Gauge 2-3/4" (cont.)

Dram Equiv.	Shot Ozs.	Load Style	Shot Sizes	Brands	Avg. Price/box	Velocity (fps)
Max	1-1/4	slug, rifled	slug	Fed.	NA	1520
Max	1-1/4	slug	slug	Lightfield		1440
Max	1-1/4	saboted slug	attached sabot	Rem.	NA	1550
Max	1	slug, rifled	slug, magnum	Rem., Fio.	$5**	1680
Max	1	slug, rifled	slug	Win., Fed., Rem.	$4**	1610
Max	1	sabot slug	slug	Sauvestre		1640
Max	7/8	slug, rifled	slug	Rem.	NA	1800
Max	400	plat. tip	sabot slug	Win.	NA	1700
Max	385 grains	Partition Gold Slug	slug	Win.	NA	1900
Max	385 grains	Core-Lokt bonded	sabot slug	Rem.	NA	1900
Max	325 grains	Barnes Sabot	slug	Fed.	NA	1900
Max	300 grains	SST Slug	sabot slug	Hornady	NA	2050
Max	3/4	Tracer	#8 + tracer	Fio.	NA	1150
Max	130 grains	Less Lethal	.73 rubber slug	Lightfield	NA	600
Max	3/4	non-toxic	zinc slug	Win.	NA	NA
3	1-1/8	steel target	6-1/2, 7	Rem.	NA	1200
2-3/4	1-1/8	steel target	7	Rem.	NA	1145
3	1#	steel	7	Win.	$11	1235
3-1/2	1-1/4	steel	T, BBB, BB, 1, 2, 3, 4, 5, 6	Win., Fed., Rem.	$18	1275
3-3/4	1-1/8	steel	BB, 1, 2, 3, 4, 5, 6	Win., Fed., Rem., Fio.	$16	1365
3-3/4	1	steel	2, 3, 4, 5, 6, 7	Win., Fed., Rem., Fio.	$13	1390
Max	7/8	steel	7	Fio.	NA	1440

16 Gauge 2-3/4"

Dram Equiv.	Shot Ozs.	Load Style	Shot Sizes	Brands	Avg. Price/box	Velocity (fps)
3-1/4	1-1/4	magnum	2, 4, 6	Fed., Rem.	$16	1260
3-1/4	1-1/8	high velocity	4, 6, 7-1/2	Win., Fed., Rem., Fio.	$12	1295
Max	1-1/8	Bismuth	4, 5	Bis.	NA	1200
2-3/4	1-1/8	standard velocity	6, 7-1/2, 8	Fed., Rem., Fio.	$9	1185
2-1/2	1	dove	6, 7-1/2, 8, 9	Fio., Win.	NA	1165
2-3/4	1		6, 7-1/2, 8	Fio.	NA	1200
Max	15/16	steel	2, 4	Fed., Rem.	NA	1300
Max	7/8	steel	2, 4	Win.	$16	1300
3	12 pellets	buffered	1 buck	Win., Fed., Rem.	$4**	1225
Max	4/5	slug, rifled	slug	Win., Fed., Rem.	$4**	1570
Max	.92	sabot slug	slug	Sauvestre	NA	1560

20 Gauge 3" Magnum

Dram Equiv.	Shot Ozs.	Load Style	Shot Sizes	Brands	Avg. Price/box	Velocity (fps)
3	1-1/4	premium	2, 4, 5, 6, 7-1/2	Win., Fed., Rem.	$15	1185
Max	1-1/4	Wingmaster HD	4, 6	Rem.	NA	1185
3	1-1/4	turkey	4, 6	Fio.	NA	1200
Max	1-1/4	Hevi-shot	2, 4, 6	Hevi-shot	NA	1250
Max	1-1/8	high density	4, 6	Rem.	NA	1300
Max	18 pellets	buck shot	2 buck	Fed.	NA	1200
Max	24 pellets	buffered	3 buck	Win.	$5**	1150

20 Gauge 3" Magnum (cont.)

Dram Equiv.	Shot Ozs.	Load Style	Shot Sizes	Brands	Avg. Price/box	Velocity (fps)
2-3/4	20 pellets	buck	3 buck	Rem.	$4**	1200
Max	1	hypersonic	2, 3, 4	Rem.	NA	Rem.
3-1/4	1	steel	1, 2, 3, 4, 5, 6	Win., Fed., Rem.	$15	1330
Max	1	blind side	Hex, 2, 5	Win.	NA	1300
Max	7/8	steel	2, 4	Win.	NA	1300
Max	7/8	FS lead	3, 4	Fed.	NA	1500
Max	1-1/16	high density	2, 4	Win.	NA	1400
Max	1-1/16	Bismuth	2, 4, 5, 6	Bismuth	NA	1250
Mag	5/8	saboted slug	275 gr.	Fed.	NA	1900
Max	3/4	TruBall slug	slug	Fed.	NA	1700

20 Gauge 2-3/4"

Dram Equiv.	Shot Ozs.	Load Style	Shot Sizes	Brands	Avg. Price/box	Velocity (fps)
2-3/4	1-1/8	magnum	4, 6, 7-1/2	Win., Fed., Rem.	$14	1175
2-3/4	1	high velocity	4, 5, 6, 7-1/2, 8, 9	Win., Fed., Rem., Fio.	$12	1220
Max	1	Bismuth	4, 6	Bis.	NA	1200
Max	1	Hevi-shot	5	Hevi-shot	NA	1250
Max	1	Supreme H-V	4, 6, 7-1/2	Win. Rem.	NA	1300
Max	1	FS lead	4, 5, 6	Fed.	NA	1350
Max	7/8	Steel	2, 3, 4	Fio.	NA	1500
2-1/2	1	standard velocity	6, 7-1/2, 8	Win., Rem., Fed., Fio.	$6	1165
2-1/2	7/8	clays	8	Rem.	NA	1200
2-1/2	7/8	promotional	6, 7-1/2, 8	Win., Rem., Fio.	$6	1210
2-1/2	1	target	8, 9	Win., Rem.	$8	1165
Max	7/8	clays	7-1/2, 8	Win.	NA	1275
2-1/2	7/8	target	8, 9	Win., Fed., Rem.	$8	1200
Max	3/4	steel	2, 4	Rem.	NA	1425
2-1/2	7/8	steel - target	7	Rem.	NA	1200
1-1/2	7/8	low recoil	8	Win.	NA	980
Max	1	buckhammer	slug	Rem.	NA	1500
Max	5/8	Saboted Slug	Copper Slug	Rem.	NA	1500
Max	20 pellets	buffered	3 buck	Win., Fed.	$4	1200
Max	5/8	slug, saboted	slug	Win.,	$9**	1400
2-3/4	5/8	slug, rifled	slug	Rem.	$4**	1580
Max	3/4	saboted slug	copper slug	Fed., Rem.	NA	1450
Max	3/4	slug, rifled	slug	Win., Fed., Rem., Fio.	$4**	1570
Max	.9	sabot slug	slug	Sauvestre		1480
Max	260 grains	Partition Gold Slug	slug	Win.	NA	1900
Max	260 grains	Core-Lokt Ultra	slug	Rem.	NA	1900

20 Gauge 2-3/4" (cont.)

Dram Equiv.	Shot Ozs.	Load Style	Shot Sizes	Brands	Avg. Price/box	Velocity (fps)
Max	260 grains	saboted slug	platinum tip	Win.	NA	1700
Max	3/4	steel	2, 3, 4, 6	Win., Fed., Rem.	$14	1425
Max	250 grains	SST slug	slug	Hornady	NA	1800
Max	1/2	rifled, slug	slug	Rem.	NA	1800
Max	67 grains	Less lethal	2/.60 rubber balls	Lightfield	NA	900

28 Gauge 3"

Dram Equiv.	Shot Ozs.	Load Style	Shot Sizes	Brands	Avg. Price/box	Velocity (fps)
Max	7/8	tundra tungsten	4, 5, 6	Fiocchi	NA	TBD

28 Gauge 2-3/4"

Dram Equiv.	Shot Ozs.	Load Style	Shot Sizes	Brands	Avg. Price/box	Velocity (fps)
2	1	high velocity	6, 7-1/2, 8	Win.	$12	1125
2-1/4	3/4	high velocity	6, 7-1/2, 8, 9	Win., Fed., Rem., Fio.	$11	1295
2	3/4	target	8, 9	Win., Fed., Rem.	$9	1200
Max	3/4	sporting clays	7-1/2, 8-1/2	Win.	NA	1300
Max	5/8	Bismuth	4, 6	Bis.	NA	1250
Max	5/8	steel	6, 7	NA	NA	1300
Max	5/8	slug		Bren.	NA	1450

410 Bore 3"

Dram Equiv.	Shot Ozs.	Load Style	Shot Sizes	Brands	Avg. Price/box	Velocity (fps)
Max	11/16	high velocity	4, 5, 6, 7-1/2, 8, 9	Win., Fed., Rem., Fio.	$10	1135
Max	9/16	Bismuth	4	Bis.	NA	1175
Max	3/8	steel	6	NA	NA	1400
		judge	5 pellets 000 Buck	Fed.	NA	960
		judge	9 pellets #4 Buck	Fed.	NA	1100
Max	Mixed	Per. Defense	3DD/12BB	Win.	NA	750

410 Bore 2-1/2"

Dram Equiv.	Shot Ozs.	Load Style	Shot Sizes	Brands	Avg. Price/box	Velocity (fps)
Max	1/2	high velocity	4, 6, 7-1/2	Win., Fed., Rem.	$9	1245
Max	1/5	slug, rifled	slug	Win., Fed., Rem.	$4**	1815
1-1/2	1/2	target	8, 8-1/2, 9	Win., Fed., Rem., Fio.	$8	1200
Max	1/2	sporting clays	7-1/2, 8, 8-1/2	Win.	NA	1300
Max		Buckshot	5-000 Buck	Win.	NA	1135
		judge	12-bb's, 3 disks	Win.	NA	TBD
Max	Mixed	Per. Defense	4DD/16BB	Win.	NA	750
Max	42 grains	Less lethal	4/.41 rubber balls	Lightfield	NA	1150

ACCU-TEK AT-380 II ACP

Caliber: 380 ACP, 6-shot magazine. **Barrel:** 2.8" **Weight:** 23.5 oz.
Length: 6.125" overall. **Grips:** Textured black composition. **Sights:**
Blade front, rear adjustable for windage. **Features:** Made from 17-4
stainless steel, has an exposed hammer, manual firing-pin safety
block and trigger disconnect. Magazine release located on the
bottom of the grip. American made, lifetime warranty. Comes with
two 6-round stainless steel magazines and a California-approved
cable lock. Introduced 2006. Made in U.S.A. by Excel Industries.
Price: Satin stainless $289.00

ACCU-TEK HC-380

Simlar to AT-380 II except has a 13-round magazine.
Price: $330.00

ACCU-TEK LT-380

Simlar to AT-380 II except has a lightweight aluminum frame.
Weight: 15 ounces.
Price: $324.00

AKDAL GHOST SERIES

Caliber: 9x19mm 15-round double stacked magazine. **Barrel:**
4.45" **Weight:** 29.10 oz. **Length:** 7.5" overall. **Grips:** Polymer
black polycoat. **Sights:** Fixed, open type with notched rear sight
dovetailed into the slide. Adjustable sight also available. **Features:**
Compact single action pre-cocked, semiautomatic pistol with short
recoil operation and locking breech. It uses modified Browning-type
locking, in which barrel engages the slide with single lug, entering
the ejection window. Pistol also has no manual safeties; instead,
it has automatic trigger and firing pin safeties. The polymer frame
features removable backstraps (of different sizes), and an integral
accessory Picatinny rail below the barrel.
Price: $499.00

AMERICAN CLASSIC 1911-A1

Caliber: .45 ACP. 7+1 magazine capacity. **Barrel:** 5" **Grips:**
Checkered walnut. **Sights:** Fixed. **Finish:** Blue or hard chromed.
A .22 LR version is also available. Other variations include Trophy
model with adjustable sights, two-tone finish.
Price: .... $579.00 to $811.00

AMERICAN CLASSIC COMMANDER

Caliber: .45 ACP. Same features as 1911-A1 model except is
Commander size with 4.25" barrel.
Price: $616.00

AMERICAN TACTICAL IMPORTS MILITARY 1911

Caliber: .45 ACP. 7+1 magazine capacity. **Barrel:** 5" **Grips:** Textured
mahogany. **Sights:** Fixed military style. **Finish:** Blue. Also offered in
Commander and Officer's sizes and Enhanced model with additional
features.
Price: .... $500.00 to $585.00

ARMALITE AR-24

Caliber: 9mm Para., 10- or 15-shot magazine. **Barrel:** 4.671"
6-groove, right-hand cut rifling. **Weight:** 34.9 oz. **Length:** 8.27"
overall. **Grips:** Black polymer. **Sights:** Dovetail front, fixed rear,
3-dot luminous design. **Features:** Machined slide,
frame and barrel. Serrations on forestrap and backstrap, external
thumb safety and internal firing pin box, half cock. Two 15-round
magazines, pistol case, pistol lock, manual and cleaning brushes.
Manganese phosphate finish. Compact comes with two 13-round
magazines, 3.89 barrel, weighs 33.4 oz. Made in U.S.A. by
ArmaLite.
Price: AR-24 Full Size...$550.00
Price: AR-24K Compact $550.00

ARMSCOR/ROCK ISLAND ARMORY 1911A1-45 FS GI

1911-style semiauto pistol chambered in .45 ACP (8 rounds), 9mm
Parabellum, .38 Super (9 rounds). Features include checkered
plastic or hardwood grips, 5-inch barrel, parkerized steel frame and
slide, drift adjustable sights.
Price: $500.00

ARMSCOR/ROCK ISLAND ARMORY 1911A1-45 CS GI

1911-style Officer's-size semiauto pistol chambered in .45 ACP. Features plain hardwood grips, 3.5-inch barrel, parkerized steel frame and slide, drift adjustable sights.
Price: $500.00

ARMSCOR/ROCK ISLAND ARMORY 1911A2-.22 TCM

Caliber: .22 TCM, 17-round magazine. **Barrel:** 5 inches. **Weight:** 36 oz. **Length:** 8.5 inches. **Grips:** Polymer. **Sights:** Adjustable rear. **Features:** Chambered for high velocity .22 TCM rimfire cartridge.
Price: **$660.00**

ARMSCOR/ROCK ISLAND ARMORY 1911 TACTICAL II FS

Caliber: 10mm, 8-round magazine. **Barrel:** 5 inches. **Weight:** 40 oz. **Length:** 8.5 inches. **Grips:** VZ G10. **Sights:** Fiber optic front, adjustable rear. **Features:** Parkerized finish, comes with two magazines, lock and lockable hard case. Accessory rail available.
Price: **$660.00**

ARMSCOR/ROCK ISLAND ARMORY MAP1 & MAPP1

Caliber: 9mm, 16-round magazine. Browning short recoil action style pistols with: integrated front sight; Snag-free rear sight (police standard); Tanfoglio barrel; Single & double-action trigger; automatic safety on firing pin & manual on rear lever; standard hammer; side extractor; standard or ambidextrous rear safety; combat slide stop; parkerized finish for nickel steel parts; polymer frame with accessory rail.
Price: **$400.00**

ARMSCOR/ROCK ISLAND ARMORY XT22

Caliber: .22 LR, 15-round magazine std. **Barrel:** 5" **Weight:** 38 oz. The XT-22 is a combat 1911 .22 pistol. Unlike most .22 1911 conversions, this pistol is built as a complete gun. Designed for durability, it is the only .22 1911 with a forged 4140 steel slide and the only .22 1911 with a one piece 4140 chrome moly barrel.
Price: **$473.99**

AUTO-ORDNANCE 1911A1

Caliber: 45 ACP, 7-shot magazine. **Barrel:** 5" **Weight:** 39 oz. **Length:** 8.5" overall. **Grips:** Brown checkered plastic with medallion. **Sights:** Blade front, rear drift-adjustable for windage. **Features:** Same specs as 1911A1 military guns-parts interchangeable. Frame and slide blued; each radius has non-glare finish. Introduced 2002. Made in U.S.A. by Kahr Arms.
Price: 1911PKZSE Parkerized, plastic grips **$668.00**
Price: 1911PKZSEW Parkerized, wood grips...........................**$685.00**

BAER H.C. 40

Caliber: 40 S&W, 18-shot magazine. **Barrel:** 5" **Weight:** 37 oz. **Length:** 8.5" overall. **Grips:** Wood. **Sights:** Low-mount adjustable rear sight with hidden rear leaf, dovetail front sight. **Features:** Double-stack Caspian frame, beavertail grip safety, ambidextrous thumb safety, 40 S&W match barrel with supported chamber, match stainless steel barrel bushing, lowered and flared ejection port, extended ejector, match trigger fitted, integral mag well, bead blast blue finish on lower, polished sides on slide. Introduced 2008. Made in U.S.A. by Les Baer Custom, Inc.
Price: $2,960.00

BAER 1911 BOSS .45

Caliber: .45 ACP, 8+1 capacity. **Barrel:** 5" **Weight:** 37 oz. **Length:** 8.5" overall. **Grips:** Premium Checkered Cocobolo Grips. **Sights:** Low-Mount LBC Adj Sight, Red Fiber Optic Front. **Features:** Speed Trgr, Beveled Mag Well, Rounded for Tactical. Rear cocking serrations on the slide, Baer fiber optic front sight (red), flat mainspring housing, checkered at 20 lpi, extended combat safety, Special tactical package, chromed complete lower, blued slide, (2) 8-round premium magazines.
Price: $2,260.00

BAER 1911 CUSTOM CARRY

Caliber: .45 ACP, 7- or 10-shot magazine. **Barrel:** 5" **Weight:** 37 oz. **Length:** 8.5" overall. **Grips:** Checkered walnut. **Sights:** Baer improved ramp-style dovetailed front, Novak low-mount rear. **Features:** Baer forged NM frame, slide and barrel with stainless bushing. Baer speed trigger with 4-lb. pull. Partial listing shown. Made in U.S.A. by Les Baer Custom, Inc.
Price: Custom Carry 5, blued $1,920.00

Price: Custom Carry 5, stainless **$2,040.00**
Price: Custom Carry 4 Commanche length, blued **$1,995.00**
Price: Custom Carry 4 Commanche length, stainless **$2,220.00**

BAER 1911 ULTIMATE RECON

Caliber: .45 ACP, 7- or 10-shot magazine. **Barrel:** 5" **Weight:** 37 oz. **Length:** 8.5" overall. **Grips:** Checkered cocobolo. **Sights:** Baer improved ramp-style dovetailed front, Novak low-mount rear. **Features:** NM Caspian frame, slide and barrel with stainless bushing. Baer speed trigger with 4-lb. pull. Includes integral Picatinny rail and Sure-Fire X-200 light. Made in U.S.A. by Les Baer Custom, Inc. Introduced 2006.
Price: Bead blast blued **$3,070.00**
Price: Bead blast chrome **$3,390.00**

BAER 1911 PREMIER II

Caliber: .38 Super, 400 Cor-Bon, .45 ACP, 7- or 10-shot magazine. **Barrel:** 5" **Weight:** 37 oz. **Length:** 8.5" overall. **Grips:** Checkered rosewood, double diamond pattern. **Sights:** Baer dovetailed front, low-mount Bo-Mar rear with hidden leaf. **Features:** Baer NM forged steel frame and barrel with stainless bushing, deluxe Commander hammer and sear, beavertail grip safety with pad, extended ambidextrous safety; flat mainspring housing; 30 lpi checkered front strap. Made in U.S.A. by Les Baer Custom, Inc.
Price: 5" .45 ACP **$1,905.00**
Price: 5" 400 Cor-Bon **$2,090.00**
Price: 5" .38 Super **$2,270.00**
Price: 6" .45 ACP, 400 Cor-Bon, .38 Super, from **$2,090.00**
Price: Super-Tac, .45 ACP, 400 Cor-Bon, .38 Super, from **$2,395.00**

BAER 1911 S.R.P.

Caliber: .45 ACP. **Barrel:** 5" **Weight:** 37 oz. **Length:** 8.5" overall. **Grips:** Checkered walnut. **Sights:** Trijicon night sights. **Features:** Similar to the F.B.I. contract gun except uses Baer forged steel frame. Has Baer match barrel with supported chamber, complete tactical action. Has Baer Ultra Coat finish. Introduced 1996. Made in U.S.A. by Les Baer Custom, Inc.
Price: Government or Commanche length **$2,490.00**

BAER 1911 STINGER

Caliber: .45 ACP or .38 Super, 7-round magazine. **Barrel:** 5" **Weight:** 34 oz. **Length:** 8.5" overall. **Grips:** Checkered cocobolo. **Sights:** Baer dovetailed front, low-mount Bo-Mar rear with hidden leaf.

Features: Baer NM frame. Baer Commanche slide, Officer's style grip frame, beveled mag well. Made in U.S.A. by Les Baer Custom, Inc.
Price: .45 ACP ....**$1,930.00 to $1,990.00**
Price: .38 Super **$1,970.00**

BAER 1911 PROWLER III

Caliber: .45 ACP, 8-round magazine. **Barrel:** 5" **Weight:** 34 oz. **Length:** 8.5" overall. **Grips:** Checkered cocobolo. **Sights:** Baer dovetailed front, low-mount Bo-Mar rear with hidden leaf. **Features:** Similar to Premier II with tapered cone stub weight, rounded corners. Made in U.S.A. by Les Baer Custom, Inc.
Price: Blued **$2,710.00**

BERETTA M92/96 A1 SERIES

Caliber: 9mm, 15-round magazine; .40 S&W, 12 rounds (M96 A1). **Barrel:** 4.9 inches. **Weight:** 33-34 oz. **Length:** 8.5 inches. **Sights:** Fiber optic front, adjustable rear. **Features:** Same as other models in 92/96 family except for addition of accessory rail.
Price: **$725.00**

BERETTA MODEL 92FS

Caliber: 9mm Para., 10-shot magazine. **Barrel:** 4.9" **Weight:** 34 oz. **Length:** 8.5" overall. **Grips:** Checkered black plastic. **Sights:** Blade front, rear adjustable for windage. Tritium night sights available. **Features:** Double action. Extractor acts as chamber loaded indicator, squared trigger guard, grooved front and backstraps, inertia firing pin. Matte or blued finish. Introduced 1977. Made in U.S.A.
Price: With plastic grips **$650.00**

BERETTA MODEL 21 BOBCAT

Caliber: .22 LR or .25 ACP. Both double action. **Barrel:** 2.4" **Weight:** 11.5 oz.; 11.8 oz. **Length:** 4.9" overall. **Grips:** Plastic. **Features:** Available in matte black or stainless. Introduced in 1985.
Price: Black matte **$310.00**
Price: Stainless **$350.00**

BERETTA MODEL 3032 TOMCAT

Caliber: .32 ACP, 7-shot magazine. **Barrel:** 2.45" **Weight:** 14.5 oz. **Length:** 5" overall. **Grips:** Checkered black plastic. **Sights:** Blade front, drift-adjustable rear. **Features:** Double action with exposed hammer; tip-up barrel for direct

HANDGUNS Autoloaders, Service & Sport

loading/unloading; thumb safety; polished or matte blue finish. Made in U.S.A. Introduced 1996.
Price: Matte $390.00
Price: Inox $430.00

Features: Ambidextrous manual safety lever, interchangeable backstraps included, lock breech and tilt barrel system, stainless steel barrel, Picatinny rail.
Price: $600.00

BERETTA MODEL U22 NEOS
Caliber: .22 LR, 10-shot magazine. **Barrel:** 4.5" and 6" **Weight:** 32 oz.; 36 oz. **Length:** 8.8"/ 10.3" **Sights:** Target.
Features: Integral rail for standard scope mounts, light, perfectly weighted, 100 percent American made by Beretta.
Price: Blue $250.00
Price: Inox $350.00

BERETTA MODEL PX4 STORM
Caliber: 9mm Para., 40 S&W. **Capacity:** 17 (9mm Para.); 14 (40 S&W). **Barrel:** 4" **Weight:** 27.5 oz. **Grips:** Black checkered w/3 interchangeable backstraps. **Sights:** 3-dot system coated in Superluminova; removable front and rear sights. **Features:** DA/SA, manual safety/hammer decocking lever (ambi) and automatic firing pin block safety. Picatinny rail. Comes with two magazines (17/10 in 9mm Para. and 14/10 in 40 S&W). Removable hammer unit. American made by Beretta. Introduced 2005.
Price: 9mm or .40 ....$575.00
Price: .45 ACP $650.00

BERETTA MODEL M9
Caliber: 9mm Para. Capacity: 15. **Barrel:** 4.9" **Weight:** 32.2-35.3 oz. **Grips:** Plastic. **Sights:** Dot and post, low profile, windage adjustable rear. **Features:** DA/SA, forged aluminum alloy frame, delayed locking-bolt system, manual safety doubles as decocking lever, combat-style trigger guard, loaded chamber indicator. Comes with two magazines (15/10). American made by Beretta. Introduced 2005.
Price: $650.00

BERETTA MODEL M9A1
Caliber: 9mm Para. Capacity: 15. **Barrel:** 4.9" **Weight:** 32.2-35.3 oz. **Grips:** Plastic. **Sights:** Dot and post, low profile, windage adjustable rear. **Features:** Same as M9, but also includes integral Mil-Std-1913 Picatinny rail, has checkered frontstrap and backstrap. Comes with two magazines (15/10). American made by Beretta. Introduced 2005.
Price: $750.00

BERETTA MODEL PX4 STORM SUB-COMPACT
Caliber: 9mm, 40 S&W. Capacity: 13 (9mm); 10 (40 S&W). **Barrel:** 3" **Weight:** 26.1 oz. **Length:** 6.2" overall. **Grips:** NA. **Sights:** NA.

BERETTA NANO
Caliber: 9mm Para. Six-shot magazine. **Barrel:** 3.07". **Weight:** 17.7 oz. **Length:** 5.7" overall. **Grips:** Polymer. Sights: 3-dot low profile.

Prices given are believed to be accurate at time of publication however, many factors affect retail pricing so exact prices are not possible.

Features: Double-action only, striker fired. Replaceable grip frames.
Price: $475.00

Price: Thunder Matte $335.00
Price: Thunder Satin Nickel $355.00
Price: Thunder Duo-Tone $355.00
Price: Thunder Duo-Tone with Crimson Trace Laser Grips $555.00

BERSA THUNDER 9 ULTRA COMPACT/40 SERIES
Caliber: 9mm Para., 40 S&W. **Barrel:** 3.5" **Weight:** 24.5 oz. **Length:** 6.6" overall. **Features:** Otherwise similar to Thunder 45 Ultra Compact. 9mm Para. High Capacity model has 17-round capacity. 40 High Capacity model has 13-round capacity. Imported from Argentina by Eagle Imports, Inc.
Price: $500.00

BERETTA PICO
Caliber: .380 ACP, 6 rounds. **Barrel:** 2.7" **Weight:** 11.5 oz. **Length:** 5.1" overall. **Grips:** Integral with polymer frame. Interchangeable backstrap. **Sights:** White outline rear. **Features:** Adjustable, quick-change. Striker-fired, double-action only operation. Ambidextrous magazine release and slide release. Ships with two magazines, one flush, one with grip extension. Made in the USA.
Price: $399.00

BERSA THUNDER 45 ULTRA COMPACT
Caliber: .45 ACP. **Barrel:** 3.6" **Weight:** 27 oz. **Length:** 6.7" overall. **Grips:** Anatomically designed polymer. **Sights:** White outline rear. **Features:** Double action; firing pin safeties, integral locking system. Available in matte, satin nickel, gold, or duo-tone. Introduced 2003. Imported from Argentina by Eagle Imports, Inc.
Price: Thunder 45, matte blue $500.00
Price: Thunder 45, duo-tone $550.00

BOBERG XR9-S
Caliber: 9mm, 7-round magazine. **Barrel:** 3.35 inches. XR9-L has 4.2 inch barrel. **Weight:** 17.4 oz. **Length:** 5.1 inches, 5.95 (XR9-L). **Sights:** Fixed low profile. **Features:** Unique rotating barrel, locked-breech operation, with "pull-push" feeding system utilizing a claw-type loader attached to the slide to pull rounds from the magazine. Black polymer frame with stainless steel barrel. Available with all black or platinum finish.
Price: $1,099.00
Price: (XR-9L)..$1,349.00

BERSA THUNDER 380 SERIES
Caliber: .380 ACP, 7 rounds. **Barrel:** 3.5" **Weight:** 23 oz. **Length:** 6.6" overall. **Features:** Otherwise similar to Thunder 45 Ultra Compact. 380 DLX has 9-round capacity. 380 Concealed Carry has 8-round capacity. Imported from Argentina by Eagle Imports, Inc.

BROWNING 1911-22 COMPACT
Caliber: .22 L.R.,10-round magazine. **Barrel:** 3.625" **Weight:** 15 oz. **Length:** 6.5" overall. **Grips:** Brown composite. **Sights:** Fixed.

Prices given are believed to be accurate at time of publication however, many factors affect retail pricing so exact prices are not possible.

69TH EDITION, 2015 ✦ **389**

Features: Slide is machined aluminum with alloy frame and matte blue finish. Blowback action and single action trigger with manual thumb and grip safetys. Works, feels and functions just like a full size 1911. It is simply scaled down and chambered in the best of all practice rounds: .22 LR for focus on the fundamentals.
Price: $600.00

BROWNING 1911-22 A1
Caliber: .22 L.R.,10-round magazine. **Barrel:** 4.25" **Weight:** 16 oz. **Length:** 7.0625" overall. **Grips:** Brown composite. **Sights:** Fixed. **Features:** Slide is machined aluminum with alloy frame and matte blue finish. Blowback action and single action trigger with manual thumb and grip safetys. Works, feels and functions just like a full size 1911. It is simply scaled down and chambered in the best of all practice rounds: .22 LR for focus on the fundamentals.
Price: $600.00

BROWNING 1911-22 POLYMER WITH RAIL
Caliber: .22 L.R.,10-round magazine. **Barrel:** 4.25" or 3.625" (Compact model, shown). **Weight:** 14 oz. overall. **Features:** Other features are similar to standard 1911-22 except for this model's composite/polymer frame, extended grip safety, stipled black laminated grip, skeleton trigger and hammer. Available with accessory rail (shown).
Price: $640.00
Price: With Rail $670.00

BROWNING 1911-22 POLYMER DESERT TAN
Caliber: .22 L.R.,10-round magazine. **Barrel:** 4.25" or 3.625" **Weight:** 13-14 oz. overall. **Features:** Other features are similar to standard 1911-22 except for this model's composite/polymer frame. Also available with pink composite grips.
Price: $580.00

BROWNING HI-POWER
Caliber: 9mm, 13-round magazine. **Barrel:** 4.625 inches. **Weight:** 32 oz. **Length:** 7.75 inches. **Grips:** Checkered walnut (standard model), textured and grooved polymer (Mark III). **Sights:** Fixed low-profile 3-dot (Mark III), fixed or adjustable low profile (standard model). **Features:** Single-action operation with ambidextrous thumb safety, forged steel frame and slide. Made in Belgium.
Price: Mark III..$1,070.00
Price: Fixed Sights..$1,080.00

Price: Standard, Adjustable sights $1,160.00

BROWNING BUCK MARK CAMPER UFX
Caliber: .22 LR with 10-shot magazine. **Barrel:** 5.5" tapered bull. **Weight:** 34 oz. **Length:** 9.5" overall. **Grips:** Overmolded Ultragrip Ambidextrous. **Sights:** Pro-Target adjustable rear, ramp front. **Features:** Matte blue receiver, matte blue or stainless barrel.
Price: Camper UFX... $390.00
Price: Camper UFX stainless $430.00

BROWNING BUCK MARK HUNTER
Caliber: .22 LR with 10-shot magazine. **Barrel:** 7.25" heavy tapered bull. **Weight:** 38 oz. **Length:** 11.3" overall. **Grips:** Cocobolo target.

Prices given are believed to be accurate at time of publication however, many factors affect retail pricing so exact prices are not possible.

Sights: Pro-Target adjustable rear, Tru-Glo/Marble's fiber-optic front. Integral scope base on top rail. Scope in photo is not included.
Features: Matte blue.
Price: $500.00

BROWNING BUCK PRACTICAL URX
Caliber: .22 LR with 10-shot magazine. **Barrel:** 5.5" tapered bull. **Weight:** 34 oz. **Length:** 9.5" overall. **Grips:** Ultragrip RX Ambidextrous. **Sights:** Pro-Target adjustable rear, Tru-Glo/Marble's fiber-optic front. **Features:** Matte gray receiver, matte blue barrel.
Price: $440.00

BROWNING BUCK MARK PLUS UDX
Caliber: .22 LR with 10-shot magazine. **Barrel:** 5.5" slab sided. **Weight:** 34 oz. **Length:** 9.5" overall. **Grips:** Walnut Ultragrip DX Ambidextrous. **Sights:** Pro-Target adjustable rear, Tru-Glo/Marble's fiber-optic front. **Features:** Matte blue.
Price: $540.00

BUSHMASTER XM-15 PATROLMAN'S AR PISTOL
Caliber: 5.56/223, 30-round. **Barrel:** 7" or 10.5" stainless steel with A2-type flash hider, knurled free-float handguard. **Weight:** 5.2 to 5.7 lbs. (4.9 to 5.5 lbs., Enhanced model). **Length:** 23" to 26.5" **Grips:** A2 pistol grip with standard triggerguard. **Features:** AR-style semi-auto pistol. Enhanced model has Barnes Precision free-float lightweight quad rail, Magpul MOE pistol grip and triggerguard.
Price: $973.00
Price: Enhanced.................................... $1,229.00

CHIAPPA 1911-22
A faithful replica of the famous John Browning 1911A1 pistol.
Caliber: .22 LR. **Barrel:** 5". **Weight:** 33.5 oz. **Length:** 8.5". **Grips:** Two-piece wood. **Sights:** Fixed. **Features:** Fixed barrel design, 10-shot magazine. Available in black, OD green or tan finish. Target and Tactical models have adjustable sights.
Price: .... $300 to $419

CHIAPPA M9-22 STANDARD
Caliber: .22 LR. **Barrel:** 5" **Weight:** 2.3 lbs. **Length:** 8.5" **Grips:** Black molded plastic or walnut. **Sights:** Fixed front sight and windage adjustable rear sight. **Features:** The M9-9mm has been a U.S. standard-issue service pistol since 1990. Chiappa's M9-22 is a replica of this pistol in 22 LR. The M9-22 has the same weight and feel as its 9mm counterpart but has an affordable 10 shot magazine for the 22 long rifle cartridge which makes it a true rimfire reproduction. Comes standard with steel trigger, hammer assembly and a 1/2-28 threaded barrel.
Price: $369.00

CHIAPPA M9-22 TACTICAL
Caliber: .22 LR. **Barrel:** 5" **Weight:** 2.3 lbs. **Length:** 8.5" **Grips:** Black molded plastic. **Sights:** Fixed front sight and Novak style rear sites. **Features:** The M9-22 Tactical model has Novak style rear sites and comes with a fake suppressor (this ups the "cool factor" on the range and extends the barrel to make it even more accurate). It also has a 1/2 x 28 thread adaptor which can be used by those with a legal suppressor.
Price: $419.00

CHRISTENSEN ARMS 1911 SERIES
Caliber: .45 ACP, .40 S&W, 9mm. **Barrel:** 3.7", 4.3", 5.5" **Features:** All models are built on a titanium frame with hand-fitted slide, match-grade barrel, tritium night sights, G10 Operator grip panels.
Price: $3,195

CITADEL M-1911
Caliber: .45 ACP, .38 Super, 9mm, .22 LR. **Capacity:** 7 (.45), 8 (9mm, .38), or 10 rounds (.22). **Barrel:** 5 or 3.5 inches (.45 & 9mm only). **Weight:** 2.3 lbs. **Length:** 8.5" **Grips:** Checkered wood or Hogue wrap-around polymer. **Sights:** Low-profile combat fixed rear, blade front. **Finish:** Matte black, brushed or polished nickel. **Features:** Extended grip safety, ambidextrous safety and slide release. Built by Armscor (Rock Island Armory) in the Philippines and imported by Legacy Sports.
Price: Matte black.................................. $592.00
Price: Matte black, Hogue grips $630.00

Prices given are believed to be accurate at time of publication however, many factors affect retail pricing so exact prices are not possible.

69TH EDITION, 2015 ⊕ **391**

Price: Brushed nickel..$681.00
Price: Polished nickel...$700.00
Price: Matte black, .22 LR......................................$310.00
Price: Matte black, .22 LR, Hogue grips, fiber-optic sights......$592.00

CIMARRON MODEL 1911
Caliber: .45 ACP **Barrel:** 5 inches. **Weight:** 37.5 oz. **Length:** 8.5"
overall. **Grips:** Checkered walnut. **Features:** A faithful reproduction
of the original pattern of the Model 1911 with Parkerized finish and
lanyard ring.
Price: $541.00

COBRA ENTERPRISES FS32, FS380
Caliber: .32 ACP, .380 ACP, 7-shot magazine. **Barrel:** 3.5" **Weight:**
2.1 lbs. **Length:** 6-3/8" overall. **Grips:** Black composition. **Sights:**
Fixed. **Features:** Choice of bright chrome, satin nickel or black
finish. Introduced 2002. Made in U.S.A. by Cobra Enterprises of
Utah, Inc.
Price: .... $129.00 to $165.00

COBRA ENTERPRISES PATRIOT SERIES
Caliber: .380, 9mm or .45 ACP; 6, 7, or 10-shot magazine. **Barrel:**
3.3" **Weight:** 20 oz. **Length:** 6" overall. **Grips:** Black polymer.
Sights: Rear adjustable. **Features:** Stainless steel or black melonite
slide with load indicator; Semi-auto locked breech, DAO. Made in
U.S.A. by Cobra Enterprises of Utah, Inc.
Price: .... $349.00 to $395.00

COBRA ENTERPRISES CA32, CA380
Caliber: .32 ACP, .380 ACP. **Barrel:** 2.8" **Weight:** 17 oz. **Length:** 5.4"
Grips: Black molded synthetic. **Sights:** Fixed. **Features:** Choice
of black, satin nickel, or chrome finish. Made in U.S.A. by Cobra
Enterprises of Utah, Inc.
Price: $157.00

COBRA DENALI
Caliber: .380 ACP, 5 rounds. **Barrel:** 2.8" **Weight:** 22 oz. **Length:** 5.4"
Grips: Black molded synthetic integral with frame. **Sights:** Fixed.
Features: Made in U.S.A. by Cobra Enterprises of Utah, Inc.
Price: ....NA

COLT MODEL 1991 MODEL O
Caliber: .45 ACP, 7-shot magazine. **Barrel:** 5" **Weight:** 38 oz. **Length:**
8.5" overall. **Grips:** Checkered black composition. **Sights:** Ramped
blade front, fixed square notch rear, high profile. **Features:** Matte
finish. Continuation of serial number range used on original G.I.
1911A1 guns. Comes with one magazine and molded carrying case.
Introduced 1991.
Price: Blue $928.00
Price: Stainless $989.00

COLT XSE SERIES MODEL O
Caliber: .45 ACP, 8-shot magazine. **Barrel:** 5" **Grips:** Checkered,
double diamond rosewood. **Sights:** Drift-adjustable 3-dot combat.
Features: Brushed stainless finish; adjustable, two-cut aluminum
trigger; extended ambidextrous thumb safety; upswept beavertail
with palm swell; elongated slot hammer. Introduced 1999. From
Colt's Mfg. Co., Inc.
Price: XSE Government $1,072.00

COLT XSE LIGHTWEIGHT COMMANDER
Caliber: .45 ACP, 8-shot. **Barrel:** 4.25" **Weight:** 26 oz. **Length:** 7.75"
overall. **Grips:** Double diamond checkered rosewood. **Sights:**
Fixed, glare-proofed blade front, square notch rear; 3-dot system.
Features: Brushed stainless slide, nickeled aluminum frame;
McCormick elongated slot enhanced hammer, McCormick two-cut
adjustable aluminum hammer. Made in U.S.A. by Colt's Mfg. Co., Inc.
Price: $1,072.00

COLT DEFENDER
Caliber: .45 ACP (7-round magazine), 9mm (8-round). **Barrel:** 3"
Weight: 22-1/2 oz. **Length:** 6.75 overall. **Grips:** Pebble-finish rubber
wraparound with finger grooves. **Sights:** White dot front, snag-free
Colt competition rear. **Features:** Stainless finish; aluminum frame;
combat-style hammer; Hi Ride grip safety, extended manual safety,
disconnect safety. Introduced 1998. Made in U.S.A. by Colt's Mfg.
Co., Inc.
Price: 07000D, stainless $1,046.00

COLT SERIES 70
Caliber: .45 ACP. **Barrel:** 5" **Weight:** 37.5 oz. **Length:** 8.5" **Grips:**
Rosewood with double diamond checkering pattern. **Sights:** Fixed.
Features: Custom replica of the Original Series 70 pistol with a
Series 70 firing system, original rollmarks. Introduced 2002. Made in
U.S.A. by Colt's Mfg. Co., Inc.
Price: Blued $1,043.00
Price: Stainless $1,078.00

COLT 38 SUPER
Caliber: .38 Super. **Barrel:** 5" **Weight:** 36.5 oz. **Length:** 8.5" **Grips:**
Checkered rubber (stainless and blue models); wood with double
diamond checkering pattern (bright stainless model). **Sights:** 3-dot.
Features: Beveled magazine well, standard thumb safety and
service-style grip safety. Introduced 2003. Made in U.S.A. by Colt's
Mfg. Co., Inc.
Price: Blued $951.00
Price: Stainless $1,311.00

Prices given are believed to be accurate at time of publication however, many factors affect retail pricing so exact prices are not possible.

COLT MUSTANG POCKETLITE
Caliber: .380 ACP. Six-shot magazine. **Barrel:** 2.75". **Weight:** 12.5 oz. **Length:** 5.5". **Grips:** Black composite. **Finish:** Brushed stainless. **Features:** Thumb safety, firing-pin safety block. Introduced 2012.
Price: $649.00

COLT NEW AGENT
Caliber: .45 ACP (7+1), 9mm (8+1). **Barrel:** 3" **Weight:** 25 oz. **Length:** 6.75" overall. **Grips:** Double diamond slim fit. **Sights:** Snag free trench style. **Features:** Semi-auto pistol with blued finish and enhanced black anodized aluminum receiver. Skeletonized aluminum trigger, series 80 firing system, front strap serrations, beveled magazine well. Also available in a double-action-only version (shown), in .45 ACP only.
Price: $1,046.00

COLT RAIL GUN
Caliber: .45 ACP (8+1). **Barrel:** NA. **Weight:** NA. **Length:** 8.5" **Grips:** Rosewood double diamond. **Sights:** White dot front and Novak rear. **Features:** 1911-style semi-auto. Stainless steel frame and slide, front and rear slide serrations, skeletonized trigger, integral; accessory rail, Smith & Alexander upswept beavertail grip palm swell safety, tactical thumb safety, National Match barrel.
Price: .... $1,141.00 to $1,223.00

COLT SPECIAL COMBAT GOVERNMENT CARRY MODEL
Caliber: .45 ACP (8+1), .38 Super (9+1). **Barrel:** 5" **Weight:** NA.

Length: 8.5". **Grips:** Black/silver synthetic. **Sights:** Novak front and rear night. **Features:** 1911-style semi-auto. Skeletonized three-hole trigger, slotted hammer, Smith & Alexander upswept beavertail grip palm swell safety and extended magazine well, Wilson tactical ambidextrous safety. Available in blued, hard chrome, or blue/satin nickel finish, depending on chambering. Marine Pistol has Desert Tan Cerakoted stainless steel finish, lanyard loop.
Price: $2,095.00
Price: Marine Pistol... $1,995.00

CZ 75 B
Caliber: 9mm Para., .40 S&W, 10-shot magazine. **Barrel:** 4.7" **Weight:** 34.3 oz. **Length:** 8.1" overall. **Grips:** High impact checkered plastic. **Sights:** Square post front, rear adjustable for windage; 3-dot system. **Features:** Single action/double action design; firing pin block safety; choice of black polymer, matte or high-polish blue finishes. All-steel frame. B-SA is a single action with a drop-free magazine. Imported from the Czech Republic by CZ-USA.
Price: 75 B $625.00
Price: 75 B, stainless $783.00
Price: 75 B-SA $661.00

CZ 75 BD DECOCKER
Similar to the CZ 75B except has a decocking lever in place of the safety lever. All other specifications are the same. Introduced 1999. Imported from the Czech Republic by CZ-USA.
Price: 9mm Para., black polymer $612.00

CZ 75 B COMPACT
Similar to the CZ 75 B except has 14-shot magazine in 9mm Para., 3.9 barrel and weighs 32 oz. Has removable front sight, non-glare ribbed slide top. Trigger guard is squared and serrated; combat hammer. Introduced 1993. Imported from the Czech Republic by CZ-USA.
Price: 9mm Para., black polymer $631.00
Price: 9mm Para., dual tone or satin nickel $651.00
Price: 9mm Para. D PCR Compact, alloy frame $651.00

CZ P-07 DUTY

Caliber: .40 S&W, 9mm Luger (16+1). **Barrel:** 3.8" **Weight:** 27.2 oz. **Length:** 7.3" overall. **Grips:** Polymer black polycoat. **Sights:** Blade front, fixed groove rear. **Features:** The ergonomics and accuracy of the CZ 75 with a totally new trigger system. The new Omega trigger system simplifies the CZ 75 trigger system, uses fewer parts and improves the trigger pull. In addition, it allows users to choose between using the handgun with a decocking lever (installed) or a manual safety (included) by a simple parts change. The polymer frame design of the Duty and a new sleek slide profile (fully machined from bar stock) reduce weight, making the P-07 Duty a great choice for concealed carry.
Price: $524.00

CZ P-09 DUTY

High-capacity version of P-07. **Caliber:** 9mm, .40 S&W. **Magazine capacity:** 19 rounds (9mm), 15 (.40). **Features:** Accessory rail, interchangeable grip backstraps, ambidextrous decocker can be converted to manual safety.
Price: $544.00

CZ 75 TACTICAL SPORT

Similar to the CZ 75 B except the CZ 75 TS is a competition ready pistol designed for IPSC standard division (USPSA limited division). Fixed target sights, tuned single-action operation, lightweight polymer match trigger with adjustments for take-up and overtravel, competition hammer, extended magazine catch, ambidextrous manual safety, checkered walnut grips, polymer magazine well, two tone finish. Introduced 2005. Imported from the Czech Republic by CZ-USA.
Price: 9mm Para., 20-shot mag. $1,310.00
Price: .40 S&W, 16-shot mag. $1,310.00

CZ 75 SP-01

Similar to NATO-approved CZ 75 Compact P-01 model. Features an integral 1913 accessory rail on the dust cover, rubber grip panels, black polycoat finish, extended beavertail, new grip geometry with checkering on front and back straps, and double or single action operation. Introduced 2005. The Shadow variant designed as an IPSC "production" division competition firearm. Includes competition hammer, competition rear sight and fiber-optic front sight, modified slide release, lighter recoil and main spring for use with "minor power factor" competition ammunition. Includes polycoat finish and

slim walnut grips. Finished by CZ Custom Shop. Imported from the Czech Republic by CZ-USA.
Price: SP-01 9mm Para., black polymer, 19+1, Standard $680.00
Price: SP-01 9mm Para., black polymer, 19+1, Shadow....$1,710.00

CZ 85 B/85 COMBAT

Same gun as the CZ 75 except has ambidextrous slide release and safety levers; non-glare, ribbed slide top; squared, serrated trigger guard; trigger stop to prevent overtravel. Introduced 1986. The CZ 85 Combat features a fully adjustable rear sight, extended magazine release, ambidextrous slide stop and safety catch, drop free magazine and overtravel adjustment. Imported from the Czech Republic by CZ-USA.
Price: 9mm Para., black polymer $628.00
Price: Combat, black polymer $702.00
Price: Combat, dual-tone, satin nickel $732.00

CZ 97 B

Caliber: .45 ACP, 10-shot magazine. **Barrel:** 4.85" **Weight:** 40 oz. **Length:** 8.34" overall. **Grips:** Checkered walnut. **Sights:** Fixed. **Features:** Single action/double action; full-length slide rails; screw-in barrel bushing; linkless barrel; all-steel construction; chamber loaded indicator; dual transfer bars. Introduced 1999. Imported from the Czech Republic by CZ-USA.
Price: Black polymer $707.00
Price: Glossy blue $727.00

CZ 97 BD DECOCKER

Similar to the CZ 97 B except has a decocking lever in place of the safety lever. Tritium night sights. Rubber grips. All other specifications are the same. Introduced 1999. Imported from the Czech Republic by CZ-USA.
Price: 9mm Para., black polymer $816.00

CZ 2075 RAMI/RAMI P

Caliber: 9mm Para., .40 S&W. **Barrel:** 3". **Weight:** 25 oz. **Length:** 6.5" overall. **Grips:** Rubber. **Sights:** Blade front with dot, white outline rear drift adjustable for windage. **Features:** Single-action/double-action; alloy or polymer frame, steel slide; has laser sight mount.

Prices given are believed to be accurate at time of publication however, many factors affect retail pricing so exact prices are not possible.

Imported from the Czech Republic by CZ-USA.
Price: 9mm Para., alloy frame, 10 and 14-shot magazines **$671.00**
Price: 40 S&W, alloy frame, 8-shot magazine **$671.00**
Price: RAMI P, polymer frame, 9mm Para., 40 S&W **$612.00**

CZ P-01

Caliber: 9mm Para., 14-shot magazine. **Barrel:** 3.85". **Weight:** 27 oz. **Length:** 7.2" overall. **Grips:** Checkered rubber. **Sights:** Blade front with dot, white outline rear drift adjustable for windage. **Features:** Based on the CZ 75, except with forged aircraft-grade aluminum alloy frame. Hammer forged barrel, decocker, firing-pin block, M3 rail, dual slide serrations, squared triggerguard, re-contoured trigger, lanyard loop on butt. Serrated front and back strap. Introduced 2006. Imported from the Czech Republic by CZ-USA.
Price: CZ P-01 ....**$627.00**

DAN WESSON DW RZ-10

Caliber: 10mm, 9-shot. **Barrel:** 5". **Grips:** Diamond checkered cocobolo. **Sights:** Bo-Mar style adjustable target sight. **Weight:** 38.3 oz. **Length:** 8.8" overall. **Features:** Stainless-steel frame and serrated slide. Series 70-style 1911, stainless-steel frame, forged stainless-steel slide. Commander-style match hammer. Reintroduced 2005. Made in U.S.A. by Dan Wesson Firearms, distributed by CZ-USA.
Price: 10mm, 8+1 ....**$1,350.00**

DAN WESSON DW RZ-45 HERITAGE

Similar to the RZ-10 Auto except in .45 ACP with 7-shot magazine. Weighs 36 oz., length is 8.8" overall.
Price: 10mm, 8+1 ....**$1,298.00**

DAN WESSON VALOR 1911

Caliber: .45 ACP, 8-shot. **Barrel:** 5". **Grips:** Slim Line G10. **Sights:** Heinie ledge straight eight adjustable night sights. **Weight:** 2.4 lbs. **Length:** 8.8" overall. **Features:** The defensive style Valor, is a base stainless 1911 with our matte black "Duty" finish. This finish is a ceramic base coating that has set the standard for all coating tests. Other features include forged stainless frame and match barrel with 25 LPI checkering and undercut triggerguard, adjustable defensive night sites, and Slim line VZ grips. Made in U.S.A. by Dan Wesson Firearms, distributed by CZ-USA.
Price: **$2,012.00**

DAN WESSON SPECIALIST

Caliber: .45 ACP, 8-shot magazine. **Barrel:** 5". **Grips:** G10 VZ Operator II. **Sights:** Single amber tritium dot rear, green lamp with white target ring front sight. **Features:** Integral Picatinny rail, 25 lpi front strap checkering, undercut triggerguard, ambidextrous thumb safety, extended mag release and detachable two-piece mag well.
Price: **$1,870.00**

DAN WESSON V-BOB

Caliber: .45 ACP 8-shot magazine. **Barrel:** 4.25". **Weight:** 34 oz. **Length:** 8". **Grips:** Slim Line G10. **Sights:** Heinie Ledge Straight-Eight Night Sights. **Features:** Black matte or stainless finish. Bobtail forged grip frame with 25 lpi checkering front and rear.
Price: **$2,077.00**

DESERT EAGLE 1911 G

Caliber: .45 ACP 8-shot magazine. **Barrel:** 5" or 4.33" (DE1911C Commander size), or 3.0" (DE1911U Undercover). **Grips:** Double diamond checkered wood. **Features:** Extended beavertail grip safety, checkered flat mainspring housing, skeletonized hammer and trigger, extended mag release and thumb safety, stainless full-length guide road, enlarged ejection port, beveled mag well and high profile sights. Comes with two 8-round magazines.
Price: DE1911G, C..**$874.00**
Price: DE1911G Tactical rail **$1,091.00**
Price: DE1911U **$946.00**

DESERT EAGLE 1911 UNDERCOVER

Caliber: .45 ACP, 6-round magazine. **Barrel:** 3 inches. **Weight:** 25.8 oz. **Length:** 6.85 inches. **Grips:** Double diamond checkered. **Sights:** Blade front, adjustable rear. **Features:** Checkered front and back strap, high-rise beavertail safety, skeleton hammer and trigger. Aluminum alloy frame, steel slide. Series 70 configuration. Imported from Israel by Magnum Research, Inc.
Price: **$946.00**

DESERT EAGLE MARK XIX

Caliber: .357 Mag., 9-shot; .44 Mag., 8-shot; .50 AE, 7-shot. **Barrel:** 6", 10", interchangeable. **Weight:** .357 Mag.-62 oz.; .44 Mag.-69 oz.; .50 AE-72 oz. **Length:** 10.25" overall (6" bbl.). **Grips:** Polymer; rubber available. **Sights:** Blade on ramp front, combat-style rear. Adjustable available. **Features:** Interchangeable barrels; rotating three-lug bolt; ambidextrous safety; adjustable trigger. Military epoxy finish. Satin, bright nickel, chrome, brushed, matte or black-oxide finishes available. 10 barrel extra. Imported from Israel by

Prices given are believed to be accurate at time of publication however, many factors affect retail pricing so exact prices are not possible.

69TH EDITION, 2015 ✦ **395**

Magnum Research, Inc.
Price: Black-6, 6" barrel **$1,594.00**
Price: Black-10, 10" barrel **$1,683.00**

MICRO DESERT EAGLE
Caliber: .380 ACP, 6-rounds. **Barrel:** 2.22. **Weight:** 14 oz. **Length:** 4.52 overall. **Grips:** NA. **Sights:** Fixed low-profile. **Features:** Small-frame DAO pocket pistol. Steel slide, aluminum alloy frame, nickel-teflon finish.
Price: **$467.00**

DESERT BABY EAGLE II
Caliber: 9mm Para., .40 S&W, .45 ACP, 10- or 15-round magazines. **Barrel:** 3.64", 3.93", 4.52" **Weight:** 26.8 to 39.8 oz. **Length:** 7.25" to 8.25" overall. **Grips:** Polymer. **Sights:** Drift-adjustable rear, blade front. **Features:** Steel slide; choice of steel or polymer frame; slide-mounted decocking safety. Reintroduced in 2011. Imported from Israel by Magnum Research, Inc.
Price: .... **$619.00 to $656.00**

DESERT EAGLE MR9, MR40
Caliber: 9mm Para., (15-round magazine) or .40 S&W (11 rounds). **Barrel:** 4.5". **Weight:** 25 oz. **Length:** 7.6" overall. **Sights:** Three-dot rear sight adjustable for windage, interchangeable front sight blades of different heights. **Features:** Polymer frame, locked breech,

striker-fired design with decocker/safety button on top of slide, three replaceable grip palm swells, Picatinny rail. Made in Germany by Walther and imported by Magnum Research. Introduced in 2014.
Price: **$559.00**

DIAMONDBACK DB380
Caliber: .380, 6+1-shot capacity. **Barrel:** 2.8". **Weight:** 8.8 oz.
Features: A "ZERO-Energy" striker firing system with a mechanical firing pin block, steel magazine catch, windage-adjustable sights. Available in several finishes including black, black/stainless two-tone, and several bright colors.
Price: .... **$394.00 to $500.00**
Price: : With Crimson Trace Laser grips **$655.00**

DIAMONDBACK DB9
Caliber: 9mm, 6+1-shot capacity. **Barrel:** 3".
Weight: 11 oz. **Length:** 5.60". **Features:** Other features similar to DB380 model. DB9 FS introduced in 2014 is full-size variant with 4.75-inch barrel, 15-round magazine.
Price: .... **$431.00 to $525.00**
Price: DB9 FS **$483.00**

DOUBLESTAR 1911
Caliber: .45 ACP, 8-shot magazine. **Barrel:** 5". **Weight:** 40 oz. **Grips:** Cocobolo wood. **Sights:** Novak LoMount 2 white-dot rear, Novak

Prices given are believed to be accurate at time of publication however, many factors affect retail pricing so exact prices are not possible.

white-dot front. **Features:** Single-action, M1911-style with forged frame and slide of 4140 steel, stainless steel barrel machined from bar stock by Storm Lake, funneled mag well, accessory rail, black Nitride or nickel plated finish.

Price: Black..**$2,000.00**
Price: Nickel plated...**$2,150.00**

EAA WITNESS FULL SIZE

Caliber: 9mm Para., .38 Super, 18-shot magazine; .40 S&W, 10mm, 15-shot magazine; .45 ACP, 10-shot magazine. **Barrel:** 4.5". **Weight:** 35.33 oz. **Length:** 8.1" overall. **Grips:** Checkered rubber. **Sights:** Undercut blade front, open rear adjustable for windage. **Features:** Double-action/single-action trigger system; round triggerguard; frame-mounted safety. Available with steel or polymer frame. Also available with interchangeable .45 ACP and .22 LR slides. Steel frame introduced 1991. Polymer frame introduced 2005. Imported from Italy by European American Armory.

Price: Steel frame **$607.00**
Price: Polymer frame **$571.00**
Price: 45/22 .22 LR, full-size steel frame, blued **$752.00**

EAA WITNESS COMPACT

Caliber: 9mm Para., 14-shot magazine; .40 S&W, 10mm, 12-shot magazine; .45 ACP, 8-shot magazine. **Barrel:** 3.6" **Weight:** 30 oz. **Length:** 7.3" overall. **Features:** Available with steel or polymer frame (shown). All polymer frame Witness pistols are capable of being converted to other calibers. Otherwise similar to Full Size Witness. Imported from Italy by European American Armory.

Price: Polymer frame **$571.00**
Price: Steel frame **$607.00**

EAA WITNESS-P CARRY

Caliber: 9mm, 17-shot magazine; 10mm, 15-shot magazine; .45 ACP, 10-shot magazine. **Barrel:** 3.6". **Weight:** 27 oz. **Length:** 7.5" overall. **Features:** Otherwise similar to Full Size Witness. Polymer frame introduced 2005. Imported from Italy by European American Armory.

Price: **$691.00**

EAA WITNESS PAVONA COMPACT POLYMER

Caliber: .380 ACP (13-round magazine), 9mm (13) or .40 S&W (9). **Barrel:** 3.6". **Weight:** 30 oz. **Length:** 7" overall. **Features:** Designed primarily for women with fine-tuned recoil and hammer springs for easier operation, a polymer frame with integral checkering, contoured lines and in black, charcoal, blue, purple, or magenta with silver or gold sparkle.

Price: ....**$476.00 to $528.00**

EAA WITNESS ELITE 1911

Caliber: .45 ACP (8-round magazine). **Barrel:** 5". **Weight:** 32 oz. **Length:** 8.58" overall. **Features:** Full-size 1911-style pistol with either steel or polymer frame.

Price: **$580.00**

ED BROWN CLASSIC CUSTOM

Caliber: .45 ACP, 7 shot. **Barrel:** 5". **Weight:** 40 oz. **Grips:** Cocobolo wood. **Sights:** Bo-Mar adjustable rear, dovetail front. **Features:** Single-action, M1911 style, custom made to order, stainless frame and slide available. Special mirror-finished slide.

Price: **$3,495.00**

ED BROWN KOBRA AND KOBRA CARRY

Caliber: .45 ACP, 7-shot magazine. **Barrel:** 5" (Kobra); 4.25" (Kobra

Prices given are believed to be accurate at time of publication however, many factors affect retail pricing so exact prices are not possible.

69TH EDITION, 2015 ⊕ **397**

Carry). **Weight:** 39 oz. (Kobra); 34 oz. (Kobra Carry). **Grips:** Hogue exotic wood. **Sights:** Ramp, front; fixed Novak low-mount night sights, rear. **Features:** Has snakeskin pattern serrations on forestrap and mainspring housing, dehorned edges, beavertail grip safety.
Price: Kobra K-SS $2,495.00
Price: Kobra Carry $2,745.00

ED BROWN KOBRA CARRY LIGHTWEIGHT
Caliber: .45 ACP, 7-shot magazine. **Barrel:** 4.25" (Commander model slide). **Weight:** 27 oz. **Grips:** Hogue exotic wood. **Sights:** 10-8 Performance U-notch plain black rear sight with .156 notch, for fast aquisition of close targets. Fixed dovetail front night sight with high visibility white outlines. **Features:** Aluminum frame and Bobtail™ housing. Matte finished Gen III coated slide for low glare, with snakeskin on rear of slide only. Snakeskin pattern serrations on forestrap and mainspring housing, dehorned edges, beavertail grip safety. "LW" insignia on slide, which stands for "Lightweight".
Price: Kobra Carry Lightweight $3,120.00

ED BROWN EXECUTIVE
Similar to other Ed Brown products, but with 25-lpi checkered frame and mainspring housing.
Price: .... $2,695.00 - $2,945.00

ED BROWN SPECIAL FORCES
Similar to other Ed Brown products, but with ChainLink treatment on forestrap and mainspring housing. Entire gun coated with Gen III finish. "Square cut" serrations on rear of slide only. Dehorned.

Introduced 2006.
Price: From $2,495.00

ED BROWN SPECIAL FORCES CARRY
Similar to the Special Forces basic models. Features a 4.25" Commander model slide, single stack commander Bobtail frame. Weighs approx. 35 oz. Fixed dovetail 3-dot night sights with high visibility white outlines.
Price: From $2,745.00

EXCEL ARMS ACCELERATOR MP-22
Caliber: .22 WMR, 9-shot magazine. **Barrel:** 8.5" bull barrel. **Weight:** 54 oz. **Length:** 12.875" overall. **Grips:** Textured black composition. **Sights:** Fully adjustable target sights. **Features:** Made from 17-4 stainless steel, comes with aluminum rib, integral Weaver base, internal hammer, firing-pin block. American made, lifetime warranty. Comes with two9-round stainless steel magazines and a California-approved cable lock. .22 WMR Introduced 2006. Made in U.S.A. by Excel Arms.
Price: $455.00

FN FNS SERIES
Caliber: 9mm, 17-shot magazine, .40 S&W (14-shot magazine). **Barrel:** 4". **Weight:** 25 oz. (9mm), 27.5 oz. (.40). **Length:** 7.25". **Grips:** Integral polymer with two interchangeable backstrap inserts. **Features:** Striker-fired, double action with manual safety, accessory rail, ambidextrous controls, 3-dot Night Sights.
Price: $699.00

FN FNX SERIES
Caliber: 9mm, 17-shot magazine, .40 S&W (14-shot), .45 ACP (10 or 14-shot). **Barrel:** 4" (9mm and .40), 4.5" .45. **Weight:** 22 to 32 oz (.45). **Length:** 7.4, 7.9" (.45). **Features:** Double-action/single-action

Prices given are believed to be accurate at time of publication however, many factors affect retail pricing so exact prices are not possible.

operation with decocking/manual safety lever. Has external extractor with loaded-chamber indicator, front and rear cocking serrations, fixed 3-dot combat sights.
Price: $699.00

FN FNX .45 TACTICAL
Similar to standard FNX .45 except with 5.3" barrel with threaded muzzle, polished chamber and feed ramp, enhanced high-profile night sights, slide cut and threaded for red-dot sight (not included), MIL-STD 1913 accessory rail, ring-style hammer.
Price: $1,400.00

FN FIVE-SEVEN
Caliber: 5.7x28mm, 10- or 20-round magazine capacity. **Barrel:** 4.8". **Weight:** 23 oz. **Length:** 8.2" **Features:** Adjustable three-dot system. Single-action polymer frame model chambered for low-recoil 5.7x28mm cartridge.
Price: $1,299.00

GLOCK 17/17C
Caliber: 9mm Para., 17/19/33-shot magazines. **Barrel:** 4.49". **Weight:** 22.04 oz. (without magazine). **Length:** 7.32" overall. **Grips:** Black polymer. **Sights:** Dot on front blade, white outline rear adjustable for windage. **Features:** Polymer frame, steel slide; double-action trigger with "Safe Action" system; mechanical firing pin safety, drop safety; simple takedown without tools; locked breech, recoil operated action. ILS designation refers to Internal Locking System. Adopted by Austrian armed forces 1983. NATO approved 1984. Imported from Austria by Glock, Inc. USA.
Price: From $599.00

GLOCK GEN4 SERIES
In 2010 a new series of Generation Four pistols was introduced with several improved features. These included a multiple backstrap system offering three different size options, short, medium or large frame; reversible and enlarged magazine release; dual recoil springs; and RTF (Rough Textured Finish) surface. As of 2012, the following models were available in the Gen4 series: Models 17, 19, 21, 22, 23, 26, 27, 31, 32, 34, 35, 37. Price: Same as standard models
Price: ....N/A

GLOCK 17 GEN4
25TH ANNIVERSARY LIMITED EDITION
This special gun features an emblem built into the grip signifying the 25 years GLOCK has been in the United States (1986 - 2011).

The top of the slide, in front of the rear sight is marked "25 Years of GLOCK Perfection in USA". It comes complete with two magazines, a speed loader, cable lock, cleaning rod and brush, two interchangeable backstraps, a limited edition silver GLOCK case, and a letter of authenticity! Each gun is identified by the special prefix of 25YUSA. Similar to Model G17 but with multiple backstrap system allowing three options: a short frame version, medium frame or large frame; reversible, enlarged magazine release catch; dual recoil spring assembly; new Rough Textured Frame (RTF) surface designed to enhance grip traction.
Price: $850.00

GLOCK 19/19C
Caliber: 9mm Para., 15/17/19/33-shot magazines. **Barrel:** 4.02". **Weight:** 20.99 oz. (without magazine). **Length:** 6.85" overall. Compact version of Glock 17. Pricing the same as Model 17. Imported from Austria by Glock, Inc.
Price: $699.00
Price: 19C Compensated $675.00

GLOCK 20/20C 10MM
Caliber: 10mm, 15-shot magazines. **Barrel:** 4.6". **Weight:** 27.68 oz. (without magazine). **Length:** 7.59" overall. **Features:** Otherwise similar to Model 17. Imported from Austria by Glock, Inc. Introduced 1990.
Price: From $700.00

GLOCK MODEL 20 SF SHORT FRAME
Caliber: 10mm. **Barrel:** 4.61" with hexagonal rifling. **Weight:** 27.51 oz. **Length:** 8.07" overall. **Sights:** Fixed. **Features:** Otherwise similar to Model 20 but with short-frame design, extended sight radius.
Price: $664.00

GLOCK 21/21C
Caliber: .45 ACP, 13-shot magazines. **Barrel:** 4.6". **Weight:** 26.28 oz. (without magazine). **Length:** 7.59" overall. **Features:** Otherwise similar to Model 17. Imported from Austria by Glock, Inc. Introduced 1991. SF version has tactical rail, smaller diameter grip, 10-round magazine capacity. Introduced 2007.
Price: Fixed sight, from $700.00

GLOCK 22/22C
Caliber: .40 S&W, 15/17-shot magazines. **Barrel:** 4.49". **Weight:** 22.92 oz. (without magazine). **Length:** 7.32" overall. **Features:** Otherwise similar to Model 17, including pricing. Imported from

Austria by Glock, Inc. Introduced 1990.
Price: Fixed sight, from **$641.00**

GLOCK 23/23C
Caliber: .40 S&W, 13/15/17-shot magazines. **Barrel:** 4.02". **Weight:** 21.16 oz. (without magazine). **Length:** 6.85" overall. **Features:** Otherwise similar to Model 22, including pricing. Compact version of Glock 22. Imported from Austria by Glock, Inc. Introduced 1990.
Price: **$641.00**
Price: 23C Compensated **$694.00**

GLOCK 26
Caliber: 9mm Para. 10/12/15/17/19/33-shot magazines. **Barrel:** 3.46". **Weight:** 19.75 oz. **Length:** 6.29" overall. Subcompact version of Glock 17. Pricing the same as Model 17. Imported from Austria by Glock, Inc.
Price: **$599.00**

GLOCK 27
Caliber: .40 S&W, 9/11/13/15/17-shot magazines. **Barrel:** 3.46". **Weight:** 19.75 oz. (without magazine). **Length:** 6.29 overall. **Features:** Otherwise similar to Model 22, including pricing. Subcompact version of Glock 22. Imported from Austria by Glock, Inc. Introduced 1996.
Price: **$750.00**

GLOCK 29
Caliber: 10mm, 10/15-shot magazines. **Barrel:** 3.78". **Weight:** 24.69 oz. (without magazine). **Length:** 6.77" overall. **Features:** Otherwise similar to Model 20, including pricing. Subcompact version of Glock 20. Imported from Austria by Glock, Inc. Introduced 1997.
Price: Fixed sight **$672.00**

GLOCK MODEL 29 SF SHORT FRAME
Caliber: 10mm. **Barrel:** 3.78" with hexagonal rifling. **Weight:** 24.52 oz. **Length:** 6.97" overall. **Sights:** Fixed. **Features:** Otherwise similar to Model 29 but with short-frame design, extended sight radius.
Price: **$660.00**

GLOCK 30
Caliber: .45 ACP, 9/10/13-shot magazines. **Barrel:** 3.78". **Weight:** 23.99 oz. (without magazine). **Length:** 6.77" overall. **Features:** Otherwise similar to Model 21, including pricing. Subcompact version of Glock 21. Imported from Austria by Glock, Inc. Introduced 1997. SF version has tactical rail, octagonal rifled barrel with a

1:15.75 rate of twist, smaller diameter grip, 10-round magazine capacity. Introduced 2008.
Price: **$700.00**

GLOCK 30S
Variation of Glock 30 with a Model 36 slide on a Model 30SF frame (short frame). **Caliber:** .45 ACP, 10-round magazine. **Barrel:** 3.78 inches. **Weight:** 20 oz. **Length:** 7 inches.
Price: **$637.00**

GLOCK 31/31C
Caliber: .357 Auto, 15/17-shot magazines. **Barrel:** 4.49". **Weight:** 23.28 oz. (without magazine). **Length:** 7.32" overall. **Features:** Otherwise similar to Model 17. Imported from Austria by Glock, Inc.
Price: From **$641.00**

GLOCK 32/32C
Caliber: .357 Auto, 13/15/17-shot magazines. **Barrel:** 4.02". **Weight:** 21.52 oz. (without magazine). **Length:** 6.85" overall. **Features:** Otherwise similar to Model 31. Compact. Imported from Austria by Glock, Inc.
Price: **$669.00**

GLOCK 33
Caliber: .357 Auto, 9/11/13/15/17-shot magazines. **Barrel:** 3.46". **Weight:** 19.75 oz. (without magazine). **Length:** 6.29" overall. **Features:** Otherwise similar to Model 31. Subcompact. Imported from Austria by Glock, Inc.
Price: From **$641.00**

GLOCK 34
Caliber: 9mm Para. 17/19/33-shot magazines. **Barrel:** 5.32". **Weight:** 22.9 oz. **Length:** 8.15" overall. **Features:** Competition version of Glock 17 with extended barrel, slide, and sight radius dimensions. Imported from Austria by Glock, Inc.
Price: Adjustable sight, from **$648.00**

GLOCK 35
Caliber: .40 S&W, 15/17-shot magazines. **Barrel:** 5.32. **Weight:** 24.52 oz. (without magazine). **Length:** 8.15 overall. **Sights:** Adjustable. **Features:** Otherwise similar to Model 22. Competition version of Glock 22 with extended barrel, slide, and sight radius dimensions. Imported from Austria by Glock, Inc. Introduced 1996.
Price: **$648.00**

GLOCK 36
Caliber: .45 ACP, 6-shot magazines. **Barrel:** 3.78. **Weight:** 20.11 oz. (without magazine). **Length:** 6.77 overall. **Sights:** Fixed. **Features:** Single-stack magazine, slimmer grip than Glock 21/30. Subcompact. Imported from Austria by Glock, Inc. Introduced 1997.
Price: **$616.00**

GLOCK 37
Caliber: .45 GAP, 10-shot magazines. **Barrel:** 4.49. **Weight:** 25.95 oz. (without magazine). **Length:** 7.32 overall. **Features:** Otherwise similar to Model 17. Imported from Austria by Glock, Inc. Introduced 2005.
Price: **$614.00**

GLOCK 38
Caliber: .45 GAP, 8/10-shot magazines. **Barrel:** 4.02. **Weight:**

24.16 oz. (without magazine). **Length:** 6.85 overall. **Features:** Otherwise similar to Model 37. Compact. Imported from Austria by Glock, Inc.

Price: **$614.00**

GLOCK 39

Caliber: .45 GAP, 6/8/10-shot magazines. **Barrel:** 3.46. **Weight:** 19.33 oz. (without magazine). **Length:** 6.3 overall. **Features:** Otherwise similar to Model 37. Subcompact. Imported from Austria by Glock, Inc.

Price: **$614.00**

GLOCK 41

Caliber: .45 ACP, 13-round magazine capacity. **Barrel:** 5.31". **Weight:** 27 oz. **Length:** 8.9" overall. **Features:** This is a long-slide .45 ACP Gen4 model introduced in 2014. Operating features are the same as other Glock models.

Price: **$775.00**

GLOCK 42

Caliber: .380 ACP, 6-round magazine capacity. **Barrel:** 3.25" **Weight:** 13.8 oz. **Length:** 5.9" overall. **Features:** This single-stack, slimline sub-compact is the smallest pistol Glock has ever made. This is also the first Glock pistol made in the USA.

Price: **$480.00**

HECKLER & KOCH USP

Caliber: 9mm Para., 15-shot magazine; .40 S&W, 13-shot magazine;

45 ACP, 12-shot magazine. **Barrel:** 4.25-4.41. **Weight:** 1.65 lbs. **Length:** 7.64-7.87 overall. **Grips:** Non-slip stippled black polymer. **Sights:** Blade front, rear adjustable for windage. **Features:** New HK design with polymer frame, modified Browning action with recoil reduction system, single control lever. Special "hostile environment" finish on all metal parts. Available in SA/DA, DAO, left- and right-hand versions. Introduced 1993. 45 ACP Introduced 1995. Imported from Germany by Heckler & Koch, Inc.

Price: USP .45 ....**$1,033.00**
Price: USP .40 and USP 9mm **$952.00**

HECKLER & KOCH USP COMPACT

Caliber: 9mm Para., 13-shot magazine; .40 S&W and .357 SIG, 12-shot magazine; .45 ACP, 8-shot magazine. Similar to the USP except the 9mm Para., 357 SIG, and 40 S&W have 3.58 barrels, measure 6.81 overall, and weigh 1.47 lbs. (9mm Para.). Introduced 1996. 45 ACP measures 7.09 overall. Introduced 1998. Imported from Germany by Heckler & Koch, Inc.

Price: USP Compact .45 ....**$1,040.00**
Price: USP Compact 9mm
     Para., .40 S&W **$992.00**

HECKLER & KOCH USP45 TACTICAL

Caliber: .40 S&W, 13-shot magazine; .45 ACP, 12-shot magazine. **Barrel:** 4.90-5.09. **Weight:** 1.9 lbs. **Length:** 8.64 overall. **Grips:** Non-slip stippled polymer. **Sights:** Blade front, fully adjustable target rear. **Features:** Has extended threaded barrel with rubber O-ring; adjustable trigger; extended magazine floorplate; adjustable trigger stop; polymer frame. Introduced 1998. Imported from Germany by Heckler & Koch, Inc.

Price: USP Tactical .45 ....**$1,352.00**
Price: USP Tactical .40 ....**$1,333.00**

HECKLER & KOCH USP COMPACT TACTICAL

Caliber: .45 ACP, 8-shot magazine. Similar to the USP Tactical except measures 7.72 overall, weighs 1.72 lbs. Introduced 2006. Imported

Prices given are believed to be accurate at time of publication however, many factors affect retail pricing so exact prices are not possible.

69TH EDITION, 2015 ✛ **401**

from Germany by Heckler & Koch, Inc.
Price: USP Compact Tactical $1,352.00

HECKLER & KOCH HK45

Caliber: .45 ACP, 10-shot magazine. **Barrel:** 4.53". **Weight:** 1.73 lbs.
Length: 7.52" overall. **Grips:** Ergonomic with adjustable grip panels.
Sights: Low profile, drift adjustable. **Features:** Polygonal rifling,
ambidextrous controls, operates on improved Browning linkless
recoil system. Available in Tactical and Compact variations.
Price: USP Tactical .45 .... **$1,193.00 to $1,392.00**

HECKLER & KOCH MARK 23 SPECIAL OPERATIONS

Caliber: .45 ACP, 12-shot magazine. **Barrel:** 5.87. **Weight:** 2.42 lbs.
Length: 9.65 overall. **Grips:** Integral with frame; black polymer.
Sights: Blade front, rear drift adjustable for windage; 3-dot.
Features: Civilian version of the SOCOM pistol. Polymer frame;
double action; exposed hammer; short recoil, modified Browning
action. Introduced 1996. Imported from Germany by Heckler &
Koch, Inc.
Price: $2,139.00

HECKLER & KOCH P30 AND P30L

Caliber: 9mm and .40 S&W with 13 or 15-shot magazines.
Barrel: 3.86" or 4.45" (P30L). **Weight:** 26 to 27.5 oz. **Length:**
6.95, 7.56" overall. **Grips:** Interchangeable panels. **Sights:**
Open rectangular notch rear sight with contrast points (no
radioactive). **Features:** Ergonomic features include a special
grip frame with interchangeable backstraps inserts and lateral
plates, allowing the pistol to be individually adapted to any
user. Browning type action with modified short recoil operation.
Ambidextrous controls include dual slide releases, magazine
release levers, and a serrated decocking button located on
the rear of the frame (for applicable variants). A Picatinny rail
molded into the front of the frame. The extractor serves as a
loaded-chamber indicator.

Price: P30 ....$1,054.00
Price: P30L Variant 2 Law Enforcement Modification
(LEM) enhanced DAO $1,108.00
Price: P30L Variant 3 Double Action/Single Action
(DA/SA) with Decocker $1,108.00

HECKLER & KOCH P2000

Caliber: 9mm Para., 13-shot magazine; .40 S&W and .357 SIG, 12-
shot magazine. **Barrel:** 3.62. **Weight:** 1.5 lbs. **Length:** 7 overall.
Grips: Interchangeable panels. **Sights:** Fixed Patridge style, drift
adjustable for windage, standard 3-dot. **Features:** Incorporates
features of HK USP Compact pistol, including Law Enforcement
Modification (LEM) trigger, double-action hammer system,
ambidextrous magazine release, dual slide-release levers, accessory
mounting rails, recurved, hook trigger guard, fiber-reinforced
polymer frame, modular grip with exchangeable back straps, nitro-
carburized finish, lock-out safety device. Introduced 2003. Imported
from Germany by Heckler & Koch, Inc.
Price: $992.00

HECKLER & KOCH P2000 SK

Caliber: 9mm Para., 10-shot magazine; .40 S&W and .357 SIG,
9-shot magazine. **Barrel:** 3.27. **Weight:** 1.3 lbs. **Length:** 6.42
overall. **Sights:** Fixed Patridge style, drift adjustable. **Features:**
Standard accessory rails, ambidextrous slide release, polymer
frame, polygonal bore profile. Smaller version of P2000. Introduced
2005. Imported from Germany by Heckler & Koch, Inc.
Price: $1,037.00

HELLCAT II

Caliber: .380 ACP, magazine capacity 6 rounds. **Barrel:** 2.75 inches.
Weight: 9.4 oz. **Length:** 5.16 inches. **Grips:** Integral polymer.
Sights: Fixed. **Features:** Polymer frame, double-action only. Several
finishes available including black, desert tan, pink, blaze orange.
Made in U.S.A. by I.O., Inc.
Price: $250.00

Prices given are believed to be accurate at time of publication however, many factors affect retail pricing so exact pricing is not possible.

HI-POINT FIREARMS MODEL 9MM COMPACT

Caliber: 9mm Para., 8-shot magazine. **Barrel:** 3.5. **Weight:** 25 oz. **Length:** 6.75 overall. **Grips:** Textured plastic. **Sights:** Combat-style adjustable 3-dot system; low profile. **Features:** Single-action design; frame-mounted magazine release; polymer frame. Scratch-resistant matte finish. Introduced 1993. Comps are similar except they have a 4 barrel with muzzle brake/compensator. Compensator is slotted for laser or flashlight mounting. Introduced 1998. Made in U.S.A. by MKS Supply, Inc.
Price: C-9 9mm $189.00

HI-POINT FIREARMS MODEL 380 POLYMER

Similar to the 9mm Compact model except chambered for .380 ACP, 8-shot magazine, adjustable 3-dot sights. Weighs 25 oz. Polymer frame. Action locks open after last shot. Includes 10-shot and 8-shot magazine; trigger lock.
Price: CF-380 ....$151.00

HI-POINT FIREARMS 40 AND 45 SW/POLY

Caliber: .40 S&W, 8-shot magazine; .45 ACP (9-shot). **Barrel:** 4.5. **Weight:** 32 oz. **Length:** 7.72 overall. **Sights:** Adjustable 3-dot. **Features:** Polymer frames, last round lock-open, grip mounted magazine release, magazine disconnect safety, integrated accessory rail, trigger lock. Introduced 2002. Made in U.S.A. by MKS Supply, Inc.
Price: $199.00

HIGH STANDARD VICTOR .22

Caliber: .22 Long Rifle (10 rounds) or .22 Short (5 rounds). **Barrel:** 4.5"-5.5". **Weight:** 45 oz.-46 oz. **Length:** 8.5"-9.5" overall. **Grips:** Freestyle wood. **Sights:** Frame mounted, adjustable. **Features:** Semi-auto with drilled and tapped barrel, tu-tone or blued finish.
Price: $905.00

HIGH STANDARD 10X CUSTOM .22

Similar to the Victor model but with precision fitting, black wood grips, 5.5 barrel only. High Standard Universal Mount, 10-shot magazine, barrel drilled and tapped, certificate of authenticity. Overall length is 9.5". Weighs 44 oz. to 46 oz. From High Standard

Custom Shop.
Price: $1,275.00

HIGH STANDARD SUPERMATIC TROPHY .22

Caliber: .22 Long Rifle (10 rounds) or .22 Short (5 rounds/Citation version), not interchangable. **Barrel:** 5.5", 7.25". **Weight:** 44 oz., 46 oz. **Length:** 9.5", 11.25" overall. **Grips:** Wood. **Sights:** Adjustable. **Features:** Semi-auto with drilled and tapped barrel, tu-tone or blued finish with gold accents.
Price: 5.5 .... $905.00

HIGH STANDARD OLYMPIC MILITARY .22

Similar to the Supermatic Trophy model but in .22 Short only with 5.5" bull barrel, five-round magazine, aluminum alloy frame, adjustable sights. Overall length is 9.5", weighs 42 oz.
Price: $1,010.00

HIGH STANDARD SUPERMATIC CITATION SERIES .22

Similar to the Supermatic Trophy model but with heavier trigger pull, 10" barrel, and nickel accents. 22 Short conversion unit available. Overall length 14.5", weighs 52 oz.
Price: $945.00

HIGH STANDARD SUPERMATIC TOURNAMENT .22

Caliber: .22 LR. **Barrel:** 5.5" bull barrel. **Weight:** 44 oz. **Length:** 9.5" overall. **Features:** Limited edition; similar to High Standard Victor model but with rear sight mounted directly to slide.
Price: $905.00

HIGH STANDARD SPORT KING .22

Caliber: .22 LR. **Barrel:** 4.5" or 6.75" tapered barrel. **Weight:** 40 oz. to 42 oz. **Length:** 8.5" to 10.75". **Features:** Sport version of High Standard Supermatic. Two-tone finish, fixed sights.
Price: $835.00

HI-STANDARD SPACE GUN

Semiauto pistol chambered in .22 LR. Recreation of famed competition

Prices given are believed to be accurate at time of publication however, many factors affect retail pricing so exact prices are not possible.

69TH EDITION, 2015 ⊕ **403**

"Space Gun" from 1960s. Features include 6.75- 8- or 10-inch barrel; 10-round magazine; adjustable sights; barrel weight; adjustable muzzle brake; blue-black finish with gold highlights.
Price: **$1,275.00**

ITHACA 1911
Caliber: .45 ACP, 7-round capacity. **Barrel:** 5". **Weight:** 41 oz. **Length:** 8.75" **Sights:** Fixed combat or fully adjustable target. **Grips:** Checkered cocobolo with Ithaca logo. **Features:** Classic 1911A1-style pistol with enhanced features including match-grade barrel, lowered and flared ejection port, skeletonized hammer and trigger, full-length two-piece guide rod, hand-fitted barrel bushing, extended beavertail grip safety, checkered front strap.
Price: **$1,799.00**

IVER JOHNSON EAGLE
Series of 1911-style pistols made in typical variations including full-size (Eagle), Commander (Hawk), Officer's (Thrasher) sizes in .45 ACP and 9mm. Many finishes available including Cerakote, polished stainless, pink and several "snakeskin" variations.
Price: .... **$608.00 to $959.00**

KAHR CM SERIES
Caliber: 9mm (6+1), .40 S&W (6+1). .45 ACP (5+1). CM45 Model is shown. **Barrel:** 3", 3.25"(45). **Weight:** 15.9 to 17.3 oz. **Length:** 5.42 overall. **Grips:** Textured polymer with integral steel rails molded into frame. **Sights:** CM9093 - Pinned in polymer sight; PM9093 - Drift adjustable, white bar-dot combat. **Features:** A conventional rifled barrel instead of the match grade polygonal barrel on Kahr's PM series; the CM slide stop lever is MIM (metal-injection-molded) instead of machined; the CM series slide has fewer machining operations and uses simple engraved markings instead of roll marking and finally the CM series are shipped with one magazine instead of two magazines. The slide is machined from solid 416 stainless slide with a matte finish, each gun is shipped with one 6-round stainless steel magazine with a flush baseplate. Magazines are USA made, plasma welded, tumbled to remove burrs and feature Wolff Gunsprings. The magazine catch in the polymer frame

is all metal and will not wear out on the stainless steel magazine after extended use.
Price: **$460.00**

KAHR CT40/CT45 SERIES
Caliber: .40 S&W (6+1) .45 ACP (7+1). **Barrel:** 4 inches. **Weight:** 23.7 oz. **Length:** 5.42 overall. **Grips:** Textured polymer with integral steel rails molded into frame. **Sights:** Drift adjustable, white bar-dot combat. **Features:** A conventional rifled barrel instead of the match grade polygonal barrel on Kahr's PM series; the CM slide stop lever is MIM (metal-injection-molded) instead of machined; the CM series slide has fewer machining operations and uses simple engraved markings instead of roll marking and finally the CM series are shipped with one magazine instead of two magazines. The slide is machined from solid 416 stainless slide with a matte finish, each gun is shipped with one 6-round stainless steel magazine with a flush baseplate. Magazines are USA made, plasma welded, tumbled to remove burrs and feature Wolff Gunsprings. The magazine catch in the polymer frame is all metal and will not wear out on the stainless steel magazine after extended use
Price: **$460.00**

KAHR K SERIES
Caliber: K9: 9mm Para., 7-shot; K40: .40 S&W, 6-shot magazine. **Barrel:** 3.5. **Weight:** 25 oz. **Length:** 6 overall. **Grips:** Wraparound

Prices given are believed to be accurate at time of publication however, many factors affect retail pricing so exact prices are not possible.

textured soft polymer. **Sights:** Blade front, rear drift adjustable for windage; bar-dot combat style. **Features:** Trigger-cocking double-action mechanism with passive firing pin block. Made of 4140 ordnance steel with matte black finish. Contact maker for complete price list. Introduced 1994. Made in U.S.A. by Kahr Arms.

Price: K9093C K9, matte stainless steel **$855.00**
Price: K9093NC K9, matte stainless steel w/tritium
    night sights **$985.00**
Price: K9094C K9 matte blackened stainless steel **$891.00**
Price: K9098 K9 Elite 2003, stainless steel **$932.00**
Price: K4043 K40, matte stainless steel **$855.00**
Price: K4043N K40, matte stainless steel w/tritium
    night sights **$985.00**
Price: K4044 K40, matte blackened stainless steel **$891.00**
Price: K4048 K40 Elite 2003, stainless steel **$932.00**

KAHR MK SERIES MICRO

Similar to the K9/K40 except is 5.35 overall, 4 high, with a 3.08 barrel. Weighs 23.1 oz. Has snag-free bar-dot sights, polished feed ramp, dual recoil spring system, DA-only trigger. Comes with 5-round flush baseplate and 6-shot grip extension magazine. Introduced 1998. Made in U.S.A. by Kahr Arms.

Price: M9093 MK9, matte stainless steel **$855.00**
Price: M9093N MK9, matte stainless steel, tritium
    night sights **$958.00**
Price: M9098 MK9 Elite 2003, stainless steel **$932.00**
Price: M4043 MK40, matte stainless steel **$855.00**
Price: M4043N MK40, matte stainless steel, tritium
    night sights **$958.00**
Price: M4048 MK40 Elite 2003, stainless steel **$932.00**

KAHR P SERIES

Caliber: 380 ACP, 9x19, 40 S&W, 45 ACP. Similar to K9/K40 steel frame pistol except has polymer frame, matte stainless steel slide. Barrel length 3.5"; overall length 5.8"; weighs 17 oz. Includes two 7-shot magazines, hard polymer case, trigger lock. Introduced 2000. Made in U.S.A. by Kahr Arms.

Price: KP9093 9mm Para. **$739.00**
Price: KP4043 .40 S&W **$739.00**
Price: KP4543 .45 ACP **$805.00**
Price: KP3833 .380 ACP (2008)..**$649.00**

KAHR PM SERIES

Caliber: 9x19, .40 S&W, .45 ACP. Similar to P-Series pistols except has smaller polymer frame (Polymer Micro). Barrel length 3.08"; overall length 5.35"; weighs 17 oz. Includes two 7-shot magazines, hard polymer case, trigger lock. Introduced 2000. Made in U.S.A. by Kahr Arms.

Price: PM9093 PM9 ....**$786.00**
Price: PM4043 PM40 ....**$786.00**
Price: PM4543 (2007) **$855.00**

KAHR T SERIES

Caliber: T9: 9mm Para., 8-shot magazine; T40: .40 S&W, 7-shot magazine. **Barrel:** 4". **Weight:** 28.1-29.1 oz. **Length:** 6.5" overall. **Grips:** Checkered Hogue Pau Ferro wood grips. **Sights:** Rear: Novak low profile 2-dot tritium night sight, front tritium night sight. **Features:** Similar to other Kahr makes, but with longer slide and barrel upper, longer butt. Trigger cocking DAO; lock breech; "Browning-type" recoil lug; passive striker block; no magazine disconnect. Comes with two magazines. Introduced 2004. Made in U.S.A. by Kahr Arms.

Price: KT9093 T9 matte stainless steel **$831.00**
Price: KT9093-NOVAK T9, "Tactical 9," Novak night sight **$968.00**
Price: KT4043 40 S&W **$831.00**

KAHR TP SERIES

Caliber: TP9: 9mm Para., 7-shot magazine; TP40: 40 S&W, 6-shot magazine. **Barrel:** 4". **Weight:** 19.1-20.1 oz. **Length:** 6.5-6.7" overall. **Grips:** Textured polymer. Similar to T-series guns, but with polymer frame, matte stainless steel slide. Comes with two magazines. TP40s introduced 2006. Made in U.S.A. by Kahr Arms.

Price: TP9093 TP9 ....**$697.00**
Price: TP9093-Novak TP9
    (Novak night sights)...**$838.00**
Price: TP4043 TP40 ....**$697.00**
Price: TP4043-Novak (Novak night sights) **$838.00**
Price: TP4543 (2007) **$697.00**
Price: TP4543-Novak (4.04 barrel, Novak night sights) **$838.00**

KAHR CW SERIES

Caliber: 9mm Para., 7-shot magazine; .40 S&W and .45 ACP, 6-shot magazine. **Barrel:** 3.5-3.64". **Weight:** 17.7-18.7 oz. **Length:** 5.9-6.36" overall. **Grips:** Textured polymer. Similar to P-Series, but CW Series have conventional rifling, metal-injection-molded slide stop lever, no front dovetail cut, one magazine. CW40 introduced 2006. Made in U.S.A. by Kahr Arms.
Price: CW9093 CW9 ....$485.00
Price: CW4043 CW40 ....$485.00
Price: CW4543 CW45 ....$485.00

KAHR P380

Very small double action only semiauto pistol chambered in .380 ACP. Features include 2.5-inch Lothar Walther barrel; black polymer frame with stainless steel slide; drift adjustable white bar/dot combat/sights; optional tritium sights; two 6+1 magazines. Overall length 4.9 inches, weight 10 oz. without magazine.
Price: Standard sights $649.00

KAHR CW380

Caliber: .380 ACP, six-round magazine. **Barrel:** 2.58 inches. **Weight:** 11.5 oz. **Length:** 4.96 inches. **Grips:** Textured integral polymer. **Sights:** Fixed white-bar combat style. **Features:** Double-action only.
Price: $419.00

KEL-TEC P-11

Caliber: 9mm Para., 10-shot magazine. **Barrel:** 3.1. **Weight:** 14 oz.

Length: 5.6 overall. **Grips:** Checkered black polymer. **Sights:** Blade front, rear adjustable for windage. **Features:** Ordnance steel slide, aluminum frame. Double-action-only trigger mechanism. Introduced 1995. Made in U.S.A. by Kel-Tec CNC Industries, Inc.
Price: From $340.00

KEL-TEC PF-9

Caliber: 9mm Para.; 7 rounds. **Weight:** 12.7 oz. **Sights:** Rear sight adjustable for windage and elevation. **Barrel Length:** 3.1. **Length:** 5.85. **Features:** Barrel, locking system, slide stop, assembly pin, front sight, recoil springs and guide rod adapted from P-11. Trigger system with integral hammer block and the extraction system adapted from P-3AT. MIL-STD-1913 Picatinny rail. Made in U.S.A. by Kel-Tec CNC Industries, Inc.
Price: From $340.00

KEL-TEC P-32

Caliber: .32 ACP, 7-shot magazine. **Barrel:** 2.68. **Weight:** 6.6 oz. **Length:** 5.07 overall. **Grips:** Checkered composite. **Sights:** Fixed. **Features:** Double-action-only mechanism with 6-lb. pull; internal slide stop. Textured composite grip/frame.
Price: From $326.00

KEL-TEC P-3AT

Caliber: .380 ACP; 7-rounds. **Weight:** 7.2 oz. **Length:** 5.2. **Features:** Lightest .380 ACP made; aluminum frame, steel barrel.
Price: From $331.00

KEL-TEC PLR-16

Caliber: 5.56mm NATO; 10-round magazine. **Weight:** 51 oz. **Sights:** Rear sight adjustable for windage, front sight is M-16 blade. **Barrel:** 9.2. **Length:** 18.5. **Features:** Muzzle is threaded 1/2-28 to accept standard attachments such as a muzzle brake. Except for the barrel, bolt, sights, and mechanism, the PLR-16 pistol is made of high-impact glass fiber reinforced polymer. Gas-operated semi-auto. Conventional gas-piston operation with M-16 breech locking system. MIL-STD-1913 Picatinny rail. Made in U.S.A. by Kel-Tec CNC Industries, Inc.
Price: Blued $682.00

KEL-TEC PLR-22

Semi-auto pistol chambered in .22 LR; based on centerfire PLR-16 by same maker. Blowback action, 26-round magazine. Open sights and picatinny rail for mounting accessories; threaded muzzle. Over-all length is 18.5", weighs 40 oz.
Price: $400.00

Prices given are believed to be accurate at time of publication however, many factors affect retail pricing so exact prices are not possible.

KEL-TEC PMR-30
Caliber: .22 Magnum (.22WMR) 30-rounds. **Barrel:** 4.3. **Weight:** 13.6 oz. **Length:** 7.9 overall. **Grips:** Glass reinforced Nylon (Zytel). **Sights:** Dovetailed aluminum with front & rear fiber optics. **Features:** Operates on a unique hybrid blowback/locked-breech system. It uses a double stack magazine of a new design that holds 30 rounds and fits completely in the grip of the pistol. Dual opposing extractors for reliability, heel magazine release to aid in magazine retention, Picatinny accessory rail under the barrel, Urethane recoil buffer, captive coaxial recoil springs. The barrel is fluted for light weight and effective heat dissipation. PMR30 disassembles for cleaning by removal of a single pin.
Price: $436.00

KIMBER MICRO CDP
Caliber: .380 ACP, 6-shot magazine. **Barrel:** 2.75". **Weight:** 17 oz. **Grips:** Double diamond rosewood. Mini 1911-style single action with no grip safety.
Price: $1,121.00

KIMBER AEGIS II
Caliber: 9mm (9-shot magazine, 8-shot (Ultra model). **Barrel:** 3", 4" or 5". **Weight:** 25 to 38 oz. **Grips:** Scale-textured zebra wood. **Sights:** Tactical wedge 3-dot green night sights. **Features:** Made in the Kimber Custom Shop. Two-tone satin silver/matte black finish. Service Melt treatment that rounds and blends edges. Available in three frame sizes: Custom (shown), Pro and Ultra.
Price: $1,331.00

KIMBER COVERT II
Caliber: .45 ACP (7-shot magazine). **Barrel:** 3", 4" or 5". **Weight:** 25 to 31 oz. **Grips:** Crimson Trace laser with camo finish. **Sights:** Tactical wedge 3-dot night sights. **Features:** Made in the Kimber Custom Shop. Desert tan frame and matte black slide finishes. Available in three frame sizes: Custom, Pro (shown) and Ultra.
Price: $1,657.00

KIMBER CUSTOM II
Caliber: .45 ACP. **Barrel:** 5". **Weight:** 38 oz. **Length:** 8.7" overall. **Grips:** Checkered black rubber, walnut, rosewood. **Sights:** Dovetailed front and rear, Kimber low profile adj. or fixed sights. **Features:** Slide, frame and barrel machined from steel or stainless steel. Match grade barrel, chamber and trigger group. Extended thumb safety, beveled magazine well, beveled front and rear slide

MICRO CARRY
Caliber: .380 ACP, 6-round magazine. **Barrel:** 2.75 inches. **Weight:** 13.4 oz. **Length:** 5.6 inches **Grips:** Black synthetic, double diamond. **Sights:** Fixed low profile. **Finish:** Blue or stainless. **Features:** Aluminum frame, steel slide, carry-melt treatment, full-length guide rod.
Price: $651.00

serrations, high ride beavertail grip safety, checkered flat mainspring housing, kidney cut under triggerguard, high cut grip, match grade stainless steel barrel bushing, polished breech face, Commander-style hammer, lowered and flared ejection port, Wolff springs, bead blasted black oxide or matte stainless finish. Introduced in 1996. Custom TLE II (Tactical Law Enforcement) has tritium night sights, threaded barrel. Made in U.S.A. by Kimber Mfg., Inc.
Price: Custom II $871.00
Price: Custom TLE II..$1,080.00

KIMBER STAINLESS II
Same features as Custom II except has stainless steel frame.
Price: Stainless II $998.00
Price: Stainless II w/night sights..$1,126.00

KIMBER PRO CARRY II
Similar to Custom II, has aluminum frame, 4 bull barrel fitted directly to the slide without bushing. Introduced 1998. Made in U.S.A. by Kimber Mfg., Inc.
Price: Pro Carry II, 45 ACP $919.00
Price: Pro Carry II, 9mm $960.00
Price: Pro Carry II
    w/night sights $1,067.00

KIMBER SOLO CARRY
Caliber: 9mm, 6-shot magazine. **Barrel:** 2.7. **Weight:** 17 oz. **Length:** 5.5 overall. **Grips:** Black synthetic, Checkered/smooth. **Sights:** Fixed low-profile dovetail-mounted 3-dot system. **Features:** Single action striker-fired trigger that sets a new standard for small pistols. A premium finish that is self-lubricating and resistant to salt and moisture. Ergonomics that ensure comfortable shooting. Ambidextrous thumb safety, slide release lever and magazine release button are pure 1911 – positive, intuitive and fast. The thumb safety provides additional security not found on most small pistols. Available with Crimson Trace Laser grips. Also available in stainless.
Price: .... $815.00 to $904.00
Price: With Crimson Trace Laser Grips.................................$1,223.00

KIMBER COMPACT STAINLESS II
Similar to Pro Carry II except has stainless steel frame, 4-inch bbl., grip is .400 shorter than standard, no front serrations. Weighs 34 oz. 45 ACP only. Introduced in 1998. Made in U.S.A. by Kimber Mfg., Inc.
Price: $1,052.00

KIMBER RAPTOR II
Caliber: .45 ACP (8-shot magazine, 7-shot (Ultra and Pro models). **Barrel:** 3", 4" or 5". **Weight:** 25 to 31 oz. **Grips:** Thin milled rosewood. **Sights:** Tactical wedge 3-dot night sights. **Features:** Made in the Kimber Custom Shop. Matte black or satin silver finish. Available in three frame sizes: Custom (shown), Pro and Ultra.
Price: .... $1,295.00 to $1,568.00

KIMBER ULTRA CARRY II
Lightweight aluminum frame, 3 match grade bull barrel fitted to slide without bushing. Grips .4 shorter. Low effort recoil. Weighs 25 oz. Introduced in 1999. Made in U.S.A. by Kimber Mfg., Inc.
Price: Stainless Ultra Carry II .45 ACP................................. $1,016.00
Price: Stainless Ultra Carry II 9mm Para.
    .... $1,021.00
Price: Stainless Ultra Carry II .45 ACP
    with night sights $1,136.00

KIMBER GOLD MATCH II
Similar to Custom II models. Includes stainless steel barrel with match grade chamber and barrel bushing, ambidextrous thumb safety, adjustable sight, premium aluminum trigger, hand-checkered

Prices given are believed to be accurate at time of publication however, many factors affect retail pricing so exact prices are not possible.

double diamond rosewood grips. Barrel hand-fitted for target accuracy. Made in U.S.A. by Kimber Mfg., Inc.

Price: Gold Match II **$1,345.00**
Price: Gold Match Stainless II .45 ACP **$1,519.00**
Price: Gold Match Stainless II
9mm Para. (2008) **$1,563.00**

KIMBER TEAM MATCH II
Similar to Gold Match II. Identical to pistol used by U.S.A. Shooting Rapid Fire Pistol Team, available in .45 ACP and 9mm. Standard features include 30 lines-per-inch front strap extended and beveled magazine well, red, white and blue Team logo grips. Introduced 2008.
Price: .45 ACP **$1,868.00**
Price: 9mm **$1,878.00**

KIMBER CDP II SERIES
Similar to Custom II, but designed for concealed carry. Aluminum

frame. Standard features include stainless steel slide, fixed Meprolight tritium 3-dot (green) dovetail-mounted night sights, match grade barrel and chamber, 30 LPI front strap checkering, two-tone finish, ambidextrous thumb safety, hand-checkered double diamond rosewood grips. Introduced in 2000. Made in U.S.A. by Kimber Mfg., Inc.

Price: Ultra CDP II 9mm Para. (2008) **$1,371.00**
Price: Ultra CDP II .45 ACP **$1,331.00**
Price: Compact CDP II .45 ACP **$1,331.00**
Price: Pro CDP II .45 ACP.......................................**$1,331.00**
Price: Custom CDP II
(5" barrel, full length grip) **$1,331.00**

KIMBER ECLIPSE II SERIES
Caliber: .45 ACP, 10mm (Target II only). Similar to Custom II and other stainless Kimber pistols. Stainless slide and frame, black oxide, two-tone finish. Gray/black laminated grips. 30 lpi front strap checkering. All models have night sights; Target versions have Meprolight adjustable Bar/Dot version. Made in U.S.A. by Kimber Mfg., Inc.

Price: Eclipse Ultra II (3" barrel, short grip) **$1,289.00**
Price: Eclipse Pro II (4" barrel, full-length grip) **$1,289.00**
Price: Eclipse Pro Target II (4" barrel, full-length grip,
adjustable sight) **$1,289.00**
Price: Eclipse Custom II 10mm **$1,376.00**
Price: Eclipse Target II (5" barrel, full-length grip,
adjustable sight) **$1,393.00**

KIMBER TACTICAL ENTRY II
Caliber: 45 ACP, 7-round magazine. **Barrel:** 5". **Weight:** 40 oz. **Length:** 8.7" overall. **Features:** 1911-style semiauto with checkered frontstrap, extended magazine well, night sights, heavy steel frame, tactical rail.
Price: **$1,490.00**

KIMBER TACTICAL CUSTOM HD II
Caliber: .45 ACP, 7-round magazine. **Barrel:** 5" match-grade. **Weight:** 39 oz. **Length:** 8.7" overall. **Features:** 1911-style semiauto with night sights, heavy steel frame.
Price: **$1,387.00**

KIMBER SUPER CARRY PRO
1911-syle semiauto pistol chambered in .45 ACP. Features include 8-round magazine; ambidextrous thumb safety; carry melt profiling; full length guide rod; aluminum frame with stainless slide; satin silver finish; super carry serrations; 4-inch barrel; micarta laminated grips; tritium night sights.
Price: **$1,596.00**

KIMBER SUPER CARRY HD SERIES
Designated as HD (Heavy Duty), each is chambered in .45 ACP

and features a stainless steel slide and frame, premium KimPro II™ finish and night sights with cocking shoulder for one-hand operation. Like the original Super Carry pistols, HD models have directional serrations on slide, front strap and mainspring housing for unequaled control under recoil. A round heel frame and Carry Melt treatment make them comfortable to carry and easy to conceal.

SUPER CARRY ULTRA HD™
Caliber: .45 ACP, 7-shot magazine. **Barrel:** 3. **Weight:** 32 oz. **Length:** 6.8 overall. **Grips:** G-10, Checkered with border. **Sights:** Night sights with cocking shoulder radius (inches): 4.8. **Features:** Rugged stainless steel slide and frame with KimPro II finish. Aluminum match grade trigger with a factory setting of approximately 4-5 pounds.
Price: $1,699.00

SUPER CARRY PRO HD™
Caliber: .45 ACP, 8-shot magazine. **Barrel:** 4. **Weight:** 35 oz. **Length:** 7.7 overall. **Grips:** G-10, Checkered with border. **Sights:** Night sights with cocking shoulder radius (inches): 5.7. **Features:** Rugged stainless steel slide and frame with KimPro II finish. Aluminum match grade trigger with a factory setting of approximately 4-5 pounds.
Price: $1,699.00

SUPER CARRY CUSTOM HD™
Caliber: .45 ACP, 8-shot magazine. **Barrel:** 5. **Weight:** 38 oz. **Length:** 8.7 overall. **Grips:** G-10, Checkered with border. **Sights:** Night sights with cocking shoulder radius (inches): 4.8. **Features:** Rugged stainless steel slide and frame with KimPro II finish. Aluminum match grade trigger with a factory setting of approximately 4-5 pounds.
Price: $1,699.00

KIMBER ULTRA CDP II
Compact 1911-syle pistol chambered in .45 ACP or 9mm. Features include 7-round magazine (9 in 9mm); ambidextrous thumb safety; carry melt profiling; full length guide rod; aluminum frame with stainless slide; satin silver finish; checkered frontstrap; 3-inch barrel; rosewood double diamond Crimson Trace lasergrips grips; tritium 3-dot night sights.
Price: $1,331.00

KIMBER STAINLESS ULTRA TLE II
1911-syle semiauto pistol chambered in .45 ACP. Features include

7-round magazine; full-length guide rod; aluminum frame with stainless slide; satin silver finish; checkered frontstrap; 3-inch barrel; tactical gray double diamond grips; tritium 3-dot night sights.
Price: **$1,253.00**

LIONHEART LH9 MKII
Caliber: 9mm, 15-round magazine. LH9C Compact, 10 rounds. **Barrel:** 4.1 inches. **Weight:** 26.5 oz. **Length:** 7.5 inches **Grips:** One piece black polymer with textured design. **Sights:** Fixed low profile. Novak LoMount sights available. **Finish:** Cerakote Graphite Black or Patriot Brown. **Features:** Hammer-forged heat-treated steel slide, hammer-forged aluminum frame. Double-action PLUS action.
Price: **$695.00**
Price: Novak sights..**$749.00**

KIMBER ROYAL II
Caliber: .45 ACP, 7-shot magazine. **Barrel:** 5". **Weight:** 38 oz. **Length:** 8.7" overall. **Grips:** Solid bone-smooth. **Sights:** Fixed low profile. **Features:** A classic full-size pistol wearing a charcoal blue finish complimented with solid bone grip panels. Front and rear serrations. Aluminum match-grade trigger with a factory setting of approximately 4-5 pounds.
Price: **$2,020.00**

NIGHTHAWK CUSTOM
Manufacturer of a wide range of 1911-style pistols in Government Model (full-size), Commander and Officer's frame sizes. **Caliber:** .45 ACP, 7 or 8-round magazine; 9mm, 9 or 10 rounds. **Barrel:** 3.8, 4.25 or 5 inches. **Weight:** 28 to 41 ounces, depending on model. Shown is T4 model, introduced in 2013 and available only in 9mm. Several models are based on designs by custom gunsmith Richard Heinie including a long-slide 10mm with a 6-inch barrel. Numerous models are available, many on custom order, with optional features, and combinations of various finishes, sights and grip styles.
Price: From .... **$3,200.00 to $3,995.00**

KIMBER MASTER CARRY PRO
Caliber: .45 ACP, 8-round magazine. **Barrel:** 4 inches. **Weight:** 28 oz. **Length:** 7.7 inches **Grips:** Crimson Trace Laser. **Sights:** Fixed low profile. **Features:** Matte black KimPro slide, aluminum round heel frame, full-length guide rod.
Price: **$1,568.00**

NORTH AMERICAN ARMS GUARDIAN DAO
Caliber: .25 NAA, .32 ACP, .380 ACP, .32 NAA, 6-shot magazine. **Barrel:** 2.49. **Weight:** 20.8 oz. **Length:** 4.75 overall. **Grips:** Black

polymer. **Sights:** Low profile fixed. **Features:** Double-action only mechanism. All stainless steel construction. Introduced 1998. Made in U.S.A. by North American Arms.
Price: From .... **$402.00 to $479.00**

OLYMPIC ARMS MATCHMASTER 5 1911

Caliber: .45 ACP, 7-shot magazine. **Barrel:** 5" stainless steel. **Weight:** 40 oz. **Length:** 8.75" overall. **Grips:** Smooth walnut with laser-etched scorpion icon. **Sights:** Ramped blade, LPA adjustable rear. **Features:** Matched frame and slide, fitted and head-spaced barrel, complete ramp and throat jobs, lowered and widened ejection port, beveled mag well, hand-stoned-to-match hammer and sear, lightweight long-shoe over-travel adjusted trigger, shaped and tensioned extractor, extended thumb safety, wide beavertail grip safety and full-length guide rod. Made in U.S.A. by Olympic Arms, Inc.
Price: **$1,034.00**

OLYMPIC ARMS ENFORCER 1911

Caliber: .45 ACP, 6-shot magazine. **Barrel:** 4" bull stainless steel. **Weight:** 35 oz. **Length:** 7.75" overall. **Grips:** Smooth walnut with etched black widow spider icon. **Sights:** Ramped blade front, LPA adjustable rear. **Features:** Compact Enforcer frame. Bushingless bull barrel with triplex counter-wound self-contained recoil system. Matched frame and slide, fitted and head-spaced barrel, complete ramp and throat jobs, lowered and widened ejection port, beveled mag well, hand-stoned-to-match hammer and sear, lightweight longshoe over-travel adjusted trigger, shaped and tensioned extractor, extended thumb safety, wide beavertail grip safety and full length guide rod. Made in U.S.A. by Olympic Arms.
Price: **$1,033.50**

OLYMPIC ARMS MATCHMASTER 6 1911

Caliber: .45 ACP, 7-shot magazine. **Barrel:** 6" stainless steel. **Weight:** 44 oz. **Length:** 9.75" overall. **Grips:** Smooth walnut with laser-etched scorpion icon. **Sights:** Ramped blade, LPA adjustable rear. **Features:** Matched frame and slide, fitted and head-spaced barrel, complete ramp and throat jobs, lowered and widened ejection port, beveled mag well, hand-stoned-to-match hammer and sear, lightweight long-shoe over-travel adjusted trigger, shaped and tensioned extractor, extended thumb safety, wide beavertail grip safety and full length guide rod. Made in U.S.A. by Olympic Arms, Inc.
Price: **$1,104.00**

OLYMPIC ARMS COHORT

Caliber: .45 ACP, 7-shot magazine. **Barrel:** 4" bull stainless steel. **Weight:** 36 oz. **Length:** 7.75" overall. **Grips:** Fully checkered walnut. **Sights:** Ramped blade front, LPA adjustable rear. **Features:** Full-size 1911 frame. Bushingless bull barrel with triplex counter-wound self-contained recoil system. Matched frame and slide, fitted and head-spaced barrel, complete ramp and throat jobs, lowered and widened ejection port, beveled mag well, hand-stoned-to-match hammer and sear, lightweight long-shoe over-travel adjusted trigger, shaped and tensioned extractor, extended thumb safety, wide beavertail grip safety and full length guide rod. Made in U.S.A. by Olympic Arms.
Price: **$973.70**

Prices given are believed to be correct at time of publication however, many factors affect retail pricing so exact prices are not possible.

ejection port, beveled mag well, hand-stoned-to-match hammer and sear, lightweight long-shoe over-travel adjusted trigger, shaped and tensioned extractor, extended thumb safety, wide beavertail grip safety and full length guide rod. Entire pistol is fitted and assembled, then disassembled and subjected to the color case hardening process. Made in U.S.A. by Olympic Arms, Inc.

Price: Constable, 4" barrel, 35 oz. . . .**$1,163.50**
Price: Westerner, 5" barrel, 39 oz. . . .**$1,163.50**
Price: Trail Boss, 6" barrel, 43 oz. . . .**$1,234.00**

OLYMPIC ARMS BIG DEUCE

Caliber: .45 ACP, 7-shot magazine. **Barrel:** 6" stainless steel. **Weight:** 44 oz. **Length:** 9.75" overall. **Grips:** Double diamond checkered exotic cocobolo wood. **Sights:** Ramped blade front, LPA adjustable rear. **Features:** Carbon steel parkerized slide with satin bead blast finish full size frame. Matched frame and slide, fitted and head-spaced barrel, complete ramp and throat jobs, lowered and widened ejection port, beveled mag well, hand-stoned-to-match hammer and sear, lightweight long-shoe over-travel adjusted trigger, shaped and tensioned extractor, extended thumb safety, wide beavertail grip safety and full length guide rod. Made in U.S.A. by Olympic Arms.

Price: **$1,163.50**

OLYMPIC ARMS SCHUETZEN WORKS 1911

Caliber: .45 ACP, 7-shot magazine. **Barrel:** 4, 5.2", bull stainless steel. **Weight:** 35-38 oz. **Length:** 7.75-8.75" overall. **Grips:** Double diamond checkered exotic cocobolo wood. **Sights:** Ramped blade, LPA adjustable rear. **Features:** Carbon steel parkerized slide with satin bead blast finish full size frame. Matched frame and slide, fitted and head-spaced barrel, complete ramp and throat jobs, lowered and widened ejection port, beveled mag well, hand-stoned-to-match hammer and sear, lightweight long-shoe over-travel adjusted trigger, shaped and tensioned extractor, extended thumb safety, wide beavertail grip safety and full length guide rod. Custom made by Olympic Arms Schuetzen Pistol Works. Parts are hand selected and fitted by expert pistolsmiths. Several no-cost options to choose from. Made in U.S.A. by Olympic Arms Schuetzen Pistol Works.

Price: Journeyman, 4" bull barrel, 35 oz. **$1,293.50**
Price: Street Deuce, 5.2" bull barrel, 38 oz. **$1,293.50**

OLYMPIC ARMS WESTERNER SERIES 1911

Caliber: .45 ACP, 7-shot magazine. **Barrel:** 4, 5, 6" stainless steel. **Weight:** 35-43 oz. **Length:** 7.75-9.75" overall. **Grips:** Smooth ivory laser-etched Westerner icon. **Sights:** Ramped blade, LPA adjustable rear. **Features:** Matched frame and slide, fitted and head-spaced barrel, complete ramp and throat jobs, lowered and widened

Prices given are believed to be accurate at time of publication however, many factors affect retail pricing so exact prices are not possible.

69TH EDITION, 2015 ✛ **413**

OLYMPIC ARMS OA-93 AR

Caliber: 5.56 NATO. **Barrel:** 6.5" button-rifled stainless steel. **Weight:** 4.46 lbs. **Length:** 17" overall. **Sights:** None. **Features:** Olympic Arms integrated recoil system on the upper receiver eliminates the buttstock, flat top upper, free floating tubular match handguard, threaded muzzle with flash suppressor. Made in U.S.A. by Olympic Arms, Inc.
Price: $1,268.00

OLYMPIC ARMS K23P AR

Caliber: 5.56 NATO. **Barrel:** 6.5" button-rifled chrome-moly steel. **Length:** 22.25" overall. **Weight:** 5.12 lbs. **Sights:** Adjustable A2 rear, elevation adjustable front post. **Features:** A2 upper with rear sight, free floating tubular match handguard, threaded muzzle with flash suppressor, receiver extension tube with foam cover, no bayonet lug. Made in U.S.A. by Olympic Arms, Inc. Introduced 2007.
Price: $973.70

OLYMPIC ARMS K23P-A3-TC AR

Caliber: 5.56 NATO. **Barrel:** 6.5" button-rifled chrome-moly steel. **Length:** 22.25" overall. **Weight:** 5.12 lbs. **Sights:** Adjustable A2 rear, elevation adjustable front post. **Features:** Flat-top upper with detachable carry handle, free floating FIRSH rail handguard, threaded muzzle with flash suppressor, receiver extension tube with foam cover, no bayonet lug. Made in U.S.A. by Olympic Arms, Inc. Introduced 2007.
Price: $1,118.20

OLYMPIC ARMS WHITNEY WOLVERINE

Caliber: .22 LR, 10-shot magazine. **Barrel:** 4.625" stainless steel. **Weight:** 19.2 oz. **Length:** 9" overall. **Grips:** Black checkered with fire/safe markings. **Sights:** Ramped blade front, dovetail rear. **Features:** Polymer frame with natural ergonomics and ventilated rib. Barrel with 6-groove 1x16 twist rate. All metal magazine shell. Made in U.S.A. by Olympic Arms.
Price: $294.00

PARA USA BLACK OPS SERIES

Caliber: .45 ACP, single (8 round) or double-stack magazine (14 rounds). **Barrel:** 5 inches. **Weight:** 39 oz. **Grips:** VZ G10. **Sights:** Fixed night sights or adjustable. Stainless receiver with IonBond finish.
Price: .... $1,257.00 to $1,325.00

PARA USA BLACK OPS RECON

Caliber: 9mm, 18-round double-stack magazine. **Barrel:** 4.25 inches. **Weight:** 34 oz. **Grips:** VZ G10. **Sights:** Trijicon night sights. **Features:** Stainless receiver with IonBond finish.
Price: $1,299.00

PARA USA EXPERT SERIES

Caliber: .45 ACP, 7+1-round capacity, 9mm (8+1). **Barrel:** 5" stainless. **Weight:** 39 oz. **Length:** 8.5" overall. **Grips:** Checkered Polymer. **Sights:** Dovetail Fixed, 3-White Dot. **Features:** The Para "Expert" is an entry level 1911 pistol that will allow new marksmen to own a pistol with features such as, Lowered and flared ejection port, beveled magazine well, flat mainspring housing, grip safety contoured for spur hammer. Model 1445 has double-stack frame, 14-round magazine.
Price: $663.00
Price: Carry $799.00
Price: Commander...$799.00
Price: 1445 Model................................. $884.00 to $919.00

PARA USA LDA SERIES

Caliber: 9mm, .45 ACP. **Capacity:** 9 rounds (9mm), 7 rounds (.45) for Officer model; 8 and 6 round capacity for Agent model, which has shorter grip. Double-action only design with PARA's exclusive LDA (Light Double Action) trigger. **Barrel:** 3 inches. **Sights:** Trijicon night sights. **Grips:** VZ Gator.
Price: Officer $1,025.00
Price: Agent $1,025.00

PARA USA WARTHOG

Caliber: .45 ACP, 10-round magazine. **Barrel:** 3 inches. **Sights:**

2-dot rear combat, Green fiber optic front. **Features:** Double-stack aluminum frame, adjustable skeletonized trigger, black nitride or satin stainless finish. Comes with two 10-round magazines.
Price: (black) **$884.00**
Price: (stainless) **$919.00**

PARA ELITE SERIES

Caliber: .45 ACP, 9mm (Elite LS Hunter only). **Capacity:** 6, 7 or 8 rounds; 9 rounds (9mm LS Hunter). **Barrel:** 3, 4 or 5 inches (.45 models), 6 inches (9mm LS Hunter). **Features:** Pro Model has Ed Brown mag well, HD extractor, checkered front strap and mainspring housing, Trijicon sights.
Price: Elite Standard **$949.00**
Price: Agent 3.5" **$949.00**
Price: Officer 4" **$949.00**
Price: Commander 4.5" **$949.00**
Price: Target **$949.00**
Price: Pro, LS Hunter **$1,249.00**
Price: Pro Stainless **$1,249.00**

PARA CUSTOM SERIES

Caliber: .45 ACP, .40 S&W, 9mm. Magazine capacity: 8 to 18 rounds, depending on model. **Barrel:** 3" (Executive Carry), 5". **Weight:** 26 or 40 oz. **Grips:** Polymer. **Sights:** Night sights or adjustable rear with fiber optic front. **Finish:** Stainless steel.
Price: Executive Carry **$1,399.00**
Price: Pro Comp 9, Pro Comp 40 .... **$1,299.00**
Price: Pro Custom 14.45 .... **$1,449.00**
Price: Pro Custom 16.40 .... **$1,449.00**

PHOENIX ARMS HP22, HP25

Caliber: .22 LR, 10-shot (HP22), .25 ACP, 10-shot (HP25). **Barrel:** 3". **Weight:** 20 oz. **Length:** 5.5" overall. **Grips:** Checkered composition. **Sights:** Blade front, adjustable rear. **Features:** Single action, exposed hammer; manual hold-open; button magazine release. Available in satin nickel, matte blue finish. Introduced 1993. Made in U.S.A. by Phoenix Arms.
Price: With gun lock **$145.00**

Price: HP Range kit with 5" bbl., locking case and accessories (1 Mag) **$188.00**
Price: HP Deluxe Range kit with 3" and 5" bbls., 2 mags, case **$224.00**

REMINGTON R1

Caliber: .45 (7-shot magazine). **Barrel:** 5". **Weight:** 38.5 oz. **Grips:** Double diamond walnut. **Sights:** Fixed, dovetail front and rear, 3-dot. **Features:** Flared and lowered ejection port. Comes with two magazines.
Price: **$729.00**
Price: (stainless) **$789.00**

REMINGTON R1 ENHANCED

Same features as standard R1 except 8-shot magazine, stainless satin black oxide finish, wood laminate grips and adjustable rear sight. Other features include forward slide serrations, fiber optic front sight. Available with threaded barrel.
Price: **$940.00**
Price: Stainless **$999.00**
Price: Threaded barrel **$1,140.00**

REMINGTON R1 CARRY

Caliber: .45 ACP. **Barrel:** 5 or 4.25 inches (Carry Commander). **Weight:** 35 to 39 oz. **Grips:** Cocobolo. **Sights:** Novak-type drift-adjustable

Prices given are believed to be accurate at time of publication however, many factors affect retail pricing so exact prices are not possible.

69TH EDITION, 2015 ⊕ **415**

rear, tritium-dot front sight. **Features:** Skeletonized trigger. Comes with one 8-round and one 7-round magazine.
Price: **$1,299.00**

REMINGTON R51

Caliber: 9mm+P rated, 6-shot magazine. **Barrel:** 3.4". **Weight:** 22 oz. **Length:** 6.6" overall **Grips:** Black synthetic, checkered/smooth. **Sights:** Fixed low-profile 3-dot system. Skeletonized trigger. **Features:** Grip safety only, fixed barrel/locked breech operating system allows a lighter recoil spring, which is placed around the barrel. This is the reason for the gun's thin design. Width of the frame is one inch. Based on the Pedersen design of the original Model 51 .32/.380 pistol made from 1918 to 1926, with numerous improvements. Introduced in 2014.
Price: **$420.00**

REPUBLIC FORGE 1911

Caliber: .45 ACP, 9mm, .38 Super, .40 S&W, 10mm. A manufacturer of custom 1911-style pistols offered in a variety of configurations, finishes and frame sizes, including single and double-stack models with many options. Made in Texas.
Price: From **$2,795.00**

ROCK RIVER ARMS LAR-15/LAR-9

Caliber: .223/5.56mm NATO or 9mm Para. **Barrel:** 7", 10.5". Wilson chrome moly, 1:9 twist, A2 flash hider, 1/2-28 thread. **Weight:** 5.1 lbs. (7" barrel), 5.5 lbs. (10.5" barrel). **Length:** 23" overall. **Stock:** Hogue rubber grip. **Sights:** A2 front. **Features:** Forged A2 or A4 upper, single stage trigger, aluminum free-float tube, one magazine. From Rock River Arms, Inc.
Price: LAR-15 7" AR2110 .... $1,060.00
Price: LAR-15 10.5" AR2122 .... $1,055.00
Price: LAR-9 7" 9MM2110X $1,210.00
Price: LAR-9 10.5" 9mm2122X............................. $1,205.00

ROBERTS DEFENSE 1911 SERIES

Caliber: : .45 ACP (8+1 rounds). **Barrel:** 5, 4.25 or 3.5 inches. **Weight:** 26 to 38 oz. **Sights:** Novak-type drift-adjustable rear, tritium-dot or fiber optic front sight. **Features:** Skeletonized trigger. Offered in three model variants with many custom features and options. Made in Wisconsin by Roberts Defense.

Price: Recon **$1,499.00**
Price: Super Grade **$1,549.00**
Price: Operator **$1,649.00**

ROHRBAUGH R9

Caliber: 9mm Parabellum, .380 ACP. **Barrel:** 2.9". **Weight:** 12.8 oz. **Length:** 5.2" overall. **Features:** Very small double-action-only semiauto pocket pistol. Stainless steel slide with matte black aluminum frame. Available with or without sights. Available with all-black (Stealth) and partial Diamond Black (Stealth Elite) finish.
Price: **$1,149.00**

RUGER SR9 /SR40

Caliber: 9mm Para. (17 round magazine), .40 S&W (15). **Barrel:** 4.14". **Weight:** 26.25, 26.5 oz. **Grips:** Glass-filled nylon in two color options—black or OD Green, w/flat or arched reversible backstrap. **Sights:** Adjustable 3-dot, built-in Picatinny-style rail. **Features:** Semi-auto in six configurations, striker-fired, through-hardened stainless steel slide, brushed or blackened stainless slide with black grip frame or blackened stainless slide with OD Green grip frame, ambidextrous manual 1911-style safety, ambi. mag release, mag disconnect, loaded chamber indicator, Ruger camblock design to absorb recoil, comes with two magazines. 10-shot mags available. Introduced 2008. Made in U.S.A. by Sturm, Ruger & Co.
Price: SR9 (17-Round), SR9-10 (SS) **$529.00**

RUGER SR9C /SR40C COMPACT

Caliber: 9mm or .40 S&W. **Barrel:** 3.4 " (SR9C), 3.5" (SR40C). **Features:** Features include 1911-style ambidextrous manual safety;

Prices given are believed to be accurate at time of publication however, many factors affect retail pricing so exact prices are not possible.

internal trigger bar interlock and striker blocker; trigger safety; magazine disconnector; loaded chamber indicator; two magazines, one 10-round and the other 17-round; 3.5-inch barrel; 3-dot sights; accessory rail; brushed stainless or blackened allow finish. Weight 23.40 oz.

Price: $525.00

RUGER SR45
Caliber: .45 ACP, 10-round magazine. **Barrel:** 4.5 inches. **Weight:** 30 oz. **Length:** 8 inches. **Grips:** Glass-filled nylon with reversible flat/arched backstra. **Sights:** Adjustable 3-dot. **Features:** Same features as SR9, SR4D.

Price: $529.00

RUGER LC9
Caliber: 9mm luger, 7+1 capacity. **Barrel:** 3.12 **Weight:** 17.10 oz. **Grips:** Glass-filled nylon. **Sights:** Adjustable 3-dot. **Features:** Double-action-only, hammer-fired, locked-breech pistol with a smooth trigger pull. Control and confident handling of the Ruger LC9 are accomplished through reduced recoil and aggressive frame checkering for a positive grip in all conditions. The Ruger LC9 features smooth "melted" edges for ease of holstering, carrying and drawing. Made in U.S.A. by Sturm, Ruger & Co.

Price: $449.00
Price: LaserMax laser grips $529.00

RUGER LC380
Caliber: .380 ACP. Other specifications and features identical to LC9.
Price: $449.00

Price: LaserMax laser grips $529.00
Price: Crimson Trace Laserguard $629.00

RUGER LCP
Caliber: .380 (6-shot magazine). **Barrel:** 2.75". **Weight:** 9.4 oz. **Length:** 5.16". **Grips:** Glass-filled nylon. **Sights:** Fixed, LaxerMax or Crimson Trace.
Price: $379.00
Price: Stainless steel slide $429.00
Price: Laser Max $449.00
Price: Crimson Trace Laserguard $559.00

RUGER MARK III SERIES
Caliber: .22 LR, 10-shot magazine. **Barrel:** 4.5, 4.75, 5.5, 6, or 6-7/8". **Weight:** 33 oz. (4.75" bbl.). **Length:** 9" (4.75" bbl.). **Grips:** Checkered composition grip panels. **Sights:** Fixed, fiber-optic front, fixed rear. **Features:** Updated design of original Standard Auto and Mark II series. Hunter models have lighter barrels. Target models have cocobolo grips; bull, target, competition, and hunter barrels; and adjustable sights. Introduced 2005. Modern successor of the first Ruger pistol of 1949.
Price: Standard $389.00
Price: Target (blue) $459.00
Price: Target (stainless) $569.00
Price: Hunter $679.00
Price: Hunter (target grips).....................................$729.00
Price: Competition $659.00

Prices given are believed to be accurate at time of publication however, many factors affect retail pricing so exact prices are not possible.

69TH EDITION, 2015 ◆ **417**

RUGER 22/45 MARK III PISTOL

Similar to other .22 Mark III autos except has Zytel grip frame that matches angle and magazine latch of Model 1911 Government Model pistol. Available in 4.0" standard barrel; 4.5, 5.5, 6-7/8" bull barrels. Comes with extra magazine, plastic case, and lock. Introduced 1992. 22/45 LITE model introduced in 2013 with 4.4" barrel, weight of 23 ounces, fixed front and adjustable rear sights.

Price: Standard model 5.5" barrel $359.00
Price: 4" bull barrel, adjustable sights $359.00
Price: 4.5" threaded bull barrel, Picatinny rails $449.00
Price: 5.5" bull blued barrel, Target model with adj. sights $399.00
Price: 5.5" stainless bull barrel, adj. sights $475.00
Price: 22/45 Lite $499.00

RUGER SR22

Caliber: .22 LR (10-shot magazine). **Barrel:** 3.5". **Weight:** 17.5 oz. **Length:** 6.4". **Sights:** Adjustable 3-dot. **Features:** Ambidextrous manual safety/decocking lever and mag release. Comes with two interchangeable rubberized grips and two magazines. Black or silveranodize finish. Available with threaded barrel.

Price: Black $399.00
Price: Silver $419.00
Price: Threaded barrel $439.00

RUGER SR1911

Caliber: .45 (8-shot magazine). **Barrel:** 5". **Weight:** 39 oz. **Length:** 8.6". **Grips:** Slim checkered hardwood. **Sights:** Novak LoMount Carry rear, standard front. **Features:** Based on Series 70 design. Flared and lowed ejection port. Extended mag release, thumb safety and slide-stop lever, oversized grip safety, checkered backstrap on the flat mainspring housing. Comes with one 7-shot and one 8-shot magazine.

Price: $829.00

RUGER SR1911 CMD

Commander-size version of SR1911. **Caliber:** .45 ACP. **Barrel:** 4.25 inches. **Weight:** 36.4 oz. Other specifications and features are identical to SR1911.

Price: $829.00

SEECAMP LWS 32/380 STAINLESS DA

Caliber: .32 ACP, .380 ACP Win. Silvertip, 6-shot magazine. **Barrel:** 2", integral with frame. **Weight:** 10.5 oz. **Length:** 4-1/8" overall. **Grips:** Glass-filled nylon. **Sights:** Smooth, no-snag, contoured slide and barrel top. **Features:** Aircraft quality 17-4 PH stainless steel. Inertia-operated firing pin. Hammer fired double-action-only. Hammer automatically follows slide down to safety rest position after each shot, no manual safety needed. Magazine safety disconnector. Polished stainless. Introduced 1985. From L.W. Seecamp.

Price: .32...$446.25
Price: .380..$795.00

SIG SAUER 250 SERIES

Caliber: 9mm Para., .357 SIG, .380 ACP, .40 S&W and .45 ACP. **Barrel:** 3.1, 3.9 or 4.7". **Weight:** 24.6 oz. **Length:** 7.2" overall. **Grips:** Interchangeable polymer. **Sights:** Fixed. Siglite night sights optional. **Features:** Modular polymer frame design allows for immediate change in caliber. Available in full, compact and subcompact sizes. Six different grip combinations for each size. Introduced 2008. From SIG Sauer, Inc.

Price: P250 .... $570.00 to $642.00

SIG SAUER 1911

Caliber: .45 ACP, 8-10 shot magazine. **Barrel:** 3.3, 4.25, 5". **Weight:** 28 to 40 oz. **Length:** 6.8 to 8.65" overall. **Grips:** Checkered wood, rosewood, aluminum or synthetic. **Sights:**

Novak night sights. Blade front, drift adjustable rear for windage. **Features:** Hand-fitted dehorned stainless-steel frame and slide; match-grade barrel, hammer/sear set and trigger; 25-lpi front strap checkering, 20-lpi mainspring housing checkering. Beavertail grip safety with speed bump, extended thumb safety, firing pin safety and hammer intercept notch. Introduced 2005. XO series has contrast sights, Ergo Grip XT textured polymer grips. Target line features adjustable target night sights, match barrel, custom wood grips, non-railed frame in stainless or Nitron finishes. TTT series is two-tone 1911 with Nitron slide and black controls on stainless frame. Includes burled maple grips, adjustable combat night sights. STX line available from Sig Sauer Custom Shop; two-tone 1911, non-railed, Nitron slide, stainless frame, burled maple grips. Polished cocking serrations, flat-top slide, magwell. Carry line has Novak night sights, lanyard attachment point, gray diamondwood or rosewood grips, 8+1 capacity. Compact series has 6+1 capacity, 7.7 OAL, 4.25" barrel, slim-profile wood grips, weighs 30.3 oz. RCS line is Customs Shop version with anti-snag dehorning. Stainless or Nitron finish, Novak night sights, slim-profile gray diamondwood or rosewood grips. 6+1 capacity. 1911 C3 is a 6+1 compact .45 ACP, rosewood custom wood grips, two-tone and Nitron finishes. Weighs about 30 ounces unloaded, lightweight alloy frame. Now offered in more than 30 different models with numerous options for frame size, grips, finishes, sight arrangements and other features.

Price: Nitron	....	**$1,099.99**
Price: Stainless	....	**$1,113.00**
Price: XO Black	....	**$1,050.00**
Price: Target Nitron	....	**$1,113.00**
Price: TTT	....	**$1,170.00**
Price: STX	....	**$1,213.00**
Price: Carry Nitron	....	**$1,099.00**
Price: RCS Nitron	....	**$1,170.00**
Price: C3	....	**$1,042.00**
Price: Ultra Two-Tone	....	**$1,156.00**
Price: Nightmare	....	**$1,242.00**
Price: Scorpion	....	**$1,213.00**
Price: Scorpion TB	....	**$1,285.00**
Price: Model 1911-22-B w/custom wood grips	....	**$460.00**

SIG SAUER P210
Caliber: 9mm, 8-shot magazine. **Barrel:** 4.7". **Weight:** 37.4 oz.

Length: 8.5" overall. **Grips:** Custom wood. **Sights:** Post and notch and adjustable target sights. **Features:** Introduced in 2011. Improved and updated version of original P210 imported by Sigarms from 1987 to 2007. The carbon steel slide, machined from solid billet steel, now features a durable Nitron coating, and the improved beavertail adorns the Nitron coated, heavy-style, carbon steel frame. The P210 Legend also offers an improved manual safety, internal drop safety, side magazine release, and custom wood grips. Super Target has 6-inch barrel, ergonomic custom wood grips with integral mag well, 1911 style safety and slide catch levers.
Price: P210-9-LEGEND **$2,428.00**
Price: P210-9-LEGEND-TGT
   w/adjustable target sights **$2,642.00**
Price: P210-9-LEGEND Super Target **$3,993.00**

SIG SAUER P220
Caliber: .45 ACP, (7- or 8-shot magazine). **Barrel:** 4.4". **Weight:** 27.8 oz. **Length:** 7.8" overall. **Grips:** Checkered black plastic. **Sights:** Blade front, drift adjustable rear for windage. Optional Siglite night sights. **Features:** Double action. Stainless-steel slide, Nitron finish, alloy frame, M1913 Picatinny rail; safety system of decocking lever, automatic firing pin safety block, safety intercept notch, and trigger bar disconnector. Squared combat-type trigger guard. Slide stays open after last shot. Introduced 1976. P220 SAS Anti-Snag has dehorned stainless steel slide, front Siglite Night Sight, rounded trigger guard, dust cover, Custom Shop wood grips. Equinox line is Custom Shop product with Nitron stainless-steel slide with a black hard-anodized alloy frame, brush-polished flats and nickel accents. Truglo tritium fiber-optic front sight, rear Siglite night sight, gray laminated wood grips with checkering and stippling. From SIG SAUER, Inc.
Price: P220 Two-Tone, matte-stainless slide,
   black alloy frame **$1,110.00**
Price: P220 Elite Stainless **$1,396.00**
Price: P220 Two-Tone SAO, single action, from **$1,108.00**
Price: P220 DAK **$1,015.00**
Price: P220 Equinox **$1,253.00**
Price: P220 Elite Dark **$1,253.00**
Price: P220 Elite Dark, threaded barrel **$1,316.00**

SIG SAUER P220 CARRY
Caliber: .45 ACP, 8-shot magazine. **Barrel:** 3.9". **Weight:** NA. **Length:** 7.1" overall. **Grips:** Checkered black plastic. **Sights:** Blade front,

drift adjustable rear for windage. Optional Siglite night sights. **Features:** Similar to full-size P220, except is "Commander" size. Single stack, DA/SA operation, Nitron finish, Picatinny rail, and either post and dot contrast or 3-dot Siglite night sights. Introduced 2005. Many variations availble. From SIG SAUER, Inc.
Price: P220 Carry, from $1,015.00
w/night sights $1,108.00
Price: P220 Carry Elite Stainless $1,396.00

SIG SAUER P224
Caliber: 9mm, .357 SIG, .40 S&W. **Magazine Capacity:** 11 rounds (9mm), 10 rounds (.357 and .40). **Barrel:** 3.5" inches. **Weight:** 25 oz. **Length:** 6.7" inches. **Grips:** Hogue G-10. **Sights:** SIGlite night sights. **Features:** Ultra-compact, double-stack design with features and operating controls of other SIG models. Available in SAS, nickel, Equinox and Extreme variations.
Price: .... $1,108.00 to $1,243.00

SIG SAUER P226
Similar to the P220 pistol except has 4.4" barrel, measures 7.7" overall, weighs 34 oz. Chambered in 9mm, .357 SIG, or .40 S&W. X-Five series has factory tuned single-action trigger, 5" slide and barrel, ergonomic wood grips with beavertail, ambidextrous thumb safety and stainless slide and frame with magwell, low-profile adjustable target sights, front cocking serrations and a 25-meter fac-

tory test target. More than 25 variations available. Snap-on modular grips. From SIG SAUER, Inc.
Price: From $1,015.00

SIG SAUER P227
Same general specifications and features as P226 except chambered for .45 ACP and has double-stack magazine. **Magazine Capacity:** 10 rounds.
Price: $1,015.00

SIG SAUER P229 DA
Similar to the P220 except chambered for 9mm Para. (10- or 15-round magazines), .40 S&W, (10- or 12-round magazines). Has 3.86" barrel, 7.1" overall length and 3.35" height. Weight is 32.4 oz. Introduced 1991. Snap-on modular grips. Frame made in Germany, stainless steel slide assembly made in U.S.; pistol assembled in U.S. Many variations available. From SIG SAUER, Inc.
Price: P229, from $1,015.00
Price: Scorpion Threaded Bbl...............................$1,356.00
Price: P229 Enhanced Elite $1,175.00

SIG SAUER SP2022
Caliber: 9mm Para., .357 SIG, .40 S&W, 10-, 12-, or 15-shot magazines. **Barrel:** 3.9". **Weight:** 30.2 oz. **Length:** 7.4" overall. **Grips:** Composite and rubberized one-piece. **Sights:** Blade front, rear adjustable for windage. Optional Siglite night sights. **Features:** Polymer frame, stainless steel slide; integral frame accessory rail; replaceable steel frame rails; left- or right-handed magazine release, two interchangeable grips. From SIG SAUER, Inc.
Price: $570.00

SIG SAUER P232 PERSONAL SIZE
Caliber: .380 ACP, 7-shot; .22 LR, 10-shot. **Barrel:** 3.6". **Weight:** 17.6-22.4 oz. **Length:** 6.6" overall. **Grips:** Checkered black composite. **Sights:** Blade front, rear adjustable for windage. **Features:** Double action/single action or DAO. Blow-back operation, stationary barrel. Introduced 1997. From SIG SAUER, Inc.
Price: .380 ACP .... $749.00 to $809.00
Price: .22 LR $427.00

SIG SAUER P238
Caliber: .380 ACP (9mm short), 6-7-shot magazine. **Barrel:** 2.7". **Weight:** 15.4 oz. **Length:** 5.5" overall. **Grips:** Hogue® G-10 and Rosewood grips. **Sights:** Contrast / SIGLITE night sights. **Features:** All metal beavertail-style frame.

Prices given are believed to be accurate at time of publication however, many factors affect retail pricing so exact prices are not possible.

Price: $679.00
Price: P238 Lady w/rosewood grips $752.00
Price: P238 Gambler w/rosewood grip $752.00
Price: P238 Extreme w/X-Grip extended magazine $752.00
Price: P238 Diamond Plate w/diamond plate detailed slide ... $752.00

SIG SAUER P290 RS

Caliber: 9mm, 6/8-shot magazine. **Barrel:** 2.9". **Weight:** 20.5 oz. **Length:** 5.5" overall. **Grips:** Polymer. **Sights:** Contrast / SIGLITE night sights. **Features:** Unlike many small pistols, the P290 features drift adjustable sights in the standard SIG SAUER dovetails. This gives shooters the option of either standard contrast sights or SIGLITE® night sights. The slide is machined from a solid billet of stainless steel and is available in a natural stainless or a durable Nitron® coating. A reversible magazine catch is left-hand adjustable. Interchangeable grip panels allow for personalization as well as a custom fit. In addition to the standard polymer inserts, optional panels will be available in aluminum, G10 and wood.

Price: Model 290 RS $570.00
Price: Model 290 RS Enhanced...$613.00
Price: Model 290 RS Two-Tone with laser sight $685.00
Price: Model 290 RS Rainbow or Pink $613.00

SIG SAUER P239

Caliber: 9mm Para., 8-shot, .357 SIG, .40 S&W, 7-shot magazine. **Barrel:** 3.6". **Weight:** 25.2 oz. **Length:** 6.6" overall. **Grips:** Checkered black composite. **Sights:** Blade front, rear adjustable for windage. Optional Siglite night sights. **Features:** SA/DA or DAO;

---

blackened stainless steel slide, aluminum alloy frame. Introduced 1996. Made in U.S.A. by SIG SAUER, Inc.
Price: $993.00

SIG SAUER P320

Caliber: 9mm, .357 SIG, .40 S&W. Magazine capacity 15 or 16 rounds (9mm), 13 or 14 rounds (.357 or .40). **Barrel:** 3.9 (Carry model) or 4.7" (Full size). **Weight:** 26 to 30 oz. **Length:** 7.2 or 8.0 inches overall. **Grips:** Interchangeable black composite. **Sights:** Blade front, rear adjustable for windage. Optional Siglite night sights. **Features:** Striker-fired double-action only, Nitron finish slide, black polymer frame. Frame size and calibers are interchangeable. Introduced 2014. A .45 ACP version is expected by 2015. Made in U.S.A. by SIG SAUER, Inc.
Price: Full size $713.00
Price: Carry (shown) $713.00

SIG SAUER MOSQUITO

Caliber: .22 LR, 10-shot magazine. **Barrel:** 3.9". **Weight:** 24.6 oz. **Length:** 7.2" overall. **Grips:** Checkered black composite. **Sights:** Blade front, rear adjustable for windage. **Features:** Blowback operated, fixed barrel, polymer frame, slide-mounted ambidextrous safety. Introduced 2005. Made in U.S.A. by SIG SAUER, Inc.
Price: Mosquito, from $408.00

SIG SAUER P522

Semiauto blowback pistol chambered in .22 LR. Pistol version of SIG522 rifle. Features include a 10-inch barrel; lightweight polymer lower receiver with pistol grip; ambi mag catch; aluminum upper; faux gas valve; birdcage; 25-round magazine; quad rail or "clean" handguard; optics rail.
Price: $587.00

SIG SAUER P938

Caliber: 9mm (6-shot magazine). **Barrel:** 3.9". **Weight:** 16 oz. **Length:** 5.9". **Grips:** Rosewood, Blackwood, Hogue Extreme, Hogue Diamondwood. **Sights:** Siglite night sights or Siglite rear with Tru-Glo front. **Features:** Slightly larger version of P238 with 9mm chambering.
Price: $823.00

SPHINX

Caliber: 9mm Para., .45 ACP., 10-shot magazine. **Barrel:** 4.43".
Weight: 39.15 oz. **Length:** 8.27" overall. **Grips:** Textured polymer.
Sights: Fixed Trijicon Night Sights. **Features:** CNC engineered from
stainless steel billet; grip frame in stainless steel, titanium or high-
strength aluminum. Integrated accessory rail, high-cut beavertail,
decocking lever. Made in Switzerland. Imported by Sabre Defence
Industries.
Price: .45 ACP (2007) **$2,990.00**
Price: 9mm Para. Standard, titanium w/decocker **$2,700.00**

SMITH & WESSON M&P SERIES

Caliber: .22 LR, 9mm, .357 Sig, .40 S&W. **Magazine capacity, full-
size models:** 12 rounds (.22), 17 rounds (9mm), 15 rounds (.40).
Compact models: 12 (9mm), 10 (.40). **Barrel:** 4.25, 3.5 inches.
Weight: 24, 22 oz. **Length:** 7.6, 6.7 inches. **Grips:** Polymer with
three interchangeable palmswell grip sizes. **Sights:** 3 white-dot
system with low-profile rear. **Features:** Zytel polymer frame with
stainless steel slide, barrel and structural components. VTAC (Viking
Tactics) model has Flat Dark Earth finish, VTAC Warrior sights.
Compact models available with Crimson Trace Lasergrips.
Price: **$569.00**
Price: VTAC **$779.00**
Price: CT **$829.00**
Price: .22 LR **$419.00**

SPHINX SDP

Caliber: 9mm (15-shot magazine). **Barrel:** 3.7". **Weight:** 27.5 oz.
Length: 7.4". **Sights:** Defiance Day & Night Green fiber/tritium
front, tritium 2-dot red rear. **Features:** Double/single action with
ambidextrous decocker, integrated slide postion safety, aluminum
MIL-STD 1913 Picatinny rail, Blued alloy/steel or stainless.
Aluminum and polymer frame, machined steel slide. Offered in
several variations. Made in Switzerland
Price: **$1,350.00**

SMITH & WESSON M&P PRO SERIES C.O.R.E.

Caliber: 9mm, .40 S&W. Magazine capacity: 17 rounds (9mm),
15 rounds (.40). **Barrel:** 4.25" (M&P9, M&P40), or 5" (M&P9L,
M&P40L.) **Features:** Based on the Pro series line of competition-
ready firearms, the C.O.R.E. models (Competition Optics Ready
Equipment) feature a slide engineered to accept six popular
competition optics (Trijicon RMR, Leupold Delta Point, Jpoint,
Doctor, C-More STS, Insight MRDS). Sight not included. Other
features identical to standard M&P9 and M&P40 models.
Price: **$769.00**

Prices given are believed to be accurate at time of publication however, many factors affect retail pricing so exact prices are not possible.

SMITH & WESSON M&P 45

M&P model offered in three frame sizes and chambered in .45 ACP. **Magazine capacity:** 8 or 10 rounds. **Barrel length:** 4 or 4.5 inches. **Weight:** 26, 28 or 30 oz. **Finish:** Black or Dark Earth Brown.
Price: .... $599.00 to $619.00

SMITH & WESSON M&P SHIELD

Ultra-compact, single-stack variation of M&P series. **Caliber:** 9mm, .40 S&W. Comes with one 6-round and one 7-round magazine. **Barrel:** 3.1 inches. **Length:** 6.I inches. **Weight:** 19 oz. **Sights:** 3-white-dot system with low-profile rear.
Price: $449.00

SMITH & WESSON MODEL SD9 VE/SD40 VE SERIES

Caliber: 9mm Para., .40 S&W; 16-shot magazine (9mm), 14 (.40). **Barrel:** 4 inches. **Weight:** 24.7 oz. **Length:** 7.2". **Grips:** Integral. **Sights:** White dot front, fixed rear; 3-dot system. **Features:** Enhanced and improved version of SD9 and SD40 with ergonomic textured grip, aggressive front and back strap texturing, front and rear slide serrations, two-tone finish with stainless steel slide, black polymer frame.
Price: $389.00

SMITH & WESSON MODEL SW1911

Caliber: .45 ACP, 9mm. **Magazine capacity:** 8 rounds (.45), 7 rounds

(sub compact .45), 10 rounds (9mm). **Barrel:** 3, 4.25, 5 inches. **Weight:** 26.5 to 41.7 oz. **Length:** 6.9 to 8.7 inches. **Grips:** Wood, wood laminate or synthetic. Crimson Trace Lasergrips available. **Sights:** Low profile white dot, tritium night sights or adjustable. **Finish:** Black matte, stainless or two-tone. **Features:** Offered in three different frame sizes. Skeletonized trigger. Accessory rail on some models. Compact models have round butt frame. Pro Series have 30 lpi checkered front strap, oversized external extractor, extended mag well, full-length guide rod, ambidextrous safety.
Price: Standard model .... **$979.00 to $1,399.00**
Price: Compact SC series **$1,449.00**
Price: Crimson Trace grips **$1,149.00**
Price: Pro Series **$1,609.00**

SMITH & WESSON BODYGUARD® 380

Caliber: .380 Auto, 6+1 round capacity. **Barrel:** 2.75". **Weight:** 11.85 oz. **Length:** 5.25". **Grips:** Polymer. **Sights:** Integrated laser sights with front: stainless steel, rear: drift adjustable. **Features:** The frame of the Bodyguard is made of reinforced polymer, as is the magazine base plate and follower, magazine catch, and the trigger. The slide, sights, and guide rod are made of stainless steel, with the slide and sights having a Melonite hard coating.
Price: **$419.00**

SPRINGFIELD ARMORY EMP ENHANCED MICRO

Caliber: 9mm Para., 40 S&W; 9-round magazine. **Barrel:** 3" stainless steel match grade, fully supported ramp, bull. **Weight:** 26 oz. **Length:** 6.5" overall. **Grips:** Thinline cocobolo hardwood. **Sights:** Fixed low profile combat rear, dovetail front, 3-dot tritium. **Features:** Two 9-round stainless steel magazines with slam pads, long aluminum match-grade trigger adjusted to 5 to 6 lbs., forged aluminum alloy frame, black hardcoat anodized; dual spring full-length guide rod, forged satin-finish stainless steel slide. Introduced 2007. From Springfield Armory.
Price: 9mm Para. Compact Bi-Tone **$1,345.00**
Price: 40 S&W Compact Bi-Tone..**$1,345.00**

Price: Service Black 9mm Para./.40 S&W, fixed sights **$578.00**
Price: Service Dark Earth .45 ACP, fixed sights **$607.00**
Price: Service Black .45 ACP, external thumb safety **$636.00**
Price: Sub-Compact OD Green 9mm Para./.40 S&W,
fixed sights **$549.00**
Price: Compact .45 ACP, 4" barrel, Bi-Tone finish **$666.00**
Price: V-10 Ported Black 9mm Para./40 S&W **$608.00**
Price: Tactical Black .45 ACP, fixed sights **$629.00**
Price: Service Bi-Tone .40 S&W, Trijicon night sights **$695.00**

SPRINGFIELD ARMORY XD POLYMER
Caliber: 9mm Para., .40 S&W, .45 ACP. **Barrel:** 3", 4", 5". **Weight:**
20.5-31 oz. **Length:** 6.26-8" overall. **Grips:** Textured polymer.
Sights: Varies by model; Fixed sights are dovetail front and rear steel
3-dot units. **Features:** Three sizes in X-Treme Duty (XD) line: Sub-
Compact (3" barrel), Service (4" barrel), Tactical (5" barrel). Three
ported models available. Ergonomic polymer frame, hammer-forged
barrel, no-tool disassembly, ambidextrous magazine release, visual/
tactile loaded chamber indicator, visual/tactile striker status indicator,
grip safety, XD gear system included. Introduced 2004. XD 45
introduced 2006. Compact line introduced 2007. Compacts ship with
one extended magazine (13) and one compact magazine (10). Made
in Croatia and imported by Springfield Armory.

SPRINGFIELD ARMORY XDM SERIES
Calibers: 9mm, .40 S&W, .45 ACP. **Barrel:** 3.8 or 4.5". **Sights:**
Fiber optic front with interchangeable red and green filaments,
adjustable target rear. **Grips:** Integral polymer with three optional
backstrap designs. **Features:** Variation of XD design with improved
ergonomics, deeper and longer slide serrations, slightly modified
grip contours and texturing. Black polymer frame, forged steel slide.
Black and two-tone finish options.
Price: .... **$697.00 to $732.00**

SPRINGFIELD ARMORY XD-S
Caliber: 9mm, .45 ACP. Same features as XDM except has single-
stack magazine for thinner profile. **Capacity:** 7 rounds (9mm), 5
rounds (.45). An extra extended-length magazine is included (10
rounds, 9mm; 7 rounds, .45). **Barrel:** 3.3 inches. **Weight:** 21.5 oz.
Features: Black or two-tone finish.
Price: (two-tone) .... **$599.00 to $669.00**

SPRINGFIELD ARMORY MIL-SPEC 1911A1
Caliber: .45 ACP, 7-shot magazine. **Barrel:** 5". **Weight:** 39 oz.
Length: 8.5" overall. **Features:** Similar to Government Model
military .45.
Price: Mil-Spec Parkerized **$715.00**
Price: Mil-Spec Stainless Steel...**$851.00**

Prices given are believed to be accurate at time of publication however, many factors affect retail pricing so exact prices are not possible.

SPRINGFIELD ARMORY 1911A1 LOADED

Caliber: .45 ACP, 7-shot magazine. **Barrel:** 5". **Sights:** Adjustable low profile rear, dovetail front. **Finish:** Parkerized or stainless. **Features:** Delta hammer and cocobolo grips. Long aluminum match-grade trigger. Comes with two magazines.
Price: Stainless $1,118.00
Price: Parkerized $1,076.00

SPRINGFIELD ARMORY TACTICAL RESPONSE

Caliber: .45 ACP, 7-shot magazine. **Barrel:** 5". **Weight:** 42 oz. **Grips:** Checkered cocobolo wood. **Finish:** Black Armory Kote or stainless. **Features:** Checkered front strap and main-spring housing, fixed combat rear sight and matching dove-tailed front sight, tuned, polished extractor, oversize barrel link, lightweight speed trigger and combat action job, match barrel and bushing, extended ambidextrous thumb safety and fitted beavertail grip safety. Comes with two 7-shot magazines. Frame is engraved "Tactical" both sides of frame with "TRP." Available with accessory rail. TRP-Pro Model meets FBI specifications for SWAT Hostage Rescue Team.
Price: $1,800.00

STOEGER COMPACT COUGAR

Caliber: 9mm, 13+1 round capacity. **Barrel:** 3.6". **Weight:** 32 oz.

Length: 7". **Grips:** Wood or rubber. **Sights:** Quick read 3-dot. **Features:** Double/single action with a matte black finish. The ambidextrous safety and decocking lever is easily accessible to the thumb of a right-handed or left-handed shooter. Based on classic Beretta design. Manufactured in Turkey.
Price: $469.00

STI DUTY ONE SERIES

Caliber: .45 ACP, .40 S&W, 9mm. Available in three frame sizes: Full-size with 5.1" bbl. (Duty One 5), Commander size with 4.4" bbl. (Duty One 4) and Compact size with 3" bbl. (Duty One 3). Features include integral tactical rail and 30 lpi checkered frontstrap; milled tactical rail on the dust cover of the frame; ambidextrous thumb safeties; high rise beavertail grip safety; lowered and flared ejection port; fixed rear sight; front and rear cocking serrations; blue matte finish, fully supported STI International ramped bull barrel.
Price: $1,384.00

STI EAGLE

1911-style semiauto pistol chambered in .45 ACP, .38 Super, .357 SIG, 9mm, .40 S&W. Features include modular steel frame with polymer grip; high capacity double-stack magazines; scalloped slide with front and rear cocking serrations; dovetail front sight and STI adjustable rear sight; stainless steel STI hi-ride grip safety and stainless steel STI ambi-thumb safety; 5- or 6-inch STI stainless steel fully supported, ramped bull barrel or the traditional bushing barrel; blued or stainless finish.
Price: $2,123.00
Price: $2,243.00

Prices given are believed to be accurate at time of publication however, many factors affect retail pricing so exact prices are not possible.

69TH EDITION, 2015 ✦ 425

STI TOTAL ECLIPSE

Compact double-stack 1911-style semiauto pistol chambered in 9x19mm, .40 S&W, and .45 ACP. Magazine capacity is 13 rounds (9mm), 12 (.40), 9 (.45). Features include 3-inch slide with rear cocking serrations, oversized ejection port; 2-dot tritium night sights recessed into the slide; high-capacity polymer grip; single sided blued thumb safety; bobbed, high-rise, blued, knuckle relief beavertail grip safety; 3.2-inch barrel.

Price: **$1,843.00**

STI ESCORT

1911-style similar to STI Eclipse but with single-stack aluminum alloy frame.

Price: **$1,185.00**

TAURUS MODEL 1911

Caliber: .45 ACP, 8+1 capacity, 9mm, 9+1 capacity. **Barrel:** 5". **Weight:** 33 oz. **Length:** 8.5". **Grips:** Checkered black. **Sights:** Heinie straight 8. **Features:** SA. Blue, stainless steel, duotone blue, and blue/gray finish. Standard/picatinny rail, standard frame, alloy frame, and alloy/picatinny rail. Introduced in 2007. Imported from Brazil by Taurus International.

Price: 1911B, Blue **$853.00**
Price: 1911SS, Stainless Steel **$927.00**
Price: 1911 DT, Duotone Blue **$906.00**

TAURUS MODEL PT-22/PT-25

Caliber: .22 LR, 8-shot (PT-22); .25 ACP, 9-shot (PT-25). **Barrel:** 2.75". **Weight:** 12.3 oz. **Length:** 5.25" overall. **Grips:** Smooth rosewood or mother-of-pearl. **Sights:** Fixed. **Features:** Double action. Tip-up barrel for loading, cleaning. Blue, nickel, duo-tone or blue with gold accents. Introduced 1992. Made in U.S.A. by Taurus International.

Price: PT-22B or PT-25B, checkered
    wood grips...**$282.00**

TAURUS PT2011 DT

Caliber: 9mm, .40 S&W. **Magazine capacity:** 9mm (13 rounds), .40 S&W (11 rounds). **Barrel:** 3.2 inches. **Weight:** 24 oz. Features: Single/double-action with trigger safety.

Price: **$589.00**
Price: (stainless)...**$605.00**

TAURUS MODEL 22PLY SMALL POLYMER FRAME

Similar to Taurus Models PT-22 and PT-25 but with lightweight polymer frame. Features include .22 LR (9+1) or .25 ACP (8+1) chambering. 2.33" tip-up barrel, matte black finish, extended magazine with finger lip, manual safety. Overall length is 4.8". Weighs 10.8 oz.

Price: **$276.00**

TAURUS MODEL 24/7

Caliber: 9mm Para., .40 S&W, .45 ACP. **Barrel:** 4". **Weight:** 27.2 oz. **Length:** 7-1/8". **Grips:** "Ribber" rubber-finned overlay on polymer. **Sights:** Adjustable. **Features:** SA/DA; accessory rail, four safeties, blue or stainless finish. One-piece guide rod, flush-fit magazine, flared bushingless barrel, Picatinny accessory rail, manual safety, user changeable sights, loaded chamber indicator, tuned ejector and lowered port, one piece guide rod and flat wound captive spring. Introduced 2003. Long Slide models have 5" barrels, measure 8-1/8" overall, weigh 27.2 oz. Imported from Brazil by Taurus International.

Price: 40BP, .40 S&W, blued, 10+1 or 15+1 ....**$528.00**
Price: 24/7-PRO Standard Series: 4" barrel; stainless,
    duotone or blued finish **$528.00**
Price: 24/7-PRO Compact Series; 3.2" barrel; stainless,
    titanium or blued finish **$544.00**

TAURUS 24/7 G2

Double/single action semiauto pistol chambered in 9mm Parabellum (15+1), .40 S&W (13+1), and .45 ACP (10+1). Features include blued or stainless finish; "Strike Two" capability; new trigger safety; low-profile adjustable rear sights for windage and elevation; ambidextrous magazine release; 4.2-inch barrel; Picatinny rail; polymer frame; polymer grip with metallic inserts and three interchangeable backstraps. Also offered in compact model with shorter grip frame and 3.5-inch barrel.

Price: **$544.00**

Prices given are believed to be accurate at time of publication however, many factors affect retail pricing so exact prices are not possible.

TAURUS MODEL 92

Caliber: 9mm Para., 10- or 17-shot mags. **Barrel:** 5". **Weight:** 34 oz. **Length:** 8.5" overall. **Grips:** Checkered rubber, rosewood, mother-of-pearl. **Sights:** Fixed notch rear. 3-dot sight system. Also offered with micrometer-click adjustable night sights. **Features:** Double action, ambidextrous 3-way hammer drop safety, allows cocked & locked carry. Blue, stainless steel, blue with gold highlights, stainless steel with gold highlights, forged aluminum frame, integral key-lock. .22 LR conversion kit available. Imported from Brazil by Taurus International.
Price: 92B **$638.00**
Price: 92SS **$653.00**

TAURUS MODEL 111 G2

Caliber: 9mm, .40 S&W (140 G2). Magazine capacity 12+1 (9m), 10+1 (.40). **Barrel:** 3.2" **Weight:** 22 oz. **Grips:** Checkered polymer. **Sights:** 3-dot fixed; night sights available. **Features:** Traditional single/double-action, matte stainless or blue steel slide, Picatinny rail, black polymer frame, manual safety, loaded chamber indicator, integral key-lock. From Taurus International.
Price: Blued **$436.00**
Price: Stainless **$450.00**

TAURUS 140 MILLENNIUM PRO
Caliber: .40 S&W, 10-shot mag. **Barrel:** 3.25. **Weight:** 18.7 oz. **Grips:**

Checkered polymer. **Sights:** 3-dot fixed; night sights available.
Features: Double action only; matte stainless or blue steel slide, black polymer frame, manual safety, integral key-lock action. From Taurus International.
Price: 140BP **$436.00**

TAURUS 145 MILLENNIUM PRO

Caliber: .45 ACP, 10-shot mag. **Barrel:** 3.27". **Weight:** 23 oz. **Grips:** Checkered polymer. **Sights:** 3-dot fixed; night sights available.
Features: Double-action only, matte stainless or blue steel slide, black polymer frame, manual safety, integral key-lock. Compact model is 6+1 with a 3.25" barrel, weighs 20.8 oz. From Taurus International.
Price: 145BP, blued **$436.00**
Price: 145SSP, stainless, ... **$450.00**

TAURUS MODEL 709 G2 SLIM

Caliber: 9mm., 7+1-shot magazine. **Barrel:** 3". **Weight:** 19 oz. **Length:** 6" overall. **Grips:** Black. **Sights:** Low profile. **Features:** Single-action only operation.

Price: Matte black **$404.00**
Price: Stainless **$504.00**

TAURUS SLIM 740

Caliber: .40 cal., 6+1-shot magazine. **Barrel:** 3.2". **Weight:** 19 oz. **Length:** 6.24" overall. **Grips:** Polymer Grips. **Features:** Double action with stainless steel finish.

Price: **$504.00**

THOMPSON CUSTOM 1911A1
Caliber: .45 ACP, 7-shot magazine. **Barrel:** 4.3". **Weight:** 34 oz.

Prices given are believed to be accurate at time of publication however, many factors affect retail pricing so exact prices are not possible.

69TH EDITION, 2015 ✛ **427**

Length: 8" overall. **Grips:** Checkered laminate grips with a Thompson bullet logo inlay. **Sights:** Front and rear sights are black with serrations and are dovetailed into the slide. **Features:** Machined from 420 stainless steel, matte finish. Thompson bullet logo on slide. Flared ejection port, angled front and rear serrations on slide, 20-lpi checkered mainspring housing and frontstrap. Adjustable trigger, combat hammer, stainless steel full-length recoil guide rod, extended beavertail grip safety; extended magazine release; checkered slide-stop lever. Made in U.S.A. by Kahr Arms.
Price: 1911TC $813.00

THOMPSON TA5 1927A-1 LIGHTWEIGHT DELUXE
Caliber: .45 ACP, 50-round drum magazine. **Barrel:** 10.5", 1:16 right-hand twist. **Weight:** 94.5 oz. **Length:** 23.3" overall. **Grips:** Walnut, horizontal foregrip. **Sights:** Blade front, open rear adjustable. **Features:** Based on Thompson machine gun design. Introduced 2008. Made in U.S.A. by Kahr Arms.
Price: TA5 (2008)... $1,284.00

TRISTAR 100 /120 SERIES
Caliber: 9mm, .40 S&W (C-100 only). **Magazine capacity:** 15 (9mm), 11 (.40). **Barrel:** 3.7 to 4.7 inches. **Weight:** 26 to 30 oz. **Grips:** Checkered polymer. **Sights:** Fixed. **Finish:** Blue or chrome. **Features:** Alloy or steel frame. Single/double action. A series of pistols based on the CZ-75 design. Imported from Turkey.
Price: .... $459.00 to $499.00

WALTHER P99 AS
Caliber: 9mm, .40 S&W. Offered in two frame sizes, standard and compact. **Magazine capacity:** 15 or 10 rounds (9mm), 10 or 8 rounds (.40). **Barrel:** 3.5 or 4 inches. **Weight:** 21 to 26 oz. **Length:** 6.6 to 7.1 inches. **Grips:** Polymer with interchangeable backstrap inserts. **Sights:** Adjustable rear, blade front with three interchangeable inserts of different heights. **Features:** Double action with trigger safety, decocker, internal striker safety, loaded chamber indicator. Made in Germany.
Price: $629.00

WALTHER PK380
Caliber: .380 ACP (8-shot magazine). **Barrel:** 3.66". **Weight:** 19.4 oz. **Length:** 6.5". **Sights:** Three-dot system, drift adjustable rear. **Features:** Double action with external hammer, ambidextrous mag release and manual safety. Picatinny rail. Black frame with black or nickel slide.
Price: $399.00
Price: Nickel slide $449.00

WALTHER PPK
Caliber: .380 ACP. **Capacity:** 6+1. **Barrel:** 3.3 inches **Weight:** 22 oz. **Length:** 6.1 inches **Grips:** Checkered plastic. **Sights:** Fixed. **Features:** Available in blue or stainless finish. Made in the U.S.A.
Price: $699.00

WALTHER PPK/S
Caliber: .22 LR or .380 ACP. **Capacity:** 10+1 (.22), 7+1 (.380). Made in Germany. **Features:** identical to PPK except for grip length and magazine capacity.
Price: (.380).. $699.00
Price: (.22 blue) $399.00
Price: (.22 stainless).. $429.00

WALTHER PPQ M2
Caliber: 9mm, (15 round magazine), .40 S&W (11). **Barrel:** 4 or 5". **Weight:** 24 oz. **Length:** 7.1, 8.1". **Sights:** Drift adjustable. **Features:** Quick Defense trigger, firing pin block, ambidextrous slide lock and mag release, Picatinny rail. Comes with two extra magazines, two interchangeable frame backstraps and hard case. Navy SD model has threaded 4.6" barrel.
Price: $649.00
Price: Navy SD.. $699.00

Prices given are believed to be accurate at time of publication however, many factors affect retail pricing so exact prices are not possible.

WALTHER PPS
Caliber: 9mm Para., 40 S&W. 6-, 7-, 8-shot magazines for 9mm Para.; 5-, 6-, 7-shot magazines for 40 S&W. **Barrel:** 3.2". **Weight:** 19.4 oz. **Length:** 6.3" overall. **Stocks:** Stippled black polymer. **Sights:** Picatinny-style accessory rail, 3-dot low-profile contoured sight. **Features:** PPS-"Polizeipistole Schmal," or Police Pistol Slim. Measures 1.04 inches wide. Ships with 6- and 7-round magazines. Striker-fired action, flat slide stop lever, alternate backstrap sizes. QuickSafe feature decocks striker assembly when backstrap is removed. Loaded chamber indicator. Introduced 2008.
Price: $629.00

WALTHER PPX
Caliber: 9mm, .40 S&W. **Capacity:** 16 rounds (9mm), 14 rounds (.40). **Barrel:** 4 inches. **Weight:** 27.2 oz. **Length:** 7.3 inches. **Grips:** Textured polymer integral with frame. **Sights:** Fixed. **Finish:** Black or black/stainless two-tone. Threaded barrel is optional.
Price: $449.00
Price: Stainless two-tone.......................................$499.00

WALTHER P22
Caliber: .22 LR. **Barrel:** 3.4, 5". **Weight:** 19.6 oz. (3.4), 20.3 oz. (5). **Length:** 6.26, 7.83". **Sights:** Interchangeable white dot, front, 2-dot adjustable, rear. **Features:** A rimfire version of the Walther P99 pistol, available in nickel slide with black frame, or Desert Camo or Digital Pink Camo frame with black slide.
Price: From $379.00
Price: Nickel slide/black frame, or black slide/camo frame $449.00

WILSON COMBAT ELITE PROFESSIONAL
Caliber: 9mm Para., .38 Super, .40 S&W; .45 ACP. **Barrel:** Compensated 4.1" hand-fit, heavy flanged cone match grade. **Weight:** 36.2 oz. **Length:** 7.7" overall. **Grips:** Cocobolo. **Sights:** Combat Tactical yellow rear tritium inserts, brighter green tritium front insert. **Features:** High-cut front strap, 30-lpi checkering on front strap and flat mainspring housing, High-Ride Beavertail grip safety. Dehorned, ambidextrous thumb safety, extended ejector, skeletonized ultralight hammer, ultralight trigger, Armor-Tuff finish on frame and slide. Introduced 1997. Made in U.S.A. by Wilson Combat. This manufacturer offers more than 100 different 1911 models ranging in price from about $2,800 to $5,000.
Price: From $3,650.00

Prices given are believed to be accurate at time of publication however, many factors affect retail pricing so exact prices are not possible.

69TH EDITION, 2015 ✦ **429**

BAER 1911 ULTIMATE MASTER COMBAT

Caliber: .38 Super, 400 Cor-Bon, .45 ACP (others available), 10-shot magazine. **Barrel:** 5, 6"; Baer NM. **Weight:** 37 oz. **Length:** 8.5" overall. **Grips:** Checkered cocobolo. **Sights:** Baer dovetail front, low-mount Bo-Mar rear with hidden leaf. **Features:** Full-house competition gun. Baer forged NM blued steel frame and double serrated slide; Baer triple port, tapered cone compensator; fitted slide to frame; lowered, flared ejection port; Baer reverse recoil plug; full-length guide rod; recoil buff; beveled magazine well; Baer Commander hammer, sear; Baer extended ambidextrous safety, extended ejector, checkered slide stop, beavertail grip safety with pad, extended magazine release button; Baer speed trigger. Made in U.S.A. by Les Baer Custom, Inc.
Price: .45 ACP Compensated $2,880.00
Price: .38 Super Compensated $3,140.00

BAER 1911 NATIONAL MATCH HARDBALL

Caliber: .45 ACP, 7-shot magazine. **Barrel:** 5". **Weight:** 37 oz. **Length:** 8.5" overall. **Grips:** Checkered walnut. **Sights:** Baer dovetail front with under-cut post, low-mount Bo-Mar rear with hidden leaf. **Features:** Baer NM forged steel frame, double serrated slide and barrel with stainless bushing; slide fitted to frame; Baer match trigger with 4-lb. pull; polished feed ramp, throated barrel; checkered front strap, arched mainspring housing; Baer beveled magazine well; lowered, flared ejection port; tuned extractor; Baer extended ejector, checkered slide stop; recoil buff. Made in U.S.A. by Les Baer Custom, Inc.
Price: $1,960.00

BAER 1911 PPC OPEN CLASS

Designed for NRA Police Pistol Combat matches. **Caliber:** .45 ACP, 9mm. **Barrel:** 6 inches, fitted to frame. **Sights:** Adjustable PPC rear, dovetail front. **Grips:** Checkered cocobola. **Features:** Lowered and flared ejection port, extended ejector, polished feed ramp, throated barrel, front strap checkered at 30 lpi, flat serrated mainspring housing, Commander hammer, front and rear slide serrations. 9mm has supported chamber.
Price: $2,350.00

BAER 1911 BULLSEYE WADCUTTER

Similar to National Match Hardball except designed for wadcutter loads only. Polished feed ramp and barrel throat; Bo-Mar rib on slide; full length recoil rod; Baer speed trigger with 3-1/2-lb. pull; Baer deluxe hammer and sear; Baer beavertail grip safety with pad; flat mainspring housing checkered 20 lpi. Blue finish; checkered walnut grips. Made in U.S.A. by Les Baer Custom, Inc.
Price: From $2,140.00

COLT GOLD CUP TROPHY

Caliber: .45 ACP, 8-shot + 1 magazine. **Barrel:** 5". **Weight:** NA. **Length:** 8.5". **Grips:** Checkered rubber composite with silver-plated medallion. **Sights:** (O5070X) Dovetail front, Champion rear; (O5870CS) Patridge Target Style front, Champion rear. **Features:** Adjustable aluminum trigger, Beavertail grip safety, full length recoil spring and target recoil spring, available in blued finish and stainless steel.
Price: (blued) $1,158.00
Price: (stainless) $1,180.00

COLT SPECIAL COMBAT GOVERNMENT

Caliber: .45 ACP, .38 Super. **Barrel:** 5". **Weight:** 39 oz. **Length:** 8.5". **Grips:** Rosewood w/double diamond checkering pattern. **Sights:** Clark dovetail, front; Bo-Mar adjustable, rear. **Features:** A competition-ready pistol with enhancements such as skeletonized trigger, upswept grip safety, custom tuned action, polished feed ramp. Blue or satin nickel finish. Introduced 2003. Made in U.S.A. by Colt's Mfg. Co.
Price: $2,095.00

COMPETITOR SINGLE-SHOT

Caliber: .22 LR through .50 Action Express, including belted magnums. **Barrel:** 14" standard; 10.5" silhouette; 16" optional. **Weight:** About 59 oz. (14 bbl.). **Length:** 15.12" overall. **Grips:** Ambidextrous; synthetic (standard) or laminated or natural wood. **Sights:** Ramp front, adjustable rear. **Features:** Rotary cannon-type action cocks on opening; cammed ejector; interchangeable barrels, ejectors. Adjustable single stage trigger, sliding thumb safety and trigger safety. Matte blue finish. Introduced 1988. From Competitor Corp., Inc.
Price: 14, standard calibers, synthetic grip $660.00

Prices given are believed to be accurate at time of publication however, many factors affect retail pricing so exact pricing is not possible.

CZ 75 TS CZECHMATE
Caliber: 9mm Luger, 20-shot magazine. **Barrel:** 130mm. **Weight:** 1360 g **Length:** 266 mm overall. **Features:** The handgun is custom-built, therefore the quality of workmanship is fully comparable with race pistols built directly to IPSC shooters wishes. Individual parts and components are excellently match fitted, broke-in and tested. Every handgun is outfitted with a four-port compensator, nut for shooting without a compensator, the slide stop with an extended finger piece, the slide stop without a finger piece, ergonomic grip panels from aluminium with a new type pitting and side mounting provision with the C-More red dot sight. For the shooting without a red dot sight there is included a standard target rear sight of Tactical Sports type, package contains also the front sight.
Price: $3,220.00

CZ 75 TACTICAL SPORTS
Caliber: 9mm Luger and .40 S&W, 17-20-shot magazine capacity. **Barrel:** 114mm. **Weight:** 1270 g **Length:** 225 mm overall. **Features:** semi-automatic handgun with a locked breech. This pistol model is designed for competition shooting in accordance with world IPSC (International Practical Shooting Confederation) rules and regulations. The pistol allow rapid and accurate shooting within a very short time frame.The CZ 75 TS pistol model design stems from the standard CZ 75 model. However, this model feature number of special modifications, which are usually required for competitive handguns: - single-action trigger mechanism (SA) - match trigger made of plastic featuring option for trigger travel adjustments before discharge (using upper screw), and for overtravel (using bottom screw). The adjusting screws are set by the manufacturer - sporting hammer specially adapted for a reduced trigger pull weight - an extended magazine catch - grip panels made of walnut wood - guiding funnel made of plastic for quick inserting of the magazine into pistol's frame. Glossy blue slide, silver polycoat frame. Packaging includes 3 pcs of magazines.
Price: .... $1,152.00 to $1,310.00

CZ 85 COMBAT
Caliber: 9mm Luger, 16-shot magazine. **Barrel:** 114mm. **Weight:** 1000 g **Length:** 206 mm overall. **Features:** The CZ 85 Combat modification was created as an extension to the CZ 85 model in its standard configuration with some additional special elements. The rear sight is adjustable for elevation and windage, and the trigger for overtravel regulation. An extended magazine catch, elimination of the magazine brake and ambidextrous controlling elements directly predispose this model for sport shooting competitions. Characteristic features of all versions A universal handgun for both left-handers and right-handers,. The selective SA/DA firing mechanism, a large capacity double-column magazine, a comfortable grip and balance in either hand lead to good results at instinctive shooting (without aiming). Low trigger pull weight and high accuracy of fire. A long service life and outstanding reliability - even when using various types of cartridges. The slide stays open after the last cartridge has been fired, suitable for COMBAT shooting. The sights are fitted with a three-dot illuminating system for better aiming in poor visibility conditions. The COMBAT version features an adjustable rear sight by means of micrometer screws.
Price: $664.00

DAN WESSON CHAOS
Caliber: 9mm Luger, 21-shot magazine capacity. **Barrel:** 5". **Weight:** 3.20 lbs. **Length:** 8.75" overall. **Features:** A double-stack 9mm designed for three-gun competition.
Price: $3,829.00

DAN WESSON HAVOC
Caliber: 9mm Luger & .38 Super, 21-shot magazine capacity. **Barrel:** 4.25". **Weight:** 2.20 lbs. **Length:** 8" overall. **Features:** The HAVOC is based on an "All Steel" Hi-capacity version of the 1911 frame. It comes ready to dominate Open IPSC/USPSA division. The C-more mounting system offers the lowest possible mounting configuration possible, enabling extremely fast target acquisition. The barrel and compensator arrangement pairs the highest level of accuracy with the most effective compensator available.
Price: $4,299.00

DAN WESSON MAYHEM
Caliber: .40 S&W, 18-shot magazine capacity. **Barrel:** 6". **Weight:** 2.42 lbs. **Length:** 8.75" overall. **Features:** The MAYHEM is based on an "All Steel" Hi-capacity version of the 1911 frame. It comes ready to dominate Limited IPSC/USPSA division or fulfill the needs of anyone looking for a superbly accurate target grade 1911. Taking weight away from where you don't want it and adding it to where you do want it was the first priority in designing this handgun. The 6" bull barrel and the tactical rail add to the static weight "good weight". We wanted a 6" long slide for the added sight radius and the enhanced pointability, but that would add to the "bad weight" so the 6" slide has been lightened to equal the weight of a 5". The result is a 6" long slide that balances and feels like a 5" but shoots like a 6". The combination of the all steel frame with industry leading parts delivers the most well balanced, softest shooting 6" limited gun on the market.
Price: $3,899.00

DAN WESSON TITAN
Caliber: 10mm, 21-shot magazine capacity. **Barrel:** 4.25". **Weight:** 1.62 lbs. **Length:** 8" overall. **Features:** The TITAN is based on an "All Steel" Hi-capacity version of the 1911 frame. Turning the most well known defensive pistol "1911" into a true combat handgun was

Prices given are believed to be accurate at time of publication however, many factors affect retail pricing so exact prices are not possible.

69TH EDITION, 2015 ✦ **431**

no easy task. The rugged HD night sights are moved forward and recessed deep in the slide yielding target accuracy and extreme durability. The Snake Scale serrations' aggressive 25 lpi checkering, and the custom competition G-10 grips ensure controllability even in the harshest of conditions. The combination of the all steel frame, bull barrel, and tactical rail enhance the balance and durability of the most formidable target grade Combat handgun on the market.
Price: **$3,829.00**

EAA WITNESS ELITE GOLD TEAM
Caliber: 9mm Para., 9x21, .38 Super, .40 S&W, .45 ACP. **Barrel:** 5.1". **Weight:** 44 oz. **Length:** 10.5" overall. **Grips:** Checkered walnut, competition-style. **Sights:** Square post front, fully adjustable rear. **Features:** Triple-chamber cone compensator; competition SA trigger; extended safety and magazine release; competition hammer; beveled magazine well; beavertail grip. Hand-fitted major components. Hard chrome finish. Match-grade barrel. From E.A.A. Custom Shop. Introduced 1992. Limited designed for IPSC Limited Class competition. Features include full-length dust-cover frame, funneled magazine well, interchangeable front sights. Stock (2005) designed for IPSC Production Class competition. Match introduced 2006. Made in Italy, imported by European American Armory.
Price: Gold Team **$2,336.00**
Price: Pro Limited, 4.75" barrel........................... **$1,119.00**
Price: Stock, 4.5" barrel, hard-chrome finish.......... **$1,102.00**
Price: Match, 4.75" barrel, two-tone finish **$778.00**

FREEDOM ARMS MODEL 83 .22 FIELD GRADE SILHOUETTE CLASS
Caliber: .22 LR, 5-shot cylinder. **Barrel:** 10". **Weight:** 63 oz. **Length:** 15.5" overall. **Grips:** Black micarta. **Sights:** Removable Patridge front blade; Iron Sight Gun Works silhouette rear, click adjustable for windage and elevation (optional adj. front sight and hood). **Features:** Stainless steel, matte finish, manual sliding-bar safety system; dual firing pins, lightened hammer for fast lock time, pre-set trigger stop. Introduced 1991. Made in U.S.A. by Freedom Arms.
Price: Silhouette Class **$2,376.00**

FREEDOM ARMS MODEL 83 CENTERFIRE SILHOUETTE MODELS
Caliber: 357 Mag., .41 Mag., .44 Mag.; 5-shot cylinder. **Barrel:** 10", 9" (.357 Mag. only). **Weight:** 63 oz. (41 Mag.). **Length:** 15.5", 14.5" (.357 only). **Grips:** Pachmayr Presentation. **Sights:** Iron Sight Gun Works silhouette rear sight, replaceable adjustable front sight blade with hood. **Features:** Stainless steel, matte finish, manual sliding-

bar safety system. Made in U.S.A. by Freedom Arms.
Price: Silhouette Models, from **$2,091.00**

HIGH STANDARD SUPERMATIC TROPHY TARGET
Caliber: .22 LR, 9-shot mag. **Barrel:** 5.5" bull or 7.25" fluted. **Weight:** 44-46 oz. **Length:** 9.5-11.25" overall. **Stock:** Checkered hardwood with thumbrest. **Sights:** Undercut ramp front, frame-mounted micro-click rear adjustable for windage and elevation; drilled and tapped for scope mounting. **Features:** Gold-plated trigger, slide lock, safety-lever and magazine release; stippled front grip and backstrap; adjustable trigger and sear. Barrel weights optional. From High Standard Manufacturing Co., Inc.
Price: 5.5", adjustable sights **$935.00**
Price: 7.25", adjustable sights **$985.00**

HIGH STANDARD VICTOR TARGET
Caliber: .22 LR, 10-shot magazine. **Barrel:** 4.5" or 5.5" polished blue; push-button takedown. **Weight:** 46 oz. **Length:** 9.5" overall. **Stock:** Checkered walnut with thumbrest. **Sights:** Undercut ramp front, micro-click rear adjustable for windage and elevation. Also available with scope mount, rings, no sights. **Features:** Stainless steel frame. Full-length vent rib. Gold-plated trigger, slide lock, safety-lever and magazine release; stippled front grip and backstrap; polished blue slide; adjustable trigger and sear. Comes with barrel weight. From High Standard Manufacturing Co., Inc.
Price: 4.5" or 5.5" barrel, vented sight rib,
  universal scope base **$935.00**

KIMBER SUPER MATCH II
Caliber: .45 ACP, 8-shot magazine. **Barrel:** 5". **Weight:** 38 oz. **Length:**

8.7" overall. **Grips:** Rosewood double diamond. **Sights:** Blade front, Kimber fully adjustable rear. **Features:** Guaranteed to shoot 1" groups at 25 yards. Stainless steel frame, black KimPro slide; two-piece magazine well; premium aluminum match-grade trigger; 30 lpi front strap checkering; stainless match-grade barrel; ambidextrous safety; special Custom Shop markings. Introduced 1999. Made in U.S.A. by Kimber Mfg., Inc.
Price: $2,313.00

KIMBER RIMFIRE TARGET
Caliber: .22 LR, 10-shot magazine. **Barrel:** 5". **Weight:** 23 oz. **Length:** 8.7" overall. **Grips:** Rosewood, Kimber logo, double diamond checkering, or black synthetic double diamond. **Sights:** Blade front, Kimber fully adjustable rear. **Features:** Bumped beavertail grip safety, extended thumb safety, extended magazine release button. Serrated flat top slide with flutes, machined aluminum slide and frame, matte black or satin silver finishes, 30 lines-per-inch checkering on frontstrap and under trigger guard; aluminum trigger, test target, accuracy guarantee. No slide lock-open after firing the last round in the magazine. Introduced 1999. Made in U.S.A. by Kimber Mfg., Inc.
Price: $871.00

RUGER MARK III TARGET
Caliber: .22 LR, 10-shot magazine. **Barrel:** 5.5" to 6-7/8". **Weight:** 41 to 45 oz. **Length:** 9.75" to 11-1/8" overall. **Grips:** Checkered cocobolo/laminate. **Sights:** .125 blade front, micro-click rear, adjustable for windage and elevation, loaded chamber indicator; integral lock, magazine disconnect. Plastic case with lock included.
Price: (bull barrel, blued) $459.00
Price: (bull barrel, stainless) $569.00
Price: Competition (stainless slabside barrel) $659.00

SMITH & WESSON MODEL 41 TARGET
Caliber: .22 LR, 10-shot clip. **Barrel:** 5.5", 7". **Weight:** 41 oz. (5.5" barrel). **Length:** 10.5" overall (5.5" barrel). **Grips:** Checkered walnut with modified thumbrest, usable with either hand. **Sights:** 1/8" Patridge on ramp base; micro-click rear adjustable for windage and elevation. **Features:** 3/8" wide, grooved trigger; adjustable trigger stop drilled and tapped.
Price: .... $1,369.00 to $1,619.00

SMITH & WESSON MODEL 22A
Caliber: .22 LR, 10-shot magazine. **Barrel:** 4", 5.5" bull. **Weight:** 28-39 oz. **Length:** 9.5" overall. **Grips:** Dymondwood with ambidextrous

thumbrests and flared bottom or rubber soft touch with thumbrest. **Sights:** Patridge front, fully adjustable rear. **Features:** Sight bridge with Weaver-style integral optics mount; alloy frame, stainless barrel and slide; blue/black finish. Introduced 1997. The 22S is similar to the Model 22A except has stainless steel frame. Introduced 1997. Made in U.S.A. by Smith & Wesson.
Price: from $339.00
Price: Realtree APG camo finish............................... $369.00

SPRINGFIELD ARMORY TROPHY MATCH
Similar to Springfield Armory's Full Size model, but designed for bullseye and action shooting competition. Available with a Service Model 5 frame with matching slide and barrel in 5" and 6" lengths. Fully adjustable sights, checkered frame front strap, match barrel and bushing. In .45 ACP only. From Springfield Inc.
Price: $1,605.00

STI APEIRO
1911-style semiauto pistol chambered in 9x19, .40 S&W, and .45 ACP. Features include Schuemann "Island" barrel; patented modular steel frame with polymer grip; high capacity double-stack magazine; stainless steel ambidextrous thumb safeties and knuckle relief high-rise beavertail grip safety; unique sabertooth rear cocking serrations; 5-inch fully ramped, fully supported "island" bull barrel, with the sight milled in to allow faster recovery to point of aim; custom engraving on the polished sides of the (blued) stainless steel slide; stainless steel magwell; STI adjustable rear sight and Dawson fiber optic front sight; blued frame.
Price: $2,934.00

STI EAGLE 5.0, 6.0
Caliber: 9mm Para., 9x21, .38 & .40 Super, .40 S&W, 10mm, .45 ACP, 10-shot magazine. **Barrel:** 5", 6" bull. **Weight:** 34.5 oz. **Length:** 8.62" overall. **Grips:** Checkered polymer. **Sights:** STI front, Novak or Heinie rear. **Features:** Standard frames plus 7 others; adjustable match trigger; skeletonized hammer; extended grip safety with locator pad. Introduced 1994. Made in U.S.A. by STI International.
Price: (5.0 Eagle).. $2,123.00
Price: (6.0 Eagle).. $2,243.00

STI EXECUTIVE
Caliber: .40 S&W. **Barrel:** 5" bull. **Weight:** 39 oz. **Length:** 8-5/8".

Prices given are believed to be accurate at time of publication however, many factors affect retail pricing so exact pricing is not possible.

69TH EDITION, 2015 ◆ **433**

Grips: Gray polymer. **Sights:** Dawson fiber optic, front; STI adjustable rear. **Features:** Stainless mag. well, front and rear serrations on slide. Made in U.S.A. by STI.
Price: $2,638.00

STI STEELMASTER
Caliber: 9mm minor, comes with one 126mm magazine. **Barrel:** 4.15". **Weight:** 38.9 oz. **Length:** 9.5" overall. **Features:** Based on the renowned STI race pistol design, the SteelMaster is a shorter and lighter pistol that allows for faster target acquisition with reduced muzzle flip and dip. Designed to shoot factory 9mm (minor) ammo, this gun delivers all the advantages of a full size race pistol in a smaller, lighter, faster reacting, and less violent package. The Steelmaster is built on the patented modular steel frame with polymer grip. It has a 4.15" classic slide which has been flat topped. Slide lightening cuts on the front and rear further reduce weight while "Sabertooth" serrations further enhance the aesthtics of this superior pistol. It also uses the innovative Trubor compensated barrel which has been designed to eliminate misalignment of the barrel and compensator bore or movement of the compensator on the barrel. The shorter Trubor barrel system in the SteelMaster gives an even greater reduction in muzzle flip, and the shorter slide decreases overall slide cycle time allowing the shooter to achieve faster follow up shots. The SteelMaster is mounted with a C-More, 6-minute, red-dot scope with blast shield and thumb rest. Additional enhancements include aluminum magwell, stainless steel ambidextrous safeties, stainless steel high rise grip safety, STI's "Spur" hammer, STI's RecoilMaster guide rod system, and checkered front strap and mainspring housing.
Price: $3,048.00

STI TROJAN
Caliber: 9mm Para., .38 Super, .40 S&W, .45 ACP. **Barrel:** 5", 6". **Weight:** 36 oz. **Length:** 8.5". **Grips:** Rosewood. **Sights:** STI front with STI adjustable rear.
Features: Stippled front strap, flat top slide, one-piece steel guide rod.
Price: (Trojan 5) $1,222.00
Price: (Trojan 6, not available in .38 Super) $1,555.00

STI TRUBOR
Caliber: 9mm 'Major', 9x23, .38 Super - USPSA, IPSC. **Barrel:** 5" with integrated compensator. **Weight:** 41.3 oz. (including scope and mount) **Length:** 10.5" overall. **Features:** Built on the patented modular steel frame with polymer grip, the STI Trubor utilizes the Trubor compensated barrel which is machined from ONE PIECE of 416, Rifle Grade, Stainless Steel. The Trubor is designed to eliminate misalignment of the barrel and compensator bore or movement of the compensator along the barrel threads, giving the shooter a more consistent performance and reduced muzzle flip. True to 1911 tradition, the Trubor has a classic scalloped slide with front and rear cocking serrations on a forged steel slide (blued) with polished sides, aluminum magwell, stainless steel ambidextrous safeties, stainless steel high rise grip safety, full length guide rod, checkered front strap, and checkered mainspring housing. With mountedC-More Railway sight included with the pistol.
Price: $3,048.00

Prices given are believed to be accurate at time of publication however, many factors affect retail pricing so exact prices are not possible.

CHARTER ARMS BULLDOG

Caliber: .44 Special. **Barrel:** 2.5". **Weight:** NA. **Sights:** Blade front, notch rear. **Features:** 6-round cylinder, soft-rubber pancake-style grips, shrouded ejector rod, wide trigger and hammer spur. American made by Charter Arms.
Price: Blued $405.00
Price: Stainless $418.00
Price: Target Bulldog, 4" barrel, 23 oz. $470.00
Price: Heller Commemortaive stainless 2.5 .... $1,595.00

CHARTER ARMS OFF DUTY

Caliber: .38 Spec. **Barrel:** 2". **Weight:** 12.5 oz. **Sights:** Blade front, notch rear. **Features:** 5-round cylinder, aluminum casting, DAO. American made by Charter Arms.
Price: Aluminum $400.00

CHARTER PANTHER BRONZE & BLACK CAMO STANDARD

Caliber: .22 Mag.- 5-round cylinder. **Barrel:** 1-1/8". **Weight:** 6 oz. **Grip:** Compact. **Sights:** Fixed. **Features:** 2-tone bronze & black with aluminum frame. American made by Charter Arms.
Price: $429.00

CHARTER ARMS PINK LADY

Caliber: .32 H&R Magnum, .38 Special +P. **Barrel:** 2". **Weight:** 12 oz. **Grips:** Rubber Pachmayr-style. **Sights:** Fixed. **Features:** Snubnose, five-round cylinder. Pink anodized aluminum alloy frame.
Price: $422.00
Price: Lavender Lady, lavender frame $410.00
Price: Goldfinger, gold anodized frame, matte black barrel and cylinder assembly $410.00

CHARTER ARMS CHIC LADY & CHIC LADY DAO

Caliber: .38 special - 5-round cylinder. **Barrel:** 2". **Weight:** 12 oz. **Grip:** Combat. **Sights:** Fixed. **Features:** 2-tone pink & stainless with aluminum frame. American made by Charter Arms.
Price: Chic Lady $478.00
Price: Chic Lady DAO $478.00

CHARTER COUGAR UNDERCOVER LITE

Caliber: .38 special +P - 5-round cylinder. **Barrel:** 2". **Weight:** 12 oz. **Grip:** Full. **Sights:** Fixed. **Features:** 2-tone pink & stainless with aluminum frame. Constructed of tough aircraft-grade aluminum and steel, the Undercover Lite offers rugged reliability and comfort. This ultra-lightweight 5-shot .38 Special features a 2" barrel, fixed sights and traditional spurred hammer. American made by Charter Arms.
Price: $429.00

CHARTER ARMS PIT BULL

Caliber: .40 S&W, 5-round cylinder. **Barrel:** 21.3". **Weight:** 20 oz. **Sights:** Fixed rear, ramp front. **Grips:** Rubber. **Features:** Matte stainless steel frame. Five-shot cylinder does not require moon clips.
Price: 9mm... $497.00
Price: .40 S&W.. $484.00

CHARTER ARMS SOUTHPAW

Caliber: .38 Special +P. **Barrel:** 2". **Weight:** 12 oz. **Grips:** Rubber Pachmayr-style. **Sights:** NA. **Features:** Snubnose, five-round cylinder, matte black aluminum alloy frame with stainless steel cylinder. Cylinder latch and crane assembly are on right side of frame for convenience to left-hand shooters.
Price: $415.00

CHARTER ARMS CRIMSON UNDERCOVER

Caliber: .38 special +P - 5-round cylinder. **Barrel:** 2". **Weight:** 16 oz. **Grip:** Crimson Trace™. **Sights:** Fixed. **Features:** Stainless finish & frame. American made by Charter Arms.
Price: $572.00

CHARTER ARMS UNDERCOVER

Caliber: .38 Spec. +P. **Barrel:** 2". **Weight:** 12 oz. **Sights:** Blade front, notch rear. **Features:** 6-round cylinder. American made by Charter Arms.
Price: Blued $342.00

Prices given are believed to be accurate at time of publication however, many factors affect retail pricing so exact pricing is not possible.

69TH EDITION, 2015 ⊕ **435**

CHARTER ARMS UNDERCOVER SOUTHPAW

Caliber: .38 Spec. +P. **Barrel:** 2". **Weight:** 12 oz. **Sights:** NA. **Features:** Cylinder release is on the right side and the cylinder opens to the right side. Exposed hammer for both single and double-action firing. 5-round cylinder. American made by Charter Arms.
Price: Aluminum..$428.00
Price: Pink SS $447.00

CHARTER ARMS UNDERCOVER LITE, RED & BLACK STANDARD

Caliber: .38 special +P - 5-round cylinder. **Barrel:** 2". **Weight:** 12 oz. **Grip:** Standard. **Sights:** Fixed. **Features:** 2-tone red & black with aluminum frame. American made by Charter Arms.
Price: $410.00

CHIAPPA RHINO

Caliber: .357 Magnum, 9x21mm, .40 S&W. **Features:** 2-, 4-, 5- or 6-inch barrel; fixed or adjustable sights; visible hammer or hammerless design. Weight 24 to 33 oz. Walnut or synthetic grips with black frame; hexagonal-shaped cylinder. Unique design fires from bottom chamber of cylinder.
Price: .... $819.00 to $989.00

COBRA SHADOW

Caliber: .38 Spec. +P. **Capacity:** 5 rounds. **Barrel:** 1-7/8". **Weight:** 15 oz. Aluminum frame with stainless steel barrel and cylinder. **Length:** 6 3/8". **Grips:** Rosewood, black rubber or Crimson Trace Laser. **Features:** Black anodized, titanium anodized, or custom colors including gold, red, pink and blue.
Price: $369.00
Price: Rosewood grips $434.00
Price: Crimson Trace Laser grips...$625.00

COMANCHE II-A

Caliber: .38 Special, 6 shot. **Barrel:** 3 or 4". **Weight:** 33, 35 oz. **Length:** 8, 8.5" overall. **Grips:** Rubber. **Sights:** Fixed. **Features:** Blued finish, alloy frame. Distributed by SGS Importers.
Price: $236.95

DAN WESSON 715

Caliber: .357 Magnum, 6-shot cylinder. **Barrel:** Six-inch heavy barrel with full lug. **Weight:** 38 oz. **Length:** 8, 8.5" overall. **Grips:** Hogue rubber with finger grooves. **Sights:** Adjustable rear, interchangeable front blade. **Features:** Stainless steel. Interchangeable barrel assembly. Reintroduced in 2014.
Price: $1,168.00

EAA WINDICATOR

Caliber: .38 Spec., 6-shot; .357 Mag., 6-shot. **Barrel:** 2", 4". **Weight:** 30 oz. (4"). **Length:** 8.5" overall (4" bbl.). **Grips:** Rubber with finger grooves. **Sights:** Blade front, fixed rear. **Features:** Swing-out cylinder; hammer block safety; blue or nickel finish. Introduced 1991. Imported from Germany by European American Armory.
Price: .38 Spec. 2" barrel, alloy frame $325.00
Price: .38 Spec. 4" barrel, alloy frame $342.00
Price: .357 Mag, 2" barrel, steel frame $343.00
Price: .357 Mag, 4" barrel, steel frame $360.00
Price: .357 Mag, 2" barrel, steel frame, nickel finish $405.00
Price: .357 Mag, 4" barrel, steel frame, nickel finish $422.00

KORTH USA

Caliber: .22 LR, .22 WMR, .32 S&W Long, .38 Spec., .357 Mag., 9mm Para. **Barrel:** 3", 4", 5.25", 6". **Weight:** 36-52 oz. Grips, Combat, Sport: Walnut, Palisander, Amboinia, Ivory. Grips, Target: German Walnut, matte with oil finish, adjustable ergonomic competition style. **Sights:** Adjustable Patridge (Sport) or Baughman (Combat), interchangeable and adjustable rear w/Patridge front (Target) in blue and matte. **Features:** DA/SA, 3 models, over 50 configurations, externally adjustable trigger stop and weight, interchangeable cylinder, removable wide-milled trigger shoe on Target model. Deluxe models are highly engraved editions. Available finishes include high polish blue finish, plasma coated in high polish or matted silver, gold, blue, or charcoal. Many deluxe options available. 6-shot. From Korth USA.
Price: From $8,000.00
Price: Deluxe Editions, from $12,000.00

ROSSI R461/R462

Caliber: .357 Mag. **Barrel:** 2". **Weight:** 26-35 oz. **Grips:** Rubber. **Sights:** Fixed. **Features:** DA/SA, +P rated frame, blue carbon or high polish stainless steel, patented Taurus Security System, 6-shot.
Price: Blue carbon finish...$391.00
Price: Stainless finish..$455.00

Prices given are believed to be accurate at time of publication however, many factors affect retail pricing so exact prices are not possible.

RUGER GP-100

Caliber: .357 Mag., 6-shot cylinder. **Barrel:** 3" full shroud, 4" full shroud, 6" full shroud. **Weight:** 36 to 45 oz. **Sights:** Fixed; adjustable on 4" and 6" full shroud barrels. **Grips:** Ruger Santoprene Cushioned Grip with Goncalo Alves inserts. **Features:** Uses action, frame features of both the Security-Six and Redhawk revolvers. Full length, short ejector shroud. Satin blue and stainless steel.
Price: Blued $699.00
Price: Satin stainless $759.00

ROSSI MODEL R971/R972

Caliber: 357 Mag. +P, 6-shot. **Barrel:** 4", 6". **Weight:** 32 oz. **Length:** 8.5 or 10.5" overall. **Grips:** Rubber. **Sights:** Blade front, adjustable rear. **Features:** Single/double action. Patented key-lock Taurus Security System; forged steel frame. Introduced 2001. Made in Brazil by Amadeo Rossi. Imported by BrazTech/Taurus.
Price: Model R971 (blued finish,
        4" bbl.) **$455.00**
Price: Model R972 (stainless steel finish, 6" bbl.) **$511.00**

ROSSI MODEL 851

Similar to Model R971/R972, chambered for .38 Spec. +P. Blued finish, 4-inch barrel. Introduced 2001. Made in Brazil by Amadeo Rossi. From BrazTech/Taurus.
Price: $389.00

RUGER GP-100 MATCH CHAMPION

Caliber: .357 Mag., 6-shot cylinder. **Barrel:** 4.2" half shroud, slab sided. **Weight:** 38 oz. **Sights:** Fixed rear, fiber optic front. **Grips:** Hogue Stippled Hardwood. **Features:** Satin stainless steel finish.
Price: Blued $899.00

RUGER LCR
Caliber: .22 LR (8-shot cylinder), .22 WMR, .38 Special and .357 Mag., 5-shot cylinder. **Barrel:** 1-7/8". **Weight:** 13.5 oz. –17.10 oz.

Prices given are believed to be accurate at time of publication however, many factors affect retail pricing so exact prices are not possible.

69TH EDITION, 2015 ✦ **437**

Length: 6-1/2" overall. **Grips:** Hogue® Tamer™ or Crimson Trace® Lasergrips®. **Sights:** Pinned ramp front, U-notch integral rear.
Features: The Ruger Lightweight Compact Revolver (LCR), a 13.5 ounce, small frame revolver with a smooth, easy-to-control trigger and highly manageable recoil. Packed with the latest technological advances and features required by today's most demanding shooters.

Price: .22 LR, .22 WMR, iron sights	$529.00
Price: .38/.357, iron sights	$599.00
Price: .22 LR, Crimson Trace Laser grip	$799.00
Price: .38/.357, Crimson Trace Laser grip	$879.00

RUGER LCRX

This model has the same features as the standard LCR model except the LCRx has visible hammer. Introduced 2014.

Price: .22 LR, .22 WMR, iron sights	$529.00
Price: .38/.357, iron sights	$599.00
Price: .22 LR, Crimson Trace Laser grip	$799.00
Price: .38/.357, Crimson Trace Laser grip	$879.00

RUGER SP-101

Caliber: .22 LR, 6-shot; .38 Spec. +P, .357 Mag., 5-shot. **Barrel:** 2.25", 3-1/16", 4.2". **Weight:** 25 to 30 oz. **Sights:** Adjustable rear/fiber optic front on 4.2" barrel guns, fixed on others. **Grips:** Ruger Cushioned Grip with inserts. **Features:** Compact, small frame, double-action revolver. Full-length ejector shroud. Stainless steel finish only. Available with enclosed hammer on 2.25" barrel model. Introduced 1988.

Price: Fixed sights	$659.00
Price: Adjustable rear, fiber optic front sights	$699.00

RUGER REDHAWK

Caliber: .44 Rem. Mag., .45 Colt, 6-shot. **Barrel:** 4", 5.5", 7.5". **Weight:** About 54 oz. (7.5" bbl.). **Length:** 13" overall (7.5" barrel). **Grips:** Square butt cushioned grip panels. **Sights:** Interchangeable Patridge-type front, rear adjustable for windage and elevation. **Features:** Stainless steel, brushed satin finish, blued ordnance steel. 9.5" sight radius. Introduced 1979.

Price: KRH-44, stainless, 7.5" barrel	$989.00
Price: KRH-44R, stainless 7.5" barrel w/scope mount	$989.00
Price: KRH-445, stainless 5.5" barrel	$989.00
Price: KRH-444, stainless 4" barrel (2007)	$989.00
Price: KRH-45-4, Hogue Monogrip, .45 Colt (2008)	$989.00

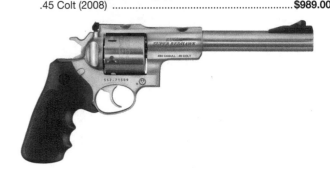

RUGER SUPER REDHAWK

Caliber: .44 Rem. Mag., .454 Casull, 6-shot cylinder. **Barrel:** 2.5" (Alaskan), 7.5" or 9.5". **Weight:** 44 to 58 oz. **Length:** 13" overall

Prices given are believed to be accurate at time of publication however, many factors affect retail pricing so exact prices are not possible.

(7.5" barrel). **Grips:** Hogue Tamer Monogrip. **Features:** Similar to standard Redhawk except has heavy extended frame with Ruger Integral Scope Mounting System on wide topstrap. Wide hammer spur lowered for better scope clearance. Incorporates mechanical design features and improvements of GP-100. Ramp front sight base has Redhawk-style Interchangeable Insert sight blades, adjustable rear sight. Alaskan model has 2.5-inch barrel. Satin stainless steel and low-glare stainless finishes. Introduced 1987.
Price: .44 Magnum $1,049.00
Price: .454 Casull..$1,079.00
Price: .454 Alaskan $1,079.00
Price: .44 Mag. Alaskan..................................$1,079.00

SMITH & WESSON GOVERNOR™
Caliber: .410 Shotshell (2 1/2"), .45 ACP, .45 Colt; 6 rounds. **Barrel:** 2.75". **Length:** 7.5", (2.5" barrel). **Grip:** Synthetic. **Sights:** Front: Dovetailed tritium night sight or black ramp, rear: fixed. **Grips:** Synthetic. **Finish:** Matte Black or matte silver (Silver Edition). **Weight:** 29.6 oz. **Features:** Capable of chambering a mixture of .45 Colt, .45 ACP and .410 gauge 2½-inch shotshells, the Governor is suited for both close and distant encounters, allowing users to customize the load to their preference. Scandium Alloy frame, stainless steel cylinder. Packaged with two full-moon clips and three 2-shot clips.
Price: Silver Edition..$809.00
Price: Matte black with Tritium night sights $869.00
Price: Matte black w/Crimson Trace® Laser Grip $1,119.00

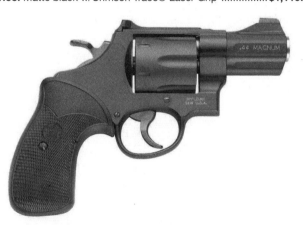

SMITH & WESSON J-FRAME
The smallest S&W wheelguns come in a variety of chamberings, barrel lengths, and materials, as noted in the individual model listings.

SMITH & WESSON 60LS/642LS LADYSMITH
Caliber: .38 Spec. +P, .357 Mag., 5-shot. **Barrel:** 1-7/8" (642LS); 2-1/8" (60LS) **Weight:** 14.5 oz. (642LS); 21.5 oz. (60LS); **Length:** 6.6" overall (60LS). **Grips:** Wood. **Sights:** Black blade, serrated ramp front, fixed notch rear. **Features:** 60LS model has a Chiefs Special-style frame. 642LS has Centennial-style frame, frosted matte finish,

smooth combat wood grips. Introduced 1996. Comes in a fitted carry/storage case. Introduced 1989. Made in U.S.A. by Smith & Wesson.
Price: (642LS) $499.00
Price: (60LS) $759.00

SMITH & WESSON MODEL 63
Caliber: .22 LR, 8-shot. **Barrel:** 5". **Weight:** 26 oz. **Length:** 7.5" overall. **Grips:** Black synthetic. **Sights:** Hi-Viz fiber optic front sight, adjustable black blade rear sight. **Features:** Stainless steel construction throughout. Made in U.S.A. by Smith & Wesson.
Price: $769.00

SMITH & WESSON MODEL 442/637/638/642 AIRWEIGHT
Caliber: .38 Spec. +P, 5-shot. **Barrel:** 1-7/8", 2-1/2". **Weight:** 15 oz. **Length:** 6-3/8" overall. **Grips:** Soft rubber. **Sights:** Fixed, serrated ramp front, square notch rear. **Features:** A family of J-frame .38 Special revolvers with aluminum-alloy frames. Model 637; Chiefs Special-style frame with exposed hammer. Introduced 1996. Models 442, 642; Centennial-style frame, enclosed hammer. Model 638, Bodyguard style, shrouded hammer. Comes in a fitted carry/storage case. Introduced 1989. Made in U.S.A. by Smith & Wesson.
Price: From $469.00

SMITH & WESSON MODELS 637 CT/638 CT/642 CT
Similar to Models 637, 638 and 642 but with Crimson Trace Laser Grips.
Price: $699.00

Prices given are believed to be accurate at time of publication however, many factors affect retail pricing so exact prices are not possible.

69TH EDITION, 2015 ⊕ **439**

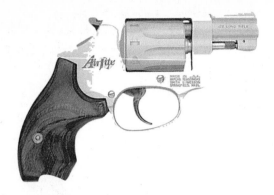

SMITH & WESSON MODEL 317 AIRLITE

Caliber: .22 LR, 8-shot. **Barrel:** 1-7/8". **Weight:** 10.5 oz. **Length:** 6.25" overall (1-7/8" barrel). **Grips:** Rubber. **Sights:** Serrated ramp front, fixed notch rear. **Features:** Aluminum alloy, carbon and stainless steels, Chiefs Special-style frame with exposed hammer. Smooth combat trigger. Clear Cote finish. Model 317 Kit Gun has adjustable rear sight, fiber optic front. Introduced 1997.
Price: $699.00
Price: Kit Gun $759.00

SMITH & WESSON MODEL 340/340PD AIRLITE SC CENTENNIAL

Caliber: .357 Mag., 38 Spec. +P, 5-shot. **Barrel:** 1-7/8". **Weight:** 12 oz. **Length:** 6-3/8" overall (1-7/8" barrel). **Grips:** Rounded butt rubber. **Sights:** Black blade front, rear notch **Features:** Centennial-style frame, enclosed hammer. Internal lock. Matte silver finish. Scandium alloy frame, titanium cylinder, stainless steel barrel liner. Made in U.S.A. by Smith & Wesson.
Price: Model 340 ....$1,019.00

SMITH & WESSON MODEL 351PD

Caliber: .22 Mag., 7-shot. **Barrel:** 1-7/8". **Weight:** 10.6 oz. **Length:** 6.25" overall (1-7/8" barrel). **Sights:** HiViz front sight, rear notch. **Grips:** Wood. **Features:** Seven-shot, aluminum-alloy frame. Chiefs Special-style frame with exposed hammer. Nonreflective matte-black finish. Internal lock. Made in U.S.A. by Smith & Wesson.
Price: $759.00

SMITH & WESSON MODEL 360/360PD AIRLITE CHIEF'S SPECIAL

Caliber: .357 Mag., .38 Spec. +P, 5-shot. **Barrel:** 1-7/8". **Weight:** 12 oz. **Length:** 6-3/8" overall (1-7/8" barrel). **Grips:** Rounded butt

rubber. **Sights:** Black blade front, fixed rear notch. **Features:** Chief's Special-style frame with exposed hammer. Internal lock. Scandium alloy frame, titanium cylinder, stainless steel barrel. Made in U.S.A. by Smith & Wesson.
Price: 360PD $1,019.00

SMITH & WESSON BODYGUARD® 38

Caliber: .38 S&W Special +P; 5 rounds. **Barrel:** 1.9". **Weight:** 14.3 oz. **Length:** 6.6". **Grip:** Synthetic. **Sights:** Front: Black ramp, Rear: fixed, integral with backstrap. Plus: Integrated laser sight. **Grips:** Synthetic. **Finish:** Matte Black. **Features:** The first personal protection series that comes with an integrated laser sight.
Price: $509.00

SMITH & WESSON MODEL 640 CENTENNIAL DA ONLY

Caliber: .357 Mag., .38 Spec. +P, 5-shot. **Barrel:** 2-1/8". **Weight:** 23 oz. **Length:** 6.75" overall. **Grips:** Uncle Mike's Boot grip. **Sights:** Serrated ramp front, fixed notch rear. **Features:** Stainless steel. Fully concealed hammer, snag-proof smooth edges. Internal lock.
Price: $729.00

SMITH & WESSON MODEL 649 BODYGUARD

Caliber: .357 Mag., .38 Spec. +P, 5-shot. **Barrel:** 2-1/8". **Weight:** 23 oz. **Length:** 6-5/8" overall. **Grips:** Uncle Mike's Combat. **Sights:** Black pinned ramp front, fixed notch rear. **Features:** Stainless steel construction, satin finish. Internal lock. Bodyguard style, shrouded hammer. Made in U.S.A. by Smith & Wesson.
Price: $729.00

SMITH & WESSON K-FRAME/L-FRAME

The K-frame series are mid-size revolvers and the L-frames are slightly larger.

SMITH & WESSON MODEL 10 CLASSIC
Caliber: .38 Special, 6-round cylinder. Features include a bright blue steel frame and cylinder, checkered wood grips, 4-inch barrel, and fixed sights. The oldest model in the Smith & Wesson line, its basic design goes back to the original Military & Police Model of 1905.
Price: $739.00

SMITH & WESSON MODEL 17 MASTERPIECE CLASSIC
Caliber: .22 LR. **Capacity:** 6 rounds. **Barrel:** 6 inches. **Weight:** 40 oz. **Grips:** Checkered wood. **Sights:** Pinned Patridge front, Micro Adjustable rear. Updated variation of K-22 Masterpiece of the 1930s.
Price: $989.00

SMITH & WESSON MODEL 48 CLASSIC
Same specifications as Model 17 excet chambered in .22 Magnum (.22 WMR) and is available with a 4 or 6-inch barrel.
Price: .... $949.00 to $989.00

SMITH & WESSON MODEL 64/67
Caliber: .38 Spec. +P, 6-shot. **Barrel:** 3". **Weight:** 33 oz. **Length:** 8-7/8" overall. **Grips:** Soft rubber. **Sights:** Fixed, 1/8 serrated ramp front, square notch rear. Model 67 issimilar to Model 64 except for adjustable sights. **Features:** Satin finished stainless steel, square butt.
Price: From .... $689.00 to $749.00

SMITH & WESSON MODEL 66
Caliber: .357 Magnum. **Capacity:** 6 rounds. **Barrel:** 4.25". **Weight:** 36.6 oz. **Grips:** Synthetic. **Sights:** White outline adjustable rear, red ramp front. **Features:** Return in 2014 of the famous K-frame "Combat Magnum" with stainless finish.
Price: $849.00

SMITH & WESSON MODEL 69
Caliber: ..44 Magnum. **Capacity:** 5 rounds. **Barrel:** 4.25". **Weight:** 37 oz. **Grips:** Checkered wood. **Sights:** White outline adjustable rear, red ramp front. **Features:** L-frame with stainless finish, 5-shot cylinder, introduced in 2014.
Price: $989.00

SMITH & WESSON MODEL 617
Caliber: .22 LR, 10-shot cylinder **Barrel:** 6". **Weight:** 44 oz. **Length:** 11-1/8". **Grips:** Soft rubber. **Sights:** Patridge front, adjustable rear. Drilled and tapped for scope mount. **Features:** Stainless steel with satin finish. Introduced 1990.
Price: From $829.00

SMITH & WESSON MODEL 386 XL HUNTER
Single/double action L-frame revolver chambered in .357 Magnum. Features include 6-inch full-lug barrel, 7-round cylinder, Hi-Viz fiber optic front sight, adjustable rear sight, scandium frame, stainless steel cylinder, black matte finish, synthetic grips.
Price: $1,019.00

SMITH & WESSON MODEL 686/686 PLUS
Caliber: .357 Mag., .38 S&W Special; 6 rounds. **Barrel:** 2.5", 4", 6". **Weight:** 35 oz. (2.5" barrel). **Length:** 7.5", (2.5" barrel). **Grips:** Rubber. **Sights:** White outline adjustable rear, red ramp front. **Features:** Satin stainless frame and cylinder. Plus series guns have 7-shot cylinders. Introduced 1996. Powerport (PP) has Patridge front, adjustable rear sight. Introduced early 1980s. Stock Service Revolver (SSR) intr. 2007. **Capacity:** 6. **Barrel:** 4". **Sights:** Interchangeable front, adjustable rear. **Grips:** Wood. **Finish:** Satin stainless frame and cylinder. **Weight:** 38.3 oz. **Features:** Chamfered charge holes, custom barrel w/recessed crown, bossed mainspring. High-hold ergonomic grip. Made in U.S.A. by Smith & Wesson.
Price: 686 ....$829.00
Price: Plus, 7 rounds $849.00
Price: SSR $999.00

SMITH & WESSON MODEL 686 PLUS PRO SERIES
Single/double-action L-frame revolver chambered in .357 Magnum. Features include 5-inch barrel with tapered underlug, 7-round

cylinder, satin stainless steel frame and cylinder, synthetic grips, interchangeable and adjustable sights.
Price: $1,059.00

SMITH & WESSON MODEL 986 PRO
Single/double-action L-frame revolver chambered in 9mm. Features similar to 686 PLUS Pro Series including 7-round cylinder, 5-inch tapered underlug barrel, satin stainless finish, synthetic grips, adjustable rear and Patridge blade front sight.
Price: $1,149.00

SMITH & WESSON M&P R8
Caliber: .357 Mag., 8-round cylinder. **Barrel:** 5", half lug with accessory rail. **Weight:** 36.3 oz. **Length:** 10.5" **Grips:** Black synthetic. **Sights:** Adjustable v-notch rear, interchangeable front. **Features:** Scandium alloy frame, stainless steel cylinder.
Price: $1,329.00

SMITH & WESSON N-FRAME
These large-frame models introduced the .357, .41 and .44 Magnums to the world.

SMITH & WESSON MODEL 25 CLASSIC
Caliber: .45 Colt. **Capacity:** Six rounds. **Barrel:** 6.5 inches. **Weight:** 45 oz. **Grips:** Checkered wood. **Sights:** Pinned Patridge front, Micro Adjustable rear.
Price: $1,009.00

SMITH & WESSON MODEL 27 CLASSIC
Caliber: .357 Magnum. **Capacity:** Six rounds. **Barrel:** 4 or 6.5 inches. **Weight:** 41.2 oz. **Grips:** Checkered wood. **Sights:** Pinned Patridge front, Micro Adjustable rear. Updated variation of the first magnum revolver, the .357 Magnum of 1935.
Price: (6.5") $1,019.00

SMITH & WESSON MODEL 57 CLASSIC
Caliber: .41 Magnum. Six rounds. **Barrel:** 6 inches. **Weight:** 48 oz. **Grips:** Checkered wood. **Sights:** Pinned red ramp, Micro Adjustable rear.
Price: $1,009.00

SMITH & WESSON MODEL 29 CLASSIC
Caliber: .44 Mag, 6-round. **Barrel:** 6.5". **Weight:** 48.5 oz. **Length:** 12". **Grips:** Altamont service walnut. **Sights:** Adjustable white-outline rear, red ramp front. **Features:** Carbon steel frame, polished-blued or nickel finish. Has integral key lock safety feature to prevent accidental discharges. Alo available with 3" barrel. Original Model 29 made famous by "Dirty Harry" character created in 1971 by Clint Eastwood.
Price: $1,240.00

SMITH & WESSON MODEL 329PD ALASKA BACKPACKER
Caliber: .44 Mag., 6-round. **Barrel:** 2.5". **Weight:** 26 oz. **Length:** 9.5". **Grips:** Synthetic. **Sights:** Adj. rear, HiViz orange-dot front. **Features:** Scandium alloy frame, blue/black finish, stainless steel cylinder.
Price: From $1,159.00

SMITH & WESSON MODEL 625/625JM
Caliber: .45 ACP, 6-shot. **Barrel:** 4", 5". **Weight:** 43 oz. (4" barrel). **Length:** 9-3/8" overall (4" barrel). **Grips:** Soft rubber; wood optional. **Sights:** Patridge front on ramp, S&W micrometer click rear adjustable for windage and elevation. **Features:** Stainless steel construction with .400 semi-target hammer, .312 smooth combat trigger; full lug barrel. Glass beaded finish. Introduced 1989. Jerry Miculek Professional (JM) Series has .265-wide grooved trigger, special wooden Miculek Grip, five full moon clips, gold bead Patridge front sight on interchangeable front sight base, bead blast finish. Unique serial number run. Mountain Gun has 4" tapered barrel, drilled and tapped, Hogue Rubber Monogrip, pinned black ramp front sight, micrometer click-adjustable rear sight, satin stainless frame and barrel, weighs 39.5 oz.
Price: 625JM $1,074.00

SMITH & WESSON MODEL 629
Caliber: .44 Magnum, .44 S&W Special, 6-shot. **Barrel:** 4", 5", 6.5". **Weight:** 41.5 oz. (4" bbl.). **Length:** 9-5/8" overall (4" bbl.). **Grips:** Soft rubber; wood optional. **Sights:** 1/8 red ramp front, white outline rear, internal lock, adjustable for windage and elevation. Classic similar to standard Model 629, except Classic has full-lug 5" barrel, chamfered front of cylinder, interchangeable red ramp front sight with adjustable white outline rear, Hogue grips with S&W monogram, drilled and tapped for scope mounting. Factory accurizing and endurance packages. Introduced 1990. Classic Power Port has Patridge front sight and adjustable rear sight. Model 629CT has 5" barrel, Crimson Trace Hoghunter Lasergrips, 10.5 OAL, 45.5 oz. weight. Introduced 2006.
Price: From $949.00

SMITH & WESSON MODEL 329 XL HUNTER
Similar to Model 386 XL Hunter but built on large N-frame and chambered in .44 Magnum. Other features include 6-round cylinder and 6.5"-barrel.
Price: $1,138.00

SMITH & WESSON X-FRAME
These extra-large X-frame S&W revolvers push the limits of bigbore handgunning.

SMITH & WESSON MODEL 500
Caliber: 500 S&W Mag., 5 rounds. **Barrel:** 4", 6-1/2", 8-3/8". **Weight:** 72.5 oz. **Length:** 15" (8-3/8" barrel). **Grips:** Hogue Sorbothane Rubber. **Sights:** Interchangeable blade, front, adjustable rear. **Features:** Recoil compensator, ball detent cylinder latch, internal lock. 6.5"-barrel model has orange-ramp dovetail Millett front sight, adjustable black rear sight, Hogue Dual Density Monogrip, .312 chrome trigger with over-travel stop, chrome tear-drop hammer, glassbead finish. 10.5"-barrel model has red ramp front sight, adjustable rear sight, .312 chrome trigger with overtravel stop, chrome tear drop hammer with pinned sear, hunting sling. Compensated Hunter has .400 orange ramp dovetail front sight, adjustable black blade rear sight, Hogue Dual Density Monogrip, glassbead finish w/black clear coat. Made in U.S.A. by Smith & Wesson.
Price: From $1,249.00

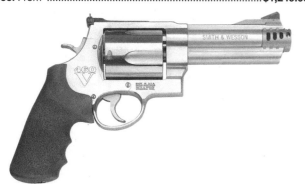

SMITH & WESSON MODEL 460V
Caliber: 460 S&W Mag., 5-shot. Also chambers .454 Casull, .45 Colt. **Barrel:** 7-1/2", 8-3/8" gain-twist rifling. **Weight:** 62.5 oz. **Length:** 11.25". **Grips:** Rubber. **Sights:** Adj. rear, red ramp front. **Features:** Satin stainless steel frame and cylinder, interchangeable compensator. 460XVR (X-treme Velocity Revolver) has black blade front sight with interchangeable green Hi-Viz tubes, adjustable rear sight. 7.5"-barrel version has Lothar-Walther barrel, 360-degree recoil compensator, tuned Performance Center action, pinned sear, integral Weaver base, non-glare surfaces, scope mount accessory kit for mounting full-size scopes, flashed-chromed hammer and trigger, Performance Center gun rug and shoulder sling. Interchangeable Hi-Viz green dot front sight, adjustable black rear sight, Hogue Dual Density Monogrip, matte-black frame and shroud finish with glass-bead cylinder finish, 72 oz. Compensated Hunter has tear drop chrome hammer, .312 chrome trigger, Hogue Dual Density Monogrip, satin/matte stainless finish, HiViz interchangeable front sight, adjustable black rear sight. XVR introduced 2006.
Price: 460V $1,519.00
Price: 460XVR, from $1,519.00

SUPER SIX CLASSIC BISON BULL
Caliber: .45-70 Government, 6-shot. **Barrel:** 10" octagonal with 1:14 twist. **Weight:** 6 lbs. **Length:** 17.5"overall. **Grips:** NA. **Sights:** Ramp front sight with dovetailed blade, click-adjustable rear. **Features:** Manganese bronze frame. Integral scope mount, manual crossbolt safety.
Price: $1,500.00

TAURUS MODEL 17 TRACKER
Caliber: .17 HMR, 7-shot. **Barrel:** 6.5". **Weight:** 45.8 oz. **Grips:** Rubber. **Sights:** Adjustable. **Features:** Double action, matte stainless, integral key-lock.
Price: From $539.00

TAURUS MODEL 44SS
Caliber: .44 Mag., 5-shot. **Barrel:** 4" ported. **Weight:** 34 oz. **Grips:** Rubber. **Sights:** Adjustable. **Features:** Double-action. Integral key-lock. Introduced 1994. Finish: Matte stainless. Imported from Brazil by Taurus International Manufacturing, Inc.
Price: From $693.00

TAURUS MODEL 65
Caliber: .357 Mag., 6-shot. **Barrel:** 4" full underlug. **Weight:** 38 oz. **Length:** 10.5" overall. **Grips:** Soft rubber. **Sights:** Fixed. **Features:** Double action, integral key-lock. Matte blue or stainless. Imported by Taurus International.
Price: Blue $499.00
Price: Stainless $547.00

TAURUS MODEL 66
Similar to Model 65, 4" or 6" barrel, 7-shot cylinder, adjustable rear sight. Integral key-lock action. Imported by Taurus International.
Price: From $555.00

TAURUS MODEL 82 SECURITY
Caliber: .38 Spec., 6-shot. **Barrel:** 4", heavy. **Weight:** 36.5 oz. **Length:** 9-1/4" overall. **Grips:** Soft black rubber. **Sights:** Serrated ramp front, square notch rear. **Features:** Double action, solid rib, integral key-lock. Imported by Taurus International.
Price: From $481.00

TAURUS MODEL 85 FS
Caliber: .38 Spec., 5-shot. **Barrel:** 2". **Weight:** 16.5-21 oz. **Grips:** Rubber. **Sights:** Ramp front, square notch rear. **Features:** Blue, stainless, two-tone. Alloy, aluminum or polymer frame. Rated for +P ammo. Integral keylock. Imported by Taurus International.
Price: From $299.00

TAURUS MODEL 85 VIEW

Caliber: .38 Spec., 5-shot. **Barrel:** 1.41". **Weight:** 9.1 oz. **Grips:** Rubber. **Sights:** Fixed. **Features:** Lexan polycarbon thermoplastic clear sideplate on right side of frame shows inner workings of the revolver's mechanism. Aluminum frame with silver or pink finish. Cylinder and barrel are made of titanium. Small grip is designed for discrete concealed carry. Integral keylock. Inroduced in 2014. Imported by Taurus International.
Price: From $599.00

TAURUS 380 MINI

Caliber: .380 ACP (5-shot cylinder w/moon clip). **Barrel:** 1.75". **Weight:** 15.5 oz. **Length:** 5.95". **Grips:** Rubber. **Sights:** Adjustable rear, fixed front. **Features:** Double-action-only. Available in blued or stainless finish. Five Star (moon) clips included.
Price: Blued $443.00
Price: Stainless $447.00

TAURUS MODEL 94

Caliber: .22 LR, 9-shot cylinder; .22 Mag, 8-shot cylinder. **Barrel:** 2", 4", 5". **Weight:** 18.5-27.5 oz. **Grips:** Soft black rubber. **Sights:** Serrated ramp front, click-adjustable rear. **Features:** Double action, integral key-lock. Introduced 1989. Imported by Taurus International.
Price: From $369.00

TAURUS MODEL 4510 JUDGE SERIES

Caliber: 2-1/2"-.410/.45 LC, 3"-.410/.45 LC. **Barrel:** 3", 6.5" (blued finish). **Weight:** 35.2 oz., 22.4 oz. **Length:** 7.5". **Grips:** Ribber rubber. **Sights:** Fiber Optic. **Features:** DA/SA. Matte Stainless and Ultra-Lite Stainless finish. Introduced in 2007. Imported from Brazil by Taurus International.
Price: Matte Stainless $654.00
Price: Blued $608.00

TAURUS JUDGE PUBLIC DEFENDER POLYMER

Single/double action revolver chambered in .45 Colt/.410 (2-1/2"). Features include 5-round cylinder; polymer frame; Ribber rubber-feel grips; fiber-optic front sight; adjustable rear sight; blued or stainless cylinder; shrouded hammer with cocking spur; blued finish; 2.5-inch barrel. Weight 27 oz.
Price: $515.00

TAURUS JUDGE PUBLIC DEFENDER ULTRA-LITE

Single/double action revolver chambered in .45 Colt/.410 (2-1/2"). Features include 5-round cylinder; lightweight aluminum frame; Ribber rubber-feel grips; fiber-optic front sight; adjustable rear sight; blued or stainless cylinder; shrouded hammer with cocking spur; blued finish; 2.5-inch barrel. Weight 20.7 oz.
Price: $668.00

TAURUS RAGING JUDGE MAGNUM

Single/double-action revolver chambered for .454 Casull, .45 Colt, 2.5-inch and 3-inch .410. Features include 3- or 6-inch barrel; fixed sights with fiber-optic front; blued or stainless steel finish; vent rib for scope mounting (6-inch only); cushioned Raging Bull grips.
Price: $1,038.00

TAURUS MODEL 627 TRACKER

Caliber: .357 Mag., 7-shot. **Barrel:** 4 or 6.5". **Weight:** 28.8, 41 oz. **Grips:** Rubber. **Sights:** Fixed front, adjustable rear. **Features:** Double-action. Stainless steel, Shadow Gray or Total Titanium; vent

Prices given are believed to be accurate at time of publication however, many factors affect retail pricing so exact prices are not possible.

rib (steel models only); integral key-lock action. Imported by Taurus International.
Price: From **$670.00**

TAURUS MODEL 444 ULTRA-LIGHT
Caliber: .44 Mag, 5-shot. **Barrel:** 2.5 or 4". **Weight:** 28.3 oz. **Grips:** Cushioned inset rubber. **Sights:** Fixed red-fiber optic front, adjustable rear. **Features:** UltraLite titanium blue finish, titanium/alloy frame built on Raging Bull design. Smooth trigger shoe, 1.760 wide, 6.280 tall. Barrel rate of twist 1:16, 6 grooves. Introduced 2005. Imported by Taurus International.
Price: **$792.00**

TAURUS MODEL 444/454 RAGING BULL SERIES
Caliber: .44 Mag., .454 Casull. **Barrel:** 2.25, 5, 6.5, 8-3/8". **Weight:** 53-63 oz. **Length:** 12" overall (6.5" barrel). **Grips:** Soft black rubber. **Sights:** Patridge front, adjustable rear. **Features:** Double-action, ventilated rib, integral key-lock. Most models have ported barrels. Introduced 1997. Imported by Taurus International.
Price: .44 Mag. from .... **$752.00 to $840.00**
Price: .454 Casull from .... **$1,012.00 to $1,070.00**

TAURUS MODEL 605 PLY
Caliber: .357 Mag., 5-shot. **Barrel:** 2". **Weight:** 20 oz. **Grips:**

Rubber. **Sights:** Fixed. **Features:** Polymer frame steel cylinder. Blued or stainless. Introduced 1995. Imported by Taurus International.
Price: Blue **$460.00**
Price: Stainless **$507.00**

TAURUS MODEL 608
Caliber: .357 Mag., 38 Spec., 8-shot. **Barrel:** 4, 6.5, 8-3/8". **Weight:** 44-57 oz. **Length:** 9-3/8" overall. **Grips:** Soft black rubber. **Sights:** Adjustable. **Features:** Double-action, integral key-lock action. Available in blue or stainless. Introduced 1995. Imported by Taurus International.
Price: From **$702.00**

TAURUS MODEL 617
Caliber: .357 Mag., 7-shot. **Barrel:** 2". **Weight:** 28.3 oz. **Length:** 6.75" overall. **Grips:** Soft black rubber. **Sights:** Fixed. **Finish:** Stainless steel. **Features:** Integral key-lock. Available with porting, concealed hammer. Introduced 1998. Imported by Taurus International.
Price: **$571.00**

TAURUS MODEL 650 CIA
Caliber: .357 Mag., or .38 Special +P only. 5-shot. **Barrel:** 2". **Weight:** 24.5 oz. **Grips:** Rubber. **Sights:** Ramp front, square notch rear. **Features:** Double-action only, blue finish, integral key-lock, internal hammer. Introduced 2001. From Taurus International.
Price: : .38 Spl. **$474.00**
Price: : .357 Mag. **$513.00**

TAURUS MODEL 817 ULTRA-LITE
Caliber: .38 Spec., 7-shot. **Barrel:** 2". **Weight:** 21 oz. **Length:** 6.5" overall. **Grips:** Soft rubber. **Sights:** Fixed. **Features:** Double-action, integral key-lock. Stainless finish. Rated for +P ammo. Introduced 1999. Imported from Brazil by Taurus International.
Price: From **$555.00**

TAURUS MODEL 941
Caliber: .22 WMR, 8-shot. **Barrel:** 2", 4", 5". **Weight:** 27.5 oz. (4" barrel). **Grips:** Soft black rubber. **Sights:** Serrated ramp front, rear adjustable. **Features:** Double-action, integral key-lock. Blued or stainless finish. Introduced 1992. Imported by Taurus International.
Price: Blue **$465.00**
Price: Stainless **$513.00**

TAURUS MODEL 970 TRACKER
Caliber: .22 LR, 7-shot. **Barrel:** 6". **Weight:** 53.6 oz. **Grips:** Rubber. **Sights:** Adjustable. **Features:** Double barrel, heavy barrel with ventilated rib; matte stainless finish, integral key-lock. Introduced 2001. From Taurus International.
Price: **$472.00**

Prices given are believed to be accurate at time of publication however, many factors affect retail pricing so exact prices are not possible.

CIMARRON 1872 OPEN TOP

Caliber: .38, .44 Special, .44 Colt, .44 Russian, .45 LC, .45 S&W Schofield. **Barrel:** 5.5" and 7.5". **Grips:** Walnut. **Sights:** Blade front, fixed rear. **Features:** Replica of first cartridge-firing revolver. Blue finish; Navy-style brass or steel Army-style frame. Introduced 2001 by Cimarron F.A. Co.

Price: Navy model...$493.00
Price: Army $519.00

CIMARRON 1875 OUTLAW

Caliber: .357, .38 Special, .44 W.C.F., .45 Colt, .45 ACP. **Barrel:** 5-1/2" and 7-1/2". **Weight:** 2.5-2.6 lbs. **Grip:** 1-piece walnut. **Features:** Standard blue finish with color case hardened frame. Replica of 1875 Remington model. Available with dual .45 Colt/.45 ACP cylinder.

Price: $559.00
Price: Dual Cyl. $660.00

CIMARRON MODEL 1890

Caliber: .357, .38 special, .44 W.C.F., .45 Colt, .45 ACP. **Barrel:** 5-1/2". **Weight:** 2.4-2.5 lbs. **Grip:** 1-piece walnut. **Features:** Standard blue finish with standard blue frame. Replica of 1890 Remington model. Available with dual .45 Colt/.45 ACP cylinder.

Price: $576.00
Price: Dual Cyl. $577.00

CIMARRON BISLEY MODEL SINGLE-ACTION

Caliber: .357 Mag., .44 WCF, .44 Spl., .45. Similar to Colt Bisley, special grip frame and triggerguard, knurled wide-spur hammer, curved trigger. Introduced 1999. Imported by Cimarron F.A. Co.

Price: From $615.00

CIMARRON LIGHTNING SA

Caliber: .22 LR, .32-20/32 H&R dual cyl. combo, .38 Special, .41 Colt. **Barrel:** 3.5", 4.75", 5.5". **Grips:** Smooth or checkered walnut. **Sights:** Blade front. **Features:** Replica of the Colt 1877 Lightning DA. Similar to Cimarron Thunderer, except smaller grip frame to fit smaller hands. Standard blue, charcoal blue or nickel finish with forged, old model, or color case-hardened frame. Dual cylinder model available with .32-30/.32 H&R chambering. Introduced 2001. From Cimarron F.A. Co.

Price: .22 LR $502.00
Price: .38 Spl $532.00
Price: .41 Colt...$548.00
Price: .32-30/.32 H&R Dual cylinder $628.00

CIMARRON MAN WITH NO NAME

Caliber: .45 LC. **Barrel:** 4-3/4" and 5-1/2". **Weight:** 2.66-2.76 lbs. **Grip:** 1-piece walnut with silver rattle snake inlay in both sides. **Features:** Standard blue finish with case hardened pre-war frame.

An accurate copy of the gun used by our nameless hero in the classic Western movies "Fist Full Of Dollars" & "For A Few Dollars More".

Price: $774.00

CIMARRON MODEL P SAA

Caliber: .32 WCF, .38 WCF, .357 Mag., .44 WCF, .44 Spec., .45 Colt, and .45 ACP. **Barrel:** 4.75, 5.5, 7.5". **Weight:** 39 oz. **Length:** 10" overall (4.75" barrel). **Grips:** Walnut. **Sights:** Blade front. **Features:** Old model black-powder frame with Bullseye ejector, or New Model frame. Imported by Cimarron F.A. Co.

Price: From $550.00

CIMARRON MODEL .P JR.

Caliber: 32-20, .32 H&R. **Barrel:** 3.5, 4.75, 5.5". **Grips:** Checkered walnut. **Sights:** Blade front. **Features:** Styled after 1873 Colt Peacemaker, except 20 percent smaller. Blue finish with color case-hardened frame; Cowboy action. Introduced 2001. From Cimarron F.A. Co.

Price: $550.00

CIMARRON ROOSTER SHOOTER

Caliber: .357, .45 Colt and .44 W.C.F. **Barrel:** 4-3/4". **Weight:** 2.5 lbs. **Grip:** 1-piece orange finger grooved. **Features:** A replica of John Wayne's Colt Single Action Army model used in many of his great Westerns including his Oscar winning performance in "True Grit", where he brings the colorful character Rooster Cogburn to life.

Price: $909.00

CIMARRON THUNDERER

Caliber: .357 Mag., .44 WCF, .45 Colt, 6-shot. **Barrel:** 3.5", 4.75", with ejector. **Weight:** 38 oz. (3.5" barrel). **Grips:** Smooth or checkered walnut. **Sights:** Blade front, notch rear. **Features:** Thunderer grip. Blue/case hardened or stainless finish. Introduced 1993. Imported by Cimarron F.A. Co.

Price: .... $561.00 to $722.00

Prices given are believed to be accurate at time of publication however, many factors affect retail pricing so exact prices are not possible.

CIMARRON U.S.V. ARTILLERY MODEL SINGLE-ACTION
Caliber: .45 Colt. **Barrel:** 5.5". **Weight:** 39 oz. **Length:** 11.5" overall.
Grips: Walnut. **Sights:** Fixed. **Features:** U.S. markings and cartouche, case-hardened frame and hammer. Imported by Cimarron F.A. Co.
Price: Blue finish $594.00
Price: Original finish $701.00

COLT NEW FRONTIER
Caliber: .44 Special and .45 Colt. **Barrel:** 4-3/4", 5-1/2",and 7-1/2".
Grip: Walnut. **Features:** The legend of Colt continues in the New Frontier®, Single Action Army. From 1890 to 1898, Colt manufactured a variation of the venerable Single Action Army with a uniquely different profile. The "Flattop Target Model" was fitted with an adjustable leaf rear sight and blade front sights. Colt has taken this concept several steps further to bring shooters a reintroduction of a Colt classic. The New Frontier has that sleek flattop design with an adjustable rear sight for windage and elevation and a target ready ramp style front sight. The guns are meticulously finished in Colt Royal Blue on both the barrel and cylinder, with a case-colored frame.
Price: $1,455.00

COLT SINGLE-ACTION ARMY
Caliber: .357 Mag., .45 Colt, 6-shot. **Barrel:** 4.75", 5.5", 7.5".
Weight: 40 oz. (4.75" barrel). **Length:** 10.25" overall (4.75" barrel).
Grips: Black Eagle composite. **Sights:** Blade front, notch rear.
Features: Available in full nickel finish with nickel grip medallions, or Royal Blue with color case-hardened frame. Reintroduced 1992. Sheriff's Model and Frontier Six introduced 2008, available in nickel in 2010.
Price: Blue $1,349.00
Price: Stainless $1,551.00

EAA BOUNTY HUNTER SA
Caliber: .22 LR/.22 WMR, .357 Mag., .44 Mag., .45 Colt, 6-shot.
10-shot cylinder available for .22LR/.22WMR. **Barrel:** 4.5", 7.5".
Weight: 2.5 lbs. **Length:** 11" overall (4-5/8" barrel). **Grips:** Smooth walnut. **Sights:** Blade front, grooved topstrap rear. **Features:** Transfer bar safety; 3-position hammer; hammer-forged barrel. Introduced 1992. Imported by European American Armory
Price: Centerfire, blue or case-hardened..................$478.00
Price: Centerfire, nickel $515.00
Price: .22 LR/.22 WMR, blue $343.00
Price: .22LR/.22WMR, nickel $380.00
Price: .22 LR/.22WMR, 10-round cylinder $485.00

EMF MODEL 1873 FRONTIER MARSHAL
Caliber: .357 Mag., .45 Colt. **Barrel:** 4.75", 5.5", 7.5". **Weight:** 39 oz. **Length:** 10.5" overall. **Grips:** One-piece walnut. **Sights:** Blade front, notch rear. **Features:** Bright brass triggerguard and backstrap, color case-hardened frame, blued barrel and cylinder. Introduced 1998. Imported from Italy.
Price: $485.00

EMF HARTFORD SINGLE-ACTION
Caliber: .357 Mag., 32-20, .38-40, .44-40, .44 Spec., .45 Colt. **Barrel:** 4.75", 5.5", 7.5". **Weight:** 45 oz. **Length:** 13" overall (7.5" barrel). **Grips:** Smooth walnut. **Sights:** Blade front, fixed rear. **Features:** : Identical to the original Colts. All major parts serial numbered using original Colt-style lettering, numbering. Bullseye ejector head and color case-hardening on old model frame and hammer. Introduced 1990. Imported by E.M.F. Co.
Price: Old Model $489.90
Price: Case-hardened New Model frame $489.90

EMF GREAT WESTERN II EXPRESS SINGLE-ACTION
Same as the regular model except uses grip of the Colt Lightning revolver. Barrel lengths of 4.75". Introduced 2006. Imported by E.M.F. Co.
Price: Stainless, Ultra Ivory grips $715.00
Price: Walnut grips $690.00

EMF 1875 OUTLAW
Caliber: .357 Mag., .44-40, .45 Colt. **Barrel:** 7.5", 9.5". **Weight:** 46 oz. **Length:** 13.5" overall. **Grips:** Smooth walnut. **Sights:** Blade front, fixed groove rear. **Features:** Authentic copy of 1875 Remington with firing pin in hammer; color case-hardened frame, blue cylinder, barrel, steel backstrap and triggerguard. Also available in nickel, factory engraved. Imported by E.M.F. Co.
Price: All calibers $520.00

Prices given are believed to be accurate at time of publication however, many factors affect retail pricing so exact prices are not possible.

69TH EDITION, 2015 ✦ **447**

HANDGUNS Single-Action Revolvers

EMF 1873 GREAT WESTERN II
Caliber: .357, .45 Colt, .44/40. **Barrel:** 3.5, 4.75, 5.5, 7.5". **Weight:** 36 oz. **Length:** 11" (5.5" barrel). **Grips:** Walnut. **Sights:** Blade front, notch rear. **Features:** Authentic reproduction of the original 2nd Generation Colt single-action revolver. Standard and bone case hardening. Coil hammer spring. Hammer-forged barrel.
Price: 1873 Californian $530.00
Price: 1873 Paladin $560.00
Price: 1873 Stainless steel, ivory-like grips $720.00
Price: 1873 Stainless steel, checkered walnut grips $660.00

FREEDOM ARMS MODEL 83 PREMIER GRADE
Caliber: .357 Mag., 41 Mag., .44 Mag., .454 Casull, .475 Linebaugh, .500 Wyo. Exp., 5-shot. **Barrel:** 4.75", 6", 7.5", 9" (.357 Mag. only), 10" (except .357 Mag. and 500 Wyo. Exp.) **Weight:** 53 oz. (7.5" bbl. in .454 Casull). **Length:** 13" (7.5" bbl.). **Grips:** Impregnated hardwood. **Sights:** Adjustable rear with replaceable front sight. Fixed rear notch and front blade. **Features:** Stainless steel construction with brushed finish; manual sliding safety bar. Micarta grips optional. 500 Wyo. Exp. Introduced 2006. Lifetime warranty. Made in U.S.A. by Freedom Arms, Inc.
Price: From $2,370.00

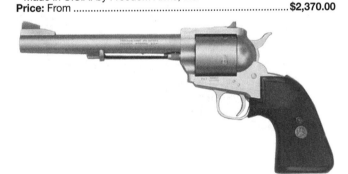

FREEDOM ARMS MODEL 83 FIELD GRADE
Caliber: .22 LR, .357 Mag., .41 Mag., .44 Mag., .454 Casull, .475 Linebaugh, .500 Wyo. Exp., 5-shot. **Barrel:** 4.75", 6", 7.5", 9" (.357 Mag. only), 10" (except .357 Mag. and .500 Wyo. Exp.) **Weight:** 56 oz. (7.5" bbl. in .454 Casull). **Length:** 13.1" (7.5" bbl.). **Grips:** Pachmayr standard, impregnated hardwood or Micarta optional. **Sights:** Adjustable rear with replaceable front sight. Model 83 frame. All stainless steel. Introduced 1988. Made in U.S.A. by Freedom Arms Inc.
Price: From $1,985.00

FREEDOM ARMS MODEL 97 PREMIER GRADE
Caliber: .17 HMR, .22 LR, .32 H&R, .357 Mag., 6-shot; .41 Mag., .44 Special, .45 Colt, 5-shot. **Barrel:** 4.25", 5.5", 7.5", 10" (.17 HMR, .22 LR, .32 H&R). **Weight:** 40 oz. (5.5" .357 Mag.). **Length:** 10.75" (5.5" bbl.). **Grips:** Impregnated hardwood; Micarta optional. **Sights:** Adjustable rear, replaceable blade front. Fixed rear notch and front blade. **Features:** Stainless steel construction, brushed finish, automatic transfer bar safety system. Introduced in 1997. Lifetime warranty. Made in U.S.A. by Freedom Arms.
Price: From $1,995.00

HERITAGE ROUGH RIDER
Caliber: .17 HMR, .17 LR, .32 H&R, .32 S&W, .32 S&W Long, .357 Mag., .44-40, .45 LC, .22 LR, .22 LR/.22 WMR combo, 6-shot. **Barrel:** 2.75, 3.5, 4.75, 5.5, 6.5, 7.5, 9". **Weight:** 31 to 38 oz. **Length:** NA. **Grips:** Exotic cocobolo laminated wood or mother-of-pearl; bird's-head models offered. **Sights:** Blade front, fixed rear. Adjustable sight on 4.75", 6.5" and 9" models. **Features:** Hammer block safety. Transfer bar with Big Bores. High polish blue, black satin, silver satin, case-hardened and stainless finish. Introduced 1993. Made in U.S.A. by Heritage Mfg., Inc.
Price: From $240.00

LEGACY SPORTS PUMA M-1873
Caliber: .22 LR / .22 Mag. **Barrel:** 4.75", 5.5" and 7.5". **Weight:** 2.2 lbs. - 2.4 lbs. **Grips:** Wood or plastic. **Features:** With the frame size and weight of a Single Action Army revolver, the M-1873 makes a great practice gun for Cowboy Action or an ideal carry gun for camping, hiking or fishing. The M-1873 loads from a side gate and at the half cock position just like a centerfire "Peacemaker", but is chambered for .22 LR or .22 magnum rounds. The hammer is made

Prices given are believed to be accurate at time of publication however, many factors affect retail pricing so exact prices are not possible.

to traditional SAA appearance and feel. A key-operated, hammer block safety is standard on the left side of the recoil shield. The M-1873 is offered in matte black or antiqued finish. Construction is of alloy and steel.

Price: .... **$189.00 to $340.00**

MAGNUM RESEARCH BFR SINGLE ACTION

Caliber: .44 Magnum, .444 Marlin, .45/70, .45 Colt/.410, .450 Marlin, .454 Casull, .460 S&W Magnum, .480 Ruger/.475 Linebaugh, .500 S&W, .30/30 Winchester. **Barrel:** 6.5", 7.5" and 10". **Weight:** 3.6 lbs. - 5.3 lbs. **Grips:** Black rubber. **Sights:** Rear sights are the same configuration as the Ruger revolvers. Many aftermarket rear sights will fit the BFR. Front sights are machined by Magnum in four heights and anodized flat black. The four heights accommodate all shooting styles, barrel lengths and calibers. All sights are interchangeable with each BFR's. **Features:** Crafted in the U.S.A., the BFR single action 5-shot stainless steel revolver frames are CNC machined inside and out from a "pre-heat treated" investment casting. This is done to prevent warping and dimensional changes or shifting that occurs during the heat treat process. Magnum Research designed the frame with large calibers and large recoil in mind, built to close tolerances to handle the pressure of true big-bore calibers. The BFR is equipped with a transfer bar safety feature that allows the gun to be carried safely with all five chambers loaded.

Price: **$1,050.00**

NORTH AMERICAN ARMS MINI

Caliber: .22 Short, 22 LR, 22 WMR, 5-shot. **Barrel:** 1-1/8", 1-5/8". **Weight:** 4 to 6.6 oz. **Length:** 3-5/8" to 6-1/8" overall. **Grips:** Laminated wood. **Sights:** Blade front, notch fixed rear. **Features:** All stainless steel construction. Polished satin and matte finish. Engraved models available. From North American Arms.

Price: .22 Short, .22 LR **$209.00**
Price: .22 WMR **$219.00**

NORTH AMERICAN ARMS MINI-MASTER

Caliber: .22 LR, .22 WMR, 5-shot cylinder. **Barrel:** 4" **Weight:** 10.7

oz. **Length:** 7.75" overall. **Grips:** Checkered hard black rubber. **Sights:** Blade front, white outline rear adjustable for elevation, or fixed. **Features:** Heavy vented barrel; full-size grips. Non-fluted cylinder. Introduced 1989.

Price: .... **$284.00 to $349.00**

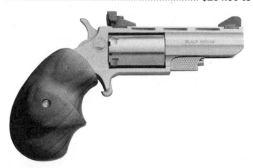

NORTH AMERICAN ARMS BLACK WIDOW

Similar to Mini-Master, 2" heavy vent barrel. Built on .22 WMR frame. Non-fluted cylinder, black rubber grips. Available with Millett Low Profile fixed sights or Millett sight adjustable for elevation only. Overall length 5-7/8", weighs 8.8 oz. From North American Arms.
Price: Adjustable sight, .22 LR or .22 WMR **$309.00**
Price: Fixed sight, .22 LR or .22 WMR **$274.00**

NORTH AMERICAN ARMS "THE EARL" SINGLE-ACTION

Caliber: .22 Magnum with .22 LR accessory cylinder, 5-shot cylinder. **Barrel:** 4" octagonal. **Weight:** 6.8 oz. **Length:** 7-3/4" overall. **Grips:** Wood. **Sights:** Barleycorn front and fixed notch rear. **Features:** Single-action mini-revolver patterned after 1858-style Remington percussion revolver. Includes a spur trigger and a faux loading lever that serves as cylinder pin release.
Price: ....**$289.00** (.22 Magnum only); **$324.00** (convertible)

RUGER NEW MODEL SINGLE SIX SERIES

Caliber: .22 LR, .17 HMR. **Capacity:** Six rounds. Convertible and Hunter models come with extra cylinder for .22 WMR. **Barrel:** 4.62, 5.5, 6.5 or 9.5 inches. **Weight:** 35 to 42 ounces. **Grips:** Black checkered hard rubber, black laminate or hardwood (stainless model only). Single-Six .17 Model available only with 6.5-inch barrel, blue finish, rubber grips. Hunter Model available only with 7.5-inch barrel, black laminate grips.
Price: (stainless) .... **$569.00 to $639.00**
Price: (Hunter) **$799.00**

RUGER SINGLE-TEN AND RUGER SINGLE-NINE SERIES

Caliber: .22 LR, .22 WMR. **Capacity:** 10 (.22 LR Single-Ten), 9 (.22 Mag Single-Nine). **Barrel:** 5.5 inches (Single-Ten), 6.5 inches (Single-Nine). **Weight:** 38 to 39 ounces. **Grips:** Hardwood Gunfighter. **Sights:** Williams Adjustable Fiber Optic.
Price: **$639.00**

RUGER NEW MODEL BLACKHAWK

Caliber: .30 Carbine, .357 Mag./.38 Spec., .41 Mag., .44 Special, .45 Colt, 6-shot. **Barrel:** 4-5/8", 5.5", 6.5", 7.5" (.30 carbine and .45 Colt). **Weight:** 36 to 45 oz. **Lengths:** 10-3/8" to 13.5" **Grips:** Rosewood or black checkered. **Sights:** 1/8 ramp front, micro-click rear adjustable for windage and elevation. **Features:** Rosewood grips, Ruger transfer bar safety system, independent firing pin, hardened chrome-moly steel frame, music wire springs through-out. Case and lock included. Convertibles come with extra cylinder.
Price: **$609.00**

Prices given are believed to be accurate at time of publication however, many factors affect retail pricing so exact prices are not possible.

69TH EDITION, 2015 ✦ **449**

Price: (Convertible, .357/9mm) $679.00
Price: (Convertible, .45 Colt/.45 ACP) $679.00
Price: (Stainless, .357 only)................................$729.00
Price: (Flattop frame, .44 Spl. only) $609.00

RUGER BISLEY SINGLE-ACTION

Similar to standard Blackhawk, hammer is lower with smoothly curved, deeply checkered wide spur. The trigger is strongly curved with wide smooth surface. Longer grip frame. Adjustable rear sight, ramp-style front. Unfluted cylinder and roll engraving, adjustable sights. Chambered for .44 Mag. and .45 Colt; 7.5" barrel; overall length 13.5"; weighs 48-51 oz. Plastic lockable case. Orig. fluted cylinder introduced 1985; discontinued 1991. Unfluted cylinder introduced 1986.
Price: RB-44W (.44 Mag.), RB45W (.45 Colt) **$799.00**

RUGER NEW MODEL SUPER BLACKHAWK

Caliber: .44 Mag., 6-shot. **Barrel:** 4-5/8", 5.5", 7.5", 10.5" bull. **Weight:** 45-55 oz. **Length:** 10.5" to 16.5" overall. **Grips:** Rosewood. **Sights:** 1/8 ramp front, micro-click rear adjustable for windage and elevation. **Features:** Ruger transfer bar safety system, fluted or unfluted cylinder, steel grip and cylinder frame, round or square back trigger guard, wide serrated trigger, wide spur hammer. With case and lock.
Price: **$739.00**

RUGER NEW MODEL SUPER BLACKHAWK HUNTER

Caliber: .44 Mag., 6-shot. **Barrel:** 7.5", full-length solid rib, unfluted

cylinder. **Weight:** 52 oz. **Length:** 13-5/8" **Grips:** Black laminated wood. **Sights:** Adjustable rear, replaceable front blade. **Features:** Reintroduced Ultimate SA revolver. Includes instruction manual, high-impact case, set 1 medium scope rings, gun lock, ejector rod as standard. Bisley-style frame available.
Price: (Hunter, Bisley Hunter) **$859.00**

RUGER NEW VAQUERO SINGLE-ACTION

Caliber: .357 Mag., .45 Colt, 6-shot. **Barrel:** 4-5/8", 5.5", 7.5". **Weight:** 39-45 oz. **Length:** 10.5" overall (4-5/8" barrel). **Grips:** Rubber with Ruger medallion. **Sights:** Fixed blade front, fixed notch rear. **Features:** Transfer bar safety system and loading gate interlock. Blued model color case-hardened finish on frame, rest polished and blued. Engraved model available. Gloss stainless. Introduced 2005.
Price: **$739.00**

RUGER NEW MODEL BISLEY VAQUERO

Similar to New Vaquero but with Bisley-style hammer and grip frame. Chambered in .357 and .45 Colt. Features include a 5.5" barrel, simulated ivory grips, fixed sights, six-shot cylinder. Overall length is 11.12", weighs 45 oz.
Price: **$809.00**

RUGER NEW BEARCAT SINGLE-ACTION

Caliber: .22 LR, 6-shot. **Barrel:** 4" **Weight:** 24 oz. **Length:** 9" overall. **Grips:** Smooth rosewood with Ruger medallion. **Sights:** Blade front, fixed notch rear. **Features:** Reintroduction of the Ruger Bearcat with slightly lengthened frame, Ruger transfer bar safety system. Available in blue only. Rosewood grips. Introduced 1996 (blued), 2003 (stainless). With case and lock.
Price: SBC-4, blued **$569.00**
Price: KSBC-4, satin stainless **$619.00**

UBERTI 1851-1860 CONVERSION

Caliber: .38 Spec., .45 Colt, 6-shot engraved cylinder. **Barrel:** 4.75, 5.5, 7.5, 8" **Weight:** 2.6 lbs. (5.5" bbl.). **Length:** 13" overall (5.5" bbl.). **Grips:** Walnut. **Features:** Brass backstrap, triggerguard; color case-hardened frame, blued barrel, cylinder. Introduced 2007. Imported from Italy by Stoeger Industries.
Price: 1851 Navy **$549.00**
Price: 1860 Army **$579.00**

Prices given are believed to be accurate at time of publication however, many factors affect retail pricing so exact prices are not possible.

HANDGUNS Single-Action Revolvers

UBERTI 1871-1872 OPEN TOP
Caliber: .38 Spec., .45 Colt, 6-shot engraved cylinder. **Barrel:** 4.75, 5.5, 7.5". **Weight:** 2.6 lbs. (5.5" bbl.). **Length:** 13" overall (5.5" bbl.). **Grips:** Walnut. **Features:** Blued backstrap, triggerguard; color case-hardened frame, blued barrel, cylinder. Introduced 2007. Imported from Italy by Stoeger Industries.
Price: .... **$532.00 to $552.00**

UBERTI 1873 CATTLEMAN SINGLE-ACTION
Caliber: .45 Colt; 6-shot fluted cylinder. **Barrel:** 4.75, 5.5, 7.5". **Weight:** 2.3 lbs. (5.5" bbl.). **Length:** 11" overall (5.5" bbl.). **Grips:** Styles: Frisco (pearl styled); Desperado (buffalo horn styled); Chisholm (checkered walnut); Gunfighter (black checkered), Cody (ivory styled), one-piece walnut. **Sights:** Blade front, groove rear. **Features:** Steel or brass backstrap, triggerguard; color case-hardened frame, blued barrel, cylinder. NM designates New Model plunger style frame; OM designates Old Model screw cylinder pin retainer. Imported from Italy by Stoeger Industries.
Price: 1873 Cattleman Frisco **$809.00**
Price: 1873 Cattleman Desperado (2006) **$819.00**
Price: 1873 Cattleman Chisholm (2006) **$549.00**
Price: 1873 Cattleman NM, blued 4.75" barrel **$619.00**
Price: 1873 Cattleman NM, Nickel finish, 7.5" barrel ..**$819.00**
Price: 1873 Cattleman Cody.................................**$819.00**

UBERTI 1873 CATTLEMAN BIRD'S HEAD SINGLE ACTION
Caliber: .357 Mag., .45 Colt; 6-shot fluted cylinder. **Barrel:** 3.5, 4,

4.75, 5.5". **Weight:** 2.3 lbs. (5.5" bbl.). **Length:** 10.9" overall (5.5" bbl.). **Grips:** One-piece walnut. **Sights:** Blade front, groove rear. **Features:** Steel or brass backstrap, triggerguard; color case-hardened frame, blued barrel, cylinder. Imported from Italy by Stoeger Industries.
Price: **$569.00**

UBERTI CATTLEMAN .22
Caliber: .22 LR. **Capacity:** 6 or 12 rounds. **Barrel:** 5.5 inches **Grips:** One-piece walnut. **Sights:** Fixed. **Features:** Blued and case hardened finish, steel or brass backstrap/triggerguard.
Price: (brass backstrap, triggerguard) **$509.00**
Price: (steel backstrap, triggerguard)........................**$529.00**
Price: (12-shot model, steel backstrap, triggerguard) **$559.00**

UBERTI 1873 BISLEY SINGLE-ACTION
Caliber: .357 Mag., .45 Colt (Bisley); .22 LR and .38 Spec. (Stallion), both with 6-shot fluted cylinder. **Barrel:** 4.75, 5.5, 7.5". **Weight:** 2 to 2.5 lbs. **Length:** 12.7" overall (7.5" barrel). **Grips:** Two-piece walnut. **Sights:** Blade front, notch rear. **Features:** Replica of Colt's Bisley Model. Polished blue finish, color case-hardened frame. Introduced 1997. Imported by Stoeger Industries.
Price: 1873 Bisley, 7.5" barrel **$599.00**

UBERTI 1873 BUNTLINE AND REVOLVER CARBINE SINGLE-ACTION
Caliber: .357 Mag., .44-40, .45 Colt; 6-shot fluted cylinder **Barrel:** 18" **Length:** 22.9 to 34" **Grips:** Walnut pistol grip or rifle stock. **Sights:** Fixed or adjustable. **Features:** Imported from Italy by Stoeger Industries.
Price: 1873 Revolver Carbine, 18" barrel, 34" OAL **$729.00**
Price: 1873 Catttleman Buntline Target, 18" barrel, 22.9" OAL **$639.00**

UBERTI OUTLAW, FRONTIER, AND POLICE
Caliber: .45 Colt, 6-shot fluted cylinder. **Barrel:** 5.5", 7.5". **Weight:** 2.5 to 2.8 lbs. **Length:** 10.8" to 13.6" overall. **Grips:** Two-piece smooth walnut. **Sights:** Blade front, notch rear. **Features:** Cartridge version of 1858 Remington percussion revolver. Nickel and blued finishes. Imported by Stoeger Industries.
Price: 1875 Outlaw, nickel finish **$629.00**
Price: 1875 Frontier, blued finish **$539.00**
Price: 1890 Police, blued finish **$549.00**

UBERTI 1870 SCHOFIELD-STYLE TOP BREAK
Caliber: .38, .44 Russian, .44-40, .45 Colt, 6-shot cylinder. **Barrel:** 3.5, 5, 7". **Weight:** 2.4 lbs. (5" barrel) **Length:** 10.8" overall (5" barrel). **Grips:** Two-piece smooth walnut or pearl. **Sights:** Blade front, notch rear. **Features:** Replica of Smith & Wesson Model 3 Schofield. Single-action, top break with automatic ejection. Polished blue finish (first model). Introduced 1994. Imported by Stoeger Industries.
Price: No. 3-2nd Model, nickel finish **$1,369.00**

Prices given are believed to be accurate at time of publication however, many factors affect retail pricing so exact prices are not possible.

69TH EDITION, 2015 ✦ 451

AMERICAN DERRINGER MODEL 1
Caliber: All popular handgun calibers plus .45 Colt/.410 Shotshell. **Capacity:** Two rounds, (.45-70 model is single shot). **Barrel:** 3 inches. **Overall length:** 4.82 inches. **Weight:** 15 oz. **Features:** Manually operated hammer-block safety automatically disengages when hammer is cocked.
Price: .... $600.00 to $800.00

AMERICAN DERRINGER MODEL 8
Caliber: .45 Colt/.410 shotshell. **Capacity:** Two rounds. **Barrel:** 8 inches. **Weight:** 24 oz.
Price: $915.00
Price: High polish finish $1,070.00

AMERICAN DERRINGER DA38
Caliber: .38 Special, .357 Magnum, 9mm Luger. **Barrel:** 3.3 inches. **Weight:** 14.5 oz. **Features:** Double-action operation with hammer-block thumb safety. Barrel, receiver and all internal parts are made from stainless steel.
Price: .... $690.00 to $750.00

BOND ARMS TEXAS DEFENDER DERRINGER
Caliber: Available in more than 10 calibers, from .22 LR to .45 LC/.410 shotshells. **Barrel:** 3". **Weight:** 20 oz. **Length:** 5". **Grips:** Rosewood. **Sights:** Blade front, fixed rear. **Features:** Interchangeable barrels, stainless steel firing pins, cross-bolt safety, automatic extractor for rimmed calibers. Stainless steel construction, brushed finish. Right or left hand.
Price: $415.00
Price: Interchangeable barrels, .22 LR thru .45 LC, 3 ......$139.00
Price: Interchangeable barrels, .45 LC, 3.5 ..... $159.00 to $189.00

BOND ARMS RANGER
Caliber: .45 LC/.410 shotshells. **Barrel:** 4.25" **Weight:** 23.5 oz. **Length:** 6.25" **Features:** Similar to Snake Slayer except no triggerguard. Intr. 2008. From Bond Arms.
Price: $649.00

BOND ARMS CENTURY 2000 DEFENDER
Caliber: .45 LC/.410 shotshells. **Barrel:** 3.5" **Weight:** 21 oz. **Length:**

5.5". **Features:** Similar to Defender series.
Price: $435.00

BOND ARMS COWBOY DEFENDER
Caliber: From .22 LR to .45 LC/.410 shotshells. **Barrel:** 3". **Weight:** 19 oz. **Length:** 5.5". **Features:** Similar to Defender series. No trigger guard.
Price: $415.00

BOND ARMS SNAKE SLAYER
Caliber: .45 LC/.410 shotshell (2.5" or 3"). **Barrel:** 3.5". **Weight:** 21 oz. **Length:** 5.5". **Grips:** Extended rosewood. **Sights:** Blade front, fixed rear. **Features:** Single-action; interchangeable barrels; stainless steel firing pin. Introduced 2005.
Price: $489.00

BOND ARMS SNAKE SLAYER IV
Caliber: .45 LC/.410 shotshell (2.5" or 3"). **Barrel:** 4.25". **Weight:** 22 oz. **Length:** 6.25". **Grips:** Extended rosewood. **Sights:** Blade front, fixed rear. **Features:** Single-action; interchangeable barrels; stainless steel firing pin. Introduced 2006.
Price: $519.00

CHARTER ARMS DIXIE DERRINGERS
Caliber: .22 LR, .22 WMR. **Barrel:** 1.125". **Weight:** 6 oz. **Length:** 4" overall. **Grips:** Black polymer. **Sights:** Blade front, fixed notch rear. **Features:** Stainless finish. Introduced 2006. Made in U.S.A. by Charter Arms.
Price: $215.00

COBRA BIG-BORE DERRINGERS
Caliber: .22 WMR, .32 H&R Mag., .38 Spec., 9mm Para., .380 ACP. **Barrel:** 2.75". **Weight:** 14 oz. **Length:** 4.65" overall. **Grips:** Textured black or white synthetic or laminated rosewood. **Sights:** Blade front, fixed notch rear. **Features:** Alloy frame, steel-lined barrels, steel breech block. Plunger-type safety with integral hammer block. Black, chrome or satin finish. Introduced 2002. Made in U.S.A. by Cobra Enterprises of Utah, Inc.
Price: $187.00

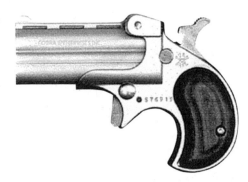

COBRA STANDARD SERIES DERRINGERS
Caliber: .22 LR, .22 WMR, .25 ACP, .32 ACP. **Barrel:** 2.4". **Weight:** 9.5 oz. **Length:** 4" overall. **Grips:** Laminated wood or pearl. **Sights:** Blade front, fixed notch rear. **Features:** Choice of black powder coat, satin nickel or chrome finish. Introduced 2002. Made in U.S.A. by Cobra Enterprises of Utah, Inc.
Price: $169.00

Prices given are believed to be accurate at time of publication however, many factors affect retail pricing so exact prices are not possible.

COBRA LONG-BORE DERRINGERS
Caliber: .22 WMR, .38 Spec., 9mm Para. **Barrel:** 3.5". **Weight:** 16 oz. **Length:** 5.4" overall. **Grips:** Black or white synthetic or rosewood. **Sights:** Fixed. **Features:** Chrome, satin nickel, or black Teflon finish. Introduced 2002. Made in U.S.A. by Cobra Enterprises of Utah, Inc.
Price: **$187.00**

COBRA TITAN
.45 LC/.410 DERRINGER
Caliber: .45 LC, .410 or 9mm, 2-round capacity. **Barrel:** 3-1/2". **Weight:** 16.4 oz. **Grip:** Rosewood. **Features:** The Titan is a powerhouse derringer designed to shoot a .45 Long Colt or the wide range of personal protection .410 shells with additional calibers to follow soon. Standard finshes include: satin stainless, black stainless, and brushed stainless. Made in U.S.A. by Cobra Enterprises of Utah, Inc.
Price: $419.00

COMANCHE SUPER SINGLE-SHOT
Caliber: .45 LC/.410 **Barrel:** 10". **Sights:** Adjustable. **Features:** Blue finish, not available for sale in CA, MA. Distributed by SGS Importers International, Inc.
Price: $200.00

HEIZER PS1 POCKET SHOTGUN
Caliber: .45 Colt or .410 shotshell. Single-shot. **Barrel:** Tip-up, 3.25 inches. **Weight:** 22 oz. **Length:** 5.6 inches. **Width:** .742 inches **Height:** 3.81 inches. **Features:** Available in several finishes.

Standard model is matte stainless or black. Also offered in Hedy Jane series for the women in pink or in two-tone combinations of stainless and pink, blue, green, purple. Made in the U.S.A. by Heizer Industries.
Price: **$499.00**

MAXIMUM SINGLE-SHOT
Caliber: .22 LR, .22 Hornet, .22 BR, .22 PPC, 223 Rem., 22-250, 6mm BR, 6mm PPC, 243, 250 Savage, 6.5mm-35M, 270 MAX, 270 Win., 7mm TCU, 7mm BR, 7mm-35, 7mm INT-R, 7mm-08, 7mm Rocket, 7mm Super-Mag., 30 Herrett, 30 Carbine, 30-30, 308 Win., 30x39, 32-20, 350 Rem. Mag., .357 Mag., .357 Maximum, 358 Win., 375 H&H, .44 Mag., .454 Casull. **Barrel:** 8.75", 10.5", 14". **Weight:** 61 oz. (10.5" bbl.); 78 oz. (14" bbl.). **Length:** 15", 18.5" overall (with 10.5" and 14" bbl., respectively). **Grips:** Smooth walnut stocks and fore-end. Also available with 17-finger-groove grip. **Sights:** Ramp front, fully adjustable open rear. **Features:** Falling block action; drilled and tapped for M.O.A. scope mounts; integral grip frame/receiver; adjustable trigger; Douglas barrel (interchangeable). Introduced 1983. Made in U.S.A. by M.O.A. Corp.
Price: **$865.00**

PUMA BOUNTY HUNTER
Caliber: .44/40, .44 Mag. and .45 Colt, 6-shot magazine capacity. **Barrel:** 12". **Weight:** 4.5 lbs. **Length:** 24". **Stock:** Walnut. **Sights:** Fixed sights. **Features:** A piece of 1950's TV nostalgia, the Bounty Hunter is a reproduction of the gun carried by Western character Josh Randall in the series "Wanted: Dead or Alive." The Bounty Hunter is based on the Winchester Model 92 carbine design, but is considered by Federal Law to be a pistol, because it is built from the ground up as a handgun. The Bounty Hunter has a teardrop shaped loop lever and is built with the same fit, finish and high-grade Italian walnut stocks as the Puma M-92 and M-86 rifles. Manufactured in the U.S.A. by Chiappa Firearms of Dayton, OH.
Price: .45LC, Case Hardened/Blued **$1,372.00**
Price: .44/40, Case Hardened/Blued **$1,372.00**
Price: .44 Mag., Case Hardened/Blued **$1,372.00**

ROSSI MATCHED PAIR , "DUAL THREAT PERFORMER"
Caliber: .22LR, .45 Colt and .410 ga. 2.5" shotshells, single-shot. **Sights:** Fiber optic front sights, adjustable rear. **Features:** Two-in-one pistol system with sinle-shot simplicity. Removable choke and cushioned grip with a Taurus Security System.
Price: **$336.00**

ROSSI RANCH HAND

Caliber: .38/.357, .45 Colt or .44 magnum, 6-shot. **Weight:** 4 lbs. **Length:** 24" overall. **Stock:** Brazilian hardwood. **Sights:** Adjustable buckhorn. **Features:** Matte blue or case hardened finish with oversized lever loop to accomodate gloved hands. Equipped with classic buckhorn sights for fast target aquisition and a Taurus Security Sytem.
Price: $676.00

ROSSI WIZARD

Caliber: .243 Win. or .22-.250 Rem. with other calibers coming soon, single-shot. **Barrel:** 11" **Length:** 20.4" **Features:** Offered in blue finish, additional features include pistol grip with custom grooves for fast handling and comfort, manual safety with "S" mark for visual confirmation, hammer extension, scope rail and the unique onboard Taurus Security System. Pistol offers outstanding and reliable performance in a versatile package. Its ingenious break-open barrel system changes quickly by unscrewing the front swivel with no tools needed.
Price: $336.00

THOMPSON/CENTER ENCORE

Calibers: .17 HMR, .22 LR, .204 Ruger, .223, .22-250, .243, .270., 7mm-08, .308, .20-06, .44 Mag., .45 Colt/.410, .45-70 Govt., .460 S&W, .500 S&W. Single shot, break-open design. **Barrel:** 15 inches, 12 inches (.44 Mag., .45 Colt). **Weight:** 4.25 to 4.5 lbs. **Grip:** Walnut on blued models, rubber on stainless. Matching fore-end. **Sights:** Adjustable rear, ramp front. **Features:** Interchangeable barrels, adjustable trigger. Pro Hunter has "Swing Hammer" to allow reaching the hammer when the gun is scoped. Other Pro Hunter features include fluted barrel.
Price: ....$679.00 to $769.00
Price: (Pro Hunter) $1,199.00

THOMPSON/CENTER G2 CONTENDER

A second generation Contender pistol maintaining the same barrel interchangeability with older Contender barrels and their corresponding forends (except Herrett fore-end). The G2 frame will not accept old-style grips due to the change in grip angle. Incorporates an automatic hammer block safety with built-in interlock. Features include trigger adjustable for overtravel, adjustable rear sight; ramp front sight blade, blued steel finish.
Price: $809.00

ARMALITE M15A2 CARBINE

Caliber: .223 Rem., 30-round magazine. **Barrel:** 16" heavy chrome lined; 1:9" twist. **Weight:** 7 lbs. **Length:** 35-11/16" overall. **Stock:** Green or black composition. **Sights:** Standard A2. **Features:** Upper and lower receivers have push-type pivot pin; hard coat anodized; A2-style forward assist; M16A2-type raised fence around magazine release button. Made in U.S.A. by ArmaLite, Inc.
Price: Green **$1,174.00**
Price: Black **$1,174.00**

ARMALITE M15A4 CARBINE

Caliber: .223 Rem., 30-round magazine. **Barrel:** 16" heavy chrome lined; 1:7" twist, flash suppressor. **Weight:** 6.8 lbs. **Length:** 36" overall. **Stock:** Green or black composition. **Sights:** Standard A2. **Features:** Forged flattop receiver with Picatinny rail, 8-inch handguard, anodize aluminum supper/lower receiver, flip-up sights.
Price: **$1,589.00**

ARMALITE AR-10A4 SPECIAL PURPOSE

Caliber: .243, .308 Win., 10- and 20-round magazine. **Barrel:** 20" chrome-lined, 1:11.25" twist. **Weight:** 9.6 lbs. **Length:** 41" overall. **Stock:** Green or black composition. **Sights:** Detachable handle, front sight, or scope mount available; comes with international style flattop receiver with Picatinny rail. **Features:** Forged upper receiver with case deflector. Receivers are hard-coat anodized. Introduced 1995. Made in U.S.A. by ArmaLite, Inc.
Price: Green **$1,557.00**
Price: Black..**$1,557.00**

ARMALITE AR-10A2

Utilizing the same 20" double-lapped, heavy barrel as the ArmaLite AR10A4 Special Purpose Rifle. Offered in .308 Win. only. Made in U.S.A. by ArmaLite, Inc.
Price: AR-10A2 rifle or carbine **$1,561.00**

ARSENAL, INC. SLR-107F

Caliber: 7.62x39mm. **Barrel:** 16.25". **Weight:** 7.3 lbs. **Stock:** Left-side folding polymer stock. **Sights:** Adjustable rear. **Features:** Stamped receiver, 24mm flash hider, bayonet lug, accessory lug, stainless steel heat shield, two-stage trigger. Introduced 2008. Made in U.S.A. by Arsenal, Inc.
Price: SLR-107FR, includes scope rail **$1,099.00**

ARSENAL, INC. SLR-107CR

Caliber: 7.62x39mm. **Barrel:** 16.25". **Weight:** 6.9 lbs. **Stock:** Left-side folding polymer stock. **Sights:** Adjustable rear. **Features:** Stamped receiver, front sight block/gas block combination, 500-meter rear sight, cleaning rod, stainless steel heat shield, scope rail, and removable muzzle attachment. Introduced 2007. Made in U.S.A. by Arsenal, Inc.
Price: SLR-107CR **$1,119.00**

ARSENAL, INC. SLR-106CR

Caliber: 5.56 NATO. **Barrel:** 16.25", Steyr chrome-lined barrel, 1:7 twist rate. **Weight:** 6.9 lbs. **Stock:** Black polymer folding stock with cutout for scope rail. Stainless-steel heatshield handguard. **Sights:** 500-meter rear sight and rear sight block calibrated for 5.56 NATO. Warsaw Pact scope rail. **Features:** Uses Arsenal, Bulgaria, Mil-Spec receiver, two-stage trigger, hammer and disconnector. Polymer magazines in 5- and 10-round capacity in black and green, with Arsenal logo. Others are 30-round black waffles, 20- and 30-round versions in clear/smoke waffle, featuring the "10" in a double-circle logo of Arsenal, Bulgaria. Ships with 5-round magazine, sling, cleaning kit in a tube, 16" cleaning rod, oil bottle. Introduced 2007. Made in U.S.A. by Arsenal, Inc.
Price: SLR-106CR **$1,200.00**

AUTO-ORDNANCE 1927A-1 THOMPSON

Caliber: .45 ACP. **Barrel:** 16.5". **Weight:** 13 lbs. **Length:** About 41" overall (Deluxe). **Stock:** Walnut stock and vertical fore-end. **Sights:** Blade front, open rear adjustable for windage. **Features:** Recreation of Thompson Model 1927. Semiauto only. Deluxe model has finned barrel, adjustable rear sight and compensator; Standard model has plain barrel and military sight. Available with 100-round drum or 30-round stick magazine. From Auto-Ordnance Corp
Price: Deluxe w/stick magazine.............................**$1,420.00**
Price: Deluxe w/drum magazine.............................**$1,699.00**
Price: Lightweight model w/stick mag...................**$1,200.00**

AUTO-ORDNANCE THOMPSON M1/M1-C

Similar to the 1927 A-1 except is in the M-1 configuration with side cocking knob, horizontal fore-end, smooth unfinned barrel, sling swivels on butt and fore-end. Matte-black finish. Introduced 1985.
Price: M1 semiauto carbine...................................**$1,334.00**
Price: M1-C lightweight semiauto **$1,200.00**

AUTO-ORDNANCE 1927 A-1 COMMANDO

Similar to the 1927 A-1 except has Parkerized finish, black-finish wood butt, pistol grip, horizontal fore-end. Comes with black nylon sling. Introduced 1998. Made in U.S.A. by Auto-Ordnance Corp.
Price: T1-C...**$1,393.00**

AUTO ORDNANCE M1 CARBINE

Caliber: .30 Carbine (15-shot magazine). **Barrel:** 18". **Weight:** 5.4 to 5.8 lbs. **Length:** 36.5". **Stock:** Wood or polymer. **Sights:** Blade front, flip-style rear. A faithful recreation of the military carbine.
Price: **$816.00**

BARRETT MODEL 82A-1 SEMI-AUTOMATIC

Caliber: .416 Barret, 50 BMG, 10-shot detachable box magazine. **Barrel:** 29". **Weight:** 28.5 lbs. **Length:** 57" overall. **Stock:** Composition with energy-absorbing recoil pad. **Sights:** Scope optional. **Features:** Semiautomatic, recoil operated with recoiling barrel. Three-lug locking bolt; muzzle brake. Adjustable bipod. Introduced 1985. Made in U.S.A. by Barrett Firearms.
Price: From **$8,900.00**

BARRETT M107A1

Caliber: 50 BMG. 10-round detachable magazine. **Barrel:** 20 or 29 inches. **Sights:** 27-inch optics rail with flip-up iron sights. **Weight:**

Prices given are believed to be accurate at time of publication however, many factors affect retail pricing so exact prices are not possible.

69TH EDITION, 2015 ✛ 455

30.9 lbs. **Finish:** Flat Dark Earth. Features: Four-port cylindrical muzzle brake. Quick-detachable Barrett QDL Suppressor. Adjustable bipod and monopod.
Price: $12,000.00

BARRETT MODEL REC7
Caliber: 5.56 (.223), 6.8 Rem. SPC. 30-round magazine. **Barrel:** 16 inches. **Sights:** ARMS rear, folding front. Weight: 28.7 lbs. **Features:** AR-style configuration with standard 17-4 stainless piston system, two-position forward venting gas plug, chrome-lined gas block, A2 flash hider, 6-postion MOE stock.
Price: $1,950.00

BENELLI R1
Caliber: .30-06 (4+1), .300 Win Mag (3+1), .338 Win Mag (3+1). **Weight:** 7.1 lbs. **Length:** 43.75" to 45.75". **Stock:** Select satin walnut or synthetic. **Sights:** None. **Features:** Auto-regulating gas-operated system, three-lug rotary bolt, interchangeable barrels, optional recoil pads. Introduced 2003. Imported from Italy by Benelli USA.
Price: .... $1,379.00 to $1,689.00

BENELLI MR1
Gas-operated semiauto rifle chambered in 5.56 NATO. Features include 16-inch, 1:9 twist, hard chrome-lined barrel, synthetic stock with pistol grip, rotating bolt, military-style aperture sights with picatinny rail. Comes equipped with 5-round detachable magazine but accepts M16 magazines.
Price: $1,339.00

BERETTA CX4/PX4 STORM CARBINE
Caliber: 9mm Para., .40 S&W, .45 ACP. **Weight:** 5.75 lbs. **Barrel Length:** 16.6", chrome lined, rate of twist 1:16 (.40 S&W) or 1:10 (9mm Para.). **Length:** NA. **Stock:** Black synthetic. **Sights:** Ghost ring. **Features:** Introduced 2005. Imported from Italy by Beretta USA.
Price: $900.00

BROWNING BAR SAFARI AND SAFARI W/BOSS SEMI-AUTO
Caliber: Safari: .25-06 Rem., .270 Win., 7mm Rem. Mag., .30-06

Spfl., .308 Win., .300 Win. Mag., .338 Win. Mag. Safari w/BOSS: .270 Win., 7mm Rem. Mag., .30-06 Spfl., .300 Win. Mag., .338 Win. Mag. **Barrel:** 22-24" round tapered. **Weight:** 7.4-8.2 lbs. **Length:** 43-45" overall. **Stock:** French walnut pistol grip stock and fore-end, hand checkered. **Sights:** No sights. **Features:** Has new bolt release lever; removable trigger assembly with larger triggerguard; redesigned gas and buffer systems. Detachable 4-round box magazine. Scroll-engraved receiver is tapped for scope mounting. BOSS barrel vibration modulator and muzzle brake system available. Mark II Safari introduced 1993. Made in Belgium.
Price: BAR MK II Safari, from $1,300.00
Price: BAR Safari w/BOSS, from $1,500.00

BROWNING BAR SHORTTRAC/LONGTRAC
Caliber:(ShortTrac models) .270 WSM, 7mm WSM, .300 WSM, .243 Win., .308 Win., .325 WSM; (LongTrac models) .270 Win., .30-06 Spfl., 7mm Rem. Mag., .300 Win. Mag. **Barrel:** 23". **Weight:** 6 lbs. 10 oz. to 7 lbs. 4 oz. **Length:** 41.5" to 44". **Stock:** Satin-finish walnut, pistol-grip, fluted fore-end. **Sights:** Adj. rear, bead front standard, no sights on BOSS models (optional). **Features:** Designed to handle new WSM chamberings. Gas-operated, blued finish, rotary bolt design (LongTrac models).
Price: BAR ShortTrac, .243 Win., .308 Win. from $1,230.00
Price: BAR ShortTrac Left-Hand, intr. 2007, from $1,270.00
Price: BAR ShortTrac Mossy Oak New Break-up
.... $1,260.00 to $1,360.00
Price: BAR LongTrac Left Hand, .270 Win., .30-06 Spfl., from $1,270.00
Price: BAR LongTrac, from $1,200.00
Price: BAR LongTrac Mossy Oak Break Up, from $1,360.00

BROWNING BAR STALKER
Caliber: .243 Win., 7mm-08, .308 Win., .270 Win., .30-06 Spfl., .270 WSM, 7mm WSM, .300 WSM, .300 Win. Mag., .338 Win. Mag. **Barrel:** 20-24". **Weight:** 7.1-7.75 LBS. **Length:** 41-45" overall. **Stock:** Black composite stock and forearm. **Sights:** Hooded front and adjustable rear. **Features:** Gas-operated action with seven-lug rotary bolt; dual action bars; 2-, 3- or 4-shot magazine (depending on cartridge). Introduced 2001. Imported by Browning.
Price: BAR ShortTrac or LongTrac Stalker, from...................$1,350.00
Price: BAR Lightweight Stalker, from.....................$1,260.00

BUSHMASTER 300 AAC BLACKOUT
Caliber: .300 AAC. M4-style AR platform chambered for cartridge that duplicates 7.62x39 ballistics. **Features:** Utilizes regular AR magazines at full capacity. Muzzlebrake. Magpul stock and grip.
Price: $1,471.00

BUSHMASTER 308 HUNTER
Caliber: .308 Win / 7.62 NATO., 5-round magazine. **Barrel:** 20". **Weight:** 8-1/2 lbs. **Length:** 38-1/4" overall. **Stock:** Standard A2 stock with Hogue® rubberized pistol grip. **Sights:** Two ¾" mini-risers for optics mounting. **Features:** Bushmaster .308 Rifles were developed for the Hunter who intends to immediately add optics (scope, red dot or holographic sight) to the rifle. The premium 20" heavy fluted profile barrel is chrome lined in both bore and chamber to provide Bushmaster accuracy, durability and maintenance ease.
Price: .308 Hunter. $1,685.00

BUSHMASTER ACR

Caliber: 5.56mm, 6.5mm, 6.8mm., 30-round polymer magazine. **Barrel:** All three calibers are availaible with 10-1/2", 14-1/2", 16-1/2" and 18" barrels. **Weight:** 14-1/2" bbl. 7 lbs.. **Length:** 14-1/5" bbl. with stock folded: 25-3/4", with stock deployed (mid) 32-5/8", 10.5" bbl. with stock folded: 21-5/16", with stock deployed (mid): 27-7/8", with stock deployed and extended: 31-3/4". Folding Stock Length of Pull - 3". **Stock:** Fixed high-impact composite A-frame stock with rubber buttpad and sling mounts (ORC & A-TACS®) **Features:** Cold hammer-forged barrels with melonite coating for extreme long life. A2 birdcage-type hider to control muzzle flash and adjustable, two-position, gas piston-driven system for firing suppressed or unsuppressed, supported by hardened internal bearing rails. The Adaptive Combat Rifle (ACR) features a tool-less, quick-change barrel system available in 10.5", 14.5" and 16.5" and in multiple calibers. Multi-caliber bolt carrier assembly quickly and easily changes from .223/5.56mm NATO to 6.8mm Rem SPC (spec II chamber). Free-floating MIL-STD 1913 monolithic top rail for optic mounting. Fully ambidextrous controls including magazine release, bolt catch and release, fire selector and nonreciprocating charging handle. High-impact composite handguard with heat shield – accepts rail inserts. High-impact composite lower receiver with textured magazine well and modular grip storage. Fire Control – Semi and Full Auto two-stage standard AR capable of accepting drop-in upgrade. Magazine – Optimized for MagPul PMAG Accepts standard NATO/M-16 magazines.
Price: Basic ORC Configuration **$2,343.00**
Price: A-TACS Basic Configuration **$2,540.00**
Price: Basic Folder Configuration...**$2,490.00**
Price: Basic State Compliant Configuration **$2,343.00**

BUSHMASTER VARMINTER

Caliber: .223 Rem., 5-shot. **Barrel:** 24", 1:9" twist, fluted, heavy, stainless. **Weight:** 8.75 lbs. **Length:** 42.25". **Stock:** Rubberized pistol grip. **Sights:** 1/2" scope risers. **Features:** Gas-operated, semiauto, two-stage trigger, slotted free floater fore-end, lockable hard case.
Price: **$1,430.00**

BUSHMASTER 6.8 SPC/7.62X39 PATROLMAN'S CARBINE

Caliber: 6.8 SPC, 26-shot mag. **Barrel:** 16" M4 profile. **Weight:** 6.57 lbs. **Length:** 32.75" overall. **Features:** Semiauto AR-style with Izzy muzzlebrake, six-position telestock. Available in A2 (fixed carry handle) or A3 (removable carry handle) configuration.
Price: **$1,391.00**

BUSHMASTER ORC CARBINE

Caliber: 5.56/.223. **Barrel:** 16" M4 profile. **Weight:** 6 lbs. **Length:** 32.5" overall. **Features:** AR-style carbine with chrome-lined barrel, fixed carry handle, receiver-length picatinny optics rail, heavy oval M4-style handguards.
Price: **$1,391.00**

BUSHMASTER 11.5" BARREL CARBINE

Caliber: 5.56/.223, 30-shot mag. **Barrel:** 11.5". **Weight:** 6.46 lbs. or 6.81 lbs. **Length:** 31.625" overall. **Features:** AR-style carbine with chrome-lined barrel with permanently attached BATF-approved 5.5" flash suppressor, fixed or removable carry handle, optional optics rail.
Price: **$1,215.00**

BUSHMASTER HEAVY-BARRELED CARBINE

Caliber: 5.56/.223. **Barrel:** 16". **Weight:** 6.93 lbs. to 7.28 lbs. **Length:** 32.5" overall. **Features:** AR-style carbine with chrome-lined heavy

profile vanadium steel barrel, fixed or removable carry handle, six-position telestock.
Price: **$1,215.00**

BUSHMASTER MODULAR CARBINE

Caliber: 5.56/.223, 30-shot mag. **Barrel:** 16". **Weight:** 7.3 lbs. **Length:** 36.25" overall. **Features:** AR-style carbine with chrome-lined chrome-moly vanadium steel barrel, skeleton stock or six-position telestock, clamp-on front sight and detachable flip-up dual aperature rear.
Price: **$1,745.00**

BUSHMASTER 450 RIFLE AND CARBINE

Caliber: .450 Bushmaster. **Barrel:** 20" (rifle), 16" (carbine), five-round mag. **Weight:** 8.3 lbs. (rifle), 8.1 lbs. (carbine). **Length:** 39.5" overall (rifle), 35.25" overall (carbine). **Features:** AR-style with chrome-lined chrome-moly barrel, synthetic stock, Izzy muzzlebrake.
Price: Carbine **$1,485.00**
Price: Rifle...**$1,500.00**

BUSHMASTER GAS PISTON

Caliber: .223, 30-shot mag. **Barrel:** 16". **Weight:** 7.46 lbs. **Length:** 32.5" overall. **Features:** Semiauto AR-style with telescoping stock, carry handle, piston assembly rather than direct gas impingement.
Price: **$1,795.00**

BUSHMASTER TARGET

Caliber: 5.56/.223, 30-shot mag. **Barrel:** 20 or 24-inch heavy or standard. **Weight:** 8.43 lbs. to 9.29 lbs. **Length:** 39.5" or 43.5" overall. **Features:** Semiauto AR-style with chrome-lined or stainless steel 1:9" twist barrel, fixed or removable carry handle, manganese phosphate finish.
Price: **$1,195.00**

BUSHMASTER M4A3 TYPE CARBINE

Caliber: 5.56/.223, 30-shot mag. **Barrel:** 16". **Weight:** 6.22 to 6.7 lbs. **Length:** 31 to 32.5 inches overall. **Features:** AR-style carbine with chrome-moly vanadium steel barrel, Izzy-type flash hider, six-position telestock, various sight options, standard or multi-rail handguard, fixed or removable carry handle.
Price: **$1,270.00**
Price: Patrolman's Carbine: Standard mil-style sights **$1,270.00**
Price: State Compliance Carbine **$1,270.00**

CENTURY INTERNATIONAL AES-10 HI-CAP

Caliber: 7.62x39mm. 30-shot magazine. **Barrel:** 23.2". **Weight:** NA. **Length:** 41.5" overall. **Stock:** Wood grip, fore-end. **Sights:** Fixed notch rear, windage-adjustable post front. **Features:** RPK-style, accepts standard double-stack AK-type mags. Side-mounted scope mount, integral carry handle, bipod. Imported by Century Arms Int'l.
Price: AES-10, from **$450.00**

CENTURY INTERNATIONAL GP WASR-10 HI-CAP

Caliber: 7.62x39mm. 30-shot magazine. **Barrel:** 16.25", 1:10 right-hand twist. **Weight:** 7.2 lbs. **Length:** 34.25" overall. **Stock:** Wood laminate or composite, forend. **Sights:** Fixed notch rear, windage-adjustable post front. **Features:** Two 30-rd. detachable box magazines, cleaning kit, bayonet. Version of AKM rifle; U.S.-parts added for BATFE compliance. Threaded muzzle, folding stock, bayonet lug, compensator, Dragunov stock available. Made in Romania by Cugir Arsenal. Imported by Century Arms Int'l.
Price: GP WASR-10, from.......................................**$450.00**

CENTURY INTERNATIONAL M70AB2 SPORTER

Caliber: 7.62x39mm. 30-shot magazine. **Barrel:** 16.25". **Weight:** 7.5 lbs. **Length:** 34.25" overall. **Stocks:** Metal grip, wood fore-end. **Sights:** Fixed notch rear, windage-adjustable post front. **Features:** Two 30-rd. double-stack magazine, cleaning kit, compensator, bayonet lug and bayonet. Paratrooper-style Kalashnikov with under-folding stock. Imported by Century Arms Int'l.

Prices given are believed to be accurate at time of publication however, many factors affect retail pricing so exact prices are not possible.

69TH EDITION, 2015 ✛ 457

Price: M70AB2, from $480.00

COLT MATCH TARGET MODEL
Caliber: .223 Rem., 5-shot magazine. **Barrel:** 16.1", 20" or 24". **Weight:** 7.1 to 8.5 lbs. **Length:** 34.5" to 39" overall. **Stock:** Composition stock, grip, forend. **Sights:** Post front, rear adjustable for windage and elevation. **Features:** 5-round detachable box magazine, flash suppressor, sling swivels. Forward bolt assist included. Introduced 1991. Made in U.S.A. by Colt's Mfg. Co., Inc.
Price: Match Target HBAR MT6601......................................$1,230.00

COLT CARBINE
Caliber: .223, 9mm. Capacity 10, 20 or 30 rounds. **Barrel:** 16.1 or 20 inches. Offered in a wide range of AR configurations and finishes.
Price: From...$1,136.00

COLT LE901
Caliber: .308. Capacity 20 rounds. **Barrel:** 16.1" heavy. **Weight:** 9.4 lbs. **Stock:** 4-position collapsible. **Sights:** Mil-Spec Flip-Up. **Features:** One piece upper receiver, fully floated barrel, ambidextrous controls, bayonet lug and flash hider.
Price: $2,493.00

DANIEL DEFENSE AR SERIES
Caliber: 5.56 NATO/.223. 20-round Magpul PMAG magazine. **Barrel:** 18 inches. Flash suppressor. **Weight:** 7.4 lbs. **Length:** 34.75" to 37.85" overall. **Stock:** Glass-filled polymer with Soft Touch overmolding. Pistol grip. **Sights:** None. **Features:** Lower receiver is Mil Spec with enhanced and flared magazine well, QD swivel attachment point. Upper receiver has M4 feed ramps. Lower and upper CNC machined of 7075-T6 aluminum, hard coat anodized. One of many AR variants offered by Daniel Defense. Made in the U.S.A.
Price: $2,199.00

DPMS VARMINT SERIES
Caliber: .204 Ruger, .223. **Barrel:** 16", 20" or 24" bull or fluted profile. **Weight:** 7.75 to 11.75 lbs. **Length:** 34.5" to 42.25" overall. **Stock:** Black Zytel composite. **Sights:** None. **Features:** Flattop receiver with Picatinny top rail; hardcoat anodized receiver; aluminum free-float tube handguard; many options. From DPMS Panther Arms.
Price: .... $1,059.00 to $1,269.00

DPMS PRAIRIE PANTHER
Semiauto AR-style rifle chambered in 5.56 NATO or 6.8 SPC. Features include 20-inch 416 stainless fluted heavy 1:8" barrel; phosphated steel bolt; free-floated carbon fiber handguard; flattop upper with Picatinny rail; aluminum lower; two 30-round magazines; skeletonized Zytel stock; Choice of matte black or one of several camo finishes.
Price: .... **$1,269.00 to $1,289.00**

DPMS REPR
Semiauto AR-style rifle chambered in .308 Win./7.62 NATO. Features include 18-inch 416 stainless steel 1:10" twist barrel; phosphated steel bolt; 4-rail free-floated handguard; no sights; aluminum lower; bipoad; two 19-round magazines; Coyote Brown camo finish overall. Scope not included.
Price: $2,549.00

DPMS MK12
Caliber: .308 Win./7.62 NATO. **Barrel:** 18 inches. **Weight:** 8.5 lbs. **Sights:** Midwest Industry flip-up. **Features:** 4-rail free floating handguard, flash hider, extruded 7029 T6 A3 Flattop receiver.
Price: $1,759.00

DPMS 3G2
Caliber: .223/5.56. **Barrel:** 16 inches. **Weight:** 7.1 lbs. **Stock:** Magpul STR with Hogue rubber pistol grip. **Sights:** Magpul Gen 2 BUS. **Features:** Miculek Compensator, two-stage fire control. M111 Modular handguard allows placement of sights on top rail or 45-degree angle.
Price: $1,239.00

DPMS LITE HUNTER
Caliber: .243, .260 Rem., .308, .338 Federal. **Barrel:** 20 inches, stainless. **Weight:** 8 pounds. **Stock:** Standard A2. **Features:** Two-stage match trigger. Hogue pistol grip. Optics ready top rail.
Price: $1,499.00

DPMS .300 AAC BLACKOUT
Caliber: .300 AAC Blackout. **Barrel:** 16-inch heavy 4150 chrome-lined. **Weight:** 7 pounds. **Stock:** Adjustable 6-position.
Price: $1,199.00

DPMS ORACLE
Caliber: .223/5.56 or .308/7.62. **Barrel:** 16 inches. **Weight:** 6.2 (.223), 8.3 (308). Standard AR-15 fire control with A3 flattop receiver. **Finish:** Matte black or A-TACS camo.
Price: .223..$739, $849 (A-TACS)
Price: .308............................. $1,099, $1,189 (A-TACS)

DSA SA58 CONGO, PARA CONGO
Caliber: .308 Win. **Barrel:** 18" w/short Belgian short flash hider. **Weight:** 8.6 lbs. (Congo); 9.85 lbs. (Para Congo). **Length:** 39.75" **Stock:** Synthetic w/military grade furniture (Congo); Synthetic with nonfolding steel para stock (Para Congo). **Sights:** Elevation adjustable protected post front sight, windage adjustable rear peep (Congo); Belgian type Para Flip Rear (Para Congo). **Features:** FAL-style rifle with fully adjustable gas system, high-grade steel upper receiver with carry handle. Made in U.S.A. by DSA, Inc.
Price: Congo $1,975.00
Price: Para Congo $2,200.00

DSA SA58 STANDARD
Caliber: .308 Win. **Barrel:** 21" bipod cut w/threaded flash hider. **Weight:** 8.75 lbs. **Length:** 43". **Stock:** Synthetic, X-Series or optional folding para stock. **Sights:** Elevation-adjustable post front, windage-adjustable rear peep. **Features:** Fully adjustable short gas system, high-grade steel or 416 stainless upper receiver. Made in U.S.A. by DSA, Inc.
Price: From $1,700.00

DSA SA58 CARBINE
Caliber: .308 Win. **Barrel:** 16.25" bipod cut w/threaded flash hider. **Features:** Carbine variation of FAL-style rifle. Other features identical to SA58 Standard model. Made in U.S.A. by DSA, Inc.
Price: $1,700.00

DSA SA58 TACTICAL CARBINE
Caliber: .308 Win. **Barrel:** 16.25" fluted with A2 flash hider. **Weight:** 8.25 lbs. **Length:** 36.5". **Stock:** Synthetic, X-Series or optional

folding para stock. **Sights:** Elevation-adjustable post front, windage-adjustable match rear peep. **Features:** Shortened fully adjustable short gas system, high grade steel or 416 stainless upper receiver. Made in U.S.A. by DSA, Inc.
Price: $1,975.00

DSA SA58 MEDIUM CONTOUR
Caliber: .308 Win. **Barrel:** 21" w/threaded flash hider. **Weight:** 9.75 lbs. **Length:** 43". **Stock:** Synthetic military grade. **Sights:** Elevation-adjustable post front, windage-adjustable match rear peep. **Features:** Gas-operated semiauto with fully adjustable gas system, high grade steel receiver. Made in U.S.A. by DSA, Inc.
Price: $1,700.00

DSA ZM4 AR SERIES
Caliber: .223/5.56 NATO. Standard Flattop rifle features include 20-inch, chrome moly heavy barrel with A2 flash hider. **Weight:** 9 pounds. **Features:** Mil-Spec forged lower receiver, forged flattop or A2 upper. Fixed A2 stock. Carbine variations are also available with 16-inch barrels and many options.
Price: ....From $788.00

EXCEL ARMS ACCELERATOR
Caliber: .17 HMR, .22 WMR, 5.7x28mm, 9-shot magazine. **Barrel:** 18" fluted stainless steel bull barrel. **Weight:** 8 lbs. **Length:** 32.5" overall. **Grips:** Textured black polymer. **Sights:** Fully adjustable target sights. **Features:** Made from 17-4 stainless steel, aluminum shroud w/ Weaver rail, manual safety, firing-pin block, last-round bolt-hold-open feature. Four packages with various equipment available. American made, lifetime warranty. Comes with one 9-round stainless steel magazine and a California-approved cable lock. Introduced 2006. Made in U.S.A. by Excel Arms.
Price: MR-17 .17 HMR $672.00
Price: MR-22 .22 WMR $538.00

EXCEL ARMS X-SERIES
Caliber: .22 LR, 5.7x28mm (10 or 25-round); .30 Carbine (10 or 20-round magazine). **Barrel:** 18". **Weight:** 6.25 lbs. **Length:** 34 to 38". **Features:** Available with or without adjustable iron sights. Blow-back action (5.57x28) or delayed blow-back (.30 Carbine).
PRICE: .22 LR..$504.00
PRICE: 5.7x28.................................... $795.00 to $916.00

FNH FNAR
Caliber: .308 Win., 10 or 20-shot magazine. **Barrel:** 18" standard or 20" heavy contour. **Weight:** 8.125 lbs. **Length:** 37.5" overall. **Stock:** Adjustable for comb height, length of pull, cast-on and cast-off. **Sights:** None furnished. Optical rail atop receiver, three accessory rails on fore-end. **Features:** Based on BAR design.
Price: $1,699.00

FNH SCAR 16S
Caliber: 5.56mm/.223. **Capacity:** 10 or 30 rounds. **Barrel:** 16.25".

Prices given are believed to be accurate at time of publication however, many factors affect retail pricing so exact prices are not possible.

69TH EDITION, 2015 ✦ **459**

Weight: 7.25 lbs. **Length:** 27.5 to 37.5 " (extended stock). **Stock:** Telescoping, side-folding polymer. Adjustable cheekpiece, A2 style pistol grip. **Sights:** Adjustable folding front and rear. **Features:** Hard anodized aluminum receiver with four accessory rails. Ambidextrous safety and mag release. Charging handle can be mounted on right or left side. Semiauto version of newest service rifle of U.S. Special Forces.
Price: **$2,995.00**

FNH SCAR 17S
Caliber: 7.62x51mm/.308. **Capacity:** 10 or 30 rounds. **Barrel:** 16.25".
Weight: 8 lbs. **Length:** 28.5 to 38.5 " (extended stock). **Features:** Other features the same as SCAR 16S.
Price: **$3,349.00**

FRANKLIN ARMORY 3 GR-L
Caliber: 5.56mm/.223. **Capacity:** 10 or 30 rounds. **Barrel:** 18" fluted with threaded muzzle crown. **Weight:** 7.25 lbs. **Stock:** Magpul PRS. Adjustable comb and length of pull. **Features:** Hard anodized Desert Smoke upper receiver with full length Picatinny rail. One of many AR type rifles and carbines offered by this manufacturer. Made in the U.S.A.
Price: **$2,240.00**

HECKLER & KOCH MODEL MR556A1
Caliber: .223 Remington/5.56 NATO, 10+1 capacity. **Barrel:** 16.5". Weight: 8.9 lbs. **Length:** 33.9"-37.68". **Stock:** Black Synthetic Adjustable. **Features:** Uses the gas piston system found on the HK 416 and G26, which does not introduce propellant gases and carbon fouling into the rifle's interior.
Price: **$3,295.00**

HECKLER & KOCH MODEL MR762A1
Caliber: Similar to Model MR556A1 except chambered for 7.62x51mm/.308 Win. cartridge. **Weight:** 10 lbs. w/empty magazine. **Length:** 36 to 39.5". Variety of optional sights are available. Stock has five adjustable positions.
Price: **$3,995.00**

HI-POINT 9MM CARBINE
Caliber: 9mm Para. .40 S&W, (10-shot magazine); .45 ACP (9-shot). **Barrel:** 16.5" (17.5" for .40 S&W and .45). **Weight:** 4.5 lbs. **Length:** 31.5" overall. **Stock:** Black polymer, camouflage. **Sights:** Protected post front, aperture rear. Integral scope mount. **Features:** Grip-mounted magazine release. Black or chrome finish. Sling swivels. Available with laser or red-dot sights, RGB 4X scope, forward grip.

Introduced 1996. Made in U.S.A. by MKS Supply, Inc.
Price: 9mm (995TS) from **$286.00**
Price: .40 S&W (4095TS) from **$315.00**
Price: .45 ACP (4595TS) from **$319.00**

KEL-TEC RFB
Caliber: 7.62 NATO/.308. 20-round FAL-type magazine. **Barrel:** 18" with threaded muzzle, A2-style flash hider. **Weight:** 8 lbs. **Features:** A bullpup short-stroke gas piston operated carbine with ambidextrous controls, reversible operating handle, Mil-Spec Picatinny rail.
Price: **$1,880.00**

KEL-TEC SU-16 SERIES
Caliber: 5.56 NATO/.223. 10-round magazine capacity. **Barrel:** 16 or 18.5". **Weight:** 4.5 to 5 lbs. **Features:** Offering in several rifle and carbine variations.
Price: **$665.00**

LARUE TACTICAL OBR
Caliber: 5.56 NATO/.223, 7.62 NATO/.308 Win. **Barrel:** 16.1, 18 or 20 inches. **Weight:** 7.5 to 9.25 lbs. **Features:** Manufacturer of several models of AR-style rifles and carbines. Optimized Battle Rifle (OBR) series is made in both NATO calibers. Many AR-type options available. Made in the U.S.A.
Price: OBR 5.56 ....**$2,245.00**
Price: OBR 7.62 ....**$3,370.00**

LEWIS MACHINE & TOOL (LMT)
Caliber: 5.56 NATO/.223, 7.62 NATO/.308 Win. **Barrel:** 16.1, 18 or 20 inches. **Weight:** 7.5 to 9.25 lbs. **Features:** Manufacturer of a wide range of AR-style carbines with many options. SOPMOD stock, gas piston operating system, monolithic rail platform, tactical sights. Made in the U.S.A. by Lewis Machine & Tool.
Price: Standard 16 ....**$1,594.00**
Price: Comp 16, flattop receiver **$1,685.00**
Price: CQB Series from..**$2,100.00**
Price: Sharpshooter Weapons System.......................**$5,198.00**

LES BAER CUSTOM ULTIMATE AR 223
Caliber: .223. **Barrel:** 18", 20", 22", 24". **Weight:** 7.75 to 9.75 lb. **Length:** NA. **Stock:** Black synthetic. **Sights:** None furnished; Picatinny-style flattop rail for scope mounting. **Features:** Forged receiver; Ultra

Prices given are believed to be accurate at time of publication however, many factors affect retail pricing so exact prices are not possible.

single-stage trigger (Jewell two-stage trigger optional); titanium firing pin; Versa-Pod bipod; chromed National Match carrier; stainless steel, hand-lapped and cryo-treated barrel; guaranteed to shoot 1/2 or 3/4 MOA, depending on model. Made in U.S.A. by Les Baer Custom Inc.

Price: Super Varmint Model...**$2,390.00**
Price: Super Match Model (introduced 2006) **$2,490.00**
Price: M4 Flattop model **$2,360.00**
Price: Police Special 16" (2008) **$1,690.00**
Price: IPSC Action Model **$2,640.00**

LR 300S
Caliber: 5.56 NATO, 30-shot magazine. **Barrel:** 16.5"; 1:9" twist. **Weight:** 7.4-7.8 lbs. **Length:** NA. **Stock:** Folding. **Sights:** YHM flip front and rear. **Features:** Flattop receive, full length top picatinny rail. Phantom flash hider, multi sling mount points, field strips with no tools. Made in U.S.A. from Z-M Weapons.
Price: AXL, AXLT **$2,139.00**
Price: NXL **$2,208.00**

MERKEL MODEL SR1 SEMI-AUTOMATIC
Caliber: .223, .308 Win., .30-06, .300 Win Mag., 7x64, 8x57IS, 9.3x62. **Features:** Streamlined profile, checkered walnut stock and fore-end, 19.7" (308) or 20.8" (300 SM) barrel, two- or five-shot detachable box magazine. Adjustable front and rear iron sights with Weaver-style optics rail included. Imported from Germany by Merkel USA.
Price: **$1,595.00**

OLYMPIC ARMS K9, K10, K40, K45 PISTOL-CALIBER AR15 CARBINES
Caliber: 9mm Para., 10mm, .40 S&W, .45 ACP; 32/10-shot modified magazines. **Barrel:** 16" button rifled stainless steel, 1x16" twist rate. **Weight:** 6.73 lbs. **Length:** 31.625" overall. **Stock:** A2 grip, M4 6-point collapsible stock. **Features:** A2 upper with adjustable rear sight, elevation adjustable front post, bayonet lug, sling swivel, threaded muzzle, flash suppressor, carbine length handguards. Made in U.S.A. by Olympic Arms, Inc.
Price: K9GL, 9mm Para., Glock lower **$1,157.00**
Price: K10, 10mm, modified 10-round Uzi magazine............**$1,006.20**
Price: K40, .40 S&W, modified 10-round Uzi magazine **$1,006.20**
Price: K45, .45 ACP, modified 10-round Uzi magazine **$1,006.20**

OLYMPIC ARMS K3B SERIES AR15 CARBINES
Caliber: 5.56 NATO, 30-shot magazines. **Barrel:** 16" button rifled chrome-moly steel, 1x9" twist rate. **Weight:** 5-7 lbs. **Length:** 31.75" overall. **Stock:** A2 grip, M4 6-point collapsible buttstock. **Features:** A2 upper with adjustable rear sight, elevation adjustable front post, bayonet lug, sling swivel, threaded muzzle, flash suppressor, carbine-length handguards. Made in U.S.A. by Olympic Arms, Inc.
Price: K3B base model, A2 upper **$815.00**
Price: K3B-M4 M4 contoured barrel & handguards **$1,103.70**
Price: K3B-M4-A3-TC A3 upper, M4 barrel, FIRSH rail
      handguard **$1,246.70**
Price: K3B-CAR 11.5" barrel with 5.5" permanent flash
      suppressor..**$1,033.50**
Price: K3B-FAR 16" featherweight contoured barrel.............**$1,071.20**

OLYMPIC ARMS PLINKER PLUS AR15 MODELS
Caliber: 5.56 NATO, 30-shot magazine. **Barrel:** 16" or 20" button-rifled chrome-moly steel, 1x9" twist. **Weight:** 7.5-8.5 lbs. **Length:** 35.5"-

39.5" overall. **Stock:** A2 grip, A2 buttstock with trapdoor. **Sights:** A1 windage rear, elevation-adjustable front post. **Features:** A1 upper, fiberlite handguards, bayonet lug, threaded muzzle and flash suppressor. Made in U.S.A. by Olympic Arms, Inc.
Price: Plinker Plus..**$713.70**
Price: Plinker Plus 20..**$843.70**

OLYMPIC ARMS GAMESTALKER
Sporting AR-style rifle chambered in .223, .243 and .25 WSSM and .300 OSSM. Features include forged aluminum upper and lower; flat top receiver with Picatinny rail; gas block front sight; 22-inch stainless steel fluted barrel; free-floating slotted tube handguard; camo finish overall; ACE FX skeleton stock.
Price: **$1,359.00**

REMINGTON MODEL R-15 MODULAR REPEATING
Caliber: .204 Ruger, .223 and .30 Rem. AR, five-shot magazine. **Barrel:** 18" (carbine), 22", 24". **Weight:** 6.75 to 7.75 lbs. **Length:** 36.25" to 42.25". **Stock:** Camo. **Features:** AR-style with optics rail, aluminum alloy upper and lower.
Price: R-15 Hunter: .30 Rem. AR, 22" barrel, Realtree AP HD
      camo **$1,327.00**
Price: R-15 VTR SS Varmint, 24" stainless steel barrel **$1,529.00**

REMINGTON MODEL R-25 MODULAR REPEATING
Caliber: .243, 7mm-08, .308 Win., four-shot magazine. **Barrel:** 20" chrome-moly. **Weight:** 7.75 lbs. **Length:** 38.25" overall. **Features:** AR-style semiauto with single-stage trigger, aluminum alloy upper and lower, Mossy Oak Treestand camo finish overall.
Price: **$1,697.00**

REMINGTON MODEL 750 WOODSMASTER
Caliber: .243 Win., .270 Win., .308 Win., .30-06 Spfl., 4-shot magazine. **Barrel:** 22" round tapered, 18.5" (carbine version). **Weight:** 7.2 to 7.5 lbs. **Length:** 42.6" overall. **Stock:** Restyled American walnut fore-end and stock with machine-cut checkering. Satin finish. **Sights:** Gold bead front sight on ramp; step rear sight with windage adjustable. **Features:** Gas-operated action, SuperCell recoil pad. Positive cross-bolt safety. Receiver tapped for scope mount. Introduced 2006. The latest variation of the classic semiauto Remington 740 of 1955. Made in U.S.A. by Remington Arms Co.
Price: 750 Woodsmaster **$1,004.00**
Price: 750 Woodsmaster Carbine (18.5" bbl.) **$1,004.00**

Prices given are believed to be accurate at time of publication however, many factors affect retail pricing so exact prices are not possible.

69TH EDITION, 2015 ✦ 461

ROCK RIVER ARMS LAR SERIES
Caliber: .223/5.56, .308/7.62, 6.8 SPC, .458 SOCOM, 9mm and .40 S&W. These AR-15 type rifles and carbines are available with a very wide range of options. Virtually any AR configuration is offered including tactical, hunting and competition models. Some models are available in left-hand versions.
Price: .... $1,010.00 to $1,600.00

RUGER SR-556
AR-style semiauto rifle chambered in 5.56 NATO. Feature include two-stage piston; quad rail handguard; Troy Industries sights; black synthetic fixed or telescoping buttstock; 16.12-inch 1:9" twist steel barrel with birdcage; 10- or 30-round detachable box magazine; black matte finish overall.

Price: $1,995.00
Price: SR-556E, basic model $1,375.00
Price: SR-762 .... $2,195.00

RUGER MINI-14
Caliber: .223 Rem., 5-shot detachable box magazine. **Barrel:** 18.5". Rifling twist 1:9". **Weight:** 6.75 to 7 lbs. **Length:** 37.25" overall. **Stock:** American hardwood, steel reinforced, or synthetic. **Sights:** Protected blade front, fully adjustable Ghost Ring rear. **Features:** Fixed piston gas-operated, positive primary extraction. New buffer system, redesigned ejector system. Ruger S100RM scope rings included on Ranch Rifle. Heavier barrels added in 2008, 20-round magazine added in 2009.
Price: .... $909.00 to $1,069.00
Price: Mini-14/5, Ranch Rifle, blued, wood stock $909.00 to $959.00
Price: K-Mini-14/5, Ranch Rifle, stainless, scope rings $979.00
Price: K-Mini-6.8/5P, All-Weather Ranch Rifle, stainless, synthetic stock $979.00
Price: Mini-14 Target Rifle: laminated thumbhole stock, heavy crowned 22" stainless steel barrel, other refinements $1,149.00
Price: Mini-14 ATI Stock: Tactical version of Mini-14 but with six-position collapsible stock or folding stock, grooved pistol grip. Multiple picatinny optics/accessory rails $989.00
Price: Mini-14 Tactical Rifle: Similar to Mini-14 but with 16.12" barrel with flash hider, black synthetic stock, adjustable sights $989.00

RUGER MINI THIRTY
Similar to the Mini-14 rifle except modified to chamber the 7.62x39 Russian service round. **Weight:** 6.75 lbs. Has 6-groove barrel with 1:10" twist, Ruger Integral Scope Mount bases and protected blade front, fully adjustable Ghost Ring rear. Detachable 5-shot staggered box magazine. 20-round magazines available. Stainless w/synthetic

stock. Introduced 1987.
Price: Stainless, scope rings .... $979.00 to $1,039.00

SIG-SAUER 556
Caliber: .223 Rem., 30-shot detachable box magazine. **Barrel:** 16". Rifling twist 1:9". **Weight:** 6.8 lbs. **Length:** 36.5" overall. **Stock:** Polymer, folding style. **Sights:** Flip-up front combat sight, adjustable for windage and elevation. **Features:** Based on SG 550 series rifle. Two-position adjustable gas piston operating rod system, accepts standard AR magazines. Polymer forearm, three integrated Picatinny rails, forward mount for right- or left-side sling attachment. Aircraft-grade aluminum alloy trigger housing, hard-coat anodized finish; two-stage trigger, ambidextrous safety, 30-round polymer magazine, battery compartments, pistol-grip rubber-padded watertight adjustable buttstock with sling-attachment points. SIG 556 SWAT model has flat-top Picatinny railed receiver, tactical quad rail. SIG 556 HOLO sight options include front combat sight, flip-up rear sight, and red-dot style holographic sighting system with four illuminated reticle patterns. DMR features a 24" military grade cold hammer-forged heavy contour barrel, 5.56mm NATO, target crown. Imported by Sig Sauer, Inc.
Price: From .... $1,266.00 to $1,272.00

SIG-SAUER SIG516 GAS PISTON
AR-style rifle chambered in 5.56 NATO. Features include 14.5-, 16-, 18- or 20-inch chrome-lined barrel; free-floating, aluminum quad rail fore-end with four M1913 Picatinny rails; threaded muzzle with a standard (0.5x28TPI) pattern; aluminum upper and lower receiver is machined; black anodized finish; 30-round magazine; flattop upper; various configurations available.
Price: .... $1,666.00 to $2,399.00

SIG SAUER M400 VARMINTER/PREDATOR SERIES
Caliber: .223/5.56 NATO. AR Flattop design. **Barrel:** 18 or 22-inch heavy stainless match grade with Hogue free-floated fore-end. **Features:** Two-stage Geissele match trigger, Hogue grip, ambidextrous controls, Magpul MOE stock.
Price: $1,234.00

SIG-SAUER SIG716 TACTICAL PATROL
AR-10 type rifle chambered in 7.62 NATO/.308 Winchester. Features include gas-piston operation with 3-round-position (4-position optional) gas valve; 16-, 18- or 20-inch chrome-lined barrel with threaded muzzle and nitride finish; free-floating aluminum quad rail

Prices given are believed to be accurate at time of publication however, many factors affect retail pricing so exact pricing is not possible.

fore-end with four M1913 Picatinny rails; telescoping buttstock; lower receiver is machined from a 7075-T6 Aircraft grade aluminum forging; upper receiver, machined from 7075-T6 aircraft grade aluminum with integral M1913 Picatinny rail.

Price: .... **$2,132.00 to $2,666.00**

SMITH & WESSON M&P15
Caliber: 5.56mm NATO/.223, 30-shot steel magazine. **Barrel:** 16", 1:9" twist. **Weight:** 6.74 lbs., w/o magazine. **Length:** 32-35" overall. **Stock:** Black synthetic. **Sights:** Adjustable post front sight, adjustable dual aperture rear sight. **Features:** 6-position telescopic stock, thermo-set M4 handguard. 14.75" sight radius. 7-lbs. (approx.) trigger pull. 7075 T6 aluminum upper, 4140 steel barrel. Chromed barrel bore, gas key, bolt carrier. Hard-coat black-anodized receiver and barrel finish. Introduced 2006. Made in U.S.A. by Smith & Wesson.
Price: From .... **$839.00 to $1,949.00**
Price: Sport Model **$739.00**

SMITH & WESSON M&P15-300
Caliber: .300 Whisper/.300 AAC Blackout. Other specifications the same of 5.56 models.
Price: **$1,119.00**

SMITH & WESSON MODEL M&P15 VTAC
Caliber: .223 Remington/5.56 NATO, 30-round magazine. **Barrel:** 16". **Weight:** 6.5 lbs. **Length:** 35" extended, 32" collapsed, overall. **Features:** Six-position CAR stock. Surefire flash-hider and G2 light with VTAC light mount; VTAC/JP handguard; JP single-stage match trigger and speed hammer; three adjustable picatinny rails; VTAC padded two-point adjustable sling.

Price: **$1,949.00**

SMITH & WESSON M&P15PC CAMO
Caliber: 223 Rem/5.56 NATO, A2 configuration, 10-round mag. **Barrel:** 20" stainless with 1:8" twist. **Weight:** 8.2 lbs. **Length:** 38.5" overall. **Features:** AR-style, no sights but integral front and rear optics rails. Two-stage trigger, aluminum lower. Finished in Realtree Advantage Max-1 camo.
Price: **$1,539.00**

SMITH & WESSON M&P10
Caliber: .308 Win. **Capacity:** 10 rounds. **Barrel:** 18 inches. **Weight:** 7.7 pounds. **Features:** 6-position CAR stock, black hard anodized finish. Camo finish hunting model available w/5-round magazine.
Price: **$1,619.00**
Price: (Camo) **$1,729.00**

SPRINGFIELD ARMORY M1A
Caliber: 7.62mm NATO (.308), 5- or 10-shot box magazine. **Barrel:** 25-1/16" with flash suppressor, 22" without suppressor. **Weight:** 9.75 lbs. **Length:** 44.25" overall. **Stock:** American walnut with walnut-colored heat-resistant fiberglass handguard. Matching walnut handguard available. Also available with fiberglass stock. **Sights:** Military, square blade front, full click-adjustable aperture rear. **Features:** Commercial equivalent of the U.S. M-14 service rifle with no provision for automatic firing. From Springfield Armory
Price: SOCOM 16 .... **$1,855.00**
Price: SOCOM II, from **$2,090.00**
Price: Scout Squad, from **$1,726.00**
Price: Standard M1A, from **$1,608.00**
Price: Loaded Standard, from **$1,759.00**
Price: National Match, from **$2,249.00**

Price: Super Match (heavy premium barrel) about **$2,818.00**
Price: Tactical, from **$3,780.00**

STAG ARMS MODEL 3
Caliber: 5.56 NATO., 30-shot magazine capacity. **Barrel:** 16". **Stock:** Six position collapsible stock. **Sights:** N/A. **Features:** A short barrel with a chrome lined bore and a 6 position collapsible stock. It uses a gas-operated firing system, so the recoil is delayed until the round exits the barrel. Although it doesn't have any sights, it does have a Diamondhead Versa Rail System, which allows users to add Picatinny rails to the top, bottom and sides. The Picatinny rail allows for easy mounting of optics and accessories. Features the Diamondhead Versa Rail System; and right and left handed models are available. Perfect for modification, the Stag Arms Model 3 AR 15 is made to mil-spec requirements to give you the most authentic experience possible.
Price: **$895.00**

STONER SR-15 M-5
Caliber: .223. **Barrel:** 20". **Weight:** 7.6 lbs. **Length:** 38" overall. **Stock:** Black synthetic. **Sights:** Post front, fully adjustable rear (300-meter sight). **Features:** Modular weapon system; two-stage trigger. Black finish. Introduced 1998. Made in U.S.A. by Knight's Mfg.
Price: **$1,925.00**

STONER SR-25 CARBINE
Caliber: 7.62 NATO, 10-shot steel magazine. **Barrel:** 16" free-floating **Weight:** 7.75 lbs. **Length:** 35.75" overall. **Stock:** Black synthetic. **Sights:** Integral Weaver-style rail. Scope rings, iron sights optional. **Features:** Shortened, nonslip handguard; removable carrying handle. Matte black finish. Introduced 1995. Made in U.S.A. by Knight's Mfg. Co.
Price: **$3,597.00**

STONER SR-30
Caliber: .300 Blackout. **Barrel:** 16" **Weight:** 7.75 lbs. **Features:** QDC flash suppressor, micro front and rear iron sights, ambidextrous controls, fully adjustable stock.
Price: **$2,723.00**

TAURUS CT G2 CARBINE
Caliber: .40 S&W, 9 mm and .45 ACP. Capacity is 10 rounds. **Barrel:** 16". **Weight:** 6.6 lbs. **Length:** 36" overall. **Stock:** Aluminum & Polymer. **Sights:** Adjustable rear sight and fixed front sight. **Features:** Full length Picatinny rail, ambidextrous slide catch, two-position safety. Made in U.S.A. by Knight's Mfg. Co.
Price: **$879.00**

WILSON COMBAT TACTICAL
Caliber: 5.56mm NATO, accepts all M-16/AR-15 Style Magazines, includes one 20-round magazine. **Barrel:** 16.25", 1:9" twist, match-grade fluted. **Weight:** 6.9 lbs. **Length:** 36.25" overall. **Stock:** Fixed or collapsible. **Features:** Free-float ventilated aluminum quad-rail handguard, Mil-Spec parkerized barrel and steel components, anodized receiver, precision CNC-machined upper and lower receivers, 7075 T6 aluminum forgings. Single stage JP Trigger/ Hammer Group, Wilson Combat Tactical Muzzle Brake, nylon tactical rifle case. M-4T version has flat-top receiver for mounting optics, OD green furniture, 16.25" match-grade M-4 style barrel. SS-15 Super Sniper Tactical Rifle has 1-in-8 twist, heavy 20" match-grade fluted stainless steel barrel. Made in U.S.A by Wilson Combat.
Price: .... **$2,225.00 to $2,450.00**

Prices given are believed to be accurate at time of publication however, many factors affect retail pricing so exact prices are not possible.

69TH EDITION, 2015 ✛ **463**

BIG HORN ARMORY MODEL 89 RIFLE AND CARBINE

Lever action rifle or carbine chambered for .500 S&W Magnum. Features include 22-or 18-inch barrel; walnut or maple stocks with pistol grip; aperture rear and blade front sights; recoil pad; sling swivels; enlarged lever loop; magazine capacity 5 (rifle) or 7 (carbine) rounds.

Price: **$2,424.00**

BROWNING BLR

Action: Lever action with rotating bolt head, multiple-lug breech bolt with recessed bolt face, side ejection. Rack-and-pinion lever. Flush-mounted detachable magazines, with 4+1 capacity for magnum cartridges, 5+1 for standard rounds. **Barrel:** Button-rifled chrome-moly steel with crowned muzzle. **Stock:** Buttstocks and forends are American walnut with grip and forend checkering. Recoil pad installed. **Trigger:** Wide-groove design, trigger travels with lever. Half-cock hammer safety; fold-down hammer. **Sights:** Gold bead on ramp front; low-profile square-notch adjustable rear. **Features:** Blued barrel and receiver, high-gloss wood finish. Receivers are drilled and tapped for scope mounts, swivel studs included. Action lock provided. Introduced 1996. Imported from Japan by Browning.

BROWNING BLR LIGHTWEIGHT W/PISTOL GRIP, SHORT AND LONG ACTION; LIGHTWEIGHT '81, SHORT AND LONG ACTION

Calibers: Short Action, 20" Barrel: .22-250 Rem., .243 Win., 7mm-08 Rem., .308 Win., .358, .450 Marlin. Calibers: Short Action, 22" Barrel: .270 WSM, 7mm WSM, .300 WSM, .325 WSM. Calibers: Long Action 22" Barrel: .270 Win., .30-06. Calibers: Long Action 24" Barrel: 7mm Rem. Mag., .300 Win. Mag. **Weight:** 6.5-7.75 lbs. **Length:** 40-45" overall. **Stock:** New checkered pistol grip and Schnabel forearm. Lightweight '81 differs from Pistol Grip models with a Western-style straight grip stock and banded forearm. Lightweight w/Pistol Grip Short Action and Long Action introduced 2005. Model '81 Lightning Long Action introduced 1996.

Price: Lightweight w/Pistol Grip Short Action, from **$1,020.00**
Price: Lightweight w/Pistol Grip Long Action **$1,100.00**
Price: Lightweight '81 Short Action **$960.00**
Price: Lightweight '81 Long Action **$1,040.00**
Price: Lightweight '81 Takedown Short Action, from **$1,040.00**
Price: Lightweight '81 Takedown Long Action, from **$1,120.00**
Price: Lightweight stainless . . . . **$1,100.00 to $1,180.00**
Price: Stainless Takedown . . . . **$1,230.00 to $1,300.00**
Price: Gold Medallion w/nickel finish,
engraving . . . . **$1,470.00 to $1,550.00**

CIMARRON 1860 HENRY CIVIL WAR MODEL

Caliber: .44 WCF, .45 LC; 12-shot magazine. **Barrel:** 24" (rifle). **Weight:** 9.5 lbs. **Length:** 43" overall (rifle). **Stock:** European walnut. **Sights:** Bead front, open adjustable rear. **Features:** Brass receiver and buttplate. Uses original Henry loading system. Copy of the original rifle. Charcoal blue finish optional. Introduced 1991. Imported by Cimarron F.A. Co.

Price: From **$1,533.78**

CIMARRON 1866 WINCHESTER REPLICAS

Caliber: .38 Spec., .357, .45 LC, .32 WCF, .38 WCF, .44 WCF. **Barrel:** 24" (rifle), 20" (short rifle), 19" (carbine), 16" (trapper). **Weight:** 9 lbs. **Length:** 43" overall (rifle). **Stock:** European walnut. **Sights:** Bead front, open adjustable rear. **Features:** Solid brass receiver, buttplate, fore-end cap. Octagonal barrel. Copy of the original Winchester '66 rifle. Introduced 1991. Imported by Cimarron F.A. Co.

Price: 1866 Short Rifle, 20" barrel, from **$1,143.00**
Price: 1866 Carbine, 19" barrel, from **$1,156.00**
Price: 1866 Trapper, 16" barrel, from **$1,104.00**

CIMARRON 1873 SHORT

Caliber: .357 Mag., .38 Spec., .32 WCF, .38 WCF, .44 Spec., .44 WCF, .45 Colt. **Barrel:** 20" tapered octagon. **Weight:** 7.5 lbs. **Length:** 39" overall. **Stock:** Walnut. **Sights:** Bead front, adjustable semi-buckhorn rear. **Features:** Has half "button" magazine. Original-type markings, including caliber, on barrel and elevator and "Kings" patent. From Cimarron F.A. Co.

Price: **$1,272.00**

CIMARRON 1873 DELUXE SPORTING

Similar to the 1873 Short Rifle except has 24" barrel with half-magazine.
Price: **$1,338.00**

CIMARRON 1873 LONG RANGE

Caliber: .44 WCF, .45 Colt. **Barrel:** 30", octagonal. **Weight:** 8.5 lbs. **Length:** 48" overall. **Stock:** Walnut. **Sights:** Blade front, semi-buckhorn ramp rear. Tang sight optional. **Features:** Color case-hardened frame; choice of modern blue-black or charcoal blue for other parts. Barrel marked "Kings Improvement." From Cimarron F.A. Co.

Price: **$1,284.10**

EMF 1860 HENRY

Caliber: .44-40 or .45 Colt. **Barrel:** 24". **Weight:** About 9 lbs. **Length:** About 43.75" overall. **Stock:** Oil-stained American walnut. **Sights:** Blade front, rear adjustable for elevation. **Features:** Reproduction of the original Henry rifle with brass frame and buttplate, rest blued. Imported by EMF.

Price: Brass frame **$1,150.00**
Price: Case-hardened frame **$1,285.00**

EMF 1866 YELLOWBOY LEVER ACTIONS

Caliber: .38 Spec., .44-40, .45 LC. **Barrel:** 19" (carbine), 24" (rifle). **Weight:** 9 lbs. **Length:** 43" overall (rifle). **Stock:** European walnut. **Sights:** Bead front, open adjustable rear. **Features:** Solid brass frame, blued barrel, lever, hammer, buttplate. Imported from Italy by EMF.

Price: Rifle. **$1,050.00**
Price: Border Rifle, Short **$1,075.00**

EMF MODEL 1873 LEVER-ACTION

Caliber: .32/20, .357 Mag., .38/40, .44-40, .45 Colt. **Barrel:** 18", 20", 24", 30". **Weight:** 8 lbs. **Length:** 43.25" overall. **Stock:** European walnut. **Sights:** Bead front, rear adjustable for windage and elevation. **Features:** Color case-hardened frame (blue on carbine). Imported by EMF.

Price: **$1,180.00**

EMF MODEL 1873 REVOLVER CARBINE

Caliber: .357 Mag., .45 Colt. **Barrel:** 18". **Weight:** 4 lbs., 8 oz. **Length:** 43-3/4" overall. **Stock:** One-piece walnut. **Sights:** Blade front, notch rear. **Features:** Color case-hardened frame, blue barrel, backstrap and triggerguard. Introduced 1998. Imported from Italy by EMF.

Price: Standard **$1,040.00**

HENRY ORIGINAL RIFLE

Caliber: .44-40 (13-round magazine). **Barrel:** 24". **Weight:** 9 lbs. **Stock:** Straight-grip fancy American walnut with hardened brass buttplate. **Sights:** Folding ladder rear with blade front. **Finish:** Hardened brass receiver with blued steel barrel. **Features:** Virtually identical to the original 1860 version except for the caliber. Each serial number has prefix "BTH" in honor of Benjamin Tyler Henry, the inventor of the lever-action repeating rifle that went on to become the most legendary firearm in American history. Introduced 2014 by Henry Repeating Arms. Made in the U.S.A.

PRICE: **$2,300.00**

Prices given are believed to be accurate at time of publication however, many factors affect retail pricing so exact prices are not possible.

HENRY .45-70
Caliber: .45-70 (4-shot magazine). **Barrel:** 18.5". **Weight:** 7 lbs. **Stock:** Pistol grip walnut. **Sights:** XS Ghost Rings with blade front.
PRICE: $850.00

HENRY BIG BOY LEVER-ACTION CARBINE
Caliber: .44 Magnum, standard model; .357 Magnum, .45 Colt, Deluxe II only. 10-shot tubular magazine. **Barrel:** 20" octagonal, 1:38" right-hand twist. **Weight:** 8.68 lbs. **Length:** 38.5" overall. **Stock:** Straight-grip American walnut, brass buttplate. **Sights:** Marbles full adjustable semi-buckhorn rear, brass bead front. **Features:** Brasslite receiver not tapped for scope mount. Made in U.S.A. by Henry Repeating Arms.
Price: .44 Magnum, walnut, blued barrel..................................**$899.95**
Price: Deluxe II .45 Colt, .357 Mag., engraved receiver **$1,995.95**

HENRY .30/30 LEVER-ACTION CARBINE
Same as the Big Boy except has straight grip American walnut, .30-30 only, 6-shot. Receivers are drilled and tapped for scope mount. Made in U.S.A. by Henry Repeating Arms.
Price: H009 Blued receiver, round barrel..................................**$749.95**
Price: H009B Brass receiver, octagonal barrel........................**$949.95**

MARLIN MODEL 336C LEVER-ACTION CARBINE
Caliber: .30-30 or .35 Rem., 6-shot tubular magazine. **Barrel:** 20" Micro-Groove. **Weight:** 7 lbs. **Length:** 38.5" overall. **Stock:** Checkered American black walnut, capped pistol grip. Mar-Shield finish; rubber buttpad; swivel studs. **Sights:** Ramp front with Wide-Scan hood, semi-buckhorn folding rear adjustable for windage and elevation. **Features:** Hammer-block safety. Receiver tapped for scope mount, offset hammer spur; top of receiver sandblasted to prevent glare. Includes safety lock. The latest variation of Marlin's classic lever gun that originated in 1937.
Price: $592.00

MARLIN MODEL 336SS LEVER-ACTION CARBINE
Same as the 336C except receiver, barrel and other major parts are machined from stainless steel. .30-30 only, 6-shot; receiver tapped for scope. Includes safety lock.
Price: $727.00

MARLIN MODEL 336W LEVER-ACTION
Similar to the Model 336C except has walnut-finished, cut-checkered Maine birch stock; blued steel barrel band has integral sling swivel; no front sight hood; comes with padded nylon sling; hard rubber buttplate. Introduced 1998. Includes safety lock. Made in U.S.A. by Marlin.
Price: $500.00

MARLIN 336BL
Lever action rifle chambered for .30-30. Features include 6-shot full length tubular magazine; 18-inch blued barrel with Micro-Groove rifling (12 grooves); big-loop finger lever; side ejection; blued steel receiver; hammer block safety; brown laminated hardwood pistol-grip stock with fluted comb; cut checkering; deluxe recoil pad; blued swivel studs.
Price: $622.00

MARLIN MODEL XLR LEVER-ACTION RIFLES
Similar to Model 336C except has an 24" stainless barrel with Ballard-type cut rifling, stainless steel receiver and other parts, laminated hardwood stock with pistol grip, nickel-plated swivel studs. Chambered for .30-30 Win. with Hornady spire-pointed Flex-Tip cartridges. Includes safety lock. Introduced 2006.
Price: Model 336XLR **$905.00**

MARLIN MODEL .308 MX, .338 MX
Caliber: .308 Marlin Express or .338 Marlin Express. **Barrel:** 24" stainless steel. **Weight:** 7.5 lbs. **Length:** 42.5" overall. **Features:**

Stainless steel receiver, lever and magazine tube. American black walnut stock and fore-end. .338 MXLR model has black/gray laminated checkered stock and fore-end. Hooded ramp front sight and adjustable semibuckhorn rear; drilled and tapped for scope mounts. Receiver-mounted crossbolt safety.
Price: .338 MXLR.. **$905.00**
Price: .308 or .338 MX **$686.00**

MARLIN MODEL 1894
Caliber: .44 Spec./.44 Mag., 10-shot tubular magazine. **Barrel:** 20" Ballard-type rifling. **Weight:** 6 lbs. **Length:** 37.5" overall. **Stock:** Checkered American black walnut, straight grip and forend. Mar-Shield finish. Rubber rifle buttpad; swivel studs. **Sights:** Wide-Scan hooded ramp front, semibuckhorn folding rear adjustable for windage and elevation. **Features:** Hammer-block safety. Receiver tapped for scope mount, offset hammer spur, solid top receiver sand blasted to prevent glare. Includes safety lock.
Price: $708.00

MARLIN MODEL 1894C CARBINE
Similar to the standard Model 1894 except chambered for .38 Spec./.357 Mag. with full-length 9-shot magazine, 18.5" barrel, hammer-block safety, hooded front sight. Introduced 1983. Includes safety lock.
Price: $708.00

MARLIN MODEL 1894 COWBOY
Caliber: .357 Mag., .44 Mag., .45 Colt, 10-shot magazine. **Barrel:** 20" tapered octagon, deep cut rifling. **Weight:** 7.5 lbs. **Length:** 41.5" overall. **Stock:** Straight grip American black walnut, hard rubber buttplate, Mar-Shield finish. **Sights:** Marble carbine front, adjustable Marble semibuckhorn rear. **Features:** Squared finger lever; straight grip stock; blued steel fore-end tip. Designed for Cowboy Shooting events. Introduced 1996. Includes safety lock. Made in U.S.A. by Marlin.
Price: $1,010.00

MARLIN MODEL 1894SS
Similar to Model 1894 except has stainless steel barrel, receiver, lever, guard plate, magazine tube and loading plate. Nickel-plated swivel studs.
Price: $829.00

MARLIN 1894 DELUXE
Lever action rifle chambered in .44 Magnum/.44 Special. Features include 10-shot tubular magazine; squared finger lever; side ejection; richly polished deep blued metal surfaces; solid top receiver; hammer block safety; #1 grade fancy American black walnut straight-grip stock and forend; cut checkering; rubber rifle buttpad; Mar-Shield finish; blued steel fore-end cap: swivel studs; deep-cut Ballard-type rifling (6 grooves).
Price: $950.00

MARLIN 1894CSS
Lever action rifle chambered in .357 Magnum/.38 Special. Features include 9-shot tubular magazine; stainless steel receiver, barrel, lever, trigger and hammer; squared finger lever; side ejection; solid top receiver; hammer block safety; American black walnut straight-grip stock and fore-end; cut checkering; rubber rifle buttpad; Mar-Shield finish.
Price: $829.00

Prices given are believed to be accurate at time of publication however, many factors affect retail pricing so exact prices are not possible.

69TH EDITION, 2015 ✦ **465**

MARLIN MODEL 1895 LEVER-ACTION

Caliber: .45-70 Govt., 4-shot tubular magazine. **Barrel:** 22", round. **Weight:** 7.5 lbs. **Length:** 40.5" overall. **Stock:** Checkered American black walnut, full pistol grip. Mar-Shield finish; rubber buttpad; quick detachable swivel studs. **Sights:** Bead front with Wide-Scan hood, semibuckhorn folding rear adjustable for windage and elevation. **Features:** Hammer-block safety. Solid receiver tapped for scope mounts or receiver sights; offset hammer spur. Includes safety lock.
Price: **$675.00**

MARLIN MODEL 1895G GUIDE GUN LEVER-ACTION

Similar to Model 1895 with deep-cut Ballard-type rifling; straight-grip walnut stock. Overall length is 37", weighs 7 lbs. Introduced 1998. Includes safety lock. Made in U.S.A. by Marlin.
Price: **$680.00**

MARLIN MODEL 1895GS GUIDE GUN

Similar to Model 1895G except receiver, barrel and most metal parts are machined from stainless steel. Chambered for .45-70 Govt., 4-shot, 18.5" barrel. Overall length is 37", weighs 7 lbs. Introduced 2001. Includes safety lock. Made in U.S.A. by Marlin.
Price: **$813.00**

MARLIN MODEL 1895 SBLR

Similar to Model 1895GS Guide Gun but with stainless steel barrel (18.5"), receiver, large loop lever and magazine tube. Black/gray laminated buttstock and forend, XS ghost ring rear sight, hooded ramp front sight, receiver/barrel-mounted top rail for mounting accessory optics. Chambered in .45-70 Government. Overall length is 42.5", weighs 7.5 lbs.
Price: **$1,039.00**

MARLIN MODEL 1895 COWBOY LEVER-ACTION

Similar to Model 1895 except has 26" tapered octagon barrel with Ballard-type rifling, Marble carbine front sight and Marble adjustable semi-buckhorn rear sight. Receiver tapped for scope or receiver sight. Overall length is 44.5", weighs about 8 lbs. Introduced 2001. Includes safety lock. Made in U.S.A. by Marlin.
Price: **$785.00**

MARLIN MODEL 1895XLR LEVER-ACTION

Similar to Model 1895 except has an 24" stainless barrel with Ballard-type cut rifling, stainless steel receiver and other parts, laminated hardwood stock with pistol grip, nickel-plated swivel studs. Chambered for .45-70 Govt. with Hornady Evolution spire-pointed Flex-Tip cartridges. Includes safety lock. Introduced 2006.
Price: (Model 1895MXLR)..**$816.00**

MARLIN 1895GBL

Lever action rifle chambered in .45-70 Government. Features include 6-shot, full-length tubular magazine; 18-1/2-inch barrel with deep-cut Ballard-type rifling (6 grooves); big-loop finger lever; side ejection; solid-top receiver; deeply blued metal surfaces; hammer block safety; pistol-grip two-tone brown laminate stock with cut checkering; ventilated recoil pad; Mar-Shield finish, swivel studs.

Price: **$713.00**

MOSSBERG 464 LEVER ACTION

Caliber: .30-30 Win., 6-shot tubular magazine. **Barrel:** 20" round. **Weight:** 6.7 lbs. **Length:** 38.5" overall. **Stock:** Hardwood with straight or pistol grip, quick detachable swivel studs. **Sights:** Folding rear sight, adjustable for windage and elevation. **Features:** Blued receiver and barrel, receiver drilled and tapped, two-position top-tang safety. Available with straight grip or semi-pistol grip. Introduced 2008. From O.F. Mossberg & Sons, Inc.
Price: **$513.00**

NAVY ARMS 1873 RIFLE

Caliber: .357 Mag., .45 Colt, 12-shot magazine. **Barrel:** 20", 24.25", full octagonal. **Stock:** Deluxe checkered American walnut. **Sights:** Gold bead front, semi-buckhorn rear. **Features:** Turnbull color case-hardened frame, rest blued. Full-octagon barrel. Available exclusively from Navy Arms.
Price: **$2,500.00**

PUMA BOUNTY HUNTER

Caliber: .44/40, .44 Mag. and .45 Colt, 6-shot magazine capacity. **Barrel:** 12". **Weight:** 4.5 lbs. **Length:** 24". **Stock:** Walnut. **Sights:** Fixed sights. **Features:** A piece of 1950's TV nostalgia, the Bounty Hunter is a reproduction of the gun carried by Western character Josh Randall in the series "Wanted: Dead or Alive." The Bounty Hunter is based on a Winchester Model 92 rifle, but is considered by Federal Law as a pistol, because it is built from the ground up as a handgun. The Bounty Hunter features a 12" barrel and 6-round tubular magazine. At just 24" OAL, the Bounty Hunter makes an ideal pack gun or camp defense pistol. The Bounty Hunter has a teardrop shaped loop lever and is built with the same fit, finish and high-grade Italian walnut stocks as our Puma M-92 and M-86 rifles. Manufactured in the U.S.A. by Chiappa Firearms of Dayton, OH.
Price: .45LC, Case Hardened/Blued.....................................**$1,372.00**
Price: .44/40, Case Hardened/Blued **$1,372.00**
Price: .44 Mag., Case Hardened/Blued **$1,372.00**

PUMA MODEL 92S AND CARBINES

Caliber: .17 HMR (XP and Scout models, only; intr. 2008), .38 Spec./.357 Mag., .44 Mag., .45 Colt, .454 Casull, .480 Ruger (.44-40 in 20" octagonal barrel). **Barrel:** 16" and 20" round; 20" and 24" octagonal. 1:30" rate of twist (exc. .17 HMR is 1:9"). **Weight:** 7.7 lbs. **Stock:** Walnut stained hardwood. **Sights:** Blade front, V rear, buckhorn sights sold separately. **Features:** Finishes available in blue/blue, blue/case colored and stainless/stainless with matching crescent buttplates. .454 and .480 calibers have rubber recoil pads. Full-length magazines, thumb safety. Large lever loop or HiViz sights available on select models. Magazine capacity is 12 rounds with 24" bbl.; 10 rounds with 20" barrel; 8 rounds in 16" barrel. Introduced in 2002. Scout includes long-eye-relief scope, rail, elevated cheekpiece, intr. 2008. XP chambered in .17 HMR, .38 Spec./.357 Mag. and .44 Mag., loads through magazine tube or loading gate, intr. 2008. Imported from Brazil by Legacy Sports International.
Price: From **$959.00**
Price: Scout Model, w/2.5x32 Nikko-Stirling Nighteater scope, intr. 2008, from.................................**$739.00**
Price: XP Model, tube feed magazine, intr. 2008, from **$613.00**

REMINGTON MODEL 7600 PUMP ACTION

Caliber: .243 Win., .270 Win., .30-06 Spfl., .308. **Barrel:** 22" round tapered. **Weight:** 7.5 lbs. **Length:** 42.6" overall. **Stock:** Cut-checkered walnut pistol grip and fore-end, Monte Carlo with full cheekpiece. Satin or high-gloss finish. Also, black synthetic. **Sights:** Gold bead front sight on matted ramp, open step adjustable sporting rear. **Features:** Redesigned and improved version of the Model 760. Detachable 4-shot magazine. Crossbolt safety. Receiver tapped for scope mount. Introduced 1981.
Price: 7600 Wood **$918.00**
Price: 7600 Synthetic...**$771.00**

ROSSI R92 LEVER-ACTION CARBINE

Caliber: .38 Special/.357 Mag, .44 Mag., .44-40 Win., .45 Colt, .454 Casull. **Barrel:** 16" or 20" with round barrel, 20" or 24" with octagon barrel. **Weight:** 4.8 lbs. to 7 lbs. **Length:** 34 to 41.5 inches. **Features:** Blued or stainless finish. Various options available

Prices given are believed to be accurate at time of publication however, many factors affect retail pricing so exact prices are not possible.

in selected chamberings (large lever loop, fiber-optic sights, cheekpiece, etc.).

Price: Blued **$624.00**
Price: Stainless **$650.00**
Price: .454 Casull **$754.00**

ROSSI RIO GRANDE
Caliber: .30-30 or .45-70 or .410 shotshell. **Barrel:** 20". **Weight:** 7 lbs. **Sights:** Adjustable rear, post front. **Stock:** Hardwood or camo.
Price: **$643.00**

UBERTI 1873 SPORTING RIFLE
Caliber: .357 Mag., .44-40, .45 Colt. **Barrel:** 16.1" round, 19" round or 20", 24.25" octagonal. **Weight:** Up to 8.2 lbs. **Length:** Up to 43.3" overall. **Stock:** Walnut, straight grip and pistol grip. **Sights:** Blade front adjustable for windage, open rear adjustable for elevation. **Features:** Color case-hardened frame, blued barrel, hammer, lever, buttplate, brass elevator. Imported by Stoeger Industries.
Price: Carbine 19" bbl. **$1,219.00**
Price: Trapper 16.1" bbl. **$1,259.00**
Price: Carbine 18" half oct. bbl. **$1,309.00**
Price: Short Rifle 20" bbl. **$1,259.00**
Price: Sporting Rifle, 24.25" bbl. **$1,259.00**
Price: Special Sporting Rifle, A-grade walnut **$1,399.00**

UBERTI 1866 YELLOWBOY CARBINE, SHORT, RIFLE
Caliber: .38 Spec., .44-40, .45 Colt. **Barrel:** 24.25", octagonal. **Weight:** 8.2 lbs. **Length:** 43.25" overall. **Stock:** Walnut. **Sights:** Blade adjustable for windage, rear adjustable for elevation. **Features:** Frame, buttplate, fore-end cap of polished brass, balance charcoal blued. Imported by Stoeger Industries.
Price: 1866 Yellowboy Carbine, 19" round barrel **$1,119.00**
Price: 1866 Yellowboy Short Rifle, 20" octagonal barrel **$1,169.00**
Price: 1866 Yellowboy Rifle, 24.25" octagonal barrel **$1,169.00**

UBERTI 1860 HENRY
Caliber: .44-40, .45 Colt. **Barrel:** 24.25", half-octagon. **Weight:** 9.2 lbs. **Length:** 43.75" overall. **Stock:** American walnut. **Sights:** Blade front, rear adjustable for elevation. Imported by Stoeger Industries.
Price: 1860 Henry Trapper, 18.5" barrel, brass frame **$1,429.00**
Price: 1860 Henry Rifle Iron Frame, 24.25" barrel **$1,459.00**

UBERTI LIGHTNING
Caliber: .357 Mag., .45 Colt, 10+1. Slide action operation. **Barrel:** 20" to 24.25". **Stock:** Satin-finished walnut. **Finish:** Case-hardened. Introduced 2006. Imported by Stoeger Industries.
Price: **$1,259.00**

WINCHESTER MODEL 94 SHORT RIFLE
Caliber: .30-30, .38-55. **Barrel:** 20". **Weight:** 6.75 lbs. **Sights:** Semi-buckhorn rear, gold bead front. **Stock:** Walnut with straight grip. Fore-

end has black grip cap. Also available in Trail's End takedown design in .450 Marlin or .30-30.
Price: **$1,230.00**
Price: (Takedown) **$1,460.00**

WINCHESTER MODEL 94 CARBINE
Same general specifications as M94 Short Rifle except for curved buttplate and fore-end barrelband.
Price: **$1,200.00**

WINCHESTER MODEL 94 SPORTER
Caliber: .30-30, .38-55. **Barrel:** 24". **Weight:** 7.5 lbs. **Features:** Same features of Model 94 Short Rifle except for crescent butt and steel buttplate, 24" half-round, half-octagon barrel, checkered stock.

Price: **$1,400.00**

WINCHESTER 1873 SHORT RIFLE
Caliber: .357 Magnum, .44-40, .45 Colt. Tubular magazine holds 10 rounds (.44-40, .45 Colt), 11 rounds (.38 Special). **Barrel:** 20 inches. **Weight:** 7.25 lbs. **Sights:** Marble semi-buckhorn rear, gold bead front. Tang is drilled and tapped for optional peep sight. **Stock:** Satin finished, straight-grip walnut with steel crescent buttplate and steel fore-end cap. Tang safety. A modern version of the "Gun That Won the West."
Price: **$1,300.00**

WINCHESTER MODEL 1886 SHORT RIFLE
Caliber: .45-70 or .49-90. **Barrel:** 24". **Weight:** 8.4 lbs. **Sights:** Adjustable buckhorn rear, blade front. **Stock:** Grade 1 walnut with crescent butt.
Price **$1,340.00**

WINCHESTER MODEL 1892 CARBINE
Caliber: .357 Mag., .44 Mag., .44-40, .45 Colt. **Barrel:** 20 inches. **Weight:** 6 lbs. **Stock:** Satin finished walnut with straight grip, steel fore-end strap. **Sights:** Marble semi-buckhorn rear, gold bead front. Other features include saddle ring and tang safety. Available with large loop lever.
Price: Large loop lever **$1,260.00**
Price: 1892 Short Rifle **$1,070.00**

Prices given are believed to be accurate at time of publication however, many factors affect retail pricing so exact prices are not possible.

69TH EDITION, 2015 ✦ **467**

ARMALITE AR-30A1

Caliber: .300 Win. Mag., .338 Lapua. Bolt-action with five-round capacity. **Barrel:** 24 inches (.300 Win.), 26 inches (.338 Lapua), competition grade. **Weight:** 12.8 lbs. **Length:** 46 inches. **Stock:** Standard fixed. **Sights:** None. Accessory top rail included. **Features**: Muzzlebrake, ambidextrous magazine release, large ejection port makes single loading easy, V-block patented bedding system, bolt-mounted safety locks firing pin. Target versions have adjustable stock.
Price: .... $3,264.00 to $3,599.00

ARMALITE AR-50A1

Caliber: .50 BMG, .416 Barrett. Bolt-action single-shot. **Barrel:** 30 inches with muzzlebrake. National Match model (shown) has 33-inch fluted barrel. **Weight:** 34.1 lbs. **Stock:** Three-section. Extruded fore-end, machined vertical grip, forged and machined buttstock that is vertically adjustable. National Match model (.50 BMG only) has V-block patented bedding system, Armalite Skid System to ensure straight-back recoil.
Price: $3,359.00
Price: National Match $4,230.00

BARRETT MODEL 95

Caliber: 50 BMG, 5-shot magazine. **Barrel:** 29". **Weight:** 23.5 lbs. **Length:** 45" overall. **Stock:** Energy-absorbing recoil pad. **Sights:** Scope optional. **Features:** Bolt-action, bullpup design. Disassembles without tools; extendable bipod legs; match-grade barrel; muzzlebrake. Introduced 1995. Made in U.S.A. by Barrett Firearms Mfg., Inc.
Price: From $6,500.00

BARRETT MODEL 98B

Caliber: .338 Lapua Magnum (10-shot magazine). **Barrel:** 27" fluted or 20". **Weight:** 13.5 lbs. **Length:** 49.8". Comes with two magazines, bipod, monopod, side accessory rail, hard case.
PRICE: $4,850.00

BARRETT MRAD

Caliber: .338 Lapua Magnum. **Magazine capacity:** 10 rounds. **Barrel:** 20, 24 or 26 inches, fluted or heavy. **Features:** User interchangeable barrel system, folding stock, adjustable cheekpiece, 5-position length of pull adjustment button, match-grade trigger, 22-inch optics rail.
Price: .... $5,850.00 to $6,000.00

BLASER R93 PROFESSIONAL

Caliber: .22-250 Rem., .243 Win., 6.5x55, .270 Win., 7x57, 7mm-08

Rem., .308 Win., .30-06 Spfl., .257 Wby. Mag., 7mm Rem. Mag., .300 Win. Mag., .300 Wby. Mag., .338 Win. Mag., .375H&H, 416 Rem. Mag. **Barrel:** 22" (standard calibers), 26" (magnum). **Weight:** 7 lbs. **Length:** 40" overall (22" barrel). **Stock:** Two-piece European walnut. **Sights:** None furnished; drilled and tapped for scope mounting. **Features:** Straight pull-back bolt action with thumb-activated safety slide/cocking mechanism; interchangeable barrels and bolt heads. LRS (Long Range Sporter) is competition model with many competition features including fluted barrel, adjustable trigger and stock. Imported from Germany by Blaser USA.
Price: From $3,145.00
Price: LRS from.. $4,405.00
Price: R-93 Synthetic from $1,800.00

BROWNING AB3 COMPOSITE STALKER

Caliber: .270, 7mm Rem. Mag., .30-06, .300 Win. Mag. or .308 Win. **Barrel:** 22 inches, 26 for magnums. **Weight:** 6.8 lbs. **Stock:** Matte black synthetic. **Sights:** None. Picatinny rail scope mount included. **Features:** Based on A-Bolt action. General specifications are the same as A-Bolt Medallion.
Price: $600.00

BROWNING A-BOLT MEDALLION

Calibers: 7mm Rem. Mag., .300 Win. Mag. **Barrel:** 26" **Weight:** 7.1 lbs. **Length:** 46.75" overall. **Stock:** Select walnut with rosewood grip cap and fore-end cap. Checkered grip and fore-end. Gloss finish. **Features:** High polish blue metal finish. Sixty-degree bolt lift, top tang safety. Medallion White Gold model has maple stock, octagonal barrel and is available in most popular calibers. Limited production.
Price: .... $1,110.00 to $1,269.00
Price: w/Boss (magnum calibers), from................................ $1,270.00

BROWNING X-BOLT HOG STALKER

Caliber: .223 or .308 Win. **Barrel:** 20 inches, medium heavy. **Weight:** 6.8 to 7 pounds. **Stock:** Composite black or Realtree Max-1 camo. **Sights:** None. Picatinny rail scope mount included.
Price: $1,200.00

BROWNING X-BOLT HUNTER

Calibers: .223, .22-250, .243 Win., .25-06 Rem., .270 Win., .270 WSM, .280 Rem., 7mm Rem. Mag., 7mm WSM, 7mm-08 Rem., .308 Win., .30-06 Spfl., .300 Win. Mag., .300 WSM, .325 WSM, .338 Win. Mag., .375 H&H Mag. **Barrels:** 22", 23", 24", 26", varies by model. Matte blued or stainless free-floated barrel, recessed muzzle crown. **Weight:** 6.3-7 lbs. **Stock:** Hunter and Medallion models have wood stocks; Composite Stalker and Stainless Stalker models have composite stocks. Inflex Technology recoil pad. **Sights:** None, drilled and tapped receiver, X-Lock scope mounts. **Features:** Adjustable three-lever Feather Trigger system, polished hard-chromed steel components, factory pre-set at 3.5 lbs., alloy trigger housing. Bolt unlock button, detachable rotary magazine, 60-degree bolt lift, three locking lugs, top-tang safety, sling swivel studs. Introduced 2008.
Price: Standard calibers $900.00
Price: Magnum calibers $950.00

Prices given are believed to be accurate at time of publication however, many factors affect retail pricing so exact prices are not possible.

CENTERFIRE RIFLES Bolt-Action

BROWNING X-BOLT MICRO HUNTER
Similar to Browning X-Bolt Hunter but with compact dimensions.
Calibers: .22-250, .243, .7mm-08, .308 Win., .270 WSM, .300 WSM.
Barrel: 20" or 22". **Weight:** 5.9 lbs. Length of pull: 13-15/16".
Price: Standard chamberings $900.00
Price: Magnum $950.00

BROWNING X-BOLT MICRO MIDAS
Caliber: .243 Win., 7mm-08 Rem., .308 Win., .22-250 Rem. **Barrel:** 20".
Weight: 6 lbs.1 oz. **Length:** 37-5/8" to 38-1/8" overall. **Stock:** Satin
finish checkered walnut stock. **Sights:** Hooded front and adjustable
rear. **Features:** Steel receiver with low-luster blued finish. Glass
bedded, drilled and tapped for scope mounts. Barrel is free-floating
and hand chambered with target crown. Bolt-action with adjustable
Feather Trigger™ and detachable rotary magazine. Compact 12-1/2"
length of pull for smaller shooters, designed to fit smaller-framed
shooters like youth and women. This model has all the same features
as the full-size model with sling swivel studs installed and Inflex
Technology recoil pad. (Scope and mounts not included).
Price: $860.00

BROWNING X-BOLT VARMINT STALKER
Similar to Browning X-Bolt Stalker but with medium-heavy free-
floated barrel, target crown, composite stock. Chamberings available:
.223, .22-250, .243 Winchester and .308 Winchester only
Price: $1,170.00

BUSHMASTER BA50 BOLT-ACTION
Caliber: 50 Browning BMG. **Barrel:** 30" (rifle), 22" (carbine), 10-round
mag. **Weight:** 30 lbs. (rifle), 27 lbs. (carbine). **Length:** 58" overall
(rifle), 50" overall (carbine). **Features:** Free-floated Lothar Walther
barrel with muzzlebrake, Magpul PRS adjustable stock.
Price: $5,500.00

CARBON ONE BOLT-ACTION
Caliber: .22-250 to .375H&H. **Barrel:** Up to 28". **Weight:** 5.5 to
7.25 lbs. **Length:** Varies. **Stock:** Synthetic or wood. **Sights:** None
furnished. **Features:** Choice of Remington, Browning or Winchester
action with free-floated Christensen graphite/epoxy/steel barrel,
trigger pull tuned to 3 to 3.5 lbs. Made in U.S.A. by Christensen
Arms.
Price: Carbon One Hunter Rifle, 6.5 to 7 lbs. $1,775.00
Price: Carbon One Custom, 5.5 to 6.5 lbs., Shilen trigger ...$3,900.00
Price: Carbon Extreme $2,450.00

CENTURY INTERNATIONAL M70 SPORTER DOUBLE-TRIGGER BOLT ACTION
Caliber: .22-250 Rem., .270 Win., .300 Win. Mag., .308 Win., 24"
barrel. **Weight:** 7.95 lbs. **Length:** 44.5". **Sights:** Flip-up U-notch rear
sight, hooded blade front sight. **Features:** Mauser M98-type action;
5-rd fixed box magazine. .22-250 has hinged floorplate. Monte Carlo
stock, oil finish. Adjustable trigger on double-trigger models. .300
Win. Mag. has 3-rd. fixed box magazine. .308 Win. holds 5 rounds.
.300 and .308 have buttpads. Manufactured by Zastava in Yugoslavia,
imported by Century International
Price: M70 Sporter Double-Trigger...$500.00
Price: M70 Sporter Double-Trigger .22-250 ....$475.00
Price: M70 Sporter Single-Trigger .300 Win. Mag. $475.00
Price: M70 Sporter Single/Double Trigger .308 Win. $500.00

CHEYTAC M-200
Caliber: 408 CheyTac, 7-round magazine. **Barrel:** 30". **Length:** 55",
stock extended. **Weight:** 27 lbs. (steel barrel); 24 lbs. (carbon-fiber
barrel). **Stock:** Retractable. **Sights:** None, scope rail provided.

Features: CNC-machined receiver, attachable Picatinny rail M-1913,
detachable barrel, integral bipod, 3.5-lb. trigger pull, muzzlebrake.
Made in U.S. by CheyTac, LLC.
Price: $13,795.00

COOPER MODEL 21
Caliber: .17 Rem., .19-223, Tactical 20, .204 Ruger, .222 Rem., .222
Rem. Mag., .223 Rem, .223 Rem A.I., 6x45, 6x47. **Barrel:** 22" or
24" in Classic configurations, 24"-26" in Varminter configurations.
Weight: 6.5-8.0 lbs., depending on type. **Stock:** AA-AAA select claro
walnut, 20 lpi checkering. **Sights:** None furnished. **Features:** Three
front locking-lug, bolt-action, single-shot. Action: 7.75" long, Sako
extractor. Button ejector. Fully adjustable single-stage trigger. Options
include wood upgrades, case-color metalwork, barrel fluting, custom
LOP, and many others.
Price: From $1,695.00

COOPER MODEL 22
Caliber: .22-250 Rem., .22-250 Rem. AI, .25-06 Rem., .25-06 Rem. AI,
.243 Win., .243 Win. AI, .220 Swift, .250/3000 AI, .257 Roberts, .257
Roberts AI, 7mm-08 Rem., 6mm Rem., .260 Rem., 6x284, 6.5x284,
.22 BR, 6mm BR, .308 Win. **Barrel:** 24" or 26" stainless match in
Classic configurations. 24" or 26" in Varminter configurations. **Weight:**
7.5 to 8.0 lbs. depending on type. **Stock:** AA-AAA select claro walnut,
20 lpi checkering. **Sights:** None furnished. **Features:** Three front
locking-lug bolt-action single shot. Action: 8.25" long, Sako-style
extractor. Button ejector. Fully adjustable single-stage trigger. Options
include wood upgrades, case-color metalwork, barrel fluting, custom
LOP, and many others.
Price: From $1,695.00

COOPER MODEL 38
Caliber: 17 Squirrel, 17 He Bee, 17 Ackley Hornet, 17 Mach IV, 19
Calhoon, 20 VarTarg, 221 Fireball, .22 Hornet, .22 K-Hornet, .22
Squirrel, 218 Bee, 218 Mashburn Bee. **Barrel:** 22" or 24" in Classic
configurations, 24" or 26" in Varminter configurations. **Weight:** 6.5-8.0
lbs. depending on type. **Stock:** AA-AAA select claro walnut, 20 lpi
checkering. **Sights:** None furnished. **Features:** Three front locking-
lug bolt-action single shot. Action: 7" long, Sako-style extractor. Button
ejector. Fully adjustable single-stage trigger. Options include wood
upgrades, case-color metalwork, barrel fluting, custom LOP, and
many others.
Price: From $1,695.00

COOPER MODEL 56
Caliber: .257 Weatherby Mag., .264 Win. Mag., .270 Weatherby
Mag., 7mm Remington Mag., 7mm Weatherby Mag., 7mm Shooting
Times Westerner, .300 Holland & Holland, .300 Winchester Mag.,
.300 Weatherby Mag., .308 Norma Mag., 8mm Rem. Mag., .338
Win. Mag., .340 Weatherby V. Three-shot magazine. **Barrel:** 22" or
24" in Classic configurations, 24" or 26" in Varminter configurations.
Weight: 7.75-8 lbs. depending on type. **Stock:** AA-AAA select
claro walnut, 20 lpi checkering. **Sights:** None furnished. **Features:**
Three front locking-lug bolt-action single shot. Action: 7" long, Sako-
style extractor. Button ejector. Fully adjustable single-stage trigger.
Options include wood upgrades, case-color metalwork, barrel
fluting, custom LOP, and many others.
Price: Classic. $1,518.00
Price: Custom Classic. $1,618.00
Price: Western Classic. $1,518.00
Price: Jackson Game. $1,618.00
Price: Jackson Hunter. $1,518.00
Price: Excalibur. $1,618.00

CZ 527 LUX BOLT-ACTION
Caliber: .17 Hornet, .204 Ruger, .22 Hornet, .222 Rem., .223 Rem.,
detachable 5-shot magazine. **Barrel:** 23.5"; standard or heavy
barrel. **Weight:** 6 lbs., 1 oz. **Length:** 42.5" overall. **Stock:** European
walnut with Monte Carlo. **Sights:** Hooded front, open adjustable
rear. **Features:** Improved mini-Mauser action with non-rotating claw
extractor; single set trigger; grooved receiver. Imported from the
Czech Republic by CZ-USA.

Prices given are believed to be accurate at time of publication however, many factors affect retail pricing so exact prices are not possible.

69TH EDITION, 2015 ⊕ 469

Price: Brown laminate stock.....................................$718.00
Price: Model FS, full-length stock, cheekpiece $827.00

CZ 527 AMERICAN BOLT-ACTION

Similar to the CZ 527 Lux except has classic-style stock with 18 lpi checkering; free-floating barrel; recessed target crown on barrel. No sights furnished. Introduced 1999. Imported from the Czech Republic by CZUSA.
Price: From $711.00

CZ 550 AMERICAN CLASSIC

Caliber: .22-250 Rem., .243 Win., 6.5x55, 7x57, 7x64, .308 Win., 9.3x62, .270 Win., 30-06. **Barrel:** Free-floating barrel; recessed target crown. **Weight:** 7.48 lbs. **Length:** 44.68" overall. **Stock:** American classic style stock with 18 lpi checkering or FS (Mannlicher). **Sights:** No sights furnished. **Features:** Improved Mauser-style action with claw extractor, fixed ejector, square bridge dovetailed receiver; single set trigger. Introduced 1999. Imported from the Czech Republic by CZ-USA.
Price: FS (full stock) $894.00
Price: American, from $827.00

CZ 550 SAFARI MAGNUM/AMERICAN SAFARI MAGNUM

Similar to CZ 550 American Classic. Chambered for .375H&H Mag., .416 Rigby, .458 Win. Mag., .458 Lott. Overall length is 46.5"; barrel length 25"; weighs 9.4 lbs., 9.9 lbs (American). Hooded front sight, express rear with one standing, two folding leaves. Imported from the Czech Republic by CZ-USA.
Price: $1,179.00
Price: American $1,261.00
Price: American Kevlar $1,714.00

CZ 550 VARMINT

Similar to CZ 550 American Classic. Chambered for .308 Win. and .22-250. Kevlar, laminated stocks. Overall length is 46.7"; barrel length 25.6"; weighs 9.1 lbs. Imported from the Czech Republic by CZ-USA.
Price: $841.00
Price: Kevlar $1,037.00
Price: Laminated $966.00

CZ 550 MAGNUM H.E.T.

Similar to CZ 550 American Classic. Chambered for .338 Lapua, .300 Win. Mag., .300 RUM. Overall length is 52"; barrel length 28"; weighs 14 lbs. Adjustable sights, satin blued barrel. Imported from the Czech Republic by CZ-USA.
Price: $3,673.00

CZ 550 ULTIMATE HUNTING

Similar to CZ 550 American Classic. Chambered for .300 Win Mag. Overall length is 44.7"; barrel length 23.6"; weighs 7.7 lbs. Imported from the Czech Republic by CZ-USA.
Price: $4,242.00

CZ 750 SNIPER

Caliber: .308 Winchester, 10-shot magazine. **Barrel:** 26". **Weight:** 11.9 lbs. **Length:** 48" overall. **Stock:** Polymer thumbhole. **Sights:** None furnished; permanently attached Weaver rail for scope mounting. **Features:** 60-degree bolt throw; oversized triggerguard and bolt handle for use with gloves; full-length equipment rail on fore-end; fully adjustable trigger. Introduced 2001. Imported from the Czech Republic by CZ-USA.
Price: $2,404.00

DAKOTA 76 TRAVELER TAKEDOWN

Caliber: .257 Roberts, .25-06 Rem., 7x57, .270 Win., .280 Rem., .30-

06 Spfl., .338-06, .35 Whelen (standard length); 7mm Rem. Mag., .300 Win. Mag., .338 Win. Mag., .416 Taylor, .458 Win. Mag. (short magnums); 7mm, .300, .330, .375 Dakota Magnums. **Barrel:** 23". **Weight:** 7.5 lbs. **Length:** 43.5" overall. **Stock:** Medium fancy-grade walnut in classic style. Checkered grip and fore-end; solid buttpad. **Sights:** None furnished; drilled and tapped for scope mounts. **Features:** Threadless disassembly. Uses modified Model 76 design with many features of the Model 70 Winchester. Left-hand model also available. Introduced 1989. African chambered for .338 Lapua Mag., .404 Jeffery, .416 Rigby, .416 Dakota, .450 Dakota, 4-round magazine, select wood, two stock cross-bolts. 24" barrel, weighs 9-10 lbs. Ramp front sight, standing leaf rear. Introduced 1989. Made in U.S.A. by Dakota Arms, Inc.
Price: Classic $7,240.00
Price: Safari $9,330.00
Price: African $10,540.00

DAKOTA 76 CLASSIC

Caliber: .257 Roberts, .270 Win., .280 Rem., .30-06 Spfl., 7mm Rem. Mag., .338 Win. Mag., .300 Win. Mag., .375H&H, .458 Win. Mag. **Barrel:** 23". **Weight:** 7.5 lbs. **Length:** 43.5" overall. **Stock:** Medium fancy grade walnut in classic style. Checkered pistol grip and fore-end; solid buttpad. **Sights:** None furnished; drilled and tapped for scope mounts. **Features:** Has many features of the original Winchester Model 70. One-piece rail triggerguard assembly; steel gripcap. Model 70-style trigger. Many options available. Left-hand rifle available at same price. Introduced 1988. From Dakota Arms, Inc.
Price: From $6,030.00

DAKOTA MODEL 97 BOLT-ACTION

Caliber: .22-250 to .330. **Barrel:** 22" to 24". **Weight:** 6.1 to 6.5 lbs. **Length:** 43" overall. **Stock:** Fiberglass. **Sights:** Optional. **Features:** Matte blue finish, black stock. Right-hand action only. Introduced 1998. Made in U.S.A. by Dakota Arms, Inc.
Price: From $3,720.00

HOWA M-1500 RANCHLAND COMPACT

Caliber: .223 Rem., .22-250 Rem., .243 Win., .308 Win. and 7mm-08. **Barrel:** 20" #1 contour, blued finish. **Weight:** 7 lbs. **Stock:** Hogue Overmolded in black, OD green, Coyote Sand colors. 13.87" LOP. **Sights:** None furnished; drilled and tapped for scope mounting. **Features:** Three-position safety, hinged floorplate, adjustable trigger, forged one-piece bolt, M-16 style extractor, forged flat-bottom receiver. Also available with Nikko-Stirling Nighteater 3-9x42 riflescope. Introduced in 2008. Imported from Japan by Legacy Sports International.
Price: Rifle Only, (2008)..$585.00
Price: Rifle with 3-9x42 Nighteater scope (2008) $700.00

HOWA M-1500 THUMBHOLE SPORTER

Caliber: .204, .223 Rem., .22-250 Rem., .243 Win., 6.5x55 (2008) .25-06 Rem., .270 Win., 7mm Rem. Mag., .308 Win., .30-06 Spfl., .300 Win. Mag., .338 Win. Mag., .375 Ruger. Similar to Camo Lightning except stock. **Weight:** 7.6 to 7.7 lbs. **Stock:** S&K laminated wood in nutmeg (brown/black) or pepper (grey/black) colors, raised comb with forward taper, flared pistol grip and scalloped thumbhole. **Sights:** None furnished; drilled and tapped for scope mounting. **Features:** Three-position safety, hinged floorplate, adjustable trigger, forged one-piece bolt, M-16 style extractor, forged flat-bottom receiver. Introduced in 2001. Imported from Japan by Legacy Sports International.
Price: Blue/Nutmeg, standard calibers................. $649.00 to $669.00
Price: Stainless/Pepper, standard calibers............ $749.00 to $769.00

Prices given are believed to be accurate at time of publication however, many factors affect retail pricing so exact prices are not possible.

HOWA M-1500 VARMINTER SUPREME AND THUMBHOLE VARMINTER SUPREME

Caliber: .204, .223 Rem., .22-250 Rem., .243 Win., .308 Win. **Stock:** Varminter Supreme: Laminated wood in nutmeg (brown), pepper (grey) colors, raised comb and rollover cheekpiece, full pistol grip with palm-filling swell and broad beavertail forend with six vents for barrel cooling. Thumbhole Varminter Supreme similar, adds a high, straight comb, more vertical pistol grip. **Sights:** None furnished; drilled and tapped for scope mounting. **Features:** Three-position safety, hinged floorplate, adjustable trigger, forged one-piece bolt, M-16 style extractor, forged flat-bottom receiver, hammer forged bull barrel and recessed muzzle crown; overall length, 43.75", 9.7 lbs. Introduced 2001. Barreled actions imported by Legacy Sports International; stocks by S&K Gunstocks.

Price: Varminter Supreme, Blue/Nutmeg...................................$679.00
Price: Varminter Supreme, Stainless/Pepper...........................$779.00
Price: Thumbhole Varminter Supreme, Blue/Nutmeg..............$773.00
Price: Thumbhole Varminter Supreme, Stainless/Pepper $813.00

HOWA/HOGUE M-1500 COMPACT HEAVY BARREL VARMINTER

Chambered in .223 Rem., 308 Win., has 20" #6 contour heavy barrel, recessed muzzle crown. **Stock:** Hogue Overmolded, black, or OD green; ambidextrous palm swells. **Sights:** None furnished; drilled and tapped for scope mounting. **Length:** 44.0" overall. **Features:** Three-position safety, hinged floorplate, adjustable trigger, forged one-piece bolt, M-16 style extractor, forged flat bottom receiver, aluminum pillar bedding and free-floated barrels. **Weight:** 9.3 lbs. Introduced 2008. Imported from Japan by Legacy Sports International.

Price: From $559.00

HOWA/AXIOM M-1500

Caliber: .204, .223 Rem., .22-250 Rem., .243 Win., 6.5x55 (2008), .25-06 Rem. (2008), .270 Win., .308 Win., .30-06 Spfl., 7mm Rem., .300 Win. Mag., .338 Win. Mag., .375 Ruger standard barrel; .204, .223 Rem., .243 Win. and .308 Win. heavy barrel. **Barrel:** Howa barreled action, 22" contour standard barrel, 20" #6 contour heavy barrel, and 24" #6 contour heavy barrel. **Weight:** 8.6-10 lbs. **Stock:** Knoxx Industries Axiom V/S synthetic, black or camo. Adjustable length of pull from 11.5" to 15.5". **Sights:** None furnished; drilled and tapped for scope mounting. **Features:** Three-position safety, adjustable trigger, hinged floorplate, forged receiver with large recoil lug, forged one-piece bolt with dual locking lugs. Introduced in 2007. Standard-barrel scope packages come with 3-10x42 Nikko-Stirling Nighteater scope, rings, bases (2008). Heavy barrels come with 4-16x44 Nikko-Stirling scope. Imported from Japan by Legacy Sports International

Price: Axiom Standard Barrel, black stock, from.....................$799.00
Price: Axiom 20" and 24" Varminter, black or
camo stock, from $853.00
Price: Axiom 20" and 24" Varminter, camo stock
w/scope (2008), from...$993.00

H-S PRECISION PRO-SERIES

Caliber: 30 chamberings, 3- or 4-round magazine. **Barrel:** 20", 22", 24" or 26", sporter contour Pro-Series 10X match-grade stainless steel barrel. Optional muzzlebrake on 30 cal. or smaller. **Weight:** 7.5 lbs. **Length:** NA. **Stock:** Pro-Series synthetic stock with full-length bedding block chassis system, sporter style. **Sights:** None; drilled and tapped for bases. **Features:** Accuracy guarantee: up to 30 calibers, 1/2 minute of angle (3 shots at 100 yards), test target supplied. Stainless steel action, stainless steel floorplate with detachable magazine, matte black Teflon finish. Made in U.S.A. by H-S Precision, Inc.

Price: $2,760.00

KENNY JARRETT RIFLES

Caliber: Custom built in virtually any chambering including .223 Rem., .243 Improved, .243 Catbird, 7mm-08 Improved, .280 Remington, .280 Ackley Improved, 7mm Rem. Mag., .284 Jarrett, .30-06 Springfield, .300 Win. Mag., .300 Jarrett, .323 Jarrett, .338 Jarrett, .375 H&H, .416 Rem., .450 Rigby, other modern cartridges.

Numerous options regarding barrel type and weight, stock styles and material. **Features:** Tri-Lock receiver. Talley rings and bases. Accuracy guarantees and custom loaded ammunition. Newest series is the Shikar featuring 28-year aged American Black walnut hand-checkered stock with Jarrett-designed stabilizing aluminum chassis. Accuracy guaranteed to be ½ MOA with standard calibers, 7/10 MOA with magnums.

Price: Shikar Series..$9,640.00
Price: Signature Series $7,640.00
Price: Wind Walker $7,380.00
Price: Original Beanfield (customer's receiver) $5,380.00
Price: Professional Hunter $10,400.00
Price: SA/Custom..$6,630.00

KIMBER MODEL 8400

Caliber: .25-06 Rem., .270 Win., 7mm, .30-06 Spfl., .300 Win. Mag., .338 Win. Mag., or .325 WSM, 4 shot. **Barrel:** 24". **Weight:** 6 lbs., 3 oz. to 6 lbs., 10 oz. **Length:** 43.25". **Stock:** Claro walnut or Kevlar-reinforced fiberglass. **Sights:** None; drilled and tapped for bases. **Features:** Mauser claw extractor, two-position wing safety, action bedded on aluminum pillars and fiberglass, free-floated barrel, match-grade adjustable trigger set at 4 lbs., matte or polished blue or matte stainless finish. Introduced 2003. Sonora model (2008) has brown laminated stock, hand-rubbed oil finish, chambered in .25-06 Rem., .30-06 Spfl., and .300 Win. Mag. Weighs 8.5 lbs., measures 44.50" overall length. Front swivel stud only for bipod. Stainless steel bull barrel, 24" satin stainless steel finish. Made in U.S.A. by Kimber Mfg. Inc.

Price: Classic..$1,223.00
Price: Classic Select Grade, French walnut stock (2008)......$1,427.00
Price: SuperAmerica, AAA walnut stock...............................$2,240.00
Price: Police Tactical, synthetic stock, fluted barrel
(.300 Win. Mag. only) .... $1,495.00 to $2,650.00

KIMBER MODEL 8400 CAPRIVI

Similar to 8400 bolt rifle, but chambered for .375 H&H, .416 Remington and .458 Lott, 4-shot magazine. Stock is Claro walnut or Kevlar-reinforced fiberglass. Features twin steel crossbolts in stock, AA French walnut, pancake cheekpiece, 24 lines-per-inch wrap-around checkering, ebony forend tip, hand-rubbed oil finish, barrel-mounted sling swivel stud, 3-leaf express sights, Howell-type rear sling swivel stud and a Pachmayr Decelerator recoil pad in traditional orange color. Introduced 2008. Made in U.S.A. by Kimber Mfg. Inc.

Price: From $3,263.00
Price: Special Edition from $5,031.00

KIMBER MODEL 8400 TALKEETNA

Similar to 8400 bolt rifle, but chambered for .375 H&H, 4-shot magazine. Weighs 8 lbs., overall length is 44.5". Stock is synthetic. Features free-floating match-grade barrel with tapered match-grade chamber and target crown, three-position wing safety acts directly on the cocking piece for greatest security, and Pachmayr Decelerator. Made in U.S.A. by Kimber Mfg. Inc

Price: $2,175.00

KIMBER MODEL 84M

Caliber: .22-250 Rem., .204 Ruger, .223 Rem., .243 Win., .257 Robts., .260 Rem., 7mm-08 Rem., .308 Win., 5-shot. **Barrel:** 22", 24", 26". **Weight:** 5 lbs., 10 oz. to 10 lbs. **Length:** 41" to 45". **Stock:** Claro walnut, checkered with steel gripcap; synthetic or gray laminate. **Sights:** None; drilled and tapped for bases. **Features:** Mauser claw extractor, three-position wing safety, action bedded on aluminum pillars, free-floated barrel, match-grade trigger set at 4 lbs., matte blue finish. Includes cable lock. Introduced 2001. Montana (2008) has synthetic stock, Pachmayr Decelerator recoil pad, stainless steel 22" sporter barrel. Made in U.S.A. by Kimber Mfg. Inc.

Price: Classic $1,223.00
Price: Varmint $1,291.00
Price: Montana $1,359.00
Price: Classic Stainless, matte stainless steel receiver
and barrel $1,495.00

KIMBER MODEL 84L CLASSIC

Bolt-action rifle chambered in .270 Win. and .30-06. Features include 24-inch sightless matte blue sporter barrel; hand-rubbed A-grade walnut stock with 20 lpi panel checkering; pillar and glass bedding; Mauser claw extractor; 3-position M70-style safety; 5-round magazine; adjustable trigger.

Price: $1,172.00

KIMBER MODEL 8400 PATROL

Bolt-action tactical rifle chambered in .308 Win. Features include 20-inch 1:12" twist fluted sightless matte blue heavy barrel; black epoxy-coated laminated wood stock with 20 lpi panel checkering; pillar and glass bedding; Mauser claw extractor; 3-position M70-style safety; 5-round magazine; adjustable trigger.

Price: $1,476.00

MAGNUM RESEARCH MOUNTAIN EAGLE MAGNUM LITE

Caliber: .22-250, .223, .224, .243, .257, 7mm Rem. Mag., 7mm WSM, .280, .300 Win. Mag., .300 WSM, .30-06, 3-shot magazine. **Barrel:** 24" sport taper graphite; 26" bull barrel graphite. **Weight:** 7.1-9.2 lbs. **Length:** 44.5-48.25" overall (adjustable on Tactical model). **Stock:** Hogue OverMolded synthetic, H-S Precision Tactical synthetic, H-S Precision Varmint synthetic. **Sights:** None. **Features:** Remington Model 700 receiver. Introduced in 2001. From Magnum Research, Inc.

Price: MLR3006ST24 Hogue stock $2,295.00
Price: MLR7MMBST24 Hogue stock $2,295.00
Price: MLRT22250 H-S Tactical stock, 26" bull barrel $2,400.00
Price: MLRT300WI Tactical $2,400.00

MARLIN XL7

Caliber: .25-06 Rem., .270 Win., .30-06 Spfl., 4-shot magazine. **Barrel:** 22" 1:10" right-hand twist, recessed barrel crown. **Weight:** 6.5 lbs. **Length:** 42.5" overall. **Stock:** Black synthetic or Realtree APG-HD camo, Soft-Tech recoil pad, pillar bedded. **Sights:** None. **Features:** Pro-Fire trigger is user adjustable down to 2.5 lbs. Fluted bolt, steel sling swivel studs, high polished blued steel, checkered bolt handle, molded checkering, one-piece scope base. Introduced in 2008. From Marlin Firearms, Inc.

Price: Black Synthetic...$402.00
Price: Camouflaged $426.00

MARLIN XS7 SHORT-ACTION

Similar to Model XL7 but chambered in 7mm-08, .243 Winchester and .308 Winchester.

Price: $391.00
Price: XS7Y Youth $402.00
Price: XS7C Camo, Realtree APG HD camo stock $426.00
Price: XS7S Stainless $500.00

MERKEL KR1

Caliber: .223 Rem., .243 Rem., 6.5x55, 7mm-08, .308 Win., .270 Win., .30-06, 9.3x62, 7mm Rem. Mag., .300 Win. Mag., .270 WSM, .300 WSM, .338 Win. Mag. **Features:** Short lock, short bolt movement, take-down design with interchangeable barrel assemblies, three-position safety, detachable box magazine, fine trigger with set feature, checkered walnut pistol-grip semi-schnable stock. Adjustable iron sights with quick release mounts. Imported from Germany by Merkel USA.

Price: $1,995.00
Price: Model KR1 Stutzen Antique: case-colored receiver, Mannlicher-style stock $3,395.00

MERKEL RX HELIX

Caliber: .223 Rem., .243 Rem., 6.5x55, 7mm-08, .308 Win., .270 Win., .30-06, 9.3x62, 7mm Rem. Mag., .300 Win. Mag., .270 WSM, .300 WSM, .338 Win. Mag. **Features:** Straight-pull bolt action. Synthetic stock on Explorer model. Walnut stock available in several grades. Factory engraved models available. Takedown system allows switching calibers in minutes.

Price: Explorer, synthetic stock, from $2,995.00
Price: Walnut stock, from $3,785.00

MOSSBERG 100 ATR

Caliber: .243 Win. (2006), .270 Win., .308 Win. (2006), .30-06 Spfl., 4-round magazine. **Barrel:** 22", 1:10" twist, free-floating, button-rifled, recessed muzzle crown. **Weight:** 6.7 to 7.75 lbs. **Length:** 42"-42.75" overall. **Stock:** Black synthetic, walnut, Mossy Oak New Break Up camo, Realtree AP camo. **Sights:** Factory-installed Weaver-style scope bases; scoped combos include 3x9 factory-mounted, bore-sighted scopes. **Features:** Marinecote and matte blue metal finishes, free gun lock, side lever safety. Introduced 2005. Night Train comes with Picatinny rail and factory-mounted 4-16x50mm variable scope. From O.F. Mossberg & Sons, Inc.

Price: .... $375.00 to $425.00
Price: With scope.. $413.00 to $488.00
Price: Night Train $615.00

MOSSBERG MVP SERIES

Caliber: .223/5.56 NATO. 10-round capacity. Uses AR-style magazines. **Barrel:** 16.25 inches medium bull, 20-inch fluted sporter. **Weight:** 6.5 to 7 lbs. **Stock:** Classic black textured polymer. **Sights:** Adjustable folding rear, adjustable blade front. **Features:** Available with factory mounted 3-9x32mm scope, (4-16x50mm on Varmint model). FLEX model has 20-inch fluted sporter barrel, FLEX AR-style 6-position adjustable stock. Varmint model has laminated stock, 24-inch barrel. Thunder Ranch model has 18-inch bull barrel, OD Green synthetic stock.

Price: Patrol model...$709.00
Price: Patrol model w/scope $863.00
Price: FLEX model $966.00
Price: FLEX MODEL w/scope......................................$1,142.00
Price: Thunder Ranch model $748.00
Price: Predator model $709.00
Price: Predator model w/scope $758.00
Price: Varmint Model $732.00
Price: Varmint Model w/scope $912.00

MOSSBERG 4X4

Caliber: Most popular calibers from .22-250 to .338 Win. Mag. **Barrel:** 24" free floating with muzzlebrake. **Stock:** Gray laminate or American black walnut, with Monte Carlo cheekpiece, fore-end vents, recoil pad. Matte blue finish, adjustable trigger. Available with 3-9x50mm factory mounted scope.

Price: From **$643.00**
Price: With scope..**$693.00**

NOSLER MODEL 48 SERIES

Caliber: Offered in most popular calibers including .280 Ackley Improved and 6.5-284 wildcats. **Barrel:** 24". **Weight:** 7.25 to 8 lbs. **Stock:** Walnut or composite. Custom Model is made to order with several optional features.

Price: Legacy **$2,695.00**
Price: Trophy...**$1,995.00**
Price: Heritage or Outfitter..**$1,895.00**
Price: Patriot...**$1,695.00**
Price: Custom Model from...**$3,695.00**

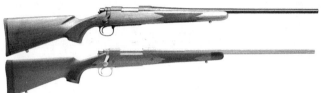

REMINGTON MODEL 700 CDL CLASSIC DELUXE

Caliber: : .223 Rem., .243 Win., .25-06 Rem., .270 Win., 7mm-08 Rem., .280 Remington, 7mm Rem. Mag., 7mm Rem. Ultra Mag., .30-06 Spfl., .300 Rem. Ultra Mag., .300 Win. Mag., .35 Whelen. **Barrel:** 24" or 26" round tapered. **Weight:** 7.4 to 7.6 lbs. **Length:** 43.6" to 46.5" overall. **Stock:** Straight-comb American walnut stock, satin finish, checkering, right-handed cheekpiece, black fore-end tip and grip cap, sling swivel studs. **Sights:** None. **Features:** Satin blued finish, jeweled bolt body, drilled and tapped for scope mounts. Hinged-floorplate magazine capacity: 4, standard calibers; 3, magnum calibers. SuperCell recoil pad, cylindrical receiver, integral extractor. Introduced 2004. CDL SF (stainless fluted) chambered for .260 Rem., .257 Wby. Mag., .270 Win., .270 WSM, 7mm-08 Rem., 7mm Rem. Mag., .30-06 Spfl., .300 WSM. Left-hand versions introduced 2008 in six calibers. Made in U.S. by Remington Arms Co., Inc.

Price: Standard Calibers from ....**$1,019.00 to $1,077.00**
Price: CDL SF from ....**$1,197.00 to $1,259.00**

REMINGTON MODEL 700 BDL

Caliber: .243 Win., .270 Win., 7mm Rem. Mag., .30-06 Spfl., .300 Rem Ultra Mag. **Barrel:** 22, 24, 26" round tapered. **Weight:** 7.25-7.4 lbs. **Length:** 41.6-46.5" overall. **Stock:** Walnut. Gloss-finish pistol grip stock with skip-line checkering, black forend tip and gripcap with white line spacers. Quick-release floorplate. **Sights:** Gold bead ramp front; hooded ramp, removable step-adjustable rear with windage screw. **Features:** Side safety, receiver tapped for scope mounts, matte receiver top, quick detachable swivels.

Price: Standard Calibers **$994.00**
Price: Magnum Calibers **$1,020.00**
Price: 50th Anniversary Edition, 7mm Rem. Mag. **$1,399.00**

REMINGTON MODEL 700 SPS

Caliber: : .22-250 Rem., 6.8 Rem SPC, .223 Rem., .243 Win., .270 Win., .270 WSM, 7mm-08 Rem., 7mm Rem. Mag., 7mm Rem. Ultra Mag., .30-06 Spfl., .308 Win., .300 WSM, .300 Win. Mag., .300 Rem. Ultra Mag. **Barrel:** 20", 24" or 26" carbon steel. **Weight:** 7 to 7.6 lbs. **Length:** 39.6" to 46.5" overall. **Stock:** Black synthetic, sling swivel studs, SuperCell recoil pad. Woodtech model has walnut decorated synthetic stock with overmolded grip patterns. Camo stock available. **Sights:** None. Introduced 2005. SPS

Stainless replaces Model 700 BDL Stainless Synthetic. **Barrel:** Bead-blasted 416 stainless steel. **Features:** Plated internal fire control component. SPS DM features detachable box magazine. Buckmaster Edition versions feature Realtree Hardwoods HD camouflage and Buckmasters logo engraved on floorplate. SPS Varmint includes X-Mark Pro trigger, 26" heavy contour barrel, vented beavertail fore-end, dual front sling swivel studs. Made in U.S. by Remington Arms Co., Inc.

Price: From ....**$724.00 to $813.00**

REMINGTON 700 SPS TACTICAL

Caliber: :.223 .300 AAC Blackout and .308 Win. **Features:** Features include 20-inch heavy-contour tactical-style barrel; dual-point pillar bedding; black synthetic stock with Hogue overmoldings; semi-beavertail fore-end; X-Mark Pro adjustable trigger system; satin black oxide metal finish; hinged floorplate magazine; SuperCell recoil pad.

Price: From ....**$788.00 to $817.00**

REMINGTON 700 VTR A-TACS CAMO

Caliber: :.223 and .308 Win. **Features:** Features include ATACS camo finish overall; triangular contour 22-inch barrel has an integral muzzlebrake; black overmold grips; 1:9" twist (.223 caliber), or 1:12" (.308) twist.
Price: **$930.00**

REMINGTON MODEL 700 VLS

Caliber: .204 Ruger, .223 Rem., .22-250 Rem., .243 Win., .308 Win. **Barrel:** 26" heavy contour barrel (0.820" muzzle O.D.), concave target-style barrel crown. **Weight:** 9.4 lbs. **Length:** 45.75" overall. **Stock:** Brown laminated stock, satin finish, with beavertail fore-end, gripcap, rubber buttpad. **Sights:** None. **Features:** Introduced 1995. Made in U.S. by Remington Arms Co., Inc.
Price: **$1,056.00**

REMINGTON MODEL 700 SENDERO SF II

Caliber: 7mm Rem. Mag., .300 Win. Mag., .300 Rem. Ultra Mag. **Barrel:** Satin stainless 26" heavy contour fluted. **Weight:** 8.5 lbs. **Length:** 45.75" overall. **Stock:** Black composite reinforced with aramid fibers, beavertail fore-end, palm swell. **Sights:** None. **Features:** Aluminum bedding block, drilled and tapped for scope mounts, hinged floorplate magazines. Introduced 1996. Made in U.S. by Remington Arms Co., Inc.
Price: **$1,465.00**

REMINGTON MODEL 700 TARGET TACTICAL

Caliber: .308 Win. **Barrel:** 26" triangular counterbored, 1:11-1/2" rifling. **Weight:** 11.75 lbs. **Length:** 45-3/4" overall. **Features:** Textured green Bell & Carlson varmint/tactical stock with adjustable comb and length of pull, adjustable trigger, satin black oxide finish on exposed metal surfaces, hinged floorplate, SuperCell recoil pad, matte blue on exposed metal surfaces.
Price: **$2,138.00**

REMINGTON MODEL 700 VTR SERIES

Caliber: .204 Ruger, .22-250, .223 Rem., .243 Win., .308 Win. **Barrel:** 22" triangular counterbored with integrated muzzlebrake. **Weight:** 7.5 lbs. **Length:** 41-5/8" overall. **Features:** Olive drab overmolded or Digital Tiger TSP Desert Camo stock with vented semi-beavertail fore-end, tactical-style dual swivel mounts for bipod, matte blue on

exposed metal surfaces.
Price: From .... **$825.00 to $980.00**

REMINGTON MODEL 700 VARMINT SF
Caliber: .22-250, .223, .220 Swift, .308 Win. **Barrel:** 26" stainless steel fluted. **Weight:** 8.5 lbs. **Length:** 45.75 inches. **Features:** Synthetic stock with ventilated forend, stainless steel/triggerguard/floorplate, dual tactical swivels for bipod attachment.
Price: **$991.00**

REMINGTON MODEL 700 MOUNTAIN SS
Calibers: .25-06, .270 Win., .280 Rem., 7mm-08, .308 Win., .30-06. **Barrel:** 22". **Length:** 40.6". **Weight:** 6.5 lbs. Satin stainless finish, Bell & Carlson Aramid Fiber stock.
Price: **$1,135.00**

REMINGTON MODEL 770 BOLT-ACTION
Caliber: .243 Win., .270 Win., 7mm Rem. Mag., 7mm-08 Rem., .308 Win., .30-06 Spfl., .300 Win. Mag. **Barrel:** 22" or 24", button rifled. **Weight:** 8.5 lbs. **Length:** 42.5" to 44.5" overall. **Stock:** Black synthetic. **Sights:** Bushnell Sharpshooter 3-9x scope mounted and bore-sighted. **Features:** Upgrade of Model 710 introduced 2001. Unique action locks bolt directly into barrel; 60-degree bolt throw; 4-shot dual-stack magazine; all-steel receiver. Introduced 2007. Stainless Camo model has Realtree camo stock, stainless metal finish. Made in U.S.A. by Remington Arms Co.
Price: **$383.00**
Price: Youth, .243 Win. **$375.00**
Price: Stainless Camo **$467.00**

REMINGTON MODEL 783
Calibers: .270 Win., 7mm Rem. Mag., .308 Win., .30-06 Sprg. **Barrel:** 22 inches. **Stock:** Synthetic. **Weight:** 7 to 7.25 lbs. **Finish:** Matte black. **Features:** Adjustable trigger with two-position trigger-block safety, magnum contour button-rifle barrel, cylindrical receiver with minimum-size ejection port, pillar-bedded stock, detachable box magazine, 90-degree bolt throw.
Price: **$451.00**
Price: Camo stock **$503.00**

REMINGTON MODEL SEVEN CDL
Calibers: .243, .260 Rem., 7mm-08, .308 Win. **Barrel:** 20". **Weight:** 6.5 lbs. **Length:** 39.25". **Stock:** Walnut with black fore-end tip, satin finish. Predator model in .223, .22-250 and .243 has Mossy Oak Brush camo stock, 22" barrel.
Price: CDL.. **$1,039.00**
Price: Predator **$895.00**
Price: Synthetic stock **$731.00**

REMINGTON 40-XB TACTICAL
Caliber: .308 Winchester. **Features:** Features include stainless steel bolt with Teflon coating; hinged floorplate; adjustable trigger; 27-1/4-inch tri-fluted 1:14" twist barrel; H-S precision pro series tactical stock, black color with dark green spiderweb; two front swivel studs; one rear swivel stud; vertical pistol grip. From the Remington Custom Shop.
Price: **$2,995.00**

REMINGTON 40-XB RANGEMASTER
Caliber: Almost any caliber from .22 BR Rem. to .300 Rem. Ultra Mag. Single-shot or repeater. **Features:** Features include stainless steel

bolt with Teflon coating; hinged floorplate; adjustable trigger; 27-1/4-inch tri-fluted 1:14" twist barrel; walnut stock. From the Remington Custom Shop.
Price: **$2,595.00**

REMINGTON 40-XS TACTICAL - 338LM SYSTEM
Caliber: .338 Lapua Magnum. **Features:** Features include 416 stainless steel Model 40-X 24-inch 1:12" twist barreled action; black polymer coating; McMillan A3 series stock with adjustable length of pull and adjustable comb; adjustable trigger and Sunny Hill heavy-duty, all-steel triggerguard; Harris bipod with quick adjust swivel lock; Leupold Mark IV 3.5-10x40mm long-range M1 scope with Mil Dot reticle; Badger Ordnance all-steel Picatinny scope rail and rings. From the Remington Custom Shop.
Price: **$4,950.00**

ROCK ISLAND ARMORY TCM
Caliber: .22 TCM. 5-round capacity magazine, interchangeable with .22 TCM 17-round pistol magazine. **Barrel:** 22.75 inches. **Weight:** 6 pounds. Chambered for .22 TCM cartridge introduced in 2013. Manufactured in the Philippines and imported by Armscor Precision International.
Price: **$450.00**

RUGER AMERICAN RIFLE
Caliber: .22-250, .243, 7mm-08, .308, .270 Win., .30-06 (4-shot rotary magazine). **Barrel:** 22" or 18" (Compact). **Length:** 42.5". **Weight:** 6.25 lbs. **Stock:** Black composite. **Finish:** Matte black or matte stainless (All Weather model). **Features:** Tang safety, hammer-forged free-floating barrel. Available with factory mounted Redfield Revolution 4x scope.
Price: Standard or compact.................... **$449.00**
Price: All-weather model, standard or compact...................... **$529.00**
Price: With scope................................... **$679.00**

RUGER COMPACT MAGNUM
Caliber: .338 RCM, .300 RCM; 3-shot magazine. **Barrel:** 20". **Weight:** 6.75 lbs. **Length:** 39.5-40" overall. **Stock:** American walnut and black synthetic; stainless steel and Hawkeye Matte blued finishes. **Sights:** Adjustable Williams "U" notch rear sight and brass bead front sight. **Features:** Based on a shortened .375 Ruger case, the .300 and .338 RCMs match the .300 and .338 Win. Mag. in performance; RCM stock is 1/2 inch shorter than standard M77 Hawkeye stock; LC6 trigger; steel floorplate engraved with Ruger logo and "Ruger Compact Magnum"; Red Eagle recoil pad; Mauser-type controlled feeding; claw extractor; 3-position safety; hammer-forged steel barrels; Ruger scope rings. Walnut stock includes extensive cut-checkering and rounded profiles. Intr. 2008. Made in U.S.A. by Sturm, Ruger & Co.
Price: **$929.00**

RUGER GUNSITE SCOUT RIFLE
Caliber: .308 WIN., 10-shot magazine capacity. **Barrel:** 16.5". **Weight:** 7 lbs. **Length:** 38-39.5". **Stock:** Black laminate. **Sights:** Front post sight and rear adjustable. **Features:** Gunsite Scout Rifle is a credible rendition of Col. Jeff Cooper's "fighting carbine" Scout Rifle. The Ruger Gunsite Scout Rifle is a new platform in the Ruger M77 family. While the Scout Rifle has M77 features such as controlled round feed and integral scope mounts (scope rings included), the 10-round detachable box magazine is the first clue this isn't your grandfather's Ruger rifle. The Ruger Gunsite Scout Rifle has a 16.5 medium

Prices given are believed to be accurate at time of publication however, many factors affect retail pricing so exact prices are not possible.

contour, cold hammer-forged, alloy steel barrel with a Mini-14 protected nonglare post front sight and receiver mounted, adjustable ghost ring rear sight for out-of-the-box usability. A forward mounted Picatinny rail offers options in mounting an assortment of optics – including Scout Scopes available from Burris and Leupold, for "both eyes open" sighting and super-fast target acquisition.

Price: **$1,039.00**
Price: (stainless) **$1,099.00**

RUGER ROTARY MAGAZINE RIFLE

Caliber: .17 Hornet, .22 Hornet, .357 Magnum, . 44 Magnum (capacity 4 to 6 rounds). **Barrel:** 18.5" (.357 and .44 Mag,), 20 or 24" (.17 Hornet and .22 Hornet). **Weight:** 5.5 to 7.5 lbs. **Stock:** American walnut, black synthetic, Next G1 Vista Camo or Green Mountain laminate.

Price: 77/17, Green Mtn. Laminate stock **$969.00**
Price: 77/22, Green Mtn. Laminate stock **$969.00**
Price: 77/22, walnut stock **$899.00**
Price: 77/357, 77/44, black synthetic stock **$969.00**
Price: 77/44, Next G1 Vista Camo **$999.00**

RUGER GUIDE GUN

Calibers: .30-06, .300 Ruger Compact Mag., .300 Win. Mag., .338 RCM, .338 Win. Mag., .375 Ruger. **Capacity:** 3 or 4 rounds. **Barrel:** 20 inches with barrelband sling swivel and removable muzzlebrake. **Weight:** 8 to 8.12 pounds. **Stock:** Green Mountain Laminate. **Finish:** Hawkeye matte stainless. **Sights:** Adjustable rear, bead front. Introduced 2013.

Price: **$1,199.00**

RUGER HAWKEYE

Caliber: .204 Ruger, .223 Rem., .22-250 Rem., .243 Win., .25-06 Rem., .270 Win., .280 Rem., 6.5 Creedmoor, 7mm/08, 7mm Rem. Mag., .308 Win., .30-06 Spfl., .300 Win. Mag., .338 Win. Mag., .375 Ruger, .416 Ruger, 4-shot magazine, except 3-shot magazine for magnums; 5-shot magazine for .204 Ruger and .223 Rem. **Barrel:** 22", 24". **Weight:** 6.75 to 8.25 lbs. **Length:** 42-44.4" overall. **Stock:** American walnut, laminate or synthetic. Magnum Hunter has Green Hogue stock. **Sights:** None furnished. Receiver has Ruger integral

scope mount base, Ruger 1" rings. **Features:** Includes Ruger LC6 trigger, new red rubber recoil pad, Mauser-type controlled feeding, claw extractor, 3-position safety, hammer-forged steel barrels, Ruger scope rings. Walnut stocks have wrap-around cut checkering on the forearm, and more rounded contours on stock and top of pistol grips. Matte stainless all-weather version features synthetic stock. Hawkeye African chambered in .375 Ruger and has 23" blued barrel, checkered walnut stock, windage-adjustable shallow "V" notch rear sight, white bead front sight. Introduced 2007.

Price: Standard, right- and left-hand **$899.00**
Price: All-Weather **$899.00**
Price: Compact **$899.00**
Price: Laminate Compact **$969.00**
Price: Compact Magnum **$969.00**
Price: African **$1,199.00**
Price: Magnum Hunter **$1,099.00**
Price: VT Varmint Target **$1,029.00**
Price: Predator **$1,029.00**

SAKO A7 AMERICAN

Caliber: .270 WSM, .300 WSM. **Barrel:** 24-3/8". **Weight:** 6 lbs., 13 oz. **Length:** 44-5/16" overall. **Features:** Stainless barrel and receiver, black composite stock with sling swivels and recoil pad, two-position safety, adjustable trigger, detachable 3+1 box magazine.

Price: From **$1,375.00**

SAKO TRG-22 TACTICAL RIFLE

Caliber: .308 Winchester (TRG-22). **Features:** Features include target grade Cr-Mo or stainless barrels with muzzlebrake; three locking lugs; 60° bolt throw; adjustable two-stage target trigger; adjustable or folding synthetic stock; receiver-mounted integral 17mm axial optics rails with recoil stop-slots; tactical scope mount for modern three-turret tactical scopes (30 and 34 mm tube diameter); optional bipod.
Price: **$3,450.00**

SAKO MODEL 85

Caliber: .22-250 Rem., .243 Win., .25-06 Rem., .260, 6.5x55mm, .270 Win., .270 WSM, 7mm-08 Rem., 7x64, .308 Win., .30-06; 7mm WSM, .300 WSM, .338 Federal, 8x57IS, 9.3x62. **Barrel:** 22.4", 22.9", 24.4". **Weight:** 7.75 lbs. **Length:** NA. **Stock:** Polymer, laminated or high-grade walnut, straight comb, shadow-line cheekpiece. **Sights:** None furnished. **Features:** Controlled-round feeding, adjustable trigger, matte stainless or nonreflective satin blue. Offered in a wide range of variations and models. Introduced 2006. Imported from Finland by Beretta USA.

Price: Grey Wolf **$1,600.00**
Price: Black Bear **$1,850.00**
Price: Kodiak **$1,925.00**
Price: Varmint Laminated **$2,000.00**
Price: Classic **$2,200.00**
Price: Bavarian .... **$2,200.00 - $2,300.00**
Price: Bavarian carbine, Full-length stock **$2,400.00**
Price: Brown Bear **$2,175.00**

SAKO 85 FINNLIGHT

Similar to Model 85 but chambered in .243 Win., .25-06, .260 Rem., .270 Win., .270 WSM, .300 WSM, .30-06, .308 Win., 6.5x55mm, 7mm Rem Mag., 7mm-08. Weighs 6 lbs., 3 oz. to 6 lbs. 13 oz. Stainless steel barrel and receiver, black synthetic stock
Price: **$1,600.00**

SAVAGE AXIS SERIES

Caliber: .243 WIN., 7mm-08 REM., .308 WIN., .25-06 REM., .270 WIN, .30-06 SPFLD., .223 REM., .22-250 REM. **Barrel:** 22". **Weight:**

Prices given are believed to be accurate at time of publication however, many factors affect retail pricing so exact prices are not possible.

69TH EDITION, 2015 ✦ **475**

6.5 lbs. **Length:** 43.875". **Stock:** Black synthetic or camo, including pink/black Muddy Girl. **Sights:** Drilled and tapped for scope mounts. Several models come with factory mounted Weaver Kaspa 3-9x40 scope. **Features:** Available with black matte or stainless finish
Price: From .... **$363.00 to $525.00**

SAVAGE MODEL 25
Caliber: .17 Hornet, .22 Hornet, .222 Rem., .204 Ruger, .223 Rem., 4-shot magazine. **Barrel:** 24", medium-contour fluted barrel with recessed target crown, free-floating sleeved barrel, dual pillar bedding. **Weight:** 8.25 lbs. **Length:** 43.75" overall. **Stock:** Brown laminate with beavertail-style fore-end. **Sights:** Weaver-style bases installed. **Features:** Diameter-specific action built around the .223 Rem. bolthead dimension. Three locking lugs, 60-degree bolt lift, AccuTrigger adjustable from 2.5 to 3.25 lbs. Model 25 Classic Sporter has satin lacquer American walnut with contrasting fore-end tip, wraparound checkering, 22" blued barrel. **Weight:** 7.15 lbs. **Length:** 41.75". Introduced 2008. Made in U.S.A. by Savage Arms, Inc.
Price: From .... **$567.00 to $775.00**

SAVAGE CLASSIC SERIES MODEL 14/114
Caliber: .243 Win., 7mm-08 Rem., .308 Win., .270 Win., 7mm Rem. Mag., .30-06 Spfl., .300 Win. Mag., 3- or 4-shot magazine. **Barrel:** 22" or 24". **Weight:** 7 to 7.5 lbs. **Length:** 41.75" to 43.75" overall (Model 14 short action); 43.25" to 45.25" overall (Model 114 long action). **Stock:** Satin lacquer American walnut with ebony fore-end, wraparound checkering, Monte Carlo Comb and cheekpiece. **Sights:** None furnished. Receiver drilled and tapped for scope mounting. **Features:** AccuTrigger, matte blued barrel and action, hinged floorplate.
Price: **$922.00**

SAVAGE MODEL 12 SERIES VARMINT
Caliber: .204 Ruger, .223 Rem., .22-250 Rem.; 4-shot magazine. **Barrel:** 26" stainless barreled action, heavy fluted, free-floating and button-rifled barrel. **Weight:** 10 lbs. **Length:** 46.25" overall. **Stock:** Dual pillar bedded, low profile, black synthetic or laminated stock with extra-wide beavertail fore-end. **Sights:** None furnished; drilled and tapped for scope mounting. **Features:** Recessed target-style muzzle. AccuTrigger, oversized bolt handle, detachable box magazine, swivel studs. Model 112BVSS has heavy target-style prone laminated stock with high comb, Wundhammer palm swell, internal box magazine. Model 12VLP DBM has black synthetic stock, detachable magazine, and additional chamberings in .243, .308 Win., .300 Win. Mag. Model 12FV has blued receiver. Model 12BTCSS has brown laminate vented thumbhole stock. Made in U.S.A. by Savage Arms, Inc.
Price: From .... **$732.00 to $1,465.00**

SAVAGE MODEL 16/116 WEATHER WARRIORS
Caliber: .204 Ruger, .223 Rem., .22-250 Rem., .243 Win., 6.5 Creedmoor, 6.5-284 Norma, 7mm-08 Rem., .308 Win., .270 WSM, 7mm WSM, .300 WSM (short action Model 16), 2- or 4-shot magazine; .270 Win., 7mm Rem. Mag., .30-06 Spfl., .300 Win. Mag., .338 Win. Mag. (long action Model 114), 3- or 4-shot magazine. **Barrel:** 22", 24"; stainless steel with matte finish, free-floated barrel. **Weight:** 6.5 to 6.75 lbs. **Length:** 41.75" to 43.75" overall (Model 16); 42.5" to 44.5" overall (Model 116). **Stock:** Graphite/fiberglass filled composite. **Sights:** None furnished; drilled and tapped for scope mounting. **Features:** Quick-detachable swivel studs; laser-etched bolt. Left-hand models available. Model 116FSS introduced 1991; 116FSAK introduced 1994. Made in U.S.A. by Savage Arms, Inc.
Price: From .... **$885.00 to $966.00**

SAVAGE MODEL 11/111 HUNTER SERIES
Caliber: .223 Rem., .22-250 Rem., .243 Win., 6.5 Creedmoor, .260 Rem., 6.5x284 Norma, .338 Lapua, 7mm-08 Rem., .308 Win., 2- or 4-shot magazine; .25-06 Rem., .270 Win., 7mm Rem. Mag., .30-06 Spfl., .300 Win. Mag., (long action Model 111), 3- or 4-shot magazine. **Barrel:** 20", 22" or 24"; blued free-floated barrel. **Weight:** 6.5 to 6.75 lbs. **Length:** 41.75" to 43.75" overall (Model 11); 42.5" to 44.5" overall (Model 111). **Stock:** Graphite/fiberglass filled composite or hardwood. **Sights:** Ramp front, open fully adjustable rear; drilled and tapped for scope

mounting. **Features:** Three-position top tang safety, double front locking lugs. Introduced 1994. Made in U.S.A. by Savage Arms, Inc.
Price: From .... **$560.00 to $1,104.00**

SAVAGE MODEL 10 BAS LAW ENFORCEMENT
Caliber: .308 Win., (10 BAS), .300 Win., .338 Lapua (110 BA). **Barrel:** 24" or 26" fluted heavy with muzzlebrake **Weight:** 13.4 to 15.6 lbs. **Length:** 45". **Features:** Bolt-action repeater based on Model 10 action but with M4-style collapsible buttstock, pistol grip with palm swell, all-aluminum Accustock, Picatinny rail for mounting optics.
Price: **$2,375.00**
Price: 110 BA... **$2,561.00**

SAVAGE MODEL 10FP/110FP LAW ENFORCEMENT SERIES
Caliber: .223 Rem., .308 Win. (Model 10), 4-shot magazine; .25-06 Rem., .300 Win. Mag., (Model 110), 3- or 4-shot magazine. **Barrel:** 24"; matte blued free-floated heavy barrel and action. **Weight:** 6.5 to 6.75 lbs. **Length:** : 41.75" to 43.75" overall (Model 10); 42.5" to 44.5" overall (Model 110). **Stock:** Black graphite/fiberglass composition, pillar-bedded, positive checkering. **Sights:** None furnished. Receiver drilled and tapped for scope mounting. **Features:** Black matte finish on all metal parts. Double swivel studs on the forend for sling and/or bipod mount. Right- or left-hand. Model 110FP introduced 1990. Model 10FP introduced 1998. Model 10FCPXP has HS Precision black synthetic tactical stock with molded alloy bedding system, Leupold 3.5-10x40mm black matte scope with Mil Dot reticle, Farrell Picatinny Rail Base, flip-open lens covers, 1.25" sling with QD swivels, Harris bipod, Storm heavy-duty case. Made in U.S.A. by Savage Arms, Inc.
Price: Model 10FP, 10FLP (left hand), 110FP **$775.00**
Price: Model 10FP folding Choate stock..................................**$896.00**
Price: Model 10FCP McMillan, McMillan fiberglass tactical stock **$1,545.00**
Price: Model 10FCP-HS HS Precision, HS Precision tactical stock...**$1,277.00**
Price: Model 10FPXP-HS Precision...................................**$2,715.00**
Price: Model 10FCP **$925.00**
Price: Model 10FLCP, left-hand model, standard stock or Accu-Stock **$975.00**
Price: Model 10FCP SR.. **$1,250.00**
Price: Model 10 Precision Carbine **$952.00**

Prices given are believed to be accurate at time of publication however, many factors affect retail pricing so exact prices are not possible.

SAVAGE MODEL 10 PREDATOR SERIES
Caliber: .204 Ruger. .223, .22-250, .243, .260 Rem., 6.5 Creedmoor, 6.5x284 Norma. **Barrel:** 22", medium-contour. **Weight:** 7.25 lbs. **Length:** 43" overall. **Stock:** Synthetic with rounded fore-end and oversized bolt handle. **Features:** Entirely covered in either Mossy Oak Brush or Realtree Hardwoods Snow pattern camo. Also features AccuTrigger, AccuStock, detachable box magazine.
Price: **$971.00**

SAVAGE MODEL 12 PRECISION TARGET SERIES BENCHREST
Caliber: .308 Win., 6.5x284 Norma, 6mm Norma BR. **Barrel:** 29" ultra-heavy. **Weight:** 12.75 lbs. **Length:** 50" overall. **Stock:** Gray laminate. **Features:** New Left-Load, Right-Eject target action, Target AccuTrigger adjustable from approx 6 oz. to 2.5 lbs, oversized bolt handle, stainless extra-heavy free-floating and button-rifled barrel.
Price: **$1,629.00**

SAVAGE MODEL 12 PRECISION TARGET PALMA
Similar to Model 12 Benchrest but in .308 Win. only, 30" barrel, multi-adjustable stock, weighs 13.3 lbs.
Price: **$2,085.00**

SAVAGE MODEL 12 F CLASS TARGET RIFLE
Similar to Model 12 Benchrest but chambered in 6 Norma BR, 30" barrel, weighs 13.3 lbs.
Price: **$1,600.00**

SAVAGE MODEL 12 F/TR TARGET RIFLE
Similar to Model 12 Benchrest but in .308 Win. only, 30" barrel, weighs 12.65 lbs.
Price: **$1,381.00**

STEVENS MODEL 200
Caliber: .223, .22-250, .243, 7mm-08, .308 Win. (short action) or .25-06, .270 Win., .30-06, 7mm Rem. Mag., .300 Win. Mag. **Barrel:** 22" (short action) or 24" (long action blued). **Weight:** 6.5 lbs. **Length:** 41.75" overall. **Stock:** Black synthetic or camo. **Sights:** None. **Features:** Free-floating and button-rifled barrel, top loading internal box magazine, swivel studs.
Price: (standard)... **$421.00**
Price: (camo).. **$439.00**
Price: Model 200XP Long or Short Action
     Package Rifle with 4x12 scope **$449.00**
Price: Model 200XP Camo, camo stock **$499.00**

STEYR MANNLICHER CLASSIC
Caliber: .222 Rem., .223 Rem., .243 Win., .25-06 Rem., .308 Win., 6.5x55, .270 Win., .270 WSM, 7x64 Brenneke, 7mm-08 Rem., .30-06 Spfl., 8x57IS, 9.3x62, 7mm Rem. Mag., .300 WSM, .300 Win. Mag., .330 Wby. Mag.; 4-shot magazine. **Barrel:** 23.6" standard; 26" magnum; 20" full stock standard calibers. **Weight:** 7 lbs. **Length:** 40.1" overall. **Stock:** Hand-checkered fancy European oiled walnut with standard fore-end. **Sights:** Ramp front adjustable for elevation, V-notch rear adjustable for windage. **Features:** Single adjustable trigger; 3-position roller safety with "safe-bolt" setting; drilled and tapped for Steyr factory scope mounts. Introduced 1997. Imported from Austria by Steyr Arms, Inc.

Price: Half stock, standard calibers................... **$3,799.00**
Price: Full stock, standard calibers..................... **$4,199.00**

STEYR PRO HUNTER
Similar to the Classic Rifle except has ABS synthetic stock with adjustable butt spacers, straight comb without cheekpiece, palm swell, Pachmayr 1" swivels. Special 10-round magazine conversion kit available. Introduced 1997. Imported from Austria by Steyr Arms, Inc.
Price: From **$1,500.00**

STEYR SCOUT
Caliber: .308 Win., 5-shot magazine. **Barrel:** 19", fluted. **Weight:** NA. **Length:** NA. **Stock:** Gray Zytel. **Sights:** Pop-up front & rear, Leupold M8 2.5x28 IER scope on Picatinny optic rail with Steyr mounts. **Features:** luggage case, scout sling, two stock spacers, two magazines. Introduced 1998. Imported from Austria by Steyr Arms, Inc.
Price: From **$2,199.00**

STEYR SSG08
Caliber: 7.62x51mmNATO (.308Win) or 7.62x63B (.300 Win Mag)., 10-shot magazine capacity. **Barrel:** 508mm or 600mm. **Weight:** 5.5 kg - 5.7 kg. **Length:** 1090mm - 1182mm. **Stock:** Dural aluminium foldingstock black with .280 mm long UIT-rail and various Picatinny rails. **Sights:** Front post sight and rear adjustable. **Features:** The STEYR SSG 08 features high-grade alumnium folding stock, adjustable cheekpiece and buttplate with height marking, and an ergonomical exchangeable pistol grip. The STEYR SSG 08 also features a Versa-Pod, a muzzlebrake, a Picatinny rail, a UIT rail on stock and various Picatinny rails on fore-end, and a 10-round HC-magazine. SBSrotary bolt action with four frontal locking lugs, arranged in pairs.Cold-hammer-forged barrels are available in standard or compact lengths.
Price: **$5,899.00**

STEYR SSG 69 PII
Caliber: .22-250 Rem., .243 Win., .308 Win., detachable 5-shot rotary magazine. **Barrel:** 26". **Weight:** 8.5 lbs. **Length:** 44.5" overall. **Stock:** Black ABS Cycolac with spacers for length of pull adjustment. **Sights:** Hooded ramp front adjustable for elevation, V-notch rear adjustable for windage. **Features:** Sliding safety; NATO rail for bipod; 1" swivels; Parkerized finish; single or double-set triggers. Imported from Austria by Steyr Arms, Inc.
Price: **$1,889.00**

THOMPSON/CENTER DIMENSION
Caliber: .204 Ruger, .223 Rem., .22-250 Rem., .243 Win., .270 Win., 7mm Rem. Mag., .308 Win., .30-06 Springfield, .300 Win. Mag., 3-round magazine. **Barrel:** 22 or 24". **Weight:** NA. **Stock:** Textured grip composite with adjustment spacers. **Features:** Calibers are interchangeable between certain series or "families" – .204/.223; .22-250/.243/7mm-08/.308; .270/.30-06; 7mm Rem. Mag./.300 Win. Mag. Introduced in 2012.
Price: **$689.00**

THOMPSON/CENTER VENTURE
Caliber: .270 Win., 7mm Rem. Mag., .30-06 Springfield, .300 Win.

Mag., 3-round magazine. **Barrel:** 24". **Weight:** NA. **Length:** NA. **Stock:** Composite. **Sights:** NA. **Features:** Nitride fat bolt design, externally adjustable trigger, two-position safety, textured grip. Introduced 2009.
Price: **$537.00**

THOMPSON/CENTER VENTURE MEDIUM ACTION

Bolt action rifle chambered in .204, .22-250, .223, .243, 7mm-08, .308 and 30TC. Features include a 24-inch crowned medium weight barrel, classic styled composite stock with inlaid traction grip panels, adjustable 3.5 to 5-pound trigger along with a drilled and tapped receiver (bases included). 3+1 detachable nylon box magazine. **Weight:** 7 lbs. **Length:** 43.5 inches.
Price: **$537.00**

THOMPSON/CENTER VENTURE PREDATOR PDX

Bolt action rifle chambered in .204, .22-250, .223, .243, .308. Similar to Venture Medium action but with heavy, deep-fluted 22-inch barrel and Max-1 camo finish overall. **Weight:** 8 lbs. **Length:** 41.5 inches.
Price: From **$638.00**

TIKKA T3 HUNTER

Caliber: .243 Win., .270 Win., 7mm Rem. Mag., .308 Win., .30-06 Spfl., .300 Win. Mag. **Stock:** Walnut. **Sights:** None furnished. **Barrel:** 22-7/16", 24-3/8". **Features:** Detachable magazine, aluminum scope rings. Left-hand model available. Introduced 2005. Imported from Finland by Beretta USA.
Price: **$745.00**

TIKKA T3 STAINLESS SYNTHETIC

Similar to the T3 Hunter except stainless steel, synthetic stock. Available in .243 Win., .25-06, .270 Win., .308 Win., .30-06 Spfl., .270 WSM, .300 WSM, 7mm Rem. Mag., .300 Win. Mag., .338 Win. Mag. Introduced 2005.
Price: **$625.00**

TIKKA T3 LITE

Similar to the T3 Hunter, available in .204 Ruger, .222 Rem., .223 Rem., .22-250 Rem., .243 Win., .25-06 Rem., .260 Rem., 6.5x66, 7mm-08, 7x64, 7mm. Rem. Mag., 8x57IS, .270 Win., .270 WSM, .308 Win., .30-06 Sprg., .300 Win. Mag., .300 WSM, .338 Federal, .338 Win. Mag., 9.3x62. Synthetic stock. Barrel lengths vary from 22-7/16" to 24-3/8". Made in Finland by Sako. Imported by Beretta USA.
Price: **$750.00**
Price: Left-hand **$800.00**

ULTRA LIGHT ARMS

Caliber: Custom made in virtually every current chambering. **Barrel:** Douglas, length to order. **Weight:** 4.75 to 7.5 lbs. **Length:** Varies. **Stock:** Kevlar graphite composite, variety of finishes. **Sights:** None furnished; drilled and tapped for scope mounts. **Features:** Timney trigger, hand-lapped action, button-rifled barrel, hand-bedded action, recoil pad, sling-swivel studs, optional Jewell trigger. Made in U.S.A. by New Ultra Light Arms.
Price: Model 20 (short action)..............................**$3,500.00**
Price: Model 24 (long action) **$3,100.00**
Price: Model 28 (magnum action) **$3,900.00**
Price: Model 40 (.300 Wby. Mag., .416 Rigby) **$3,900.00**

WEATHERBY MARK V

Caliber: Deluxe version comes in all Weatherby calibers plus .243 Win.,

.270 Win., 7mm-08 Rem., .30-06 Spfl., .308 Win. **Barrel:** 24", 26", 28". **Weight:** 6.75 to 10 lbs. **Length:** 44" to 48.75" overall. **Stock:** Walnut, Monte Carlo with cheekpiece; high luster finish; checkered pistol grip and fore-end; recoil pad. **Sights:** None furnished. **Features:** 4 models with Mark V action and wood stocks; other common elements include cocking indicator; adjustable trigger; hinged floorplate, thumb safety; quick detachable sling swivels. Ultramark has hand-selected exhibition-grade walnut stock, maplewood/ebony spacers, 20-lpi checkering. Chambered for .257 and .300 Wby Mags. Lazermark same as Mark V Deluxe except stock has extensive oak leaf pattern laser carving on pistol grip and fore-end; chambered in Wby. Magnums—.257, .270 Win., 7mm., .300, .340, with 26" barrel. Introduced 1981. Sporter is same as the Mark V Deluxe without the embellishments. Metal has low-luster blue, stock is Claro walnut with matte finish, Monte Carlo comb, recoil pad. Chambered for these Wby. Mags: .257, .270 Win., 7mm, .300, .340. Other chamberings: 7mm Rem. Mag., .300 Win. Introduced 1993. Six Mark V models come with synthetic stocks. Ultra Lightweight rifles weigh 5.75 to 6.75 lbs.; 24", 26" fluted stainless barrels with recessed target crown; Bell & Carlson stock with CNC-machined aluminum bedding plate and tan "spider web" finish, skeletonized handle and sleeve. Available in .243 Win., Wby. Mag., .25-06 Rem., .270 Win., 7mm-08 Rem., 7mm Rem. Mag., .308 Win., .280 Rem., .30-06 Spfl., .300 Win. Mag. Wby. Mag chamberings: .240, .257, .270 Win., 7mm, .300. Introduced 1998. Accumark uses Mark V action with heavy-contour 26" and 28" stainless barrels with black oxidized flutes, muzzle diameter of .705". No sights, drilled and tapped for scope mounting. Stock is composite with matte gel-coat finish, full-length aluminum bedding Hasblock. Weighs 8.5 lbs. Chambered for these Wby. Mags: .240, .257, .270, 7mm, .300, .340, .338-378, .30-378. Other chamberings: .22-250, .243 Win., .25-06 Rem., .270 Win., .308 Win., 7mm Rem. Mag., .300 Win. Mag. Introduced 1996. SVM (Super Varmint Master) has 26" fluted stainless barrel, spiderweb-pattern tan laminated synthetic stock, fully adjustable trigger. Chambered for .223 Rem., .22-250 Rem., .243. Mark V Synthetic has lightweight injection-molded synthetic stock with raised Monte Carlo comb, checkered grip and fore-end, custom floorplate release. Weighs 6.5-8.5 lbs., 24-28" barrels. Available in .22-250 Rem., .243 Win., .25-06 Rem., .270 Win., 7mm-08 Rem., 7mm Rem. Mag, .280 Rem., .308 Win., .30-06 Spfl., .300 Win. Mag., .375 H&H Mag., and these Wby. Magnums: .240, .257, .270 Win., 7mm, .300, .30-378, .338-378, .340. Introduced 1997. Fibermark composites are similar to other Mark V models except has black Kevlar and fiberglass composite stock and bead-blast blue or stainless finish. Chambered for 9 standard and magnum calibers. Introduced 1983; reintroduced 2001. SVR comes with 22" button-rifled chrome-moly barrel, .739" muzzle diameter. Composite stock w/bedding block, gray spiderweb pattern. Made in U.S.A. From Weatherby.
Price: Mark V Deluxe **$2,400.00**
Price: Mark V Ultramark..**$3,200.00**
Price: Mark V Lazermark **$2,600.00**
Price: Mark V Sporter **$1,600.00**
Price: Mark V Ultra Lightweight **$2,100.00**
Price: Mark V Accumark ....**$2,100.00 to $2,400.00**
Price: Mark V Fibermark **$1,500.00**

WEATHERBY VANGUARD II SERIES

Caliber: .240, .257, and .300 Wby Mag. **Barrel:** 24" barreled action, matte black. **Weight:** 7.5 to 8.75 lbs. **Length:** 44" to 46-3/4" overall. **Stock:** Raised comb, Monte Carlo, injection-molded composite stock. **Sights:** None furnished. **Features:** One-piece forged, fluted bolt body with three gas ports, forged and machined receiver, adjustable trigger, factory accuracy guarantee. Vanguard Stainless has 410-Series stainless steel barrel and action, bead blasted matte metal finish. Vanguard Deluxe has raised comb, semi-fancy-grade Monte Carlo walnut stock with maplewood spacers, rosewood fore-end and grip cap, polished action with high-gloss-blued metalwork. Vanguard Synthetic Package includes Vanguard

Prices given are believed to be accurate at time of publication however, many factors affect retail pricing so exact prices are not possible.

Synthetic rifle with Bushnell Banner 3-9x40mm scope mounted and boresighted, Leupold Rifleman rings and bases, Uncle Mikes nylon sling, and Plano PRO-MAX injection-molded case. Sporter has Monte Carlo walnut stock with satin urethane finish, fineline diamond point checkering, contrasting rosewood fore-end tip, matte-blued metalwork. Sporter SS metalwork is 410 Series bead-blasted stainless steel. Vanguard Youth/Compact has 20" No. 1 contour barrel, short action, scaled-down nonreflective matte black hardwood stock with 12.5" length of pull, and full-size, injection-molded composite stock. Chambered for .223 Rem., .22-250 Rem., .243 Win., 7mm-08 Rem., .308 Win. Weighs 6.75 lbs.; OAL 38.9". Sub-MOA Matte and Sub-MOA Stainless models have pillar-bedded Fiberguard composite stock (Aramid, graphite unidirectional fibers and fiberglass) with 24" barreled action; matte black metalwork, Pachmayr Decelerator recoil pad. Sub-MOA Stainless metalwork is 410 Series bead-blasted stainless steel. Sub-MOA Varmint guaranteed to shoot 3-shot group of .99" or less when used with specified Weatherby factory or premium (non-Weatherby calibers) ammunition. Hand-laminated, tan Monte Carlo composite stock with black spiderwebbing; CNC-machined aluminum bedding block, 22" No. 3 contour barrel, recessed target crown. Varmint Special has tan injection-molded Monte Carlo composite stock, pebble grain finish, black spiderwebbing. 22" No. 3 contour barrel (.740" muzzle dia.), bead blasted matte black finish, recessed target crown. Back Country has two-stage trigger, pillar-bedded Bell & Carlson stock, 24-in. fluted barrel, three-position safety. WBY-X Series comes with choice of several contemporary camo finishes (Bonz, Black Reaper, Kryptek) and is primarily targeted to younger shooters. Made in U.S.A. From Weatherby.

Price: Vanguard Synthetic **$649.00**
Price: Vanguard Synthetic DBM .... **$749.00 to $899.00**
Price: Vanguard Stainless **$799.00**
Price: Vanguard Deluxe, 7mm Rem. Mag., .300 Win. Mag. ...**$1,149.00**
Price: Vanguard Synthetic Package, .25-06 Rem.....................**$999.00**
Price: Vanguard Sporter **$849.00**
Price: Vanguard Youth/Compact **$599.00**
Price: Vanguard S2 Back Country **$1,399.00**
Price: Vanguard WBY-X Series **$749.00**
Price: Vanguard Black Reaper **$749.00**
Price: Vanguard RC (Range Certified)..................................**$1,199.00**
Price: Vanguard Varmint Special **$849.00**

WINCHESTER MODEL 70

Caliber: Varies by model. Available in virtually all popular calibers. **Barrel:** Blued, or free-floating, fluted stainless hammer-forged barrel, 22", 24", 26". Recessed target crown. **Weight:** 6.75 to 7.25 lbs. **Length:** 41" to 45.75 " overall. **Stock:** Walnut (three models) or Bell and Carlson composite; textured charcoal-grey matte finish, Pachmayr Decelerator recoil pad. **Sights:** None. **Features:** Claw extractor, three-position safety, M.O.A. three-lever trigger system, factory-set at 3.75 lbs. Super Grade features fancy grade walnut stock, contrasting black fore-end tip and pistol grip cap, and sculpted shadowline cheekpiece. Featherweight Deluxe has angled-comb walnut stock, Schnabel fore-end, satin finish, cut checkering. Extreme Weather SS has composite stock, drop @ comb, 0.5"; drop @ heel, 0.5". Made in U.S.A. From Winchester Repeating Arms.

Price: Extreme Weather SS..**$1,200.00**
Price: Super Grade **$1,300.00**

WINCHESTER MODEL 70 COYOTE LIGHT

Caliber: .22-250, .243 Winchester, .308 Winchester, .270 WSM, .300 WSM and .325 WSM, five-shot magazine (3-shot in .270 WSM, .300 WSM and .325 WSM). **Barrel:** 22" fluted stainless barrel (24" in .270 WSM, .300 WSM and .325 WSM). **Weight:** 7.5 lbs. **Length:** NA. **Features:** Composite Bell and Carlson stock, Pachmayr Decelerator pad. Controlled round feeding. No sights but drilled and tapped for mounts.
Price: **$1,099.00**

WINCHESTER MODEL 70 FEATHERWEIGHT

Caliber: .22-250, .243, 7mm-08, .308, .270 WSM, 7mm WSM, .300 WSM, .325 WSM, .25-06, .270, .30-06, 7mm Rem. Mag., .300 Win. Mag., .338 Win. Mag. Capacity 5 rounds (short action) or 3 rounds (long action). **Barrel:** 22" blued barrel (24" in magnum chamberings). **Weight:** 6-1/2 to 7-1/4 lbs. **Length:** NA. **Features:** Satin-finished checkered Grade I walnut stock, controlled round feeding. Pachmayr Decelerator pad. No sights but drilled and tapped for scope mounts.
Price: **$880.00**

WINCHESTER MODEL 70 SPORTER

Caliber: .270 WSM, 7mm WSM, .300 WSM, .325 WSM, .25-06, .270, .30-06, 7mm Rem. Mag., .300 Win. Mag., .338 Win. Mag. Capacity 5 rounds (short action) or 3 rounds (long action). **Barrel:** 22", 24" or 26" blued. **Weight:** 6-1/2 to 7-1/4 lbs. **Length:** NA. **Features:** Satin-finished checkered Grade I walnut stock with sculpted cheekpiece, controlled round feeding. Pachmayr Decelerator pad. No sights but drilled and tapped for scope mounts.
Price: .... **$880.00 to $920.00**

WINCHESTER MODEL 70 ULTIMATE SHADOW

Caliber: .243, .308, .270 WSM, 7mm WSM, .300 WSM, .325 WSM, .270, .30-06, 7mm Rem. Mag., .300 Win. Mag. Capacity 5 rounds (short action) or 3 rounds (long action). **Barrel:** 22" matte stainless (24" or 26" in magnum chamberings). **Weight:** 6-1/2 to 7-1/4 lbs. **Length:** NA. **Features:** Synthetic stock with WinSorb recoil pad, controlled round feeding. Pachmayr Decelerator pad. No sights but drilled and tapped for scope mounts.
Price: .... **$760.00 to $970.00**

WINCHESTER MODEL 70 ALASKAN

Caliber: .30-06, .300 Win. Mag., .338 Win. Mag., .375 H&H Magnum. **Barrel:** 25 inches. **Weight:** 8.8 pounds. **Sights:** Folding adjustable rear, hooded brass bead front. **Stock:** Satin finished Monte Carlo with cut checkering. **Features:** Integral recoil lug, Pachmayr Decelerator recoil pad.
Price: **$1,270.00**

WINCHESTER MODEL 70 SAFARI EXPRESS

Caliber: .375 H&H Magnum, .416 Remington, .458 Winchester. **Barrel:** 24 inches. **Weight:** 9 pounds. **Sights:** Fully adjustable rear, hooded brass bead front. **Stock:** Satin finished Monte Carlo with cut checkering, deluxe cheekpiece. **Features:** Forged steel receiver with double integral recoil lugs bedded front and rear, dual steel crossbolts, Pachmayr Decelerator recoil pad.
Price: **$1,420.00**

ARMALITE AR-50
Caliber: .50 BMG **Barrel:** 31". **Weight:** 33.2 lbs. **Length:** 59.5" **Stock:** Synthetic. **Sights:** None furnished. **Features:** A single-shot bolt-action rifle designed for long-range shooting. Available in left-hand model. Made in U.S.A. by Armalite.
Price: $3,359.00

BALLARD 1875 1 1/2 HUNTER
Caliber: Various calibers. **Barrel:** 26-30". **Weight:** NA **Length:** NA. **Stock:** Hand-selected classic American walnut. **Sights:** Blade front, Rocky Mountain rear. **Features:** Color case-hardened receiver, breechblock and lever. Many options available. Made in U.S.A. by Ballard Rifle & Cartridge Co.
Price: $3,250.00

BALLARD 1875 #3 GALLERY SINGLE SHOT
Caliber: Various calibers. **Barrel:** 24-28" octagonal with tulip. **Weight:** NA. **Length:** NA. **Stock:** Hand-selected classic American walnut. **Sights:** Blade front, Rocky Mountain rear. **Features:** Color case-hardened receiver, breechblock and lever. Many options available. Made in U.S.A. by Ballard Rifle & Cartridge Co.
Price: $3,300.00

BALLARD 1875 #4 PERFECTION
Caliber: Various calibers. **Barrel:** 30" or 32" octagon, standard or heavyweight. **Weight:** 10.5 lbs. (standard) or 11.75 lbs. (heavyweight bbl.) **Length:** NA. **Stock:** Smooth walnut. **Sights:** Blade front, Rocky Mountain rear. **Features:** Rifle or shotgun-style buttstock, straight grip action, single or double-set trigger, "S" or right lever, hand polished and lapped Badger barrel. Made in U.S.A. by Ballard Rifle & Cartridge Co.
Price: $3,950.00

BALLARD 1875 #7 LONG RANGE
Caliber: .32-40, .38-55, .40-65, .40-70 SS, .45-70 Govt., .45-90, .45-110. **Barrel:** 32", 34" half-octagon. **Weight:** 11.75 lbs. **Length:** NA. **Stock:** Walnut; checkered pistol grip shotgun butt, ebony fore-end cap. **Sights:** Globe front. **Features:** Designed for shooting up to 1,000 yards. Standard or heavy barrel; single or double-set trigger; hard rubber or steel buttplate. Introduced 1999. Made in U.S.A. by Ballard Rifle & Cartridge Co.
Price: From $3,600.00

BALLARD 1875 #8 UNION HILL
Caliber: Various calibers. **Barrel:** 30" half-octagon. **Weight:** About 10.5 lbs. **Length:** NA. **Stock:** Walnut; pistol grip butt with cheekpiece. **Sights:** Globe front. **Features:** Designed for 200-yard offhand shooting. Standard or heavy barrel; double-set triggers; full loop lever; hook Schuetzen buttplate. Introduced 1999. Made in U.S.A. by Ballard Rifle & Cartridge Co.
Price: From $4,175.00

BALLARD MODEL 1885 LOW WALL SINGLE SHOT RIFLE
Caliber: Various calibers. **Barrel:** 24-28". **Weight:** NA. **Length:** NA. **Stock:** Hand-selected classic American walnut. **Sights:** Blade front, sporting rear. **Features:** Color case-hardened receiver, breechblock and lever. Many options available. Made in U.S.A. by Ballard Rifle & Cartridge Co.
Price: $3,300.00

BALLARD MODEL 1885 HIGH WALL STANDARD SPORTING SINGLE SHOT
Caliber: Various calibers. **Barrel:** Lengths to 34". **Weight:** NA. **Length:** NA. **Stock:** Straight-grain American walnut. **Sights:** Buckhorn or flattop rear, blade front. **Features:** Faithful copy of original Model 1885 High Wall; parts interchange with original rifles; variety of options available. Introduced 2000. Made in U.S.A. by Ballard Rifle & Cartridge Co.
Price: $3,300.00

BALLARD MODEL 1885 HIGH WALL SPECIAL SPORTING SINGLE SHOT
Caliber: Various calibers. **Barrel:** 28-30" octagonal. **Weight:** NA. **Length:** NA. **Stock:** Hand-selected classic American walnut. **Sights:** Blade front, sporting rear. **Features:** Color case-hardened receiver, breechblock and lever. Many options available. Made in U.S.A. by Ballard Rifle & Cartridge Co.
Price: $3,600.00

BARRETT MODEL 99 SINGLE SHOT
Caliber: .50 BMG., .416 Barrett. **Barrel:** 33". **Weight:** 25 lbs. **Length:** 50.4" overall. **Stock:** Anodized aluminum with energy-absorbing recoil pad. **Sights:** None furnished; integral M1913 scope rail. **Features:** Bolt action; detachable bipod; match-grade barrel with high-efficiency muzzlebrake. Introduced 1999. Made in U.S.A. by Barrett Firearms.
Price: From .... $3,850.00 to $4,100.00

BROWN MODEL 97D SINGLE SHOT
Caliber: Available in most factory and wildcat calibers from .17 Ackley Hornet to .375 Winchester. **Barrel:** Up to 26", air gauged match grade. **Weight:** About 5 lbs., 11 oz. **Stock:** Sporter style with pistol grip, cheekpiece and Schnabel fore-end. **Sights:** None furnished; drilled and tapped for scope mounting. **Features:** Falling-block action gives rigid barrel-receiver matting; polished blue/black finish. Hand-fitted action. Standard and custom made-to-order rifles with many options. Made in U.S.A. by E. Arthur Brown Co., Inc.
Price: Standard model $999.00
Price: Custom model $1,350.00

C. SHARPS ARMS MODEL 1875 TARGET & SPORTING RIFLE
Caliber: .38-55, .40-65, .40-70 Straight or Bottlenecks, .45-70, .45-90. **Barrel:** 30" heavy tapered round. **Weight:** 11 lbs. **Length:** NA. **Stock:** American walnut. **Sights:** Globe with post front sight. **Features:** Long Range Vernier tang sight with windage adjustments. Pistol grip stock with cheek rest; checkered steel buttplate. Introduced 1991. From C. Sharps Arms Co.
Price: Without sights...$1,325.00
Price: With blade front & Buckhorn rear barrel sights $1,420.00
Price: With standard Tang & Globe w/post & ball front sights $1,615.00
Price: With deluxe vernier Tang & Globe w/spirit level & aperture sights $1,730.00
Price: With single set trigger, add $125.00

C. SHARPS ARMS 1875 CLASSIC SHARPS
Similar to New Model 1875 Sporting Rifle except 26", 28" or 30" full octagon barrel, crescent buttplate with toe plate, Hartford-style fore-end with cast German silver nose cap. Blade front sight, Rocky Mountain buckhorn rear. Weighs 10 lbs. Introduced 1987. From C. Sharps Arms Co.
Price: $1,670.00

Prices given are believed to be accurate at time of publication however, many factors affect retail pricing so exact prices are not possible.

C. SHARPS ARMS 1874 BRIDGEPORT SPORTING
Caliber: .38-55 to .50-3.25. **Barrel:** 26", 28", 30" tapered octagon. **Weight:** 10.5 lbs. **Length:** 47". **Stock:** American black walnut; shotgun butt with checkered steel buttplate; straight grip, heavy fore-end with Schnabel tip. **Sights:** Blade front, buckhorn rear. Drilled and tapped for tang sight. **Features:** Double-set triggers. Made in U.S.A. by C. Sharps Arms.
Price: **$1,895.00**

C. SHARPS ARMS NEW MODEL 1885 HIGHWALL
Caliber: .22 LR, .22 Hornet, .219 Zipper, .25-35 WCF, .32-40 WCF, .38-55 WCF, .40-65, .30-40 Krag, .40-50 ST or BN, .40-70 ST or BN, .40-90 ST or BN, .45-70 Govt. 2-1/10" ST, .45-90 2-4/10" ST, .45-100 2-6/10" ST, .45-110 2-7/8" ST, .45-120 3-1/4" ST. **Barrel:** 26", 28", 30", tapered full octagon. **Weight:** About 9 lbs., 4 oz. **Length:** 47" overall. **Stock:** Oil-finished American walnut; Schnabel-style forend. **Sights:** Blade front, buckhorn rear. Drilled and tapped for optional tang sight. **Features:** Single trigger; octagonal receiver top; checkered steel buttplate; color case-hardened receiver and buttplate, blued barrel. Many options available. Made in U.S.A. by C. Sharps Arms Co.
Price: From **$1,850.00**

C. SHARPS ARMS CUSTOM NEW MODEL 1877 LONG RANGE TARGET
Caliber: .44-90 Sharps/Rem., .45-70 Govt., .45-90, .45-100 Sharps. **Barrel:** 32", 34" tapered round with Rigby flat. **Weight:** About 10 lbs. **Stock:** Walnut checkered. Pistol grip/fore-end. **Sights:** Classic long range with windage. **Features:** Custom production only.
Price: From **$7,250.00**

CIMARRON U.S. SHOOTING TEAM CREEDMOOR SHARPS
Caliber: .45-70. **Barrel:** 34" round. **Weight:** 11.5 pounds. **Length:** NA. **Stock:** European walnut. **Sights:** Blade front, Creedmoor rear. **Features:** Color case-hardened frame, blued barrel. Hand-checkered grip and fore-end; hand-rubbed oil finish. A percentage of the sale of this rifle that was used to win the first organized shooting event in the United States, will be given to the USA Shooting Team to support their efforts to continue the country's legacy in international shooting sports. Made in Italy by Chiappa. Imported by Cimarron F.A. Co.
Price: From **$1,559.70**

CIMARRON BILLY DIXON 1874 SHARPS SPORTING
Caliber: .45-70, .45-90, .50-70. **Barrel:** 32" tapered octagonal. **Weight:** NA. **Length:** NA. **Stock:** European walnut. **Sights:** Blade front, Creedmoor rear. **Features:** Color case-hardened frame, blued barrel. Hand-checkered grip and fore-end; hand-rubbed oil finish. Made by Pedersoli. Imported by Cimarron F.A. Co.
Price: From **$1,987.70**

CIMARRON MODEL 1885 HIGH WALL
Caliber: .38-55, .40-65, .45-70 Govt., .45-90, .45-120, .30-40 Krag, .348 Winchester, .405 Winchester. **Barrel:** 30" octagonal. **Weight:** NA. **Length:** NA. **Stock:** European walnut. **Sights:** Bead front, semi-buckhorn rear. **Features:** Replica of the Winchester 1885 High Wall rifle. Color case-hardened receiver and lever, blued barrel. Curved buttplate. Optional double-set triggers. Introduced 1999. Imported by Cimarron F.A. Co.
Price: From **$1,065.00**
Price: With pistol grip, from **$1,250.00**

CIMARRON MODEL 1885 LOW WALL
Caliber: .22 Hornet, .32-20, .38-40, .44-40, .45 Colt. **Barrel:** 30" octagonal. **Weight:** NA. **Length:** NA. **Stock:** European walnut. **Sights:** Bead front, semi-buckhorn rear. **Features:** Replica of the Winchester 1885 Low Wall rifle. Color case-hardened receiver, blued barrel. Curved buttplate. Optional double-set triggers. Introduced

1999. Imported by Cimarron F.A. Co.
Price: From **$1,003.00**

CIMARRON ADOBE WALLS ROLLING BLOCK
Caliber: .45-70 Govt. **Barrel:** 30" octagonal. **Weight:** 10-1/3 lbs. **Length:** NA. **Stock:** Hand-checkered European walnut. **Sights:** Bead front, semi-buckhorn rear. **Features:** Color case-hardened receiver, blued barrel. Curved buttplate. Double-set triggers. Made by Pedersoli. Imported by Cimarron F.A. Co.
Price: From **$1,740.00**

DAKOTA ARMS MODEL 10
Caliber: Most rimmed and rimless commercial calibers. **Barrel:** 23". **Weight:** 6 lbs. **Length:** 39.5" overall. **Stock:** Medium fancy grade walnut in classic style. Standard or full-length Mannlicher-style. Checkered grip and fore-end. **Sights:** None furnished. Drilled and tapped for scope mounting. **Features:** Falling block action with underlever. Top tang safety. Removable trigger plate for conversion to single set trigger. Introduced 1990. Made in U.S.A. by Dakota Arms.
Price: From **$5,260.00**
Price: Deluxe from **$6,690.00**

DAKOTA ARMS SHARPS
Calibers: Virtually any caliber from .17 Ackley Hornet to .30-40 Krag. Features include a 26" octagon barrel, XX-grade walnut stock with straight grip and tang sight. Many options and upgrades are available.
Price: From **$4,490.00**

EMF PREMIER 1874 SHARPS
Caliber: .45-70, .45-110, .45-120. **Barrel:** 32", 34". **Weight:** 11-13 lbs. **Length:** 49", 51" overall. **Stock:** Pistol grip, European walnut. **Sights:** Blade front, adjustable rear. **Features:** Superb quality reproductions of the 1874 Sharps Sporting Rifles; case-hardened locks; double-set triggers; blue barrels. Imported from Pedersoli by EMF.
Price: Business Rifle **$1,499.90**
Price: Down Under Sporting Rifle, Patchbox, heavy barrel .. **$2,249.90**
Price: Silhouette, pistol-grip **$1,799.90**
Price: Super Deluxe Hand Engraved **$3,500.00**

H&R ULTRA VARMINT/ULTRA HUNTER
Caliber: .204 Ruger, .22-250 Rem., .223 Rem., .243 Win., .25-06 Rem., .308 Win., .30-06, .45-70 Govt. **Barrel:** 22" to 26" heavy taper. **Weight:** About 7.5 lbs. **Stock:** Laminated birch with Monte Carlo comb or skeletonized polymer. Thumbhole stock available on some models. **Sights:** None furnished. Drilled and tapped for scope mounting. **Features:** Break-open action with side-lever release, positive ejection. Scope mount. Blued receiver and barrel. Swivel studs. Introduced 1993. Ultra Hunter introduced 1995. From H&R 1871, Inc.
Price: Ultra Varmint Fluted, 24" bull barrel, polymer stock....... **$517.00**
Price: Ultra Hunter Rifle, 26" bull barrel in .25-06 Rem., laminated stock **$381.00**
Price: Ultra Varmint Rifle, 22" bull barrel in .223 Rem., laminated stock **$381.00**

H&R ULTRA HUNTER WITH THUMBHOLE STOCK
Caliber: .45-70 Govt. **Barrel:** 24". **Weight:** 8 lbs. **Length:** 40". **Features:** Stainless steel barrel and receiver with scope mount rail, hammer

Prices given are believed to be accurate at time of publication however, many factors affect retail pricing so exact prices are not possible.

69TH EDITION, 2015 ◈ **481**

extension, cinnamon laminate thumbhole stock.
Price: **$590.00**

H&R HANDI-RIFLE/SLUG GUN COMBOS
Chamber: .44 Magnum w/12 gauge, .357 Mag. w/ 20 gauge. **Barrel:** 22" for rifle barrels, 28" for 12 ga., 30" for 20 gauge. **Weight:** 7-8 lbs. **Length:** 38" overall (both rifle chamberings). **Features:** Each model comes with one rifle barrel and one shotgun barrel in the combinations listed. High density black polymer buttstock and fore-end with molded grip patterns. Monte Carlo comb, sling swivels, recoil pad. No sights but each barrel has top mounted accessory rail.
Price: **$590.00**

H&R BUFFALO CLASSIC
Caliber: .45 Colt or .45-70 Govt. **Barrel:** 32" heavy. **Weight:** 8 lbs. **Length:** 46" overall. **Stock:** Cut-checkered American black walnut. **Sights:** Williams receiver sight; Lyman target front sight with 8 aperture inserts. **Features:** Color case-hardened Handi-Rifle action with exposed hammer; color case-hardened crescent buttplate; 19th century checkering pattern. Introduced 1995. Made in U.S.A. by H&R 1871, Inc.
Price: Buffalo Classic Rifle...............................**$479.00**

H&R HANDI-RIFLE
Caliber: .204 Ruger, .22 Hornet, .223 Rem., .243 Win., .30-30, .270 Win., .280 Rem., 7mm-08 Rem., .308 Win., 7.62x39 Russian, .30-06 Spfl., .357 Mag., .35 Whelen, .44 Mag., .45-70 Govt., .500 S&W. **Barrel:** From 20" to 26", blued or stainless. **Weight:** 5.5 to 7 lbs. **Stock:** Walnut-finished hardwood or synthetic. **Sights:** Vary by model, but most have ramp front, folding rear, or are drilled and tapped for scope mount. **Features:** Break-open action with side-lever release. Swivel studs on all models. Blue finish. Introduced 1989. From H&R 1871, Inc.
Price: **$314.00**
Price: Synthetic stock **$323.00**
Price: Thumbhole stock **$341.00**
Price: Superlight model **$323.00**

H&R SURVIVOR
Caliber: 223 Rem., .308 Win. **Barrel:** 20" to 22" bull contour. **Weight:** 6 lbs. **Length:** 34.5" to 36" overall. **Stock:** Black polymer, thumbhole design. **Sights:** None furnished; scope mount provided. **Features:** Receiver drilled and tapped for scope mounting. Stock and fore-end have storage compartments for ammo, etc.; comes with integral swivels and black nylon sling. Introduced 1996. Made in U.S.A. by H&R 1871, Inc.
Price: Blue or nickel finish **$327.00**

KRIEGHOFF HUBERTUS SINGLE-SHOT
Caliber: .222, .22-250, .243 Win., .270 Win., .308 Win., .30-06 Spfl., 5.6x50R Mag., 5.6x52R, 6x62R Freres, 6.5x57R, 6.5x65R, 7x57R, 7x65R, 8x57JRS, 8x75RS, 9.3x74R, 7mm Rem. Mag., .300 Win. Mag. **Barrel:** 23.5". Shorter lengths available. **Weight:** 6.5 lbs. **Length:** 40.5" **Stock:** High-grade walnut. **Sights:** Blade front, open rear. **Features:** Break-open loading with manual cocking lever on top tang; takedown; extractor; Schnabel forearm; many options. Imported from Germany by Krieghoff International Inc.
Price: Hubertus single shot, from **$6,495.00**
Price: Hubertus, magnum calibers **$7,495.00**

MEACHAM HIGHWALL SILHOUETTE OR SCHUETZEN
Caliber: Any rimmed cartridge. **Barrel:** 26-34". **Weight:** 8-15 lbs. **Sights:** None. Tang drilled for Win. base, 3/8 dovetail slot front. **Stock:** Fancy eastern walnut with cheekpiece; ebony insert in forearm tip. **Features:** Exact copy of 1885 Winchester. With most Winchester factory options available, including double-set triggers. Introduced 1994. Made in U.S.A. by Meacham T&H Inc.
Price: From **$5,800.00**

MERKEL K1 MODEL LIGHTWEIGHT STALKING
Caliber: .243 Win., .270 Win., 7x57R, .308 Win., .30-06 Spfl., 7mm Rem. Mag., .300 Win. Mag., 9.3x74R. **Barrel:** 23.6". **Weight:** 5.6 lbs. unscoped. **Stock:** Satin-finished walnut, fluted and checkered; sling-swivel studs. **Sights:** None (scope base furnished). **Features:** Franz Jager single-shot break-open action, cocking/uncocking slide-type safety, matte silver receiver, selectable trigger pull weights, integrated, quick detach 1" or 30mm optic mounts (optic not included). Imported from Germany by Merkel USA.
Price: Jagd Stutzen Carbine **$3,795.00**

MERKEL K-2 CUSTOM SINGLE-SHOT "WEIMAR" STALKING
Caliber: .308 Win., .30-06 Spfl., 7mm Rem. Mag., .300 Win. Mag. . **Features:** Franz Jager single-shot break-open action, cocking. Uncocking slide safety, deep relief engraved hunting scenes on silvered receiver, octagon barrel, deluxe walnut stock. Includes front and rear adjustable iron sights, scope rings. Imported from Germany by Merkel USA.
Price: Jagd Stutzen Carbine **$15,595.00**

MILLER ARMS
Calibers: Virtually any caliber from .17 Ackley Hornet to .416 Remington. Falling block design with 24" premium match-grade barrel, express sights, XXX-grade walnut stock and fore-end with 24 lpi checkering. Made in several styles including Classic, Target and Varmint. Many options and upgrades are available. From Dakota Arms.
Price: From **$4,995.00**

ROSSI SINGLE-SHOT SERIES
Caliber: .223 Rem., .243 Win., .44 Magnum. **Barrel:** 22" **Weight:** 6.25 lbs. **Stocks:** Black Synthetic. **Sights:** Adjustable sights, drilled and tapped for scope. **Features:** Single-shot break open, positive ejection, internal transfer bar mechanism, manual external safety, trigger block system, Taurus Security System, Matte blue finish.
Price: **$307.00**

ROSSI MATCHED PAIRS
Gauge/Caliber: 12 gauge, 20 gauge, .410 bore shotgun; .223 Rem, .243 Win., .270 Win., .30-06, .308 Win., .50 (black powder). **Barrel:** 23", 28". **Weight:** 5-6.3 lbs. **Stocks:** Wood or black synthetic. **Sights:**

Bead front on shotgun barrel, fully adjustable front and rear on rifle barrel, drilled and tapped for scope, fully adjustable fiber-optic sights (black powder). **Features:** Single-shot break open, internal transfer bar mechanism, manual external safety, blue finish, trigger block system, Taurus Security System. Rimfire models are also available.
Price: **$352.00**

RUGER NO. 1-A LIGHT SPORTER
Caliber: .280 Rem. **Barrel:** 22". **Weight:** 7.25 lbs. **Length:** 38.5". **Stock:** Checkered American walnut with Alexander Henry style fore-end. **Sights:** Adjustable rear, bead front. **Features:** Under-lever falling-block design with automatic ejector, top tang safety. Starting with 2014, Ruger now chambers each No. 1 model only in one caliber. This caliber is expected to change each year.
Price: **$1,399.00**

RUGER NO. 1-V VARMINTER
Caliber: .220 Swift. **Barrel:** 26" heavy barrel. **Weight:** 8.5 lbs. **Length:** 38.5". **Stock:** Checkered American walnut with semi-beavertail fore-end. **Sights:** None. Barrel ribbed for target scope block, with 1" Ruger scope rings. **Features:** Under-lever falling-block design with automatic ejector, top tang safety. Starting with 2014, Ruger now chambers each No. 1 model only in one caliber. This caliber is expected to change each year.
Price: **$1,399.00**

RUGER NO. 1 RSI INTERNATIONAL
Caliber: .257 Roberts. **Barrel:** 20 inches. **Weight:** 7 lbs. **Length:** 38.5". **Stock:** Checkered American walnut with full-length International-style fore-end with loop sling swivel. **Sights:** Adjustable folding leaf rear sight on quarter-rib, ramp front with gold bead. **Features:** Under-lever falling-block design with automatic ejector, top tang safety. Starting with 2014, Ruger now chambers each No. 1 model only in one caliber. This caliber is expected to change each year.
Price: **$1,399.00**

RUGER NO. 1-H TROPICAL RIFLE
Caliber: .450/400 Nitro Express. **Barrel:** 24" heavy contour. **Weight:** 9.25 lbs. **Length:** 38.5". **Stock:** Checkered American walnut with Alexander Henry-style fore-end. **Sights:** Adjustable folding leaf rear sight on quarter-rib, ramp front with dovetail gold bead. **Features:**

Under-lever falling-block design with automatic ejector, top tang safety. Starting with 2014, Ruger now chambers each No. 1 model only in one caliber. This caliber is expected to change each year.
Price: **$1,399.00**

RUGER NO. 1-S MEDIUM SPORTER
Caliber: 9.3x62. **Barrel:** 20" **Weight:** 7.25 lbs. **Length:** 38.5". **Stock:** Checkered American walnut with Alexander Henry-style fore-end. **Sights:** Adjustable folding leaf rear sight on quarter-rib, ramp front sight base and dovetail-type gold bead front sight. **Features:** Under-lever falling-block design with automatic ejector, top tang safety. Starting with 2014, Ruger now chambers each No. 1 model only in one caliber. This caliber is expected to change each year.
Price: **$1,399.00**

SHILOH CO. SHARPS 1874 LONG RANGE EXPRESS
Caliber: .38-55, .40-50 BN, .40-70 BN, .40-90 BN, .40-70 ST, .40-90 ST, .45-70 Govt. ST, .45-90 ST, .45-110 ST, .50-70 ST, .50-90 ST. **Barrel:** 34" tapered octagon. **Weight:** 10.5 lbs. **Length:** 51" overall. **Stock:** Oil-finished walnut (upgrades available) with pistol grip, shotgun-style butt, traditional cheek rest, Schnabel forend. **Sights:** Customer's choice. **Features:** Re-creation of the Model 1874 Sharps rifle. Double-set triggers. Made in U.S.A. by Shiloh Rifle Mfg. Co.
Price: **$1,959.00**
Price: Sporter Rifle No. 1 (similar to above except with 30" barrel, blade front, buckhorn rear sight) **$1,959.00**
Price: Sporter Rifle No. 3 (similar to No. 1 except straight-grip stock, standard wood) **$1,854.00**

SHILOH CO. SHARPS 1874 QUIGLEY
Caliber: .45-70 Govt., .45-110. **Barrel:** 34" heavy octagon. **Stock:** Military-style with patch box, standard-grade American walnut. **Sights:** Semi-buckhorn, interchangeable front and midrange vernier tang sight with windage. **Features:** Gold inlay initials, pewter tip, Hartford collar, case color or antique finish. Double-set triggers.
Price: **$3,396.00**

SHILOH CO. SHARPS 1874 SADDLE
Caliber: .38-55, .40-50 BN, .40-65 Win., .40-70 BN, .40-70 ST, .40-90 BN, .40-90 ST, .44-77 BN, .44-90 BN, .45-70 Govt. ST, .45-90 ST, .45-100 ST, .45-110 ST, .45-120 ST, .50-70 ST, .50-90 ST. **Barrel:** 26" full or half octagon. **Stock:** Semi-fancy American walnut. Shotgun style with cheek rest. **Sights:** Buckhorn and blade. **Features:** Double-set trigger, numerous custom features can be added.
Price: **$1,907.00**

SHILOH CO. SHARPS 1874 MONTANA ROUGHRIDER
Caliber: .38-55, .40-50 BN, .40-65 Win., .40-70 BN, .40-70 ST, .40-90

Prices given are believed to be accurate at time of publication however, many factors affect retail pricing so exact prices are not possible.

69TH EDITION, 2015 ⊕ **483**

BN, .40-90 ST, .44-77 BN, .44-90 BN, .45-70 Govt. ST, .45-90 ST, .45-100 ST, .45-110 ST, .45-120 ST, .50-70 ST, .50-90 ST. **Barrel:** 30" full or half octagon. **Stock:** American walnut in shotgun or military style. **Sights:** Buckhorn and blade. **Features:** Double-set triggers, numerous custom features can be added.
Price: $1,959.00

SHILOH CO. SHARPS CREEDMOOR TARGET
Caliber: .38-55, .40-50 BN, .40-65 Win., .40-70 ST, .40-90 BN, .40-90 ST, .44-77 BN, .44-90 BN, .45-70 Govt. ST, .45-90 ST, .45-100 ST, .45-110 ST, .45-120 ST, .50-70 ST, .50-90 ST. **Barrel:** 32", half round-half octagon. **Stock:** Extra fancy American walnut. Shotgun style with pistol grip. **Sights:** Customer's choice. **Features:** Single trigger, AA finish on stock, polished barrel and screws, pewter tip.
Price: $2,825.00

THOMPSON/CENTER ENCORE PROHUNTER PREDATOR RIFLE
Caliber: .204 Ruger, .223 Remington, .22-250 and .308 Winchester. **Barrel:** 28-inch deep-fluted interchangeable. **Length:** 42.5 inches. **Weight:** 7 3/4 lbs. **Stock:** Composite buttstock and fore-end with non-slip inserts in cheekpiece, pistol grip and fore-end. Realtree Advantage Max-1 camo finish overall. Scope is not included.
Price: $882.00

THOMPSON/CENTER ENCORE PRO HUNTER KATAHDIN CARBINE
Caliber: .45-70 Govt., .460 S&W Mag., .500 S&W Mag. **Barrel:** 28-inch deep-fluted interchangeable. **Length:** 34.5 inches. **Weight:** 7 lbs. **Stock:** Flex-Tech with Simms recoil pad. Grooved and textured grip surfaces. **Sights:** Adjustable rear peep, fiber optic front.
Price: $852.00

UBERTI 1874 SHARPS SPORTING
Caliber: .45-70 Govt. **Barrel:** 30", 32", 34" octagonal. **Weight:** 10.57 lbs. with 32" barrel. **Length:** 48.9" with 32" barrel. **Stock:** Walnut. **Sights:** Dovetail front, Vernier tang rear. **Features:** Cut checkering, case-colored finish on frame, buttplate, and lever. Imported by Stoeger Industries.
Price: Standard Sharps.....................................$1,809.00
Price: Special Sharps..$2,019.00
Price: Deluxe Sharps...$3,129.00
Price: Down Under Sharps $2,579.00
Price: Long Range Sharps $2,579.00
Price: Buffalo Hunter Sharps $2,469.00
Price: Sharps Cavalry Carbine............................$1,809.00
Price: Sharps Extra Deluxe $4,999.00
Price: Sharps Hunter $1,639.00

UBERTI 1885 HIGH-WALL SINGLE-SHOT
Caliber: .45-70 Govt., .45-90, .45-120. **Barrel:** 28" to 32". **Weight:** 9.3 to 9.9 lbs. **Length:** 44.5" to 47" overall. **Stock:** Walnut stock and fore-end. **Sights:** Blade front, fully adjustable open rear. **Features:** Based on Winchester High-Wall design by John Browning. Color case-hardened frame and lever, blued barrel and buttplate. Imported by Stoeger Industries.
Price: From .... $1,009.00 to $1,279.00

UBERTI SPRINGFIELD TRAPDOOR RIFLE/CARBINE
Caliber: .45-70 Govt., single shot **Barrel:** 22 or 32.5 inches. **Features:** Blue steel receiver and barrel, case-hardened breechblock and buttplate. **Sights:** Creedmoor style.
Price: Springfield Trapdoor Carbine, 22" barrel $1,669.00
Price: Springfield Trapdoor Army, 32.5" barrel $1,949.00

WINCHESTER MODEL 1885 HIGH WALL HUNTER
Caliber: .220 Swift, .270 Win., .270 WSM, .30-06, .300 WSM, .300 Win. Mag. **Barrel:** 28 inches full octagon, without sights, drilled and tapped for scope mounts. **Length:** 44 inches. **Stock:** Checkered walnut with Pachmayr Decelerator recoil pad and Schnabel fore-end.
Price: $1,600.00

DRILLINGS, COMBINATION / DOUBLE GUNS

BERETTA S686/S689 O/U RIFLE SERIES
Calibers: .30-06, 9.3x74R. **Barrels:** 23 inches. O/U boxlock action. Single or double triggers. EELL Grade has better wood, moderate engraving.
Price: .... $4,200.00 to $9,000.00
Price: EELL Diamond Sable grade, from $12,750.00

BRNO MODEL 802 COMBO GUN
Caliber/Gauge: .243 Win./12 ga. Over/under. **Barrels:** 23.6". **Weight:** 7.6 lbs. **Length:** 41". **Stock:** European walnut. **Features:** Double trigger, shotgun barrel is improved-modified chokes. Imported by CZ USA.
Price: $2,181.00

EAA MP94 COMBO GUN
Caliber/Gauge: Over/under style with 12-gauge shotgun barrel over

either a .223 or .308 rifle barrel. **Barrels:** 19.7". **Stock:** Checkered walnut. **Sights:** Adjustable rear, ramp front with bead. Picatinny or 11mm scope rail. **Features:** Four choke tubes for shotgun barrel. Double triggers. Made by Baikal and imported by European American Armory. Also available in .410/.22 LR model.
Price: $790.00
Price: .410/.22 model..$562.00

EAA MP221 DOUBLE RIFLE
Caliber: .30-06 or .45-70 side-by-side double rifle. **Barrels:** 23.5". **Stock:** Checkered walnut. **Sights:** Adjustable rear, ramp front with bead. Picatinny or 11mm scope rail. **Features:** Double triggers, extractors, adjustable barrel regulation. Imported by European American Armory.
Price: $1,155.00

FAUSTI CLASS EXPRESS
Caliber: .30-06, .30R Blaser, 8x57 JRS, 9.3x74R, .444 Marlin,

.45-70 Govt. Over/under. **Barrels:** 24". **Weight:** 7.5 lbs. **Length:** 41". **Stock:** Oil-finished Grade A walnut. Pistol grip, Bavarian or Classic. **Sights:** Folding leaf rear, fiber optic front adjustable for elevation. **Features:** Inertia single or double trigger, automatic ejectors. Made in Italy and imported by Fausti USA.
Price: $4,990.00

HOENIG ROTARY ROUND ACTION DOUBLE
Caliber: Most popular calibers. Over/under design. **Barrel:** 22" to 26". **Stock:** English Walnut. **Sights:** Swivel hood front with button release (extra bead stored in trap door gripcap), express-style rear on quarter-rib adjustable for windage and elevation; scope mount. **Features:** Round action opens by rotating barrels, pulling forward. Inertia extractor system, rotary safety blocks strikers. Single lever quick-detachable-e scope mount. Simple takedown without removing fore-end. Introduced 1997. Made in U.S.A. by George Hoenig.
Price: From $22,500.00

HOENIG ROTARY ROUND ACTION COMBINATION
Caliber: Most popular calibers and shotgun gauges. Over/under design with rifle barrel atop shotgun barrel. **Barrel:** 26". **Weight:** 7 lbs. **Stock:** English Walnut to customer specs. **Sights:** Front ramp with button release blades. Foldable aperture tang sight windage and elevation adjustable. Quarter-rib with scope mount. **Features:** Round action opens by rotating barrels, pulling forward. Inertia extractor; rotary safety blocks strikers. Simple takedown without removing forend. Made in U.S.A. by George Hoenig.
Price: $27,500.00

HOENIG VIERLING FOUR-BARREL COMBINATION
Caliber/gauge: Two 20-gauge shotgun barrels with one rifle barrel chambered for .22 Long Rifle and another for .223 Remington.
Price: $50,000.00

KRIEGHOFF CLASSIC DOUBLE
Caliber: 7x57R, 7x65R, .308 Win., .30-06 Spfl., 8x57 JRS, 8x75RS, 9.3x74R, 375NE, 500/416NE, 470NE, 500NE. **Barrel:** 23.5". **Weight:** 7.3 to 11 lbs. **Stock:** High grade European walnut. Standard model has conventional rounded cheekpiece, Bavaria model has Bavarian-style cheekpiece. **Sights:** Bead front with removable, adjustable wedge (.375 H&H and below), standing leaf rear on quarter-rib. **Features:** Boxlock action; double triggers; short opening angle for fast loading; quiet extractors; sliding, self-adjusting wedge for secure bolting; Purdey-style barrel extension; horizontal firing pin placement. Many options available. Introduced 1997. Imported from Germany by Krieghoff International.
Price: $10,995.00
Price: Engraved sideplates, add...........................$4,000.00
Price: Extra set of rifle barrels, add $6,300.00
Price: Extra set of 20-ga., 28" shotgun barrels, add $4,400.00

KRIEGHOFF CLASSIC BIG FIVE DOUBLE RIFLE
Similar to the standard Classic except available in .375 H&H, .375 Flanged Mag. N.E., .416 Rigby, .458 Win., 500/416 NE, 470 NE, 500 NE. Has hinged front trigger, nonremovable muzzle wedge, Universal Trigger System, Combi Cocking Device, steel triggerguard, specially weighted stock bolt for weight and balance. Many options available. Introduced 1997. Imported from Germany by Krieghoff International.
Price: $13,995.00
Price: Engraved sideplates, add $4,000.00
Price: Extra set of 20-ga. shotgun barrels, add....................$5,000.00
Price: Extra set of rifle barrels, add $6,300.00

LEBEAU-COURALLY EXPRESS SXS
Caliber: 7x65R, 8x57JRS, 9.3x74R, .375 H&H, .470 N.E. **Barrel:** 24" to 26". **Weight:** 7.75 to 10.5 lbs. **Stock:** Fancy French walnut with cheekpiece. **Sights:** Bead on ramp front, standing left express rear on quarter-rib. **Features:** Holland & Holland-type sidelock with automatic ejectors; double triggers. Built to order only. Imported from Belgium by Wm. Larkin Moore and Griffin & Howe.
Price: $45,000.00

MERKEL DRILLINGS
Caliber/Gauge: : 12, 20, 3" chambers, 16, 2-3/4" chambers; .22 Hornet, 5.6x50R Mag., 5.6x52R, .222 Rem., .243 Win., 6.5x55, 6.5x57R, 7x57R, 7x65R, .308 Win., .30-06 Spfl., 8x57JRS, 9.3x74R, .375 H&H. **Barrel:** 25.6". **Weight:** 7.9 to 8.4 lbs. depending upon caliber. **Stock:** Oil-finished walnut with pistol grip; cheekpiece on 12-, 16-gauge. **Sights:** Blade front, fixed rear. **Features:** Double barrel locking lug with Greener crossbolt; scroll-engraved, case-hardened receiver; automatic trigger safety; Blitz action; double triggers. Imported from Germany by Merkel USA.
Price: Model 96K (manually cocked rifle system), from.........$8,495.00
Price: Model 96K engraved (hunting series on receiver) $9,795.00

MERKEL BOXLOCK DOUBLE
Caliber: 5.6x52R, .243 Winchester, 6.5x55, 6.5x57R, 7x57R, 7x65R, .308 Win., .30-06 Springfield, 8x57 IRS, 9.3x74R. **Barrel:** 23.6". **Weight:** 7.7 oz. **Length:** NA. **Stock:** Walnut, oil finished, pistol grip. **Sights:** Fixed 100 meter. **Features:** Anson & Deeley boxlock action with cocking indicators, double triggers, engraved color case-hardened receiver. Introduced 1995. Imported from Germany by Merkel USA.
Price: Model 140-2, from....................................$11,995.00
Price: Model 141 Small Frame SXS Rifle; built on smaller frame, chambered for 7mm Mauser, .30-06, or 9.3x74R $8,195.00
Price: Model 141 Engraved; fine hand-engraved hunting scenes on silvered receiver $9,495.00

RIZZINI EXPRESS 90L
Caliber: .308 Win., .30-06 Spfl., 7x65R, 9.3x74R, 8x57 JRS, .444 Marlin. **Barrel:** 24". **Weight:** 7.5 lbs. **Length:** 40" overall. **Stock:** Select European walnut with satin oil finish; English-style cheekpiece. **Sights:** Ramp front, quarter-rib with express sight. **Features:** Over/under with color case-hardened boxlock action; automatic ejectors; single selective trigger; polished blue barrels. Extra 20-gauge shotgun barrels available. Imported from Italy by Fierce Products.
Price: With case..$4,500.00

Prices given are believed to be accurate at time of publication however, many factors affect retail pricing so exact prices are not possible.

69TH EDITION, 2015 ✛ **485**

ANSCHUTZ RX22
Caliber: .22 LR. AR-style semiautomatic rifle with blowback operation. **Barrel:** 16.5". **Features:** Available in several styles and colors including black, Desert Tan. Fixed or folding stock, adjustable trigger, military-type folding iron sights. Made in Germany and imported by Steyr Arms Inc.
Price: $895.00

AMERICAN TACTICAL IMPORTS GSG-522
Semiauto tactical rifle chambered in .22 LR. Features include 16.25-inch barrel; black finish overall; polymer fore-end and buttstock; backup iron sights; receiver-mounted Picaatinny rail; 10-round magazine. Several other rifle and carbine versions available.
Price: $451.00

BROWNING BUCK MARK SEMI-AUTO
Caliber: .22 LR, 10+1. **Action:** A rifle version of the Buck Mark Pistol; straight blowback action; machined aluminum receiver with integral rail scope mount; manual thumb safety. **Barrel:** Recessed crowns. **Stock:** Stock and forearm with full pistol grip. **Features:** Action lock provided. Introduced 2001. Four model name variations for 2006, as noted below. **Sights:** FLD Target, FLD Carbon, and Target models have integrated scope rails. Sporter has Truglo/Marble fiber-optic sights. Imported from Japan by Browning.
Price: FLD Target, 5.5 lbs., bull barrel, laminated stock $720.00
Price: Target, 5.4 lbs., blued bull barrel, wood stock $700.00
Price: Sporter, 4.4 lbs., blued sporter barrel w/sights $700.00

BROWNING SA-22 SEMI-AUTO 22
Caliber: .22 LR. Tubular magazine in buttstock hold 11 rounds. **Barrel:** 19.375". **Weight:** 5 lbs. 3 oz. **Length:** 37" overall. **Stock:** Checkered select walnut with pistol grip and semi-beavertail fore-end. **Sights:** Gold bead front, folding leaf rear. **Features:** Engraved receiver with polished blue finish; crossbolt safety; easy takedown for carrying or storage. The Grade VI is available with either grayed or blued receiver with extensive engraving with gold-plated animals: right side pictures a fox and squirrel in a woodland scene; left side shows a beagle chasing a rabbit. On top is a portrait of the beagle. Stock and fore-end are of high-grade walnut with a double-bordered cut checkering design. Introduced 1987. Imported from Japan by Browning.
Price: Grade I, scroll-engraved blued receiver $700.00
Price: Grade VI BL, gold-plated engraved blued receiver $1,580.00

CITADEL M-1 CARBINE
Caliber: .22LR., 10-round magazines. **Barrel:** 18". **Weight:** 4.8 lbs. **Length:** 35". **Stock:** Wood or synthetic in black or several camo patterns. **Features:** Built to the exacting specifications of the G.I. model used by U.S. infantrymen in both WWII theaters of battle and in Korea. Used by officers as well as tankers, drivers, artillery crews, mortar crews, and other personnel. Weight, barrel length and OAL are the same as the "United States Carbine, Caliber .30, M1," its official military designation. Made in Italy by Chiappa. Imported by Legacy Sports.
Price: Synthetic stock, black. $316.00
Price: Synthetic stock, camo. $368.00
Price: Wood stock. $400.00

CZ MODEL 512
Caliber: .22 LR/.22 WMR, 5-round magazines. **Barrel:** 20.5". **Weight:** 5.9 lbs. **Length:** 39.3". **Stock:** Beech. **Sights:** Adjustable. **Features:** The modular design is easily maintained, requiring only a coin as a tool for field stripping. The action of the 512 is composed of an aluminum alloy upper receiver that secures the barrel and bolt assembly and a fiberglass reinforced polymer lower half that houses the trigger mechanism and detachable magazine. The 512 shares the same magazines and scope rings with the CZ 455 bolt-action rifle.
Price: .22 LR $480.00
Price: .22 WMR... $510.00

HENRY U.S. SURVIVAL AR-7 22
Caliber: .22 LR, 8-shot magazine. **Barrel:** 16" steel lined. **Weight:** 2.25 lbs. **Stock:** ABS plastic. **Sights:** Blade front on ramp, aperture rear. **Features:** Takedown design stores barrel and action in hollow stock. Light enough to float on water. Dark gray or camo finish. Comes with two magazines. Introduced 1998. From Henry Repeating Arms Co.
Price: H002B Black finish $290.00
Price: H002C Camo finish $350.00

KEL-TEC SU-22CA
Caliber: .22 LR. 26-round magazine. **Barrel:** 16.1". **Weight:** 4 lbs. **Length:** 34" **Features:** Blowback action, crossbolt safety, adjustable front and rear sights with integral picatinny rail. Threaded muzzle, 26-round magazine.
Price: $440.00

MAGNUM RESEARCH MAGNUMLITE
Caliber: .22 WMR or .22 LR, 10-shot magazine. **Barrel:** 17" graphite. **Weight:** 4.45 lbs. **Length:** 35.5" overall. **Stock:** Hogue OverMolded synthetic or walnut. **Sights:** Integral scope base. **Features:** Magnum Lite graphite barrel, French grey anodizing, match bolt, target trigger. .22 LR rifles use factory Ruger 10/22 magazines. 4-5 lbs. average trigger pull. Graphite carbon-fiber barrel. Introduced: 2007. From Magnum Research, Inc.
Price: .22 LR $665.00
Price: .22 WMR... $791.00

MARLIN MODEL 60
Caliber: .22 LR, 14-shot tubular magazine. **Barrel:** 19" round tapered. **Weight:** About 5.5 lbs. **Length:** 37.5" overall. **Stock:** Press-checkered, laminated Maine birch with Monte Carlo, full pistol grip; black synthetic or Realtree Camo. **Sights:** Ramp front, open adjustable rear. Matted receiver is grooved for scope mount. **Features:** Last-shot bolt hold-open. Available with factory mounted 4x scope.

Prices given are believed to be accurate at time of publication however, many factors affect retail pricing so exact prices are not possible.

RIMFIRE RIFLES Autoloaders

Price: Laminate..$199.00
Price: Model 60C camo $232.00
Price: Synthetic...$191.00

MARLIN MODEL 60SS SELF-LOADING RIFLE
Same as the Model 60 except breech bolt, barrel and outer magazine tube are made of stainless steel; most other parts are either nickel-plated or coated to match the stainless finish. Monte Carlo stock is of black/gray Maine birch laminate, and has nickel-plated swivel studs, rubber buttpad. Introduced 1993.
Price: $300.00

MARLIN 70PSS PAPOOSE STAINLESS
Caliber: .22 LR, 7-shot magazine. **Barrel:** 16.25" stainless steel, Micro-Groove rifling. **Weight:** 3.25 lbs. **Length:** 35.25" overall. **Stock:** Black fiberglass-filled synthetic with abbreviated forend, nickel-plated swivel studs, molded-in checkering. **Sights:** Ramp front with orange post, cut-away Wide Scan hood; adjustable open rear. Receiver grooved for scope mounting. **Features:** Takedown barrel; crossbolt safety; manual bolt hold-open; last shot bolt hold-open; comes with padded carrying case. Introduced 1986. Made in U.S.A. by Marlin.
Price: $345.00

MARLIN MODEL 795
Caliber: .22. **Barrel:** 18" with 16-groove Micro-Groove rifling. **Sights:** Ramp front sight, adjustable rear. Receiver grooved for scope mount. **Stock:** Black synthetic, hardwood, synthetic thumbhole, solid pink, pink camo, or Mossy Oak New Break-up camo finish. **Features:** 10-round magazine, last shot hold-open feature. Introduced 1997. SS is similar to Model 795 except stainless steel barrel. Most other parts nickel-plated. Adjustable folding semi-buckhorn rear sights, ramp front high-visibility post and removable cutaway wide scan hood. Made in U.S.A. by Marlin Firearms Co.
Price: $183.00
Price: Stainless $262.00

MOSSBERG MODEL 702 PLINKSTER
Caliber: .22 LR, 10-round detachable magazine. **Barrel:** 18" free-floating. **Weight:** 4.1 to 4.6 lbs. **Sights:** Adjustable rifle. Receiver grooved for scope mount. **Stock:** Solid pink or pink marble finish synthetic. **Features:** Ergonomically placed magazine release and safety buttons, crossbolt safety, free gun lock. Made in U.S.A. by O.F. Mossberg & Sons, Inc.
Price: $182.00

MOSSBERG MODEL 702 PLINKSTER AUTOLOADING RIFLE WITH MUZZLE BRAKE
Semiauto rifle chambered in .22 LR. Features include a black synthetic stock with Schnabel, 10-round detachable box magazine, 21-inch matte blue barrel with muzzlebrake, receiver grooved for scope mount.
Price: $294.00

MOSSBERG MODEL 702 PLINKSTER DUCK COMMANDER
Caliber: .22 LR. Similar to standard model except synthetic stock has Realtree Max-5 camo finish, Duck Dynasty logo.
Price: $274.00

MOSSBERG MODEL 715T SERIES
Caliber: .22 LR with 10 or 25-round magazine. AR-style offered in several models. **Barrel:** 16.25 or 18 inches with A2-style muzzlebrake. **Weight:** 5.5 lbs. **Features:** Flattop or A2 style carry handle. Available with several camo patterns including Mossy Oak Brush, Muddy Girl, Realtree Max-5 finish with Duck Dynasty logo.
Price: Black finish $375.00

Price: Muddy Girl camo...................................$430.00
Price: Mossy Oak camo...................................$435.00
Price: Duck Commander $509.00

REMINGTON MODEL 552 BDL DELUXE SPEEDMASTER
Caliber: .22 Short (20 rounds), Long (17) or LR (15) tubular magazine. **Barrel:** 21" round tapered. **Weight:** 5.75 lbs. **Length:** 40" overall. **Stock:** Walnut. Checkered grip and fore-end. **Sights:** Adjustable rear, ramp front. **Features:** Positive crossbolt safety in triggerguard, receiver grooved for tip-off mount. Operates with .22 Short, Long or Long Rifle cartridges. Classic design introduced in 1957.
Price: $667.00

REMINGTON 597
Caliber: .22 LR, 10-shot clip; or .22 WMR, 8-shot clip. **Barrel:** 20". **Weight:** 5.5 lbs. **Length:** 40" overall. **Stock:** Black synthetic or camo coverage in several patterns. TVP has laminated, contoured thumbhole stock. **Sights:** Big game. **Features:** Matte black metal finish or stainless, nickel-plated bolt. Receiver is grooved and drilled and tapped for scope mounts. Introduced 1997. Made in U.S.A. by Remington.
Price: Standard model, synthetic stock $213.00
Price: Synthetic w/Scope $257.00
Price: Camo from $306.00
Price: Stainless TVP from $595.00
Price: Laminated stock, heavy barrel .22 WMR only $645.00

RUGER 10/22 AUTOLOADING CARBINE
Caliber: .22 LR, 10-shot rotary magazine. **Barrel:** 18.5" round tapered (16.12", compact model). **Weight:** 5 lbs. (4.5, compact). **Length:** 37.25", 34" (compact) overall. **Stock:** American hardwood with pistol grip and barrelband, or synthetic. **Sights:** Brass bead front, folding leaf rear adjustable for elevation. **Features:** Available with satin black or stainless finish on receiver and barrel. Detachable rotary magazine fits flush into stock, crossbolt safety, receiver tapped and grooved for scope blocks or tip-off mount. Scope base adaptor furnished with each rifle. Made in U.S.A. by Sturm, Ruger & Co.
Price: Wood stock $279.00
Price: Synthetic stock $279.00
Price: Stainless, synthetic stock $309.00
Price: Compact model, fiber-optic front sight $329.00

RUGER 10/22 DELUXE SPORTER
Same specificaions as 10/22 Carbine except has American walnut stock with hand-checkered pistol grip and fore-end, straight buttplate, sling swivels, 18.9" barrel, and no barrelband.
Price: $379.00

RUGER 10/22-T TARGET RIFLE
Similar to the 10/22 except has 20" heavy, hammer-forged barrel with tight chamber dimensions, improved trigger pull. **Weight:** 7.5 lbs. **Stock:** Black or brown laminated hardwood, dimensioned for optical sights. No iron sights supplied. Introduced 1996.
Price: From $529.00
Price: Stainless from.......................................$569.00

RUGER 10/22VLEH TARGET TACTICAL RIFLE
Caliber: .22 LR. **Features:** Features include precision-rifled, cold

Prices given are believed to be accurate at time of publication however, many factors affect retail pricing so exact prices are not possible.

69TH EDITION, 2015 ⊕ **487**

hammer-forged, spiral-finished 16-1/8-inch crowned match barrel; Hogue OverMolded stock, 10/22T target trigger, precision-adjustable bipod for steady shooting from the bench; 10-round rotary magazine. **Weight:** 6-7/8 lbs.
Price: $579.00

RUGER 10/22 50TH ANNIVERSARY MODEL
Caliber: .22 LR. **Barrel:** 16 1/8". **Weight:** 5 lbs. **Features:** Introduced in 2014 to commemorate 50 years of the 10/22. Features include a black composite stock with interchangeable modules for changing comb height and length of pull, stainless steel receiver and barrel with satin finish, 16-1/8-inch barrel with flash suppressor, accessory rail, precision-adjustable bipod for steady shooting from the bench, and 10-round rotary magazine. This design was the winning entry in a contest conducted by Ruger.
Price: $379.00

RUGER SR-22 RIFLE
AR-style semiauto rifle chambered in .22 LR, based on 10/22 action. Features include all-aluminum chassis replicating the AR-platform dimensions between the sighting plane, buttstock height and grip; Picatinny rail optic mount includes a six-position, telescoping M4-style buttstock (on a Mil-Spec diameter tube); Hogue Monogrip pistol grip; buttstocks and grips interchangeable with any AR-style compatible option; round, mid-length handguard mounted on a standard-thread AR-style barrel nut; precision-rifled, cold hammer forged 16-1/8-inch alloy steel barrel capped with an SR-556/Mini-14 flash suppressor.
Price: $649.00

SAVAGE MODEL 64G
Caliber: .22 LR, 10-shot magazine. **Barrel:** 20", 21". **Weight:** 5.5 lbs. **Length:** 40", 41". **Stock:** Walnut-finished hardwood with Monte Carlo-type comb, checkered grip and fore-end. **Sights:** Bead front, open adjustable rear. Receiver grooved for scope mounting. **Features:** Thumb-operated rotating safety. Blue finish. 64 SS has stainless finish. Side ejection, bolt hold-open device. Introduced 1990. Made in Canada, from Savage Arms.
Price: 64 G $221.00
Price: 64 F..$175.00
Price: 64 FSS...$254.00
Price: 64 TR-SR..$348.00

SMITH & WESSON M&P15-22 SERIES
Caliber: .22 LR. 10 or 25-round magazine. **Barrel:** 15.5", 16" or 16.5" **Stock:** 6-position telescoping or fixed. **Features:** A rimfire verson of

AR-derived M&P tactical autoloader. Operates with blowback action. Quad-mount picatinny rails, plain barrel or compensator, alloy upper and lower, matte black metal finish. Many optional camo and color finishes available, including Tan & Black, Flat Dark Earth, Realtree APG camo, Pink Platinum, Purple Platinum, Harvest Moon Orange and others.
Price: Standard..$499.00
Price: Pink, Purple, Platinum finish...$559.00
Price: Realtree APG Camo $589.00
Price: MOE Model with Magpul sights, stock and grip $609.00
Price: Performance Center upgrades, threaded barrel.............$789.00

THOMPSON/CENTER .22 LR CLASSIC
Caliber: .22 LR, 8-shot magazine. **Barrel:** 22" match-grade. **Weight:** 5.5 pounds. **Length:** 39.5" overall. **Stock:** Satin-finished American walnut with Monte Carlo-type comb and pistol gripcap, swivel studs. **Sights:** Ramp-style front and fully adjustable rear, both with fiber optics. **Features:** All-steel receiver drilled and tapped for scope mounting; barrel threaded to receiver; thumb-operated safety; triggerguard safety lock included. New .22 Classic Benchmark TGT target rifle variant has 18" heavy barrel, brown laminated target stock, blued with matte finish, 10-shot magazine and no sights; drilled and tapped.
Price: T/C .22 LR Classic (blue)..$396.00
Price: T/C .22 LR Classic Benchmark $505.00

UMAREX COLT TACTICAL RIMFIRE M4 OPS CARBINE
Blowback semiauto rife chambered in .22 LR, styled to resemble Colt M16. Features include 16.2-inch barrel; front sight adjustable for elevation; adjustable rear sight; alloy lower; adjustable telestock; flattop receiver with removable carry handle; 10- or 30-round detachable magazine. Made in Germany by Walther, under licenses from Colt. Manufactured by Walther. Imported by Umarex.
Price: $599.00

UMAREX COLT TACTICAL RIMFIRE M4 CARBINE
Blowback semiauto rifle chambered in .22 LR, styled to resemble Colt M4. Features include 16.2-inch barrel; front sight adjustable for elevation; adjustable rear sight; alloy lower; adjustable telestock; flattop receiver with optics rail; 10- or 30-round detachable magazine. Manufactured by Walther. Imported by Umarex.
Price: $699.00

UMAREX H&K 416-22
Blowback semiauto rife chambered in .22 LR, styled to resemble H&K 416. Features include metal upper and lower receivers; RIS – rail interface system; retractable stock; pistol grip with storage compartment; on-rail sights; rear sight adjustable for wind and elevation; 16.1-inch barrel; 10- or 20-round magazine. Also available in pistol version with 9-inch barrel. Manufactured by Walther. Imported by Umarex.
Price: $675.00

UMAREX H&K MP5 A5
Blowback semiauto rifle chambered in .22 LR, styled to resemble H&K MP5. Features include metal receiver; compensator; bolt catch; NAVY pistol grip; on-rail sights; rear sight adjustable for wind and elevation; 16.1-inch barrel; 10- or 25-round magazine. Also available in pistol version with 9-inch barrel. Also available with SD-type fore-end. Manufactured by Walther. Imported by Umarex.
Price: $525.00

BROWNING BL-22

Action: Short-throw lever action, side ejection. Rack-and-pinion lever. Tubular magazines, with 15+1 capacity for .22 LR. **Barrel:** Recessed muzzle. **Stock:** Walnut, two-piece straight-grip Western style. **Trigger:** Half-cock hammer safety; fold-down hammer. **Sights:** Bead post front, folding-leaf rear. Steel receiver grooved for scope mount. **Weight:** 5-5.4 lbs. **Length:** 36.75-40.75" overall. **Features:** Action lock provided. Introduced 1996. FLD Grade II Octagon has octagonal 24" barrel, silver nitride receiver with scroll engraving, gold-colored trigger. FLD Grade I has satin-nickel receiver, blued trigger, no stock checkering. FLD Grade II has satin-nickel receivers with scroll engraving; gold-colored trigger, cut checkering. Both introduced 2005. Grade I has blued receiver and trigger, no stock checkering. Grade II has gold-colored trigger, cut checkering, blued receiver with scroll engraving. Imported from Japan by Browning.

Price: BL-22 Grade I/II, from.....................................**$620.00**
Price: BL-22 FLD Grade I/II, from ....**$660.00 to $750.00**
Price: BL-22 FLD, Grade II Octagon **$980.00**
Price: Grade II Maple stock **$780.00**

HENRY LEVER-ACTION RIFLES

Caliber: .22 Long Rifle (15 shot), .22 Magnum (11 shots), .17 HMR (11 shots). **Barrel:** 18.25" round. **Weight:** 5.5 to 5.75 lbs. **Length:** 34" overall (.22 LR). **Stock:** Walnut. **Sights:** Hooded blade front, open adjustable rear. **Features:** Polished blue finish; full-length tubular magazine; side ejection; receiver grooved for scope mounting. Introduced 1997. Made in U.S.A. by Henry Repeating Arms Co.

Price: H001 Carbine .22 LR.....................................**$360.00**
Price: H001L Carbine .22 LR, Large Loop Lever......................**$375.00**
Price: H001Y Youth model (33" overall, 11-round .22 LR) **$360.00**
Price: H001M .22 Magnum, 19.25" octagonal barrel, deluxe
  walnut stock **$500.00**
Price: H001V .17 HMR, 20" octagonal barrel, Williams Fire
  Sights..**$500.00**

HENRY LEVER-ACTION OCTAGON FRONTIER MODEL

Same as Lever rifles except chambered in .17 HMR, .22 Short/Long/LR, .22 Magnum. **Barrel:** 20" octagonal. **Sights:** Marble's full adjustable semi-buckhorn rear, brass bead front. **Weight:** 6.25 lbs. Made in U.S.A. by Henry Repeating Arms Co.

Price: H001T Lever Octagon **$450.00**
Price: H001TM Lever Octagon .22 Magnum...........................**$550.00**

HENRY GOLDEN BOY .22 LEVER ACTION

Caliber: .17 HMR, .22 LR (16-shot), .22 Magnum. **Barrel:** 20" octagonal. **Weight:** 6.25 lbs. **Length:** 38" overall. **Stock:** American walnut. **Sights:** Blade front, open rear. **Features:** Brasslite receiver, brass buttplate, blued barrel and lever. Introduced 1998. Made in U.S.A. from Henry Repeating Arms Co.

Price: H004 .22 LR...**$550.00**
Price: H004M .22 Magnum **$595.00**
Price: H004V .17 HMR **$615.00**
Price: H004DD .22 LR Deluxe, engraved receiver................**$1,585.00**

HENRY PUMP-ACTION .22 PUMP

Caliber: .22 LR, 15-shot. **Barrel:** 18.25". **Weight:** 5.5 lbs. **Length:** NA. **Stock:** American walnut. **Sights:** Bead on ramp front, open adjustable rear. **Features:** Polished blue finish; receiver grooved for scope mount; grooved slide handle; two barrelbands. Introduced 1998. Made in U.S.A. from Henry Repeating Arms Co.

Price: H003T .22 LR...**$550.00**
Price: H003TM .22 Magnum.....................................**$595.00**

MARLIN MODEL 39A GOLDEN

Caliber: .22, S (26), L (21), LR (19), tubular magazine. **Barrel:** 24" Micro-Groove. **Weight:** 6.5 lbs. **Length:** 40" overall. **Stock:** Checkered American black walnut; Mar-Shield finish. Swivel studs; rubber buttpad. **Sights:** Bead ramp front with detachable Wide-Scan hood, folding rear semi-buckhorn adjustable for windage and elevation. **Features:** Hammer block safety; rebounding hammer. Takedown action, receiver tapped for scope mount (supplied), offset hammer spur, gold-colored steel trigger. The 39 series certainly deserve the term "classic" since it has been in continuous production longer than any other rifle in the America, since 1922.
Price: **$709.00**

MOSSBERG MODEL 464 RIMFIRE

Caliber: .22 LR. **Barrel:** 20" round blued. **Weight:** 5.6 lbs. **Length:** 35-3/4" overall. **Features:** Adjustable sights, straight grip stock, 14-shot tubular magazine, plain hardwood straight stock and fore-end.
Price: **$485.00**
Price: SPX...**$513.00**

REMINGTON 572 BDL DELUXE FIELDMASTER PUMP

Caliber: .22 S (20), L (17) or LR (15), tubular magazine. **Barrel:** 21" round tapered. **Weight:** 5.5 lbs. **Length:** 40" overall. **Stock:** Walnut with checkered pistol grip and slide handle. **Sights:** Big game. **Features:** Crossbolt safety; removing inner magazine tube converts rifle to single shot; receiver grooved for tip-off scope mount. Another classic rimfire, this model was been in production since 1955.
Price: **$723.00**

Prices given are believed to be accurate at time of publication however, many factors affect retail pricing so exact prices are not possible.

69TH EDITION, 2015 ✦ **489**

ANSCHUTZ MODEL 64 MP

Caliber: .22 LR. **Magazine capacity:** 5 rounds. **Barrel:** 25.6 inch heavy match. **Weight:** About 9 pounds. **Stock:** Multipurpose hardwood with beavertail fore-end. **Sights:** None. Drilled and tapped for scope or receiver sights. **Features:** Model 64S BR (benchrest) has 20" heavy barrel, adjustable two-stage match-grade trigger, flat beavertail stock, weighs 9.5 pounds. Imported from Germany by Steyr Arms

Price: $1,399.00
Price: Model 64 S BR $1,539.00

ANSCHUTZ 1416D/1516D CLASSIC

Caliber: .22 LR (1416D888), .22 WMR (1516D), 5-shot clip. **Barrel:** 22.5". **Weight:** 6 lbs. **Length:** 41" overall. **Stock:** European hardwood with walnut finish; classic style with straight comb, checkered pistol grip and fore-end. **Sights:** Hooded ramp front, folding leaf rear. **Features:** Uses Match 64 action. Adjustable single-stage trigger. Receiver grooved for scope mounting. Imported from Germany by Steyr Arms.

Price: 1416D KL, .22 LR $1,099.00
Price: 1416D KL Classic left-hand $1,199.00
Price: 1516D KL, .22 WMR...................................$1,169.00
Price: 1416D, thumbhole stock $1,599.00

ANSCHUTZ 1710D CUSTOM

Caliber:.22 LR, 5-shot clip. **Barrel:** 23.75 or 24.25" heavy contour. **Weight:** 6.5 to 7-3/8 lbs. **Length:** 42.5" overall. **Stock:** Select European walnut. **Sights:** Hooded ramp front, folding leaf rear; drilled and tapped for scope mounting. **Features:** Match 54 action with adjustable single-stage trigger; roll-over Monte Carlo cheekpiece, slim fore-end with Schnabel tip, Wundhammer palm swell on pistol grip, rosewood gripcap with white diamond insert; skip-line checkering on grip and fore-end. Introduced 1988. Imported from Germany by Steyr Arms.

Price: $2,089.00

BROWNING T-BOLT RIMFIRE

Caliber: .22 LR, .17 HMR, .22 WMR, 10-round rotary box Double Helix magazine. **Barrel:** 22", free-floating, semi-match chamber, target muzzle crown. **Weight:** 4.8 lbs. **Length:** 40.1" overall. **Stock:** Walnut, maple or composite. **Sights:** None. **Features:** Straight-pull bolt-action, three-lever trigger adjustable for pull weight, dual action screws, sling swivel studs. Crossbolt lockup, enlarged bolt handle, one-piece dual extractor with integral spring and red cocking indicator band, gold-tone trigger. Top-tang, thumb-operated two-position safety, drilled and tapped for scope mounts. Varmint model has raised Monte Carlo comb, heavy barrel, wide forearm. Introduced 2006. Imported from Japan by Browning. Left-hand models added in 2009.

Price: .22 LR, from................................. $750.00 to $780.00
Price: .17 HMR/.22 WMR, from .... $790.00 to $830.00

COOPER MODEL 57-M REPEATER

Caliber: .22 LR, .22 WMR, .17 HMR. **Barrel:** 22" or 24". **Weight:** 6.5-7.5 lbs. **Stock:** Claro walnut, 22 lpi hand checkering. **Sights:** None

furnished. **Features:** Three rear locking lug, repeating bolt-action with 5-shot magazine for .22 LR; 4-shot magazine for .22 WMR and 17 HMR. Fully adjustable trigger. Left-hand models add $150 to base rifle price. 1/4"-group rimfire accuracy guarantee at 50 yards; 0.5"-group centerfire accuracy guarantee at 100 yards. Options include wood upgrades, case-color metalwork, barrel fluting, custom LOP, and many others.

Price: Classic $1,995.00
Price: LVT $2,075.00
Price: Custom Classic $2,595.00
Price: Western Classic $3,295.00
Price: TRP-3 (.22 LR only, benchrest style) $1,895.00
Price: Jackson Squirrel Rifle $2,125.00
Price: Jackson Hunter (synthetic) $1,895.00
Price: Mannlicher AAA Claro walnut stock $4,395.00

CZ 452 LUX

Caliber: .22 LR, .22 WMR, 5-shot detachable magazine. **Barrel:** 24.8". **Weight:** 6.6 lbs. **Length:** 42.63" overall. **Stock:** Walnut with checkered pistol grip. **Sights:** Hooded front, fully adjustable tangent rear. **Features:** All-steel construction, adjustable trigger, polished blue finish. Imported from the Czech Republic by CZ-USA.

Price: .22 LR, .22 WMR $450.00

CZ 452 VARMINT RIFLE

Similar to the Lux model except has heavy 20.8" barrel; stock has beavertail fore-end; weighs 7 lbs.; no sights furnished. Available in .22 LR, .22 WMR, .17HMR, .17M2. Imported from the Czech Republic by CZ-USA.

Price: From $497.00

CZ 452 AMERICAN

Similar to the CZ 452 M 2E Lux except has classic-style stock of Circassian walnut; 22.5" free-floating barrel with recessed target crown; receiver dovetail for scope mounting. No open sights furnished. Introduced 1999. Imported from the Czech Republic by CZ-USA.

Price: .22 LR, .22 WMR $463.00

CZ 455 AMERICAN

Caliber: .17 HMR, .22 LR, .22 WMR (5-round magazine). **Barrel:** 20.5". **Weight:** 6.1 lbs. **Length:** 38.2". **Stock:** Walnut. **Sights:** None. Intergral 11mm dovetail scope base. **Features:** Adjustable trigger. Six versions available including blue laminate with thumbhole stock, Varmint model with .866" heavy barrel, full-length Mannlicher walnut stock, and others. American Combo Package includes interchangeable barrel to switch calibers.

Price: from .... $421.00 to $565.00

DAVEY CRICKETT SINGLE SHOT

Caliber: .22 LR, 122 WMR, single-shot. **Barrel:** 16-1/8". **Weight:** About 2.5 lbs. **Length:** 30" overall. **Stock:** American walnut. **Sights:** Post on ramp front, peep rear adjustable for windage and elevation. **Features:** Drilled and tapped for scope mounting using special

Chipmunk base ($13.95). Engraved model also available. Made in U.S.A. Introduced 1982. Formerly Chipmunk model. From Keystone Sporting Arms.
Price: From $120.00

HENRY MINI BOLT YOUTH RIFLE
Caliber: .22 LR, single-shot youth gun. **Barrel:** 16" stainless, 8-groove rifling. **Weight:** 3.25 lbs. **Length:** 30", LOP 11.5". **Stock:** Synthetic, pistol grip, wraparound checkering and beavertail forearm. Available in black finish or bright colors. **Sights:** William Fire sights. **Features:** One-piece bolt configuration manually operated safety.
Price: $275.00

MARLIN MODEL XT-17 SERIES
Caliber: .17 HRM. **Magazine capacity:** 4 and 7-shot, two magazines included. **Barrel:** 22 inches. **Weight:** 6 pounds. **Stock:** Black synthetic with palm swell, stippled grip areas, or walnut-finished hardwood with Monte Carlo comb. Laminated stock available. **Sights:** Adjustable rear, ramp front. Drilled and tapped for scope mounts. **Features:** Adjustable trigger. Blue or stainless finish.
Price: .... $269.00 to $300.00
Price: Laminate thumbhole stock $464.00

MARLIN MODEL XT-22 SERIES
Caliber: .22 Short, Long, Long Rifle. Available with 7-shot detachable box magazine or tubular magazine (17 to 22 rounds). **Barrel:** 22 inches. Varmint model has heavy barrel. **Weight:** 6 lbs. **Stock:** Black synthetic, walnut-finished hardwood, walnut or camo. Tubular model available with two-tone brown laminated stock. **Finish:** Blue or stainless. **Sights:** Adjustable rear, ramp front. Some models have folding rear sight with a hooded or high visibility orange front sight. **Features:** Pro-Fire Adjustable Trigger, Micro-Groove rifling, thumb safety with red cocking indicator. The XT-22M series is chambered for .22 WMR. Made in U.S.A. by Marlin Firearms Co.
Price: From .... $221.00 to $340.00
Price: XT-22M .... $240.00 to $270.00
Price: XT-22MTSL (.22 WMR w/laminated stock)................... $379.00

MARLIN MODEL XT-22 YOUTH SERIES SINGLE SHOT
Caliber: .22 Short, Long or Long Rifle. **Barrel:** 16.25 inches. **Weight:** 4 lbs. **Stock:** Black synthetic, walnut or hardwood. **Sights:** Adjustable rear, ramp front. **Features:** Blue or stainless steel finish. Designed exclusively for young shooters. It features a shorter stock, shorter trigger reach, smaller grip and a raised comb; making it easier for a youth to acquire and hold the proper sight picture. These guns also feature a reduced bolt release force, for smoother loading and to prevent jams.
Price: .... $219.00 to $239.00

MEACHAM LOW-WALL
Caliber: Any rimfire cartridge. **Barrel:** 26-34". **Weight:** 7-15 lbs. **Sights:** none. Tang drilled for Win. base, 3/8" dovetail slot front. **Stock:** Fancy eastern walnut with cheekpiece; ebony insert in forearm tip. **Features:** Exact copy of 1885 Winchester. With most Winchester factory options available including double-set triggers. Introduced 1994. Made in U.S.A. by Meacham T&H Inc.
Price: From $4,999.00

MOSSBERG MODEL 817
Caliber: .17 HMR, 5-round magazine. **Barrel:** 21"; free-floating bull

barrel, recessed muzzle crown. **Weight:** 4.9 lbs. (black synthetic), 5.2 lbs. (wood). **Stock:** Black synthetic or wood; length of pull, 14.25". **Sights:** Factory-installed Weaver-style scope bases. **Features:** Blued or brushed chrome metal finishes, crossbolt safety, gun lock. Introduced 2008. Made in U.S.A. by O.F. Mossberg & Sons, Inc.
Price: .... $212.00 to $253.00

MOSSBERG MODEL 801/802
Caliber: .22 LR, 10-round detachable magazine. **Barrel:** 18" free-floating. Varmint model has 21" heavy barrel. **Weight:** 4.1 to 4.6 lbs. **Sights:** Adjustable rifle. Receiver grooved for scope mount. **Stock:** Black synthetic. **Features:** Ergonomically placed magazine release and safety buttons, crossbolt safety, free gun lock. 801 Half Pint has 12.25" length of pull, 16" barrel, and weighs 4 lbs. Hardwood stock; removable magazine plug.
Price: Plinkster...$223.00
Price: Half Pint...$223.00
Price: Varmint...$223.00

NEW ULTRA LIGHT ARMS 20RF
Caliber: .22 LR, single-shot or repeater. **Barrel:** Douglas, length to order. **Weight:** 5.25 lbs. **Length:** Varies. **Stock:** Kevlar/graphite composite, variety of finishes. **Sights:** None furnished; drilled and tapped for scope mount. **Features:** Timney trigger, hand-lapped action, button-rifled barrel, hand-bedded action, recoil pad, sling-swivel studs, optional Jewell trigger. Made in U.S.A. by New Ultra Light Arms.
Price: 20 RF single shot.......................................$1,800.00
Price: 20 RF repeater $1,850.00

ROSSI MATCHED PAIR SINGLE-SHOT/SHOTGUN
Caliber: .17 HMR rifle with interchangeable 12 or 20-gauge shotgun barrel. **Barrel:** 23" (rifle), 28" (shotgun). **Weight:** 5.25 to 6.25 lbs. **Stock:** Hardwood (brown or black finish). **Sights:** Fully adjustable front and rear. **Features:** Break-open breech, transfer-bar manual safety. Youth Model has .17 HMR or .22 LR rifle barrel with interchangeable .410 shotgun. Introduced 2001. Imported by BrazTech International.
Price: From $298.00
Price: Youth model from $245.00

RUGER 77/22 RIMFIRE
Caliber: .22 LR, 10-shot magazine; .22 WMR, 9-shot magazine. **Barrel:** 20" or 24" (stainless model only). **Weight:** 6.0 to 6.5 lbs. (20" bbl.); 7.5 lbs. (24" bbl.). **Length:** 39.25" overall (20" bbl.). **Stock:** Checkered American walnut or synthetic, stainless sling swivels. **Sights:** Plain barrel with integral scope mounting system complete with 1-inch Ruger rings. **Features:** Mauser-type action uses Ruger's famous rotary magazine. Three-position safety, simplified bolt stop, patented bolt-locking system. Uses the dual-screw barrel attachment system of the 10/22 rifle.
Price: Blue finish w/walnut or synthetic stock $899.00
Price: Stainless steel w/walnut stock $969.00

RUGER 77/17 RIMFIRE
Caliber: .17 HMR, 9-shot rotary magazine. **Barrel:** 22" to 24". **Weight:** 6.5-7.5 lbs. **Length:** 41.25-43.25" overall. **Stock:** Checkered American walnut, laminated hardwood; stainless sling swivels. **Sights:** None. Integral scope mounting system with 1-inch Ruger rings. **Features:** Mauser-type action uses Ruger's rotary magazine. Three-position safety, simplified bolt stop, patented bolt-locking system. Uses the dual-screw barrel attachment system of the 10/22 rifle. Introduced 2002.
Price: Blue finish w/walnut stock..$899.00
Price: Stainless steel w/laminate stock $969.00

SAVAGE MARK II BOLT-ACTION
Caliber: .22 LR, .17 HMR, 10-shot magazine. **Barrel:** 20.5". **Weight:** 5.5 lbs. **Length:** 39.5" overall. **Stock:** Walnut-finished hardwood with Monte Carlo-type comb, checkered grip and fore-end. Camo or OD Green stock available. **Sights:** Bead front, open adjustable rear.

Prices given are believed to be accurate at time of publication however, many factors affect retail pricing so exact pricing is not possible.

69TH EDITION, 2015 ✦ **491**

Receiver grooved for scope mounting. **Features:** Thumb-operated rotating safety. Blue finish. Introduced 1990. Made in Canada, from Savage Arms, Inc.

Price: .... **$228.00 to $280.00**
Price: Varmint w/heavy barrel **$242.00**
Price: Camo stock **$280.00**
Price: OD Green stock **$291.00**

SAVAGE MARK II-FSS STAINLESS RIFLE

Similar to the Mark II except has stainless steel barreled action and black synthetic stock with positive checkering, swivel studs, and 20.75" free-floating and button-rifled barrel with detachable magazine. Weighs 5.5 lbs. Introduced 1997. Imported from Canada by Savage Arms, Inc.

Price: **$336.00**

SAVAGE MODEL 93G MAGNUM BOLT-ACTION

Caliber: .22 WMR, 5-shot magazine. **Barrel:** 20.75". **Weight:** 5.75 lbs. **Length:** 39.5" overall. **Stock:** Walnut-finished hardwood with Monte Carlo-type comb, checkered grip and fore-end. **Sights:** Bead front, adjustable open rear. Receiver grooved for scope mount. **Features:** Thumb-operated rotary safety. Blue finish. Introduced 1994. Made in Canada, from Savage Arms.

Price: Model 93G **$272.00**
Price: Model 93F (as above with black graphite/fiberglass stock) **$252.00**
Price: Model 93 BSEV, thumbhole stock **$627.00**

SAVAGE MODEL 93FSS MAGNUM RIFLE

Similar to Model 93G except stainless steel barreled action and black synthetic stock with positive checkering. Weighs 5.5 lbs. Introduced 1997. Imported from Canada by Savage Arms, Inc.

Price: **$306.00**

SAVAGE MODEL 93FVSS MAGNUM

Similar to Model 93FSS Magnum except 21" heavy barrel with recessed target-style crown, satin-finished stainless barreled action, black graphite/fiberglass stock. Drilled and tapped for scope mounting; comes with Weaver-style bases. Introduced 1998. Imported from Canada by Savage Arms, Inc.

Price: **$347.00**

SAVAGE B-MAG

Caliber: .17 Winchester Super Magnum. Rotary magazine holds 8 rounds. **Stock:** Synthetic. **Weight:** 4.5 pounds. Chambered for new Winchester .17 Super Magnum rimfire cartridge that propels a 20-grain bullet at approximately 3,000 fps. **Features:** Adjustable AccuTrigger, rear locking lugs, new and different bolt-action rimfire design that cocks on close of bolt. New in 2013.

Price: **$359.00**
Price: Stainless steel receiver and barrel...............................**$408.00**

SAVAGE BRJ SERIES

Similar to Mark II, Model 93 and Model 93R17 rifles but features spiral fluting pattern on a heavy barrel, blued finish and Royal Jacaranda wood laminate stock.

Price: Mark II BRJ, .22 LR **$456.00**
Price: Model 93 BRJ, .22 Mag..**$464.00**
Price: Model 93 R17 BRJ, .17 HMR **$464.00**

SAVAGE TACTICAL RIMFIRE SERIES

Similar to Savage Model BRJ series semiauto rifles but with matte finish and a tactical-style wood stock.

Price: Mark II TR, .22 LR..**$469.00**
Price: Mark II TRR, .22 LR, three-way accessory rail **$539.00**
Price: Model 93R17 TR, .17 HMR **$477.00**
Price: Model 93R17 TRR, .17 HMR, three-way accessory rail.**$536.00**

THOMPSON/CENTER HOTSHOT YOUTH

Single-shot dropping-barrel rifle chambered in .22 Long Rifle. Features include a crowned 19-inch steel barrel, exposed hammer, synthetic fore-end and buttstock, peep sight (receiver drilled and tapped for optics), three stock pattern options (black, Realtree AP and pink AP). Overall weight 3 lbs., 11.5-inch length of pull.

Price: .... **$219.00 to $249.00**

WINCHESTER MODEL 1885 LOW WALL HUNTER RIMFIRE

Caliber: .17 Winchester Super Magnum, .17 HMR, .22 LR, .22 WMR. **Barrel:** 24-inch octagon. **Weight:** 7.5 pounds. **Stock:** Oil finished Grade I walnut, checkered with Schnabel fore-end. **Sights:** Gold bead front, semi-buckhorn rear. **Finish:** Gloss blue. Single-shot lever-operated recreation of classic Model 1885 design.

Price: **$1,470.00**

Prices given are believed to be accurate at time of publication however, many factors affect retail pricing so exact pricing are not possible.

ANSCHUTZ 1903 MATCH

Caliber: .22 LR, single-shot. **Barrel:** 21.25". **Weight:** 8 lbs. **Length:** 43.75" overall. **Stock:** Walnut-finished hardwood with adjustable cheekpiece; stippled grip and fore-end. **Sights:** None furnished. **Features:** Uses Anschutz Match 64 action. A medium weight rifle for intermediate and advanced Junior Match competition. Available from Champion's Choice.
Price: Right-hand..**$1,195.00**

ANSCHUTZ 64-MP R SILHOUETTE

Caliber: .22 LR, 5-shot magazine. **Barrel:** 21.5", medium heavy; 7/8" diameter. **Weight:** 8 lbs. **Length:** 39.5" overall. **Stock:** Walnut-finished hardwood, silhouette-type. **Sights:** None furnished. **Features:** Uses Match 64 action. Designed for metallic silhouette competition. Stock has stippled checkering, contoured thumb groove with Wundhammer swell. Two-stage #5098 trigger. Slide safety locks sear and bolt. Introduced 1980. Available from Champion's Choice.
Price: 64-MP R **$1,100.00**
Price: 64-S BR Benchrest.....................................**$1,327.00**

ANSCHUTZ 2007 MATCH RIFLE

Uses same action as the Model 2013, but has a lighter barrel. European walnut stock in right-hand, true left-hand or extra-short models. Sights optional. Available with 19.6" barrel with extension tube, or 26", both in stainless or blue. Introduced 1998. Available from Champion's Choice.
Price: Right-hand, blue, no sights **$2,595.00**

ANSCHUTZ 1827BT FORTNER BIATHLON

Caliber: .22 LR, 5-shot magazine. **Barrel:** 21.7". **Weight:** 8.8 lbs. with sights. **Length:** 40.9" overall. **Stock:** European walnut with cheekpiece, stippled pistol grip and fore-end. **Sights:** Optional globe front specially designed for Biathlon shooting, micrometer rear with hinged snow cap. **Features:** Uses Super Match 54 action and nine-way adjustable trigger; adjustable wooden buttplate, biathlon butthook, adjustable hand-stop rail. Uses Anschutz/Fortner system straight-pull bolt action, blued or stainless steel barrel. Introduced 1982. Available from Champion's Choice.
Price: From about **$3,195.00**

ANSCHUTZ SUPER MATCH SPECIAL MODEL 2013

Caliber: .22 LR, single-shot. **Barrel:** 25.9". **Weight:** 13 lbs. **Length:** 41.7" to 42.9". **Stock:** Adjustable aluminum. **Sights:** None furnished. **Features:** 2313 aluminum-silver/blue stock, 500mm barrel, fast lock time, adjustable cheekpiece, heavy action and muzzle tube, w/ handstop and standing riser block. Introduced in 1997. Available from Champion's Choice.
Price: From about **$3,995.00**

ANSCHUTZ 1912 SPORT

Caliber: .22 LR. **Barrel:** 26" match. **Weight:** 11.4 lbs. **Length:** 41.7" overall. **Stock:** Non-stained thumbhole stock adjustable in length with adjustable buttplate and cheekpiece adjustment. Flat fore-end raiser block 4856 adjustable in height. Hook buttplate. **Sights:** None furnished. **Features:** "Free rifle" for women. Smallbore model 1907 with 1912 stock: Match 54 action. Delivered with: Hand stop 6226, fore-end raiser block 4856, screwdriver, instruction leaflet with test target. Available from Champion's Choice.
Price: **$2,795.00**

ANSCHUTZ 1913 SUPER MATCH RIFLE

Same as the Model 1911 except European walnut International-type stock with adjustable cheekpiece, or color laminate, both available with straight or lowered fore-end, adjustable aluminum hook buttplate, adjustable hand stop, weighs 13 lbs., 46" overall. Stainless or blue barrel. Available from Champion's Choice.
Price: Right-hand, blue, no sights, walnut stock..................**$3,290.00**

ANSCHUTZ 1907 STANDARD MATCH RIFLE

Same action as Model 1913 but with 7/8" diameter 26" barrel (stainless or blue). Length is 44.5" overall, weighs 10.5 lbs. Choice of stock configurations. Vented fore-end. Designed for prone and position shooting ISU requirements; suitable for NRA matches. Also available with walnut flat-forend stock for benchrest shooting. Available from Champion's Choice.
Price: Right-hand, blue, no sights **$2,185.00**

ARMALITE AR-10(T)

Caliber: .308 Win., 10-shot magazine. **Barrel:** 24" target-weight Rock 5R custom. **Weight:** 10.4 lbs. **Length:** 43.5" overall. **Stock:** Green or black composition; N.M. fiberglass handguard tube. **Sights:** Detachable handle, front sight, or scope mount available. Comes with international-style flattop receiver with Picatinny rail. **Features:** National Match two-stage trigger. Forged upper receiver. Receivers hard-coat anodized. Introduced 1995. Made in U.S.A. by ArmaLite, Inc.
Price: Black **$1,912.00**
Price: AR-10, .338 Federal **$1,912.00**

ARMALITE AR-10 NATIONAL MATCH

Caliber: .308/7.62 NATO. **Barrel:** 20", triple-lapped Match barrel, 1:10" twist rifling. **Weight:** 11.5 lbs. **Length:** 41". **Features:** Stainless steel flash suppressor, two-stage National Match trigger. Forged flattop receiver with Picatinny rail and forward assist.
Price: **$2,365.00**

ARMALITE M15A4(T) EAGLE EYE

Caliber: .223 Rem., 10-round magazine. **Barrel:** 24" heavy stainless; 1:8" twist. **Weight:** 9.2 lbs. **Length:** 42-3/8" overall. **Stock:** Green or black butt, N.M. fiberglass handguard tube. **Sights:** One-piece international-style flattop receiver with Weaver-type rail, including case deflector. **Features:** Detachable carry handle, front sight and scope mount (30mm or 1") available. Upper and lower receivers have push-type pivot pin, hard coat anodized. Made in U.S.A. by ArmaLite, Inc.
Price: Green or black furniture.............................**$1,296.00**

ARMALITE M15 A4 CARBINE 6.8 & 7.62X39

Caliber: 6.8 Rem., 7.62x39. **Barrel:** 16" chrome-lined with flash suppressor. **Weight:** 7 lbs. **Length:** 26.6". **Features:** Front and rear picatinny rails for mounting optics, two-stage tactical trigger, anodized aluminum/phosphate finish.
Price: **$1,107.00**

BLASER R93 LONG RANGE SPORTER 2

Caliber: .308 Win., 10-shot detachable box magazine. **Barrel:** 24". **Weight:** 10.4 lbs. **Length:** 44" overall. **Stock:** Aluminum with synthetic lining. **Sights:** None furnished; accepts detachable scope mount. **Features:** Straight-pull bolt action with adjustable trigger; fully adjustable stock; quick takedown; corrosion resistant finish. Introduced 1998. Imported from Germany by Blaser USA.
Price: **$3,848.00**

Prices given are believed to be accurate at time of publication however, many factors affect retail pricing so exact prices are not possible.

69TH EDITION, 2015 ✦ **493**

BUSHMASTER A2/A3 TARGET
Caliber: 5.56mm, .223 Rem., 30-round magazine. **Barrel:** 20", 24". **Weight:** 8.43 lbs. (A2); 8.78 lbs. (A3). **Length:** 39.5" overall (20" barrel). **Stock:** Black composition; A2 type. **Sights:** Adjustable post front, adjustable aperture rear. **Features:** Patterned after Colt M-16A2. Chrome-lined barrel with manganese phosphate exterior. Available in stainless barrel. Made in U.S.A. by Bushmaster Firearms Co.
Price: (A3 type) **$1,135.00**

BUSHMASTER DCM-XR COMPETITION
Caliber: 5.56mm, .223 Rem., 10-round magazine. **Barrel:** 20" extra-heavy (1" diameter) barrel with 1:8" twist for heavier competition bullets. **Weight:** About 12 lbs. with balance weights. **Length:** 38.5". **Stock:** NA. **Sights:** A2 rear sight. **Features:** Has special competition rear sight with interchangeable apertures, extra-fine 1/2- or 1/4-MOA windage and elevation adjustments; specially ground front sight post in choice of three widths. Full-length handguards over free-floater barrel tube. Introduced 1998. Made in U.S.A. by Bushmaster Firearms, Inc.
Price: A2 .... **$1,150.00**
Price: A3 .... **$1,250.00**

BUSHMASTER VARMINTER
Caliber: 5.56mm. **Barrel:** 24", fluted. **Weight:** 8.4 lbs. **Length:** 42.25" overall. **Stock:** Black composition, A2 type. **Sights:** None furnished; upper receiver has integral scope mount base. **Features:** Chrome-lined .950" extra heavy barrel with counter-bored crown, manganese phosphate finish, free-floating aluminum handguard, forged aluminum receivers with push-pin takedown, hard anodized mil-spec finish. Competition trigger optional. Made in U.S.A. by Bushmaster Firearms, Inc.
Price: **$1,360.00**

COLT MATCH TARGET COMPETITION HBAR RIFLE
Caliber: .223 Rem. **Barrel:** 20" match. **Weight:** 8.5 lbs. **Sights:** QD carry handle has 600-meter adjustable rear sight. Receiver accepts Weaver-type scope rings. **Features:** Flattop receiver for scope mounting, stainless steel heavy barrel, tubular handguard, and free-floating barrel. Matte black finish. Made in U.S.A. by Colt's Mfg. Co., Inc.
Price: Model MT6700C **$1,230.00**

COLT M2012
Caliber: .308 Win. or .260 Rem. 5- or 10-round magazine. **Barrel:** 22" match-grade fluted, heavy or medium heavy, stainless or chrome-moly. **Weight:** 8.5 to 13.2 lbs. **Stock:** Custom forged aluminum, custom Manners composite, or gray laminated hardwood. **Features:** Timney single-stage adjustable trigger, Cooper Firearms muzzle brake, matte black, gray or Coyote Tan finish.
Price: From .... **$2,796.00 to $3,195.00**

COLT ACCURIZED RIFLE
Caliber: .223 Rem. **Barrel:** 24" stainless match. **Features:** Features flattop receiver for scope mounting, stainless steel heavy barrel, tubular handguard, and free-floating barrel. Matte black finish. Weighs

9.25 lbs. Made in U.S.A. by Colt's Mfg. Co., Inc.
Price: Model CR6724 .... **$1,374.00 to $1,653.00**

OLYMPIC ARMS UM ULTRAMATCH AR15
Caliber: .223 Rem. minimum SAAMI spec, 30-shot magazine. **Barrel:** 20" or 24" bull broach-cut Ultramatch stainless steel 1x10" twist rate. **Weight:** 8-10 lbs. **Length:** 38.25" overall. **Stock:** A2 grip, A2 buttstock with trapdoor. **Sights:** None, flattop upper and gas block with rails. **Features:** Flattop upper, free-floating tubular match handguard, Picatinny gas block, crowned muzzle and factory trigger job. Premium model adds pneumatic recoil buffer, Harris S-series bipod, hand selected premium receivers and William Set Trigger. Made in U.S.A. by Olympic Arms, Inc
Price: UM-1, 20" Ultramatch **$1,332.50**
Price: UM-1P **$1,623.70**

OLYMPIC ARMS ML-2 MULTIMATCH AR15 CARBINES
Caliber: .223 Rem. minimum SAAMI spec, 30-shot magazine. **Barrel:** 16" broach-cut Ultramatch stainless steel 1x10" twist rate. **Weight:** 7-8 lbs. **Length:** 34-36" overall. **Stock:** A2 grip and varying buttstock. **Sights:** None. **Features:** The ML-2 includes bull diameter barrel, flattop upper, free-floating tubular match handguard, Picatinny gas block, crowned muzzle and A2 buttstock with trapdoor. Made in U.S.A. by Olympic Arms, Inc.
Price: ML-2 .... **$1,253.20**

OLYMPIC ARMS K8 TARGETMATCH AR15
Caliber: 5.56 NATO, .223 WSSM, .243 WSSM, .25 WSSM, 30/7-shot magazine. **Barrel:** 20", 24" bull button-rifled stainless/chrome-moly steel 1x9"/1x10" twist rate. **Weight:** 8-10 lbs. **Length:** 38"-42" overall. **Stock:** A2 grip, A2 buttstock with trapdoor. **Sights:** None. **Features:** Barrel has satin bead-blast finish; flattop upper, free-floating tubular match handguard, Picatinny gas block, crowned muzzle and "Targetmatch" pantograph on lower receiver. K8-MAG model uses Winchester Super Short Magnum cartridges. Includes 24" bull chrome-moly barrel, flattop upper, free-floating tubular match handguard, Picatinny gas block, crowned muzzle and 7-shot magazine. Made in U.S.A. by Olympic Arms, Inc.
Price: K8 .... **$908.70**
Price: K8-MAG **$1,363.70**

REMINGTON 40-XB RANGEMASTER TARGET
Caliber: 15 calibers from .220 Swift to .300 Win. Mag. **Barrel:** 27.25". **Weight:** 11.25 lbs. **Length:** 47" overall. **Stock:** American walnut, laminated thumbhole or Kevlar with high comb and beavertail fore-end stop. Rubber nonslip buttplate. **Sights:** None. Scope blocks installed. **Features:** Adjustable trigger. Stainless barrel and action. Receiver drilled and tapped for sights. Model 40-XB Tactical (2008) chambered in .308 Win., comes with guarantee of 0.75-inch maximum 5-shot groups at 100 yards. **Weight:** 10.25 lbs. Includes Teflon-coated stainless button-rifled barrel, 1:14" twist, 27.25-inch long, three longitudinal flutes. Bolt-action repeater, adjustable 40-X trigger and precision machined aluminum bedding block. Stock is H-S Precision Pro Series synthetic tactical stock, black with green web finish, vertical pistol grip. From Remington Custom Shop.
Price: 40-XB KS, aramid fiber stock, single shot **$2,863.00**
Price: 40-XB KS, aramid fiber stock, repeater **$3,014.00**

Prices given are believed to be accurate at time of publication however, many factors affect retail pricing so exact prices are not possible.

COMPETITION RIFLES Centerfire & Rimfire

Price: 40-XB Tactical .308 Win. **$2,927.00**
Price: 40-XB Thumbhole Repeater **$3,014.00**

REMINGTON 40-XBBR KS
Caliber: Five calibers from .22 BR to .308 Win. **Barrel:** 20" (light varmint class), 24" (heavy varmint class). **Weight:** 7.25 lbs. (light varmint class); 12 lbs. (heavy varmint class). **Length:** 38" (20" bbl.), 42" (24"bbl.). **Stock:** Aramid fiber. **Sights:** None. Supplied with scope blocks. **Features:** Unblued benchrest with stainless steel barrel, trigger adjustable from 1-1/2 lbs. to 3.5 lbs. Special 2-oz. trigger extra cost. Scope and mounts extra.
Price: Single shot.. **$3,950.00**

REMINGTON 40-XC KS TARGET
Caliber: 7.62 NATO, 5-shot. **Barrel:** 24", stainless steel. **Weight:** 11 lbs. without sights. **Length:** 43.5" overall. **Stock:** Aramid fiber. **Sights:** None furnished. **Features:** Designed to meet the needs of competitive shooters. Stainless steel barrel and action.
Price: **$3,000.00**

REMINGTON 40-XR CUSTOM SPORTER
Caliber: .22 LR, .22 WM. **Barrel:** 24" stainless steel, no sights. **Weight:** 9.75 lbs. **Length:** 40". **Features:** Model XR-40 Target rifle action. Many options available in stock, decoration or finish.
Price: Single shot.. **$4,500.00**

SAKO TRG-22 BOLT-ACTION
Caliber: .308 Win., 10-shot magazine, .338 Lapua, 5-shot magazine. **Barrel:** 26". **Weight:** 10.25 lbs. **Length:** 45.25" overall. **Stock:** Reinforced polyurethane with fully adjustable cheekpiece and buttplate. **Sights:** None furnished. Optional quick-detachable, one-piece scope mount base, 1" or 30mm rings. **Features:** Resistance-free bolt, free-floating heavy stainless barrel, 60-degree bolt lift. Two-stage trigger is adjustable for length, pull, horizontal or vertical pitch. TRG-42 has similar features but has long action and is chambered for .338 Lapua. Imported from Finland by Beretta USA.
Price: TRG-22 folding stock **$3,540.00**
Price: TRG-42 .... **$4,445.00**

SPRINGFIELD ARMORY M1A SUPER MATCH
Caliber: .308 Win. **Barrel:** 22", heavy Douglas Premium. **Weight:** About 11 lbs. **Length:** 44.31" overall. **Stock:** Heavy walnut competition stock with longer pistol grip, contoured area behind the rear sight, thicker butt and fore-end, glass bedded. **Sights:** National Match front and rear. **Features:** Has figure-eight-style operating rod guide. Introduced 1987. From Springfield Armory.
Price: About **$2,900.00**

SPRINGFIELD ARMORY M1A/M-21 TACTICAL MODEL
Similar to M1A Super Match except special sniper stock with adjustable cheekpiece and rubber recoil pad. Weighs 11.6 lbs. From Springfield Armory.
Price: **$3,555.00**

STI SPORTING COMPETITION
AR-style semiauto rifle chambered in 5.56 NATO. Features include 16-inch 410 stainless 1:8" twist barrel; mid-length gas system; Nordic Tactical Compensator and JP Trigger group; custom STI Valkyrie handguard and gas block; flattop design with picatinny rail; anodized finish with black Teflon coating. Also available in Tactical configuration.
Price: **$1,455.00**

TIME PRECISION .22 RF BENCH REST
Caliber: .22 LR, single-shot. **Barrel:** Shilen match-grade stainless. **Weight:** 10 lbs. with scope. **Length:** NA. **Stock:** Fiberglass. Pillar bedded. **Sights:** None furnished. **Features:** Shilen match trigger removable trigger bracket, full-length steel sleeve, aluminum receiver. Introduced 2008. Made in U.S.A. by Time Precision.
Price: **$2,200.00**

Prices given are believed to be accurate at time of publication however, many factors affect retail pricing so exact prices are not possible.

69TH EDITION, 2015 ✛ 495

BENELLI ETHOS

Gauge: 12. 3" chamber. Magazine capacity 4+1. **Barrel:** 28" (Full, Mod., Imp. Cyl., Imp. Mod., Cylinder choke tubes). **Weight:** 6.5 lbs. **Length:** 49.5" overall (28" barrel). **Stock:** Select AA European walnut with satin finish. **Sights:** Red bar fiber optic front, with three interchangeable inserts, metal middle bead. **Features:** Utilizes Benelli's Intertia Driven system. Recoil is reduced by Progressive Comfort recoil reduction system within the buttstock. Cycles all 3-inch loads from light 7/8 oz. up to 3-inch magnums. Also available with nickel-plated engraved receiver. Imported from Italy by Benelli USA, Corp.
Price: **$1,999.00**
Price: Engraved nickel-plated (shown) **$2,199.00**

BENELLI LEGACY

Gauge: 12, 20, 28. 3" chamber (12, 20), 2 ¾" (28). **Barrel:** 24", 26", 28" (Full, Mod., Imp. Cyl., Imp. Mod., cylinder choke tubes). Mid-bead sight. **Weight:** 5.8 to 7.4 lbs. **Length:** 49-5/8" overall (28" barrel). **Stock:** Select AA European walnut with satin finish. **Features:** Uses the rotating bolt inertia recoil operating system with a two-piece steel/aluminum etched receiver (bright on lower, blue upper). Drop adjustment kit allows the stock to be custom fitted without modifying the stock. Introduced 1998. Ultralight model has gloss-blued finish receiver. Weight is 6.0 lbs., 24" barrel, 45.5" overall length. WeatherCoat walnut stock. Introduced 2006. Imported from Italy by Benelli USA, Corp.
Price: Legacy (12 and 20 gauge) **$1,799.00**
Price: Legacy (28 gauge) **$2,039.00**
Price: Legacy Sport **$2,439.00**

BENELLI LEGACY SPORT

Gas-operated semiauto shotgun chambered for 12, 20 (2-3/4- and 3-inch) gauge. Features include Inertia Driven system; sculptured lower receiver with classic game scene etchings; highly polished blued upper receiver; AA-Grade walnut stock; gel recoil pad; ported 24- or 26-inch barrel, Crio chokes. Weight 7.4 to 7.5 lbs.
Price: **$2,369.00**

BENELLI ULTRA LIGHT

Gauge: 12, 20, 28. 3" chamber (12, 20), 2 ¾" (28). **Barrel:** 24", 26". Mid-bead sight. **Weight:** 5.2 to 6 lbs. **Features:** Similar to Legacy line. Drop adjustment kit allows the stock to be custom fitted without modifying the stock. WeatherCoat walnut stock. Lightened receiver, shortened magazine tube, carbon-fiber rib and grip cap. Introduced 2008. Imported from Italy by Benelli USA, Corp.
Price: 12 and 20 gauge..**$1,699.00**
Price: 28 gauge..**$1,799.00**

BENELLI M2 FIELD

Gauge: 20 ga., 12 ga., 3" chamber. **Barrel:** 21", 24", 26", 28". **Weight:** 5.4 to 7.2 lbs. **Length:** 42.5 to 49.5" overall. **Stock:** Synthetic, Advantage

Max-4 HD, Advantage Timber HD, APG HD. **Sights:** Red bar. **Features:** Uses the Inertia Driven bolt mechanism. Vent rib. Comes with set of five choke tubes. Imported from Italy by Benelli USA.
Price: Synthetic stock 12 ga. **$1,499.00**
Price: Camo stock 12 ga. **$1,549.00**
Price: Synthetic stock 20 ga. **$1,499.00**
Price: Camo stock 20 ga. **$1,599.00**
Price: Rifled slug ....**$1,469.00 to $1,589.00**
Price: Left-hand 12 ga. **$1409**
Price: Left-hand model 20 ga. **$1519**

BENELLI MONTEFELTRO

Gauge: 12 and 20 ga. Full, Imp. Mod., Mod., Imp. Cyl., Cyl. choke tubes. **Barrel:** 24", 26", 28". **Weight:** 5.3 to 7.1 lbs. **Stock:** Checkered walnut with satin finish. **Length:** 43.6 to 49.5" overall. **Features:** Uses the Inertia Driven rotating bolt system with a simple inertia recoil design. Finish is blue. Introduced 1987.
Price: Standard Model **$1,139.00**
Price: Left Hand Model **$1,229.00**
Price: Silver **$1,779.00**

BENELLI SUPER BLACK EAGLE II

Gauge: 12, 3 ½-inch chamber. **Barrel:** 24", 26", 28" (Cyl. Imp. Cyl., Mod., Imp. Mod., Full choke tubes). **Weight:** 7.1 to 7.3 lbs. **Length:** 45.6 to 49.6" overall. **Stock:** European walnut with satin finish, polymer, or camo. Adjustable for drop. **Sights:** Red bar front. **Features:** Uses Benelli inertia recoil bolt system. Vent rib. Advantage Max-4 HD, Advantage Timber HD camo patterns. Features ComforTech stock. Introduced 1991. Left-hand models available. Imported from Italy by Benelli USA.
Price: Satin walnut **$1,569.00**
Price: Camo stock .... **$1,680.00 to $1,899.00**
Price: Black Comfortech synthetic stock **$1,799.00**
Price: Left hand, camo stock **$1,999.00**
Price: Left hand, Comfortech synthetic **$1,899.00**
Price: Turkey edition w/pistol grip stock...............**$1,999.00**

BENELLI SUPER BLACK EAGLE II WATERFOWL EDITION

Gauge: 12, (3+1 capacity), chambered for 2 ¾", 3" and 3 1/4" ammunition. **Barrel:** 28". **Weight:** 7.3 lbs. **Length:** 49.6". **Features:** Lengthened and polished forcing cone, Rob Roberts Custom choke tubes, Realtree Max-4 camo finish, Hi Viz front sight, metal middle bead. From the Benelli Performance Shop.
Price: **$2,669.00**

BENELLI CORDOBA

Gauge: 20; 12; 3" chamber. **Barrel:** 28" and 30", ported, 10mm sporting rib. **Weight:** 7.2 to 7.3 lbs. **Length:** 49.6 to 51.6". **Features:** Designed for high-volume sporting clays and Argentina dove shooting. Inertia-driven action, Extended Sport CrioChokes, 4+1 capacity. Ported. Imported from Italy by Benelli USA.
Price: Field Models .... **$2,069.00 to $2,099.00**
Price: Performance Shop Model .... **$2,719.00 to $2,829.00**

BENELLI SUPERSPORT & SPORT II

Gauge: 20; 12; 3" chamber. **Barrel:** 28" and 30", ported, 10mm sporting

rib. **Weight:** 7.2 to 7.3 lbs. **Length:** 49.6 to 51.6". **Stock:** Carbon fiber, ComforTech (Supersport) or walnut (Sport II). **Sights:** Red bar front, metal midbead. Sport II is similar to the Legacy model except has nonengraved dual tone blue/silver receiver, ported wide-rib barrel, adjustable buttstock, and functions with all loads. Walnut stock with satin finish. Introduced 1997. **Features:** Designed for high-volume sporting clays. Inertia-driven action, Extended CrioChokes, 4+1 capacity. Ported. Imported from Italy by Benelli USA.
Price: Supersport $2,199.00
Price: Sport II $1,899.00

BENELLI VINCI
Gauge: 12, 3-inch chamber. Gas-operated action. Features include modular disassembly; interchangeable choke tubes; 24- to 28-inch ribbed barrel; black, MAX-4HD or APG HD finish; synthetic contoured stocks; optional Steady-Grip model. Weight is 6.7 to 6.9 lbs.
Price: .... **$1,449.00 to $2,199.00**

BENELLI SUPER VINCI
Gauge: 12 - 2-3/4", 3" and 3-1/2" chamber. **Barrel:** 26" and 28" barrels. **Weight:** 6.9-7 lbs. **Length:** 48.5"-50.5". **Stock:** Black synthetic, Realtree Max4 and Realtree APG. **Features:** 3+1 capacity, Crio Chokes: C,IC,M,IM,F. Length of Pull: 14-3/8". Drop at Heel: 2". Drop at Comb: 1-3/8". Type of **Sights:** Red bar front sight and metal bead mid-sight. Minimum recommended load: 3-dram, 1-1/8 oz. loads (12-ga.). Receiver drilled and tapped for scope mounting. Imported from Italy by Benelli USA., Corp.
Price: Black Synthetic Comfortech $1,799.00
Price: Camo $1,899.00

BERETTA A300 OUTLANDER
Gauge: 12, 3-inch chamber. **Capacity:** 3+1. Operates with 2 ¾" shells. **Barrel:** 28 inches with Mobilechoke system. **Stock:** Synthetic, camo or wood. **Weight:** 7.1 pounds. Based on A400 design but at a lower price. A300 Xtrema model is chambered for 3.5-inch 12-gauge Magnum.
Price: ....**$775.00 to $850.00**
Price: Xtrema $1,350.00

BERETTA A400 XPLOR UNICO
Self-regulation gas-operated shotgun chambered to shoot all 12-ga, loads from 2-3/4 to 3.5 inches. Features include optional Kick-Off hydraulic damper; 26- or 28-inch "Steelium" barrel with interchangeable choke tubes; anodized aluminum receiver; sculpted, checkered walnut buttstock and fore-end.
Price: **$1,755.00**
Price: With Kick-Off recoil reduction system.........................$1,855.00

BERETTA A400 XPLOR LIGHT
Gauge: 12-gas operated. 3" chamber. **Barrel:** 26, 28, 30" barrel. **Weight:** 6.25 to 6.4 lbs.. **Stock:** Walnut and polymer. **Features:** The A400 Light combines Beretta's exclusive Blink operating system, self compensating exhaust valve and self cleaning piston, steelium barrel design with 1/4" x 1/4" ventilated rib and Optima-Choke HP, also fitted with the Micro-Core recoil pad. The stock is a wood-oil finish with a mix of walnut and polymer to maximize performance from the fore-end insert to the trigger guard. Also available with Beretta's improved Kick-Off damper system. Imported from Italy by Benelli USA, Corp.
Price: $1,620.00

BERETTA A400 XCEL SPORTING
Gauge: 12-gas operated, 3" chamber. **Barrel:** 28, 30 or 32". **Weight:** 7.5 lbs. **Stock:** Walnut and polymer. **Features:** In addition to A400 specifications and features, the Sporting model has aqua blue receiver. Optional Gun Pod electronic system gives digital read-out of air temperature, ammunition pressure, number of rounds fired.
Price: $1,745.00

BERETTA A400 ACTION
Gauge: 12, 20 (3") or 28 (2 ¾" chamber). **Barrel:** 28, 30 barrel. **Weight:** 5.3 (28 ga.) to 6.7 lbs. **Stock:** Walnut and polymer combination. **Features:** Gas-operating Blink operating system can reportedly fire 4 rounds in less than one second. Hydraulic recoil reduction system reduces felt recoil up to 70 percent.
Price: $1,550.00

BREDA GRIZZLY
Gauge: 12, 3.5" chamber. **Barrel:** 28". **Weight:** 7.2 lbs. **Stock:** Black synthetic or Advantage Timber with matching metal parts. **Features:** Chokes tubes are Mod., IC, Full; inertia-type action, four-round magazine.
Price: Blued/black $1,826.00
Price: Advantage Timber Camo...$2,121.00

BREDA XANTHOS
Gauge: 12, 3" chamber. **Barrel:** 28". **Weight:** 6.5 lbs. **Stock:** High grade walnut. **Features:** Chokes tubes are Mod., IC, Full; inertia-type action, four-round magazine, spark engraving with hand-engraved details and hand-gilding figures on receiver. Blued, Grey or Chrome finishes.
Price: Blued $2,309.00
Price: Grey $2,451.00
Price: Chrome..$3,406.00

BREDA ECHO
Gauge: 12, 20. 3" chamber. **Barrel:** 28". **Weight:** 6.0-6.5 lbs. **Stock:** Walnut. **Features:** Chokes tubes are Mod., IC, Full; inertia-type action, four-round magazine, blue, grey or nickel finishes, modern engraving, fully checkered pistol grip.
Price: Blued, 12 ga. $1,897.00
Price: Grey, 12 ga $1,969.00
Price: Nickel, 12 ga. $2,214.00
Price: Nickel, 20 ga. $2,214.00

BREDA ALTAIR
Gauge: 12, 20. 3" chamber. **Barrel:** 28". **Weight:** 5.7-6.1 lbs. **Stock:** Oil-rubbed walnut. **Features:** Chokes tubes are Mod., IC, Full; gas-actuated action, four-round magazine, blued finish, lightweight frame.
Price: Blued, 12 ga. $1,320.00
Price: Grey, 20 ga. $1,320.00

BROWNING A5
Gauge: 12, 3 or 3.5-inch chamber. **Barrel:** 26, 28 or 30". **Weight:** 6.6 to 7 lbs. **Length:** 47.25 to 51.5". **Stock:** Gloss finish walnut with 22 lpi checkering, black synthetic or camo. Adjustable for cast and drop. **Features:** Operates on Kinematic short-recoil system, totally different than the classic Auto-5 long-recoil action manufactured from 1903-1999. Lengthened forcing cone, three choke tubes (IC, M, F), flat ventilated rib, brass bead front sight, ivory middle bead. Available in Mossy Oak Duck Blind or Break-up Infinity camo. Ultimate Model has satin finished aluminum alloy receiver with light engraving of pheasants on left side, mallards on the right. Glossy blue finish, Grade III oil-finished walnut stock,
Price: A5 Hunter $1,580.00
Price: A5 Hunter 3.5" $1,700.00
Price: A5 Stalker (synthetic) $1,420.00
Price: A5 Stalker 3.5" $1,580.00
Price: A5 Ultimate $1,920.00

BROWNING MAXUS HUNTER
Gauge: 12 ga., 3" & 3-1/2" chamber. **Barrel:** 26", 28" & 30" flat ventilated rib with fixed cylinder choke; stainless Steel; Matte finish. **Weight:** 7 lbs. 2 ozs. **Length:** 40.75". **Stock:** Gloss finish walnut stock with close radius pistol grip, sharp 22 lines-per-inch checkering,

Prices given are believed to be accurate at time of publication however, many factors affect retail pricing so exact prices are not possible.

69TH EDITION, 2015 ⊕ **497**

speed Lock Forearm, shim adjustable for length of pull, cast and drop. **Features:** Vector Prolengthened forcing cone, three Invector-Pluschoke tubes, Inflex Technology recoil pad, ivory front bead sight, One 1/4" stock spacer. Strong, lightweight aluminum alloy receiver with durable satin nickel finish & laser engraving (pheasant on the right, mallard on the left).
Price: 3" chamber..$1,500.00
Price: 3-1/2" chamber $1,640.00

BROWNING MAXUS MOSSY OAK BOTTOMLAND
Gauge: 12 ga., 3-1/2" chamber. **Barrel:** 28" flat ventilated rib. **Weight:** 6 lbs. 15 ozs. Length: 49.25". **Stock:** Composite stock with close radius pistol grip; Speed Lock forearm; textured gripping surfaces; shim adjustable for length of pull, cast and drop; Mossy Oak Bottomlandcamo finish; Dura-Touch Armor Coating. **Features:** Vector Prolengthened forcing cone; three Invector Pluschoke tubes (F,M,IC); Inflex Technology recoil pad; ivory front bead sight; one 1/4" stock spacer.
Price: $1,539.00

BROWNING MAXUS MOSSY OAK DUCK BLIND
Gauge: 12 ga., 3" & 3-1/2" chamber. **Barrel:** 26"& 28" flat ventilated rib with fixed cylinder choke; stainless Steel; Matte finish. **Weight:** 6 lbs. 14 ozs.-6 lbs. 15 ozs. Length: 47.25"-49.25". **Stock:** Composite stock with close radius pistol grip, Speed Lock forearm, textured gripping surfaces, Mossy Oak Duck Blind camo finish, Dura-Touch Armor Coating. **Features:** Vector Prolengthened forcing cone, three Invector-Pluschoke tubes, Inflex Technology recoil pad, ivory front bead sight, One 1/4" stock spacer. Strong, lightweight aluminum alloy receiver. Gas-operated autoloader, new Power Drive Gas System reduces recoil and cycles a wide range of loads.
Price: 3" chamber..$1,470.00
Price: 3-1/2" chamber $1,600.00

BROWING MAXUS SPORTING
Gauge: 12 ga., 3" chamber. **Barrel:** 28" & 30" flat ventilated rib. **Weight:** 7 lbs. 2 ozs. Length: 49.25"-51.25". **Stock:** Gloss finish high grade walnut stock with close radius pistol grip , Speed Lock forearm, shim adjustable for length of pull, cast and drop. **Features:** This new model is sure to catch the eye, with its laser engraving of game birds transforming into clay birdson the lightweight alloy receiver. Quail are on the right side, and a mallard duck on the left. The Power Drive Gas System reduces recoil and cycles a wide array of loads. It's available in a 28" or 30" barrel length. The high grade walnut stock and forearm are generously checkered, finished with a deep, high gloss. The stock is adjustable and one 1/4" stock spacer is included. For picking up either clay or live birds quickly, the HiViz Tri-Comp fiber-optic front sight with mid-bead ivory sight does a great job, gathering light on the most overcast days. Vector Prolengthened forcing cone, five Invector-Pluschoke tubes, Inflex Technology recoil pad ,HiViz Tri-Comp fiber-optic front sight, ivory mid-bead sight, one ¼" stock spacer.
Price: $1,700.00

BROWNING MAXUS SPORTING CARBON FIBER
Gauge: 12 ga., 3" chamber. **Barrel:** 28" & 30" flat ventilated rib. **Weight:** 6 lbs. 15 ozs. - 7 lbs. Length: 49.25"-51.25". **Stock:** Composite stock with close radius pistol grip, Speed Lock forearm, textured gripping surfaces, shim adjustable for length of pull, cast and drop, carbon fiber finish, Dura-Touch Armor Coating. **Features:** Strong, lightweight aluminum alloy, carbon fiber finish on top and

bottom The stock is finished with Dura-Touch Armor Coating for a secure, non-slip grip when the gun is wet. It has the Browning exclusive Magazine Cut-Off, a patented Turn-Key Magazine Plug and Speed Load Plus. It will be an impossible task to locate an autoloading shotgun for the field with such shooter-friendly features as the Browning Maxus, especially with this deeply finished look of carbon fiber and the Dura-Touch Armor Coating feel. Vector Prolengthened forcing cone, five Invector-Pluschoke tubes, Inflex Technology recoil pad, HiViz Tri-Comp fiber-optic front sight, ivory mid-bead sight, one 1/4" stock spacer.
Price: $1,500.00

BROWNING RIFLED DEER STALKER
Gauge: 12 ga., 3" chamber. **Barrel:** 22" thick-walled, fully rifled for slug ammunition only. **Weight:** 7 lbs. 3 ozs. Length: 43.25". **Stock:** Composite stock with close radius pistol grip, Speed Lock forearm, textured gripping surfaces, shim adjustable for length of pull, cast and drop, matte black finish Dura-Touch Armor Coating. **Features:** Stock is adjustable for length of pull, cast and drop. Cantilever scope mount, one 1/4" stock spacer.
Price: $1,470.00

BROWNING SILVER
Gauge: 12, 3" or 3-1/2" chamber; 20, 3" chamber. **Barrel:** 12 ga.-26", 28", 30", Invector Plus choke tubes. **Weight:** 7 lbs., 9 oz. (12 ga.), 6 lbs., 7 oz. (20 ga.). **Stock:** Satin finish walnut. **Features:** Active Valve gas system, semi-humpback receiver. Invector Plus choke system, three choke tubes. Imported by Browning.
Price: Silver Hunter, 12 ga., 3.5" chamber..........................$1,340.00
Price: Silver Hunter, 20 ga., 3" chamber, intr. 2008 ....$1,180.00
Price: Silver Sporting, 12 ga., 2-3/4" chamber, intr. 2009 .... $1,300.00
Price: Silver Sporting Micro, 12 ga., 2-3/4" chamber, intr. 2008 ....$1,300.00
Price: Silver Rifled Deer, Mossy Oak New Break-Up, 12 ga., 3" chamber, intr. 2008................$1,419.00
Price: Silver Rifled Deer Stalker, 12 ga., 3" chamber, intr. 2008 ....$1,280.00
Price: Silver Rifled Deer Satin, satin-finished aluminum alloy receiver and satin-finished walnut buttstock and fore-end $1,340.00
Price: Silver Stalker, black composite buttstock and fore-end $1,179.00

CZ MODEL 712/720
Gauge: 12, 20 (4+1 capacity). **Barrel:** 26". **Weight:** 6.3 lbs. **Stock:** Turkish walnut with 14.5" length of pull. **Features:** Chrome-lined barrel with 3-inch chamber, ventilated rib, five choke tubes. Matte black finish.
Price: $499

SHOTGUNS Autoloaders

ESCORT WATERFOWL EXTREME SEMIAUTO
Gauge: 12 or 20 ga., 2-3/4" through 3-1/2" chamber, multi 5+1 capacity. **Barrel:** 28". **Weight:** 7.4 lbs. Length: 48". **Stock:** Composite stock with close radius pistol grip; Speed Lock forearm; textured gripping surfaces; shim adjustable for length of pull, cast and drop; Realtree Max4 or AP camo finish; Dura-Touch Armor Coating. **Sights:** HiVis MagniSightfiber optic, magnetic sight to enhance sight acquisition in low light conditions. **Features:** The addition of non-slip grip pads on the fore-end and pistol grip provide a superior hold in all weather conditions. Smart-Valve gas pistons regulate gas blowback to cycle every round – from 2.75 inch range loads through 3.5 inch heavy magnums. Escorts also have Fast-loading systems that allow one-handed round changes without changing aiming position. Avery Outdoors' KW1 or Buck Brush camo patterns available.

Price:		
Black/Synthetic		$551.00
Realtree Camo		$736.00
3.5" Black/Synthetic		$649.00
3.5" Realtree Camo		$815.00

ESCORT SEMI-AUTO
Gauge: 12, 20; 3" or 3.5" chambers. **Barrel:** 22" (Youth), 26" and 28". **Weight:** 6.7-7.8 lbs. **Stock:** Polymer in black, Shadow Grass or Obsession camo finish, Turkish walnut, select walnut. **Sights:** Optional HiViz Spark front. **Features:** Black-chrome or dipped-camo metal parts, top of receiver dovetailed for sight mounts, gold plated trigger, trigger guard safety, magazine cut-off. Three choke tubes (IC, M, F) except the Waterfowl/Turkey Combo, which adds a .665 turkey choke to the standard three. Waterfowl/Turkey combo is two-barrel set, 24"/26" and 26"/28". Several models have Trio recoil pad. Models are: AS, AS Select, AS Youth, AS Youth Select, PS, PS Spark and Waterfowl/Turkey. Introduced 2002. Camo introduced 2003. Youth, Slug and Obsession camo introduced 2005. Imported from Turkey by Legacy Sports International.
Price: .... $425.00 to $589.00

FABARM XLR5 VELOCITY
Gauge: 12. **Barrel:** 30 or 32". **Weight:** 8.4 to 9.9 lbs. Gas-operated model designed for competition shooting. Features include a unique adjustable rib that allows a more upright shooting position. There is also an adjustable trigger shoe, magazine cap adjustable weight system. Five interchangeable choke tubes. Field grade versions available.
Price: From .... $2,700.00 to $3,245.00

FRANCHI AFFINITY
Gauge: 12, 20. Three-inch chamber also handles 2 ¾ inch shells. **Barrel:** 26, 28 inches or 30 inches (12 ga.), 26 inches (20 ga.). 30-inch barrel available only on 12-gauge Sporting model. **Weight:** 5.6 to 6.8 pounds. **Stock:** Black synthetic or Realtree Camo.

Price:		
Synthetic		$849.00
Camo		$949.00
Sporting		$1,149.00

FRANCHI INTENSITY
Gauge: 12, 3.5" chamber. **Barrel:** 26", 28", 30" (IC, Mod., Full choke tubes). **Weight:** 6.8 lbs. **Stock:** Black synthetic or camo.

Price:		
Synthetic		$1,099.00
Camo		$1,199.00

FRANCHI FENICE
Gauge: 20 or 28. **Barrel:** 26", 28". **Weight:** 5.5 to 5.7 lbs. **Stock:** Oil finished, checkered AA walnut. **Features:** Light scroll engraving on silver finish receiver. Limited availability.
Price: Camo $1,359.00

FRANCHI 48AL FIELD AND DELUXE
Gauge: 20 or 28, 2-3/4" chamber. **Barrel:** 24", 26", 28" (Full, Cyl., Mod., choke tubes). **Weight:** 5.4 to 5.7 lbs. **Length:** 42.25" to 48". **Stock:** Walnut with checkered grip and fore-end. **Features:** Long recoil-operated action. Chrome-lined bore; cross-bolt safety. Imported from Italy by Benelli USA.

Price:		
Al Field 20 ga.		$899.00
Al Field 28 ga.		$999.00
Al Field Deluxe 20 ga.		$1,149.00
Al Field Deluxe 28 ga.		$1,249.00

HARRINGTON & RICHARDSON EXCELL
Gauge: 12, 3" chamber. **Barrel:** 28", 22" (Turkey). Ventilated rib with four screw-in choke tubes (IC, M, IM, F). **Weight:** About 7 lbs. **Stock:** Black synthetic or camo. Imported by H&R 1871, Inc.

Price:		
Synthetic		$499.00
Waterfowl, camo finish		$579.00
Turkey, camo finish, 22" barrel, fiber optic sights		$579.00

MOSSBERG 930
Gauge: 12, 3" chamber, 4-shot magazine. **Barrel:** 24", 26", 28", over-bored to 10-gauge bore dimensions; factory ported, Accu-Choke tubes. **Weight:** 7.5 lbs. **Length:** 44.5" overall (28" barrel). **Stock:** Walnut or synthetic. Adjustable stock drop and cast spacer system. **Sights:** Turkey Taker fiber-optic, adjustable windage and elevation. Front bead fiber-optic front on waterfowl models. **Features:** Self-regulating gas system, dual gas-vent system and piston, EZ-Empty magazine button, cocking indicator. Interchangeable Accu-Choke tube set (IC, Mod, Full) for waterfowl and field models. XX-Full turkey Accu-Choke tube included with turkey models. Ambidextrous thumb-operated safety, Uni-line stock and receiver. Receiver drilled and tapped for scope base attachment, free gun lock. Introduced 2008. From O.F. Mossberg & Sons, Inc.

Price:		
Turkey, from		$736.00
Waterfowl, from		$736.00
Combo, from		$700.00
Field, from		$633.00
Slugster, from		$606.00
Turkey Pistolgrip; full pistolgrip stock, matte black or Mossy Oak Obsession camo finish overall		$828.00
Tactical; 18.5" tactical barrel, black synthetic stock and matte black finish		$683.00
SPX; no muzzle brake, M16-style front sight, ghost ring rear sight, full pistolgrip stock, eight-round extended magazine		$787.00
Home Security/Field Combo; 18.5" Cylinder bore barrel and 28" ported Field barrel; black synthetic stock and matte black finish		$604.00

MOSSBERG MODEL 935 MAGNUM
Gauge: 12; 3" and 3.5» chamber, interchangeable. **Barrel:** 22", 24», 26», 28». **Weight:** 7.25 to 7.75 lbs. **Length:** 45" to 49" overall. **Stock:** Synthetic. **Features:** Gas-operated semiauto models in blued or camo finish. Fiber optics sights, drilled and tapped receiver, interchangeable Accu-Mag choke tubes.

Price:		
935 Magnum Turkey: Realtree Hardwoods, Mossy Oak New Break-up or Mossy Oak Obsession camo overall, 24" barrel		$815.00
935 Magnum Turkey Pistolgrip; full pistolgrip stock		$925.00
935 Magnum Grand Slam: 22" barrel, Realtree Hardwoods or Mossy Oak New Break-up camo overall		$832.00
935 Magnum Flyway: 28" barrel and Advantage Max-4 camo overall		$870.00
935 Magnum Waterfowl: 26"or 28" barrel, matte black, Mossy Oak New Break-up, Advantage Max-4 or Mossy Oak Duck Blind cam overall		$682.00
935 Magnum Turkey/Deer Combo: interchangeable 24" Turkey barrel, Mossy Oak New Break-up camo overall		$901.00
935 Magnum Waterfowl/Turkey Combo: 24" Turkey and 28" Waterfowl barrels, Mossy Oak New Break-up finish overall		$901.00

Prices given are believed to be accurate at time of publication however, many factors affect retail pricing so exact prices are not possible.

69TH EDITION, 2015 ⊕ **499**

MOSSBERG SA-20

Gauge: 20. 20" (Tactical), 26" or 28". **Weight:** 5.5 to 6 lbs. **Stock:** Black synthetic. Gas operated action, matte blue finish. Tactical model has ghost-ring sight, accessory rail.
Price: From .... $518.00 to $595.00

REMINGTON MODEL 11-87 SPORTSMAN

Gauge: 12, 20, 3" chamber. **Barrel:** 26", 28", RemChoke tubes. Standard contour, vent rib. **Weight:** About 7.75 to 8.25 lbs. Length: 46" to 48" overall. **Stock:** Black synthetic or Mossy Oak Break Up Mossy Oak Duck Blind, and Realtree Hardwoods HD and AP Green HD camo finishes. **Sights:** Single bead front. **Features:** Matte-black metal finish, magazine cap swivel studs. Sportsman Deer gun has 21-inch fully rifled barrel, cantilever scope mount.
Price: .... $804.00 to $929.00

REMINGTON 11-87 SPORTSMAN SUPER MAG SYNTHETIC

Semiauto shotgun chambered in 12-ga. 3-1/2-inch. Features include black matte synthetic stock and fore-end; rubber overmolded grip panels on the stock and fore-end; black padded sling; HiViz sights featuring interchangeable light pipe; 28-inch vent rib barrel; SuperCell recoil pad; RemChoke.
Price: From .... $859.00 to $998.00

REMINGTON 11-87 SPORTSMAN SUPER MAG SHURSHOT TURKEY

Similar to 11-87 Sportsman Super Mag Synthetic but with ambidextrous ShurShot pistol-grip stock; full Realtree APG HD coverage; 23-inch barrel with fully adjustable TruGlo rifle sights. Wingmaster HD Turkey Choke included.
Price: $972.00

REMINGTON MODEL 1100 50TH ANNIVERSARY EDITION

To celebrate the 50th anniversary of the famous Model 1100 gas-operated autoloading shotgun, Remington announces a Limited Edition 12-gauge model. Features include a machine-cut engraved receiver with gold-filled retriever, quail and duck images; a high-grade walnut stock with high gloss finish, white diamond grip cap and white-line spacers (features that were popular in 1963); 28-inch light-contour barrel with twin bead sights and Rem Choke. Shipped in a green Remington hard case.
Price: $1999

REMINGTON MODEL 1100 COMPETITION MODELS

Gauge: .410 bore, 28, 20, 12. **Barrel:** 26", 27", 28", 30" light target contoured vent rib barrel with twin bead target sights. **Stock:** Semi-fancy American walnut stock and fore-end, cut checkering, high

gloss finish. **Features:** Classic Trap has 30-inch barrel and weighs approximately 8.25 pounds. Sporting Series is available in all four gauges with 28-inch barrel in 12 and 20 gauge, 27 inch in 28 and .410. **Weight:** 6.25 to 8 pounds. Competion Synthetic model has synthetic stock with adjustable comb, case and length. Five Briley Target choke tubes. High-gloss blued barrel, Nickel-Teflon finish on receiver and internal parts. **Weight:** 8.1 pounds.
Price: Classic Trap $1,270.00
Price: Sporting Series, from $1,211.00
Price: Competition Synthetic: $1,242.00

REMINGTON MODEL 1100 TAC-4

Similar to Model 1100 but with 18" or 22" barrel with ventilated rib; 12 gauge 2-3/4"only; standard black synthetic stock or Knoxx SpecOps SpeedFeed IV pistolgrip stock; RemChoke tactical choke tube; matte black finish overall. Length is 42-1/2" and weighs 7-3/4 lbs.
Price: $1,015.00

REMINGTON VERSA MAX SERIES

Gauge: 12 ga., 2 3/4", 3", 3 1/2" chamber. **Barrel:** 26" and 28" flat ventilated rib. **Weight:** 7.5 lbs.-7.7 lbs. Length: 40.25". **Stock:** Synthetic. **Features:** Reliably cycles 12-gauge rounds from 2 3/4" to 3 1/2" magnum. Versaport gas system regulates cycling pressure based on shell length. Reduces recoil to that of a 20-gauge. Self-cleaning - Continuously cycled thousands of rounds in torture test. Synthetic stock and fore-end with grey overmolded grips. Drilled and tapped receiver. Enlarged trigger guard opening and larger safety for easier use with gloves. TriNyte Barrel and Nickel Teflon plated internal components offer extreme corrosion resistance. Includes 5 Flush Mount Pro Bore Chokes (Full, Mod, Imp Mod Light Mod, IC)
Price: Sportsman, from $1,025.00
Price: Synthetic, from $1,399.00
Price: Tactical, from $1,399.00
Price: Waterfowl, from $1,599.00
Price: Camo, from $1,599.00
Price: Zombie Green or Pink, from $1,599.00

SKB MODEL IS300

Gauge: 12, 2-3/4 and 3-inch loads. Magazine capacity: 4+1. Inertia-driven operating system. **Barrel:** 26, 28 or 30 inches with 3 choke tubes IC, M, F. **Stock:** Black synthetic, oil-finished walnut or camo. **Weight:** 6.7 to 7.3 pounds. **Features:** Target models have adjustable stock dimensions including cast and drop. Made in Turkey and imported by GU, Inc.
Price: Synthetic $625.00
Price: Walnut or Camo Field $715.00
Price: Walnut Target $870.00

STOEGER MODEL 2000

Gauge: 12, 3" chamber, set of five choke tubes (C, IC, M, F, XFT). **Barrel:** 24", 26", 28", 30". **Stock:** Walnut, synthetic, Timber HD, Max-4. **Sights:** Red bar front. **Features:** Inertia-recoil. Minimum recommended load: 3 dram, 1-1/8 oz. Imported by Benelli USA.
Price: Walnut $499.00
Price: Synthetic $499.00
Price: Max-4 .... $549.00
Price: Black synthetic pistol grip (2007) $499.00
Price: APG HD camo pistol grip (2007), 18.5" barrel $549.00

STOEGER MODEL 3000

Gauge: 12, 2-3/4 and 3-inch loads. Minimum recommended load 3-dram, 1-1/8 ounces. **Magazine capacity:** 4+1. Inertia-driven operating system. **Barrel:** 26 or 28 inches with 3 choke tubes IC, M, XF. **Weight:** 7.4 to 7.5 pounds. **Finish:** Black synthetic or camo (Realtree APG or Max-4).
Price: Synthetic $529.00
Price: Camo $599.00

STOEGER MODEL 3500
Gauge: 12. 2 3/4, 3 and 3 1/2-inch loads. Minimum recommended load 3-dram, 1-1/8 ounces. **Barrel:** 24, 26 or 28 inches. Other features similar to Model 3000. Choke tubes for IC, M, XF. **Weight:** 7.4 to 7.5 pounds. **Finish:** Black synthetic or camo (Realtree APG or Max-4).
Price: Synthetic $629.00
Price: Camo $719.00

TRISTAR VIPER
Gauge: 12, 20; shoots 2-3/4" or 3" interchangeably. **Barrel:** 26", 28" barrels (carbon fiber only offered in 12-ga. 28" and 20-ga. 26"). **Stock:** Wood, black synthetic, Mossy Oak Duck Blind camouflage, faux carbon fiber finish (2008) with the new Comfort Touch technology. **Features:** Magazine cut-off, vent rib with matted sight plane, brass front bead (camo models have fiber-optic front sight), five round magazine-shot plug included, and 3 Beretta-style choke tubes (IC, M, F). Viper synthetic, Viper camo have swivel studs. Five-year warranty. Viper Youth models have shortened length of pull and 24" barrel. Imported by Tristar Sporting Arms Ltd.
Price: From $469.00
Price: Camo models (2008), from $569.00

WEATHERBY SA-SERIES
Gauge: 12 ga. & 20 ga., 3" chamber. **Barrel:** 26" and 28" flat ventilated rib. **Weight:** 6.5 lbs. **Stock:** Wood and synthetic. **Features:** The SA-08 is a reliable workhorse that lets you move from early season dove loads to late fall's heaviest waterfowl loads in no time. Available with wood and synthetic stock options in 12 and 20 gauge models, including a scaled-down youth model to fit 28 ga. Comes with 3 application-specific choke tubes (SK/IC/M). Made in Turkey.
Price: SA-08 Upland $799.00
Price: SA-08 Synthetic (New 2011) $599.00
Price: SA-08 Waterfowler 3.0 .... $749.00
Price: SA-08 Synthetic Youth $599.00
Price: SA-08 Deluxe.. $799.00

WINCHESTER SUPER X3
Gauge: 12, 3" and 3.5" chambers. **Barrel:** 26", 28", .742" back-bored; Invector Plus choke tubes. **Weight:** 7 to 7.25 lbs. **Stock:** Composite, 14.25"x1.75"x2". Mossy Oak New Break-Up camo with Dura-Touch Armor Coating. Pachmayr Decelerator buttpad with hard heel insert, customizable length of pull. **Features:** Alloy magazine tube, gunmetal grey Perma-Cote UT finish, self-adjusting Active Valve gas action, lightweight recoil spring system. Electroless nickel-plated bolt, three choke tubes, two length-of-pull stock spacers, drop and cast adjustment spacers, sling swivel studs. Introduced 2006. Made in Belgium, assembled in Portugal by U.S. Repeating Arms Co.
Price: Field $1,070.00
Price: Black Shadow .... $1,000.00 to $1,070.00 (3.5")
Price: Universal Hunter .... $1,160.00 to $1,230.00 (3.5")
Price: Waterfowl Hunter $1,200.00
Price: Sporting, Adj. comb $1,700.00
Price: Cantilever Buck $1,150.00

BENELLI SUPERNOVA
Gauge: 12; 3.5" chamber. **Barrel:** 24", 26", 28". **Length:** 45.5-49.5". **Stock:** Synthetic; Max-4 , Timber, APG HD (2007). **Sights:** Red bar front, metal midbead. **Features:** 2-3/4", 3" chamber (3-1/2" 12 ga. only). Montefeltro rotating bolt design with dual action bars, magazine cut-off, synthetic trigger assembly, adjustable combs, shim kit, choice of buttstocks. 4-shot magazine. Introduced 2006. Imported from Italy by Benelli USA.
Price: $549.00
Price: Camo stock $669.00
Price: Rifle slug model .... $829.00 to $929.00

BENELLI NOVA
Gauge: 12, 20. **Barrel:** 24", 26", 28". **Stock:** Black synthetic, Max-4, Timber and APG HD. **Sights:** Red bar. **Features:** 2-3/ 4", 3" chamber (3-1/2" 12 ga. only). Montefeltro rotating bolt design with dual action bars, magazine cut-off, synthetic trigger assembly, 4-shot magazine. Introduced 1999. Field & Slug Combo has 24" barrel and rifled bore; open rifle sights; synthetic stock; weighs 8.1 lbs. Imported from Italy by Benelli USA.
Price: Max-5 camo stock..$559.00
Price: H20 model, black synthetic, matte nickel finish.............$669.00
Price: Tactical, 18.5" barrel, Ghost Ring sight.........................$459.00
Price: Black synthetic youth stock, 20 ga. $469.00

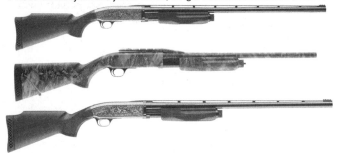

BROWNING BPS
Gauge: 10, 12, 3-1/2" chamber; 12, 16, or 20, 3" chamber (2-3/4" in target guns), 28, 2-3/4" chamber, 5-shot magazine, .410, 3" chamber. **Barrel:** 10 ga.-24" Buck Special, 28", 30", 32" Invector; 12, 20 ga.-22", 24", 26", 28", 30", 32" (Imp. Cyl., Mod. or Full), .410-26" barrel. (Imp. Cyl., Mod. and Full choke tubes.) Also available with Invector choke tubes, 12 or 20 ga.; Upland Special has 22" barrel with Invector tubes. BPS 3" and 3-1/2" have back-bored barrel. **Weight:** 7 lbs., 8 oz. (28" barrel). Length: 48.75" overall (28" barrel). **Stock:** 14.25"x1.5"x2.5". Select walnut, semi-beavertail fore-end, full pistol grip stock. **Features:** All 12 gauge 3" guns except Buck Special and game guns have back-bored barrels with Invector Plus choke tubes. Bottom feeding and ejection; receiver top safety, high post vent rib. Double action bars eliminate binding. Vent rib barrels only. All 12 and 20 gauge guns with 3" chamber available with fully engraved receiver flats at no extra cost. Each gauge has its own unique game scene. Introduced 1977. Stalker is same gun as the standard BPS except all exposed metal parts have a matte blued finish and the stock has a black finish with a black recoil pad. Available in 10 ga. (3-1/2") and 12 ga. with 3" or 3-1/2" chamber, 22", 28", 30" barrel with Invector choke system. Introduced 1987. Rifled Deer Hunter is similar to the standard BPS except has newly designed receiver/magazine tube/barrel mounting system to eliminate play, heavy 20.5" barrel with rifle-type sights with adjustable rear, solid receiver scope mount, "rifle" stock dimensions for scope or open sights, sling swivel studs. Gloss or matte finished wood with checkering, polished blue metal. Medallion model has additional engraving on receiver, polished blue finish, AA/AAA grade walnut stock with checkering. All Purpose model has

Realtree AP camo on stock and fore-end, HiVis fiber optic sights. Introduced 2013. Imported from Japan by Browning.
Price: Field, Stalker models....................................$700.00
Price: Camo coverage $820.00
Price: Deer Hunter $830.00
Price: Deer Hunter Camo......................................$870.00
Price: All Purpose $930.00
Price: Magnum Hunter (3.5") ....$800.00 to $1,030.00
Price: Medallion $830.00

BROWNING BPS 10 GAUGE SERIES
Similar to the standard BPS except completely covered with Mossy Oak Shadow Grass camouflage. Available with 26" and 28" barrel. Introduced 1999. Imported by Browning
Price: Mossy Oak camo...$950.00
Price: Synthetic stock, Stalker...................................$800.00

BROWNING BPS NWTF TURKEY SERIES
Similar to the standard BPS except has full coverage Mossy Oak Break-Up Infinity camo finish on synthetic stock, fore-end and exposed metal parts. Offered in 12 gauge, 3" or 3-1/2" chamber, or 10 gauge; 24" bbl. has extra-full choke tube and HiViz fiber-optic sights. Introduced 2001. From Browning.
Price: 12 ga., 3"...$950.00
Price: 3.5"...$1,030.00

BROWNING BPS MICRO MIDAS
Gauge: 12, 20, 28 ga. or .410 bore, 24 or 26". Three Invector choke tubes for 12 and 20 gauge, standard tubes for 28 and .410. **Stock:** Walnut with pistol grip and recoil pad. Satin finished and scaled down to fit smaller statured shooters. Length of pull is 13.25". Two spacers included for stock length adjustments. **Weight:** 7 to 7.8 lbs.
Price: .... $700.00 to $740.00

BROWING BPS HIGH CAPACITY
Gauge: .410 bore. 3" chamber. 5-round magazine. **Barrel:** 20" fixed Cylinder choke; stainless Steel; Matte finish. **Weight:** 6 lbs. **Length:** 40.75". **Stock:** Black composite on All Weather with matte finish. **Features:** Forged and machined steel; satin nickel finish. Bottom ejection; dual steel action bars; top tang safety. HiViz Tactical fiber-optic front sight; stainless internal mechanism; swivel studs installed.
Price: Synthetic...$800.00

CZ 612
Gauge: 12. Chambered for all shells up to 3 ½ inches. **Capacity:** 5+1, magazine plug included with Wildfowl Magnum. **Barrel length:** 18.5 inches (Home Defense), 20 (HC-P), 26 inches (Wildfowl Mag). **Weight:** 6 to 6.8 pounds. **Stock:** Polymer. **Finish:** Matte black or full camo (Wildfowl Mag.) HC-P model has pistol grip stock, fiber optic front sight and ghost-ring rear. Home Defense Combo comes with extra 26-inch barrel.
Price: Wildfowl Magnum $428.00
Price: Home Defense .... $304.00 to $409.00

ESCORT PUMP SERIES
Gauge: 12, 20; 3" chamber. **Barrel:** 18" (AimGuard, Home Defense and MarineGuard), 22" (Youth Pump), 26", and 28" lengths. **Weight:** 6.7-7.0 lbs. **Stock:** Polymer in black, Shadow Grass camo or Obsession camo finish. Two adjusting spacers included. Youth model

has Trio recoil pad. **Sights:** Bead or Spark front sights, depending on model. AimGuard and MarineGuard models have blade front sights. **Features:** Black-chrome or dipped camo metal parts, top of receiver dovetailed for sight mounts, gold plated trigger, trigger guard safety, magazine cut-off. Three choke tubes (IC, M, F) except AimGuard/MarineGuard which are cylinder bore. Models include: FH, FH Youth, AimGuard and Marine Guard. Introduced in 2003. Imported from Turkey by Legacy Sports International.
Price: .... **$379.00 to $393.00**

HARRINGTON & RICHARDSON (H&R) PARDNER PUMP
Gauge: 12, 20.3-inch chamber. **Barrel:** 21 to 28 inches. **Weight:** 6.5 to 7.5 lbs. **Stock:** Synthetic or hardwood. Ventilated recoil pad and grooved fore-end. **Features:** Steel receiver, double action bars, crossbolt safety, easy takedown, ventilated rib, screw-in choke tubes.
Price: From ....**$231.00 to $259.00**

IAC MODEL 97T TRENCH GUN
Gauge: 12, 2 ¾" chamber. Replica of Winchester Model 1897 Trench Gun. **Barrel:** 20" with cylinder choke. **Stock:** Hand rubbed American walnut. **Features:** Metal hand guard, bayonet lug. Imported from China by International Arms Corp.
Price: **$465.00**

ITHACA MODEL 37 FEATHERWEIGHT
Gauge: 12, 20, 16, 28 (4+1 capacity). **Barrel:** 26, 28 or 30" with 3" chambers (12 and 20 ga.), plain or ventiltated rib. **Weight:** 6.1 to 7.6 lbs. **Stock:** Fancy grade black walnut with Pachmayr Decelerator recoil pad. Checkered fore-end made of matching walnut. **Features:** Receiver machined from a single block of steel or aluminum. Barrel is steel shot compatible. Three Briley choke tubes provided. Available in several variations including turkey, home defense, tactical and high-grade.
Price: 12, 16 or 20 ga. from **$849.00**
Price: 28 ga. from **$1,149.00**
Price: Turkey Slayer w/synthetic stock from...........................**$899.00**
Price: Trap Series 12 ga..**$999.00**

ITHACA DEERSLAYER III SLUG
Gauge: 12, 20; 3" chamber. **Barrel:** 26" fully rifled, heavy fluted with 1:28 twist for 12 ga.; 1:24 for 20 ga. **Weight:** 8.14 lbs. to 9.5 lbs. with scope mounted. **Length:** 45.625" overall. **Stock:** Fancy black walnut stock and fore-end. **Sights:** NA. **Features:** Updated, slug-only version of the classic Model 37. Bottom ejection, blued barrel and receiver.
Price: **$1,289.00**

MAVERICK ARMS MODEL 88
Gauge: 12, 20. 3" chamber. **Barrel:** 26" or 28", Accu-Mag choke tubes for steel or lead shot. **Weight:** 7.25 lbs. **Stock:** Black synthetic with recoil pad. **Features:** Crossbolt safety, aluminum alloy receiver. Economy model of Mossberg Model 500 series. Available in several variations including Youth, Slug and Special Purpose (home defense) models.
Price: **$298.00**

MOSSBERG MODEL 835 ULTI-MAG
Gauge: 12, 3-1/2" chamber. **Barrel:** Ported 24" rifled bore, 24", 28", Accu-Mag choke tubes for steel or lead shot. **Weight:** 7.75 lbs. **Length:** 48.5" overall. **Stock:** 14"x1.5"x2.5". Dual Comb. Cut-checkered hardwood or camo synthetic; both have recoil pad. **Sights:** White

bead front, brass mid-bead; fiber-optic rear. Turkey Thug has red dot sight. **Features:** Shoots 2-3/4", 3" or 3-1/2" shells. Back-bored and ported barrel to reduce recoil, improve patterns. Ambidextrous thumb safety, twin extractors, dual slide bars. Mossberg Cablelock included. Introduced 1988.
Price: Turkey **$600.00**
Price: Turkey Thug **$708.00**
Price: Waterfowl **$513.00**
Price: Slugster **$638.00**
Price: Duck Commander **$693.00**

MOSSBERG MODEL 500 SPORTING SERIES
Gauge: 12, 20, .410, 3" chamber. **Barrel:** 18.5" to 28" with fixed or Accu-Choke, plain or vent rib. **Weight:** 6-1/4 lbs. (.410), 7-1/4 lbs. (12). **Length:** 48" overall (28" barrel). **Stock:** 14"x1.5"x2.5". Walnut-stained hardwood, black synthetic, Mossy Oak Advantage camouflage. Cut-checkered grip and fore-end. **Sights:** White bead front, brass mid-bead; fiber-optic. **Features:** Ambidextrous thumb safety, twin extractors, disconnecting safety, dual action bars. Quiet Carry fore-end. Many barrels are ported. FLEX series has many modular options and accessories including barrels and stocks. From Mossberg.
Price: Turkey, from **$466.00**
Price: Waterfowl, from **$537.00**
Price: Combo, from **$593.00**
Price: FLEX Duck Commander.....................................**$835.00**
Price: FLEX Hunting..**$770.00**
Price: FLEX All Purpose...**$682.00**
Price: Field, from **$401.00**
Price: Slugster, from **$434.00**

MOSSBERG 510 MINI BANTAM
Gauge: 20 & .410 ga., 3" chamber. **Barrel:** 18 1/2 " vent-rib. **Weight:** 5 lbs. **Length:** 34 3/4". **Stock:** Synthetic with optional Mossy Oak Break-Up Infinity, Muddy Girl pink/black camo. **Features:** Available in either 20 gauge or .410 bore, the Mini features an 18 1/2 " vent-rib barrel with dual-bead sights. Parents don't have to worry about their young shooter growing out of this gun too quick, the adjustable classic stock can be adjusted from 10 1/2" to 11 1/2" length of pull so the Mini can grow with your youngster. This adjustability also helps provide a proper fit for young shooters and allowing for a more safe and enjoyable shooting experience.
Price: From **$466.00**

MOSSBERG MODEL 500 BANTAM PUMP
Same as the Model 500 Sporting Pump except 12 or 20 gauge, 22" vent rib Accu-Choke barrel with choke tube set; has 1" shorter stock, reduced length from pistol grip to trigger, reduced fore-end reach. Introduced 1992.
Price: **$414.00**
Price: Combo with extra slug barrel, camo finish....................**$534.00**

REMINGTON MODEL 870 WINGMASTER
Gauge: 12, 20, 28 ga., .410 bore. **Barrel:** 25", 26", 28" 30" (RemChokes). **Weight:** 7-1/4 lbs. **Length:** 46", 48". **Stock:** Walnut,

Prices given are believed to be accurate at time of publication however, many factors affect retail pricing so exact prices are not possible.

69TH EDITION, 2015 ✦ **503**

hardwood. **Sights:** Single bead (Twin bead Wingmaster). **Features:** Light contour barrel. Double action bars, cross-bolt safety, blue finish. LW is 28 gauge and .410-bore only, 25" vent rib barrel with RemChoke tubes, high-gloss wood finish. Gold-plated trigger, American B Grade walnut stock and fore-end, high-gloss finish, fleur-de-lis checkering. A classic American shotgun first introduced in 1950.
Price: .... $830.00 to $929.00

REMINGTON MODEL 870 AMERICAN CLASSIC
Gauge: 12, 20 or 28 gauge. **Barrel:** 25" (28 ga), 26" (20 ga.), 28" (12 ga.) with ventilated rib and Rem Choke system. **Weight:** 6 to 7 lbs. Commemorating one of the most popular firearms in history, this model features a B-grade American walnut stock, a high polish blue finish, and machine-cut engraved receiver with gold filled banner reading "American Classic." Other features in keeping with those that were popular in the 1950s include ventilated recoil pad with white line spacer and a diamond grip cap.
Price: $1,249.00

REMINGTON MODEL 870 MARINE MAGNUM
Similar to 870 Wingmaster except all metal plated with electroless nickel, black synthetic stock and fore-end. Has 18" plain barrel (cyl.), bead front sight, 7-shot magazine. Introduced 1992. XCS version with TriNyte corrosion control introduced 2007.
Price: $841.00

REMINGTON MODEL 870 CLASSIC TRAP
Similar to Model 870 Wingmaster except has 30" vent rib, light contour barrel, singles, mid- and long-handicap choke tubes, semi-fancy American walnut stock, high-polish blued receiver with engraving. Chamber 2.75". From Remington Arms Co.
Price: $1,098.00

REMINGTON MODEL 870 EXPRESS
Similar to Model 870 Wingmaster except laminate, synthetic black, or camo stock with solid, black recoil pad and pressed checkering on grip and fore-end. Outside metal surfaces have black oxide finish. Comes with 26" or 28" vent rib barrel with mod. RemChoke tube. ShurShot Turkey (2008) has ShurShot synthetic pistol-grip thumbhole design, extended fore-end, Mossy Oak Obsession camouflage, matte black metal finish, 21" vent rib barrel, twin beads, Turkey Extra Full Rem Choke tube. Receiver drilled and tapped for mounting optics. ShurShot FR CL (Fully Rifled Cantilever, 2008) includes compact 23" fully-rifled barrel with integrated cantilever scope mount.
Price: .... $417.00 to $629.00

REMINGTON MODEL 870 EXPRESS SUPER MAGNUM
Similar to Model 870 Express except 28" vent rib barrel with 3-1/2" chamber, vented recoil pad. Introduced 1998. Model 870 Express Super Magnum Waterfowl (2008) is fully camouflaged with Mossy Oak Duck Blind pattern, 28-inch vent rib Rem Choke barrel, "Over Decoys" Choke tube (.007") fiber-optic HiViz single bead front sight; front and rear sling swivel studs, padded black sling.
Price: $629.00

REMINGTON MODEL 870 EXPRESS TACTICAL
Similar to Model 870 but in 12 gauge only (2-2/4" and 3" interchangeably) with 18.5" barrel, Tactical RemChoke extended/ported choke tube, black synthetic buttstock and fore-end, extended magazine tube, gray powdercoat finish overall. 38.5" overall length, weighs 7.5 lbs.
Price: $601.00
Price: Model 870 TAC Desert Recon; desert camo stock and sand-toned metal surfaces $692.00
Price: Tactical Magpul $898.00

REMINGTON MODEL 870 SPS SHURSHOT SYNTHETIC SUPER SLUG
Gauge: 12; 2-3/4" and 3" chamber, interchangeable. **Barrel:** 25.5" extra-heavy, fully rifled pinned to receiver. **Weight:** 7-7/8 lbs. Length: 47" overall. **Features:** Pump-action model based on 870 platform. SuperCell recoil pad. Drilled and tapped for scope mounts with Weaver rail included. Matte black metal surfaces, Mossy Oak Treestand Shurshot buttstock and fore-end.
Price: $829.00
Price: 870 SPS ShurShot Synthetic Turkey; adjustable sights and APG HD camo buttstock and fore-end $681.00

REMINGTON 870 EXPRESS SYNTHETIC SUPER MAG TURKEY-WATERFOWL CAMO
Pump action shotgun chambered in 12-ga., 2-3/4 to 3-1/2 inch. Features include full Mossy Oak Bottomland camo coverage; 26-inch barrel with HiViz fiber-optics sights; Wingmaster HD Waterfowl and Turkey Extra Full RemChokes; SuperCell recoil pad; drilled and tapped receiver.
Price: $629.00

REMINGTON 870 EXPRESS SYNTHETIC TURKEY CAMO
Pump action shotgun chambered for 2-3/4 and 3-inch 12-ga. Features include 21-inch vent rib bead-sighted barrel; standard Express finish on barrel and receiver; Turkey Extra Full RemChoke; synthetic stock

Prices given are believed to be accurate at time of publication however, many factors affect retail pricing so exact prices are not possible.

with integrated sling swivel attachment.
Price: $492.00

REMINGTON 870 SUPER MAG TURKEY-PREDATOR CAMO WITH SCOPE

Pump action shotgun chambered in 12-ga., 2-3/4 to 3-1/2 inch. Features include 20-inch barrel; TruGlo red/green selectable illuminated sight mounted on pre-installed Weaver-style rail; black padded sling; Wingmaster HDTurkey/Predator RemChoke; full Mossy Oak Obsession camo coverage; ShurShot pistol grip stock with black overmolded grip panels; TruGlo 30mm Red/Green Dot Scope pre-mounted.
Price: $679.00

REMINGTON MODEL 887 NITRO MAG

Gauge: 12; 3.5", 3", and 2-3/4" chambers. **Barrel:** 28". **Features:** Pump-action model based on the Model 870. Interchangeable shells, black matte ArmoLokt rustproof coating throughout. SuperCell recoil pad. Solid rib and Hi-Viz front sight with interchangeable light tubes. Black synthetic stock with contoured grip panels.
Price: $436.00
Price: Model 887 Nitro Mag Waterfowl, camo $532.00

REMINGTON 887 NITRO MAG CAMO COMBO

Pump action shotgun chambered in 12-ga., 2-3/4 to 3-1/2 inch. Features include 22-inch turkey barrel with HiViz fiber-optic rifle sights and 28-inch waterfowl with a HiViz sight; extended Waterfowl and Super Full Turkey RemChokes are included; SuperCell recoil pad; synthetic stock and fore-end with specially contoured grip panels; full camo coverage.
Price: $728.00

STEVENS MODEL 350/320

Gauge: 12, 3-inch chamber, 5+1 capacity. **Barrel:** 18.25" with interchangeable choke tubes. Features include all-steel barrel and receiver; bottom-load and ejection design; black synthetic stock.
Price: Security Model $276.00
Price: Field Model 320 with 28-inch barrel $251.00
Price: Combo Model with Field and Security barrels $307.00

STOEGER P-350

Gauge: 12. Designed to fire any 12-gauge ammunition. **Capacity:**

4+1. **Barrel:** 18.5, 20, 24, 26 or 28 inches, with ventilated rib. **Weight:** 6.6 to 7 pounds. **Stock:** Black synthetic, or Realtree APG or Max-4 camo in standard stock configuration. Also available with vertical pistol-style handgrip.
Price: ....$349 to $479

WEATHERBY PA-08 SERIES

Gauge: 12 ga. chamber. **Barrel:** 26" and 28" flat ventilated rib. **Weight:** 6.5 lbs. -7 lbs. **Stock:** Walnut. **Features:** The PA-08 # Walnut stock with gloss finish, all metalwork is gloss black for a distinctive look, vented top rib dissipates heat and aids in target acquisition. Comes with 3 application-specific choke tubes (IC/M/F). Upland/Slug Gun combo includes 24" rifled barrel. Made in Turkey.
Price: PA-08 Upland $449.00
Price: PA-08 Upland/Slug combo........................$649.00
Price: PA-08 Synthetic..$399.00
Price: PA-08 Synthetic Waterfowler.....................$399.00
Price: PA-08 Synthetic Turkey $399.00

WEATHERBY PA-459 TURKEY

Gauge: 12, 3-inch chamber. Barrel: 21.25 inches. Stock: Synthetic with Mothwing Spring Mimicry camo, rubber texturized grip areas. Vertical pistol grip. **Sights:** Ghost ring rear, fiber optic front. Picatinny rail. Features: Mothwing Spring Mimicry camo.
Price: $549.00

WINCHESTER SUPER X (SXP)

Gauge: 12, 3" or 3.5" chambers; 20 gauge, 3". **Barrel:** 18"; 26" and 28" barrels are .742" back-bored, chrome plated; Invector Plus choke tubes. **Weight:** 6 .5 to 7 lbs. **Stock:** Walnut or composite. **Features:** Rotary bolt, four lugs, dual steel action bars. Walnut Field has gloss-finished walnut stock and forearm, cut checkering. Black Shadow Field has composite stock and forearm, non-glare matte finish barrel and receiver. SXP Defender has composite stock and forearm, chromed plated, 18" cylinder choked barrel, non-glare metal surfaces, five-shot magazine, grooved forearm. Reintroduced 2009. Made in U.S.A. from Winchester Repeating Arms Co.
Price: Black Shadow Field, 3" $380.00
Price: Black Shadow Field, 3.5" $430.00
Price: SXP Defender...........................$350.00 to $400.00
Price: Waterfowl Hunter 3" $460.00
Price: Waterfowl Hunter 3.5" $500.00
Price: Turkey Hunter 3.5" $520.00
Price: Black Shadow Deer $520.00
Price: Trap..$480.00

Prices given are believed to be accurate at time of publication however, many factors affect retail pricing so exact prices are not possible.

69TH EDITION, 2015 ✦ **505**

BERETTA DT10 TRIDENT

Gauge: 12, 2-3/4", 3" chambers. **Barrel:** 28", 30", 34"; competition-style vent rib; fixed or Optima choke tubes. **Weight:** 8 lbs. **Stock:** High-grade walnut stock with oil finish; hand-checkered grip and fore-end, adjustable stocks available. **Features:** Detachable, adjustable trigger group, raised and thickened receiver, fore-end iron has adjustment nut to guarantee wood-to-metal fit. Introduced 2000. Imported from Italy by Beretta USA.

Price: DT10 Trident Trap, adjustable stock............................$8,650.00
Price: DT10 Trident Skeet..$8,050.00
Price: DT10 Trident Sporting, from $7,500.00

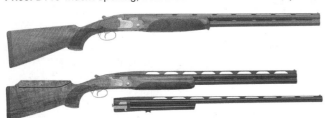

BERETTA SERIES 682 GOLD E SKEET, TRAP, SPORTING

Gauge: 12, 2-3/4" chambers. **Barrel:** skeet-28"; trap-30" and 32", Imp. Mod. & Full and Mobilchoke; trap mono shotguns-32" and 34" Mobilchoke; trap top single guns-32" and 34" Full and Mobilchoke; trap combo sets-from 30" O/U, to 32" O/U, 34" top single. **Stock:** Close-grained walnut, hand checkered. **Sights:** White Bradley bead front sight and center bead. **Features:** Receiver has Greystone gunmetal gray finish with gold accents. Trap Monte Carlo stock has deluxe trap recoil pad. Various grades available. Imported from Italy by Beretta USA.

Price: 682 Gold E Trap with adjustable stock........................$4,800.00
Price: 682 Gold E Sporting $4,600.00
Price: 682 Gold E Skeet, adjustable stock $4,800.00

BERETTA 686 ONYX

Gauge: 12, 20, 28; 3", 3.5" chambers. **Barrel:** 26", 28" (Mobilchoke tubes). **Weight:** 6.8-6.9 lbs. **Stock:** Checkered American walnut. **Features:** Intended for the beginning sporting clays shooter. Has wide, vented target rib, radiused recoil pad. Polished black finish on receiver and barrels. Introduced 1993. Imported from Italy by Beretta U.S.A.

Price: White Onyx $2,240.00
PPrice: White Onyx Sporting $2,460.00

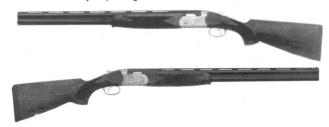

BERETTA 686/687 SILVER PIGEON SERIES

Gauge: 12, 20, 28, 3" chambers (2-3/4" 28 ga.). .410 bore, 3" chamber. **Barrel:** 26", 28". **Weight:** 6.8 lbs. **Stock:** Checkered walnut. **Features:** Interchangeable barrels (20 and 28 ga.), single selective gold-plated trigger, boxlock action, auto safety, Schnabel fore-end.

Price: 686 Silver Pigeon Grade I..$2,240.00
Price: 687 Silver Pigeon Grade III $3,430.00
Price: 687 Silver Pigeon Grade V...$4,075.00

BERETTA MODEL 692 SPORTING

Gauge: 12, 3-inch chamber. **Barrels:** 30 inches with long forcing cones of approximately 14 inches. Receiver is ½-inch wider than 682 model for improved handling. **Stock:** Hand rubbed oil finished select walnut with Schnabel fore-end. Features include selective single adjustable trigger, manual safety, tapered 8mm to 10mm rib.

Price: $4,755.00
Price: Skeet $5,225.00

BERETTA DT11

Gauge: 12. 3-inch chambers. Competition model offered in Sporting, Skeet and Trap models. **Barrels:** 30, 32, 34 inches. Top rib has hollowed bridges. **Stock:** Hand-checkered buttstock and fore-end. Hand-rubbed oil, Tru-Oil or wax finish. Adjustable comb on skeet and trap models. Newly designed receiver, top lever, safety/selector button.

Price: From $8,999

BERETTA SV10 PERENNIA

Gauge: 12, 20. 3-inch chambers. **Barrels:** 26 or 28 inches. **Weight:** 6.5 to 7.3 pounds. **Stock:** Oil-finished walnut with semi-beavertail fore-end, newly designed fore-end latching system. Kick-Off recoil reduction system is optional. Ejection system can be set to automatic or extractors only. Floral engraving. Perennia III model has higher-grade wood, removable trigger group, and more engraving. Also available in SV10 Prevail Sporting and Trap models.

Price: Perennia I $2,890.00
Price: Perennia III $3,950.00
Price: Prevail Sporting $3,300.00
Price: Prevail Trap $3,000.00

BERETTA ULTRALIGHT

Gauge: 12, 2-3/4" chambers. **Barrel:** 26", 28", Mobilchoke tubes. **Weight:** About 5 lbs., 13 oz. **Stock:** Select American walnut with checkered grip and fore-end. **Features:** Low-profile aluminum alloy receiver with titanium breech face insert. Electroless nickel receiver with game scene engraving. Single selective trigger; automatic safety. Introduced 1992. Ultralight Deluxe except has matte electroless nickel finish receiver with gold game scene engraving; matte oil-finished, select walnut stock and fore-end. Imported from Italy by Beretta U.S.A.

Price: $2,550.00

BLASER F3 SUPERSPORT

Gauge: 12 ga., 3" chamber. **Barrel:** 32". **Weight:** 9 lbs. **Stock:** Adustable semi-custom, turkish walnut wood grade: 4. **Features:** The latest addition to the F3 family is the F3 SuperSport. The perfect blend of overall weight, balance and weight distribution make the F3 SuperSport the ideal competitor. Briley Spectrum-5 chokes, free floating barrels, adjustable barrel hanger system on o/u, chrome plated barrels full length, revolutionary ejector ball system, barrels finished in a powder coated nitride, selectable competition trigger.

Price: From $8,689.00

BROWNING CYNERGY

Gauge: .410, 12, 20, 28. **Barrel:** 26", 28", 30", 32". **Stock:** Walnut or composite. **Sights:** White bead front most models; HiViz Pro-Comp sight on some models; mid bead. **Features:** Mono-Lock hinge,

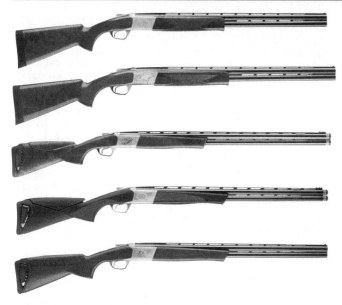

recoil-reducing interchangeable Inflex recoil pad, silver nitride receiver; striker-based trigger, ported barrel option. Models include: Cynergy Sporting, Adjustable Comb; Cynergy Sporting Composite CF; Cynergy Field, Composite; Cynergy Classic Sporting; Cynergy Classic Field; Cynergy Camo Mossy Oak New Shadow Grass; Cynergy Camo Mossy Oak New Break-Up; and Cynergy Camo Mossy Oak Brush. Imported from Japan by Browning.

Price: Field Grade Model, 12 ga. $2,800.00
Price: Field, small gauges...$2,860.00
Price: Feather model, from $2,900.00
Price: Sporting, from..$4,020.00
Price: Sporting w/adjustable comb $4,500.00
Price: Sporting composite w/adjustable comb $3,870.00
Price: Classic Field, Sporting from .... **$2,540.00 to $3,640.00**
Price: Classic Field Grade III, from.....................................$4,000.00
Price: Classic Field Grade VI, from.....................................$6,100.00
Price: Trap model..$4,280.00
Price: Trap w/adjustable comb...$4,280.00

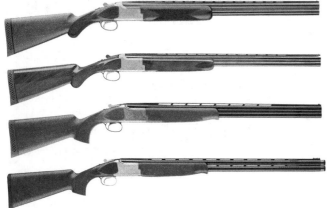

BROWNING CITORI SERIES
Gauge: 12, 20, 28 and .410. **Barrel:** 26", 28" in 28 and .410. Offered with Invector choke tubes. All 12 and 20 gauge models have back-bored barrels and Invector Plus choke system. **Weight:** 6 lbs., 8 oz. (26" .410) to 7 lbs., 13 oz. (30" 12 ga.). **Length:** 43" overall (26" bbl.). **Stock:** Dense walnut, hand checkered, full pistol grip, beavertail fore-end. Field-type recoil pad on 12 ga. field guns and trap and skeet models. **Sights:** Medium raised beads, German nickel silver. **Features:** Barrel selector integral with safety, automatic ejectors, three-piece takedown. Citori 625 Field (intr. 2008) includes Vector Pro extended forcing cones, new wood checkering patterns, silver-nitride finish with high-relief engraving, gloss oil finish with Grade II/III walnut with radius pistol grip, Schnabel forearm, 12 gauge, three Invector Plus choke tubes. Citori 625 Sporting (intr. 2008) includes standard

and adjustable combs, 32", 30", and 28" barrels, five Diamond Grade extended Invector Plus choke tubes. Triple Trigger System allows adjusting length of pull and choice of wide checkered, narrow smooth, and wide smooth canted trigger shoe. HiViz Pro-Comp fiber-optic front sights. Imported from Japan by Browning.

Price: Lightning, from $1,990.00
Price: White Lightning, from $2,070.00
Price: Superlight Feather $2,390.00
Price: Lightning Feather, combo 20 and 28 ga. $3,580.00
Price: 625 Field, 12, 20 or 28 ga. and 410. Weighs
     6 lbs. 12 oz. to 7 lbs. 14 oz. $2,630.00
Price: 625 Sporting, 12, 20 or 28 ga. and 410,
     standard comb, intr. 2008...$3,550.00

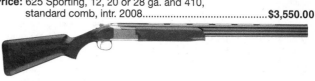

BROWNING 725 CITORI
Gauge: 12, 3" chambers. **Barrel:** 26, 28, 30". **Weight:** 7.25 to 7.6 lbs. **Length:** 43.75 to 50". **Stock:** Gloss oil finish grade II/III walnut. Features include a new receiver that is significantly lower in profile than other 12-gauge Citori models. Other features include a mechanical trigger, Vector Pro lengthened forcing cones, three Invector-DS choke tubes, silver nitride finish with high relief engraving.

Price: 725 Field $2,470.00
Price: 725 Sporting...$3,140.00

BROWNING CITORI HIGH GRADE SERIES
Similar to standard Citori except has engraved hunting scenes and gold inlays, high-grade, hand-oiled walnut stock and forearm. Introduced 2000. From Browning.

Price: Grade III Lightning, engraved gray receiver,
     introduced 2005, from $4,670.00
Price: Grade VI Lightning, engraved gray or blue receiver,
     introduced 2005, from $7,340.00

BROWNING CITORI XT TRAP
Gauge: 12. **Barrels:** 30" or 32", Invector-Plus choke tubes, adjustable comb and buttplate. **Features:** Engraved silver nitride receiver with gold highlights, vented side barrel rib. Introduced 1999. Imported by Browning.

Price: XT Trap $2,960.00
Price: XT Trap w/adjustable comb.......................................$3,390.00
Price: XT Trap Gold w/adjustable comb, introduced 2005....$5,720.00

CAESAR GUERINI ELLIPSE
Gauge: 12, 20, 28 gauge, also 20/28 gauge combo. Some models are available in 410 bore. **Barrels:** All standard lengths from 26 to 32 inches. **Weight:** 5.5 to 8.8 lbs. **Stock:** High grade walnut with hand-rubbed oil finish. **Features:** A wide range of over/under models designed for the field, sporting clays, skeet and trap shooting. The models listed below are representative of some of the different models and variants. Many optional features are offered including high grade wood and engraving, and extra sets of barrels. Made it Italy and imported by Caesar Guerini USA.

Price: Ellipse $4,325.00

Price: Ellipse Curve..$6,795.00
Price: Ellipse EVO Sporting $6,695.00
Price: Magnus...$4,530.00
Price: Maxum..$6,175.00
Price: Forum..$10,300.00
Price: Woodlander $3,350.00
Price: Invictus Sporting.....................................$6,750.00

CONNECTICUT SHOTGUN A10 AMERICAN

Gauge: 12, 20, 28, 2 ¾" chambers, .410, 3-inches. Sidelock design. **Barrels:** 26, 28, 30 or 32" with choice of fixed or interchangeable chokes. **Weight:** 6.3 lbs. **Stock:** Hand rubbed oil finished, hand checkered at 24 lines per inch. Black, English or Turkish walnut offered in numerous grades. Pistol or Price of Wales grip, short or long tang. **Features:** Low profile, shallow frame full sidelock. Single-selective trigger, automatic ejectors. Engraved models available. Made in the U.S.A. by Connecticut Shotgun Mfg. Co.
Price: 12 gauge from $8,995.00
Price: Smaller gauges from $9,495.00

CONNECTICUT SHOTGUN MODEL 21 O/U

Gauge: 20, 3" chambers. **Barrels:** 26" to 32" chrome-lined, back-bored with extended forcing cones. **Weight:** 6.3 lbs. **Stock:** A Fancy (2X) American walnut, standard point checkering, choice of straight or pistol grip. Higher grade walnut is optional. **Features:** The over/under version of Conn. Shotgun's replica of the Winchester Model 21 side-by-side, built using the same machining, tooling, techniques and finishes. Low profile shallow frame with blued receiver. Pigeon and Grand American grades are available. Made in the U.S.A. by Connecticut Shotgun Mfg. Co.
Price: From $2,995.00

CZ SPORTER

Gauge: 12, 3" chambers. **Barrel:** 30", 32" chrome-lined, back-bored with extended forcing cones. **Weight:** 8.5 lbs. **Length:** NA. **Stock:** Neutral cast stock with an adjustable comb, trap style fore-end, pistol grip and ambidextrous palm swells. No. 3 grade Circassian walnut. At lowest position, drop at comb: 1-5/8"; drop at heel: 2-3/8"; length of pull: 14-1/2". **Features:** Designed for Sporting Clays and FITASC competition. Hand engraving, satin black-finished receiver. Tapered adjustable rib with center bead and a red fiber-optic front bead, 10 choke tubes with wrench, single selective trigger, automatic ejectors, thin rubber pad with slick plastic top. Introduced 2008. Made in the Czech Repubic and imported by CZ-USA.
Price: $2,250.00
Price: Standard grade...$1,899.00

CZ CANVASBACK

Gauge: 12, 20, 3" chambers; 28 ga., .410 bore. **Barrel:** 26", 28". **Weight:** 7.3 lbs. **Length:** NA. **Stock:** Round-knob pistol grip, Schnabel fore-end, Turkish walnut. **Features:** Single selective trigger, set of 5 screw-in chokes, black chrome finished receiver. From CZ-USA.
Price: 12 or 20 ga. $827.00
Price: 28 or .410 ....$959.00

CZ MALLARD

Gauge: 12, 20, 28, .410, 3" chambers. **Barrel:** 26". **Weight:** 7.7 lbs. **Length:** NA. **Stock:** Round-knob pistol grip, Schnabel fore-end, Turkish walnut. **Features:** Double triggers and extractors, coin finished receiver, multi chokes. From CZ-USA.
Price: $583.00

CZ REDHEAD

Gauge: 12, 20, .410 (3" chambers), 28 (2 3/4"). **Barrel:** 28". **Weight:** 7.4 lbs. **Length:** NA. **Stock:** Round-knob pistol grip, Schnabel fore-end, Turkish walnut. **Features:** Single selective triggers and extractors (12 & 20 ga.), screw-in chokes (12, 20, 28 ga.) choked IC and Mod (.410), coin finished receiver, multi chokes. From CZ-USA.
Price: Deluxe $953.00
Price: Mini (28, .410) $960.00
Price: Target $1,389.00

CZ SUPER SCROLL COMBO

Gauge: 20 and 28 combo. **Barrels:** 30 inches for both gauges with five choke tubes for each set. **Stock:** Grave V Turkish walnut with Schnabel fore-end, rounded grip. **Weight:** 6.7 pounds. **Features:** Ornate hand-engraved scrollwork on receiver, faux sideplates, triggerguard and mono-block. Comes in a custom-fitted aluminum case.
Price: $3,899.00

CZ UPLAND STERLING

Gauge: 12, 3-inch chambers. **Barrels:** 28 inches with ventilated rib, fiber optic sight, five choke tubes. **Stock:** Turkish walnut with stippled gripping surfaces. **Weight:** 7.5 pounds. Lady Sterling has smaller stock dimensions.
Price: $999.00
Price: Lady Sterling..$1,281.00

CZ WINGSHOOTER

Gauge: 12, 20, 28 & .410 ga., 2-3/4" chamber. **Barrel:** 28" flat ventilated rib. **Weight:** 6.3 lbs. **Length:** 45.5". **Stock:** Turkish walnut. **Features:** This colorful Over and Under shotgun has the same old world craftsmanship as all of our shotguns but with a new stylish look. This elegant hand engraved work of art is available in four gauges and its eye-catching engraving will stand alone in the field or range. 12 and 20 gauge models have auto ejectors, while the 28 gauge and .410 have extractors only. Heavily engraved scroll work with special side plate design, mechanical selective triggers, box Lock frame design, 18 LPI checkering, coil spring operated hammers, chrome lined, 5 interchangeable choke tubes and special engraved skeleton butt plate.
Price: 12 or 20 ga. $999.00
Price: 28 ga. or .410 ....$1,040.00

ESCORT OVER/UNDER

Gauge: 12, 3" chamber. **Barrel:** 28". **Weight:** 7.4 lbs. **Stock:** Walnut or select walnut with Trio recoil pad; synthetic stock with adjustable comb. Three adjustment spacers. **Sights:** Bronze front bead. **Features:** Blued barrels, blued or nickel receiver. Trio recoil pad. Five interchangeable chokes (SK, IC, M, IM, F); extractors or ejectors (new, 2008), barrel selector. Hard case available. Introduced 2007. Imported from Turkey by Legacy Sports International.
Price: From $641.00

FAUSTI CLASSIC ROUND BODY

Gauge: 16, 20, 28. **Barrels:** 28 or 30". **Weight:** 5.8 to 6.3 lbs. **Length:** 45.5 to 47.5". **Stock:** Turkish walnut Prince of Wales style with oil finish. Features include automatic ejectors, single selective trigger, laser-engraved receiver.
Price: 20 gauge...$4,950.00
Price: 16, 28 gauge, .410...$5,540.00

FAUSTI CALEDON

Gauge: 12, 16, 20, 28 and .410 bore. **Barrels:** 26, 28 or 30". **Weight:** 5.8 to 7.3 lbs. **Stock:** Turkish walnut with oil finish, round pistol grip. **Features:** Automatic ejectors, single selective trigger, laser-engraved receiver. Coin finish receiver with gold inlays.
Price: 12 or 20 ga. $1,999.00
Price: 16, 28, .410...$2,569.00

FN SC-1

Gauge: 12. 2-3/4" chamber. **Barrels:** 28 or 30 inches, ported

Prices given are believed to be accurate at time of publication however, many factors affect retail pricing so exact prices are not possible.

with ventilated rib, Invector-Plus extended choke tubes. **Stock:** Laminated black or blue with adjustable comb and length-of-pull. **Weight:** 8 pounds.
Price: **$2,449.00**

FRANCHI ASPIRE
Gauge: 28 or .410. **Barrels:** 28 inches with ventilated rib and fiber optic front sight. **Stock:** Oil-finished checkered walnut with rounded pistol grip. **Weight:** 5.8 pounds. **Features:** Slim, round-action receiver with case-colored finish.
Price: **$2,299.00**

FRANCHI INSTINCT SERIES
Gauge: 12, 20 with 3" chambers. Barrels: 26 or 28". **Weight:** 5.3 to 6.4 lbs. Length: 42.5 to 44.5". **Stock:** AA-grade satin walnut (LS), A-grade (L) with rounded pistol grip and recoil pad. Single trigger, automatic ejectors, tang safety, choke tubes. LS model has aluminum alloy receiver, L model has steel receiver.
Price: (Instinct L) **$1,149.00**
Price: (Instinct LS) **$1,349.00**

KOLAR SPORTING CLAYS
Gauge: 12, 2-3/4" chambers. **Barrel:** 30", 32", 34"; extended choke tubes. **Stock:** 14-5/8"x2.5"x1-7/8"x1-3/8". French walnut. Four stock versions available. **Features:** Single selective trigger, detachable, adjustable for length; overbored barrels with long forcing cones; flat tramline rib; matte blue finish. Made in U.S. by Kolar.
Price: Standard...**$9,595.00**
Price: Prestige..**$14,190.00**
Price: Elite Gold...**$16,590.00**
Price: Legend...**$17,090.00**
Price: Select...**$22,590.00**
Price: Custom .... **Price on request**

KOLAR AAA COMPETITION TRAP
Gauge: 12. Similar to the Sporting Clays gun except has 32" O/U /34" Unsingle or 30" O/U /34" Unsingle barrels as an over/under, unsingle, or combination set. Stock dimensions are 14.5"x2.5"x1.5"; American or French walnut; step parallel rib standard. Contact maker for full listings. Made in U.S.A. by Kolar.
Price: Single bbl. from **$8,495.00**
Price: O/U from..**$11,695.00**

KOLAR AAA COMPETITION SKEET
Similar to the Sporting Clays gun except has 28" or 30" barrels with Kolarite AAA sub gauge tubes; stock of American or French walnut with matte finish; flat tramline rib; under barrel adjustable for point of impact. Many options available. Contact maker for complete listing. Made in U.S.A. by Kolar.
Price: Max Lite, from..**$12,995.00**

KRIEGHOFF K-80 SPORTING CLAYS
Gauge: 12. **Barrel:** 28", 30", 32", 34" with choke tubes. **Weight:** About 8 lbs. **Stock:** #3 Sporting stock designed for gun-down shooting. **Features:** Standard receiver with satin nickel finish and classic scroll engraving. Selective mechanical trigger adjustable for position. Choice of tapered flat or 8mm parallel flat barrel rib. Free-floating barrels. Aluminum case. Imported from Germany by Krieghoff International, Inc.
Price: Standard grade with five choke tubes, from **$11,395.00**

KRIEGHOFF K-80 SKEET
Gauge: 12, 2-3/4" chambers. **Barrel:** 28", 30", 32", (skeet & skeet), optional choke tubes). **Weight:** About 7.75 lbs. **Stock:** American skeet or straight skeet stocks, with palm-swell grips. Walnut. **Features:** Satin gray receiver finish. Selective mechanical trigger adjustable for position. Choice of ventilated 8mm parallel flat rib or ventilated

8-12mm tapered flat rib. Introduced 1980. Imported from Germany by Krieghoff International, Inc.
Price: Standard, skeet chokes...**$10,595.00**
Price: Skeet Special (28", 30", 32" tapered flat rib,
   skeet & skeet choke tubes) **$9,100.00**

KRIEGHOFF K-80 TRAP
Gauge: 12, 2-3/4" chambers. **Barrel:** 30", 32" (Imp. Mod. & Full or choke tubes). **Weight:** About 8.5 lbs. **Stock:** Four stock dimensions or adjustable stock available; all have palm-swell grips. Checkered European walnut. **Features:** Satin nickel receiver. Selective mechanical trigger, adjustable for position. Ventilated step rib. Introduced 1980. Imported from Germany by Krieghoff International, Inc.
Price: K-80 O/U (30", 32", Imp. Mod. & Full), from...............**$8,850.00**
Price: K-80 Unsingle (32", 34", Full), standard, from..........**$10,080.00**
Price: K-80 Combo (two-barrel set), standard, from **$13,275.00**

KRIEGHOFF K-20
Similar to the K-80 except built on a 20-gauge frame. Designed for skeet, sporting clays and field use. Offered in 20, 28 and .410; 28", 30" and 32" barrels. Imported from Germany by Krieghoff International Inc.
Price: K-20, 20 gauge, from..**$11,395.00**
Price: K-20, 28 gauge, from..**$12,395.00**
Price: K-20, .410, from..**$12,395.00**

LEBEAU-COURALLY BOSS-VEREES
Gauge: 12, 20, 2-3/4" chambers. **Barrel:** 25" to 32". **Weight:** To customer specifications. **Stock:** Exhibition-quality French walnut. **Features:** Boss-type sidelock with automatic ejectors; single or double triggers; chopper lump barrels. A custom gun built to customer specifications. Imported from Belgium by Wm. Larkin Moore.
Price: From **$96,000.00**

LJUTIC LM-6 SUPER DELUXE
Gauge: 12. **Barrel:** 28" to 34", choked to customer specs for live birds, trap, international trap. **Weight:** To customer specs. **Stock:** To customer specs. Oil finish, hand checkered. **Features:** Custom-made gun. Hollow-milled rib, pull or release trigger, push-button opener in front of trigger guard. From Ljutic Industries.
Price: Super Deluxe LM-6 O/U **$19,995.00**
Price: Over/Under combo (interchangeable single barrel,
   two trigger guards, one for single trigger,
   one for doubles)..**$27,995.00**
Price: Extra over/under barrel sets, 29"-32"..........................**$6,995.00**

MERKEL MODEL 2001EL O/U
Gauge: 12, 20, 3" chambers, 28, 2-3/4" chambers. **Barrel:** 12-28"; 20, 28 ga.-26.75". **Weight:** About 7 lbs. (12 ga.). **Stock:** Oil-finished walnut; English or pistol grip. **Features:** Self-cocking Blitz boxlock action with cocking indicators; Kersten double cross-bolt lock; silver-grayed receiver with engraved hunting scenes; coil spring ejectors; single selective or double triggers. Imported from Germany by Merkel USA.
Price: **$9,995.00**
Price: Model 2001EL Sporter; full pistol grip stock **$9,995.00**

MERKEL MODEL 2000CL
Similar to Model 2001EL except scroll-engraved case-hardened receiver; 12, 20, 28 gauge. Imported from Germany by Merkel USA.
Price: **$8,495.00**
Price: Model 2016 CL; 16 gauge **$8,495.00**

SHOTGUNS Over/Unders

MOSSBERG SILVER RESERVE II
Gauge: 12, 3-inch chambers. **Barrels:** 28 inches with ventilated rib, choke tubes. **Stock:** Select black walnut with satin finish. **Sights:** Metal bead. Available with extractors or automatic ejectors. Also offered in Sport model with ported barrels with wide rib, fiber optic front and middle bead sights. Super Sport has extra wide high rib, optional adjustable comb.
Price: Field $736.00
Price: Field w/ejectors $824.00
Price: Sport...$905.00
Price: Sport w/ejectors $1,019.00
Price: Super Sport w/ejectors............................$1,108.00
Price: Super Sport w/ejectors, adj. comb $1,216.00

PERAZZI MX8/MX8 TRAP/SKEET
Gauge: 12, 20 2 ¾" chambers. **Barrel:** Trap: 29.5" (Imp. Mod. & Extra Full), 31.5" (Full & Extra Full). Choke tubes optional. Skeet: 27-5/8" (skeet & skeet). **Weight:** About 8.5 lbs. (trap); 7 lbs., 15 oz. (skeet). **Stock:** Interchangeable and custom made to customer specs. **Features:** Has detachable and interchangeable trigger group with flat V springs. Flat 7/16" vent rib. Many options available. Imported from Italy by Perazzi U.S.A., Inc.
Price: Trap from $9,861.00
Price: Skeet from $9,861.00

PERAZZI MX8
Gauge: 12, 20 2 ¾" chambers. **Barrel:** 28-3/8" (Imp. Mod. & Extra Full), 29.5" (choke tubes). **Weight:** 7 lbs., 12 oz. **Stock:** Special specifications. **Features:** Has single selective trigger; flat 7/16" x 5/16" vent rib. Many options available. Imported from Italy by Perazzi U.S.A., Inc.
Price: Standard, from $9,861.00
Price: Sporting, from $9,861.00
Price: SC3 Grade (variety of engraving patterns) from $21,000.00
Price: SCO Grade (more intricate engraving/inlays) from ...$36,000.00

PERAZZI MX12 HUNTING
Gauge: 12, 2-3/4" chambers. **Barrel:** 26.75", 27.5", 28-3/8", 29.5" (Mod. & Full); choke tubes available in 27-5/8", 29.5" only (MX12C). **Weight:** 7 lbs., 4 oz. **Stock:** To customer specs; interchangeable. **Features:** Single selective trigger; coil springs used in action; Schnabel fore-end tip. Imported from Italy by Perazzi U.S.A., Inc.
Price: From $11,698.00
Price: MX12C (with choke tubes) from $12,316.00

PERAZZI MX20 HUNTING
Similar to the MX12 except 20 ga. frame size. Non-removable trigger group. Available in 20, 28, .410 with 2-3/4" or 3" chambers. 26" standard, and choked Mod. & Full. Weight is 6 lbs., 6 oz. Imported from Italy by Perazzi U.S.A., Inc.
Price: From $11,900.00
Price: MX20C (with choke tubes) from $13,700.00

PERAZZI MX10
Gauge: 12, 2-3/4" chambers. **Barrel:** 29.5", 31.5" (fixed chokes). **Weight:** NA. **Stock:** Walnut; cheekpiece adjustable for elevation and cast. **Features:** Adjustable rib; vent side rib. Externally selective trigger. Available in single barrel, combo, over/under trap, skeet, pigeon and sporting models. Introduced 1993. Imported from Italy by Perazzi U.S.A., Inc.
Price: From $11,900.00

PERAZZI MX2000S
Gauge: 12, 20. **Barrels:** 29.5, 30.75, 31.5 inches with fixed I/M and Full chokes, or interchangeable. Competition model with features similar to MX8.
Price: $12,500.00

PERAZZI MX15 UNSINGLE TRAP
Gauge: 12, 20. **Barrel:** 34 inches with fixed Full choke. **Features:** Bottom single barrel with 6-notch adjustable rib, adjustable stock, drop-out trigger. , or interchangeable. Competition model with features similar to MX8.
Price: $8,395.00

PIOTTI BOSS
Gauge: 12, 20. **Barrel:** 26" to 32", chokes as specified. **Weight:** 6.5 to 8 lbs. **Stock:** Dimensions to customer specs. Best quality figured walnut. **Features:** Essentially a custom-made gun with many options. Introduced 1993. Imported from Italy by Wm. Larkin Moore.
Price: From $75,000.00

RIZZINI OMNIMUM
Gauge: 12, 20. **Barrels:** 26.5, 28 or 30 inches with choke tubes, ventilated rib. **Stock:** Walnut with pistol grip, Schnabel fore-end. **Features:** Entry level Rizzini over/under boxlock with blue or coin finish, scroll engraving, automatic ejectors and single-selective trigger.
Price: From $2,632.00

RIZZINI S790 EMEL
Gauge: 20, 28, .410. **Barrel:** 26", 27.5" (Imp. Cyl. & Imp. Mod.). **Weight:** About 6 lbs. **Stock:** 14"x1.5"x2-1/8". Extra fancy select walnut. **Features:** Boxlock action with profuse engraving; automatic ejectors; single selective trigger; silvered receiver. Comes with Nizzoli leather case. Introduced 1996. Made in Italy by Battista Rizzini and distributed by Wm. Larkin Moore & Co.
Price: From $14,600.00

RIZZINI S792 EMEL
Similar to S790 EMEL except dummy sideplates with extensive engraving coverage. Nizzoli leather case. Introduced 1996. Made in Italy by Battista Rizzini and distributed by Wm. Larkin Moore & Co.
Price: From $15,500.00

RIZZINI UPLAND EL
Gauge: 12, 16, 20, 28, .410. **Barrel:** 26", 27.5", Mod. & Full, Imp. Cyl. & Imp. Mod. choke tubes. **Weight:** About 6.6 lbs. **Stock:** 14.5"x1-1/2"x2.25". **Features:** Boxlock action; single selective trigger; ejectors; profuse engraving on silvered receiver. Comes with fitted case. Introduced 1996. Made in Italy by Battista Rizzini and distributed by Wm. Larkin Moore & Co.
Price: From $5,200.00

RIZZINI ARTEMIS
Gauge: 12, 16, 20, 28, .410. Same as Upland EL model except dummy sideplates with extensive game scene engraving. Fancy European walnut stock. Fitted case. Introduced 1996. Imported from Italy by Fierce Products and by Wm. Larkin Moore & Co.
Price: From $4,196.00

RIZZINI S782 EMEL
Gauge: 12, 2-3/4" chambers. **Barrel:** 26", 27.5" (Imp. Cyl. & Imp. Mod.). **Weight:** About 6.75 lbs. **Stock:** 14.5"x1.5"x2.25". Extra fancy select walnut. **Features:** Boxlock action with dummy sideplates, extensive engraving with gold inlaid game birds, silvered receiver, automatic

ejectors.

Prices given are believed to be accurate at time of publication however, many factors affect retail pricing so exact prices are not possible.

ejectors, single selective trigger. Nizzoli leather case. Introduced 1996. Made in Italy by Battista Rizzini and distributed by Wm. Larkin Moore & Co.
Price: From $18,800.00

RUGER RED LABEL
Gauge: 12. 3-inch chambers. **Barrels:** 26, 28 or 30 inches with ventilated rib. Back bored with two-inch forcing cones. Five steel-shot compatible Briley choke tubes (IC, M, F, Skt, Skt). **Stock:** Checkered American walnut with soft Pachmayr pad, slim tapered fore-end. **Weight:** 7.5 to 7.9 lbs. **Features:** Single selective mechanical trigger, two-position safety/barrel selector. Custom molded semi-soft case. Re-introduced in 2014 with improved inner workings, new center of gravity.
Price: $1,399.00

SKB 590 FIELD
Gauge: 12, 20 with 3" chambers. **Barrel:** 26", 28", 30". Three SKB Competion choke tubes (IC, M, F). Lengthened forcing cones. **Stock:** Oil finished walnut with Pachmayr recoil pad. **Weight:** 7.1 to 7.9 lbs. **Sights:** NA. **Features:** Boxlock action, bright blue finish with laser engraved receiver. Automatic ejectors, single trigger with selector switch incorporated in thumb-operated tang safety. Youth Model has 13" length of pull. Imported from Turkey by GU, Inc.
Price: $1,300.00

SKB 90TSS
Gauge: 12, 20 with 2 ¾-inch chambers. **Barrel:** 28, 30, 32 inches. Three SKB Competion choke tubes (SK, IC, M for Skeet and Sporting Models; IM, M, F for Trap). Lengthened forcing cones. **Stock:** Oil finished walnut with Pachmayr recoil pad. **Weight:** 7.1 to 7.9 lbs. **Sights:** Ventilated rib with target sights. **Features:** Boxlock action, bright blue finish with laser engraved receiver. Automatic ejectors, single trigger with selector switch incorporated in thumb-operated tang safety. Sporting and Trap models have adjustable comb and buttpad system. Imported from Turkey by GU, Inc.
Price: Skeet $1,470.00
Price: Sporting Clays, Trap...............................$1,720.00

STEVENS MODEL 512 GOLD WING
Gauge: 12, 20, 28, .410; 2-3/4" and 3" chambers. **Barrel:** 26", 28". **Weight:** 6 to 8 lbs. **Sights:** NA. **Features:** Five screw-in choke tubes with 12, 20, and 28 gauge; .410 has fixed M/IC chokes. Black chrome, sculpted receiver with a raised gold pheasant, laser engraved trigger guard and fore-end latch. Turkish walnut stock finished in satin lacquer and beautifully laser engraved with fleur-de-lis checkering on the side panels, wrist and Schnabel forearm.
Price: $689.00

STOEGER CONDOR
Gauge: 12, 20, 2-3/4" 3" chambers; 16, .410. **Barrel:** 22", 24", 26", 28", 30". **Weight:** 5.5 to 7.8 lbs. **Sights:** Brass bead. **Features:** IC, M, or F screw-in choke tubes with each gun. Oil finished hardwood with pistol grip and fore-end. Auto safety, single trigger, automatic extractors.
Price: From .... $449.00 to $669.00
Price: Combo with 12 and 20 ga. barrel sets $899.00

TRISTAR FIELD HUNTER
Gauge: 12. **Barrels:** 26 or 28 inches. **Weight:** 7.2 to 7.4 pounds. Features similar to Setter series plus automatic ejectors, higher-grade wood, chrome-lined barrels, fiber-optic front sight, five choke tubes.
Price: $729.00

TRISTAR HUNTER EX
Gauge: 12, 20, 28, .410. **Barrel:** 26", 28". **Weight:** 5.7 lbs. (.410); 6.0 lbs. (20, 28), 7.2-7.4 lbs. (12). Chrome-lined steel mono-block barrel, five Beretta-style choke tubes (SK, IC, M, IM, F). Length: NA. **Stock:** Walnut, cut checkering. 14.25"x1.5"x2-3/8". **Sights:** Brass front sight. **Features:** All have extractors, engraved receiver, sealed actions, self-adjusting locking bolts, single selective trigger, ventilated rib. 28 ga. and .410 built on true frames. Five-year warranty. Imported from Italy by Tristar Sporting Arms Ltd.
Price: From $630.00

TRISTAR SETTER
Gauge: 12, 20 with 3-inch chambers. **Barrels:** 28" (12 ga.), 26" (20 ga.) with ventilated rib, three Beretta-style choke tubes. **Weight:** 6.3 to 7.2 pounds. **Stock:** High gloss wood. Single selective trigger, extractors.
Price: $559.00

WEBLEY & SCOTT O/U SERIES
Gauge: 12, 20, 28, .410. **Barrels:** 26, 28, 30", five interchangeable choke tubes. **Weight:** 5.5 to 7.5 lbs. **Stock:** Checkered Turkish walnut with recoil pad. **Features:** Automatic ejectors, single selective trigger, ventilated rib, tang selector/safety. 2000 Premium Model has higher-grade select walnut stock, color case hardening. 3000 Sidelock Model is a high-grade gun with 7-pin sidelocks, oil-finished premium-grade walnut stock with checkered butt, jeweled monobloc walls, and comes with high quality, fleeced line lockable case. Made in Turkey and imported by Centurion International.
Price: 900 Sporting...$1,250.00
Price: 2000 Premium $2,500.00
Price: 3000 Sidelock...$6,000.00

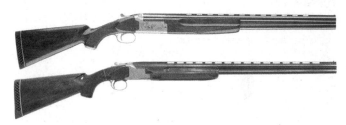

WINCHESTER MODEL 101
Gauge: 12, 2-3/4", 3" chambers. **Barrel:** 28", 30", 32", ported, Invector Plus choke system. **Weight:** 7 lbs. 6 oz. to 7 lbs. 12. oz. **Stock:** Checkered high-gloss grade II/III walnut stock, Pachmayr Decelerator sporting pad. **Features:** Chrome-plated chambers; back-bored barrels; tang barrel selector/safety; Signature extended choke tubes. Model 101 Field comes with solid brass bead front sight, three tubes, engraved receiver. Model 101 Sporting has adjustable trigger, 10mm runway rib, white mid-bead, Tru-Glo front sight, 30" and 32" barrels. Camo version of Model 101 Field comes with full-coverage Mossy Oak Duck Blind pattern. Model 101 Pigeon Grade Trap has 10mm steel runway rib, mid-bead sight, interchangeable fiber-optic front sight, porting and vented side ribs, adjustable trigger shoe, fixed raised comb or adjustable comb, Grade III/IV walnut, 30" or 32" barrels, molded ABS hard case. Reintroduced 2008. Made in Belgium by FN.
Price: Field $1,870.00
Price: Sporting..$2,320.00
Price: Pigeon Grade Trap.....................................$2,470.00
Price: Pigeon Grade Trap w/adj. comb................$2,630.00

ARRIETA SIDELOCK DOUBLE

Gauge: 12, 16, 20, 28, .410. **Barrel:** Length and chokes to customer specs. **Weight:** To customer specs. **Stock:** To customer specs. Straight English with checkered butt (standard), or pistol grip. Select European walnut with oil finish. **Features:** Essentially custom gun with myriad options. H&H pattern hand-detachable sidelocks, selective automatic ejectors, double triggers (hinged front) standard. Some have self-opening action. Finish and engraving to customer specs. Imported from Spain by Quality Arms, Wm. Larking Moore and others.

Price: Model 557..$6,970.00
Price: Model 570..$7,350.00
Price: Model 578..$8,200.00
Price: Model 600 Imperial...$12,125.00
Price: Model 801..$19,850.00
Price: Model 802..$19,850.00
Price: Model 803..$15,000.00
Price: Model 931..$36,000.00

AYA MODEL 4/53

Gauge: 12, 16, 20, 28, 410. **Barrel:** 26", 27", 28", 30". **Weight:** To customer specifications. Length: To customer specifications. **Features:** Hammerless boxlock action; double triggers; light scroll engraving; automatic safety; straight grip oil finished walnut stock; checkered butt. Made in Spain. Imported by New England Custom Gun Service.

Price: $3,895.00
Price: No. 2..$5,895.00
Price: No. 2 Rounded Action.....................................$6,299.00

AYA MODEL ADARRA

Gauge: 12, 16, 20, 28, 410. **Barrel:** 26", 28". **Weight:** Approx. 6.7 lbs. **Features:** Hammerless boxlock action; double triggers; light scroll engraving; automatic safety; straight grip oil finished walnut stock; checkered butt. Made in Spain. Imported by New England Custom Gun Service.

Price: $4,800.00

BERETTA 481 PARALELLO

Gauge: 12, 3" chamber. **Barrel:** 26", 28", 30". **Weight:** 7.1 lbs. **Stock:** English-style straight grip, splinter fore-end. Select European walnut, checkered, oil finish. **Features:** Round action, Optima-Choke Tubes. Automatic ejection or mechanical extraction. Firing-pin block safety, manual or automatic, open top-lever safety. Imported from Italy by Beretta U.S.A.

Price: $5,350.00

CIMARRON 1878 COACH GUN

Gauge: 12. 3-inch chambers. **Barrels:** 20 or 26 inches. **Weight:** 8 to 9 pounds. **Stock:** Hardwood. External hammers, double triggers. Finish: Blue, Cimarron "USA", Cimarron "Original."

Price: Blue .... $575.00 (20") to $594.00 (26")
Price: Original .... $675.00 to $694.00
Price: USA .... $832.00 to $851.00

CIMARRON 1881 HAMMERLESS

Gauge: 12. 3-inch chambers. **Barrels:** 20, 22, 26, 28 or 30 inches. **Stock:** Standard or Deluxe wood with rounded pistol grip. Single trigger, extractors, bead front sight.

Price: Deluxe..$722.00 to $761.00

CONNECTICUT SHOTGUN MANUFACTURING CO. RBL

Gauge: 12, 16, 20. **Barrel:** 26", 28" 30", 32". **Weight:** NA. **Length:** NA. **Stock:** NA. **Features:** Round-action SxS shotguns made in the USA. Scaled frames, five TruLock choke tubes. Deluxe fancy grade walnut buttstock and fore-end. Quick Change recoil pad in two lengths.

Various dimensions and options available depending on gauge.
Price: 12 gauge $3,795.00
Price: 16 gauge $3,795.00
Price: 20 gauge Special Custom Model $7,995.00

CONNECTICUT SHOTGUN MANUFACTURING CO. MODEL 21

Gauge: 12, 16, 20, 28, .410. A faithful re-creation of the famous Winchester Model 21. Many options and upgrades are available. Each frame is machined from specially produced proof steel. The 28 and .410 guns are available on the standard frame or on a newly engineered small frame. These are custom guns and are made to order to the buyer's individual specifications, wood, stock dimensions, barrel lengths, chokes, finishes and engraving.

Price: 12, 16 or 20 gauge from $15,000.00
Price: 28 or .410 from $18,000.00

CZ BOBWHITE, RINGNECK

Gauge: 12, 20, 28, .410. (5 screw-in chokes in 12 and 20 ga. and fixed chokes in IC and Mod in .410). **Barrel:** 26 or 28". **Weight:** 6.5 lbs. **Stock:** Turkish walnut with straight English-style grip and double triggers (Bobwhite) or conventional American pistol grip with a single trigger (Ringneck). Both are hand checkered 20 lpi. **Features:** Both color case-hardened shotguns are hand engraved.

Price: Bobwhite $789.00
Price: Bobwhite 28 or .410 ....$974.00
Price: Ringneck...$1,036.00
Price: Ringneck Target...$1,298.00

CZ HAMMER COACH

Gauge: 12, 3" chambers. **Barrel:** 20". **Weight:** 6.7 lbs. **Features:** Following in the tradition of the guns used by the stagecoach guards of the 1880's, this cowboy gun features double triggers, 19th century color case-hardening and fully functional external hammers.

Price: $922.00
Price: Classic model w/30" bbls.................................$963.00

EMF OLD WEST HAMMER

Gauge: 12. **Barrel:** 20". **Weight:** 8 lbs. **Length:** 37" overall. **Stock:** Smooth walnut with steel butt place. **Sights:** Large brass bead. **Features:** Colt-style exposed hammers rebounding type; blued receiver and barrels; cylinder bore. Introduced 2006. Imported from China for EMF by TTN.

Price: $474.90

FAUSTI DEA SERIES

Gauge: 12, 16, 20, 28, .410. **Barrel:** 26, 28, or 30 inches. **Weight:** 6 to 6.8 lbs. **Stock:** AAA walnut, oil finished. Straight grip, checkered butt, classic fore-end. **Features:** Automatic ejectors, single non-selective trigger. Duetto model is in 28 gauge with extra set of .410 barrels. Made in Italy and imported by Fausti, USA.

Price: 12 or 20 ....$3,350.00
Price: 16, 28, .410..$3,990.00
Price: Duetto $5,300.00
Price: Round action $5,899.00

FOX, A.H.

Gauge: 16, 20, 28, .410. **Barrel:** Length and chokes to customer specifications. Rust-blued Chromox or Krupp steel. **Weight:** 5-1/2 to 6.75 lbs. **Stock:** Dimensions to customer specifications. Hand-checkered Turkish Circassian walnut with hand-rubbed oil finish. Straight, semi or full pistol grip; splinter, Schnabel or beavertail fore-end; traditional pad, hard rubber buttplate or skeleton butt. **Features:** Boxlock action with automatic ejectors; double or Fox single selective

Prices given are believed to be accurate at time of publication however, many factors affect retail pricing so exact prices are not possible.

trigger. Scalloped, rebated and color case-hardened receiver; hand finished and handengraved. Grades differ in engraving, inlays, grade of wood, amount of hand finishing. Introduced 1993. Made in U.S. by Connecticut Shotgun Mfg.

Price: CE Grade $19,500.00
Price: XE Grade $22,000.00
Price: DE Grade $25,000.00
Price: FE Grade $30,000.00
Price: 28/.410 CE Grade $21,500.00
Price: 28/.410 XE Grade $24,000.00
Price: 28/.410 DE Grade $27,000.00
Price: 28/.410 FE Grade $32,000.00

GARBI MODEL 101

Gauge: 12, 16, 20, 28. **Barrel:** 26", 28", choked to customer specs. **Weight:** 5-1/2 to 7.5 lbs. **Stock:** 14.5"x2.25"x1.5". Select European walnut. Straight grip, checkered butt, classic fore-end. **Features:** Sidelock action, automatic ejectors, double triggers standard. Color case-hardened action, coin finish optional. Single trigger; beavertail fore-end, etc. optional. Hand engraved with scroll engraving. Imported from Spain by Wm. Larkin Moore.

Price: From $14,650.00

GARBI MODEL 103A, 103B

Similar to the Garbi Model 101 except has Purdey-type fine scroll and rosette engraving. Model 103B has nickel-chrome steel barrels, H&H-type easy opening mechanism; other mechanical details remain the same. Imported from Spain by Wm. Larkin Moore.

Price: Model 103A. From $21,000.00
Price: Model 103B. From $28,360.00

GARBI MODEL 200

Similar to the Garbi Model 101 except has heavy-duty locks, magnum proofed. Very fine Continental-style floral and scroll engraving, well figured walnut stock. Other mechanical features remain the same. Imported from Spain by Wm. Larkin Moore.

Price: $24,100.00

MERKEL MODEL 47E, 147E

Gauge: 12, 3" chambers, 16, 2.75" chambers, 20, 3" chambers. **Barrel:** 12, 16 ga.-28"; 20 ga.-26.75" (Imp. Cyl. & Mod., Mod. & Full). **Weight:** About 6.75 lbs. (12 ga.). **Stock:** Oil-finished walnut; straight English or pistol grip. **Features:** Anson & Deeley-type boxlock action with single selective or double triggers, automatic safety, cocking indicators. Color case-hardened receiver with standard arabesque engraving. Imported from Germany by Merkel USA.

Price: Model 47E (H&H ejectors) $4,595.00
Price: Model 147E (as above with ejectors)............$5,795.00

MERKEL MODEL 47EL, 147EL

Similar to Model 47E except H&H style sidelock action with cocking indicators, ejectors. Silver-grayed receiver and sideplates have arabesque engraving, engraved border and screws (Model 47E), or fine hunting scene engraving (Model 147E). Limited edition. Imported from Germany by Merkel USA.

Price: Model 47EL $7,195.00
Price: Model 147EL $7,695.00

MERKEL MODEL 280EL, 360EL

Similar to Model 47E except smaller frame. Greener cross bolt with double under-barrel locking lugs, fine engraved hunting scenes on silver-grayed receiver, luxury-grade wood, Anson and Deeley boxlock action. H&H ejectors, single-selective or double triggers. Introduced 2000. Imported from Germany by Merkel USA.

Price: Model 280EL (28 gauge, 28" barrel, Imp. Cyl. and Mod. chokes).. $7,695.00
Price: Model 360EL (.410, 28" barrel, Mod. and Full chokes)... $7,695.00
Price: Model 280EL Combo $11,195.00

MERKEL MODEL 280SL AND 360SL

Similar to Model 280EL and 360EL except has sidelock action, double triggers, English-style arabesque engraving. Introduced 2000. Imported from Germany by Merkel USA.

Price: Model 280SL (28 gauge, 28" barrel, Imp. Cyl. and Mod. chokes)..............................$10,995.00
Price: Model 360SL (.410, 28" barrel, Mod. and Full chokes)...$10,995.00

MERKEL MODEL 1620

Gauge: 16. **Features:** Greener crossbolt with double under-barrel locking lugs, scroll-engraved case-hardened receiver, Anson and Deeley boxlock action, Holland & Holland ejectors, English-style stock, single selective or double triggers, or pistol grip stock with single selective trgger. Imported from Germany by Merkel USA.

Price: $4,995.00
Price: Model 1620E; silvered, engraved receiver $5,995.00
Price: Model 1620 Combo; 16- and 20-gauge two-barrel set $7,695.00
Price: Model 1620EL; upgraded wood $7,695.00
Price: Model 1620EL Combo; 16- and 20-gauge two-barrel set $11,195.00

MOSSBERG SILVER RESERVE II SXS

Gauge: 12, 20, 28. **Barrels:** 26 or 28 inches with front bead sight, five choke tubes. **Stock:** Select black walnut. **Weight:** 6.5 to 7.5 pounds. Side-by-side companion to over/under model with same Silver Reserve name. Blue barrels, silver receiver with scroll engraving. Single non-selective trigger with standard extractors.

Price: $1,067.00

PIOTTI KING NO. 1

Gauge: 12, 16, 20, 28, .410. **Barrel:** 25" to 30" (12 ga.), 25" to 28" (16, 20, 28, .410). To customer specs. Chokes as specified. **Weight:** 6.5 lbs. to 8 lbs. (12 ga. to customer specs.). **Stock:** Dimensions to customer specs. Finely figured walnut; straight grip with checkered butt with classic splinter fore-end and hand-rubbed oil finish standard. Pistol grip, beavertail fore-end. **Features:** Holland & Holland pattern sidelock action, automatic ejectors. Double trigger; non-selective single trigger optional. Coin finish standard; color case-hardened optional. Top rib; level, file-cut; concave, ventilated optional. Very fine, full coverage scroll engraving with small floral bouquets. Imported from Italy by Wm. Larkin Moore.

Price: From $40,900.00

PIOTTI LUNIK SIDE-BY-SIDE SHOTGUN

Similar to the Piotti King No. 1 in overall quality. Has Renaissance-style large scroll engraving in relief. Best quality Holland & Holland-pattern sidelock ejector double with chopper lump (demi-bloc) barrels. Other mechanical specifications remain the same. Imported from Italy by Wm. Larkin Moore.

Price: From $43,825.00

PIOTTI PIUMA

Gauge: 12, 16, 20, 28, .410. **Barrel:** 25" to 30" (12 ga.), 25" to 28" (16, 20, 28, .410). **Weight:** 5-1/2 to 6-1/4 lbs. (20 ga.). **Stock:** Dimensions to customer specs. Straight grip stock with walnut checkered butt, classic splinter fore-end, hand-rubbed oil finish are standard; pistol grip, beavertail fore-end, satin luster finish optional. **Features:** Anson & Deeley boxlock ejector double with chopper lump barrels. Level, file-cut rib, light scroll and rosette engraving, scalloped frame. Double triggers; single non-selective optional. Coin finish standard, color case-hardened optional. Imported from Italy by Wm. Larkin Moore.

Price: From $20,800.00

SKB 200 SERIES

Gauge: 12, 20, .410, 3" chambers; 28, 2¾-inches. **Barrel:** 26", 28". Five choke tubes provided (F, IM, M, IC, SK). **Stock:** Hand checkered and oil finished Turkish walnut. Price of Wales grip and beavertail fore-end. **Weight:** 6 to 7 lbs. **Sights:** Brass bead. **Features:** Boxlock with platform lump barrel design. Polished bright blue finish with charcoal color case hardening on receiver. Manual safety, automatic ejectors, single selective trigger. 200 HR target model has high ventilated rib, full pistol grip. 250 model has decorative color case hardened sideplates. Imported from Turkey by GU, Inc.

Price: 12, 20 ga...$2,100.00
Price: 28, .410..$2,250.00
Price: 200 HR 12, 20 ga...$2,500.00
Price: 200 HR 28, .410...$2,625.00
Price: 250 12, 20 ga...$2,600.00
Price: 250 28, .410...$2,725.00

Prices given are believed to be accurate at time of publication however, many factors affect retail pricing so exact prices are not possible.

69TH EDITION, 2015 ✛ **513**

SKB 7000SL SIDELOCK
Gauge: 12, 20. **Barrel:** 28", 30". Five choke tubes provided (F, IM, M, IC, SK). **Stock:** Premium Turkish walnut with hand-rubbed oil finish, fine-line hand checkering, Price of Wales grip and beavertail fore-end. **Weight:** 6 to 7 lbs. **Sights:** Brass bead. **Features:** Sidelock design with Holland & Holland style seven-pin removable locks with safety sears. Bison Bone Charcoal case hardening, hand engraved sculpted sidelock receiver. Manual safety, automatic ejectors, single selective trigger. Available by special order only. Imported from Turkey by GU, Inc.
Price: From $6,700.00

STOEGER UPLANDER
Gauge: 12, 20, .410, 3" chambers; 28, 2-3/4 chambers. **Barrel:** 22", 24", 26", 28". **Weight:** 6.5 to 7.3 lbs. **Sights:** Brass bead. **Features:** Double trigger, IC & M choke tubes included with gun. Other choke tubes available. Tang auto safety, extractors, black plastic buttplate. Imported by Benelli USA.
Price: Standard...$499.00
Price: Supreme (single trigger, AA-grade wood) $539.00
Price: Longfowler (12 ga., 30" bbl.) $499.00
Price: Home Defense (20 or 12 ga., 20" bbl., tactical sights) ..$499.00
Price: Double Defense (20 ga.) fiber optic sight, accessory rail$499.00

STOEGER COACH GUN
Gauge: 12, 20, 2-3/4", 3" chambers. **Barrel:** 20". **Weight:** 6.5 lbs. **Stock:**

Brown hardwood, classic beavertail fore-end. **Sights:** Brass bead. **Features:** Double or single trigger, IC & M choke tubes included, others available. Tang auto safety, extractors, black plastic buttplate. Imported by Benelli USA.
Price: .... $449.00 to $499.00

WEBLEY & SCOTT SXS SERIES
Gauge: 12, 20. **Barrels:** 28 inches, five interchangeable choke tubes. **Weight:** 6.5 to 7.5 lbs. **Stock:** Oil finished, hand-checkered Turkish walnut with recoil pad, splinter fore-end. **Features:** Automatic ejectors, single selective trigger, ventilated rib, tang selector/safety, charcoal case hardened receiver, English scroll engraving. 3000 Model is a high-grade gun with hand-rubbed oil-finished premium-grade walnut stock with checkered butt, jeweled monobloc walls, higher grade English scroll engraving, and comes with high quality, fleeced line lockable case. Made in Turkey and imported by Centurion International.
Price: Model 2000...$2,500.00
Price: Model 3000...$6,000.00

BERETTA DT10 TRIDENT TRAP TOP SINGLE

Gauge: 12, 3" chamber. **Barrel:** 34"; five Optima Choke tubes (Full, Full, Imp. Modified, Mod. and Imp. Cyl.). **Weight:** 8.8 lbs. **Stock:** High-grade walnut; adjustable. **Features:** Detachable, adjustable trigger group; Optima Bore for improved shot pattern and reduced recoil; slim Optima Choke tubes; raised and thickened receiver for long life. Introduced 2000. Imported from Italy by Beretta USA.
Price: $8,650.00

BROWNING BT-99 TRAP

Gauge: 12. **Barrel:** 30", 32", 34". **Stock:** Walnut; standard or adjustable. **Weight:** 7 lbs. 11 oz. to 9 lbs. **Features:** Back-bored single barrel; interchangeable chokes; beavertail forearm; extractor only; high rib.
Price: BT-99 w/conventional comb, 32" or 34" barrels **$1,430.00**
Price: BT-99 w/adjustable comb, 32" or 34" barrels **$1,680.00**
Price: BT-99 Golden Clays w/adjustable comb, 32" or
    34" barrels **$4,340.00**
Price: BT-99 Grade III ....**$2,540.00 to $2,840.00**

BROWNING A-BOLT SHOTGUN HUNTER

Gauge: 12 ga. 3" chamber. **Barrel:** 22". **Weight:** 7 lbs. 2 ozs. **Length:** 43.75". **Stock:** Satin finish walnut stock and forearm – checkered. **Features:** Drilled and tapped for scope mounts, 60° bolt action lift, detachable two-round magazine, and top-tang safety. Sling swivel studs installed, recoil pad, TRUGLO/Marble's fiber-optic front sight with rear sight adjustable for windage and elevation.
Price: **$1,280.00**
Price: Medallion **$1,580.00**

BROWNING A-BOLT SHOTGUN, MOSSY OAK BREAK-UP INFINITY

Gauge: 12 ga. 3" chamber. **Barrel:** 22". **Weight:** 7 lbs. 2 ozs. **Length:** 43.75". **Stock:** Composite stock and forearm, textured gripping surfaces, Mossy Oak Break-Up Infinitycamo finish • Dura-Touch Armor Coating. **Features:** Drilled and tapped for scope mounts, 60° bolt action lift, detachable two-round magazine, and top-tang safety. Sling swivel studs installed, rrecoil pad, TRUGLO/Marble's fiber-optic front sight with rear sight adjustable for windage and elevation.
Price: From **$1.300.00**

BROWNING A-BOLT SHOTGUN STALKER

Gauge: 12 ga. 3" chamber. **Barrel:** 22". **Weight:** 7 lbs. **Length:** 43.75". **Stock:** Composite stock and forearm, textured gripping surfaces, Dura-Touch Armor Coating. **Features:** Drilled and tapped for scope mounts, 60° bolt action lift, detachable two-round magazine, and top-tang safety. Sling swivel studs installed, rrecoil pad, TRUGLO/Marble's fiber-optic front sight with rear sight adjustable for windage and elevation.
Price: From **$1,150.00**

HARRINGTON & RICHARDSON ULTRA SLUG HUNTER/TAMER

Gauge: 12, 20 ga., 3" chamber, .410. **Barrel:** 20" to 24" rifled. **Weight:** 6 to 9 lbs. **Length:** 34.5" to 40". **Stock:** Hardwood, laminate, or polymer with full pistol grip; semi-beavertail fore-end. **Sights:** Gold bead front. **Features:** Break-open action with side-lever release,

automatic ejector. Introduced 1994. From H&R 1871, LLC.
Price: Ultra Slug Hunter, blued, hardwood $291.00
Price: Ultra Slug Hunter Youth, blued, hardwood, 13-1/8"
    LOP $291.00
Price: Ultra Slug Hunter Deluxe, blued, laminated $291.00
Price: Tamer .410 bore, stainless barrel, black
    polymer stock $193.00

HARRINGTON & RICHARDSON ULTRA LITE SLUG HUNTER

Gauge: 12, 20 ga., 3" chamber. **Barrel:** 24" rifled. **Weight:** 5.25 lbs. **Length:** 40". **Stock:** Hardwood with walnut finish, full pistol grip, recoil pad, sling swivel studs. **Sights:** None; base included. **Features:** Youth Model, available in 20 ga. has 20" rifled barrel. Deluxe Model has checkered laminated stock and fore-end. From H&R 1871, LLC.
Price: $194.00

HARRINGTON & RICHARDSON ULTRA SLUG HUNTER THUMBHOLE STOCK

Similar to the Ultra Lite Slug Hunter but with laminated thumbhole stock and weighs 8.5 lbs.
Price: $401.00

HARRINGTON & RICHARDSON PARDNER AND TRACKER II

Gauge: 10, 12, 16, 20, 28, .410, up to 3.5" chamber for 10 and 12 ga. 16, 28, 2-3/4" chamber. **Barrel:** 24" to 30". **Weight:** Varies from 5 to 9.5 lbs. **Length:** Varies from 36" to 48". **Stock:** Walnut-finished hardwood with full pistol grip, synthetic, or camo finish. **Sights:** Bead front on most. **Features:** Transfer bar ignition; break-open action with side-lever release.
Price: Pardner, all gauges, hardwood stock, 26" to 32"
    blued barrel, Mod. or Full choke....................................$206.00
Price: Turkey model, 10/12 ga., camo finish
    or black....................................**$277.00 to $322.00**
Price: Youth Turkey, 20 ga., camo finish or black....................**$192.00**
Price: Waterfowl, 10 ga., camo finish or hardwood................. **$227.00**
Price: Tracker II slug gun, 12/20 ga., hardwood......................**$291.00**

KRIEGHOFF K-80 SINGLE BARREL TRAP GUN

Gauge: 12, 2-3/4" chamber. **Barrel:** 32" or 34" Unsingle. Fixed Full or choke tubes. **Weight:** About 8-3/4 lbs. **Stock:** Four stock dimensions or adjustable stock available. All hand-checkered European walnut. **Features:** Satin nickel finish. Selective mechanical trigger adjustable for finger position. Tapered step vent rib. Adjustable point of impact.
Price: Standard grade Full Unsingle, from............................**$10,595.00**

KRIEGHOFF KX-6 TRAP GUN

Gauge: 12, 2-3/4" chamber. **Barrel:** 32", 34"; choke tubes. **Weight:** About 8.5 lbs. **Stock:** Factory adjustable stock. European walnut. **Features:** Ventilated tapered step rib. Adjustable position trigger, optional release trigger. Fully adjustable rib. Satin gray electroless nickel receiver. Fitted aluminum case. Imported from Germany by Krieghoff International, Inc.
Price: $5,495.00

Prices given are believed to be accurate at time of publication however, many factors affect retail pricing so exact prices are not possible.

69TH EDITION, 2015 ◈ **515**

LJUTIC MONO GUN SINGLE BARREL

Gauge: 12 only. **Barrel:** 34", choked to customer specs; hollow-milled rib, 35.5" sight plane. **Weight:** Approx. 9 lbs. **Stock:** To customer specs. Oil finish, hand checkered. **Features:** Custom gun. Pull or release trigger; removable trigger guard contains trigger and hammer mechanism; Ljutic pushbutton opener on front of trigger guard. From Ljutic Industries.

Price: Std., med. or Olympic rib, custom bbls.,
fixed choke. **$7,495.00**
Price: Stainless steel mono gun **$8,495.00**

LJUTIC LTX PRO 3 DELUXE MONO GUN

Deluxe, lightweight version of the Mono gun with high quality wood, upgrade checkering, special rib height, screw-in chokes, ported and cased.

Price: **$8,995.00**
Price: Stainless steel model...**$9,995.00**

ROSSI CIRCUIT JUDGE

Revolving shotgun chambered in .410 (2-1/2- or 3-inch/.45 Colt. Based on Taurus Judge handgun. Features include 18.5-inch barrel; fiber optic front sight; 5-round cylinder; hardwood Monte Carlo stock.

Price: **$669.00**

ROSSI SINGLE-SHOT

Gauge: 12, 20, .410. **Barrel:** 22" (Youth), 28". **Weight:** 3.75-5.25 lbs. Stocks: Wood. **Sights:** Bead front sight, fully adjustable fiber optic sight on Slug and Turkey. **Features:** Single-shot break open, 8 models available, positive ejection, internal transfer bar mechanism, trigger block system, Taurus Security System, blued finish, Rifle Slug has ported barrel.

Price: From **$171.00**

ROSSI TUFFY

Gauge: .410. **Barrel:** 18-1/2". **Weight:** 3 lbs. **Length:** 29.5" overall. **Features:** Single-shot break-open model with black synthetic thumbhole stock in blued or stainless finish.

Price: **$205.00**

ROSSI MATCHED PAIRS

Gauge/Caliber: 12, 20, .410, .22 Mag, .22LR, .17HMR, .223 Rem, .243 Win, .270 Win, .30-06, .308 Win. **Barrel:** 23", 28". **Weight:** 5-6.3 lbs. Stocks: Wood or black synthetic. **Sights:** Bead front on shotgun barrel, fully adjustable front and rear on rifle barrel, drilled and tapped for scope, fully adjustable fiber optic sights (black powder). **Features:** Single-shot break open, 27 models available, internal transfer bar mechanism, manual external safety, blue finish, trigger block system, Taurus Security System, youth models available.

Price: Rimfire/Shotgun, from **$245.00**
Price: Centerfire/Shotgun **$345.00**

SKB CENTURY III TRAP

Single-shot, break-open 12 gauge with 2 ¾" chamber, SKB Competition Choke Tube System with three choke tubes. **Barrel:** 30 or 32 inches with lengthened forcing cone. **Stock:** Oil finished Grade II Turkish walnut, right or left-hand cast, Pachmayr SXT recoil pad. Adjustable comb and buttplate system is available. Imported from Turkey by GU, Inc.

Price: **$1,150.00**
Price: Adjustable comb **$1,300.00**
Price: Adjustable comb and buttstock **$1,430.00**

TAR-HUNT RSG-12 PROFESSIONAL RIFLED SLUG GUN

Gauge: 12, 2-3/4" or 3" chamber, 1-shot magazine. **Barrel:** 23", fully rifled with muzzle brake. **Weight:** 7.75 lbs. **Length:** 41.5" overall. **Stock:** Matte black McMillan fiberglass with Pachmayr Decelerator pad. **Sights:** None furnished; comes with Leupold windage or Weaver bases. **Features:** Uses rifle-style action with two locking lugs; two-position safety; Shaw barrel; single-stage, trigger; muzzle brake. Many options available. All models have area-controlled feed action. Introduced 1991. Made in U.S. by Tar-Hunt Custom Rifles, Inc.

Price: 12 ga. Professional model **$2,895.00**
Price: Left-hand model **$3,000.00**

TAR-HUNT RSG-16 ELITE

Similar to RSG-12 Professional except 16 gauge; right- or left-hand versions.

Price: **$2,895.00**

TAR-HUNT RSG-20 MOUNTAINEER SLUG GUN

Similar to the RSG-12 Professional except chambered for 20 gauge (2-3/4" and 3" shells); 23" Shaw rifled barrel, with muzzle brake; two-lug bolt; one-shot blind magazine; matte black finish; McMillan fiberglass stock with Pachmayr Decelerator pad; receiver drilled and tapped for Rem. 700 bases. Right- or left-hand versions. Weighs 6.5 lbs. Introduced 1997. Made in U.S.A. by Tar-Hunt Custom Rifles, Inc.

Price: **$2,895.00**

BENELLI M3 CONVERTIBLE

Gauge: 12, 2-3/4", 3" chambers, 5-shot magazine. **Barrel:** 19.75" (Cyl.). **Weight:** 7 lbs., 4oz. **Length:** 41" overall. **Stock:** High-impact polymer with sling loop in side of butt; rubberized pistol grip on stock. **Sights:** Open rifle, fully adjustable. Ghost ring and rifle type. **Features:** Combination pump/auto action. Alloy receiver with inertia recoil rotating locking lug bolt; matte finish; automatic shell release lever. Introduced 1989. Imported by Benelli USA. Price with pistol grip, open rifle sights.
Price: With ghost ring sights, pistol grip stock **$1,589.00**

BENELLI M2 TACTICAL

Gauge: 12, 2-3/4", 3" chambers, 5-shot magazine. **Barrel:** 18.5" IC, M, F choke tubes. **Weight:** 6.7 lbs. **Length:** 39.75" overall. **Stock:** Black polymer. **Sights:** Rifle type ghost ring system, tritium night sights optional. **Features:** Semiauto intertia recoil action. Cross-bolt safety; bolt release button; matte-finish metal. Introduced 1993. Imported from Italy by Benelli USA.
Price: from .... **$1,239.00 to $1,359.00**

BENELLI M4 TACTICAL

Gauge: 12, 3" chamber. **Barrel:** 18.5". **Weight:** 7.8 lbs. **Length:** 40" overall. **Stock:** Synthetic. **Sights:** Ghost Ring rear, fixed blade front. **Features:** Auto-regulating gas-operated (ARGO) action, choke tube, Picatinny rail, standard and collapsible stocks available, optional LE tactical gun case. Introduced 2006. Imported from Italy by Benelli USA.
Price: From **$1,899.00**

CITADEL LE TACTICAL

Gauge: 12 ga., 3" chamber. **Barrel:** 22". **Weight:** 5.8 lbs -7.15 lbs. **Length:** 49". **Stock:** Composite stock with close radius pistol grip; Speed Lock forearm; textured gripping surfaces; shim adjustable for length of pull, cast and drop; Mossy Oak Bottomland camo finish; Dura-Touch Armor Coating. **Features:** These pump action shotguns are built in the U.S.A. Using a common receiver and trigger group, the Citadel LE comes in four models: Spec-Ops, Talon, Pistol Grip with Heat Shield and Standard. All models feature a lightweight receiver, 7 +1 magazine capacity, 20 inch barrel, ergonomic fore-end, quick feed short stroke pump and rifle style sights. The Spec-Ops model features the Blackhawk Spec-Ops stock, which is adjustable for 4 inches of LOP, and estimated at absorbing up to 70% of felt recoil. The Spec-Ops gets you on target quickly – and keeps you there shot after shot. The Talon model also offers 70% felt recoil reduction with a skeletonized thumbhole stock from Blackhawk that permits free hand movement with even the heaviest of gloves, and a short, 13.5 inch LOP. The Pistol Grip and Standard models offer a traditional, synthetic stock with a fixed, 13.5 inch LOP.
Price: Standard Stock **$466.00**
Price: Spec-Ops **$632.00**
Price: Talon **$632.00**
Price: Pistol grip with heat shield **$495.00**

INTERSTATE ARMS 982 T

Gauge: 12; 3" chamber. **Barrel:** 18.5" with fixed Cylinder choke. **Stock:** Black synthetic. Pistol grip. **Sights:** Ghost ring read, bead front. **Features:** Imported by Interstate Arms Corporation (IAC).
Price: **$300.00**

KEL-TEC KSG BULL-PUP TWIN-TUBE

The shotgun bears a stunning resemblance to the South African designed Neostead pump action scattergun. The operator is able to move a switch located near the top of the grip to select the right or left tube, or move the switch to the center to eject a shell without chambering another round. The bull-pup design results in an overall length of only 26" with an 18.5" barrel while the bottom eject design makes the firearm truly ambidextrous. The incredibly short overall length makes it more nimble than a sawed off shotgun, and with a 14+1 capacity with 2 3/4" you don't sacrifice ammunition capacity to get a small package. Optional accessories include a factory installed Picatinny rail with flip-up sights and a pistol grip.
Price: **$1,200.00**

MOSSBERG MODEL 500 SPECIAL PURPOSE

Gauge: 12, 20, .410, 3" chamber. **Barrel:** 18.5", 20" (Cyl.). **Weight:** 7 lbs. **Stock:** Walnut-finished hardwood or black synthetic. **Sights:** Metal bead front. **Features:** Available in 6- or 8-shot models. Top-mounted safety, double action slide bars, swivel studs, rubber recoil pad. Blue, Parkerized, Marinecote finishes. Mossberg Cablelock included. The HS410 Home Security model chambered for .410 with 3" chamber; has pistol grip fore-end, thick recoil pad, muzzle brake and has special spreader choke on the 18.5" barrel. Overall length is 37.5", weight is 6.25 lbs. Blue finish; synthetic field stock. Mossberg Cablelock and video included. Mariner model has Marinecote metal finish to resist rust and corrosion. Synthetic field stock; pistol grip kit included. 500 Tactical 6-shot has black synthetic tactical stock. Introduced 1990.
Price: Rolling Thunder, 6-shot **$537.00**
Price: HS410 Home Security **$502.00**
Price: Tactical.. **$583.00 to $630.00**
Price: 500 Blackwater SPX...**$478.00**
Price: 500 Chainsaw pistol grip only; removable top handle ...**$525.00**
Price: JIC **$435.00**
Price: Road Blocker...**$544.00**

MOSSBERG MODEL 590 SPECIAL PURPOSE

Gauge: 12, 20, .410 3" chamber, 9 shot magazine. **Barrel:** 20" (Cyl.). **Weight:** 7.25 lbs. **Stock:** Synthetic field or Speedfeed. **Sights:** Metal bead front or Ghost Ring. **Features:** Top-mounted safety, double slide action bars. Comes with heat shield, bayonet lug, swivel studs, rubber recoil pad. Blue, Parkerized or Marinecote finish. Mossberg Cablelock included. From Mossberg.
Price: Special Purpose 9-shot **$537.00**
Price: Tactical Light Fore-End..**$677.00**
Price: Tactical Tri-Rail **$640.00**

MOSSBERG 930 SPECIAL PURPOSE SERIES

Gauge: 12 ga., 3" chamber. **Barrel:** 28" flat ventilated rib. **Weight:** 7.3 lbs. **Length:** 49". **Stock:** Composite stock with close radius pistol grip; Speed Lock forearm; textured gripping surfaces; shim adjustable for length of pull, cast and drop; Mossy Oak Bottomland camo finish; Dura-Touch Armor Coating. **Features:** 930 Special Purpose shotguns feature a self-regulating gas system that vents excess gas to aid in recoil reduction and eliminate stress on critical components. All 930 autoloaders chamber both 2 3/4 inch and 3-inch 12-gauge shotshells with ease—from target loads, to non-toxic magnum loads, to the latest sabot slug ammo. Magazine capacity is 7+1 on models with extended magazine tube, 4+1 on models without. To complete the package, each Mossberg 930 includes a set of specially designed spacers for quick adjustment of the horizontal and vertical angle of the stock, bringing a custom-feel fit to every shooter. All 930 Special Purpose models feature a drilled and tapped receiver, factory-ready for Picatinny rail, scope base or optics installation. 930 SPX models conveniently come with a factory-mounted Picatinny rail and LPA/M16-Style Ghost Ring combination sight right out of the box. Other sighting options include a basic front bead, or white-dot front sights. Mossberg 930 Special Purpose shotguns are available in a variety of configurations; 5-shot tactical barrel, 5-shot with muzzle brake, 8-shot pistol-grip, and even a 5-shot security / field combo.

Price: Tactical 5-Shot...$683.00
Price: Blackwater Series..$865.00
Price: Home Security...$612.00
Price: Standard Stock...$787.00
Price: Pistol Grip 8-shot $883.00
Price: 5-shot Combo w/extra 18.5" barrel................$679.00

REMINGTON MODEL 870 PUMP AND MODEL 1100 AUTOLOADER TACTICAL SHOTGUNS

Gauge: 870: 12, 2-3/4 or 3" chamber; 1100: 2-3/4". **Barrel:** 18", 20", 22" (Cyl or IC). **Weight:** 7.5-7.75 lbs. **Length:** 38.5-42.5" overall. **Stock:** Black synthetic, synthetic Speedfeed IV full pistol-grip stock, or Knoxx Industries SpecOps stock w/recoil-absorbing spring-loaded cam and adjustable length of pull (12" to 16", 870 only). **Sights:** Front post w/dot only on 870; rib and front dot on 1100. **Features:** R3 recoil pads, LimbSaver technology to reduce felt recoil, 2-, 3- or 4-shot extensions based on barrel length; matte-olive-drab barrels and receivers. Model 1100 Tactical is available with Speedfeed IV pistol grip stock or standard black synthetic stock and fore-end. Speedfeed IV model has an 18" barrel with two-shot extension. Standard synthetic-stocked version is equipped with 22" barrel and four-shot extension. Introduced 2006. From Remington Arms Co.

Price: 870 Express Tactical Knoxx 20 ga. $555.00
Price: 870 Express Magpul......................................$898.00
Price: 870 Special Purpose Marine (nickel) $829.00
Price: 870 Express Blackhawk Spec Ops $638.00
Price: 1100 TAC-4 ....$1,015.00

REMINGTON 870 EXPRESS TACTICAL A-TACS CAMO

Pump action shotgun chambered for 2-3/4- and 3-inch 12-ga. Features include full A-TACS digitized camo; 18-1/2-inch barrel; extended ported Tactical RemChoke; SpeedFeed IV pistol-grip stock with SuperCell recoil pad; fully adjustable XS Ghost Ring Sight rail with removable white bead front sight; 7-round capacity with factory-installed 2-shot extension; drilled and tapped receiver; sling swivel stud.

Price: $720.00

REMINGTON 887 NITRO MAG TACTICAL

Pump action shotgun chambered in 12-ga., 2-3/4 to 3-1/2 inch. Features include 18-1/2-inch barrel with ported, extended tactical RemChoke; 2-shot magazine extension; barrel clamp with integral Picatinny rails; ArmorLokt coating; synthetic stock and fore-end with specially contour grip panels.

Price: $534.00

TACTICAL RESPONSE TR-870 STANDARD MODEL

Gauge: 12, 3" chamber, 7-shot magazine. **Barrel:** 18" (Cyl). **Weight:** 9 lbs. **Length:** 38" overall. **Stock:** Fiberglass-filled polypropolene with non-snag recoil absorbing butt pad. Nylon tactical fore-end houses flashlight. **Sights:** Trak-Lock ghost ring sight system. Front sight has Tritium insert. **Features:** Highly modified Remington 870P with Parkerized finish. Comes with nylon three-way adjustable sling, high visibility non-binding follower, high performance magazine spring, Jumbo Head safety, and Side Saddle extended 6-shot shell carrier on left side of receiver. Introduced 1991. From Scattergun Technologies, Inc.

Price: Standard model, from................................$1,540.00
Price: Border Patrol model, from $1,135.00
Price: Professional Model 13" bbl. (Law enf., military only)...$1,550.00

TRISTAR COBRA

Gauge: 12, 3". **Barrel:** 28". **Weight:** 6.7 lbs. Three Beretta-style choke tubes (IC, M, F). **Length:** NA. **Stock:** Matte black synthetic stock and forearm. **Sights:** Vent rib with matted sight plane. **Features:** Five-year warranty. Cobra Tactical Pump Shotgun magazine holds 7, return spring in forearm, 20" barrel, Cylinder choke. Introduced 2008. Imported by Tristar Sporting Arms Ltd.

Price: Tactical.. $319.00 to $429.00

TRISTAR TECH 12 AUTO/PUMP

Gauge: 12. 3-inch chamber. 20-inch ported barrel with fixed cylinder choke. Capable of operating in pump-action or semi-auto model with the turn of a dial. **Stock:** Pistol-grip synthetic with matte black finish. **Weight:** 7.4 lbs. **Sights:** Ghost-ring rear, raised bridge fiber-optic front. Picatinny rail.

Price: $689

WINCHESTER SXP EXTREME DEFENDER

Gauge: 12. 3-inch chamber. Pump action. **Barrel:** 18-inches with chrome-plated chamber and bore, "door breaching" ported choke tube. **Stock:** Adjustable military-style buttstock with vertical pistol grip. **Sights:** Ghost-ring rear integrated with Picatinny rail. Matte black finish.

Price: $560.00
Price: Marine Model with hard chrome metal finish $620.00

CABELA'S HOWDAH HUNTER 20-GAUGE PISTOL
Gauge: 20. **Barrels:** Cylinder bored, 11.25 in. **Weight:** 4.5 lbs. **Length:** 17.25 in. **Stock:** American walnut with checkered grip. **Sights:** Brass bead front sight. **Features:** Blued barrels, swamped barrel rib, engraved, color case-hardened locks and hammers, captive steel ramrod. Available with detachable shoulder stock, case, holster and mold. Made by Pedersoli. Imported by Cabela's, Dixie Gun Works, Taylor's and others.
Price: Cabela's 20-gauge $700.00

CHARLESTON UNDERHAMMER MATCH PERCUSSION PISTOL
Caliber: .36. **Barrel:** 9.5 in., browned octagonal, rifled. **Weight:** 2.25 lbs. **Length:** 16.75 in. overall. **Stocks:** Walnut grip. **Sights:** Blade front, open rear, adjustable for elevation. **Features:** Percussion, under-hammer ignition, adjustable trigger, no half cock. No ramrod. Made by Pedersoli. Imported by Dixie Gun Works.
Price: Dixie, FH0332 .... $915.00

CVA OPTIMA PISTOL
Caliber: .50. **Barrel:** 14 in., 1:28-in. twist, Cerakote finish. **Weight:** 3.7 lbs. **Length:** 19 in. **Stocks:** Black synthetic, Realtree Xtra Green. **Ramrod:** Aluminum. **Sights:** Scope base mounted. **Features:** Break-open action, all stainless construction, quick-removal breech plug for 209 primer. From CVA.
Price: Stainless steel, black synthetic $330.00
Price: Stainless steel, Realtree Xtra Green, ... $380.00

DRAGOON PISTOL U.S. MODEL OF 1858 WITH DETACHABLE SHOULDER STOCK
Caliber: .58. **Barrel:** 12 in. **Weight:** 3.75 lbs., with shoulder stock 5.5 lbs. **Length:** 18.25 in. overall pistol. **Stocks:** Walnut pistol and shoulder stock. **Sights:** Flip-up blued steel rear, blade steel front. **Features:** Percussion, musket-cap nipple, case-hardened lock, brass furniture. Captive steel ramrod. Shoulder stock included. Made by Palmetto. Imported by Dixie Gun Works.
Price: Dixie Gun Works, with shoulder stock PH1000… $600.00

FRENCH AN IX, AN XIII AND GENDARMERIE NAPOLEONIC PISTOLS
Caliber: .69. **Barrel:** 8.25 in. **Weight:** 3 lbs. **Length:** 14 in. overall. **Stocks:** Walnut. **Sights:** None. **Features:** Flintlock, case-hardened lock, brass furniture, buttcap, lock marked "Imperiale de S. Etienne." Steel ramrod. Other Napoleonic pistols include half-stocked "AN XIII" and Gendarmerie with 5.25-inch barrel. Made by Pedersoli. Imported by Dixie Gun Works.
Price: Dixie Gun Works FH0890 .... $740.00
Price: Dixie Gun Works AN XIII FHO895................................. $710.00
Price: Dixie Gun Works Gendarmerie FHO954........................ $665.00

HARPER'S FERRY 1805 PISTOL
Caliber: .58. **Barrel:** 10 in. **Weight:** 2.5 lbs. **Length:** 16 in. overall. **Stocks:** Walnut. **Sights:** Fixed. **Features:** Flintlock. Case-hardened lock, brass-mounted German silver-colored barrel. Wooden ramrod. Replica of the first U.S. government made flintlock pistol. Made by Pedersoli. Imported by Dixie Gun Works.
Price: Dixie Gun Works RH0225.. $565.00
Price: Dixie Gun Works Kit RH0411....................................... $433.00

HOWDAH HUNTER PISTOLS
Caliber: .50, 20 gauge, .58 **Barrels:** 11.25 in., blued, rifled in .50 and .58 calibers **Weight:** 4.25 to 5 lbs. **Length:** 17.25 in. **Stocks:** American walnut with checkered grip. **Sights:** Brass bead front sight. **Features:** Blued barrels, swamped barrel rib, engraved, color case-hardened locks and hammers, captive steel ramrod. Available with detachable shoulder stock, case, holster and mold. Made by Pedersoli. Imported by Dixie Gun Works, and individual models by Cabela's, Taylor's and others.
Price: Dixie, 50X50, PH0572 .... $850.00
Price: Dixie, 58XD58, PH09024 .... $875.00
Price: Dixie, 20X20 gauge, PH0581...................................... $815.00
Price: Dixie, 50X20 gauge, PH0581...................................... $850.00
Price: Dixie, 50X50, Kit, PK0952 .... $640.00
Price: Dixie, 50X20, Kit, PK1410.. $675.00
Price: Dixie, 20X20, Kit, PK0954.. $640.00

KENTUCKY PISTOL
Caliber: .45, .50, .54 **Barrel:** 10.25 in. **Weight:** 2.5 lbs. **Length:** 15.4 in. overall. **Stocks:** Walnut with smooth rounded birds-head grip. **Sights:** Fixed. **Features:** Available in flint or percussion ignition in various calibers. Case-hardened lock, blued barrel, drift-adjustable rear sights, blade front. Wooden ramrod. Kit guns of all models available from Dixie Gun Works. Made by Pedersoli. Imported by Dixie Gun Works, EMF and others.
Price: .45 Percussion, Dixie, PH0440 .... $375.00
Price: .45 Flint, Dixie, PH0430 .... $410.00
Price: .45 Flint, Dixie, Kit FH0320 .... $299.00
Price: .50 Flint, Dixie, PH0935 .... $435.00
Price: .50 Percussion, Dixie, PH0930 .... $395.00
Price: .54 Flint, Dixie, PH0080 .... $440.00
Price: .54 Percussion, Dixie,PH0330 .... $395.00
Price: .54 Percussion, Dixie, Kit PK0436 .... $283.00
Price: .45 Flint, Navy Moll, brass buttcap, Dixie, PK0436 ...... $610.00
Price: .45 Percussion, Navy Moll, brass buttcap,
    Dixie, PK0903 ....$565.00

LE PAGE PERCUSSION DUELING PISTOL
Caliber: .44 (Pedersoli), .45 (Armi, Chiappa). **Barrel:** 10.25 in. browned octagon, rifled. **Weight:** 2.5 lbs. **Length:** 16.6 in. overall. **Stocks:** Walnut, rounded checkered butt (Pedersoli), fluted butt (Armi). **Sights:** Blade front, open-style rear. **Features:** Single set trigger (Pedersoli), double set (Armi) trigger. Browned barrel (Dixie International). Bright barrel, silver-plated brass furniture (Armi). External ramrod. Made by Pedersoli, Armi, Chiappa. Imported by Dixie Gun Works.
Price: Dixie, Pedersoli, PH0431 ....$925.00
Price: Dixie, International, Pedersoli, PH0231 ....$1,250.00
Price: Dixie, Armi, PH0310 .... $627.00

LYMAN PLAINS PISTOL
Caliber: .50 or .54. **Barrel:** 8 in.; 1:30-in. twist, both calibers. **Weight:** 50 oz. **Length:** 15 in. overall. **Stocks:** Walnut. **Sights:** Blade front, square-notch rear adjustable for windage. **Features:** Polished brass triggerguard and ramrod tip, color case-hardened coil spring lock, spring-loaded trigger, stainless steel nipple, blackened iron furniture.

Prices given are believed to be accurate at time of publication however, many factors affect retail pricing so exact pricing are not possible.

69TH EDITION, 2015 ✦ **519**

Hooked patent breech, detachable belt hook. Introduced 1981. From Lyman Products.
Price: Finished **$370.00**
Price: Kit **$310.00**

MORTIMER TARGET PISTOL
Caliber: .44. **Barrel:** 10 in., bright octagonal on Standard, browned on Deluxe, rifled. **Weight:** 2.25 lbs. **Length:** 16 in. overall. Stocks: Walnut, checkered saw-handle grip on Deluxe. **Sights:** Blade front, open-style rear. **Features:** Percussion or flint, single set trigger, sliding hammer safety, engraved lock on Deluxe. Wooden ramrod. Made by Pedersoli. Imported by Dixie Gun Works
Price: Dixie, Flint, FH0316 ....**$1,175.00**
Price: Dixie, Percussion, PH0231 ....**$1,095.00**
Price: Dixie, Deluxe, FH0950 ....**$2,200.00**

PEDERSOLI MANG TARGET PISTOL
Caliber: .38. **Barrel:** 10.5 in., octagonal; 1:15-in. twist. **Weight:** 2.5 lbs. **Length:** 17.25 in. overall. Stocks: Walnut with fluted grip. **Sights:** Blade front, open rear adjustable for windage. **Features:** Browned barrel, polished breech plug, remainder color case-hardened. Made by Pedersoli. Imported by Dixie Gun Works.
Price: PH0503.. **$1,750.00**

PHILADELPHIA DERRINGER
Caliber: .45. **Barrel:** 3.1 in., browned, rifled. **Weight:** .5 lbs. **Length:** 6.215 in. Grips: European walnut checkered. **Sights:** V-notch rear, blade front. **Features:** Back-hammer percussion lock with engraving, single trigger. From Pedersoli. Sold by Dixie Gun Works.
Price: Dixie, PH0913 .... **$550.00**
Price: Dixie, Kit PK0863 .... **$385.00**

QUEEN ANNE FLINTLOCK PISTOL
Caliber: .50. **Barrel:** 7.5 in., smoothbore. Stocks: Walnut. **Sights:** None. **Features:** Flintlock, German silver-colored steel barrel, fluted brass triggerguard, brass mask on butt. Lockplate left in the white. No ramrod. Introduced 1983. Made by Pedersoli. Imported by Dixie Gun Works.
Price: Dixie, RH0211.. **$470.00**
Price: Dixie, Kit, FH0421 .... **$470.00**

REMINGTON RIDER DERRINGER
Caliber: 4.3 mm (BB lead balls only). **Barrel:** 2.1 in., blued, rifled. **Weight:** .25 lbs. **Length:** 4.75 in. Grips: All-steel construction. **Sights:** V-notch rear, bead front. **Features:** Fires percussion cap only – no powder. Available as case-hardened frame or polished white. From Pedersoli. Sold by Dixie Gun Works.
Price: Dixie, Casehardened PH0923 . ... **$210.00**

SCREW BARREL PISTOL
Caliber: .44. **Barrel:** 2.35 in., blued, rifled. **Weight:** .5 lbs. **Length:** 6.5 in. Grips: European walnut. **Sights:** None. **Features:** Percussion, boxlock with center hammer, barrel unscrews for loading from rear, folding trigger, external hammer, combination barrel and nipple

wrench furnished. From Pedersoli. Sold by Dixie Gun Works.
Price: Dixie, PH0530 .... **$210.00**
Price: Dixie, PH0545 .... **$165.00**

TRADITIONS KENTUCKY PISTOL
Caliber: .50. **Barrel:** 10 in., 1:20 in. twist. **Weight:** 2.75 lbs. **Length:** 15 in. Stocks: Hardwood full stock. **Sights:** Brass blade front, square notch rear adjustable for windage. **Features:** Polished brass finger spur-style triggerguard, stock cap and ramrod tip, color case-hardened leaf spring lock, spring-loaded trigger, No. 11 percussion nipple, brass furniture. From Traditions, and as kit from Bass Pro and others.
Price: Finished **$241.00**
Price: Kit **$206.00**

TRADITIONS PIRATE PISTOL
Caliber: .50. **Barrel:** 10 in., round armory-bright steel, 1:20 in. twist. **Weight:** 2.75 lbs. **Length:** 15 in. Stocks: Hardwood rounded bag-style grip with skull-crushing brass grip cap, fullstock. **Sights:** Square-notched rear adjustable for windage, brass blade front. **Features:** Flint, armory-bright polished lock, single trigger, polished brass triggerguard, stock cap and ramrod tip, color case-hardened leaf spring lock, spring-loaded trigger. From Traditions, and as kit from Bass Pro and others.
Price: Finished, flint **$400.00**
Price: Kit, flint **$334.00**

TRADITIONS TRAPPER PISTOL
Caliber: .50. **Barrel:** 9.75 in., octagonal, blued, hooked patent breech, 1:20 in. twist. **Weight:** 2.75 lbs. **Length:** 15.5 in. Stocks: Hardwood, modified saw-handle style grip, halfstock. **Sights:** Brass blade front, rear sight adjustable for windage and elevation. **Features:** Percussion or flint, double set triggers, polished brass triggerguard, stock cap and ramrod tip, color case-hardened leaf spring lock, spring-loaded trigger, No. 11 percussion nipple, brass furniture. From Traditions and as a kit from Bass Pro and others.
Price: Finished, percussion.. **$325.00**
Price: Finished, flint **$362.00**
Price: Kit, percussion **$295.00**
Price: Kit, flint **$355.00**

TRADITIONS VEST POCKET DERRINGER
Caliber: .31. **Barrel:** 2.35 in., round brass, smoothbore. **Weight:** .75 lbs. **Length:** 4.75 in. Grips: Simulated ivory. **Sights:** Front bead. **Features:** Replica of riverboat gambler's derringer. No. 11 percussion cap nipple, brass frame and barrel, spur trigger, external hammer. From Traditions.
Price: **$193.00**
Price: Dixie, White, PH0920 .... **$210.00**

TRADITIONS VORTEK PISTOL
Caliber: .50. **Barrel:** 13 in., 1:28 in. twist, Cerakote finish. **Weight:** 3.25 lbs. **Length:** 18 in. Stocks: Hardwood, black synthetic, Reaper Buck camo. Ramrod: Solid aluminum. **Sights:** LPA steel, 1-4X24mm scope. **Features:** Vortek break-open action with removable trigger group, quick-removal breech plug for 209 primer, over-molded stocks. From Traditions.
Price: Select hardwood, Cerakote finish **$398.00**
Price: Select hardwood, Cerakote finish 1-4X24 scope.......... **$486.00**
Price: Black Synthetic, Cerakote finish................................ **$318.00**
Price: Select hardwood, Cerakote finish 1-4X24 scope.......... **$412.00**
Price: Synthetic, Reaper Buck camo **$368.00**
Price: Select, Reaper Buck camo 1-4X24 scope **$462.00**

Prices given are believed to be accurate at time of publication however, many factors affect retail pricing so exact prices are not possible.

ARMY COLT 1860 PERCUSSION REVOLVER

Caliber: .44. **Barrel:** 8 in. **Weight:** 2.75 lbs. **Length:** 13.25 in. overall. **Grips:** One-piece walnut. **Sights:** Brass blade front, hammer notch rear. **Features:** Steel or case-hardened frame, brass triggerguard, case-hardened creeping loading lever. Many models and finishes are available for this pistol. Made by Pietta and Uberti. Imported by Cabela's, Cimarron, Dixie Gun Works, EMF, Taylor's, Uberti U.S.A. and others.
Price: Dixie, standard model with brass triggerguard RH0705 **$260.00**
Price: Dixie, standard model kit RK0965 .... **$234.00**
Price: Dixie, half-fluted cylinder cut for shoulder stock RH0125 ....
   $234.00
Price: Dixie, 5.5 in. Sheriff's model RH0975 .... **$305.00**

ARMY COLT 1862 POLICE SNUBNOSE (THUNDERER) PERCUSSION REVOLVER

Caliber: .44, six-shot. **Barrel:** 3 in. **Weight:** 1.5 lbs. **Length:** 9.2 in. overall. **Grips:** Varnished birds-head walnut. **Sights:** Brass pin front, hammer notch rear. **Features:** Steel or case-hardened frame, steel triggerguard, no loading. Ramrod: Brass loading rod. Made by Uberti. Imported by EMF, Taylor's, Uberti U.S.A.
Price: from **$402.00**

BABY DRAGOON 1848, 1849 POCKET, WELLS FARGO PERCUSSION REVOLVER

Caliber: .31. **Barrel:** 3 in., 4 in., 5 in., 6 in.; seven-groove; RH twist. **Weight:** About 21 oz. **Grips:** Varnished walnut. **Sights:** Brass pin front, hammer notch rear. **Features:** No loading lever on Baby Dragoon or Wells Fargo models. Unfluted cylinder with stagecoach holdup scene, cupped cylinder pin, no grease grooves, one safety pin on cylinder and slot in hammer face, straight (flat) mainspring. Made by Uberti. Imported by Cimarron, Dixie Gun Works, EMF, Uberti U.S.A. and others.
Price: from .... **$310.00 to $346.00**

COLT 1847 WALKER PERCUSSION REVOLVER

Caliber: .44 **Barrel:** 9 in. **Weight:** 4.5 lbs. **Length:** 15.7 in. overall. **Grips:** One-piece hardwood. **Sights:** Brass blade front, hammer notch rear. **Features:** Copy of Sam Colt's first U.S. contract revolver. Engraved cylinder, case-hardened hammer and loading lever. Blued finish. Made by Uberti, imported by Cabela's, Cimarron, Dixie Gun Works, EMF, Taylor's, Uberti U.S.A. and others.
Price: Dixie, standard model, blued steel RH0450 .... **$410.00**
Price: Dixie, standard model, blued steel kit RH0450 .... **$340.00**

COLT 1848 DRAGOON PERCUSSION REVOLVERS

Caliber: .44 **Barrel:** 7.5 in. **Weight:** 4.1 lbs. **Grips:** One-piece walnut. **Sights:** Brass blade front, hammer notch rear. **Features:** Copy of Eli Whitney's design for Colt using Walker parts and improved loading lever latch. Blued barrel, backstrap and triggerguard. Made in Italy by Uberti. Imported by Dixie Gun Works, Taylor's, Uberti U.S.A. and others.
Price: 1848 Whitneyville Dragoon, ... **$385.00**
Price: 1848 Dragoon, 1st-3rd models, ... **$385.00**
Price: 1848 Dragoon, 3rd. model, cut for stock **$410.00**

COLT TEXAS PATTERSON PERCUSSION REVOLVER

Caliber: .36 **Barrel:** 9 in. tapered octagon. **Weight:** 2.75 lbs. **Length:** 13.75 in. **Grips:** One-piece walnut. **Sights:** Brass pin front, hammer notch rear. **Features:** Folding trigger, blued steel furniture, frame and barrel; engraved scene on cylinder. Ramrod: Loading tool provided. Made by Pietta. Imported by Dixie Gun Works.
Price: Dixie RH0600 .... **$560.00**

DANCE AND BROTHERS PERCUSSION REVOLVER

Caliber: .44 **Barrel:** 7.4 in., round. **Weight:** 2.5 lbs. **Length:** 13 in. overall. **Grip:** Two-piece walnut. **Sights:** Fixed. **Features:** Reproduction of the C.S.A. revolver. Brass frame and triggerguard. Made by Pietta. From Dixie Gun Works, Cabela's and others.
Price: Dixie Gun Works RH0120 .... **$343.00**

DIXIE WYATT EARP PERCUSSION REVOLVER

Caliber: .44 **Barrel:** 12 in., octagon. **Weight:** 46 oz. **Length:** 18 in. overall. **Grips:** One-piece hardwood. **Sights:** Fixed. **Features:** Highly polished brass frame, backstrap and triggerguard; blued barrel and cylinder; case-hardened hammer, trigger and loading lever. Navy-size shoulder stock requires minor fitting. Made by Pietta. From Dixie Gun Works, EMF.
Price: RH0130 .... **$225.00**

GRISWOLD AND GUNNISON PERCUSSION REVOLVER

Caliber: .36 **Barrel:** 7.5 in., round. **Weight:** 2.5 lbs. **Length:** 13.25 in. **Grip:** One-piece walnut. **Sights:** Fixed. **Features:** Reproduction of the C.S.A. revolver. Brass frame and triggerguard. Made by Pietta. From Cabela's and others.
Price: Cabelas **$210.00**

LEACH AND RIGDON PERCUSSION REVOLVER

Caliber: .36. **Barrel:** 7.5 in., octagon to round. **Weight:** 2.75 lbs. **Length:** 13 in. **Grip:** One-piece walnut. **Sights:** Hammer notch and pin front. **Features:** Steel frame. Reproduction of the C.S.A. revolver. Brass backstrap and triggerguard. Made by Uberti. From Dixie Gun Works and others.
Price: Dixie Gun Works RH0611 .... **$340.00**

LEMAT PERCUSSION REVOLVER

Caliber: .44/20 ga. **Barrel:** 6.75 in. (revolver); 4-7/8 in. (single shot). **Weight:** 3 lbs., 7 oz. **Length:** 14 in. overall. **Grips:** Hand-checkered walnut. **Sights:** Post front, hammer notch rear. **Features:** Exact reproduction with all-steel construction; 44-cal. 9-shot cylinder, 20-gauge single barrel; color case-hardened hammer with selector; spur triggerguard; ring at butt; lever-type barrel release. Made by Pietta. From Dixie Gun Works.
Price: LeMat Navy with knurled pin barrel release **$925.00**
Price: LeMat Calvary with trigger spur and lanyard ring **$925.00**
Price: LeMat Army with cross pin barrel selector **$925.00**

NAVY MODEL COLT 1851 PERCUSSION REVOLVER

Caliber: .36, .44, 6-shot. **Barrel:** 7.5 in. **Weight:** 44 oz. **Length:** 13 in. overall. **Grips:** Walnut. **Sights:** Post front, hammer notch rear. **Features:** Many authentic and non-authentic variations are offered that include, brass backstrap and triggerguard, steel or brass frame options, some have 1st Model square-back triggerguard, engraved cylinder with navy battle scene; case-hardened hammer, loading lever. Cartridge conversion pistols and cylinders are also available from Cimarron and Taylor's. Made by Uberti and Pietta. Imported by Cabela's, Cimarron, EMF, Dixie Gun Works, Taylor's, Traditions (.44 only), Uberti U.S.A. and others.

Price: Brass frame (Dixie Gun Works RH0100).........................**$240.00**
Price: Steel frame (Dixie Gun Works RH844)...........................**$245.00**
Price: Confederate Navy (Cabela's) **$180.00**
Price: Cartridge conversion cylinders .38 Spl. and .45 LC .... **$240-$300.00**

NAVY COLT 1861 PERCUSSION REVOLVER

Caliber: .36 **Barrel:** 8 in. **Weight:** 2.75 lbs. **Length:** 13.25 in. overall. Grips: One-piece walnut. **Sights:** Brass blade front, hammer notch rear. **Features:** Steel or case-hardened frame, brass triggerguard, case-hardened creeping loading lever. Many models and finishes are available for this pistol. Made by Pietta and Uberti. Imported by Cabela's, Cimarron, Dixie Gun Works, EMF, Taylor's, Uberti U.S.A. and others.

Price: Dixie, standard model with brass triggerguard RH0841 **$315.00**
Price: Dixie, Sheriff's 5.5 in. barrel RK0975 .... **$205.00**

NEW MODEL 1858 REMINGTON ARMY PERCUSSION REVOLVER

Caliber: .36 or .44, 6-shot. **Barrel:** Standard 8 in., and 5.5 to 12 in. **Weight:** Standard 2 lbs. **Length:** Standard 13.5 in. Grips: Walnut, two-piece. **Sights:** Standard blade front, groove-in-frame rear; adjustable on some models. **Features:** Many variations of this gun are available. Also available as the Army Model Belt Revolver in .36 cal., a shortened and lightened version of the .44 model. Target Model (Uberti U.S.A.) has fully adjustable target rear sight, target front, .36 or .44. Imported by Cabela's, Cimarron F.A. Co., EMF, Taylor's, Traditions (.44 only), Uberti U.S.A. and others.

Price: Steel frame, Dixie RH0220 .... **$323.00**
Price: Steel frame kit, Dixie, oversized grips and frame RV0440...**$245.00**
Price: Stainless steel Model 1858, Cabela's, Traditions **$390.00**
Price: Target Model, adj. rear sight (Cabela's, Traditions) **$480.00**
Price: Sheriff's Model, .44, steel frame (Cabela's, Traditions) . **$280.00**
Price: Brass frame Cabela's, Traditions,................................. **$285.00**
Price: Buffalo model, brass frame, .44-cal. (Cabela's) **$250.00**
Price: Traditions Redi-Pak, steel frame, accessories **$336.00**
Price: 1858 Target Carbine 18 in. barrel Dixie PR0338........... **$565.00**

NEW MODEL POCKET REMINGTON PERCUSSION REVOLVER

Caliber: .31, 5-shot. **Barrel:** 3.5 in. **Weight:** 1 lb. **Length:** 7.6 in. Grips: Walnut, two-piece. **Sights:** Pin front, groove-in-frame rear. **Features:** Spur trigger; iron, brass or nickel-plated frame. Made by Pietta. Imported by Dixie Gun Works, EMF, Taylor's and others.

Price: Brass frame, Dixie PH0407 .... **$243.00**
Price: Steel frame, Dixie PH0370.. **$288.00**
Price: Nickel-plated, Dixie PH0409 .... **$288.00**

NORTH AMERICAN COMPANION PERCUSSION REVOLVER

Caliber: .22 **Barrel:** 1-1/8 in. **Weight:** 5.1 oz. **Length:** 4 in. overall. Grips: Laminated wood. **Sights:** Blade front, notch rear. **Features:**

All stainless steel construction. Uses No. 11 percussion caps. Comes with bullets, powder measure, bullet seater, leather clip holster, gun rag. Long Rifle frame. Introduced 1996. Made in U.S. by North American Arms.

Price: Long Rifle frame **$234.00**

NORTH AMERICAN EARL PERCUSSION REVOLVER

Caliber: .22 **Barrel:** 4 in. **Weight:** 9.4 oz. **Length:** 7.75 in. **Sights:** Post front, notch rear. **Features:** All stainless steel construction. No. 11 percussion caps. Nonfunctional loading lever. Comes with bullets, powder measure, bullet seater, leather clip holster, gun rag. Introduced 1996. Magnum frame. Introduced 2012. Made in U.S. by North American Arms.

Price: Magnum frame **$309.00**

NORTH AMERICAN SUPER COMPANION PERCUSSION REVOLVER

Caliber: .22 **Barrel:** 1-5/8 in. **Weight:** 7.2 oz. **Length:** 5-1/8 in. Grips: Laminated wood. **Sights:** Blade font, notched rear. **Features:** All stainless steel construction. No. 11 percussion caps. Comes with bullets, powder measure, bullet seater, leather clip holster, gun rag. Introduced 1996. Larger "Magnum" frame. Made in U.S. by North American Arms.

Price: Magnum frame **$244.00**

POCKET POLICE COLT 1862 PERCUSSION REVOLVER

Caliber: .36, 5-shot. **Barrel:** 4.5 in., 5.5 in., 6.5 in., 7.5 in. **Weight:** 26 oz. **Length:** 12 in. overall (6.5 in. bbl.). Stocks: Walnut. **Sights:** Fixed. **Features:** Round tapered barrel; half-fluted and rebated cylinder; case-hardened frame, loading lever and hammer; silver or brass triggerguard and backstrap. Made by Uberti. Imported by Cimarron, Dixie Gun Works, Taylor's, Uberti U.S.A. and others.

Price: Dixie Gun Works RH0422... **$340.00**
Price: EMF NY Metropolitan Police, silver fixtures, lanyard ring...**$375.00**

ROGERS & SPENCER PERCUSSION REVOLVER

Caliber: .44 **Barrel:** 7.5 in. **Weight:** 47 oz. **Length:** 13.75 in. overall. Stocks: Walnut. **Sights:** Cone front, integral groove-in-frame for rear. **Features:** Accurate reproduction of a Civil War design. Solid frame, extra-large nipple cut-out on rear of cylinder; loading lever and cylinder easily removed for cleaning. From Dixie Gun Works and others.

Price: **$450.00**

SHERIFF MODEL COLT 1851 PERCUSSION REVOLVER

Caliber: .44, 6-shot. **Barrel:** 5.5 in. **Weight:** 40 oz. **Length:** 10.5 in. overall. Grips: Walnut. **Sights:** Fixed. **Features:** Steel frame, brass backstrap and triggerguard; engraved navy scene; case-hardened frame, hammer, loading lever. Made by Uberti. Imported by EMF.

Price: Steel frame **$169.95**

Prices given are believed to be accurate at time of publication however, many factors affect retail pricing so exact pricing is not possible.

SPILLER & BURR PERCUSSION REVOLVER
Caliber: .36 **Barrel:** 7 in., octagon. **Weight:** 2.5 lbs. **Length:** 12.5 in. overall. **Grip:** Two-piece walnut. **Sights:** Fixed. **Features:** Reproduction of the C.S.A. revolver. Brass frame and triggerguard. Also available as a kit. Made by Pietta. From Dixie Gun Works, Traditions and others.
Price: Dixie Gun Works RH0120 .... **$263.00**
Price: Dixie Gun Works kit RH0300 .... **$233.00**

STARR DOUBLE-ACTION 1858 ARMY REVOLVER
Caliber: .44 **Barrel:** 6 in. tapered round. **Weight:** 3 lbs. **Length:** 11.75 in. Stocks: Walnut one-piece. **Sights:** Hammer notch rear, dovetailed front. **Features:** Double-action mechanism, round tapered barrel, all blued frame and barrel. Made by Pietta. Imported by Dixie Gun Works and others.
Price: Dixie Gun Works RH460 .... **$540.00**

STARR SINGLE-ACTION ARMY REVOLVER
Caliber: .44 **Barrel:** 8 in. tapered round. **Weight:** 3 lbs. **Length:** 13.5 in. Stocks: Walnut one-piece. **Sights:** Hammer notch rear, dovetailed front. **Features:** Single-action mechanism, round tapered barrel, all blued frame and barrel. Made by Pietta. Imported by Cabela's, Dixie Gun Works and others.
Price: Dixie Gun Works RH460 .... **$515.00**

WALKER 1847 PERCUSSION REVOLVER
Caliber: .44, 6-shot. **Barrel:** 9 in. **Weight:** 84 oz. **Length:** 15.5 in. overall. Stocks: Walnut. **Sights:** Fixed. **Features:** Case-hardened frame, loading lever and hammer; iron backstrap; brass triggerguard; engraved cylinder. Imported by Cabela's, Cimarron, Taylor's and others.
Price: Case-hardened frame.. **$450.00**

BROWN BESS MUSKET, SECOND MODEL

Caliber: .75. **Barrel:** 42 in., round, smoothbore. **Weight:** 9 lbs. **Length:** 57.75 in. **Stock:** European walnut, fullstock. **Sights:** Steel stud on front serves as bayonet lug. **Features:** Flintlock using one-inch flint with optional brass flash guard (SCO203), steel parts all polished armory bright, brass furniture. Lock marked Grice, 1762 with crown and GR. Made by Pedersoli. Imported by Cabela's, Dixie Gun Works, others.

Price: Dixie Complete gun FR0810	**$1,380.00**
Price: Dixie Kit Gun FR0825	**$1,050.00**
Price: Cabela's Complete gun	**$1,100.00**
Price: Dixie Trade Gun, 30.5-in. barrel, browned FR0665	**$1,400.00**
Price: Dixie Trade Gun Kit FR0600	**$950.00**
Price: Dixie Trade Musket , 30.5-in. barrel, browned FR3170	**$1,050.00**
Price: Dixie Trade Musket Kit FR3370	**$995.00**

CABELA'S BLUE RIDGE RIFLE

Caliber: .32, .36, .45, .50, .54. **Barrel:** 39 in., octagon. **Weight:** 7.75 lbs. **Length:** 55 in. overall. **Stock:** American black walnut. **Sights:** Blade front, rear drift adjustable for windage. **Features:** Color case-hardened lockplate and cock/hammer, brass triggerguard and buttplate; double set, double-phased triggers. From Cabela's.

Price: Percussion	**$569.99**
Price: Flintlock	**$599.99**

CABELA'S KODIAK EXPRESS DOUBLE RIFLE

Caliber: .50, .54, .58, .72. **Barrel:** 1:48 in. twist. **Weight:** 9.3 lbs. **Length:** 45.25 in. overall. **Stock:** European walnut, oil finish. **Sights:** Fully adjustable double folding-leaf rear, ramp front. **Features:** Percussion. Barrels regulated to point of aim at 75 yards; polished and engraved lock, top tang and triggerguard. From Cabela's.

Price: .50, .54, .58 calibers	**$929.99**
Price: .72 caliber	**$959.99**

CABELA'S TRADITIONAL HAWKEN

Caliber: .50, 54. **Barrel:** 29 in. **Weight:** 9 lbs. **Stock:** Walnut. **Sights:** Blade front, open adjustable rear. **Features:** Flintlock or percussion. Adjustable double-set triggers. Polished brass furniture, color case-hardened lock. Imported by Cabela's.

Price: Percussion, right hand or left hand	**$339.99**
Price: Flintlock, right hand	**$399.99**

CVA OPTIMA V2 BREAK-ACTION RIFLE

Caliber: .45, .50. **Barrel:** 28 in. fluted. **Weight:** 8.8 lbs. **Stock:** Ambidextrous solid composite in standard or thumbhole. **Sights:** Adj. fiber-optic. **Features:** Break-action, stainless No. 209 breech plug, aluminum loading rod, cocking spur, lifetime warranty.

Price: CR4002 (.50-cal., blued/Realtree HD)	**$398.95**
Price: CR4002X (.50-cal., stainless/Realtree HD)	**$456.95**
Price: CR4003X (.45-cal., stainless/Realtree HD)	**$456.95**
Price: CR4000T (.50-cal), blued/black fiber grip thumbhole)	**$366.95**
Price: CR4000 (.50-cal., blued/black fiber grip)	**$345.95**
Price: CR4002T (.50-cal., blued/Realtree HD thumbhole)	**$432.95**
Price: CR4002S (.50-cal., stainless/Realtree HD thumbhole)	**$422.95**
Price: CR4000X (.50-cal., stainless/black fiber grip thumbhole)	**$451.95**
Price: CR4000S (.50-cal., stainless/black fiber grip)	**$400.95**

CVA OPTIMA 209 MAGNUM BREAK-ACTION RIFLE

Similar to Optima Elite but with 26-in. bbl., nickel or blue finish, .50 cal.

Price:	**$317.00 to $409.00**

CVA WOLF 209 MAGNUM BREAK-ACTION RIFLE

Similar to Optima 209 Mag. but with 24-in. barrel, weighs 7 lbs., in .50 cal. only.

Price:	**$247.00 to $329.00**

CVA APEX

Caliber: .45, .50. **Barrel:** 27 in., 1:28 in. twist. **Weight:** 8 lbs. **Length:** 42 in. **Stock:** Synthetic. **Features:** Ambidextrous with rubber grip panels in black or Realtree APG camo, crush-zone recoil pad, reversible hammer spur, quake claw sling, lifetime warranty.

Price: CR4010S (.50-cal., stainless/black)	**$738.00**

CVA ACCURA

Similar to Apex but weighs 7.3 lbs., in stainless steel or matte blue finish, cocking spur.

Price: PR3106S (.50-cal, stainless steel/Realtree APG thumbhole)	**$495.95**
Price: PR3107S (.45-cal., stainless steel/Realtree APG thumbhole)	**$495.95**
Price: PR 3104S (.50-cal., stainless steel/black fiber grip thumbhole)	**$438.95**
Price: PR3100 (.50-cal., blued/black fiber grip)	**$345.95**
Price: PR3100S (.50-cal., stainless steel/black fibergrip)	**$403.95**
Price: PR3102S (.50-cal., stainless steel/Realtree APG)	**$460.95**

CVA BUCKHORN 209 MAGNUM

Caliber: .50. **Barrel:** 24 in. **Weight:** 6.3 lbs. **Sights:** Illuminator fiber optic. **Features:** Grip-dot stock, thumb-actuated safety, drilled and tapped for scope mounts.

Price: Black stock, blue barrel	**$177.00**

DIXIE 1803 HARPERS FERRY FLINTLOCK RIFLE

Caliber: .54. **Barrel:** 35.5 in., smoothbore. **Weight:** 9.5 lbs. **Length:** 29.5 in. overall. **Stock:** Halfstock, walnut w/oil finish. **Sights:** Blade front, notched rear. **Features:** Color case-hardened lock, browned barrel, with barrel key. Made by Euro Arms. Imported by Dixie Gun Works.

Price: FR0171	**$1,050.00**

DIXIE 1816 FLINTLOCK MUSKET

Caliber: .69. **Barrel:** 42 in., smoothbore. **Weight:** 9.75 lbs. **Length:** 56-7/8 in. overall. **Stock:** Walnut w/oil finish. **Sights:** Blade front. **Features:** All metal finished in "National Armory Bright," three barrelbands w/springs, steel ramrod w/button-shaped head. Made by Pedersoli. Imported by Dixie Gun Works.

Price: FR0305	**$1,460.00**
Price: PR3180, Percussion conversion	**$1,425.00**

DIXIE DELUXE CUB RIFLE

Caliber: .32, .36, .45. **Barrel:** 28 in. octagonal. **Weight:** 6.5 lbs. **Length:** 44 in. overall. **Stock:** Walnut. **Sights:** Fixed. **Features:** Each gun available in either flint or percussion ignition. Short rifle for small game and beginning shooters. Brass patchbox and furniture. Kit guns available in .32 or .36 calibers in percussion ($690) or flint ($710). From Dixie Gun Works.

Price: Deluxe Cub (.32-cal. flint) PR3130	**$890.00**
Price: Deluxe Cub (.36-cal. flint) FR3135	**$890.00**
Price: Deluxe Cub kit (.32-cal. percussion) PK3360	**$690.00**
Price: Deluxe Cub kit (.36-cal. percussion) PK3365	**$690.00**
Price: Deluxe Cub (.45-cal. percussion) PR0768	**$850.00**
Price: Deluxe Cub (.32-cal. percussion) PR3140	**$850.00**
Price: Deluxe Cub (.36-cal. percussion) PR3145	**$850.00**

DIXIE EARLY AMERICAN JAEGER RIFLE

Caliber: .54. **Barrel:** 27.5 in. octagon, 1:24 in. twist. **Weight:** 8.25 lbs. **Length:** 43.5 in. overall. **Stock:** American walnut; sliding wooden patchbox on butt. **Sights:** Notch rear, blade front. **Features:** Flintlock or percussion. Conversion kits available, and recommended converting percussion guns to flintlocks using kit LO1102 at $209.00. Browned steel furniture. Made by Pedersoli. Imported by Dixie Gun Works.

Price: Percussion, PR0835	**$1,295.00**
Price: Flint, PR0835	**$1,375.00**

Prices given are believed to be accurate at time of publication however, many factors affect retail pricing so exact prices are not possible.

Price: Percussion, kit gun, PK0146 .... $1,075.00
Price: Flint, kit gun, PKO143 .... $1,075.00

DIXIE HAWKEN RIFLE
Caliber: .50 and .54. **Barrel:** 29.5 in. octagonal, 1:48 in. twist. **Weight:** 9 or 8.5 lbs. **Length:** 45.5 in. overall. **Stock:** European walnut, halfstock. **Sights:** Rear click adjustable for windage and elevation, blade front. **Features:** Percussion and flintlock, brass patchbox, double-set triggers, one barrel key. Flint gun available for left-handed shooters. Both flint and percussion guns available as kit guns. Made by Pedersoli. Imported by Dixie Gun Works.
Price: Percussion, .50 PR0502 .... $465.00
Price: Percussion, .54 PR0507 .... $450.00
Price: Flint, .50 FR1332 .... $525.00
Price: Flint, .50 left hand, FR1336 .... $525.00
Price: Flint, .50 left hand, kit, FR1345 .... $450.00

DIXIE JAPANESE TANEGASHIMA MATCHLOCK
Caliber: .50. **Barrel:** 53 in. **Weight:** 8.75 lbs. **Length:** 53 in. overall. **Stock:** Japanese cherry with drilled hole on bottom for wooden ramrod. **Sights:** Post front, block rear. **Features:** A replica of the snapping matchlock guns used in Japan from the 17th to 19th centuries. Brass lock with ball trigger, and brass lockplate and hammer. Pan has pivoting cover. Browned barrel. Case-hardened lock. Made by Miroku. Imported by Dixie Gun Works.
Price: Dixie MM0005 .... $1,100.00

DIXIE J.P. MURRAY ARTILLERY CARBINE
Caliber: .58. **Barrel:** 23.5 in. **Weight:** 8 lbs. **Length:** 39.5 in. **Stock:** European walnut. **Sights:** Blade front, fixed notch rear. **Features:** Percussion musket-cap ignition. Reproduction of the original Confederate carbine. Lock marked "J.P. Murray, Columbus, Georgia." Blued barrel. Made Euro Arms. Imported by Dixie Gun Works and others.
Price: Dixie, PRO173 . ... $1,100.00

DIXIE PEDERSOLI 1857 MAUSER RIFLE
Caliber: .54. **Barrel:** 39.75 in. **Weight:** 9.5 lbs. **Length:** 52 in. overall. **Stock:** European walnut. **Sights:** Blade front, rear steel adjustable for windage and elevation. **Features:** Percussion musket-cap ignition. Color case-hardened lockplate marked "Konigi.Wurt Fabrik." Armory bright steel barrel. Made by Pedersoli. Imported by Dixie Gun Works.
Price: Dixie PR1330 .... $1,595.00

DIXIE PENNSYLVANIA RIFLE
Caliber: .45 and .50. **Barrel:** 41.5 in. octagonal, .45/1:48, .50/1:56 in. twist. **Weight:** 8.5, 8.75 lbs. **Length:** 56 in. overall. **Stock:** European walnut, full-length stock. **Sights:** Notch rear, blade front. **Features:** Flintlock or percussion, brass patchbox, double-set triggers. Also available as kit guns for both calibers and ignition systems. Made by Pedersoli. Imported by Dixie Gun Works.
Price: Percussion, .45, PF1070 .... $995.00
Price: Flint, .45, PF1060 .... $995.00
Price: Percussion, .50, PR3205 .... $995.00
Price: Flint, .45, PR3200 .... $995.00

DIXIE POTSDAM 1809 PRUSSIAN MUSKET
Caliber: .75 **Barrel:** 41.2 in. round, smoothbore. **Weight:** 9 lbs. **Length:** 56 in. **Stock:** European walnut, fullstock. **Sights:** Brass lung on upper barrelband. **Features:** Flintlock using one-inch flint. Steel parts all polished armory bright, brass furniture. Lock marked "Potsdam over G.S." Made by Pedersoli. Imported by Dixie Gun Works.
Price: Dixie FR3175 .... $1,495.00

DIXIE SHARPS NEW MODEL 1859 MILITARY RIFLE AND CARBINE
Caliber: .54. **Barrel:** 30 in., 6-groove, 1:48 in. twist. **Weight:** 9 lbs. **Length:** 45.5 in. overall. **Stock:** Oiled walnut. **Sights:** Blade front,

---

ladder-style rear. **Features:** Blued barrel, color case-hardened barrelbands, receiver, hammer, nose cap, lever, patchbox cover and buttplate. Introduced 1995. Rifle made by Armi Sport (Chiappa) and carbine by Pedersoli. Rifle imported from Italy by Dixie Gun Works and carbine by Dixie and Cabela's.
Price: Rifle PR0862 .... $1,095.00
Price: Carbine (22-in. barrel, 39-1/4 in. long, 8 lbs.) PR0982 $1,400.00

DIXIE SMITH CARBINE
Caliber: .50. **Barrel:** 21.5 in., 3-groove, 1:66 in. twist. **Weight:** 7.75 lbs. **Length:** 39 in. **Stock:** Oiled walnut. **Sights:** Blade front, ladder-style rear. **Features:** Hinged breech that drops barrel to allow loading of pre-loaded brass or plastic cartridges fired by a musket cap. Blued barrel, color case-hardened receiver and hammer. Cavalry Carbine has saddle bar and ring, Artillery Carbine has sling swivel on buttstock and barrelband. Rifle made by Pietta. Imported from Italy by Dixie Gun Works.
Price: Dixie Cavalry Carbine PR0220 .... $925.00
Price: Dixie Artillery Carbine PR0223 .... $925.00

DIXIE TRYON RIFLE
Caliber: .50. **Barrel:** 32 in. octagonal, 1:48 in. twist. **Weight:** 9.5 lbs. **Length:** 49 in. overall. **Stock:** European walnut, halfstock. **Sights:** Elevation-adjustable rear with stair-step notches, blade front. **Features:** Percussion, brass patchbox, double-set triggers, two barrel keys. Made by Pedersoli. Imported by Dixie Gun Works.
Price: Percussion, PR0860 .... $995.00
Price: Percussion, kit, PR0255 .... $890.00

DIXIE ZOUAVE RIFLE
Caliber: .58. **Barrel:** 33 in. **Weight:** 9.5 lbs. **Length:** 49 in. **Stock:** European walnut. **Sights:** Blade front, three-leaf military rear. **Features:** Percussion musket-cap ignition. Case-hardened lock and blued barrel. One-piece solid barrel and bolster. Made in Italy by Armi Sport. Imported by Dixie Gun Works, others.
Price: PF0340 .... $950.00

ENFIELD MUSKETOON P1861
Caliber: .58. **Barrel:** 33 in. **Weight:** 9 lbs. **Length:** 35 in. overall. **Stock:** European walnut. **Sights:** Blade front, flip-up rear with elevator marked to 700 yards. **Features:** Reproduction of the original cavalry version of the Enfield rifle. Percussion musket-cap ignition. Blued barrel with steel barrelbands, brass furniture. Case-hardened lock. Euro Arms version marked London Armory with crown. Pedersoli version has Birmingham stamp on stock and Enfield and Crown on lockplate. Made by Euro Arms, Pedersoli. Imported by Cabela's, Dixie Gun Works and others.
Price: Cabelas, Pedersoli $900.00
Price: Dixie Euro Arms PR0343 .... $1,050.00

ENFIELD THREE-BAND P1853 RIFLE
Caliber: .58. **Barrel:** 39 in. **Weight:** 10.25 lbs. **Length:** 52 in. overall. **Stock:** European walnut. **Sights:** Blade front, flip-up rear with elevator marked to 800 yards. **Features:** Reproduction of the original three-band rifle. Percussion musket-cap ignition. Blued barrel with steel barrelbands, brass furniture. Case-hardened lock. Lockplate marked "London Armory Co. and Crown." Made by Euro Arms, Armi Sport (Chiappa), Pedersoli. Imported by Cabela's, Dixie Gun Works and others.
Price: Cabela's, Pedersoli $930.00
Price: Dixie Armi Sport/Chiappa PR1130 .... $858.00
Price: Dixie Euro Arms PR0340 .... $1,200.00

ENFIELD TWO-BAND P1858 RIFLE
Caliber: .58. **Barrel:** 24 in. **Weight:** 7.75 lbs. **Length:** 43.25 in. overall. **Stock:** European walnut. **Sights:** Blade front, flip-up rear with elevator marked to 1,000 yards. **Features:** Reproduction of the original two-band rifle. Percussion musket-cap ignition. Blued barrel with steel barrelbands, brass furniture. Case-hardened lock. Lockplate marked "1858 Enfield and Crown." Made by Euro Arms, Pedersoli, Chiappa. Imported by Cabela's, Dixie Gun Works and others.
Price: Cabela's, Pedersoli $930.00
Price: Dixie Euro Arms PR1135 .... $825.00
Price: Dixie Chiappa 150th Aniv. Mod. PR0106 .... $750.00

KNIGHT BIGHORN
Caliber: .50. **Barrel:** 26 in., 1:28 in. twist. **Weight:** 7 lbs. 3 oz. **Length:** 44.5 in. overall. **Stock:** G2 straight or thumbhole, Carbon Knight straight or thumbhole or black composite thumbhole with recoil pad,

---

Prices given are believed to be accurate at time of publication however, many factors affect retail pricing so exact prices are not possible.

69TH EDITION, 2015 ⊕ **525**

sling swivel studs. **Ramrod:** Carbon core with solid brass extendable jag. **Sights:** Fully adjustable metallic fiber optic. **Features:** Uses four different ignition systems (included): #11 nipple, musket nipple, bare 208 shotgun primer and 209 Extreme shotgun primer system (Extreme weatherproof full plastic jacket system); vented breech plug, striker fired with one-piece removable hammer assembly. With recommended loads, guaranteed to have 4-inch, three-shot groups at 200 yards. Also available as Western gun with exposed ignition. Made in U.S. by Knight Rifles (Modern Muzzleloading).
Price: Standard stock $460.00

KNIGHT DISC EXTREME
Caliber: .50, .52. **Barrel:** 26 in., fluted stainless, 1:28 in. twist. **Weight:** 7 lbs. 14 oz. to 8 lbs. **Length:** 45 in. overall. **Stock:** Carbon Knight straight or thumbhole with blued or SS; G2 thumbhole; left-handed Nutmeg thumbhole. **Ramrod:** Solid brass extendable jag. **Sights:** Fully adjustable metallic fiber optics. **Features:** Bolt-action rifle, full plastic jacket ignition system, #11 nipple, musket nipple, bare 208 shotgun primer. With recommended loads, guaranteed to have 4-inch, three-shot groups at 200 yards. Also available as Western gun with exposed ignition. Made in U.S. by Knight Rifles (Modern Muzzleloading).
Price: .... $560.00 to $930.00

KNIGHT HPX
Caliber: .50, .45-70 Govt. or .444 Marlin. **Barrel:** 26 in. as muzzleloader, 24 in. as centerfire. **Length:** 43.5 in./muzzleloader, 39.5 in./centerfire. **Ignition:** Full Plastic Jacket or bare 209 primer. **Stock:** Shadow gray laminated wood, G2 Camo or composite straight. **Weight:** 8 lbs./muzzleloader, 7.8 lbs./cartridge. **Features:** Break-open rifle with stainless steel action, quick-release trigger assembly, vented breech plug and stainless steel Dyna-coated barrel. **Ramrod:** Carbon core with solid brass extendable jag. **Sights:** Williams fiber-optic sights. **Finish:** Stainless steel. With recommended loads, guaranteed to have 4-inch, three-shot groups at 200 yards. Made in U.S. by Knight Rifles (Modern Muzzleloading).
Price: To be determined, about $900

KNIGHT LITTLEHORN
Caliber: .50. **Barrel:** 22 in., 1:28 in. twist. **Weight:** 6.7 lbs. **Length:** 39 in. overall. **Stock:** 12.5-in. length of pull, G2 straight or pink Realtree AP HD. **Ramrod:** Carbon core with solid brass extendable jag. **Sights:** Fully adjustable Williams fiber optic. **Features:** Uses four different ignition systems (included): Full Plastic Jacket, #11 nipple, musket nipple or bare 209 shotgun primer; vented breech plug, striker fired with one-piece removable hammer assembly. **Finish:** Stainless steel. With recommended loads, guaranteed to have 4-inch, three-shot groups at 200 yards. Also available as Western gun with exposed ignition. Made in U.S. by Knight Rifles (Modern Muzzleloading).
Price: $500.00

KNIGHT MOUNTAINEER FOREST GREEN
Caliber: .45, .50, .52. **Barrel:** 27 in. fluted stainless steel, free floated. **Weight:** 8 lbs. (thumbhole stock), 8.3 lbs. (straight stock). **Length:** 45.5 inches. **Sights:** Fully adjustable metallic fiber optic. **Features:** Bolt-action rifle, adjustable match-grade trigger, aluminum ramrod with carbon core, solid brass extendable jag, vented breech plug. **Ignition:** Full plastic jacket, #11 nipple, musket nipple, bare 208 shotgun primer. With recommended loads, guaranteed to have 4-inch, three-shot groups at 200 yards. Also available as Western gun with exposed ignition. Made in U.S. by Knight Rifles (Modern Muzzleloading).
Price: .... $670.00 to $950.00

KNIGHT ULTRA-LITE
Caliber: .50. **Barrel:** 24 in. **Ignition:** 209 Primer with Full Plastic Jacket, musket cap or #11 nipple, bare 208 shotgun primer; vented breech

plug. **Stock:** Black, tan or olive green Kevlar spider web. **Weight:** 6 lbs. **Features:** Bolt-action rifle. **Ramrod:** Carbon core with solid brass extendable jag. **Sights:** With or without Williams fiber-optic sights, drilled and tapped for scope mounts. **Finish:** Stainless steel. With recommended loads, guaranteed to have 4-inch, three-shot groups at 200 yards. Also available as Western version with exposed ignition. Made in U.S. by Knight Rifles (Modern Muzzleloading).
Price: $900

KNIGHT VISION
Caliber: .50. **Barrel:** 24 in. **Length:** 44 in. **Ignition:** Full Plastic Jacket. **Stock:** Black composite. **Weight:** 7.9 lbs. **Features:** Break-open rifle with carbon-steel barrel and all new machined steel action. With recommended loads, guaranteed to have 4-inch, three-shot groups at 200 yards. **Ramrod:** Carbon core with solid brass extendable jag. **Sights:** Weaver sight bases attached and Williams fiber-optic sights provided. **Finish:** Blued steel. Made in U.S. by Knight Rifles (Modern Muzzleloading).
Price: To be determined, about $450

KNIGHT WOLVERINE
Caliber: .50. **Barrel:** 22 in. stainless steel, 1:28 in. twist. **Weight:** 6.9 lbs. **Length:** 40.5 overall. **Stock:** Realtree Hardwoods straight, CarbonKnight straight. **Ramrod:** Carbon core with solid brass extendable jag. **Sights:** Fully adjustable Williams fiber optic. **Features:** Ignition systems (included): #11 nipple, musket nipple, bare 208 shotgun primer; vented breech plug, striker fired with one-piece removable hammer assembly. **Finish:** Stainless steel. With recommended loads, guaranteed to have 4-inch, three-shot groups at 200 yards. Also available as Western gun with exposed ignition. Made in U.S. by Knight Rifles (Modern Muzzleloading).
Price: $500.00
Price: Thumbhole stock $480.00

LHR REDEMPTION RIFLE
Caliber: .50. **Barrel:** 24 or 20 in. nitride finished, tapered barrel. **Weight:** 6.75 or 6.25 lbs. **Length:** 44 in. or 40 in. **Stock:** Walnut, black synthetic, G2-Vista Camo. **Finish:** Armornite nitride. **Features:** Break-open action, sliding hammerless cocking mechanism, optional pellet or loose powder, easy removable breech plugs retained by external collar, aluminum frame with steel mono-block to retain barrel, recoil pad. **Sights:** Williams fiber-optic sights furnished, drilled and tapped for scope. A similar model has five 21-in. interchangeable rifle barrels, a 20-gauge shotgun barrel and a 20-gauge rifled-slug barrel. Made in the U.S. by LHR Sporting Arms. Available through dealers or you may order from the factory.
Price: .50 ca. 24-in. barrel, black synthetic stock $620.00
Price: .50 cal. 24-in. barrel, G2 camo stock $670.00
Price: .50 cal. 24-in. barrel, walnut stock $820.00
Price: .50 ca. 20-in. barrel, black synthetic stock $620.00
Price: .50 cal. 20-in. barrel, G2 camo stock $670.00
Price: .50 cal. 20-in. barrel, walnut stock $820.00

LYMAN DEERSTALKER RIFLE
Caliber: .50, .54. **Barrel:** 24 in., octagonal, 1:48 in. rifling. **Weight:** 10.4 lbs. **Stock:** Walnut with black rubber buttpad. **Sights:** Lyman #37MA beaded front, fully adjustable fold-down Lyman #16A rear. **Features:** Percussion and flintlock ignition. Stock has less drop for quick sighting. All metal parts are blackened, with color case-hardened lock, single trigger. Comes with sling and swivels. Available in flint or percussion. Introduced 1990. From Lyman.
Price: .50-cal. flintlock $480.00
Price: Left-hand flintlock $483.00
Price: .54-cal. flintlock $483.00
Price: Percussion blue $480.00

BLACKPOWDER MUSKETS & RIFLES

LYMAN GREAT PLAINS RIFLE
Caliber: .50, .54. **Barrel:** 32 in., 1:60in. twist. **Weight:** 11.6 lbs. **Stock:** Walnut. **Sights:** Steel blade front, buckhorn rear adjustable for windage and elevation, and fixed notch primitive sight included. **Features:** Percussion or flint ignition. Blued steel furniture. Stainless steel nipple. Coil spring lock, Hawken-style triggerguard and double-set triggers. Round thimbles recessed and sweated into rib. Steel wedge plates and toe plate. Introduced 1979. From Lyman.
Price: Percussion $518.00
Price: Flintlock $455.00
Price: Left-hand percussion $650.00
Price: Left-hand flintlock $670.00

LYMAN GREAT PLAINS HUNTER MODEL
Similar to Great Plains model except 1:32 in. twist, shallow-groove barrel and comes drilled and tapped for Lyman 57GPR peep sight.
Price: Percussion $520.00
Price: Flintlock $540.00

LYMAN MUSTANG
Caliber: .50. **Barrel:** 26 in., 1:28 twist. Ignition: 209 primer. **Weight:** 7 lbs. **Stock:** Ultra Grade wood finish, checkered, rubber recoil pad. Ramrod: Solid aluminum. **Sights:** Fiber-optic front and rear. **Features:** Hammerless break-open action for 209 shotshell primer and up to 150-grain charges. Imported by Lyman.
Price: $410.00

LYMAN TRADE RIFLE
Caliber: .50, .54. **Barrel:** 28 in. octagon, 1:48 in. twist. **Weight:** 10.8 lbs. **Length:** 45 in. overall. **Stock:** European walnut. **Sights:** Blade front, open rear adjustable for windage, or optional fixed sights. **Features:** Fast-twist rifling for conical bullets. Polished brass furniture with blue steel parts, stainless steel nipple. Hook breech, single trigger, coil spring percussion lock. Steel barrel rib and ramrod ferrules. Introduced 1980. From Lyman.
Price: Percussion...$400.00
Price: Flintlock $400.00

PEDERSOLI 1776 CHARLEVILLE MUSKET
Caliber: .69. **Barrel:** 44.75 in. round, smoothbore. **Weight:** 10.5 lbs. **Length:** 60 in. **Stock:** European walnut, fullstock. **Sights:** Steel stud on upper barrelband. **Features:** Flintlock using one-inch flint. Steel parts all polished armory bright, brass furniture. Lock marked Charleville. Made by Pedersoli. Imported by Cabela's, Dixie Gun Works, others.
Price: Dixie Complete gun FR1045.....................................$1,425.00
Price: Dixie Kit Gun FK3440 ....$1,140.00
Price: Dixie French Model 1777 Complete gun FR0930 ...... $1,450.00
Price: Dixie French Currige An IX Charleville FR0157 .... $1,450.00

PEDERSOLI 1795 SPRINGFIELD MUSKET
Caliber: .69. **Barrel:** 44.75 in., round, smoothbore. **Weight:** 10.5 lbs. **Length:** 57.25 in. **Stock:** European walnut, fullstock. **Sights:** Brass stud on upper barrelband. **Features:** Flintlock using one-inch flint. Steel parts all polished armory bright, brass furniture. Lock marked US Springfield. Made by Pedersoli. Imported by Cabela's, Dixie Gun Works, others.
Price: Dixie Complete gun FR3210.......................................$1,495.00

PEDERSOLI 1841 MISSISSIPPI RIFLE
Caliber: .58. **Barrel:** 33 inches. **Weight:** 9.5 lbs. **Length:** 48.75 in. overall. **Stock:** European walnut. **Sights:** Blade front, notched rear. **Features:** Percussion musket-cap ignition. Reproduction of the original one-band rifle with large brass patchbox. Color case-hardened lockplate with browned barrel. Made by Pedersoli. Imported by Cabela's.
Price: Cabela's...$850.00

PEDERSOLI 1861 SPRINGFIELD RIFLE
Caliber: .58. **Barrel:** 40 inches. **Weight:** 10 lbs. **Length:** 55.5 in. overall. **Stock:** European walnut. **Sights:** Blade front, three-leaf military rear. **Features:** Reproduction of the original three-band rifle. Percussion musket-cap ignition. Lockplate marked 1861 with eagle and U.S. Springfield. Armory bright steel. Made by Armi Sport/Chiappa, Pedersoli. Imported by Cabela's, Dixie Gun Works, others.
Price: Cabela's, Pedersoli.....................................$980.00
Price: Dixie Armi Sport/Chiappa PR3180 ....$1,150.00

PEDERSOLI BRISTLEN MORGES AND WAADTLANDER TARGET RIFLES
Caliber: .44, .45. **Barrel:** 29.5 in. tapered octagonal, hooked breech. **Weight:** 15.5 lbs. **Length:** 48.5 in. overall. **Stock:** European walnut, halfstock with hooked buttplate and detachable palm rest. **Sights:** Creedmoor rear on Morges, Swiss Diopter on Waadtlander, hooded front sight notch. **Features:** Percussion back-action lock, double set, double-phase triggers, one barrel key, muzzle protector. Specialized bullet molds for each gun. Made by Pedersoli. Imported by Dixie Gun Works.
Price: Percussion, .44 Bristlen Morges PR0165 .... $2,995.00
Price: Percussion, .45 Waadtlander PR0183 .... $2,995.00

PEDERSOLI COOK & BROTHER CONFEDERATE CARBINE
Caliber: .58. **Barrel:** 24 inches. **Weight:** 7.5 lbs. **Length:** 40.25 in. **Stock:** Select oil-finished walnut. **Features:** Percussion musket-cap ignition. Color case-hardened lock, browned barrel. Buttplate, triggerguard, barrelbands, sling swivels and nose cap of polished brass. Lock marked with stars and bars flag on tail and Athens, Georgia. Made by Pedersoli. Imported by Dixie Gun Works, others.
Price: Pedersoli...$1,100.00

PEDERSOLI COUNTRY HUNTER
Caliber: .50. **Barrel:** 26 in. octagonal. **Weight:** 6 lbs. **Length:** 41.75 in. overall. **Stock:** European walnut, halfstock. **Sights:** Rear notch, blade front. **Features:** Percussion, one barrel key. Made by Pedersoli. Imported by Dixie Gun Works.
Price: Percussion, .50 PR3155 .... $595.00

PEDERSOLI KENTUCKY RIFLE
Caliber: .32, .45 and .50. **Barrel:** 35.5 in. octagonal. **Weight:** 7.5 (.50 cal.) to 7.75 lbs. (.32 cal.) **Length:** 51 in. overall. **Stock:** European walnut, full-length stock. **Sights:** Notch rear, blade front. **Features:** Flintlock or percussion, brass patchbox, double-set triggers. Also available as kit guns for all calibers and ignition systems. Made by Pedersoli. Imported by Dixie Gun Works.
Price: Percussion, .32, PR3115 .... $695.00
Price: Flint, .32, FR3100 .... $750.00
Price: Percussion, .45, FR3120 .... $695.00
Price: Flint, .45, FR3105 .... $750.00
Price: Percussion, .50, FR3125 .... $695.00
Price: Flint, .50, FR3110 .... $750.00

PEDERSOLI KODIAK DOUBLE RIFLES AND COMBINATION GUN
Caliber: .50, .54 and .58 **Barrel:** 28.5 in.; 1:24/1:24/1:48 in. twist. **Weight:** 11.25/10.75/10 lbs. **Stock:** Straight grip European walnut. **Sights:** Two adjustable rear, steel ramp with brass bead front. **Features:** Percussion ignition, double triggers, sling swivels. A .72-caliber express rifle and a .50-caliber/12-gauge shotgun combination gun are also available. Blued steel furniture. Stainless steel nipple. Made by Pedersoli. Imported by Dixie Gun Works and some models by Cabela's and others.
Price: Rifle 50X50 PR0970...$1,495.00
Price: Rifle 54X54 PR0975 ....$1,495.00
Price: Rifle 58X58 PR0980...$1,495.00
Price: Combo 50X12 gauge PR0990 ....$1,350.00
Price: Express Rifle .72 caliber PR0916 ....$1,525.00

PEDERSOLI MORTIMER RIFLE & SHOTGUN
Caliber: .54, 12 gauge. **Barrel:** 36 in., 1:66 in. twist, and cylinder bore. **Weight:** 10 lbs. rifle, 9 lbs. shotgun. **Length:** 52.25 in. **Stock:** Halfstock walnut. **Sights:** Blued steel rear with flip-up leaf, blade front. **Features:** Percussion and flint ignition. Blued steel furniture. Single trigger. Lock with hammer safety and "waterproof pan" marked Mortimer. A percussion .45-caliber target version of this gun is available with a peep sight on the wrist, and a percussion shotgun version is also offered. Made by Pedersoli. Imported by Dixie.
Price: Flint Rifle, FR0151 ....$1,475.00
Price: Flint Shotgun FS0155..$1,425.00

Prices given are believed to be accurate at time of publication however, many factors affect retail pricing so exact prices are not possible.

69TH EDITION, 2015 ✛ 527

BLACKPOWDER MUSKETS & RIFLES

Price: Percussion .45-cal. Whitworth rifle, PR0175$ **1,550.00**
Price: Percussion Shotgun PS3160 .... **$1,275.00**

PEDERSOLI ROCKY MOUNTAIN & MISSOURI RIVER HAWKEN RIFLES

Caliber: .54 (Rocky Mountain), .45 and .50 in Missouri River. **Barrel:** 34.75 in. octagonal with hooked breech; Rocky Mountain 1:65 in. twist; Missouri River 1:47 twist in .45 cal., and 1:24 twist in .50 cal. **Weight:** 10 lbs. **Length:** 52 in. overall. **Stock:** Maple or walnut, halfstock. **Sights:** Rear buckhorn with push elevator, silver blade front. **Features:** Percussion, brass furniture, double triggers, two barrel keys. Made by Pedersoli. Imported by Dixie Gun Works, others.
Price: Rocky Mountain, Maple PR3430 .... **$1,325.00**
Price: Rocky Mountain, Walnut PR3435 .... **$1,125.00**
Price: Missouri River, .50 Walnut PR3415 .... **$1,250.00**
Price: Missouri River, .50 Maple PR3410 .... **$1,475.00**
Price: Missouri River, .45 Walnut PR3405 .... **$1,250.00**
Price: Missouri River, .45 Maple PR3080 .... **$1,475.00**

PEDERSOLI ZOUAVE RIFLE

Caliber: .58 percussion. **Barrel:** 33 inches. **Weight:** 9.5 lbs. **Length:** 49 inches. **Stock:** European walnut. **Sights:** Blade front, three-leaf military rear. **Features:** Percussion musket-cap ignition. One-piece solid barrel and bolster. Brass-plated patchbox. Made in Italy by Pedersoli. Imported by Cabela's, others.
Price: **$930.00**

RICHMOND 1861 RIFLE

Caliber: .58. **Barrel:** 40 inches. **Weight:** 9.5 lbs. **Length:** 55.5 in. overall. **Stock:** European walnut. **Sights:** Blade front, three-leaf military rear. **Features:** Reproduction of the original three-band rifle. Percussion musket-cap ignition. Lock marked C. S. Richmond, Virginia. Armory bright. Made by Pedersoli, Euro Arms. Imported by Cabela's, Dixie Gun Works and others.
Price: Cabela's **$950.00**
Price: From Dixie Gun Works, Made by Euro Arms
    PR0846 .... **$1,150.00**

SECOND MODEL BROWN BESS MUSKET

Caliber: .75. **Barrel:** 42 in., round, smoothbore. **Weight:** 9 lbs. **Length:** 57.75 in. **Stock:** European walnut, fullstock. **Sights:** Steel stud on front serves as bayonet lug. **Features:** Flintlock using one-inch flint with optional brass flash guard (SCO203). Steel parts all polished armory bright, brass furniture. Lock marked Grice, 1762 with crown and GR. Made by Pedersoli. Imported by Cabela's, Dixie Gun Works, others.
Price: Dixie Complete gun FR0810 .... **$1,380.00**
Price: Dixie Kit Gun FR0825 .... **$1,050.00**
Price: Cabela's Complete gun **$1,100.00**
Price: Dixie Trade Gun, 30.5-in. barrel, browned FR0665 .... **$1,400.00**
Price: Dixie Trade Gun Kit FR0600 .... **$950.00**
Price: Dixie Trade Musket, 30.5-in. barrel, browned FR3170 **$1,050.00**
Price: Dixie Trade Musket Kit FR3370 .... **$995.00**

THOMPSON/CENTER BONE COLLECTOR

Similar to the Triumph Magnum but with added FlexTech technology and Energy Burners to a shorter stock. Also added is Thompson/Center's premium fluted barrel with Weather Shield and their patented Power Rod.
Price: .... **$600.00 to $800.00**

THOMPSON/CENTER ENCORE PRO HUNTER

Caliber: .50 as muzzleloading barrel. **Barrel:** 26 in., Weather Shield with relieved muzzle on muzzleloader; interchangeable with 14 centerfire calibers. **Weight:** 7 lbs. **Length:** 40.5 in. overall. **Stock:** Interchangeable American walnut butt and forend, black composite, FlexTech recoil-reducing camo stock as thumbhole or straight, rubber over-molded stock and fore-end. **Ramrod:** Solid aluminum. **Sights:** TruGlo fiber optic front and rear. **Features:** Blue or stainless steel. Uses the frame of the Encore centerfire pistol; break-open design using triggerguard spur; stainless steel universal breech plug; uses #209 shotshell primers. Made in U.S. by Thompson/Center Arms.
Price: Stainless with camo stock **$772.00**

Price: Blue, composite stock and forend **$637.00**
Price: Stainless, composite stock and forend **$713.00**
Price: All camo Realtree Hardwoods **$729.00**

THOMPSON/CENTER IMPACT MUZZLELOADING RIFLE

Caliber: .50-caliber. **Barrel:** 26 in., 1:28 twist, Weather Shield finish. **Weight:** 6.5 lbs. **Length:** 41.5 in. **Stock:** Straight Realtree Hardwoods HD or black composite. **Features:** Sliding-hood, break-open action, #209 primer ignition, removable breech plug, synthetic stock adjustable from 12.5 to 13.5 in., adjustable fiber-optic sights, aluminum ramrod, camo, QLA relieved muzzle system.
Price: Impact Camo, Weather Shield, Black .... **$249.00 to $269.00**

THOMPSON/CENTER TRIUMPH MAGNUM MUZZLELOADER

Caliber: .50. **Barrel:** 28 in. Weather Shield coated. **Weight:** 6.5 lbs. **Stock:** FlexTech recoil-reducing. Black composite or Realtree AP HD camo straight, rubber over-molded stock and fore-end. **Sights:** Fiber optic. **Ramrod:** Solid aluminum. **Features:** Break-open action. Quick Detachable Speed Breech XT plug, #209 shotshell primer ignition, easy loading QLA relieved muzzle, Cabela's, Bass Pro. Made in U.S. by Thompson/Center Arms.
Price: .... **$450.00 to $650.00**

TRADITIONS BUCKSTALKER

Caliber: .50. **Barrel:** 24 in., Cerakote finished, Accelerator Breech Plug. **Weight:** 6 lbs. **Length:** 40 in. **Stock:** Synthetic, G2 Vista camo or black. **Sights:** Fiber-optic rear. **Features:** Break-open action, matte-finished action and barrel. **Ramrod:** Solid aluminum.
Price: Steel, .50 cal., synthetic black, blued **$218.00**
Price: Steel, .50 cal., synthetic stock, Cerakote **$249.00**
Price: Steel, .50 cal., synthetic stock, G2-Vista **$293.00**
Price: Steel, .50 cal., synthetic stock, G2-Vista with scope **$364.00**

TRADITIONS CROCKETT RIFLE

Caliber: .32. **Barrel:** 32 in., 1:48 in. twist. **Weight:** 6.75 lbs. **Length:** 49 in. overall. **Stock:** Beech, inletted toe plate. **Sights:** Blade front, fixed rear. **Features:** Set triggers, hardwood halfstock, brass furniture, color case-hardened lock. Percussion. From Traditions.
Price: Percussion **$509.00**
Price: Kit, percussion, hardwood, Armory bright,
    unfinished brass **$438.00**

TRADITIONS DEERHUNTER RIFLE SERIES

Caliber: .50. **Barrel:** 24 in., Cerakote finish, octagonal, 15/16 in. flats, 1:48 in. twist. **Weight:** 6 lbs. **Length:** 40 in. overall. **Stock:** Stained hardwood or All-Weather composite with rubber buttpad, sling swivels. **Ramrod:** Synthetic polymer. **Sights:** Lite Optic blade front, adjustable rear fiber optics, offset hammer spur. **Features:** Flint or percussion with color case-hardened lock. Hooked breech, oversized triggerguard, blackened furniture, PVC ramrod. Drilled and tapped for scope mounting. Imported by Traditions, Inc.
Price: Flintlock, .50 cal., hardwood, 1:48 in. twist **$377.00**
Price: Percussion, .50 cal., synthetic/blued **$266.00**
Price: Flintlock, .50 cal., synthetic/blued **$323.00**
Price: Flintlock, .50 cal., Cerakote **$309.00**
Price: Flintlock, .50 cal., Cerakote Realtree Xtra **$399.00**
Price: Redi-Pak, .50 cal. flintlock **$367.00**

      Prices given are believed to be accurate at time of publication however, many factors affect retail pricing so exact prices are not possible.

Price: Flintlock, left-handed hardwood, .50 cal. **$414.00**
Price: .50 cal., hardwood/blued **$319.00**
Price: Kit, perc., hardwood, Armory bright, unfinished brass.. **$295.00**

TRADITIONS EVOLUTION BOLT-ACTION BLACKPOWDER RIFLE
Caliber: .50 percussion. **Barrel:** 26 in., 1:28 in. twist, Cerakote finished barrel and action. **Length:** 39 in. **Sights:** Steel Williams fiber-optic sights. **Weight:** 7 to 7.25 lbs. **Length:** 45 in. overall. **Features:** Bolt action, cocking indicator, thumb safety, shipped with adaptors for No. 11 caps, musket caps and 209 shotgun primer ignition, sling swivels. Ramrod: Aluminum, sling studs. Available with exposed ignition as a Northwest Gun.
Price: .50-cal. synthetic black, Cerakote................................. **$310.00**

TRADITIONS HAWKEN WOODSMAN RIFLE
Caliber: .50. **Barrel:** 28 in., blued, 15/16 in. flats. **Weight:** 7 lbs., 11 oz. **Length:** 44.5 in. overall. **Stock:** Walnut stained hardwood. **Sights:** Beaded blade front, hunting-style open rear adjustable for windage and elevation. **Features:** Percussion only. Brass patchbox and furniture. Double-set triggers. Flint or percussion. From Traditions.
Price: Percussion **$474.00**
Price: Flintlock **$510.00**
Price: Kit, perc., hardwood, Armory bright, unfinished brass.. **$370.00**

TRADITIONS KENTUCKY RIFLE
Caliber: .50. **Barrel:** 33.5 in., 7/8 in. flats, 1:66 in. twist. **Weight:** 7 lbs. **Length:** 49 in. overall. **Stock:** Beech, inletted toe plate. **Sights:** Blade front, fixed rear. **Features:** Full-length, two-piece stock; brass furniture; color case-hardened lock. Flint or percussion. From Traditions, Bass Pro and others.
Price: Percussion **$421.00**
Price: Percussion, Bass Pro **$400.00**
Price: Flintlock **$480.00**
Price: Kit, perc., hardwood, Armory bright, unfinished brass.. **$314.00**

TRADITIONS PA PELLET FLINTLOCK
Caliber: .50. **Barrel:** 26 in., blued, 1:48 in. twist., Cerakote. **Weight:** 7 lbs. **Length:** 45 in. **Stock:** Hardwood, synthetic and synthetic break-up, sling swivels. **Sights:** Fiber optic. **Features:** New flintlock action, removable breech plug, available as left-hand model with hardwood stock.
Price: Hardwood, blued... **$459.00**
Price: Hardwood left hand, blued **$478.00**
Price: Synthetic Realtree Xtra camo, Cerakote barrel **$471.00**
Price: Synthetic Realtree Xtra camo, frame and barrel........... **$500.00**

TRADITIONS PENNSYLVANIA RIFLE
Caliber: .50. **Barrel:** 40.25 in., 7/8 in. flats, 1:66 in. twist, octagon. **Weight:** 9 lbs. **Length:** 57.5 in. overall. **Stock:** Walnut. **Sights:** Blade front, adjustable rear. **Features:** Single-piece walnut stock, brass patchbox and ornamentation. Double-set triggers. Flint or percussion. From Traditions.
Price: Percussion **$782.00**
Price: Flintlock **$814.00**

TRADITIONS PURSUIT ULTRALIGHT MUZZLELOADER
Caliber: .50. **Barrel:** 26 in., chromoly tapered, fluted barrel with premium Cerakote finish, Accelerator Breech Plug. **Weight:** 5.5 lbs. **Length:** 42 in. **Stock:** Rubber over-molded Soft Touch camouflage, straight and thumbhole stock options. **Sights:** 3-9x40 scope with medium rings and bases, mounted and bore sighted by a factory trained technician. **Features:** Break-open action, Williams fiber-optic sights.
Price: Steel, blued, Cerakote................................. **$338.00**
Price: Steel, Mossy Oak Infinity **$397.00**

Price: Steel, Reaper Buck Camo, scope **$454.00**
Price: Steel, Realtree Xtra, scope.. **$530.00**

TRADITIONS TENNESSEE RIFLE
Caliber: .50. **Barrel:** 24 in., octagon, 15/16 in. flats, 1:66 in. twist. **Weight:** 6 lbs. **Length:** 40.5 in. overall. **Stock:** Stained beech. **Sights:** Blade front, fixed rear. **Features:** One-piece stock has brass furniture, cheekpiece, double-set trigger, V-type mainspring. Flint or percussion. From Traditions.
Price: Percussion **$395.00**
Price: Flintlock **$448.00**

TRADITIONS TRACKER 209 IN-LINE RIFLE
Caliber: .50. **Barrel:** 24 in., blued or Cerakote, 1:28 in. twist. **Weight:** 6 lbs., 4 oz. **Length:** 43 in. **Stock:** Black synthetic. Ramrod: Synthetic, high-impact polymer. **Sights:** Lite Optic blade front, adjustable rear. **Features:** Striker-fired action, thumb safety, adjustable trigger, rubber buttpad, sling swivel studs. Takes 150 grains of Pyrodex pellets, one-piece breech system takes 209 shotshell primers. Drilled and tapped for scope. Legal for use in Northwest. From Traditions.
Price: **$184.00**

TRADITIONS VORTEK STRIKERFIRE
Caliber: .50 **Barrel:** 28 in., chromoly, tapered, fluted barrel. **Weight:** 6.25 lbs. **Length:** 44 in. **Stock:** Over-molded soft-touch straight stock, removable buttplate for in-stock storage. **Finish:** Premium Cerakote and Realtree Xtra. **Features:** Break-open action, sliding hammerless cocking mechanism, drop-out trigger assembly, speed load system, accelerator breech plug, recoil pad. **Sights:** Optional 3-9x40 muzzleloader scope.
Price: Synthetic black Hogue Over-mold, Cerakote barrel...... **$493.00**
Price: Synthetic Realtree Xtra camo, Cerakote barrel **$583.00**
Price: Synthetic Realtree Xtra camo frame and barrel, scope. **$649.00**

TRADITIONS VORTEK STRIKERFIRE LDR
Caliber: .50 **Barrel:** 30 in., chromoly, tapered, fluted barrel. **Weight:** 6.8 lbs. **Length:** 46 in. **Stock:** Over-molded soft-touch straight stock, removable buttplate for in-stock storage. **Finish:** Premium Cerakote and Realtree Xtra. **Features:** Break-open action, sliding hammerless cocking mechanism, drop-out trigger assembly, speed load system, accelerator breech plug, recoil pad. **Sights:** Optional 3-9x40 muzzleloader scope.
Price: Synthetic black Hogue Over-mold, Cerakote barrel...... **$561.00**
Price: Synthetic Realtree Xtra camo, Cerakote barrel **$583.00**
Price: Synthetic Realtree Xtra camo, Cerakote barrel **$471.00**
Price: Synthetic Realtree Xtra camo frame and barrel, scope. **$649.00**

TRADITIONS VORTEK STRIKERFIRE NORTHWEST MODEL
Caliber: .50. **Barrel:** 28 or 30 in. chromoly tapered, fluted barrel. **Weight:** 6.25 or 6.8 lbs. **Length:** 46 or 48 in. **Stock:** Synthetic black, over-molded soft-touch straight stock, removable buttplate for in-stock storage. **Finish:** Premium Cerakote. **Features:** Break-open action, sliding hammerless cocking mechanism, drop-out trigger assembly, speed load system, accelerator breech plug, recoil pad. **Sights:** Williams fiber-optic sights.
Price: Northwest, synthetic black, Cerakote barrel **$530.00**
Price: Northwest, synthetic Realtree Xtra Camo, soft touch .. **$589.00**

TRADITIONS VORTEK ULTRALIGHT
Caliber: .50. **Barrel:** 28 in., chromoly, tapered, fluted barrel. **Weight:** 6.25 lbs. **Length:** 44 in. **Stock:** Over-molded soft-touch straight stock. **Finish:** Premium Cerakote, Realtree AP, Reaper Buck. **Features:** Break-open action, hammer cocking mechanism, drop-out trigger

assembly, speed load system, accelerator breech plug, recoil pad. **Sights:** Optional 3-9x40 muzzleloader scope.
Price: Synthetic black Hogue Over-mold, Cerakote barrel...... **$440.00**
Price: Synthetic Reaper Buck camo Hogue, Cerakote barrel   **$524.00**
Price: Synthetic Realtree AP camo, Cerakote barrel...............**$508.00**
Price: Synthetic Realtree AP camo frame and barrel, scope .. **$629.00**

TRADITIONS VORTEK ULTRALIGHT LDR
Caliber: .50. **Barrel:** 30 in., chromoly tapered, fluted barrel. **Weight:** 6.8 lbs. **Length:** 46 in. **Stock:** Over-molded soft-touch straight stock. Finish: Premium Cerakote, Realtree AP, Reaper Buck. **Features:** Break-open action, hammer cocking mechanism, drop-out trigger assembly, speed load system, accelerator breech plug, recoil pad. **Sights:** Optional 3-9x40 muzzleloader scope.
Price: Synthetic black Hogue Over-mold, Cerakote barrel.......**$458.00**
Price: Synthetic Reaper Buck camo Hogue, Cerakote barrel   **$544.00**
Price: Synthetic Realtree AP camo, Cerakote barrel.............. **$524.00**
Price: Synthetic Realtree AP camo frame and barrel, scope .. **$629.00**

TRADITIONS VORTEK ULTRALIGHT NORTHWEST MAGNUM
Caliber: .50. **Barrel:** 28 or 30 in. chromoly tapered, fluted barrel. **Weight:** 6.25 or 6.8 lbs. **Length:** 44 or 46 in. **Stock:** Over-molded, soft-touch, straight or thumbhole stock. Finish: Premium Cerakote and Realtree AP. **Features:** Break-open action, hammer cocking mechanism, musket-cap ignition, drop-out trigger assembly, speed load system, accelerator breech plug, recoil pad. **Sights:** Williams fiber-optic sights.
Price: Synthetic black Hogue Over-mold, Cerakote barrel...... **$470.00**
Price: Synthetic Realtree AP Thumbhole, Hogue, Cerakote .. **$531.00**
Price: Synthetic Realtree AP camo, Cerakote barrel.............. **$531.00**
Price: Synthetic, Black, LDR, Hogue, 30-in. barrel, Cerakote **$500.00**

Prices given are believed to be accurate at time of publication however, many factors affect retail pricing so exact prices are not possible.

BAKER CAVALRY SHOTGUN

Gauge: 20. **Barrels:** 11.25 inches. **Weight:** 5.75 pounds. **Length:** 27.5 in. overall. **Stock:** American walnut. **Sights:** Bead front. **Features:** Reproduction of shotguns carried by Confederate cavalry. Single non-selective trigger, back-action locks. No. 11 percussion musket-cap ignition. Blued barrel with steel furniture. Case-hardened lock. Pedersoli also makes a 12-gauge coach-length version of this back-action-lock shotgun with 20-inch barrels, and a full-length version in 10, 12 and 20 gauge. Made by Pedersoli. Imported by Cabela's and others.

Price: Cabela's, Pedersoli..$900.00

CABELA'S HOWDAH HUNTER 20-GAUGE PISTOL

Gauge: 20. **Barrels:** Cylinder bored, 11.25 in. **Weight:** 4.5 lbs. **Length:** 17.25 in. **Stock:** American walnut with checkered grip. **Sights:** Brass bead front sight. **Features:** Blued barrels, swamped barrel rib, engraved, color case-hardened locks and hammers, captive steel ramrod. Available with detachable shoulder stock, case, holster and mold. Made by Pedersoli. Imported by Cabela's, Dixie Gun Works, Taylor's and others.

Price: Cabela's 20-gauge $700.00

KNIGHT TK-2000 TURKEY SHOTGUN

Gauge: 12. **Ignition:** #209 primer with Full Plastic Jacket, musket cap or No. 11. Striker-fired with one-piece removable hammer assembly. **Barrel:** 26 inches. Choke: Extra-full and improved cylinder available. **Stock:** Realtree Xtra Green straight or thumbhole. **Weight:** 7.7 pounds. **Sights:** Williams fully adjustable rear, fiber-optic front. **Features:** Striker-fired action, receiver is drilled and tapped for scope, adjustable trigger, removable breech plug, double-safety system. Made in U.S. by Knight Rifles (Modern Muzzleloading).

Price: ....$410.00 to $420.00

PEDERSOLI KODIAK MK III RIFLE-SHOTGUN COMBINATION GUN

Gauge: .50 caliber/12 gauge. **Barrels:** 28.5 in. **Weight:** 10.75 lbs. **Stock:** Straight grip, European walnut. **Sights:** Two adjustable rear, steel ramp with brass bead. **Features:** Percussion ignition, double

triggers, sling swivels, 12-gauge cylinder bored barrel. Blued steel furniture. Stainless steel nipple. Made by Pedersoli. Imported by Dixie Gun Works, and some models by Cabela's and others.

Price: Combo 50X12 gauge PR0990 ....$1,350.00

PEDERSOLI MAGNUM PERCUSSION SHOTGUN & COACH GUN

Gauge: 10, 12, 20 **Barrel:** Chrome-lined blued barrels, 25.5 in. Imp. cyl. and Mod. **Weight:** 7.25, 7, 6.75 lbs. **Length:** 45 in. overall. **Stock:** Hand-checkered walnut, 14-in. pull. **Features:** Double triggers, light hand engraving, case-hardened locks, sling swivels. Made by Pedersoli. From Dixie Gun Works, others.

Price: 10-ga. PS1030 .... $1,125.00
Price: 10-ga. kit PS1040 .... $975.00
Price: 12-ga. PS0930.. $1,125.00
Price: 12-ga. Kit PS0940 .... $875.00
Price: 12-ga. Coach gun, 25.5-in. barrels, CylXCyl. PS0914 .... $1,050.00
Price: 20-ga. PS0334.. $1,100.00

PEDERSOLI MORTIMER SHOTGUN

Gauge: 12. **Barrel:** 36 in., 1:66 in., cylinder bore. **Weight:** 9 pounds. **Length:** 52.25 in. **Stock:** Halfstock walnut. **Sights:** Bead front. **Features:** Percussion and flint ignition. Single trigger. Lock with hammer safety and "waterproof pan" on flintlock gun. Lock marked Mortimer. Rifle versions of this gun are also available. Made by Pedersoli. Imported by Dixie.

Price: Flint Shotgun FS0155...$1,425.00
Price: Percussion Shotgun PS3160......................................$1,275.00

PEDERSOLI OLD ENGLISH SHOTGUN

Gauge: 12 **Barrels:** Browned, 28.5 in. Cyl. and Mod. **Weight:** 7.5 lbs. **Length:** 45 in. overall. **Stock:** Hand-checkered American maple, cap box, 14-in. pull. **Features:** Double triggers, light hand engraving on lock, cap box and tang, swivel studs for sling attachment. Made by Pedersoli. From Dixie Gun Works, others.

Price: PR4090 .... $1,750.00

AIRFORCE TALON P

AIRFORCE TALON P
Caliber: .25, single shot. **Barrel:** 12". **Weight:** 3.5 lbs. **Length:** 24.2".
Features: Quick-detachable air tank with adjustable power. Lothar Walther 12" match barrel, optional combo packages available, 3,000 psi fill pressure and automatic safety. Air tank capacity-231 cc. Can be charged using a high pressure air supply form a scuba tank or hand filled with an air pump. Muzzle velocity adjustable from 500 to 900 fps.
Price: **$435.50**

ARS HUNTING MASTER AR6 AIR PISTOL
Caliber: .22 (.177 + 20 special order). **Barrel:** 12" rifled. **Weight:** 3 lbs. **Length:** 18.25 overall. **Power:** NA. **Grips:** Indonesian walnut with checkered grip. **Sights:** Adjustable rear, blade front. **Features:** 6 shot repeater with rotary magazine, single or double action, receiver grooved for scope, hammer block and trigger block safeties.
Price: **$659.00**

BEEMAN 2004 MAGNUM AIR PISTOL
Caliber: .177 **Barrel:** 7.4". **Weight:** 1.7 lbs. **Length:** 10" overall. **Power:** Top lever cocking, single stroke pneumatic. **Grips:** Polymer. **Sights:** Front and rear fiber-optic sights with red-dot sight. **Features:** Grooved for scope mounting with dry-fire feature for practice.
Price: **$45.00**

BEEMAN 2004K AIR PISTOL
Caliber: .177 **Barrel:** 9.17". **Weight:** 2.1 lbs. **Power:** Pneumatic single-shot. **Grips:** Polymer. **Features:** Comes with 250 count pellets and safety glasses. 410 fps.
Price: **$55.00**

BEEMAN 2006 PNEUMATIC AIR PISTOL
Caliber: .177 **Barrel:** 7.4". **Weight:** 1.7 lbs. **Length:** 9.6" overall. **Power:** Single-stroke pneumatic with over-lever barrel cocking. **Grips:** Polymer. **Sights:** Front and rear fiber-optic sights with red-dot sight. **Features:** Polymer frame, automatic safety, two-stage trigger and built-in muzzle brake. 410 fps.
Price: **$55.00**

BEEMAN P1 MAGNUM AIR PISTOL
Caliber: .177, 20. **Barrel:** 8.4". **Weight:** 2.5 lbs. **Length:** 11" overall. **Power:** Top lever cocking; spring-piston. **Grips:** Checkered walnut. **Sights:** Blade front, square notch rear with click micrometer adjustments for windage and elevation. Grooved for scope mounting. **Features:** Dual power for .177 and 20 cal.; low setting gives 350-400 fps; high setting 500-600 fps. All Colt 45 auto grips fit gun. Dry-firing feature for practice. Optional wood shoulder stock. Imported by Beeman.
Price: . . . . **$530.00 to $565.00**

BEEMAN P3 PNEUMATIC AIR PISTOL
Caliber: .177. **Barrel:** NA. **Weight:** 1.7 lbs. **Length:** 9.6" overall. **Power:** Single-stroke pneumatic; overlever barrel cocking. **Grips:** Reinforced polymer. **Sights:** Front and rear fiber-optic sights. **Features:** Velocity 410 fps. Polymer frame; automatic safety; two-stage trigger; built-in muzzle brake.
Price: **$290.00**

BEEMAN/FEINWERKBAU P44
Caliber: .177, single shot. **Barrel:** 9.17". **Weight:** 2.10 lbs. **Length:**

16.54" overall. **Power:** Pre-charged pneumatic. **Grips:** Walnut grip. **Sights:** front and rear sights. **Features:** 500 fps, sighting line adjustable from 360 to 395mm, adjustable 3-D grip in three sizes, adjustable match trigger, delivered in special transport case.
Price: **$2,000.00**
Price: Left-hand model **$2,100.00**

BEEMAN/FEINWERKBAU P56
Caliber: .177, 5-shot magazine. **Barrel:** 8.81". **Weight:** 2.43 lbs. **Length:** 16.54" overall. **Power:** Pre-charged pneumatic. **Grips:** Walnut Morini grip. **Sights:** front and rear sights. **Features:** 500 fps, match-adjustable trigger, adjustable rear sight, front sight accepts interchangeable inserts, delivered in special transport case.
Price: **$2,400.00**

BEEMAN/FWB 103 AIR PISTOL
Caliber: .177. **Barrel:** 10.1," 12-groove rifling. **Weight:** 2.5 lbs. **Length:** 16.5" overall. **Power:** Single-stroke pneumatic, underlever cocking. **Grips:** Stippled walnut with adjustable palm shelf. **Sights:** Blade front, open rear adjustable for windage and elevation. Notch size adjustable for width. Interchangeable front blades. **Features:** Velocity 510 fps. Fully adjustable trigger. Cocking effort 2 lbs. Imported by Beeman.
Price: Right-hand **$2,110.00**
Price: Left-hand **$2,350.00**

BEEMAN HW70A AIR PISTOL
Caliber: .177. **Barrel:** 6-1/4", rifled. **Weight:** 38 oz. **Length:** 12-3/4" overall. **Power:** Spring, barrel cocking. **Grips:** Plastic, with thumbrest. **Sights:** Hooded post front, square notch rear adjustable for windage and elevation. Comes with scope base. **Features:** Adjustable trigger, 31-lb. cocking effort, 440 fps MV; automatic barrel safety. Imported by Beeman.
Price: **$335.00**

BENJAMIN MARAUDER PCP PISTOL
Caliber: .22 **Weight:** 2.7 lbs. **Length:** 18" overall. **Power:** Precharged pneumatic 3,000 psi multi-shot (8-round rotary magazine) bolt action. **Grips:** Synthetic. **Features:** Rifled, shrouded steel barrel, two-stage trigger, includes both pistol grips and a carbine stock and is built in America. 700 fps.
Price: **$395.00**

BENJAMIN MARAUDER WOODS WALKER PCP PISTOL
Caliber: .22 **Weight:** 2.7 lbs. **Length:** 18" overall. **Power:** Precharged pneumatic 3,000 psi multi-shot (eight-round rotary magazine) bolt action. **Grips:** Synthetic. **Sights:** CenterPoint Multi-Tac Quick Aim Sight. **Features:** Rifled, steel shrouded barrel, includes both pistol grips and a carbine stock. Two-stage trigger, Realtree AP camo finish and is built in America. Up to 700 fps.
Price: **$510.00**

BENJAMIN TRAIL NP BREAK BARREL PISTOL
Caliber: .177, single shot. **Weight:** 3.43 lbs. **Length:** 16" overall. **Power:** Nitro Piston with cocking aid for easier cocking. **Grips:** Synthetic. **Sights:** Fiber-optic front, fully adjustable rear. **Features:** Velocity to 625 fps. Rifled steel barrel.
Price: **$95.00**

BENJAMIN & SHERIDAN CO2

BENJAMIN & SHERIDAN CO2 PISTOLS
Caliber: .22, single shot. **Barrel:** 6-3/8", brass. **Weight:** 1 lb. 12 oz. **Length:** 9" overall. **Power:** 12-gram CO2 cylinder. **Grips:** American Hardwood. **Sights:** High ramp front, fully adjustable notched rear. **Features:** Velocity to 500 fps. Turnbolt action with cross-bolt safety. Gives about 40 shots per CO2 cylinder. Black or nickel finish. Made

Prices given are believed to be accurate at time of publication however, many factors affect retail pricing so exact prices are not possible.

in U.S. by Crosman Corp.
Price: EB22 (.22) **$118.59**

BENJAMIN & SHERIDAN PNEUMATIC PELLET PISTOLS
Caliber: .177, .22, single shot. **Barrel:** 9-3/8", rifled brass. **Weight:** 2 lbs., 8 oz. **Length:**12.25" overall. **Power:** Underlever pnuematic, hand pumped. **Grips:** American Hardwood. **Sights:** High ramp front, fully adjustable notch rear. **Features:** Velocity to 525 fps (variable). Bolt action with cross-bolt safety. Choice of black or nickel finish. Made in U.S. by Crosman Corp.
Price: Black finish, HB17 (.177), HB22 (.22) **$133.59**

BERETTA MODEL 84FS

BERETTA MODEL 84FS CO2 PISTOL
Caliber: .177 **Barrel:** 3.6" **Weight:** 1.4 lbs. **Power:** CO2 valve system with blowback slide cycle action. **Sights:** Fixed. **Features:** Velocity to 360 fps. Made by Umarex.
Price: **$99.00**

BROWNING BUCK MARK URX

BROWNING BUCK MARK URX AIR PISTOL
Caliber: .177 **Barrel:** 5.25" **Weight:** 1.5 lbs. **Power:** Single-shot break-barrel pellet pistol. **Sights:** Fixed. **Features:** Velocity to 360 fps. Made by Umarex.
Price: **$50.00**

COLT PYTHON

COLT PYTHON CO2 PISTOL
Caliber: .177 **Barrel:** 5.5" **Weight:** 2.6 lbs. **Power:** CO2 valve system with swing-out cylinder, removable casings and functioning ejector. **Sights:** Fixed. **Features:** Velocity to 400 fps. Made by Umarex.
Price: **$99.00**

CROSMAN MODEL 1088

CROSMAN 1088 REPEATAIR PISTOL
Caliber: .177, 8-shot pellet clip. **Barrel:** Rifled steel. **Weight:** 17 oz. **Length:** 7.75" overall. **Power:** CO2 Powerlet. **Grips:** Checkered black plastic. **Sights:** Fixed blade front, adjustable rear. **Features:** Velocity about 430 fps. Single or double semi-automatic action. From Crosman.
Price: **$60.00**

CROSMAN 2240
Caliber: .22. **Barrel:** Rifled steel. **Weight:** 1 lb. 13 oz. **Length:** 11.125". **Power:** CO2. **Grips:** NA. **Sights:** Blade front, rear adjustable. **Features:** Ergonomically designed ambidextrous grip fits the hand for perfect balance and comfort with checkering and a thumbrest on both grip panels. From Crosman.
Price: **$69.00**

CROSMAN 2300S CO2 TARGET PISTOL
Caliber: .177 **Weight:** 2.7 lbs. **Length:** 16" **Power:** Single-shot, bolt action, CO2 Powerlet powered. **Sights:** Front fixed sight and Williams notched rear sight. **Features:** Meets IHMSA rules for Production Class Silhouette Competitions. Lothar Walter barrel, adjustable trigger, adjustable hammer, stainless steel bolt, 60 shots per Powerlet.
Price: **$254.00**

CROSMAN 2300T CO2 TARGET PISTOL
Caliber: .177 **Weight:** 2.6 lbs. **Length:** 16" **Power:** Single-shot, bolt action, CO2 Powerlet powered. **Sights:** Front fixed sight and LPA rear sight. **Features:** Adjustable trigger, designed for shooting clubs and organizations that teach pistol shooting and capable of firing 40 shots per Powerlet.
Price: **$160.00**

CROSMAN 3576 REVOLVER
Caliber: .177, pellets. **Barrel:** Rifled steel. **Weight:** 2 lbs. **Length:** 11.38". **Power:** CO2. **Grips:** NA. **Sights:** Blade front, rear adjustable. **Features:** Semi-auto 10-shot with revolver styling and finger-molded grip design, 6" barrel for increased accuracy. From Crosman.
Price: **$80.00**

CROSMAN C11
Caliber: .177, 18-shot BB or pellet. **Weight:** 1.4 lbs. **Length:** 8.5". **Power:** 12g CO2. **Sights:** Fixed. **Features:** Compact semi-automatic BB pistol. Velocity up to 480 fps. Under barrel weaver style rail.
Price: **$60.00**

CROSMAN C41 CO2 PISTOL
Caliber: .177, 18-shot BB. **Weight:** 2 lbs. **Length:** 8.5" **Power:** 12g CO2. **Sights:** Fixed. **Features:** Compact semiautomatic BB pistol. Velocity up to 480 fps.
Price: **$65.00**

CROSMAN C-TT
Caliber: BB, 18-shot magazine. **Length:** 8". Semi-auto CO2-powered

---

CROSMAN C-TT

repeater styled after Russian Tarev TT-30. Metal frame and polymer grip.
Price: **$100.00**

CROSMAN PRO77
Caliber: .177, 17-shot BB. **Weight:** 1.31 lbs. **Length:** 6.75". **Power:** 12g CO2. **Sights:** Fixed. **Features:** Compact pistol with realistic recoil. Under the barrel weaver style rail. Velocity up to 325 fps.
Price: Pro77CS **$90.00**

CROSMAN PUMPMASTER CLASSIC

CROSMAN PUMPMASTER CLASSIC PISTOL
Caliber: .22 **Weight:** 2 lbs. **Length:** 13.6" **Power:** Single-shot bolt-action pneumatic pump pistol. **Sights:** Front fixed sight and adjustable rear sight. **Features:** Control velocity with easy-pump forearm. Velocity up to 600 fps.
Price: **$60.00**

CROSMAN SURVIVALIST CO2 PISTOL
Caliber: .177, 20-shot BB. **Weight:** 1.1 lbs. **Length:** 6.9" **Power:** CO2-powered. **Sights:** Fixed. **Features:** Compact semiautomatic, under-barrel Weaver-style rail and holster included. Velocity up to 495 fps.
Price: **$40.00**

CROSMAN T4
Caliber: .177, 8-shot BB or pellet. **Weight:** 1.32 lbs. **Length:** 8.63". **Power:** 12g CO2. **Sights:** Fixed front, windage adjustable rear. **Features:** Shoots BBs or pellets. Easy patent-pending CO2 piercing mechanism. Under the barrel weaver style rail.
Price: T4CS **$90.00**
Price: T4OPS, includes adjustable Red Dot sight, barrel compensator, and pressure operated tactical flashlight. Comes in foam padeed, hard sided protective case **$167.99**

CROSMAN VIGILANTE CO2 REVOLVER
Caliber: .177, pellets and BB. **Barrel:** 6" rifled steel. **Weight:** 2 lbs. **Length:** 11.38" **Power:** CO2-powered. **Sights:** Blade front sight and adjustable rear sight. **Features:** Semiauto 10-shot pellet clip and 6-shot BB clip with revolver styling and finger-molded grip design.
Price: **$90.00**

DAISY POWERLINE MODEL 15XT AIR PISTOL
Caliber: .177 BB, 15-shot built-in magazine. **Barrel:** NA. **Weight:** NA. **Length:** 7.21". **Power:** CO2. **Grips:** NA. **Sights:** NA. **Features:** Velocity 480 fps. Made in the U.S.A. by Daisy Mfg. Co.
Price: **$39.99**
Price: With electronic point sight **$54.99**

DAISY MODEL 717 AIR PISTOL
Caliber: .177, single shot. **Weight:** 2.25 lbs. **Length:** 13-1/2" overall.

DAISY MODEL 717

Grips: Molded checkered woodgrain with contoured thumbrest. **Sights:** Blade and ramp front, open rear with windage and elevation adjustments. **Features:** Single pump pneumatic pistol. Rifled steel barrel. Crossbolt trigger block. Muzzle velocity 395 fps. From Daisy Mfg. Co.
Price: **$200.00**

DAISY MODEL 747 TRIUMPH AIR PISTOL
Caliber: .177, single shot. **Weight:** 2.35 lbs. **Length:** 13-1/2" overall. **Grips:** Molded checkered woodgrain with contoured thumbrest. **Sights:** Blade and ramp front, open rear with windage and elevation adjustments. **Features:** Single pump pneumatic pistol. Lothar Walther rifled high-grade steel barrel; crowned 12 lands and grooves, right-hand twist. Precision bore sized for match pellets. Muzzle velocity 395 fps. From Daisy Mfg. Co.
Price: **$264.99**

DAISY POWERLINE 201
Caliber: .177 BB or pellet. **Weight:** 1 lb. **Length:** 9.25" overall. **Sights:** Blade and ramp front, fixed open rear. **Features:** Spring-air action, trigger-block safety and smooth-bore steel barrel. Muzzle velocity 230 fps. From Daisy Mfg. Co.
Price: **$29.99**

DAISY POWERLINE 340
Caliber: BB **Features:** Spring-air action, 200-shot BB reservoir with a 13-shot Speed-load Clip located in the grip.
Price: **$24.99**

DAISY POWERLINE 693 AIR PISTOL
Caliber: .177, single shot. **Weight:** 1.10 lbs. **Length:** 7.9" overall. **Grips:** Molded checkered. **Sights:** Blade and ramp front, fixed open rear. **Features:** Semi-automoatic BB pistol with a nickel finish and smooth bore steel barrel. Muzzle veocity 449 fps. From Daisy Mfg. Co.
Price: **$76.99**

DAISY POWERLINE 5170

DAISY POWERLINE 5170 CO2 PISTOL
Caliber: .177 BB. **Weight:** 1 lb. **Length:** 9.5" overall. **Sights:** Blade and ramp front, open rear. **Features:** CO2 semi-automatic action, manual trigger-block safety, upper and lower rails for mounting sights and other accessories and a smooth-bore steel barrel. Muzzle velocity 520 fps. From Daisy Mfg. Co.
Price: **$59.99**

DAISY POWERLINE 5501 CO2 BLOWBACK PISTOL
Caliber: .177, BB. **Weight:** 1 lb. **Length:** 9.5" overall. **Sights:** Blade and ramp front, open rear. **Features:** CO2 semi-automatic blow-back action, manual trigger-block safety, and a smooth-bore steel barrel. Muzzle velocity 430 fps. From Daisy Mfg. Co.
Price: **$89.99**

Prices given are believed to be accurate at time of publication however, many factors affect retail pricing so exact prices are not possible.

EAA/BAIKAL IZH-46M TARGET AIR PISTOL
Caliber: .177, single shot. **Barrel:** 10". **Weight:** 2.4 lbs. **Length:** 16.8" overall. **Power:** Underlever single-stroke pneumatic. **Grips:** Adjustable wooden target. **Sights:** Micrometer fully adjustable rear, blade front. **Features:** Velocity about 440 fps. Hammer-forged, rifled barrel. Imported from Russia by European American Armory.
Price: **$560.00**

GAMO MP-9 CO2 PISTOL
Caliber: .177, BB **Weight:** 3 lbs. **Power:** CO2 cartridge. **Sights:** NA. **Features:** Blow-back semiautomatic replica of the B&T MP-9 9mm submachine gun. Shoots both pellets or BBs using the same magazine, Weaver-style tactical rails, ambidextrous compact design, foldable stock, 16-shot double magazine and manual safety. 450 fps.
Price: **$149.95**

GAMO P-23, P-23 LASER PISTOL
Caliber: .177, 12-shot. **Barrel:** 4.25". **Weight:** 1 lb. **Length:** 7.5". **Power:** CO2 cartridge, semi-automatic, 410 fps. **Grips:** Plastic. **Sights:** NA. **Features:** Walther PPK cartridge pistol copy, optional laser sight. Imported from Spain by Gamo.
Price: . . . . **$89.95**, (with laser) **$139.95**

GAMO P-900 IGT AIR PISTOL
Caliber: .177 **Weight:** 1.3 lbs. **Power:** CO2 cartridge. **Features:** Break-barrel single-shot, ergonomic design, rubberized grip, rifled steel barrel and manual safety. 400 fps.
Price: **$79.95**

GAMO PT-25 BLOWBACK CO2 PISTOL
Caliber: .177 **Weight:** 1.5 lbs. **Power:** CO2 cartridge **Features:** Semiautomatic design, iron sights, 16-shot double magazine, manual safety. 450 fps.
Price: . . . . **$ 106.95**

GAMO PT-25 BLOWBACK TACTICAL CO2 PISTOL
Caliber: .177 **Weight:** 1.5 lbs. **Power:** CO2 cartridge **Sights:** Gamo red-dot. **Features:** Semiautomatic design, mounting rail on top and bottom, flashlight mounted on bottom rail, 16-shot double magazine, manual safety. 560 fps.
Price: . . . . **$ 189.95**

GAMO PT-80, PT-80 LASER PISTOL
Caliber: .177, 8-shot. **Barrel:** 4.25". **Weight:** 1.2 lbs. **Length:** 7.2". **Power:** CO2 cartridge, semi-automatic, 410 fps. **Grips:** Plastic. **Sights:** 3-dot. **Features:** Optional laser sight and walnut grips available. Imported from Spain by Gamo.
Price: . . . . **$89.95**, (with laser) **$159.95**
Price: (with walnut grip) **$119.95**

GAMO PT-85 BLOWBACK CO2 PISTOL
Caliber: .177 **Weight:** 1.5 lbs. **Power:** CO2 cartridge **Features:** Semiautomatic design, iron sights, 16-shot double magazine, manual safety. 450 fps.
Price: . . . . **$ 139.95**

GAMO PT-85 BLOWBACK SOCOM CO2 PISTOL
Caliber: .177 **Weight:** 2.32 lbs. **Power:** CO2 cartridge **Features:** Semiautomatic design, Quad rail included, 16 shot double magazine, manual safety. 560 fps.
Price: . . . . **$ 139.95**

GAMO PT-85 BLOWBACK TACTICAL CO2 PISTOL
Caliber: .177 **Weight:** 3.3 lbs. **Power:** CO2 cartridge **Features:** Semiautomatic design, compensator, rifled steel barrel, manual safety, 16-shot double magazine, quad rail, laser and light included. 560 fps.
Price: . . . . **$ 269.95**

HAMMERLI AP-40

HAMMERLI AP-40 AIR PISTOL
Caliber: .177. **Barrel:** 10". **Weight:** 2.2 lbs. **Length:** 15.5". **Power:** NA. **Grips:** Adjustable orthopedic. **Sights:** Fully adjustable micrometer. **Features:** Sleek, light, well balanced and accurate.
Price: **$1,725.00**

MAGNUM RESEARCH DESERT EAGLE
Caliber: .177, 8-shot pellet. 5.7" rifled. **Weight:** 2.5 lbs. 11" overall. **Power:** 12g CO2. **Sights:** Fixed front, adjustable rear. Velocity of 425 fps. 8-shot rotary clip. Double or single action. The first .177 caliber air pistol with BLOWBACK action. Big and weighty, designed in the likeness of the real Desert Eagle. Made by Umarex.
Price: **$220.00**

MAGNUM BABY DESERT
Caliber: .177, 15-shot BB. 4" **Weight:** 1.0 lbs. 8-1/4" overall. **Power:** 12g CO2. **Sights:** Fixed front and rear. Velocity of 420 fps. Double action BB repeater. Comes with bonus Picatinny top rail and built-in bottom rail. Made by Umarex.
Price: **$50.00**

MARKSMAN 200K AIR PISTOL
Caliber: .177 **Weight:** 2.10 lbs. **Length:** 12-3/4" overall. **Power:** Spring barrel cocking BB repeater capable of shooting pellets, darts or bolts in single shot manner. **Grips:** Plastic checkered. **Sights:** blade front and square notch rear. **Features:** 18-shot BB reservoir, includes kit with holster, high-impact shooting glasses, BB speedloader with 300 BBs, 50 wadcutter pellets and six mohair darts. .
Price: **$40.00**

MARKSMAN 1010C AIR PISTOL
Caliber: .177 **Barrel:** 8.81" **Weight:** 2.43 lbs. **Length:** 10" overall. **Power:** Spring piston capable of shooting pellets, darts or bolts. **Grips:** Checkered. **Sights:** Blade front and open rear. **Features:** 18-shot BB reservoir. 230 fps.
Price: **$30.00**

MARKSMAN 2002 AIR PISTOL
Caliber: .177 **Barrel:** 7.4" **Weight:** 2.5 lbs. **Length:** 10" overall. **Power:** Spring piston capable of shooting pellets, darts or bolts. **Grips:** Checkered. **Features:** 18-shot BB reservoir. 200 fps.
Price: **$25.00**

MORINI CM 162 EL MATCH AIR PISTOLS
Caliber: .177, single shot. **Barrel:** 9.4". **Weight:** 32 oz. **Length:** 16.1" overall. **Power:** Scuba air. **Grips:** Adjustable match type. **Sights:** Interchangeable blade front, fully adjustable match-type rear. **Features:** Power mechanism shuts down when pressure drops to a preset level. Adjustable electronic trigger.
Price: **$1,075.00**

RUGER MARK I

RUGER MARK I
Caliber: .177. **Barrel:** 6.5". **Weight:** 48 oz. **Sights:** Fiber optic front, open rear. Spring-piston operated pellet pistol up to 500 fps velocity with lead pellets, 600 fps with alloy. Made by Umarex.
Price: **$75.00**

RWS 9B/9N AIR PISTOLS
Caliber: .177, single shot. **Barrel:** 8". **Weight:** 2.38 lbs. **Length:** 10.4". **Power:** 550 fps. **Grips:** Right hand with thumbrest. **Sights:** Adjustable. **Features:** Spring-piston powered. Black or nickel finish.
Price: 9B/9N **$150.00**

RWS MODEL LP8 MAGNUM AIR PISTOL
Caliber: .177 **Weight:** 3.2 lbs. **Power:** Spring-piston operated. **Grips:**

Combat style. **Sights:** Fiber-optic front and rear sights are fully adjustable in the rear. **Features:** Ambidextrous safety catch engages when pistol is cocked, muzzlebrake, fully grooved 11mm scope rail atop the receiver. 700 fps.
Price: **$259.00**

SMITH & WESSON 586 & 686
Caliber: .177, 10-shot pellet. Rifled. **Power:** 12g CO2. **Sights:** Fixed front, adjustable rear. 10-shot rotary clip. Double or single action. Replica revolvers that duplicate both weight and handling. Made by Umarex.
Price: 4" barrel, 2.5 lbs, 400 fps **$239.99**
Price: 6" barrel, 2.8 lbs, 425 fps **$259.99**
Price: 8" barrel, 3.0 lbs, 460 fps **$247.65**
Price: S&W 686 Nickel, 6" barrel, 2.8 lbs, 425 fps **$269.95**

SMITH & WESSON M&P CO2 PISTOL
Caliber: .177, BB. **Barrel:** 4.24" smoothbore. **Weight:** 1.5 lbs. **Length:** 7.5" overall. **Power:** CO2-powered repeater. **Sights:** Blade front and ramp rear fiber optic. **Features:** Integrated accessory rail, drop-free 19-shot BB magazine, manual safety, double-action only, synthetic frame and available in dark earth brown or black color. 480 fps. Made by Umarex.
Price: **$39.99**

STEYR LP10P MATCH AIR PISTOL
Caliber: .177, single shot. **Barrel:** 9". **Weight:** 38.7 oz. **Length:** 15.3" overall. **Power:** Scuba air. **Grips:** Adjustable Morini match, palm shelf, stippled walnut. **Sights:** Interchangeable blade in 4mm, 4.5mm or 5mm widths, adjustable open rear, interchangeable 3.5mm or 4mm leaves. **Features:** Velocity about 500 fps. Adjustable trigger, adjustable sight radius from 12.4" to 13.2". With compensator. Recoil elimination.
Price: **$1,400.00**

TECH FORCE SS2 OLYMPIC COMPETITION AIR PISTOL
Caliber: .177 pellet, single shot. **Barrel:** 7.4". **Weight:** 2.8 lbs. **Length:** 16.5" overall. **Power:** Spring piston, sidelever. **Grips:** Hardwood. **Sights:** Extended adjustable rear, blade front accepts inserts. **Features:** Velocity 520 fps. Recoilless design; adjustments allow duplication of a firearm's feel. Match-grade, adjustable trigger; includes carrying case. Imported from China by Compasseco, Inc.
Price: **$295.00**

TECH FORCE 35 AIR PISTOL
Caliber: .177 pellet, single shot. **Weight:** 2.86 lbs. **Length:** 14.9" overall. **Power:** Spring-piston, underlever. **Grips:** Hardwood. **Sights:** Micrometer adjustable rear, blade front. **Features:** Velocity 400 fps. Grooved for scope mount; trigger safety. Imported from China by Compasseco, Inc.
Price: **$39.95**

TECH FORCE S2-1 AIR PISTOL
Similar to Tech Force 8 except basic grips and sights for plinking.
Price: **$29.95**

UMAREX LEGENDS MAKAROV ULTRA
Caliber: .177 **Barrel:** 3.5" **Weight:** 1.4 lbs. **Power:** CO2 valve system with blowback slide cycle action. **Sights:** Fixed. **Features:** Metal frame and classic Russian replica design. 350 fps.
Price: **$89.99**

WALTHER CP99 COMPACT
Caliber: .177, 17-shot steel BB semi-auto. **Barrel:** 3". **Weight:** 1.7 lbs. **Length:** 6-1/2" overall. **Power:** 12g CO2. **Sights:** Fixed front and rear. **Features:** Velocity of 345 fps. Realistic recoil, blowback action. Heavyweight steel construction. Built-in Picatinny mount. Made by Umarex.
Price: **$83.08**

WALTHER LP300 MATCH PISTOL
Caliber: .177 **Weight:** 1,018 g. **Length:** 236mm. **Power:** Recharged pneumatic single-shot pistol. **Grips:** Adjustable. **Sights:** Integrated front with three different widths, adjustable rear. **Features:** Adjustable grip and trigger. Made by Umarex.
Price: **$1,800.00**

WALTHER PPK/S
Caliber: .177, 15-shot steel BB. **Barrel:** 3-1/2". **Weight:** 1.2 lbs. **Length:** 6-1/4" overall. **Power:** 12g CO2. **Sights:** Fixed front and rear. **Features:** Velocity of 295 fps. Lookalike of one of the world's most famous pistols. Realistic recoil. Heavyweight steel construction. Made by Umarex.
Price: **$71.92**
Price: With laser sight **$94.23**
Price: With BiColor pistol, targets, shooting glasses, BBs **$84.62**

WALTHER PPS

WALTHER PPS PISTOL
Caliber: .177 **Barrel:** 3" **Weight:** 1.2 lbs. **Power:** CO2 valve system with blowback slide cycle action. **Sights:** Fixed. **Features:** Velocity of 350 fps. Metal replica frame and 18-round capacity. Made by Umarex.
Price: **$75.99**

WINCHESTER MODEL 11

WINCHESTER MODEL 11
Caliber: BB. CO2-powered pistol with 16-round removable magazine. **Weight:** 30 ozs. **Features:** Can be fired double or single action. Slide stays open after last shot. Dimensions and operating controls the same as 1911 pistol. Made by Daisy.
Price: **$119.99**

AIRFORCE CONDOR

AIRFORCE CONDOR RIFLE
Caliber: .177, .22 single shot. **Barrel:** 24" rifled. **Weight:** 6.5 lbs. **Length:** 38.75" overall. **Power:** Pre-charged pneumatic. **Stock:** NA. **Sights:** Intended for scope use, fiber-optic open sights optional. **Features:** Lothar Walther match barrel, adjustable power levels from 600-1,300 fps. 3,000 psi fill pressure. Automatic safety. Air tank volume: 490cc. An integral extended scope rail allows easy mounting of the largest air-gun scopes. Operates on high-pressure air from scuba tank or hand pump. Manufactured in the U.S.A by AirForce Airguns.
Price: **$689.50**
Price: With 4-16x50 scope, Spin-Lock tank, hand pump . . . **$1,006.00**

AIRFORCE CONDOR SS AIR RIFLE
Caliber: .177, .20, .22, .25 **Barrel:** 18" **Weight:** 6.1 lbs. **Length:** 38.125" overall. **Power:** Pre-charged. **Sights:** Designed for a scope, but fiber-optic open sights are optional. **Features:** Pneumatic single-shot with 3,000 PSI fill pressure. Lothar Walther match-grade rifled barrel, air tank volume - 490cc. Sound-Loc technology helps to reduce the firing report. Air can be charged from either a scuba tank or replenished by a hand pump. The Condor SS is manufactured in the USA by AirForce Airguns. Adjustable power level from 600 to 1,300 fps.
Price: **$717.00**

AIRFORCE ESCAPE AIR RIFLE
Caliber: .22, .25 **Barrel:** 24" **Weight:** 5.3 lbs. **Length:** Adjustable 34.5" to 39" overall. **Power:** Pre-charged. **Sights:** Designed for a scope, but fiber-optic open sights are optional. **Features:** Pneumatic single-shot with 3,000 PSI fill pressure. Lothar Walther match-grade rifled barrel, air tank volume - 490cc. Air can be charged from either a scuba tank or replenished by a hand pump. Adjustable power level from 800 to 1,300 fps.
Price: **$640.00**

AIRFORCE ESCAPE SS AIR RIFLE
Caliber: .22, .25 **Barrel:** 12" **Weight:** 4.3 lbs. **Length:** Adjustable 27.75" to 32.25" overall. **Power:** Pre-charged. **Sights:** Designed for a scope, but fiber-optic open sights are optional. **Features:** Pneumatic single-shot with 3,000 PSI fill pressure. Lothar Walther match-grade rifled barrel, automatic safety, air tank volume—213cc. Air can be charged from either a scuba tank or replenished by a hand pump. Adjustable power level from 500 to 1,200 fps.
Price: **$630.00**

AIRFORCE ESCAPE UL AIR RIFLE
Caliber: .22, .25 **Barrel:** 18" **Weight:** 4.25 lbs. **Length:** Adjustable 28.5" to 33" overall. **Power:** Pre-charged. **Sights:** Designed for a scope, but fiber-optic open sights are optional. **Features:** Pneumatic single-shot with 3,000 PSI fill pressure. Lothar Walther match-grade rifled barrel, automatic safety, air tank volume—213cc. Air can be charged from either a scuba tank or replenished by a hand pump. Adjustable power level from 800 to 1,200 fps.
Price: **$590.00**

AIRFORCE TALON AIR RIFLE
Caliber: .177, .20, .22, .25, single shot. **Barrel:** 18" rifled. **Weight:** 5.5 lbs. **Length:** 32.6". **Power:** Pre-charged pneumatic. **Stock:** NA. **Sights:** Intended for scope use, fiber-optic open sights optional. **Features:** Lothar Walther match barrel, adjustable power levels from 400-1,000 fps, 3,000 psi fill pressure. Automatic safety. Air tank volume: 490cc. Operates on high-pressure air from scuba tank or hand pump. Manufactured in the U.S.A. by AirForce Airguns.
Price: **$562.50**

AIRFORCE TALON SS AIR RIFLE
Caliber: .177, .20, .22, .25 single shot. **Barrel:** 12" rifled. **Weight:** 5.25 lbs. **Length:** 32.75". **Power:** Pre-charged pneumatic. **Stock:** NA. **Sights:** Intended for scope use, fiber-optic open sights optional. **Features:** Lothar Walther match barrel, adjustable power levels from 400-1,000 fps. 3,000 psi fill pressure. Automatic safety. Chamber in front of barrel strips away air turbulence, protects muzzle and reduces firing report. Air tank volume: 490cc. Operates on high-pressure air from scuba tank or hand pump. Manufactured in the U.S.A. by AirForce Airguns.
Price: **$599.50**

AIRROW MODEL A-8SRB STEALTH AIR RIFLE
Caliber: .177, .22, .25, 9-shot. **Barrel:** 20"; rifled. **Weight:** 6 lbs. **Length:** 34" overall. **Power:** CO2 or compressed air; variable power. **Stock:** Telescoping CAR-15-type. **Sights:** Variable 3.5-10x scope. **Features:** Velocity 1100 fps in all calibers. Pneumatic air trigger. All aircraft aluminum and stainless steel construction. Mil-spec materials and finishes. From Swivel Machine Works, Inc.
Price: About **$2,299.00**

AIRROW MODEL A-8S1P STEALTH AIR RIFLE
Caliber: #2512 16" arrow. **Barrel:** 16". **Weight:** 4.4 lbs. **Length:** 30.1" overall. **Power:** CO2 or compressed air; variable power. **Stock:** Telescoping CAR-15-type. **Sights:** Scope rings only. 7 oz. rechargeable cylinder and valve. **Features:** Velocity to 650 fps with 260-grain arrow. Pneumatic air trigger. Broadhead guard. All aircraft aluminum and stainless steel construction. Mil-spec materials and finishes. A-8S Models perform to 2,000 PSIG above or below water levels. Waterproof case. From Swivel Machine Works, Inc.
Price: **$1,699.00**

BEEMAN 1051 TETON AIR RIFLE
Caliber: .177, .22 **Barrel:** 21-1/2". **Weight:** 9 lbs. **Length:** 42.13" overall. **Power:** Break-barrel spring gun. **Stock:** European hardwood. **Sights:** Fiber-optic front and rear. Grooved for scope mounting. 4x32mm scope and mounts. **Features:** 2-stage adjustable RS2 match trigger and manual safety. 1,140 fps (.177) and 945 fps (.22).
Price: **$150.00**

BEEMAN 1071 WOLVERINE AIR RIFLE
Caliber: .177, .20, .22 **Barrel:** 19.6" **Weight:** 8.5 lbs. **Length:** 45.2" overall. **Power:** Spring piston barrel cocking system. **Stock:** All weather synthetic. **Sights:** 4x32mm scope. **Features:** Twelve-groove rifled barrel. 1,140 fps (.177) and 945 fps (.22).
Price: **$150.00**

BEEMAN 1072 GRIZZLY X2 DUAL CALIBER AIR RIFLE
Caliber: .177, .22 **Barrel:** 19.6" **Weight:** 6.1 lbs. **Length:** 40.2" overall. **Power:** Spring piston. **Stock:** European hardwood. **Sights:** 4x32mm scope, fiber optics front and rear. **Features:** RS2 2-stage adjustable trigger. 1,200 fps (.177) and 950 fps (.22).
Price: **$200.00**

BEEMAN 1074 KODIAK X2 DUAL CALIBER AIR RIFLE
Caliber: .177, .22, interchangeable barrels. **Weight:** 7.3 lbs. **Length:** 43" overall. **Power:** Spring break-barrel cocking system. **Stock:** European hardwood. **Sights:** 4x32mm scope. **Features:** Adjustable X2 trigger, automatic safety. 1,200 fps (.177) and 950 fps (.22).
Price: **$200.00**

BEEMAN 1077 SILVER KODIAK X2 DUAL CALIBER AIR RIFLE
Caliber: .177, .22 **Barrel:** 19.6" **Weight:** 8.8 lbs. **Power:** Gas-spring piston air with single-stroke barrel cocking. **Stock:** Laminated wood. **Sights:** Tunnel front, click-adjustable rear. **Features:** 12-groove rifled barrel. 1,200 fps (.177) and 959 fps (.22).
Price: **$225.00**

BEEMAN 1086 BEAR CLAW AIR RIFLE
Caliber: .177, .22 **Barrel:** 16.1" **Weight:** 8.6 lbs. **Power:** Spring-piston barrel cocking system. **Stock:** Stained European hardwood thumbhole ambidextrous (right or left hand) stock with rubber buttpad. **Sights:** 3-9x32mm scope. **Features:** Adjustable metal RS3 2-stage trigger. 1,200 fps.
Price: **$225.00**

BEEMAN 1192 BEAR CLAW X2 DUAL CALIBER AIR RIFLE
Caliber: .177, .22 **Weight:** 10.8 lbs. **Length:** 47.5" overall. **Power:** Break barrel spring system. **Stock:** European hardwood. **Sights:** 3-9x32 AO scope. **Features:** Adjustable metal RS3 2-stage trigger, ported muzzlebrake, interchangeable barrels. 1,200 fps (.177) and 950 fps (.22).
Price: **$250.00**

BEEMAN HW100
Caliber: .177 or .22, 14-shot magazine. **Barrel:** 21-1/2". **Weight:** 9 lbs. **Length:** 42.13" overall. **Power:** Pre-charged. **Stock:** Walnut Sporter checkering on the pistol grip & forend; walnut thumbhose with lateral finger grooves on the forend & stippling on the pistol grip. **Sights:** None. Grooved for scope mounting. **Features:** 1140 fps .177 caliber; 945 fps .22 caliber. 14-shot magazine, quick-fill cylinder. Two-stage adjustable match trigger and manual safety.
Price: From **$1,470.00**

BEEMAN MACH 12.5 AIR RIFLE
Caliber: .177, .22 **Weight:** 10.6 lbs. **Length:** 47.3" overall. **Power:** Single-shot break barrel spring system. **Stock:** Checkered European hardwood. **Sights:** 3-9x40mm AO/TT scope. **Features:** RS3 2-stage trigger, ported barrel with muzzlebrake. 1,400 fps (.177) and 1,200 fps (.22).
Price: **$300.00**

BEEMAN R1 AIR RIFLE
Caliber: .177, .20 or .22, single shot. **Barrel:** 19.6", 12-groove rifling. **Weight:** 8.5 lbs. **Length:** 45.2" overall. **Power:** Spring-piston, barrel cocking. **Stock:** Walnut-stained beech; cut-checkered pistol grip; Monte Carlo comb and cheekpiece; rubber buttpad. **Sights:** Tunnel front with interchangeable inserts, open rear click-adjustable for windage and elevation. Grooved for scope mounting. **Features:** Velocity 940-1000 fps (.177), 860 fps (20), 800 fps (.22). Non-drying nylon piston and breech seals. Adjustable metal trigger. Milled steel safety. Right- or left-hand stock. Adjustable cheekpiece and buttplate at extra cost. Custom and Super Laser versions available. Imported by Beeman.
Price: Right-hand **$729.95**
Price: Left-hand **$789.95**

BEEMAN R1 CARBINE
Caliber: .177,. 20, .22 single shot. **Barrel:** 16.1". **Weight:** 8.6 lbs. **Length:** 41.7" overall. **Power:** Spring-piston, barrel cocking. **Stock:** Stained beech; Monte Carlo comb and checkpiece; cut checkered pistol grip; rubber buttpad. **Sights:** Tunnel front with interchangeable inserts, open adjustable rear; receiver grooved for scope mounting. **Features:** Velocity up to 1000 fps (.177). Non-drying nylon piston and breech seals. Adjustable metal trigger. Machined steel receiver end cap and safety. Right- or left-hand stock. Imported by Beeman.
Price: .177, 20, .22, right-hand **$749.95**

BEEMAN R7 AIR RIFLE
Caliber: .177, .20, single shot. **Barrel:** 17". **Weight:** 6.1 lbs. **Length:** 40.2" overall. **Power:** Spring-piston. **Stock:** Stained beech. **Sights:** Hooded front, fully adjustable micrometer click open rear. **Features:** Velocity to 700 fps (.177), 620 fps (20). Receiver grooved for scope mounting; double-jointed cocking lever; fully adjustable trigger; checkered grip. Imported by Beeman.
Price: .177 .... **$470.00**
Price: .20 .... **$500.00**

BEEMAN R9 AIR RIFLE
Caliber: .177, .20, single shot. **Barrel:** NA. **Weight:** 7.3 lbs. **Length:** 43" overall. **Power:** Spring-piston, barrel cocking. **Stock:** Stained hardwood. **Sights:** Tunnel post front, fully adjustable open rear. **Features:** Velocity to 1000 fps (.177), 800 fps (20). Adjustable Rekord trigger; automatic safety; receiver dovetailed for scope mounting. Imported from Germany by Beeman Precision Airguns.
Price: **$470.00**

BEEMAN R11 MKII

BEEMAN R11 MKII AIR RIFLE
Caliber: .177, single shot. **Barrel:** 19.6". **Weight:** 8.6 lbs. **Length:** 43.5" overall. **Power:** Spring-piston, barrel cocking. **Stock:** Walnut-stained beech; adjustable buttplate and cheekpiece. **Sights:** None furnished. Has dovetail for scope mounting. **Features:** Velocity 910-940 fps. All-steel barrel sleeve. Imported by Beeman.
Price: **$700.00**

BEEMAN RX-2 GAS-SPRING MAGNUM AIR RIFLE
Caliber: .177, .20, .22, .25, single shot. **Barrel:** 19.6", 12-groove rifling. **Weight:** 8.8 lbs. **Power:** Gas-spring piston air; single stroke barrel cocking. **Stock:** Laminated wood stock. **Sights:** Tunnel front, click-adjustable rear. **Features:** Velocity adjustable to about 1200 fps. Imported by Beeman.
Price: .177, right-hand **$889.95**
Price: .20, right-hand **$909.95**
Price: .22, right-hand **$889.95**
Price: .25, right-hand **$909.95**

BEEMAN/FEINWERKBAU 700 P MATCH RIFLE
Caliber: .177, single shot. **Barrel:** 16.6". **Weight:** 10.8 lbs. Aluminum; 9.9 lbs. Wood. **Length:** 43.3-46.25" Aluminum; 43.7" Wood. **Power:** Pre-charged pneumatic. **Stock:** Aluminum stock P laminated hardwood. **Sights:** Tunnel front sight with interchangeable inserts, click micrometer match aperture rear sight. **Features:** Velocity 570 fps. Recoilless action. Anatomical grips can be tilted and pivoted to the barrel axis. Adjustable buttplate and cheekpiece.
Price: Aluminum 700, right, blue or silver **$2,775.00**
Price: Aluminum 700, universal. **$2,910.00**

BEEMAN/FEINWERKBAU P70 FIELD TARGET
Caliber: .177, single shot. **Barrel:** 24.6". **Weight:** 10.6 lbs. **Length:** 43.3" overall. **Power:** Pre-charged pneumatic. **Stock:** Aluminum stock (red or blue) anatomical grips, buttplate & cheekpiece. **Sights:** None, receiver grooved for scope mounting. **Features:** 870 fps velocity. At 50 yards, this air rifle is capable of achieving 1/2-inch groups. Match adjustable trigger. 2001 US Field Target National Champion.
Price: P70FT, precharged, right (red or blue) **$3,819.95**
Price: P70FT, precharged, left (red or blue) **$3,964.95**

BEEMAN/HW97 AIR RIFLE
Caliber: .177, .20, .22, single shot. **Barrel:** 17.75". **Weight:** 9.2 lbs. **Length:** 44.1" overall. **Power:** Spring-piston, underlever cocking. **Stock:** Walnut-stained beech; rubber buttpad. **Sights:** None. Receiver grooved for scope mounting. **Features:** Velocity 830 fps (.177). Fixed barrel with fully opening, direct loading breech. Adjustable trigger. Imported by Beeman Precision Airguns.
Price: .177 .... **$725.00**
Price: .20, .22 .... **$750.00**

BENJAMIN & SHERIDAN PNEUMATIC

BENJAMIN & SHERIDAN PNEUMATIC (PUMP-UP) AIR RIFLE
Caliber: .177 or .22, single shot. **Barrel:** 19-3/8", rifled brass. **Weight:** 5-1/2 lbs. **Length:** 36-1/4" overall. **Power:** Underlever pneumatic, hand pumped. **Stock:** American walnut stock and forend. **Sights:** High ramp front, fully adjustable notched rear. **Features:** Variable velocity to 800 fps. Bolt action with ambidextrous push-pull safety. Black or nickel finish. Made in the U.S.A. by Benjamin. Also manufactured under the Sheridan brand.
Price: Model 397 (.177) **$170.00**
Price: Model 392 (.20) **$170.00**
Price: Sheridan CB9 (.22) **$200.00**

BENJAMIN MARAUDER PCP AIR RIFLE
Caliber: .177, .22, .25 **Weight:** 8.2 lbs. **Length:** 42.87" overall. **Power:** Multishot bolt-action precharged pneumatic 3,000 psi hunting rifle. **Stock:** Hardwood or synthetic, ambidextrous with adjustable cheekpiece. **Features:** Shrouded rifled steel barrel, adjustable two-stage match-grade trigger with eight or 10-round magazine, ambidextrous bolt.
Price: .177, .22 .... **$700.00**
Price: .25 .... **$750.00**

BENJAMIN ROGUE .357 CALIBER MULTI-SHOT AIR RIFLE
Caliber: .357, 6-shot mag (optional single-shot tray). **Features:** Electronic precharged pneumatic (ePCP), Bolt-action, 2-stage adjustable electronic trigger with dual electronic switches, Ambidextrous synthetic stock w/adjustable buttstock & sling swivel studs, 11mm, Adjustable power, Up to 900 fps (250 ft-lbs. max),

Prices given are believed to be accurate at time of publication however, many factors affect retail pricing so exact prices are not possible.

BENJAMIN ROGUE .357 CALIBER MULTI-SHOT

3000 psi (206 bar) max fill pressure (delivers full-power shots with as little as 1000 psi), Shrouded for stealthy hunting, Up to 20 shots at 100 ft-lbs. when filled to 3000 psi, Built-in manometer (air pressure gauge), Weaver bipod rail, LCD screen for EPiC controls on left side of gun, includes fill adapter. Made in the U.S. by Benjamin Sheridan Co.
Price: **$1,349.00**

BENJAMIN TITAN XS NP BREAK BARREL AIR RIFLE

Caliber: .177 **Weight:** 8.3 lbs. **Length:** 44.5" overall. **Power:** Single-shot Nitro Piston powered break barrel. **Stock:** Synthetic ambidextrous thumbhole. **Sights:** 4x32mm scope. **Features:** Rifled steel barrel, adjustable two-stage trigger, Picatinny mounting rail. 1,250 fps. 18 ft-lbs.
Price: . . . . **$ 232.00**

BENJAMIN TRAIL NITRO PISTON 2 BREAK BARREL AIR RIFLE

Caliber: .177, .22 **Weight:** 8.3 lbs. **Length:** 46.25" overall. **Power:** Break barrel single shot–Patent Pending Nitro Piston 2. **Stock:** Hardwood, black synthetic or Realtree Xtra camo. **Sights:** CenterPoint 3-9x32mm scope. **Features:** Clean Break Trigger (CBT), integrated sound suppression system. 1,200 fps in .177 and 1,400 fps in .22.
Price: .177 Trail NP Synthetic **$350.00**
Price: .22 Trail NP Synthetic **$350.00**
Price: .22 Trail NP Hardwood **$350.00**
Price: .22 Trail NP Realtree Xtra **$380.00**

BENJAMIN VARMINT POWER PACK BREAK BARREL

Caliber: .22 **Power:** Single-shot Nitro Pistol powered break barrel. **Stock:** Ambidextrous synthetic stock with raised cheekpiece. **Sights:** Red Class IIIa fast-acquisition laser. **Features:** Rifled steel barrel, two-stage adjustable trigger, Picatinny mounting rail, recoil-proof 90 lumen LED flashlight. 21 ft-lbs. 950 fps.
Price: .177 Trail NP Synthetic **$250.00**

BERETTA CX4 STORM

BERETTA CX4 STORM

Caliber: .177, 30-shot semiauto. 17-1/2", rifled. **Weight:** 5.25 lbs. **Length:** 30.75" overall. **Power:** 88g CO2. **Stock:** Replica style. **Sights:** Adjustable front and rear. Blowback action. Velocity of 600 fps. Accessory rails. Made by Umarex.
Price: **$375.00**

BSA MAGNUM SUPERSPORT AIR RIFLE, CARBINE

Caliber: .177, .22, .25, single shot. **Barrel:** 18-1/2". **Weight:** 6 lbs., 8 oz. **Length:** 41" overall. **Power:** Spring-air, barrel cocking. **Stock:** Oil-finished hardwood; Monte Carlo with cheekpiece, recoil pad. **Sights:** Ramp front, micrometer adjustable rear. Maxi-Grip scope rail. **Features:** Velocity 950 fps (.177), 750 fps (.22), 600 fps (.25). Patented Maxi-Grip scope rail protects optics from recoil; automatic anti-beartrap plus manual tang safety. Muzzle brake standard. Imported for U.K.
Price: **$194.95**
Price: Carbine, 14" barrel, muzzle brake **$214.95**

BSA METEOR AIR RIFLE

Caliber: .177, .22, single shot. **Barrel:** 18-1/2". **Weight:** 6 lbs. **Length:** 41" overall. **Power:** Spring-air, barrel cocking. **Stock:** Oil-finished hardwood. **Sights:** Ramp front, micrometer adjustable rear. **Features:** Velocity 650 fps (.177), 500 fps (.22). Automatic anti-beartrap; manual tang safety. Receiver grooved for scope mounting. Imported from U.K.
Price: Rifle **$144.95**
Price: Carbine **$164.95**

BSA R-10 MK2 PCP AIR RIFLE

Caliber: .17, .22 **Barrel:** 18" **Weight:** 7.3 lbs. **Power:** Pre-charged pneumatic (3,365 psi maximum fill pressure) bolt action. **Stock:** Oiled walnut Monte Carlo stock with right-hand raised cheekpiece and checkered grip and fore-end. **Sights:** No sights, aluminum 11mm dovetail grooves for scope installation. **Features:** Sling swivel studs, rifled steel hammer-forged free-floated fully shrouded barrel, two-stage adjustable trigger, adjustable buttplate, manual safety, 10-round capacity, up to 50 shots per fill in .17 and up to 45 shots per fill in .22 caliber. 1,000 fps in .17 and 900 fps in .22.
Price: **$1,299.99**

BSA SCORPION 1200 SE AIR RIFLE

Caliber: .177, .22 **Barrel:** 24" **Weight:** 8.75 lbs. **Power:** Pre-charged pneumatic (3,364 psi maximum fill pressure) bolt action. **Stock:** Synthetic ambidextrous stock with twin raised cheekpieces. **Sights:** No sights, aluminum 11mm dovetail grooves for scope installation. **Features:** Rifled steel hammer-forged free-floated barrel, 2-stage adjustable trigger, ventilated rubber buttplate, manual safety, 10-round removable rotary self-indexing magazine, built-in manometer (air pressure gauge). 1,200 fps in .17 and 1,000 fps in .22.
Price: **$975.95**

BSA SCORPION SE AIR RIFLE

Caliber: .17, .22, .25 **Barrel:** 18.5" **Weight:** 7.7 lbs. **Power:** Pre-charged pneumatic (3,365 psi maximum fill pressure) bolt action. **Stock:** Ambidextrous Monte Carlo Beech wood. **Sights:** No sights, aluminum 11mm dovetail grooves for scope installation. **Features:** Rifled steel hammer-forged free-floated barrel, 2-stage adjustable trigger, ventilated rubber buttplate, manual safety, 10-round removable rotary self-indexing magazine (10 round capacity in .17 and .22 and 8-round capacity in .25 caliber), with up to 40-shots per fill in .17 and up to 30 shots per fill in .22 and .25 calibers, built-in manometer (air pressure gauge). 1,000 fps in .17 caliber, 820 fps in .22 caliber and 700 fps in .25 caliber.
Price: **$949.99**

BSA SUPERTEN MK3 AIR RIFLE

Caliber: .177, .22 10-shot repeater. **Barrel:** 17-1/2". **Weight:** 7 lbs., 8 oz. **Length:** 37" overall. **Power:** Precharged pneumatic via buddy bottle. **Stock:** Oil-finished hardwood; Monte Carlo with cheekpiece, cut checkered grip; adjustable recoil pad. **Sights:** No sights; intended for scope use. **Features:** Velocity 1000+ fps (.177), 1000+ fps (.22). Patented 10-shot indexing magazine, bolt-action loading. Left-hand version also available. Imported from U.K.
Price: **$800.00**

BSA SUPERTEN MK3 BULLBARREL

Caliber: .177, .22, .25, single shot. **Barrel:** 18-1/2". **Weight:** 8 lbs., 8 oz. **Length:** 43" overall. **Power:** Spring-air, underlever cocking. **Stock:** Oil-finished hardwood; Monte Carlo with cheekpiece, checkered at grip; recoil pad. **Sights:** Ramp front, micrometer adjustable rear. Maxi-Grip scope rail. **Features:** Velocity 950 fps (.177), 750 fps (.22), 600 fps (.25). Patented rotating breech design. Maxi-Grip scope rail protects optics from recoil; automatic anti-beartrap plus manual safety. Imported from U.K.
Price: Rifle, MKII Carbine (14" barrel, 39-1/2" overall) **$349.95**

BSA ULTRA SE MULTISHOT AIR RIFLE

Caliber: .17, .22, .25 **Barrel:** 12" **Weight:** 5.9 lbs. **Length:** 32" **Power:** Pre-charged pneumatic (3,365 psi maximum fill pressure) bolt action. **Stock:** Synthetic ambidextrous Monte Carlo stock with textured grip and forearm. **Sights:** No sights, aluminum 11mm dovetail grooves for scope installation. **Features:** Match-grade cold-hammer-forged steel barrel equipped with a muzzlebrake, two-stage adjustable match-grade trigger, manual safety, built-in pressure gauge, rubber buttplate. 10-round capacity (eight rounds in .25 caliber).
Price: **$899.99**

CROSMAN CHALLENGER PCP COMPETITION

CROSMAN CHALLENGER PCP COMPETITION AIR RIFLE

Caliber: .177 **Weight:** 7.1 lbs. **Length:** 41.5" overall. **Power:**

Precharged pneumatic sporting class single-shot air rifle, which operates on either compressed air or CO2. **Stock:** Synthetic. **Sights:** Diopter front sight and Precision Diopter rear sight. **Features:** Rifled steel floated Lothar Walther barrel, two-stage match-grade trigger and is built in America.
Price: $630.00

CROSMAN M4-177

CROSMAN M4-177
Caliber: .177 pellet or BB. Removable 5-shot magazine. **Weight:** 3.5 lbs. **Length:** 34". **Sights:** Windage-adjustable flip-up rear, elevation-adjustable front. **Features:** Rifled barrel, adjustable stock, pneumatic multi-pump operation gives up to 660 fps muzzle velocity. Bolt-action variation of AR-style rifle. Also available in kit form.
Price: $75.00

CROSMAN MARINES USMC MOS 0311 RIFLEMAN
Caliber: .177, BB **Weight:** 3.5 lbs. **Length:** 34". **Power:** Pneumatic multi-pump bolt-action variation of AR-style rifles. **Sights:** Dual aperture windage-adjustable flip-up rear and elevation-adjustable front sight. **Features:** Rifled barrel, adjustable stock, removable five-shot magazine and 350 BB reservoir. 660 fps with BBs and 700 fps with alloy pellets.
Price: $100.00

CROSMAN MODEL 664SB POWERMASTER AIR RIFLE
Caliber: .177 (single shot pellet) or BB, 200-shot reservoir. **Barrel:** 20", rifled steel. **Weight:** 2 lbs. 15 oz. **Length:** 38-1/2" overall. **Power:** Pneumatic; hand-pumped. **Stock:** Wood-grained ABS plastic; checkered pistol grip and forend. **Sights:** Fiber-optic front, fully adjustable open rear. **Features:** Velocity about 645 fps. Bolt action, cross-bolt safety. From Crosman.
Price: $105.50

CROSMAN MODEL 760 PUMPMASTER AIR RIFLE
Caliber: .177 pellets (single shot) or BB (200-shot reservoir). **Barrel:** 19-1/2", rifled steel. **Weight:** 2 lbs., 12 oz. **Length:** 33.5" overall. **Power:** Pneumatic, hand-pump. **Stock:** Walnut-finished ABS plastic stock and forend. **Features:** Velocity to 590 fps (BBs, 10 pumps). Short stroke, power determined by number of strokes. Fiber-optic front sight and adjustable rear sight. Cross-bolt safety. From Crosman.
Price: Model 760 . . . . $48.00

CROSMAN MODEL 1077 REPEATAIR RIFLE
Caliber: .177 pellets, 12-shot clip. **Barrel:** 20.4", rifled steel. **Weight:** 3 lbs., 11 oz. **Length:** 37" overall. **Power:** CO2 Powerlet. **Stock:** Textured synthetic. **Sights:** Fiber-optic front sight and fully adjustable rear. **Features:** Velocity 625 fps. Removable 12-shot clip. True semiautomatic action. From Crosman.
Price: $90.00

CROSMAN MODEL 2100 CLASSIC AIR RIFLE
Caliber: .177 pellets (single shot), or BB (200-shot BB reservoir). **Barrel:** 21", rifled. **Weight:** 4 lbs., 13 oz. **Length:** 39-3/4" overall. **Power:** Pump-up, pneumatic. **Stock:** Wood-grained checkered synthetic. **Features:** 755 fps with BBs and 725 fps with pellets. Cross-bolt safety; concealed reservoir holds over 200 BBs. From Crosman.
Price: Model 2100B $69.99

CROSMAN MODEL 2260 AIR RIFLE
Caliber: .22, single shot. **Barrel:** 24". **Weight:** 4 lbs., 12 oz. **Length:** 39.75" overall. **Power:** CO2 Powerlet. **Stock:** Hardwood. **Sights:** Blade front, adjustable rear open or peep. **Features:** Variable pump power; three pumps give 395 fps, six pumps 530 fps, 10 pumps 600 fps (average). Full-size adult air rifle. From Crosman.
Price: $83.84

CROSMAN MODEL NITRO VENOM AIR RIFLE
Caliber: .177, .22 **Weight:** 7.4 lbs. **Length:** 44.5" **Power:** Single shot Nitro Venom Piston design. **Stock:** Hardwood or synthetic

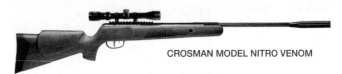

CROSMAN MODEL NITRO VENOM

ambidextrous stock with a raised cheekpiece and modified beavertail forearm. **Sights:** 4x32mm scope. **Features:** Precision rifled barrel with fluted muzzlebrake and sculpted rubber recoil pad. The rifle is equipped with a scope quick-lock mounting system for quick and easy optic mounting. 1,200 fps and 18 foot-pounds of energy (.177). 950 fps and 21 foot-pounds of energy (.22).
Price: .177 . . . . $170.00
Price: .22 . . . . $180.00

CROSMAN MODEL NITRO
VENOM DUSK

CROSMAN MODEL NITRO VENOM DUSK AIR RIFLE
Caliber: .177 & .22. **Features:** Nitro Venom air rifle feature precision, rifled barrel with fluted muzzle brake and sculpted rubber recoil pad. The rifle is equipped with a CenterPoint 3-9x32mm precision scope and a quick-lock mounting system for quick and easy optic mounting. The ambidextrous hardwood stock with raised cheek piece and modified, beavertail forearm. Crosman Nitro Venom air rifle delivers serious hunting power with muzzle energy up to 21 fps and up to 1200 fps. Take one on a hunt to experience the power, stability and stealth of Nitro Piston® technology.
Price: .177 . . . . $209.99

CROSMAN MODEL TRAIL NP
ALL WEATHER

Price: .22 . . . . N/A

CROSMAN MODEL TRAIL NP ALL WEATHER & LAMINATED HARDWOOD AIR RIFLES
Caliber: .177, .22 & .25, up to 1200 fps (.177), 950 fps (.22) & 900 fps (.25). **Weight:** 6.65 lbs. - 8 lbs. **Length:** 43" overall. **Features:** The Nitro Venom Dusk air rifle features a precision, rifled barrel with fluted muzzle break and sculpted rubber recoil pad. The rifle is equipped with a CenterPoint 3-9x32mm precision scope and a quick-lock mounting system for quick and easy optic mounting. The ambidextrous synthetic stock has a raised cheek piece and modified, beavertail forearm. Crosman Nitro Venom air rifles delivers serious hunting power with muzzle energy up to 18 fpe and up to 1200 fps.. Take one on a hunt to experience the power, stability and stealth of Nitro Piston® technology. The .22 caliber series is equiped with various harwood and laminated thumbhole and standard stocks and also models with bull barrels, imposing 23 ft-lbs of muzzle energy provides 16% more downrange energy than a .177 cal. The new XL725 provides 24% more downrange energy than a .177 caliber offers. This is the most powerful Nitro Piston® break barrel available.
Price: .177 Trail NP $247.00
Price: .177 Trail NP XL 1500 . . . . $247.00
Price: .22 Trail NP All Weather $247.00
Price: .22 Trail NP Hardwood $299.00
Price: .22 Trail NP All Weather with Realtree APG $279.95
Price: .22 Trail NP All Weather 495fps $299.00
Price: .22 Trail NP Laminated Hardwood . . . . N/A
Price: .22 Trail NP XL 1100 . . . . $359.00
Price: .25 Trail NP XL 725 . . . . $329.00

CROSMAN MTR77 NP TACTICAL BREAK BARREL AIR RIFLE
Caliber: .177 **Weight:** 5.8 lbs. **Length:** 40" overall. **Power:** Single-shot Nitro Piston modern sporting rifle design. **Stock:** Textured synthetic all-weather tactical style. **Sights:** 4x32mm scope.

Features: Rifled steel barrel, adjustable trigger and provides 18 foot-pounds of energy.
Price: **$200.00**

CROSMAN TR77 NPS TACTICAL BREAK BARREL AIR RIFLE
Caliber: .177 **Weight:** 5.8 lbs. **Length:** 40" overall. **Power:** Single-shot Nitro Piston. **Stock:** Compact, tactical-style, textured synthetic. **Sights:** 4x32mm scope. **Features:** Rifled steel barrel, 1,000 fps.
Price: **$160.00**

DAISY 1938 RED RYDER AIR RIFLE
Caliber: BB, 650-shot repeating action. **Barrel:** Smoothbore steel with shroud. **Weight:** 2.2 lbs. **Length:** 35.4" overall. **Stock:** Wood stock burned with Red Ryder lariat signature. **Sights:** Post front, adjustable open rear. **Features:** Walnut forend. Saddle ring with leather thong. Lever cocking. Gravity feed. Controlled velocity. 350 fps. From Daisy Mfg. Co.
Price: **$39.99**

DAISY AVANTI MODEL 887 GOLD MEDALIST
Caliber: .177 **Barrel:** Lothar Walther rifled high-grade steel, crowned, 12 lands and grooves, right hand twist. Precision bore sized for match pellets. **Weight:** 7.3 lbs. **Length:** 39.5" overall. **Power:** CO2 power single shot bolt. **Stock:** Laminated hardwood. **Sights:** Front globe sight with changeable aperture inserts: rear diopter sight with micrometer click adjustment for windage and elevation. **Features:** Velocity to 500 fps. Crossbolt trigger block safety. Includes rail adapter. From Daisy Mfg. Co.
Price: **$699.00**

DAISY AVANTI MODEL 888 MEDALIST
Caliber: .177 **Barrel:** Lothar Walther rifled high-grade steel, crowned, 12 lands and grooves, right-hand twist. Precision bore sized for match pellets. **Weight:** 6.9 lbs. **Length:** 38.5" overall. **Power:** CO2 single shot bolt. **Stock:** Sporter-style multicolored laminated hardwood. **Sights:** Hooded front with interchangeable aperture inserts; micrometer adjustable rear peep sight. **Features:** Velocity to 500 fps. Crossbolt trigger block safety. From Daisy Mfg. Co.
Price: **$469.99**

DAISY MODEL 105 BUCK AIR RIFLE
Caliber: .177 or BB. **Barrel:** Smoothbore steel. **Weight:** 1.6 lbs. **Length:** 29.8" overall. **Power:** Lever cocking, spring air. **Stock:** Stained solid wood. **Sights:** TruGlo fiber-optic, open fixed rear. **Features:** Velocity to 275. Crossbolt trigger block safety. From Daisy Mfg. Co.
Price: **$29.99**

DAISY MODEL 753 ELITE
Caliber: .177, pellet. **Barrel:** Lothar Walther rifled high-grade steel barrel, crowned, 12 lands and grooves, right-hand twist. Precision bore sized for match pellets. **Weight:** 6.4 lbs. **Length:** 39.75" overall. **Power:** Recoilless single pump pneumatic, straight pull bolt. **Stock:** Full length match-style hardwood stock with raised cheek piece and adjustable length. **Sights:** Front globe sight with changeable aperture inserts, diopter rear sight with micrometer adjustable rear. **Features:** Velocity to 510 fps. Crossbolt trigger block safety with red indicator. From Daisy Mfg. Co.
Price: **$450.00**

DAISY MODEL 840B GRIZZLY AIR RIFLE
Caliber: .177 pellet single shot; or BB 350-shot. **Barrel:** 19", smoothbore, steel. **Weight:** 2.25 lbs. **Length:** 36.8" overall. **Power:** Single pump pneumatic. **Stock:** Molded wood-grain stock and forend. **Sights:** Ramp front, open, adjustable rear. **Features:** Muzzle velocity 320 fps (BB), 300 fps (pellet). Steel buttplate; straight pull bolt action; cross-bolt safety. Forend forms pump lever. From Daisy Mfg. Co.
Price: **$44.99**
Price: (840C in Mossy Oak Breakup Camo) **$49.99**

DAISY MODEL 853 LEGEND
Caliber: .177, pellet. **Barrel:** Lothar Walther rifled high-grade steel barrel, crowned, 12 lands and grooves, right-hand twist. Precision bore sized for match pellets. **Weight:** 5.5 lbs. **Length:** 38.5" overall. **Power:** Single-pump pneumatic, straight pull-bolt. **Stock:** Full-length, sporter-style hardwood with adjustable length. **Sights:** Hooded front with interchangeable aperture inserts; micrometer adjustable rear. **Features:** Velocity to 510 fps. Crossbolt trigger block safety with red indicator. From Daisy Mfg. Co.
Price: **$400.00**

DAISY MODEL 4841 GRIZZLY
Caliber: .177 pellet single-shot. **Barrel:** NA. **Weight:** NA. **Length:** 36.8" overall. **Power:** Single pump pneumatic. **Stock:** Composite camo. **Sights:** Blade and ramp front a fixed Model 840 Daisy scope. **Features:** Muzzle velocity 350 fps. From Daisy Mfg. Co.
Price: **$59.99**

DAISY POWERLINE MODEL 35 AIR RIFLE
Caliber: .177, BB. **Weight:** 3.1 lbs. **Length:** 34.5" overall. **Power:** Multi-pump pneumatic. **Stock:** Molded synthetic with checkering. **Sights:** Blade ramp front sight and adjustable rear. **Features:** Smoothbore steel barrel. 625 fps.
Price: **$39.99**
Price: (Camo) **$49.99**

DAISY POWERLINE® 500 BREAK BARREL
Caliber: .177 pellet, single shot. **Barrel:** Rifled steel. **Weight:** 6.6 lbs. **Length:** 45.7" overall. **Stock:** Stained solid wood. **Sights:** Truglo® fiber-optic front, micro-adjustable open rear, adjustable 4x32 riflescope. **Features:** Auto rear-button safety. Velocity to 490 fps. Made in U.S.A. by Daisy Mfg. Co.
Price: **$120.99**

DAISY POWERLINE® 800 BREAK BARREL
Caliber: .177 pellet, single shot. **Barrel:** Rifled steel. **Weight:** 6.6 lbs. **Length:** 46.7" overall. **Stock:** Black composite. **Sights:** Truglo fiber-optic front, micro-adjustable open rear, adjustable 4x32 riflescope. **Features:** Auto rear-button safety. Velocity to 800 fps. Made in U.S.A. by Daisy Mfg. Co.
Price: **$120.99**

DAISY POWERLINE® 880 AIR RIFLE
Caliber: .177 pellet or BB, 50-shot BB magazine, single shot for pellets. **Barrel:** Rifled steel. **Weight:** 3.7 lbs. **Length:** 37.6" overall. **Power:** Multi-pump pneumatic. **Stock:** Molded wood grain; Monte Carlo comb. **Sights:** Hooded front, adjustable rear. **Features:** Velocity to 800 fps. (BB). Variable power (velocity, range) increase with pump strokes; resin receiver with dovetailed scope mount. Made in U.S.A. by Daisy Mfg. Co.
Price: **$49.99**

DAISY POWERLINE® 901 AIR RIFLE
Caliber: .177. **Barrel:** Rifled steel. **Weight:** 3.7 lbs. **Length:** 37.5" overall. **Power:** Multi-pump pneumatic. **Stock:** Advanced composite. **Sights:** Fiber-optic front, adjustable rear. **Features:** Velocity to 750 fps. (BB); advanced composite receiver with dovetailed mounts for optics. Made in U.S.A. by Daisy Mfg. Co.
Price: **$60.99**

DAISY POWERLINE® 1000 BREAK BARREL
Caliber: .177 pellet, single shot. **Barrel:** Rifled steel. **Weight:** 6.6 lbs. **Length:** 46.7" overall. **Stock:** Black composite. **Sights:** Truglo® fiber-optic front, micro-adjustable open rear, adjustable 4x32 riflescope. **Features:** Auto rear-button safety. Velocity to 750 fps (BB). Made in U.S.A. by Daisy Mfg. Co.
Price: **$231.99**

DAISY POWERLINE® TARGETPRO 953 AIR RIFLE
Caliber: .177 pellets, single shot. **Weight:** 6.40 lbs. **Length:** 39.75" overall. **Power:** Pneumatic single-pump cocking lever; straight-pull bolt. **Stock:** Full-length, match-style black composite. **Sights:** Front and rear fiber optic. **Features:** Rifled high-grade steel barrel with 1:15 twist. Max. Muzzle Velocity of 560 fps. From Daisy Mfg. Co.
Price: **$119.99**

DIANA MODEL 34 PREMIUM AIR RIFLE
Caliber: .177, .22 **Weight:** 7.5 lbs. **Length:** 46" overall. **Power:** Break-barrel single-shot. **Stock:** Monte Carlo stock with checkered forearm, pistol grip and soft rubber pad. **Sights:** Metal with interchangeable front sight inserts. **Features:** 1,000 fps in .177 and 800 fps in .22.
Price: **$439.99**

DIANA MODEL 52 AIR RIFLE
Caliber: .177, .22, .25 **Barrel:** 17.3" **Weight:** 9.4 lbs. **Length:** 45" overall. **Power:** Side-cocking, spring-piston design. **Stock:** Walnut stained beechwood with cheekpiece and fine checkering on forearm and pistol grip. **Sights:** Adjustable. **Features:** Two-stage adjustable trigger, rubber buttplate, 11mm scope rail. 1,150 fps in .177; 850 fps in .22, 610 in .25.
Price: (.177 & .22) **$549.99**
Price: (.25) **$599.99**

DIANA MODEL 56 TARGET HUNTER AIR RIFLE
Caliber: .177, .22, .25 **Weight:** 11.1 lbs. **Length:** 44" overall. **Power:** Recoiless spring gun. **Stock:** Monte Carlo stock with cheekpiece, adjustable rear buttpad for elevation, ambidextrous thumbhole design. **Features:** Upgraded metal safety catch, upgraded 2-stage all metal trigger assembly, muzzle stabilizer. 1,000 fps in .177; 900 fps in .22; 610 fps in .25.
Price: (.177 & .22) **$859.99**
Price: (.25) **$919.99**

DIANA MODEL 440 TARGET HUNTER AIR RIFLE
Caliber: .177, .22 **Barrel:** 15.4" **Weight:** 9 lbs. **Length:** 41" overall. **Power:** Break-barrel single shot. **Stock:** Thumbhole hardwood. **Features:** Scope rail, two-stage adjustable trigger, auto safety and rifled barrel. 870 fps in .177 and 670 fps in .22.
Price: **$639.99**

DIANA MODEL 470 TARGET HUNTER AIR RIFLE
Caliber: .177, .22 **Barrel:** 18" **Weight:** 9.4 lbs. **Length:** 45" overall. **Power:** Break-barrel single shot. **Stock:** Ambidextrous thumbhole hardwood, adjustable buttplate for elevation. **Features:** Upgraded two-stage adjustable trigger assembly with all-metal parts, rifled barrel. 1,150 fps in .177 and 930 fps in .22.
Price: **$659.99**

DIANA MODEL P1000 PCP AIR RIFLE
Caliber: .177, .22 **Weight:** 7.9 lbs. **Length:** 38" overall. **Power:** Precharged pneumatic airgun. **Stock:** Monte Carlo, two-piece hunting style. **Features:** 14-shot magazine, single-shot adapter, 300-bar steel cylinder, TO6-metal trigger with automatic safety, 11-mm top rail. 1,150 fps in .177 and 950 fps in .22.
Price: **$1,169.99**

DIANA MODEL P1000 PCP TARGET HUNTER AIR RIFLE
Caliber: .177, .22 **Weight:** 8.2 lbs. **Length:** 38" overall. **Power:** Precharged pneumatic airgun. **Stock:** Monte Carlo, two-piece hunting style. **Features:** 14-shot magazine, single-shot adapter, 300-bar steel cylinder, TO6-metal trigger with automatic safety, 11-mm top rail. 1,150 fps in .177 and 950 fps in .22.
Price: **$1,219.99**

EAA/BAIKAL IZH61 AIR RIFLE
Caliber: .177 pellet, 5-shot magazine. **Barrel:** 17.8". **Weight:** 6.4 lbs. **Length:** 31" overall. **Power:** Spring-piston, side-cocking lever. **Stock:** Black plastic. **Sights:** Adjustable rear, fully hooded front. **Features:** Velocity 490 fps. Futuristic design with adjustable stock. Imported from Russia by European American Armory.
Price: **$122.65**

GAMO BIG CAT AIR RIFLES
Caliber: .177, .22 **Weight:** 6.1 lbs. **Power:** Break-barrel spring action. **Stock:** Ambidextrous all-weather black synthetic. **Sights:** 4x32mm scope. **Features:** Two-stage adjustable trigger, fluted polymer jacketed precision rifled steel barrel, rubber recoil pad. .177 – 1,200 fps and .22 – 975 fps.
Price: (.177) **$199.95**
Price: (.22) **$189.95**

GAMO BIG CAT 1400 AIR RIFLE
Caliber: .177 **Weight:** 6.61 lbs. **Power:** Break-barrel spring action. **Stock:** Ambidextrous all-weather synthetic. **Sights:** 4x32mm scope. **Features:** Two-stage adjustable trigger, fluted polymer jacketed precision rifled steel barrel, rubber recoil pad. 1,400 fps.
Price: **$199.95**

GAMO BONE COLLECTOR BULL WHISPER AIR RIFLE
Caliber: .177, .22 **Weight:** 6.2 lbs. **Power:** Break-barrel spring action. **Stock:** Ambidextrous all-weather synthetic green and black colored. **Sights:** 4x32mm scope. **Features:** Two-stage adjustable trigger, fluted polymer jacketed precision rifled steel barrel, rubber recoil pad. 1,300 fps in .177; 975 fps in .22.
Price: **$279.95**

GAMO BONE COLLECTOR IGT AIR RIFLE
Caliber: .177 **Weight:** 6.1 lbs. **Power:** Break-barrel spring action. **Stock:** Ambidextrous all-weather synthetic green and black colored. **Sights:** 4x32mm scope. **Features:** Two-stage adjustable trigger, fluted polymer jacketed precision rifled steel barrel, rubber recoil pad. 1,300 fps.
Price: **$249.95**

GAMO BUCKMASTER SQUIRREL TERMINATOR AIR RIFLE
Caliber: .177 **Weight:** 6.1 lbs. **Power:** Break-barrel spring airgun. **Stock:** Ambidextrous all-weather synthetic. **Sights:** 4x32mm scope. **Features:** Two-stage adjustable trigger, turbo stabilizing system, fluted polymer jacketed rifled steel barrel, rubber recoil pad. 1,275 fps.
Price: **$219.95**

GAMO CAMO ROCKET IGT AIR RIFLE
Caliber: .177 **Weight:** 6.1 lbs. **Power:** Break-barrel spring action. **Stock:** Ambidextrous all-weather synthetic black thumbhole style. **Sights:** Fiber optics front and rear and 4x32mm scope. **Features:** Two-stage adjustable trigger, fluted polymer jacketed precision rifled steel barrel, rubber recoil pad. 1,300 fps.
Price: **$248.95**

GAMO HUNTER AIR RIFLES
Caliber: .177. **Barrel:** NA. **Weight:** 6.5 to 10.5 lbs. **Length:** 43.5-48.5". **Power:** Single-stroke pneumatic, 850-1,000 fps. **Stock:** Wood. **Sights:** Varies by model **Features:** Adjustable two-stage trigger, rifled barrel, raised scope ramp on receiver. Realtree camo model available.
Price: Sport **$250.00**
Price: Pro **$300.00**

GAMO HUNTER EXTREME SE (SPECIAL EDITION) AIR RIFLE
Caliber: .177 **Weight:** 6.61 lbs. **Power:** Break-barrel spring action. **Stock:** Hardwood. **Sights:** 4x32mm scope. **Features:** Two-stage adjustable trigger, fluted polymer jacketed precision rifled steel barrel, rubber recoil pad. 1,650 fps.
Price: **$549.95**

GAMO RECON G2 WHISPER AIR RIFLE
Caliber: .177 **Weight:** 4.64 lbs. **Power:** Break-barrel spring action. **Stock:** Ambidextrous all-weather synthetic. **Sights:** Illuminated green dot. **Features:** Two-stage adjustable trigger, fluted polymer jacketed rifled steel barrel, rubber recoil pad. 750 fps.
Price: **$119.95**

GAMO SHADOW FOX

GAMO SHADOW AIR RIFLES
Caliber: .177. **Barrel:** 18", fluted polymer bull. **Weight:** 6.1 to 7.15 lbs. **Length:** 43" to 43.3". **Power:** Single-stroke pneumatic, 850-1,000 fps. **Stock:** Tough all-weather molded synthetic. **Sights:** NA. **Features:** Single shot, manual safety,
Price: Sport **$219.95**
Price: Hunter **$219.95**
Price: Big Cat 1200 . . . . **$169.95**
Price: Fox **$279.95**

GAMO SHAWN MICHAELS SHOWSTOPPER AIR RIFLE
Caliber: .177 **Weight:** 6.61 lbs. **Power:** Break-barrel spring action. **Stock:** Ambidextrous all-weather synthetic. **Sights:** 4x32mm scope. **Features:** Two-stage adjustable trigger, fluted polymer jacketed precision rifled steel barrel, rubber recoil pad. 1,400 fps.
Price: **$249.95**

GAMO SILENT CAT AIR RIFLE
Caliber: .177 **Weight:** 5.28 lbs. **Power:** Break-barrel spring action. **Stock:** Ambidextrous all-weather synthetic black thumbhole style. **Sights:** 4x32mm scope and fiber optics front and rear. **Features:** Two-stage adjustable trigger, fluted polymer jacketed precision rifled steel barrel, rubber recoil pad. 1,300 fps.
Price: **$249.95**

GAMO SILENT STALKER AIR RIFLE
Caliber: .177 **Weight:** 6.1 lbs. **Power:** Break-barrel spring action. **Stock:** Ambidextrous all-weather synthetic. **Sights:** 4x32mm scope. **Features:** Two-stage adjustable trigger, fluted polymer jacketed precision rifled steel barrel, rubber recoil pad. 1,300 fps.
Price: **$229.95**

GAMO SILENT STALKER WHISPER AIR RIFLE
Caliber: .177, .22 **Weight:** 6.61 lbs. **Power:** Break-barrel spring action. **Stock:** Ambidextrous all-weather synthetic. **Sights:** 3-9x40mm scope. **Features:** Two-stage adjustable trigger, fluted polymer

GAMO SILENT STALKER WHISPER

jacketed precision rifled steel barrel, rubber recoil pad, flashlight with pressure switch. .177 – 1,300 fps and .22 – 975 fps.
Price: **$310.95**

GAMO VARMINT HUNTER AIR RIFLE
Caliber: .177 **Weight:** 7 lbs. **Power:** Break-barrel spring airgun. **Stock:** Ambidextrous all-weather synthetic. **Sights:** 4x32mm scope. **Features:** Two-stage adjustable trigger, fluted polymer jacketed rifled steel barrel, rubber recoil pad. 1,250 fps.
Price: **$249.95**

GAMO VARMINT HUNTER HP AIR RIFLE
Caliber: .177 **Weight:** 6.1 lbs. **Power:** Break-barrel spring action. **Stock:** Ambidextrous all-weather synthetic green. **Sights:** Laser and 4x32mm scope. **Features:** Two-stage adjustable trigger, fluted polymer jacketed precision rifled steel barrel, rubber recoil pad, flashlight with pressure switch. 1,400 fps.
Price: **$299.95**

GAMO VARMINT STALKER AIR RIFLE
Caliber: .177 **Weight:** 6.1 lbs. **Power:** Break-barrel spring action. **Stock:** Ambidextrous all-weather synthetic black thumbhole style. **Sights:** 4x32mm scope. **Features:** Two-stage adjustable trigger, fluted polymer jacketed precision rifled steel barrel, rubber recoil pad. 1,250 fps.
Price: **$244.95**

GAMO WHISPER

GAMO WHISPER AIR RIFLES
Caliber: .177, .22. **Barrel:** 18", fluted polymer bull. **Weight:** 5.28 to 7.4 lbs. **Length:** 45.7" to 46". **Stock:** Tough all-weather molded synthetic. **Sights:** Fiber-optic front with sight guard, adjustable rear. **Features:** Single shot, manual trigger safety. Non-removable noise dampener (with up to 52 percent reduction).
Price: Whisper. **$279.95**
Price: Whisper Deluxe **$319.95**
Price: Whisper VH (Varmint Hunter/Whisper in one rifle) **$329.95**
Price: Whisper .22 .... **$299.95**
Price: CSI Camo (.177) **$329.95**
Price: CSI Camo (.22) **$329.95**

GAMO WHISPER AIR RIFLE
Caliber: .177 **Weight:** 8 lbs. **Power:** Break-barrel spring action. **Stock:** Ambidextrous all-weather synthetic pistol grip style. **Sights:** 3-9x40mm scope. **Features:** Two-stage adjustable trigger, fluted polymer jacketed precision rifled steel barrel, rubber recoil pad. 1,100 fps.
Price: **$329.95**

GAMO WHISPER FUSION AIR RIFLE
Caliber: .177 **Weight:** 6.61 lbs. **Power:** Break-barrel spring action. **Stock:** Ambidextrous all-weather synthetic. **Sights:** 3-9x40mm scope. **Features:** Two-stage adjustable trigger, fluted polymer jacketed precision rifled steel barrel, rubber recoil pad, adjustable comb for height. 1,300 fps.
Price: **$309.95**

GAMO WHISPER FUSION PRO AIR RIFLE
Caliber: .177, .22 **Weight:** 6.61 lbs. **Power:** Break-barrel spring action. **Stock:** Ambidextrous all-weather synthetic. **Sights:** 3-9x40mm scope and fiber optics front and rear. **Features:** Two-stage adjustable trigger, fluted polymer jacketed precision rifled steel barrel, rubber recoil pad. .177 – 1,400 and .22 – 1,000 fps.
Price: **$329.95**

GAMO WHISPER G2 AIR RIFLE
Caliber: .177, .22. **Weight:** 6.3 lbs. **Stock:** Ambidextrous all weather synthetic. **Sights:** 4x32mm scope and fiber optics front and rear. **Features:** Two-stage adjustable trigger, turbo stabilizing system, fluted polymer jacketed rifled steel barrel, adjustable cheekpiece,

rubber recoil pad. .177 - 1,250 fps and .22 - 975 fps.
Price: **$269.95**

HAMMERLI 850 AIR MAGNUM
Caliber: .177, .22, 8-shot repeater. 23-1/2", rifled. **Weight:** 5.8 lbs. 41" overall. **Power:** 88g CO2. **Stock:** All-weather polymer, Monte Carlo, textured grip and forearm. **Sights:** Hooded fiber optic front, fiber optic adjustable rear. Velocity of 760 fps (.177), 655 (22). Blue finish. Rubber buttpad. Bolt-action. Scope compatible.
Price: .177, .22 .... **$370.00**

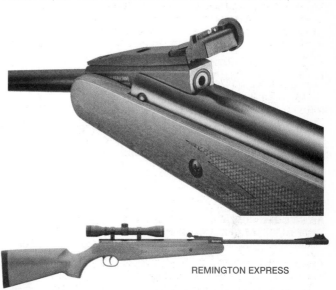

REMINGTON EXPRESS

REMINGTON EXPRESS AIR RIFLE/SCOPE COMBO
Caliber: .177, .22. **Weight:** 9.5 lbs. **Power:** Spring-piston system break-barrel action. **Stock:** Checkered hardwood. **Sights:** Fiber-optic front sight and fully adjustable rear and 4x32mm scope. **Features:** Feel of a Remington Model 700 rifle, two-stage precision trigger, automatic safety. 1,000 fps and 16 ft-lbs of energy.
Price: **$209.95**

RUGER TALON HUNTER

RUGER TALON HUNTER RIFLE
Caliber: .22 **Weight:** 9.85 lbs. **Barrel:** 18.7" **Power:** Spring-piston operated. **Sights:** Fiber-optic front sight and rear, and 3-9x32 scope. **Features:** Includes sling, sling swivels, SilencAir muzzle suppressor. 800 fps with lead pellets and 1,000 fps with alloy pellets.
Price: **$209.95**

RWS MODEL 34
Caliber: .177, .22, single shot. **Barrel:** 19-1/2", rifled. **Weight:** 7.3 lbs. **Length:** 45" overall. **Power:** Spring-air, break-barrel cocking. **Stock:** Wood. **Sights:** Hooded front, adjustable rear. **Features:** Velocity of 1000 fps (.177), 800 (.22). 33 lbs. cocking effort. Blued finish. Scope compatible.
Price: **$259.00**

RWS MODEL 34 BREAKBARREL MAGNUM AIR RIFLE
Caliber: .177, .22 **Weight:** 7.5 lbs. **Barrel:** Rifled 19" **Length:** 45" **Power:** Single-shot with spring-air break-barrel cocking. **Sights:** Front sight and rear, and scope rails. **Features:** Adjustable two-stage trigger set at 3.3 lbs., automatic safety. .177 –1,000 fps and .22 – 800 fps.
Price: **$252.50**

RWS MODEL 34 MEISTERSCHUTZE PRO COMPACT AIR RIFLE
Caliber: .177 **Weight:** 7.75 lbs. **Barrel:** Rifled 15.75" **Length:** 42.25" **Power:** Break-barrel single-shot. **Stock:** Ambidextrous hardwood. Sights: 3-9x40mm scope. **Features:** Ambidextrous auto safety. two-stage adjustable trigger. 1,000 fps.
Price: **$289.00**

RWS MODEL 34P

STOEGER X50

RWS MODEL 34P
Caliber: .177, .22, single shot. 19-3/4", rifled. **Weight:** 7.7 lbs. 46" overall. **Power:** Spring-air, break-barrel cocking. **Stock:** Synthetic black. **Sights:** Ramp fiber optic front, adjustable fiber optic rear. Velocity of 1000 fps (.177), 800 (.22). 33 lbs. cocking effort. Blued finish. Scope compatible. Automatic safety.
Price: .177, .22 .... **$243.00**

RWS MODEL 34 PANTHER AIR RIFLE
Caliber: .177, .22 **Weight:** 7.7 lbs. **Length:** 46" **Power:** Break-barrel single-shot. **Stock:** Injected molded plastic. **Sights:** Tru-Glo open sights. **Features:** .177 – 1,000 fps and .22 – 740 fps.
Price: **$240.00**

RWS MODEL 34 PANTHER PRO COMPACT AIR RIFLE
Caliber: .177 **Weight:** 8 lbs. **Barrel:** Rifled 15.75" **Length:** 42.125" **Power:** Break-barrel single-shot. **Stock:** Ambidextrous all-weather synthetic black. **Sights:** 3-9x40mm scope. **Features:** Ambidextrous auto safety, two-stage adjustable trigger, receiver and barrel are matte finished. 1,000 fps.
Price: **$247.00**

RWS MODEL 48 SIDE COCKING MAGNUM AIR RIFLE
Caliber: .177, .22, single shot. **Barrel:** 17" rifled. **Weight:** 8.5 lbs. **Length:** 42" overall. **Power:** Spring-air, side-lever cocking. **Stock:** Wood. **Sights:** Adjustable front, adjustable rear. **Features:** Adjustable trigger, velocity of 1,100 fps (.177), 900 (.22). 39 lbs. cocking effort. Blued finish. Scope compatible. Automatic safety.
Price: .177, .22 .... **$377.00**

RWS MODEL 54 SIDE COCKING MAGNUM AIR RIFLE
Caliber: .177, .22 **Weight:** 9 lbs. **Length:** 43" overall. **Power:** Side lever cocking system. **Stock:** Monte Carlo style with cheekpiece and checkering. **Sights:** Adjustable rear sight and scope rail. **Features:** When rifle is fired the action moves back slightly within the stock to absorb the recoil. Auto safety, adjustable trigger.
Price: .177, .22 .... **$558.00**

RWS MODEL 350 MAGNUM AIR RIFLE
Caliber: .177, .22 **Weight:** 8.5 lbs. **Length:** 48" overall. **Power:** Break-barrel spring piston system. **Stock:** Walnut stained hardwood with shadow-line raised cheekpiece and hand checkering on forearm and pistol grip. **Sights:** Micro-click adjustable Diana sights with hooded aperture in front that will accept interchangeable sight inserts. Scope mounting rail. **Features:** Cocking-activated safety, adjustable trigger and rubber recoil pad. .177 – 1,250 fps and .22 – 1,000 fps.
Price: .177, .22 .... **$378.00**

RWS MODEL 350 PANTHER MAGNUM AIR RIFLE
Caliber: .177, .22 **Weight:** 8.2 lbs. **Length:** 48" overall. **Power:** Break-barrel spring piston system. **Stock:** Black synthetic stock equipped with an ambidextrous cheekpiece and texturing on grip and forearm. **Features:** .177 – 1,250 fps and .22 – 1,000 fps.
Price: .177, .22 .... **$340.00**

RWS MODEL 350 PRO COMPACT AIR RIFLE
Caliber: .177, .22 **Barrel:** 15.75" rifled. **Weight:** 8.5 lbs. **Length:** 44.625" overall. **Power:** Break-barrel spring piston system. **Stock:** Walnut stained hardwood. **Sights:** 3-9x40mm scope. **Features:** This is a shortened version of the RWS Model 350 Feuerkraft air rifle. Ambidextrous auto safety, two-stage adjustable trigger, large muzzlebrake. .177 – 1,100 fps .22 – 900 fps.
Price: **$389.00**

RWS MODEL 460 MAGNUM
Caliber: .177, .22, single-shot. **Barrel:** 18-7/16", rifled. **Weight:** 8.3 lbs. **Length:** 45" overall. **Power:** Spring-air, underlever cocking. **Stock:** American Sporter, checkered grip and forearm. **Sights:** Ramp front, adjustable rear. **Features:** Velocity of 1,100 fps (.177), 930 (.22). 36 lbs. cocking effort. Blue finish. Rubber buttpad. Top-side loading port. Scope compatible.
Price: .177, .22 .... **$502.99**

STOEGER X50 AIR RIFLE
Caliber: .177, .22, .25 **Barrel:** 16.5" **Weight:** 8.9 lbs. **Power:** Break-action, spring and piston mechanism, single-shot. **Stock:** Matte black lightweight synthetic or hardwood stock with nonslip rubber buttpad, and checkered grip panels and fore-end. **Sights:** 3-9x40mm scope and red fiber-optic front sight and fully adjustable rear sight with green fiber-optic inserts. **Features:** Automatic safety, two-stage adjustable trigger. .177 – 1,500 fps, .22 – 1,200 fp, .25 – 900 fps.
Price: **$319.00**

TECH FORCE 6 AIR RIFLE
Caliber: .177 pellet, single shot. **Barrel:** 14". **Weight:** 6 lbs. **Length:** 35.5" overall. **Power:** Spring-piston, sidelever action. **Stock:** Paratrooper-style folding, full pistol grip. **Sights:** Adjustable rear, hooded front. **Features:** Velocity 800 fps. All-metal construction; grooved for scope mounting. Imported from China by Compasseco, Inc.
Price: **$69.95**

TECH FORCE 99 AIR RIFLE
Caliber: .177, .22, single shot. **Barrel:** 18", rifled. **Weight:** 8 lbs. **Length:** 44.5" overall. **Power:** Spring piston. **Stock:** Beech wood; raised cheek piece and checkering on pistol grip and forearm, plus soft rubber recoil pad. **Sights:** Insert type front. **Features:** Velocity 1,100 fps (.177; 900 fps: .22); fixed barrel design has an underlever cocking mechanism with an anti-beartrap lock and automatic safety. Imported from China by Compasseco, Inc.
Price: 177 or .22 caliber **$152.96**

TECH FORCE TF8 AIR RIFLE & COMBO PACKAGE
Caliber: .177 **Weight:** 6.6 lbs. (rifle alone) **Length:** 40" overall. **Power:** Spring-piston, break-barrel, single-shot. **Stock:** Ambidextrous Monte Carlo hardwood stock with checkered grip and forearm. **Sights:** 11mm grooved dovetail for scope mounting. **Features:** Rifled barrel, automatic safety, rubber buttplate, muzzlebrake for extra cocking leverage. 800 fps.
Price: **$149.95**
Price: (Combo Pkg. with 4x32 AO Scope): **$195.95**

TECH FORCE TF12 AIR RIFLE & COMBO PACKAGES
Caliber: .177, .22 **Weight:** 6.85 lbs. (rifle alone) **Length:** 44.25" overall. **Power:** Spring-piston, break-barrel, single-shot. **Stock:** Ambidextrous Monte Carlo hardwood stock with checkered grip and forearm. **Sights:** 11mm grooved dovetail for scope mounting. **Features:** Rifled barrel, automatic safety, rubber buttplate, muzzlebrake for extra cocking leverage. Combo packages include a selection of riflescopes. 800 fps.
Price: **$199.99**
Price: (Combo Pkg. with 3-9x32 AO Scope): **$249.99**
Price: (Combo Pkg. with 4-12x40 AO Scope): **$279.99**
Price: (Combo Pkg. with 4-12x40 AO/IR Scope): **$299.99**

TECH FORCE TF20 CONTENDER & COMBO PACKAGE
Caliber: .177, .22 **Weight:** 5.7 lbs. (rifle alone) **Length:** 40" overall. **Power:** Spring pneumatic, under-lever, single-shot with 18 lbs. of effort needed for cocking. **Sights:** fixed front sight and adjustable rear. **Features:** Ergonomic design. 600 fps.
Price: **$50.96**
Price: (Combo Pkg. with 4x32mm scope): **$93.46**

TECH FORCE TF49 CONTENDER COMBO PACKAGE
Caliber: .177, .22 **Weight:** 7 lbs. **Length:** 45" overall. **Power:** Spring pneumatic, under-lever, single-shot. **Stock:** Monte Carlo with low raised cheekpiece. **Sights:** Fixed front sight and adjustable rear, and 4x20 scope. **Features:** : 650 fps.
Price: **$67.96**

TECH FORCE TF59 AIR RIFLE & COMBO PACKAGE
Caliber: .177, .22 **Weight:** 7 lbs. **Length:** 42.3" overall. **Power:** Spring-piston, break-barrel, under-lever, single-shot. **Features:** Sized for an adult, wood and metal construction, two-stage adjustable trigger with an anti-beartrap mechanism, and a cocking effort of 28 lbs. 730 fps.
Price: **$84.96**
Price: (Combo Pkg. with 2-7x32mm Scope) **$135.96**

Prices given are believed to be accurate at time of publication however, many factors affect retail pricing so exact prices are not possible.

AIRGUNS—Long Guns

TECH FORCE TF89 AIR RIFLE & COMBO PACKAGE
Caliber: .177, .22 **Barrel:** 17.9" **Weight:** 7.72 lbs. **Length:** 46.1"
overall. **Power:** Spring pneumatic, single-shot. **Stock:** Beech wood
checkered. **Sights:** Fixed front sight and adjustable rear. **Features:**
Muzzlebrake, ventilated recoil pad, scope stop, grooved receiver for
scope mounting, and cocking effort of 28 lbs. 1,100 fps.
Price: **$189.95**
Price: (Combo Pkg. with 3-12x44mm Scope) **$279.95**

TECH FORCE TF97 AIR RIFLE & COMBO PACKAGE
Caliber: .177, .22 **Barrel:** 16" **Weight:** 8 lbs. **Length:** 40" overall.
Power: Spring pneumatic, under-lever, single-shot. **Stock:** Beech
wood, Monte Carlo. **Sights:** Fixed front sight and adjustable rear.
Features: Ventilated recoil pad, scope stop, grooved receiver for
scope mounting, and cocking effort of 12 lbs. 700 fps.
Price: **$89.95**
Price: (Combo Pkg. with 2-7x32mm Scope) **$135.95**

UMAREX OCTANE

UMAREX OCTANE RIFLE
Caliber: .22 **Barrel:** 19.5" **Weight:** 9.5 lbs. **Power:** ReAxis Gas-piston
operated pellet rifle. **Sights:** Fiber-optic front and rear sights, and
3-9x40mm scope with LockDown mounting rail. **Features:** SilencAir
muzzle suppressor. 1,050 fps with lead pellets.
Price: **$259.99**

UMAREX
STEEL FORCE

UMAREX STEEL FORCE CO2 RIFLE
Caliber: .177, BB **Barrel:** 7.5" **Weight:** 3.37 lbs. **Power:** CO2-powered
M4-style "full-auto" six-shot burst BB rifle. **Sights:** Flip-up fixed sights.
Features: 300-round reservoir and a 30-round built-in magazine.
Price: **$129.99**

WALTHER LGV
COMPETITION ULTRA

WALTHER LGV COMPETITION ULTRA AIR RIFLE
Caliber: .177 **Barrel:** 15.7" **Weight:** 10.1 lbs. **Power:** Super Silent-
Vibration Reduction Technology spring operated. **Sights:** Tru-Glo®
fiber-optic sights. **Features:** 1,000 fps with lead pellets. Made by
Umarex.
Price: **$839.99**

WALTHER LEVER ACTION
Caliber: .177, 8-shot lever action. **Barrel:** 19", rifled. **Weight:** 7.5 lbs.
Length: 38" overall. **Power:** Two 12g CO2. **Stock:** Wood. **Sights:**

WALTHER LEVER ACTION

Fixed front, adjustable rear. **Features:** Classic design. Velocity of 630
fps. Scope compatible. Made by Umarex.
Price: **$500.00**
Price: Nickel finish. **$600.00**

WINCHESTER MODEL 1029S
Caliber: .177 pellet. Single shot. **Weight:** 6.6 lbs. **Length:** 46.7". Rifled
steel barrel. Composite stock with thumbhole grip. Thumb safety.
Comes with 3-9x32 scope. Distributed by Daisy.
Price: **$250.00**

WINCHESTER
MODEL 1400 CS

WINCHESTER MODEL 1400 CS AIR RIFLE
Caliber: .177 **Weight:** 9 lbs. **Length:** 51.2" overall. **Power:** Break-
barrel spring air rifle, single-shot. **Stock:** Camo composite. **Sights:**
3-9x32mm scope. **Features:** Rifled steel barrel with sound
suppressor, thumb safety engages when rifle is cocked. 1,400 fps.
Distributed by Daisy.
Price: **$229.99**

WINCHESTER
MODEL M14

WINCHESTER MODEL M14
Caliber: .177. CO2 semi-automatic. 16-round capacity. Maximum
velocity 700 fps. **Weight:** 4.4 pounds. **Sights:** Adjustable rear, blade
front. Rifled steel barrel, brown composite stock. Distributed by Daisy.
Price: **$220.00**

WINCHESTER
MODEL MP4

WINCHESTER MODEL MP4 CO2 RIFLE
Caliber: .177, BB **Weight:** 5.8 lbs. **Length:** 46.5" overall. **Power:** CO2
semiautomatic with a 16-shot reversible rotary magazine. **Stock:**
Composite collapsible. **Sights:** Flip-down front and adjustable flip-
down rear sights. **Features:** Metal receiver, integral rail system with
extended top rail, manual safety and rifled steel barrel, 700 fps.
Distributed by Daisy.
Price: **$199.99**

Prices given are believed to be accurate at time of publication however, many factors affect retail pricing so exact prices are not possible.

69TH EDITION, 2015 ✦ **545**

THE 2015 GUN DIGEST
web directory

The *Gun Digest* Web Directory is now in its 16th year of publication and grows with every edition. The firearms industry is doing a remarkably good job of adapting to e-commerce. Most major sites now include Facebook, Twitter and industry blog options for the informed consumer.

The world has become a mobile, Internet culture, and that's why web directories like our own have become such essential references. The focus of our directory is on companies that have a proven track record of product success and have been in business for several years.

The following index of web addresses is offered to our readers as a convenient jumping-off point. Half the fun is just exploring what's out there. Considering that most of the web pages have hot links to other firearms-related web pages, the Internet trail just goes on and on once you've taken the initial step to go online. So welcome to the digital world of firearms, where a journey of a thousand sites begins with a single click.

Here are a few pointers: If the website you desire is not listed, try using the full name of the company or product, typed without spaces, between www.- and-.com, for example, www.krause.com. Probably 95 percent of current websites are based on this simple, self-explanatory format.

The other option is to go directly to the dominant search engines, www.google.com and www.bing.com, and enter the name of the company or product for which you are searching. This is also an invaluable method of finding companies that have recently changed their web addresses.

Finally, make it a point to access www.YouTube.com for short videos on the subjects you are pursuing. Firearms enthusiasts and companies have posted literally thousands of firearms-related videos—some good, some bad—but always interesting. Many of the how-to gunsmithing videos, in particular, are excellent. Just be very specific when you type in the subject to be searched.

—*The Editors*

AMMUNITION AND COMPONENTS

Accurate Arms Co. Inc **www.accuratepowder.com**
ADCO/Nobel Sport Powder **www.adcosales.com**
Advanced Armament Corp. **www.300aacblackout.com**
Aguila Ammunition **www.aguilaammo.com**
Alexander Arms **www.alexanderarms.com**
Allegiance Ammunition **www.allegianceammunition.com**
Alliant Powder **www.alliantpowder.com**
American Ammunition **www.a-merc.com**
American Derringer Co. **www.amderringer.com**
American Pioneer Powder **www.americanpioneerpowder.com**
American Specialty Ammunition **www.americanspeciality-ammo.com**
Ammo Depot **www.ammodepot.com**
Ammo Guide **www.ammoguide.com**
Arizona Ammunition, Inc. **www.arizonaammunition.com**
Armscor **www.us.armscor.com**
Ballistic Products Inc. **www.ballisticproducts.com**
Barnaul Cartridge Plant **www.barnaulpatron.ru**

Barnes Bullets **www.barnesbullets.com**
Barrett Firearms Mfg. Co. **www.barrett.net**
Baschieri & Pellagri **www.baschieri-pellagri.com**
Beartooth Bullets **www.beartoothbullets.com**
Bell Brass **www.bellbrass.com**
Berger Bullets, Ltd. **www.bergerbullets.com**
Berry's Mfg., Inc. **www.berrysmfg.com**
Big Bore Bullets of Alaska **www.awloo.com/bbb/index.htm**
Big Bore Express **www.powerbeltbullets.com**
Bismuth Cartridge Co. **www.bismuth-notox.com**
Black Dawge Cartridge **www.blackdawgecartridge.com**
Black Hills Ammunition, Inc. **www.black-hills.com**
Black Hills Shooters Supply **www.bhshooters.com**
BlackHorn209 **www.blackhorn209.com**
Brenneke of America Ltd. **www.brennekeusa.com**
Buffalo Arms **www.buffaloarms.com**
Buffalo Bore Ammunition **www.buffalobore.com**
Calhoon, James, Bullets **www.jamescalhoon.com**

Cartuchos Saga www.saga.es
Cast Performance Bullet www.castperformance.com
CBC www.cbc.com.br
CCI/Speer www.cci-ammunition.com
Centurion Ordnance www.aguilaammo.com
Century International Arms www.centuryarms.com
Cheaper Than Dirt www.cheaperthandirt.com
Cheddite France www.cheddite.com
Claybuster Wads www.claybusterwads.com
Clean Shot Powder www.cleanshot.com
Cole Distributing www.cole-distributing.com
Combined Tactical Systems www.less-lethal.com
Cor-Bon/Glaser www.cor-bon.com
Cowboy Bullets www.cowboybullets.com
Cutting Edge Bullets www.cuttingedgebullets.com
D.Dupleks, Ltd. www.ddupleks.lv
Defense Technology Corp. www.defense-technology.com
Denver Bullet Co. denbullets@aol.com
Dillon Precision www.dillonprecision.com
Dionisi Cartridge www.dionisi.com
DKT, Inc. www.dktinc.com
D.L. Unmussig Bullets .14,.17 &.20 cal (804)320-1165
Double Tap Ammunition www.doubletapammo.com
Down Range Mfg. www.downrangemfg.com
Dynamic Research Technologies www.drtammo.com
Dynamit Nobel RWS Inc. www.dnrws.com
E. Arthus Brown Co. wwweabco.com
EcoSlug www.eco-slug.com
Elephant/Swiss Black Powder www.elephantblackpowder.com
Eley Ammunition www.eleyusa.com
Eley Hawk Ltd. www.eleyhawk.com
Environ-Metal www.hevishot.com
Estate Cartridge www.estatecartridge.com
Extreme Shock Munitions www.extremeshockusa.com
Federal Cartridge Co. www.federalpremium.com
Fiocchi of America www.fiocchiusa.com
Fowler Bullets www.benchrest.com/fowler
Gamebore Cartridge www.gamebore.com
GaugeMate www.gaugemate.com
Garrett Cartridges hammerhead.creator@gmail.com
Gentner Bullets www.benchrest.com/gentner/
Glaser Safety Slug, Inc. www.corbon.com
GOEX Inc. www.goexpowder.com
GPA www.cartouchegpa.com
Graf & Sons www.grafs.com
Grizzly Cartridge Co. www.grizzlycartridge.com
H&K Associates www.6mmhagar.com
Haendler & Natermann www.hn-sport.de
Hawk Bullets www.hawkbullets.com
Herter's Ammuniition www.cabelas.com
Hevi.Shot www.hevishot.com
High Precision Down Range www.hprammo.com
Hi-Tech Ammunition www.iidbs.com/hitech
Hodgdon Powder www.hodgdon.com
Hornady www.hornady.com
HSM Ammunition www.thehuntingshack.com
Hull Cartridge www.hullcartridge.com
Huntington Reloading Products www.huntingtons.com
Impact Bullets www.impactbullets.com
IMR Smokeless Powders www.imrpowder.com
International Cartridge Corp www.iccammo.com

Israel Military Industries www.imisammo.co.il
ITD Enterprise www.itdenterpriseinc.com
Jagemann Technologies www.jagemanntech.com
James Calhoon www.jamescalhoon.com
Kent Cartridge America www.kentgamebore.com
Knight Bullets www.benchrest.com/knight/
Kynoch Ammunition www.kynochammunition.com
Lapua www.lapua.com
Lawrence Brand Shot www.metalico.com
Lazzeroni Arms Co. www.lazzeroni.com
Leadheads Bullets www.proshootpro.com
Leigh Defense www.leighdefense.com
Liberty Ammunition www.liberty
Lightfield Ammunition Corp www.lightfieldslugs.com
Lomont Precision Bullets www.klomont.com/kent
Lost River Ballistic Technologies, Inc. www.lostriverballistic.com
Lyman www.lymanproducts.com
Magkor Industries. www.magkor.com
Magnum Muzzleloading Products www.mmpsabots.com
Magnus Bullets www.magnusbullets.com
MagSafe Ammunition www.realpages.com/magsafeammo
Magtech www.magtechammunition.com
Masterclass Bullet Co. www.mastercast.com
Maxam www.maxam-outdoors.com
Meister Bullets www.meisterbullets.com
Midway USA www.midwayusa.com
Miltex, Inc. www.miltexusa.com
Mitchell Mfg. Co. www.mitchellsales.com
MK Ballistic Systems www.mkballistics.com
Mullins Ammunition www.mullinsammunition.com
National Bullet Co. www.nationalbullet.com
Navy Arms www.navyarms.com
Nobel Sport www.nobelsportammo.com
Norma www.norma.cc
North Fork Technologies www.northforkbullets.com
Nosler Bullets, Inc. www.nosler.com
Old Western Scrounger www.ows-ammunition.com
One Shot, Inc. www.oneshotmunitions.com
Oregon Trail/Trueshot Bullets www.trueshotbullets.com
Pattern Control www.patterncontrol.com
PCP Ammunition www.pcpammo.com
Pierce Munitions www.piercemunitions.com
Piney Mountain Ammunition www.pineymountainammunitionco.com
PMC www.pmcammo.com
PolyCase Ammunition www.polycaseammo.com
Polywad www.polywad.com
PowerBelt Bullets www.powerbeltbullets.com
PPU Ammunition www.prvipartizan.com
PR Bullets www.prbullet.com
Precision Ammunition www.precisionammo.com
Precision Reloading www.precisionreloading.com
Pro Grade Ammunition www.progradeammo.com
Pro Load Ammunition www.proload.com
Prvi Partizan Ammunition www.prvipartizan.com
Quality Cartridge www.qual-cart.com
Rainier Ballistics www.rainierballistics.com
Ram Shot Powder www.ramshot.com
Rare Ammunition www.rareammo.com
Reloading Specialties Inc. www.reloadingspecialties.com
Remington www.remington.com
Rio Ammunition www.rioammo.com

Rocky Mountain Cartridge www.rockymountaincartride.com
RUAG Ammotec www.ruag.com
RWS www.ruag-usa.com
Samco Global Arms www.samcoglobal.com
Sauvestre Ammunition www.centuryarms.com
SBR Ammunition www.sbrammunition.com
Scharch Mfg. www.scharch.com
Schuetzen Powder www.schuetzenpowder.com
Sellier & Bellot www.sellier-bellot.cz
Shilen www.shilen.com
Sierra www.sierrabullets.com
Silver State Armory www.ssarmory.com
Simunition. www.simunition.com
SinterFire, Inc. www.sinterfire.com
Spectra Shot www.spectrashot.com
Speer Ammunition www.speer-ammo.com
Speer Bullets www.speer-bullets.com
Sporting Supplies Int'l Inc. www.ssiintl.com
Starline www.starlinebrass.com
Superior Ballistics www.superiorballistics.com
Swift Bullets Co. www.swiftbullet.com
Tannerite www.tannerite.com
Tascosa Cartridge Co. www.tascosacartridge.com
Ted Nugent Ammunition www.americantactical.us
Ten-X Ammunition www.tenxammo.com
Top Brass www.topbrass.com
Triton Cartridge www.a-merc.com
Trueshot Bullets www.trueshotbullets.com
Tru-Tracer www.trutracer.com
TulAmmo www.tulammousa.com
Ultramax Ammunition www.ultramaxammunition.com
Vihtavuori Lapua www.vihtavuori-lapua.com
Weatherby www.weatherby.com
West Coast Bullets www.westcoastbullet.com
Western Powders Inc. www.westernpowders.com
Widener's Reloading & Shooters Supply www.wideners.com
Winchester Ammunition www.winchester.com
Windjammer Tournament Wads www.windjammer-wads.com
Wolf Ammunition www.wolfammo.com
Woodleigh Bullets www.woodleighbullets.com.au
Zanders Sporting Goods www.gzanders.com

CASES, SAFES, GUN LOCKS AND CABINETS

Ace Case Co. www.acecase.com
AG English Sales Co. www.agenglish.com
All Americas' Outdoors www.innernet.net/gunsafe
Alpine Cases www.alpinecases.com
Aluma Sport by Dee Zee www.deezee.com
American Security Products www.amsecusa.com
Americase www.americase.com
Assault Systems www.elitesurvival.com
Avery Outdoors, Inc. www.averyoutdoors.com
Bear Track Cases www.beartrackcases.com
Bore-Stores www.borestores.com
Boyt Harness Co. www.boytharness.com
Bulldog Gun Safe Co. www.gardall.com
Burglar Bomb www.burglarbomb.com
Campbell Industrial Supply www.gun-racks.com
Cannon Safe Co. www.cannonsafe.com
CCL Security Products www.cclsecurity.com
Concept Development Corp. www.saf-t-blok.com

Doskocil Mfg. Co. www.doskocilmfg.com
Fort Knox Safes www.ftknox.com
Franzen Security Products www.securecase.com
Frontier Safe Co. www.frontiersafe.com
Goldenrod Dehumidifiers www.goldenroddehumidifiers.com
Granite Security Products www.granitesafe.com
Gunlocker Phoenix USA Inc. www.gunlocker.com
Gun Storage Solutions www.storemoreguns.com
GunVault www.gunvault.com
Hakuba USA Inc. www.hakubausa.com
Heritage Safe Co. www.heritagesafecompany.com
Hide-A-Gun www.hideagun.net
Homak Safes www.homak.com
Hunter Company www.huntercompany.com
Integrity Gunbags www.integrity-gunbags.com
Knouff & Knouff, Inc. www.kkair.com
Knoxx Industries www.knoxx,com
Kolpin Mfg. Co. www.kolpin.com
Liberty Safe & Security www.libertysafe.com
LockSfa www.locksfa.com
Morton Enterprises www.uniquecases.com
New Innovative Products www.starlightcases
Noble Security Systems Inc. www.noble.co.ll
Phoenix USA Inc. www.gunlocker.com
Plano Molding Co. www.planomolding.com
Plasticase, Inc. www.nanuk.com
Rhino Safe www.rhinosafe.com
Rotary Gun Racks www.gun-racks.com
Sack-Ups www.sackups.com
Safe Tech, Inc. www.safrgun.com
Secure Firearm Products www.securefirearmproducts.com
Securecase www.securecase.com
Shot Lock Corp. www.shotlock.com
SKB Cases www.skbcases.com
Smart Lock Technology Inc. www.smartlock.com
Snap Safe www.snapsafe.com
Sportsmans Steel Safe Co. www.sportsmansteelsafes.com
Stack-On Products Co. www.stack-on.com
Starlight Cases www.starlightcases.com
Strong Case www.strongcasebytnb.com
Sun Welding www.sunwelding.com
Technoframes www.technoframes.com
Titan Gun Safes www.titangunsafes.com
T.Z. Case Int'l www.tzcase.com
U.S. Explosive Storage www.usexplosivestorage.com
Versatile Rack Co. www.versatilegunrack.com
V-Line Industries www.vlineind.com
Winchester Safes www.winchestersafes.com
Ziegel Engineering www.ziegeleng.com
Zonetti Armor www.zonettiarmor.com

CHOKE DEVICES, RECOIL REDUCERS, SUPPRESSORS AND ACCURACY DEVICES

Advanced Armament Corp. www.advanced-armament.com
100 Straight Products www.100straight.com
Answer Products Co. www.answerrifles.com
AWC Systems Technology www.awcsystech.com
Briley Mfg www.briley.com
Carlson's www.choketube.com
Colonial Arms www.colonialarms.com

Comp-N-Choke www.comp-n-choke.com
Elite Iron www.eliteiron.net
Gemtech www.gem-tech.com
KDF, Inc. www.kdfguns.com
Kick's Industries www.kicks-ind.com
LimbSaver www.limbsaver.com
Mag-Na-Port Int'l Inc. www.magnaport.com
Metro Gun www.metrogun.com
Patternmaster Chokes www.patternmaster.com
Poly-Choke www.poly-choke.com
SilencerCo www.silencerco.com
Sims Vibration Laboratory www.limbsaver.com
SRT Arms www.srtarms.com
SureFire www.surefire.com
SWR Mfg. www.swrmfg.com
Teague Precision Chokes www.teague.ca
Truglo www.truglo.com
Trulock Tool www.trulockchokes.com
Vais Arms, Inc. www.muzzlebrakes.com

CHRONOGRAPHS AND BALLISTIC SOFTWARE

Barnes Ballistic Program www.barnesbullets.com
Ballisticard Systems www.ballisticards.com
Competition Electronics www.competitionelectronics.com
Competitive Edge Dynamics www.cedhk.com
Hodgdon Shotshell Program www.hodgdon.com
Lee Shooter Program www.leeprecision.com
Load From A Disk www.loadammo.com
NECO www.neconos.com
Oehler Research Inc. www.oehler-research.com
PACT www.pact.com
Pjsa Ballistics Pejsa@sprintmail.com
ProChrony www.competitionelectronics.com
Quickload www.neconos.com
RCBS Load www.rcbs.com
Shooting Chrony Inc www.shootingchrony.com
Sierra Infinity Ballistics Program www.sierrabullets.com
Winchester Ballistics Calculator www.winchester.com

CLEANING PRODUCTS

Ballistol USA www.ballistol.com
Battenfeld Technologies www.battenfeldtechnologies.com
Birchwood Casey www.birchwoodcasey.com
Blue Wonder www.bluewonder.com
Bore Tech www.boretech.com
Break-Free, Inc. www.break-free.com
Bruno Shooters Supply www.brunoshooters.com
Butch's Bore Shine www.lymanproducts.com
C.J. Weapons Accessories www.cjweapons.com
Clenzoil www.clenzoil.com
Corrosion Technologies www.corrosionx.com
Dewey Mfg. www.deweyrods.com
DuraCoat www.lauerweaponry.com
Eezox Inc. www.xmission.com
Emby Enterprises www.alltemptacticallube.com
Extreme Gun Care www.extremeguncare.com
G96 www.g96.com
Gun Butter www.gunbutter.com
Gun Cleaners www.guncleaners.com
Gunslick Gun Care www.gunslick.com

Gunzilla www.topduckproducts.com
Hollands Shooters Supply www.hollandgun.com
Hoppes www.hoppes.com
Hydrosorbent Products www.dehumidify.com
Inhibitor VCI Products www.theinhibitor.com
Iosso Products www.iosso.com
Jag Brush www.jagbrush.com
KG Industries www.kgcoatings.com
Kleen-Bore Inc. www.kleen-bore.com
L&R Ultrasonics www.lrultrasonics.com
Lyman www.lymanproducts.com
Mil-Comm Products www.mil-comm.com
Militec-1 www.militec-1.com
Montana X-Treme www.montanaxtreme.com
MPT Industries www.mptindustries.com
Mpro7 Gun Care www.mp7.com
Old West Snake Oil www.oldwestsnakeoil.com
Otis Technology, Inc. www.otisgun.com
Outers www.outers-guncare.com
Ox-Yoke Originals Inc. www.oxyoke.com
Parker-Hale Ltd. www.parker-hale.com
Prolix Lubricant www.prolixlubricant.com
ProShot Products www.proshotproducts.com
ProTec Lubricants www.proteclubricants.com
Rigel Products www.rigelproducts.com
Rusteprufe Labs www.rusteprufe.com
Sagebrush Products www.sagebrushproducts.com
Sentry Solutions Ltd. www.sentrysolutions.com
Shooters Choice Gun Care www.shooters-choice.com
Silencio www.silencio.com
Slip 2000 www.slip2000.com
Southern Bloomer Mfg. www.southernbloomer.com
Stony Point Products www.uncle-mikes.com
Tetra Gun www.tetraproducts.com
The TM Solution thetmsolution@comsast.net
Top Duck Products www.topduckproducts.com
Triangle Patch www.trianglepatch.com
Wipe-Out www.sharpshootr.com
World's Fastest Gun Bore Cleaner www.michaels-oregon.com

FIREARM AUCTION SITES

A&S Auction Co. www.asauction.com
Alderfer Austion www.alderferauction.com
Amoskeag Auction Co. www.amoskeagauction.com
Antique Guns www.antiqueguns.com
Auction Arms www.auctionarms.com
Batterman's Auctions www.battermans.com
Bonhams & Butterfields www.bonhams.com/usarms
Cowan's www.cowans.com
Fontaine's Auction Gallery www.fontainesauction.net
Guns America www.gunsamerica.com
Gun Broker www.gunbroker.com
Guns4Pennies www.guns4pennies.com
Guns International www.gunsinternational.com
Heritage Auction Galleries www.ha.com
James D. Julia, Inc. www.jamesdjulia.com
Little John's Auction Service www.littlejohnsauctionservice.com
Morphy Auctions www.morphyauctions.com
Poulin Auction Co. www.poulinantiques.com
Rock Island Auction Co. www.rockislandauction.com
Wallis & Wallis www.wallisandwallis.org

FIREARM MANUFACTURERS AND IMPORTERS

Accuracy Int'l North America www.accuracyinternational.com
Accuracy Rifle Systems www.mini-14.net
Adcor Defense www.adcorindustries.com
Advanced Weapons Technology www.AWT-Zastava.com
AIM www.aimsurplus.com
AirForce Airguns www.airforceairguns.com
Air Gun Inc. www.airrifle-china.com
Airguns of Arizona www.airgunsofarizona.com
Airgun Express www.airgunexpress.com
Akkar Sporting Arms www.akkar-usa.com
Alchemy Arms www.alchemyltd.com
Alexander Arms www.alexanderarms.com
America Remembers www.americaremembers.com
American Classic www.americanclassic1911.com
American Derringer Corp. www.amderringer.com
American Rifle Co. www.americanrifleco.com
American Spirit Arms Corp. www.gunkits.com
American Tactical Imports www.americantactical.us
American Western Arms www.awaguns.com
Anics Corp. www.anics.com
Anschutz www.anschutz-sporters.com
Answer Products Co. www.answerrifles.com
AR-7 Industries www.ar-7.com
Ares Defense Systems www.aresdefense.com
Armalite www.armalite.com
Armi Sport www.armisport.com
Armory USA www.globaltraders.com
Armscor USA www.armscor.com
Arrieta www.arrietashotguns.com
Arsenal Inc. www.arsenalinc.com
Atlanta Cutlery Corp. www.atlantacutlery.com
ATA Arms www.ataarms.com
Auto-Ordnance Corp. www.tommygun.com
Aya www.aya-fineguns.com
Baikal www.baikalinc.ru/eng/
Badger Ordnance www.badgerordnance.com
Ballard Rifles www.ballardrifles.com
Barrett Firearms Mfg. www.barrettrifles.com
Bat Machine Co. www.batmachine.com
Beeman Precision Airguns www.beeman.com
Benelli USA Corp. www.benelliusa.com
Benjamin Sheridan www.crosman.com
Beretta U.S.A. Corp. www.berettausa.com
Bernardelli www.bernardelli.com
Bersa www.bersa.com
Bighorn Arms www.bighornarms.com
Blaser Jagdwaffen Gmbh www.blaser.de Bleiker www.bleiker.ch
Bluegrass Armory www.bluegrassarmory.com
Bond Arms www.bondarms.com
Borden Rifles, Inc. www.bordenrifles.com
Boss & Co. www.bossguns.co.uk
Bowen Classic Arms www.bowenclassicarms.com
Briley Mfg www.briley.com
BRNO Arms www.cz-usa.com
Brown, McKay www.mckaybrown.com
Brown, Ed Products www.edbrown.com
Browning www.browning.com
BRP Corp. www.brpguns.com
BSA Guns www.bsagunusa.com

BUL Ltd. www.bultransmark.com
Bushmaster Firearms www.bushmaster.com
BWE Firearms www.bwefirearms.com
Cabot Guns www.cabotguns.com
Caesar Guerini USA www.gueriniusa.com
Carbon 15 www.professional-ordnance.com
Caspian Arms, Ltd. www.caspianarmsltd.com
Casull Arms Corp. www.casullarms.com
CDNN Sports www.cdnnsports.com
Century Arms www.centuryarms.com
Chadick's Ltd. www.chadicks-ltd.com
Champlin Firearms www.champlinarms.com
Chapuis Arms www.doubleguns.com/chapuis.htm
Charles Daly www.charlesdaly-us.com
Charter Arms www.charterfirearms.com
CheyTac USA www.cheytac.com
Chiappa Firearms www.chiappafirearms.com
Christensen Arms www.christensenarms.com
Cimarron Firearms Co. www.cimarron-firearms.com
Clark Custom Guns www.clarkcustomguns.com
Cobra Enterprises www.cobrapistols.com
Cogswell & Harrison www.cogswell.co.uk/home.htm
Collector's Armory, Ltd. www.collectorsarmory.com
Colt's Mfg Co. www.colt.com
Connecticut Shotgun Mfg. Co. www.connecticutshotgun.com
Connecticut Valley Arms www.cva.com
Coonan, Inc. www.coonaninc.com
Cooper Firearms www.cooperfirearms.com
Core Rifle Systems www.core15.com
Corner Shot www.cornershot.com
CPA Rifles www.singleshotrifles.com
Crosman www.crosman.com
C.Sharp Arms Co. www.csharparms.com
CVA www.cva.com
Cylinder & Slide Shop www.cylinder-slide.com
Czechpoint USA www.czechpoint-usa.com
CZ USA www.cz-usa.com
Daisy Mfg Co. www.daisy.com
Dakota Arms Inc. www.dakotaarms.com
Dan Wesson Firearms www.danwessonfirearms.com
Daniel Defense, Inc. www.danieldefense.com
Detonics USA www.detonicsdefense.com
Diana www.diana-airguns.de
Dixie Gun Works www.dixiegunworks.com
Dlask Arms Corp. www.dlask.com
DoubleTap www.heizerdefense.com
DPMS, Inc. www.dpmsinc.com
D.S. Arms, Inc. www.dsarms.com
Dumoulin www.dumoulin-herstal.com
EAA Corp. www.eaacorp.com
Eagle Imports, Inc. www.bersa-llama.com
Ed Brown Products www.edbrown.com
EDM Arms www.edmarms.com
EMF Co. www.emf-company.com
Entreprise Arms www.entrerprise.com
E. R. Shaw www.ershawbarrels.com
European American Armory Corp. www.eaacorp.com
Evans, William www.williamevans.com
Excel Arms www.excelarms.com
Fabarm www.fabarm.com
Falcon Pneumatic Systems www.falcon-airguns.co.uk

Fausti USA www.faustiusa.com
Firestorm www.bersa.com
Flodman Guns www.flodman.com
FN Herstal www.fnherstal.com
FNH USA www.fnhusa.com
Franchi www.franchiusa.com
Franklin Armory www.franklinarmory.com
Freedom Arms www.freedomarms.com
Freedom Group, Inc. www.freedom-group.com
Galazan www.connecticutshotgun.com
Gambo Renato www.renatogamba.it
Gary Reeder Custom Guns www.reeder-customguns.com
Gibbs Rifle Company www.gibbsrifle.com
Glock www.glock.com
Griffin & Howe www.griffinhowe.com
Grizzly Big Boar Rifle www.largrizzly.com
GSI Inc. www.gsifirearms.com
Gunbroker.com www.gunbroker.com
Hammerli www.haemmerli.info/en/home.html
Hatsan Arms Co. www.hatsan.com.tr
Heckler and Koch www.hk-usa.com
Henry Repeating Arms Co. www.henryrepeating.com
Heritage Mfg. www.heritagemfg.com
Heym www.heym-waffenfabrik.de
High Standard Mfg. www.highstandard.com
Hi-Point Firearms www.hi-pointfirearms.com
Holland & Holland www.hollandandholland.com
H&R 1871 Firearms www.hr1871.com
H-S Precision www.hsprecision.com
Hunters Lodge Corp. www.hunterslodge.com
IAR Inc. www.iar-arms.com
International Military Antiques, Inc. www.ima-usa.com
Inter Ordnance www.ioinc-us.com
Israel Weapon Industries (IWI) www.israel-weapon.com
ISSC, LLC www.issc-at
Iver Johnson Arms www.iverjohnsonarms.com
IMZ www.imzcorp.com
James River Armory www.jamesriverarmory.com
Jarrett Rifles, Inc. www.jarrettrifles.com
J&G Sales, Ltd. www.jgsales.com
Johannsen Express Rifle www.johannsen-jagd.de
Jonathan Arthur Ciener www.22lrconversions.com
JP Enterprises, Inc. www.jprifles.com
Kahr Arms/Auto-Ordnance www.kahr.com
KDF, Inc. www.kdfguns.com
Kel-Tec CNC Ind., Inc. www.kel-tec.com
Keystone Sporting Arms www.keystonesportingarmsllc.com
Kifaru www.kifaru.net
Kimber www.kimberamerica.com
Knight's Armament Co. www.knightsarmco.com
Knight Rifles www.knightrifles.com
Korth www.korthwaffen.de
Krebs Custom Guns www.krebscustom.com
Kriss www.kriss-usa.com
Krieghoff Int'l www.krieghoff.com
KY Imports, Inc. www.kyimports.com
K-VAR www.k-var.com
Lanber www.lanber.net
L.A.R. Mfg www.largrizzly.com
Lazzeroni Arms Co. www.lazzeroni.com
Legacy Sports International www.legacysports.com

Les Baer Custom, Inc. www.lesbaer.com
Lewis Machine & Tool Co. www.lewismachine.net
LHR Sporting Arms www.lhrsportingarms.com
Linebaugh Custom Sixguns www.sixgunner.com/linebaugh
Ljutic www.ljuticgun.com
LMT Defense www.lmtdefense.com
LRB Arms www.lrbarms.com
Lyman www.lymanproducts.com
LWRC Int'l www.lwrci.com
Magnum Research www.magnumresearch.com
Majestic Arms www.majesticarms.com
Marksman Products www.marksman.com
Marlin www.marlinfirearms.com
MasterPiece Arms www.masterpiecearms.com
Mauser www.mauser.com
McMillan Bros Rifle Co. www.mcmfamily.com
Meacham Rifles www.meachamrifles.com
Merkel www.merkel-usa.com
Metro Arms www.metroarms.com
Milkor USA www.milkorusainc.com
Miller Precision Arms www.shopmillerprecisionarms.com
Miltech www.miltecharms.com
Mitchell's Mausers www.mausers.org
Montana Rifle Co. www.montanarifleco.com
Mossberg www.mossberg.com
Navy Arms www.navyarms.com
Nesika www.nesika.com
New England Arms Corp. www.newenglandarms.com
New England Custom Gun Svc, Ltd. www.newenglandcustom-gun.com
New Ultra Light Arms www.newultralight.com
Nighthawk Custom www.nighthawkcustom.com
Noreen Firearms www.onlylongrange.com
North American Arms www.northamericanarms.com
Nosler Bullets, Inc. www.nosler.com
Nowlin Mfg. Inc. www.nowlinguns.com
O.F. Mossberg & Sons www.mossberg.com
Ohio Ordnance Works www.ohioordnanceworks.com
Olympic Arms www.olyarms.com
Osprey Defense www.gaspiston.com
Panther Arms www.dpmsinc.com
Para-USA www.para-usa.com
Pedersoli Davide & Co. www.davide-pedersoli.com
Perazzi www.perazzi.com
Pietta www.pietta.it
Pistol Dynamics www.pistoldynamics.com
PKP Knife-Pistol www.sanjuanenterprise.com
Power Custom www.powercustom.com
Precision Small Arm Inc. www.precisionsmallarms.com
Primary Weapons Systems www.primaryweapons.com
Professional Arms www.professional-arms.com
Proof Research www.proofresearch.com
PTR Industries www.ptr91.com
Purdey & Sons www.purdey.com
Pyramid Air www.pyramidair.com
RAAC www.raacfirearms.com
Red Jacket Firearms www.redjacketfirearms.com
Remington www.remington.com
Rhineland Arms, Inc. www.rhinelandarms.com
Rigby www.johnrigbyandco.com
Rizzini USA www.rizziniusa.com
RM Equipment, Inc. www.40mm.com

Robar Companies, Inc. www.robarguns.com
Robinson Armament Co. www.robarm.com
Rock River Arms, Inc. www.rockriverarms.com
Rogue Rifle Co. Inc. www.chipmunkrifle.com
Rohrbaugh Firearms www.rohrbaughfirearms.com
Rossi Arms www.rossiusa.com
RPM www.rpmxlpistols.com
Russian American Armory www.raacfirearms.com
RUAG Ammotec www.ruag.com
Sabatti SPA www.sabatti.com
Saco Defense www.sacoinc.com
Safari Arms www.olyarms.com
Safety Harbor Firearms www.safetyharborfirearms.com
Sako www.berettausa.com
Samco Global Arms Inc. www.samcoglobal.com
Sarco www.sarcoinc.com
Sarsilmaz Silah San www.sarsilmaz.com
Sauer & Sohn www.sauer.de
Savage Arms Inc. www.savagearms.com
Scattergun Technologies Inc. www.wilsoncombat.com
Schmeisser Gmbh www.schmeisser-germany.de
Searcy Enterprises www.searcyent.com
Sharps Rifle Companies www.asquareco.com
Shaw www.ershawbarrels.com
Shiloh Rifle Mfg. www.shilohrifle.com
Sig Sauer, Inc. www.sigsauer.com
Simpson Ltd. www.simpsonltd.com
SKB Shotguns www.skbshotguns.com
Smith & Wesson www.smith-wesson.com
SOG International, Inc. soginc@go-concepts.com
Sphinx System www.sphinxarms.com
Springfield Armory www.springfield-armory.com
SSK Industries www.sskindustries.com
Stag Arms www.stagarms.com
Steyr Arms, Inc. www.steyrarms.com
STI International www.stiguns.com
Stoeger Industries www.stoegerindustries.com
Strayer-Voigt Inc. www.sviguns.com
Sturm, Ruger & Company www.ruger-firearms.com
Super Six Classic www.bisonbull.com
Surgeon Rifles www.surgeonrifles.com
Tactical Rifles www.tacticalrifles.com
Tactical Solutions www.tacticalsol.com
Tar-Hunt Slug Guns, Inc. www.tar-hunt.com
Taser Int'l www.taser.com
Taurus www.taurususa.com
Taylor's & Co., Inc. www.taylorsfirearms.com
Tempco Mfg. Co. www.tempcomfg.com
The 1877 Sharps Co. www.1877sharps.com
Thompson Center Arms www.tcarms.com
Tikka www.berettausa.com
TNW, Inc. www.tnwfirearms.com
Traditions www.traditionsfirearms.com
Tristar Sporting Arms www.tristarsportingarms.com
Turnbull Mfg. Co. www.turnbullmfg.com
Uberti www.uberti.com
Ultralite 50 www.ultralite50.com
Ultra Light Arms www.newultralight.com
Umarex www.umarex.com
U.S. Armament Corp. www.usarmamentcorp.com
U.S. Fire Arms Mfg. Co. www.usfirearms.com

Uselton Arms, Inc. www.useltonarmsinc.com
Valkyrie Arms www.valkyriearms.com
Verney-Carron www.verney-carron.com
Volquartsen Custom Ltd. www.volquartsen.com
Vulcan Armament www.vulcanarmament.com
Walther USA www.waltherarms.com
Weatherby www.weatherby.com
Webley and Scott Ltd. www.webley.co.uk
Westley Richards www.westleyrichards.com
Widley www.widleyguns.com
Wild West Guns www.wildwestguns.com
William Larkin Moore & Co. www.doublegun.com
Wilson Combat www.wilsoncombat.com
Winchester Rifles and Shotguns www.winchesterguns.com

GUN PARTS, BARRELS, AFTERMARKET ACCESSORIES

300 Below www.300below.com
Accuracy International of North America www.accuracyinternational.org
Accuracy Speaks, Inc. www.accuracyspeaks.com
Accurary Systems www.accuracysystemsinc.com
Accurate Airguns www.accurateairguns.com
Adam Arms www.adamarms.net
Advanced Barrel Systems www.carbonbarrels.com
Advantage Arms www.advantagearms.com
Aim Surplus www.aimsurplus.com
AK-USA www.ak-103.com
American Spirit Arms Corp. www.gunkits.com
Amhurst-Depot www.amherst-depot.com
AMT Gun Parts www.amt-gunparts.com
Apex Gun Parts www.apexgunparts.com
Armatac Industries www.armatac.com
Armscorp USA Inc. www.armscorpusa.com
Arthur Brown Co. www.eabco.com
Asia Sourcing Corp. www.asiasourcing.com
Barnes Precision Machine www.barnesprecision.com
Bar-Sto Precision Machine www.barsto.com
Battenfeld Technologies www.battenfeldtechnologies.com
Bellm TC's www.bellmtcs.com
Belt Mountain Enterprises www.beltmountain.com
Bergara Barrels www.bergarabarrels.com
Beyer Barrels www.beyerbarrels.com
Bill Wiseman & Co. www.wisemanballistics.com
Bravo Company USA www.bravocompanyusa.com
Briley www.briley.com
Brownells www.brownells.com
B-Square www.b-square.com
Buffer Technologies www.buffertech.com
Bullberry Barrel Works www.bullberry.com
Bulldog Barrels www.bulldogbarrels.com
Bushmaster Firearms/Quality Parts www.bushmaster.com
Butler Creek Corp www.butler-creek.com
Cape Outfitters Inc. www.capeoutfitters.com
Cavalry Arms www.cavalryarms.com
Caspian Arms Ltd. www.caspianarms.com
CDNN Sports www.cdnnsports.com
Cheaper Than Dirt www.cheaperthandirt.com
Chesnut Ridge www.chestnutridge.com
Chip McCormick Corp www.chipmccormickcorp.com
Choate Machine & Tool Co. www.riflestock.com

Christie's Products www.1022cental.com
Cierner, Jonathan Arthur www.22lrconversions.com
CJ Weapons Accessories www.cjweapons.com
Colonial Arms www.colonialarms.com
Comp-N-Choke www.comp-n-choke.com
Cylinder & Slide Shop www.cylinder-slide.com
Daniel Defense www.danieldefense.com
Dave Manson Precision Reamers www.mansonreamers.com
Digi-Twist www.fmtcorp.com
Dixie Gun Works www.dixiegun.com
Douglas Barrels www.benchrest.com/douglas/
DPMS www.dpmsinc.com
D.S.Arms www.dsarms.com
eBay www.ebay.com
E. Arthur Brown Co. www.eabco.com
Ed Brown Products www.edbrown.com
EFK Marketing/Fire Dragon Pistol Accessories www.flmfire.com
E.R. Shaw www.ershawbarrels.com
Fast Fire www.fastfire.com
FJ Fedderson Rifle Barrels www.gunbarrels.net
Forrest, Inc. www.gunmags.com
FTF Industries www.ftfindustries.com
Fulton Armory www.fulton-armory.com
Galazan www.connecticutshotgun.com
Gemtech www.gem-tech.com
Gentry, David www.gentrycustom.com
GG&G www.gggaz.com
Green Mountain Rifle Barrels www.gmriflebarrel.com
Gun Parts Corp. www.gunpartscorp.com
Guntec USA www.guntecusa.com
Harris Engineering www.harrisbipods.com
Hart Rifle Barrels www.hartbarrels.com
Hastings Barrels www.hastingsbarrels.com
Heinie Specialty Products www.heinie.com
HKS Products wwwhksspeedloaders.com
Holland Shooters Supply www.hollandgun.com
H-S Precision www.hsprecision.com
100 Straight Products www.100straight.com
I.M.A. www.ima-usa.com
Jack First Gun Shop www.jackfirstgun.com
Jarvis, Inc. www.jarvis-custom.com
J&T Distributing www.jtdistributing.com
John's Guns www.johnsguns.com
John Masen Co. www.johnmasen.com
Jonathan Arthur Ciener, Inc. www.22lrconversions.com
JP Enterprises www.jprifles.com
Keng's Firearms Specialities www.versapod.com
KG Industries www.kgcoatings.com
Kick Eez www.kickeez.com
Kidd Triggers www.coolguyguns.com
King's Gunworks www.kingsgunworks.com
Knoxx Industries www.knoxx.com
Krieger Barrels www.kriegerbarrels.com
K-VAR Corp. www.k-var.com
LaRue Tactical www.laruetactical.com
Les Baer Custom, Inc. www.lesbaer.com
Lilja Barrels www.riflebarrels.com
Lone Wolf Dist. www.lonewolfdist.com
Lothar Walther Precision Tools Inc. www.lothar-walther.de
M&A Parts, Inc. www.m-aparts.com
MAB Barrels www.mab.com.au

Magna-Matic Defense www.magna-matic-defense.com
Magpul Industries Corp. www.magpul.com
Majestic Arms www.majesticarms.com
Marvel Products, Inc. www.marvelprod.com
MEC-GAR USA www.mec-gar.com
Mech Tech Systems www.mechtechsys.com
Mesa Tactical www.mesatactical.com
Michaels of Oregon Co. www.michaels-oregon.com
Midway USA www.midwayusa.com
New England Custom Gun Service www.newenglandcustomgun.com
NIC Industries www.nicindustries.com
North Mfg. Co. www.rifle-barrels.com
Numrich Gun Parts Corp. www.gunpartscorp.com
Osprey Defense LLC www.gaspiston.com
Pachmayr www.pachmayr.com
Pac-Nor Barrels www.pac-nor.com
Power Custom, Inc. www.powercustom.com
Point Tech Inc. pointec@ibm.net
Precision Reflex www.pri-mounts.com
Promag Industries www.promagindustries.com
RCI-XRAIL www.xrailbyrci.com
Red Star Arms www.redstararms.com
River Bank Armory www.riverbankarmory.com
Rock Creek Barrels www.rockcreekbarrels.com
Rocky Mountain Arms www.bearcoat.com
Royal Arms Int'l www.royalarms.com
R.W. Hart www.rwhart.com
Sage Control Ordnance www.sageinternationalltd.com
Sarco Inc. www.sarcoinc.com
Scattergun Technologies Inc. www.wilsoncombat.com
Schuemann Barrels www.schuemann.com
Score High Gunsmithing www.scorehi.com
Seminole Gunworks Chamber Mates www.chambermates.com
Shaw Barrels www.ershawbarrels.com
Shilen www.shilen.com
SilencerCo www.silencerco.com
Silencio www.silencio.com
Sims Vibration Laboratory www.limbsaver.com
Slide Fire www.slidefire.com
Smith & Alexander Inc. www.smithandalexander.com
Speed Shooters Int'l www.shooternet.com/ssi
Sprinco USA Inc. sprinco@primenet.com
Springfield Sporters, Inc. www.ssporters.com
STI Int'l www.stiguns.com
S&S Firearms www.ssfirearms.com
SSK Industries www.sskindustries.com
Sun Devil Mfg. www.sundevilmfg.com
Sunny Hill Enterprises www.sunny-hill.com
Tac Star www.lymanproducts.com
Tactical Innovations www.tacticalinc.com
Tactical Solutions www.tacticalsol.com
Tactilite www.tactilite.com
Tapco www.tapco.com
Tennessee Guns Intl. www.tnguns.com
Trapdoors Galore www.trapdoors.com
Triple K Manufacturing Co. Inc. www.triplek.com
Ultimak www.ultimak.com
U.S.A. Magazines Inc. www.usa-magazines.com
Verney-Carron SA www.verney-carron.com
Vintage Ordnance www.vintageordnance.com
Vltor Weapon Systems www.vltor.com

Volquartsen Custom Ltd. **www.volquartsen.com**
W.C. Wolff Co. **www.gunsprings.com**
Waller & Son **www.wallerandson.com**
Weigand Combat Handguns **www.weigandcombat.com**
Western Gun Parts **www.westerngunparts.com**
Wilson Arms **www.wilsonarms.com**
Wilson Combat **www.wilsoncombat.com**
Wisner's Inc. **www.wisnerinc.com**
Z-M Weapons **www.zmweapons.com/home.htm**

GUNSMITHING SUPPLIES AND INSTRUCTION

4-D Products **www.4-dproducts.com**
American Gunsmithing Institute **www.americangunsmith.com**
Baron Technology **www.baronengraving.com**
Battenfeld Technologies **www.battenfeldtechnologies.com**
Bellm TC's **www.bellmtcs.com**
Blue Ridge Machinery & Tools **www.blueridgemachinery.com**
Brownells, Inc. **www.brownells.com**
B-Square Co. **www.b-square.com**
Cerakote Firearm Coatings **www.cerakoteguncoatings.com**
Clymer Mfg. Co. **www.clymertool.com**
Craftguard Metal Finishing **crftgrd@aol.com**
Dem-Bart **www.dembartco.com**
Doug Turnbull Restoration **www.turnbullrestoration,com**
Du-Lite Corp. **www.dulite.com**
DuraCoat Firearm Finishes **www.lauerweaponry.com**
Dvorak Instruments **www.dvorakinstruments.com**
Gradiant Lens Corp. **www.gradientlens.com**
Grizzly Industrial **www.grizzly.com**
Gunline Tools **www.gunline.com**
Harbor Freight **www.harborfreight.com**
JGS Precision Tool Mfg. LLC **www.jgstools.com**
Mag-Na-Port International **www.magnaport.com**
Manson Precision Reamers **www.mansonreamers.com**
Midway USA **www.midwayusa.com**
Murray State College **www.mscok.edu**
New England Custom Gun Service **www.newenglandcustomgun.com**
Olympus America Inc. **www.olympus.com**
Pacific Tool & Gauge **www.pacifictoolandgauge.com**
Penn Foster Career School **www.pennfoster.edu**
Pennsylvania Gunsmith School **www.pagunsmith.edu**
Piedmont Community College **www.piedmontcc.edu**
Precision Metalsmiths, Inc. **www.precisionmetalsmiths.com**
Rail Vise Technologies **www.railvise.com**
Sonoran Desert Institute **www.sdi.edu**
Trinidad State Junior College **www.trinidadstate.edu**

HANDGUN GRIPS

Ajax Custom Grips, Inc. **www.ajaxcustomgrips.com**
Altamont Co. **www.altamontco.com**
Aluma Grips **www.alumagrips.com**
Badger Custom Grips **www.badgercustomgrips.com**
Barami Corp. **www.hipgrip.com**
Blu Magnum Grips **www.blumagnum.com**
Buffalo Brothers **www.buffalobrothers.com**
Crimson Trace Corp. **www.crimsontrace.com**
Decal Grip **www.decalgrip.com**
Eagle Grips **www.eaglegrips.com**
Falcon Industries **www.ergogrips.net**
Herrett's Stocks **www.herrettstocks.com**

Hogue Grips **www.getgrip.com**
Kirk Ratajesak **www.kgratajesak.com**
Lett Custom Grips **www.lettgrips.com**
N.C. Ordnance **www.gungrip.com**
Nill-Grips USA **www.nill-grips.com**
Pachmayr **www.pachmayr.com**
Pearce Grips **www.pearcegrip.com**
Rio Grande Custom Grips **www.riograndecustomgrips.com**
Trausch Grips Int. Co. **www.trausch.com**
Tyler-T Grips **www.t-grips.com**
Uncle Mike's **www.uncle-mikes.com**

HOLSTERS AND LEATHER PRODUCTS

Active Pro Gear **www.activeprogear.com**
Akah **www.akah.de**
Aker Leather Products **www.akerleather.com**
Alessi Distributor R&F Inc. **www.alessiholsters.com**
Alfonso's of Hollywood **www.alfonsogunleather.com**
Armor Holdings **www.holsters.com**
Bagmaster **www.bagmaster.com**
Bandara Gunleather **www.bandaragunleather.com**
Bianchi International **www.bianchi-intl.com**
Black Dog Machine **www.blackdogmachinellc.net**
Blackhawk Outdoors **www.blackhawk.com**
Blackhills Leather **www.blackhillsleather.com**
Boyt Harness Co. **www.boytharness.com**
Brigade Gun Leather **www.brigadegunleather.com**
Center of Mass **www.comholsters.com**
Chimere **www.chimere.com**
Clipdraw **www.clipdraw.com**
Conceal It **www.conceal-it.com**
Concealment Shop Inc. **www.theconcealmentshop.com**
Coronado Leather Co. **www.coronadoleather.com**
Covert Carry **www.covertcarry.com**
Creedmoor Sports, Inc. **www.creedmoorsports.com**
Cross Breed Holsters **www.crossbreedholsters.com**
Custom Leather Wear **www.customleatherwear.com**
Deep Conceal **www.deepconceal.com**
Defense Security Products **www.thunderwear.com**
Dennis Yoder **www.yodercustomleather.com**
DeSantis Holster **www.desantisholster.com**
Diamond Custom Leather **www.diamondcustomleather.com**
Dillon Precision **www.dillonprecision.com**
Don Hume Leathergoods, Inc. **www.donhume.com**
Elite Survival **www.elitesurvival.com**
Ernie Hill International **www.erniehill.com**
Fist **www.fist-inc.com**
Fobus USA **www.fobusholster.com**
Front Line Ltd. **frontlin@internet-zahav.net**
Frontier Gun Leather **www.frontiergunleather.com**
Galco **www.usgalco.com**
Gilmore's Sports Concepts **www.gilmoresports.com**
Gould & Goodrich **www.gouldusa.com**
Gunmate Products **www.gun-mate.com**
Hellweg Ltd. **www.hellwegltd.com**
Hide-A-Gun **www.hide-a-gun.com**
High Noon Holsters **www.highnoonholsters.com**
Holsters.com **www.holsters.com**
Horseshoe Leather Products **www.horseshoe.co.uk**
Hunter Co. **www.huntercompany.com**
JBP/Master's Holsters **www.jbpholsters.com**

Kirkpatrick Leather Company www.kirkpatrickleather.com
KJ Leather www.kbarjleather.com
KNJ www.knjmfg.com
Kramer Leather www.kramerleather.com
Law Concealment Systems www.handgunconcealment.com
Levy's Leathers Ltd. www.levysleathers.com
Mernickle Holsters www.mernickleholsters.com
Michaels of Oregon Co. www.michaels-oregon.com
Milt Sparks Leather www.miltsparks.com
Mitch Rosen Extraordinary Gunleather www.mitchrosen.com
N82 Tactical www.n82tactical.com
Old World Leather www.gun-mate.com
Pacific Canvas & Leather Co. paccanadleather@directway.com
Pager Pal www.pagerpal.com
Phalanx Corp. www.smartholster.com
Purdy Gear www.purdygear.com
PWL www.pwlusa.com
Rumanya Inc. www.rumanya.com
S.A. Gunleather www.elpasoleather.com
Safariland Ltd. Inc. www.safariland.com
Shooting Systems Group Inc. www.shootingsystems.com
Skyline Tool Works www.clipdraw.com
Solerial Leather www.solerialleather.com
Stellar Rigs www.stellarrigs.com
Strictly Anything Inc. www.strictlyanything.com
Strong Holster Co. www.strong-holster.com
Tex Shoemaker & Sons www.texshoemaker.com
The Belt Co. www.conceal-it.com
The Leather Factory Inc. lflandry@flash.net
The Outdoor Connection www.outdoorconnection.com
Top-Line USA inc. www.toplineusa.com
Tuff Products www.tuffproducts.com
Triple K Manufacturing Co. www.triplek.com
Wilson Combat www.wilsoncombat.com

MISCELLANEOUS SHOOTING PRODUCTS

Aero Peltor www.aearo.com
American Body Armor www.americanbodyarmor.com
American Tactical Imports www.americantactical.com
Ammo-Up www.ammoupusa.com
Armor Holdings Products www.armorholdings.com
AutoGun Tracker www.autoguntracker.com
Battenfeld Technologies www.battenfeldtechnologies.com
Beamhit www.beamhit.com
Beartooth www.beartoothproducts.com
Bodyguard by S&W www.yourbodyguard.com
Burnham Brothers www.burnhambrothers.com
Collectors Armory www.collectorsarmory.com
Dalloz Safety www.cdalloz.com
Deben Group Industries Inc. www.deben.com
Decot Hy-Wyd Sport Glasses www.sportyglasses.com
Defense Technology www.safariland.com/lesslethal
E.A.R., Inc. www.earinc.com
First Choice Armor www.firstchoicearmor.com
Gunstands www.gunstands.com
Howard Leight Hearing Protectors www.howardleight.com
Hunters Specialities www.hunterspec.com
Johnny Stewart Wildlife Calls www.hunterspec.com
Joseph Chiarello Gun Insurance www.guninsurance.com
Mec-Gar USA www.mec-gar.com
Merit Corporation www.meritcorporation.com

Michaels of Oregon Co. www.michaels-oregon.com
MPI Outdoors www.mpioutdoors.com
MT2, LLC www.mt2.com
MTM Case-Gard www.mtmcase-gard.com
North Safety Products www.northsafety-brea.com
Oakley, Inc. www.usstandardissue.com
Plano Molding www.planomolding.com
Practical Air Rifle Training Systems www.smallarms.com
Pro-Ears www.pro-ears.com
Second Chance Body Armor Inc. www.secondchance.com
Silencio www.silencio.com
SilencerCo www.silencerco.com
Smart Lock Technologies www.smartlock.com
SportEAR www.sportear.com
STRAC, Inc. www.stractech.com
Surefire www.surefire.com
Taser Int'l www.taser.com
Vyse-Gelatin Innovations www.gelatininnovations.com
Walker's Game Ear Inc. www.walkersgameear.com

MUZZLELOADING FIREARMS AND PRODUCTS

American Pioneer Powder www.americanpioneerpowder.com
Armi Sport www.armisport.com
Barnes Bullets www.barnesbullets,com
Black Powder Products www.bpiguns.com
Buckeye Barrels www.buckeyebarrels.com
Cabin Creek Muzzleloading www.cabincreek.net
CVA www.cva.com
Caywood Gunmakers www.caywoodguns.com
Davide Perdsoli & Co. www.davide-pedersoli.com
Dixie Gun Works, Inc. www.dixiegun.com
Elephant/Swiss Black Powder www.elephantblackpowder.com
Goex Black Powder www.goexpowder.com
Green Mountain Rifle Barrel Co. www.gmriflebarrel.com
Gunstocks Plus www.gunstocksplus.com
Gun Works www.thegunworks.com
Harvester Muzzleloading www.harvestermuuzzleloading.com
Honorable Company of Horners www.hornguild.org
Hornady www.hornady.com
Jedediah Starr Trading Co. www.jedediah-starr.com
Jim Chambers Flintlocks www.flintlocks.com
Kahnke Gunworks www.powderandbow.com/kahnke/
Knight Rifles www.knightrifles.com
Knob Mountain Muzzleloading www.knobmountainmuzzleloading.com
The leatherman www.blackpowderbags.com
Log Cabin Shop www.logcabinshop.com
L&R Lock Co. www.lr-rpl.com
Lyman www.lymanproducts.com
Magkor Industries www.magkor.com
MDM Muzzleloaders www.mdm-muzzleloaders.com
Middlesex Village Trading www.middlesexvillagetrading.com
Millennium Designed Muzzleloaders www.mdm-muzzleloaders.com
MSM, Inc. www.msmfg.com
Muzzleloader Builders Supply www.muzzleloadersbuilderssupply.com
Muzzleload Magnum Products www.mmpsabots.com
Muzzleloading Shotguns www.muzzleloadingshotguns.com
Muzzleloading Technologies, Inc. www.mtimuzzleloading.com
Navy Arms www.navyarms.com
Northwest Trade Guns www.northstarwest.com
Nosler, Inc. www.nosler.com
October Country Muzzleloading www.oct-country.com

Ox-Yoke Originals Inc. **www.rmcoxyoke.com**
Pacific Rifle Co. **pacificrifle@aol.com**
Palmetto Arms **www.palmetto.it**
Pecatonica River **www.longrifles-pr.com**
Pietta **www.pietta.it**
Powerbelt Bullets **www.powerbeltbullets.com**
PR Bullets **www.prbullets.com**
Precision Rifle Dead Center Bullets **www.prbullet.com**
R.E. Davis Co. **www.redaviscompany.com**
Rightnour Mfg. Co. Inc. **www.rmcsports.com**
The Rifle Shop **therifleshoppe.com**
Savage Arms, Inc. **www.savagearms.com**
Schuetzen Powder **www.schuetzenpowder.com**
TDC **www.tdcmfg.com**
Tennessee Valley Muzzleloading **www.avsia.com/tvm**
Thompson Center Arms **www.tcarms.com**
Tiger Hunt Stocks **www.gunstockwood.com**
Track of the Wolf **www.trackofthewolf.com**
Traditions Performance Muzzleloading **www.traditionsfirearms.com**
Vernon C. Davis & Co. **www.stonewallcreekoutfitters.com**

PUBLICATIONS, VIDEOS AND CD'S

Arms and Military Press **www.skennerton.com**
A&J Arms Booksellers **www.ajarmsbooksellers.com**
American Cop **www.americancopmagazine.com**
American Firearms Industry **www.amfire.com**
American Gunsmithing Institute **www.americangunsmith.com**
American Handgunner **www.americanhandgunner.com**
American Hunter **www.nrapublications.org**
American Pioneer Video **www.americanpioneervideo.com**
American Rifleman **www.nrapublications.org**
American Shooting Magazine **www.americanshooting.com**
Backwoodsman **www.backwoodsmanmag.com**
Black Powder Cartridge News **www.blackpowderspg.com**
Blue Book Publications **www.bluebookinc.com**
Combat Handguns **www.combathandguns.com**
Concealed Carry **www.uscca.us**
Cornell Publications **www.cornellpubs.com**
Countrywide Press **www.countrysport.com**
Field & Stream **www.fieldandstream.com**
Fouling Shot **www.castbulletassoc.org**
Fur, Fish & Game **www.furfishgame.com**
George Shumway Publisher **www.shumwaypublisher.com**
Gray's Sporting Journal **www.grayssportingjournal.com**
Gun Digest Magazine **www.gundigest.com**
Gun Digest Books **www.gundigeststore.com**
Gun Dog **www.gundogman.com**
Gun Video **www.gunvideo.com**
Guns & Ammo **www.gunsandammo.com**
Guns of the Old West **www.gunsoftheoldwest.com**
Gun Mag **www.thegunmag.com**
Gun World **www.gunworld.com**
Handguns **www.handgunsmag.com**
Handloader **www.riflemagazine.com**
Hendon Publishing Co. **www.hendonpub.com**
Heritage Gun Books **www.gunbooks.com**
Krause Publications **www.krausebooks.com**
Law and Order **www.hendonpub.com**
Man at Arms **www.gunandswordcollector.com**
Muzzle Blasts **www.nmlra.org**
Muzzleloader **www.muzzleloadermag.com**

On-Target Productions **www.ontargetdvds.com**
Outdoor Channel **www.outdoorchannel.com**
Outdoor Life **www.outdoorlife.com**
Paladin Press **www.paladin-press.com**
Police and Security News **www.policeandsecuritynews.com**
Police Magazine **www.policemag.com**
Precision Shooting **www.precisionshooting.com**
Primitive Arts Video **www.primitiveartsvideo.com**
Pursuit Channel **www.pursuitchannel.com**
Recoil Magazine **www.recoilmag.com**
Rifle and Handloader Magazines **www.riflemagazine.com**
Rifle Shooter Magazine **www.rifleshootermag.com**
Safari Press Inc. **www.safaripress.com**
Schiffer Publishing **www.schifferbooks.com**
Scurlock Publishing **www.muzzleloadingmag.com**
Shoot! Magazine **www.shootmagazine.com**
Shooting Illustrated **www.nrapublications.org**
Shooting Industry **www.shootingindustry.com**
Shooting Times Magazine **www.shootingtimes.com**
Shooting Sports Retailer **www.shootingsportsretailer.com**
Shooting Sports USA **www.nrapublications.org**
Shooting Sportsman **www.shootingsportsman.com**
Shotgun News **www.shotgunnews.com**
Shotgun Report **www.shotgunreport.com**
Shotgun Sports Magazine **www.shotgun-sports.com**
Single Shot Exchange **www.singleshotexchange.com**
Single Shot Rifle Journal **www.assra.com**
Small Arms Review **www.smallarmsreview.com**
Small Caliber News **www.smallcaliber.com**
Sporting Classics **www.sportingclassics.com**
Sporting Clays Web Edition **www.sportingclays.net**
Sports Afield **www.sportsafield.com**
Sportsman's Channel **www.thesportsmanchannel.com**
Sportsmen on Film **www.sportsmenonfilm.com**
Successful Hunter **www.riflemagazine.com**
SWAT Magazine **www.swatmag.com**
The Sixgunner **www.sskindustries.com**
Varmint Hunter **www.varminthunter.org**
VSP Publications **www.gunbooks.com**

RELOADING TOOLS

21st Century Shooting **www.21stcenturyshooting.com**
Ballisti-Cast Mfg. **www.ballisti-cast.com**
Battenfeld Technologies **www.battenfeldtechnologies.com**
Bruno Shooters Supply **www.brunoshooters.com**
Buffalo Arms **www.buffaloarms.com**
CabineTree **www.castingstuff.com**
Camdex, Inc. **www.camdexloader.com**
CH/4D Custom Die **www.ch4d.com**
Colorado Shooters Supply **www.hochmoulds.com**
Corbin Mfg & Supply Co. **www.corbins.com**
Dillon Precision **www.dillonprecision.com**
Forster Precision Products **www.forsterproducts.com**
Gracey Trimmer **www.matchprep.com**
GSI International, Inc. **www.gsiinternational.com**
Hanned Line **www.hanned.com**
Harrell's Precision **www.harrellsprec.com**
Holland's Shooting Supplies **www.hollandgun.com**
Hornady **www.hornady.com**
Hunter's Supply, Inc. **www.hunters-supply.com**
Huntington Reloading Products **www.huntingtons.com**

J & J Products Co. www.jandjproducts.com
Lead Bullet Technology www.lbtmoulds.com
Lee Precision, Inc. www.leeprecision.com
Littleton Shotmaker www.leadshotmaker.com
Load Data www.loaddata.com
Lyman www.lymanproducts.com
Magma Engineering www.magmaengr.com
Mayville Engineering Co. (MEC) www.mecreloaders.com
Midway www.midwayusa.com
Moly-Bore www.molybore.com
Montana Bullet Works www.montanabulletworks.com
MTM Case-Guard www.mtmcase-guard.com
NECO www.neconos.com
NEI www.neihandtools.com
Neil Jones Custom Products www.neiljones.com
New Lachaussee SA www.lachaussee.com
Ponsness/Warren www.reloaders.com
Precision Reloading www.precisionreloading.com
Quinetics Corp. www.quineticscorp.com
Ranger Products www.pages.prodigy.com/rangerproducts. home.htm
Rapine Bullet Mold Mfg Co. www.bulletmoulds.com
RCBS www.rcbs.com
Redding Reloading Equipment www.redding-reloading.com
Russ Haydon's Shooting Supplies www.shooters-supply.com
Sinclair Int'l Inc. www.sinclairintl.com
Stoney Point Products Inc www.stoneypoint.com
Thompson Bullet Lube Co. www.thompsonbulletlube.com
Vickerman Seating Die www.castingstuff.com
Wilson (L.E. Wilson) www.lewilson.com

RESTS— BENCH, PORTABLE, ATTACHABLE

Accu-Shot www.accu-shot.com
Battenfeld Technolgies www.battenfeldtechnologies.com
Bench Master www.bench-master.com
B-Square www.b-square.com
Bullshooter www.bullshooterssightingin.com
Center Mass, Inc. www.centermassinc.com
Desert Mountain Mfg. www.benchmasterusa.com
DOA Tactical www.doatactical.com
Harris Bipods www.harrisbipod.com
KFS Industries www.versapod.com
Kramer Designs www.snipepod.com
L Thomas Rifle Support www.ltsupport.com
Level-Lok www.levellok.com
Midway www.midwayusa.com
Predator Sniper Styx www.predatorsniperstyx.com
Ransom International www.ransom-intl.com
Rotary Gun Racks www.gun-racks.com
R.W. Hart www.rwhart.com
Sinclair Intl, Inc. www.sinclairintl.com
Shooters Ridge www.shooterridge.com
Shooting Bench USA www.shootingbenchusa.com
Target Shooting www.targetshooting.com
Varmint Masters www.varmintmasters.com
Versa-Pod www.versapod.com

SCOPES, SIGHTS, MOUNTS AND ACCESSORIES

Accumount www.accumounts.com
Accusight www.accusight.com
ADCO www.shooters.com/adco/index/htm

Adirondack Opitcs www.adkoptics.com
Advantage Tactical Sight www.advantagetactical.com
Aimpoint www.aimpoint.com
Aim Shot, Inc. www.aimshot.com
Aimtech Mount Systems www.aimtech-mounts.com
Alpec Team, Inc. www.alpec.com
Alpen Outdoor Corp. www.alpenoutdoor.com
American Technologies Network, Corp. www.atncorp.com
AmeriGlo, LLC www.ameriglo.net
ArmaLaser www.armalaser.com
Armament Technology, Inc. www.armament.com
ARMS www.armsmounts.com
Aro-Tek, Ltd. www.arotek.com
ATN www.atncorp.com
Badger Ordnance www.badgerordnance.com
Barrett www.barrettrifles.com
Beamshot-Quarton www.beamshot.com
BKL Technologies, Inc. www.bkltech.com
BSA Optics www.bsaoptics.com
B-Square Company, Inc. www.b-square.com
Burris www.burrisoptics.com
Bushnell Performance Optics www.bushnell.com
Carl Zeiss Optical Inc. www.zeiss.com
Carson Optical www.carson-optical.com
CenterPoint Precision Optics www.centerpointoptics.com
Centurion Arms www.centurionarms.com
C-More Systems www.cmore.com
Conetrol Scope Mounts www.conetrol.com
Crimson Trace Corp. www.crimsontrace.com
Crossfire L.L.C. www.amfire.com/hesco/html
Cylinder & Slide, Inc. www.cylinderslide.com
DCG Supply Inc. www.dcgsupply.com
D&L Sports www.dlsports.com
DuraSight Scope Mounting Systems www.durasight.com
EasyHit, Inc. www.easyhit.com
EAW www.eaw.de
Elcan Optical Technologies www.armament.com, www.elcan.com
Electro-Optics Technologies www.eotechmdc.com/holosight
EoTech www.eotech-inc.com
Europtik Ltd. www.europtik.com
Fujinon, Inc. www.fujinon.com
GG&G www.w.gggaz.com
Gilmore Sports www.gilmoresports.com
Gradient Lens Corp. www.gradientlens.com
Hakko Co. Ltd. www.hakko-japan.co.jp
Hahn Precision www.hahn-precision.com
Hesco www.hescosights.com
Hi-Lux Optics www.hi-luxoptics.com
Hitek Industries www.nightsight.com
HIVIZ www.hivizsights.com
Hollands Shooters Supply www.hollandguns.com
Horus Vision www.horusvision.com
Hunter Co. www.huntercompany.com
Huskemaw Optics www.huskemawoptics.com
Innovative Weaponry, Inc. www.ptnightsights.com
Insight www.insighttechnology.com
Ironsighter Co. www.ironsighter.com
ITT Night Vision www.ittnightvision.com
Kahles www.kahlesoptik.com
KenSight www.kensight.com
Knight's Armament www.knightarmco.com

Kowa Optimed Inc. **www.kowascope.com**
Kwik-Site Co. **www.kwiksitecorp**
L-3 Communications-Eotech **www.l-3com.com**
LaRue Tactical **www.laruetactical.com**
Laser Bore Sight **www.laserboresight.com**
Laser Devices Inc. **www.laserdevices.com**
Lasergrips **www.crimsontrace.com**
LaserLyte **www.laserlytesights.com**
LaserMax Inc. **www.lasermax.com**
Laser Products **www.surefire.com**
Leapers, Inc. **www.leapers.com**
Leather**wood www.hi-luxoptics.com**
Legacy Sports **www.legacysports.com**
Leica Camera Inc. **www.leica-camera.com/usa**
Leupold **www.leupold.com**
Lewis Machine & Tool **www.lewismachine.net**
LightForce/NightForce USA **www.nightforcescopes.com**
Lyman **www.lymanproducts.com**
Lynx **www.b-square.com**
Matech **www.adcofirearms.com**
Marble's Gunsights **www.marblearms.com**
MDS, Inc. **www.mdsincorporated.com**
Meopta **www.meopta.com**
Meprolight **www.kimberamerica.com**
Micro Sight Co. **www.microsight.com**
Millett **www.millettsights.com**
Miniature Machine Corp. **www.mmcsight.com**
Mini-Scout-Mount **www.amegaranges.com**
Minox USA **www.minox.com**
Montana Vintage Arms **www.montanavintagearms.com**
Moro Vision **www.morovision.com**
Mounting Solutions Plus **www.mountsplus.com**
NAIT **www.nait.com**
Newcon International Ltd. **www.newcon-optik.com**
Night Force Optics **www.nightforcescopes.com**
Night Optics USA, Inc. **www.nightoptics.com**
Night Owl Optics **www.nightowloptics.com**
Night Vision Systems **www.nightvisionsystems.com**
Nikon Inc. **www.nikonhunting.com**
Nitehog **www.nitehog.com**
Novak Sights **www.novaksights.com**
North American Integrated Technologies **www.nait.com**
O.K. Weber, Inc. **www.okweber.com**
Optolyth-Optic **www.optolyth.de Osprey Optics www.osprey-optics.com**
Pentax Corp. **www.pentaxlightseeker.com**
Precision Reflex **www.pri-mounts.com**
Pride Fowler, Inc. **www.rapidreticle.com**
Premier Reticles **www.premierreticles.com**
Redfield **www.redfield.com**
Rifle Electronics **www.theriflecam.com**
R&R Int'l Trade **www.nightoptic.com**
Schmidt & Bender **www.schmidt-bender.com**
Scopecoat **www.scopecoat.com**
Scopelevel **www.scopelevel.com**
Scout Scopes **www.scoutscopes.com**
Segway Industries **www.segway-industries.com**
Shepherd Scope Ltd. **www.shepherdscopes.com**
SIG Sauer **www.sigsauer.com**
Sightmark **www.sightmark.com**
Sightron **www.sightron.com**
Simmons **www.simmonsoptics.com**

S&K **www.scopemounts.com**
Springfield Armory **www.springfield-armory.com**
Steiner **www.steiner-binoculars.com**
Steve Earle Products **www.steveearleproducts.com**
Sun Optics USA **www.sunopticsusa.com**
Sure-Fire **www.surefire.com**
Swarovski/Kahles **www.swarovskioptik.com**
SWATSCOPE **www.swatscope.com**
Swift Optics **www.swiftoptics.com**
Talley Mfg. Co. **www.talleyrings.com**
Tasco **www.tascosales.com**
Tech Sights **www.tech-sights.com**
Trijicon Inc. **www.trijicon.com**
Troy Industries **www.troyind.com**
Truglo Inc. **www.truglo.com**
Ultimak **www.ultimak.com**
UltraDot **www.ultradotusa.com**
Unertl Optical Co. **www.unertlopics.com**
U.S. Night Vision **www.usnightvision.com**
U.S. Optics Technologies Inc. **www.usoptics.com**
Valdada-IOR Optics **www.valdada.com**
Viridian Green Laser Sights **www.viridiangreenlaser.com**
Vortex Optics **www.vortexoptics.com**
Warne **www.warnescopemounts.com**
Weaver Mounts **www.weaver-mounts.com**
Weaver Scopes **www.weaveroptics.com**
Wilcox Industries Corp **www.wilcoxind.com**
Williams Gun Sight Co. **www.williamsgunsight.com**
Wilson Combat **www.wilsoncombat.com**
XS Sight Systems **www.xssights.com**
Zeiss **www.zeiss.com**

SHOOTING ORGANIZATIONS, SCHOOLS AND RANGES

Amateur Trapshooting Assoc. **www.shootata.com**
American Custom Gunmakers Guild **www.acgg.org**
American Gunsmithing Institute **www.americangunsmith.com**
American Pistolsmiths Guild **www.americanpistol.com**
American Shooting Sports Council **www.assc.com**
American Single Shot Rifle Assoc. **www.assra.com**
American Snipers **www.americansnipers.org**
Antique Shooting Tool Collector's Assoc. **www.oldshootingtools. org**
Armed Citizens Alliance **www.armedcitizensalliance.com**
Assoc. of Firearm & Tool Mark Examiners **www.afte.org**
BATFE **www.atf.ustreas.gov**
Blackwater Lodge and Training Center **www.blackwaterlodge.com**
Boone and Crockett Club **www.boone-crockett.org**
Browning Collectors Assn. **www.browningcollectors.com**
Buckmasters, Ltd. **www.buckmasters.com**
Cast Bullet Assoc. **www.castbulletassoc.org**
Citizens Committee for the Right to Keep & Bear Arms **www.ccrkba.org**
Civilian Marksmanship Program **www.odcmp.com**
Colorado School of Trades **www.gunsmith-school.com**
Colt Collectors Assn. **www.coltcollectors.org**
Contemporary Longrifle Assoc. **www.longrifle.com**
Cylinder & Slide Pistolsmithing Schools **www.cylinder-slide.com**
Ducks Unlimited **www.ducks.org**
4-H Shooting Sports Program **www.4-hshootingsports.org**
Fifty Caliber Institute **www.fiftycal.com**
Fifty Caliber Shooters Assoc. **www.fcsa.org**

Firearms Coalition **www.firearmscoalition.com**
Front Sight Firearms Training Institute **www.frontsight.com**
German Gun Collectors Assoc. **www.germanguns.com**
Gun Clubs **www.associatedgunclubs.org**
Gun Owners' Action League **www.goal.org**
Gun Owners of America **www.gunowners.org**
Gun Trade Asssoc. Ltd. **www.brucepub.com/**gta
Gunsite Training Center, Inc. **www.gunsite.com**
Handgun Hunters International **www.sskindustries.com**
Hunting and Shooting Sports Heritage Fund **www.huntand-shoot.org**
I.C.E. Training **www.icetraining.com**
IWA **www.iwa.info**
International Defense Pistol Assoc. **www.idpa.com**
International Handgun Metallic Silhouette Assoc. **www.ihmsa. org**
International Hunter Education Assoc. **www.ihea.com**
Int'l Law Enforcement Educators and Trainers Assoc. **www.ileeta.com**
International Single Shot Assoc. **www.issa-schuetzen.org**
Jews for the Preservation of Firearms Ownership **www.jpfo.org**
Mule Deer Foundation **www.muledeer.org**
Muzzle Loaders Assoc. of Great Britain **www.mlagb.com**
National 4-H Shooting Sports **www.4-hshootingsports.org**
National Association of Sporting Goods Wholesalers **www. nasgw.org**
National Benchrest Shooters Assoc. **www.benchrest.com**
National Defense Industrial Assoc. **www.ndia.org**
National Firearms Act Trade & Collectors Assoc. **www.nfatca.org**
National Muzzle Loading Rifle Assoc. **www.nmlra.org**
National Reloading Manufacturers Assoc **www.reload-nrma.com**
National Rifle Assoc. **www.nra.org**
National Rifle Assoc. ILA **www.nraila.org**
National Shooting Sports Foundation **www.nssf.org**
National Skeet Shooters Association **www.nssa-nsca.com**
National Sporting Clays Assoc. **www.nssa-nsca.com**
National Tactial Officers Assoc. **www.ntoa.org**
National Wild Turkey Federation **www.nwtf.com**
NICS/FBI **www.fbi.gov**
North American Hunting Club **www.huntingclub.com**
Order of Edwardian Gunners (Vintagers) **www.vintagers.org**
Outdoor Industry Foundation **www.outdoorindustryfoundation. org**
Pennsylvania Gunsmith School **www.pagunsmith.com**
Piedmont Community College **www.piedmontcc.edu**
Quail Unlimited **www.qu.org**
Remington Society of America **www.remingtonsociety.com**
Right To Keep and Bear Arms **www.rkba.org**
Rocky Mountain Elk Foundation **www.rmef.org**
Ruger Collector's Association **www.rugercollectorsassociation.com**
SAAMI **www.saami.org**
Safari Club International **www.scifirstforhunters.org**
Scholastic Clay Target Program **www.nssf.org/sctp**
Scholastic Shooting Sports Foundation **www.shootsctp.com**
Second Amendment Foundation **www.saf.org**
Second Amendment Sisters **www.2asisters.org**
Shooting for Women Alliance **www.shootingforwomenalliance.com**
Shooting Ranges Int'l **www.shootingranges.com**
Sig Sauer Academy **www.sigsauer.com**
Single Action Shooting Society **www.sassnet.com**
Smith & Wesson Collector's Assoc. **www.theswca.org**
Steel Challenge Pistol Tournament **www.steelchallenge.com**
Students for Second Amendment **www.sf2a.org**
Sturgis Economic Development Corp. **www.sturgisdevelopment.com**
Suarez Training **www.warriortalk.com**
S&W Academy and Nat'l Firearms Trng. Center **www.sw-academy.com**

Tactical Defense Institute **www.tdiohio.com**
Tactical Life **www.tactical-life.com**
Ted Nugent United Sportsmen of America **www.tednugent.com**
Thunder Ranch **www.thunderranchinc.com**
Trapshooters Homepage **www.trapshooters.com**
Trinidad State Junior College **www.trinidadstate.edu**
United Sportsmen's Youth Foundation **www.usyf.com**
Universal Shooting Academy **www.universalshootingacademy.com**
U.S. Concealed Carry Association **www.uscca.us**
U.S. Int'l Clay Target Assoc. **www.usicta.com**
U.S. Fish and Wildlife Service **www.fws.gov**
U.S. Practical Shooting Assoc. **www.uspsa.org**
U.S. Sportsmen's Alliance **www.ussportsmen.org**
USA Shooting **www.usashooting.com**
Varmint Hunter's Assoc. **www.varminthunter.org**
Winchester Arms Collectors Assoc. **www.winchestercollector.com**
Women Hunters **www.womanhunters.com**

STOCKS, GRIPS, FOREARMS

10/22 Fun Gun **www.1022fungun.com**
Ace, Ltd. **www.aceltdusa.com**
Advanced Technology **www.atigunstocks.com**
Battenfeld Technologies **www.battenfeldtechnologies.com**
Bell & Carlson, Inc. **www.bellandcarlson.com**
Boyd's Gunstock Industries, Inc. **www.boydsgunstocks.com**
Butler Creek Corp **www.butler-creek.com**
Cadex **www.vikingtactics.com**
Calico Hardwoods, Inc. **www.calicohardwoods.com**
Choate Machine **www.riflestock.com**
Command Arms **www.commandarms.com**
C-More Systems **www.cmore.com**
D&L Sports **www.dlsports.com**
Duo Stock **www.duostock.com**
E.Arthur Brown Co. **www.eabco.com**
Elk Ridge Stocks **www.reamerrentals.com/elk_ridge.htm**
FAB Tactical **www.botachtactical.com**
Fajen **www.battenfeldtechnologies.com**
Falcon Ergo Grip **www.ergogrips.com**
Great American Gunstocks **www.gunstocks.com**
Grip Pod **www.grippod.com**
Gun Stock Blanks **www.gunstockblanks.com**
Herrett's Stocks **www.herrettstocks.com**
High Tech Specialties **www.bansnersrifle.com/hightech**
Hogue Grips **www.getgrip.com**
Holland's Shooting Supplies **www.hollandgun.com**
Knight's Mfg. Co. **wwwknightarmco.com**
Knoxx Industries **www.blackhawk.com**
KZ Tactical **www.kleyzion.com**
LaRue Tactical **www.laruetactical.com**
Laser Stock **www.laserstock.com**
Lewis Machine & Tool **www.lewismachine.net**
Lone Wolf **proofresearch.com**
Magpul **www.magpul.com**
Manners Composite Stocks **www.mannerstocks.com**
McMillan Fiberglass Stocks **www.mcmfamily.com**
MPI Stocks **www.mpistocks.com**
Precision Gun Works **www.precisiongunstocks.com**
Ram-Line **www.outers-guncare.com**
Richards Microfit Stocks **www.rifle-stocks.com**
Rimrock Rifle Stock **www.rimrockstocks.com**
Royal Arms Gunstocks **www.imt.net/**~royalarms

Speedfeed www.safariland.com
TacStar/Pachmayr www.tacstar.com
Tango Down www.tangodown.com
TAPCO www.tapco.com
Slide Fire www.slidefire.com
Stocky's www.newriflestocks.com
Surefire www.surefire.com
Tiger-Hunt Curly Maple Gunstocks www.gunstockwood.com
UTG Pro www.leapers.com
Vltor www.vltor.com
Wenig Custom Gunstocks Inc. www.wenig.com
Wilcox Industries www.wilcoxind.com
Yankee Hill www.yhm.net

TARGETS AND RANGE EQUIPMENT

Action Target Co. www.actiontarget.com
Advanced Interactive Systems www.ais-sim.com
Advanced Training Systems www.atsusa.biz
Alco Target www.alcotarget.com
Arntzen Targets www.arntzentargets.com
Birchwood Casey www.birchwoodcasey.com
Bullet Proof Electronics www.thesnipertarget.com
Caswell Meggitt Defense Systems www.mds-caswell.com
Champion Traps & Targets www.championtarget.com
Custom Metal Products www.custommetalprod.com
Handloader/Victory Targets www.targetshandloader.com
Just Shoot Me Products www.ballistictec.com
Laser Shot www.lasershot.com
MGM Targets www.mgmtargets.com
Mountain Plains Industries www.targetshandloader.com
MTM Products www.mtmcase-gard.com
National Muzzleloading Rifle Assoc. www.nmlra.org
National Target Co. www.nationaltarget.com
Newbold Target Systems www.newboldtargets.com
PJL Targets www.pjltargets.com
Porta Target, Inc. www.portatarget.com
Range Management Services Inc. www.casewellintl.com
Range Systems www.range-systems.com
Reactive Target Systems Inc. chrts@primenet.com
Rolling Steel Targets www.rollingsteeltargets.com
Savage Range Systems www.savagerangesystems.com
ShatterBlast Targets www.daisy.com
Super Trap Bullet Containment Systems www.supertrap.com
Thompson Target Technology www.thompsontarget.com
Tombstone Tactical Targets www.tombstonetactical.com
Unique Tek www.uniquetek.com
Visible Impact Targets www.crosman.com
White Flyer www.whiteflyer.com

TRAP AND SKEET SHOOTING EQUIPMENT AND ACCESSORIES

Atlas Trap Co www.atlastraps.com
Auto-Sporter Industries www.auto-sporter.com
Claymaster Traps www.claymaster.com
Do-All Traps, Inc. www.dooalloutdoors.com
Laporte USA www.laporte-shooting.com
Outers www.blount.com
Promatic, Inc. www.promatic.biz
Trius Products Inc. www.triustraps.com
White Flyer www.whiteflyer.com

TRIGGERS

American Trigger Corp. www.americantrigger.com
Brownells www.brownells.com
Chip McCormick Corp. www.chipmccormickcorp.com
E-Z Pull Triggers www.ezpulltriggerassist.com
Geissele Automatics, LLC www.ar15triggers.com
Huber Concepts www.huberconcepts.com
Jard, Inc. www.jardinc.com
Jewell Triggers (512)353-2999
Kidd Triggers. www.coolguyguns.com
Shilen www.shilen.com
Spec-Tech Industries, Inc. www.spec-tech-industries
Timney Triggers www.timneytriggers.com
Williams Trigger Specialties www.williamstriggers.com

MAJOR SHOOTING WEBSITES AND LINKS

24 Hour Campfire www.24hourcampfire.com
Accurate Shooter www.6mmbr.com
Alphabetic Index of Links www.gunsgunsguns.com
Ammo Guide www.ammoguide.com
Auction Arms www.auctionarms.com
Benchrest Central www.benchrest.com
Big Game Hunt www.biggamehunt.net
Bullseye Pistol www.bullseyepistol.com
Firearms History www.researchpress.co.uk/firearms
Glock Talk www.glocktalk.com
Gun Broker Auctions www.gunbroker.com
Gun Industry www.gunindustry.com
Gun Blast www.gunblast.com
Gun Boards www.gunboards.com
GunsAmerica.com www.gunsamerica.com
Guns & Ammo Forum http://forums.gunsandammo.com
Guns Unified Nationally Endorsing Dignity www.guned.com
Gun Shop Finder www.gunshopfinder.com
GUNS and Hunting www.gunsandhunting.com
Hunt and Shoot (NSSF) www.huntandshoot.org
Keep and Bear Arms www.keepandbeararms.com
Leverguns www.leverguns.com
Load Swap www.loadswap.com
Long Range Hunting www.longrangehunting.com
National Firearms Museum www.nramuseum.org
Outdoor Press Room www.outdoorpressroom.com
Real Guns www.realguns.com
Ruger Forum www.rugerforum.com
SavageShooters www.savageshooters.com
Shooters Forum www.shootersforum.com
Shotgun Sports Resource Guide www.shotgunsports.com
Shotgun World www.shotgunworld.com
Sixgunner www.sixgunner.com
Sniper's Hide www.snipershide.com
Sportsman's Web www.sportsmansweb.com
Surplus Rifles www.surplusrifle.com
Tactical-Life www.tactical-life.com
The Gun Room www.doublegun.com
Wing Shooting USA www.wingshootingusa.org

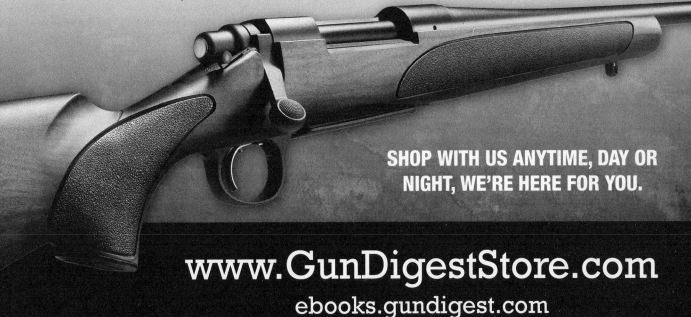

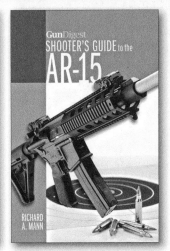

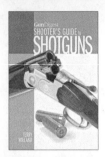

GUN DIGEST SHOOTERS GUIDE TO SHOTGUNS
U2146 • $19.99

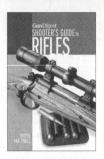

GD SHOOTER'S GUIDE TO RIFLES
V6631 • $19.99

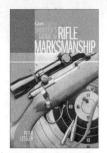

GUN DIGEST SHOOTER'S GUIDE TO RIFLE MARKSMANSHIP
U2928 • $19.99

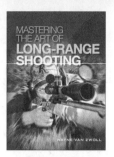

Mastering the Art of Long-Range Shooting
U2148 • $29.99

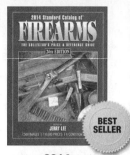

2014 STANDARD CATALOG OF FIREARMS
U5072 • $42.99

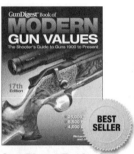

Gun Digest Book of Modern Gun Values
U5559 • $34.99

GD BOOK OF THE REMINGTON 870
V8197 • $32.99

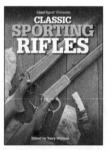

GUN DIGEST PRESENTS CLASSIC SPORTING RIFLES
W7930 • $24.99

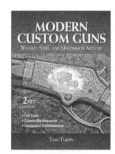

Modern Custom Guns
U3979 • $59.99

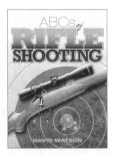

ABCs of Rifle Shooting
U8579 • $27.99

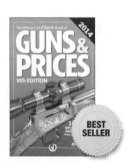

The Official Gun Digest Book of Guns & Prices 2014
U8735 • $25.99

GD ILLUSTRATED GUIDE TO MODERN FIREARMS
V9118 • $32.99

Gun Safety in the Home
T0031 • $15.99

Gun Digest Guide to Maintaining & Accessorizing Firearms
T0033 • $32.99

Gun Digest Shooter's Guide to the AR-15
U7713 • $19.99

Gun Digest Guide to Modern Shotgunning
U9369 • $32.99

Newhall Shooting: A Tactical Analysis
T1794 • $24.99

To order, go to www.GunDigestStore.com.

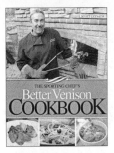

**THE SPORTING CHEF'S
BETTER VENISON
COOKBOOK**
U1948 • $24.99

COOKING GAME
U2929 • $9.99

**VENISON WISDOM
COOKBOOK**
Z8928 • $14.99

**WE KILL IT
WE GRILL IT**
V6707 • $9.99

**301
VENISON RECIPES**
VR01 • $10.95

**ADVENTURE
BOWHUNTER**
V9708 • $34.99

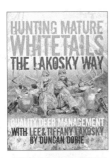

**HUNTING MATURE
WHITETAILS
THE LAKOSKY WAY**
W4542 • $29.99

**DEER & DEER
HUNTING'S GUIDE
TO BETTER
BOW HUNTING**
V6706 • $9.99

**STRATEGIES FOR
WHITETAILS**
WTLDD • $24.99

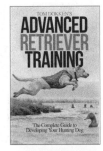

**TOM DOKKEN'S
ADVANCED RETRIEVER
TRAINING**
U1863 • $22.99

**Trophy Whitetails with Pat
and Nicole Reeve**
U3680 • $31.99

**LEGENDARY
WHITETAILS**
W7618 • $29.99

GUT IT. CUT IT. COOK IT.
Z5014 • $24.99

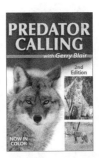

**PREDATOR CALLING
WITH GERRY BLAIR**
Z0740 • $19.99

The Rut Hunters
U7573 • $31.99

Game Cookery
U7125 • $24.99

**The Mountain Man
Cookbook**
U9370 • $12.99

**TOM DOKKEN'S
RETRIEVER TRAINING**
Z3235 • $19.99

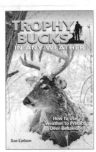

**TROPHY BUCKS
IN ANY WEATHER**
Z1781 • $21.99

To order, go to www.GunDigestStore.com.

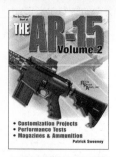
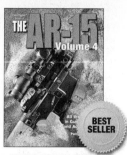
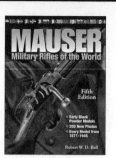
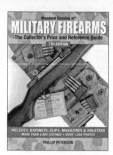
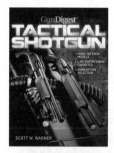
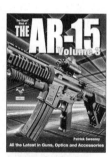
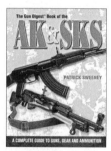

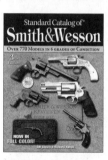
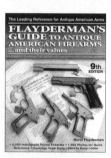

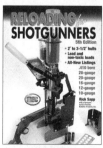
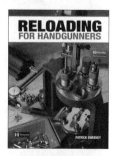

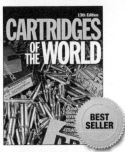
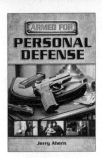

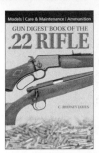

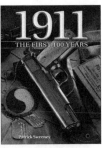

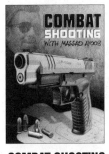

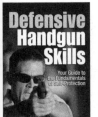

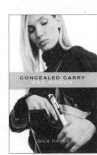

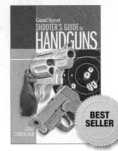

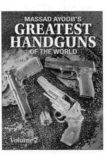
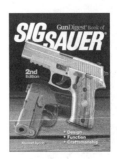

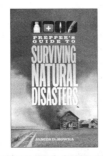

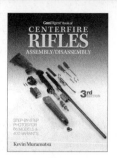

GUN DIGEST BOOK OF CENTERFIRE RIFLES ASSEMBLY/ DISASSEMBLY 3RD ED.
U2620 • $34.99

GD BOOK OF SHOTGUNS ASSEM/DISSASEM, 3RD ED.
V6630 • $36.99

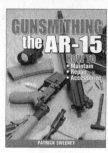

GUNSMITHING THE AR-15
Z6613 • $27.99

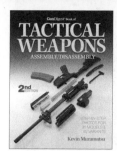

Gun Digest Book of Tactical Weapons Assembly/Disassembly
U3671 • $29.99

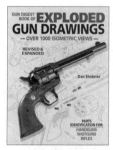

GUN DIGEST BOOK OF EXPLODED GUN DRAWINGS
Y0047 • $37.99

GUN DIGEST BOOK OF REVOLVERS ASSEMBLY/DISASSEMBLY
Y0773 • $34.99

GUN DIGEST BOOK OF AUTOMATIC PISTOL ASSEMBLY / DISSASEMBLY
W7933 • $39.99

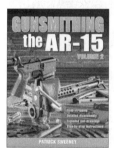

Gunsmithing the AR-15 Volume 2
U7714 • $29.99

CUSTOMIZE THE RUGER 10/22
NGRTT • $29.99

CUSTOM RIFLES: MASTERY OF WOOD & METAL
V8196 • $59.99

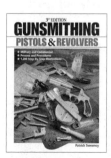

GUNSMITHING: PISTOLS & REVOLVERS
Z5056 • $29.99

GUN DIGEST BOOK OF RIMFIRE RIFLES ASSEMBLY/DISASSEMBLY
W1577 • $34.99

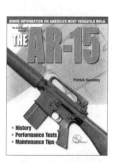

GUN DIGEST BOOK OF THE AR-15
GDAR • $27.99

To order, go to www.GunDigestStore.com.

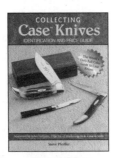
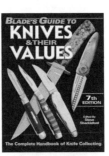